Philip's World Maps

The reference maps which form the main body of this atlas have been prepared in accordance with the highest standards of international cartography to provide an accurate and detailed representation of the Earth. The scales and projections used have been carefully chosen to give balanced coverage of the world, while emphasizing the most densely populated and economically significant regions. A hallmark of Philip's mapping is the use of hill shading and relief colouring to create a graphic impression of landforms: this makes the maps exceptionally easy to read. However, knowledge of the key features employed in the construction and presentation of the maps will enable the reader to derive the fullest benefit from the atlas.

MAP SEQUENCE

The atlas covers the Earth continent by continent: first Europe; then its land neighbour Asia (mapped north before south, in a clockwise sequence), then Africa, Australia and Oceania, North America and South America. This is the classic arrangement adopted by most cartographers since the 16th century. For each continent, there are maps at a variety of scales. First, physical relief and political maps

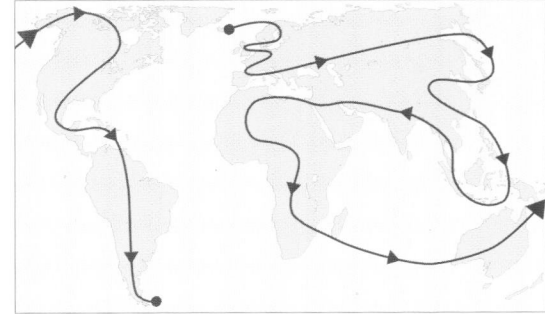

of the whole continent; then a series of larger-scale maps of the regions within the continent, each followed, where required, by still larger-scale maps of the most important or densely populated areas. The governing principle is that by turning the pages of the atlas, the reader moves steadily from north to south through each continent, with each map overlapping its neighbours.

MAP PRESENTATION

With very few exceptions (e.g. for the Arctic and Antarctic), the maps are drawn with north at the top, regardless of whether they are presented upright or sideways on the page. In the borders will be found the map title; a locator diagram showing the area covered and the page numbers for maps of adjacent areas; the scale; the projection used; the degrees of latitude and longitude; and the letters and figures used in the index for locating place names and geographical features. Physical relief maps also have a height reference panel identifying the colours used for each layer of contouring.

MAP SYMBOLS

Each map contains a vast amount of detail which can only be conveyed clearly and accurately by the use of symbols. Points and circles of varying sizes locate and identify the relative importance of towns and cities; different styles of type are employed for administrative, geographical and regional place names to aid identification. A variety of pictorial symbols denote landscape features such as glaciers, marshes and coral reefs, and man-made structures including roads, railways, airports, canals and dams. International borders are shown by red lines. Where neighbouring countries are in dispute, for example in parts of the Middle East, the maps show the *de facto* boundary between nations, regardless of the legal or historical situation. The symbols are explained on the first page of the *World Maps* section of the atlas.

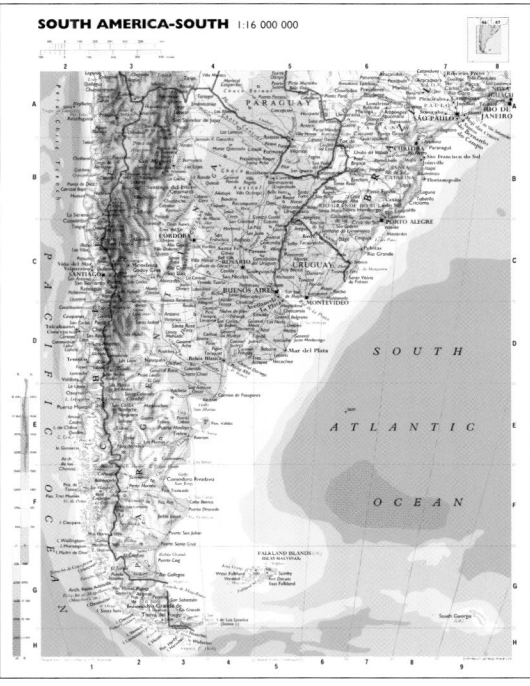

SOUTH AMERICA-SOUTH 1:16 000 000

MAP SCALES

1:16 000 000
1 inch = 252 statute miles

The scale of each map is given in the numerical form known as the 'representative fraction'. The first figure is always one, signifying one unit of distance on the map; the second figure, usually in millions, is the number by which the map unit must be multiplied to give the equivalent distance on the Earth's surface. Calculations can easily be made in centimetres and kilometres, by dividing the Earth units figure by 100 000 (i.e. deleting the last five 0s). Thus 1:1 000 000 means 1 cm = 10 km. The calculation for inches and miles is more laborious, but 1 000 000 divided by 63 360 (the number of inches in a mile) shows that 1:1 000 000 means approximately 1 inch = 16 miles. The table below provides distance equivalents for scales down to 1:50 000 000.

LARGE SCALE		
1:1 000 000	1 cm = 10 km	1 inch = 16 miles
1:2 500 000	1 cm = 25 km	1 inch = 39.5 miles
1:5 000 000	1 cm = 50 km	1 inch = 79 miles
1:6 000 000	1 cm = 60 km	1 inch = 95 miles
1:8 000 000	1 cm = 80 km	1 inch = 126 miles
1:10 000 000	1 cm = 100 km	1 inch = 158 miles
1:15 000 000	1 cm = 150 km	1 inch = 237 miles
1:20 000 000	1 cm = 200 km	1 inch = 316 miles
1:50 000 000	1 cm = 500 km	1 inch = 790 miles
SMALL SCALE		

MEASURING DISTANCES

Although each map is accompanied by a scale bar, distances cannot always be measured with confidence because of the distortions involved in portraying the curved surface of the Earth on a flat page. As a general rule, the larger the map scale (i.e. the lower the number of Earth units in the representative fraction), the more accurate and reliable will be the distance measured. On small-scale maps such as those of the world and of entire continents, measurement may only

be accurate along the 'standard parallels', or central axes, and should not be attempted without considering the map projection.

MAP PROJECTIONS

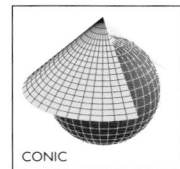  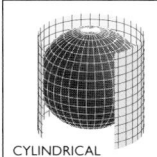

CONIC   AZIMUTHAL   CYLINDRICAL

Unlike a globe, no flat map can give a true scale representation of the world in terms of area, shape and position of every region. Each of the numerous systems that have been devised for projecting the curved surface of the Earth on to a flat page involves the sacrifice of accuracy in one or more of these elements. The variations in shape and position of landmasses such as Alaska, Greenland and Australia, for example, can be quite dramatic when different projections are compared.

For this atlas, the guiding principle has been to select projections that involve the least distortion of size and distance. The projection used for each map is noted in the border. Most fall into one of three categories – conic, azimuthal or cylindrical – whose basic concepts are shown above. Each involves plotting the forms of the Earth's surface on a grid of latitude and longitude lines, which may be shown as parallels, curves or radiating spokes.

LATITUDE AND LONGITUDE

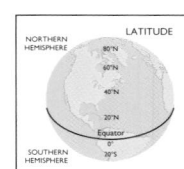 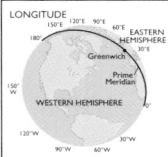 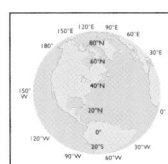

Accurate positioning of individual points on the Earth's surface is made possible by reference to the geometrical system of latitude and longitude. Latitude *parallels* are drawn west–east around the Earth and numbered by degrees north and south of the Equator, which is designated 0° of latitude. Longitude *meridians* are drawn north–south and numbered by degrees east and west of the *prime meridian*, 0° of longitude, which passes through Greenwich in England. By referring to these co-ordinates and their subdivisions of minutes (1/60th of a degree) and seconds (1/60th of a minute), any place on Earth can be located to within a few hundred metres. Latitude and longitude are indicated by blue lines on the maps; they are straight or curved according to the projection employed. Reference to these lines is the easiest way of determining the relative positions of places on different maps, and for plotting compass directions.

NAME FORMS

For ease of reference, both English and local name forms appear in the atlas. Oceans, seas and countries are shown in English throughout the atlas; country names may be abbreviated to their commonly accepted form (e.g. Germany, not The Federal Republic of Germany). Conventional English forms are also used for place names on the smaller-scale maps of the continents. However, local name forms are used on all large-scale and regional maps, with the English form given in brackets only for important cities – the large-scale map of Russia and Central Asia thus shows Moskva (Moscow). For countries which do not use a Roman script, place names have been transcribed according to the systems adopted by the British and US Geographic Names Authorities. For China, the Pin Yin system has been used, with some more widely known forms appearing in brackets, as with Beijing (Peking). Both English and local names appear in the index, the English form being cross-referenced to the local form.

Contents

World Statistics

Countries	x
Cities	xi
Climate	xii–xiii
Physical Dimensions	xiv–xv
Regions in the News	xvi

The Earth In Space

The Universe	2–3
Star Charts and Constellations	4–7
The Solar System	8–9
The Earth: Time and Motion	10–11
The Earth from Space	12–13
The Dynamic Earth	14–15
Earthquakes and Volcanoes	16–17
Forces of Nature	18–19
Oceans and Ice	20–21
The Earth's Atmosphere	22–23
Climate and Weather	24–25
Water and Land Use	26–27
The Natural World	28–29
The Human World	30–31
Languages and Religions	32–33
International Organizations	34–35
Agriculture	36–37
Energy and Minerals	38–39
World Economies	40–41
Trade and Commerce	42–43
Travel and Communications	44–45
The World Today	46–47

World Maps

Map Symbols	**1**
The World: Political 1:71 100 000	**2–3**
Arctic Ocean 1:31 100 000	**4**
Antarctica 1:31 100 000	**5**

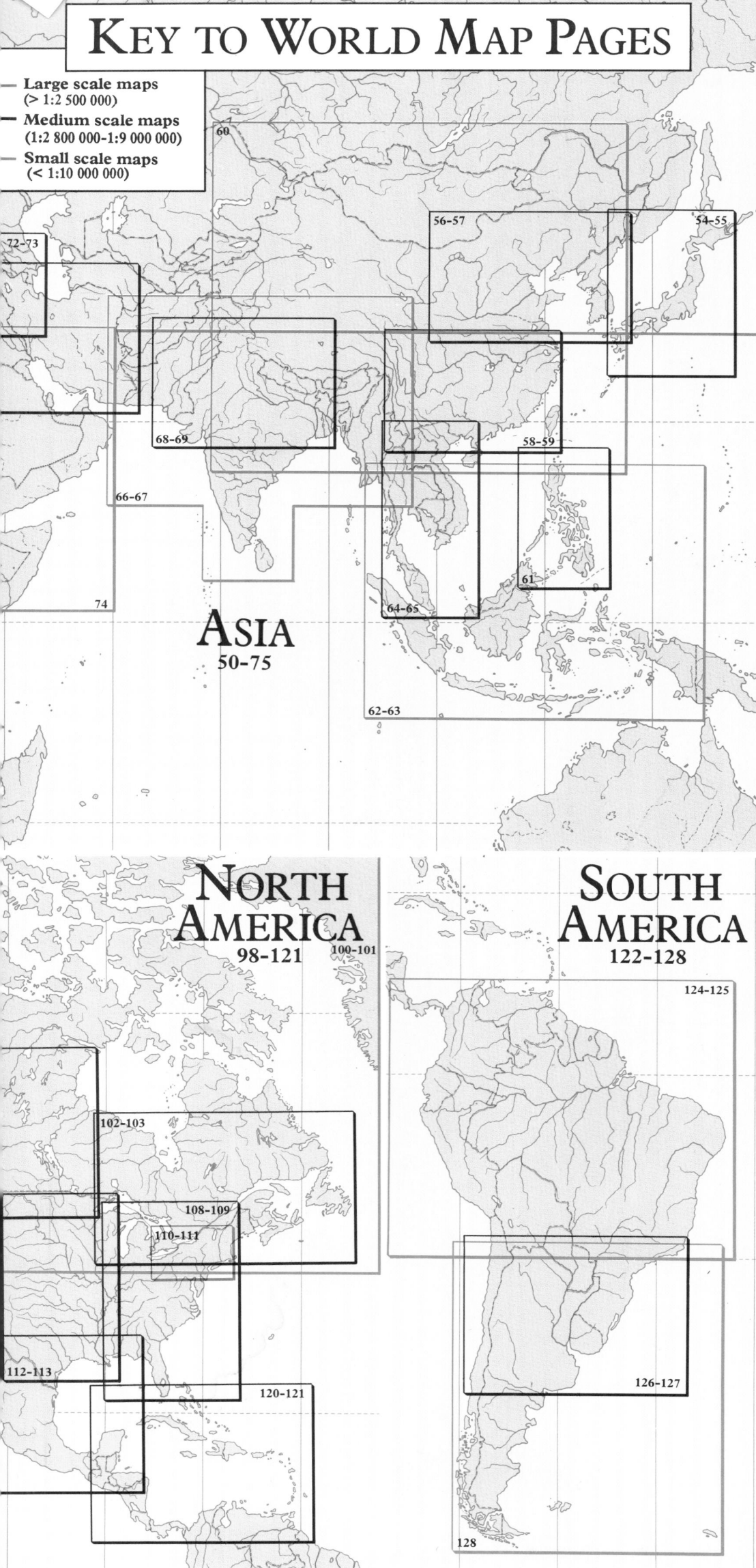

KEY TO WORLD MAP PAGES

- Large scale maps
  (> 1:2 500 000)
- Medium scale maps
  (1:2 800 000–1:9 000 000)
- Small scale maps
  (< 1:10 000 000)

60

56-57

54-55

72-73

68-69

66-67

58-59

61

64-65

74

ASIA
50-75

62-63

NORTH
AMERICA
98-121   100-101

SOUTH
AMERICA
122-128

124-125

102-103

108-109

110-111

112-113

126-127

120-121

128

COUNTRY INDEX

Afghanistan	66	Kuwait	70–71
Albania	40	Kyrgyzstan	50
Algeria	78		
Angola	84–85	Laos	64
Argentina	126, 128	Latvia	46
Armenia	73	Lebanon	75
Australia	92–95	Lesotho	88–89
Austria	26–27	Liberia	82
Azerbaijan	73	Libya	79
		Lithuania	46
Bahamas	120–121	Luxembourg	17
Bahrain	71		
Bangladesh	67	Macedonia	40
Barbados	121	Madagascar	89
Belarus	46–47	Malawi	87
Belgium	17	Malaysia	62–63
Belize	120	Mali	78, 82–83
Benin	83	Malta	36
Bhutan	67	Mauritania	78, 82
Bolivia	124	Mauritius	77
Bosnia-		Mexico	118–119
Herzegovina	29, 40	Moldova	43
Botswana	88–89	Mongolia	60
Brazil	124–127	Morocco	78
Brunei	78	Mozambique	85, 87
Bulgaria	40–41		
Burkina Faso	82–83	Namibia	88
Burma	67	Nepal	69
Burundi	86	Netherlands	17
		New Zealand	91
Cambodia	64–65	Nicaragua	120
Cameroon	84	Niger	83
Canada	100–101	Nigeria	83
Central African		Northern Ireland	15
Republic	84	Norway	8–9
Chad	79		
Chile	124, 128	Oman	74
China	56–60		
Colombia	124	Pakistan	68
Congo	84	Panama	120
Congo, Dem. Rep.		Papua New Guinea	90
of the	84–85	Paraguay	126–127
Costa Rica	120	Peru	124
Croatia	29, 42	Philippines	61
Cuba	120–121	Poland	44–45
Cyprus	36	Portugal	34–35
Czech Republic	26–27	Puerto Rico	121
Denmark	11	Qatar	71
Djibouti	74		
Dominican		Romania	42–43
Republic	121	Russia	50–51
		Rwanda	86
Ecuador	124		
Egypt	80	Saudi Arabia	74
El Salvador	120	Scotland	14
England	12–13	Senegal	82
Equatorial Guinea	84	Sierra Leone	82
Eritrea	80–81	Singapore	65
Estonia	46	Slovak Republic	27
Ethiopia	74, 81	Slovenia	29
		Somali Republic	74
Fiji	91	South Africa	88–89
Finland	8–9	Spain	32–35, 37
France	18–21	Sri Lanka	66
French Guiana	125	Sudan	79, 81
		Surinam	124–125
Gabon	84	Swaziland	89
Gambia	82	Sweden	8–9
Georgia	73	Switzerland	25
Germany	24–25	Syria	72–73
Ghana	82-83		
Greece	38–41	Taiwan	59
Greenland	4	Tajikistan	50
Guatemala	120	Tanzania	86–87
Guinea	82	Thailand	64–65
Guinea-Bissau	82	Togo	83
Guyana	124	Trinidad and	
		Tobago	121
Haiti	121	Tunisia	78–79
Honduras	120	Turkey	72–73
Hungary	42	Turkmenistan	50
Iceland	8	Uganda	86
India	66–69	Ukraine	47
Indonesia	62–63	United Arab Emirates	71
Iran	70–71	United Kingdom	12–15
Iraq	70–71	USA	106–117
Irish Republic	15	Uruguay	126–127
Israel	75	Uzbekistan	50
Italy	28–31		
Ivory Coast	82	Venezuela	124
		Vietnam	64–65
Jamaica	120		
Japan	54–55	Wales	12–13
Jordan	75		
		Yemen	74
Kazakstan	50	Yugoslavia	40, 42
Kenya	86		
Korea, North	57	Zambia	84–85, 87
Korea, South	57	Zimbabwe	87

PHILIP'S

CONCISE WORLD ATLAS

PHILIP'S

CONCISE WORLD ATLAS

TWELFTH EDITION

IN ASSOCIATION WITH
THE ROYAL GEOGRAPHICAL SOCIETY
WITH THE INSTITUTE OF BRITISH GEOGRAPHERS

THE EARTH IN SPACE
Cartography by Philip's

Text
Keith Lye

Illustrations
Stefan Chabluk

Star Charts
John Cox
Richard Monkhouse

PICTURE ACKNOWLEDGEMENTS
Corbis Sygma /Thorne Anderson 47
Robert Harding Picture Library /PHOTRI 13, /Bill Ross 41, /Adam Woolfitt 43
Hutchison Library /John Hatt 46
Image Bank /Peter Hendrie 20, /Daniel Hummel 34, /Image Makers 8 top,
/Pete Turner 39
Images Colour Library Limited 15
Japan National Tourist Organization 45
NASA/Galaxy Picture Library 8 bottom left
NPA Group, Edenbridge, UK 48
Panos Pictures /Howard Davies 35
Chris Rayner 19 top
Rex Features /SIPA Press /Scott Andrews 12
Science Photo Library /Martin Bond 14, /CNES, 1992 Distribution Spot
Image 27 top, /Luke Dodd 3, 6, /Earth Satellite Corporation 25 bottom,
/NASA 9 centre right, 9 top, 22, 23, 24, /David Parker 26, /Peter Ryan 27
below, /Jerry Schad 4, /Space Telescope Science Institute /NASA 9 centre left,
9 bottom right, /US Geological Survey 8 centre right
Space Telescope Science Institute /R. Williams /NASA 2
Starland Picture Library /NASA 8 centre left
Still Pictures /Francois Pierrel 28, /Heine Pedersen 31, 40
Tony Stone Images 33, /Glen Allison 38, /James Balog 16, /John Beatty 21,
/Neil Beer 30, /Kristin Finnegan 11, /Jeremy Horner 42, /Gary Norman 36,
/Frank Oberle 25 top, /Dennis Oda 17, /Nigel Press 37, /Donovan Reese 18,
19, /Hugh Sitton 32, /Richard Surman 44, /Michael Townsend 29, /World
Perspectives 10
Telegraph Colour Library /Space Frontiers 9 bottom left

Published in Great Britain in 2002
by Philip's,
a division of Octopus Publishing Group Limited,
2–4 Heron Quays, London E14 4JP

Copyright © 2002 Philip's

Cartography by Philip's

ISBN 0–540–08233–3

A CIP catalogue record for this book is available from the British Library.

Printed in Hong Kong

Details of other Philip's titles and services can be found on our website at:
www.philips-maps.co.uk

Philip's World Atlases are published in association with
The Royal Geographical Society (with The Institute of
British Geographers).

The Society was founded in 1830 and given a Royal
Charter in 1859 for 'the advancement of geographical
science'. It holds historical collections of national and
international importance, many of which relate to
the Society's association with and support for scientific
exploration and research from the 19th century onwards.
It was pivotal in establishing geography as a teaching and
research discipline in British universities close to
the turn of the century, and has played a key role in
geographical and environmental education ever since.

Today the Society is a leading world centre for
geographical learning – supporting education, teaching,
research and expeditions, and promoting public
understanding of the subject.

The Society welcomes those interested in geography
as members. For further information, please visit the
website at: www.rgs.org

Europe

Europe: Physical
1:17 800 000
6

Europe: Political
1:17 800 000
7

Scandinavia
1:4 400 000

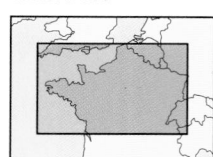

8–9

Denmark and Southern Sweden
1:2 200 000

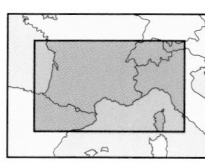

10–11

England and Wales
1:1 800 000

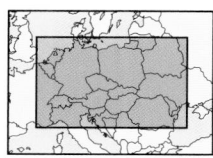

12–13

Scotland
1:1 800 000

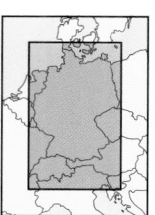

14

Ireland
1:1 800 000

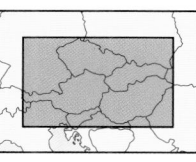

15

British Isles
1:4 400 000

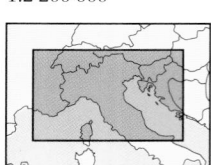

16

Netherlands, Belgium and Luxembourg
1:2 200 000

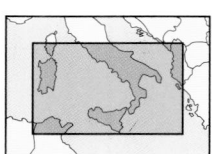

17

Northern France
1:2 200 000

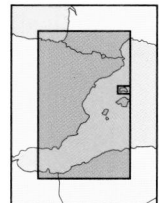

18–19

Southern France
1:2 200 000

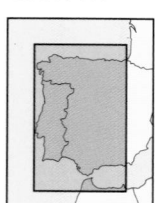

20–21

Middle Europe
1:4 400 000

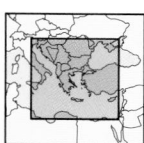

22–23

Germany and Switzerland
1:2 200 000

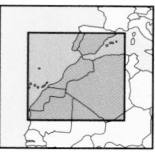

24–25

**Austria, Czech Republic
and Slovak Republic**
1:2 200 000

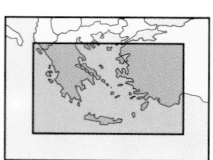

26–27

Northern Italy, Slovenia and Croatia
1:2 200 000

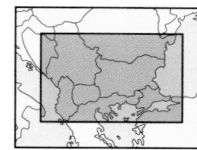

28–29

Southern Italy
1:2 200 000

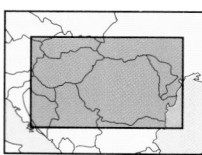

30–31

Eastern Spain
1:2 200 000

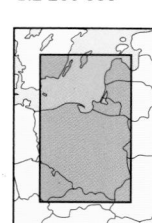

32–33

Western Spain and Portugal
1:2 200 000

34–35

Malta, Crete, Corfu, Rhodes and Cyprus
1:900 000 / 1:1 200 000

36

The Balearics, the Canaries and Madeira
1:900 000 / 1:1 800 000

37

Southern Greece and Western Turkey
1:2 200 000

38–39

Northern Greece, Bulgaria and Yugoslavia
1:2 200 000

40–41

Hungary, Romania and the Lower Danube
1:2 200 000

42–43

Poland and the Southern Baltic
1:2 200 000

44–45

Baltic States, Belarus and Ukraine
1:4 400 000

46–47

The Volga Basin and the Caucasus
1:4 400 000

48–49

Asia

Russia and Central Asia
1:17 800 000

50–51

Asia: Physical
1:44 400 000   52

Asia: Political
1:44 400 000   53

Japan
1:4 400 000

54–55

Northern China and Korea
1:5 300 000

56–57

Southern China
1:5 300 000

58–59

China
1:17 800 000

60

The Philippines
1:6 700 000

61

Indonesia and the Philippines
1:11 100 000

62–63

Mainland South-east Asia
1:5 300 000

64–65

South Asia
1:8 900 000

66–67

The Indo-Gangetic Plain
1:5 300 000

68–69

The Middle East
1:6 200 000

70–71

Turkey and Transcaucasia
1:4 400 000

72–73

Arabia and the Horn of Africa
1:13 300 000

74

The Near East
1:2 200 000

75

Africa

Africa: Physical
1:37 300 000   76

Africa: Political
1: 37 300 000   77

Northern Africa
1:13 300 000

78–79

The Nile Valley and the Nile Delta
1:7 100 000 / 1:3 600 000

80–81

West Africa
1:7 100 000

82–83

Central and Southern Africa
1:13 300 000

84–85

East Africa
1:7 100 000

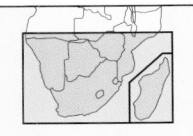

86–87

Southern Africa
1:7 100 000 / 1:7 100 000

88–89

Australia and Oceania

Australia and Oceania:
Physical and Political
1:44 400 000   90

New Zealand and Samoa, Fiji and Tonga
1:5 300 000 / 1:10 700 000

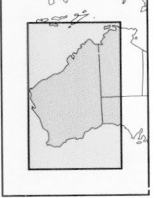

91

Western Australia
1:7 100 000

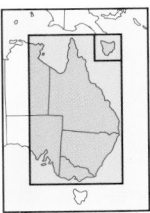

92–93

Eastern Australia
1:7 100 000

94–95

Pacific Ocean
1:48 000 000   96–97

North America

North America: Physical
1:31 100 000   98

North America: Political
1:31 100 000   99

Canada and Alaska
1:13 300 000 / 1:26 700 000

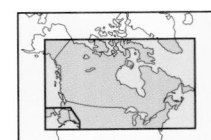

100–101

Eastern Canada
1:6 200 000

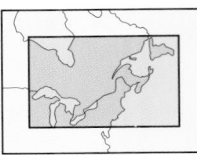

102–103

Western Canada
1:6 200 000

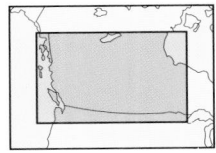

104–105

United States and Hawaii
1:10 700 000 / 1:8 900 000

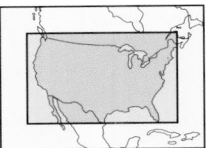

106–107

Eastern United States
1:5 300 000

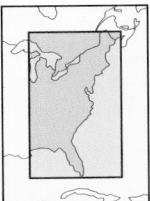

108–109

North-eastern United States
1:2 200 000

110–111

Middle United States
1:5 300 000

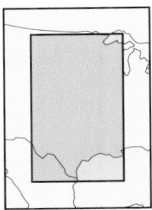

112–113

Western United States
1:5 300 000

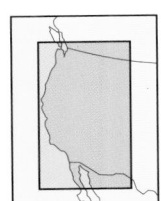

114–115

Central and Southern California
and Western Washington
1:2 200 000

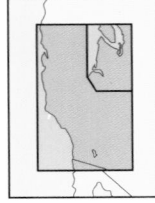

116–117

Mexico
1:7 100 000

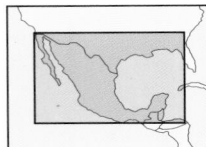

118–119

Central America and the West Indies
1:7 100 000

120–121

South America

South America: Physical
1:31 100 000   122

South America: Political
1:31 100 000   123

South America – North
1:14 200 000

124–125

Central South America
1:7 100 000

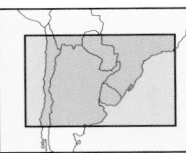

126–127

South America – South
1:14 200 000

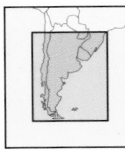

128

Index to World Maps

129–224

World Statistics: Countries

This alphabetical list includes all the countries and territories of the world. If a territory is not completely independent, the country it is associated with is named. The area figures give the total area of land, inland water and ice.

The population figures are 2001 estimates. The annual income is the Gross Domestic Product per capita† in US dollars. The figures are the latest available, usually 2000 estimates.

Country/Territory	Area km^2 Thousands	Area miles^2 Thousands	Population Thousands	Capital	Annual Income US $
Afghanistan	652	252	26,813	Kabul	800
Albania	28.8	11.1	3,510	Tirana	3,000
Algeria	2,382	920	31,736	Algiers	5,500
American Samoa (US)	0.2	0.08	67	Pago Pago	8,000
Andorra	0.45	0.17	68	Andorra La Vella	18,000
Angola	1,247	481	10,366	Luanda	1,000
Anguilla (UK)	0.1	0.04	12	The Valley	8,200
Antigua & Barbuda	0.44	0.17	67	St John's	8,200
Argentina	2,767	1,068	37,385	Buenos Aires	12,900
Armenia	29.8	11.5	3,336	Yerevan	3,000
Aruba (Netherlands)	0.19	0.07	70	Oranjestad	28,000
Australia	7,687	2,968	19,358	Canberra	23,200
Austria	83.9	32.4	8,151	Vienna	25,000
Azerbaijan	86.6	33.4	7,771	Baku	3,000
Azores (Portugal)	2.2	0.87	243	Ponta Delgada	11,040
Bahamas	13.9	5.4	298	Nassau	15,000
Bahrain	0.68	0.26	645	Manama	15,900
Bangladesh	144	56	131,270	Dhaka	1,570
Barbados	0.43	0.17	275	Bridgetown	14,500
Belarus	207.6	80.1	10,350	Minsk	7,500
Belgium	30.5	11.8	10,259	Brussels	25,300
Belize	23	8.9	256	Belmopan	3,200
Benin	113	43	6,591	Porto-Novo	1,030
Bermuda (UK)	0.05	0.02	64	Hamilton	33,000
Bhutan	47	18.1	2,049	Thimphu	1,100
Bolivia	1,099	424	8,300	La Paz/Sucre	2,600
Bosnia-Herzegovina	51	20	3,922	Sarajevo	1,700
Botswana	582	225	1,586	Gaborone	6,600
Brazil	8,512	3,286	174,469	Brasilia	6,500
Brunei	5.8	2.2	344	Bandar Seri Begawan	17,600
Bulgaria	111	43	7,707	Sofia	6,200
Burkina Faso	274	106	12,272	Ouagadougou	1,000
Burma (= Myanmar)	677	261	41,995	Rangoon	1,500
Burundi	27.8	10.7	6,224	Bujumbura	720
Cambodia	181	70	12,492	Phnom Penh	1,300
Cameroon	475	184	15,803	Yaoundé	1,700
Canada	9,976	3,852	31,593	Ottawa	24,800
Canary Is. (Spain)	7.3	2.8	1,577	Las Palmas/Santa Cruz	17,100
Cape Verde Is.	4	1.6	405	Praia	1,700
Cayman Is. (UK)	0.26	0.1	36	George Town	24,500
Central African Republic	623	241	3,577	Bangui	1,700
Chad	1,284	496	8,707	Ndjaména	1,000
Chile	757	292	15,328	Santiago	10,100
China	9,597	3,705	1,273,111	Beijing	3,600
Colombia	1,139	440	40,349	Bogotá	6,200
Comoros	2.2	0.86	596	Moroni	720
Congo	342	132	2,894	Brazzaville	1,100
Congo (Dem. Rep. of the)	2,345	905	53,625	Kinshasa	600
Cook Is. (NZ)	0.24	0.09	21	Avarua	5,000
Costa Rica	51.1	19.7	3,773	San José	6,700
Croatia	56.5	21.8	4,334	Zagreb	5,800
Cuba	111	43	11,184	Havana	1,700
Cyprus	9.3	3.6	763	Nicosia	13,800
Czech Republic	78.9	30.4	10,264	Prague	12,900
Denmark	43.1	16.6	5,353	Copenhagen	25,500
Djibouti	23.2	9	461	Djibouti	1,300
Dominica	0.75	0.29	71	Roseau	4,000
Dominican Republic	48.7	18.8	8,581	Santo Domingo	5,700
East Timor	14.9	5.7	737	Dili	N/A
Ecuador	284	109	13,184	Quito	2,900
Egypt	1,001	387	69,537	Cairo	3,600
El Salvador	21	8.1	6,238	San Salvador	4,000
Equatorial Guinea	28.1	10.8	486	Malabo	2,000
Eritrea	94	36	4,298	Asmara	710
Estonia	44.7	17.3	1,423	Tallinn	10,000
Ethiopia	1,128	436	65,892	Addis Ababa	600
Faroe Is. (Denmark)	1.4	0.54	46	Tórshavn	20,000
Fiji	18.3	7.1	844	Suva	7,300
Finland	338	131	5,176	Helsinki	22,900
France	552	213	59,551	Paris	24,400
French Guiana (France)	90	34.7	178	Cayenne	6,000
French Polynesia (France)	4	1.5	254	Papeete	10,800
Gabon	268	103	1,221	Libreville	6,300
Gambia, The	11.3	4.4	1,411	Banjul	1,100
Gaza Strip (OPT)*	0.36	0.14	1,178	–	1,000
Georgia	69.7	26.9	4,989	Tbilisi	4,600
Germany	357	138	83,030	Berlin	23,400
Ghana	239	92	19,894	Accra	1,900
Gibraltar (UK)	0.007	0.003	28	Gibraltar Town	17,500
Greece	132	51	10,624	Athens	17,200
Greenland (Denmark)	2,176	840	56	Nuuk (Godthåb)	20,000
Grenada	0.34	0.13	89	St George's	4,400
Guadeloupe (France)	1.7	0.66	431	Basse-Terre	9,000
Guam (US)	0.55	0.21	158	Agana	21,000
Guatemala	109	42	12,974	Guatemala City	3,700
Guinea	246	95	7,614	Conakry	1,300
Guinea-Bissau	36.1	13.9	1,316	Bissau	850
Guyana	215	83	697	Georgetown	4,800
Haiti	27.8	10.7	6,965	Port-au-Prince	1,800
Honduras	112	43	6,406	Tegucigalpa	2,700
Hong Kong (China)	1.1	0.4	7,211	–	25,400
Hungary	93	35.9	10,106	Budapest	11,200
Iceland	103	40	278	Reykjavik	24,800
India	3,288	1,269	1,029,991	New Delhi	2,200
Indonesia	1,890	730	227,701	Jakarta	2,900
Iran	1,648	636	66,129	Tehran	6,300
Iraq	438	169	23,332	Baghdad	2,500
Ireland	70.3	27.1	3,841	Dublin	21,600
Israel	20.6	7.96	5,938	Jerusalem	18,900
Italy	301	116	57,680	Rome	22,100
Ivory Coast (= Côte d'Ivoire)	322	125	16,393	Yamoussoukro	1,600
Jamaica	11	4.2	2,666	Kingston	3,700
Japan	378	146	126,772	Tokyo	24,900
Jordan	89.2	34.4	5,153	Amman	3,500
Kazakstan	2,717	1,049	16,731	Astana	5,000
Kenya	580	224	30,766	Nairobi	1,500
Kiribati	0.72	0.28	94	Tarawa	850
Korea, North	121	47	21,968	Pyŏngyang	1,000
Korea, South	99	38.2	47,904	Seoul	16,100
Kuwait	17.8	6.9	2,042	Kuwait City	15,000
Kyrgyzstan	198.5	76.6	4,753	Bishkek	2,700
Laos	237	91	5,636	Vientiane	1,700
Latvia	65	25	2,385	Riga	7,200
Lebanon	10.4	4	3,628	Beirut	5,000
Lesotho	30.4	11.7	2,177	Maseru	2,400
Liberia	111	43	3,226	Monrovia	1,100
Libya	1,760	679	5,241	Tripoli	8,900
Liechtenstein	0.16	0.06	33	Vaduz	23,000
Lithuania	65.2	25.2	3,611	Vilnius	7,300
Luxembourg	2.6	1	443	Luxembourg	36,400
Macau (China)	0.02	0.006	454	–	17,500
Macedonia (FYROM)	25.7	9.9	2,046	Skopje	4,400
Madagascar	587	227	15,983	Antananarivo	800
Madeira (Portugal)	0.81	0.31	259	Funchal	12,120
Malawi	118	46	10,548	Lilongwe	900
Malaysia	330	127	22,229	Kuala Lumpur	10,300
Maldives	0.3	0.12	311	Malé	2,000
Mali	1,240	479	11,009	Bamako	850
Malta	0.32	0.12	395	Valletta	14,300
Marshall Is.	0.18	0.07	71	Dalap-Uliga-Darrit	1,670
Martinique (France)	1.1	0.42	418	Fort-de-France	11,000
Mauritania	1,030	398	2,747	Nouakchott	2,000
Mauritius	2	0.72	1,190	Port Louis	10,400
Mayotte (France)	0.37	0.14	163	Mamoundzou	600
Mexico	1,958	756	101,879	Mexico City	9,100
Micronesia, Fed. States of	0.7	0.27	135	Palikir	2,000
Moldova	33.7	13	4,432	Chişinău	2,500
Monaco	0.002	0.001	32	Monaco	27,000
Mongolia	1,567	605	2,655	Ulan Bator	1,780
Montserrat (UK)	0.1	0.04	8	Plymouth	5,000
Morocco	447	172	30,645	Rabat	3,500
Mozambique	802	309	19,371	Maputo	1,000
Namibia	825	318	1,798	Windhoek	4,300
Nauru	0.02	0.008	12	Yaren District	5,000
Nepal	141	54	25,284	Katmandu	1,360
Netherlands	41.5	16	15,981	Amsterdam/The Hague	24,400
Netherlands Antilles (Neths)	0.99	0.38	212	Willemstad	11,400
New Caledonia (France)	18.6	7.2	205	Nouméa	15,000
New Zealand	269	104	3,864	Wellington	17,700
Nicaragua	130	50	4,918	Managua	2,700
Niger	1,267	489	10,355	Niamey	1,000
Nigeria	924	357	126,636	Abuja	950
Northern Mariana Is. (US)	0.48	0.18	75	Saipan	12,500
Norway	324	125	4,503	Oslo	27,700
Oman	212	82	2,622	Muscat	7,700
Pakistan	796	307	144,617	Islamabad	2,000
Palau	0.46	0.18	19	Koror	7,100
Panama	77.1	29.8	2,846	Panamá	6,000
Papua New Guinea	463	179	5,049	Port Moresby	2,500
Paraguay	407	157	5,734	Asunción	4,750
Peru	1,285	496	27,484	Lima	4,550
Philippines	300	116	82,842	Manila	3,800
Poland	313	121	38,634	Warsaw	8,500
Portugal	92.4	35.7	9,444	Lisbon	15,800
Puerto Rico (US)	9	3.5	3,939	San Juan	10,000
Qatar	11	4.2	769	Doha	20,300
Réunion (France)	2.5	0.97	733	St-Denis	4,800
Romania	238	92	22,364	Bucharest	5,900
Russia	17,075	6,592	145,470	Moscow	7,700
Rwanda	26.3	10.2	7,313	Kigali	900
St Kitts & Nevis	0.36	0.14	39	Basseterre	7,000
St Lucia	0.62	0.24	158	Castries	4,500
St Vincent & Grenadines	0.39	0.15	116	Kingstown	2,800
Samoa	2.8	1.1	179	Apia	3,200
San Marino	0.06	0.02	27	San Marino	32,000
São Tomé & Príncipe	0.96	0.37	165	São Tomé	1,100
Saudi Arabia	2,150	830	22,757	Riyadh	10,500
Senegal	197	76	10,285	Dakar	1,600
Seychelles	0.46	0.18	80	Victoria	7,700
Sierra Leone	71.7	27.7	5,427	Freetown	510
Singapore	0.62	0.24	4,300	Singapore	26,500
Slovak Republic	49	18.9	5,415	Bratislava	10,200
Slovenia	20.3	7.8	1,930	Ljubljana	12,000
Solomon Is.	28.9	11.2	480	Honiara	2,000
Somalia	638	246	7,489	Mogadishu	600
South Africa	1,220	471	43,586	C. Town/Pretoria/Bloem.	8,500
Spain	505	195	38,432	Madrid	18,000
Sri Lanka	65.6	25.3	19,409	Colombo	3,250
Sudan	2,506	967	36,080	Khartoum	1,000
Surinam	163	63	434	Paramaribo	3,400
Swaziland	17.4	6.7	1,104	Mbabane	4,000
Sweden	450	174	8,875	Stockholm	22,200
Switzerland	41.3	15.9	7,283	Bern	28,600
Syria	185	71	16,729	Damascus	3,100
Taiwan	36	13.9	22,370	Taipei	17,400
Tajikistan	143.1	55.2	6,579	Dushanbe	1,140
Tanzania	945	365	36,232	Dodoma	710
Thailand	513	198	61,798	Bangkok	6,700
Togo	56.8	21.9	5,153	Lomé	1,500
Tonga	0.75	0.29	104	Nuku'alofa	2,200
Trinidad & Tobago	5.1	2	1,170	Port of Spain	9,500
Tunisia	164	63	9,705	Tunis	6,500
Turkey	779	301	66,494	Ankara	6,800
Turkmenistan	488.1	188.5	4,603	Ashkhabad	4,300
Turks & Caicos Is. (UK)	0.43	0.17	18	Cockburn Town	7,300
Tuvalu	0.03	0.01	11	Fongafale	1,100
Uganda	236	91	23,986	Kampala	1,100
Ukraine	603.7	233.1	48,760	Kiev	3,850
United Arab Emirates	83.6	32.3	2,407	Abu Dhabi	22,800
United Kingdom	243.3	94	59,648	London	22,800
United States of America	9,373	3,619	278,059	Washington, DC	36,200
Uruguay	177	68	3,360	Montevideo	9,300
Uzbekistan	447.4	172.7	25,155	Tashkent	2,400
Vanuatu	12.2	4.7	193	Port-Vila	1,300
Vatican City	0.0004	0.0002	0.89	Vatican City	N/A
Venezuela	912	352	23,917	Caracas	6,200
Vietnam	332	127	79,939	Hanoi	1,950
Virgin Is. (UK)	0.15	0.06	21	Road Town	16,000
Virgin Is. (US)	0.34	0.13	122	Charlotte Amalie	15,000
Wallis & Futuna Is. (France)	0.2	0.08	15	Mata-Utu	2,000
West Bank (OPT)*	5.86	2.26	2,091	–	1,500
Western Sahara	266	103	251	El Aaiún	N/A
Yemen	528	204	18,078	Sana	820
Yugoslavia (Serbia & Montenegro)	102.3	39.5	10,677	Belgrade	2,300
Zambia	753	291	9,770	Lusaka	880
Zimbabwe	391	151	11,365	Harare	2,500

*OPT = Occupied Palestinian Territory   N/A = Not Available

† Gross Domestic Product per capita has been measured using the purchasing power parity method. This enables comparisons to be made between countries through their purchasing power (in US dollars), showing real price levels of goods and services rather than using currency exchange rates.

World Statistics: Cities

This list shows the principal cities with more than 500,000 inhabitants (only cities with more than 1 million inhabitants are included for Brazil, China, Indonesia, Japan and Russia). The figures are taken from the most recent census or estimate available, and as far as possible are the population of the metropolitan area, e.g. greater New York, Mexico or Paris. All the figures are in thousands. Local name forms have been used for the smaller cities (e.g. Kraków).

AFGHANISTAN
Kabul 1,565
ALGERIA
Algiers 1,722
Oran 664
ANGOLA
Luanda 2,250
ARGENTINA
Buenos Aires 10,990
Córdoba 1,198
Rosario 1,096
Mendoza 775
La Plata 640
San Miguel de Tucumán 622
Mar del Plata 520
ARMENIA
Yerevan 1,256
AUSTRALIA
Sydney 4,041
Melbourne 3,417
Brisbane 1,601
Perth 1,364
Adelaide 1,093
AUSTRIA
Vienna 1,560
AZERBAIJAN
Baku 1,713
BANGLADESH
Dhaka 7,832
Chittagong 2,041
Khulna 877
Rajshahi 517
BELARUS
Minsk 1,717
Homyel 502
BELGIUM
Brussels 948
BENIN
Cotonou 537
BOLIVIA
La Paz 1,126
Santa Cruz 767
BOSNIA-HERZEGOVINA
Sarajevo 526
BRAZIL
São Paulo 10,434
Rio de Janeiro 5,858
Salvador 2,443
Belo Horizonte 2,239
Fortaleza 2,141
Brasília 2,051
Curitiba 1,587
Recife 1,423
Manaus 1,406
Pôrto Alegre 1,361
Belém 1,281
Goiânia 1,093
Guarulhos 1,073
BULGARIA
Sofia 1,139
BURKINA FASO
Ouagadougou 690
BURMA (MYANMAR)
Rangoon 2,513
Mandalay 533
CAMBODIA
Phnom Penh 570
CAMEROON
Douala 1,200
Yaoundé 800
CANADA
Toronto 4,881
Montréal 3,511
Vancouver 2,079
Ottawa-Hull 1,107
Calgary 972
Edmonton 957
Québec 693
Winnipeg 685
Hamilton 681
CENTRAL AFRICAN REPUBLIC
Bangui 553
CHAD
Ndjaména 530
CHILE
Santiago 4,691
CHINA
Shanghai 15,082
Beijing 12,362
Tianjin 10,687
Hong Kong (SAR)* 6,502
Chongqing 3,870
Shenyang 3,762
Wuhan 3,520
Guangzhou 3,114
Harbin 2,505
Nanjing 2,211
Xi'an 2,115
Chengdu 1,933
Dalian 1,855
Changchun 1,810
Jinan 1,660
Taiyuan 1,642
Qingdao 1,584
Zibo 1,346
Zhengzhou 1,324
Lanzhou 1,296
Anshan 1,252
Fushun 1,246
Kunming 1,242
Changsha 1,198
Hangzhou 1,185
Nanchang 1,169
Shijiazhuang 1,159
Guiyang 1,131
Ürümqi 1,130
Jilin 1,118
Tangshan 1,110
Qiqihar 1,104
Baotou 1,033
COLOMBIA
Bogotá 6,005
Cali 1,986
Medellín 1,971
Barranquilla 1,158
Cartagena 813
Cúcuta 589
Bucaramanga 508
CONGO
Brazzaville 938
Pointe-Noire 576
CONGO (DEM. REP.)
Kinshasa 2,664
Lubumbashi 565
CROATIA
Zagreb 868
CUBA
Havana 2,204
CZECH REPUBLIC
Prague 1,203
DENMARK
Copenhagen 1,362
DOMINICAN REPUBLIC
Santo Domingo 2,135
Stgo. de los Caballeros 691
ECUADOR
Guayaquil 2,070
Quito 1,574
EGYPT
Cairo 6,800
Alexandria 3,339
El Gîza 2,222
Shubra el Kheima 871
EL SALVADOR
San Salvador 1,522
ETHIOPIA
Addis Ababa 2,316
FINLAND
Helsinki 532
FRANCE
Paris 11,175
Lyons 1,648
Marseilles 1,516
Lille 1,143
Toulouse 965
Nice 933
Bordeaux 925
Nantes 711
Strasbourg 612
Toulon 565
Douai 553
Rennes 521
Rouen 518
Grenoble 515
GEORGIA
Tbilisi 1,253
GERMANY
Berlin 3,426
Hamburg 1,705
Munich 1,206
Cologne 964
Frankfurt 644
Essen 609
Dortmund 595
Stuttgart 585
Düsseldorf 571
Bremen 547
Duisburg 529
Hanover 521
GHANA
Accra 1,781
GREECE
Athens 3,097
GUATEMALA
Guatemala 1,167
GUINEA
Conakry 1,508
HAITI
Port-au-Prince 885
HONDURAS
Tegucigalpa 814
HUNGARY
Budapest 1,885
INDIA
Mumbai (Bombay) 16,368
Kolkata (Calcutta) 13,217
Delhi 12,791
Chennai (Madras) 6,425
Bangalore 5,687
Hyderabad 5,534
Ahmadabad 4,519
Pune 3,756
Surat 2,811
Kanpur 2,690
Jaipur 2,324
Lucknow 2,267
Nagpur 2,123
Patna 1,707
Indore 1,639
Vadodara 1,492
Bhopal 1,455
Coimbatore 1,446
Ludhiana 1,395
Cochin 1,355
Vishakhapatnam 1,329
Agra 1,321
Varanasi 1,212
Madurai 1,195
Meerut 1,167
Nasik 1,152
Jabalpur 1,117
Jamshedpur 1,102
Asansol 1,090
Faridabad 1,055
Allahabad 1,050
Amritsar 1,011
Vijayawada 1,011
Rajkot 1,002
INDONESIA
Jakarta 11,500
Surabaya 2,701
Bandung 2,368
Medan 1,910
Semarang 1,366
Palembang 1,352
Tangerang 1,198
Ujung Pandang 1,092
IRAN
Tehran 6,759
Mashhad 1,887
Esfahan 1,266
Tabriz 1,191
Shiraz 1,053
Karaj 941
Ahvaz 805
Qom 778
Bakhtaran 693
IRAQ
Baghdad 3,841
As Sulaymaniyah 952
Arbil 770
Al Mawsil 664
Al Kazimiyah 521
IRELAND
Dublin 1,024
ISRAEL
Tel Aviv-Yafo 1,880
Jerusalem 591
ITALY
Rome 2,654
Milan 1,306
Naples 1,050
Turin 923
Palermo 689
Genoa 659
IVORY COAST
Abidjan 2,500
JAMAICA
Kingston 644
JAPAN
Tokyo 17,950
Yokohama 3,427
Osaka 2,599
Nagoya 2,171
Sapporo 1,822
Kobe 1,494
Kyoto 1,468
Fukuoka 1,341
Kawasaki 1,250
Hiroshima 1,126
Kitakyushu 1,011
Sendai 1,008
JORDAN
Amman 1,752
KAZAKHSTAN
Almaty 1,151
Qaraghandy 574
KENYA
Nairobi 2,000
Mombasa 600
KOREA, NORTH
Pyöngyang 2,741
Hamhung 710
Chöngjin 583
KOREA, SOUTH
Seoul 10,231
Pusan 3,814
Taegu 2,449
Inch'on 2,308
Taejön 1,272
Kwangju 1,258
Ulsan 967
Söngnam 869
Puch'on 779
Suwön 756
Anyang 590
Chönju 563
Chöngju 531
Ansan 510
P'ohang 509
KYRGYZSTAN
Bishkek 589
LAOS
Vientiane 532
LATVIA
Riga 811
LEBANON
Beirut 1,500
Tripoli 500
LIBERIA
Monrovia 962
LIBYA
Tripoli 960
LITHUANIA
Vilnius 580
MACEDONIA
Skopje 541
MADAGASCAR
Antananarivo 1,053
MALAYSIA
Kuala Lumpur 1,145
MALI
Bamako 810
MAURITANIA
Nouakchott 735
MEXICO
Mexico City 15,643
Guadalajara 2,847
Monterrey 2,522
Puebla 1,055
León 872
Ciudad Juárez 798
Tijuana 743
Culiacán 602
Mexicali 602
Acapulco 592
Mérida 557
Chihuahua 530
San Luis Potosí 526
Aguascalientés 506
MOLDOVA
Chişinău 658
MONGOLIA
Ulan Bator 673
MOROCCO
Casablanca 2,943
Rabat-Salé 1,220
Marrakesh 602
Fès 564
MOZAMBIQUE
Maputo 2,000
NEPAL
Katmandu 535
NETHERLANDS
Amsterdam 1,115
Rotterdam 1,086
The Hague 700
Utrecht 557
NEW ZEALAND
Auckland 1,090
NICARAGUA
Managua 864
NIGERIA
Lagos 10,287
Ibadan 1,432
Ogbomosho 730
Kano 674
NORWAY
Oslo 502
PAKISTAN
Karachi 9,269
Lahore 5,064
Faisalabad 1,977
Rawalpindi 1,406
Multan 1,182
Hyderabad 1,151
Gujranwala 1,125
Peshawar 988
Quetta 560
Islamabad 525
PARAGUAY
Asunción 945
PERU
Lima 6,601
Arequipa 620
Trujillo 509
PHILIPPINES
Manila 8,594
Quezon City 1,989
Caloocan 1,023
Davao 1,009
Cebu 662
Zamboanga 511
POLAND
Warsaw 1,626
Lódz 815
Kraków 740
Wroclaw 641
Poznań 580
PORTUGAL
Lisbon 2,561
Oporto 1,174
ROMANIA
Bucharest 2,028
RUSSIA
Moscow 8,405
St Petersburg 4,216
Nizhniy Novgorod 1,371
Novosibirsk 1,367
Yekaterinburg 1,275
Samara 1,170
Omsk 1,158
Kazan 1,085
Chelyabinsk 1,084
Ufa 1,082
Perm 1,025
Rostov 1,023
Volgograd 1,005
SAUDI ARABIA
Riyadh 1,800
Jedda 1,500
Mecca 630
SENEGAL
Dakar 1,905
SIERRA LEONE
Freetown 505
SINGAPORE
Singapore - 3,866
SOMALIA
Mogadishu 997
SOUTH AFRICA
Cape Town 2,350
Johannesburg 1,196
Durban 1,137
Pretoria 1,080
Port Elizabeth 853
Vanderbijlpark-Vereeniging 774
Soweto 597
Sasolburg 540
SPAIN
Madrid 3,030
Barcelona 1,615
Valencia 763
Sevilla 720
Zaragoza 608
Málaga 532
SRI LANKA
Colombo 1,863
SUDAN
Omdurman 1,271
Khartoum 925
Khartoum North 701
SWEDEN
Stockholm 727
SWITZERLAND
Zürich 733
SYRIA
Aleppo 1,813
Damascus 1,394
Homs 659
TAIWAN
T'aipei 2,596
Kaohsiung 1,435
T'aichung 858
T'ainan 708
Panch'iao 539
TAJIKISTAN
Dushanbe 524
TANZANIA
Dar-es-Salaam 1,361
THAILAND
Bangkok 7,507
TOGO
Lomé 590
TUNISIA
Tunis 1,827
TURKEY
Istanbul 8,506
Ankara 3,294
Izmir 2,554
Bursa 1,485
Adana 1,273
Konya 1,140
Mersin (Içel) 956
Gaziantep 867
Antalya 867
Kayseri 862
Diyarbakir 833
Urfa 785
Manisa 696
Kocaeli 629
Antalya 591
Samsun 590
Kahramanmaras 551
Balikesir 538
Eskisehir 519
Erzurum 512
Malatya 510
TURKMENISTAN
Ashkhabad 536
UGANDA
Kampala 954
UKRAINE
Kiev 2,621
Kharkov 1,521
Dnepropetrovsk 1,122
Donetsk 1,065
Odessa 1,027
Zaporizhzhya 863
Lviv 794
Kryvyy Rih 720
Mykolayiv 518
Mariupol 500
UNITED ARAB EMIRATES
Abu Dhabi 928
Dubai 674
UNITED KINGDOM
London 8,089
Birmingham 2,373
Manchester 2,353
Liverpool 852
Glasgow 832
Sheffield 661
Nottingham 649
Newcastle 617
Bristol 552
Leeds 529
UNITED STATES
New York 21,200
Los Angeles 16,374
Chicago-Gary 9,158
Washington-Baltimore 7,608
San Francisco-San Jose 7,039
Philadelphia-Atlantic City 6,188
Boston-Worcester 5,819
Detroit-Flint 5,456
Dallas-Fort Worth 5,222
Houston-Galveston 4,670
Atlanta 4,112
Miami-Fort Lauderdale 3,876
Seattle-Tacoma 3,554
Phoenix-Mesa 3,252
Minneapolis-St Paul 2,969
Cleveland-Akron 2,946
San Diego 2,814
St Louis 2,604
Denver-Boulder 2,582
San Juan 2,450
Tampa-Saint Petersburg 2,396
Pittsburgh 2,359
Portland-Salem 2,265
Cincinnati-Hamilton 1,979
Sacramento-Yolo 1,797
Kansas City 1,776
Milwaukee-Racine 1,690
Orlando 1,645
Indianapolis 1,607
San Antonio 1,592
Norfolk-Virginia Beach-Newport News 1,570
Las Vegas 1,563
Columbus, OH 1,540
Charlotte-Gastonia 1,499
New Orleans 1,338
Salt Lake City 1,334
Greensboro-Winston Salem-High Point 1,252
Austin-San Marcos 1,250
Nashville 1,231
Providence-Fall River 1,189
Raleigh-Durham 1,188
Hartford 1,183
Buffalo-Niagara Falls 1,170
Memphis 1,136
West Palm Beach 1,131
Jacksonville, FL 1,100
Rochester 1,098
Grand Rapids 1,089
Oklahoma City 1,083
Louisville 1,026
Richmond-Petersburg 997
Greenville 962
Dayton-Springfield 951
Fresno 923
Birmingham 921
Honolulu 876
Albany-Schenectady 876
Tucson 844
Tulsa 803
Syracuse 732
Omaha 717
Albuquerque 713
Knoxville 687
El Paso 680
Bakersfield 662
Allentown 638
Harrisburg 629
Scranton 625
Toledo 618
Baton Rouge 603
Youngstown-Warren 595
Springfield, MA 592
Sarasota 590
Little Rock 584
McAllen 569
Stockton-Lodi 564
Charleston 549
Wichita 545
Mobile 540
Columbia, SC 537
Colorado Springs 517
Fort Wayne 502
URUGUAY
Montevideo 1,379
UZBEKISTAN
Tashkent 2,118
VENEZUELA
Caracas 1,975
Maracaibo 1,706
Valencia 1,263
Barquisimeto 811
Ciudad Guayana 642
Petare 176
Maracay 459
VIETNAM
Ho Chi Minh City 4,322
Hanoi 3,056
Haiphong 783
YEMEN
Sana' 972
Aden 562
YUGOSLAVIA
Belgrade 1,598
ZAMBIA
Lusaka 982
ZIMBABWE
Harare 1,189
Bulawayo 622

* SAR = Special Administrative Region of China

World Statistics: Climate

Rainfall and temperature figures are provided for more than 70 cities around the world. As climate is affected by altitude, the height of each city is shown in metres beneath its name. For each location, the top row of figures shows the total rainfall or snow in millimetres, and the bottom row the average temperature in degrees Celsius; the average annual temperature and total annual rainfall are at the end of the rows. The map opposite shows the city locations.

CITY	JAN.	FEB.	MAR.	APR.	MAY	JUNE	JULY	AUG.	SEPT.	OCT.	NOV.	DEC.	YEAR
EUROPE													
Athens, Greece 107 m	62	37	37	23	23	14	6	7	15	51	56	71	402
	10	10	12	16	20	25	28	28	24	20	15	11	18
Berlin, Germany 55 m	46	40	33	42	49	65	73	69	48	49	46	43	603
	-1	0	4	9	14	17	19	18	15	9	5	1	9
Istanbul, Turkey 14 m	109	92	72	46	38	34	34	30	58	81	103	119	816
	5	6	7	11	16	20	23	23	20	16	12	8	14
Lisbon, Portugal 77 m	111	76	109	54	44	16	3	4	33	62	93	103	708
	11	12	14	16	17	20	22	23	21	18	14	12	17
London, UK 5 m	54	40	37	37	46	45	57	59	49	57	64	48	593
	4	5	7	9	12	16	18	17	15	11	8	5	11
Málaga, Spain 33 m	61	51	62	46	26	5	1	3	29	64	64	62	474
	12	13	16	17	19	29	25	26	23	20	16	13	18
Moscow, Russia 156 m	39	38	36	37	53	58	88	71	58	45	47	54	624
	-13	-10	-4	6	13	16	18	17	12	6	-1	-7	4
Odesa, Ukraine 64 m	57	62	30	21	34	34	42	37	37	13	35	71	473
	-3	-1	2	9	15	20	22	22	18	12	9	1	10
Paris, France 75 m	56	46	35	42	57	54	59	64	55	50	51	50	619
	3	4	8	11	15	18	20	19	17	12	7	4	12
Rome, Italy 17 m	71	62	57	51	46	37	15	21	63	99	129	93	744
	8	9	11	14	18	22	25	25	22	17	13	10	16
Shannon, Ireland 2 m	94	67	56	53	61	57	77	79	86	86	96	117	929
	5	5	7	9	12	14	16	16	14	11	8	6	10
Stockholm, Sweden 44 m	43	30	25	31	34	45	61	76	60	48	53	48	554
	-3	-3	-1	5	10	15	18	17	12	7	3	0	7
ASIA													
Bahrain 5 m	8	18	13	8	<3	0	0	0	0	0	18	18	81
	17	18	21	25	29	32	33	34	31	28	24	19	26
Bangkok, Thailand 2 m	8	20	36	58	198	160	160	175	305	206	66	5	1,397
	26	28	29	30	29	29	28	28	28	28	26	25	28
Beirut, Lebanon 34 m	191	158	94	53	18	3	<3	<3	5	51	132	185	892
	14	14	16	18	22	24	27	28	26	24	19	16	21
Bombay (Mumbai), India 11 m	3	3	3	<3	18	485	617	340	264	64	13	3	1,809
	24	24	26	28	30	29	27	27	27	28	27	26	27
Calcutta, India 6 m	10	31	36	43	140	297	325	328	252	114	20	5	1,600
	20	22	27	30	30	30	29	29	29	28	23	19	26
Colombo, Sri Lanka 7 m	89	69	147	231	371	224	135	109	160	348	315	147	2,365
	26	26	27	28	28	27	27	27	27	27	26	26	27
Harbin, China 160 m	6	5	10	23	43	94	112	104	46	33	8	5	488
	-18	-15	-5	6	13	19	22	21	14	4	-6	-16	3

CITY	JAN.	FEB.	MAR.	APR.	MAY	JUNE	JULY	AUG.	SEPT.	OCT.	NOV.	DEC.	YEAR
ASIA (continued)													
Ho Chi Minh, Vietnam 9 m	15	3	13	43	221	330	315	269	335	269	114	56	1,984
	26	27	29	30	29	28	28	28	27	27	27	26	28
Hong Kong, China 33 m	33	46	74	137	292	394	381	361	257	114	43	31	2,162
	16	15	18	22	26	28	28	28	27	25	21	18	23
Jakarta, Indonesia 8 m	300	300	211	147	114	97	64	43	66	112	142	203	1,798
	26	26	27	27	27	27	27	27	27	27	27	26	27
Kabul, Afghanistan 1,815 m	31	36	94	102	20	5	3	3	<3	15	20	10	338
	-3	-1	6	13	18	22	25	24	20	14	7	3	12
Karachi, Pakistan 4 m	13	10	8	3	3	18	81	41	13	<3	3	5	196
	19	20	24	28	30	31	30	29	28	28	24	20	26
Kazalinsk, Kazakstan 63 m	10	10	13	13	15	5	5	8	8	10	13	15	125
	-12	-11	-3	6	18	23	25	23	16	8	-1	-7	7
New Delhi, India 218 m	23	18	13	8	13	74	180	172	117	10	3	10	640
	14	17	23	28	33	34	31	30	29	26	20	15	25
Omsk, Russia 85 m	15	8	8	13	31	51	51	51	28	25	18	20	318
	-22	-19	-12	-1	10	16	18	16	10	1	-11	-18	-1
Shanghai, China 7 m	48	58	84	94	94	180	147	142	130	71	51	36	1,135
	4	5	9	14	20	24	28	28	23	19	12	7	16
Singapore 10 m	252	173	193	188	173	173	170	196	178	208	254	257	2,413
	26	27	28	28	28	28	28	27	27	27	27	27	27
Tehran, Iran 1,220 m	46	38	46	36	13	3	3	3	3	8	20	31	246
	2	5	9	16	21	26	30	29	25	18	12	6	17
Tokyo, Japan 6 m	48	74	107	135	147	165	142	152	234	208	97	56	1,565
	3	4	7	13	17	21	25	26	23	17	11	6	14
Ulan Bator, Mongolia 1,325 m	<3	<3	3	5	10	28	76	51	23	5	5	3	208
	-26	-21	-13	-1	6	14	16	14	8	-1	-13	-22	-3
Verkhoyansk, Russia 100 m	5	5	3	5	8	23	28	25	13	8	8	5	134
	-50	-45	-32	-15	0	12	14	9	2	-15	-38	-48	-17
AFRICA													
Addis Ababa, Ethiopia 2,450 m	<3	3	25	135	213	201	206	239	102	28	<3	0	1,151
	19	20	20	20	19	18	18	19	21	22	21	20	20
Antananarivo, Madag. 1,372 m	300	279	178	53	18	8	8	10	18	61	135	287	1,356
	21	21	21	19	18	15	14	15	17	19	21	21	19
Cairo, Egypt 116 m	5	5	5	3	3	<3	0	0	<3	<3	3	5	28
	13	15	18	21	25	28	28	28	26	24	20	15	22
Cape Town, S. Africa 17 m	15	8	18	48	79	84	89	66	43	31	18	10	508
	21	21	20	17	14	13	12	13	14	16	18	19	17
Jo'burg, S. Africa 1,665 m	114	109	89	38	25	8	8	8	23	56	107	125	709
	20	20	18	16	13	10	11	13	16	18	19	20	16

AFRICA (continued)

CITY	JAN.	FEB.	MAR.	APR.	MAY	JUNE	JULY	AUG.	SEPT.	OCT.	NOV.	DEC.	YEAR
Khartoum, Sudan	<3	<3	<3	<3	3	8	53	71	18	5	<3	0	158
390 m	24	25	28	31	33	34	32	31	32	32	28	25	29
Kinshasa, Congo (D.R.)	135	145	196	196	158	8	3	3	31	119	221	142	1,354
325 m	26	26	27	27	26	24	23	24	25	26	26	26	25
Lagos, Nigeria	28	46	102	150	269	460	279	64	140	206	69	25	1,836
3 m	27	28	29	28	28	26	26	25	26	26	28	28	27
Lusaka, Zambia	231	191	142	18	3	<3	<3	0	<3	10	91	150	836
1,277 m	21	22	21	21	19	16	16	18	22	24	23	22	21
Monrovia, Liberia	31	56	97	216	516	973	996	373	744	772	236	130	5,138
23 m	26	26	27	27	26	25	24	25	25	25	26	26	26
Nairobi, Kenya	38	64	125	211	158	46	15	23	31	53	109	86	958
820 m	19	19	19	19	18	16	16	16	18	19	18	18	18
Timbuktu, Mali	<3	<3	3	<3	5	23	79	81	38	3	<3	<3	231
301 m	22	24	28	32	34	35	32	30	32	31	28	23	29
Tunis, Tunisia	64	51	41	36	18	8	3	8	33	51	48	61	419
66 m	10	11	13	16	19	23	26	27	25	20	16	11	18
Walvis Bay, Namibia	<3	5	8	3	3	<3	<3	3	<3	<3	<3	<3	23
7 m	19	19	19	18	17	16	15	14	14	15	17	18	18

AUSTRALIA, NEW ZEALAND AND ANTARCTICA

CITY	JAN.	FEB.	MAR.	APR.	MAY	JUNE	JULY	AUG.	SEPT.	OCT.	NOV.	DEC.	YEAR
Alice Springs, Aust.	43	33	28	10	15	13	8	8	8	18	31	38	252
579 m	29	28	25	20	15	12	12	14	18	23	26	28	21
Christchurch, N.Z.	56	43	48	48	66	66	69	48	46	43	48	56	638
10 m	16	16	14	12	9	6	6	7	9	12	14	16	11
Darwin, Australia	386	312	254	97	15	3	<3	3	13	51	119	239	1,491
30 m	29	29	29	29	28	26	25	26	28	29	30	29	28
Mawson, Antarctica	11	30	20	10	44	180	4	40	3	20	0	0	362
14 m	0	−5	−10	−14	−15	−16	−18	−18	−19	−13	−5	−1	−11
Perth, Australia	8	10	20	43	130	180	170	149	86	56	20	13	881
60 m	23	23	22	19	16	14	13	13	15	16	19	22	18
Sydney, Australia	89	102	127	135	127	117	117	76	73	71	73	73	1,181
42 m	22	22	21	18	15	13	12	13	15	18	19	21	17

NORTH AMERICA

CITY	JAN.	FEB.	MAR.	APR.	MAY	JUNE	JULY	AUG.	SEPT.	OCT.	NOV.	DEC.	YEAR
Anchorage, USA	20	18	15	10	13	18	41	66	66	56	25	23	371
40 m	−11	−8	−5	2	7	12	14	13	9	2	−5	−11	2
Chicago, USA	51	51	66	71	86	89	84	81	79	66	61	51	836
251 m	−4	−3	2	9	14	20	23	22	19	12	5	−1	10
Churchill, Canada	15	13	18	23	32	44	46	58	51	43	39	21	402
13 m	−28	−26	−20	−10	−2	6	12	11	5	−2	−12	−22	−7
Edmonton, Canada	25	19	19	22	43	77	89	78	39	17	16	25	466
676 m	−15	−10	−5	4	11	15	17	16	11	6	−4	−10	3
Honolulu, USA	104	66	79	48	25	18	23	28	36	48	64	104	643
12 m	23	18	19	20	22	24	25	26	26	24	22	19	22
Houston, USA	89	76	84	91	119	117	99	99	104	94	89	109	1,171
12 m	12	13	17	21	24	27	28	29	26	22	16	12	21

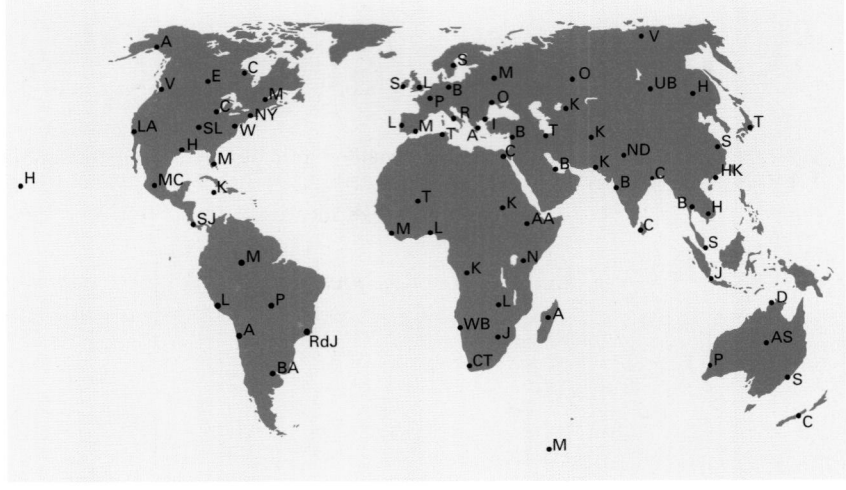

NORTH AMERICA (continued)

CITY	JAN.	FEB.	MAR.	APR.	MAY	JUNE	JULY	AUG.	SEPT.	OCT.	NOV.	DEC.	YEAR
Kingston, Jamaica	23	15	23	31	102	89	38	91	99	180	74	36	800
34 m	25	25	25	26	26	28	28	28	27	27	26	26	26
Los Angeles, USA	79	76	71	25	10	3	<3	<3	5	15	31	66	381
95 m	13	14	14	16	17	19	21	22	21	18	16	14	17
Mexico City, Mexico	13	5	10	20	53	119	170	152	130	51	18	8	747
2,309 m	12	13	16	18	19	19	17	18	18	16	14	13	16
Miami, USA	71	53	64	81	173	178	155	160	203	234	71	51	1,516
8 m	20	20	22	23	25	27	28	28	27	25	22	21	24
Montréal, Canada	72	65	74	74	66	82	90	92	88	76	81	87	946
57 m	−10	−9	−3	−6	13	18	21	20	15	9	2	−7	6
New York City, USA	94	97	91	81	81	84	107	109	86	89	76	91	1,092
96 m	−1	−1	3	10	16	20	23	23	21	15	7	2	11
St Louis, USA	58	64	89	97	114	114	89	86	81	74	71	64	1,001
173 m	0	1	7	13	19	24	26	26	22	15	8	2	14
San José, Costa Rica	15	5	20	46	229	241	211	241	305	300	145	41	1,798
1,146 m	19	19	21	21	22	21	21	21	21	20	20	19	20
Vancouver, Canada	154	115	101	60	52	45	32	41	67	114	150	182	1,113
14 m	3	5	6	9	12	15	17	17	14	10	6	4	10
Washington, DC, USA	86	76	91	84	94	99	112	109	94	74	66	79	1,064
22 m	1	2	7	12	18	23	25	24	20	14	8	3	13

SOUTH AMERICA

CITY	JAN.	FEB.	MAR.	APR.	MAY	JUNE	JULY	AUG.	SEPT.	OCT.	NOV.	DEC.	YEAR
Antofagasta, Chile	0	0	0	<3	<3	3	5	3	<3	3	<3	0	13
94 m	21	21	20	18	16	15	14	14	15	16	18	19	17
Buenos Aires, Arg.	79	71	109	89	76	61	56	61	79	86	84	99	950
27 m	23	23	21	17	13	9	10	11	13	15	19	22	16
Lima, Peru	3	<3	<3	<3	5	5	8	8	8	3	3	<3	41
120 m	23	24	24	22	19	17	17	16	17	18	19	21	20
Manaus, Brazil	249	231	262	221	170	84	58	38	46	107	142	203	1,811
44 m	28	28	28	27	28	28	28	28	29	29	29	28	28
Paraná, Brazil	287	236	239	102	13	<3	3	5	28	127	231	310	1,582
260 m	23	23	23	23	23	21	22	24	24	24	24	23	23
Rio de Janeiro, Brazil	125	122	130	107	79	53	41	43	66	79	104	137	1,082
61 m	26	26	25	24	22	21	21	21	21	22	23	25	23

World Statistics: Physical Dimensions

Each topic list is divided into continents and within a continent the items are listed in order of size. The bottom part of many of the lists is selective in order to give examples from as many different countries as possible. The order of the continents is as in the atlas, Europe through to South America. The world top ten are shown in square brackets; in the case of mountains this has not been done because the world top 30 are all in Asia. The figures are rounded as appropriate.

WORLD, CONTINENTS, OCEANS

THE WORLD	km²	miles²	%
The World	509,450,000	196,672,000	–
Land	149,450,000	57,688,000	29.3
Water	360,000,000	138,984,000	70.7
Asia	44,500,000	17,177,000	29.8
Africa	30,302,000	11,697,000	20.3
North America	24,241,000	9,357,000	16.2
South America	17,793,000	6,868,000	11.9
Antarctica	14,100,000	5,443,000	9.4
Europe	9,957,000	3,843,000	6.7
Australia & Oceania	8,557,000	3,303,000	5.7
Pacific Ocean	179,679,000	69,356,000	49.9
Atlantic Ocean	92,373,000	35,657,000	25.7
Indian Ocean	73,917,000	28,532,000	20.5
Arctic Ocean	14,090,000	5,439,000	3.9

SEAS

PACIFIC	km²	miles²
South China Sea	2,974,600	1,148,500
Bering Sea	2,268,000	875,000
Sea of Okhotsk	1,528,000	590,000
East China & Yellow	1,249,000	482,000
Sea of Japan	1,008,000	389,000
Gulf of California	162,000	62,500
Bass Strait	75,000	29,000

ATLANTIC	km²	miles²
Caribbean Sea	2,766,000	1,068,000
Mediterranean Sea	2,516,000	971,000
Gulf of Mexico	1,543,000	596,000
Hudson Bay	1,232,000	476,000
North Sea	575,000	223,000
Black Sea	462,000	178,000
Baltic Sea	422,170	163,000
Gulf of St Lawrence	238,000	92,000

INDIAN	km²	miles²
Red Sea	438,000	169,000
The Gulf	239,000	92,000

MOUNTAINS

EUROPE		m	ft
Elbrus	Russia	5,642	18,510
Mont Blanc	France/Italy	4,807	15,771
Monte Rosa	Italy/Switzerland	4,634	15,203
Dom	Switzerland	4,545	14,911
Liskamm	Switzerland	4,527	14,852
Weisshorn	Switzerland	4,505	14,780
Taschorn	Switzerland	4,490	14,730
Matterhorn/Cervino	Italy/Switz.	4,478	14,691
Mont Maudit	France/Italy	4,465	14,649
Dent Blanche	Switzerland	4,356	14,291
Nadelhorn	Switzerland	4,327	14,196
Grandes Jorasses	France/Italy	4,208	13,806
Jungfrau	Switzerland	4,158	13,642
Barre des Ecrins	France	4,103	13,461
Gran Paradiso	Italy	4,061	13,323
Piz Bernina	Italy/Switzerland	4,049	13,284
Eiger	Switzerland	3,970	13,025
Monte Viso	Italy	3,841	12,602
Grossglockner	Austria	3,797	12,457
Wildspitze	Austria	3,772	12,382
Monte Disgrazia	Italy	3,678	12,066
Mulhacén	Spain	3,478	11,411
Pico de Aneto	Spain	3,404	11,168
Marmolada	Italy	3,342	10,964
Etna	Italy	3,340	10,958
Zugspitze	Germany	2,962	9,718
Musala	Bulgaria	2,925	9,596
Olympus	Greece	2,917	9,570
Triglav	Slovenia	2,863	9,393
Monte Cinto	France (Corsica)	2,710	8,891
Galdhøpiggen	Norway	2,468	8,100
Ben Nevis	UK	1,343	4,406

ASIA		m	ft
Everest	China/Nepal	8,850	29,035
K2 (Godwin Austen)	China/Kashmir	8,611	28,251
Kanchenjunga	India/Nepal	8,598	28,208
Lhotse	China/Nepal	8,516	27,939
Makalu	China/Nepal	8,481	27,824
Cho Oyu	China/Nepal	8,201	26,906
Dhaulagiri	Nepal	8,172	26,811
Manaslu	Nepal	8,156	26,758
Nanga Parbat	Kashmir	8,126	26,660
Annapurna	Nepal	8,078	26,502
Gasherbrum	China/Kashmir	8,068	26,469
Broad Peak	China/Kashmir	8,051	26,414
Xixabangma	China	8,012	26,286
Kangbachen	India/Nepal	7,902	25,925
Jannu	India/Nepal	7,902	25,925
Gayachung Kang	Nepal	7,897	25,909
Himalchuli	Nepal	7,893	25,896
Disteghil Sar	Kashmir	7,885	25,869
Nuptse	Nepal	7,879	25,849
Khunyang Chhish	Kashmir	7,852	25,761
Masherbrum	Kashmir	7,821	25,659
Nanda Devi	India	7,817	25,646
Rakaposhi	Kashmir	7,788	25,551
Batura	Kashmir	7,785	25,541
Namche Barwa	China	7,756	25,446
Kamet	India	7,756	25,446
Soltoro Kangri	Kashmir	7,742	25,400
Gurla Mandhata	China	7,728	25,354
Trivor	Pakistan	7,720	25,328
Kongur Shan	China	7,719	25,324
Tirich Mir	Pakistan	7,690	25,229
K'ula Shan	Bhutan/China	7,543	24,747
Pik Kommunizma	Tajikistan	7,495	24,590
Demavend	Iran	5,604	18,386
Ararat	Turkey	5,165	16,945
Gunong Kinabalu	Malaysia (Borneo)	4,101	13,455
Yu Shan	Taiwan	3,997	13,113
Fuji-San	Japan	3,776	12,388

AFRICA		m	ft
Kilimanjaro	Tanzania	5,895	19,340
Mt Kenya	Kenya	5,199	17,057
Ruwenzori			
(Margherita)	Uganda/Congo (D.R.)	5,109	16,762
Ras Dashan	Ethiopia	4,620	15,157
Meru	Tanzania	4,565	14,977
Karisimbi	Rwanda/Congo (D.R.)	4,507	14,787
Mt Elgon	Kenya/Uganda	4,321	14,176
Batu	Ethiopia	4,307	14,130
Guna	Ethiopia	4,231	13,882
Toubkal	Morocco	4,165	13,665
Irhil Mgoun	Morocco	4,071	13,356
Mt Cameroon	Cameroon	4,070	13,353
Amba Ferit	Ethiopia	3,875	13,042
Pico del Teide	Spain (Tenerife)	3,718	12,198
Thabana Ntlenyana	Lesotho	3,482	11,424
Emi Koussi	Chad	3,415	11,204
Mt aux Sources	Lesotho/S. Africa	3,282	10,768
Mt Piton	Réunion	3,069	10,069

OCEANIA		m	ft
Puncak Jaya	Indonesia	5,029	16,499
Puncak Trikora	Indonesia	4,750	15,584
Puncak Mandala	Indonesia	4,702	15,427
Mt Wilhelm	Papua NG	4,508	14,790
Mauna Kea	USA (Hawaii)	4,205	13,796
Mauna Loa	USA (Hawaii)	4,169	13,681
Mt Cook (Aoraki)	New Zealand	3,753	12,313
Mt Balbi	Solomon Is.	2,439	8,002
Orohena	Tahiti	2,241	7,352
Mt Kosciuszko	Australia	2,237	7,339

NORTH AMERICA		m	ft
Mt McKinley			
(Denali)	USA (Alaska)	6,194	20,321
Mt Logan	Canada	5,959	19,551
Citlaltepetl	Mexico	5,700	18,701
Mt St Elias	USA/Canada	5,489	18,008
Popocatepetl	Mexico	5,452	17,887

NORTH AMERICA (continued)		m	ft
Mt Foraker	USA (Alaska)	5,304	17,401
Ixtaccihuatl	Mexico	5,286	17,342
Lucania	Canada	5,227	17,149
Mt Steele	Canada	5,073	16,644
Mt Bona	USA (Alaska)	5,005	16,420
Mt Blackburn	USA (Alaska)	4,996	16,391
Mt Sanford	USA (Alaska)	4,940	16,207
Mt Wood	Canada	4,848	15,905
Nevado de Toluca	Mexico	4,670	15,321
Mt Fairweather	USA (Alaska)	4,663	15,298
Mt Hunter	USA (Alaska)	4,442	14,573
Mt Whitney	USA	4,418	14,495
Mt Elbert	USA	4,399	14,432
Mt Harvard	USA	4,395	14,419
Mt Rainier	USA	4,392	14,409
Blanca Peak	USA	4,372	14,344
Longs Peak	USA	4,345	14,255
Tajumulco	Guatemala	4,220	13,845
Grand Teton	USA	4,197	13,770
Mt Waddington	Canada	3,994	13,104
Mt Robson	Canada	3,954	12,972
Chirripó Grande	Costa Rica	3,837	12,589
Pico Duarte	Dominican Rep.	3,175	10,417

SOUTH AMERICA		m	ft
Aconcagua	Argentina	6,960	22,834
Bonete	Argentina	6,872	22,546
Ojos del Salado	Argentina/Chile	6,863	22,516
Pissis	Argentina	6,779	22,241
Mercedario	Argentina/Chile	6,770	22,211
Huascaran	Peru	6,768	22,204
Llullaillaco	Argentina/Chile	6,723	22,057
Nudo de Cachi	Argentina	6,720	22,047
Yerupaja	Peru	6,632	21,758
N. de Tres Cruces	Argentina/Chile	6,620	21,719
Incahuasi	Argentina/Chile	6,601	21,654
Cerro Galan	Argentina	6,600	21,654
Tupungato	Argentina/Chile	6,570	21,555
Sajama	Bolivia	6,542	21,463
Illimani	Bolivia	6,485	21,276
Coropuna	Peru	6,425	21,079
Ausangate	Peru	6,384	20,945
Cerro del Toro	Argentina	6,380	20,932
Siula Grande	Peru	6,356	20,853
Chimborazo	Ecuador	6,267	20,561
Alpamayo	Peru	5,947	19,511
Cotapaxi	Ecuador	5,896	19,344
Pico Colon	Colombia	5,800	19,029
Pico Bolivar	Venezuela	5,007	16,427

ANTARCTICA		m	ft
Vinson Massif		4,897	16,066
Mt Kirkpatrick		4,528	14,855
Mt Markham		4,349	14,268

OCEAN DEPTHS

ATLANTIC OCEAN	m	ft	
Puerto Rico (Milwaukee) Deep	9,220	30,249	[7]
Cayman Trench	7,680	25,197	[10]
Gulf of Mexico	5,203	17,070	
Mediterranean Sea	5,121	16,801	
Black Sea	2,211	7,254	
North Sea	660	2,165	
Baltic Sea	463	1,519	
Hudson Bay	258	846	

INDIAN OCEAN	m	ft
Java Trench	7,450	24,442
Red Sea	2,635	8,454
Persian Gulf	73	239

PACIFIC OCEAN	m	ft	
Mariana Trench	11,022	36,161	[1]
Tonga Trench	10,882	35,702	[2]
Japan Trench	10,554	34,626	[3]
Kuril Trench	10,542	34,587	[4]
Mindanao Trench	10,497	34,439	[5]
Kermadec Trench	10,047	32,962	[6]

PACIFIC OCEAN (continued)

		m	ft	
Peru–Chile Trench		8,050	26,410	[8]
Aleutian Trench		7,822	25,662	[9]

ARCTIC OCEAN

		m	ft
Molloy Deep		5,608	18,399

LAND LOWS

		m	ft
Dead Sea	Asia	−411	−1,348
Lake Assal	Africa	−156	−512
Death Valley	N. America	−86	−282
Valdés Peninsula	S. America	−40	−131
Caspian Sea	Europe	−28	−92
Lake Eyre North	Oceania	−16	−52

RIVERS

EUROPE

		km	miles	
Volga	Caspian Sea	3,700	2,300	
Danube	Black Sea	2,850	1,770	
Ural	Caspian Sea	2,535	1,575	
Dnepr (Dnipro)	Black Sea	2,285	1,420	
Kama	Volga	2,030	1,260	
Don	Black Sea	1,990	1,240	
Petchora	Arctic Ocean	1,790	1,110	
Oka	Volga	1,480	920	
Belaya	Kama	1,420	880	
Dnister (Dniester)	Black Sea	1,400	870	
Vyatka	Kama	1,370	850	
Rhine	North Sea	1,320	820	
N. Dvina	Arctic Ocean	1,290	800	
Desna	Dnepr (Dnipro)	1,190	740	
Elbe	North Sea	1,145	710	
Wisla	Baltic Sea	1,090	675	
Loire	Atlantic Ocean	1,020	635	

ASIA

		km	miles	
Yangtze	Pacific Ocean	6,380	3,960	[3]
Yenisey–Angara	Arctic Ocean	5,550	3,445	[5]
Huang He	Pacific Ocean	5,464	3,395	[6]
Ob–Irtysh	Arctic Ocean	5,410	3,360	[7]
Mekong	Pacific Ocean	4,500	2,795	[9]
Amur	Pacific Ocean	4,400	2,730	[10]
Lena	Arctic Ocean	4,400	2,730	
Irtysh	Ob	4,250	2,640	
Yenisey	Arctic Ocean	4,090	2,540	
Ob	Arctic Ocean	3,680	2,285	
Indus	Indian Ocean	3,100	1,925	
Brahmaputra	Indian Ocean	2,900	1,800	
Syrdarya	Aral Sea	2,860	1,775	
Salween	Indian Ocean	2,800	1,740	
Euphrates	Indian Ocean	2,700	1,675	
Vilyuy	Lena	2,650	1,645	
Kolyma	Arctic Ocean	2,600	1,615	
Amudarya	Aral Sea	2,540	1,575	
Ural	Caspian Sea	2,535	1,575	
Ganges	Indian Ocean	2,510	1,560	
Si Kiang	Pacific Ocean	2,100	1,305	
Irrawaddy	Indian Ocean	2,010	1,250	
Tarim–Yarkand	Lop Nor	2,000	1,240	
Tigris	Indian Ocean	1,900	1,180	

AFRICA

		km	miles	
Nile	Mediterranean	6,670	4,140	[1]
Congo	Atlantic Ocean	4,670	2,900	[8]
Niger	Atlantic Ocean	4,180	2,595	
Zambezi	Indian Ocean	3,540	2,200	
Oubangi/Uele	Congo (D.R.)	2,250	1,400	
Kasai	Congo (D.R.)	1,950	1,210	
Shaballe	Indian Ocean	1,930	1,200	
Orange	Atlantic Ocean	1,860	1,155	
Cubango	Okavango Swamps	1,800	1,120	
Limpopo	Indian Ocean	1,600	995	
Senegal	Atlantic Ocean	1,600	995	
Volta	Atlantic Ocean	1,500	930	

AUSTRALIA

		km	miles
Murray–Darling	Indian Ocean	3,750	2,330
Darling	Murray	3,070	1,905
Murray	Indian Ocean	2,575	1,600
Murrumbidgee	Murray	1,690	1,050

NORTH AMERICA

		km	miles	
Mississippi–Missouri	Gulf of Mexico	6,020	3,740	[4]
Mackenzie	Arctic Ocean	4,240	2,630	
Mississippi	Gulf of Mexico	3,780	2,350	
Missouri	Mississippi	3,780	2,350	
Yukon	Pacific Ocean	3,185	1,980	
Rio Grande	Gulf of Mexico	3,030	1,880	

NORTH AMERICA (continued)

		km	miles
Arkansas	Mississippi	2,340	1,450
Colorado	Pacific Ocean	2,330	1,445
Red	Mississippi	2,040	1,270
Columbia	Pacific Ocean	1,950	1,210
Saskatchewan	Lake Winnipeg	1,940	1,205
Snake	Columbia	1,670	1,040
Churchill	Hudson Bay	1,600	990
Ohio	Mississippi	1,580	980
Brazos	Gulf of Mexico	1,400	870
St Lawrence	Atlantic Ocean	1,170	730

SOUTH AMERICA

		km	miles	
Amazon	Atlantic Ocean	6,450	4,010	[2]
Paraná–Plate	Atlantic Ocean	4,500	2,800	
Purus	Amazon	3,350	2,080	
Madeira	Amazon	3,200	1,990	
São Francisco	Atlantic Ocean	2,900	1,800	
Paraná	Plate	2,800	1,740	
Tocantins	Atlantic Ocean	2,750	1,710	
Paraguay	Paraná	2,550	1,580	
Orinoco	Atlantic Ocean	2,500	1,550	
Pilcomayo	Paraná	2,500	1,550	
Araguaia	Tocantins	2,250	1,400	
Juruá	Amazon	2,000	1,240	
Xingu	Amazon	1,980	1,230	
Ucayali	Amazon	1,900	1,180	
Marañón	Amazon	1,600	990	
Uruguay	Plate	1,600	990	

LAKES

EUROPE

		km²	miles²
Lake Ladoga	Russia	17,700	6,800
Lake Onega	Russia	9,700	3,700
Saimaa system	Finland	8,000	3,100
Vänern	Sweden	5,500	2,100
Rybinskoye Res.	Russia	4,700	1,800

ASIA

		km²	miles²	
Caspian Sea	Asia	371,800	143,550	[1]
Lake Baykal	Russia	30,500	11,780	[8]
Aral Sea	Kazakhstan/Uzbekistan	28,687	11,086	[10]
Tonlé Sap	Cambodia	20,000	7,700	
Lake Balqash	Kazakhstan	18,500	7,100	
Lake Dongting	China	12,000	4,600	
Lake Ysyk	Kyrgyzstan	6,200	2,400	
Lake Orumiyeh	Iran	5,900	2,300	
Lake Koko	China	5,700	2,200	
Lake Poyang	China	5,000	1,900	
Lake Khanka	China/Russia	4,400	1,700	
Lake Van	Turkey	3,500	1,400	

AFRICA

		km²	miles²	
Lake Victoria	E. Africa	68,000	26,000	[3]
Lake Tanganyika	C. Africa	33,000	13,000	[6]
Lake Malawi/Nyasa	E. Africa	29,600	11,430	[9]
Lake Chad	C. Africa	25,000	9,700	
Lake Turkana	Ethiopia/Kenya	8,500	3,300	
Lake Volta	Ghana	8,500	3,300	
Lake Bangweulu	Zambia	8,000	3,100	
Lake Rukwa	Tanzania	7,000	2,700	
Lake Mai-Ndombe	Congo (D.R.)	6,500	2,500	
Lake Kariba	Zambia/Zimbabwe	5,300	2,000	
Lake Albert	Uganda/Congo (D.R.)	5,300	2,000	
Lake Nasser	Egypt/Sudan	5,200	2,000	
Lake Mweru	Zambia/Congo (D.R.)	4,900	1,900	
Lake Cabora Bassa	Mozambique	4,500	1,700	
Lake Kyoga	Uganda	4,400	1,700	
Lake Tana	Ethiopia	3,630	1,400	

AUSTRALIA

		km²	miles²
Lake Eyre	Australia	8,900	3,400
Lake Torrens	Australia	5,800	2,200
Lake Gairdner	Australia	4,800	1,900

NORTH AMERICA

		km²	miles²	
Lake Superior	Canada/USA	82,350	31,800	[2]
Lake Huron	Canada/USA	59,600	23,010	[4]
Lake Michigan	USA	58,000	22,400	[5]
Great Bear Lake	Canada	31,800	12,280	[7]
Great Slave Lake	Canada	28,500	11,000	
Lake Erie	Canada/USA	25,700	9,900	
Lake Winnipeg	Canada	24,400	9,400	
Lake Ontario	Canada/USA	19,500	7,500	
Lake Nicaragua	Nicaragua	8,200	3,200	
Lake Athabasca	Canada	8,100	3,100	
Smallwood Reservoir	Canada	6,530	2,520	
Reindeer Lake	Canada	6,400	2,500	
Nettilling Lake	Canada	5,500	2,100	
Lake Winnipegosis	Canada	5,400	2,100	

SOUTH AMERICA

		km²	miles²
Lake Titicaca	Bolivia/Peru	8,300	3,200
Lake Poopo	Bolivia	2,800	1,100

ISLANDS

EUROPE

		km²	miles²	
Great Britain	UK	229,880	88,700	[8]
Iceland	Atlantic Ocean	103,000	39,800	
Ireland	Ireland/UK	84,400	32,600	
Novaya Zemlya (N.)	Russia	48,200	18,600	
W. Spitzbergen	Norway	39,000	15,100	
Novaya Zemlya (S.)	Russia	33,200	12,800	
Sicily	Italy	25,500	9,800	
Sardinia	Italy	24,000	9,300	
N.E. Spitzbergen	Norway	15,000	5,600	
Corsica	France	8,700	3,400	
Crete	Greece	8,350	3,200	
Zealand	Denmark	6,850	2,600	

ASIA

		km²	miles²	
Borneo	S. E. Asia	744,360	287,400	[3]
Sumatra	Indonesia	473,600	182,860	[6]
Honshu	Japan	230,500	88,980	[7]
Sulawesi (Celebes)	Indonesia	189,000	73,000	
Java	Indonesia	126,700	48,900	
Luzon	Philippines	104,700	40,400	
Mindanao	Philippines	101,500	39,200	
Hokkaido	Japan	78,400	30,300	
Sakhalin	Russia	74,060	28,600	
Sri Lanka	Indian Ocean	65,600	25,300	
Taiwan	Pacific Ocean	36,000	13,900	
Kyushu	Japan	35,700	13,800	
Hainan	China	34,000	13,100	
Timor	Indonesia	33,600	13,000	
Shikoku	Japan	18,800	7,300	
Halmahera	Indonesia	18,000	6,900	
Ceram	Indonesia	17,150	6,600	
Sumbawa	Indonesia	15,450	6,000	
Flores	Indonesia	15,200	5,900	
Samar	Philippines	13,100	5,100	
Negros	Philippines	12,700	4,900	
Bangka	Indonesia	12,000	4,600	
Palawan	Philippines	12,000	4,600	
Panay	Philippines	11,500	4,400	
Sumba	Indonesia	11,100	4,300	
Mindoro	Philippines	9,750	3,800	

AFRICA

		km²	miles²	
Madagascar	Indian Ocean	587,040	226,660	[4]
Socotra	Indian Ocean	3,600	1,400	
Réunion	Indian Ocean	2,500	965	
Tenerife	Atlantic Ocean	2,350	900	
Mauritius	Indian Ocean	1,865	720	

OCEANIA

		km²	miles²	
New Guinea	Indon./Papua NG	821,030	317,000	[2]
New Zealand (S.)	Pacific Ocean	150,500	58,100	
New Zealand (N.)	Pacific Ocean	114,700	44,300	
Tasmania	Australia	67,800	26,200	
New Britain	Papua NG	37,800	14,600	
New Caledonia	Pacific Ocean	19,100	7,400	
Viti Levu	Fiji	10,500	4,100	
Hawaii	Pacific Ocean	10,450	4,000	
Bougainville	Papua NG	9,600	3,700	
Guadalcanal	Solomon Is.	6,500	2,500	
Vanua Levu	Fiji	5,550	2,100	
New Ireland	Papua NG	3,200	1,200	

NORTH AMERICA

		km²	miles²	
Greenland	Atlantic Ocean	2,175,600	839,800	[1]
Baffin Is.	Canada	508,000	196,100	[5]
Victoria Is.	Canada	212,200	81,900	[9]
Ellesmere Is.	Canada	212,000	81,800	[10]
Cuba	Caribbean Sea	110,860	42,800	
Newfoundland	Canada	110,680	42,700	
Hispaniola	Dom. Rep./Haiti	76,200	29,400	
Banks Is.	Canada	67,000	25,900	
Devon Is.	Canada	54,500	21,000	
Melville Is.	Canada	42,400	16,400	
Vancouver Is.	Canada	32,150	12,400	
Somerset Is.	Canada	24,300	9,400	
Jamaica	Caribbean Sea	11,400	4,400	
Puerto Rico	Atlantic Ocean	8,900	3,400	
Cape Breton Is.	Canada	4,000	1,500	

SOUTH AMERICA

		km²	miles²
Tierra del Fuego	Argentina/Chile	47,000	18,100
Falkland Is. (East)	Atlantic Ocean	6,800	2,600
South Georgia	Atlantic Ocean	4,200	1,600
Galapagos (Isabela)	Pacific Ocean	2,250	870

World: Regions in the News

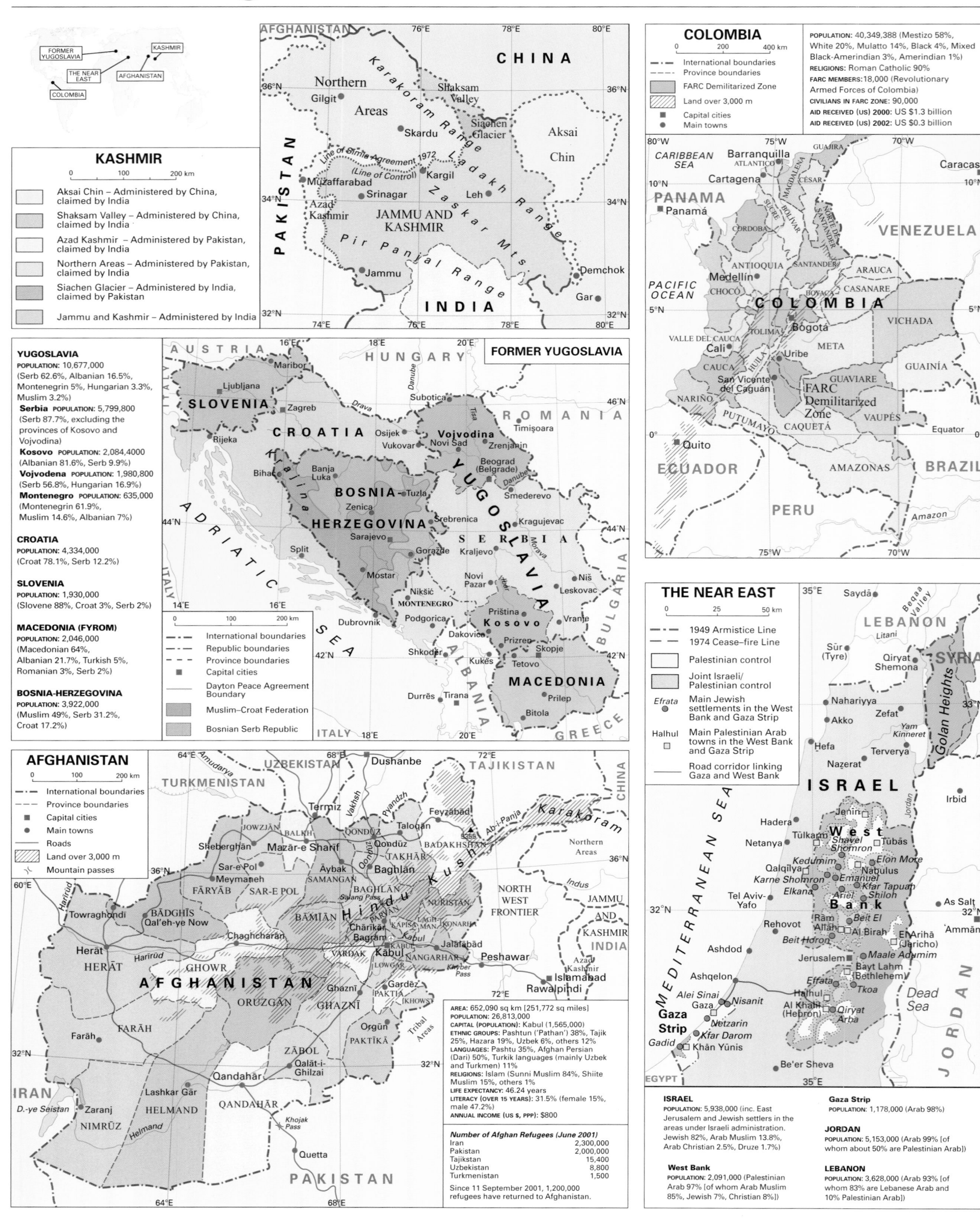

KASHMIR

0   100   200 km

- Aksai Chin – Administered by China, claimed by India
- Shaksam Valley – Administered by China, claimed by India
- Azad Kashmir – Administered by Pakistan, claimed by India
- Northern Areas – Administered by Pakistan, claimed by India
- Siachen Glacier – Administered by India, claimed by Pakistan
- Jammu and Kashmir – Administered by India

COLOMBIA

0   200   400 km

- —·—· International boundaries
- –––– Province boundaries
- FARC Demilitarized Zone
- Land over 3,000 m
- ■ Capital cities
- ● Main towns

POPULATION: 40,349,388 (Mestizo 58%, White 20%, Mulatto 14%, Black 4%, Mixed Black-Amerindian 3%, Amerindian 1%)
RELIGIONS: Roman Catholic 90%
FARC MEMBERS: 18,000 (Revolutionary Armed Forces of Colombia)
CIVILIANS IN FARC ZONE: 90,000
AID RECEIVED (US) 2000: US $1.3 billion
AID RECEIVED (US) 2002: US $0.3 billion

YUGOSLAVIA
POPULATION: 10,677,000
(Serb 62.6%, Albanian 16.5%, Montenegrin 5%, Hungarian 3.3%, Muslim 3.2%)
Serbia POPULATION: 5,799,800
(Serb 87.7%, excluding the provinces of Kosovo and Vojvodina)
Kosovo POPULATION: 2,084,4000
(Albanian 81.6%, Serb 9.9%)
Vojvodena POPULATION: 1,980,800
(Serb 56.8%, Hungarian 16.9%)
Montenegro POPULATION: 635,000
(Montenegrin 61.9%, Muslim 14.6%, Albanian 7%)

CROATIA
POPULATION: 4,334,000
(Croat 78.1%, Serb 12.2%)

SLOVENIA
POPULATION: 1,930,000
(Slovene 88%, Croat 3%, Serb 2%)

MACEDONIA (FYROM)
POPULATION: 2,046,000
(Macedonian 64%, Albanian 21.7%, Turkish 5%, Romanian 3%, Serb 2%)

BOSNIA-HERZEGOVINA
POPULATION: 3,922,000
(Muslim 49%, Serb 31.2%, Croat 17.2%)

FORMER YUGOSLAVIA

0   100   200 km

- —·—· International boundaries
- –··–··– Republic boundaries
- –––– Province boundaries
- ■ Capital cities
- ——— Dayton Peace Agreement Boundary
- Muslim–Croat Federation
- Bosnian Serb Republic

THE NEAR EAST

0   25   50 km

- –·–·– 1949 Armistice Line
- –––– 1974 Cease-fire Line
- Palestinian control
- Joint Israeli/Palestinian control
- *Efrata* ● Main Jewish settlements in the West Bank and Gaza Strip
- *Halhul* □ Main Palestinian Arab towns in the West Bank and Gaza Strip
- ——— Road corridor linking Gaza and West Bank

AFGHANISTAN

0   100   200 km

- —·—· International boundaries
- –––– Province boundaries
- ■ Capital cities
- ● Main towns
- ——— Roads
- Land over 3,000 m
- Mountain passes

AREA: 652,090 sq km [251,772 sq miles]
POPULATION: 26,813,000
CAPITAL (POPULATION): Kabul (1,565,000)
ETHNIC GROUPS: Pashtun ('Pathan') 38%, Tajik 25%, Hazara 19%, Uzbek 6%, others 12%
LANGUAGES: Pashtu 35%, Afghan Persian (Dari) 50%, Turkik languages (mainly Uzbek and Turkmen) 11%
RELIGIONS: Islam (Sunni Muslim 84%, Shiite Muslim 15%, others 1%)
LIFE EXPECTANCY: 46.24 years
LITERACY (OVER 15 YEARS): 31.5% (female 15%, male 47.2%)
ANNUAL INCOME (US $, PPP): $800

Number of Afghan Refugees (June 2001)

Iran	2,300,000
Pakistan	2,000,000
Tajikstan	15,400
Uzbekistan	8,800
Turkmenistan	1,500

Since 11 September 2001, 1,200,000 refugees have returned to Afghanistan.

ISRAEL
POPULATION: 5,938,000 (inc. East Jerusalem and Jewish settlers in the areas under Israeli administration. Jewish 82%, Arab Muslim 13.8%, Arab Christian 2.5%, Druze 1.7%)

West Bank
POPULATION: 2,091,000 (Palestinian Arab 97% [of whom Arab Muslim 85%, Jewish 7%, Christian 8%])

Gaza Strip
POPULATION: 1,178,000 (Arab 98%)

JORDAN
POPULATION: 5,153,000 (Arab 99% [of whom about 50% are Palestinian Arab])

LEBANON
POPULATION: 3,628,000 (Arab 93% [of whom 83% are Lebanese Arab and 10% Palestinian Arab])

THE EARTH
IN SPACE

THE UNIVERSE 2

STAR CHARTS AND CONSTELLATIONS 4

THE SOLAR SYSTEM 8

THE EARTH: TIME AND MOTION 10

THE EARTH FROM SPACE 12

THE DYNAMIC EARTH 14

EARTHQUAKES AND VOLCANOES 16

FORCES OF NATURE 18

OCEANS AND ICE 20

THE EARTH'S ATMOSPHERE 22

CLIMATE AND WEATHER 24

WATER AND LAND USE 26

THE NATURAL WORLD 28

THE HUMAN WORLD 30

LANGUAGES AND RELIGIONS 32

INTERNATIONAL ORGANIZATIONS 34

AGRICULTURE 36

ENERGY AND MINERALS 38

WORLD ECONOMIES 40

TRADE AND COMMERCE 42

TRAVEL AND COMMUNICATIONS 44

THE WORLD TODAY 46

The Universe

The depths of the Universe
This photograph shows some of the 1,500 or more galaxies that were recorded in the montage of photographs taken by the Hubble Space Telescope in 1995.

THE NEAREST STARS

The 20 nearest stars, excluding the Sun, with their distance from the Earth in light-years*.

Proxima Centauri	4.2
Alpha Centauri A	4.3
Alpha Centauri B	4.3
Barnard's Star	6.0
Wolf 359	7.8
Lalande 21185	8.3
Sirius A	8.7
Sirius B	8.7
UV Ceti A	8.7
UV Ceti B	8.7
Ross 154	9.4
Ross 248	10.3
Epsilon Eridani	10.7
Ross 128	10.9
61 Cygni A	11.1
61 Cygni B	11.1
Epsilon Indi	11.2
Groombridge 34 A	11.2
Groombridge 34 B	11.2
L789-6	11.2

* A light-year equals approximately 9,500 billion km [5,900 billion miles].

Just before Christmas 1995, the Hubble Space Telescope, which is in orbit about 580 km [360 miles] above the Earth, focused on a tiny area in distant space. Over a ten-day period, photographs taken by the telescope revealed unknown galaxies billions of times fainter than the human eye can see.

Because the light from these distant objects has taken so long to reach us, the photographs transmitted from the telescope and released to the media were the deepest look into space that astronomers have ever seen. The features they revealed were in existence when the Universe was less than a billion years old.

The Hubble Space Telescope is operated by the Space Telescope Science Institute in America and was launched in April 1990. The photographs it took of the Hubble Deep Field have been described by NASA as the biggest advance in astronomy since the work of the Italian scientist Galileo in the early 17th century. US scientists described these astonishing photographs as 'postcards from the edge of space and time'.

THE BIG BANG

According to research published in 2001, the Universe was created, and 'time' began, about 12,500 million (or 12.5 billion) years ago, though earlier estimates have ranged from 8 to 24 billion years. Following a colossal explosion, called the 'Big Bang', the Universe expanded in the first millionth of a second of its existence

The End of the Universe
The diagram shows two theories concerning the fate of the Universe. One theory, top, suggests that the Universe will expand indefinitely, moving into an immense dark graveyard. Another theory, bottom, suggests that the galaxies will fall back until everything is again concentrated in one point in a so-called 'Big Crunch'. This might then be followed by a new 'Big Bang'.

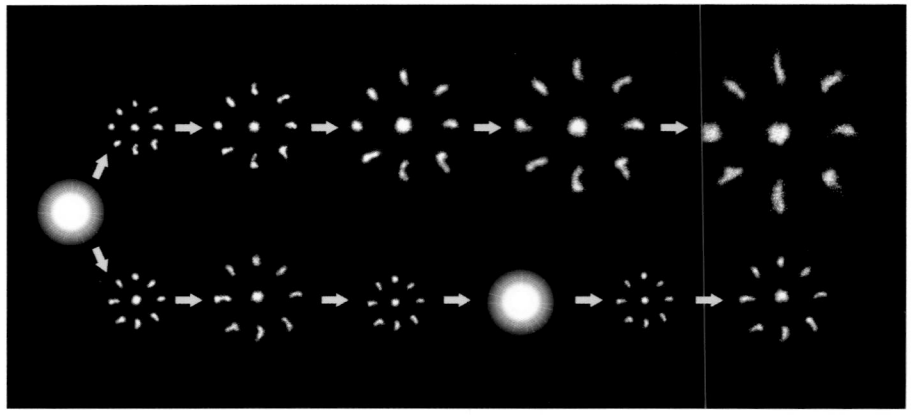

from a dimensionless point of infinite mass and density into a fireball about 30 billion km [19 million miles] across. The Universe has been expanding ever since, as demonstrated in the 1920s by Edwin Hubble, the American astronomer after whom the Hubble Space Telescope was named.

The temperature at the end of the first second was perhaps 10 billion degrees – far too hot for composite atomic nuclei to exist. As a result, the fireball consisted mainly of radiation mixed with microscopic particles of matter. Almost a million years passed before the Universe was cool enough for atoms to form.

A few billion years later, atoms in regions where matter was relatively dense began, under the influence of gravity, to move together to form proto-galaxies – masses of gas separated by empty space. The proto-galaxies were dark, because the Universe had cooled. But a few billion years later, stars began to form within the proto-galaxies as particles were drawn together. The internal pressure produced as matter condensed created the high temperatures required to cause nuclear fusion. Stars were born and later destroyed. Each generation of stars fed on the debris of extinct ones. Each generation produced larger atoms, increasing the number of different chemical elements.

The Home Galaxy
This schematic plan shows that our Solar System is located in one of the spiral arms of the Milky Way galaxy, a little less than 30,000 light-years from its centre. The centre of the Milky Way galaxy is not visible from Earth. Instead, it is masked by light-absorbing clouds of interstellar dust.

THE GALAXIES

At least a billion galaxies are scattered through the Universe, though the discoveries made by the Hubble Space Telescope suggest that there may be far more than once thought, and some estimates are as high as 100 billion. The largest galaxies contain trillions of stars, while small ones contain less than a billion.

Galaxies tend to occur in groups or clusters, while some clusters appear to be grouped in vast superclusters. Our Local Cluster includes the spiral Milky Way galaxy, whose diameter is about 100,000 light-years; one light-year, the distance that light travels in one year, measures about 9,500 billion km [5,900 billion miles]. The Milky Way is a huge galaxy, shaped like a disk with a bulge at the centre. It is larger, brighter and more massive than many other known galaxies. It contains about 100 billion stars which rotate around the centre of the galaxy in the same direction as the Sun does.

One medium-sized star in the Milky Way galaxy is the Sun. After its formation, about 5 billion years ago, there was enough leftover matter around it to create the planets, asteroids,

The Milky Way
This section of the Milky Way is dominated by Sirius, the Dog Star, top centre, in the constellation of Canis Major. Sirius is the brightest star in the sky.

moons and other bodies that together form our Solar System. The Solar System rotates around the centre of the Milky Way galaxy approximately every 225 million years.

Stars similar to our Sun are known to have planets orbiting around them. By the start of 2002, more than 70 extra-solar planets had been reported and evidence from the Hubble Space Telescope suggests that the raw materials from which planets are formed is common in dusty disks around many stars. This provokes one of the most intriguing questions that has ever faced humanity. If other planets exist in the Universe, then are they home to living organisms?

Before the time of Galileo, people thought that the Earth lay at the centre of the Universe. But we now know that our Solar System and even the Milky Way galaxy are tiny specks in the Universe as a whole. Perhaps our planet is also not unique in being the only one to support intelligent life.

Star Charts and Constellations

The Plough
The Plough, or Big Dipper, above glowing yellow clouds lit by city lights. It is part of a larger group called Ursa Major one of the best-known constellations of the northern hemisphere. The two bright stars to the lower right of the photograph (Merak and Dubhe) are known as the Pointers because they show the way to the Pole Star.

THE BRIGHTEST STARS

The 15 brightest stars visible from northern Europe. Magnitudes are given to the nearest tenth.

Sirius	−1.5
Arcturus	0.0
Vega	0.0
Capella	0.1
Rigel	0.1
Procyon	0.4
Betelgeuse	0.4
Altair	0.8
Aldebaran	0.8
Antares	1.0
Spica	1.0
Pollux	1.1
Fomalhaut	1.2
Deneb	1.2
Regulus	1.3

On a clear night, under the best conditions and far away from the glare of city lights, a person in northern Europe can look up and see about 2,500 stars. In a town, however, light pollution can reduce visibility to 200 stars or less. Over the whole celestial sphere it is possible to see about 8,500 stars with the naked eye and it is only when you look through a telescope that you begin to realize that the number of stars is countless.

SMALL AND LARGE STARS

Stars come in several sizes. Some, called neutron stars, are compact, with the same mass as the Sun but with diameters of only about 20 km [12 miles]. Larger than neutron stars are the small white dwarfs. Our Sun is a medium-sized star, but many visible stars in the night sky are giants with diameters between 10 and 100 times that of the Sun, or supergiants with diameters over 100 times that of the Sun.

Two bright stars in the constellation Orion are Betelgeuse (also known as Alpha Orionis) and Rigel (or Beta Orionis). Betelgeuse is an orange-red supergiant, whose diameter is about 400 times that of the Sun. Rigel is also a supergiant. Its diameter is about 50 times that of the Sun, but its luminosity is estimated to be over 100,000 times that of the Sun.

The stars we see in the night sky all belong to our home galaxy, the Milky Way. This name is also used for the faint, silvery band that arches across the sky. This band, a slice through our

THE CONSTELLATIONS

The constellations and their English names. Constellations visible from both hemispheres are listed.

Andromeda	Andromeda	Delphinus	Dolphin	Perseus	Perseus
Antlia	Air Pump	Dorado	Swordfish	Phoenix	Phoenix
Apus	Bird of Paradise	Draco	Dragon	Pictor	Easel
Aquarius	Water Carrier	Equuleus	Little Horse	Pisces	Fishes
Aquila	Eagle	Eridanus	River Eridanus	Piscis Austrinus	Southern Fish
Ara	Altar	Fornax	Furnace	Puppis	Ship's Stern
Aries	Ram	Gemini	Twins	Pyxis	Mariner's Compass
Auriga	Charioteer	Grus	Crane	Reticulum	Net
Boötes	Herdsman	Hercules	Hercules	Sagitta	Arrow
Caelum	Chisel	Horologium	Clock	Sagittarius	Archer
Camelopardalis	Giraffe	Hydra	Water Snake	Scorpius	Scorpion
Cancer	Crab	Hydrus	Sea Serpent	Sculptor	Sculptor
Canes Venatici	Hunting Dogs	Indus	Indian	Scutum	Shield
Canis Major	Great Dog	Lacerta	Lizard	Serpens*	Serpent
Canis Minor	Little Dog	Leo	Lion	Sextans	Sextant
Capricornus	Sea Goat	Leo Minor	Little Lion	Taurus	Bull
Carina	Ship's Keel	Lepus	Hare	Telescopium	Telescope
Cassiopeia	Cassiopeia	Libra	Scales	Triangulum	Triangle
Centaurus	Centaur	Lupus	Wolf	Triangulum Australe	
Cepheus	Cepheus	Lynx	Lynx		Southern Triangle
Cetus	Whale	Lyra	Lyre	Tucana	Toucan
Chamaeleon	Chameleon	Mensa	Table	Ursa Major	Great Bear
Circinus	Compasses	Microscopium	Microscope	Ursa Minor	Little Bear
Columba	Dove	Monoceros	Unicorn	Vela	Ship's Sails
Coma Berenices	Berenice's Hair	Musca	Fly	Virgo	Virgin
Corona Australis	Southern Crown	Norma	Level	Volans	Flying Fish
Corona Borealis	Northern Crown	Octans	Octant	Vulpecula	Fox
Corvus	Crow	Ophiuchus	Serpent Bearer		
Crater	Cup	Orion	Hunter		
Crux	Southern Cross	Pavo	Peacock	*In two halves: Serpens Caput, the*	
Cygnus	Swan	Pegasus	Winged Horse	*head, and Serpens Cauda, the tail.*	

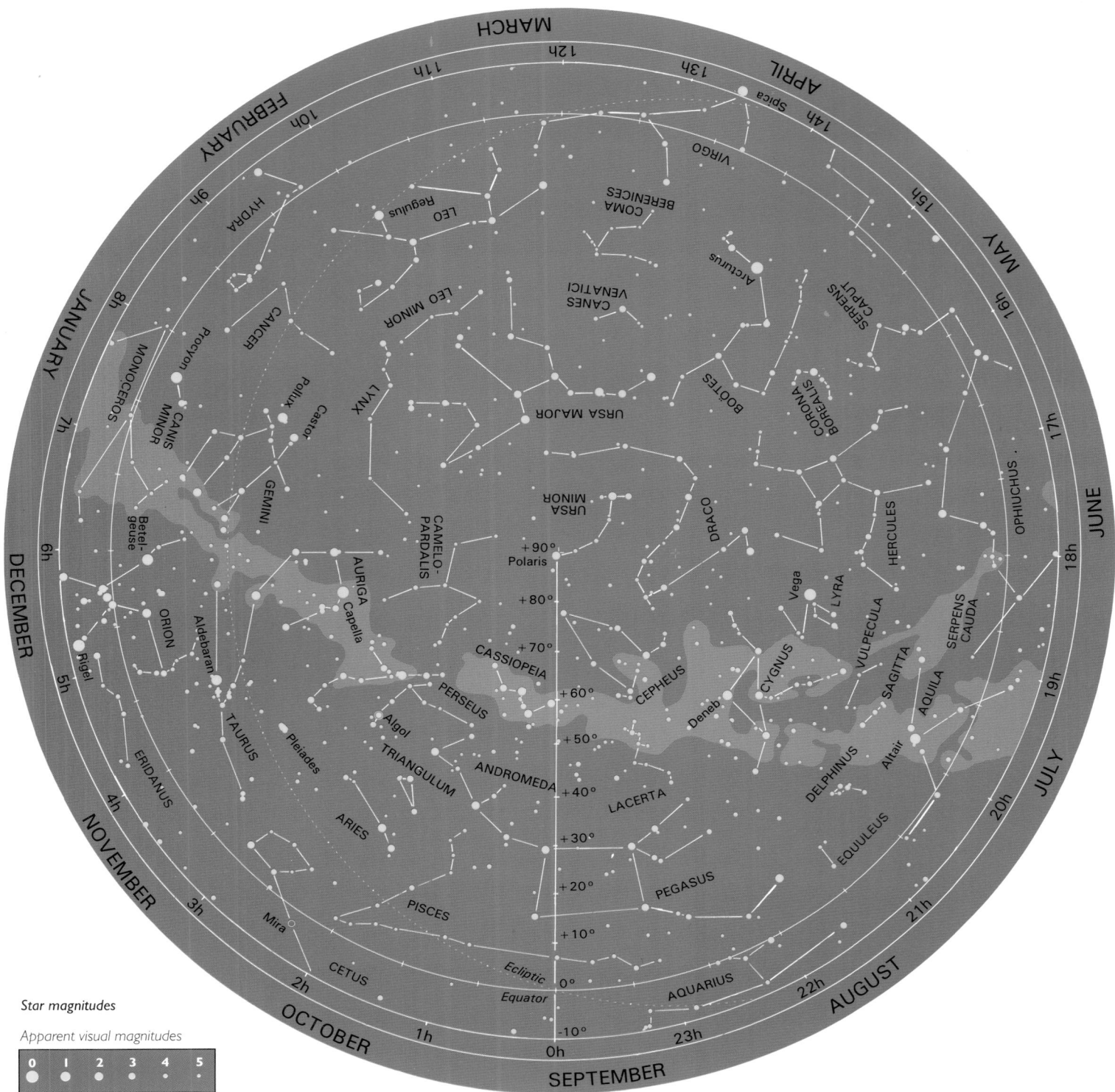

Star magnitudes

Apparent visual magnitudes

| 0 | 1 | 2 | 3 | 4 | 5 |

The Milky Way is shown in light blue on the above chart.

galaxy, contains an enormous number of stars. The nucleus of the Milky Way galaxy cannot be seen from Earth. Lying in the direction of the constellation Sagittarius in the southern hemisphere, it is masked by clouds of dust.

THE BRIGHTNESS OF STARS

Astronomers use a scale of magnitudes to measure the brightness of stars. The brightest visible to the naked eye were originally known as first-magnitude stars, ones not so bright were second-magnitude, down to the faintest visible, which were rated as sixth-magnitude. The brighter the star, the lower the magnitude. With the advent of telescopes and the development of accurate instruments for measuring brightnesses, the magnitude scale has been refined and extended.

Star chart of the northern hemisphere

When you look into the sky, the stars seem to be on the inside of a huge dome. This gives astronomers a way of mapping them. This chart shows the sky as it would appear from the North Pole. To use the star chart above, an observer in the northern hemisphere should face south and turn the chart so that the current month appears at the bottom. The chart will then show the constellations on view at approximately 11pm Greenwich Mean Time. The map should be rotated clockwise 15° for each hour before 11pm and anticlockwise for each hour after 11pm.

Very bright bodies such as Sirius, Venus and the Sun have negative magnitudes. The nearest star is Proxima Centauri, part of a multiple star system, which is 4.2 light-years away. Proxima Centauri is very faint and has a magnitude of 11.3. Alpha Centauri A, one of the two brighter members of the system, is the nearest visible star to Earth. It has a magnitude of 1.7.

These magnitudes are known as apparent magnitudes – measures of the brightnesses of the stars as they appear to us. These are the magnitudes shown on the charts on these pages. But the stars are at very different distances. The star Deneb, in the constellation Cygnus, for example, is over 1,200 light-years away. So astronomers also use absolute magnitudes – measures of how bright the stars really are. A star's absolute magnitude is the apparent magnitude it would have if it could be placed 32.6 light-years away. So Deneb, with an apparent magnitude of 1.2, has an absolute magnitude of –7.2.

The brightest star in the night sky is Sirius, the Dog Star, with a magnitude of –1.5. This medium-sized star is 8.64 light-years distant but it gives out about 20 times as much light as the Sun. After the Sun and the Moon, the brightest objects in the sky are the planets Venus, Mars and Jupiter. For example, Venus has a magnitude of up to –4. The planets have no light of their own however, and shine only because they reflect the Sun's rays. But whilst stars have fixed positions, the planets shift nightly in relation to the constellations, following a path called

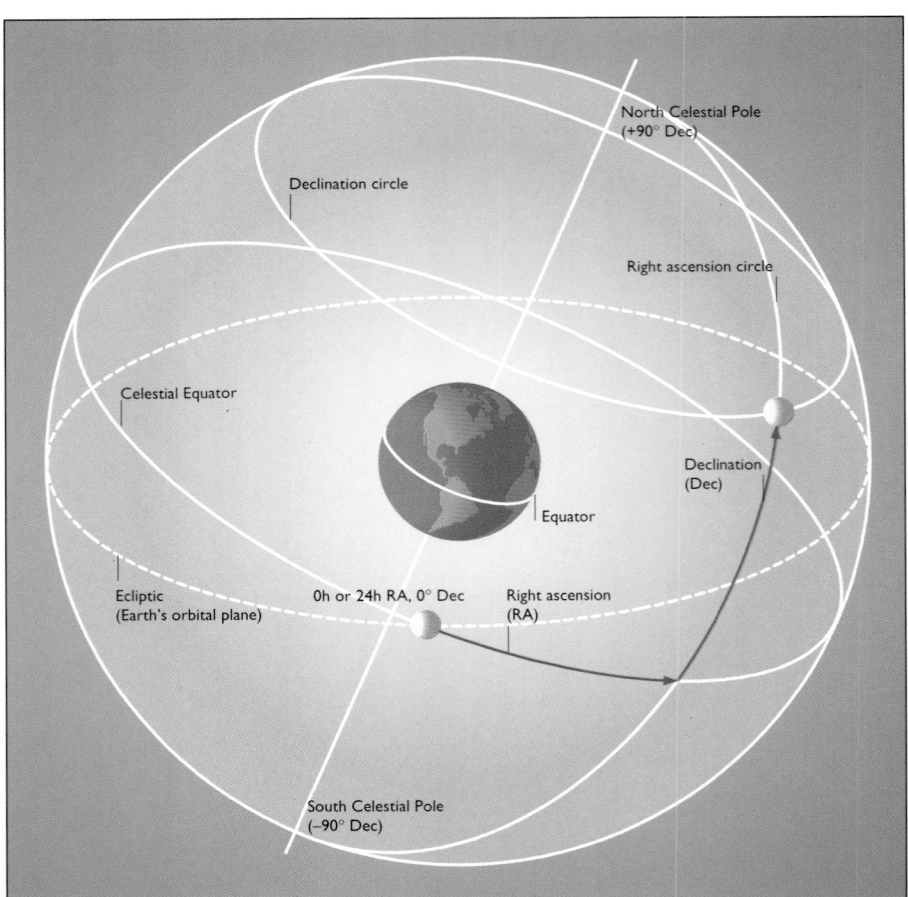

Celestial sphere

The diagram shows the imaginary surface on which astronomical positions are measured. The celestial sphere appears to rotate about the celestial poles, as though an extension of the Earth's own axis. The Earth's axis points towards the celestial poles.

the Ecliptic (shown on the star charts). As they follow their orbits around the Sun, their distances from the Earth vary, and therefore so also do their magnitudes.

While atlas maps record the details of the Earth's surface, star charts are a guide to the heavens. An observer at the Equator can see the entire sky at some time during the year, but an observer at the poles can see only the stars in a single hemisphere. As a result, star charts of both hemispheres are produced. The northern hemisphere chart is centred on the North Celestial Pole, while the southern hemisphere chart is centred on the South Celestial Pole.

In the northern hemisphere, the North Pole is marked by the star Polaris, or North Star. Polaris lies within a degree of the point where an extension of the Earth's axis meets the sky. Polaris appears to be stationary and navigators throughout history have used it as a guide. Unfortunately, the South Pole has no convenient reference point.

Star charts of the two hemispheres are bounded by the Celestial Equator, an imaginary line in the sky directly above the terrestrial Equator. Astronomical co-ordinates, which give the location of stars, are normally stated in terms of right ascension (the equivalent of longitude) and declination (the equivalent of latitude). Because the stars appear to rotate around the Earth every 24 hours, right ascension is measured eastwards in hours and minutes. Declination is measured in degrees north or south of the Celestial Equator.

The Southern Cross

The Southern Cross, or Crux, in the southern hemisphere, was classified as a constellation in the 17th century. It is as familiar to Australians and New Zealanders as the Plough (or Big Dipper) is to people in the northern hemisphere. The vertical axis of the Southern Cross points towards the South Celestial Pole.

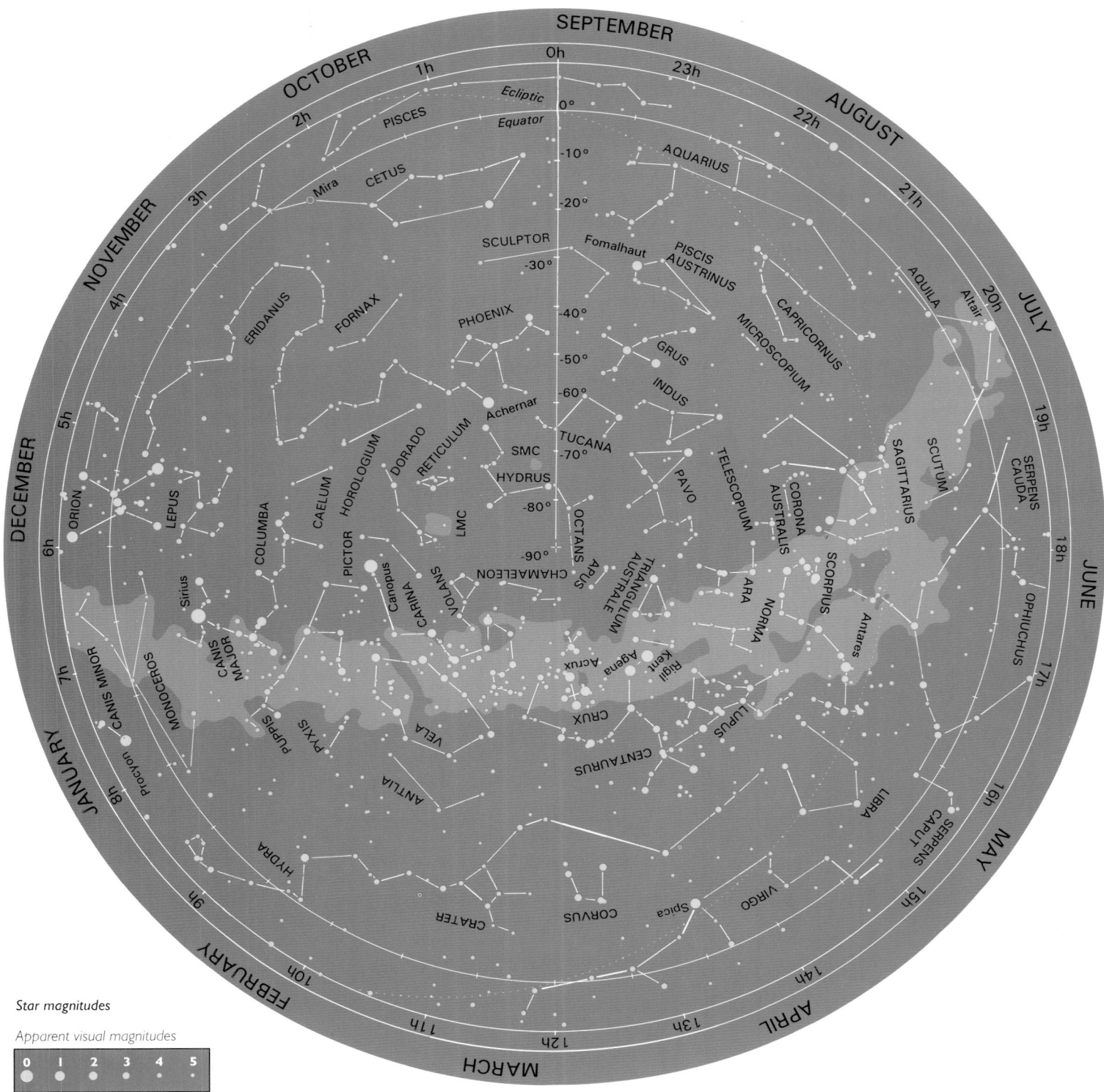

Star magnitudes

Apparent visual magnitudes

0	1	2	3	4	5

The Milky Way is shown in light blue on the above chart.

Star chart of the southern hemisphere

Many constellations in the southern hemisphere were named not by the ancients but by later astronomers. Some, including Antila (Air Pump) and Microscopium (Microscope), have modern names. The Large and Small Magellanic Clouds (LMC, SMC) are small 'satellite' galaxies of the Milky Way. To use the chart, an observer in the southern hemisphere should face north and turn the chart so that the current month appears at the bottom. The map will then show the constellations on view at approximately 11pm Greenwich Mean Time. The chart should be rotated clockwise 15° for each hour before 11pm and anticlockwise for each hour after 11pm.

CONSTELLATIONS

Every star is identifiable as a member of a constellation. The night sky contains 88 constellations, many of which were named by the ancient Greeks, Romans and other early peoples after animals and mythological characters, such as Orion and Perseus. More recently, astronomers invented names for constellations seen in the southern hemisphere, in areas not visible around the Mediterranean Sea.

Some groups of easily recognizable stars form parts of a constellation. For example, seven stars form the shape of the Plough or Big Dipper within the constellation Ursa Major. Such groups are called asterisms.

The stars in constellations lie in the same direction in space, but normally at vastly differ-ent distances. Hence, there is no real connection between them. The positions of stars seem fixed, but in fact the shapes of the constellations are changing slowly over very long periods of time. This is because the stars have their own 'proper motions', which because of the huge distances involved are imperceptible to the naked eye.

The Solar System

Although the origins of the Solar System are still a matter of debate, many scientists believe that it was formed from a cloud of gas and dust, the debris from some long-lost, exploded star. Around 5 billion years ago, material was drawn towards the hub of the rotating disk of gas and dust, where it was compressed to thermonuclear fusion temperatures. A new star, the Sun, was born, containing 99.8% of the mass of the Solar System. The remaining material was later drawn together to form the planets and the other bodies in the Solar System. Spacecraft, manned and unmanned, have greatly increased our knowledge of the Solar System since the start of the Space Age in 1957, when the Soviet Union launched the satellite Sputnik I.

THE PLANETS

Mercury is the closest planet to the Sun and the fastest moving. Space probes have revealed that its surface is covered by craters, and looks much like our Moon. Mercury is a hostile place, with no significant atmosphere and temperatures ranging between 400°C [750°F] by day and −170°C [−275°F] by night. It seems unlikely that anyone will ever want to visit this planet.

Venus is much the same size as Earth, but it is the hottest of the planets, with temperatures reaching 475°C [885°F], even at night. The reason for this scorching heat is the atmosphere, which consists mainly of carbon dioxide, a gas that traps heat thus creating a greenhouse effect. The density of the atmosphere is about 90 times that of Earth and dense clouds permanently mask the surface. Active volcanic regions discharging sulphur dioxide may account for the haze of sulphuric acid droplets in the upper atmosphere.

From planet Earth, Venus is brighter than any other star or planet and is easy to spot. It is often the first object to be seen in the evening sky and the last to be seen in the morning sky. It can even be seen in daylight.

Earth, seen from space, looks blue (because of the oceans which cover more than 70% of the planet) and white (a result of clouds in the atmosphere). The atmosphere and water make Earth the only planet known to support life. The Earth's hard outer layers, including the crust and the top of the mantle, are divided into rigid plates. Forces inside the Earth move the plates, modifying the landscape and causing earthquakes and volcanic activity. Weathering and erosion also change the surface.

Mars has many features in common with Earth, including an atmosphere with clouds and polar caps that partly melt in summer. Scientists once considered that it was the most likely planet on which other life might exist, but the two Viking space probes that went there in the 1970s found only a barren rocky surface with no trace of water. But Mars did have flowing water at one time and there are many dry channels – but these are not the fictitious 'canals'. There are also giant, dormant volcanoes.

PLANETARY DATA

Planet	Mean distance from Sun (million km)	Mass (Earth=1)	Period of orbit (Earth yrs)	Period of rotation (Earth days)	Equatorial diameter (km)	Average density (water=1)	Surface gravity (Earth=1)	Number of known satellites
Sun	–	333,000	–	25.4	1,391,000	1.41	28	–
Mercury	57.9	0.055	0.2406	58.67	4,880	5.43	0.38	0
Venus	108.2	0.815	0.6152	243.0	12,104	5.20	0.90	0
Earth	149.6	1.0	1.00	1.00	12,756	5.52	1.00	1
Mars	227.9	0.107	1.88	1.028	6,792	3.91	0.38	2
Jupiter	778.3	317.8	11.86	0.411	142,800	1.33	2.69	27
Saturn	1,426.8	95.2	29.46	0.427	120,000	0.69	1.19	30
Uranus	2,869.4	14.53	84.01	0.748	51,118	1.29	0.79	21
Neptune	4,496.3	17.14	164.8	0.710	49,528	1.64	0.98	8
Pluto	5,900.1	0.002	2447.7	6.39	2,320	2.00	0.03	1

Asteroids are small, rocky bodies. Most of them orbit the Sun between Mars and Jupiter, but some small ones can approach the Earth. The largest is Ceres, 913 km [567 miles] in diameter. There may be around a million asteroids bigger than 1 km [0.6 miles].

Jupiter, the giant planet, lies beyond Mars and the asteroid belt. Its mass is almost three times as much as all the other planets combined and, because of its size, it shines more brightly than any other planet apart from Venus and, occasionally, Mars. The four largest moons of Jupiter were discovered by Galileo. Jupiter is made up mostly of hydrogen and helium, covered by a layer of clouds. Its Great Red Spot is a high-pressure storm. Jupiter made headline news when it was struck by fragments of Comet Shoemaker–Levy 9 in July 1994. This was the greatest collision ever seen by scientists between a planet and another heavenly body. The fragments of the comet that crashed into Jupiter created huge fireballs that caused scars on the planet that remained visible for months after the event.

Saturn is structurally similar to Jupiter but it is best known for its rings. The rings measure about 270,000 km [170,000 miles] across, yet they are no more than a few hundred metres thick. Seen from Earth, the rings seem divided

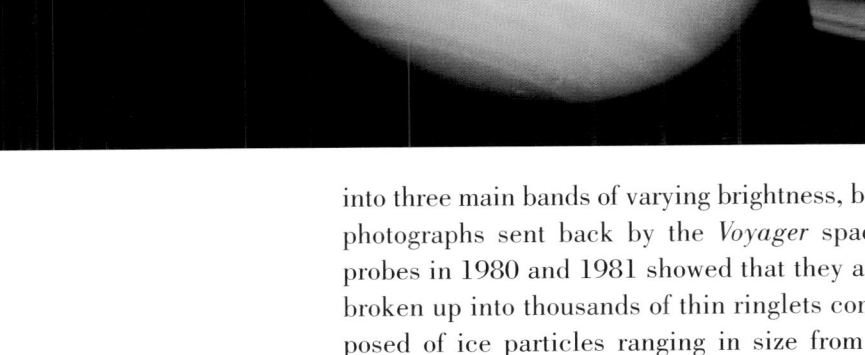

into three main bands of varying brightness, but photographs sent back by the *Voyager* space probes in 1980 and 1981 showed that they are broken up into thousands of thin ringlets composed of ice particles ranging in size from a snowball to an iceberg. The origin of the rings is still a matter of debate.

Uranus was discovered in 1781 by William Herschel who first thought it was a comet. It is broadly similar to Jupiter and Saturn in composition, though its distance from the Sun makes its surface even colder. Uranus is circled by thin rings which were discovered in 1977. Unlike the rings of Saturn, the rings of Uranus are black, which explains why they cannot be seen from Earth.

Neptune, named after the mythological sea god, was discovered in 1846 as the result of mathematical predictions made by astronomers to explain irregularities in the orbit of Uranus, its near twin. Little was known about this distant

body until *Voyager 2* came close to it in 1989. Neptune has thin rings, like those of Uranus. Among its blue-green clouds is a prominent dark spot, which rotates anticlockwise every 18 hours or so.

Pluto is the smallest planet in the Solar System, even smaller than our Moon. The American astronomer Clyde Tombaugh discovered Pluto in 1930. Its orbit is odd and it sometimes comes closer to the Sun than Neptune. The nature of Pluto, a gloomy planet appropriately named after the Greek and Roman god of the underworld, is uncertain. At Pluto's distance and beyond are many small, asteroid-like bodies the first of which was found in 1992.

Comets are small icy bodies that orbit the Sun in highly elliptical orbits. When a comet swings in towards the Sun some of its ice evaporates, and the comet brightens and may become visible from Earth. The best known is Halley's Comet, which takes 76 years to orbit the Sun.

The Earth: Time and Motion

The Earth is constantly moving through space like a huge, self-sufficient spaceship. First, with the rest of the Solar System, it moves around the centre of the Milky Way galaxy. Second, it rotates around the Sun at a speed of more than 100,000 km/h [more than 60,000 mph], covering a distance of nearly 1,000 million km [600 million miles] in a little over 365 days. The Earth also spins on its axis, an imaginary line joining the North and South Poles, via the centre of the Earth, completing one turn in a day. The Earth's movements around the Sun determine our calendar, though accurate observations of

Spring/Vernal Equinox
Northern spring, southern autumn
Summer Solstice
N
21 March
Winter Solstice
21 June
SUN
22 December
23 September
Northern summer, southern winter
Northern winter, southern summer
Autumnal Equinox
Northern autumn, southern spring
S

The Earth from the Moon

In 1969, Neil Armstrong and Edwin 'Buzz' Aldrin Junior were the first people to set foot on the Moon. This superb view of the Earth was taken by the crew of Apollo 11.

the stars made by astronomers help to keep our clocks in step with the rotation of the Earth around the Sun.

THE CHANGING YEAR

The Earth takes 365 days, 6 hours, 9 minutes and 9.54 seconds to complete one orbit around the Sun. We have a calendar year of 365 days, so allowance has to be made for the extra time over and above the 365 days. This is allowed for by introducing leap years of 366 days. Leap years are generally those, such as 1992 and 1996, which are divisible by four. Century years, however, are not leap years unless they are divisible by 400. Hence, 1700, 1800 and 1900 were not leap years, but the year 2000 was one. Leap years help to make the calendar conform with the solar year.

Because the Earth's axis is tilted by 23½°, the middle latitudes enjoy four distinct seasons. On 21 March, the vernal or spring equinox in the northern hemisphere, the Sun is directly overhead at the Equator and everywhere on Earth has about 12 hours of daylight and 12 hours of darkness. But as the Earth continues on its journey around the Sun, the northern hemisphere tilts more and more towards the Sun. Finally, on 21 June, the Sun is overhead at the Tropic of Cancer (latitude 23½° North). This is

The Seasons

The 23½° tilt of the Earth's axis remains constant as the Earth orbits around the Sun. As a result, first the northern and then the southern hemispheres lean towards the Sun. Annual variations in the amount of sunlight received in turn by each hemisphere are responsible for the four seasons experienced in the middle latitudes.

Tides

The daily rises and falls of the ocean's waters are caused by the gravitational pull of the Moon and the Sun. The effect is greatest on the hemisphere facing the Moon, causing a 'tidal bulge'. The diagram below shows that the Sun, Moon and Earth are in line when the spring tides occur. This causes the greatest tidal ranges. On the other hand, the neap tides occur when the pull of the Moon and the Sun are opposed. Neap tides, when tidal ranges are at their lowest, occur near the Moon's first and third quarters.

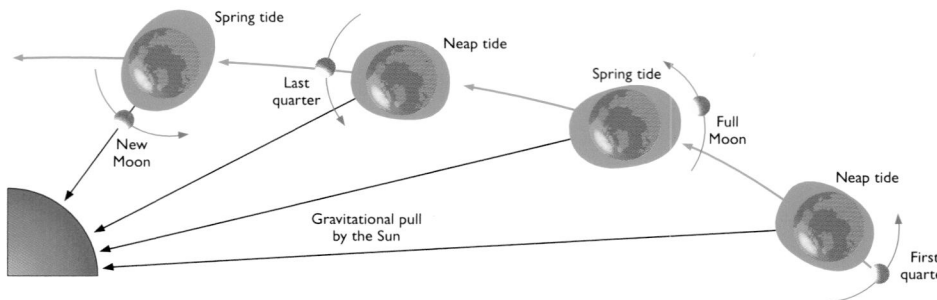

SUN DATA	
DIAMETER	1.391 × 10⁶ km
VOLUME	1.412 × 10¹⁸ km³
VOLUME (EARTH=1)	1.303 × 10⁶
MASS	1.989 × 10³⁰ kg
MASS (EARTH=1)	3.329 × 10⁶
MEAN DENSITY (WATER=1)	1.409
ROTATION PERIOD	
AT EQUATOR	25.4 days
AT POLES	about 35 days
SURFACE GRAVITY	
(EARTH=1)	28
MAGNITUDE	
APPARENT	−26.9
ABSOLUTE	+4.71
TEMPERATURE	
AT SURFACE	5,400°C [5,700 K]
AT CORE	15 × 10⁶ K

MOON DATA	
DIAMETER	3,476 km
MASS (EARTH=1)	0.0123
DENSITY (WATER=1)	3.34
MEAN DISTANCE FROM EARTH	384,402 km
MAXIMUM DISTANCE (APOGEE)	406,740 km
MINIMUM DISTANCE (PERIGEE)	356,410 km
SIDERIAL ROTATION AND REVOLUTION PERIOD	27.322 days
SYNODIC MONTH (NEW MOON TO NEW MOON)	29.531 days
SURFACE GRAVITY (EARTH=1)	0.165
MAXIMUM SURFACE TEMPERATURE	+130°C [403 K]
MINIMUM SURFACE TEMPERATURE	−158°C [115 K]

Phases of the Moon

The Moon rotates more slowly than the Earth, making one complete turn on its axis in just over 27 days. This corresponds to its period of revolution around the Earth and, hence, the same hemisphere always faces us. The interval between one full Moon and the next (and also between new Moons) is about 29½ days, or one lunar month. The apparent changes in the appearance of the Moon are caused by its changing position in relation to Earth. Like the planets, the Moon produces no light of its own. It shines by reflecting the Sun's rays, varying from a slim crescent to a full circle and back again.

the summer solstice in the northern hemisphere.

The overhead Sun then moves south again until on 23 September, the autumn equinox in the northern hemisphere, the Sun is again overhead at the Equator. The overhead Sun then moves south until, on around 22 December, it is overhead at the Tropic of Capricorn. This is the winter solstice in the northern hemisphere, and the summer solstice in the southern, where the seasons are reversed.

At the poles, there are two seasons. During half of the year, one of the poles leans towards the Sun and has continuous sunlight. For the other six months, the pole leans away from the Sun and is in continuous darkness.

Regions around the Equator do not have marked seasons. Because the Sun is high in the sky throughout the year, it is always hot or warm. When people talk of seasons in the tropics, they are usually referring to other factors, such as rainy and dry periods.

DAY, NIGHT AND TIDES

As the Earth rotates on its axis every 24 hours, first one side of the planet and then the other faces the Sun and enjoys daylight, while the opposite side is in darkness.

The length of daylight varies throughout the year. The longest day in the northern hemisphere falls on the summer solstice, 21 June, while the longest day in the southern hemisphere is on 22 December. At 40° latitude, the length of daylight on the longest day is 14 hours, 30 minutes. At 60° latitude, daylight on that day lasts 18 hours, 30 minutes. On the shortest day, 22 December in the northern hemisphere and 21 June in the southern, daylight hours at 40° latitude total 9 hours and 9 minutes. At latitude 60°, daylight lasts only 5 hours, 30 minutes in the 24-hour period.

Tides are caused by the gravitational pull of the Moon and, to a lesser extent, the Sun on the waters in the world's oceans. Tides occur twice every 24 hours, 50 minutes – one complete orbit

Total eclipse of the Sun

A total eclipse is caused when the Moon passes between the Sun and the Earth. With the Sun's bright disk completely obscured, the Sun's corona, or outer atmosphere, can be viewed.

of the Moon around the Earth.

The highest tides, the spring tides, occur when the Earth, Moon and Sun are in a straight line, so that the gravitational pulls of the Moon and Sun are combined. The lowest, or neap, tides occur when the Moon, Earth and Sun form a right angle. The gravitational pull of the Moon is then opposed by the gravitational pull of the Sun. The greatest tidal ranges occur in the Bay of Fundy in North America. The greatest mean spring range is 14.5 m [47.5 ft].

The speed at which the Earth is spinning on its axis is gradually slowing down, because of the movement of tides. As a result, experts have calculated that, in about 200 million years, the day will be 25 hours long.

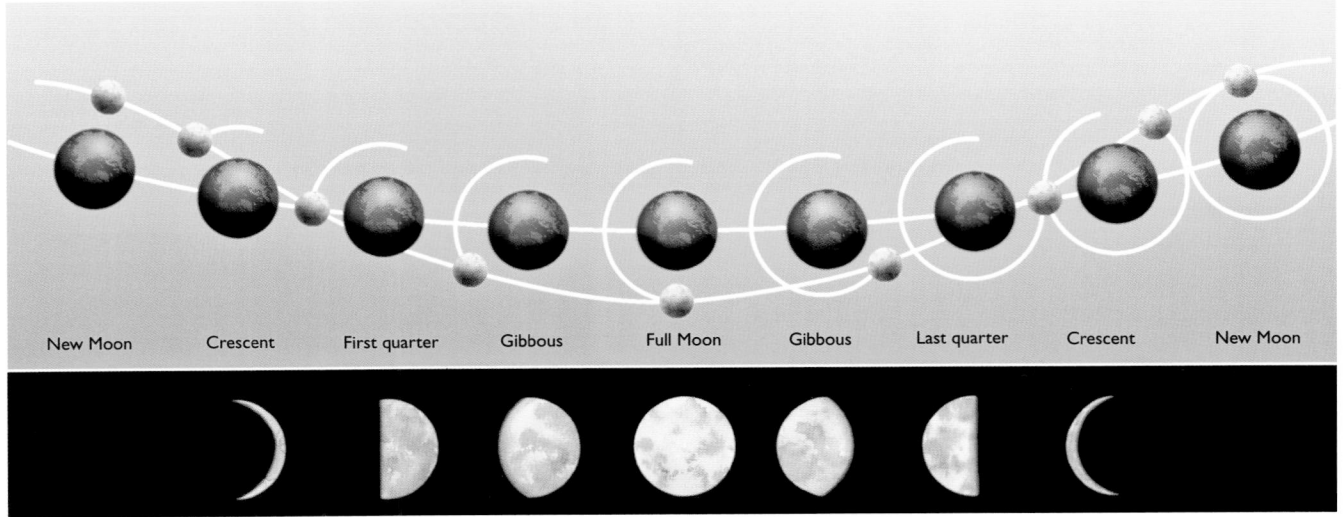

New Moon   Crescent   First quarter   Gibbous   Full Moon   Gibbous   Last quarter   Crescent   New Moon

The Earth from Space

Any last doubts about whether the Earth was round or flat were finally resolved by the appearance of the first photographs of our planet taken at the start of the Space Age. Satellite images also confirmed that map- and globe-makers had correctly worked out the shapes of the continents and the oceans.

More importantly, images of our beautiful, blue, white and brown planet from space impressed on many people that the Earth and its resources are finite. They made people realize that if we allow our planet to be damaged by such factors as overpopulation, pollution and irresponsible over-use of resources, then its future and the survival of all the living things upon it may be threatened.

VIEWS FROM ABOVE

The first aerial photographs were taken from balloons in the mid-19th century and their importance in military reconnaissance was recognized as early as the 1860s during the American Civil War.

Launch of the Space Shuttle Atlantis
Space Shuttles transport astronauts and equipment into orbit around the Earth. The American Space Shuttle Atlantis, *shown below, launched the Magellan probe, which undertook a radar mapping programme of the surface of Venus in the early 1990s.*

Since the end of World War II, photographs taken by aircraft have been widely used in map-making. The use of air photographs has greatly speeded up the laborious process of mapping land details and they have enabled cartographers to produce maps of the most remote parts of the world.

Aerial photographs have also proved useful because they reveal features that are not visible at ground level. For example, circles that appear on many air photographs do not correspond to visible features on the ground. Many of these mysterious shapes have turned out to be the sites of ancient settlements previously unknown to archaeologists.

IMAGES FROM SPACE

Space probes equipped with cameras and a variety of remote sensing instruments have sent back images of distant planets and moons. From these images, detailed maps have been produced, rapidly expanding our knowledge of the Solar System.

Photographs from space are also proving invaluable in the study of the Earth. One of the best known uses of space imagery is the study of the atmosphere. Polar-orbiting weather satellites that circle the Earth, together with geostationary satellites, whose motion is synchronized with the Earth's rotation, now regularly transmit images showing the changing patterns of weather systems from above. Forecasters use these images to track the development and the paths taken by hurricanes, enabling them to issue storm warnings to endangered areas, saving lives and reducing damage to property.

Remote sensing devices are now monitoring changes in temperatures over the land and sea, while photographs indicate the melting of ice sheets. Such evidence is vital in the study of global warming. Other devices reveal polluted areas, patterns of vegetation growth, and areas suffering deforestation.

In recent years, remote sensing devices have been used to monitor the damage being done to the ozone layer in the stratosphere, which prevents most of the Sun's harmful ultraviolet radiation from reaching the surface. The discovery of 'ozone holes', where the protective layer of ozone is being thinned by chlorofluorocarbons (CFCs), chemicals used in the manufacture of such things as air conditioners and refrigerators, has enabled governments to take concerted action to save our planet from imminent danger.

EARTH DATA

MAXIMUM DISTANCE FROM SUN (APHELION)
152,007,016 km

MINIMUM DISTANCE FROM SUN (PERIHELION)
147,000,830 km

LENGTH OF YEAR – SOLAR TROPICAL (EQUINOX TO EQUINOX)
365.24 days

LENGTH OF YEAR – SIDEREAL (FIXED STAR TO FIXED STAR)
365.26 days

LENGTH OF DAY – MEAN SOLAR DAY
24 hours, 03 minutes, 56 seconds

LENGTH OF DAY – MEAN SIDEREAL DAY
23 hours, 56 minutes, 4 seconds

SUPERFICIAL AREA
510,000,000 km^2

LAND SURFACE
149,000,000 km^2 (29.3%)

WATER SURFACE
361,000,000 km^2 (70.7%)

EQUATORIAL CIRCUMFERENCE
40,077 km

POLAR CIRCUMFERENCE
40,009 km

EQUATORIAL DIAMETER
12,756.8 km

POLAR DIAMETER
12,713.8 km

EQUATORIAL RADIUS
6,378.4 km

POLAR RADIUS
6,356.9 km

VOLUME OF THE EARTH
1,083,230 × 10^6 km^3

MASS OF THE EARTH
5.9 × 10^{21} tonnes

Satellite image of San Francisco Bay

Unmanned scientific satellites called ERTS (Earth Resources Technology Satellites), or Landsats, were designed to collect information about the Earth's resources. The satellites transmitted images of the land using different wavelengths of light in order to identify, in false colours, such subtle features as areas that contain minerals or areas covered with growing crops, that are not identifiable on simple photographs using the visible range of the spectrum. They were also equipped to monitor conditions in the atmosphere and oceans, and also to detect pollution levels. This Landsat image of San Francisco Bay covers an area of great interest to geologists because it lies in an earthquake zone in the path of the San Andreas fault.

The Dynamic Earth

The Earth was formed about 4.6 billion years [4,600 million years] ago from the ring of gas and dust left over after the formation of the Sun. As the Earth took shape, lighter elements, such as silicon, rose to the surface, while heavy elements, notably iron, sank towards the centre.

Gradually, the outer layers cooled to form a hard crust. The crust enclosed the dense mantle which, in turn, surrounded the even denser liquid outer and solid inner core. Around the Earth was an atmosphere, which contained abundant water

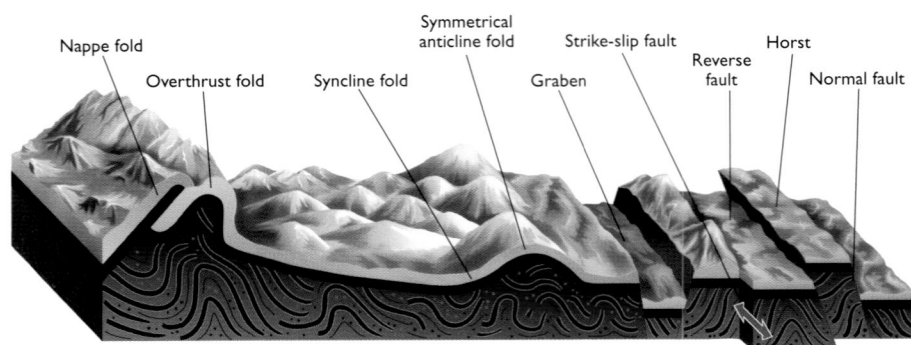

Lulworth Cove, southern England
When undisturbed by earth movements, sedimentary rock strata are generally horizontal. But lateral pressure has squeezed the Jurassic strata at Lulworth Cove into complex folds.

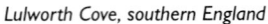

vapour. When the surface cooled, rainwater began to fill hollows, forming the first lakes and seas. Since that time, our planet has been subject to constant change – the result of powerful internal and external forces that still operate today.

THE HISTORY OF THE EARTH
From their study of rocks, geologists have pieced together the history of our planet and the life forms that evolved upon it. They have dated the oldest known crystals, composed of the mineral zircon, at 4.2 billion years. But the oldest rocks are younger, less than 4 billion years old. This is because older rocks have been weathered away by natural processes.

The oldest rocks that contain fossils, which are

evidence of once-living organisms, are around 3.5 billion years old. But fossils are rare in rocks formed in the first 4 billion years of Earth history. This vast expanse of time is called the Precambrian. This is because it precedes the Cambrian period, at the start of which, about 590 million years ago, life was abundant in the seas.

The Cambrian is the first period in the Paleozoic (or ancient life) era. The Paleozoic era is followed by the Mesozoic (middle life) era, which witnessed the spectacular rise and fall of the dinosaurs, and the Cenozoic (recent life) era, which was dominated by the evolution of mammals. Each of the eras is divided into periods, and the periods in the Cenozoic era, covering the last 65 million years, are further divided into epochs.

THE EARTH'S CHANGING FACE
While life was gradually evolving, the face of the Earth was constantly changing. By piecing together evidence of rock structures and fossils, geologists have demonstrated that around 250 million years ago, all the world's land areas were grouped together in one huge landmass called Pangaea. Around 180 million years ago, the supercontinent Pangaea, began to break up. New oceans opened up as the continents began to move towards their present positions.

Evidence of how continents drift came from studies of the ocean floor in the 1950s and 1960s. Scientists discovered that the oceans are young features. By contrast with the continents, no part of the ocean floor is more than 200 million years old. The floors of oceans older than 200 million years have completely vanished.

Studies of long undersea ranges, called ocean ridges, revealed that the youngest rocks occur along their centres, which are the edges of huge plates – rigid blocks of the Earth's lithosphere, which is made up of the crust and the solid upper layer of the mantle. The Earth's lithosphere is split into six large and several smaller

Mountain building
Lateral pressure, which occurs when plates collide, squeezes and compresses rocks into folds. Simple symmetrical upfolds are called anticlines, while downfolds are synclines. As the pressure builds up, strata become asymmetrical and they may be tilted over to form recumbent folds. The rocks often crack under the intense pressure and the folds are sheared away and pushed forward over other rocks. These features are called overthrust folds or nappes. Plate movements also create faults along which rocks move upwards, downwards and sideways. The diagram shows a downfaulted graben, or rift valley, and an uplifted horst, or block mountain.

Nappe fold · Overthrust fold · Symmetrical anticline fold · Syncline fold · Strike-slip fault · Graben · Reverse fault · Horst · Normal fault

The Himalayas seen from Nepal
The Himalayas are a young fold mountain range formed by a collision between two plates. The earthquakes felt in the region testify that the plate movements are still continuing.

Geological time scale

The geological time scale was first constructed by a study of the stratigraphic, or relative, ages of layers of rock. But the absolute ages of rock strata could not be fixed until the discovery of radioactivity in the early 20th century. Some names of periods, such as Cambrian (Latin for Wales), come from places where the rocks were first studied. Others, such as Carboniferous, refer to the nature of the rocks formed during the period. For example, coal seams (containing carbon) were formed from decayed plant matter during the Carboniferous period.

plates. The ocean ridges are 'constructive' plate margins, because new crustal rock is being formed there from magma that wells up from the mantle as the plates gradually move apart. By contrast, the deep ocean trenches are 'destructive' plate edges. Here, two plates are pushing against each other and one plate is descending beneath the other into the mantle where it is melted and destroyed. Geologists call these areas subduction zones.

A third type of plate edge is called a transform fault. Here two plates are moving alongside each other. The best known of these plate edges is the San Andreas fault in California, which separates the Pacific plate from the North American plate.

Slow-moving currents in the partly molten asthenosphere, which underlies the solid lithosphere, are responsible for moving the plates, a process called plate tectonics.

MOUNTAIN BUILDING

The study of plate tectonics has helped geologists to understand the mechanisms that are responsible for the creation of mountains. Many of the world's greatest ranges were created by the collision of two plates and the bending of the intervening strata into huge loops, or folds. For example, the Himalayas began to rise around 50 million years ago, when a plate supporting India collided with the huge Eurasian plate. Rocks on the floor of the intervening and long-vanished Tethys Sea were squeezed up to form the Himalayan Mountain Range.

Plate movements also create tension that cracks rocks, producing long faults along which rocks move upwards, downwards or sideways. Block mountains are formed when blocks of rock are pushed upwards along faults. Steep-sided rift valleys are formed when blocks of land sink down between faults. For example, the basin and range region of the south-western United States has both block mountains and down-faulted basins, such as Death Valley.

Pre-Cambrian	Lower	Paleozoic (Primary)		Upper			Mesozoic (Secondary)			Cenozoic (Tertiary, Quaternary)	Era
Pre-Cambrian	Cambrian	Ordovician	Silurian	Devonian	Carboniferous	Permian	Triassic	Jurassic	Cretaceous	Paleocene / Eocene / Oligocene / Miocene / Pliocene / Quaternary	System
			CALEDONIAN FOLDING		HERCYNIAN FOLDING					LARAMIDE FOLDING / ALPINE FOLDING	Orogeny
600	550 500	450	400	350	300	250	200	150	100	50	

Millions of years before present

Earthquakes and Volcanoes

On 26 January, 2001, an earthquake rocked north-west India and south-east Pakistan. Bhuj, in Gujarat state, suffered the worst damage. The death toll was more than 14,000, and the 'quake was felt as far away as Karachi, Delhi and Mumbai. Earlier that month, an earthquake had struck El Salvador in Central America. Around 1,200 people died, 750 of them being buried by mudslides.

THE RESTLESS EARTH

Earthquakes can occur anywhere, whenever rocks move along faults. But the most severe and most numerous earthquakes occur near the edges of the plates that make up the

San Andreas Fault, United States
Geologists call the San Andreas fault in south-western California a transform, or strike-slip, fault. Sudden movements along it cause earthquakes. In 1906, shifts of about 4.5 metres [15 ft] occurred near San Francisco, causing a massive earthquake.

Earth's lithosphere. Japan, for example, lies in a particularly unstable region above subduction zones, where plates are descending into the Earth's mantle. It lies in a zone encircling the Pacific Ocean, called the 'Pacific ring of fire'.

Plates do not move smoothly. Their edges are jagged and for most of the time they are locked together. However, pressure gradually builds up until the rocks break and the plates lurch forward, setting off vibrations ranging from slight tremors to terrifying earthquakes. The greater the pressure released, the more destructive the earthquake.

Earthquakes are also common along the ocean trenches where plates are moving apart, but they mostly occur so far from land that they do little damage. Far more destructive are the earthquakes that occur where plates are moving alongside each other. For example, the earthquakes that periodically rock south-western California are caused by movements along the San Andreas Fault.

The spot where an earthquake originates is called the focus, while the point on the Earth's surface directly above the focus is called the epicentre. Two kinds of waves, P-waves or compressional waves and S-waves or shear waves, travel from the focus to the surface where they make the ground shake. P-waves travel faster than S-waves and the time difference between their arrival at recording stations enables scientists to calculate the distance from a station to the epicentre.

Earthquakes are measured on the Richter scale, which indicates the magnitude of the shock. The most destructive earthquakes are shallow-focus, that is, the focus is within 60 km [37 miles] of the surface. A magnitude of 7.0 is a major earthquake, but earthquakes with a somewhat lower magnitude can cause tremendous damage if their epicentres are on or close to densely populated areas.

NOTABLE EARTHQUAKES
(since 1900)

Year	Location	Mag.
1906	San Francisco, USA	8.3
1906	Valparaiso, Chile	8.6
1908	Messina, Italy	7.5
1915	Avezzano, Italy	7.5
1920	Gansu, China	8.6
1923	Yokohama, Japan	8.3
1927	Nan Shan, China	8.3
1932	Gansu, China	7.6
1934	Bihar, India/Nepal	8.4
1935	Quetta, India†	7.5
1939	Chillan, Chile	8.3
1939	Erzincan, Turkey	7.9
1964	Anchorage, Alaska	8.4
1968	N. E. Iran	7.4
1970	N. Peru	7.7
1976	Guatemala	7.5
1976	Tangshan, China	8.2
1978	Tabas, Iran	7.7
1980	El Asnam, Algeria	7.3
1980	S. Italy	7.2
1985	Mexico City, Mexico	8.1
1988	N. W. Armenia	6.8
1990	N. Iran	7.7
1993	Maharashtra, India	6.4
1994	Los Angeles, USA	6.6
1995	Kobe, Japan	7.2
1995	Sakhalin Is., Russia	7.5
1996	Yunnan, China	7.0
1997	N. E. Iran	7.1
1998	N. Afghanistan	6.1
1998	N. E. Afghanistan	7.0
1999	Izmit, Turkey	7.4
1999	Taipei, Taiwan	7.6
2001	El Salvador	7.7
2001	Gujarat, India	7.7
2002	Afyon, Turkey	6.0
2002	N. Afghanistan	5.2

† *now Pakistan*

Earthquakes in subduction zones
Along subduction zones, one plate is descending beneath another. The plates are locked together until the rocks break and the descending plate lurches forwards. From the point where the plate moves – the origin – seismic waves spread through the lithosphere, making the ground shake. The earthquake in Mexico City in 1985 occurred in this way.

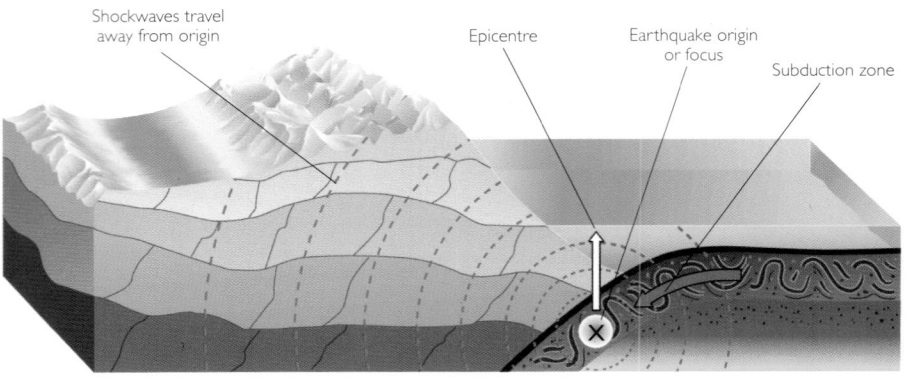

Shockwaves travel away from origin

Epicentre

Earthquake origin or focus

Subduction zone

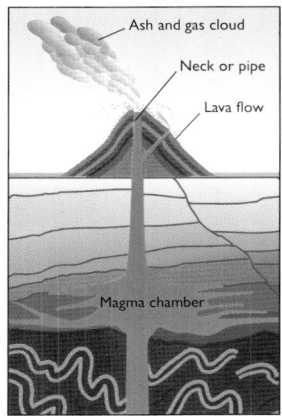

Cross-section of a volcano

Volcanoes are vents in the ground, through which magma reaches the surface. The term volcano is also used for the mountains formed from volcanic rocks. Beneath volcanoes are pockets of magma derived from the semi-molten asthenosphere in the mantle. The magma rises under pressure through the overlying rocks until it reaches the surface. There it emerges through vents as pyroclasts, ranging in size from large lumps of magma, called volcanic bombs, to fine volcanic ash and dust. In quiet eruptions, streams of liquid lava run down the side of the mountain. Side vents sometimes appear on the flanks of existing volcanoes.

Scientists have been working for years to find effective ways of forecasting earthquakes but with very limited success. Following the Kobe earthquake in 1995, many experts argued that they would be better employed developing techniques of reducing the damage caused by earthquakes, rather than pursuing an apparently vain attempt to predict them.

VOLCANIC ERUPTIONS

Most active volcanoes also occur on or near plate edges. Many undersea volcanoes along the ocean ridges are formed from magma that wells up from the asthenosphere to fill the gaps created as the plates, on the opposite sides of the ridges, move apart. Some of these volcanoes reach the surface to form islands. Iceland is a country which straddles the Mid-Atlantic Ocean Ridge. It is gradually becoming wider as magma rises to the surface through faults and vents. Other volcanoes lie alongside subduction zones. The magma that fuels them comes from the melted edges of the descending plates.

A few volcanoes lie far from plate edges. For example, Mauna Loa and Kilauea on Hawaii are situated near the centre of the huge Pacific plate. The molten magma that reaches the surface is created by a source of heat, called a 'hot spot', in the Earth's mantle.

Magma is molten rock at temperatures of about 1,100°C to 1,200°C [2,012°F to 2,192°F]. It contains gases and superheated steam. The chemical composition of magma varies. Viscous magma is rich in silica and superheated steam, while runny magma contains less silica and steam. The chemical composition of the magma affects the nature of volcanic eruptions.

Explosive volcanoes contain thick, viscous magma. When they erupt, they usually hurl clouds of ash (shattered fragments of cooled magma) into the air. By contrast, quiet volcanoes emit long streams of runny magma, or lava. However, many volcanoes are intermediate in type, sometimes erupting explosively and sometimes emitting streams of fluid lava. Explosive and intermediate volcanoes usually have a conical shape, while quiet volcanoes are flattened, resembling upturned saucers. They are often called shield volcanoes.

One dangerous type of eruption is called a *nuée ardente*, or 'glowing cloud'. It occurs when a cloud of intensely hot volcanic gases and dust particles and superheated steam are exploded from a volcano. They move rapidly downhill, burning everything in their path and choking animals and people. The blast that creates the *nuée ardente* may release the pressure inside the volcano, resulting in a tremendous explosion that hurls tall columns of ash into the air.

Kilauea Volcano, Hawaii

The volcanic Hawaiian islands in the North Pacific Ocean were formed as the Pacific plate moved over a 'hot spot' in the Earth's mantle. Kilauea on Hawaii emits blazing streams of liquid lava.

Forces of Nature

When the volcano Mount Pinatubo erupted in the Philippines in 1991, loose ash covered large areas around the mountain. During the 1990s and early 2000s, rainwater mixed with the ash on sloping land, creating *lahars*, or mudflows, which swept down river valleys burying many areas. Such incidents are not only reminders of the great forces that operate inside our planet but also of those natural forces operating on the surface, which can have dramatic effects on the land.

The chief forces acting on the surface of the Earth are weathering, running water, ice and winds. The forces of erosion seem to act slowly. One estimate suggests that an average of only 3.5 cm [1.4 in] of land is removed by natural processes every 1,000 years. This may not sound much, but over millions of years, it can reduce mountains to almost flat surfaces.

WEATHERING

Weathering occurs in all parts of the world, but the most effective type of weathering in any area depends on the climate and the nature of the rocks. For example, in cold mountain areas,

Grand Canyon, Arizona, at dusk
The Grand Canyon in the United States is one of the world's natural wonders. Eroded by the Colorado River and its tributaries, it is up to 1.6 km [1 mile] deep and 29 km [18 miles] wide.

RATES OF EROSION

	SLOW ←	WEATHERING RATE →	FAST
Mineral solubility	low (e.g. quartz)	moderate (e.g. feldspar)	high (e.g. calcite)
Rainfall	low	moderate	heavy
Temperature	cold	temperate	hot
Vegetation	sparse	moderate	lush
Soil cover	bare rock	thin to moderate soil	thick soil

Weathering is the breakdown and decay of rocks in situ. It may be mechanical (physical), chemical or biological.

---

when water freezes in cracks in rocks, the ice occupies 9% more space than the water. This exerts a force which, when repeated over and over again, can split boulders apart. By contrast, in hot deserts, intense heating by day and cooling by night causes the outer layers of rocks to expand and contract until they break up and peel away like layers of an onion. These are examples of what is called mechanical weathering.

Other kinds of weathering include chemical reactions usually involving water. Rainwater containing carbon dioxide dissolved from the air or the soil is a weak acid which reacts with limestone, wearing out pits, tunnels and networks of caves in layers of limestone rock. Water also combines with some minerals, such as the feldspars in granite, to create kaolin, a white

Rates of erosion
The chart shows that the rates at which weathering takes place depend on the chemistry and hardness of rocks, climatic factors, especially rainfall and temperature, the vegetation and the nature of the soil cover in any area. The effects of weathering are increased by human action, particularly the removal of vegetation and the exposure of soils to the rain and wind.

clay. These are examples of chemical weathering which constantly wears away rock.

RUNNING WATER, ICE AND WIND

In moist regions, rivers are effective in shaping the land. They transport material worn away by weathering and erode the land. They wear out V-shaped valleys in upland regions, while vigorous meanders widen their middle courses. The work of rivers is at its most spectacular when earth movements lift up flat areas and rejuvenate the rivers, giving them a new erosive power capable of wearing out such features as the Grand Canyon. Rivers also have a constructive role. Some of the world's most fertile regions are deltas and flood plains composed of sediments

Glaciers

During Ice Ages, ice spreads over large areas but, during warm periods, the ice retreats. The chart shows that the volume of ice in many glaciers is decreasing, possibly as a result of global warming. Experts estimate that, between 1850 and the early 21st century, more than half of the ice in Alpine glaciers has melted.

Juneau Glacier, Alaska

Like huge conveyor belts, glaciers transport weathered debris from mountain regions. Rocks frozen in the ice give the glaciers teeth, enabling them to wear out typical glaciated land features.

ANNUAL FLUCTUATIONS FOR SELECTED GLACIERS

Glacier name and location	Changes in the annual mass balance†		Cumulative total
	1970–1	1990–1	1970–90
Alfotbreen, Norway	+940	+790	+12,110
Wolverine, USA	+770	−410	+2,320
Storglaciaren, Sweden	−190	+170	−120
Djankuat, Russia	−230	−310	−1,890
Grasubreen, Norway	+470	−520	−2,530
Ürümqi, China	+102	−706	−3,828
Golubin, Kyrgyzstan	−90	−722	−7,105
Hintereisferner, Austria	−600	−1,325	−9,081
Gries, Switzerland	−970	−1,480	−10,600
Careser, Italy	−650	−1,730	−11,610
Abramov, Tajikistan	−890	−420	−13,700
Sarennes, France	−1,100	−1,360	−15,020
Place, Canada	−343	−990	−15,175

† *The annual mass balance is defined as the difference between glacier accumulation and ablation (melting) averaged over the whole glacier. Balances are expressed as water equivalent in millimetres. A plus indicates an increase in the depth or length of the glacier; a minus indicates a reduction.*

periodically dumped there by such rivers as the Ganges, Mississippi and Nile.

Running water in the form of sea waves and currents shapes coastlines, wearing out caves, natural arches, and stacks. The sea also transports and deposits worn material to form such features as spits and bars.

Glaciers in cold mountain regions flow downhill, gradually deepening valleys and shaping dramatic landscapes. They erode steep-sided U-shaped valleys, into which rivers often plunge in large waterfalls. Other features include cirques, armchair-shaped basins bounded by knife-edged ridges called *arêtes*. When several glacial cirques erode to form radial *arêtes*, pyramidal peaks like the Matterhorn are created. Deposits of moraine, rock material dumped by the glacier, are further evidence that ice once covered large areas. The work of glaciers, like other agents of erosion, varies with the climate. In recent years, global warming has been making glaciers retreat in many areas, while several of the ice shelves in Antarctica have been breaking up.

Many land features in deserts were formed by running water at a time when the climate was much rainier than it is today. Water erosion also occurs when flash floods are caused by rare thunderstorms. But the chief agent of erosion in dry areas is wind-blown sand, which can strip the paint from cars, and undercut boulders to create mushroom-shaped rocks.

Oceans and Ice

Since the 1970s, oceanographers have found numerous hot vents on the ocean ridges. Called black smokers, the vents emit dark, mineral-rich water reaching 350°C [662°F]. Around the vents are chimney-like structures formed from minerals deposited from the hot water. The discovery of black smokers did not surprise scientists who already knew that the ridges were plate edges, where new crustal rock was being formed as molten magma welled up to the surface. But what was astonishing was that the hot water contained vast numbers of bacteria, which provided the base of a food chain that included many strange creatures, such as giant worms, eyeless shrimps and white clams. Many species were unknown to science.

Little was known about the dark world beneath the waves until about 50 years ago. But through the use of modern technology such as echo-sounders, magnetometers, research ships equipped with huge drills, submersibles that can carry scientists down to the ocean floor, and satellites, the secrets of the oceans have been gradually revealed.

The study of the ocean floor led to the discovery that the oceans are geologically young features – no more than 200 million years old. It also revealed evidence as to how oceans form and continents drift because of the action of plate tectonics.

THE BLUE PLANET

Water covers almost 71% of the Earth, which makes it look blue when viewed from space. Although the oceans are interconnected, geographers divide them into four main areas: the Pacific, Atlantic, Indian and Arctic oceans. The average depth of the oceans is 3,370 m [12,238 ft], but they are divided into several zones.

Around most continents are gently sloping continental shelves, which are flooded parts of the continents. The shelves end at the continental slope, at a depth of about 200 m [656 ft]. This slope leads steeply down to the abyss. The deepest parts of the oceans are the trenches, which reach a maximum depth of 11,033 m [36,198 ft] in the Mariana Trench in the western Pacific.

Most marine life is found in the top 200 m [656 ft], where there is sufficient sunlight for plants, called phytoplankton, to grow. Below this zone, life becomes more and more scarce, though no part of the ocean, even at the bottom of the deepest trenches, is completely without living things.

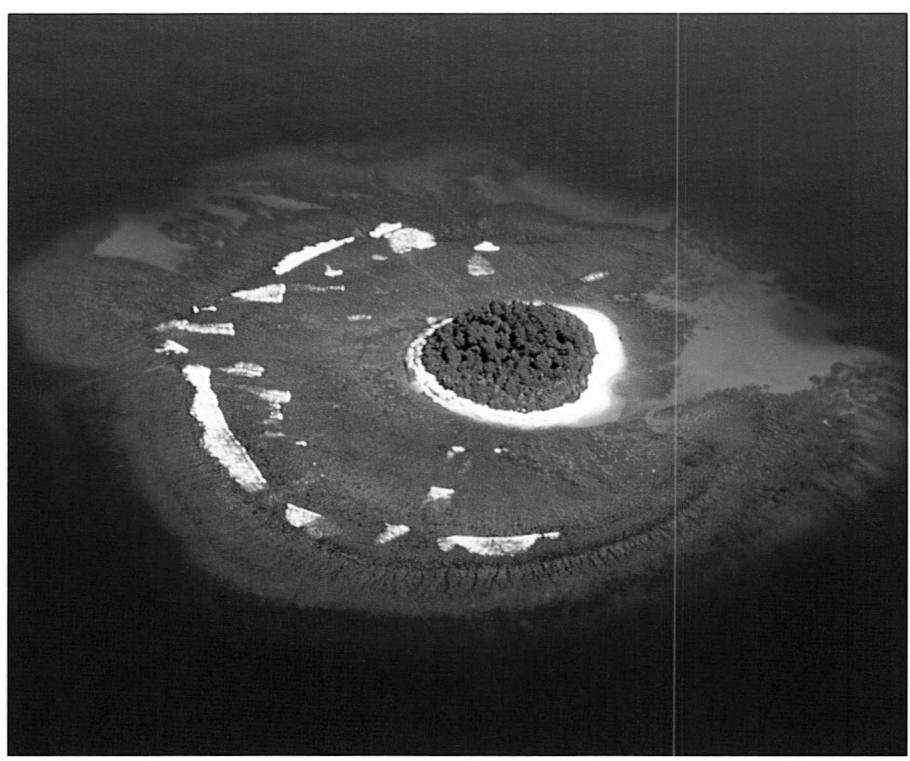

Vava'u Island, Tonga
This small coral atoll in northern Tonga consists of a central island covered by rainforest. Low coral reefs washed by the waves surround a shallow central lagoon.

Continental islands, such as the British Isles, are high parts of the continental shelves. For example, until about 7,500 years ago, when the ice sheets formed during the Ice Ages were melting, raising the sea level and filling the North Sea and the Strait of Dover, Britain was linked to mainland Europe.

By contrast, oceanic islands, such as the Hawaiian chain in the North Pacific Ocean, rise from the ocean floor. All oceanic islands are of volcanic origin, although many of them in warm parts of the oceans have sunk and are capped by layers of coral to form ring- or horseshoe-shaped atolls and coral reefs.

OCEAN WATER

The oceans contain about 97% of the world's water. Seawater contains more than 70 dissolved elements, but chloride and sodium make up 85% of the total. Sodium chloride is common salt and it makes seawater salty. The salinity of the oceans is mostly between 3.3–3.7%. Ocean water fed by icebergs or large rivers is less saline than shallow seas in the tropics, where the evaporation rate is high. Seawater is a source of salt but the water is useless for agriculture or drinking unless it is desalinated. However, land

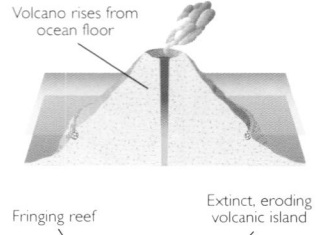

Volcano rises from ocean floor

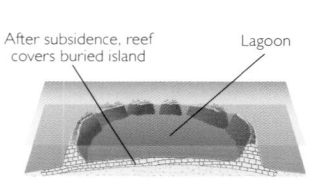

Fringing reef — Extinct, eroding volcanic island

After subsidence, reef covers buried island — Lagoon

Development of an atoll
Some of the volcanoes that rise from the ocean floor reach the surface to form islands. Some of these islands subside and become submerged. As an island sinks, coral starts to grow around the rim of the volcano, building up layer upon layer of limestone deposits to form fringing reefs. Sometimes coral grows on the tip of a central cone to form an island in the middle of the atoll.

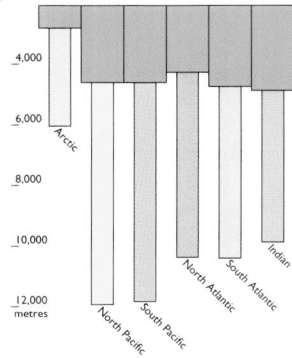

The ocean depths
The diagram shows the average depths (in dark blue) and the greatest depths in the four oceans. The North Pacific Ocean contains the world's deepest trenches, including the Mariana Trench, where the deepest manned descent was made by the bathyscaphe Trieste in 1960. It reached a depth of 10,916 metres [35,813 ft].

Relative sizes of the world's oceans:

PACIFIC	49%	ATLANTIC	26%
INDIAN	21%	ARCTIC	4%

Some geographers distinguish a fifth ocean, the Southern or Antarctic Ocean, but most authorities regard these waters as the southern extension of the Pacific, Atlantic and Indian oceans.

areas get a regular supply of fresh water through the hydrological cycle (see page 26).

The density of seawater depends on its salinity· and temperature. Temperatures vary from –2°C [28°F], the freezing point of seawater at the poles, to around 30°C [86°F] in parts of the tropics. Density differences help to maintain the circulation of the world's oceans, especially deep-sea currents. But the main cause of currents within 350 m [1,148 ft] of the surface is the wind. Because of the Earth's rotation, currents are deflected, creating huge circular motions of surface water – clockwise in the northern hemisphere and anticlockwise in the southern hemisphere.

Ocean currents transport heat from the tropics to the polar regions and thus form part of the heat engine that drives the Earth's climates. Ocean currents have an especially marked effect on coastal climates, such as north-western Europe. In the mid-1990s, scientists warned that global warming may be weakening currents, including the warm Gulf Stream which is responsible for the mild winters experienced in north-western Europe.

ICE SHEETS, ICE CAPS AND GLACIERS

Global warming is also a threat to the world's ice sheets, ice caps and glaciers that together account for about 2% of the world's water. There are two ice sheets in the world, the largest covers most of Antarctica. With the ice reaching maximum depths of 4,800 m [15,748 ft], the Antarctic ice sheet contains about 70% of the world's fresh water, with a total volume about nine times greater than the Greenland ice sheet. Smaller bodies of ice include ice caps in northern Canada, Iceland and Scandinavia. Also throughout the world in high ranges are many valley glaciers, which help to shape dramatic mountain scenery.

Only about 11,000 years ago, during the final phase of the Pleistocene Ice Age, ice covered much of the northern hemisphere. The Ice Age, which began about 1.8 million years ago, was not a continuous period of cold. Instead, it consisted of glacial periods when the ice advanced and warmer interglacial periods when temperatures rose and the ice retreated.

Some scientists believe that we are now living in an interglacial period, and that glacial conditions will recur in the future. Others fear that global warming, caused mainly by pollution, may melt the world's ice, raising sea levels by up to 55 m [180 ft]. Many fertile and densely populated coastal plains, islands and cities would vanish from the map.

Weddell Sea, Antarctica
Antarctica contains two huge bays, occupied by the Ross and Weddell seas. Ice shelves extend from the ice sheet across parts of these seas. Researchers fear that warmer weather is melting Antarctica's ice sheets at a dangerous rate, after large chunks of the Larsen ice shelf and the Ronne ice shelf broke away in 1997 and 1998 respectively. This was followed in March 2002 by the disintegration of the Larsen B ice shelf.

The Earth's Atmosphere

Since the discovery in 1985 of a thinning of the ozone layer, creating a so-called 'ozone hole', over Antarctica, many governments have worked to reduce the emissions of ozone-eating substances, notably the chlorofluorocarbons (CFCs) used in aerosols, refrigeration, air conditioning and dry cleaning.

Following forecasts that the ozone layer would rapidly repair itself as a result of controls on these emissions, scientists were surprised in early 1996 when a marked thinning of the ozone layer occurred over the Arctic, northern Europe, Russia and Canada. The damage, which was recorded as far south as southern Britain, was due to pollution combined with intense cold in the stratosphere. It was another sharp reminder of the dangers humanity faces when it interferes with and harms the environment.

The ozone layer in the stratosphere blocks out most of the dangerous ultraviolet B radiation in the Sun's rays. This radiation causes skin cancer and cataracts, as well as harming plants on the land and plankton in the oceans. The ozone layer is only one way in which the atmosphere protects life on Earth. The atmosphere also provides the air we breathe and the carbon dioxide required by plants. It is also a shield against meteors and it acts as a blanket to prevent heat radiated from the Earth escaping into space.

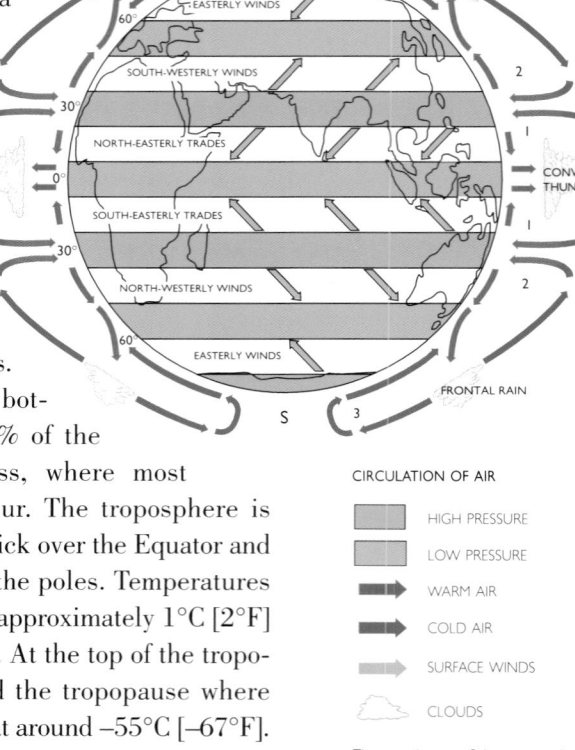

LAYERS OF AIR

The atmosphere is divided into four main layers. The troposphere at the bottom contains about 85% of the atmosphere's total mass, where most weather conditions occur. The troposphere is about 15 km [9 miles] thick over the Equator and 8 km [5 miles] thick at the poles. Temperatures decrease with height by approximately 1°C [2°F] for every 100 m [328 ft]. At the top of the troposphere is a level called the tropopause where temperatures are stable at around −55°C [−67°F]. Above the tropopause is the stratosphere, which contains the ozone layer. Here, at about 50 km [31 miles] above the Earth's surface, temperatures rise to about 0°C [32°F].

The ionosphere extends from the stratopause to about 600 km [373 miles] above the surface. Here temperatures fall up to about 80 km

CIRCULATION OF AIR

▨	HIGH PRESSURE
▨	LOW PRESSURE
➡	WARM AIR
➡	COLD AIR
➡	SURFACE WINDS
◠	CLOUDS

The circulation of the atmosphere can be divided into three rotating but interconnected air systems, or cells. The Hadley cell (figure 1 on the above diagram) is in the tropics; the Ferrel cell (2) lies between the subtropics and the mid-latitudes, and the Polar cell (3) is in the high latitudes.

Moonrise seen from orbit

This photograph taken by an orbiting Shuttle shows the crescent of the Moon. Silhouetted at the horizon is a dense cloud layer. The reddish-brown band is the tropopause, which separates the blue-white stratosphere from the yellow troposphere.

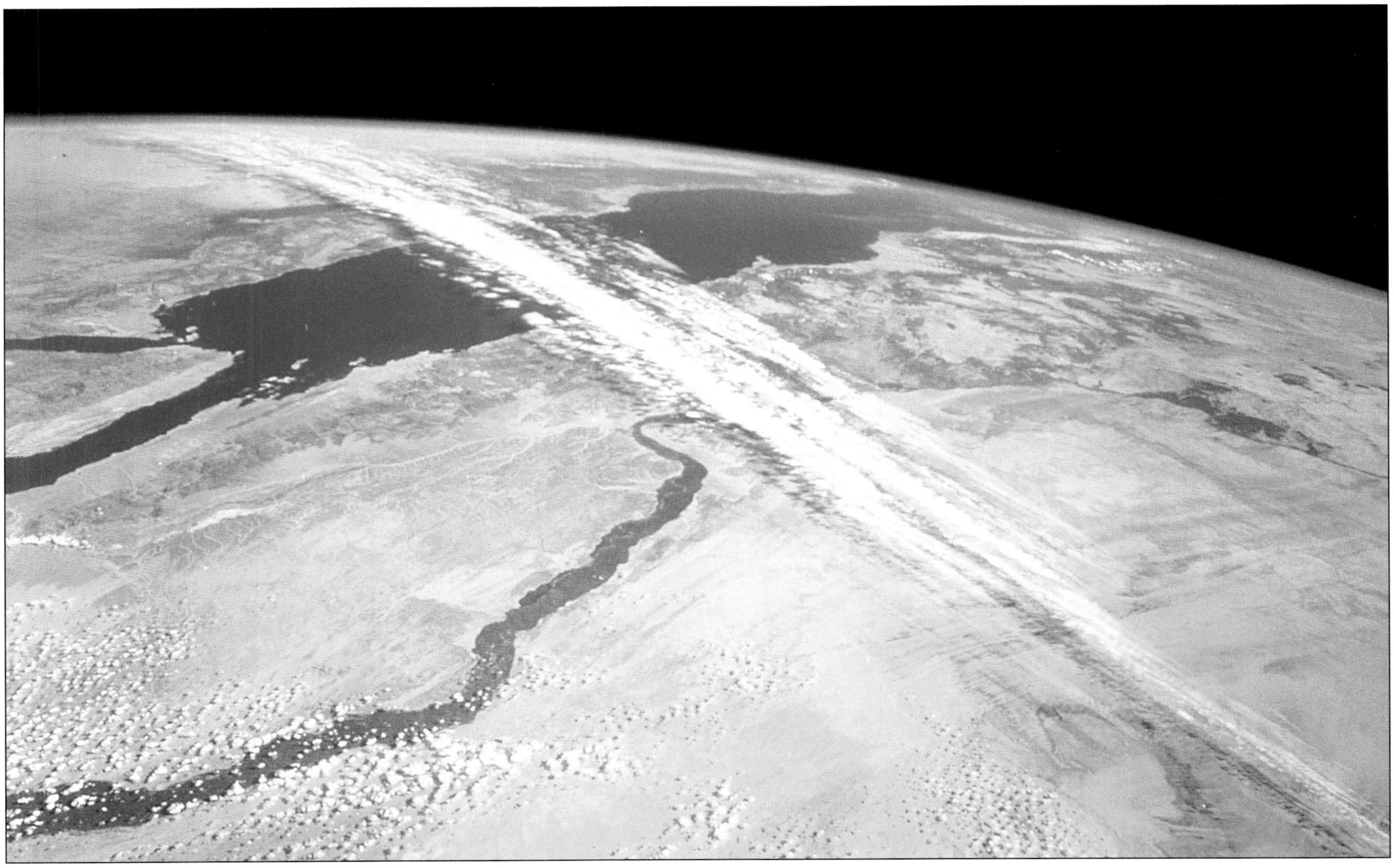

[50 miles], but then rise. The aurorae, which occur in the ionosphere when charged particles from the Sun interact with the Earth's magnetic field, are strongest near the poles. In the exosphere, the outermost layer, the atmosphere merges into space.

CIRCULATION OF THE ATMOSPHERE
The heating of the Earth is most intense around the Equator where the Sun is high in the sky. Here warm, moist air rises in strong currents, creating a zone of low air pressure: the doldrums. The rising air eventually cools and spreads out north and south until it sinks back to the ground around latitudes 30° North and 30° South. This forms two zones of high air pressure called the horse latitudes.

From the horse latitudes, trade winds blow back across the surface towards the Equator, while westerly winds blow towards the poles. The warm westerlies finally meet the polar easterlies (cold dense air flowing from the poles). The line along which the warm and cold air streams meet is called the polar front. Depressions (or cyclones) are low air pressure frontal systems that form along the polar front.

COMPOSITION OF THE ATMOSPHERE
The air in the troposphere is made up mainly of nitrogen (78%) and oxygen (21%). Argon makes up more than 0.9% and there are also minute amounts of carbon dioxide, helium, hydrogen, krypton, methane, ozone and xenon. The atmosphere also contains water vapour, the gaseous form of water, which, when it condenses around minute specks of dust and salt, forms tiny water droplets or ice crystals. Large masses of water droplets or ice crystals form clouds.

Classification of clouds

Clouds are classified broadly into cumuliform, or 'heap' clouds, and stratiform, or 'layer' clouds. Both types occur at all levels. The highest clouds, composed of ice crystals, are cirrus, cirrostratus and cirrocumulus. Medium-height clouds include altostratus, a grey cloud that often indicates the approach of a depression, and altocumulus, a thicker and fluffier version of cirrocumulus. Low clouds include stratus, which forms dull, overcast skies; nimbostratus, a dark grey layer cloud which brings almost continuous rain and snow; cumulus, a brilliant white heap cloud; and stratocumulus, a layer cloud arranged in globular masses or rolls. Cumulonimbus, a cloud associated with thunderstorms, lightning and heavy rain, often extends from low to medium altitudes. It has a flat base, a fluffy outline and often an anvil-shaped top.

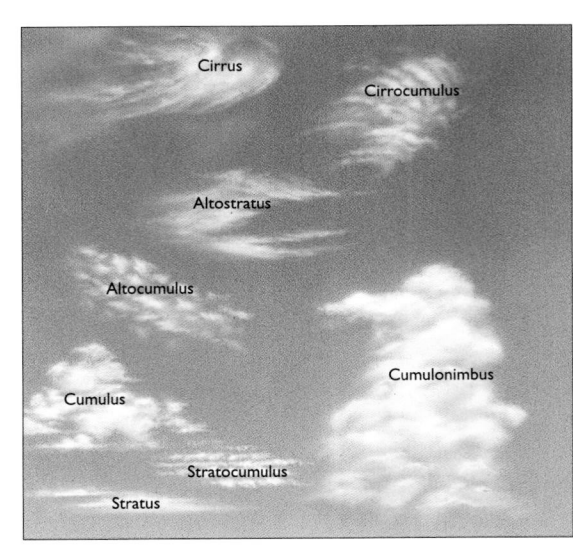

Cirrus
Cirrocumulus
Altostratus
Altocumulus
Cumulonimbus
Cumulus
Stratocumulus
Stratus

Climate and Weather

In 1992, Hurricane Andrew struck the Bahamas, Florida and Louisiana, causing record damage estimated at $30 billion. In September 1998, following heavy monsoon rains, floods submerged two-thirds of Bangladesh. The same month, in Central America, more than 7,000 people died in floods and mudslides caused by Hurricane Mitch. The economy of Honduras, already crippled by debt, was thought to have been put back by 15 to 20 years. In November 2001, violent storms in Algeria caused the deaths of more than 700 people in floods and landslides.

Every year, exceptional weather conditions cause disasters around the world. Modern forecasting techniques now give people warning of advancing storms, but the toll of human deaths continues as people are powerless in the face of the awesome forces of nature.

Weather is the day-to-day condition of the atmosphere. In some places, the weather is normally stable, but in other areas, especially the middle latitudes, it is highly variable, changing with the passing of a depression. By contrast, climate is the average weather of a place, based on data obtained over a long period.

Hurricane Elena, 1995
Hurricanes form over warm oceans north and south of the Equator. Their movements are tracked by satellites, enabling forecasters to issue storm warnings as they approach land. In North America, forecasters identify them with boys' and girls' names.

CLIMATIC FACTORS

Climate depends basically on the unequal heating of the Sun between the Equator and the poles. But ocean currents and terrain also affect climate. For example, despite their northerly positions, Norway's ports remain ice-free in winter. This is because of the warming effect of the North Atlantic Drift, an extension of the Gulf Stream which flows across the Atlantic Ocean from the Gulf of Mexico.

By contrast, the cold Benguela current which flows up the coast of south-western Africa cools the coast and causes arid conditions. This is because the cold onshore winds are warmed as they pass over the land. The warm air can hold more water vapour than cold air, giving the winds a drying effect.

The terrain affects climate in several ways. Because temperatures fall with altitude, highlands are cooler than lowlands in the same

CLIMATIC REGIONS

Tropical rainy climates
All mean monthly temperatures above 18°C [64°F].

RAINFOREST CLIMATE
MONSOON CLIMATE
SAVANNA CLIMATE

Dry climates
Low rainfall combined with a wide range of temperatures.

STEPPE CLIMATE
DESERT CLIMATE

Warm temperate rainy climates
The mean temperature is below 18°C [64°F] but above −3°C [26°F] and that of the warmest month is over 10°C [50°F].

DRY WINTER CLIMATE
DRY SUMMER CLIMATE
CLIMATE WITH NO DRY SEASON

Cold temperate rainy climates
The mean temperature of the coldest month is below 3°C [37°F] but the warmest month is over 10°C [50°F].

DRY WINTER CLIMATE
CLIMATE WITH NO DRY SEASON

Polar climates
The temperature of the warmest month is below 10°C [50°F], giving permanently frozen subsoil.

TUNDRA CLIMATE
POLAR CLIMATE

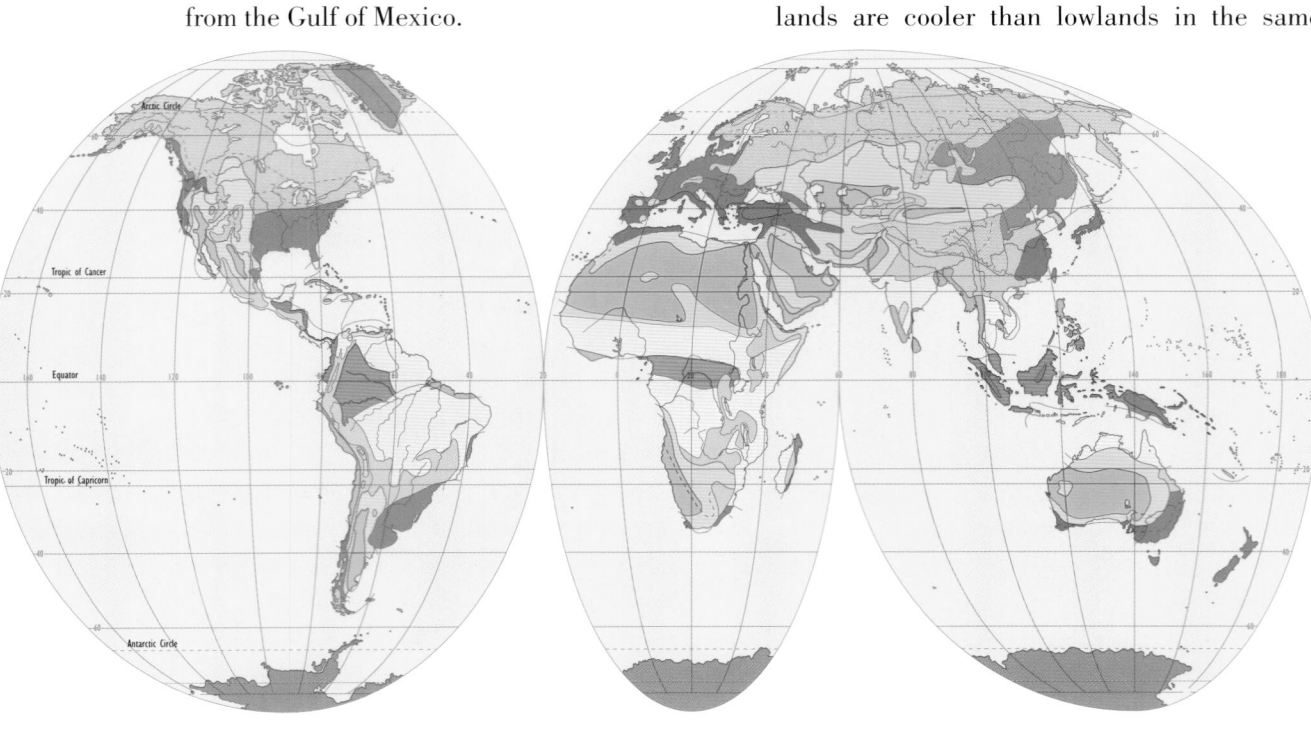

Flood damage in the United States
In June and July 1993, the Mississippi River basin suffered record floods. The photograph shows a sunken church in Illinois. The flooding along the Mississippi, Missouri and other rivers caused great damage, amounting to about $12 billion. At least 48 people died in the floods.

Floods in St Louis, United States
The satellite image, right, shows the extent of the floods at St Louis at the confluence of the Mississippi and the Missouri rivers in June and July 1993. The floods occurred when very heavy rainfall raised river levels by up to 14 m [46 ft]. The floods reached their greatest extent between Minneapolis in the north and a point approximately 150 km [93 miles] south of St Louis. In places, the width of the Mississippi increased to nearly 11 km [7 miles], while the Missouri reached widths of 32 km [20 miles]. In all, more than 28,000 sq km [10,800 sq miles] were inundated and hundreds of towns and cities were flooded. Damage to crops was estimated at $8 billion. The USA was hit again by flooding in early 1997, when heavy rainfall in North Dakota and Minnesota caused the Red River to flood. The flooding had a catastrophic effect on the city of Grand Forks, which was inundated for months.

latitude. Terrain also affects rainfall. When moist onshore winds pass over mountain ranges, they are chilled as they are forced to rise and the water vapour they contain condenses to form clouds which bring rain and snow. After the winds have crossed the mountains, the air descends and is warmed. These warm, dry winds create rain shadow (arid) regions on the lee side of the mountains.

CLIMATIC REGIONS

The two major factors that affect climate are temperature and precipitation, including rain and snow. In addition, seasonal variations and other climatic features are also taken into account. Climatic classifications vary because of the weighting given to various features. Yet most classifications are based on five main climatic types: tropical rainy climates; dry climates; warm temperate rainy climates; cold temperate rainy climates; and very cold polar climates. Some classifications also allow for the effect of altitude. The main climatic regions are sub-divided according to seasonal variations and also to the kind of vegetation associated with the climatic conditions. Thus, the rainforest climate, with rain throughout the year, differs from monsoon and savanna climates, which have marked dry seasons. Similarly, parched desert climates differ from steppe climates which have enough moisture for grasses to grow.

Water and Land Use

All life on land depends on fresh water. Yet about 80 countries now face acute water shortages. The world demand for fresh water is increasing by about 2.3% a year and this demand will double every 21 years. About a billion people, mainly in developing countries, do not have access to clean drinking water and around 10 million die every year from drinking dirty water. This problem is made worse in many countries by the pollution of rivers and lakes.

In 1995, a World Bank report suggested that wars will be fought over water in the 21st century. Relations between several countries are

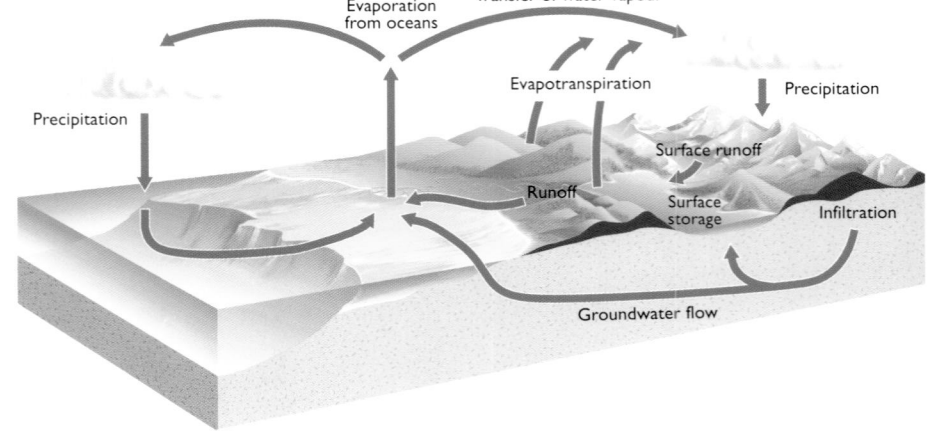

already soured by disputes over water resources. Egypt fears that Sudan and Ethiopia will appropriate the waters of the Nile, while Syria and Iraq are concerned that Turkish dams will hold back the waters of the Euphrates.

However, experts stress that while individual countries face water crises, there is no global crisis. The chief global problems are the uneven distribution of water and its inefficient and wasteful use.

THE WORLD'S WATER SUPPLY

Of the world's total water supply, 99.4% is in the oceans or frozen in bodies of ice. Most of the rest circulates through the rocks beneath our feet as ground water. Water in rivers and lakes, in the soil and in the atmosphere together make up only 0.013% of the world's water.

The freshwater supply on land is dependent on the hydrological, or water cycle which is driven by the Sun's heat. Water is evaporated from the oceans and carried into the air as invisible water vapour. Although this vapour averages less than 2% of the total mass of the atmosphere, it is the chief component from the standpoint of weather.

When air rises, water vapour condenses into visible water droplets or ice crystals, which eventually fall to earth as rain, snow, sleet, hail or frost. Some of the precipitation that reaches the ground returns directly to the atmosphere through evaporation or transpiration via plants. Much of the rest of the water flows into the rocks to become ground water or across the surface into rivers and, eventually, back to the oceans, so completing the hydrological cycle.

WATER AND AGRICULTURE

Only about a third of the world's land area is used for growing crops, while another third

Hoover Dam, United States
The Hoover Dam in Arizona controls the Colorado River's flood waters. Its reservoir supplies domestic and irrigation water to the south-west, while a hydroelectric plant produces electricity.

The hydrological cycle
The hydrological cycle is responsible for the continuous circulation of water around the planet. Water vapour contains and transports latent heat, or latent energy. When the water vapour condenses back into water (and falls as rain, hail or snow), the heat is released. When condensation takes place on cold nights, the cooling effect associated with nightfall is offset by the liberation of latent heat.

WATER DISTRIBUTION
The distribution of planetary water, by percentage.

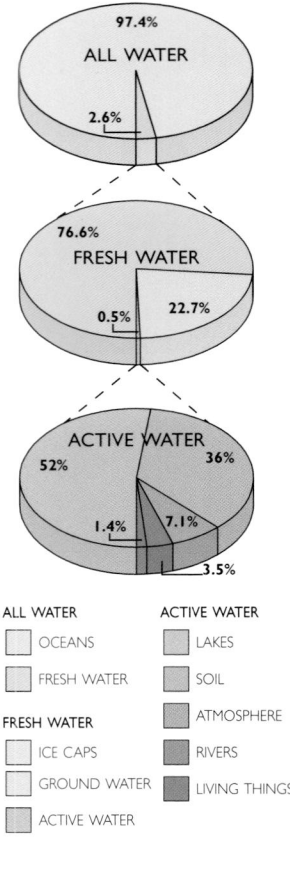

ALL WATER	ACTIVE WATER
☐ OCEANS	☐ LAKES
☐ FRESH WATER	☐ SOIL
	☐ ATMOSPHERE
FRESH WATER	☐ RIVERS
☐ ICE CAPS	☐ LIVING THINGS
☐ GROUND WATER	
☐ ACTIVE WATER	

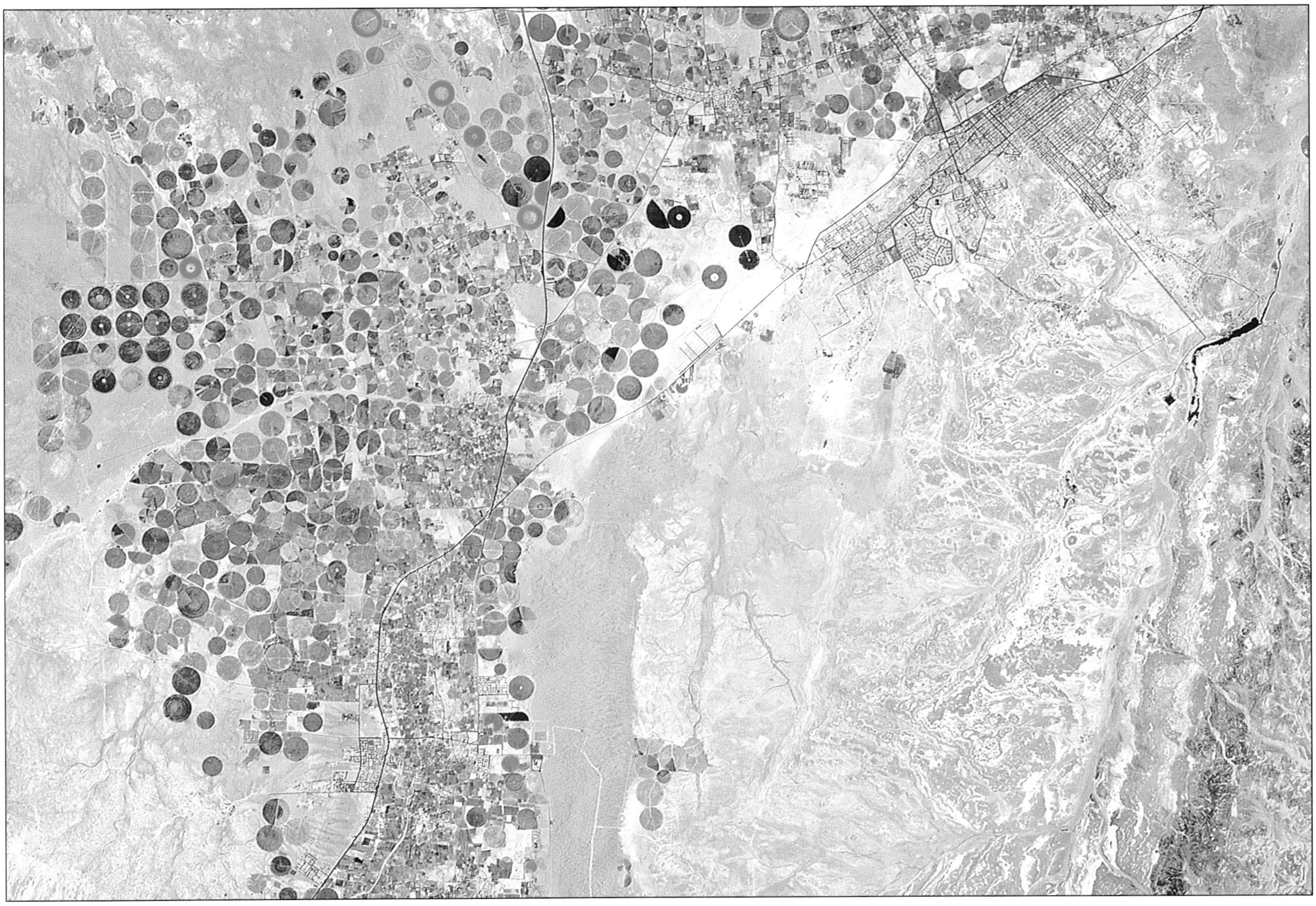

Irrigation boom

The photograph shows a pivotal irrigation boom used to sprinkle water over a wheat field in Saudi Arabia. Irrigation in hot countries often takes place at night so that water loss through evaporation is reduced. Irrigation techniques vary from place to place. In monsoon areas with abundant water, the fields are often flooded, or the water is led to the crops along straight furrows. Sprinkler irrigation has become important since the 1940s. In other types of irrigation, the water is led through pipes which are on or under the ground. Underground pipes supply water directly to the plant roots and, as a result, water loss through evaporation is minimized.

Irrigation in Saudi Arabia

Saudi Arabia is a desert country which gets its water from oases, which tap ground water supplies, and desalination plants. The sale of oil has enabled the arid countries of south-western Asia to develop their agriculture. In the above satellite image, vegetation appears brown and red.

consists of meadows and pasture. The rest of the world is unsuitable for farming, being too dry, too cold, too mountainous, or covered by dense forests. Although the demand for food increases every year, problems arise when attempts are made to increase the existing area of farmland. For example, the soils and climates of tropical forest and semi-arid regions of Africa and South America are not ideal for farming. Attempts to work such areas usually end in failure. To increase the world's food supply, scientists now concentrate on making existing farmland more productive rather than farming marginal land.

To grow crops, farmers need fertile, workable land, an equable climate, including a frost-free growing period, and an adequate supply of fresh water. In some areas, the water falls directly as rain. But many other regions depend on irrigation.

Irrigation involves water conservation through the building of dams which hold back storage reservoirs. In some areas, irrigation water comes from underground aquifers, layers of permeable and porous rocks through which ground water percolates. But in many cases, the water in the aquifers has been there for thousands of years, having accumulated at a time when the rainfall was much greater than it is today. As a result, these aquifers are not being renewed and will, one day, dry up.

Other sources of irrigation water are desalination plants, which remove salt from seawater and pump it to farms. This is a highly expensive process and is employed in areas where water supplies are extremely low, such as the island of Malta, or in the oil-rich desert countries around the Gulf, which can afford to build huge desalination plants.

LAND USE BY CONTINENT

	Forest	Permanent pasture	Permanent crops	Arable	Non-productive
North America	32.2%	17.3%	0.3%	12.6%	37.6%
South America	51.8%	26.7%	1.5%	6.6%	13.4%
Europe	33.4%	17.5%	3.0%	26.8%	19.3%
Africa	23.2%	26.6%	0.6%	5.6%	44.0%
Asia	20.2%	25.0%	1.2%	16.0%	37.8%
Oceania	23.5%	52.2%	0.1%	5.7%	18.5%

The Natural World

In 2002, a United Nations report identified more than 11,000 plant and animal species known to face a high risk of extinction, including 24% of all mammals and 12% of birds. Human activities, ranging from habitat destruction to the introduction of alien species from one area to another, are the main causes of this devastating reduction of our planet's biodiversity, which might lead to the disappearance of unique combinations of genes that could be vital in improving food yields on farms or in the production of drugs to combat disease.

Extinctions of species have occurred throughout Earth history, but today the extinction rate is estimated to be about 10,000 times the natural average. Some scientists have even compared it with the mass extinction that wiped out the dinosaurs 65 million years ago. However, the main cause of today's high extinction rate is not some natural disaster, such as the impact of an asteroid a few kilometres across, but it is the result of human actions, most notably the destruction of natural habitats for farming and other purposes. In some densely populated areas, such as Western Europe, the natural

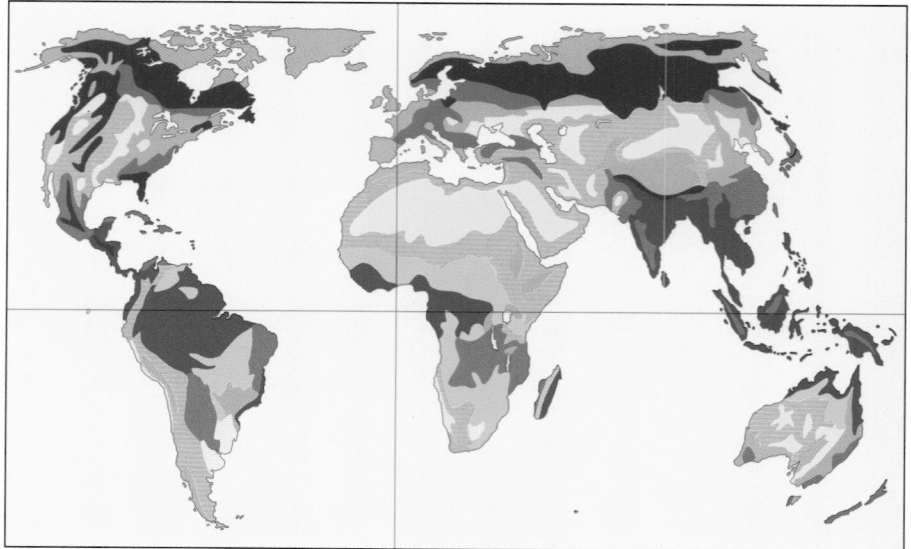

Rainforest in Rwanda

Rainforests are the most threatened of the world's biomes. Effective conservation policies must demonstrate to poor local people that they can benefit from the survival of the forests.

habitats were destroyed long ago. Today, the greatest damage is occurring in tropical rainforests, which contain more than half of the world's known species.

Modern technology has enabled people to live comfortably almost anywhere on Earth. But most plants and many animals are adapted to particular climatic conditions, and they live in association with and dependent on each other. Plant and animal communities that cover large areas are called biomes.

THE WORLD'S BIOMES

The world's biomes are defined mainly by climate and vegetation. They range from the tundra, in polar regions and high mountain regions, to the lush equatorial rainforests.

The Arctic tundra covers large areas in the polar regions of the northern hemisphere. Snow covers the land for more than half of the year and the subsoil, called permafrost, is permanently frozen. Comparatively few species can survive in this harsh, treeless environment. The main plants are hardy mosses, lichens, grasses, sedges and low shrubs. However, in summer, the tundra plays an important part in world animal geography, when its growing plants and swarms of insects provide food for migrating animals and birds that arrive from the south.

The tundra of the northern hemisphere merges in the south into a vast region of needleleaf evergreen forest, called the boreal forest or taiga. Such trees as fir, larch, pine and spruce are adapted to survive the long, bitterly cold winters of this region, but the number of plant and animal species is again small. South of the boreal forests is a zone of mixed needleleaf evergreens and broadleaf deciduous trees, which

NATURAL VEGETATION

- TUNDRA & MOUNTAIN VEGETATION
- NEEDLELEAF EVERGREEN FOREST
- MIXED NEEDLELEAF EVERGREEN & BROADLEAF DECIDUOUS TREES
- BROADLEAF DECIDUOUS WOODLAND
- MID-LATITUDE GRASSLAND
- EVERGREEN BROADLEAF & DECIDUOUS TREES & SHRUBS
- SEMI-DESERT SCRUB
- DESERT
- TROPICAL GRASSLAND (SAVANNA)
- TROPICAL BROADLEAF RAINFOREST & MONSOON FOREST
- SUBTROPICAL BROADLEAF & NEEDLELEAF FOREST

The map shows the world's main biomes. The classification is based on the natural 'climax' vegetation of regions, a result of the climate and the terrain. But human activities have greatly modified this basic division. For example, the original deciduous forests of Western Europe and the eastern United States have largely disappeared. In recent times, human development of some semi-arid areas has turned former dry grasslands into barren desert.

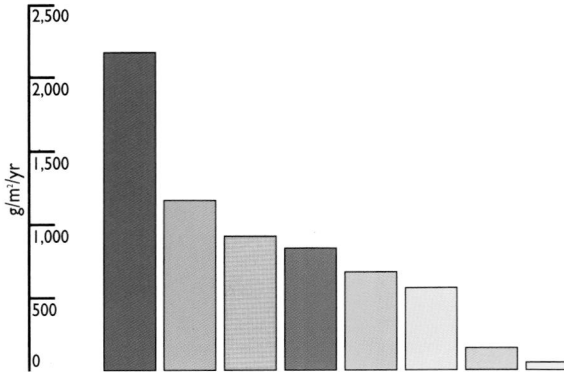

Tundra in subarctic Alaska
The Denali National Park, Alaska, contains magnificent mountain scenery and tundra vegetation which flourishes during the brief summer. The park is open between 1 June and 15 September.

shed their leaves in winter. In warmer areas, this mixed forest merges into broadleaf deciduous forest, where the number and diversity of plant species is much greater.

Deciduous forests are adapted to temperate, humid regions. Evergreen broadleaf and deciduous trees grow in Mediterranean regions, with their hot, dry summers. But much of the original deciduous forest has been cut down and has given way to scrub and heathland. Grasslands occupy large areas in the middle latitudes, where the rainfall is insufficient to support forest growth. The moister grasslands are often called prairies, while drier areas are called steppe.

The tropics also contain vast dry areas of semi-desert scrub which merges into desert, as well as large areas of savanna, which is grassland with scattered trees. Savanna regions, with their marked dry season, support a wide range of mammals.

Tropical and subtropical regions contain three types of forest biomes. The tropical rainforest, the world's richest biome measured by its plant and animal species, experiences rain and high temperatures throughout the year. Similar forests occur in monsoon regions, which have a season of very heavy rainfall. They, too, are rich in plant species, though less so than the tropical rainforest. A third type of forest is the subtropical broadleaf and needleleaf forest, found in such places as south-eastern China, south-central Africa and eastern Brazil.

NET PRIMARY PRODUCTION OF EIGHT MAJOR BIOMES

- TROPICAL RAINFORESTS
- DECIDUOUS FORESTS
- TROPICAL GRASSLANDS
- CONIFEROUS FORESTS
- MEDITERRANEAN
- TEMPERATE GRASSLANDS
- TUNDRA
- DESERTS

The net primary production of eight major biomes is expressed in grams of dry organic matter per square metre per year. The tropical rainforests produce the greatest amount of organic material. The tundra and deserts produce the least.

2,500
2,000
1,500
1,000
500
0

g/m²/yr

The Human World

Every minute, the world's population increases by between 160 and 170. While forecasts of future growth are difficult to make, most demographers are in agreement that the world's population, which passed the 6 billion mark in October 1999, would reach 8.9 billion by 2050. It was not expected to level out until 2200, when it would peak at around 11 billion. After 2200, it is expected to level out or even decline a little. The fastest rates of increase will take place in the developing countries of Africa, Asia and Latin America – the places least able to afford the enormous costs incurred by such a rapidly expanding population.

Elevated view of Ki Lung Street, Hong Kong
Urban areas of Hong Kong, a Special Administrative Region on the southern coast of China, contain busy streets overlooked by crowded apartments.

Average world population growth rates have declined from about 2% a year in the early 1960s to 1.4% in 1998. This was partly due to a decline in fertility rates – that is, the number of births to the number of women of child-bearing age – especially in developed countries where, as income has risen, the average size of families has fallen.

Declining fertility rates were also evident in many developing countries. Even Africa shows signs of such change, though its population is expected to triple before it begins to fall. Population growth is also dependent on death rates, which are affected by such factors as famine, disease and the quality of medical care.

THE POPULATION EXPLOSION

The world's population has grown steadily throughout most of human history, though certain events triggered periods of population growth. The invention of agriculture around 10,000 years ago, led to great changes in human society. Before then, most people had obtained food by hunting animals and gathering plants. Average life expectancies were probably no more than 20 years and life was hard. However, when farmers began to produce food surpluses, people began to live settled lives. This major milestone in human history led to the development of the first cities and early civilizations.

From an estimated 8 million in 8000 BC, the world population rose to about 300 million by AD 1000. Between 1000 and 1750, the rate of world population increase was around 0.1% per year, but another period of major economic and social change – the Industrial Revolution – began in the late 18th century. The Industrial Revolution led to improvements in farm technology and increases in food production. The world population began to increase quickly as industrialization spread across Europe and into North America. By 1850, it had reached 1.2 billion. The 2 billion mark was passed in the 1920s, and then the population rapidly doubled to 4 billion by the 1970s.

POPULATION FEATURES

Population growth affects the structure of societies. In developing countries with high annual rates of population increase, the large majority of the people are young and soon to become parents themselves. For example, in Kenya, which had until recently an annual rate of population growth of around 4%, just over half

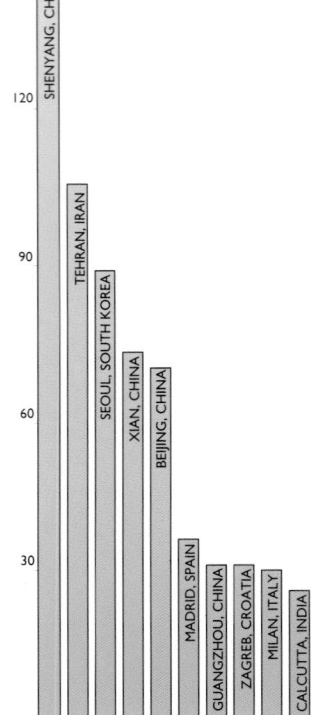

Urban air pollution
This diagram of the world's most polluted cities indicates the number of days per year when sulphur dioxide levels exceed the WHO threshhold of 150 micrograms per cubic metre.

Hong Kong's business district
By contrast with the picturesque old streets of Hong Kong, the business district of Hong Kong City, on the northern shore of Hong Kong Island, is a cluster of modern high-rise buildings. The glittering skyscrapers reflect the success of this tiny region, which has one of the strongest economies in Asia.

of the population is under 15 years of age. On the other hand, the populations of developed countries, with low population growth rates, have a fairly even spread across age groups.

Such differences are reflected in average life expectancies at birth. In rich countries, such as Australia and the United States, the average life expectancy is 77 years (74 years for men and 80 for women; women live longer, on average, than their male counterparts). As a result, an increasing proportion of the people are elderly and retired, contributing little to the economy. The reverse applies in many poor countries, where average life expectancies are below 60 years. In the early 21st century, life expectancies were falling in some southern African countries, such as Botswana, where they fell from nearly 70 to around 40 years because of the fast spread of HIV and AIDS.

Paralleling the population explosion has been a rapid growth in the number and size of cities and towns, which contained nearly half of the world's people by the 1990s. This proportion

POPULATION CHANGE 1990–2000
The population change for the years 1990–2000.

OVER 40% POPULATION GAIN
30–40% POPULATION GAIN
20–30% POPULATION GAIN
10–20% POPULATION GAIN
0–10% POPULATION GAIN
NO CHANGE OR LOSS

TOP 5 COUNTRIES
Kuwait	+75.9%
Namibia	+62.5%
Afghanistan	+60.1%
Mali	+55.5%
Tanzania	+54.6%

BOTTOM 5 COUNTRIES
Belgium	-0.1%
Hungary	-0.2%
Grenada	-2.4%
Germany	-3.2%
Tonga	-3.2%

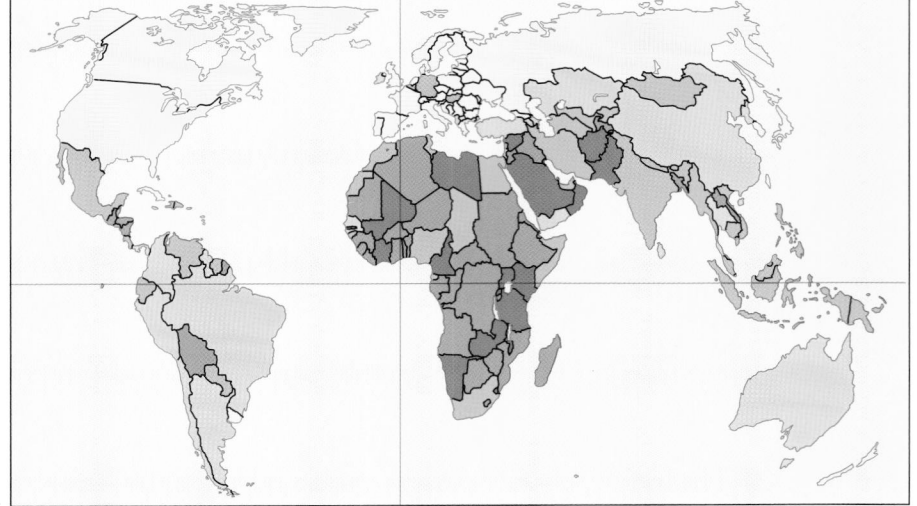

is expected to rise to nearly two-thirds by 2025.

Urbanization occurred first in areas undergoing the industrialization of their economies, but today it is also a feature of the developing world. In developing countries, people are leaving impoverished rural areas hoping to gain access to the education, health and other services available in cities. But many cities cannot provide the facilities necessitated by rapid population growth. Slums develop and pollution, crime and disease become features of everyday life.

The population explosion poses another problem for the entire world. No one knows how many people the world can support or how consumer demand will damage the fragile environments on our planet. The British economist Thomas Malthus argued in the late 18th century that overpopulation would lead to famine and war. But an increase in farm technology in the 19th and 20th centuries, combined with a green revolution, in which scientists developed high-yield crop varieties, has greatly increased food production since Malthus' time.

However, some modern scientists argue that overpopulation may become a problem in the 21st century. They argue that food shortages leading to disastrous famines will result unless population growth can be halted. Such people argue in favour of birth control programmes. China, one of the two countries with more than a billion people, has introduced a one-child family policy. Its action has slowed the growth of China's huge population.

Languages and Religions

In 1995, 90-year-old Edna Guerro died in northern California. She was the last person able to speak Northern Pomo, one of about 50 Native American languages spoken in the state. Her death marked the extinction of one of the world's languages.

This event is not an isolated incident. Language experts regularly report the disappearance of languages and some of them predict that between 20 to 50% of the world's languages will no longer exist by the end of the 21st century. Improved transport and communications are partly to blame, because they bring people from various cultures into closer and closer contact. Many children no longer speak the language of their parents, preferring instead to learn the language used at their schools. The pressures on children to speak dominant rather than minority languages are often great. In the first part of the 20th century, Native American children were punished if they spoke their native language.

The disappearance of a language represents the extinction of a way of thinking, a unique expression of the experiences and knowledge of a group of people. Language and religion together give people an identity and a sense of belonging. However, there are others who argue that the disappearance of minority languages is a step towards international understanding and economic efficiency.

THE WORLD'S LANGUAGES

Definitions of what is a language or a dialect vary and, hence, estimates of the number of languages spoken around the world range from about 3,000 to 6,000. But whatever the figure, it is clear that the number of languages far exceeds the number of countries.

RELIGIOUS ADHERENTS

Number of adherents to the world's major religions, in millions (1998).

Christian	1,980
Roman Catholic	1,300
Orthodox	240
African sects	110
Pentecostal	105
Others	225
Islam	1,300
Sunni	940
Shiite	120
Others	240
Hindu	900
Secular/Atheist/Agnostic/	
Non-religious	850
Buddhist	360
Chinese Traditional	225
Indigenous/Animist	190
Sikh	23
Yoruba	20
Juche	19
Spiritism	14
Judaism	14
Baha'i	6
Jainism	4
Shinto	4

Buddhist monks in Katmandu, Nepal

Hinduism is Nepal's official religion, but the Nepalese observe the festivals of both Hinduism and Buddhism. They also regard Buddhist shrines and Hindu temples as equally sacred.

Countries with only one language tend to be small. For example, in Liechtenstein, everyone speaks German. By contrast, more than 860 languages have been identified in Papua New Guinea, whose population is only about 4.6 million people. Hence, many of its languages are spoken by only small groups of people. In fact, scientists have estimated that about a third of the world's languages are now spoken by less than 1,000 people. By contrast, more than half of the world's population speak just seven languages.

The world's languages are grouped into families. The Indo-European family consists of languages spoken between Europe and the Indian subcontinent. The growth of European empires over the last 300 years led several Indo-European languages, most notably English, French, Portuguese and Spanish, to spread throughout much of North and South America, Africa, Australia and New Zealand.

English has become the official language in many countries which together contain more than a quarter of the world's population. It is now a major international language, surpassing in importance Mandarin Chinese, a member of the Sino-Tibetan family, which is the world's leading first language. Without a knowledge of English, businessmen face many problems when conducting international trade, especially with the United States or other English-speaking countries. But proposals that English, French, Russian or some other language should become a world language seem unlikely to be acceptable to a majority of the world's peoples.

WORLD RELIGIONS

Religion is another fundamental aspect of human culture. It has inspired much of the world's finest architecture, literature, music and painting. It has also helped to shape human cultures since prehistoric times and is responsible for the codes of ethics by which most people live.

The world's major religions were all founded in Asia. Judaism, one of the first faiths to teach that there is only one god, is one of the world's oldest. Founded in south-western Asia, it influenced the more recent Christianity and Islam, two other monotheistic religions which

MOTHER TONGUES
First-language speakers of the major languages, in millions (1999).

- MANDARIN CHINESE 885M
- SPANISH 332M
- ENGLISH 322M
- BENGALI 189M
- HINDI 182M
- PORTUGUESE 170M
- RUSSIAN 170M
- JAPANESE 125M
- GERMAN 98M
- WU CHINESE 77M

OFFICIAL LANGUAGES: % OF WORLD POPULATION	
English	27.0%
Chinese	19.0%
Hindi	13.5%
Spanish	5.4%
Russian	5.2%
French	4.2%
Arabic	3.3%
Portuguese	3.0%
Malay	3.0%
Bengali	2.9%
Japanese	2.3%

Polyglot nations

The graph, right, shows countries of the world with more than 200 languages. Although it has only about 4.6 million people, Papua New Guinea holds the record for the number of languages spoken.

Brazil (210)
Congo (Z.) (220)
Australia (230)
Mexico (240)
Cameroon (275)
India (410)
Nigeria (470)
Indonesia (701)
Papua New Guinea (862)

The Church of San Giovanni, Dolomites, Italy
Christianity has done much to shape Western civilization. Christian churches were built as places of worship, but many of them are among the finest achievements of world architecture.

now have the greatest number of followers. Hinduism, the third leading faith in terms of the numbers of followers, originated in the Indian subcontinent and most Hindus are now found in India. Another major religion, Buddhism, was founded in the subcontinent partly as a reaction to certain aspects of Hinduism. But unlike Hinduism, it has spread from India throughout much of eastern Asia.

Religion and language are powerful creative forces. They are also essential features of nationalism, which gives people a sense of belonging and pride. But nationalism is often also a cause of rivalry and tension. Cultural differences have led to racial hatred, the persecution of minorities, and to war between national groups.

International Organizations

Twelve days before the surrender of Germany and four months before the final end of World War II, representatives of 50 nations met in San Francisco to create a plan to set up a peace-keeping organization, the United Nations. Since its birth on 24 October 1945, its membership has grown from 51 to 189 in 2001.

Its first 50 years have been marked by failures as well as successes. While it has helped to prevent some disputes from flaring up into full-scale wars, the Blue Berets, as the UN troops are called, have been forced, because of their policy of neutrality, to stand by when atrocities are committed by rival warring groups.

THE WORK OF THE UN

The United Nations has six main organs. They include the General Assembly, where member states meet to discuss issues concerned with peace, security and development. The Security Council, containing 15 members, is concerned with main-taining world peace. The Secretariat, under the Secretary-General, helps the other organs to do their jobs effectively, while the Economic and Social Council works with specialized agencies to implement policies concerned with such matters as development, education and health. The Interna-tional Court of Justice, or World Court, helps to settle disputes between member nations. The sixth organ of the UN, the Trusteeship Council, was designed to bring 11 UN trust territories to inde-pendence. Its task has now been completed.

The specialized agencies do much important work. For example, UNICEF (United Nations

Food aid

International organizations supply aid to people living in areas suffering from war or famine. In Bosnia-Herzegovina, the UN Protection Force supervised the movements of food aid, as did NATO on the borders of Kosovo a few years later.

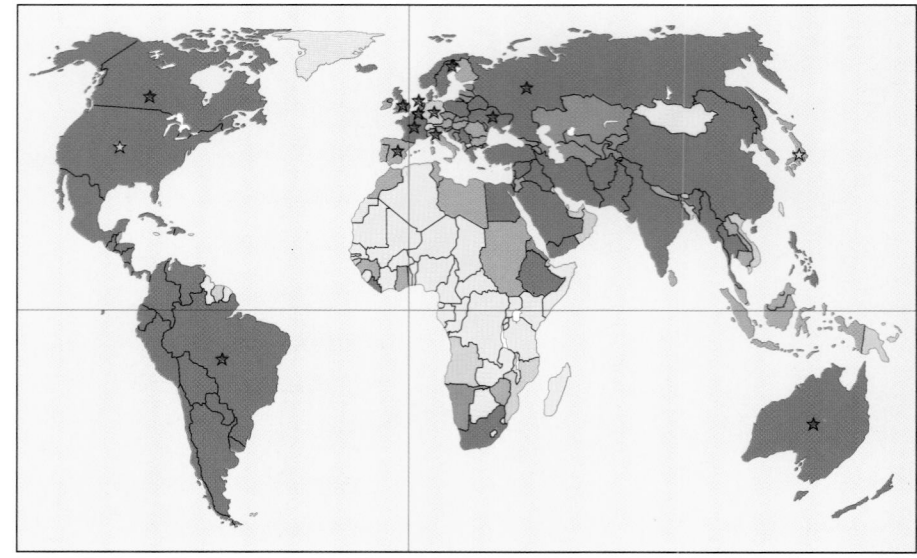

International Children's Fund) has provided health care and aid for children in many parts of the world. The ILO (International Labour Organization) has improved working conditions in many areas, while the FAO (Food and Agri-cultural Organization) has worked to improve the production and distribution of food. Among the other agencies are organizations to help refugees, to further human rights and to control the environment. The latest agency, set up in 1995, is the WTO (World Trade Organization), which took over the work of GATT (General Agreement on Tariffs and Trade).

OTHER ORGANIZATIONS

In a world in which nations have become increasingly interdependent, many other organiz-ations have been set up to deal with a variety of problems. Some, such as NATO (the North Atlantic Treaty Organization), are defence alli-ances. In the early 1990s, the end of the Cold War suggested that NATO's role might be fin-ished, but the civil war in the former Yugoslavia showed that it still has a role in maintaining peace and security.

Other organizations encourage social and economic co-operation in various regions. Some are NGOs (non-governmental organizations), such as the Red Cross and its Muslim equiva-lent, the Red Crescent. Other NGOs raise funds to provide aid to countries facing major crises, such as famine.

Some major international organizations aim at economic co-operation and the removal of trade barriers. For example, the European Union has 15 members. Its economic success and the adoption of a single currency, the euro, by 12

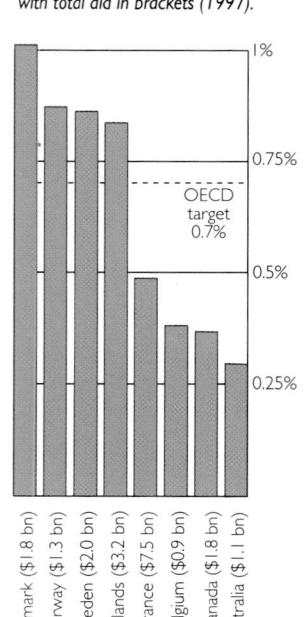

UNHCR-funded jetty, Sri Lanka

At the start of 2000, the number of people 'of concern' to the UN High Commission for Refugees totalled 22.3 million people. Sometimes, it has to provide transport facilities, such as this jetty, to get aid to the refugees.

of its members, has prompted some people to support the idea of a federal Europe. But others fear that political union might lead to a loss of national sovereignty by member states.

Other groupings include ASEAN (the Association of South-east Asian Nations) which aims to reduce trade barriers between its members (Brunei, Burma [Myanmar], Cambodia, Indonesia, Laos, Malaysia, the Philippines, Singapore, Thailand and Vietnam). APEC (the Asia-Pacific Co-operation Group), founded in 1989, aims to create a free trade zone between the countries of eastern Asia, North America, Australia and New Zealand by 2020. Meanwhile, Canada, Mexico and the United States have formed NAFTA (the North American Free Trade Agreement), while other economic groupings link most of the countries in Latin America. Another grouping with a more limited but important objective is OPEC (the Organization of Oil-Exporting Countries). OPEC works to unify policies concerning trade in oil on the world markets.

Some organizations exist to discuss matters of common interest between groups of nations. The Commonwealth of Nations, for example, grew out of links created by the British Empire. In North and South America, the OAS (Organization of American States) aims to increase understanding in the Western hemisphere. The OAU (Organization of African Unity) has a similar role in Africa, while the Arab League represents the Arab nations of North Africa and the Middle East.

COUNTRIES OF THE EUROPEAN UNION

	Total land area (sq km)	Total population (2001 est.)	GDP per capita, US$ (2000 est.)	Unemployment rate, % (2001)	Year of accession to the EU	Seats in EU parliament (1999–2004)
Austria	83,850	8,151,000	25,000	3.9%	1995	21
Belgium	30,510	10,259,000	25,300	6.9%	1958	25
Denmark	43,070	5,353,000	25,500	4.3%	1973	16
Finland	338,130	5,176,000	22,900	9.2%	1995	16
France	551,500	59,551,000	24,400	8.6%	1958	86
Germany	356,910	83,030,000	25,350	7.9%	1958	99
Greece	131,990	10,624,000	23,400	10.3%	1981	25
Ireland	70,280	3,841,000	21,600	3.8%	1973	15
Italy	301,270	57,680,000	22,100	9.4%	1958	87
Luxembourg	2,590	443,000	36,400	2.5%	1958	6
Netherlands	41,526	15,981,000	24,400	2.2%	1958	31
Portugal	92,390	9,444,000	15,800	4.4%	1986	25
Spain	504,780	38,432,000	18,000	13.0%	1986	64
Sweden	449,960	8,875,000	22,200	4.9%	1995	22
United Kingdom	243,368	59,648,000	22,800	5.1%	1973	87

Agriculture

Around the turn of the century, partly because of ongoing turmoil in the Russian economy, the increase in food production was less than the rise in world population, creating a small per capita fall in food production. Downward trends in world food production reopened an old debate – whether food production will be able to keep pace with the predicted rapid rises in the world population in the 21st century.

Some experts argue that the lower than expected production figures in the 1990s heralded a period of relative scarcity and high prices of food, which will be felt most in the poorer developing countries. Others are more optimistic. They point to the successes of the 'green revolution' which, through the use of new crop varieties produced by scientists, irrigation and the extensive use of fertilizers and pesticides,

Rice harvest, Bali, Indonesia
More than half of the world's people eat rice as their basic food. Rice grows well in tropical and subtropical regions, such as in Indonesia, India and south-eastern China.

has revolutionized food production since the 1950s and 1960s.

The green revolution has led to a great expansion in the production of many crops, including such basic foods as rice, maize and wheat. In India, its effects have been spectacular. Between 1955 and 1995, grain production trebled, giving the country sufficient food reserves to prevent famine in years when droughts or floods reduce the harvest. While once India had to import food, it is now self-sufficient.

Food Production

Agriculture, which supplies most of our food, together with materials to make clothes and other products, is the world's most important economic activity. But its relative importance has declined in comparison with manufacturing and service industries. As a result, the end of the 20th century marked the first time for 10,000 years when the vast majority of the people no longer had to depend for their living on growing crops and herding animals.

However, agriculture remains the dominant economic activity in many developing countries in Africa and Asia. For example, by the start of the 21st century, 80% or more of the people of Bhutan, Burundi, Nepal and Rwanda depended on farming for their living.

Many people in developing countries eke out the barest of livings by nomadic herding or shifting cultivation, combined with hunting, fishing and gathering plant foods. A large proportion of farmers live at subsistence level, producing little more than they require to provide the basic needs of their families.

The world's largest food producer and exporter is the United States, although agriculture employs

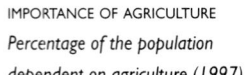

IMPORTANCE OF AGRICULTURE
Percentage of the population dependent on agriculture (1997).

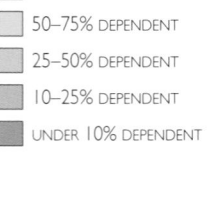

- OVER 75% DEPENDENT
- 50–75% DEPENDENT
- 25–50% DEPENDENT
- 10–25% DEPENDENT
- UNDER 10% DEPENDENT

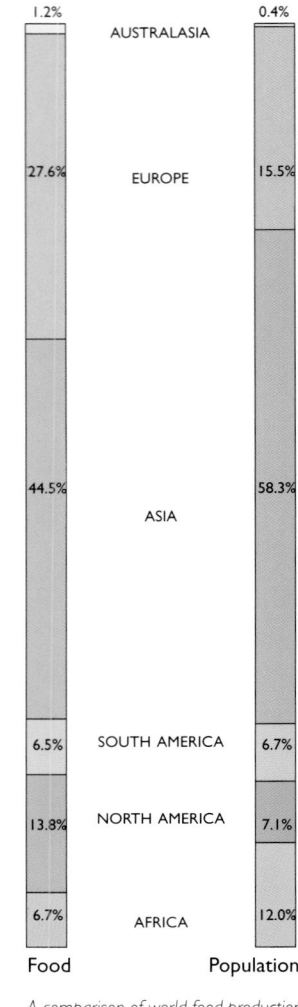

A comparison of world food production and population by continent.

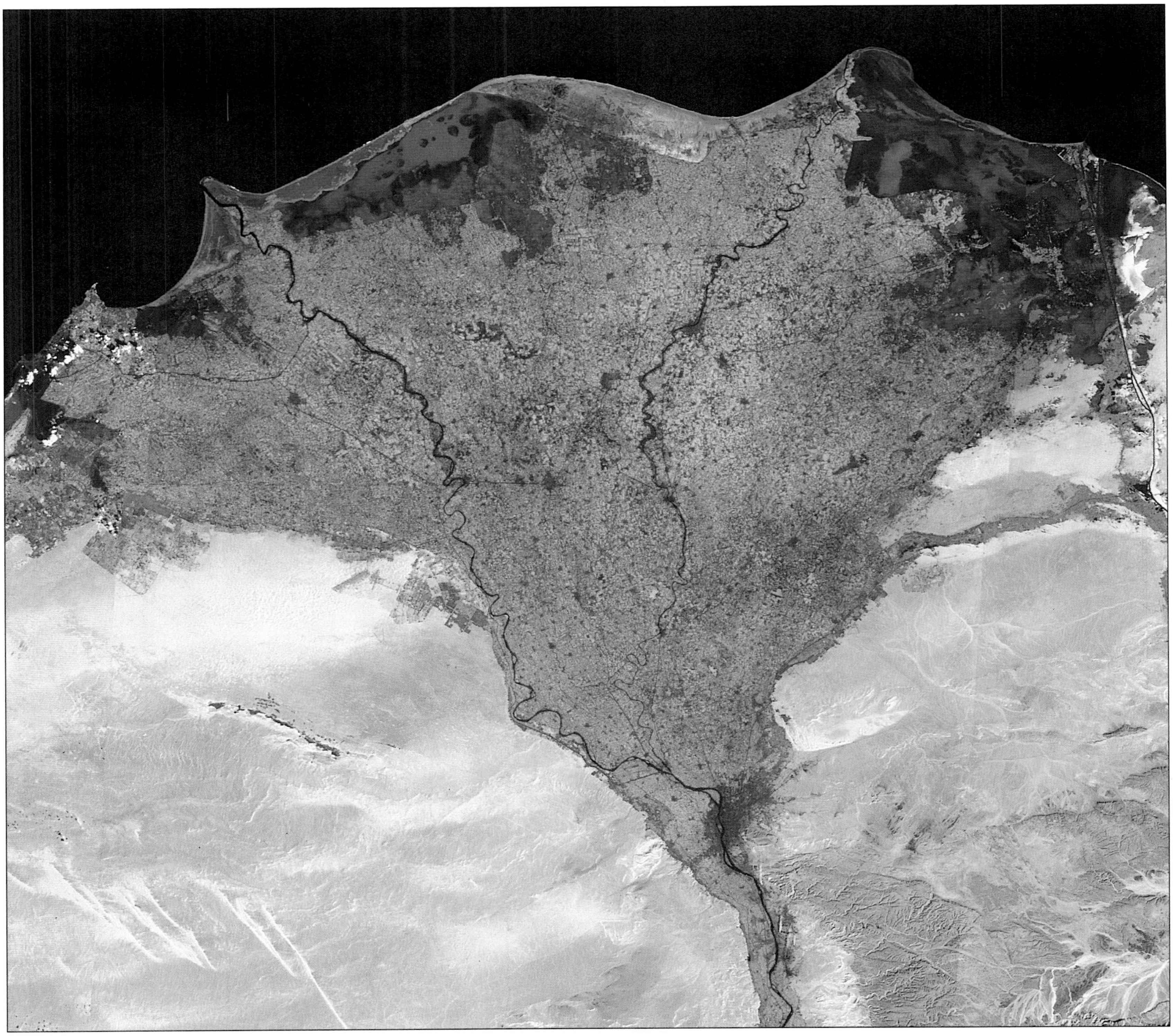

Landsat *image of the Nile delta, Egypt*

Most Egyptians live in the Nile valley and on its delta. Because much of the silt carried by the Nile now ends up on the floor of Lake Nasser, upstream of the Aswan Dam, the delta is now retreating and seawater is seeping inland. This eventuality was not foreseen when the Aswan High Dam was built in the 1960s.

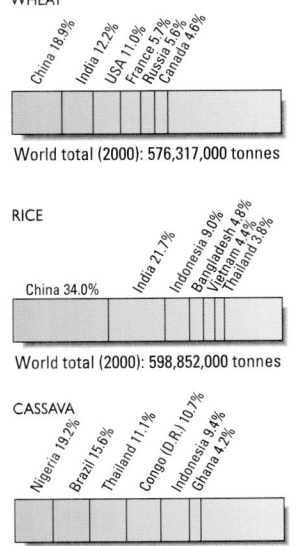

WHEAT

China 18.9% India 12.2% USA 11.0% France 5.7% Russia 5.6% Canada 4.6%

World total (2000): 576,317,000 tonnes

RICE

China 34.0% India 21.7% Indonesia 9.0% Bangladesh 4.8% Vietnam 4.4% Thailand 3.6%

World total (2000): 598,852,000 tonnes

CASSAVA

Nigeria 19.2% Brazil 15.6% Thailand 11.1% Congo (D.R.) 10.7% Indonesia 9.4% Ghana 4.2%

World total (2000): 172,737,000 tonnes

around 2% of its total workforce. The high production of the United States is explained by its use of scientific methods and mechanization, which are features of agriculture throughout the developed world.

INTENSIVE OR ORGANIC FARMING

In the early 21st century, some people were beginning to question the dependence of farmers on chemical fertilizers and pesticides. Many people became concerned that the widespread use of chemicals was seriously polluting and damaging the environment.

Others objected to the intensive farming of animals to raise production and lower prices. For example, the suggestion in Britain in 1996 that BSE, or 'mad cow disease', might be passed on to people causing CJD (Creuzfeldt-Jakob Disease) caused widespread alarm.

Such problems have led some farmers to return to organic farming, which is based on animal-welfare principles and the banning of chemical fertilizers and pesticides. The costs of organic foods are certainly higher than those produced by intensive farming, but an increasing number of consumers in the Western world are beginning to demand organic products from their retailers.

Energy and Minerals

In September 2000, Japan experienced its worst nuclear accident, when more than 400 people were exposed to harmful levels of radiation. This was the worst nuclear incident since the explosion at the Chernobyl nuclear power station, in Ukraine, in 1986. Nuclear power provides around 17% of the world's electricity and experts once thought that it would generate much of the world's energy supply. But concerns about safety and worries about the high costs make this seem unlikely. Some developed countries have already abandoned their nuclear programmes.

FOSSIL FUELS

Huge amounts of energy are needed for heating, generating electricity and for transport. In the early years of the Industrial Revolution, coal formed from organic matter buried beneath the Earth's surface, was the leading source of energy. It remains important as a raw material in the manufacture of drugs and other products and also as a fuel, despite the fact that burning coal causes air pollution and gives off carbon dioxide, an important greenhouse gas.

However, oil and natural gas, which came into wide use in the 20th century, are cheaper to produce and easier to handle than coal, while, kilogram for kilogram, they give out more heat. Oil is especially important in moving transport, supplying about 97% of the fuel required.

In 1995, proven reserves of oil were sufficient to supply the world, at current rates of production, for 43 years, while supplies of natural gas stood at about 66 years. Coal reserves are more abundant and known reserves would last 200 years at present rates of use. Although these figures must be regarded with caution, because they do not allow for future discoveries, it is clear that fossil fuel reserves will one day run out.

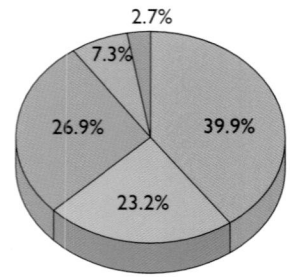

2.7%
7.3%
26.9%
39.9%
23.2%

WORLD ENERGY CONSUMPTION

- OIL
- GAS
- COAL
- NUCLEAR
- HYDRO

The diagram shows the proportion of world energy consumption in 1997 by form. Total energy consumption was 8,509.2 million tonnes of oil equivalent. Such fuels as wood, peat and animal wastes, together with renewable forms of energy, such as wind and geothermal power, are not included, although they are important in some areas.

Wind farms in California, United States
Wind farms using giant turbines can produce electricity at a lower cost than conventional power stations. But in many areas, winds are too light or too strong for wind farms to be effective.

SELECTED MINERAL PRODUCTION STATISTICS (1997)			
Bauxite		**Diamonds**	
Australia	34.9%	Australia	33.9%
Guinea	15.1%	Congo (D.R.)	18.6%
Brazil	9.8%	Botswana	17.0%
Jamaica	9.4%	Russia	16.1%
China	7.1%	S. Africa	8.5%
Gold		**Iron ore**	
S. Africa	20.5%	China	22.1%
USA	14.9%	Brazil	17.4%
Australia	13.1%	Australia	14.0%
Canada	7.0%	Ukraine	10.3%
China	6.5%	Russia	6.7%
Manganese		**Zinc**	
Ukraine	27.0%	China	16.4%
China	25.6%	Canada	14.5%
S. Africa	11.4%	Australia	14.0%
Brazil	8.0%	Peru	11.7%
Australia	7.8%	USA	8.5%

MINERAL DISTRIBUTION

The map shows the richest sources of the most important minerals. Major mineral locations are named. Undersea deposits, most of which are considered inaccessible, are not shown.

▽ GOLD
⬠ SILVER
◆ DIAMONDS
▽ TUNGSTEN
● IRON ORE
■ NICKEL
▽ CHROME
▲ MANGANESE
□ COBALT
▲ MOLYBDENUM
■ COPPER
▲ LEAD
● BAUXITE
▽ TIN
◆ ZINC
▽ MERCURY

Potash mines in Utah, United States

Potash is a mineral used mainly to make fertilizers. Much of it comes from mines where deposits formed when ancient seas dried up are exploited. Potash is also extracted from salt lakes.

ALTERNATIVE ENERGY

Other sources of energy are therefore required. Besides nuclear energy, the main alternative to fossil fuels is water power. The costs of building dams and hydroelectric power stations is high, though hydroelectric production is comparatively cheap and it does not cause pollution. But the creation of reservoirs uproots people and, in tropical rainforests, it destroys natural habitats. Hydroelectricity is also suitable only in areas with plenty of rivers and steep slopes, such as Norway, while it is unsuitable in flat areas, such as the Netherlands.

In Brazil, alcohol made from sugar has been used to fuel cars. Initially, this government-backed policy met with great success, but it has proved to be extremely expensive. Battery-run, electric cars have also been developed in the United States, but they appear to have limited use, because of the problems involved in regular and time-consuming recharging.

Other forms of energy, which are renewable and cleaner than fossil fuels, are winds, sea waves, the rise and fall of tides, and geothermal power. These forms of energy are already used to some extent. However, their contribution in global terms seems likely to remain small in the immediate future.

MINERALS FOR INDUSTRY

In addition to energy, manufacturing industries need raw materials, including minerals, and these natural resources, like fossil fuels, are being used in such huge quantities that some experts have predicted shortages of some of them before long.

Manufacturers depend on supplies of about 80 minerals. Some, such as bauxite (aluminium ore) and iron, are abundant, but others are scarce or are found only in deposits that are uneconomical to mine. Many experts advocate a policy of recycling scrap metal, including aluminium, chromium, copper, lead, nickel and zinc. This practice would reduce pollution and conserve the energy required for extracting and refining mineral ores.

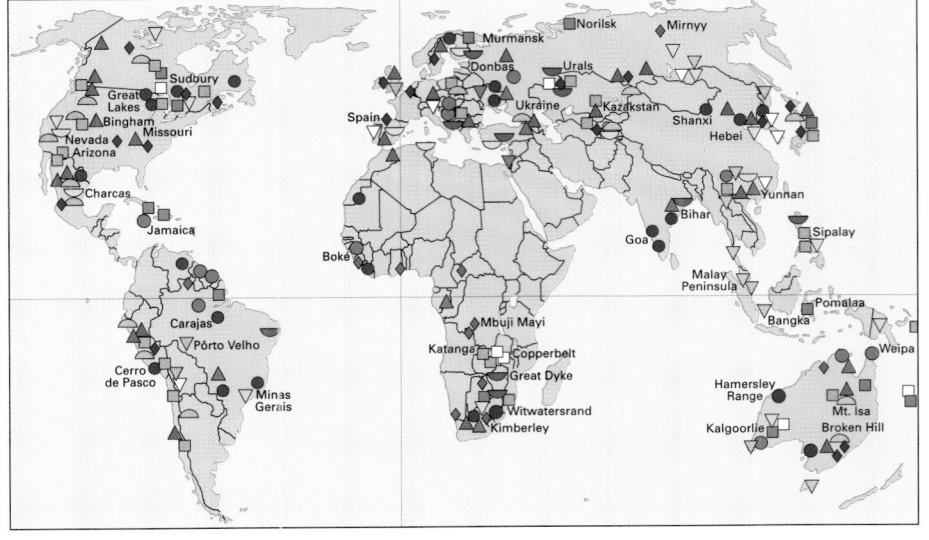

World Economies

In 1999, Tanzania had a per capita GNP (Gross National Product) of US$240, as compared with Switzerland, whose per capita GNP stood at $38,350. These figures indicate the vast gap between the economies and standards of living of the two countries.

The GNP includes the GDP (Gross Domestic Product), which consists of the total output of goods and services in a country in a given year, plus net exports – that is, the value of goods and services sold abroad less the value of foreign goods and services used in the country in the same year. The GNP divided by the population gives a country's GNP per capita. In low-income developing countries, agriculture makes a high contribution to the GNP. For example, in Tanzania, 40% of the GDP in 1999 came from

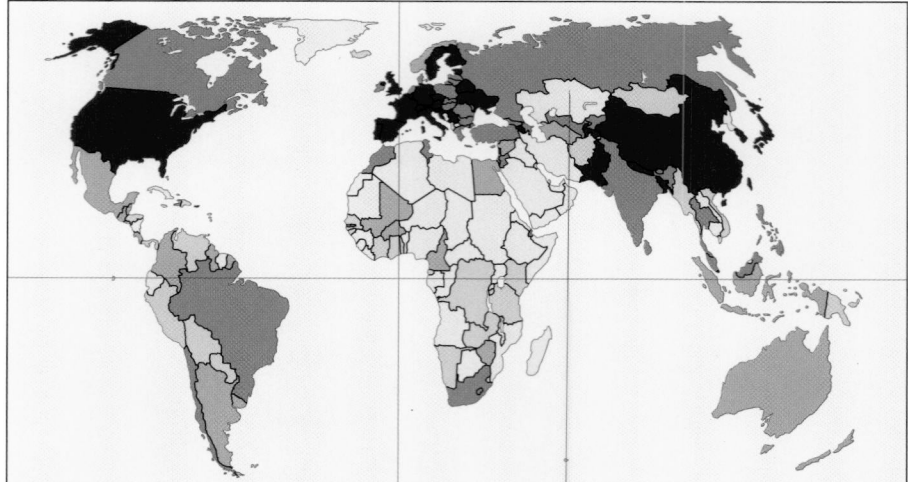

Microchip production, Taiwan
Despite its lack of resources, Taiwan is one of eastern Asia's 'tiger' economies. Its high-tech industries have helped it to achieve fast economic growth and to compete on the world market.

agriculture. On the other hand, manufacturing was small-scale and contributed only 6.6% of the GDP. By comparison, in high-income economies, the percentage contribution of manufacturing far exceeds that of agriculture.

INDUSTRIALIZATION

The Industrial Revolution began in Britain in the late 18th century. Before that time, most people worked on farms. But with the Industrial Revolution came factories, using machines that could manufacture goods much faster and more cheaply than those made by cottage industries which already existed.

The Industrial Revolution soon spread to several countries in mainland Europe and the United States and, by the late 19th century, it had reached Canada, Japan and Russia. At first, industrial development was based on such areas as coalfields or ironfields. But in the 20th century, the use of oil, which is easy to transport along pipelines, made it possible for industries to be set up anywhere.

Some nations, such as Switzerland, became industrialized even though they lacked natural resources. They depended instead on the specialized skills of their workers. This same pattern applies today. Some countries with rich natural resources, such as Mexico (with a per capita GNP in 1999 of $4,400), lag far behind Japan ($32,230) and Cyprus ($11,960), which lack resources and have to import many of the materials they need for their manufacturing industries.

SERVICE INDUSTRIES

Experts often refer to high-income countries as industrial economies. But manufacturing employs only one in six workers in the United

INDUSTRY AND TRADE
Manufactured goods (including machinery and transport) as a percentage of total exports.

- ■ OVER 75%
- ▨ 50–75%
- ▤ 25–50%
- ▢ 10–25%
- □ UNDER 10%

Eastern Asia, including Japan (98.3%), Taiwan (92.7%) and Hong Kong (93.0%), contains countries whose exports are most dominated by manufactures. But some countries in Europe, such as Slovenia (92.5%), are also heavily dependent on manufacturing.

GROSS NATIONAL PRODUCT PER CAPITA US$ (1999 ESTIMATES)		
1	Liechtenstein	50,000
2	Luxembourg	44,640
3	Switzerland	38,350
4	Bermuda	35,590
5	Norway	32,880
6	Japan	32,230
7	Denmark	32,030
8	USA	30,600
9	Singapore	29,610
10	Iceland	29,280
11	Austria	25,970
12	Germany	25,350
13	Sweden	25,040
14	Monaco	25,000
15	Belgium	24,510
16	Brunei	24,630
17	Netherlands	24,320
18	Finland	23,780
19	Hong Kong (China)	23,520
20	France	23,480

New cars awaiting transportation, Los Angeles, United States
Cars are the most important single manufactured item in world trade, followed by vehicle parts and engines. The world's leading car producers are Japan, the United States, Germany and France.

States, one in five in Britain, and one in three in Germany and Japan.

In most developed economies, the percentage of manufacturing jobs has fallen in recent years, while jobs in service industries have risen. For example, in Britain, the proportion of jobs in manufacturing fell from 37% in 1970 to 14% in 2001, while jobs in the service sector rose from just under 50% to 77%. While change in Britain was especially rapid, similar changes were taking place in most industrial economies. By the late 1990s, service industries accounted for well over half the jobs in the generally prosperous countries that made up the OECD (Organization for Economic Co-operation and Development). Instead of being called the 'industrial' economies, these countries might be better named the 'service' economies.

Service industries offer a wide range of jobs and many of them require high educational qualifications. These include finance, insurance and high-tech industries, such as computer programming, entertainment and telecommunications. Service industries also include marketing and advertising, which are essential if the cars and television sets made by manufacturers are to be sold. Another valuable service industry is tourism; in some countries, such as the Gambia, it is the major foreign exchange earner. Trade in services plays a crucial part in world economics. The share of services in world trade rose from 17% in 1980 to 22% in the 1990s.

THE WORKFORCE
Percentage of men and women between 15 and 64 years old in employment, selected countries (latest available year).

■ MEN
□ WOMEN

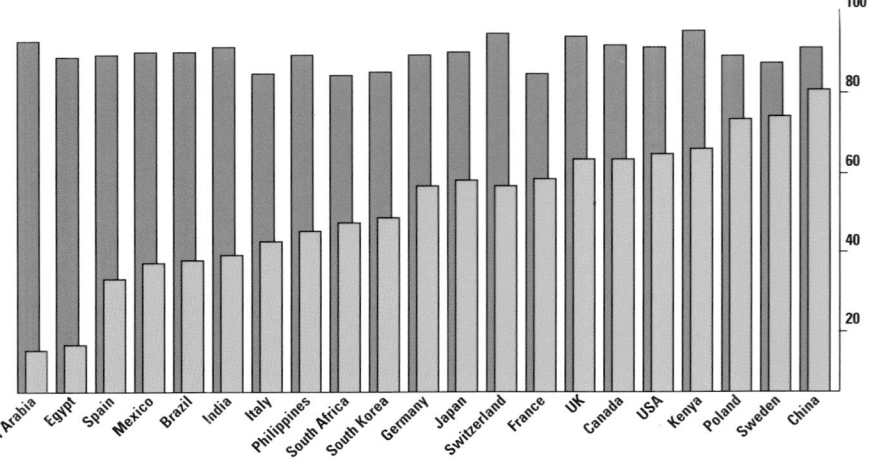

Trade and Commerce

The establishment of the WTO (World Trade Organization) on 1 January 1995 was the latest step in the long history of world trade. The WTO was set up by the eighth round of negotiations, popularly called the 'Uruguay round', conducted by the General Agreement on Tariffs and Trade (GATT). This treaty was signed by representatives of 125 governments in April, 1994. By the start of 2002, the WTO had 144 members.

GATT was first established in 1948. Its initial aim was to produce a charter to create a body called the International Trade Organization. This body never came into being. Instead, GATT, acting as an *ad hoc* agency, pioneered a series of agreements aimed at liberalizing world trade by reducing tariffs on imports and other obstacles to free trade.

GATT's objectives were based on the belief

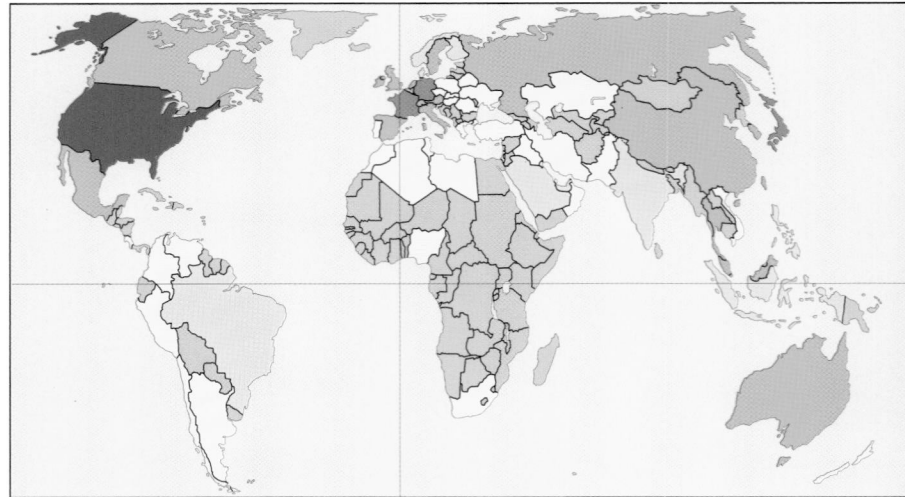

New York City Stock Exchange, United States
Stock exchanges, where stocks and shares are sold and bought, are important in channelling savings and investments to companies and governments. The world's largest stock exchange is in Tokyo, Japan.

that international trade creates wealth. Trade occurs because the world's resources are not distributed evenly between countries, and, in theory, free trade means that every country should concentrate on what it can do best and purchase from others goods and services that they can supply more cheaply. In practice, however, free trade may cause unemployment when imported goods are cheaper than those produced within the country.

Trade is sometimes an important factor in world politics, especially when trade sanctions are applied against countries whose actions incur the disapproval of the international community. For example, in the 1990s, world-wide trade sanctions were imposed on Serbia because of its involvement in the civil war in Bosnia-Herzegovina.

CHANGING TRADE PATTERNS

The early 16th century, when Europeans began to divide the world into huge empires, opened up a new era in international trade. By the 19th century, the colonial powers, who were among the first industrial powers, promoted trade with their colonies, from which they obtained unprocessed raw materials, such as food, natural fibres, minerals and timber. In return, they shipped clothes, shoes and other cheap items to the colonies.

From the late 19th century until the early 1950s, primary products dominated world trade, with oil becoming the leading item in the later part of this period. Many developing countries still depend heavily on the export of one or two primary products, such as coffee or iron ore, but overall the proportion of primary products in world trade has fallen since the 1950s. Today the most important elements in world trade are

WORLD TRADE
Percentage share of total world exports by value (1999).

- ◼ OVER 10% OF WORLD TRADE
- ◼ 5–10% OF WORLD TRADE
- ◻ 1–5% OF WORLD TRADE
- ◻ 0.5–1% OF WORLD TRADE
- ◻ 0.1–0.5% OF WORLD TRADE
- ◻ UNDER 0.1% OF WORLD TRADE

The world's leading trading nations, according to the combined value of their exports and imports, are the United States, Germany, Japan, France and the United Kingdom.

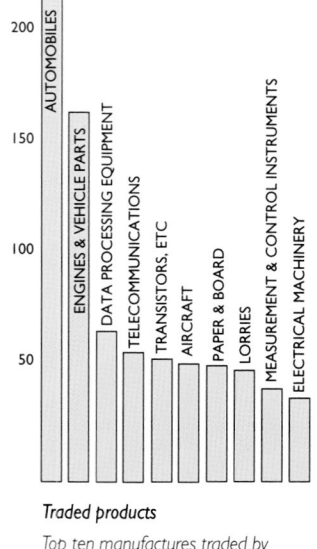

Traded products
Top ten manufactures traded by value in billions of US$ (latest available year).

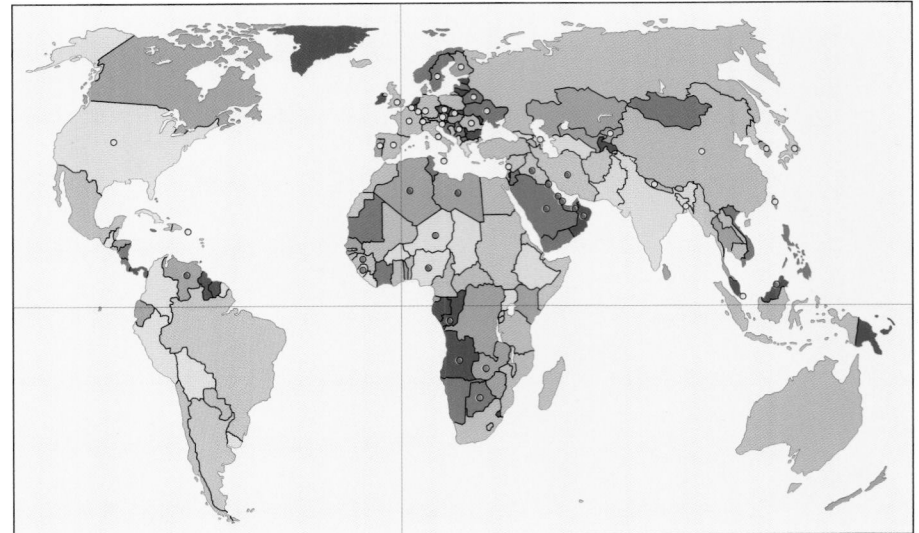

Rotterdam, Netherlands

World trade depends on transport. Rotterdam, the world's largest port, serves not only the Netherlands, but also industrial areas in parts of Germany, France and Switzerland.

DEPENDENCE ON TRADE

Value of exports as a percentage of GDP (Gross Domestic Product) 1997.

- OVER 50% GDP FROM EXPORTS
- 40–50% GDP FROM EXPORTS
- 30–40% GDP FROM EXPORTS
- 20–30% GDP FROM EXPORTS
- 10–20% GDP FROM EXPORTS
- UNDER 10% GDP FROM EXPORTS

- ○ MOST DEPENDENT ON INDUSTRIAL EXPORTS (OVER 75% OF TOTAL)
- ● MOST DEPENDENT ON FUEL EXPORTS (OVER 75% OF TOTAL)
- ● MOST DEPENDENT ON METAL & MINERAL EXPORTS (OVER 75% OF TOTAL)

manufactures and semi-manufactures, exchanged mainly between the industrialized nations.

THE WORLD'S MARKETS

Private companies conduct most of world trade, but government policies affect it. Governments which believe that certain industries are strategic, or essential for the country's future, may impose tariffs on imports, or import quotas to limit the volume of imports, if they are thought to be undercutting the domestic industries.

For example, the United States has argued that Japan has greater access to its markets than the United States has to Japan's. This might have led the United States to resort to protectionism, but instead the United States remains committed to free trade despite occasional disputes.

Other problems in international trade occur when governments give subsidies to its producers, who can then export products at low prices. Another difficulty, called 'dumping', occurs when products are sold at below the market price in order to gain a market share. One of the aims of the newly-created WTO is the phasing out of government subsidies for agricultural products, though the world's poorest countries will be exempt from many of the WTO's most severe regulations.

Governments are also concerned about the volume of imports and exports and most countries keep records of international transactions. When the total value of goods and services imported exceeds the value of goods and services exported, then the country has a deficit in its balance of payments. Large deficits can weaken a country's economy.

Travel and Communications

In the 1990s, millions of people became linked into an 'information superhighway' called the Internet. Equipped with a personal computer, an electricity supply, a telephone and a modem, people are able to communicate with others all over the world. People can now send messages by e-mail (electronic mail), they can engage in electronic discussions, contacting people with similar interests, and engage in 'chat lines', which are the latest equivalent of telephone conferences.

These new developments are likely to affect the working lives of people everywhere, enabling them to work at home whilst having many of the facilities that are available in an office. The Internet is part of an ongoing and astonishingly rapid evolution in the fields of communications and transport.

TRANSPORT

Around 200 years ago, most people never travelled far from their birthplace, but today we are much more mobile. Cars and buses now provide convenient forms of transport for many millions of people, huge ships transport massive cargoes around the world, and jet airliners, some travelling faster than the speed of sound, can transport high-value goods as well as holiday-makers to almost any part of the world.

Land transport of freight has developed greatly

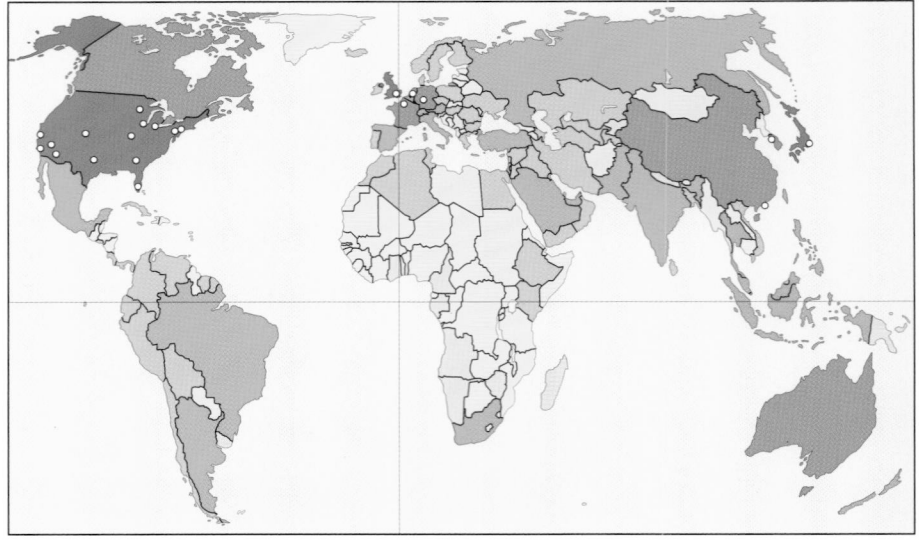

Jodrell Bank Observatory, Cheshire, England
The world's first giant radio telescope began operations at Jodrell Bank in 1957. Radio telescopes can explore the Universe as far as 16 billion light-years away.

since the start of the Industrial Revolution. Canals, which became important in the 18th century, could not compete with rail transport in the 19th century. Rail transport remains important, but, during the 20th century, it suffered from competition with road transport, which is cheaper and has the advantage of carrying materials and goods from door to door.

Road transport causes pollution and the burning of fuels creates greenhouse gases that contribute to global warming. Yet privately owned cars are now the leading form of passenger traffic in developed nations, especially for journeys of less than around 400 km [250 miles]. Car owners do not have to suffer the inconvenience of waiting for public transport, such as buses, though they often have to endure traffic jams at peak travel times.

Ocean passenger traffic is now modest, but ships carry the bulk of international trade. Huge oil tankers and bulk grain carriers now ply the oceans with their cargoes, while container ships

AIR TRAVEL – PASSENGER KILOMETRES* FLOWN (1997).

- ◼ OVER 100,000 MILLION
- ◼ 50,000–100,000 MILLION
- ◻ 10,000–50,000 MILLION
- ☐ 1,000–10,000 MILLION
- ☐ 500–1,000 MILLION
- ☐ UNDER 500 MILLION
- ○ MAJOR AIRPORTS (HANDLING OVER 25 MILLION PASSENGERS IN 2000)

* Passenger kilometres are the number of passengers (both international and domestic) multiplied by the distance flown by each passenger from the airport of origin.

SELECTED NEWSPAPER CIRCULATION FIGURES (1995)

France			**Russia**		
Le Monde		357,362	Pravda		1,373,795
Le Figaro		350,000	Ivestia		700,000
Germany			**Spain**		
Bild		4,500,000	El Pais		407,629
Süddeutsche Zeitung		402,866			
			United Kingdom		
Italy			The Sun		4,061,253
Corriera Della Sella		676,904	Daily Mirror		2,525,000
La Republica		655,321	Daily Express		1,270,642
La Stampa		436,047	The Times		672,802
			The Guardian		402,214
Japan					
Yomiuri Shimbun	(a.m. edition)	9,800,000	**United States**		
	(p.m. edition)	4,400,000	New York Times		1,724,705
Manichi Shimbun	(a.m. edition)	3,200,000	Chicago Tribune		1,110,552
	(p.m. edition)	1,900,000	Houston Chronicle		605,343

carry mixed cargoes. Containers are boxes built to international standards that contain cargo. Containers are easy to handle, and so they reduce shipping costs, speed up deliveries and cut losses caused by breakages. Most large ports now have the facilities to handle containers.

Air transport is suitable for carrying goods that are expensive, light and compact, or perishable. However, because of the high costs of air freight, it is most suitable for carrying passengers along long-distance routes around the world. Through air travel, international tourism, with people sometimes flying considerable distances, has become a major and rapidly expanding industry.

COMMUNICATIONS

After humans first began to communicate by using the spoken word, the next great stage in the development of communications was the invention of writing around 5,500 years ago.

The invention of movable type in the mid 15th century led to the mass production of books and, in the early 17th century, the first newspapers. Newspapers now play an important part in the mass communication of information, although today radio and, even more important, television have led to a decline in the circulation of newspapers in many parts of the world.

The most recent developments have occurred in the field of electronics. Artificial communications satellites now circle the planet, relaying radio, television, telegraph and telephone signals. This enables people to watch events on the far side of the globe as they are happening. Electronic equipment is also used in many other ways, such as in navigation systems used in air, sea and space, and also in modern weaponry, as shown vividly in the television coverage of such military actions as that in Afghanistan in 2001.

THE AGE OF COMPUTERS

One of the most remarkable applications of electronics is in the field of computers. Computers are now making a huge contribution to communications. They are able to process data at incredibly high speeds and can store vast quantities of information. For example, the work of weather forecasters has been greatly improved now that computers can process the enormous amount of data required for a single weather forecast. They also have many other applications in such fields as business, government, science and medicine.

Through the Internet, computers provide a free interchange of news and views around the world. But the dangers of misuse, such as the exchange of pornographic images, have led to calls for censorship. Censorship, however, is a blunt weapon, which can be used by authoritarian governments to suppress the free exchange of information that the new information super-highway makes possible.

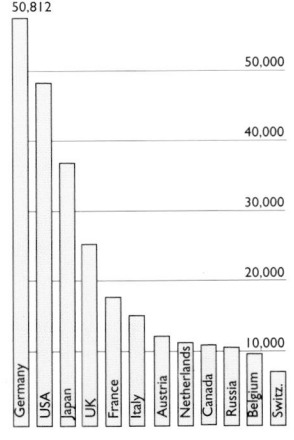

Spending on tourism
Countries spending the most on overseas tourism, US$ million (1996).

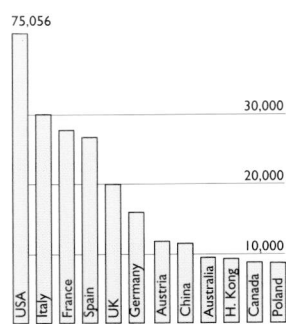

Receipts from tourism
Countries receiving the most from overseas tourism, US$ million (1996).

The World Today

The early years of the 20th century witnessed the exploration of Antarctica, the last uncharted continent. Today, less than 100 years later, tourists are able to take cruises to the icy southern continent, while almost no part of the globe is inaccessible to the determined traveller. Improved transport and images from space have made our world seem smaller.

A DIVIDED WORLD

Between the end of World War II in 1945 and the late 1980s, the world was divided, politically and economically, into three main groups: the developed countries or Western democracies, with their free enterprise or mixed economies; the centrally planned or Communist countries; and the developing countries or Third World.

This division became obsolete when the former Soviet Union and its old European allies, together with the 'special economic zones' in eastern China, began the transition from centrally planned to free enterprise economies. This left the world divided into two broad camps: the prosperous developed countries and the poorer developing countries. The simplest way of distinguishing between the groups is with reference to their per capita Gross National Products (per capita GNPs).

The World Bank divides the developing countries into three main groups. At the bottom are the low-income economies, which include China, India and most of sub-Saharan Africa. In 1999, this group contained about 40% of the

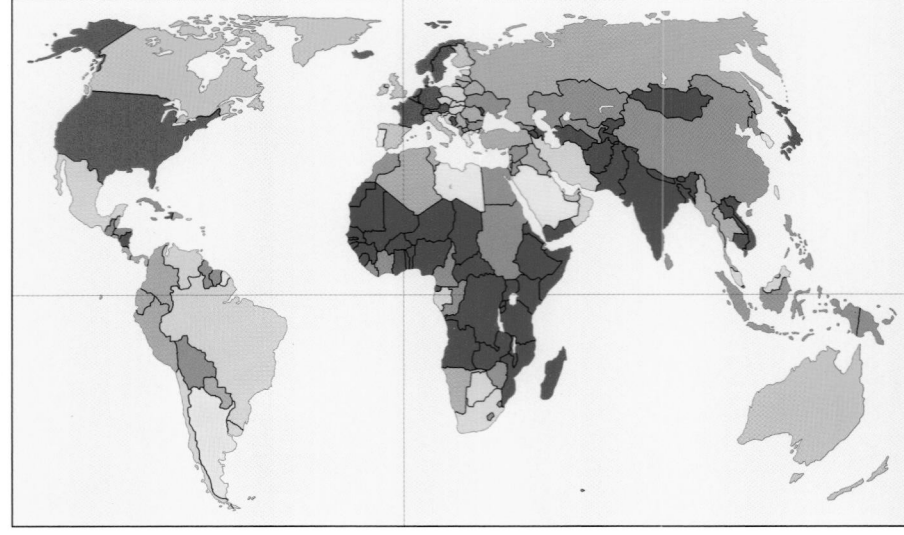

world's population, but its average per capita GNP was only US$420. The other two groups are the lower-middle-income economies, with an average per capita GNP of $1,200, and the upper-middle-income economies with an average per capita GNP of $4,870. By contrast, the high-income economies, also called the developed countries, contain only 15% of the world's population but have the high (and rising) average GNP per capita of $26,440.

ECONOMIC AND SOCIAL CONTRASTS

Economic differences are coupled with other factors, such as rates of population growth. For example, around the turn of the century, the low- and middle-income economies had a high population growth rate of 1.7%, while the growth rate in high-income economies was around 0.1%. Around 18 countries in Europe experienced a natural decrease in population in 1998.

Stark contrasts exist worldwide in the quality

GROSS NATIONAL PRODUCT PER CAPITA
The value of total production divided by the population (1999).

■ OVER 400% OF WORLD AVERAGE
▨ 200–400% OF WORLD AVERAGE
☐ 100–200% OF WORLD AVERAGE
[WORLD AVERAGE WEALTH PER PERSON US$6,316]
☐ 50–100% OF WORLD AVERAGE
▨ 25–50% OF WORLD AVERAGE
▨ 10–25% OF WORLD AVERAGE
■ UNDER 10% OF WORLD AVERAGE

RICHEST COUNTRIES

Liechtenstein	$44,640
Switzerland	$38,350
Bermuda	$35,590
Norway	$32,880
Japan	$32,230

POOREST COUNTRIES

Ethiopia	$100
Burundi	$120
Sierra Leone	$130
Guinea-Bissau	$160
Niger	$190

Porters carrying luggage for tourists, Selous Park, Tanzania
Improved and cheaper transport has led to a boom in tourism in many developing countries. Tourism provides jobs and foreign exchange, though it can undermine local cultures.

Operation Enduring Freedom, Afghanistan

A joint patrol of US Marines and Army soldiers is seen here patrolling through the village of Cem, Afghanistan, some 10 km [6 miles] from the airport near Kandahar, in January 2002.

of life. Generally, the people in Western Europe and North America are better fed, healthier and have more cars and better homes than the people in low- and middle-income economies.

In 1999, the average life expectancy at birth in sub-Saharan Africa was 47 years. By contrast, the average life expectancy in the United States and the United Kingdom was 77 years. Illiteracy in low-income economies for people aged 15 and over was 39% in 1999. But for women, the percentage of those who could not read or write was 48%. Illiteracy is relatively rare for both sexes in high-income economies.

FUTURE DEVELOPMENT

In the last 50 years, despite all the aid supplied to developing countries, much of the world still suffers from poverty and economic backwardness. Some countries are even poorer now than they were a generation ago while others have become substantially richer.

However, several factors suggest that poor countries may find progress easier in the 21st century. For example, technology is now more readily transferable between countries, while improved transport and communications make it easier for countries to take part in the world economy. But industrial development could lead to an increase in global pollution. Hence, any

strategy for global economic expansion must also take account of environmental factors.

A WORLD IN CONFLICT

The end of the Cold War held out hopes of a new world order. But ethnic, religious and other rivalries have subsequently led to appalling violence in places as diverse as the Balkan peninsula, Israel and the Palestinian territories, and Rwanda–Burundi. Then, on 11 September 2001, the attack on those symbols of the economic and military might of the United States – the World Trade Center and the Pentagon Building – demonstrated that nowhere on Earth is safe from attack by extremists prepared to sacrifice their lives in pursuit of their aims.

The danger posed by terrorist groups, such as al Qaida, or by rogue states, possibly in possession of nuclear or biological weapons, has forced many countries into new alliances to combat the terrorists and the governments that give them shelter. Many people also recognize a pressing need to understand and correct the wrongs, real or perceived, that lead people to acts of martyrdom or murderous destruction.

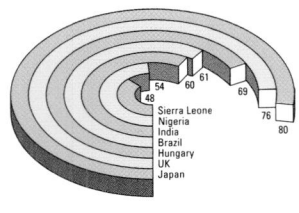

Years of life expectancy at birth, selected countries (1997).

The chart shows the contrasting range of average life expectancies at birth for a range of countries, including both low-income and high-income economies. Generally, improved health services are raising life expectancies. On average, women live longer than men, even in the poorer developing countries.

WESTERN CAPE, SOUTH AFRICA

Kansai International Airport, Japan
The new airport, opened in September 1994, is built on an artificial island in Osaka Bay. The island holds the world's biggest airport terminal at nearly 2 km [1.2 miles] long.

carry mixed cargoes. Containers are boxes built to international standards that contain cargo. Containers are easy to handle, and so they reduce shipping costs, speed up deliveries and cut losses caused by breakages. Most large ports now have the facilities to handle containers.

Air transport is suitable for carrying goods that are expensive, light and compact, or perishable. However, because of the high costs of air freight, it is most suitable for carrying passengers along long-distance routes around the world. Through air travel, international tourism, with people sometimes flying considerable distances, has become a major and rapidly expanding industry.

COMMUNICATIONS

After humans first began to communicate by using the spoken word, the next great stage in the development of communications was the invention of writing around 5,500 years ago.

The invention of movable type in the mid 15th century led to the mass production of books and, in the early 17th century, the first newspapers. Newspapers now play an important part in the mass communication of information, although today radio and, even more important, television have led to a decline in the circulation of newspapers in many parts of the world.

The most recent developments have occurred in the field of electronics. Artificial communications satellites now circle the planet, relaying radio, television, telegraph and telephone signals. This enables people to watch events on the far side of the globe as they are happening. Electronic equipment is also used in many other ways, such as in navigation systems used in air, sea and space, and also in modern weaponry, as shown vividly in the television coverage of such military actions as that in Afghanistan in 2001.

THE AGE OF COMPUTERS

One of the most remarkable applications of electronics is in the field of computers. Computers are now making a huge contribution to communications. They are able to process data at incredibly high speeds and can store vast quantities of information. For example, the work of weather forecasters has been greatly improved now that computers can process the enormous amount of data required for a single weather forecast. They also have many other applications in such fields as business, government, science and medicine.

Through the Internet, computers provide a free interchange of news and views around the world. But the dangers of misuse, such as the exchange of pornographic images, have led to calls for censorship. Censorship, however, is a blunt weapon, which can be used by authoritarian governments to suppress the free exchange of information that the new information super-highway makes possible.

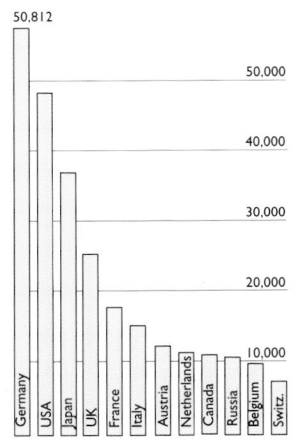

Spending on tourism
Countries spending the most on overseas tourism, US$ million (1996).

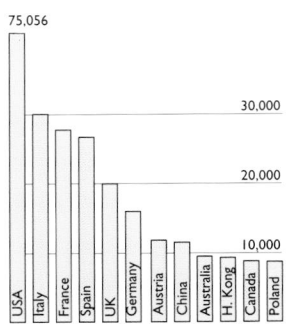

Receipts from tourism
Countries receiving the most from overseas tourism, US$ million (1996).

46

The World Today

The early years of the 20th century witnessed the exploration of Antarctica, the last uncharted continent. Today, less than 100 years later, tourists are able to take cruises to the icy southern continent, while almost no part of the globe is inaccessible to the determined traveller. Improved transport and images from space have made our world seem smaller.

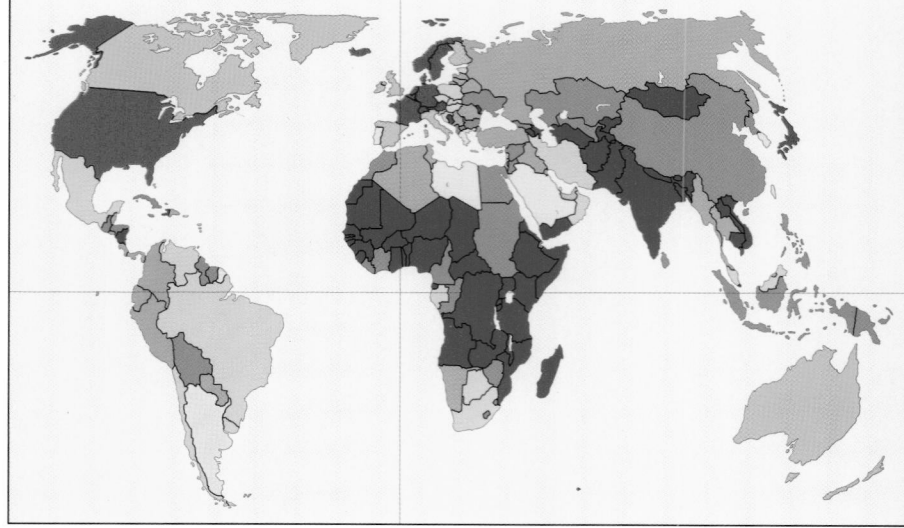

A DIVIDED WORLD

Between the end of World War II in 1945 and the late 1980s, the world was divided, politically and economically, into three main groups: the developed countries or Western democracies, with their free enterprise or mixed economies; the centrally planned or Communist countries; and the developing countries or Third World.

This division became obsolete when the former Soviet Union and its old European allies, together with the 'special economic zones' in eastern China, began the transition from centrally planned to free enterprise economies. This left the world divided into two broad camps: the prosperous developed countries and the poorer developing countries. The simplest way of distinguishing between the groups is with reference to their per capita Gross National Products (per capita GNPs).

The World Bank divides the developing countries into three main groups. At the bottom are the low-income economies, which include China, India and most of sub-Saharan Africa. In 1999, this group contained about 40% of the world's population, but its average per capita GNP was only US$420. The other two groups are the lower-middle-income economies, with an average per capita GNP of $1,200, and the upper-middle-income economies with an average per capita GNP of $4,870. By contrast, the high-income economies, also called the developed countries, contain only 15% of the world's population but have the high (and rising) average GNP per capita of $26,440.

ECONOMIC AND SOCIAL CONTRASTS

Economic differences are coupled with other factors, such as rates of population growth. For example, around the turn of the century, the low- and middle-income economies had a high population growth rate of 1.7%, while the growth rate in high-income economies was around 0.1%. Around 18 countries in Europe experienced a natural decrease in population in 1998.

Stark contrasts exist worldwide in the quality

GROSS NATIONAL PRODUCT PER CAPITA
The value of total production divided by the population (1999).

- OVER 400% OF WORLD AVERAGE
- 200–400% OF WORLD AVERAGE
- 100–200% OF WORLD AVERAGE
[WORLD AVERAGE WEALTH PER PERSON US$6,316]
- 50–100% OF WORLD AVERAGE
- 25–50% OF WORLD AVERAGE
- 10–25% OF WORLD AVERAGE
- UNDER 10% OF WORLD AVERAGE

RICHEST COUNTRIES
Liechtenstein $44,640
Switzerland $38,350
Bermuda $35,590
Norway $32,880
Japan $32,230

POOREST COUNTRIES
Ethiopia $100
Burundi $120
Sierra Leone $130
Guinea-Bissau $160
Niger $190

Porters carrying luggage for tourists, Selous Park, Tanzania
Improved and cheaper transport has led to a boom in tourism in many developing countries. Tourism provides jobs and foreign exchange, though it can undermine local cultures.

Operation Enduring Freedom, Afghanistan

A joint patrol of US Marines and Army soldiers is seen here patrolling through the village of Cem, Afghanistan, some 10 km [6 miles] from the airport near Kandahar, in January 2002.

of life. Generally, the people in Western Europe and North America are better fed, healthier and have more cars and better homes than the people in low- and middle-income economies.

In 1999, the average life expectancy at birth in sub-Saharan Africa was 47 years. By contrast, the average life expectancy in the United States and the United Kingdom was 77 years. Illiteracy in low-income economies for people aged 15 and over was 39% in 1999. But for women, the percentage of those who could not read or write was 48%. Illiteracy is relatively rare for both sexes in high-income economies.

FUTURE DEVELOPMENT

In the last 50 years, despite all the aid supplied to developing countries, much of the world still suffers from poverty and economic backwardness. Some countries are even poorer now than they were a generation ago while others have become substantially richer.

However, several factors suggest that poor countries may find progress easier in the 21st century. For example, technology is now more readily transferable between countries, while improved transport and communications make it easier for countries to take part in the world economy. But industrial development could lead to an increase in global pollution. Hence, any

strategy for global economic expansion must also take account of environmental factors.

A WORLD IN CONFLICT

The end of the Cold War held out hopes of a new world order. But ethnic, religious and other rivalries have subsequently led to appalling violence in places as diverse as the Balkan peninsula, Israel and the Palestinian territories, and Rwanda–Burundi. Then, on 11 September 2001, the attack on those symbols of the economic and military might of the United States – the World Trade Center and the Pentagon Building – demonstrated that nowhere on Earth is safe from attack by extremists prepared to sacrifice their lives in pursuit of their aims.

The danger posed by terrorist groups, such as al Qaida, or by rogue states, possibly in possession of nuclear or biological weapons, has forced many countries into new alliances to combat the terrorists and the governments that give them shelter. Many people also recognize a pressing need to understand and correct the wrongs, real or perceived, that lead people to acts of martyrdom or murderous destruction.

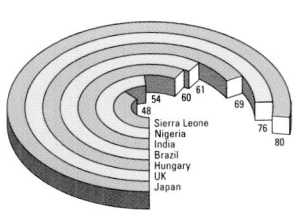

Years of life expectancy at birth, selected countries (1997).

The chart shows the contrasting range of average life expectancies at birth for a range of countries, including both low-income and high-income economies. Generally, improved health services are raising life expectancies. On average, women live longer than men, even in the poorer developing countries.

WESTERN CAPE, SOUTH AFRICA

WORLD MAPS

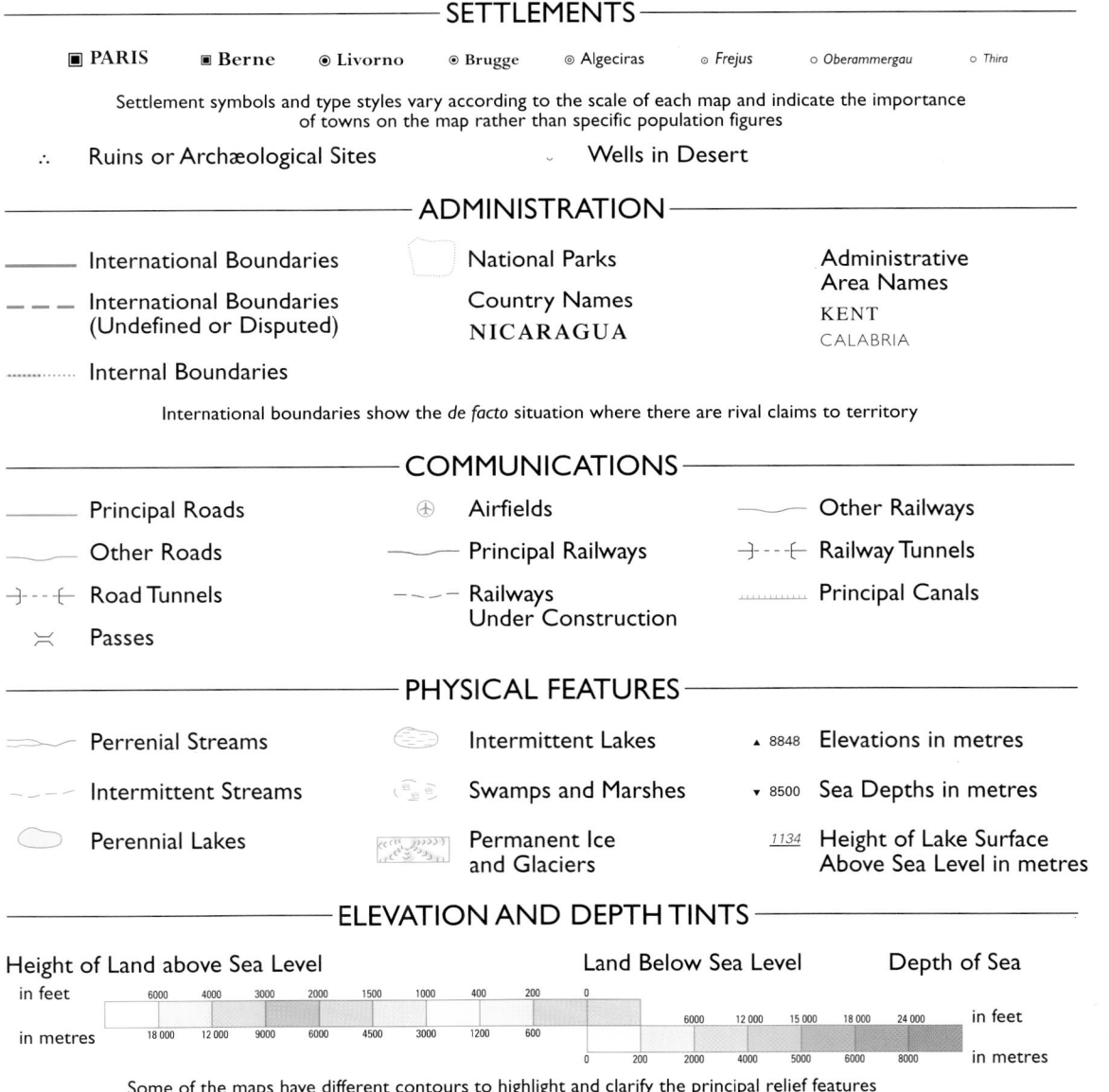

SETTLEMENTS

■ PARIS   ■ Berne   ◉ Livorno   ◉ Brugge   ◎ Algeciras   ○ Frejus   ○ Oberammergau   ○ Thira

Settlement symbols and type styles vary according to the scale of each map and indicate the importance
of towns on the map rather than specific population figures

∴ Ruins or Archæological Sites   ⌣ Wells in Desert

ADMINISTRATION

———— International Boundaries

– – – International Boundaries
(Undefined or Disputed)

·········· Internal Boundaries

⬡ National Parks

Country Names
NICARAGUA

Administrative
Area Names

KENT

CALABRIA

International boundaries show the *de facto* situation where there are rival claims to territory

COMMUNICATIONS

———— Principal Roads

———— Other Roads

+--+ Road Tunnels

⌣ Passes

⊕ Airfields

———— Principal Railways

–⌣– – Railways
Under Construction

⌣ Other Railways

+--+ Railway Tunnels

·········· Principal Canals

PHYSICAL FEATURES

⌣ Perrenial Streams

– – – Intermittent Streams

⬭ Perennial Lakes

⬭ Intermittent Lakes

Swamps and Marshes

Permanent Ice
and Glaciers

▲ 8848 Elevations in metres

▼ 8500 Sea Depths in metres

1134 Height of Lake Surface
Above Sea Level in metres

ELEVATION AND DEPTH TINTS

Height of Land above Sea Level   Land Below Sea Level   Depth of Sea

in feet   6000 4000 3000 2000 1500 1000 400 200   0
                                                              6000 12 000 15 000 18 000 24 000   in feet

in metres   18 000 12 000 9000 6000 4500 3000 1200 600
                                                              0 200 2000 4000 5000 6000 8000   in metres

Some of the maps have different contours to highlight and clarify the principal relief features

Projection: *Hammer Equal Area*

Hanoi ◉ Capital Cities

Projection : Zenithal Equidistant

West from Greenwich   East from Greenwich

COPYRIGHT GEORGE PHILIP LTD

Maximum extent of sea ice

Summer extent of sea ice

Ice caps and permanent ice shelf

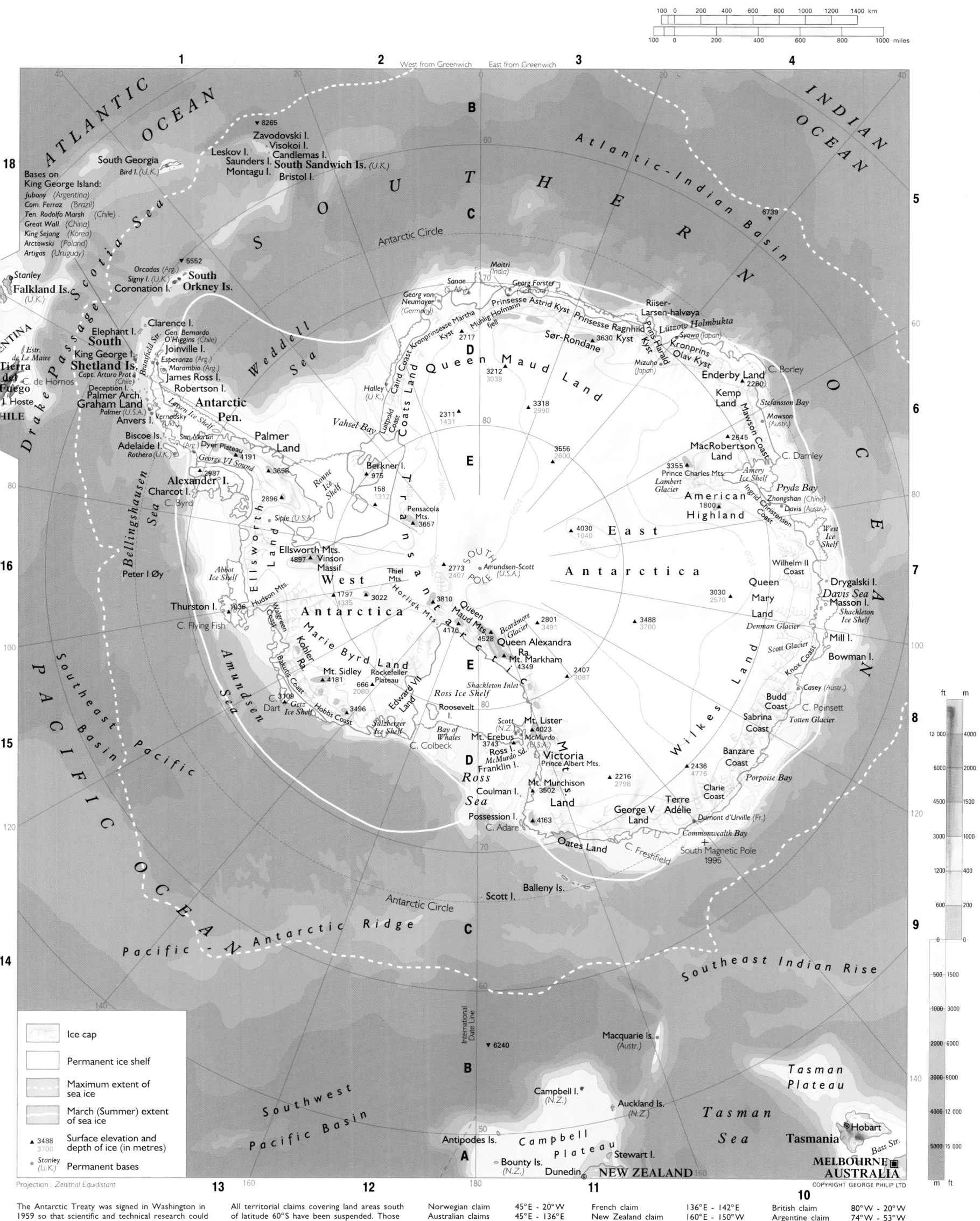

100 0 200 400 600 800 1000 1200 1400 km
100 0 200 400 600 800 1000 miles

Ice cap

Permanent ice shelf

Maximum extent of sea ice

March (Summer) extent of sea ice

▲ 3488 / 3700 **Surface elevation and depth of ice (in metres)**

● Stanley (U.K.) **Permanent bases**

Projection : Zenithal Equidistant

The Antarctic Treaty was signed in Washington in 1959 so that scientific and technical research could continue unhampered by international politics.

All territorial claims covering land areas south of latitude 60°S have been suspended. Those claims were:

Norwegian claim	45°E - 20°W
Australian claims	45°E - 136°E
	142°E - 160°E
French claim	136°E - 142°E
New Zealand claim	160°E - 150°W
Chilean claim	90°W - 53°W
British claim	80°W - 20°W
Argentine claim	74°W - 53°W

COPYRIGHT GEORGE PHILIP LTD

100 0 100 200 300 400 500 600 700 800 km
100 0 100 200 300 400 500 miles

CARTOGRAPHY BY PHILIPS.

ATLANTIC OCEAN

Norwegian Sea

North Sea

White Sea

Barents Sea

Baltic Sea

G. of Bothnia

Gulf of Bothnia

Kattegat

Skagerrak

English Channel

Bay of Biscay

Mediterranean Sea

Tyrrhenian Sea

Adriatic Sea

Ionian Sea

Ægean Sea

Black Sea

Caspian Sea

ICELAND
Reykjavik

UNITED KINGDOM
SCOTLAND Aberdeen, Dundee, Glasgow, Edinburgh, Newcastle-upon-Tyne, Leeds, Manchester, Liverpool, Sheffield, **ENGLAND**, Birmingham, **LONDON**, Bristol, Cardiff, **WALES**, Southampton, Plymouth
N. IRELAND Belfast
IRELAND Dublin, Cork

NORWAY Tromsø, Narvik, Trondheim, Bergen, Stavanger, Oslo
SWEDEN Kiruna, Luleå, Vaasa, Umeå, Sundsvall, Gävle, Uppsala, Stockholm, Örebro, Gothenburg, Göteborg, Jönköping, Malmö
FINLAND Helsinki, Turku, Tampere
DENMARK Copenhagen, Ålborg, Århus

NETHERLANDS Amsterdam, The Hague, Rotterdam
BELGIUM Brussels, Antwerp
LUX. Luxembourg
GERMANY Hamburg, Bremen, Hannover, Berlin, Magdeburg, Leipzig, Dresden, Cologne, Bonn, Essen, Dortmund, Frankfurt am Main, Wiesbaden, Nuremberg, Stuttgart, Munich
FRANCE Lille, Le Havre, Rouen, **PARIS**, Strasbourg, Nantes, Dijon, Limoges, Lyons, St.-Étienne, Bordeaux, Toulouse, Grenoble, Nice, Marseilles, Toulon
SWITZERLAND Bern, Zürich, Geneva
AUSTRIA Vienna, Linz, Salzburg, Innsbruck, Graz
LIECH.
MONACO
ANDORRA

SPAIN La Coruña, Vigo, Valladolid, Bilbao, Zaragoza, Barcelona, **Madrid**, Valencia, Alicante, Murcia, Granada, Córdoba, Málaga, Seville, Cádiz
PORTUGAL Porto, Lisbon
Gibraltar (U.K.)

ITALY Milan, Turin, Genoa, Venice, Bologna, Florence, **Rome**, Naples, Bari, Taranto, Palermo, Catania, Messina, Cagliari
SAN MARINO
MALTA Valletta
Corsica, Sardinia, Sicily

POLAND Gdańsk, Szczecin, Bydgoszcz, Poznań, Warsaw, Łódź, Wrocław, Kraków, Katowice, Lublin
CZECH REP. Prague
SLOVAK REP. Bratislava
HUNGARY Budapest, Miskolc, Debrecen
SLOVENIA Ljubljana
CROATIA Zagreb
BOSNIA-HERZ. Sarajevo, Split
YUGOSLAVIA Belgrade, **SERBIA**, Niš, **MONTE-NEGRO**
ROMANIA Cluj-Napoca, Timișoara, Brașov, Bucharest, Galați, Ploiești
BULGARIA Sofia, Plovdiv, Varna
MACEDONIA Skopje
ALBANIA Tirana
GREECE Thessaloniki, Athens, Patras, Patrai
Crete, Corfu, Rhodes

ESTONIA Tallinn
LATVIA Riga
LITHUANIA Vilnius, Kaunas, Kaliningrad (Russia)
BELARUS Minsk, Mogilev, Gomel, Brest
UKRAINE Kiev, Lvov, Zhitomir, Chernigov, Dnepropetrovsk, Donetsk, Zaporozhye, Kharkov, Kherson, Nikolayev, Odessa, Sevastopol, Crimea
MOLDOVA Kishinev

RUSSIA MOSCOW, St. Petersburg, Murmansk, Arkhangelsk, N. Dvina, Kotlas, Vologda, Yaroslavl, Kostroma, Ivanovo, Nizhniy Novgorod, Kazan, Kirov, Izhevsk, Perm, Yekaterinburg, Nizhniy Tagil, Chelyabinsk, Magnitogorsk, Ufa, Samara, Saratov, Volgograd, Penza, Tambov, Voronezh, Lipetsk, Orel, Tula, Kursk, Smolensk, Rostov, Taganrog, Krasnodar, Stavropol, Astrakhan, Makhachkala

KAZAKSTAN Uralsk

GEORGIA Tbilisi
ARMENIA Yerevan
AZERBAIJAN Baku

TURKEY Istanbul, Bursa, Ankara, İzmir, Konya, Adana, Kayseri, Samsun, Antalya, Erzurum, Diyarbakir
CYPRUS Nicosia
SYRIA Aleppo
IRAQ Baghdad
IRAN Tabriz
Atrak, Tigris, Euphrates

MOROCCO Tangier, Ceuta (Sp.), Melilla (Sp.)
ALGERIA Algiers, Oran, Constantine, Annaba
TUNISIA Tunis

Balearic Is., Ibiza, Majorca, Minorca
Pantelleria (Italy)

Rivers: Ob, Volga, Don, Dnieper, Dniester, Danube, Rhine, Rhône, Elbe, Oder, Vistula, Seine, Loire, Garonne, Ebro, Duero, Tagus, Guadiana, Guadalquivir, W. Dvina, W. Dvina, Pripet, Bug, Kama, Tiber, Po

Lakes: L. Onega, L. Ladoga, Rybinsk Res., L. Chudskoye, Vänern, Vättern, Mälar

Arctic Circle

■ LONDON Capital Cities

Projection: Bonne   West from Greenwich 0 East from Greenwich

SCANDINAVIA 1:4 400 000

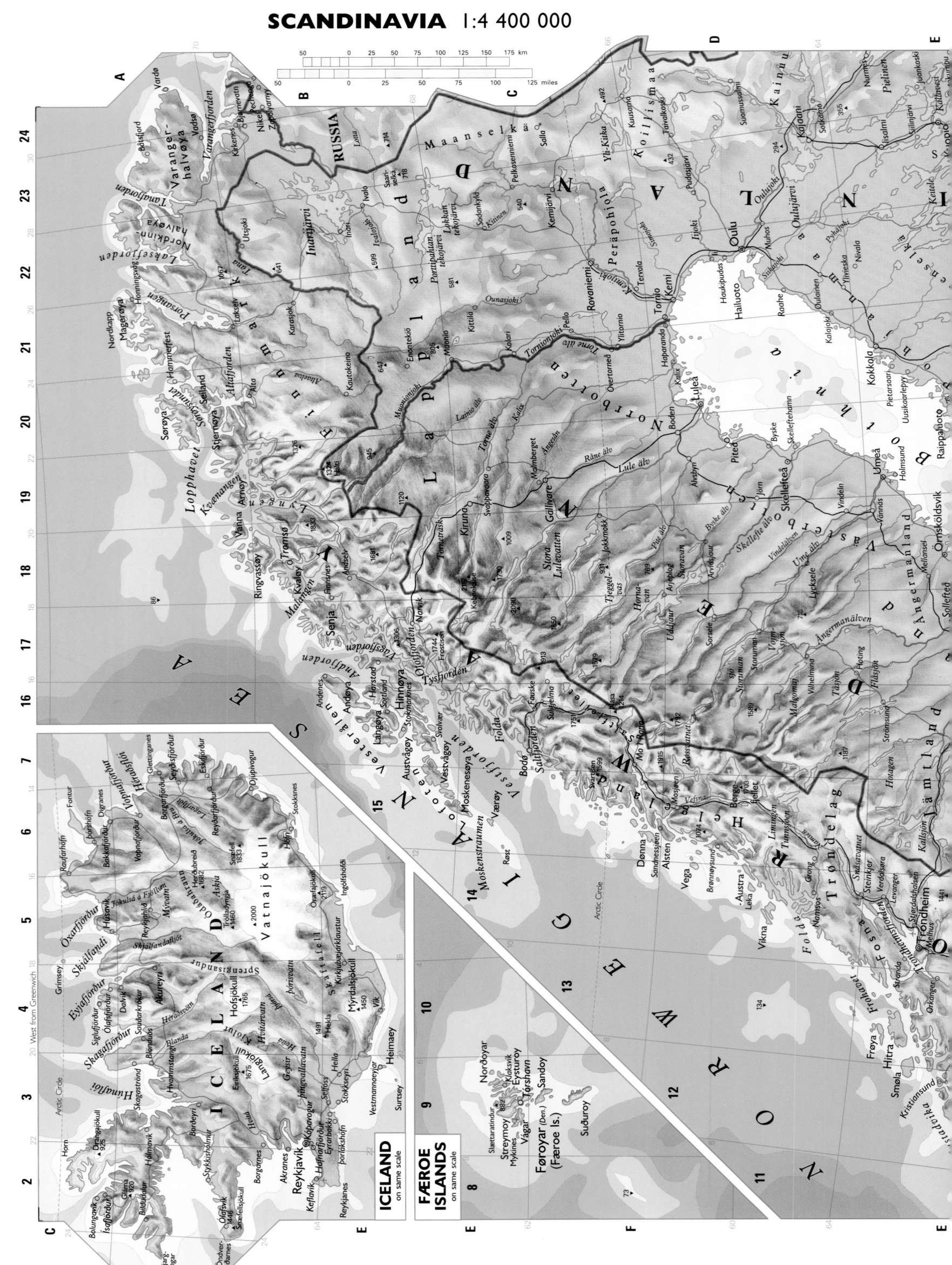

ICELAND
on same scale

FÆROE
ISLANDS
on same scale

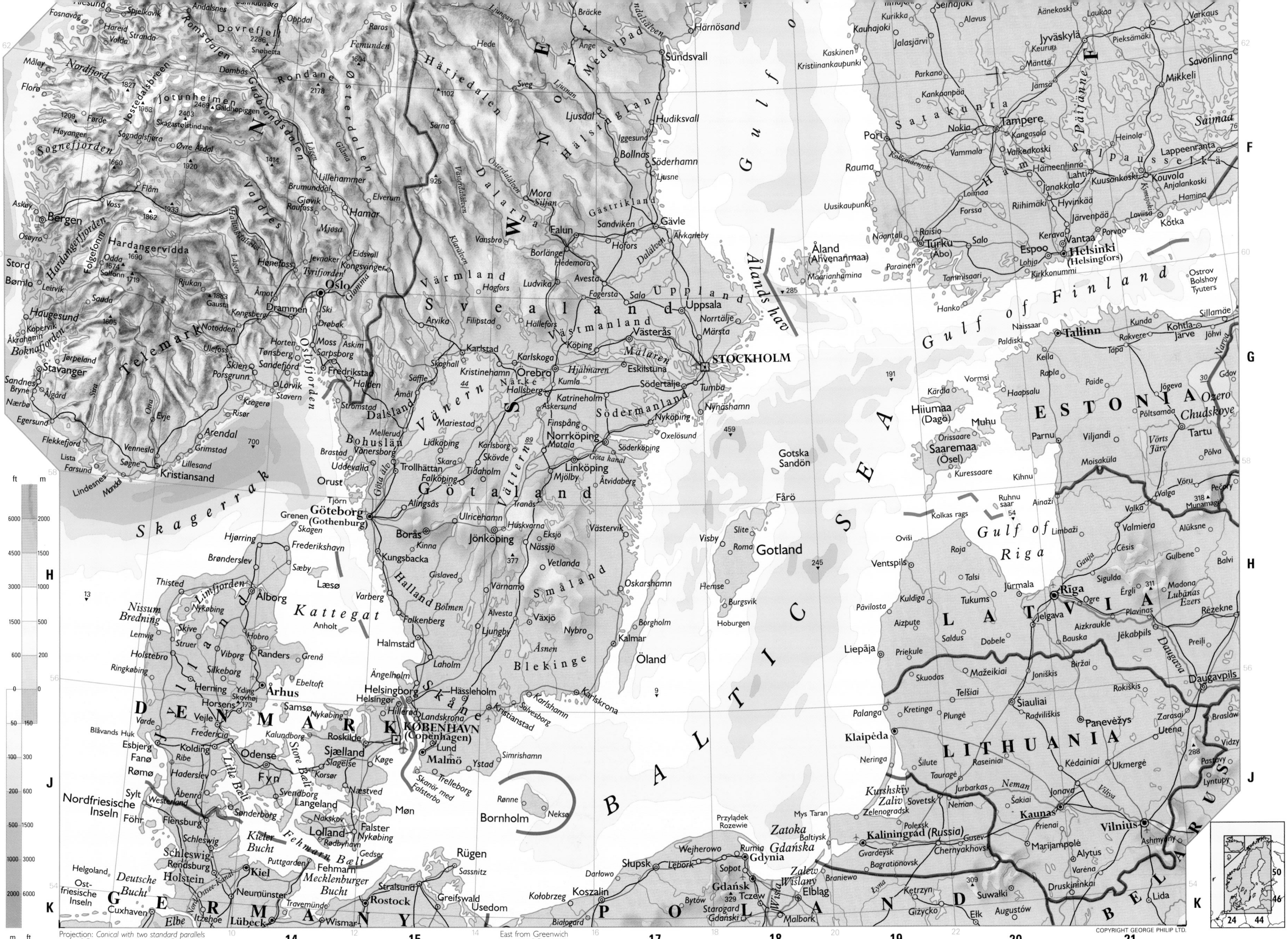

9

F   G   H   J   K

FINLAND
Saimaa
Savonlinna
Mikkeli
Lappeenranta
Kouvola
Kotka
Hamina
Kymijoki
Helsinki (Helsingfors)
Espoo Vantaa
Lahti
Hämeenlinna
Tampere
Turku (Åbo)
Pori
Rauma
Uusikaupunki

ESTONIA
Tallinn
Tartu
Pärnu
Viljandi
Paide
Rakvere
Narva
Ozero Chudskoye
Hiiumaa (Dagö)
Saaremaa (Ösel)
Kuressaare
Haapsalu

LATVIA
Riga
Jelgava
Jūrmala
Ventspils
Liepāja
Daugavpils
Valmiera
Cēsis
Rēzekne

LITHUANIA
Vilnius
Kaunas
Šiauliai
Panevėžys
Klaipėda

RUSSIA
Kaliningrad (Russia)

Gulf of Finland
Gulf of Riga
Åland (Ahvenanmaa)
Ålands hav

B A L T I C   S E A
Gotland
Visby
Öland
Bornholm
Gotska Sandön

SWEDEN
STOCKHOLM
Uppsala
Västerås
Örebro
Norrköping
Linköping
Jönköping
Gävle
Sundsvall
Härnösand
Hudiksvall
Falun
Borlänge
Mora
Karlstad
Göteborg (Gothenburg)
Borås
Halmstad
Helsingborg
Malmö
Lund
Karlskrona
Kalmar
Växjö
Dalarna
Värmland
Gotland
Småland
Blekinge
Skåne
Halland
Bohuslän

NORWAY
Oslo
Bergen
Stavanger
Kristiansand
Arendal
Drammen
Fredrikstad
Sarpsborg
Hamar
Lillehammer
Dovrefjell
Jotunheimen
Hardangervidda
Skagerrak
Oslofjorden

DENMARK
KØBENHAVN (Copenhagen)
Århus
Ålborg
Odense
Esbjerg
Randers
Kolding
Horsens
Vejle
Sjælland
Fyn
Lolland
Falster
Langeland
Bornholm
Kattegat

GERMANY
Kiel
Lübeck
Rostock
Flensburg
Rügen
Usedom
Cuxhaven
Neumünster
Schleswig
Holstein
Mecklenburger Bucht
Nordfriesische Inseln
Deutsche Bucht

POLAND
Gdańsk
Gdynia
Słupsk
Koszalin
Szczecin
Kołobrzeg
Elbląg
Malbork

Projection: Conic with two standard parallels
East from Greenwich

10 0 10 20 30 40 50 60 70 80 90 km

10 0 10 20 30 40 50 60 miles

Gulf of Bothnia

VÄSTER- NORRLANDS LÄN

Örnsköldsvik

Härnösand

Sundsvall

Medelpad

Indalsälven

Ljungan

JÄMTLANDS LÄN

Östersund

Storsjön

Härjedalen

Hälsingland

GÄVLEBORGS LÄN

Hudiksvall

Söderhamn

Gästrikland

Gävle

Sandviken

KOPPARBERGS LÄN

Dalarna

Siljan

Mora

Falun

Borlänge

Dalälven

SÖR-TRØNDELAG

Trondheim

Dovrefjell

Rondane

MØRE OG ROMSDAL

Kristiansund

Ålesund

OPPLAND

Gudbrandsdalen

Lillehammer

Gjøvik

HEDMARK

Østerdalen

Klarälven

Österdalälven

Västerdalälven

VÄRMLANDS LÄN

Karlstad

ÖREBRO LÄN

Örebro

VÄSTMANLANDS LÄN

Västerås

SÖDERMANLANDS LÄN

Eskilstuna

Mälaren

UPPSALA LÄN

Uppsala

STOCKHOLMS LÄN

STOCKHOLM

Södertälje

AKERSHUS

OSLO

Oslo

BUSKERUD

TELEMARK

VESTFOLD

ØSTFOLD

Fredrikstad

Drammen

Hallingdal

Numedal

Valdres

m 2000 1500 1000 500 200 0

ft 6000 4500 3000 1500 600 0

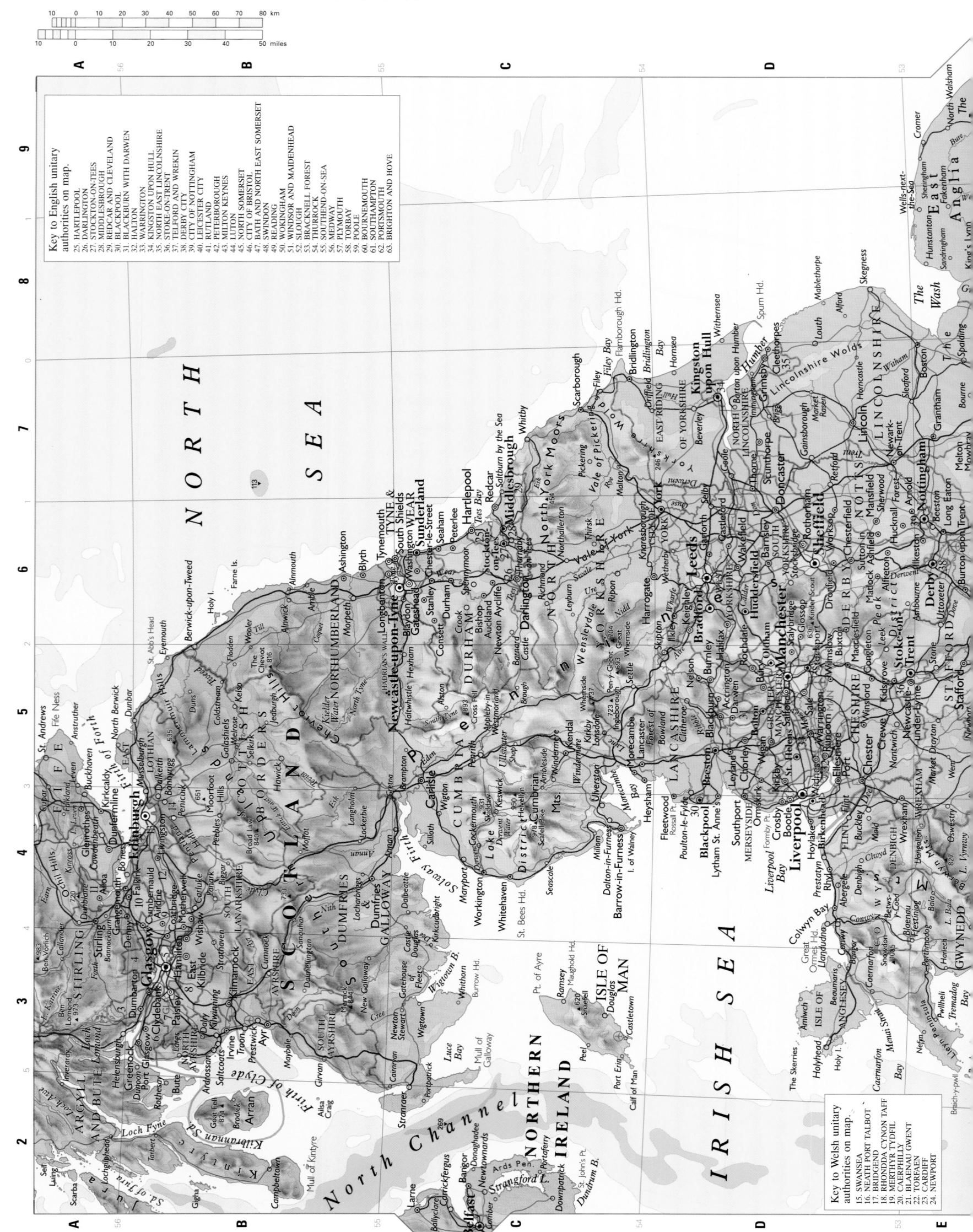

Key to English unitary authorities on map.

25. HARTLEPOOL
26. DARLINGTON
27. STOCKTON-ON-TEES
28. MIDDLESBROUGH
29. REDCAR AND CLEVELAND
30. BLACKPOOL
31. BLACKBURN WITH DARWEN
32. HALTON
33. WARRINGTON
34. KINGSTON UPON HULL
35. NORTH EAST LINCOLNSHIRE
36. NORTH LINCOLNSHIRE
37. TELFORD AND WREKIN
38. STOKE-ON-TRENT
39. DERBY CITY
40. CITY OF NOTTINGHAM
41. LEICESTER CITY
42. RUTLAND
43. PETERBOROUGH
44. LUTON
45. MILTON KEYNES
46. NORTH SOMERSET
47. CITY OF BRISTOL
48. BATH AND NORTH EAST SOMERSET
49. SWINDON
50. READING
51. WOKINGHAM
52. WINDSOR AND MAIDENHEAD
53. SLOUGH
54. BRACKNELL FOREST
55. THURROCK
56. SOUTHEND-ON-SEA
57. MEDWAY
58. PLYMOUTH
59. TORBAY
60. POOLE
61. BOURNEMOUTH
62. SOUTHAMPTON
63. PORTSMOUTH
64. BRIGHTON AND HOVE

Key to Welsh unitary authorities on map.

15. SWANSEA
16. NEATH PORT TALBOT
17. BRIDGEND
18. RHONDDA CYNON TAFF
19. MERTHYR TYDFIL
20. CAERPHILLY
21. BLAENAU GWENT
22. TORFAEN
23. CARDIFF
24. NEWPORT

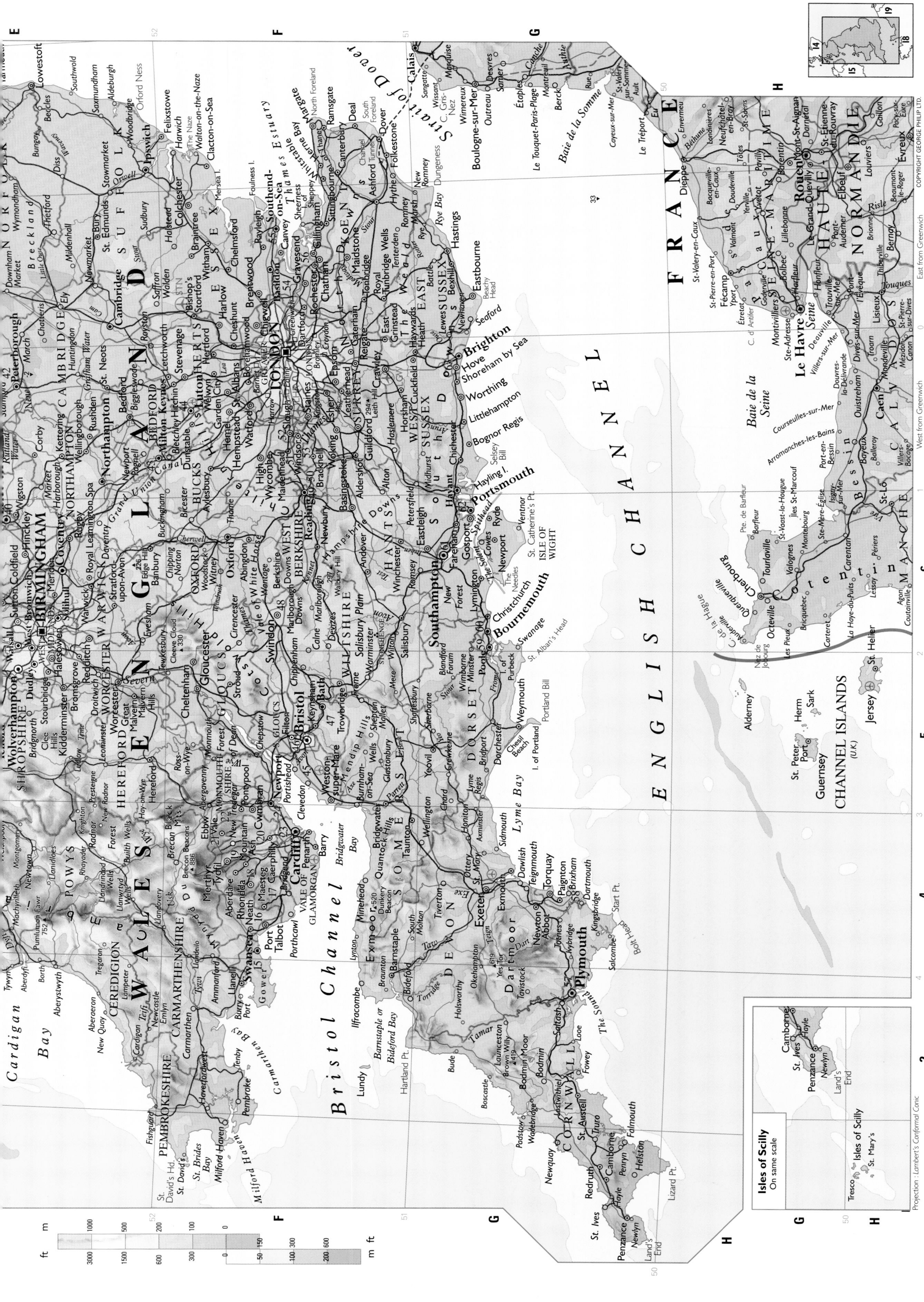

ENGLAND

WALES

FRANCE

NORMANDIE

HAUTE-SEINE-MARITIME

CALVADOS

MANCHE

English Channel

Bristol Channel

Cardigan Bay

Strait of Dover

CHANNEL ISLANDS (U.K.)

Guernsey · Jersey · Alderney · Sark · Herm

LONDON

Birmingham · **Cardiff** · **Bristol** · **Southampton** · **Portsmouth** · **Brighton** · **Bournemouth** · **Plymouth** · **Le Havre** · **Rouen** · **Caen**

NORFOLK · SUFFOLK · ESSEX · KENT · EAST SUSSEX · WEST SUSSEX · SURREY · HANTS · DORSET · DEVON · CORNWALL · SOMERSET · WILTSHIRE · BERKSHIRE · OXON · BUCKS · HERTS · CAMBRIDGE · NORTHAMPTON · WARWICK · WORCESTER · HEREFORD · SHROPSHIRE · GLOUCS · GLAMORGAN · CARMARTHENSHIRE · PEMBROKESHIRE · CEREDIGION · POWYS

Lowestoft · Southwold · Aldeburgh · Orford Ness · Felixstowe · Harwich · Clacton-on-Sea · Ipswich · Colchester · Cambridge · Peterborough · Luton · Oxford · Reading · Windsor · Guildford · Worthing · Eastbourne · Hastings · Dover · Folkestone · Canterbury · Margate · Ramsgate · Deal · Ashford · Maidstone · Chatham · Rochester · Gravesend · Southend-on-Sea · Canvey Island · Chelmsford · Braintree · Bedford · Northampton · Coventry · Gloucester · Cheltenham · Swindon · Salisbury · Winchester · Basingstoke · Andover · Chichester · Bognor Regis · Littlehampton · Christchurch · Swanage · Weymouth · Dorchester · Bridport · Exeter · Exmouth · Torquay · Paignton · Brixham · Dartmouth · Kingsbridge · Start Pt. · Salcombe · Bude · Newquay · Padstow · Wadebridge · Bodmin · Truro · St. Austell · Fowey · Falmouth · Penzance · Newlyn · Land's End · Lizard Pt. · St. Ives · Helston · Redruth · Camborne

Swansea · Neath · Merthyr Tydfil · Newport · Aberystwyth · Cardigan · Fishguard · Milford Haven · Tenby · Haverfordwest

Calais · Boulogne-sur-Mer · Étaples · Berck · Dieppe · Le Tréport · Eu · Fécamp · Étretat · Honfleur · Deauville · Trouville · Lisieux · Bayeux · Cherbourg · Valognes · Carentan · St-Lô · Coutances · Évreux · Louviers · Bernay

Isles of Scilly — On same scale
Tresco · Isles of Scilly · St. Mary's

Isle of Wight
Newport · Ryde · Cowes · Ventnor · The Needles · St. Catherine's Pt.

Projection: Lambert's Conformal Conic

COPYRIGHT GEORGE PHILIP LTD.

East from Greenwich · West from Greenwich

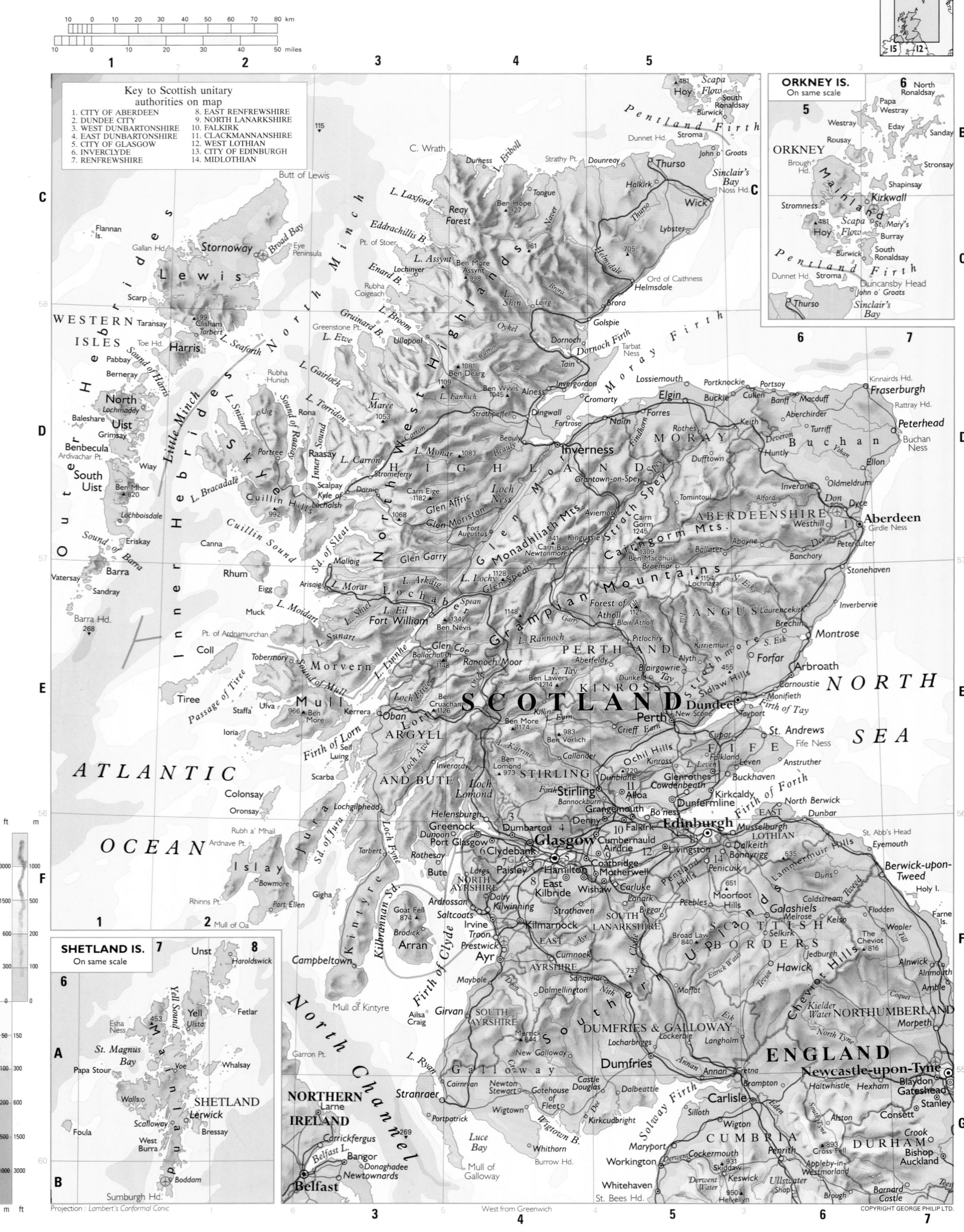

Key to Scottish unitary
authorities on map

1. CITY OF ABERDEEN
2. DUNDEE CITY
3. WEST DUNBARTONSHIRE
4. EAST DUNBARTONSHIRE
5. CITY OF GLASGOW
6. INVERCLYDE
7. RENFREWSHIRE
8. EAST RENFREWSHIRE
9. NORTH LANARKSHIRE
10. FALKIRK
11. CLACKMANNANSHIRE
12. WEST LOTHIAN
13. CITY OF EDINBURGH
14. MIDLOTHIAN

ORKNEY IS.
On same scale

SHETLAND IS.
On same scale

Projection : Lambert's Conformal Conic

West from Greenwich

COPYRIGHT GEORGE PHILIP LTD.

10 0 10 20 30 40 50 60 70 80 km
10 0 10 20 30 40 50 miles

ATLANTIC OCEAN

NORTH CHANNEL

IRISH SEA

St. George's Channel

CELTIC SEA

Firth of Clyde

Kintyre — Campbeltown — Brodick — Arran — Ailsa Craig — Cairnryan — Stranraer — Portpatrick

Mull of Oa — Rathlin I. — Fair Hd. — Ballycastle — Mts of Antrim — Garron Pt. — Trostan ▲554

Malin Hd. — Malin Pen. — Inishowen Pen. — Carndonagh — Moville — Buncrana — Portstewart — Portrush — Coleraine — Limavady — Ballymoney

Tory I. — Bloody Foreland — Horn Head — Sheep Haven — Mulroy B. — Lough Swilly — Fanad Hd. — Lough Foyle — L. Foyle — **LONDONDERRY** — Londonderry — Roe — Ballymena — Larne — Carrickfergus ▲269

Inishfree B. — Gweedore — Errigal ▲752 — Derryveagh Mts. — The Rosses — Rathmelton — Letterkenny — **DONEGAL** — Lifford — Strabane — Sawel Mt. ▲683 — Sperrin Mts. — Magherafelt — **NORTHERN** — Randalstown — Ballyclare — Antrim — Belfast L. — Bangor — Donaghadee — Newtownards

Aran I. — Crohy Hd. ▲683 — Gweebarra B. — Dawros Hd. — Glenties — Lavagh More ▲676 — Sion Mills — Newtownstewart — **TYRONE** — Cookstown — Moneymore — Coalisland — **U l s t e r** — Lurgan — **IRELAND** — Lisburn — Saintfield — Comber — Ards Pen. — Strangford L. — Portaferry

Loughros More B. — Rossan Pt. — St. John's Pt. — Donegal — **Donegal Bay** — Ballyshannon — Bundoran — Erne — Castlederg — Mourne — Omagh — Dromore — Irvinestown — Dungannon — Armagh — **NORTHERN IRELAND** — Craigavon — Portadown — Banbridge — Ballynahinch — Downpatrick — St. John's Pt. — Ballyquintin Pt.

Killybegs — Downpatrick Hd. — Killala B. — Lower L. Erne — Enniskillen — **FERMANAGH** — Upper L. Erne — Clones — **MONAGHAN** — Monaghan — Aughnacloy — Keady — Middletown — **ARMAGH** — Newry — Warrenpoint — Kilkeel — Carlingford L. — Slieve Donard ▲852 — **DOWN** — Dundrum — Dundrum B. — Newcastle

Broad Haven — Erris Hd. — Belmullet — Mullet Pen. — Inishkea North — Inishkea South — Blacksod Bay — Ballina — **SLIGO** — Sligo — Sligo Bay — Dromore West ▲544 — Slieve SGamph — Collooney — L. Allen — Belturbet — Castleblaney — Coatehill — Clones — **MONAGHAN** — Slieve Gullion ▲577 — **Dundalk** — Greenore — Dundalk Bay

Achill Hd. — Achill I. — Corraun Pen. — Clare I. — **MAYO** — Newport — L. Conn ▲806 — Nephin ▲765 — Castlebar — Knock — **ROSCOMMON** — Charlestown — Swinford — Ballyhaunis — Castlerea — L. Gowna — Granard — **MEATH** — **Drogheda** — Balbriggan

Inishturk — Clew Bay — Westport — Croagh Patrick ▲765 — Mweelrea ▲819 — Claremorris — Ballaghaderreen — Boyle — Carrick-on-Shannon — **LEITRIM** — Leitrim — **CAVAN** — Carrickmacross — Kingscourt — Oldcastle — Ceanannus Mor (Kells) — Blackwater — An Uaimh (Navan) — Rush — Lambay I.

Inishbofin — Inishshark — Killary Harbour — Ballinrobe — Lough Mask — Glennamaddy — Roscommon — Longford — **LONGFORD** — Castlepollard — L. Sheelin — Athboy — Boyne — Trim — Malahide

Clifden — Slyne Hd. — **Connemara** — Oughterard — Cong — Tuam — **GALWAY** — Athenry — **IRELAND** — Athlone — **WESTMEATH** — Moate — **Leinster** — Mullingar — Royal Canal — Maynooth — Howth Hd. — **DUBLIN** — Dun Laoghaire

Bertraghboy B. — Lough Corrib — Lough Ree — Clara — Bog — Tullamore — Edenderry — Allen — Naas — Clondalkin — **Dublin** — Bray — Greystones

Kilkieran B. — Aran Is. — Inishmore — Galway — **Galway Bay** — Black Hd. — Loughrea — Ballinasloe — **OFFALY** — Grand Canal — Daingean — Droichead Nua — **KILDARE** — Kildare — Monasterevin — Poulaphouca Res. — **WICKLOW** — Lugnaquilla ▲926

Inishmaan — Inisheer — Gort — Slieve Aughty ▲368 — Portumna — Shannon — Birr — Mountmellick — Portarlington — Port Laoise — Athy — Wicklow Mts — Rathdrum — Wicklow Hd.

Hags Hd. — Liscannor Bay — Ennistimon — Slieve Bloom ▲529 — Arderin — Roscrea — Mountrath — **LAOIS** — Carlow — Tullow — Shillelagh — Gorey — **Wicklow**

Mal Bay — Milltown Malbay — Mutton I. — **CLARE** — Tulla — Lough Derg — Nenagh — Templemore — Durrow — **CARLOW** — Muine Bheag — Bunclody — Arklow

Loop Hd. — Kilkee — Kilrush — Ennis — Sixmilebridge — Killaloe — Keeper Hill ▲694 — Thurles — **TIPPERARY** — Kilkenny — Mt. Leinster ▲796 — Enniscorthy

Shannon Airport — **Limerick** — **TIPPERARY** — Golden Vale — **KILKENNY** — Callan — Barrow — **WEXFORD** — Cahore Pt.

Mouth of the Shannon — Foynes — **LIMERICK** — Rathkeale — Tipperary — Cashel — Slievenamon ▲722 — Carrick-on-Suir — New Ross — Wexford — Wexford Harbour — Rosslare — Greenore Pt.

Kerry Hd. — Listowel — Newcastle West — Kilfinnane — Galtymore ▲920 — Galty Mts. — Caher — Clonmel — **WATERFORD** — Waterford — Tramore — Carnsore Pt.

Brandon B. — Tralee B. — Tralee — Slieve Mish ▲953 ▲853 — Maine — Abbeyfeale — Rath Luirc — Mitchelstown — Knockmealdown Mts ▲795 — Comeragh Mts ▲792 — Tramore Harbour — Saltee Is.

Smerwick Harbour — Brandon Mt. ▲953 — Dingle — Laune — Newmarket — Kanturk — Buttevant — Fermoy — **WATERFORD** — Lismore — Dungarvan — Dungarvan Harbour — Tramore B. — Hook Hd.

Great Blasket I. — Dunmore Hd. — Inishvickillane — Dingle Bay — Killorglin — **KERRY** — Killarney — L. Leane — Mallow — Blackwater — Youghal — Youghal B. — Waterford Harbour

Valencia I. — Caherciveen — Carrauntoohill ▲1041 — Macgillycuddy's Reeks — Boggeragh Mts ▲646 — **CORK** — Macroom — Blarney — Passage West — **Cork** — Midleton — Cobh — Crosshaven

Puffin I. — Great Skellig — Kenmare — Lee — Cork Harbour — Old Head of Kinsale

Ballinskelligs B. — Scariff I. — Kenmare River — Caha Mts ▲686 — Glengarriff — Dunmanway — Bandon — Bandon — Kinsale

Dursey I. — Crow Hd. — Castletown Bearhaven — Bear I. — Bantry Bay — Bantry — Clonakilty — Clonakilty B.

Mizen Hd. — Long I. — Skull — Baltimore — Sherkin I. — Skibbereen — Galley Hd.

C. Clear — Clear I.

123 ▲ — 115 ▲

Projection : Lambert's Conformal Conic

West from Greenwich

COPYRIGHT GEORGE PHILIP LTD.

ft m — 1500 500 — 600 200 — 300 100 — 50 150 — 100 300 — 200 600 — 500 1500 — 1000 3000 — 2000 6000 — m ft

50 0 25 50 75 100 125 150 175 km
50 0 25 50 75 100 125 miles

ft m
3000 1000
1500 500
600 200
0 0
50 150
100 300
200 600
500 1500
1000 3000
2000 6000
m ft

ATLANTIC OCEAN

NORWAY
Bergen
Osøyro
Stord
Bømlo
Lei
Haugesund
Kopervik
Åkrahamn
Bokna
Stavanger
Sandne
Bryne
Nærbø

Shetland Is.
Yell
Unst
Fetlar
Foula
Mainland
Lerwick
Fair Isle

Orkney Is.
Westray
Sanday
Stronsay
Mainland
Hoy
Kirkwall
South Ronaldsay

C. Wrath
Pentland Firth
Thurso
Wick
Helmsdale

SCOTLAND
Lewis
Stornoway
Harris
St. Kilda
North Minch
North Uist
Benbecula
South Uist
Outer Hebrides
Inner Hebrides
Skye
Rhum
Eigg
Coll
Tiree
Mull
Tobermory
Oban
Colonsay
Jura
Islay
Mallaig
Portree
Ullapool
Lairg
Golspie
Tain
Invergordon
Dingwall
Inverness
L. Ness
Nairn
Elgin
Buckie
Banff
Fraserburgh
Peterhead
Huntly
Inverurie
Aberdeen
Stonehaven
Aviemore
Grampian Mts.
North West Highlands
Ben Nevis 1342
Fort William
789
182
1311
Dee
Ballater
Don
Spey

Montrose
Arbroath
Forfar
Perth
Dundee
St. Andrews
Glenrothes
Kirkcaldy
Dunfermline
Stirling
L. Lomond
973
1214
L. Fyne

Greenock
Paisley
Glasgow
East Kilbride
Hamilton
Edinburgh
Clyde
Irvine
Kilmarnock
Ayr
Arran
Campbeltown
Girvan
Stranraer
Southern Uplands
840
Jedburgh
Hawick
Cheviot Hills
816
Galashiels
Berwick-upon-Tweed
Alnwick
Dumfries
Kirkcudbright
Annan
Workington
Whitehaven
Mull of Galloway
Carlisle
Hexham
Gateshead
Newcastle-upon-Tyne
South Shields
Sunderland
Durham
Hartlepool
Darlington
Redcar
Middlesbrough
Stockton-on-Tees
Scarborough
Bridlington
893
1224
316
238

NORTH SEA
16

NORTHERN IRELAND
Buncrana
Letterkenny
Lifford
Londonderry
Coleraine
Ballymena
Larne
Ballymoney
Antrim
Bangor
Belfast
Lisburn
Lurgan
Portadown
Armagh
Newry
Lough Neagh
Ulster
Donegal
Bundoran
Lower L. Erne
Enniskillen
Omagh
Clogher
Castleblayney
Malin Hd.
Aran I.
North Channel
Firth of Clyde

IRELAND
Achill I.
Ballina
Castlebar
Westport
Lough Mask
Lough Corrib
Connemara
Galway B.
Aran Is.
Galway
Ballinasloe
Roscommon
Longford
Athlone
Mullingar
Lough Ree
Ennis
Limerick
Nenagh
Thurles
Tipperary
Clonmel
Carrick-on-Suir
Waterford
Dungarvan
Youghal
Cork
Cóbh
Kinsale
Bandon
Bantry
Killarney
Tralee
Listowel
Mallow
Blackwater
Macgillycuddy's Reeks
Carrauntoohill 1041
Dingle
Valencia
C. Clear
953
Shannon
Sligo
Leitrim
Cavan
Dundalk
Drogheda
Boyne
Ceanannus Mor
Tullamore
Liffey
Dublin
Dun Laoghaire
Bray
Naas
Port Laoise
Athy
Carlow
Kilkenny
Wicklow Mts.
926
Arklow
Wexford
Rosslare
Lough Derg
Kilrush
Clones
L. Conn

UNITED KINGDOM

IRISH SEA
I. of Man
Douglas
Holyhead
Anglesey
Bangor
Colwyn Bay
Conwy
Snowdon 1085
Cambrian Mts.
Pwllheli
Cardigan Bay
Aberystwyth
Welshpool
St. George's Channel
Fishguard
Haverfordwest
Milford Haven
Pembroke
Carmarthen
Llanelli
Swansea
Neath
Port Talbot
Merthyr Tydfil
Brecon
886
Rhondda
Cwmbran
Newport
Cardiff
Barry
Bristol Channel

WALES

Barrow-in-Furness
978
Lancaster
Cumbrian Mts.
Blackpool
Preston
Blackburn
Burnley
Keighley
Bradford
Halifax
Huddersfield
Harrogate
York
Leeds
Beverley
Kingston upon Hull
Humber
Grimsby
Scunthorpe
Doncaster
Barnsley
Rotherham
Sheffield
636
Louth
Lincoln
Skegness
The Wash
Boston
Cromer
Great Yarmouth
Lowestoft
Norwich
King's Lynn
Peterborough
Thetford
Bury St. Edmunds
Ely
Cambridge
Ipswich
Felixstowe
Harwich
Colchester
Chelmsford
36

ENGLAND
Liverpool
Birkenhead
Manchester
Stockport
Oldham
Warrington
Chester
Crewe
Wrexham
Stoke-on-Trent
Stafford
Shrewsbury
Telford
Derby
Nottingham
Mansfield
Chesterfield
Grantham
Trent
Leicester
Nuneaton
Coventry
Rugby
Corby
Northampton
Bedford
Milton Keynes
BIRMINGHAM
Wolverhampton
Redditch
Royal Leamington Spa
Worcester
Hereford
Gloucester
Cheltenham
Cotswold Hills
Stevenage
Luton
Harlow
Watford
Basildon
Southend-on-Sea
Cwmbran
High Wycombe
Oxford
Hemel Hempstead
Newbury
Swindon
Bath
Bristol
Reading
Slough
LONDON
Thames
Chatham
Canterbury
Margate
Maidstone
Ashford
Dover
Folkestone
Reigate
Crawley
Guildford
Basingstoke
Winchester
Salisbury
Southampton
Portsmouth
Isle of Wight
Newport
Poole
Bournemouth
Weymouth
Worthing
Brighton
Eastbourne
Hastings
Havant
Fareham
Yeovil
Taunton
Exmoor
Barnstaple
Weston-super-Mare
Bude
Exeter
Dartmoor
Exmouth
Torbay
Newquay
Truro
St. Austell
Plymouth
Land's End
Penzance
Falmouth
Isles of Scilly
99

CELTIC SEA

ENGLISH CHANNEL

Channel Is. (U.K.)
Guernsey
St. Peter Port
Sark
Alderney
St. Helier
Jersey
C. de la Hague
Pte. de Barfleur
Cherbourg
Valognes
Cotentin
Bayeux
Caen
Le Havre
Trouville-sur-Mer
Lisieux
Elbeuf
Bolbec
Rouen
Seine
Pays de Caux
Fécamp
Dieppe
Le Tréport
Abbeville
Amiens
St-Quentin

FRANCE
Boulogne-sur-Mer
Le Touquet-Paris-Plage
33
Str. of Dover
C. Gris-Nez
Calais
Dunkerque
St-Omer
Picardie
Gravelines

NETHERLANDS
's-Gravenhage (Den Haag)
Hoek van Holland
ROTTERDAM
Dordrecht
Haarlem
Den Held
Alkm
Texel

BELGIUM
BRUSSELS (Bruxelles)
Antwerpen
Gent
Brugge
Mechelen
Oostende
Zeebrugge
Vlissingen
Tournai
Lille
Roubaix
Tourcoing
Villeneuve-d'Ascq
Béthune
Bruay-la-Buissière
Lens
Valenciennes
Cambrai

NORTH SEA

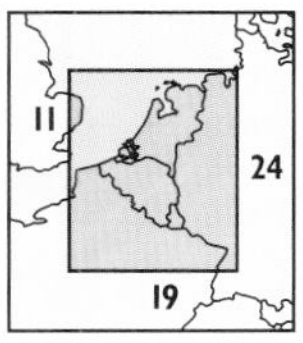
11
24
19

10 0 10 20 30 40 50 60 70 80 90 km
10 0 10 20 30 40 50 60 miles

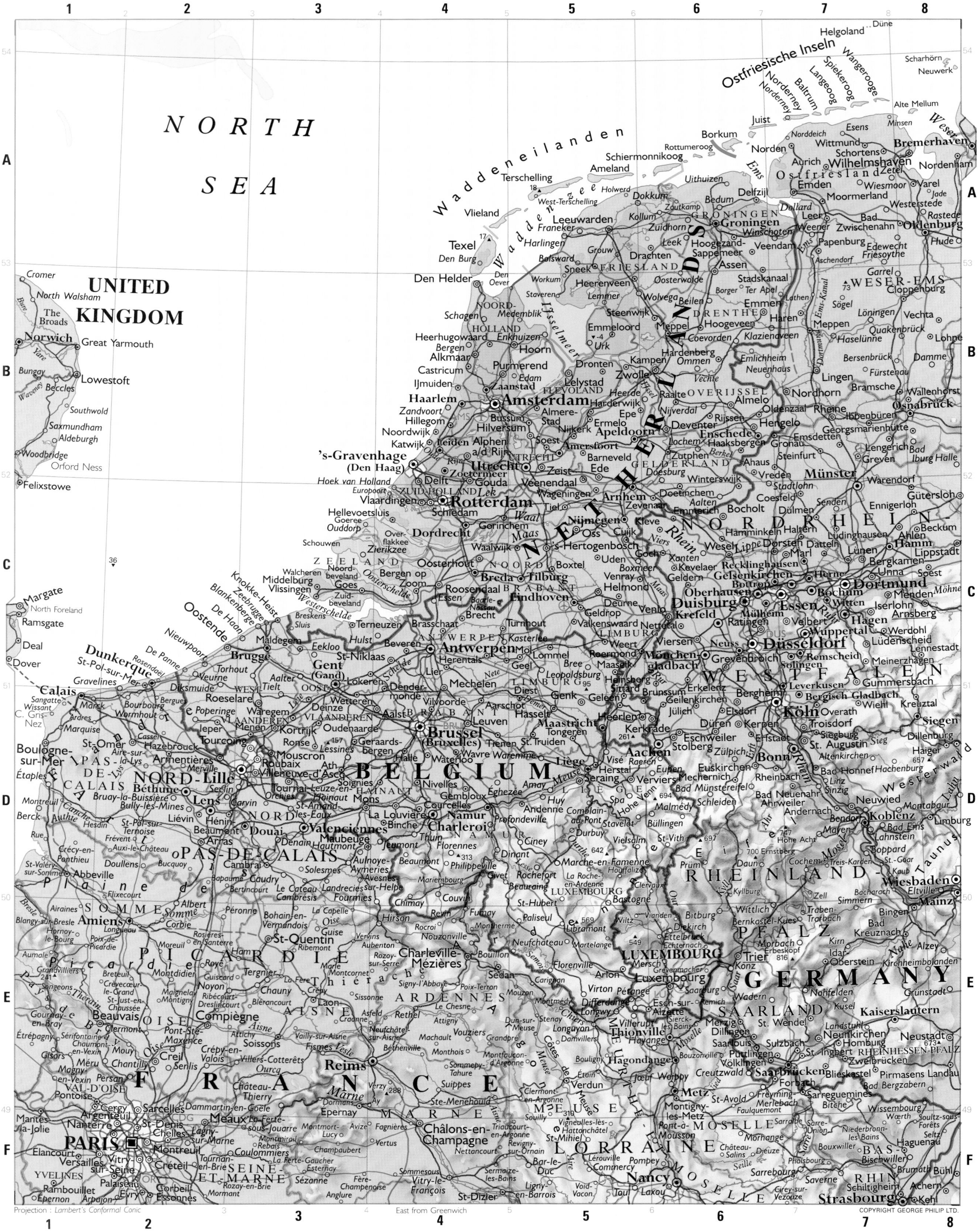
NORTH SEA
UNITED KINGDOM
NETHERLANDS
BELGIUM
LUXEMBOURG
GERMANY
FRANCE
Waddeneilanden
Ostfriesische Inseln
Amsterdam
Rotterdam
's-Gravenhage (Den Haag)
Utrecht
Antwerpen
Brussel (Bruxelles)
Gent (Gand)
Brugge
Liège
Luxembourg
Köln
Düsseldorf
Dortmund
Essen
Lille
Reims
PARIS
Projection : Lambert's Conformal Conic
East from Greenwich
COPYRIGHT GEORGE PHILIP LTD.

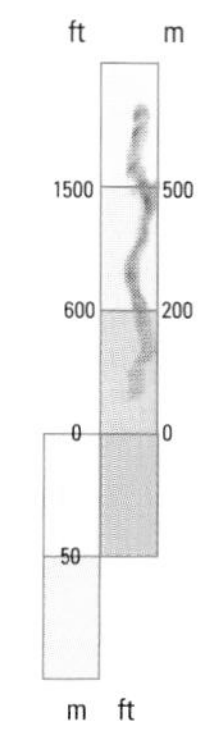
ft
m
1500
500
600
200
0
0
50
m
ft

Underlined towns give their name to the administrative area in which they stand.

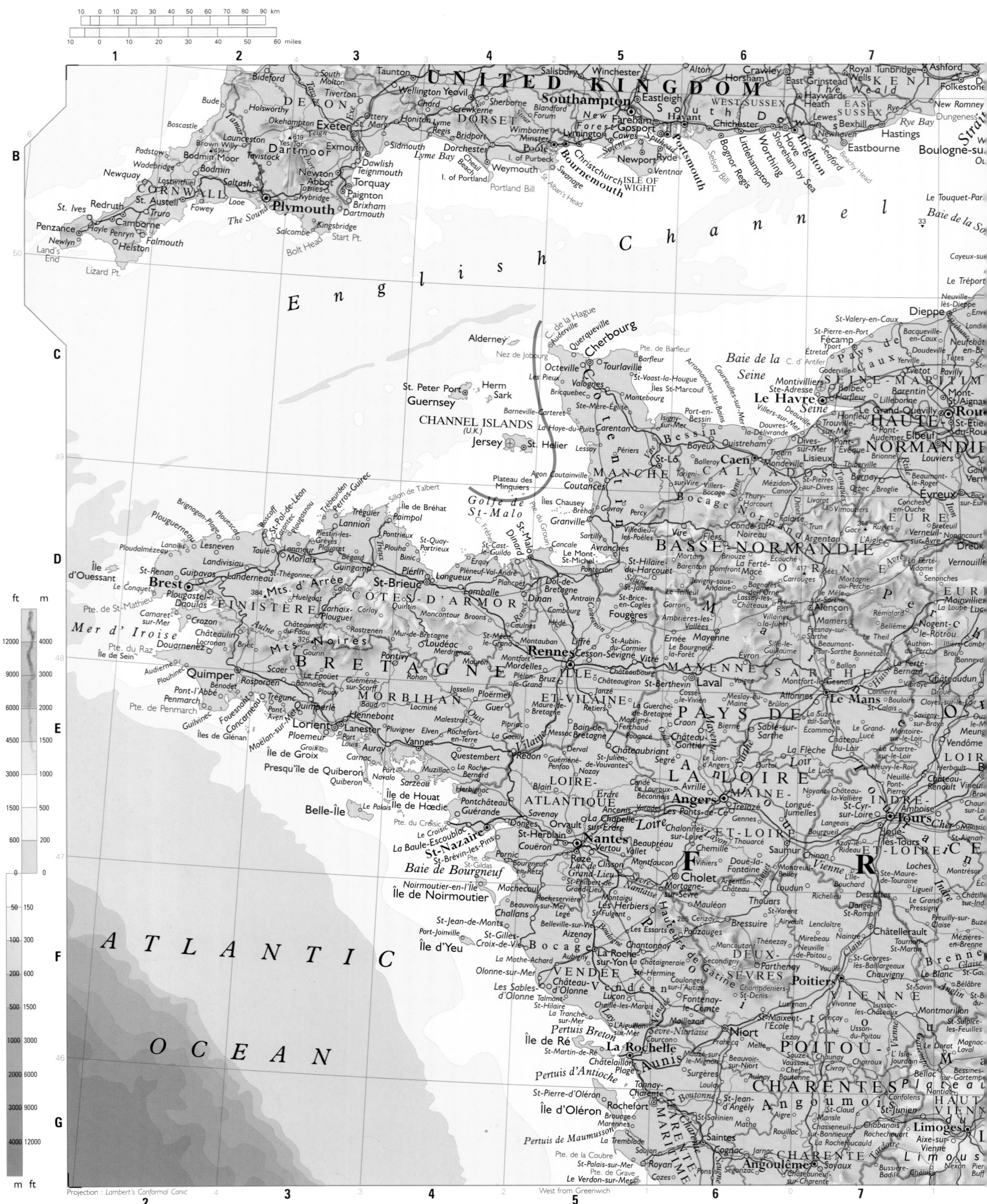

10 0 10 20 30 40 50 60 70 80 90 km
10 0 10 20 30 40 50 60 miles

ft m

12000 4000
9000 3000
6000 2000
4500 1500
3000 1000
1500 500
600 200
0 0
50 150
100 300
200 600
500 1500
1000 3000
2000 6000
3000 9000
4000 12000
m ft

Projection : Lambert's Conformal Conic

West from Greenwich

DÉPARTEMENTS IN THE PARIS AREA
1. Ville de Paris   3. Val-de-Marne
2. Seine-St-Denis   4. Hauts-de-Seine

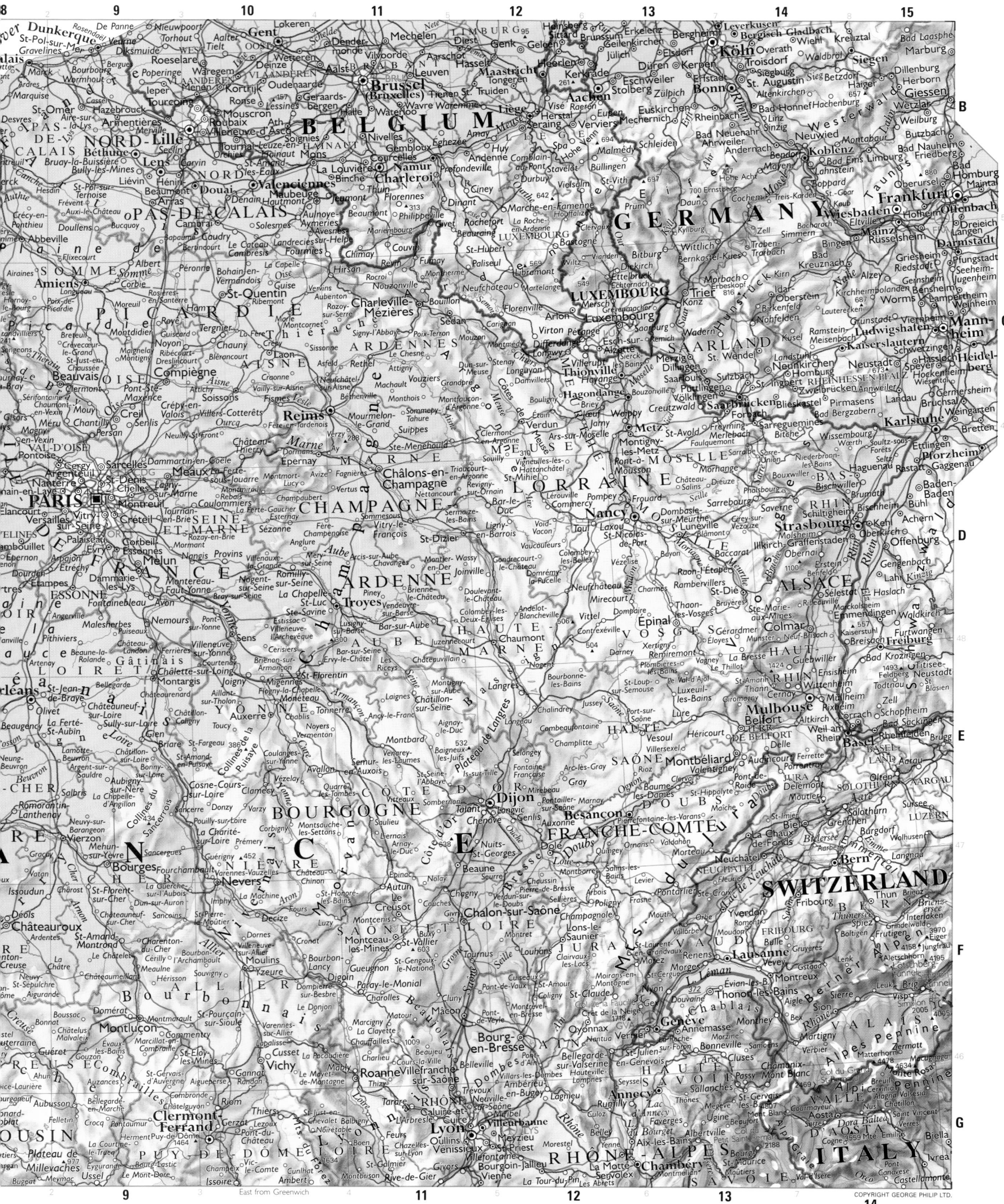

Underlined towns give their name to the
administrative area in which they stand.

East from Greenwich

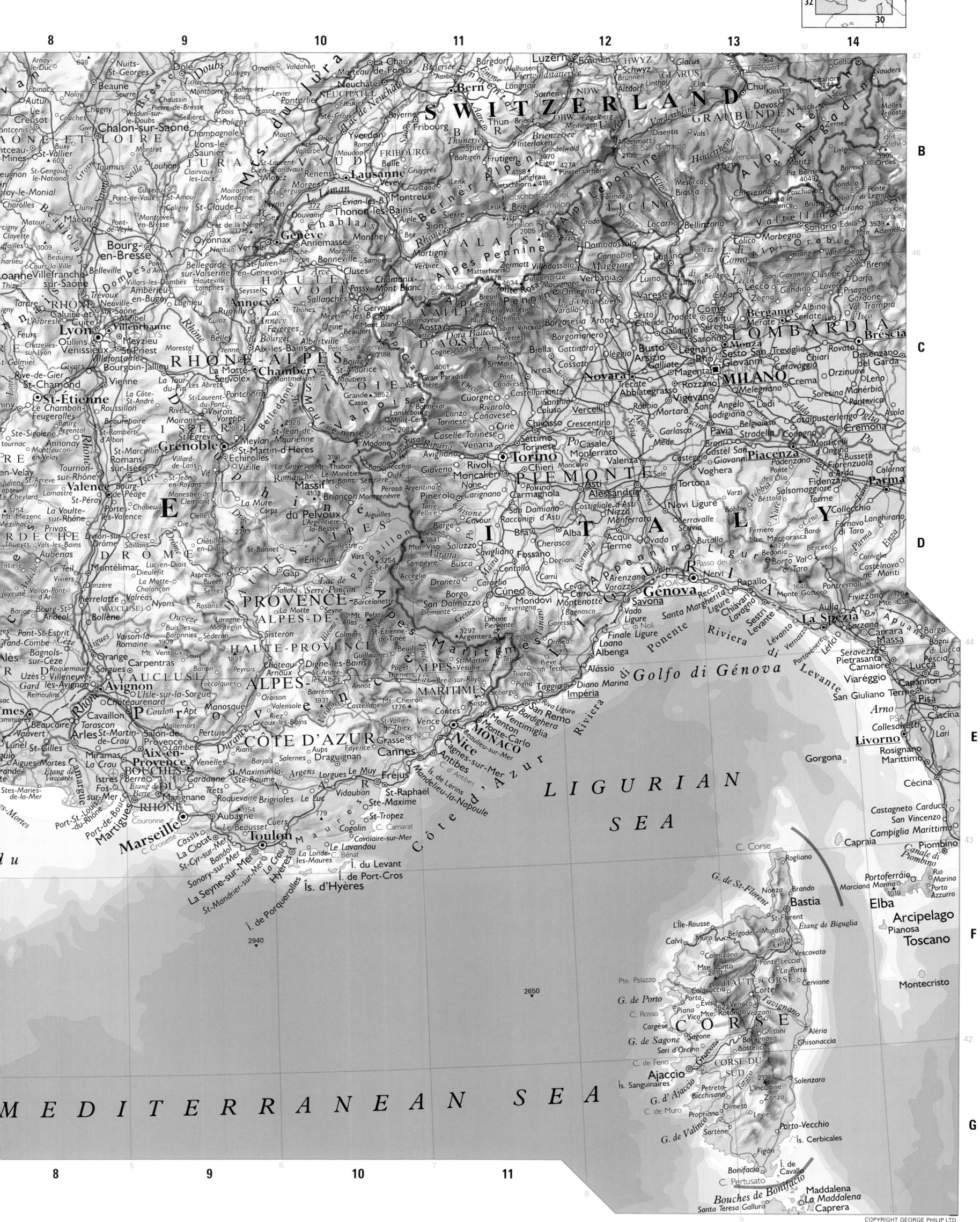

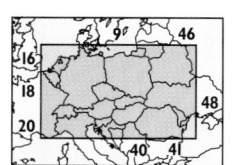

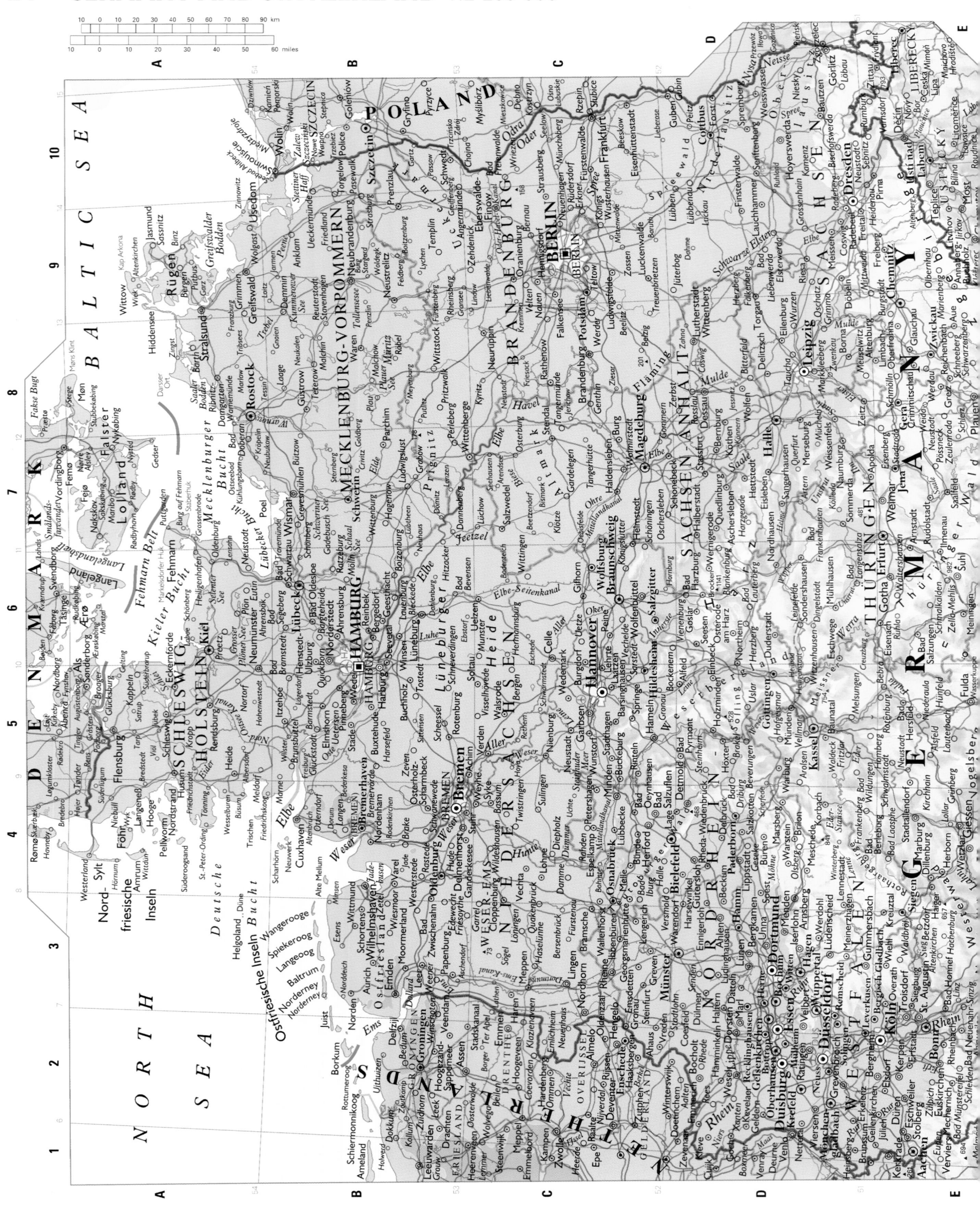

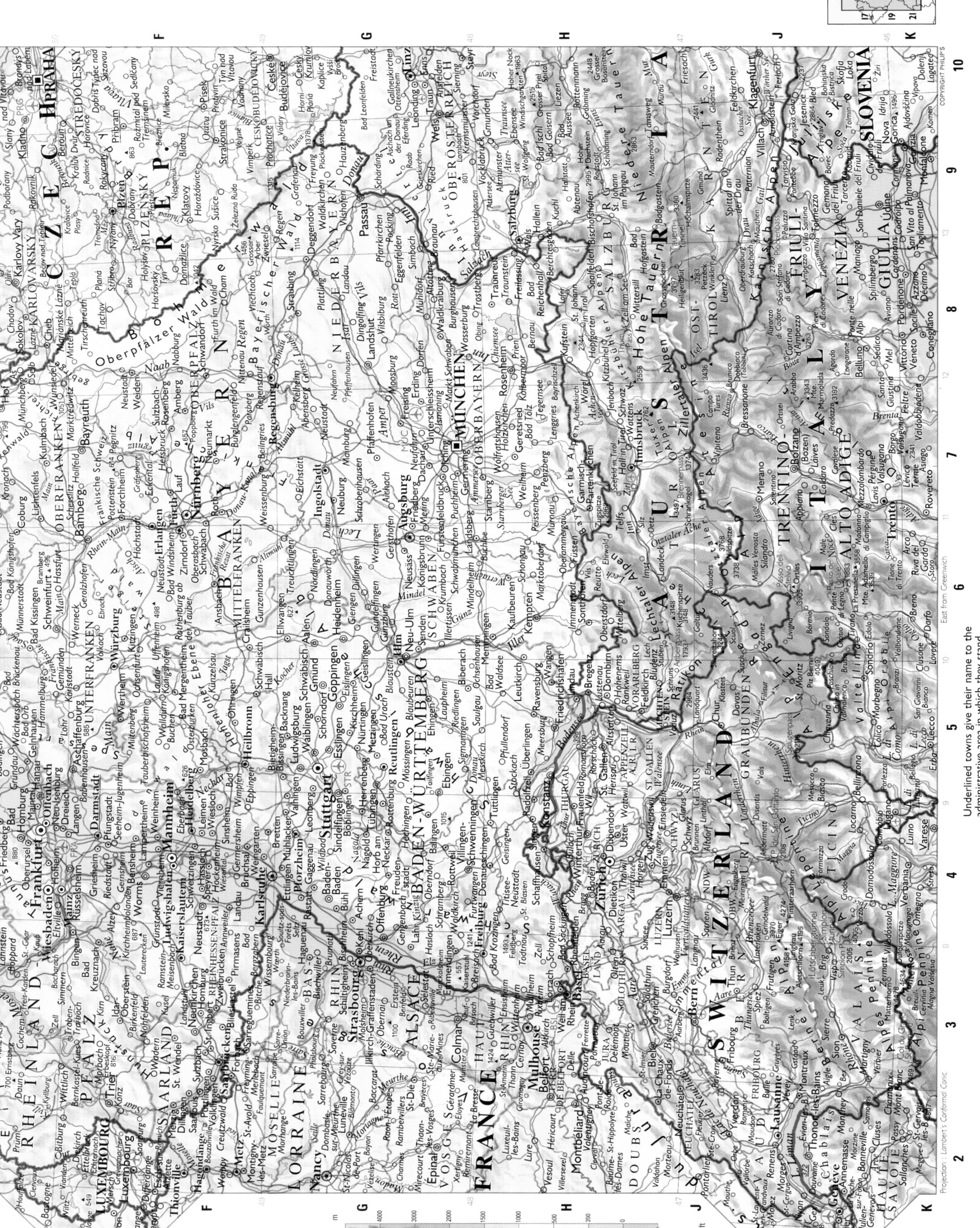

Underlined towns give their name to the
administrative area in which they stand.

East from Greenwich

Projection: Lambert's Conformal Conic

COPYRIGHT PHILIP'S

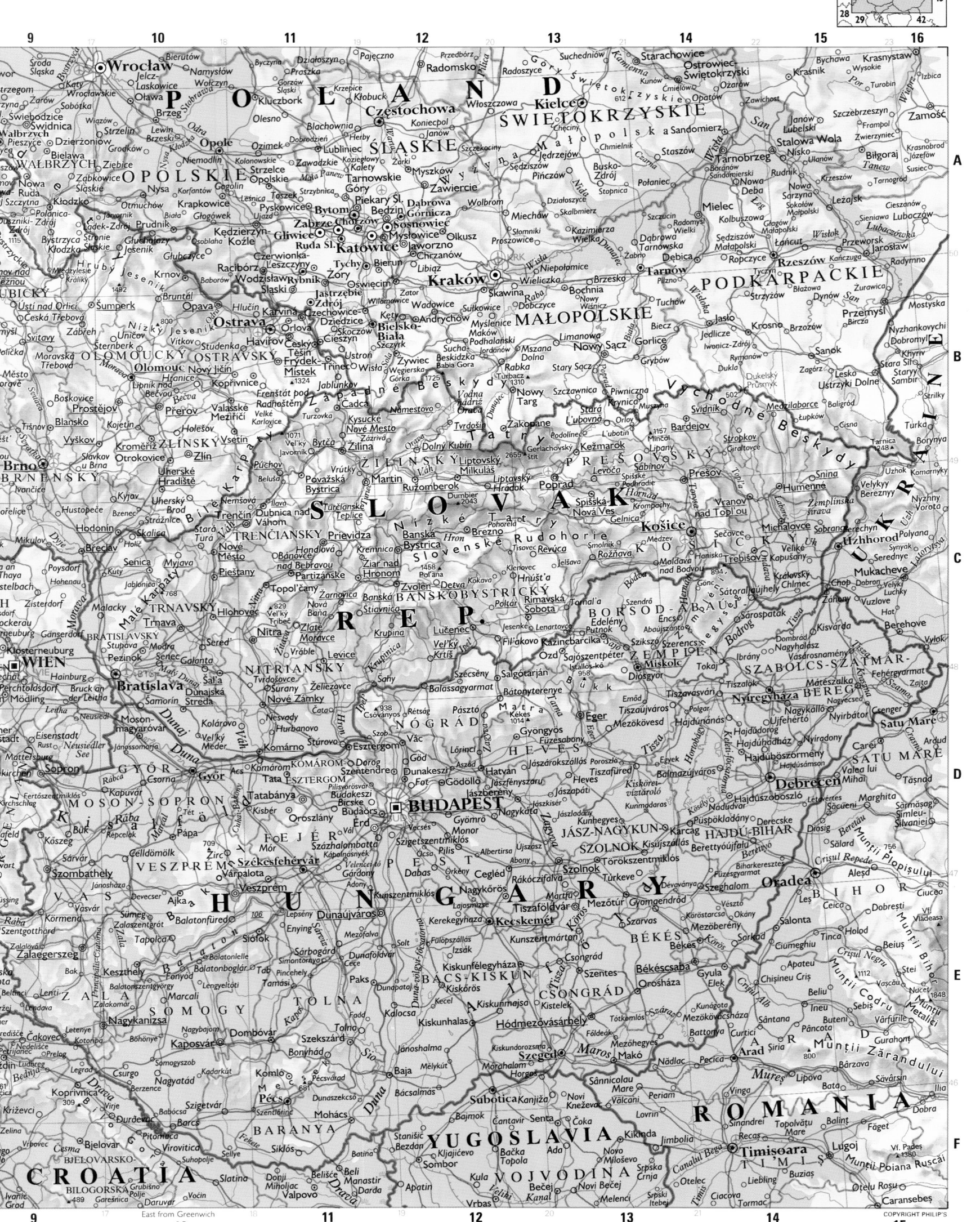

Underlined towns give their name to the
administrative area in which they stand.

Underlined towns give their name to t
administrative area in which they stand

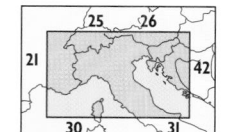

inistrative divisions in Croatia:
odsko-Posavska   4. Medimurska   8. Virovitičko-Podravska
privničko-Križevačka 6. Požeško-Slavonska   10. Zagrebačka
apinsko-Zagorska   7. Varaždinska

Inter-entity boundaries as agreed
at the 1995 Dayton Peace Agreement.

COPYRIGHT GEORGE PHILIP LTD.

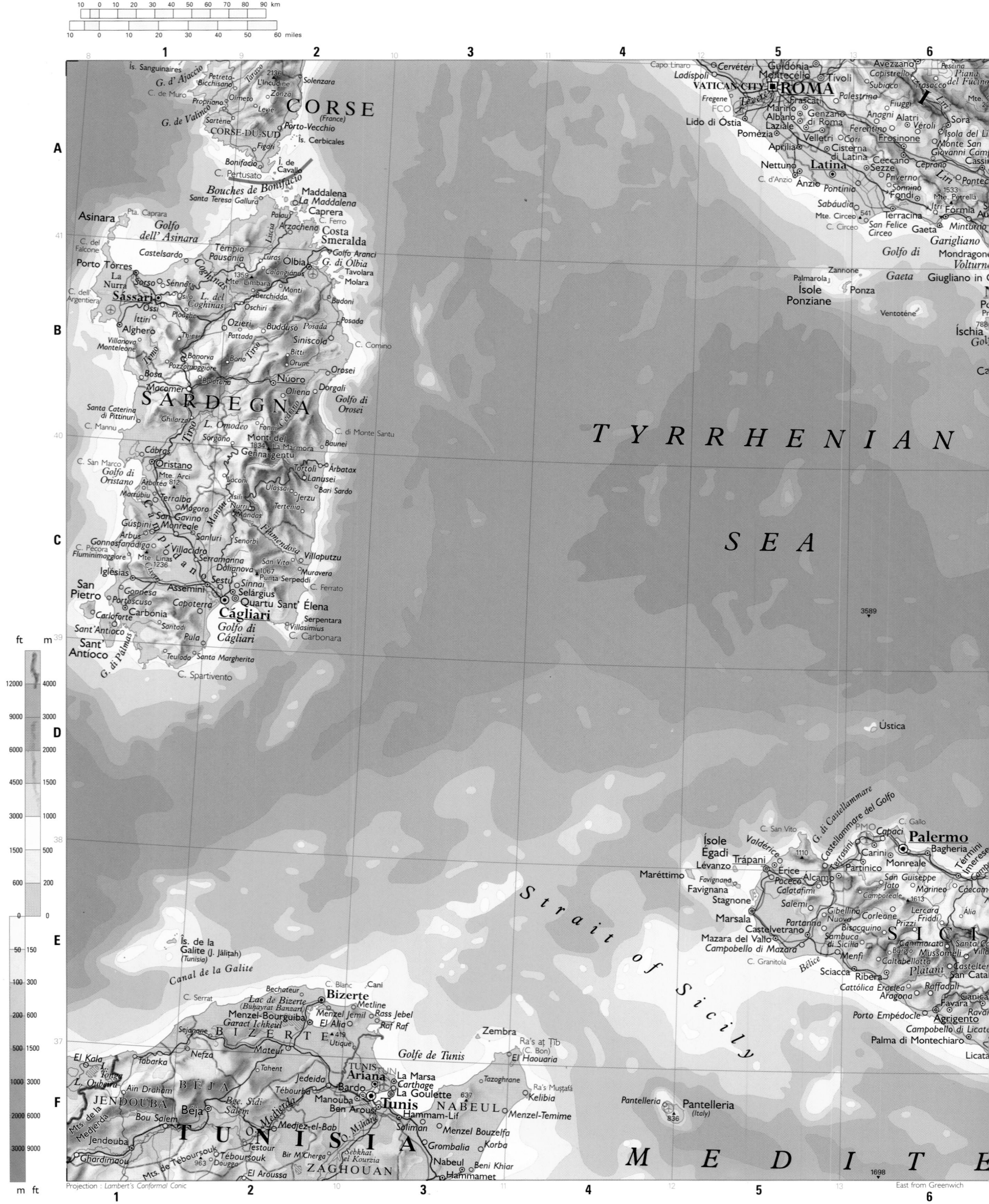

30 SOUTHERN ITALY 1:2 200 000

10 0 10 20 30 40 50 60 70 80 90 km
10 0 10 20 30 40 50 60 miles

A

Ìs. Sanguinaires
G. d'Ajaccio
Petreta-Bicchisano
Olmeto
L'Incudine
Solenzara
Zonzai
Propriano
Sartène
Levie
CORSE
(France)
C. de Muro
Figari
Porto-Vecchio
CORSE-DU-SUD
Bonifacio
Ìs. Cerbicales
I. de Cavallo
C. Pertusato
Bouches de Bonifacio
Maddalena
La Maddalena
Caprera
Santa Teresa Gallura
Palau
Arzachena
Costa
C. Ferro
Smeralda

Asinara
Pta. Caprara
Golfo dell'Asinara
Tèmpio Pausania
Golfo Aranci
G. di Olbia
Olbia
Tavolara
C. del Falcone
Luras
Lumbara
Monti
Molara
Porto Tórres
La Nurra
Castelsardo
Calangiánus
Berchidda
Budoni

B

Sorso
Sénneri
Oschiri
Posada
Algheró
Ozieri
Buddusò
Siniscola
Ìttiri
Thiesi
Pattada
Villanova Monteleone
Bonorva
Bitti
Orune
Orosei
Bosa
Pozzomaggiore
Boro Tirso
Nuoro
Macomer
Bulcotana
Dorgali
Bólotana
Oliena
Golfo di Orosei
Santa Caterina di Pittinuri
Ghilarza
L. Omodeo
Fonni
Baunei
SARDEGNA
Sòrgono
Monti del Gennargentu
C. di Monte Santu

C

C. Mannu
Òristano
Mte. Arci
La Marmora
Tortolì
Àrbatax
Cábras
Atbárea
Lanusei
Golfo di Oristano
Làconi
Ulassai
Jerzu
C. San Marco
Marrùbiu
Àsili
Nurri
Bari Sardo
Terralba
Mógora
San Gavino Monreale
Mandas
Tertenia
Sanluri
San Vito
Gúspini
Arbus
Villacidro
Serramanna
Senorbì
Villaputzu
Gonnosfanàdiga
Mte. Linas
Dòlianova
Muravera
Fluminimaggiore
Serrenti
Sèstu
Sìnnai
C. Ferrato
Iglésias
Gondesa
Assémini
Selárgius
Punta Serpeddi
San Pietro
Portoscuso
Capoterra
Quartu Sant' Élena
Carbónia
Cágliari
Serpentara
Carloforte
Santádi
Pula
Golfo di Cágliari
Villasimius
Sant'Antíoco
Teulada
Santa Margherita
C. Carbonara
Sant' Antíoco
G. di Pálmas
C. Spartivento

D

Ùstica

3589

E

Ìs. de la Galite (J. Jālitah) (Tunisia)
Canal de la Galite
C. San Vito
Ìsole Égadi
Valdérice
G. di Castellammare del Golfo
C. Gallo
Capaci
Palermo
Bagheria
Trápani
Érice
Carini
Monreale
Tèrmini Imerese
Maréttimo
Lèvanzo
Alcamo
Partinico
San Guiseppe Jato
Marineo
Caccam
Favignana
Paceco
Calatafimi
Campofelice
Favignana
Stagnone
Salemi
Gibellina Nuova
Corleone
Prizzi
Lercara Friddi
Àlia
Marsala
Partanna
Bisacquino
SICI
Mazara del Vallo
Castelvetrano
Sambuca di Sicilia
Burgo
Mussomeli
Camporeale
Santa
Campobello di Mazara
Menfi
Sciacca
Caltabellotta
Castelter
San Cata
Bélice
C. Granitola
Ribera
Platani
Cattòlica Eraclea
Raffadali
Aragona
Porto Empédocle
Favara
Canica
Campobello di Licate
Agrigento
Ravar
Palma di Montechiaro
Licata

F

El Kala
L. Tonga
L. Oubeira
Tabarka
Ìs. de la
Bechateur
C. Blanc
Cani
Nefza
Metline
Ras Jebel
Raf Raf
C. Serrat
Lac de Bizerte (Buḥayrat Banzart)
Menzel Jemil
El Alia
Zembra
Ra's at Tib (C. Bon)
Sejnane
Menzel-Bourguiba
Garaet Ichkeul
Utique
El Haouaria
BIZERTE
Mateur
Golfe de Tunis
Tazoghrane
Ra's Mustafa
Tahent
Jedeida
TUNIS
La Marsa
Kelibia
Ariana
Bardo
La Goulette
637
Manouba
NABEUL
Menzel-Temime
JENDOUBA
Medjerda
Bge. Sidi Salem
BÉJA
Béja
Ben Arous
Tunis
Hammam-Lif
Soliman
Menzel Bouzelfa
Pantelleria
Pantelleria (Italy)
Bou Salem
Medjez-el-Bab
Testour
Grombalia
Korba
836
Jendouba
Bir M'Cherga
Soliman
Nabeul
Beni Khir
Ghardimaou
Sebkhat el Kourzia
El Aroussa
963
Dougga
ZAGHOUAN
El Aroussa
TUNISIA
Hammamet
Mts. de la Medjerda
Mts. de Téboursouk
1698

T Y R R H E N I A N

S E A

Strait of Sicily

M E D I T E

Capo Linaro
Cervéteri
Guidónia
Ladispoli
Montecélio
Tivoli
Avezzano
Copistrello
Pescina
VATICAN CITY
ROMA
Palestrina
Subiaco
Trasacco
Piana del Fucino
Fregene
FCO
Tèvere
Frascati
Anagni
Alatri
Véroli
Sora
Marino
Genzano
Fiuggi
Albano
di Roma
Ferentino
Monte San
Giovanni Cam
Lido di Óstia
Laziale
Cori
Frosinone
Cassi
Pomézia
Velletri
Ceccano
Ceprano
Pontec
Aprília
Cisterna di Latina
Sezze
Privèrno
Nettuno
C. d'Anzio
Anzio
Latina
Priverno
1533
Mte. Potrella
Sabáudia
Pontínia
Fondi
Ìtri
Formia
541
Terracina
Gaeta
Minturno
Mte. Circeo
San Felice
Circeo
Gariglíano
C. Circeo
Golfo di
Mondragon
Volturn
Palmarola
Zannone
Gaeta
Giugliano in Ca
Ìsole
Ventotène
Ponza
Po
Ponziane
Íschia
Gol

ft m
12000 4000
9000 3000
6000 2000
4500 1500
3000 1000
1500 500
600 200
0 0
50 150
100 300
200 600
500 1500
1000 3000
2000 6000
3000 9000
m ft

39
38
37
41
40

ADRIATIC

SEA

IONIAN

SEA

R R A N E A N   S E A

Golfo di
Táranto

Strait of Otranto

ALBANIA

GREECE

CALABRIA

BASILICATA

Underlined towns give their name to the
administrative area in which they stand.

33

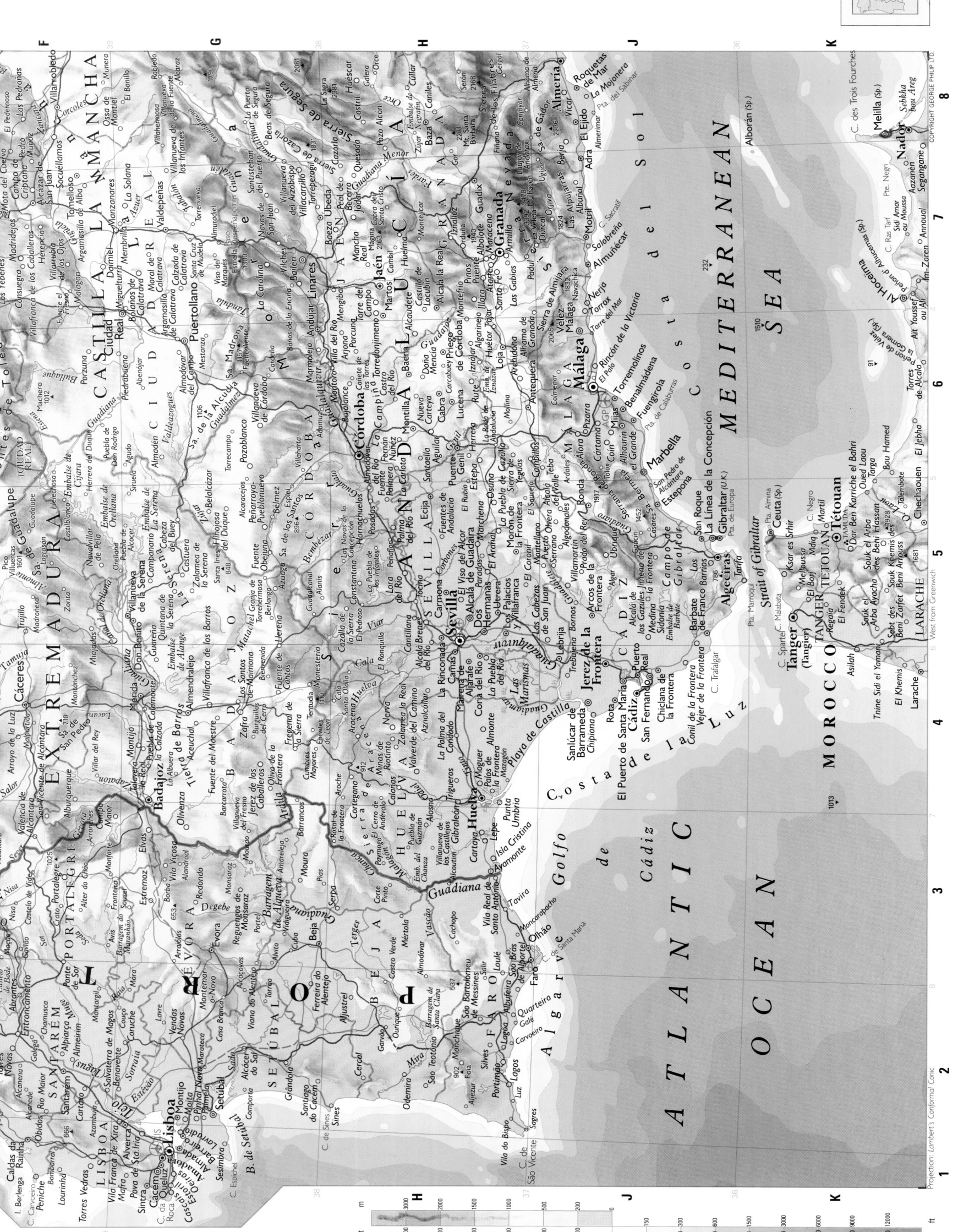

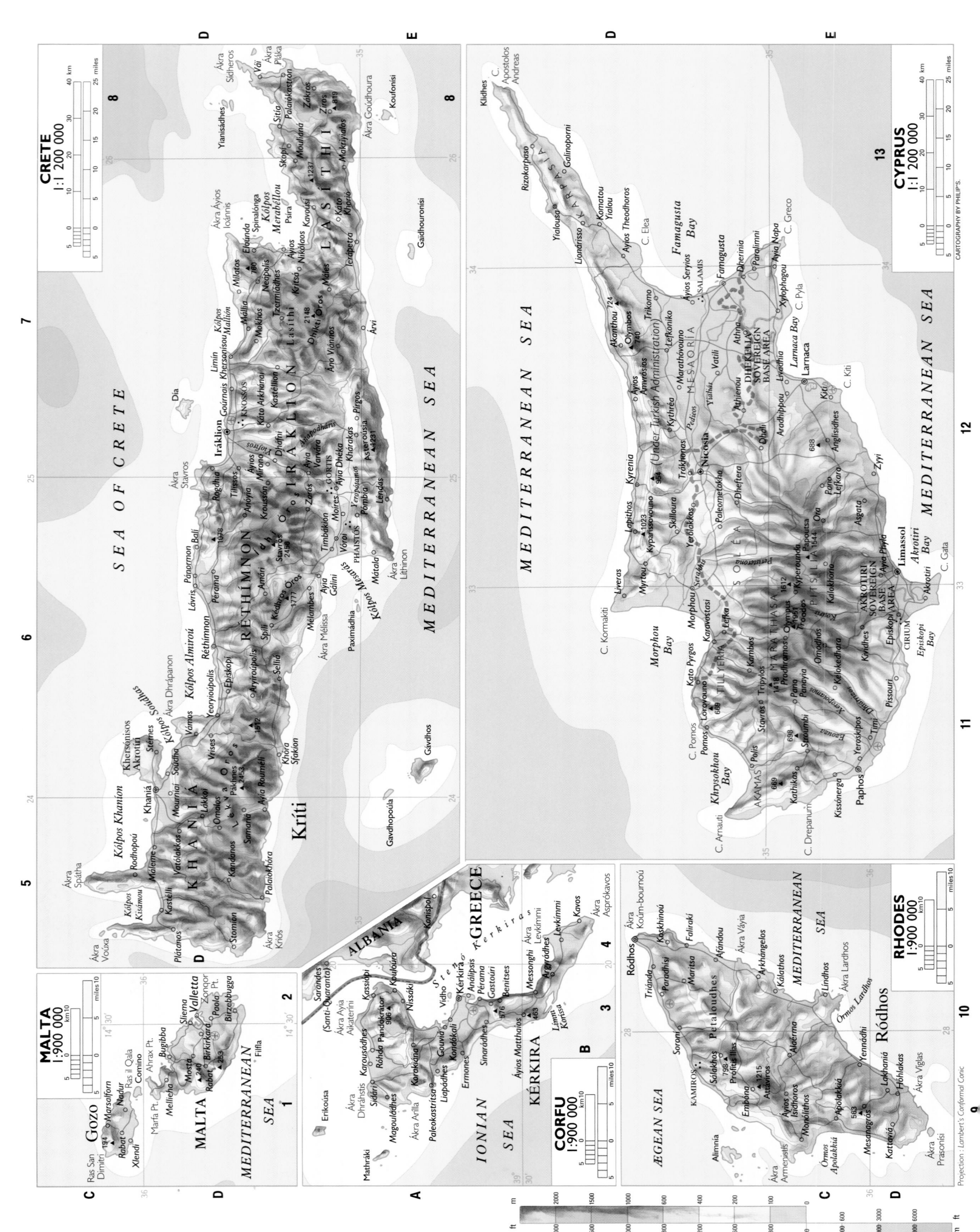

CRETE 1:1 200 000

MALTA 1:900 000

CORFU 1:900 000

RHODES 1:900 000

CYPRUS 1:1 200 000

CARTOGRAPHY BY PHILIP'S.

Projection: Lambert's Conformal Conic

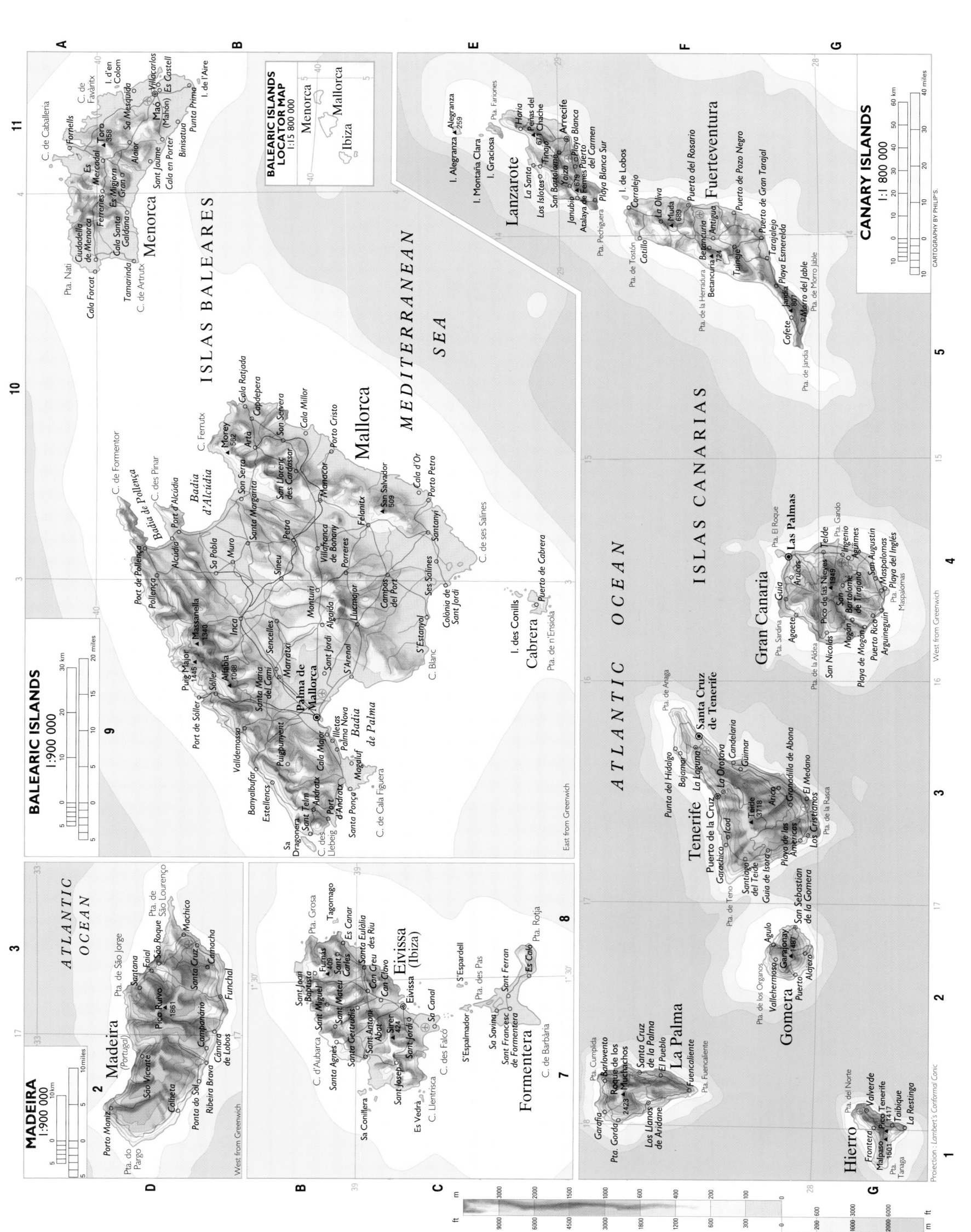

MADEIRA
1:900 000

ATLANTIC OCEAN

Madeira (Portugal)

Porto Moniz
Pta. do Pargo
São Vicente
Santana
Faial
São Roque
Pico Ruivo
1861
Santa Cruz
Caniçal
Machico
Calheta
Ponta do Sol
Ribeira Brava
Campanário
Câmara de Lobos
Funchal
Pta. de São Lourenço
Pta. de São Jorge

West from Greenwich

BALEARIC ISLANDS
1:900 000

Menorca
Pta. Nati
C. de Caballeria
Fornells
Ciudadella de Menorca
Cala Forcat
Es Mercadal
Ferreries
Cala Santa Galdana
Es Migjorn Gran
Toro 358
Mahón (Maó)
Villacarlos
Es Castell
Alaior
Sant Jaume
Cala en Porter
Binisafua
Punta Prima
I. de l'Aire
Tamarinda
C. de Arrutx

I. d'en Colom
C. de Favàritx

Pta. de Formentor
C. de Formentor
Port de Pollença
Pollença
Alcúdia
Port d'Alcúdia
Badia de Pollença
C. des Pinar
Badia d'Alcúdia
C. Ferrutx
Morey 562
Artà
Capdepera
Cala Ratjada
Son Serra
San Lorenç des Cardassar
San Servera
Cala Millor
Manacor
Porto Cristo
Santa Margarita
Petra
Sa Pobla
Muro
Sineu
Inca
Massanella 1340
Valldemossa
Puig Major 1445
Puigpunyent
Sóller
Alfàbia 1068
Santa Maria del Camí
Marratxí
Sencelles
Algaida
Villafranca de Bonany
Porreres
Montuiri
Llucmajor
Felanitx
San Salvador 509
Cala d'Or
Porto Petro
Santanyí
Ses Salines
C. de ses Salines
Colonia de Sant Jordi
S'Estanyol
Sant Jordi
S'Arenal
Badia de Palma
Palma de Mallorca
Illetas
Palma Nova
Magaluf
Cala Major
Banyalbufar
Estellencs
Sa Dragonera
C. des Llebeig
Sant Telm
Andratx
Port d'Andratx
Santa Ponça
C. de Cala Figuera

Mallorca

Port de Sóller

East from Greenwich

Eivissa (Ibiza)
C. d'Aubarca
Pta. Grosa
Sant Joan Baptista
Santa Agnès
Fornàs 409
Tagomago
Santa Gertrudis
Sant Miquel
Sant Carles
Es Canar
Santa Eulària
Can Creu des Riu
Can Clavo
Sant Antoni Abad
Sant Rafel
424
Eivissa (Ibiza)
Sant Josep
Sant Jordi
Sa Canal
Es Vedrà
C. Llentrisca
C. des Falcó
Sa Conillera

Formentera
S'Espalmador
S'Espardell
Pta. des Pas
Sa Savina
Sant Francesc de Formentera
Sant Ferran
Es Caló
Pta. Rotja
C. de Barbària

West from Greenwich

ISLAS BALEARES

MEDITERRANEAN SEA

BALEARIC ISLANDS LOCATOR MAP
1:15 800 000
Menorca
Mallorca
Ibiza

CANARY ISLANDS
1:1 800 000

Lanzarote
I. Alegranza
Alegranza 259
I. Montaña Clara
I. Graciosa
Haría
La Santa
Peñas del Chache 671
Tinajo
San Bartolomé
Los Islotes
Yaiza
Janubio
Atalaya de Femés 608
Arrecife
Playa Blanca
Puerto del Carmen
Playa Blanca Sur
Pta. Pechiguera
I. de Lobos

Fuerteventura
Corralejo
Cotillo
La Oliva
Pta. de Tostón
Puerto del Rosario
Tuineje
La Muda 689
Betancuria
Betancuria 724
Antigua
Tarajalejo
Puerto de Pozo Negro
Puerto de Gran Tarajal
Tuineje
Pta. de la Herradura
Playa Esmerelda
Cofete
Jandía 807
Morro del Jable
Pta. de Morro Jable
Pta. de Jandía

Gran Canaria
Pta. El Roque
Las Palmas
Telde
Arucas
Guía
Pta. Sardina
Agaete
Pico de las Nieves 1949
Ingenio
Aguimes
Santa Brígida
San Bartolomé de Tirajana
San Augustín
Maspalomas
Playa del Inglés
Maspalomas
Pta. de la Aldea
San Nicolás
Mogán
Playa de Mogán
Puerto Rico
Arguineguín
Pta. Gando

West from Greenwich

ISLAS CANARIAS

ATLANTIC OCEAN

Tenerife
Punta del Hidalgo
Bajamar
Pta. de Anaga
La Laguna
Santa Cruz de Tenerife
Puerto de la Cruz
La Orotava
Candelaria
Güimar
Icod
Teide 3718
Arico
Granadilla de Abona
El Medano
Garachico
Santiago del Teide
Guía de Isora
Playa de las Américas
Los Cristianos
Pta. de la Rasca
Pta. de Teno

Gomera
Pta. de los Órganos
Vallehermoso
Agulo
Garajonay 1487
San Sebastián de la Gomera
Puerto
Alajeró

La Palma
Pta. Cumplida
Barlovento
Roque de los Muchachos 2423
Santa Cruz de la Palma
El Pueblo
Garafía
Pta. Gorda
Los Llanos de Aridane
Fuencaliente
Pta. Fuencaliente

Hierro
Pta. del Norte
Frontera
Valverde
Malpaso 1501
Pico Tenerife 1417
Taibique
La Restinga
Pta. Tanaja

Cabrera
Puerto de Cabrera
Pta. de n'Ensiola
C. Blanc
I. des Conills

CARTOGRAPHY BY PHILIP'S.
Projection: Lambert's Conformal Conic

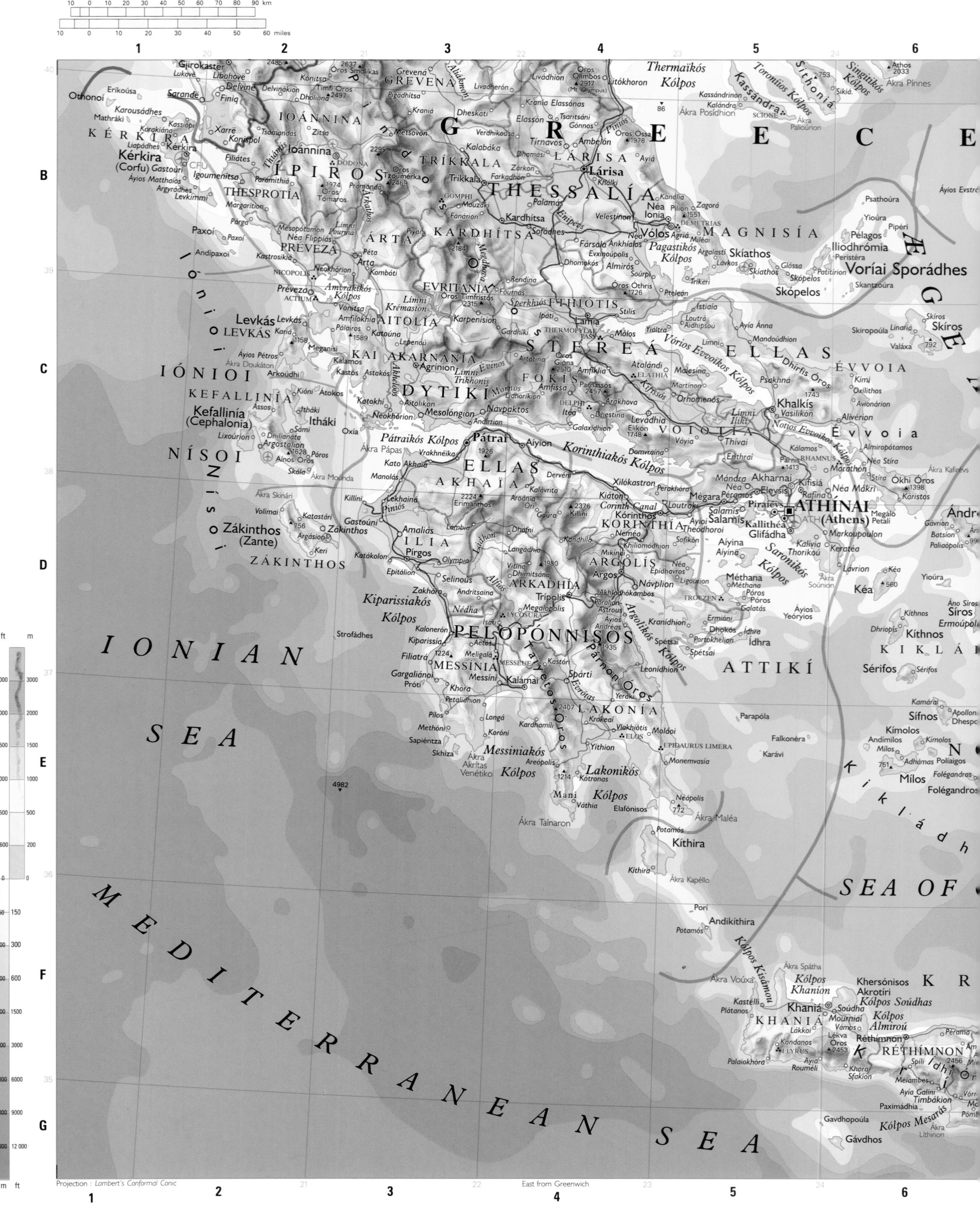

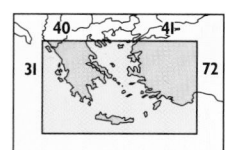

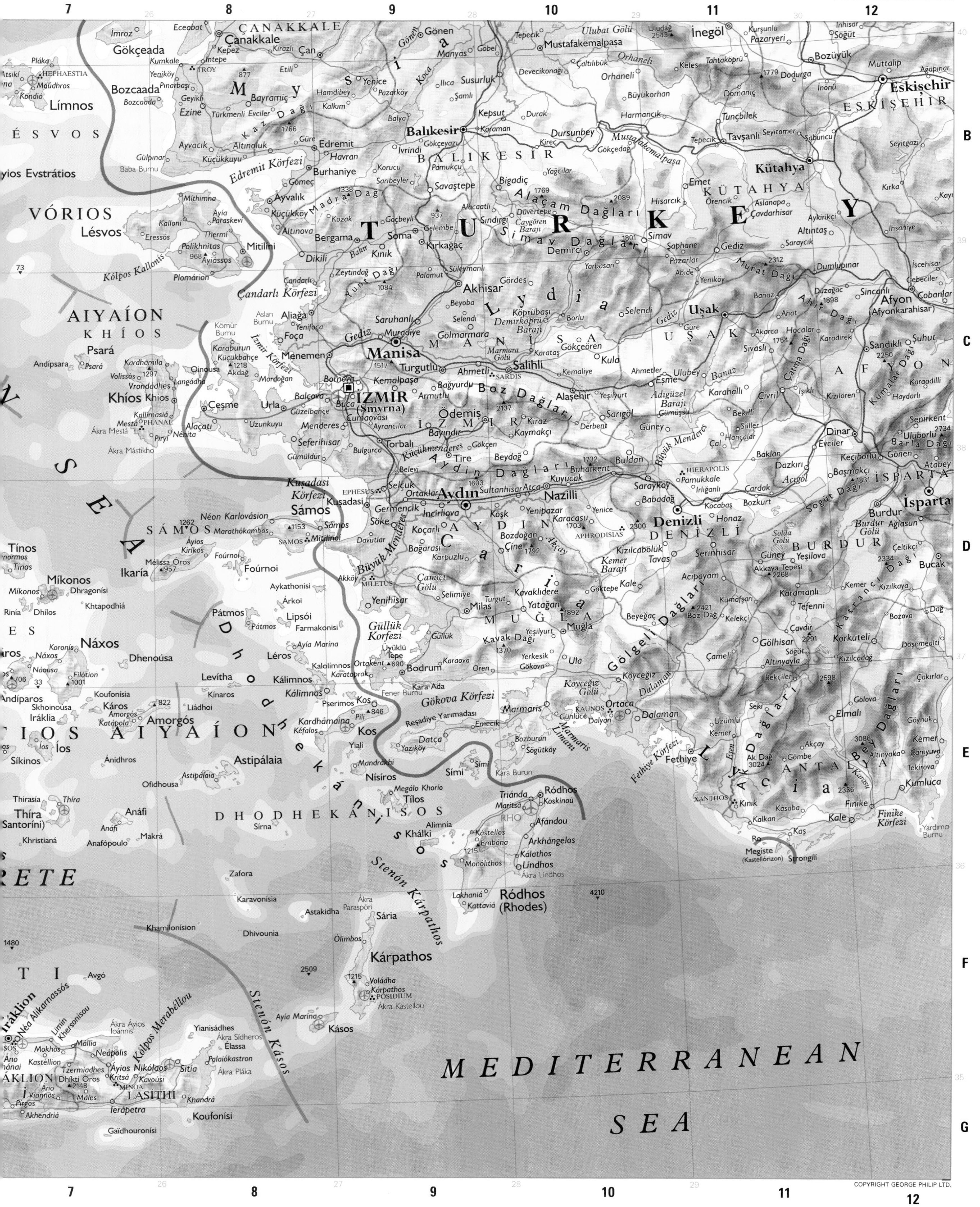

Projection : Lambert's Conformal Conic

East from Greenwich

Inter-entity boundaries as agreed
at the 1995 Dayton Peace Agreement.

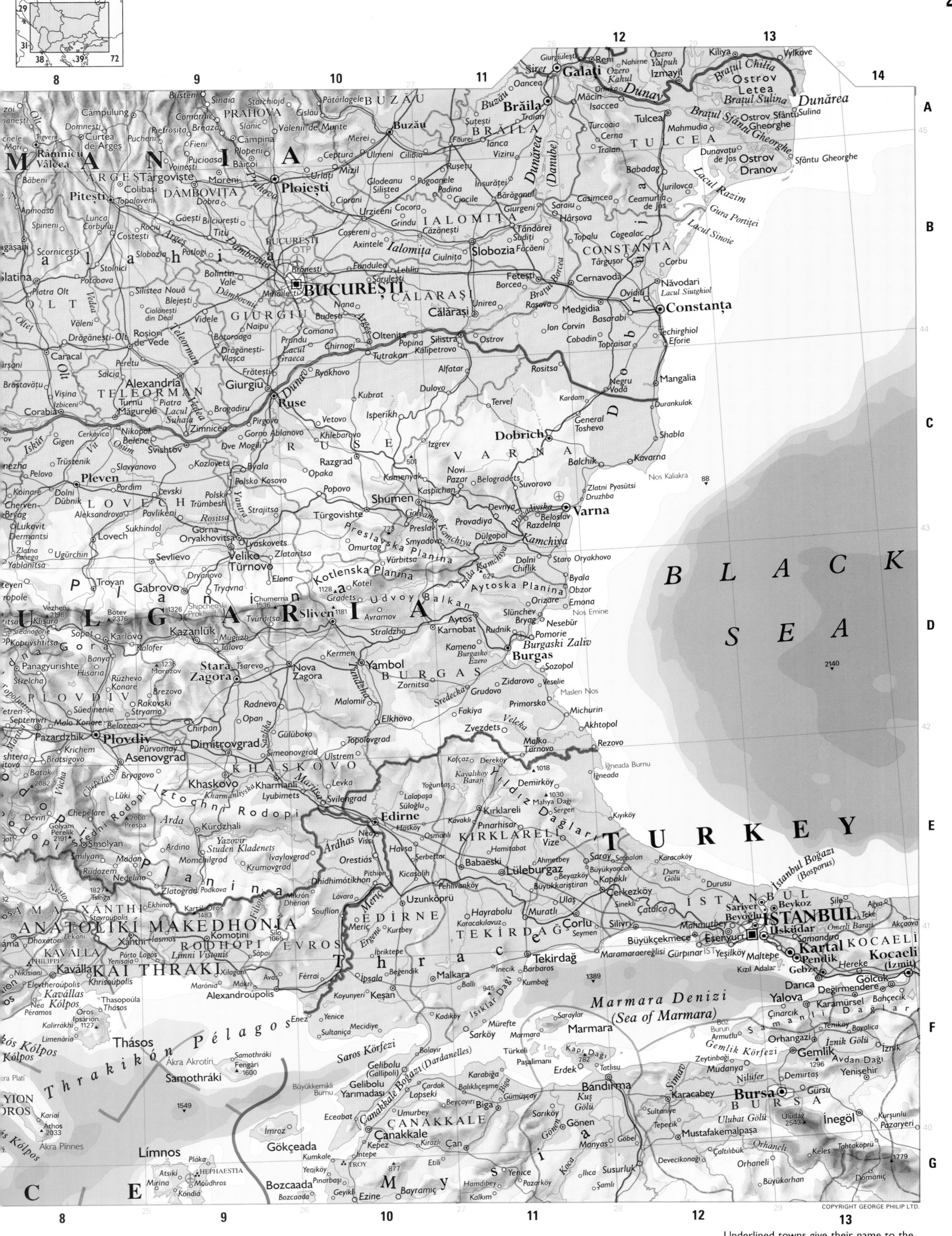

Underlined towns give their name to the
administrative area in which they stand.

COPYRIGHT GEORGE PHILIP LTD.

Administrative divisions in Croatia:
1. Brodsko-Posavska   5. Osječko-Baranjska   9. Vukovarsko-Srijemska
2. Koprivničko-Križevačka   6. Požeško-Slavonska
4. Medimurska   8. Virovitičko-Podravska

Projection : Lambert's Conformal Conic

East from Greenwich

– – – – Inter-entity boundaries as agreed
at the 1995 Dayton Peace Agreement.

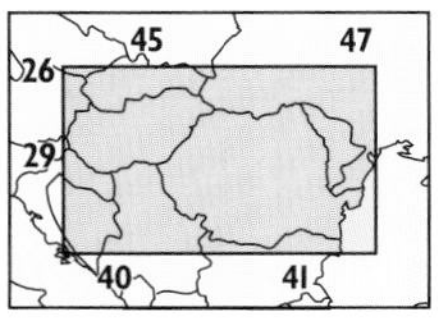

8 9 10 11 12 13 14

B

C

D

E

F

G

Major regions/countries:
UKRAINE · MOLDOVA · ROMANIA · BULGARIA

Ivano-Frankivsk · IVANO-FRANKIVSKA · Chernivtsi · CHERNIVETSKA · VINNYTSKA · Kamyanets-Podilskyy

BOTOŞANI · SUCEAVA · Suceava · Botoşani · IAŞI · Iaşi · NEAMŢ · Piatra Neamţ · Bacău · BACĂU · VASLUI · Vaslui · Bârlad

Bălţi · Chişinău (Kishinev) · MOLDOVA · Tiraspol · Tighina · ODESKA

Cluj-Napoca · CLUJ · BISTRIŢA NĂSĂUD · MUREŞ · Târgu Mureş · HARGHITA · ALBA · SIBIU · Sibiu · Mediaş · COVASNA · Sfântu Gheorghe · BRAŞOV · Braşov · VRANCEA · Focşani · GALAŢI · Galaţi · Izmayil · TULCEA · Tulcea

Craiova · DOLJ · OLT · VÂLCEA · Râmnicu Vâlcea · Târgovişte · DÂMBOVIŢA · Piteşti · ARGEŞ · PRAHOVA · Ploieşti · BUZĂU · Buzău · Brăila · BRĂILA · BUCUREŞTI · GIURGIU · Giurgiu · TELEORMAN · Alexandria · CĂLĂRAŞI · Călăraşi · IALOMIŢA · Slobozia · CONSTANŢA · Constanţa · DOBRICH

Ruse · Pleven · BULGARIA

BLACK SEA

COPYRIGHT GEORGE PHILIP LTD.

Underlined towns give their name to the
administrative area in which they stand.

COPYRIGHT PHILIP'S

Underlined towns give their name to the
administrative area in which they stand.

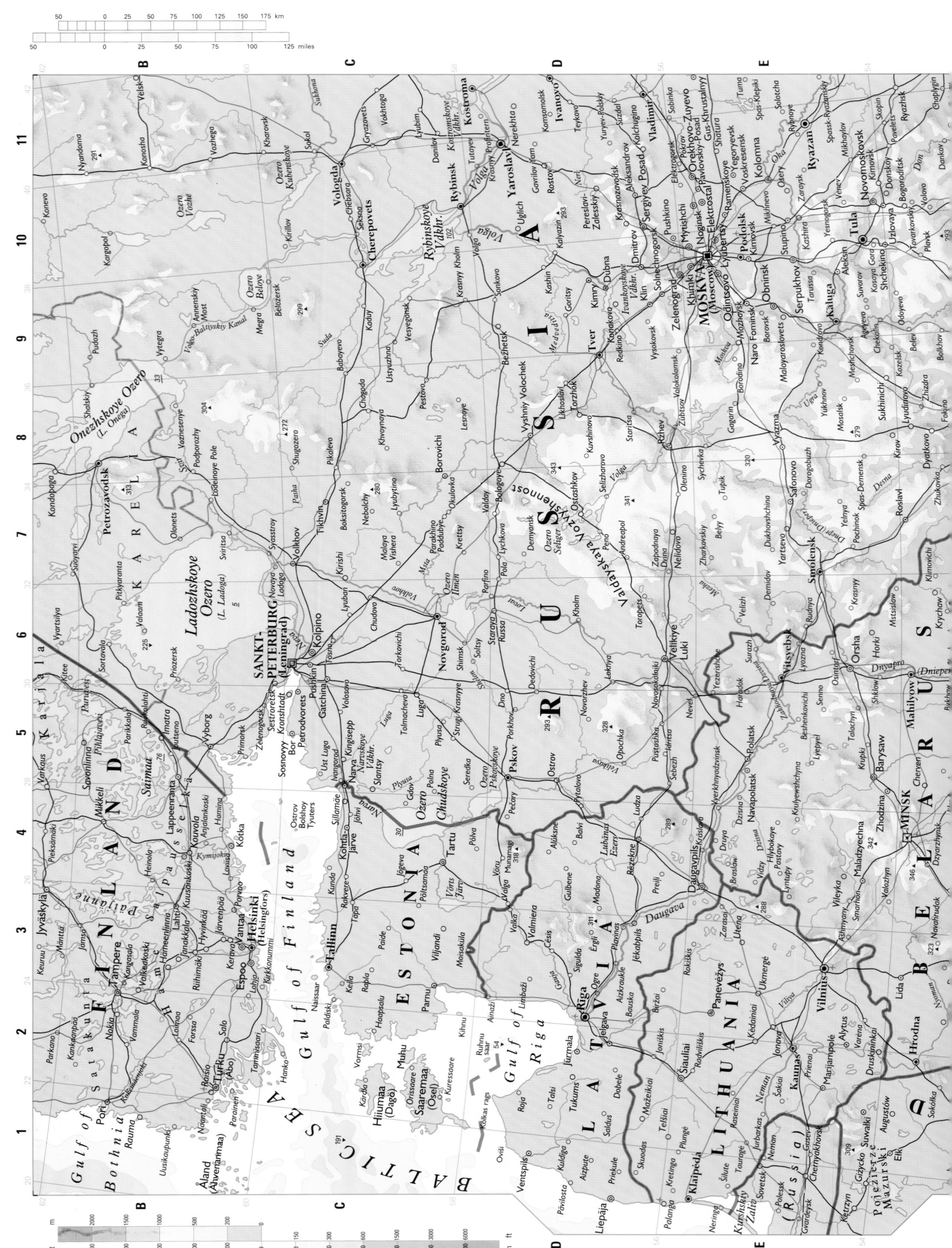

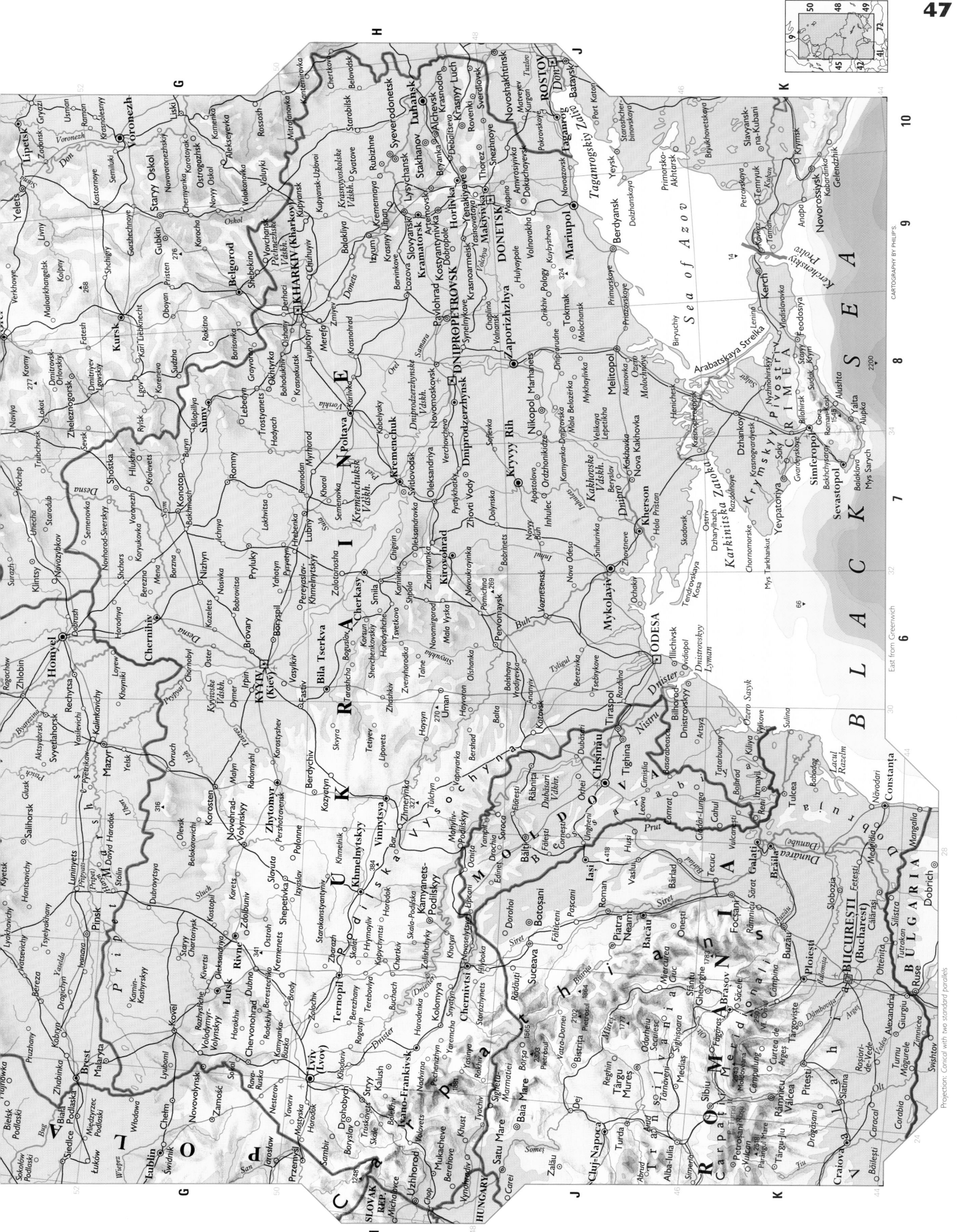

CARTOGRAPHY BY PHILIP'S.

East from Greenwich

Projection: Conical with two standard parallels

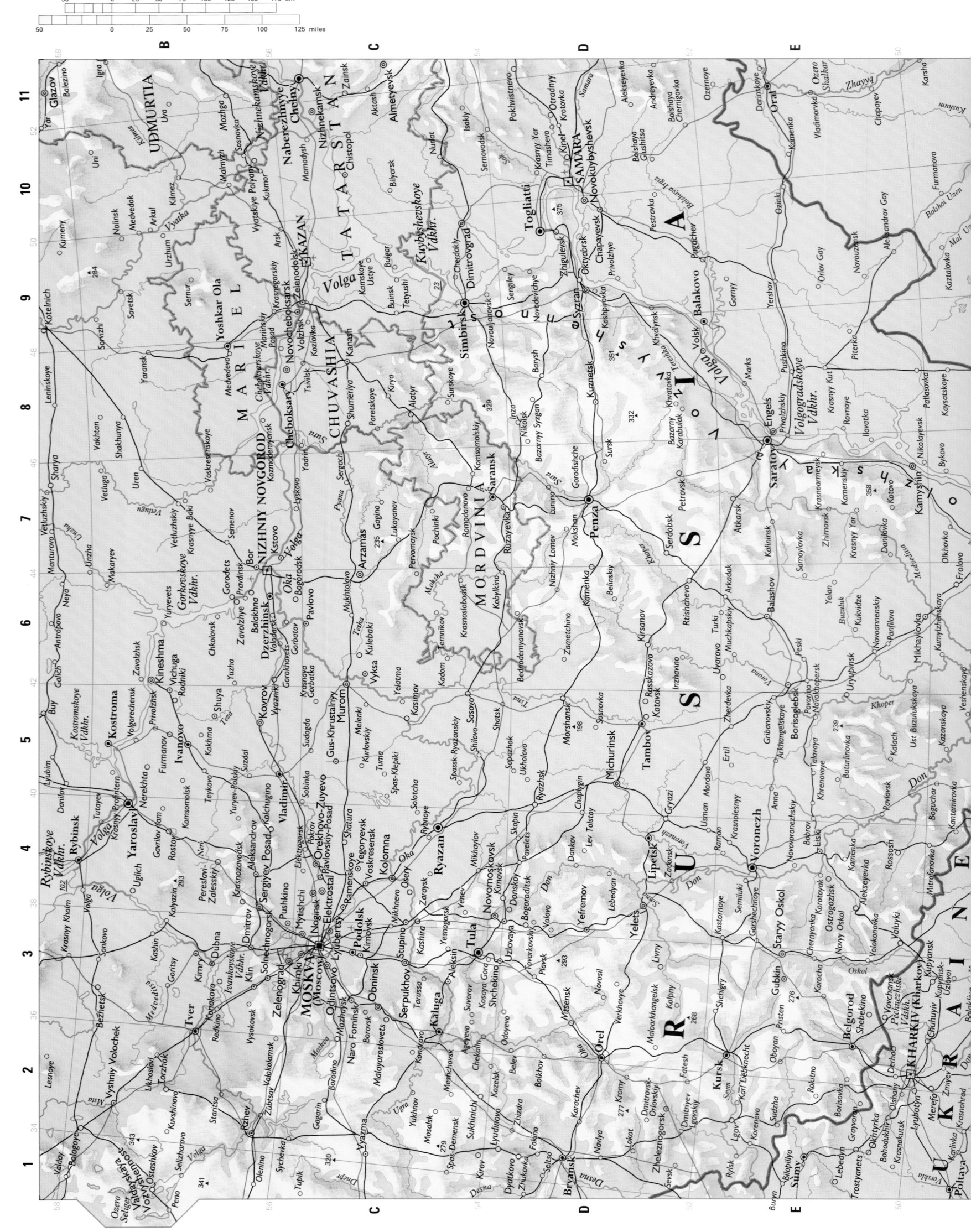

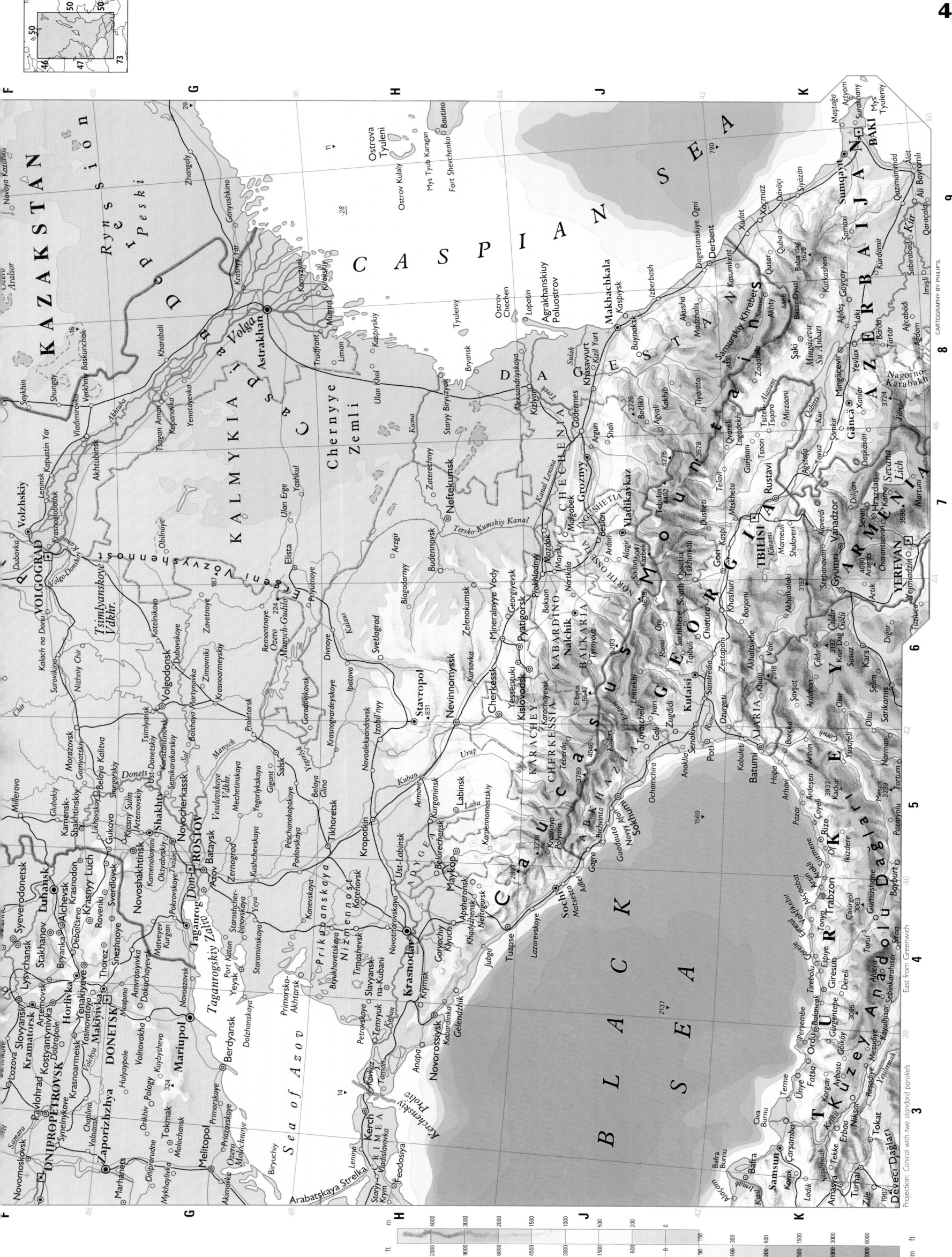

CASPIAN SEA

BLACK SEA

KAZAKSTAN

AZERBAIJAN

GEORGIA

ARMENIA

DAGESTAN

CHECHENIA

Caucasus Mountains

KALMYKIA

Sea of Azov

VOLGOGRAD

ROSTOV

DONETSK

CARTOGRAPHY BY PHILIP'S

Projection: Conical with two standard parallels

East from Greenwich

RUSSIA
1 Adygea
2 Karachey-Cherkessia
3 Kabardino-Balkaria
4 North Ossetia
5 Ingushetia
6 Chechenia
7 Dagestan
8 Mordvinia
9 Chuvashia
10 Mari El
11 Tatarstan
12 Udmurtia
13 Khakassia
AZERBAIJAN
14 Naxçivan
GEORGIA   UKRAINE
15 Ajaria   17 Crimea
16 Abkhazia

Projection: Conical Orthomorphic with two standard parallels

East from Greenwich

51

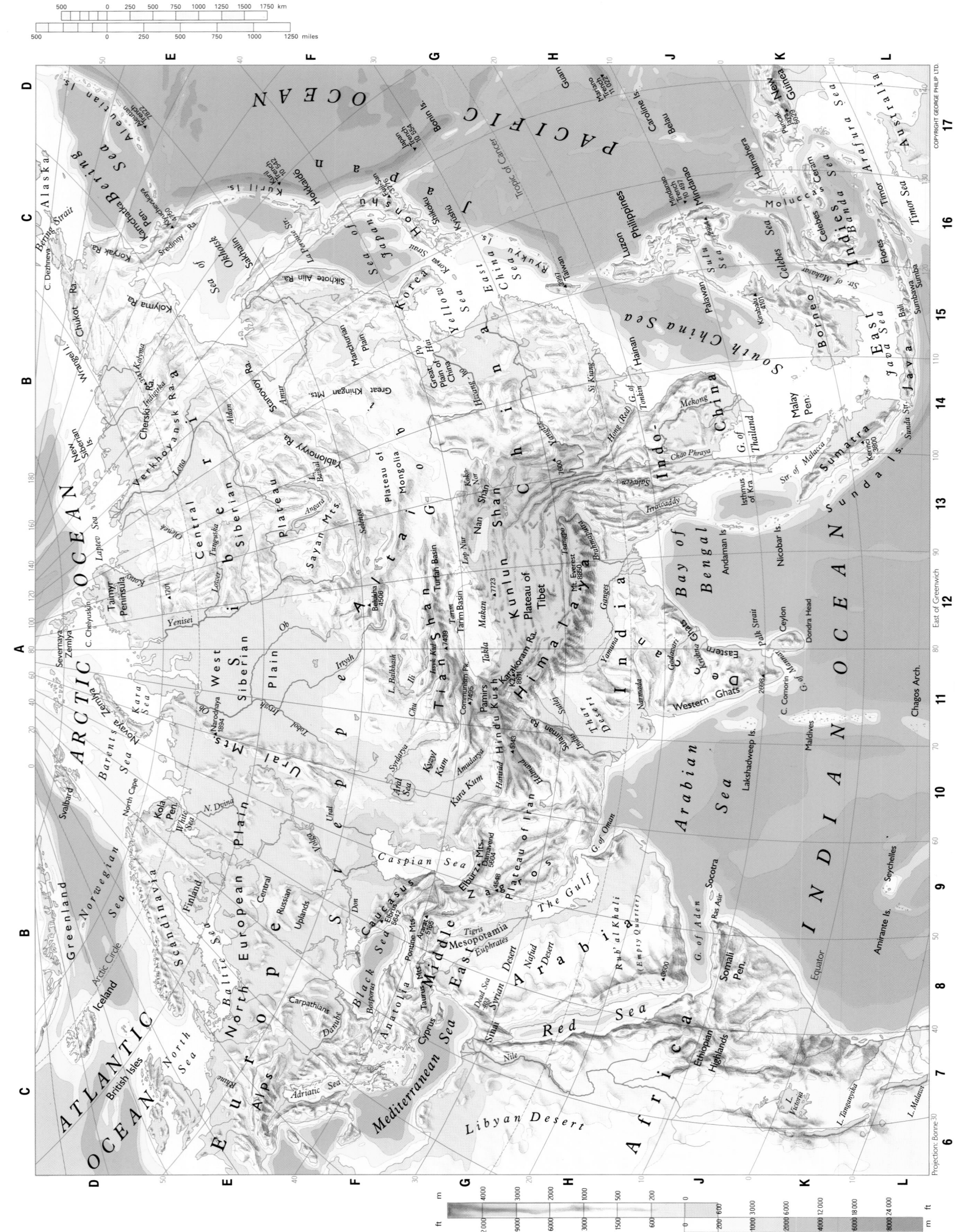

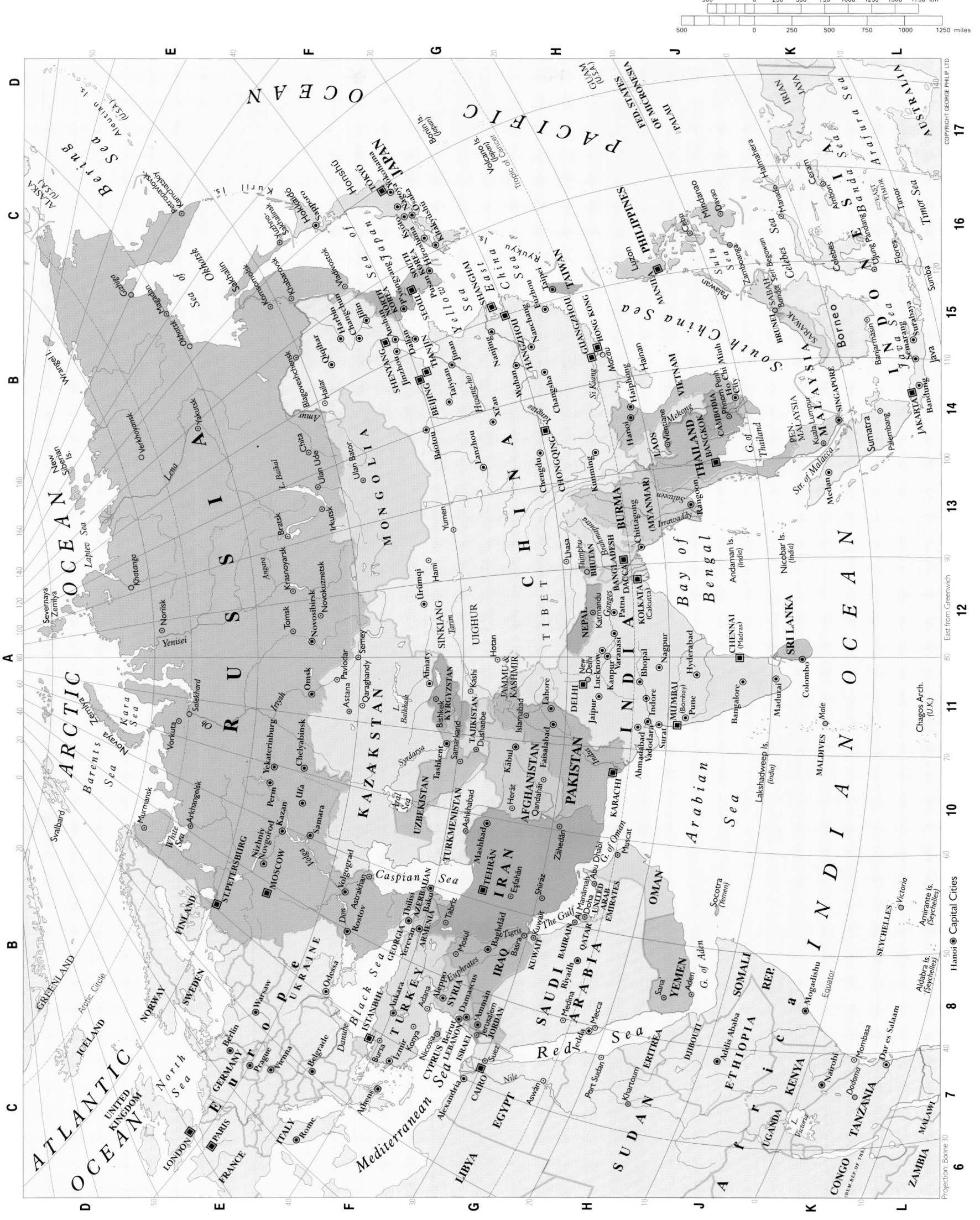

JAPAN 1:4 400 000

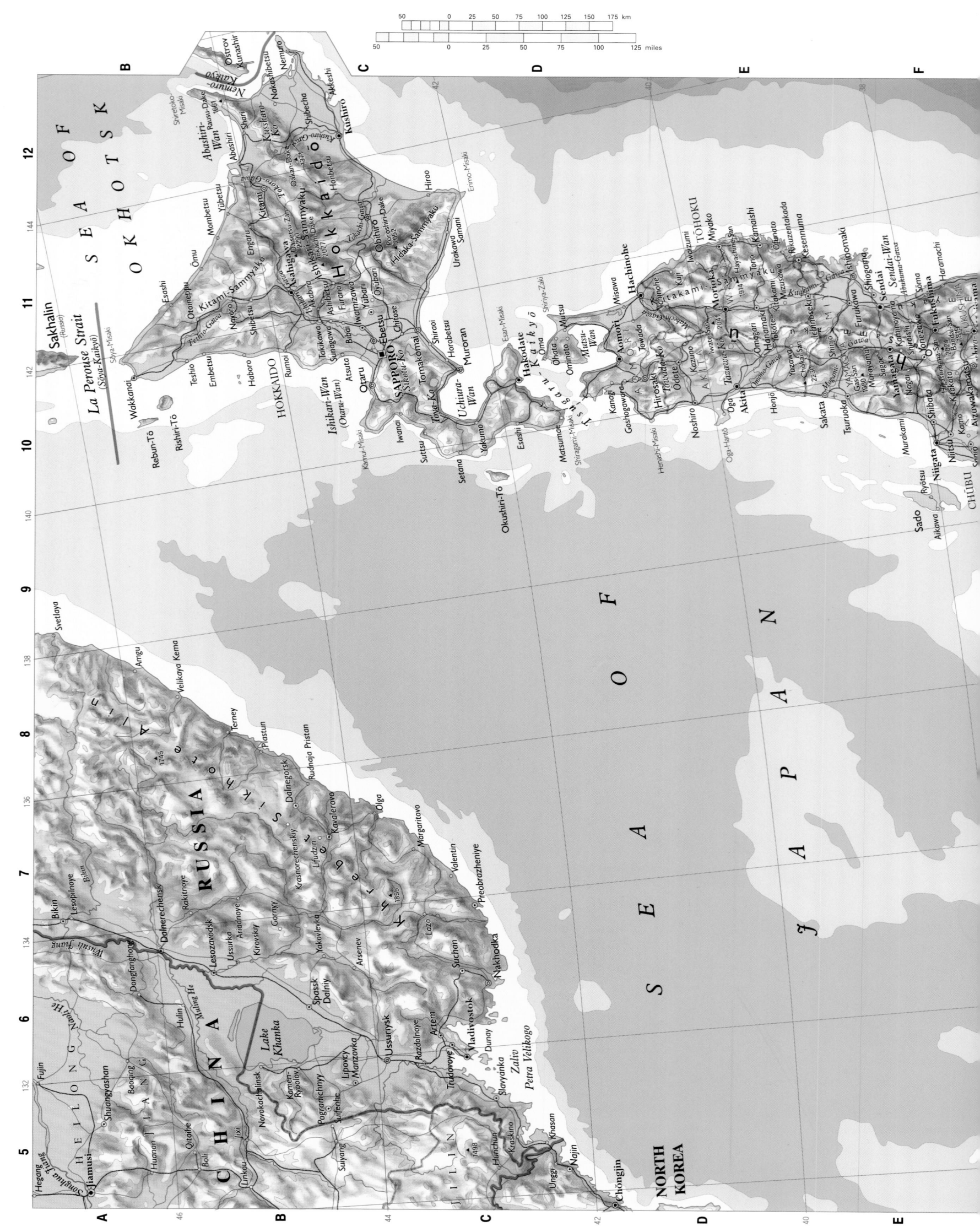

SEA OF OKHOTSK

Ostrov Kunashir

Nemuro-Kaikyō

Nokashibetsu
Nemuro
Shibecha
Akkeshi
Kushiro

Shiretoko-Misaki
Abashiri-Wan
Abashiri
Shari
Rausu-Dake
1661
Kussharo-Ko

Hiroo

Erimo-Misaki

Mombetsu
Yūbetsu
Engaru
Kitami
Tokoro-Gawa

Daisetsu-Zan
Asahi-Dake
2290
Ishikari-Sammyaku
Poroshiri-Dake
2052
Hidaka-Sammyaku
Urakawa
Samani

Ōmu
Esashi
Otoineppu
Kitami-Sammyaku
Nayoro
Asahigawa
Takikawa
Bibai
Furano
Yūbari
Ōyubari
Obihiro

TŌHOKU

Miyako
Kamaishi
Ōfunato

Rikuzentakada
Kesennuma

Ishinomaki
Sendai
Sendai-Wan

SEA OF OKHOTSK

Sakhalin
(Russia)

La Perouse Strait
(Sōya-Kaikyō)

Wakkanai

Rebun-Tō
Rishiri-Tō

Teshio
Haboro
Rumoi

HOKKAIDŌ

Ashibetsu
Iwamizawa
SAPPORO
Ebetsu
Chitose
Shiraoi

Otaru
Ishikari-Wan
(Otaru-Wan)
Kamui-Misaki
Iwanai

Suttsu
Toya-Ko
Tomakomai

Atsuta
Horobetsu
Muroran
Uchiura-Wan

Setana
Yakumo

Okushiri-Tō

Esashi
Matsumae
Shiranuka-Misaki

Esan-Misaki
Hakodate
Tsugaru-Kaikyō

Ōma
Ōhata
Mutsu
Mutsu-Wan
Ominato

Shiriya-Zaki
Misawa
Hachinohe
Noheji
Kinohe
Towada
AOMORI
Towada-Ko

Kanogi
Gosjogawara
Hirosaki
Kuroishi
Ōdate
Kazuno

Oga-Hantō
Oga
AKITA
Akita
Honjō

Noshiro

Sakata
Tsuruoka

Murakami
Niitsu
Shibata
NIIGATA

Sado
Ryōtsu
Aikawa

CHŪBU

Iwazumi
Kitakami-Gawa
Tōno
Hayachine-San
1914
MORIOKA
Iwate-San
2041

TŌHOKU

SEA OF JAPAN

RUSSIA
Sikhote Alin

Svetlaya

Amgu

Velikaya Kema
Terney
Plastun

Rudnaja Pristan
Dalnegorsk

Kavalerovo
Olga

Margaritovo

Valentin
Preobrazheniye

CHINA

HEILONGJIANG

Hegang
Fujin
Songhua Jiang
Jiamusi
Shuangyashan

Baoqing
Huanan

Qitaihe
Boli
Linkou

Wusuli Jiang
(Ussuri)

Hulin

Mishan

Dongfanghong

Hunchun

JILIN

Mudan He

Dunhua

Bikin
Lesopilnoye
Bikin

Novokachalinsk

Rokitnoye

Dalnerechensk

Lesozavodsk
Ussurka
Aradnoye
Kirovskiy
Gornyy

Spassk
Dalniy

Lake
Khanka

Kamen-Rybolov
Poganichnyy

Suifenhe

Suyang

Razdolnoye
Ussuriysk

Artem
Dunay
Vladivostok
Zaliv Petra Velikogo
Nakhodka

Trudovoye

Slavyanka
Lipovcy
Manzovka

Kraskino

Khasan

Unggi
Najin

Chongjin

NORTH KOREA

SEA OF JAPAN

La Perouse Strait

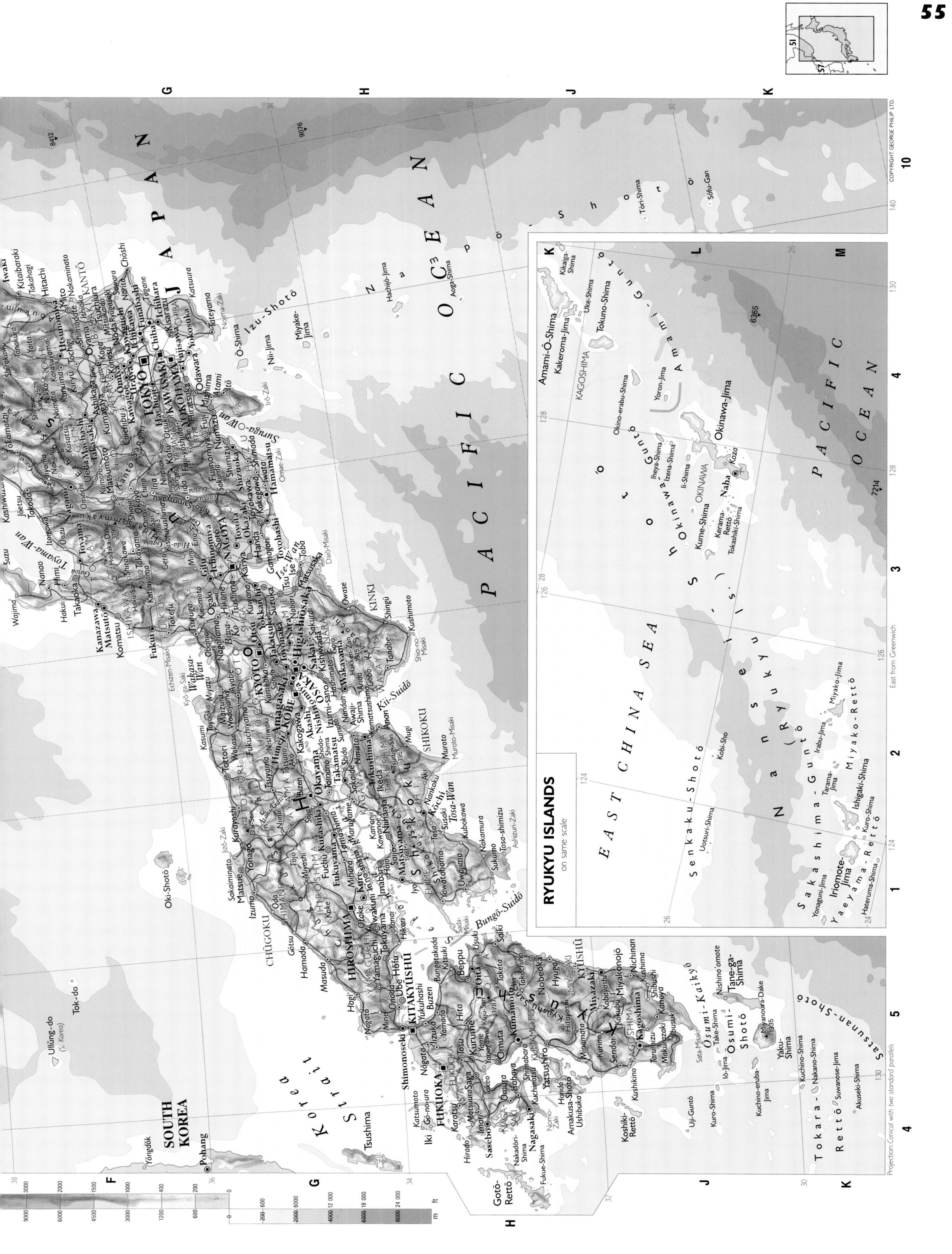

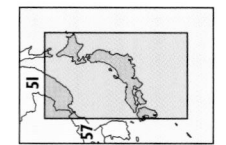

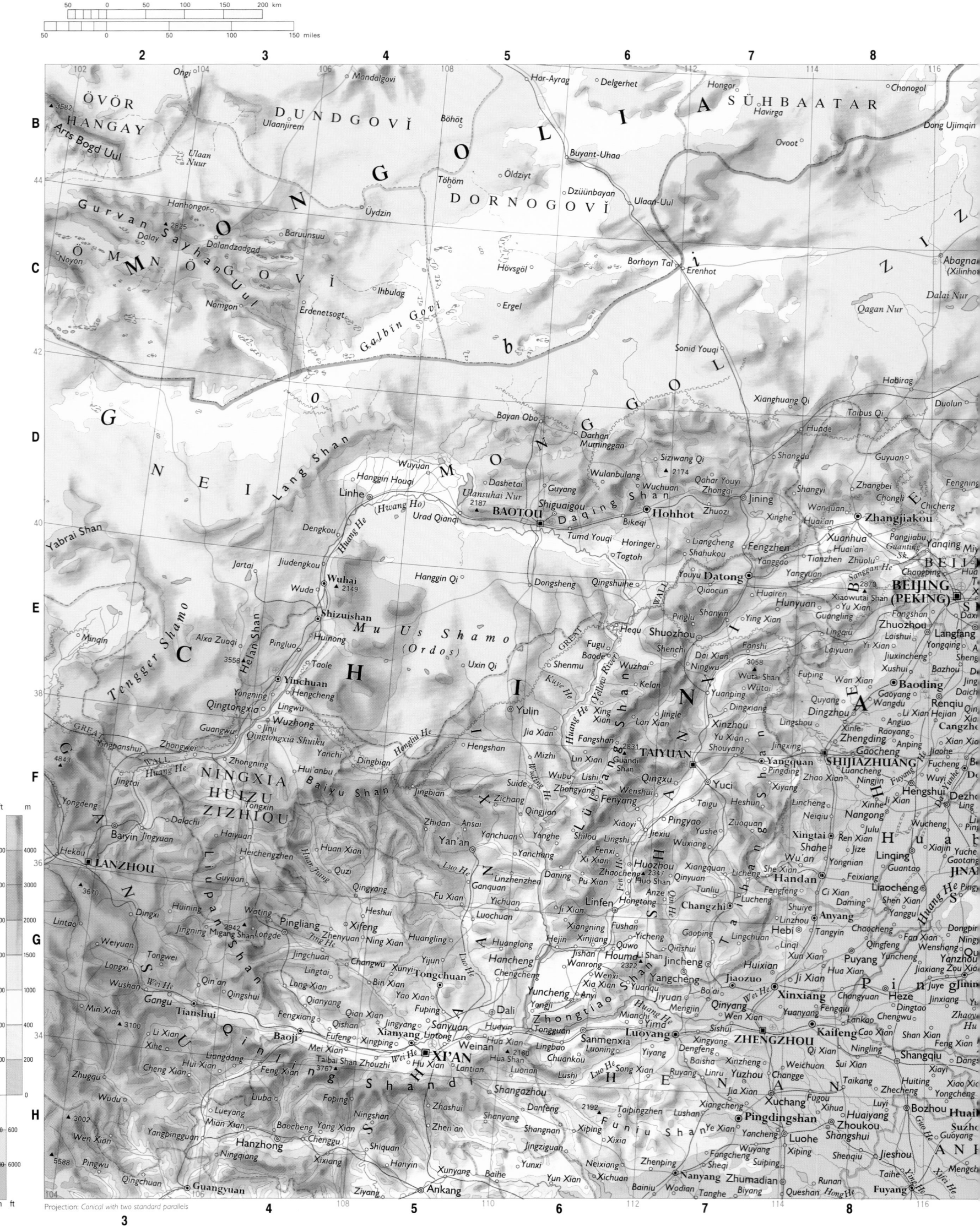

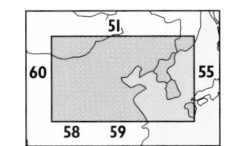

9   **10**   **11**   **12**   **13**   **14**   **15**   **16**

Horqin Youyi Qianqi
(Ulanhot)

Hulingol

HARBIN   Bin Xian
Zhenlai   Maoxing Zhaoyuan Shuangcheng Acheng   Linkou   **Jixi**
Hulin He   Da'an   Changchunling   Shangzhi   Turiy Rog
Baicheng   **HEILONGJIANG**   Ozero Khanka
Tuquan   Lalin   Yimianpo   Muling   **RUSSIA**
Taonan   Anguang   Qagan Nur Qian Gorlos   Sanchahe   Wuchang   Hengdaohezi   **Mudanjiang**   Maqiaohe
Tongyu   Fuyu   Beitaolaizhao   Yushu   Shanhetun   Hailin   Xiachengzi   Pogranichnyy
JILIN   Shenjingzi   Nong'an   Dehui   Shulan   Ning'an   Muling Suiyang Suifenhe
Jarud Qi   Zhanyu   Beizhengzhen   Fulongguan   Gangyao   Dongjingcheng   Dongning   Golenki
Zhongai   Changling   Jiutai   Wulajie   Zhangguangcai Ling   Ussuriysk
Xinkai He   Maolin   **CHANGCHUN**   **JILIN**   Jiaohe   Emu   1690   Luozigou   Razdolnoye
Bairin Zuoqi   Kailu Tongliao   Huaidezhen   Fanjiatun   Songhua Hu   Dunhua Daxinggou   Wangqing Shixian   Tavrichanka
Linxi   Bairin Youqi   Xiliao He   Shuangliao   Gongzhuling Shuangyang   Yitong   Hungsongdian   Mingyuegue   Tumen   **Vladivostok**
Xar Moron He   Jargalang   Siping   Panshi   Huadian   Longjing Yanji   Tumen   Hunchun   Slavyanka
Ongniud Qi   Bamiancheng   Liaoyuan   Hula   Huinan   Baishan   Antu   Helong   Namyang   Kraskino   Posyet
Chifeng   Laoha He   Zhangwu   Xifeng   Dongfeng   Jingyu   Fusong   Baihe 1677   Hoeryong   Unggi   Sôsura
Weichang   Wutonghaolai   Kangping   **WALL**   Hunjiang   Linjiang   Chunggang-up   Changbai Shan   Puryong   Musan   Najin
Heishui   Xiawa   Hure Qi   Faku Tiefa Kaiyuan   Shanchengzhen   Tonghua   Changbai   Paektu-san 2714   Pugôdong
1885   Ningcheng   Fuxin   Xinlitun Xinmin   Qingyuan   Huch'ang   Hupyongdong   Nanam   **Chôngjin**
Chengde   Chaoyang   Beipiao Qinghemen   **SHENYANG**   **FUSHUN**   Huanren 1845   Inpundong   Kasan-dong   Hyesan   Kyôngsông
Luanne   Heishan   Liaozhong   Tianshifu   Ji'an   Manp'o   Pungsan   Hapsu   Iryangdong   Chuuronjang
Liugou Shangbancheng   Beizhen   **Benxi**   Kanggye   Kuup-tong   Kapsan   Kilchu   Ondaejin

LIAONING
Jinzhou   Liaoyang   **ANSHAN**   Lianshanguan   Supung Shuiku   Pwon-chôsuji Pungsan 2522   Chail-bong   Kosongni   **Kimch'aek** (Songjin)
Jianchang   Jinxi   Panjin   Haicheng   Kuandian   Pyôktong Ch'osan   Kôin-dong   Changjin-chôsuji   Pupm-chôsuji   Kwangdaeri   Tanch'ôn
Xinglong   Niuzhuang   Tianzhuangtai   Cao He   Sakchu   Taegwan   Koin-dong   Changjin   Changhûngni   Pukch'ông
Shuiku   Huludao   Xingcheng   Dashiqiao   Gaizhou   Fengcheng   Xiuyan   Uiju   Pukchin   Sinhûng   Sinp'o   Sinch'ang
Zunhua   Suizhong   Xiongyuecheng   Wanfu 1131   Buyun Shan   **Dandong**   Sinûiju   Pukchin   **NORTH**   Hamhung   Sôhori
Fengrun Lulong   Liangdong   Donggou Gushan   Yongamp'o   Kusong   Kujang   Tôkch'ôn   **Hûngnam**   Tongchôn-ni
Yutian   Funing   **Qinhuangdao**   Wan   Zhuanghe   Yalu Jiang   Sônch'ôn   Chôngju Pakch'ôn   Anju   **KOREA**   Yônghûng   Tongjosôn Man   **SEA OF**
Luan Xian   Changli   Wafangdian   Pulandian   Sukch'ôn   Sunch'on   Sinchang-ni   Kowôn   Munch'ôn   **JAPAN**
Leting   Pikou   Jin Xian   **Korea**   Sunan   Songch'ôn   Kangdong   Tongyang   **Wônsan**   Anbyôn
TIANJIN SHI   Hangu   Lüshun   **DALIAN**   **Bay**   Namp'o   Chunghwa   Koksan   Sepo-ri   Singosan   Hoeyang 1638   Kansông
Tanggu   **P'YONGYANG**   Suan   Chiha-ri   Pyônggang   Changdo-ri   Sokch'o
Dagu   Miaodao Qundao   Sariwôn   Sinmak   Nam-ch'on   Kumhwa   Hwach'on-chôsuji 1578   Yangyang
Oikou   Chaeryông   Cho-do   Kûmch'on   Ch'ôrwon   Chumunjin
Huanghua   Changyôn   Sinch'ôn   Haeju   Kaesông   Panmunjôm   Ch'unch'ôn   Kangnûng
Yanshan   Penglai   Paengnyông-do   Ongjin   Yônan   Munsan Uijôngbu   Hongch'ôn   Samch'ôk
Qingyun   Longkou   Daxindian   **Yantai**   Weihai   Kanghwa   **SOUL**   Songnam   Hoengsông   Chôngsôn   Ullûng-do
Wudi   Zhanhua   **Huang He**   Huang Xian   Fushan Muping   **Puch'on**   Ichon   Wonju   Yôngwol
Huimin   Dongying Wan   Zhaoyuan Qixia   Chengshan Jiao   **INCH'ON**   Anyang   Hongch'on   Wonju   Yôngju   Ulchin
Shanghe   Binzhou   Dongying   Laizhou   Wendeng   Ansan   Suwon   Osan   Ch'ungju   Chech'on   Yôngju
Gaoyuan   **Shandong Bandao**   Laiyang   Rongcheng   P'yongt'aek   **SOUTH**   Yech'on
Zhoucun   Guangrao   923   Rushan   Ch'onan   **KOREA**   Andong   Yôngdôk
ZIBO   Huantai   Linzi   Changyi   Pingdu   Laixi   Nanhuang   Shidao   Sôsan   Yesan   Chôngju   Sangju   Uisong
Shan   Boshan   Yidu   **Weifang**   Haiyang   Hongsông   Kongju   **TAEJON**   Kimch'ôn   Kumi   **Chôngha**
Linqu   Fangzi   Gaomi   Lancun   Anmyôn-do   Nonsan   Yôngdong   Yôngch'ôn   Kyôngju   **P'ohang**
SHANDONG   Laiwu   Linqu   Anqiu   Jimo   Chengyang   Taech'ôn-ni   Kanggyông   Iri   Waegwan   **TAEGU**   Changga-Ap
Xintai   Zhucheng   1108   Jiaozhou   Kunsan   Kimje   **Chônju**   Koch'ang   Chôngdo   **Ulsan**
Mengyin   Yishui   Wulian   **QINGDAO**   Huanghou Wan   Puan   Iri   Koch'ang   Koryông   Miryang
Pingyi   Yi He   Ju Xian   Liangcheng   Chôngup   Kimhae
Rizhao   **HUANG HAI**   Namwôn   Chii-san   Chinju Masan   Kimhae
Fei Xian   Tangtou   Shijiusuo   *(Yellow Sea)*   Sagô-ri   Tamyang 1915   **Ch'angwon**   **PUSAN**
Tengzhou   Linyi   Andongwei   Songjông-ni   **KWANGJU**   Hadong   Samch'ônp'o   Tongnae   Sasuna
Teng Xian   **Zaozhuang**   Ganyu   Haizhou Wan   Naju   Sunch'on   Posong   Ch'ungmu   Yosu   Saka Tsushima
Hanzhuang   Pizhou   Lianyungang   **Mokp'o**   Changhûng   Polgyo-ri   Izuhara
Jiawang   Tancheng   Chenjiagang   Haenam   Chindo   **Korea Strait**   Iki
Xuzhou   Yaowan   Guanyun   Xiangshui   Hûksan-chedo   Karatsu
Suqian   Shuyang   Guannan   Binhai   **JAPAN**   Sasebo   Imari
Suining   Lianshui   **JIANGSU**   Funing   Cheju   Cheju-do   Kashima   Ōmura   Isahaya
Lingbi   Hongze Hu   Huai'an   Sheyang   Hallim   Onp'yông-ni   Nakadôri-Shima
Guzhen   Suzhou   Huaiyin   Liuzhuang   Taejông   Halla-san 1950   Mosûlpo   Sôgwipo   **Nagasaki**   Kuchinotsu
Wuhe   Baoying   Yancheng   Fukue-Shima
Bengbu   Gaoyou Hu   Xinghua   Dongtai
Fengyang

9   **10**   **11**   **12**   **13**   **14**   **15**

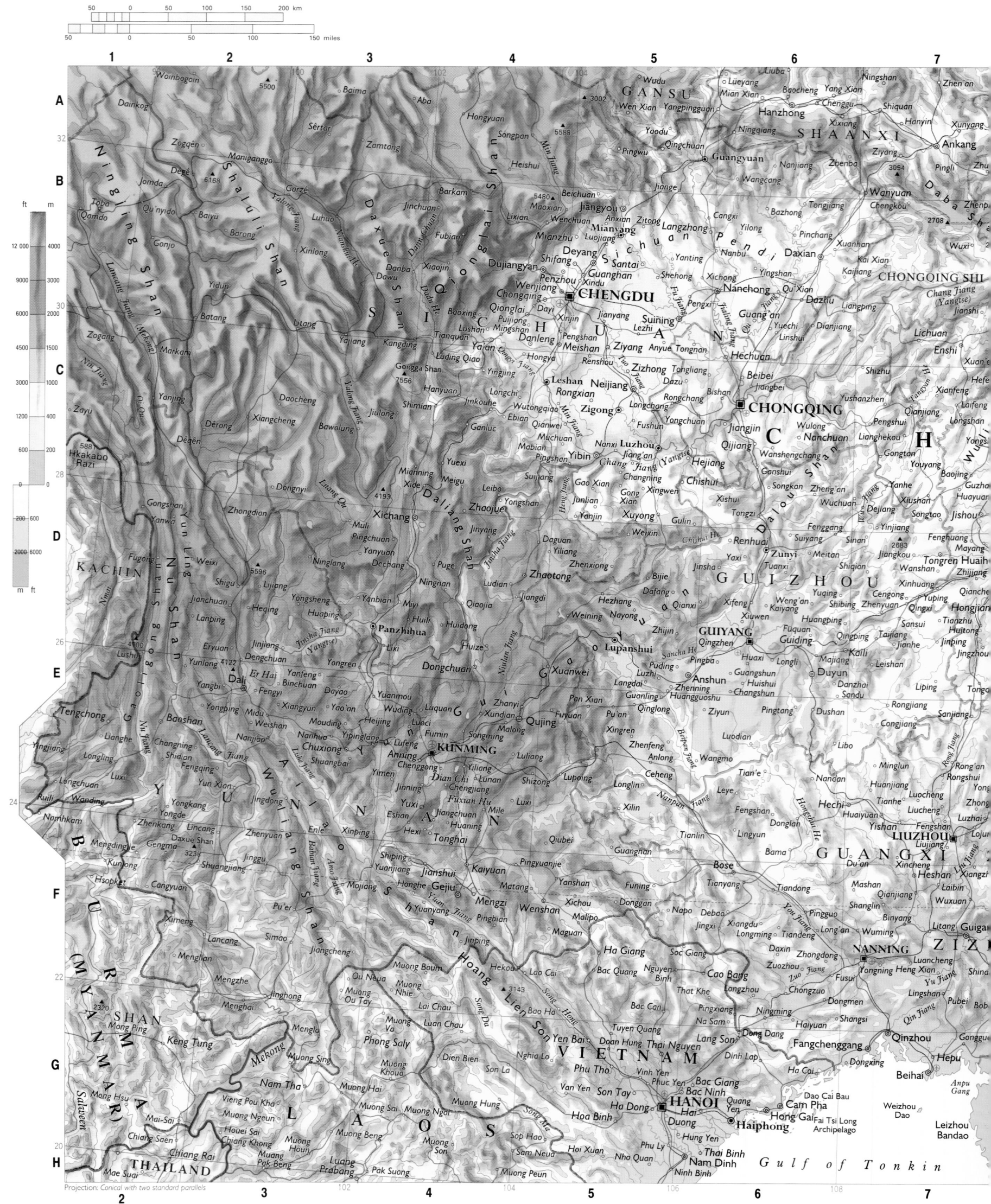

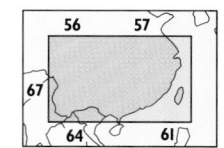

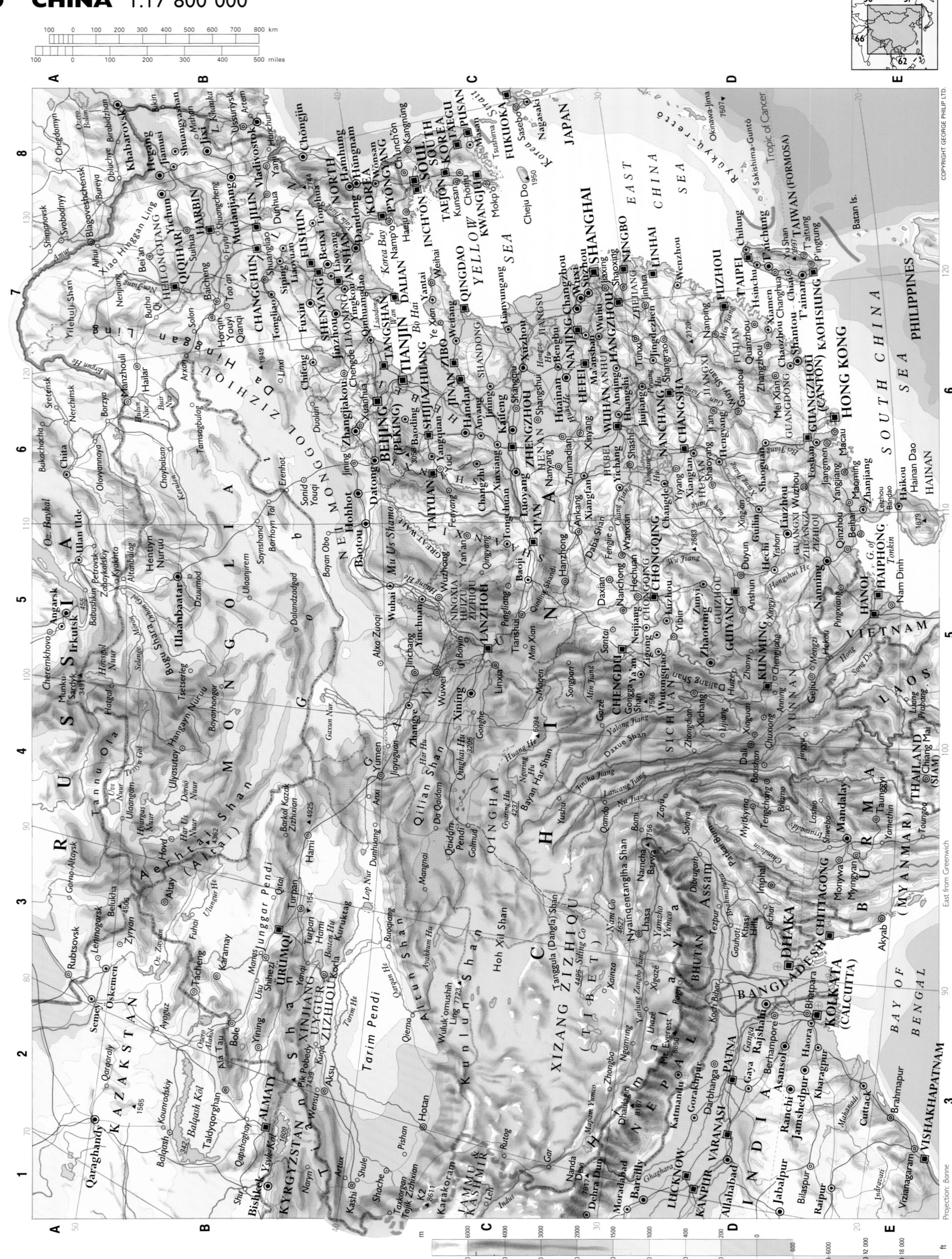

Projection: Bonne

50 0 100 150 200 250 300 km
50 0 50 100 150 200 miles

A

Itbayat I.
Batan I.

20

Balintang Channel

B

Calayan I. Babuyan I.
Dalupiri I. Babuyan Camiguin I.
Islands
Mayraira Pt. *Babuyan Channel* Fuga I.
Bacarra Bangui Claveria Aparri Santa Ana
San Nicolas Laoag Kabugao Gonzaga
Batac Gattaran
18 Cabugao 2360 Tuao Tuguegarao
Vigan Bangued *Mt. Cresta*
Santa *Cordillera Central* Cabagan 1685
Maria Roxas Ilagan
Candon Bontoc *Palanan Pt.*
Tagudin San Mateo Santiago Palanan
Balaoan *Sierra* *C. San Ildefonso*

C

PACIFIC

San Fernando Mt. Pulog Cordon
Lingayen Gulf 2928 Solano
Baguio Bayombong
Bolinao Rosario Mt. Anacuao
Alaminos 1852
Lingayen Dagupan *C. San Ildefonso*
16 San Manuel
San Carlos Bayambang San Jose Baler Bay
Santa Cruz Moncada Cuyapo Baler
Camiling Victoria
Masinloc Tarlac *Luzon*
Iba 2037 Cabanatuan
Concepcion La Gapan
1780 Paz
Mt. Pinatubo Angeles Dingalan
San Antonio San Fernando
Olongapo Orani Malabon Polillo Is.
Bataan *Manila* Caloocan Patnanongan I.
Bay Quezon City Jomalig I.
Cavite MANILA Pasay Santa Cruz *Lamon Bay*
Dasmariñas Paracale
Tagaytay Is. de Bay San Pablo Atimonan Labo
Nasugbu Lipa Lucban Daet
Balayan Lemery Lucena Calauag
Batangas Lopez Calabanga San Andres
Verde I. Pass Boac Catanauan Naga Iriga Virac
Lobo *Tayabas Bay* Nabua 2421 Tabaco
C. Calavite Marin- Ligao Mayon Vol.
Mamburao Calapan duque Legazpi Sorsogon
Mindoro Victoria Pinamalayan Burias I. Donsol Magallanes *San Bernardino Str.*
Sablayan Mt. Baco Bulan Irosin
2487 *SIBUYAN* Romblon Aroroy Ticao I. Allen
Bongabong Masbate Calbayog
Roxas Tablas I. Sibuyan I. Mandaon Milagros
San Jose Odiongan Masbate

D

OCEAN

PHILIPPINES

E

SOUTH

CHINA

SEA

F

Busuanga I. *SEA*
Culion I. Calamian Placer Catbalogan Paranas *Samar*
Group Kalibo *VISAYAN* Bilinan I. Calbiran Santa Borongan
Linapacan Str. Pandan Roxas *SEA* Calubian Rita Llorente
Linapacan I. Dao Pilar Bantayan Carigara Basey General MacArthur
Tibiao 2117 Ajuy I. Palompon Tacloban Guiuan
Cuyo West Pass Cuyo Is. Bugasong Sara Passi Cadiz Bogo Ormoc *Leyte* Dulag Homonhon I.
Cuyo *Panay* Pototan Sagay Tuburan Danao *Leyte Gulf* Abuyog
Taytay *Cuyo East Pass* San Jose Iloilo Silay Victorias San Carlos Camotes Is. Baybay
Dumaran I. Guimaras Bacolod 2450 *Camotes* Sogod Dinagat I.
Palawan Jordan La San Carlos Mandaue *Sea* San Juan
1593 Hinigaran Carlota Guihulngan Cebu Maasin Dinagat I.
Binalbagan Panaon I. Siargao I.
Irahuan Honda Bay Himamaylan *Tanon* Argao *Bohol I.* Surigao Placer
Puerto Princesa Kabankalan Carcar Bucas Grande I.
Cagayan Is. Sipalay *Str.* Bais Oslob Tagbilaran Carrascal
Mt. Mantalingajan Bais *BOHOL* L. Tandag
2085 *Negros* Tanjay Mainit 2012
Hinoba-an Dumaguete Siquijor I. Cabadbaran Lanuza
C. Bululuyan Bayawan Siaton Zamboanguita Camiguin I. Butuan Tago
Bugsuk I. Talisayan Nasipit Bayugan Marihatag
SULU Dipolog *SEA* Balingasag Esperanza Lianga
Balabac I. Dapitan Talacogon Hinatuan
Balabac *SEA* Manukan Iligan Opol Cagayan de Oro Bislig
Balambangan *Strait* Oroquieta Bay 2938 Malaybalay
Banggi Sindangan Ozamiz Iligan Marawi City Bunawan
Kudat Labason Marawi City L. Lanao Tubod
Seraja Siocon Kabasalan Pagadian *Mindanao* Tagum Cateel
Jembongan Tubod Panabo
Langkon Suba Talan Sibuco Margosatubig Malabang Baganga
Kota Belud *Sibuguey* 2815
Tenghilan Turtle Is. *Bay* Illana Parang Panabo Manay
Kota G. Kinabalu Cagayan Sulu I. Olutanga *Bay* Midsayap Pantukan
Kinabalu 4101 Cotabato Mt. Apo *Davao*
Papar *MALAYSIA* Zamboanga *Moro Gulf* Datu Piang 2954 Digos *Davao*
Melalap Pilas Isabela Pikit *Gulf*
Keningau Group Talayan Kalamansig Malita
Kuamat Basilan I. Lamitan Koronadal C. San Agustin
Pangutaran Lebak Kiamba 2083 General
Silam Group Samales Palimbang Santos
Sandakan Jolo Group *Sarangani Bay*
Borneo Parang Group Tinaca Pt.
Talipao Siasi I.
Banjaran Crocker Tawi-tawi Tapul Pata I. *CELEBES* Sarangani Is.
Semporna Group Tapul
SABAH Sibutu Group *SEA*
Telok Darvel

G

2000
1500
1000

H

600
200
0

J

INDONESIA Kep. Talaud

ft m
9000 3000
6000 2000
4500 1500
3000 1000
1200 400
600 200
0 0
200 600
4000 12 000
8000 24 000
m ft

BURMA
(MYANMAR)

Letpadan
Tharrawaddy
Insein
RANGOON
(YANGON)
Ma-ubin
Pyapon
G. of
Martaban
Kyaikkami
Ye
Thaton
Moulmein
2080

THAILAND

Thoen
Uttaradit
Sawankhalok
Loei
Nong Khai
Vientiane
(Viangchan)
Udon Thani
Nakhon
Phanom
Muang
Khammouan
Ba Don
Dong Hoi

Tak
Phitsanulok
Khon Kaen
Sakon
Nakhon
Savannakhet
Quang Tri
Hue

Natkyizin
Nam Tok
Phra Nakhon
Si Ayutthaya
Saraburi
Phetchabun
Nakhon
Sawan
Chaiyaphum
Roi Et
Ubon
Ratchathani
Pakxe
Saravan
VIETNAM
Da Nang
Hoi An

Tavoy
Maungmagan
Islands
2075
Kanchanaburi
Samut
Songkhram
BANGKOK
Nakhon
Ratchasima
Buriram
Khu Khan
Sisaket
Attapu
2598
Quang Ngai

Mali Kyun
Phet Buri
Samut Prakan
Chon Buri
Pattaya
Aranyaprathet
Sisophon
Siemreab
Kompong
Thom
Stoeng Treng
Phnom Dangrek
461
Muang
Khong
Plei Ku
Kon Tum
Bong Son
Binh Dinh
Qui Nhon
Song Cau

Kadan
Kyun
Hua Hin
Chanthaburi
Trat
Ko Chang
Pouthisat
1813
Kampong Chhnang
Kampong
Cham
Kracheh
Senmonorom
2405
Buon Me Thuot
Nha Trang
Cam Ranh

CAMBODIA

Mergui
Taninthari
Prachuap
Khiri Khan
Ko Kut
Phumi
Koh Kong
Krong
Kaoh Kong
Sre Ambel
Prey Veng
Da Lat
Phan Rang
Mui Dinh
4424

Letsôk-
aw Kyun
Bang Saphan
Bokpyin
Chumphon
Kho Khot Kra
Takey
Kampot
Kampong Saom
Kampong Saom
Svay Rieng
Long
Xuyen
My Tho
THANH PHO HO CHI MINH
Phan Thiet

Lambi Kyun
Kyunzu
Maliwun
Chaak Kampong Saom
Dao Phu Quoc
Hon Chong
Rach Gia
Sa Dec
Can Tho
Bien Hoa
Vung Tau

Zadetkyi Kyun
Ranong
Ko Phangan
Ko Samui
Mui Ca Mau
Soc Trang
Bac Lieu
Ca Mau
Con Son

Gulf
_of_
Thailand

Andaman _Sea_

Phangnga
Surat Thani
1835
Nakhon Si Thammarat
Pak Phanang
Thung Song

Phuket
Trang
Kantang
Phatthalung
Thale Luang
Songkhla

Tarutao
Hat Yai
Satun
Pattani
Narathiwat
Tumpat
Kota Baharu
Perhentian

We
Sabang
Banda Aceh
Langkawi
Alor Setar
Yala
Redang

Sigli
Meureudu
Bireuen
Pasir Mas
Sungai Petani
Butterworth
Kuala Terengganu

Lhokseumawe
ACEH
Idi
Peureulak
George Town
Pinang
Kuala Lipis
Gunong Tahan
2190
Dungun
Kemaman

Calang
Takengon
Langsa
PENINSULAR
MALAYSIA
Taiping
Ipoh
Kampar
Temerloh
Kuantan

Meulaboh
Kualasimpang
Pangkalanbrandan
G. Leuser
3381
Teluk
Intan
Kota Kubu
Baharu
Kelang
KUALA LUMPUR

Ujung Raja
Binjai
Belawan
MEDAN
Tebingtinggi
Seremban
Melaka

Tapaktuan
Kabanjahe
Tanjungbalai
Pelabuhan Kelang
Port Dickson
Muar
Keluang
Kota Tinggi
Pulau
Tioman

Simeulue
Pematangsiantar
Prapat
Bagansiapiapi
Batu
Pahat
Johor Baharu

Sinabang
Danau Toba
Tarutung
Dumai
Bengkalis
Rupat
SINGAPORE

Kepulauan
Banyak
Sibolga
Rantauprapat
Bintan
Tanjungpinang

Lahewa
Musala
Siaksriindrapura
Kepulauan
Riau

Nias
Gunungsitoli
Padangsidempuan
Pekanbaru
Bangkinang
RIAU
Lingga
Lingga

Telukdalam
UTARA
Lubuksikaping
Kampar
Pasirkuning
Singkep

Tanahmasa
Bukittinggi
Payakumbuh
Rengat
Belinyu

Kepulauan
Banyak
Tanahbala
Padangpanjang
Sawahlunto
Solok
BARAT
Muaratebo
INDONESIA

Siberut
Padang
Painan
Muarabungo
Kerinci
3805
Jambi
Muaratembesi
Muntok
Pangkalpinang
Bangka

Pulau
Pagai Utara
Sungaipenuh
Bangko
Sarolangun
Tanjungpandan
Belitung

Sabulubbek
Mukomuko
JAMBI
Manggar

Pulau Pagai
Selatan
Lubuklinggau
Curup
PALEMBANG
Sungaigerong
Toboali
Dendang

Kepulauan
Mentawai
Tebingtinggi
Sekayu
Perabumulih
Muaraenim

Bengkulu
Lahat
SELATAN

BENGKULU
Dempo
3159
Baturaja
Menggala

Manna
Martapura
Kotabumi

6073
Kotaagung
Tanjungkarang
Telukbetung
LAMPUNG
Kalianda
Serbu

Strait of Malacca
Strait of Malacca

Enggano
Merak
Serang
JAKARTA
Bogor
Sukabumi

Pulau
Krakatau
Panaitan
BANTEN
Jatinegara
Purwakarta
Cirebon
Brebes
Tegal
Pemalang
Pekalongan

Teluk Pelabuhan
Ratu
BANDUNG
Garut
Tasikmalaya
Cilacap
Kebumen
Magelang

INDIAN _OCEAN_

Java _Trench_
6650
Yogyakarta
Surakarta
Blitar
Malang
3670
3428
TENGAH
Bojonegoro
Madiun
Kediri
3265
2563
TIMUR
Probolinggo
Jember

SOUTH CHINA SEA

Paracel Is.

Nanshan I.
Loaita I.
Itu Aba I.
Sin Cowe I.

Spratly I.
Amboyna Cay

Spratly Is.

Kepulauan
Natuna
Besar
Natuna
Besar
Telukbutun
Binjai

Matak
Siantan
Subi
Kepulauan
Natuna Selatan
Serasan

Laut
Kepulauan
Anambas
Midai

Tanjung Datu

Kepulauan
Tambelan

Kepulauan
Badas

Sambas
Lundu
Bau
Serian
Kucing

Singkawang
Niut
1701
Tebakang
Bandar Sri Aman

MALAYSIA

BRUNEI
Kuala Belait
Tutong
Bandar Seri Begawan
Seria
Miri
Niah
Lawas
Limbang

Kudat
Langkon
Kota Belud
Gunong
Kinabalu
4101
Kota Kinabalu
Beaufort
Labuan
Pulau Labuan
Tenom
Melalap

SABAH

2438
Bintulu
Mukah
SARAWAK
Tanjungselor

Oya
Sibu
Kanowit
Gunung
Mulu
2240
Longnawan
2988
Tanjungredeb

Sarikei
Kapit
Longiram
Samar

Ngabang
BARAT
Sanggau
Semitau
Sintang
Putussibau
1758
2278
Purukcahu
Tenggarong
Balikpapan

Pontianak
Nangapinoh
Muarajuloi
Muaratewe

G. Saran
Nangatayap
Sukadana
Ketapang
Nangapinoh
Kualakurun

Kepulauan
Karimata
Sukaraja
TENGAH
Palangkaraya
Buntok
Tanahgrogot

Kendawangan
Pangkalanbuun
Kumai
Sampit
SELATAN
Amuntai
Tanjung
Besar
1892
Kandangan

Kualajelai
Semuda
Kualapembuang
Kualakapuas
Martapura
Banjarmasin
Barabai
Kotabaru

Tanjungpandan
Belitung
Dendang
Teluk
Sampit
Pelaihari
Pagatan
Sebuku
Karambu
Pulau Laut

KALIMANTAN

BORNEO

Selat Karimata

Greater _Sunda_ _Isla_

Tanjung Sambar
Tanjung Puting
Tg. Selatan
Satui

Java _Sea_

Kepulauan
Karimunjawa
Bawean
Kepulauan
Masalembo
Kepulauan
Masalir

Sangkapura
Kepulauan
Kangean

SEMARANG
Tuban
Bangkalan
Madura
Gresik
SURABAYA
Pasuruan

Demak
Kendal

Timor

Tulungagung
Banyuwangi
Semeru
BALI
Agung
3142
Rinjani
3726
Denpasar
Penida
Mataram
Praya
Taliwang
Lombok

NUSA TENGGARA
BARAT

Lesser

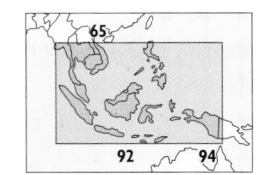

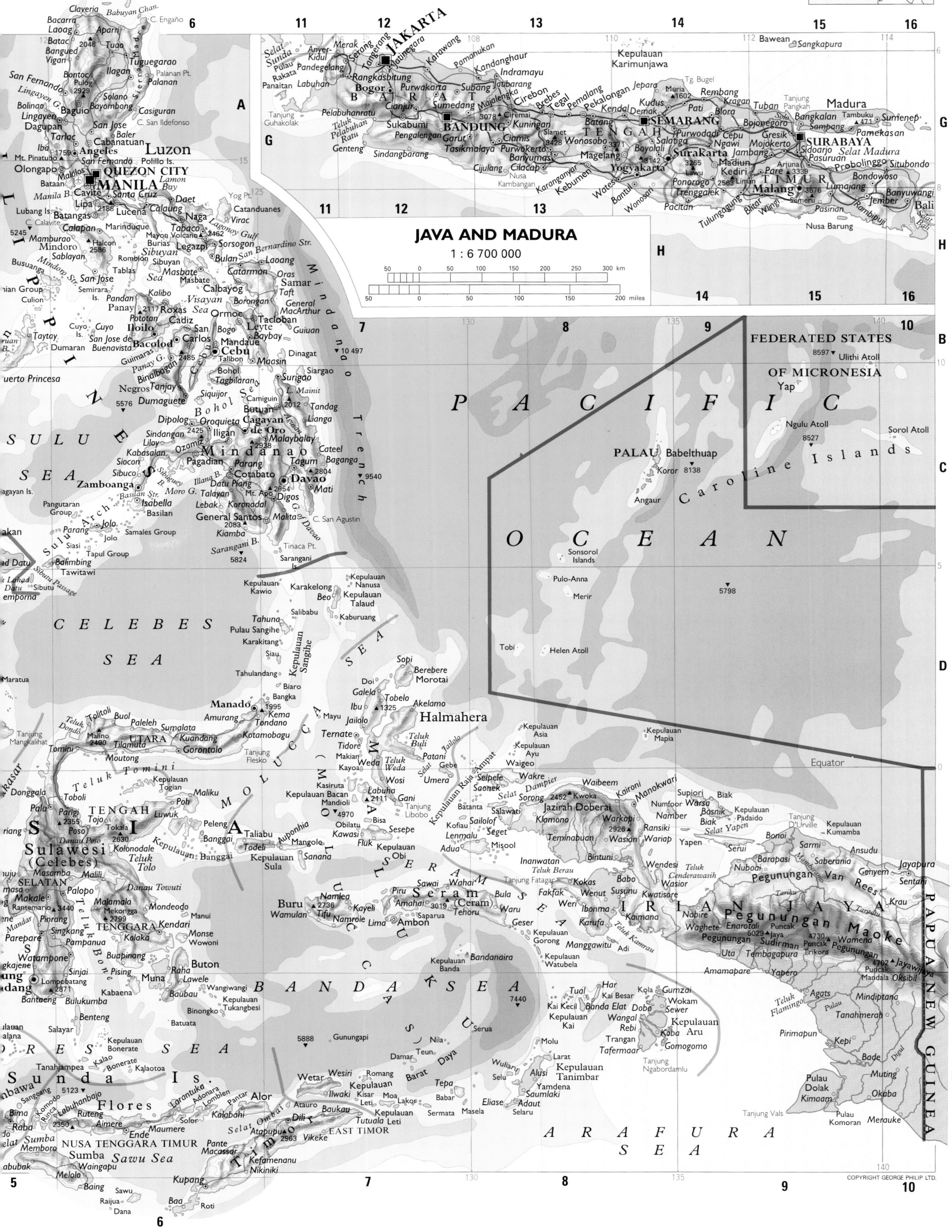

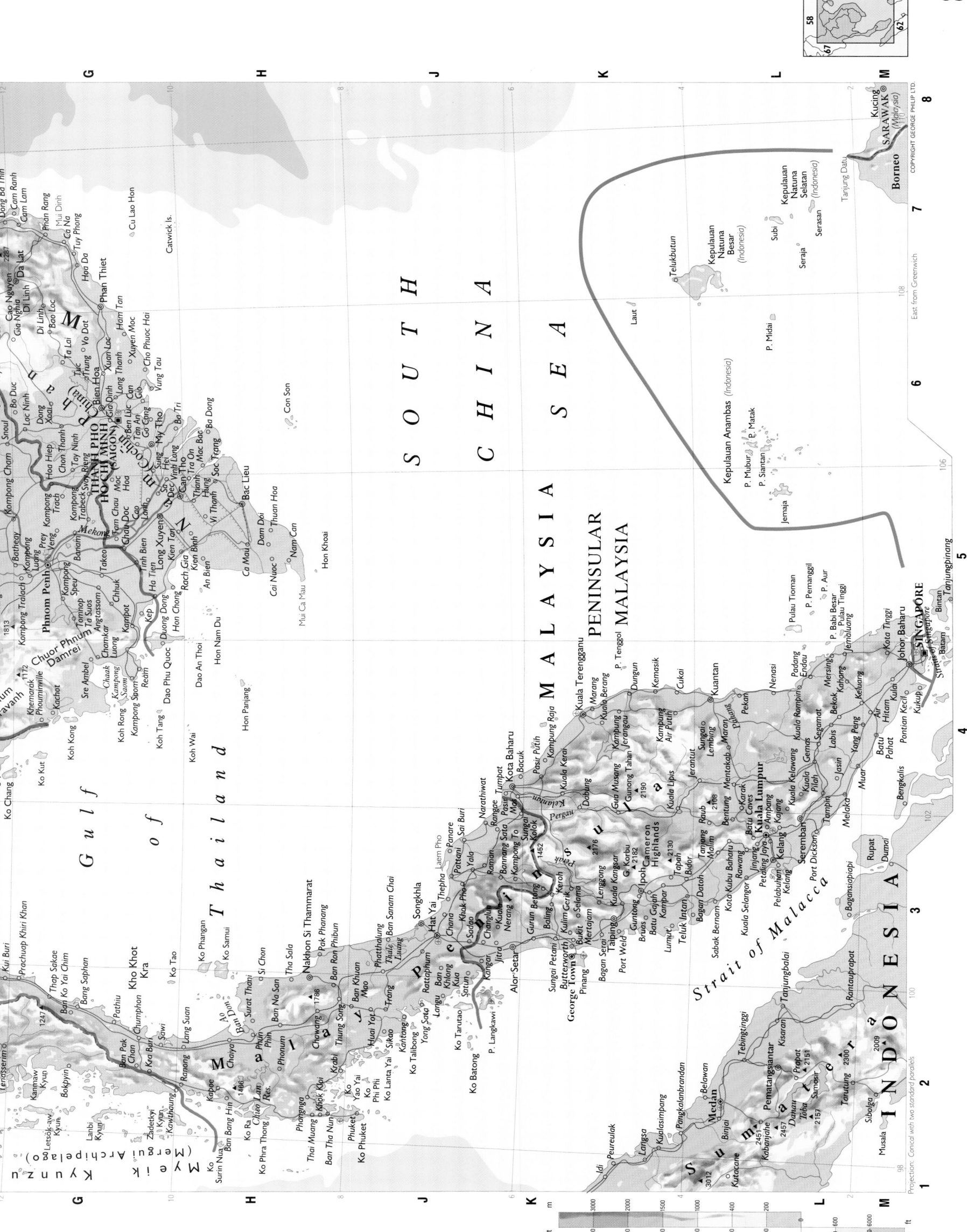

58
62
62
67
62

COPYRIGHT GEORGE PHILIP LTD.

Kucing
SARAWAK
(Malaysia)
Borneo
Tanjung Datu

Kepulauan
Natuna
Besar
(Indonesia)

Kepulauan
Natuna
Selatan
(Indonesia)

Subi
Seraja
Serasan

Telukbutun

East from Greenwich

108

Laut

Kepulauan Anambas (Indonesia)

P. Mubur
P. Matak
P. Siantan
P. Midai

Jemaja

106

S O U T H   C H I N A   S E A

Con Son

Dong Ba Thin
Cam Ranh
Cam Lam
Phan Rang
Mui Dinh
Ca Na
Tuy Phong
Hoa Da
Phan Thiet

Cu Lao Hon

Catwick Is.

Cao Nguyen 2287
Da Lat
Di Linh
Gia Nghia
Bao Loc
Ta Lai
Ta Lai

M

Hoa Hiep
Loc Ninh
Bo Duc
Dong
Xoai
Tuc
Trung
Xuan Loc
Long Thanh
Ham Tan

u

Snoul
Kompong Cham
Bathegy
Kompong
Luong
Kompong Tralach
Phnom Penh
Kompong
Speu
Takeo
Banam
Mekong
Prey
Veng
Kompong
Trabeck
Sreng
Ba Ria
Bien Hoa
THANH PHO
HO CHI MINH
(SAIGON)
Thu Dau Mot
Tay Ninh
Long Thanh
Ba Ria
Vung Tau
Cho Phuoc Hai
Ba Dong

I
N
D
O
C
H
I
N
A

1813

Chuor Phnum
Damrei
1172

Kompong
Saom
Chhuk
Chamkar
Luong
Kampot
Kep
Ha Tien
Duong Dong
Hon Chong
Rach Gia
Kien Binh
Kien Tan
Tinh Bien
Long Xuyen
Chau Doc
Tan An
Go Cong
Cao
Lonh
My Tho
Vinh Long
Tra On
Mac Bac
Soc Trang
Bac Lieu
Vi Thanh
Thuan Hoa
Nam Can
Dam Doi
Ca Mau
Cai Nuoc
Hon Khoai

Chhung
Sre Ambel
Khemarak
Phouminville
Kachot

ravanh

Ko Kong
Ko Kut
Ko Chang
Koh Kong
Kampong Saom
Redm
Chaak
Kampong
Saom
Koh Rong
Koh Tang
Koh Wai
Dao Phu Quoc
Dao An Thoi
Hon Nam Du
Hon Panjang
Hon Chong

Mui Ca Mau

G u l f   o f   T h a i l a n d

Kui Buri
Prachuap Khiri Khan
Thap Sakae
Ban Kai Chim
Bang Saphan

1247

Chumphon
Lang Suan
Ban Pak
Chan
Kra Buri
Sawi
Pathiu
Chaiya
Surat Thani

Kho Khot
Kra

Ko Phangan
Ko Samui
Ko Tao

Si Chon
Tha Sala
Nakhon Si Thammarat
Pak Phanang
Ban Na San
Ban Ron Phibun
Phatthalung

Ban Don
1786

Kanmaw Kyun
Bokpyin
Letsôk-aw
Kyun
Lanbi
Kyun
Kawthoung

K y u n z u
(Mergui Archipelago)
M e i k

Tenasserim
Bokpyin
Zádetkyi
Kyun

Thai Muang
Ko Surin Nua
Ban Bang Hin
Kapoe
Ko Ra
Ban Bang Hin
Phangnga
Ko Yao Yai
Ko Phi Phi
Phuket
Ban Tha Nun
Ko Phuket

Ranong
Kra Buri

M a l a
y

1466

Chaiya
Ban Don
Khao Luang
Phun
Phin
Thung Song
Huai Yot
Trang
Sikao
Kantang
Ko Lanta Yai
Ko Libong
Ko Talibong
Ko Tarutao
P. Langkawi
Ko Batong

Krabi
Ko Klang
Ao Luk
Ban Khuan
Yao

P e
n
i
n
s
u
l
a

Nakhon Si Thammarat
Songkhla
Hat Yai
Sadao
Yong Sata
Langu
Satun
Kangar
Jitra
Alor Setar

T h a i l a n d

Sai Buri
Laem Pho
Panare
Pattani
Yala
Raman
Thepha
Chana
Khlong Kua
Betong

Pasir Mas
Tumpat
Kota Baharu
Pasir Putih
Bacuk
Kampung Raja
Kuala Kerai
Kuala Terengganu
Marang
Kuala Berang
Kuala
Terengganu

Rangae
Narathiwat
Tak Bai
Sungai
Golok
Kuala Krai
Dabung
Gua Musang
Gunong Tahan 2190
a
l
a

M A L A Y S I A

PENINSULAR
MALAYSIA

Kampung
Ternggau
Dungun
Kemasik
Cukai
Kuantan

P. Tenggol

Gurun
Baling
Keroh
Gerik
Pergau
Lenggong
Kulim
Selama
Bukit
Mertajam
Sungai
Petani
Butterworth
George Town
Pinang
Bagan Serai
Port Weld
Taiping
Kuala Kangsar
G. Gorbu 2182
G. Korbu 2176
Ipoh
Cameron
Highlands 2130
Batu
Gajah
Bruas
Lumut
Teluk Intan
Bidor
Tapah
Tanjung
Malim
Raub
Batu
Gua Caves
Bentung
Karak
Kuala Lipis
Kuala
Lumpur
Ampang
Kuala
Kelawang
Kuala Rompin

P e r a k

1452

S e l a
n
g
o
r

Petaling Jaya
Kelang
Port Swettenham
Kelang
Klang
Kota Kubu Bahru
Rawang
Kajang
Seremban
Kuala Pilah
Jelebu
Bagan Datoh
Sabak Bernam
Kuala Selangor
Port Dickson
Tampin
Gemas
Segamat
Labis
Jasin
Melaka
Muar
Batu
Pahat
Pontian Kecil
Bengkalis

2700

Mersing
Kahong
Keluang
Kluang
Yang Peng
Air
Hitam
Kulai
Johor Baharu
SINGAPORE
Singapore
Strait of Singapore

Pulau Toman
P. Tinggi
P. Babi Besar
P. Aur
P. Pemanggil
Pulau Tioman
Padang
Endau
Nenasi
Pekan
Pahang
Jerantut
Mentakab
Kuala
Krau
Temerloh
Maran
Bekok

Kucing
Kota Tinggi
Jemaluang
Bintan
Batam
Tanjungpinang

S t r a i t   o f   M a l a c c a

Rupat
Dumai
Bagansiapiapi
Tanjungbalai

I N D O N E S I A

Peureulak
Idi
Langsa
Kualasimpang
Pangkalanbrandan
Belawan
Medan
Binjai
Tebingtinggi
Pematangsiantar
Kisaran
Rantauprapat

Musala
Sibolga
Kabanjahe
Kutacane

S u m a t e r a

3012
2451
2457
Danau
Toba
Samosir
Prapat
2009
2300
2151
2151
Tarutung

Musi

Projection: Conical with two standard parallels

ft   m
9000   3000
6000   2000
4500   1500
3000   1000
1200   400
600   200
0   0
200   600
2000   6000
m   ft

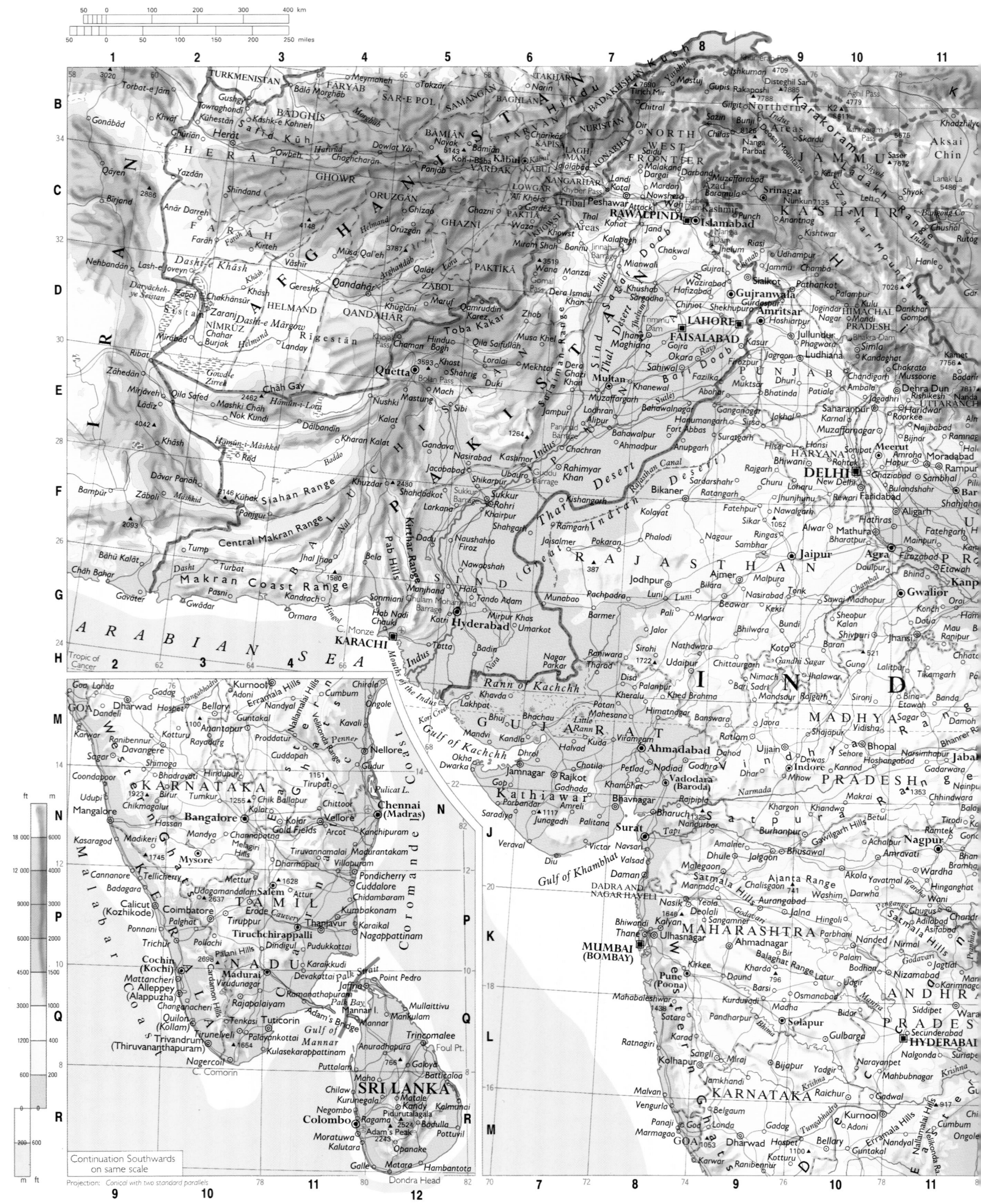

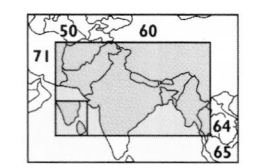

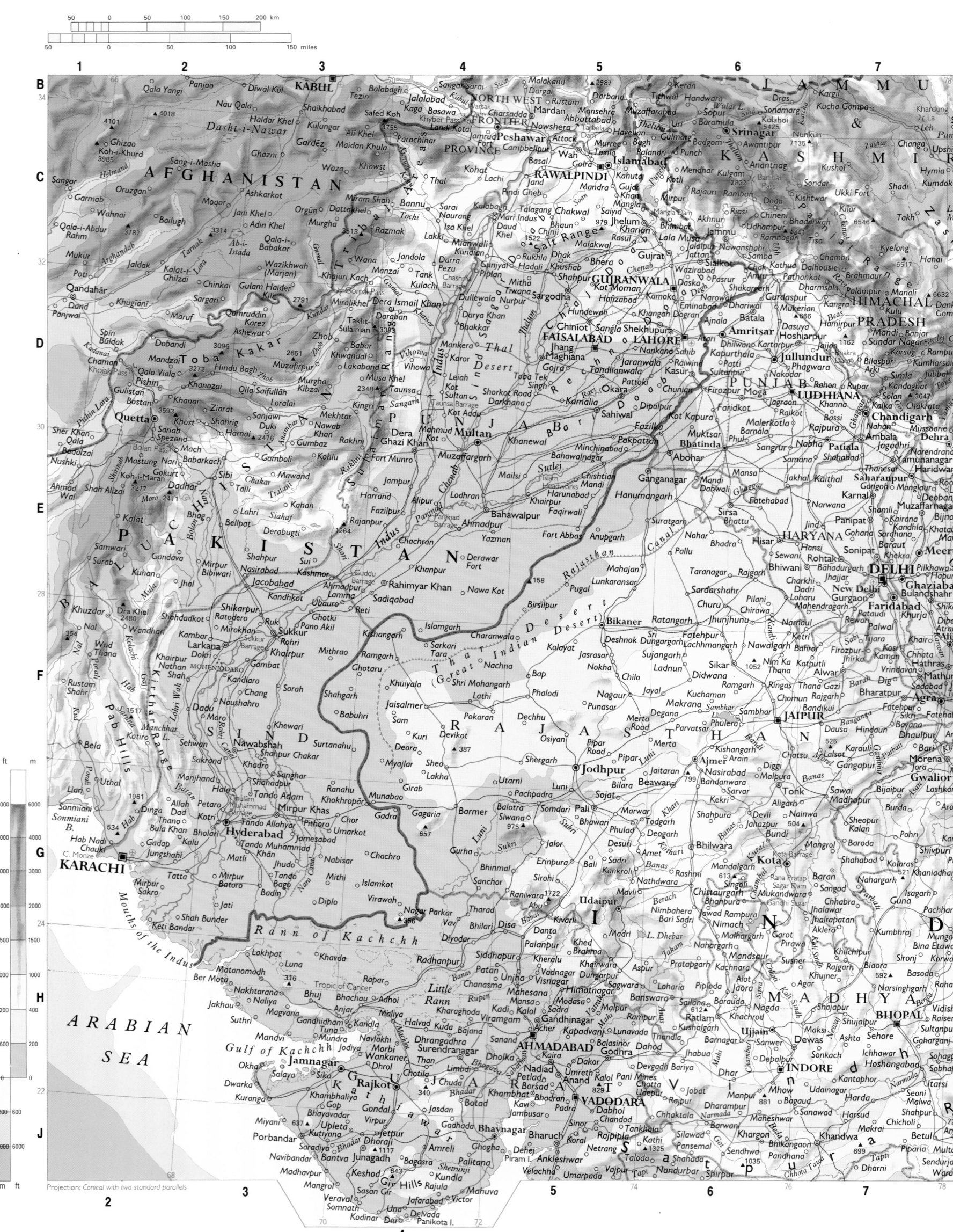

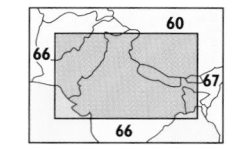

JAMMU AND KASHMIR
On same scale as Main Map

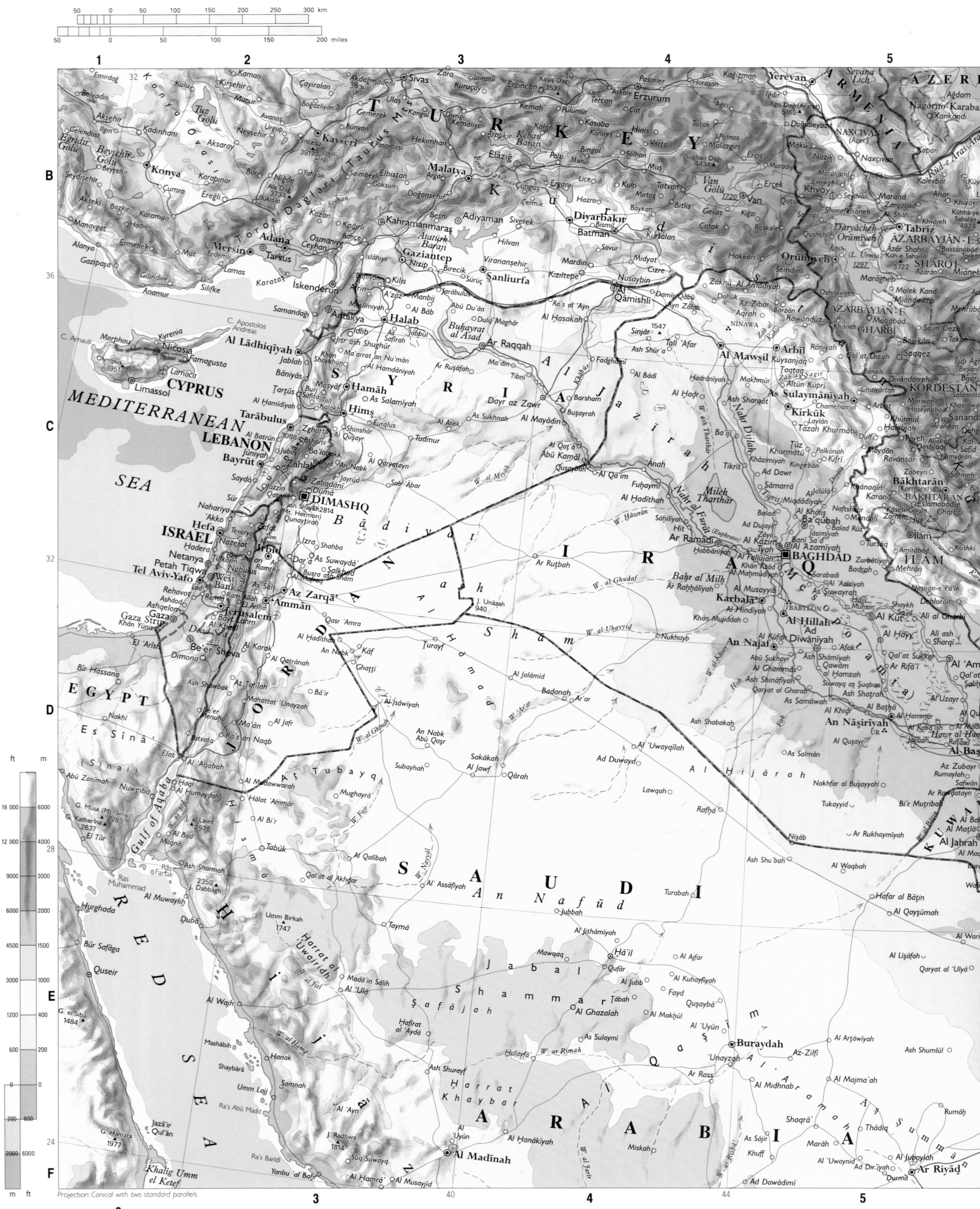

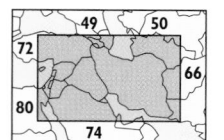

Projection: Conical with two standard parallels

– – – Division between Greeks and Turks in Cyprus; Turks to the North.

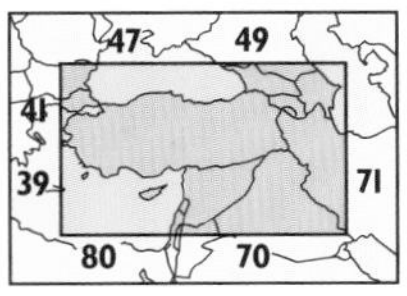

CASPIAN SEA

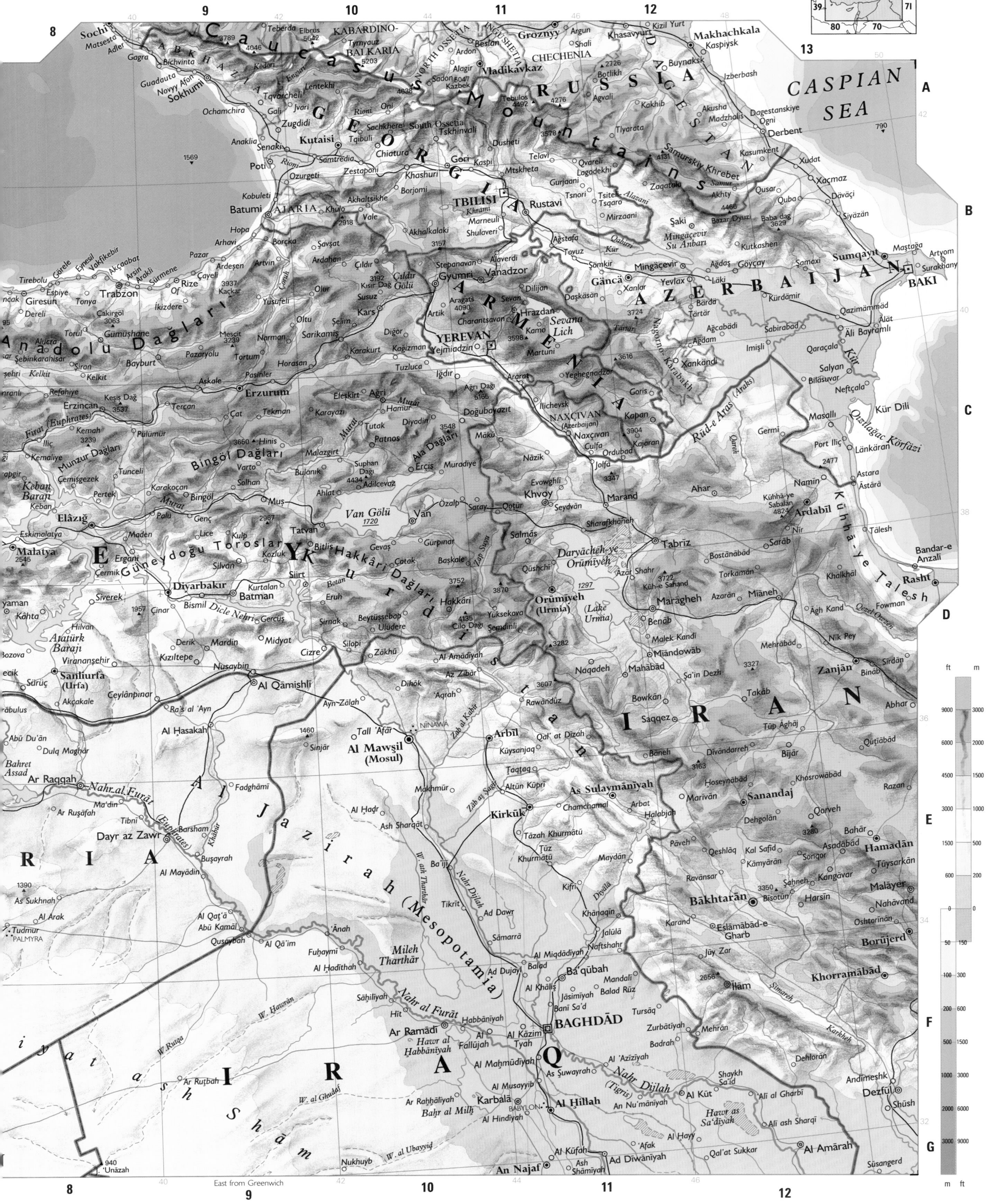

RUSSIA
GEORGIA
ARMENIA
AZERBAIJAN
TURKEY
IRAN
IRAQ
SYRIA

Caucasus Mountains

TBILISI
YEREVAN
BAKI
BAGHDAD

Sochi · Matsesta · Adler · Gagra · Bichvinta · Guadauta · Novyy Afon · Sokhum · Ochamchira · Gali · Zugdidi · Senaki · Anaklia · Poti · Kobuleti · Batumi · AJARIA

KABARDINO-BALKARIA · Tyrnyauz · Elbrus 5642 · Teberda · Nalchik · North Ossetia · Vladikavkaz · Kazbek · Alagir · Ardon · INGUSHETIA · Grozny · Argun · Shali · CHECHENIA · Botlikh · DAGESTAN · Buynaksk · Makhachkala · Kaspiysk · Izberbash · Derbent

Kutaisi · Samtredia · Ozurgeti · Rioni · Chiatura · Gori · Kaspi · Mtskheta · Khashuri · Borjomi · Akhaltsikhe · Khulo · Vale · Akhalkalaki · Marneuli · Rustavi · Shulaveri

Trabzon · Rize · Of · Gümüşhane · Bayburt · Erzurum · Erzincan · Kars · Ağrı · Iğdır · Van · Van Gölü · Elâzığ · Malatya · Diyarbakır · Batman · Siirt · Hakkâri

Gyumri · Vanadzor · Sevan · Sevana Lich · Hrazdan · Ararat · Martuni · Goris · Kapan · NAXÇIVAN · Naxçıvan · Culfa · Ordubad

Gäncä · Xanlar · Mingäçevir · Ağdam · Xankändi · Nagorno-Karabakh · Rüd-e Aras (Aras) · Sumqayıt · Maştağa · Şaki · Quba · Xaçmaz · Länkäran · Astara

Tabriz · Ardabīl · Rasht · Orūmīyeh (Urmia) · Daryācheh-ye Orūmīyeh (Lake Urmia) · Marāgheh · Mīāneh · Zanjān · Hamadān · Bākhtarān · Borūjerd · Khorramābād · Sanandaj · As Sulaymānīyah · Kirkūk · Arbīl · Al Mawşil (Mosul) · Ar Raqqah · Dayr az Zawr · Al Jazīrah (Mesopotamia) · Karbalā · An Najaf · Al Amārah

100   100   200   300   400   500   600 km
100   100   200   300   400 miles

1   35   2   40   3   45   4   50   5   55   6   60   7

LEBANON
BAYRÛT (BEIRUT)
SYRIA
DIMASHQ (DAMASCUS)
Jabal ad Durûz 1801
ISRAEL
Tel Aviv-Yafo
Ashdod
Hems
AMMAN
Bûr Sa'îd (Port Said) Gaza Strip
Qanâ es Suweis
Ismâ'îliya
El Suweis (Suez)
Jerusalem
West Bank
JORDAN
Ma'an
Elat
Al 'Aqabah
Es Sinâ'
G. Mûsa 2637
Khalîg el Suweis
EGYPT
Hurghada
2187
Bûr Safâga
Al Muwaylih
Tabûk 2578
IRAQ
Ar Rutbah
Al Najaf
Karbalâ
BAGHDÂD
Mesopotamia
Nahr Dijlah
Nahr al Furât
An Nâşirîyah
Al Amarah
Al Başrah
Abâdân
Khorramshahr
IRAN
EŞFAHÂN 4548
Ahvâz
Yazd
Birjand
Farâh
AFGHANISTAN
Zâbol
Zâhedân
Bam
Kermân
Dasht-e Lut
Daryâcheh-ye Seistan
Al Jawf
Rafhâ
Hafar al Bâtin
Al-Kuwayt
KUWAIT
J. Khârk
Bûbiyân
Kâzerûn
Büshehr
Deyyer
Jahrom
Neyrîz
Shirâz
Al Qatîf
Ad Dammâm
BAHRAIN
Al Manâmah
QATAR
Al Mubarraz
Al Hufûf
Ad Dawhah (Doha)
Dubayy (Dubai)
Abû Zaby (Abu Dhabi)
Ash Shâriqah
Ra's al-Khaymah
Ra's Musandam (Oman)
Bandâr 'Abbâs
Qeshm
Khamir
Str. of Hormuz
Gâbrik
Bampûr
The Gulf
Hasa
SAUDI
An Nafûd
Hâ'il
Burayda
'Unayzah
Hijâz
Al Wajh
Buraydah
AR RIYÂD (RIYADH)
Haraq
Al 'Ubaylah
Gulf of Oman
Suhâr
3019
Matrah
Masqat
Nazwâ
Şûr
Ra's al Hsed
Khalûf
Khalîj Maşîrah
Maşîrah
UNITED ARAB EMIRATES
OMAN
Al Madînah
Tropic of Cancer
Yanbu 'al Bahr
Ras Bânâs
Bîr Shalatein
ARABIA
Rābigh
Ras Hadarba
Halaib
Halib
Makkah (Mecca)
JIDDAH (JEDDA)
Muhammad Qol 2259
At Tâ'if 2565
Âl Lîth
Turabah
Laylá
As Sulayyil
Es Sahrâ en Nûbiya
Kosha
Delgo
3rd Cataract
Dongola
4th Cataract
Kareima
Ed Debba
Abu Hamed
Wadi Halfa
Buheirat en Naser
RED SEA
Bûr Sûdân
Suakin
Sinkat
Trinkitat
Haiya
Karora 2180
Nakfa
Adarama
Atbara
Berber
Nahr 'Atbara
Wad Hamid
Shendî
6th Cataract
5th Cataract
Abhâ
Jîzân
Farasân
Dahlak Kebir
Massawa
Zula
Kamaran
Al Luhayyah
Khamir
Al Hudaydah
Nişâb
YEMEN
2469
Shibâm
Hadramawt
Salâlah
Mirbât
Râs Fartak
Sayhût
Rub' al Khâlî (Empty Quarter)
Zufâr
Ra's al Madrakah
J. Khurîyâ Murîyâ
Omdurmân
El Khartûm (Khartoum)
Kassalâ
Khashm el Girba
Asmera
Akordat
Adigrat
-116
ERITREA
Danakil Desert
Sana'
Ta'izz
Djebel Manar 3350
Hanish
Aseb
Al Mukhâ
Bab el Mandeb
Al' Adan (Aden)
Shaqrâ
Ahwar
Al Mukallâ
Abd al Kûri
Socotra (Yemen)
Hadiboh
Gulf of Aden
Berbera
Bosaso
Ras Asir
Bereda
Erigavo 2406
El Gal
Dante
Ras Hafun
El Dueim
Wad Medanî
Gedaref
El Obeid
Umm Ruwaba
Ed Damazin
Singa
Kôstî
Gezira
Nîl el Azraq
SUDAN
Aksum
Adwa
Mekele
Ras Dashen 4620
Gonder
Lalibela 4190
L. Tana
Bâhir Dar
Debre Tabor
Debre Markos
Bure
Dese
Tendaho
Dikhil
L. Abbé
-155
DJIBOUTI
Tadjoura
Zeila
Karin
Dire Dawa
Hargeisa
Burao
Gardo
Bender Beila
Eil
Las Anod
Garoe
SOMALI REP.
Malakâl
Sobat
Sûdd
Bahr el Jebel
Nekemte
ADDIS ABEBA
3202
Debre Zeyit
Awash
Nazret
3381
Harer
Jijiga
Dembidolo
Metu
Gore
ETHIOPIA
Ziway
Asela
Shashemene
Ginir
Goba
Kebri Dehar
Ogaden
Galcaio
Jima
3686
Awasa
Yirga Alem
Mt. Batu 4307
Imi
Scebeli
Sinadogo
Obbia
Omo
L. Abaya
Dila
Kibre Mengist
Arba Minch
L. Shamo
Negele
Genale
Ferfer
El Dere
Bôr
Pibor Post
Tali Post
Juba
Mongalla
Kapoeta
Chew Bahir
375
L. Turkana
Lokitaung
Dolo
Lugh Ganana
Bardera
Belet Uen
Bur Acaba
Baidoa
INDIAN OCEAN
Yei
Arua
Gulu
Lira
Moroto
2484
219
Pakwach
Murchison Falls
Kojo Kaji
3187
Torit
Lodwar
South Horr
Mega
Moyale
El Wak
Wajir
Marsabit
Dif
Merca
MUQDISHO (MOGADISHU)
Wabi Scebeli
Giuba
UGANDA
L. Albert
Masindi
Soroti
4321
L. Kyoga
Mbale
3206
Kitale
KENYA
3084
ft m
12 000 4000
9000 3000
6000 2000
4500 1500
3000 1000
1200 400
600 200
0 0
200 600
1000 3000
2000 6000
4000 12 000
m ft

Projection: Sanson-Flamsteed's Sinusoidal

1 35 2 East from Greenwich 3 40 4 45 5 50 6

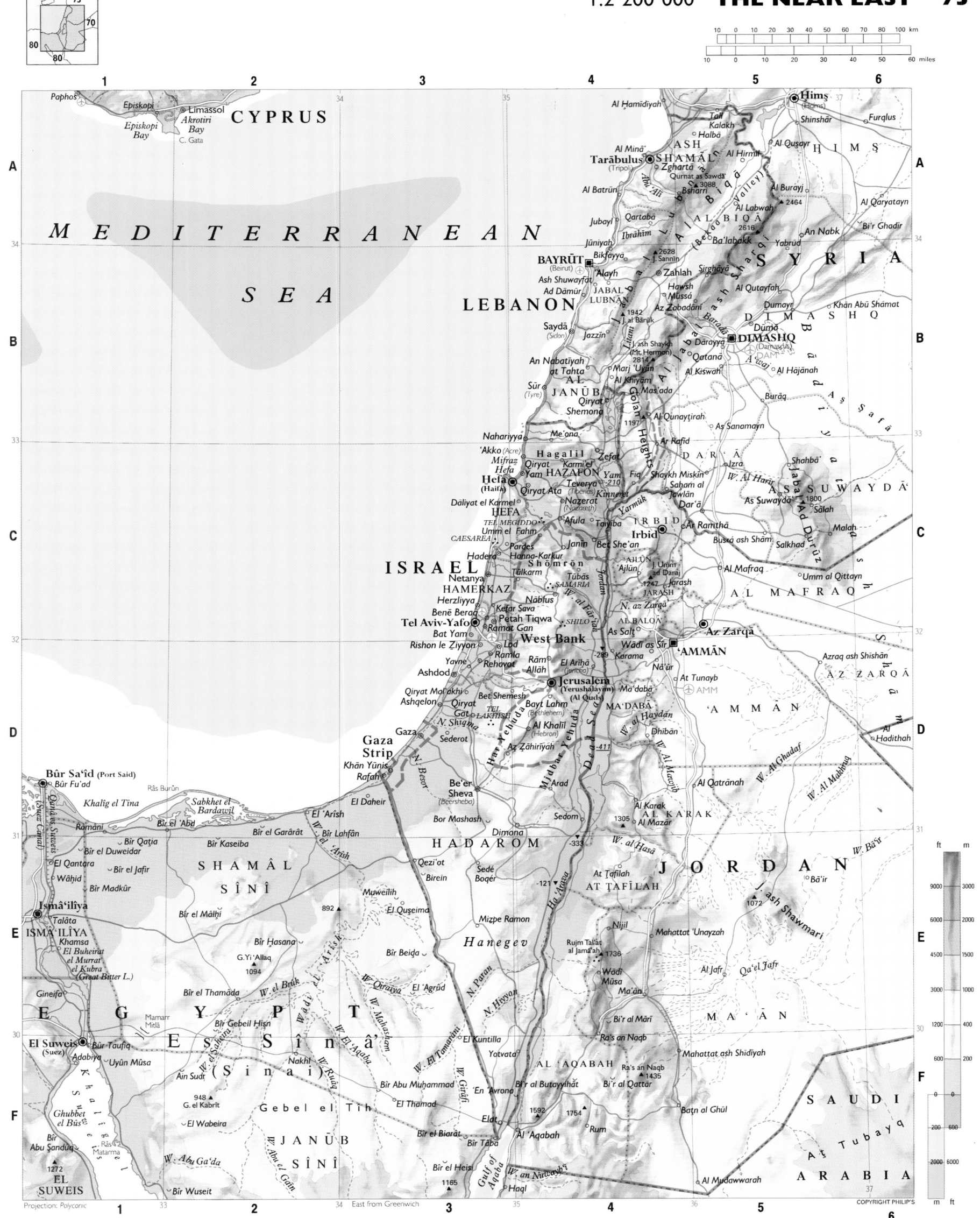

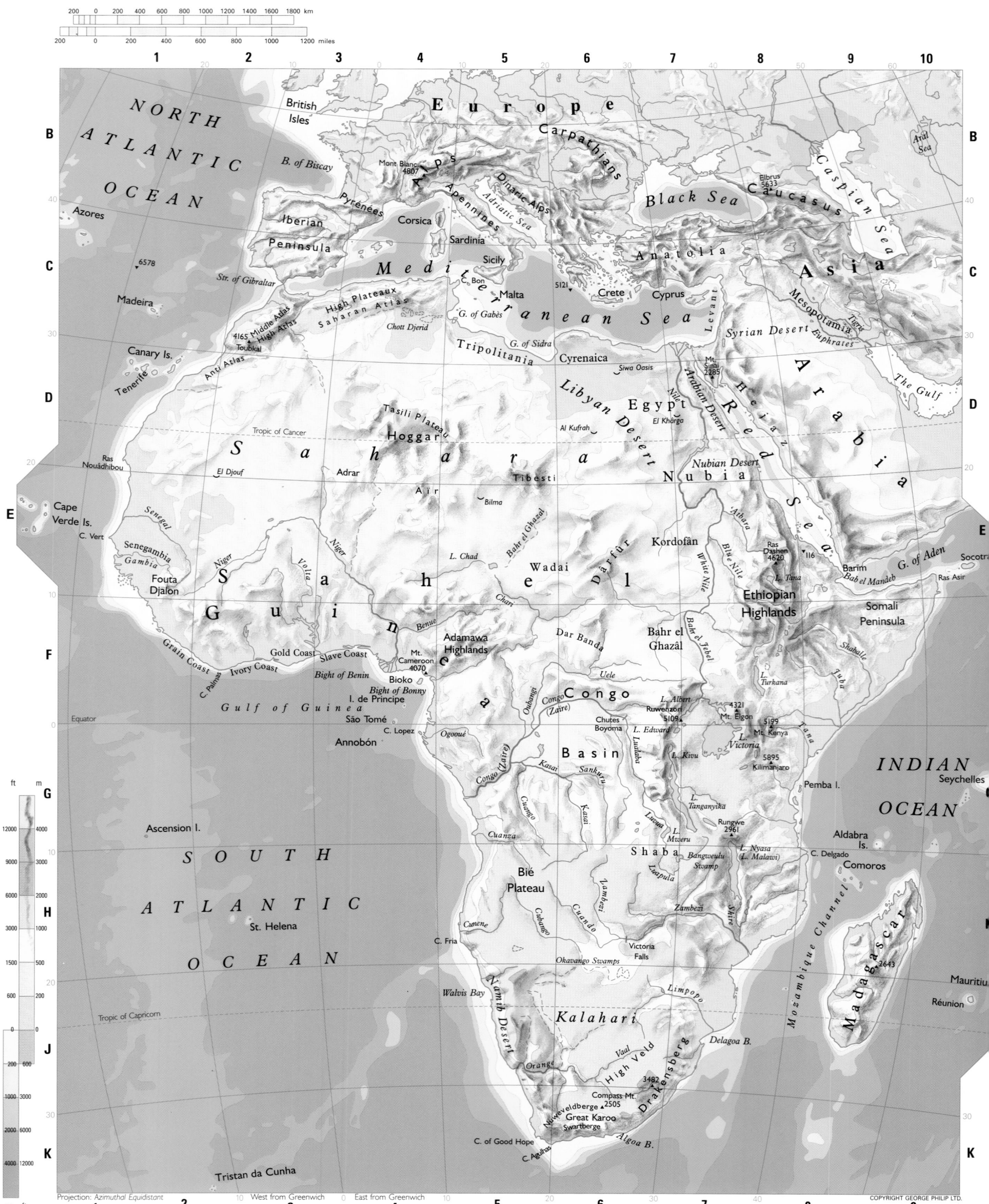

Projection: Azimuthal Equidistant

Projection: Azimuthal Equidistant

● Dakar Capital Cities

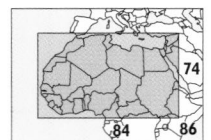

8   9   10   11   12   13   14

ariana
CARTHAGE
TUNIS   Sicilia   **TURKEY**   Antalya   **ADANA**
Bizerte   Nabeul   **GREECE**   Ródhos   Antakya   **HALAB**
Béja   Sousse   **MALTA**   Iráklion   **CYPRUS**   Al Lādhiqīyah   **A**
uan   Mahdia   Valletta   Kríti   Nicosia   **SYRIA**
   Sfax   Tarābulus   Hims
Golfe de Gabès   **M E D I T E R R A N E A N   S E A**   **LEBANON**   **IRAQ**
   Île de Djerba   **BAYRŪT**   **DIMASHQ**   Ar Rutbah   **B**
edenine   Zarzis   Zāwiyat al Baydā   Darnah   **ISRAEL**   (Beirut)   (Damascus)   Jabal ad   **Bādiyat**
houine   Zuwārah   **Tarābulus** (Tripoli)   El Mahalla el Kubra   Tel Aviv-Yafo   Hefa   Druz
   Az Zāwiyah   Al Khums   **Banghāzī**   Al Marj   Damanhūr   Ashdod   **AMMĀN**   ash Shām
hibat   Gharyān   Misrātah   Suluq   Tubruq   **EL ISKANDARĪYA**   Dumyât   Jerusalem   **JORDAN**
   Mizdah   Surt   968   Bardīyah   Salūm   (Alexandria)   **Bûr Saʿid**   West
Daraj   **Khalīj**   Ajdābiyā   Marsā   El Mansūra   Bank
âdâmis   **Tripolitania**   **Surt**   Matrûh   El Alamein   Qanâ es Suweis   Maʿân   Al Jawf
   Hūn   **C y r e n a i c a**   Tantâ   **Ismaʿilīya**   **SAUDI**
   Zillah   Al Jaghbūb   Zagazig   **El Suweis**   Elât
L I B Y A   Awjilah   Sīwa   -133   Munkhafed   **EL GIZA**   **EL QAHIRA**   Al ʿAqabah   Tabūk
   Brach   el Qattâra   Helwān   El Suweis   (Cairo)   2578   **ARABIA**   **C**
Idehan   **S a h r â'**   El Faiyûm   Es   2637
Awbārī   Sabhah   **E G Y P T**   Beni Suef   G. Musa   Al Muwaylih
   ▲1200   Maghâgha   Sinâ
   Awbārī   Marzūq   **L î b î y a**   El Minyâ   Es Sahrā   Hurghada
F e z z a n   Mallawi   Esh Sharqīya   Al Wajh
Ghat   Waw al Kabir   Manfalūt   Asyût   2187   Bûr Safâga
   Al Qatrūn   Qasr Farâfra   Tahta   Sohâg
   a   Girga   Qena   Quseir
   Sahrâ'   El Wâhât   KARNAK   **R E D**   **Hijaz**
   Rebiana   el-Dakhla   Mût   El Khârga   THEBES   El Uqsur   Al Wajh
   Al Kufrah   El Wâhât   Idfû
   Al Jawf   el-Khârga   Kom Ombo   Ras Bânâs   Yanbuʿ   **D**
   a   1082   Sadd el Aali   Aswân   al Bahr
Aozou   J. Uweinat   Buheirat   Bîr   Râbigh
Toummo   1893   ABU SIMBEL   en Naser   Shalatein
Madama   Bardai   Ma'tan   Wadi Halfa   Halaib   Ras Hadarba
Chirfa   Pic Toussidé   ▲3150   as Sarra   El Wâhât   **E s   S a h r â**   **S E A**
   3265   Tarso Emissi   el Selîma   2259
   T i b e s t i   Zouar   Kosha   **e n   N û b i y a**   Muhammad   **B**
Fachi   Emi Koussi   **S t r i p**   Delgo   Qol   **Bûr**
   3415   3rd Cataract   Abu Hamed   **Sûdân**
Bilma   **B o r k o u**   Dongola   Suakin   **E**
   Grand Erg du Bilma   Bir 'Atrun   Kareima   4th Cataract   Sinkat   Trinkitât
   Ouniânga Sérir   Ed Debba   5th Cataract   Haiya   Karora
   Faya-Largeau   **Dépression du Mourdi**   Berber   2180
   E r g   d u   D j o u r a b   Fada   1310   Atbara   Adarama   Nakfa
   E n n e d i   Wad   **ERITREA**
   Oum Chalouba   **Z a g a o u a**   Hamid   6th Cataract   Shendi   Akordat
C H A D   Malha   **S U D A N**   El Khashm el Girba
   Zigey   1954   El Wuz   **El Khartûm**   Kassalâ   **F**
Nguigmi   Biltine   Kutum   Sodiri   Omdurmân   (Khartoum)   **El**
Mao   Moussoro   Al   Umm   Ed Dueim   **Gezira**   Wâd Medanî
Bosso   **Lac Tchad**   Ati   Junaynah   Keddada   Gedaref   Gonder
Gashua   Massakory   Abéché   El Fâsher   En Nahud   El Obeid   Kôstî   1830
Geidam   Chari   Bokoro   Mongo   Goz Beïda   Nyâlâ   Umm Ruwaba   Singa   L. Tana
Maiduguri   **Ndjamena**   Massenya   Abou-Deïa   Jebel   Abû   Er Rahad   Bahir
Potiskum   Kousseri   Am Timan   Marra   Zabad   Dar
Bama   Bajoga   Massaguet   3088   El Odaiya   1325   Ed Damazin   Bure
Biu   Maroua   Bongor   **D a r f û r**   Kâdugli   Debre
Kumo   Mubi   Guider   Birao   Nyâlâ   Markos   **G**
Numan   Garoua   Logone   Sarh   Songa   Bahr el Arab   Malakâl   Nekemte
Yola   Pala   Laï   1226   3202   **ETHIOPIA**
   Moundou   Koumra   Ndélé   Saʿid   Dembidolo   3686
gashaka   Doba   Bundas   **B a h r   e l**   Gogriâl   Metu   Jima
sif   Baïbokoum   Raga   **G h a z â l**   Wâw   Gore   Jima
maoua   Bétaré   Kaga Bandoro   **C E N T R A L   A F R I C A N**   Rumbêk   Bôr   3686
Banyo   Oya   Bouar   Yalinga   **R E P U B L I C**   Tonj   Pibor Post   L. Abaya
Kumba   Ngaoundéré   Bossangoa   Ippy   Toinya   Arba Minch   **G**
EROON   Bozoum   Sibut   Bakouma   Amâdi   Tali Post   L. Shamo
   Yoko   Carnot   Bambari   Obo   El Istiwa'iya   Mongalla   Chew
   Bertoua   Bossembélé   Bangassou   Juba   Bahir
Yaoundé   Abong-Mbang   **Bangui**   Zongo   Bosobolo   Bomu   Yâmbiô   Kapoeta   3187
   Mbaïki   Libenge   Mobaye   Bondo   Yei   Kajo Kaji   Torit   Lokitaung   L.
   Mobayi   Uele   Dungu   Faradje   Ango   Turkana   **H**
   375
   COPYRIGHT GEORGE PHILIP LTD.

8   9   10   11   12   13

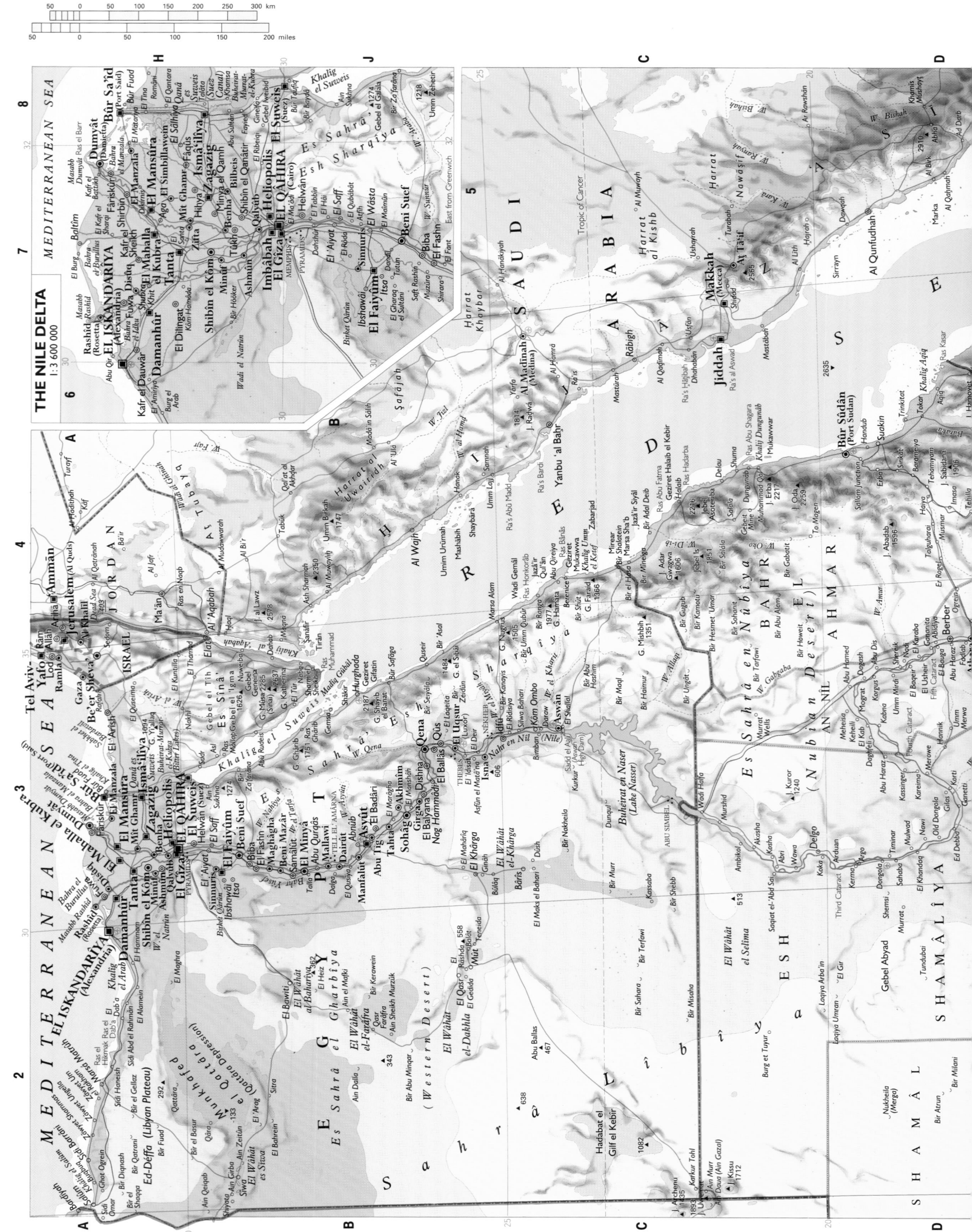

THE NILE DELTA
1:3 600 000

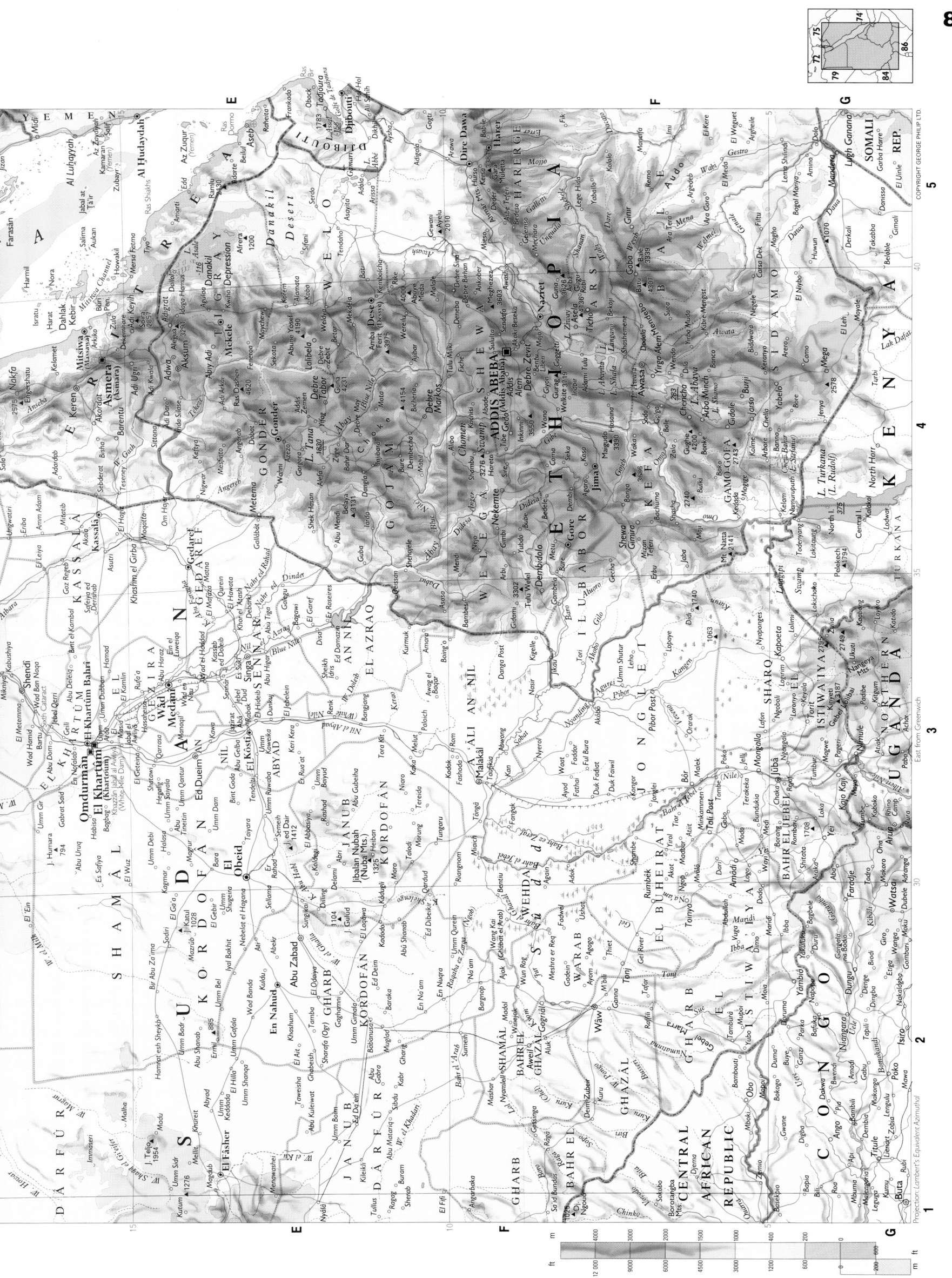

81

Projection : *Lambert's Equivalent Azimuthal*

West from Greer

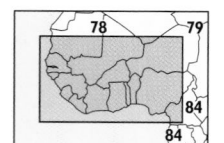

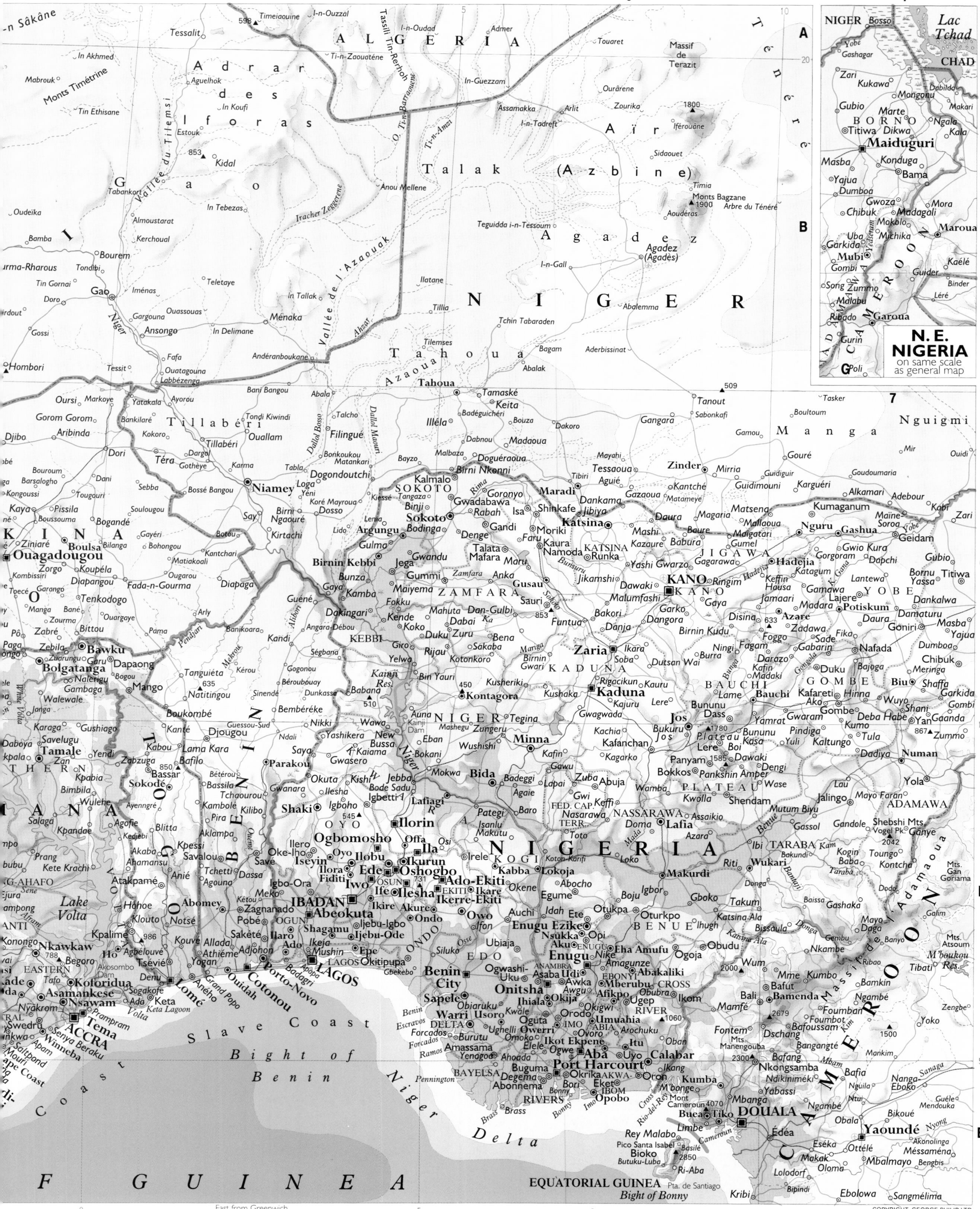

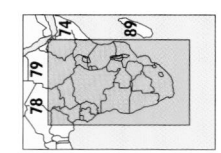

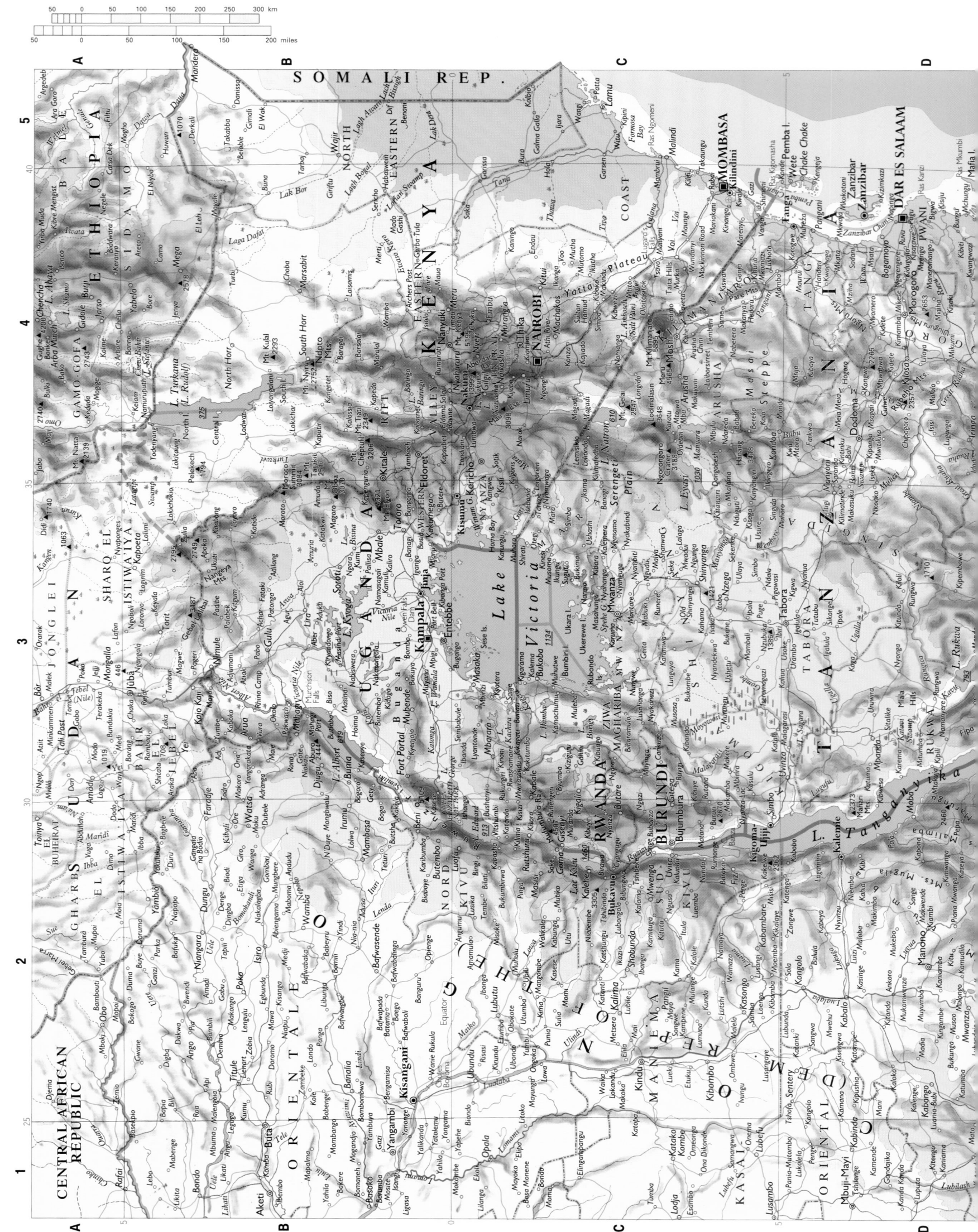

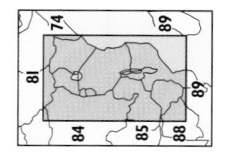

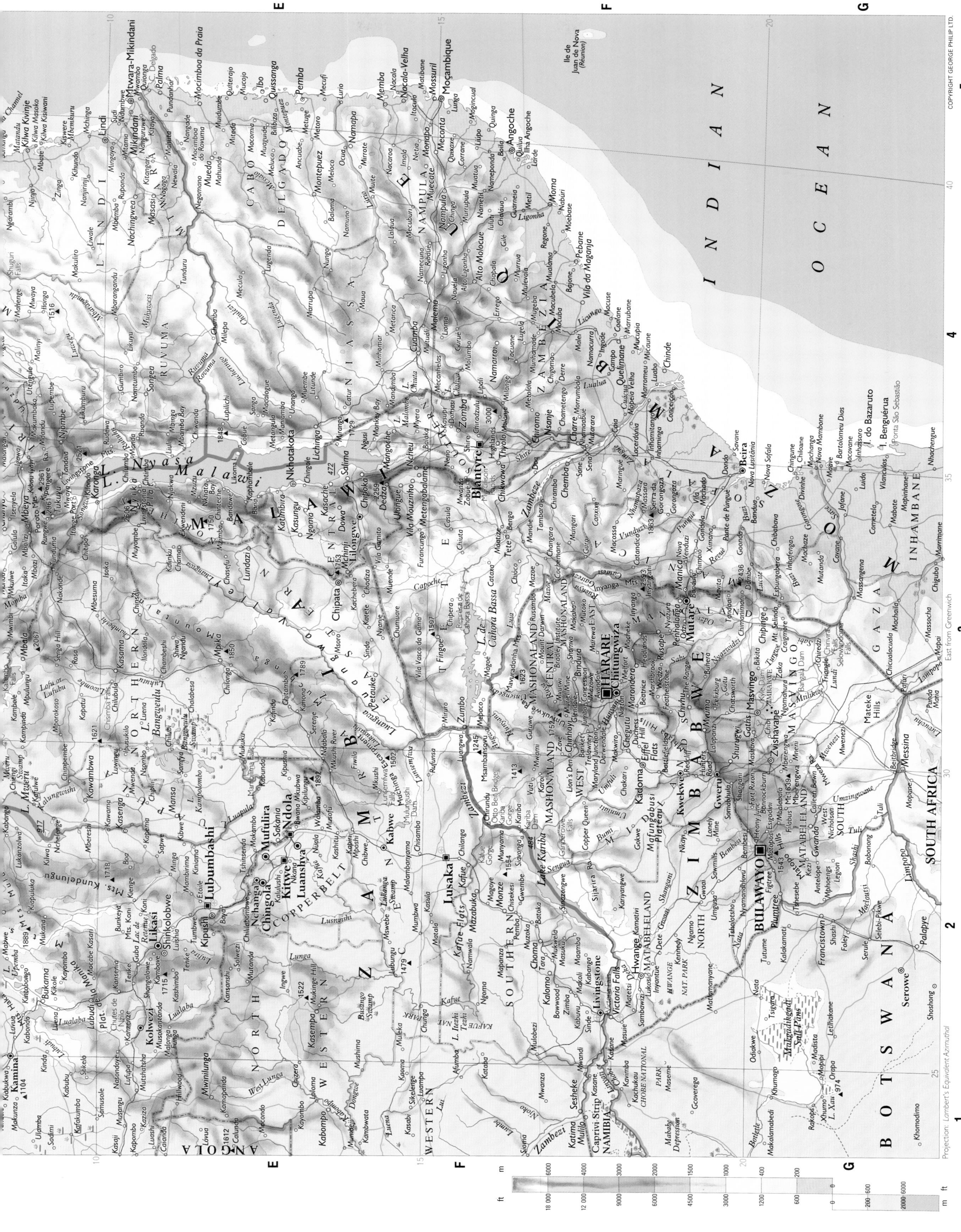

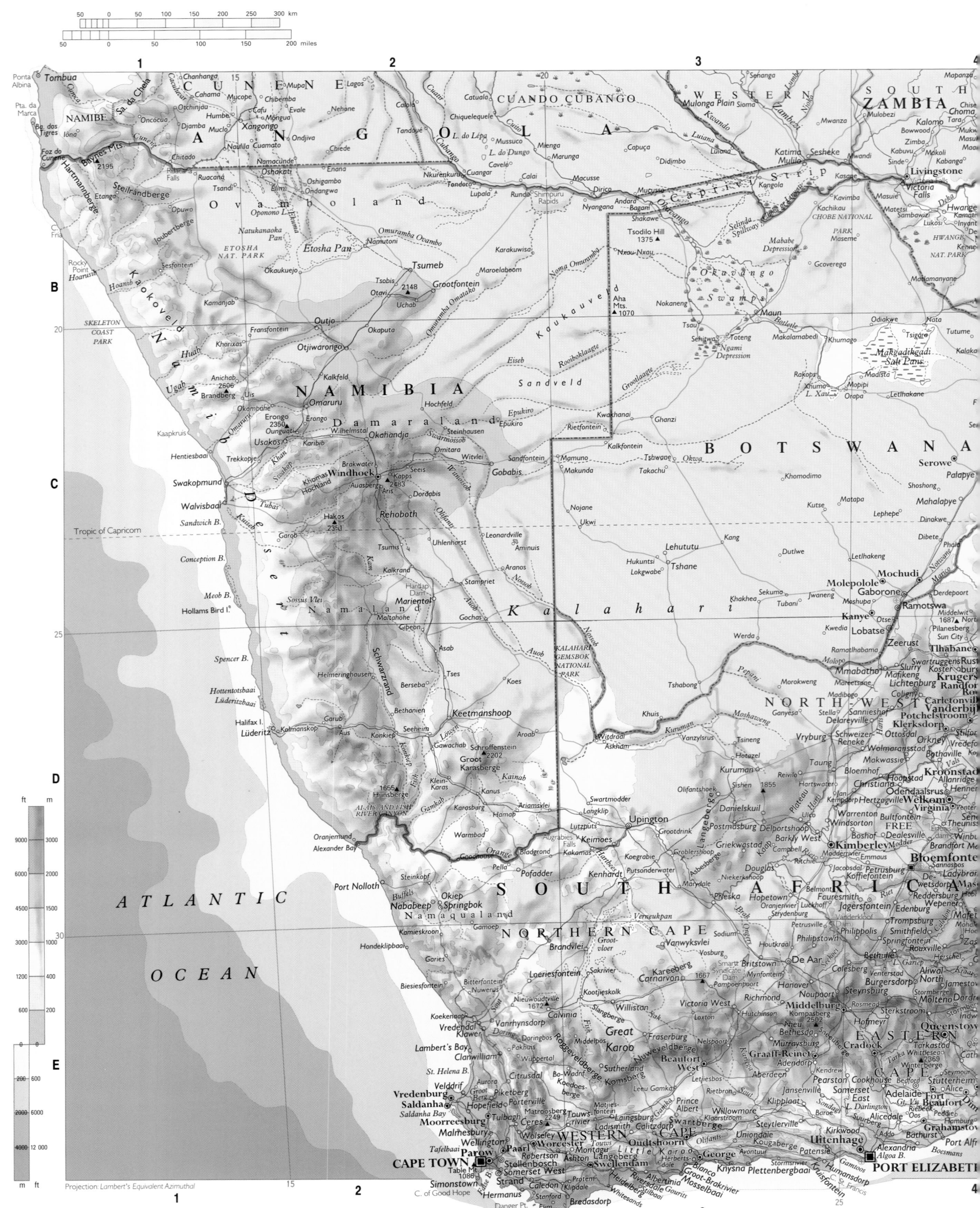

50 0 50 100 150 200 250 300 km
50 0 50 100 150 200 miles

1 **2** **3** **4**

Ponta
Albina
Tombua
Pta. da
Marca
NAMIBE
Ba. dos
Tigres
Iona
Foz do
Cunene
C.
Fria
Rocky
Point
Hoanib

CUNE NE
Chanhanga
Cahama
Mucope
Mupa
Lagos
Nehone
Evale
Chibemba
Djamba
Mucio
Xangongo
Ondjiva
Cuamato
Namacunde
Roçadas
Ruacaná
Tsandi
Oshakati
Oshigambo
Ondangwa
Elim

A N G O L A
Catuala
Calola
Cuangar
Cuito Cuanavale
Chiquelequele
Cuando
Cubango
Mussoco
L. do Lépa
Mienga
Capuça
Dirico
Macusse
Shimpuru
Rapids
Nyangana
Andara
Bagani
Shakawe

CUANDO CUBANGO
Senanga
Mulonga Plain Sioma
Luiana
Luiana
Didimbo
Mucusso
Kongola
Katima
Mulilo
Kabuyu

WESTERN
Mwanza
Mulobezi
Sesheke
Mwandi
Sinde
Masuie
Matetsi

SOUTH
ZAMBIA
Mapanza
Chisekesi
Kalomo
Tara
Bowwood
Choma
Kabuyu
Masuku
Livingstone
Victoria
Falls
Kazungula
Kasane

Natukanaoka
Pan
Oponono L.
Ovamboland
Omuramba Ocambo
Namutoni
Karakuwisa

ETOSHA
NAT. PARK
Etosha Pan
Okaukuejo
Tsumeb
Maroelaboom

Noma Omuramba
Nkurenkuru
Cuangar
Runtu
Rundu

Okavango
Capriv i Strip
Kavimba
Kachikau
Kasungula

CHOBE NATIONAL
PARK
Maseme

HWANGE
NAT. PARK
Hwange
Kamativi
Inyanti
Lukosi
Dete

Sesfontein
Kamanjab
Tsobis
Otavi
Uchab
Grootfontein
Aha
Mts.
1070
Nokaneng
Tsau
Gcoverega
Maun
Batletle

Okavango
Swamps
Sehitwa
Toteng
Ngami
Depression

Tsodilo Hill
1375

Odiakwe
Nata
Tutume
Tsigre
Makalamabedi
Khumaga

Makgadikgadi
Salt Pans
Rakops
Madisa
L. Xau
Orapa
Letlhakane

SKELETON
COAST
PARK
Khorixas
Fransfontein
Outjo
Okaputa
Otjiwarongo
Hochfeld

B

20

Kaokoveld
Hoanib
Huab
Anichab
2606
Brandberg
Okombahe
Uis
Omaruru
Erongo
2350
Ounguati
Erongo
Wilhelmstal
Okahandja
Epukiro
Epukiro

Kaukauveld
Eiseb
Rooibokiaagte
Groolaagte
Sandveld

BOTSWANA
Serowe
Palapye
Shoshong
Mahalapye
Dinokwe
Dibete

Ghanzi
Kalkfontein
Rietfontein
Kwakhanai
Xhumo
Mopipi

NAMIBIA
Khomas
Hochland
Windhoek
Kapps
Seeis
2483
Auasberg
Aris
Dordabis

Damaraland
Swartmodder
Omitara
Witvlei
Gobabis
Sandfontein
Mamuno
Makunda
Takachu

Kaapkruis
Usakos
Karibib
Khan
Trekkopje

C

Swakopmund
Walvisbaai
Sandwich B.

N a m i b
Kuiseb
Tubas
Hakos
2351
Rehoboth

D e s e r t
Garob
Tsumis
Olifants
Leonardville
Aminuis
Kang
Werda

Tropic of Capricorn
Conception B.
Uhlenhorst
Ukwi
Lehututu
Lokgwabe
Tshane
Letlhakeng

Hukuntsi
Dutlwe
Khakhea
Sekuma
Jwaneng
Meshupa
Tubani
Kwedia

Mochudi
Molepolole
Gaborone
Ramotswa
Kanye
Lobatse
Zeerust

Meob B.
Kalkrand
Stampriet
Kam
Hardap Dam
Mariental
Gibeon
Maltahohe

Namaland
Schwarzrand
Helmeringhausen
Asab
Tses
Koes
Nossob

Kalahari
Auob
Gochas
Aranos

KALAHARI
GEMSBOK
NATIONAL
PARK
Khuis
Kuruman

NORTH-WEST
Mmabatho
Mafikeng
Lichtenburg
Koster
Krugersdorp
Randfontein
Carletonville
Vanderbijl

D

Spencer B.
Hottentotsbaai
Lüderitzbaai
Halifax I.
Lüderitz
Kolmanskop
Bethanien
Berseba
Seeheim
Keetmanshoop
Löffen
Gawachab
Schroffenstein
2202
Groot
Karasberge
Kainab
Aroab
Koichas
Kanus
Karasburg
Hamab
Ariamsvlei
Swartmodder
Langklip
Askham
Kakamas
Upington
Keimoes
Grootdrink
Groblershoop
Olifantshoek
Sishen
1855
Danielskuil
Postmasburg
Delportshoop
Kuruman
Hotazel
Reivilo
Vryburg
Taung
Stella
Reneke
Schweizer
Ottosdal
Makwassie
Bloemhof
Christiana
Klerksdorp
Orkney
Odendaalsrus
Hennenman
Kroonstad
Allanridge
Welkom
Virginia
Ventersburg

Hunsberge
1655
Klein-
Karas
Gamkab
Fish
Karasburg

ALAIS AND FISH
RIVER CANYON

Oranjemund
Alexander Bay
Port Nolloth
Steinkopf
Buffels
Okiep
Nababeep
Springbok

Namaqualand
Warmbad
Orange
Goodhouse
Pella
Pofadder
Kakamas
Koegrabie
Putsonderwater
Marydale
Niekerkshoop
Douglas
Ritchie
Campbell
Modderrivier
Kimberley
Jacobsdal
Petrusburg

FREE
Bultfontein
Warrenton
Windsorton
Boshof
Dealesville
Brandfort
Bloemfontein
Ladybrand

E

30

ATLANTIC

OCEAN

Hondeklipbaai
Kamieskroon
Garies
Springbok
Gamoep
Bitterfontein
Nuwerus
Biesiesfontein
Koekenaap
Vanrhynsdorp
Nieuwoudtville
1672
Calvinia
Loeriesfontein
Sakrivier
Brandvlei
Groot-
vloer
Vanwyksvlei
Carnarvon
1667
Kareeberg
Smartt
Syndicate
Dam
Pampoenpoort
Victoria West
Richmond
Loxton
Britstown
De Aar
Hanover
Noupoort
Colesberg
Petrusville
Hopetown
Strydenburg
Oranjerivier
Luckhoff
Jagersfontein
Fauresmith
Koffiefontein
Philippolis
Springfontein
Trompsburg
Edenburg
Reddersburg
Smithfield
Rouxville
Bethulie
Aliwal
North

Doring
Klawer
Vredendal
Klawer
Citrusdal
Clanwilliam
Wupperthal
Middelpos
Sutherland
Fraserburg
Willistan
Slangberg
Beaufort
West
Nieu
Bethesda
Graaff-Reinet
Aberdeen
Murraysburg
Nelspoort
Kompasberg
2502
Pearston
Somerset
East

St. Helena B.
Lambert's Bay
Aurora
Velddrif
Vredenburg
Saldanha
Saldanha Bay
Moorreesburg
Malmesbury
Wellington
Tulbagh
Piketberg
Hopefield
Porterville
Matroosberg
2249
Ceres
Tafelbaai
Worcester
Paarl
Robertson
Parow
Stellenbosch
Somerset West
Strand

CAPE TOWN
Table Mt.
1086
Simonstown
C. of Good Hope
Danger Pt.
Hermanus
Ouoin Pt.
C. Agulhas
Caledon
Bredasdorp
Stanford

WESTERN
CAPE
Montagu
Ashton
Swellendam
Heidelberg
Klipdale
Protem
Whitesands
Riversdale
Albertinia
Mosselbaai

Great
Karoo
Little Karoo
Oudtshoorn
George
Knysna
Plettenbergbaai
Groot-Brakrivier
Humansdorp
Gouritz
Stormsrivier
Avontuur
Uniondale
Willowmore
Steytlerville
Prince
Albert
Baroe
Klipplaat
Kirkwood
Addo
Uitenhage
Alexandria
Alicedale

EASTERN
CAPE
Cradock
Tarkastad
Adendorp
Kendrew
Pearston
Bedford
Adelaide
Fort
Beaufort
Grahamstown
Port Alfred
Bathurst

PORT ELIZABETH
Algoa B.
C. St. Francis

Projection: Lambert's Equivalent Azimuthal

ft   m
9000 3000
6000 2000
4500 1500
3000 1000
1200 400
600   200
0   0
200   600
2000 6000
4000 12 000
m   ft

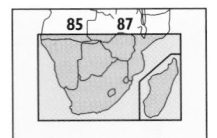

MADAGASCAR

On same scale as General Map

COPYRIGHT GEORGE PHILIP LTD.

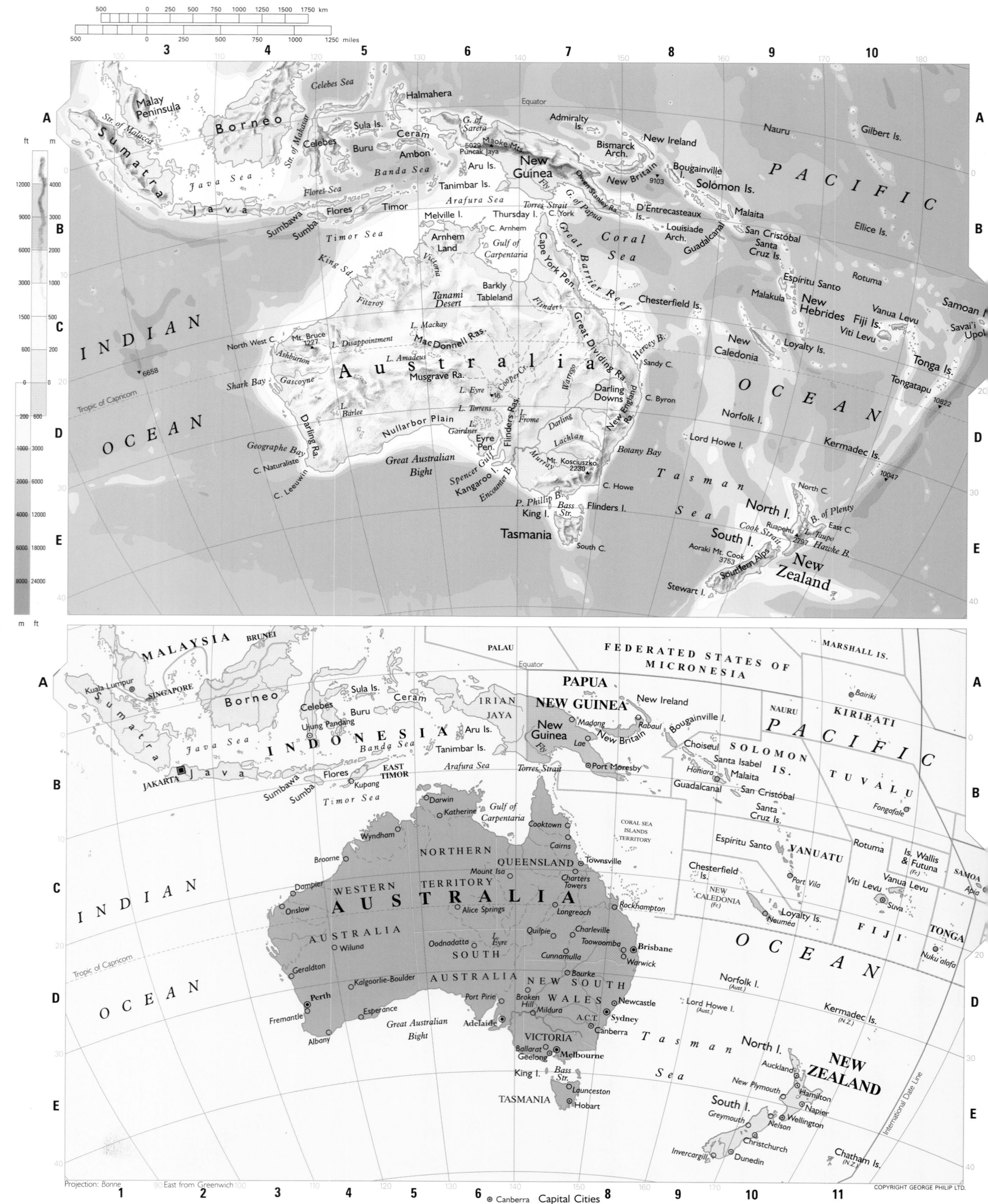

96
96 96
96

50 0 50 100 150 200 km
50 0 50 100 150 miles

PACIFIC OCEAN

TASMAN SEA

North Island

C. Reinga
C. Maria van Diemen
North C.
Houhora Heads
Rangaunu B.
Doubtless B.
Mangonui
Whangaroa Harb.
Ahipara B.
Kaitaia
Tauroa Pt.
Okaihau
B. of Islands
C. Brett
Rawene
Kaikohe
Hikurangi
Hokianga Harbour
Whangarei
Donnelly's Crossing
Whangarei Harb.
Bream Hd.
Dargaville
Waipu
Bream B.
Little Barrier I.
Great Barrier I.
Warkworth
C. Rodney
Helensville
C. Colville
Cuvier I.
Kaipara Harbour
Hauraki Gulf
Coromandel
Takapuna
Devonport
Whitianga
AUCKLAND
Manukau
Papakura
Thames
Waiuku
Pukekohe
Mercer
Mayor I.
Waihi
Waikato
Paeroa
Tauranga Harb.
Huntly
Te Aroha
White I.
C. Runaway
Morrinsville
Mount Maunganui
Bay of Plenty
East C.
Hamilton
Tauranga
Raglan
Cambridge
Te Puke
Whakatane
Te Awamutu
Kawerau
Opotiki
Hikurangi 1753
Raukumara Ra.
Kawhia Harbour
Putaruru
Rotorua
Taneatua
Waipiro
Otorohanga
Tokoroa
L. Rotorua
Murupara
Motu
Te Kuiti
Kinleith
L. Tarawera
Tolaga Bay
Mokau
Mokai
Wairakei
Taupo
Ormond
North Taranaki Bight
Ongarue
L. Taupo
Gisborne
Waitara
Taumarunui
Rangitaiki
L. Waikaremoana
New Plymouth
Inglewood
Whangamomona
Turangi
Poverty Bay
Mt. Taranaki (Mt. Egmont) 2518
Stratford
Ruapehu 2797
Nuhaka
C. Egmont
Ohakune
Waiouru
Wairoa
Opunake
Eltham
Raetihi
Waikokopu
Kapuni
Bay View
Mahia Pen.
Hawera
Waverley
Taihape
Napier
South Taranaki Bight
Patea
Mangaweka
Hawke Bay
Hastings
Wanganui
Hunterville
Waipawa
Morton
Halcombe
Waipukurau
Bulls
Feilding
Dannevirke
Palmerston North
Woodville
Foxton
Shannon
Pahiatua
Levin
Eketahuna
Otaki
C. Turnagain
Paraparaumu
Kapiti I.
Masterton
Upper Hutt
Featherston
Carterton
Petone
Greytown
Lower Hutt
Eastbourne
Martinborough
WELLINGTON
Wairarapa
Cook Strait

South Island

Southern Alps

C. Farewell
Golden B.
Collingwood
D'Urville I.
Takaka
Tasman B.
Tasman Mts.
Motueka
Karamea
Nelson
Havelock
Karamea Bight
Tadmor
Richmond
Picton
Seddonville
Matiri Ra.
Wakefield
Granity
Lyell
Murchison
Blenheim
Westport
Inangahua
Rotoroa
Seddon
Reefton
Mt. Travers 2338
Ward
Blackball
Grey
Spenser Mts.
Tapuaenuku 2885
Runanga
Lewis Pass
Greymouth
Hanmer Springs
Kaikoura
Kumara
Waiau
Hokitika
L. Brunner
Jacksons
Culverden
Waiau
Ross
Arthur's Pass
Waikari
Hurunui
Waipara
Waimak ariri
Amberley
Oxford
Rangiora
Pegasus Bay
Abut Hd.
Coleridge
Kaiapoi
Westland Bight
Springfield
New Brighton
Whitecliffs
Christchurch
Aoraki Mt. Cook 3753
Methven
Riccarton
Lyttelton
Jackson B.
Mount Cook
Staveley
Lincoln
Okuru
Tekapo
Plains
L. Ellesmere
Akaroa
Banks Pen.
Little River
Southbridge
L. Coleridge
Rangitata
Rakaia
Haast
L. Tekapo
Fairlie
Geraldine
Ashburton Bight
Mt. Aspiring 3027
Ohau
Temuka
Mt. Earnslaw 2818
L. Ohau
Wanaka L.
Hakataramea
Timaru
Milford Sd.
Sutherland Falls
Milford Sound
St. Andrews
Bligh Sound
Wanaka
Kurow
Waimate
George Sound
Arrowtown
Dunstan Mts.
Kakanui Mts.
Secretary I.
Queenstown
Cromwell
Tokarahi
Ngapara
Doubtful Sd.
Clyde
Alexandra
Oamaru
Te Anau
Kingston
Naseby
Maheno
Breaksea Sd.
L. Manapouri
Roxburgh
Hampden
Resolution I.
Mossburn
Garvie Mts.
Waikouaiti
Dusky Sd.
Lumsden
Umbrella Mts.
Palmerston
Chalky Inlet
Ohai
Kelso
Port Chalmers
Pegertes
Nightcaps
Edievale
Otago Harbour
Preservation Inlet
Clifden
Winton
Clinton
Mosgiel
Saunders C.
Te Waewae B.
Tuatapere
Hedgehope
Gore
Milton
Lawrence
Fairfield
Riverton
Orepuki
Mataura
Balclutha
Dunedin
Kaitangata
Invercargill
Wyndham
Owaka
Bluff
Tokanui
Nugget Pt.
South Invercargill
Ruapuke I.
Tahakopa
Foveaux Str.
Halfmoon Bay
Stewart I.
Southwest C.
Port Pegasus

Projection : Conical with two standard parallels
East from Greenwich
COPYRIGHT GEORGE PHILIP LTD.

SAMOA ISLANDS
1:10 700 000

SAMOA
AMERICAN SAMOA
Savai'i
Apia
Upolu
Pago Pago
Tutuila
West from Greenwich

FIJI AND TONGA ISLANDS
1:10 700 000

Wallis & Futuna (Fr.)
Futuna
Niuafo'ou (Tonga)
Thikombia
Labasa
Vanua Levu
Vanua Balavu
Yasawa Group
Taveuni
Koro
FIJI
Lautoka 1323
Levuka
Nandi
Ovalau
Lau Group
TONGA (Friendly Is.)
Viti Levu
Gau
Suva
Koro Sea
Lakeba
Vava'u
Moala
Kandavu
Tofua
Vatoa
Tofua
Tongatapu
Nuku'alofa

50 0 50 100 150 200 km
50 0 50 100 150 miles

West from Greenwich

ft m
9000 3000
6000 2000
3000 1000
1200 400
600 200
0 0
200 600
2000 12000
4000
6000 18000
m ft

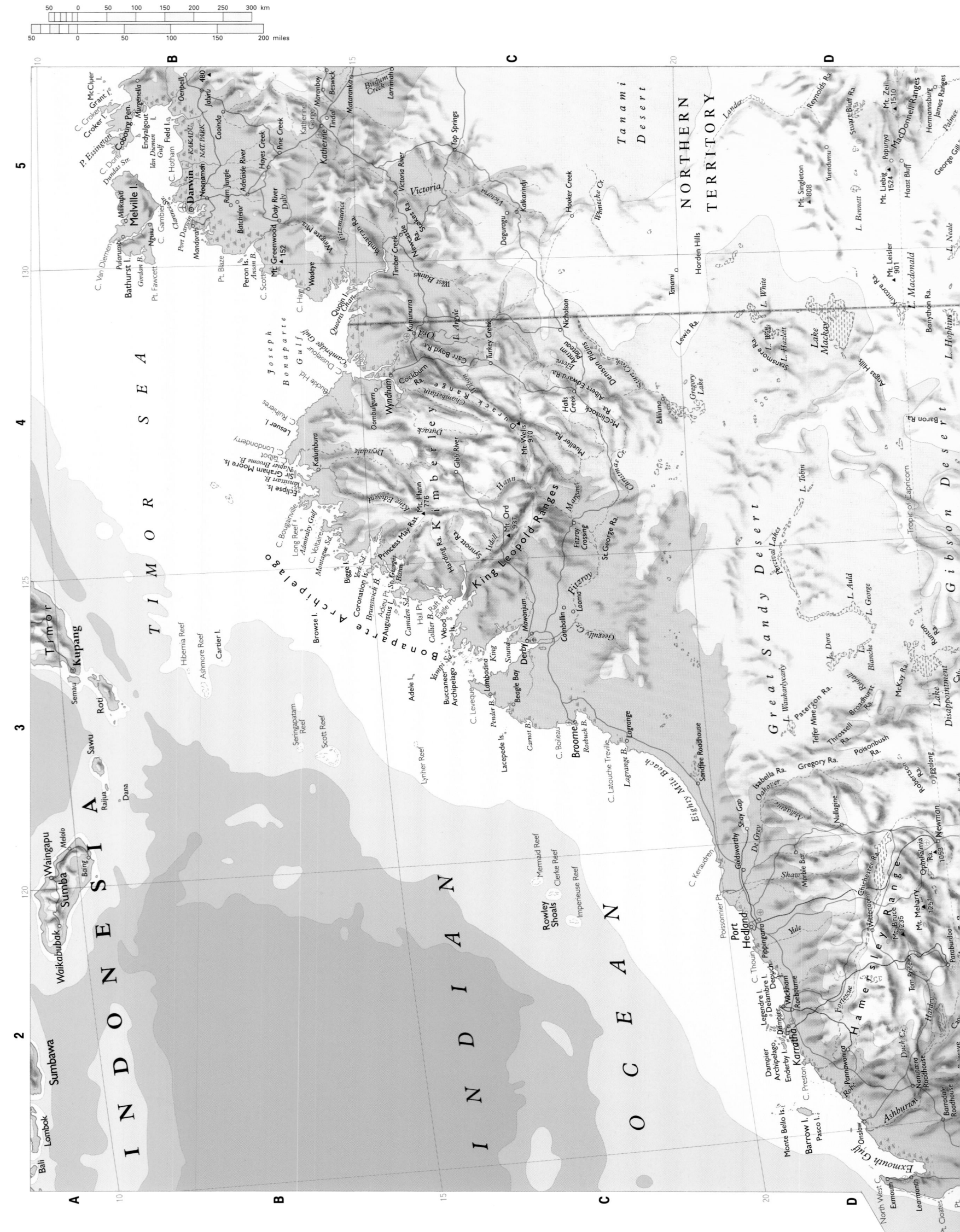

94
95
62

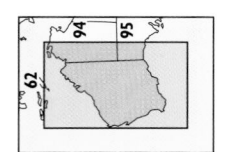

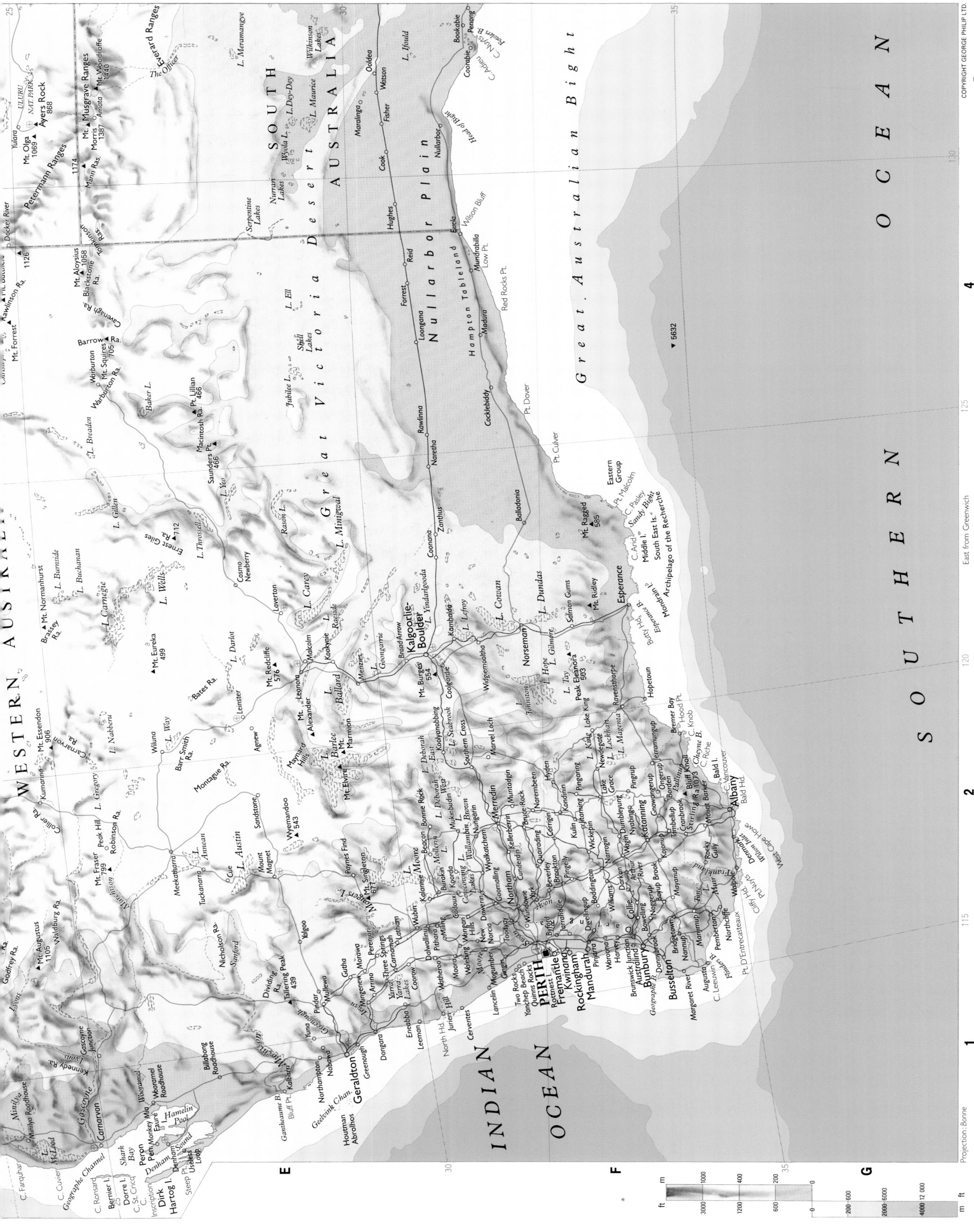

WESTERN AUSTRALIA
SOUTH AUSTRALIA
Great Victoria Desert
Nullarbor Plain
Hampton Tableland
Great Australian Bight
INDIAN OCEAN
SOUTHERN OCEAN
Ayers Rock 868
Mt. Olga 1069
ULURU NAT. PARK
Yulara
Petermann Ranges
Musgrave Ranges
Mt. Woodroffe 1440
Everard Ranges
The Officer
L. Meramangye
Mann Ras.
Docker River
Mt. Aloysius 1058
Blackstone Ra.
Cavenagh Ra.
Rawlinson Ra.
Mt. Forrest
Barrow Ra.
Warburton
Mt. Squires 705
Warburton Ra.
Baker L.
Pt. Lillian 466
Macintosh Ra.
Saunders Pt. 466
L. Breaden
L. Yeo
L. Gillen
Ernest Giles Ra. 712
L. Throssell
Rason L.
L. Minigwal
L. Carey
Cosmo Newberry
Laverton
L. Wells
L. Carnegie
L. Burnside
L. Buchanan
Mt. Normanhurst
Brassey Ra.
Mt. Eureka 499
Mt. Redcliffe 576
Leonora
Malcolm
L. Darlot
Bates Ra.
Leinster
Mt. Essendon 906
Carnarvon Ra.
L. Nabberu
Wiluna
L. Way
Barr Smith Ra.
Agnew
Montague Ra.
Sandstone
Wyemandoo 543
Mount Magnet
Cue
L. Austin
Annean
Meekatharra
Tuckanarra
Peak Hill
Robinson Ra.
Mt. Fraser 799
L. Gregory
Kumarina
Collier Ra.
Mt. Augustus 1105
Waldburg Ra.
Godfrey Ra.
Lyons
Gascoyne
Gascoyne Junction
Kennedy Ra.
Carnarvon
Minilya Roadhouse
L. MacLeod
Wooramel Roadhouse
Hamelin Pool
Shark Bay
Denham
Monkey Mia
Useless Loop
Steep Pt.
Dirk Hartog I.
Dorre I.
Bernier I.
C. Cuvier
C. Farquhar
Geographe Channel
C. Inscription
Kalbarri
Billabong Roadhouse
Murchison
Northampton
Nabawa
Geraldton
Greenough
Geelvink Chan.
Houtman Abrolhos
Gantheaume B.
Bluff Pt.
Yuna
Mullewa
Pindar
Yalgoo
Tallering Peak 439
Dividing Ra.
Nicholson Ra.
Sanford
Dongara
Eneabba
Leeman
Jurien
North Hd.
Cervantes
Lancelin
Two Rocks
Yanchep Beach
Quinns Rocks
PERTH
Fremantle
Rottnest I.
Kwinana
Rockingham
Mandurah
Pinjarra
Waroona
Harvey
Brunswick Junction
Australind
Bunbury
Collie
Donnybrook
Busselton
Geographe B.
Margaret River
Augusta
C. Leeuwin
Pemberton
Northcliffe
Manjimup
Walpole
Denmark
Albany
Mount Barker
Katanning
Narrogin
Northam
York
Merredin
Southern Cross
Kalgoorlie-Boulder
Coolgardie
Kambalda
Norseman
L. Cowan
L. Lefroy
L. Dundas
Salmon Gums
Esperance
Ravensthorpe
Hopetoun
Peak Eleanora 503
Mt. Ragged 585
Archipelago of the Recherche
Balladonia
Zanthus
Coonana
Naretha
Rawlinna
Cocklebiddy
Madura
Loongana
Forrest
Reid
Eucla
Mundrabilla
Hughes
Cook
Fisher
Watson
Ooldea
Maralinga
Nullarbor
Head of Bight
Wilson Bluff
Coorabie
Penong
Bookabie
L. Ifould
Wilkinson Lakes
Pt. Dover
Pt. Culver
Red Rocks Pt.
5632
Projection: Bonne
East from Greenwich
COPYRIGHT GEORGE PHILIP LTD.
E
F
G
1
2
3
4
5
115
120
125
130
25
30
35
m ft
1000 3000
400 1200
200 600
0 0
200 600
2000 6000
4000 12 000

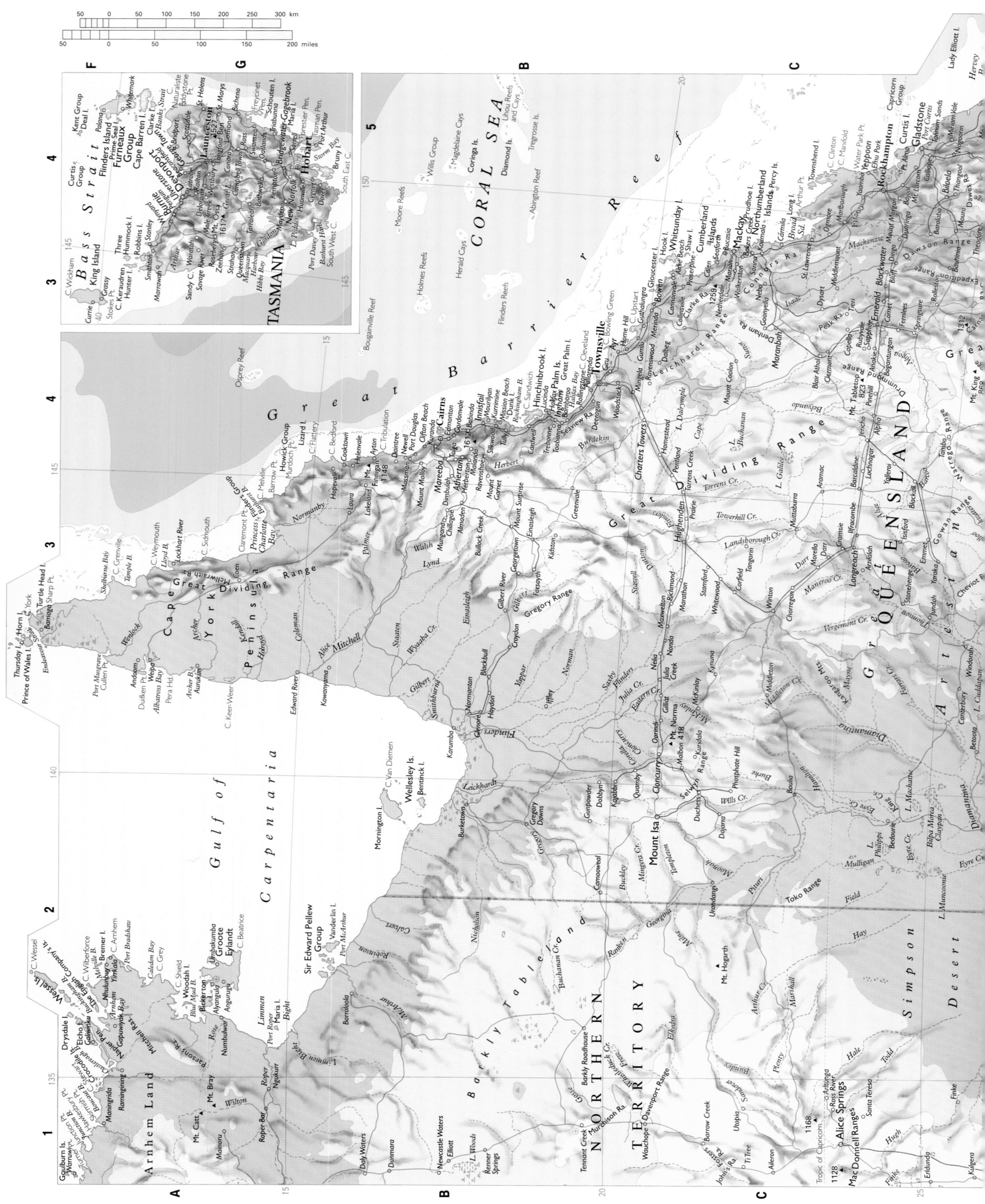

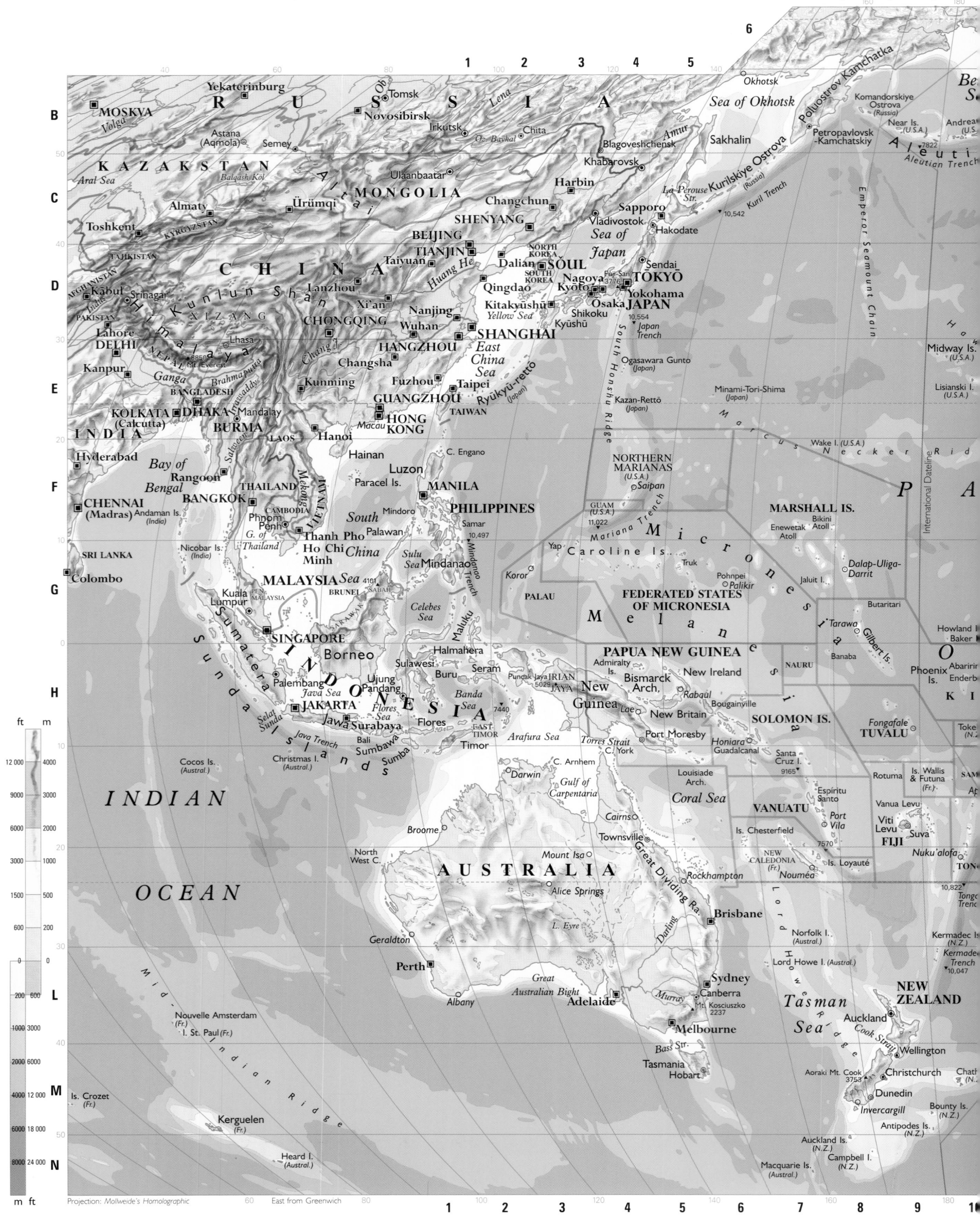

Arctic Circle

ALASKA
(U.S.A.)
Anchorage

Bristol Bay

Gulf of Alaska
Juneau

ROCKY
Prince of Wales I.
(U.S.A.) Prince Rupert
Queen Charlotte Is.
(Canada)

Vancouver
Vancouver I.
Seattle
Portland
Victoria

C A N A D A

Edmonton
Calgary
Regina
Winnipeg
L. Winnipeg

Newfoundland

N O R T H

St. Lawrence
Québec
Montréal Ottawa
Toronto
Detroit
L. Superior
L. Huron
L. Michigan
L. Ontario
Buffalo
L. Erie
Boston
St. John's

Minneapolis
Missouri

CHICAGO
Pittsburgh

NEW YORK CITY
PHILADELPHIA
Baltimore
Washington D.C.

A T L A N T I C

C. Mendocino
Salt Lake
City
Denver
Kansas City
St. Louis
Cincinnati

UNITED STATES

Sacramento
SAN FRANCISCO
4418
Colorado

Oklahoma City
Memphis
Atlanta
C. Hatteras

Bermuda
(U.K.)

6741

LOS ANGELES
San Diego

Phoenix
Dallas

Houston
San Antonio
New
Orleans

Guadalupe
(Mex.)
Ciudad
Juárez

Gulf of Mexico
Miami
BAHAMAS

Sargasso Sea

O C E A N

Tropic of Cancer

Honolulu
Oahu
4205
HAWAIIAN IS.
(U.S.A.)
Hawaii

Ridge

nston I.
.A.)

Palmyra Is.
(U.S.A.)

Teraina
Tabuaeran
Kiritimati

C I F I C

Is. Revilla Gigedo
(Mex.)

Guadalajara
MEXICO
5700
Puebla
Mérida
La Habana
CUBA
West Indies
Canal de Yucatan

Acapulco
BELIZE
GUATEMALA
Guatemala
San Salvador
EL SALVADOR
HONDURAS
Managua
NICARAGUA
JAMAICA
Kingston
HAITI
DOMINICAN REP.
9200
PUERTO
RICO
(U.S.A.)
Leeward
Is.

Caribbean Sea

BARBADOS
Windward Is.

Barranquilla
San José
COSTA
RICA
Colón
Panamá
PANAMA
Maracaibo
Caracas

I. Clipperton
(Fr.)

O

7680

E A N

Jarvis I.
(U.S.A.)

Equator

Malden I.
Starbuck I.

I. del Coco
(Costa Rica)
I. de Malpelo
(Colombia)
Medellín
Cali
COLOMBIA
Bogotá
VENEZUELA
Orinoco

B A T I

Galápagos
(Ecuador)
Quito
ECUADOR

Tongareva
Pukapuka
Manihiki
Caroline I.
Vostok I.
Flint I.
Is. Marquises

Guayaquil
C. Paliñas
Iquitos
Amazonas
BRAZIL

Suwarrow Is.
Is. de la
Société
Papeete Tahiti
Is. Tuamotu

Trujillo

6369
PERU
Nevada Ancohuma
6550

Cook Is.
(N.Z.)
Austral
Seamount Chain
FRENCH POLYNESIA
Mururoa

LIMA
Cuzco
L. Titicaca
Arequipa
6866
Peru-
Arica
La Paz
BOLIVIA

Rarotonga
Is. Tubuai
Ridge
Tropic of Capricorn

Ducie I.
Pitcairn I.
(U.K.)
Rapa

Sala-y-Gómez
(Chile)
I. de Pascua
(Chile)

Iquique
Chile
Antofagasta
PARAGUAY
8050
Trench
San Miguel
de Tucumán
Asunción

San Felix
(Chile)
San Ambrosio
(Chile)
Porto
Alegre

Arch. de
Juan Fernández
(Chile)
Córdoba
Aconcagua
6960
Valparaíso
Rosario
URUGUAY
Montevideo

East Pacific Ridge
SANTIAGO
Concepción
BUENOS
AIRES
Río de la Plata

ARGENTINA

Chile Rise
S O U T H

A T L A N T I C

Pacific-Antarctic Ridge
O C E A N
6212

Punta Arenas
Falkland Is.
(U.K.)
Est. de Magallanes
Tierra del Fuego
South Georgia
(U.K.)
C. de Hornos

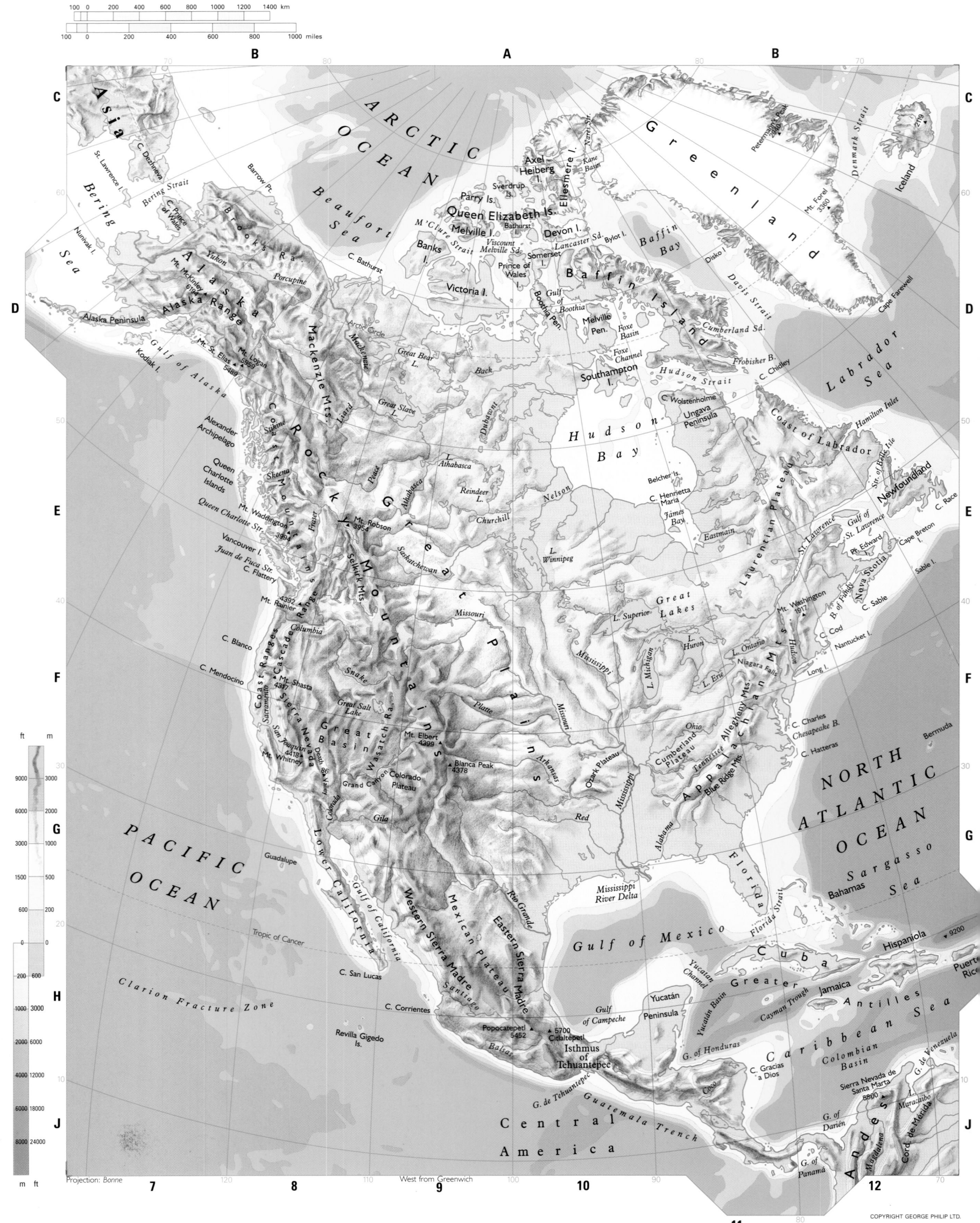

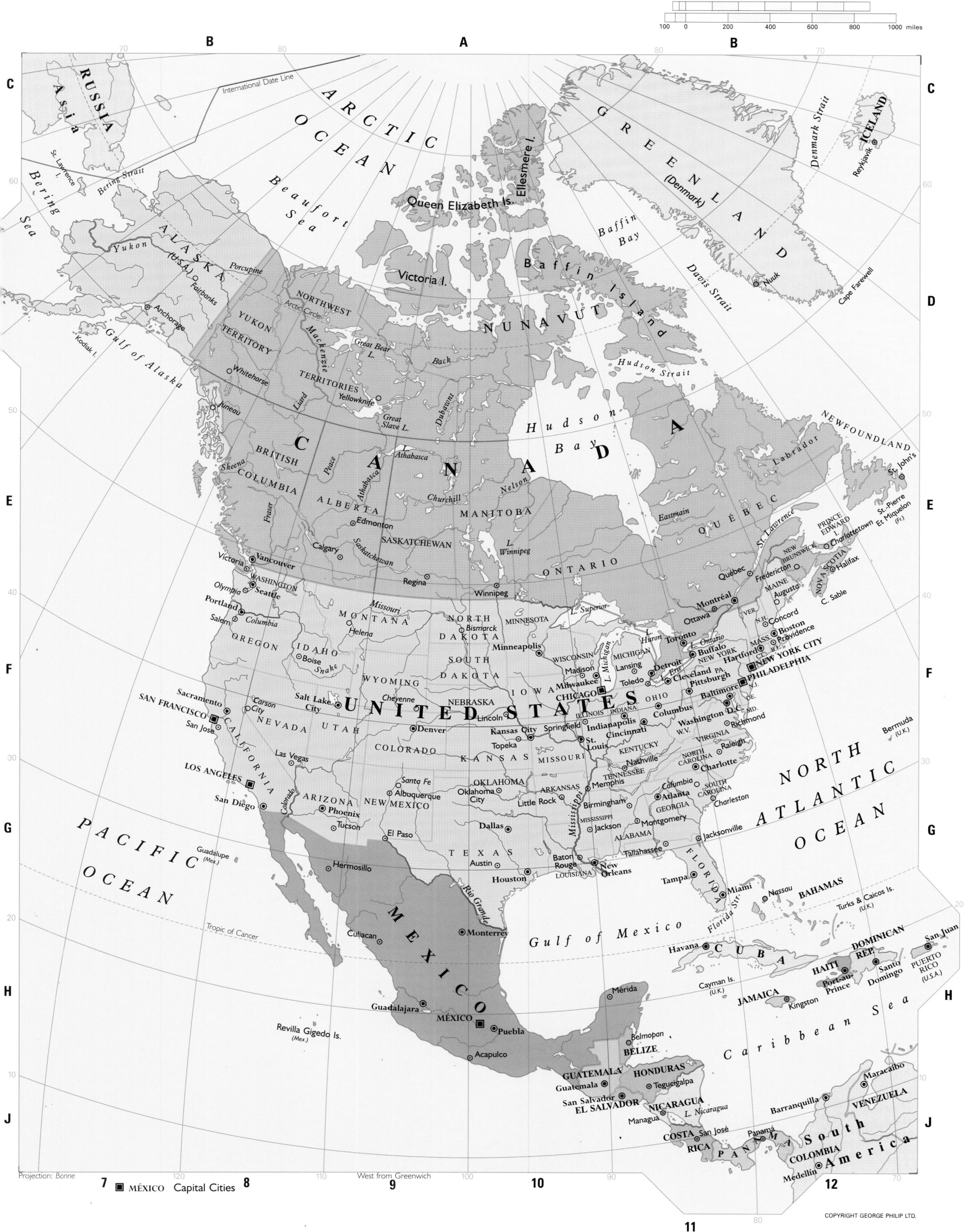

Projection: Bonne

7 ■ MÉXICO Capital Cities 8

West from Greenwich

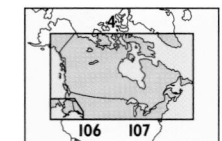

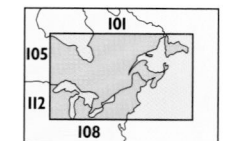

COPYRIGHT GEORGE PHILIP LTD.

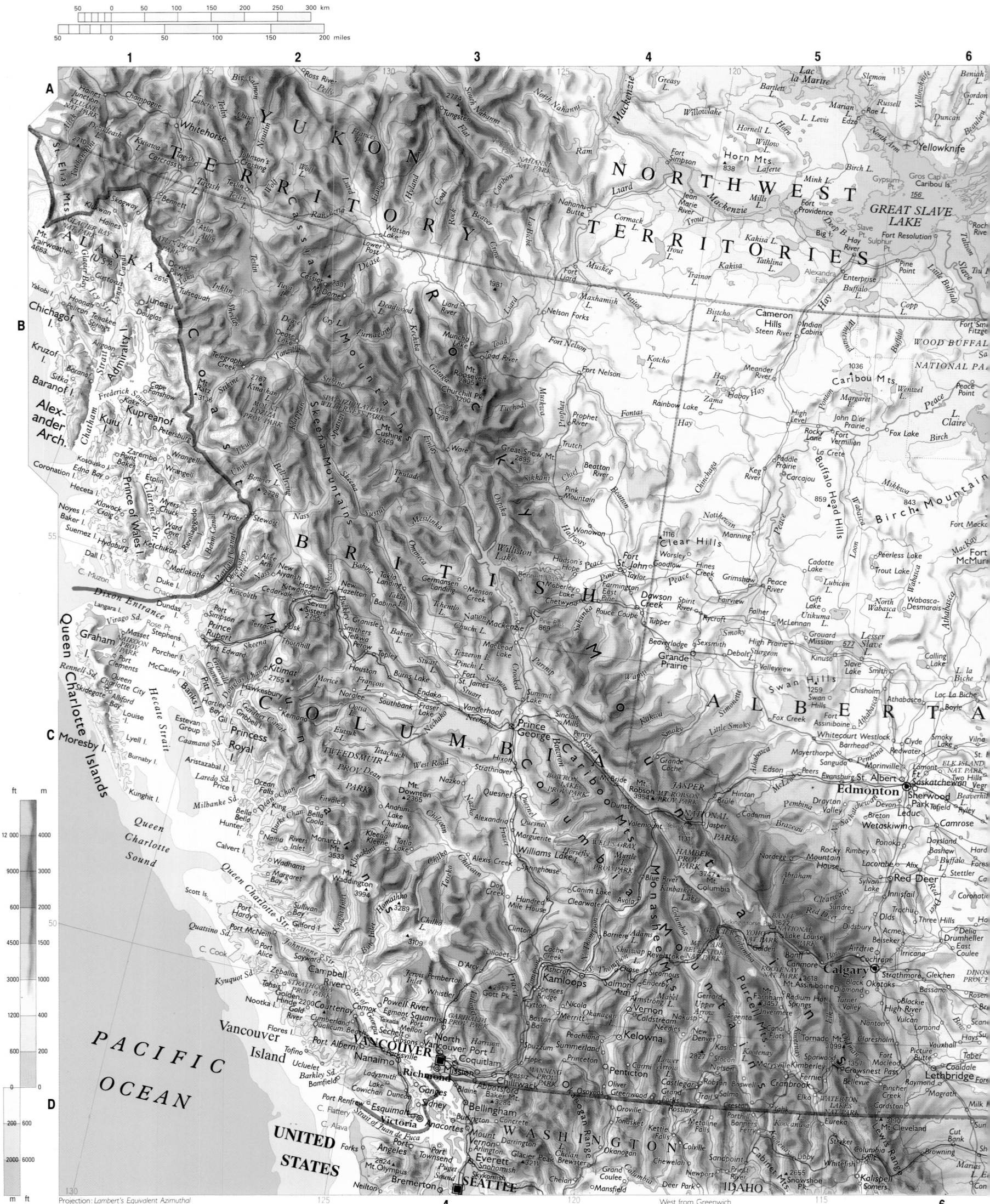

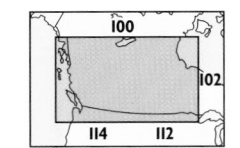

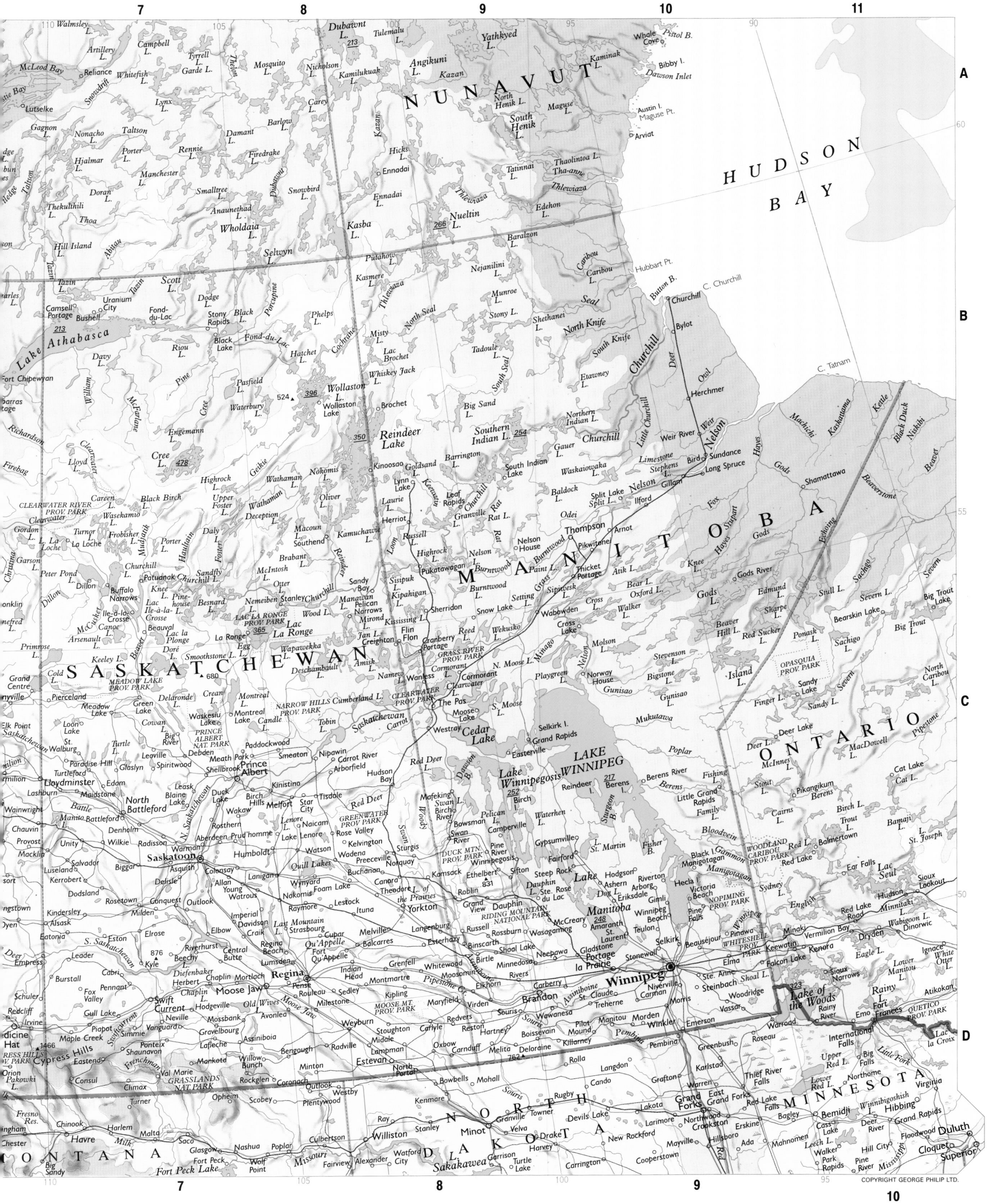

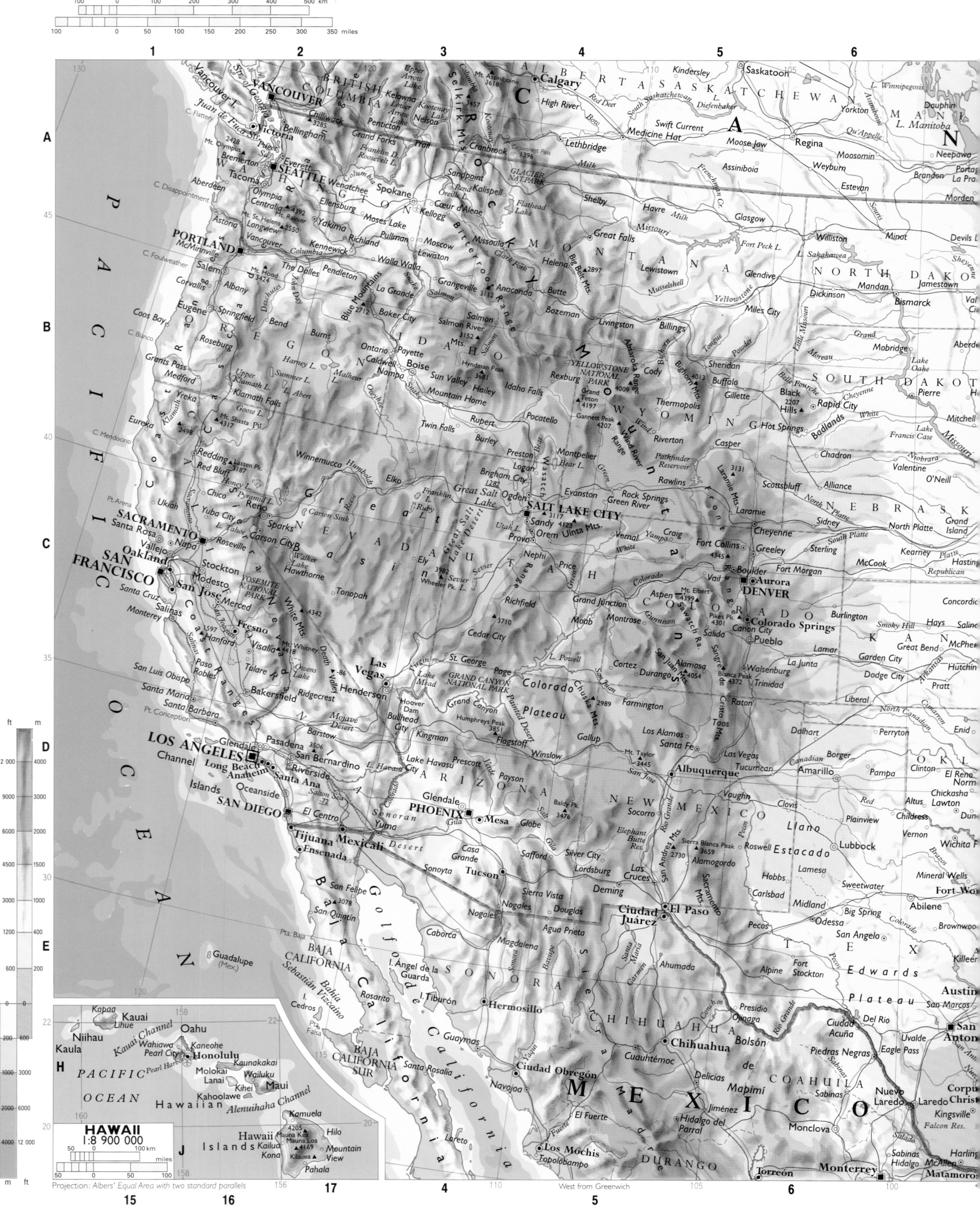

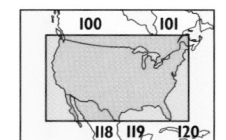

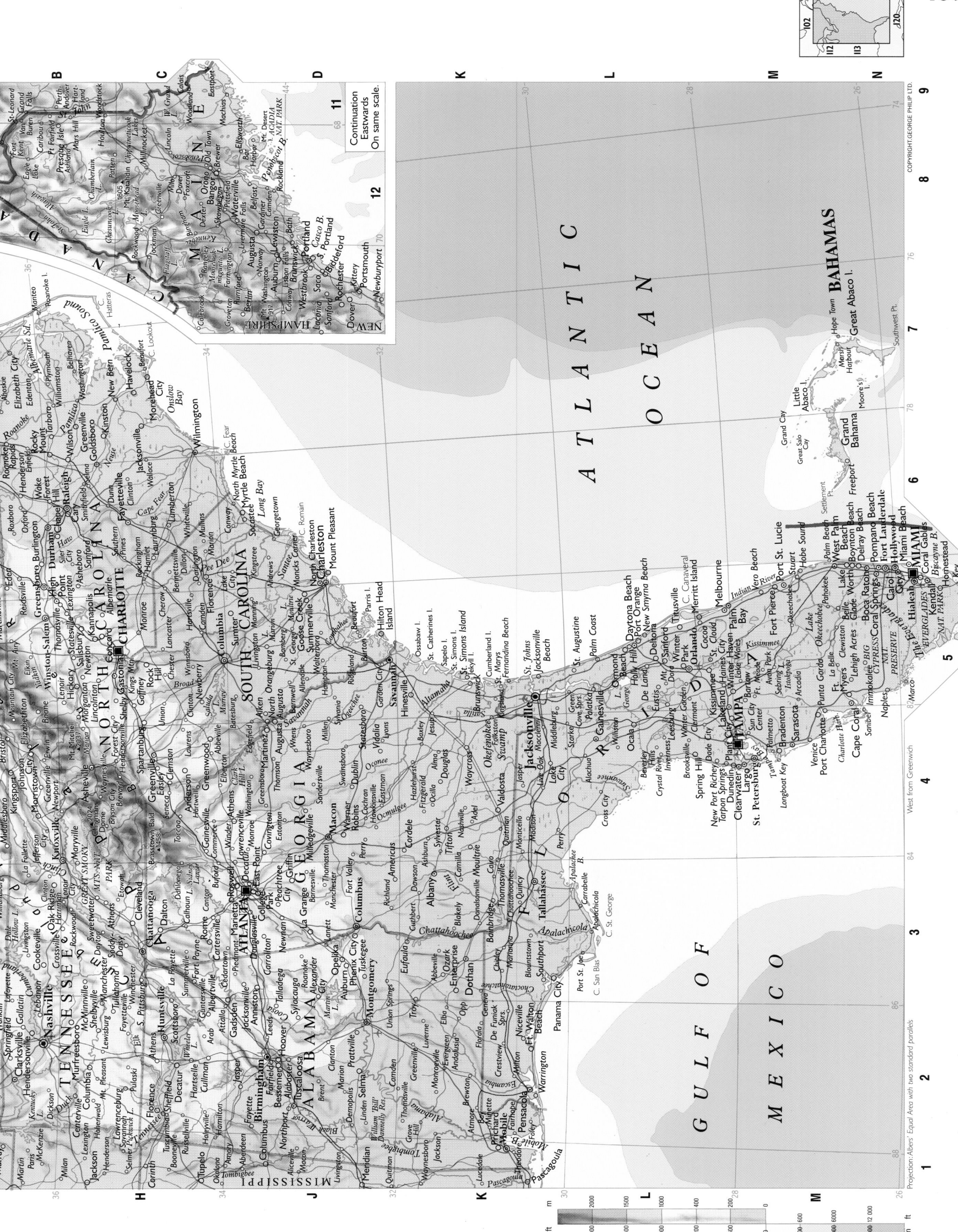

ATLANTIC

OCEAN

BAHAMAS

GULF OF

MEXICO

MAINE

NEW HAMPSHIRE

Continuation
Eastwards
On same scale.

NORTH CAROLINA

SOUTH CAROLINA

GEORGIA

FLORIDA

ALABAMA

TENNESSEE

MISSISSIPPI

Projection: Albers' Equal Area with two standard parallels

West from Greenwich

Projection: Bonne

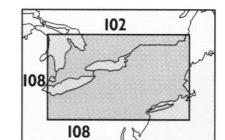

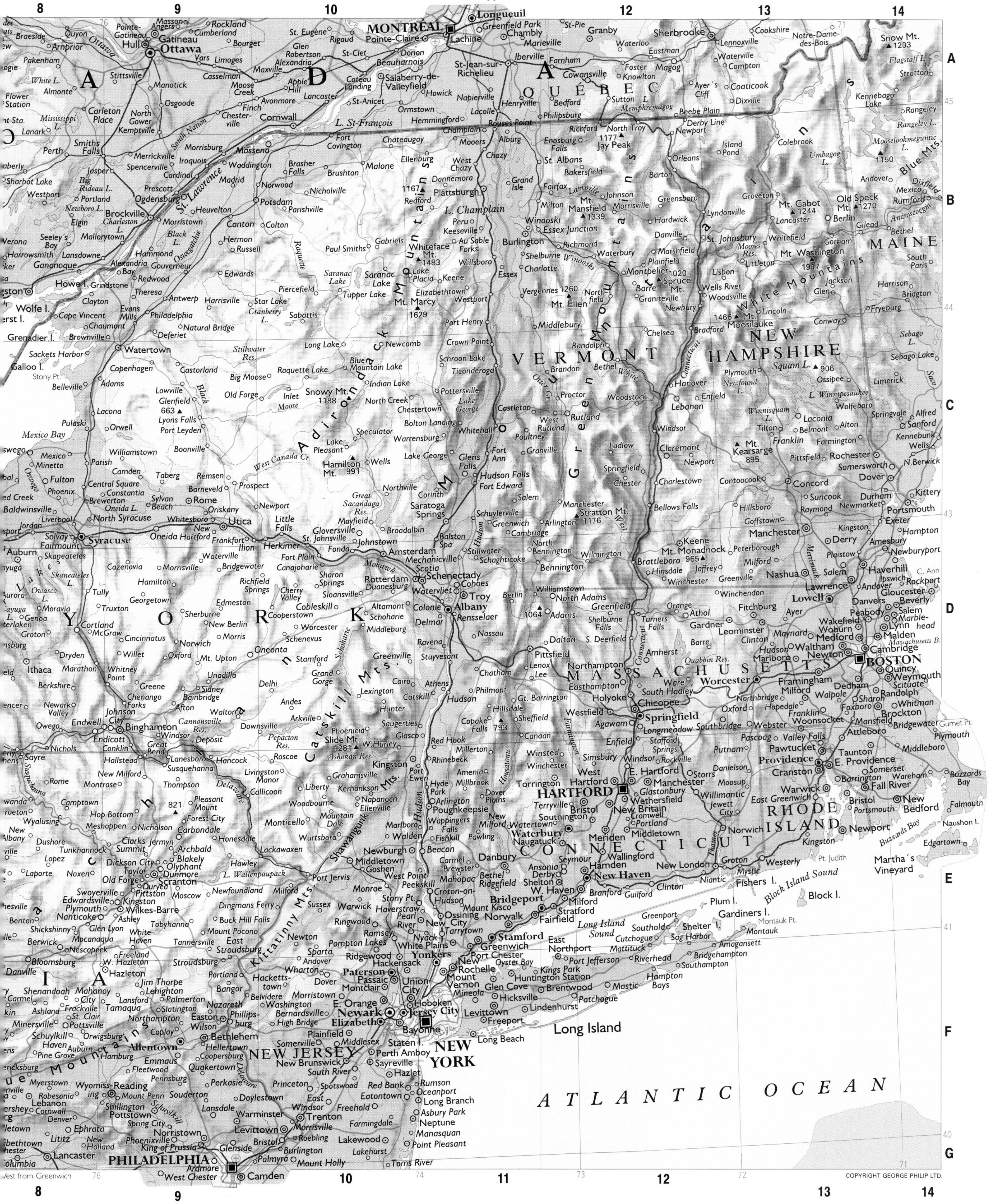

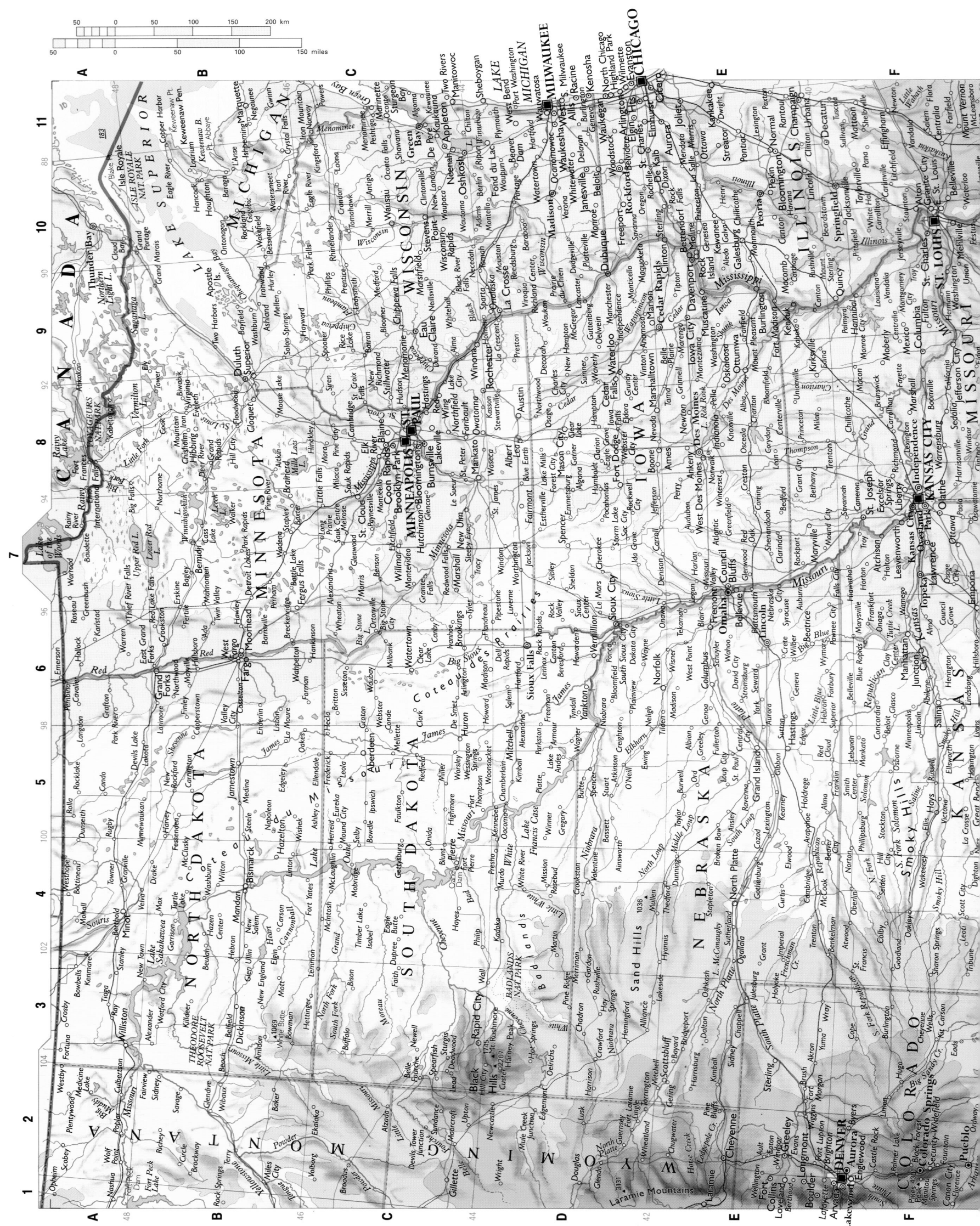

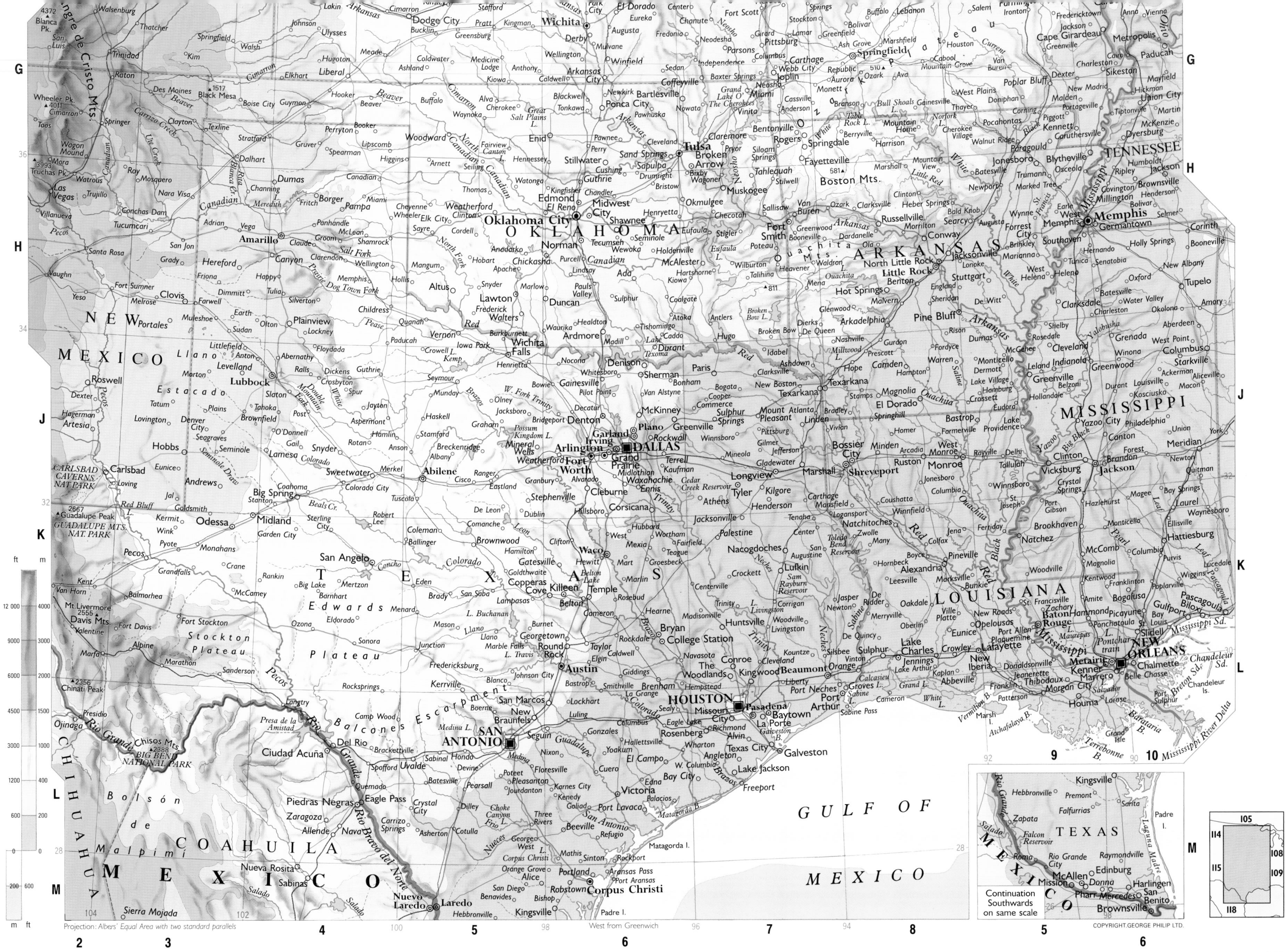

TENNESSEE

MISSISSIPPI

ARKANSAS

OKLAHOMA

LOUISIANA

TEXAS

NEW MEXICO

COAHUILA

CHIHUAHUA

MEXICO

GULF OF MEXICO

Laguna Madre

Continuation Southwards on same scale

West from Greenwich

Projection: Albers' Equal Area with two standard parallels

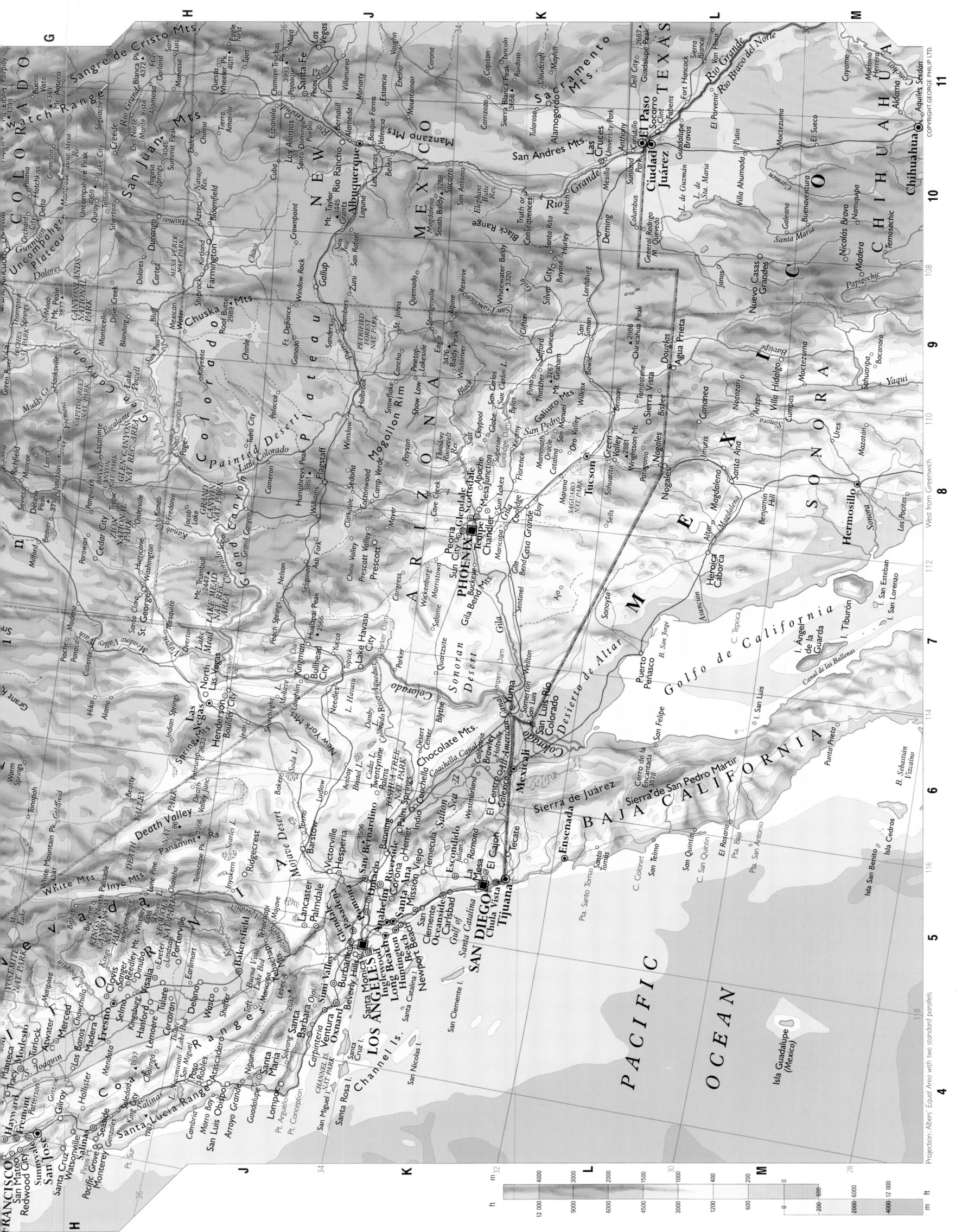

NEVADA

ARIZONA

MEXICO

BAJA CALIFORNIA

Death Valley

Amargosa Range

DESERT NATIONAL MONUMENT

Mojave Desert

Colorado Desert

Sonoran Desert

Chocolate Mts.

San Bernardino

San Gabriel Mts.

Santa Monica Mts.

Tehachapi Mts.

Temblor Range

San Rafael Mts.

Channel Islands

PACIFIC OCEAN

San Pedro Channel

Santa Barbara Channel

CHANNEL ISLANDS NATIONAL PARK

JOSHUA TREE NATIONAL PARK

Gulf of Santa Catalina

Imperial Valley

Salton Sea

Coachella Canal

Coachella Valley

Lake Mead

LAKE MEAD NATIONAL RECREATION AREA

Colorado

Las Vegas

North Las Vegas

Henderson

Boulder City

Hoover Dam

Bakersfield

LOS ANGELES

Long Beach

Santa Monica

Pasadena

Glendale

Burbank

Anaheim

Santa Ana

Riverside

San Bernardino

Ontario

Pomona

Fullerton

Irvine

Newport Beach

Huntington Beach

Torrance

Inglewood

Compton

Downey

Palmdale

Lancaster

Victorville

Barstow

Hesperia

Apple Valley

Palm Springs

Palm Desert

Indio

Coachella

Mecca

El Centro

Calexico

Mexicali

Brawley

Yuma

Tijuana

SAN DIEGO

Chula Vista

National City

Coronado

Oceanside

Carlsbad

Escondido

Vista

San Marcos

Encinitas

El Cajon

La Mesa

Santee

Lakeside

Poway

Mission Viejo

San Clemente

Santa Barbara

Ventura

Oxnard

Goleta

Santa Maria

San Luis Obispo

Lompoc

Santa Catalina I.

San Clemente I.

San Nicolas I.

Santa Cruz I.

Santa Rosa I.

San Miguel I.

Santa Barbara I.

Needles

Lake Havasu City

Kingman

Bullhead City

Parker

Blythe

Twentynine Palms

Joshua Tree

Baker

Ludlow

Amboy

Essex

Searchlight

Nipton

Pt. Conception

Pt. Arguello

West from Greenwich

Projection: Bonne

REFERENCE TO NUMBERS

1 Distrito Federal   5 México
2 Aguascalientes   6 Morelos
3 Guanajuato   7 Querétaro
4 Hidalgo   8 Tlaxcala

Projection: Bi-polar oblique Conical Orthomorphic

West from Greenwich

GULF OF MEXICO

U.S.A.
L. Okeechobee
West Palm Beach
Fort Myers
Fort Lauderdale
Boca Raton
Naples
The Everglades
C. Romano
C. Sable
Hialeah
MIAMI
Bimini Is.
Dry Tortugas (U.S.A.)
Key West
Florida Keys

West End
Grand Bahama
Freeport
Hope Town
Little Abaco I.
Great Abaco I.
Northwest Providence Channel
Nicolls Town
Berry Is.
New Providence
Nassau
Adelaide
Andros Town
Andros Island
Eleuthera
Governor's
BA
Northeast Providence Channel
Exuma Sound
Great Exuma
Great Guana Cay
Jument
Cays

Straits of Florida
LA HABANA (Havana)
MARIANAO
Guanabacoa
Bahía Honda
La Esperanza
Los Palacios
San Antonio de los Baños
Pinar del Río
Guane
La Fé
San Luis
Corrientes
I. de la Juventud
Nueva Gerona
Arch. de los Canarreos
Santa Cruz del Norte
Matanzas
Cárdenas
Jovellanos
Colón
Jagüey Grande
Güines
Cienfuegos
Santa Clara
Sagua la Grande
Caibarién
Placetas
Trinidad
Sancti Spíritus
Júcaro
Tunas de Zaza
Arch. de Jardines de la Reina
Moron
Cayo Romano
Ciego de Avila
Florida
Camagüey
Victoria de las Tunas
Golfo de Guacanayabo
Manzanillo
Bayamo
Sierra Maestra
C. Cruz
Nuevitas
Puerto Man
Puerto P
Gibara
HOLGU
Sori
2000
SANTIA
DE CU
Canal Nicholas
Cay Sal Bank
Santaren Channel
Canal Viejo de Bahama
Duncan T
Great Bahama Bank
CUBA
Greater

Canal de Yucatán
I. Desterrada
I. Pérez (Mexico)
Punta Yalkubul
Río Lagartos
Progreso
Dzilam de Bravo
El Cuyo
C. Catoche
C. San Antonio
Motul
Temax
Tizimín
DZIBILCHALTÚN
Mérida
Izamal
Espita
Cancún
Puerto Juárez
Maxcanú
Sotuta
CHICHÉN ITZÁ
Valladolid
El Diaz
Calkiní
UXMAL
Ticul
Peto
Puerto Morelos
Tenabo
Tekax
MAYAPÁN
Cozumel
Campeche
ETZNA
Hopelchén
Bolonchenticul
Vigía Chico
Isla Cozumel
Champotón
Chenkán
San José Carpizo
Felipe Carrillo Puerto
B. de la Ascensión
Ciudad del Carmen
I. de Términos
Pital
Matamoros
YUCATÁN
QUINTANA ROO
Bacalar
B. del Espíritu Santo
Palizada
Balancán
Concepción
MEXICO
CAMPECHE
Chetumal
Corozal
B. de Chetumal
Banco Chinchorro
Tenosique
Uaxactún
Orange Walk
Ambergris Cay
PALENQUE
Ocosingo
L. Petén Itzá
TIKAL
San Ignacio
Belmopan
Hondo
Belize City
Turneffe Is.
La Libertad
Flores
Benque Viejo
Middlesex
BELIZE
La Independencia
Lacantún
Sebol
Dangriga
Comitán
Maya Mts.
San Luis
Golfo de Honduras
Is. de la Bahía
Sierra de los Cuchumatanes
Cobán
L. de Izabal
Punta Gorda
Livingston
San Antonio
Monkey River
Roatán
Puerto Cortés
3993
Cuilco
GUATEMALA
Motagua
Puerto Barrios
Tela
La Ceiba
Balfate
Trujillo
Puerto Castillo
Iriona
C. Camarón
Punta Patuca
San Marcos
Huehuetenango
UTATLÁN
Santa Bárbara
San Pedro Sula
El Progreso
Yoro
Savá
Olanchito
Brus Laguna
Laguna Caratasca
Ayutla
Quezaltenango
Totonicapán
Sololá
Gualán
Zacapa
COPÁN
El Jaral
L. de Yojoa
Sulaco
Arena
Juticalpa
Catacamas
Coco (Segovia)
C. Falso
C. Gracias a Dios
Antigua
GUATEMALA
Santa Rosa de Copán
HONDURAS
Comayagua
Patuca
Puerto Cabo Gracias á Dios
Jalapa
Chiquimula
Amatitlán
La Esperanza
La Paz
Tegucigalpa
Yuscarán
Kisalaya
Mazatenango
Escuintla
Santa Ana
Suchitoto
Danlí
Cayos Miskitos (Nicaragua)
Retalhuleu
San José
Cojutepeque
Nacaóme
Ocotal
Bonanza
Pta. Gorda
Coatepeque
Ahuachapán
Sonsonate
SAN SALVADOR
Zacatecoluca
La Unión
Choluteca
Somoto
Siuna
Puerto Cabezas
Acajutla
Nueva San Salvador
Usulután
San Miguel
Cord. Isabelia
Tuma
Tungla
Cayos Roncador (U.S.A. & Colombia)
EL SALVADOR
G. de Fonseca
Puerto Morazán
El Sauce
Estelí
Jinotega
Matagalpa
San Pedro del Norte
Prinzapolca
I. de Providencia (Colombia)
Chinandega
Corinto
León
Muy Muy
Boaco
Río Grande
Cayos de Albuquerque (Colombia)
La Paz Centro
L. de Managua
NICARAGUA
Siquia
Santo Domingo
Rama
Bluefields
I. de San Andrés (Colombia)
MANAGUA
Masaya
Granada
Juigalpa
El Bluff
Is. del Maíz (Nicaragua, U.S.A.)
Diriamba
Jinotepe
Lago de Nicaragua
Cord. de Yolaina
Pta. Mico
Punta de Perlas
San Juan del Sur
I. de Ometepe
San Carlos
B. de San Juan del Norte
B. de Salinas
La Cruz
Los Chiles
San Juan
San Juan del Norte
C. Santa Elena
G. de Papagayo
Liberia
Guápiles
Siquirres
I. de San Bernar
C. Velas
Santa Cruz
COSTA RICA
Cord. Central
Limón
Santa Cruz
Nicoya
Alajuela
SAN JOSÉ
Cartago
Pta. Mona
Carmona
Puntarenas
Esparta
Bribri
Bocas del Toro
Panamá Colón
Nombre de Dios
Portobelo
Archipiélago de San Blas
Pen. de Nicoya
RICA
Pandora
C. Blanco
G. de Nicoya
Chirripó Grande
3837
Cord. de Talamanca
3374
Almirante
Boquete
L. de Chiriquí
Canal
L. Gatún
Chepo
Balboa
PANAMÁ
Serranía del Darién
Golfo del Darién
Morr
B. de Coronado
Buenos Aires
Volcán Barú
La Concepción
G. de los Mosquitos
La Chorrera
Chiman
San Miguel
La Palma
El Real
Quepos
Puerto Cortés
San Vito
David
Remedios
Río Hato
Penonomé
Arch. de las Perlas
I. del Rey
Yaviza
Pen. de Osa
Golfito
Puerto Armuelles
Aguadulce
Santiago
Chitré
Golfo de Panamá
Garachiné
G. Dulce
Pta. Burica
Soná
Las Tablas
Los Santos
Pocrí
Monte
G. de Chiriquí
I. de Coiba
I. del Cebaco
Pen. de Azuero
Pta. Mala
Tonosí
Jaqué
Punta Mariato

PACIFIC OCEAN

Swan Islands (U.S.A. & Honduras)
Mosquitia
CARI
CARI
Bajo Nuevo (Colombia)
Pedro Cays (Jamaica)
Cayman Islands (U.K.)
Cayman Brac
Little Cayman
Georgetown
Grand Cayman
7680
Montego Bay
Falmouth
St. Ann's Bay
Lucea
Negril
South Negril Pt.
JAMAICA
Cambridge
Savanna-la-Mar
Black River
Mandeville
May Pen
Spanish Town
KINGSTO
Por
A
Annotto Ba
Port Maria
Port An
Por
CART
CARTA
L. de Nicaragua

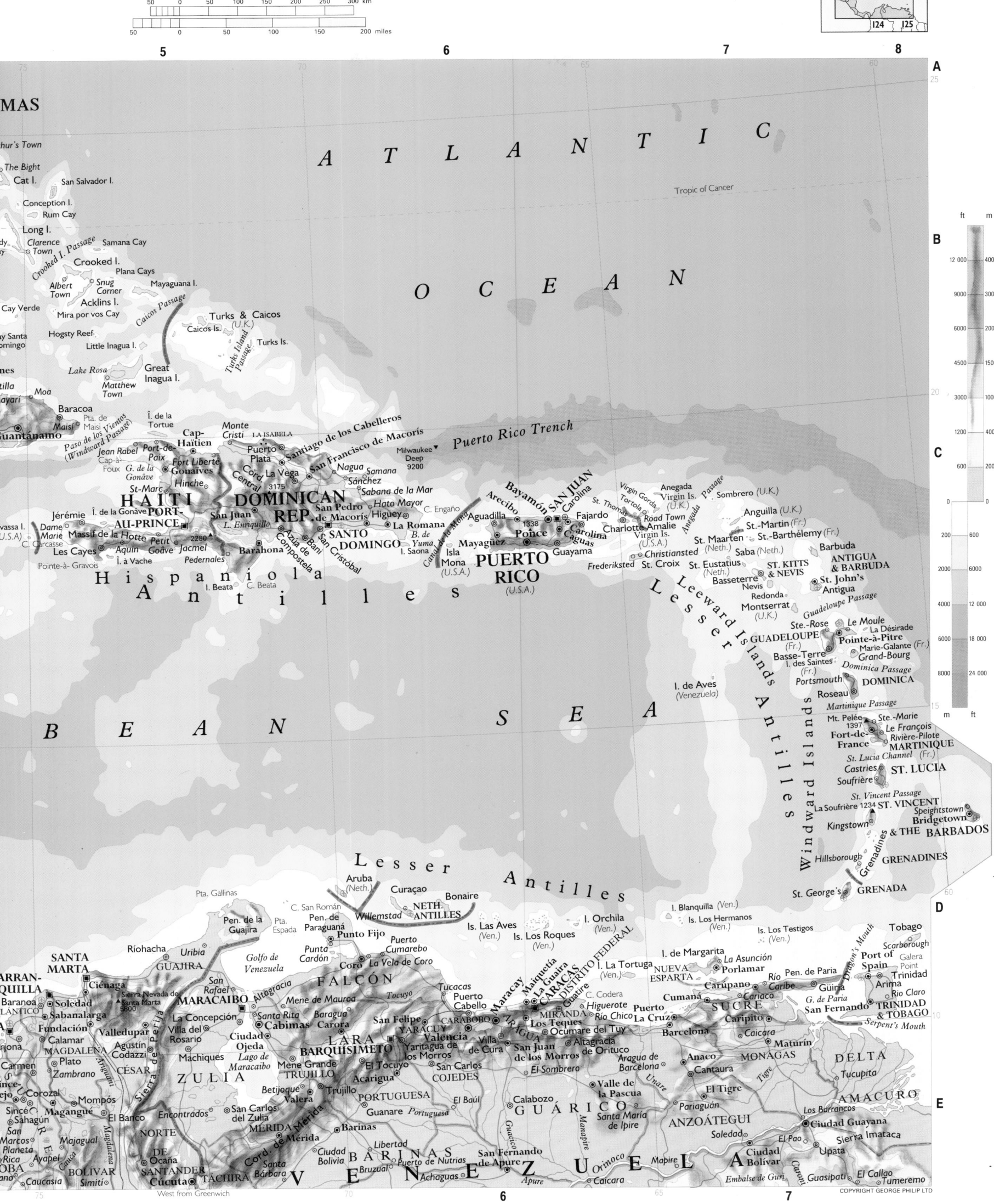

100 0   200   400   600   800 1000 1200 1400 km
100 0   200   400   600   800   1000 miles

A
NORTH
ATLANTIC
OCEAN

Tropic of Cancer

Yucatán Channel
Cuba
Greater Antilles
Turks & Caicos Is.
Gulf of Campeche
Yucatán Peninsula
Hispaniola
9200
Puerto Rico
Jamaica
Lesser Antilles
Guadeloupe
Dominica
Martinique
St. Lucia
St. Vincent
Barbados

Isthmus of Tehuantepec
G. de Honduras
C. Gracias a Dios
Cocos
L. Nicaragua
Guatemala Trench
Caribbean Sea
I. Margarita
Grenada
Tobago
Trinidad

B
ATLANTIC
OCEAN

Panama Canal
G. of Darién
C. de la Aguja
5800
Sierra Nevada de Santa Marta
L. Maracaibo
Cord. de Mérida

Gulf of Panamá
Cordillera Occidental
Cordillera Central
Magdalena
Cordillera Oriental
Llanos
Orinoco
Meta
Guiana Highlands
Mt. Roraima 2810
Sierra Pacaraima
Serra Tumucumaque
C. Orange

C
Guaviare
Caquetá
Negro
Branco
Equator
Marajó I.

C. de San Francisco
Cotopaxi 5897
Chimborazo 6267
Putumayo
Japurá
Amazon
Amazon
Tocantins

G. of Guayaquil
Napo
Marañón
Selvas
Juruá
Purus
Madeira
Tapajós
Xingu
Araguaia
Parnaíba
C. de São Roque

D
Pta. Pariñas
Pta. Negra
Ucayali
Madre de Dios
Roosevelt
Teles Pires
São Francisco
Plat. of Borborema

Huascarán 6768
Mamoré
Guaporé
Arinos
Brazilian Highlands

Chincha Alta
Chile Peru Trench
L. Titicaca
Bolivian Plateau
Nevada Ancohuma 6550
Plateau of Mato Grosso

E
PACIFIC
OCEAN
L. de Poopó
Abrolhos Bank

ft   m
Galapagos Is.

Tropic of Capricorn
San Félix
8050
Atacama Desert
Cerro Ojos del Salado 6863
Gran Chaco
Paraguay
Pilcomayo
Paraná
Serra da Mantiqueira 2890
Pico da Bandeira
C. Frio

F
San Ambrosio
Andes
Salinas Grandes
Salado
Entre Ríos
Iguaçu Falls
Uruguay
Serra do Mar

Mt. Aconcagua 6960
Sierra de Córdoba
L. Mar Chiquita
Paraná
L. dos Patos

Arch. de Juan Fernández
Pampa
Río de la Plata

G
SOUTH
ATLANTIC
OCEAN

Colorado
Bahía Blanca
Negro
G. San Matías
Valdés Peninsula
40
Argentine Basin

Chile Rise
Chiloé I.
Patagonia
Chubut

Chonos Archipelago
Mte. San Valentín 4058
Gulf of San Jorge

Taitao Peninsula
Gulf of Penas
6212

H
Wellington I.
Madre de Dios I.
Falkland Is.
West Falkland
East Falkland
South Georgia

Magellan's Str.
Santa Inés I.
Tierra del Fuego
Staten I.
Canal Cockburn
Canal Beagle
C. Horn

West from Greenwich

Projection: Lambert's Azimuthal Equal Area
CARTOGRAPHY BY PHILIP'S.

■ LIMA Capital Cities

CARTOGRAPHY BY PHILIP'S.

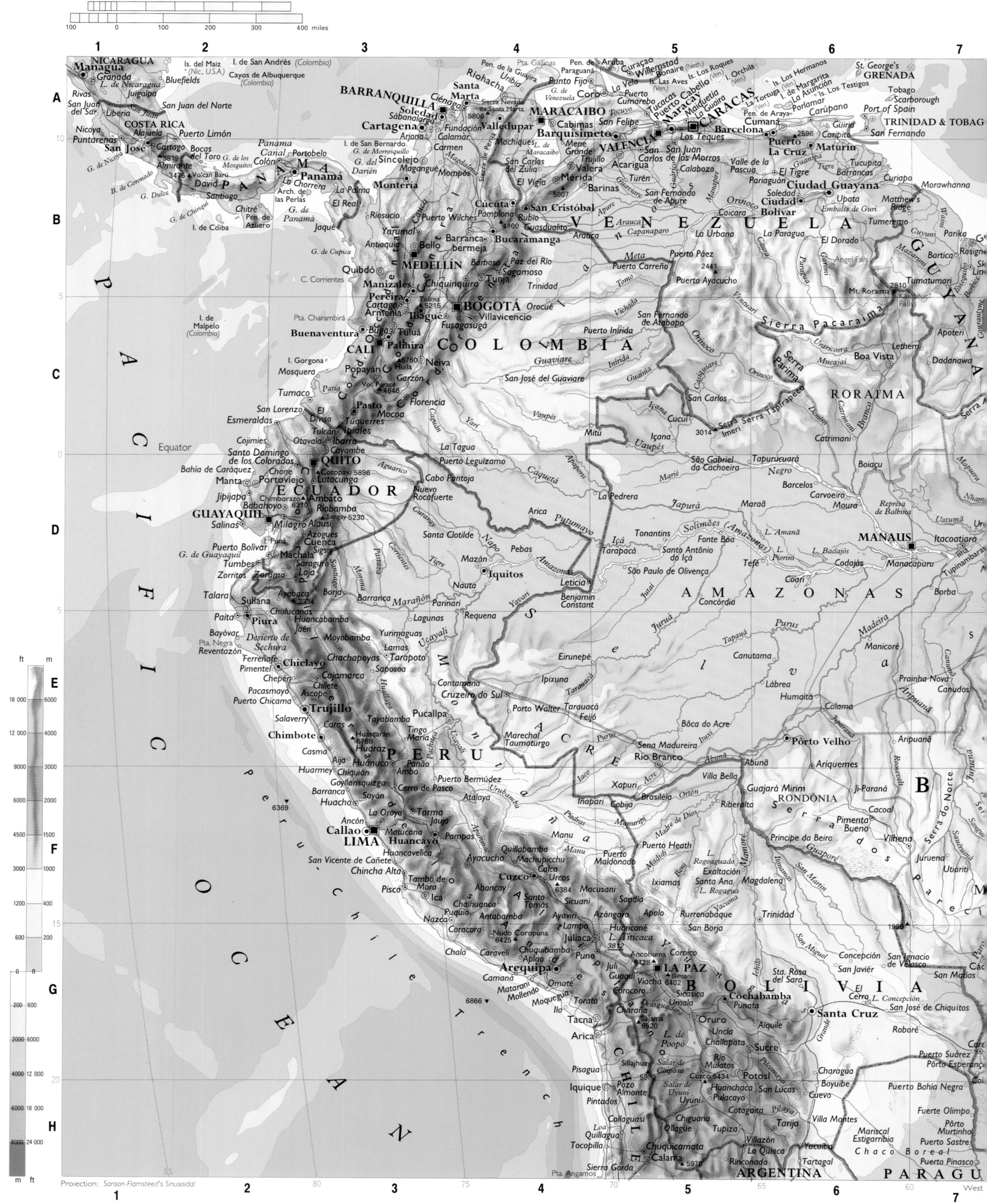

Projection: Sanson-Flamsteed's Sinusoidal

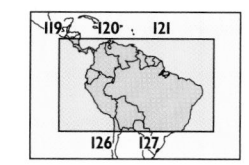

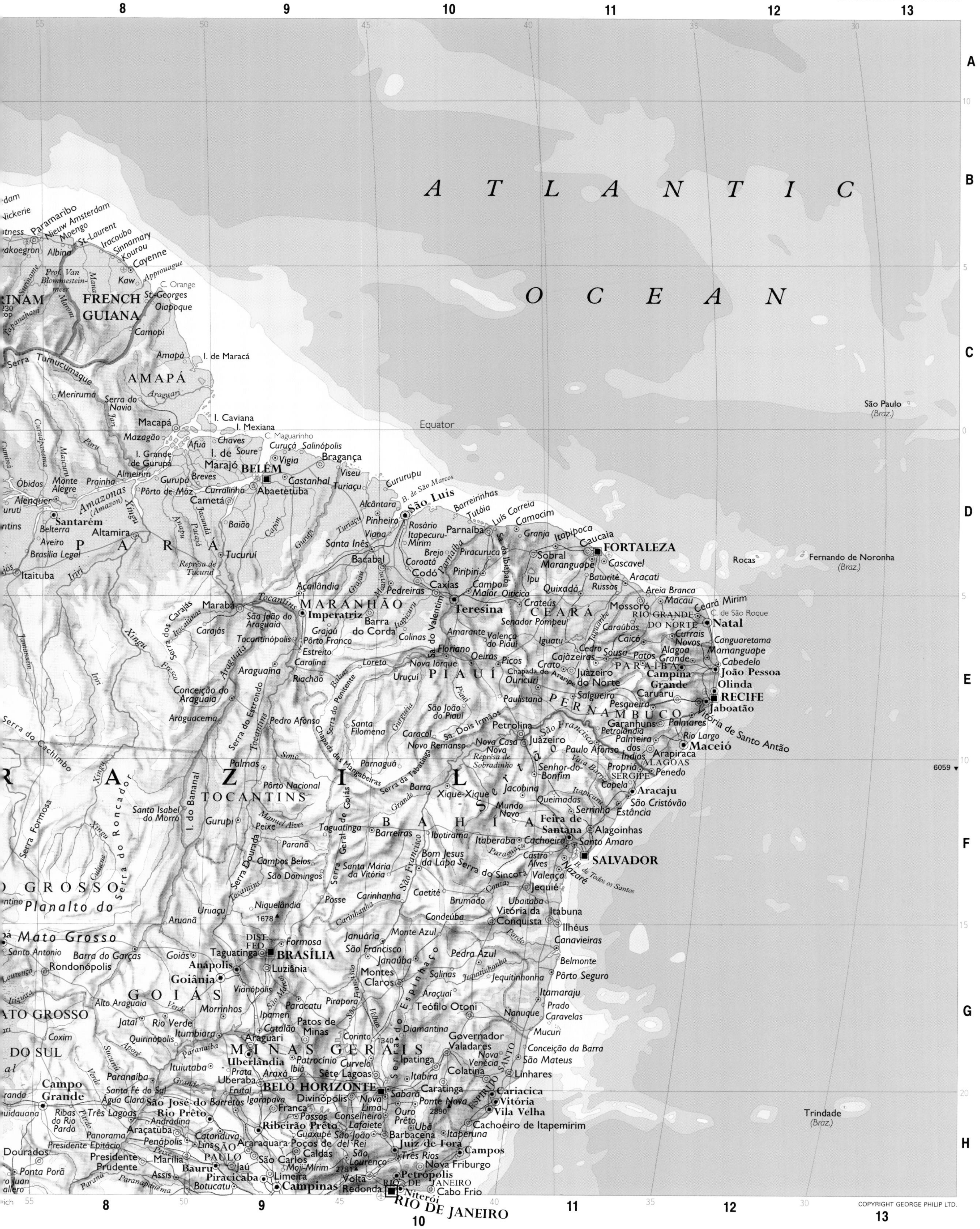

8 **9** **10** **11** **12** **13**

A

A T L A N T I C

B

O C E A N

C

São Paulo
(Braz.)

Equator

D

FRENCH
GUIANA

SURINAM

Paramaribo
Nieuw Amsterdam
Moengo
St-Laurent
Cayenne
Kourou
Sinnamary
Iracoubo
Approuague
Kaw
C. Orange
St-Georges
Oiapoque
Camopi

AMAPÁ

Serra do Navio
Macapá
Mazagão
I. Caviana
I. Mexiana
Afuá
Chaves
Curuçá Salinópolis
I. de Soure
Vigia
Bragança
Marajó BELÉM
Castanhal
Viseu
Gurupá Breves Abaetetuba
Cametá Curralinho
Turiaçu
B. de São Marcos
São Luís
Alcântara
Cururupu
Barreirinhas
Tutóia
Luís Correia
Camocim
Granja Itapipoca
Caucaia

Santarém
Altamira
Tucuruí

PARÁ

Maranhão

FORTALEZA

Fernando de Noronha
(Braz.)

Rocas

E

Marabá
São João do Araguaia
Carajás
Imperatriz
Barra do Corda
Grajaú
Tocantinópolis
Araguaína
Estreito
Carolina
Riachão
Conceição do Araguaia
Araguacema

Teresina
CEARÁ
Crateús
Iguatu

MARANHÃO

Mossoró
RIO GRANDE DO NORTE
Natal
Caicó
PARAÍBA
João Pessoa
Campina Grande
Olinda
RECIFE
Jaboatão

PERNAMBUCO

Maceió

F

BRAZIL

TOCANTINS

Palmas
Pôrto Nacional
Gurupi
Peixe
Taguatinga

BAHIA

Barra
Xique-Xique
Barreiras
Ibotirama
Itaberaba
Feira de Santana
Alagoinhas
Santo Amaro
SALVADOR

Aracaju
SERGIPE
São Cristóvão
Estância

6059

G

MATO GROSSO

Planalto do Mato Grosso

GOIÁS

Niquelândia
Formosa
DIST. FED.
BRASÍLIA
Anápolis
Goiânia
Luziânia

MINAS GERAIS

Januária
Montes Claros

Vitória da Conquista
Itabuna
Ilhéus
Canavieiras
Belmonte
Pôrto Seguro

H

Campo Grande
MATO GROSSO DO SUL

Uberlândia
Uberaba
BELO HORIZONTE
Ouro Prêto
Juiz de Fora

Governador Valadares
Teófilo Otoni

Vitória
Vila Velha

Trindade
(Braz.)

SÃO PAULO
Campinas
Volta Redonda
RIO DE JANEIRO
Niterói
Cabo Frio

8 **9** **10** **11** **12** **13**

RIO DE JANEIRO

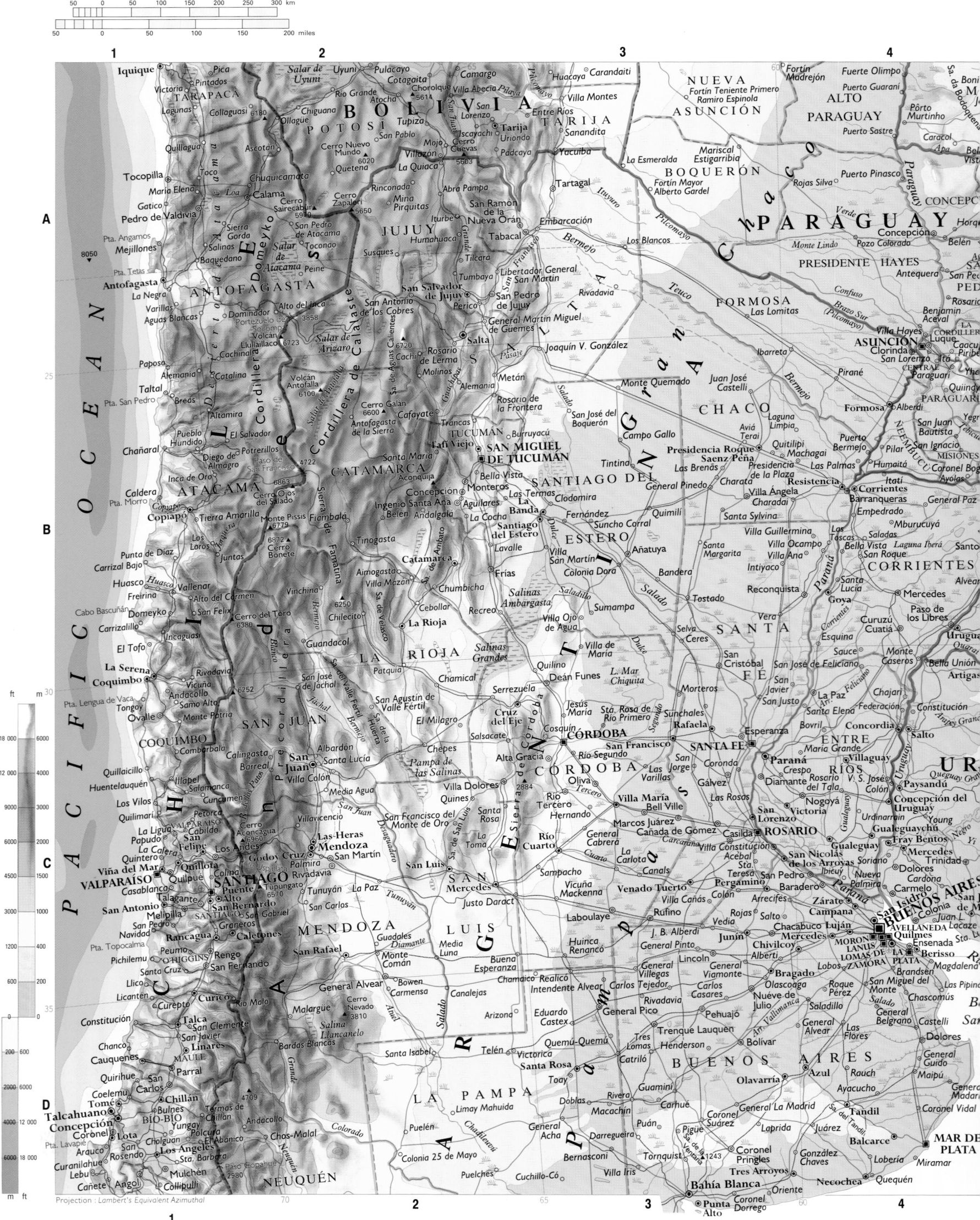

Projection : Lambert's Equivalent Azimuthal

124 125
128

5 6 7

BELO HORIZONTE
Nova Lima
Itabirito

Vitória
Itaquari
Vila Velha
Guarapari

Sidrolândia
Nioaque
Congonhas
Conselheiro
Ouro
Prêto
Ponte Nova
Pico da
Bandeira
2880
Castelo
Cachoeiro
de Itapemirim

TO GROSSO
Três Lagoas
Xavantina
Andradina
Mirassol
Olímpia
São José
do Rio Prêto
Batatais
Passos
Oliveira
Campo Belo
São João
del Rei
Ubá
Muriaé
Alegre
Itaperuna

Maracaju
Nova Alvorada
do Sul
Mirandópolis
Araçatuba
Bebedouro
Catanduva
Novo
Horizonte
Ribeirão
Prêto
Guaxupé
Três
Pontas
Lavras
Barbacena
Cataguases
Itaperuna

DO SUL
Dourados
Panorama
Presidente
Epitácio
Adamantina
Penápolis
Lins
Mococa
Casa
Branca
Alfenas
Varginha
Poços de
Juiz de Fora
Leopoldina
Cambuci
Guarus

Brilhante
Nova
Andradina
Santo
Anastácio
Tupã
Araraquara
São
Carlos
Jaboticabal
Poços de
Caldas
Pouso
Três
Corações
Dumont
Três
Rios
Paraíba do Sul
CAMPOS

Ponta Porã
Pôrto São José
Presidente
Prudente
Martinópolis
Marília
Garça
Bariri
Jaú
Rio Claro
da Boa Vista
Pinhal
Ouro Fino
Itajubá
Volta
RIO DE JANEIRO
Cabo de
São Tomé

Pedro Juan Caballero
Euclides da
Cunha Paulista
Rancharia
Paraguaçu
Paulista
Bauru
Rio Claro
Limeira
Americana
Mogi-Mirim
Redonda
Barra do Piraí
Nova Friburgo
Macaé

Ivinhema
Rosana
Assis
Santa Cruz
do Rio Pardo
Piracicaba
CAMPINAS
Botucatu
Itu
Bragança
Barra
Mansa
NOVA IGUAÇU
DUQUE DE CAXIAS
SÃO GONÇALO

Naviraí
Paranavaí
Nova
Esperança
Rolândia
Ourinhos
Avaré
Jundiaí
Taubaté
Angra dos
Reis
NITERÓI
Cabo Frio

Paranapanema
Londrina
Maringá
Apucarana
Cornélio
Procópio
Jacarèzinho
Tatuí
SÃO PAULO
Jacareí
La. de Araruama

Umuarama
Cianorte
Mandaguari
Joaquim
Távora
Ibaiti
Itapetininga
Sorocaba
SANTO ANDRÉ
Ilha Grande
Bahia da Ilha Grande

Guaíra
Goio-Erê
Campo
Mourão
Itararé
Itapeva
São Bernardo
do Campo
SANTOS

BRAZIL
Cascavel
Sa. das Araras
Pitanga
PARANÁ
Castro
Jaguariaíva
Paranapiacaba
São Vicente
Guarujá
Ilha de São Sebastião
Pta. de Boi

Foz do Iguaçu
Guarapuava
Prudentópolis
Ponta
Grossa
Apiaí
Juquiá
Itanhaém

Ciudad
del Este
Iguaçu
Laranjeiras
do Sul
Palmeira
Irati
Registro
Iguape

PARANÁ
Francisco
Beltrão
União da
Vitória
São Mateus
do Sul
Lapa
Antonina
Ilha Comprida

Bernardo
de Irigoyen
Pato Branco
Pôrto União
Rio Negro
Mafra
CURITIBA
Ilha do Cardoso

Eldorado
Palmas
Paranaguá
Matinhos
Guaratuba

MISIONES
San
Pedro
Clevelândia
Sa. da Fartura
Xanxerê
Caçador
Joinville
São Francisco do Sul

Encarnación
Chapecó
Joaçaba
Itajaí
Blumenau
Santa Cecília

Corpus
Monteagudo
Frederico
Westphalen
Campos
Novos
Brusque

Obera
Erechim
Curitibanos
Rio do Sul

Candelaria
Leandro N. Alem
Palmeira
das Missões
SANTA CATARINA
São José
Ilha de Santa Catarina

San
Javier
Santa Rosa
Lajes
Florianópolis

Apóstoles
Santo Angelo
Carazinho
São
Joaquim

São Luís
Gonzaga
Cruz Alta
Coxilha Grande
Guaporé
Vacaria
Tubarão
Laguna

Borja
Ijuí
Passo
Fundo
Bento Gonçalves
Criciúma
Cabo Santa Marta Grande

Santiago
RIO GRANDE
Caxias do Sul
Araranguá

Santa Maria
Santa Cruz
do Sul
Montenegro
Nôvo
Hamburgo
Torres

Alegrete
São
Leopoldo
Osorio

DO SUL
Cachoeira do Sul
Canoas
PÔRTO ALEGRE

Santana do
Livramento
São
Gabriel
Caçapava
do Sul
Encantadas
Rio Pardo
Viamão

Rivera
Dom Pedrito
Camaquã
Tapes

Bagé
Sa. do Canguçu
São Lourenço
do Sul
Mostardas

Pinheiro
Machado
Canguçu
Pelotas

UAY
Melo
Jaguarão
São José do Norte
Rio Grande

Río Branco
Vergara
Lagoa Mangueira
Lagoa
dos Patos

Treinta y Tres
Santa Vitória do Palmar
Chuy

ATLANTIC

OCEAN

Tropic of Capricorn

5304

West from Greenwich

COPYRIGHT GEORGE PHILIP LTD

A
B
C
D

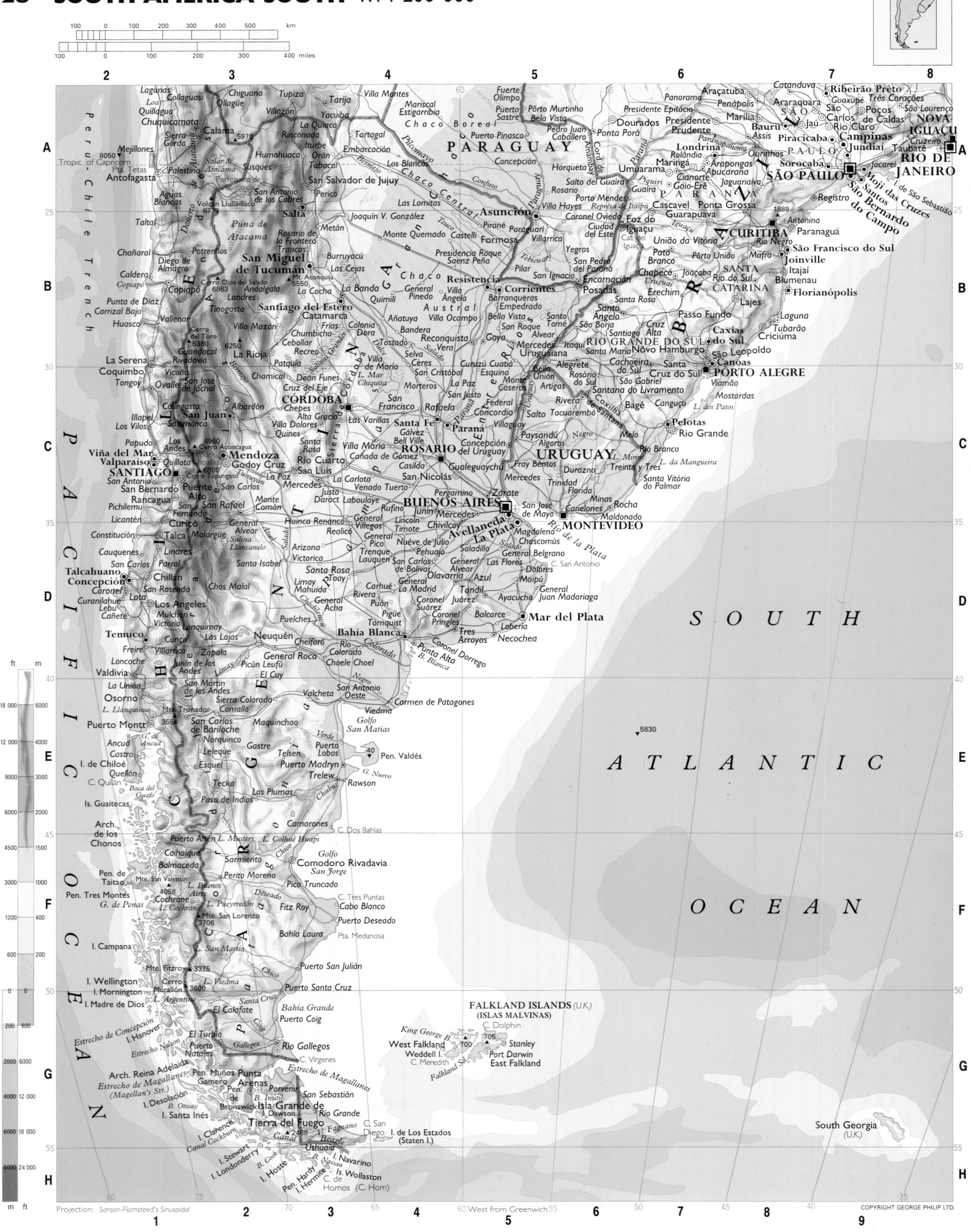

100 0 100 200 300 400 500 km
100 0 100 200 300 400 miles

| | 126 | 127 |

2   3   4   5   6   7   8

PARAGUAY

Fuerte Olimpo
Chaco Boreal
Pôrto Murtinho
Bela Vista
Pedro Juan Caballero
Ponta Porã

Lagunas
Collaguasi
Chiguana
Tupiza
Villa Montes
Mariscal Estigarribia
Panorama
Araçatuba
Penápolis
Catanduva
Ribeirão Prêto
Três Corações
São Lourenço

Loa
Quillagua
Ollagüe
Tarija
Yacuíba
Puerto Sastre
Dourados
Presidente Epitácio
Marília
Bauru
Jaú
Carlos de Caldas
Poços
São
São Lourenço

Chuquicamata
Calama
5970
La Quiaca
Humahuaca
Iturbe
Embarcación
Los Blancos
Puerto Pinasco
Concepción
Presidente Prudente
Londrina
Rolândia
Maringá
Cianorte
Arapongas
Apucarana
Jacareí
Campinas
Jundiaí
Taubaté
Cruzeiro
NOVA IGUAÇU

Mejillones
Pta. Tetas
Antofagasta
Palestina
Salar de Atacama
Volcán Llullaillaco 6739
San Antonio de los Cobres
Perico
Horqueta
Salto del Guairá
Umuarama
Goio-Erê
Guaira
Ourinhos
SÃO PAULO
Moji das Cruzes
Santos
São Bernardo do Campo
RIO DE JANEIRO

Tropic of Capricorn
8050

Aguas Blancas
San Salvador de Jujuy
Asunción
Villa Hayes
Coronel Oviedo
Foz do Iguaçu
Ciudad del Este
Cascavel
Ponta Grossa
Guarapuava
Sorocaba
Registro
I. de São Sebastião

Taltal
Chañaral
Caldera
Copiapó
Cerro Ojos del Salado 6863
Aconquija 5550
Metán
Joaquín V. González
Las Lomitas
Pirané
Paraguarí
Villarrica
Yegros
San Pedro
Encarnación
Chapecó
Pato Branco
União da Vitória
Antonina
Paranaguá
São Francisco do Sul
CURITIBA
Rio Negro

Diego de Almagro
Andalgalá
Salta
Presidencia Roque Sáenz Peña
Formosa
Pôrto União
Mafra
Joinville
SANTA CATARINA

Punta de Díaz
Carrizal Bajo
Copiapó
Londres
Catamarca
Frías
Colonia Dora
Villa Ocampo
Santo Tomé
Erechim
Rio do Sul
Blumenau
Florianópolis

Huasco
Cerro del Toro 6250
Tinogasta
Villa Mazán
La Banda
La Cocha
Bandera
Bella Vista
Reconquista
Goya
Santo Ângelo
Passo Fundo
Lajes

Vallenar
Guandacol
Chumbicha
Recreo
Curuzú Cuatiá
Uruguaiana
Itaquí
Santa Maria
Caxias do Sul
Criciúma
Tubarão

La Serena
Coquimbo
La Rioja
Patquia
Chamical
Dean Funes
San Cristóbal
La Paz
Monte Caseros
Santa Rosa
Alegrete
São Gabriel
Novo Hamburgo
São Leopoldo
Canoas
PORTO ALEGRE

Tongoy
Vicuña
Rivadavia
Chepes
L. Mar Chiquita
Morteros
Esquina
Rosário
Santana do Livramento
Santa
Cruz do Sul
Viamão

Ovalle
San José de Jáchal
CÓRDOBA
San Francisco
Rafaela
Paraná
Villaguay
Salto
Tacuarembó
Bagé
Canguçu
Pelotas

Illapel
Albardón
Alta Gracia
Las Varillas
Santa Fe
Gálvez
Concepción del Uruguay
Paysandú
Durazno
Rivera
Melo
Rio Branco
Rio Grande

Los Vilos
Calingasta
San Juan
Villa Dolores
Quines
Villa María
Bell Ville
ROSARIO
Casilda
Gualeguaychú
Fray Bentos
Mercedes
Trinidad
Florida
Treinta y Tres
L. da Mangueira

Papudo
Cerro Aconcagua 6960
Los Andes
Mendoza
San Luis
Cañada de Gómez
San Nicolás
URUGUAY
Minas
Rocha
Santa Vitória do Palmar

Viña del Mar
Valparaíso
Quillota
Godoy Cruz
La Carlota
Venado Tuerto
Pergamino
Zárate
San José de Mayo
Canelones
Maldonado

SANTIAGO
San Antonio
San Bernardo
Cerro Tupungato 6800
Puente del Inca
San Carlos
La Paz
Mercedes
Justo Daract
Laboulaye
Rufino
Junín
Mercedes
Lincoln
BUENOS AIRES
Avellaneda
La Plata
Magdalena
MONTEVIDEO

Pichilemu
Rancagua
San Fernando
San Rafael
Monte Comán
General Alvear
Huinca Renancó
General Villegas
General Pico
Nueve de Julio
Chivilcoy
Saladillo
General Belgrano
C. San Antonio

Curicó
Talca
Malargüe
Salina Llancanelo
Arizona
Victorica
Santa Rosa
Lauquen
San Carlos de Bolívar
Las Flores
Dolores
Maipú

Constitución
Linares
Chos Malal
Anzoátegui
Toay
Carhué
Olavarría
General Alvear
Tandil
General Juan Madariaga

Cauquenes
San Carlos
Parral
General Acha
Puán
Coronel Suárez
Juárez
Ayacucho
Balcarce
Lobería

Talcahuano
Concepción
Coronel
Lota
San Rosendo
Chillán
Limay Mahuida
Rivera
Coronel Pringles
Mar del Plata

Curanilahue
Lebu
Cañete
Los Angeles
Mulchén
Victoria
Lonquimay
General Roca
Bahía Blanca
Punta Alta
B. Blanca
Tres Arroyos
Necochea

SOUTH

Temuco
Freire
Villarrica
Zapala
Picún Leufú
Choele Choel
Coronel Dorrego

Valdivia
Cunco
Las Lajas
Junín de los Andes
Neuquén
Río Colorado
Río Negro

La Unión
Loncoche
San Martín de los Andes
Valcheta
San Antonio Oeste
Carmen de Patagones
5830

Osorno
Mte. Tronador 3554
Sierra Colorada
Comallo
Viedma

ATLANTIC

Puerto Montt
San Carlos de Bariloche
Ñorquinco
Maquinchao
Golfo San Matías

Ancud
G.° de Ancud
Leleque
Telsen
Puerto Lobos
Pen. Valdés

I. de Chiloé
Castro
Esquel
Puerto Madryn
Trelew
G. Nuevo

Quellón
C. Quilán
Tecka
Rawson

Is. Guaitecas
Paso de Indios
Chubut

Arch. de los Chonos
Camarones
C. Dos Bahías

OCEAN

Puerto Aisén
L. Musters
L. Colhué Huapi
Golfo San Jorge

Caihaique
Sarmiento
Comodoro Rivadavia

Balmaceda
Perito Moreno
Pico Truncado
C. Tres Puntas

Mte. San Valentín
Cochrane
Lago Buenos Aires
Deseado
Puerto Deseado

4058
L. Cochrane
L. Pueyrredón
Fitz Roy
Cabo Blanco

Pen. de Taitao
G. de Penas
Mte. San Lorenzo 3706
Bahía Laura

Pen. Tres Montes
Mte. Fitzroy 3375
Pta. Medanosa

I. Campana
Cerro Murallón 3600
L. Viedma
Puerto San Julián

I. Wellington
L. San Martín
Chico

I. Mornington
El Calafate
Santa Cruz
Puerto Santa Cruz

I. Madre de Dios
L. Argentino
Bahía Grande
Puerto Coig

Estrecho de Concepción
I. Hanover
El Turbio
Río Gallegos
Coig
C. Virgenes

Arch. Reina Adelaida
Estrecho Nelson
Puerto Natales
Gallegos

FALKLAND ISLANDS (U.K.)
(ISLAS MALVINAS)
C. Dolphin
King George B.
West Falkland
Weddell I.
C. Meredith
700
705
Stanley
Port Darwin
East Falkland
Falkland Sd.

Pen. Muñoz Gamero
Punta Arenas
Porvenir
San Sebastián

Pen. de Brunswick
B. Inútil
I. Dawson
Río Grande

I. Desolación
Isla Grande de Tierra del Fuego

I. Santa Inés
2488
C. San Diego
I. de Los Estados (Staten I.)

Estrecho de Magallanes (Magellan's Str.)
B. Otway
Ushuaia
L. Fagnano

South Georgia
(U.K.)

I. Clarence
Canal Cockburn
B. Cook
I. Navarino

I. Stewart
I. Londonderry
Canal Beagle
C. San
B. Nassau
I. Hoste
Pen. Hardy
Is. Wollaston
C. de Hornos (C. Horn)

ft   m
18 000 6000
12 000 4000
9000   3000
6000   2000
4500   1500
3000   1000
1200   400
600   200
0   0
200   600
2000   6000
4000   12000
6000   18000
m   ft

West from Greenwich

INDEX

The index contains the names of all the principal places and features shown on the World Maps. Each name is followed by an additional entry in italics giving the country or region within which it is located. The alphabetical order of names composed of two or more words is governed primarily by the first word and then by the second. This is an example of the rule:

Mīr Kūh, *Iran* **71 E8**
Mīr Shahdād, *Iran* **71 E8**
Mira, *Italy* **29 C9**
Mira por vos Cay, *Bahamas* . . **121 B5**
Miraj, *India* **66 79**

Physical features composed of a proper name (Erie) and a description (Lake) are positioned alphabetically by the proper name. The description is positioned after the proper name and is usually abbreviated:

Erie, L., *N. Amer.* **110 D4**

Where a description forms part of a settlement or administrative name however, it is always written in full and put in its true alphabetic position:

Mount Morris, *U.S.A.* **110 D7**

Names beginning with M' and Mc are indexed as if they were spelled Mac. Names beginning St. are alphabetised under Saint, but Sankt, Sint, Sant', Santa and San are all spelt in full and are alphabetised accordingly. If the same place name occurs two or more times in the index and all are in the same country, each is followed by the name of the administrative subdivision in which it is located. The names are placed in the alphabetical order of the subdivisions. For example:

Jackson, *Ky., U.S.A.* **108 G4**
Jackson, *Mich., U.S.A.* **108 D3**
Jackson, *Minn., U.S.A.* **112 D7**

The number in bold type which follows each name in the index refers to the number of the map page where that feature or place will be found. This is usually the largest scale at which the place or feature appears.

The letter and figure which are in bold type immediately after the page number give the grid square on the map page, within which the feature is situated. The letter represents the latitude and the figure the longitude.

In some cases the feature itself may fall within the specified square, while the name is outside. This is usually the case only with features which are larger than a grid square.

Rivers are indexed to their mouths or confluences, and carry the symbol ➔ after their names. A solid square ■ follows the name of a country, while an open square □ refers to a first order administrative area.

ABBREVIATIONS USED IN THE INDEX

A.C.T. – Australian Capital Territory
A.R. – Autonomous Region
Afghan. – Afghanistan
Afr. – Africa
Ala. – Alabama
Alta. – Alberta
Amer. – America(n)
Arch. – Archipelago
Ariz. – Arizona
Ark. – Arkansas
Atl. Oc. – Atlantic Ocean
B. – Baie, Bahía, Bay, Bucht, Bugt
B.C. – British Columbia
Bangla. – Bangladesh
Barr. – Barrage
Bos.-H. – Bosnia-Herzegovina
C. – Cabo, Cap, Cape, Coast
C.A.R. – Central African Republic
C. Prov. – Cape Province
Calif. – California
Cat. – Catarata
Cent. – Central
Chan. – Channel
Colo. – Colorado
Conn. – Connecticut
Cord. – Cordillera
Cr. – Creek
Czech. – Czech Republic
D.C. – District of Columbia
Del. – Delaware
Dem. – Democratic
Dep. – Dependency
Des. – Desert
Dét. – Détroit
Dist. – District
Dj. – Djebel
Domin. – Dominica

Dom. Rep. – Dominican Republic
E. – East
E. Salv. – El Salvador
Eq. Guin. – Equatorial Guinea
Est. – Estrecho
Falk. Is. – Falkland Is.
Fd. – Fjord
Fla. – Florida
Fr. – French
G. – Golfe, Golfo, Gulf, Guba, Gebel
Ga. – Georgia
Gt. – Great, Greater
Guinea-Biss. – Guinea-Bissau
H.K. – Hong Kong
H.P. – Himachal Pradesh
Hants. – Hampshire
Harb. – Harbor, Harbour
Hd. – Head
Hts. – Heights
I.(s). – Île, Ilha, Insel, Isla, Island, Isle
Ill. – Illinois
Ind. – Indiana
Ind. Oc. – Indian Ocean
Ivory C. – Ivory Coast
J. – Jabal, Jebel
Jaz. – Jazīrah
Junc. – Junction
K. – Kap, Kapp
Kans. – Kansas
Kep. – Kepulauan
Ky. – Kentucky
L. – Lac, Lacul, Lago, Lagoa, Lake, Limni, Loch, Lough
La. – Louisiana
Ld. – Land
Liech. – Liechtenstein
Lux. – Luxembourg

Mad. P. – Madhya Pradesh
Madag. – Madagascar
Man. – Manitoba
Mass. – Massachusetts
Md. – Maryland
Me. – Maine
Medit. S. – Mediterranean Sea
Mich. – Michigan
Minn. – Minnesota
Miss. – Mississippi
Mo. – Missouri
Mont. – Montana
Mozam. – Mozambique
Mt.(s) – Mont, Montaña, Mountain
Mte. – Monte
Mti. – Monti
N. – Nord, Norte, North, Northern, Nouveau
N.B. – New Brunswick
N.C. – North Carolina
N. Cal. – New Caledonia
N. Dak. – North Dakota
N.H. – New Hampshire
N.I. – North Island
N.J. – New Jersey
N. Mex. – New Mexico
N.S. – Nova Scotia
N.S.W. – New South Wales
N.W.T. – North West Territory
N.Y. – New York
N.Z. – New Zealand
Nat. – National
Nebr. – Nebraska
Neths. – Netherlands
Nev. – Nevada
Nfld. – Newfoundland
Nic. – Nicaragua
O. – Oued, Ouadi
Occ. – Occidentale

Okla. – Oklahoma
Ont. – Ontario
Or. – Orientale
Oreg. – Oregon
Os. – Ostrov
Oz. – Ozero
P. – Pass, Passo, Pasul, Pulau
P.E.I. – Prince Edward Island
Pa. – Pennsylvania
Pac. Oc. – Pacific Ocean
Papua N.G. – Papua New Guinea
Pass. – Passage
Peg. – Pegunungan
Pen. – Peninsula, Péninsule
Phil. – Philippines
Pk. – Peak
Plat. – Plateau
Prov. – Province, Provincial
Pt. – Point
Pta. – Ponta, Punta
Pte. – Pointe
Qué. – Québec
Queens. – Queensland
R. – Rio, River
R.I. – Rhode Island
Ra. – Range
Raj. – Rajasthan
Recr. – Recreational, Récréatif
Reg. – Region
Rep. – Republic
Res. – Reserve, Reservoir
Rhld-Pfz. – Rheinland-Pfalz
S. – South, Southern, Sur
Si. Arabia – Saudi Arabia
S.C. – South Carolina
S. Dak. – South Dakota
S.I. – South Island
S. Leone – Sierra Leone
Sa. – Serra, Sierra

Sask. – Saskatchewan
Scot. – Scotland
Sd. – Sound
Sev. – Severnaya
Sib. – Siberia
Sprs. – Springs
St. – Saint
Sta. – Santa
Ste. – Sainte
Sto. – Santo
Str. – Strait, Stretto
Switz. – Switzerland
Tas. – Tasmania
Tenn. – Tennessee
Terr. – Territory, Territoire
Tex. – Texas
Tg. – Tanjung
Trin. & Tob. – Trinidad & Tobago
U.A.E. – United Arab Emirates
U.K. – United Kingdom
U.S.A. – United States of America
Ut. P. – Uttar Pradesh
Va. – Virginia
Vdkhr. – Vodokhranilishche
Vdskh. – Vodoskhovyshche
Vf. – Vírful
Vic. – Victoria
Vol. – Volcano
Vt. – Vermont
W. – Wadi, West
W. Va. – West Virginia
Wall. & F. Is. – Wallis and Futuna Is.
Wash. – Washington
Wis. – Wisconsin
Wlkp. – Wielkopolski
Wyo. – Wyoming
Yorks. – Yorkshire
Yug. – Yugoslavia

A Baña

A

A Baña, *Spain* 34 C2
A Cañiza, *Spain* 34 C2
A Coruña, *Spain* 34 B2
A Estrada, *Spain* 34 C2
A Fonsagrada, *Spain* 34 B3
A Guarda, *Spain* 34 D2
A Gudiña, *Spain* 34 C3
A Rúa, *Spain* 34 C3
Aachen, *Germany* 24 E2
Aalborg = Ålborg, *Denmark* 11 G3
Aalen, *Germany* 25 G6
A'âli an Nîl □, *Sudan* 81 F3
Aalst, *Belgium* 17 D4
Aalten, *Neths.* 17 C6
Aalter, *Belgium* 17 C3
Äänekoski, *Finland* 9 E21
Aarau, *Switz.* 25 H4
Aarberg, *Switz.* 25 H3
Aare →, *Switz.* 25 H4
Aargau □, *Switz.* 25 H4
Aarhus = Århus, *Denmark* 11 H4
Aarschot, *Belgium* 17 D4
Aba, *China* 58 A3
Aba, *Dem. Rep. of the Congo* 86 B3
Aba, *Nigeria* 83 D6
Âbâ, Jazîrat, *Sudan* 81 E3
Abadab, J., *Sudan* 80 D4
Ābādān, *Iran* 71 D6
Abade, *Ethiopia* 81 F4
Ābādeh, *Iran* 71 D7
Abadin, *Spain* 34 B3
Abadla, *Algeria* 78 B5
Abaetetuba, *Brazil* 125 D9
Abagnar Qi, *China* 56 C9
Abai, *Paraguay* 127 B4
Abak, *Nigeria* 83 E6
Abakaliki, *Nigeria* 83 D6
Abakan, *Russia* 51 D10
Abala, *Niger* 83 C5
Abalak, *Niger* 83 B6
Abalemma, *Niger* 83 B6
Abana, *Turkey* 72 B6
Abancay, *Peru* 124 F4
Abano Terme, *Italy* 29 C8
Abarán, *Spain* 33 G3
Abariringa, *Kiribati* 96 H10
Abarqū, *Iran* 71 D7
Abashiri, *Japan* 54 B12
Abashiri-Wan, *Japan* 54 C12
Abaújszántó, *Hungary* 42 B6
Abava →, *Latvia* 44 A8
Ābay = Nîl el Azraq →, *Sudan* 81 D3
Abay, *Kazakstan* 50 E8
Abaya, L., *Ethiopia* 81 F4
Abaza, *Russia* 50 D9
Abbadia San Salvatore, *Italy* 29 F8
'Abbāsābād, *Iran* 71 C8
Abbay = Nîl el Azraq →, *Sudan* 81 D3
Abbaye, Pt., *U.S.A.* 108 B1
Abbé, L., *Ethiopia* 81 E5
Abbeville, *France* 19 B8
Abbeville, *Ala., U.S.A.* 109 K3
Abbeville, *La., U.S.A.* 113 L8
Abbeville, *S.C., U.S.A.* 109 H4
Abbiategrasso, *Italy* 28 C5
Abbot Ice Shelf, *Antarctica* 5 D16
Abbottabad, *Pakistan* 68 B5
Abd al Kūrī, *Ind. Oc.* 74 E5
Ābdar, *Iran* 71 D7
'Abdolābād, *Iran* 71 C8
Abdulpur, *Bangla.* 69 G13
Abéché, *Chad* 79 F10
Abejar, *Spain* 32 D2
Abekr, *Sudan* 81 E2
Abengourou, *Ivory C.* 82 D4
Abenójar, *Spain* 35 G6
Åbenrå, *Denmark* 11 J3
Abensberg, *Germany* 25 G7
Abeokuta, *Nigeria* 83 D5
Aber, *Uganda* 86 B3
Aberaeron, *U.K.* 13 E3
Aberayron = Aberaeron, *U.K.* 13 E3
Aberchirder, *U.K.* 14 D6
Abercorn = Mbala, *Zambia* 87 D3
Abercorn, *Australia* 95 D5
Aberdare, *U.K.* 13 F4
Aberdare Ra., *Kenya* 86 C4
Aberdeen, *Australia* 95 E5
Aberdeen, *Canada* 105 C7
Aberdeen, *S. Africa* 88 E3
Aberdeen, *U.K.* 14 D6
Aberdeen, *Ala., U.S.A.* 109 J1
Aberdeen, *Idaho, U.S.A.* 114 E7
Aberdeen, *Md., U.S.A.* 108 F7
Aberdeen, *S. Dak., U.S.A.* 112 C5
Aberdeen, *Wash., U.S.A.* 116 D3
Aberdeen, City of □, *U.K.* 14 D6
Aberdeenshire □, *U.K.* 14 D6
Aberdovey = Aberdyfi, *U.K.* 13 E3
Aberdyfi, *U.K.* 13 E3
Aberfeldy, *U.K.* 14 E5
Abergavenny, *U.K.* 13 F4
Abergele, *U.K.* 12 D4
Abernathy, *U.S.A.* 113 J4
Abert, L., *U.S.A.* 114 E3
Aberystwyth, *U.K.* 13 E3
Abhā, *Si. Arabia* 74 D3
Abhar, *Iran* 71 B6
Abhayapuri, *India* 69 F14
Abia □, *Nigeria* 83 D6
Abide, *Turkey* 39 C11
Abidiya, *Sudan* 80 D3
Abidjan, *Ivory C.* 82 D4
Abilene, *Kans., U.S.A.* 112 F6
Abilene, *Tex., U.S.A.* 113 J5
Abingdon, *U.K.* 13 F6
Abingdon, *U.S.A.* 109 G5
Abington Reef, *Australia* 94 B4
Abitau →, *Canada* 105 B7
Abitibi →, *Canada* 102 B3
Abitibi, L., *Canada* 102 C4
Abiy Adi, *Ethiopia* 81 E4
Abkhaz Republic = Abkhazia □, *Georgia* 49 J5
Abkhazia □, *Georgia* 49 J5
Abminga, *Australia* 95 D1
Abnûb, *Egypt* 80 B3
Åbo = Turku, *Finland* 9 F20
Abocho, *Nigeria* 83 D6
Abohar, *India* 68 D6
Aboisso, *Ivory C.* 82 D4
Abomey, *Benin* 83 D5
Abong-Mbang, *Cameroon* 84 D2
Abonnema, *Nigeria* 83 E6
Abony, *Hungary* 42 C5
Aboso, *Ghana* 82 D4
Abou-Deïa, *Chad* 79 F9
Aboyne, *U.K.* 14 D6
Abra Pampa, *Argentina* 126 A2
Abraham L., *Canada* 104 C5
Abrantes, *Portugal* 35 F2
Abreojos, Pta., *Mexico* 118 B2
Abri, *Esh Shamâliya, Sudan* 80 C3
Abri, *Janub Kordofân, Sudan* 81 E3
Abrud, *Romania* 42 D8
Abruzzo □, *Italy* 29 F10
Absaroka Range, *U.S.A.* 114 D9
Abtenau, *Austria* 26 D6
Abu, *India* 68 G5
Abū al Abyad, *U.A.E.* 71 E7
Abū al Khaşīb, *Iraq* 71 D6
Abū 'Alī, *Si. Arabia* 71 E6
Abū 'Alī →, *Lebanon* 75 A4
Abu Ballas, *Egypt* 80 C2
Abu Deleiq, *Sudan* 81 D3
Abu Dhabi = Abū Zāby, *U.A.E.* 71 E7
Abu Dis, *Sudan* 80 D3
Abu Dom, *Sudan* 81 D3
Abū Du'ān, *Syria* 70 B3
Abu el Gairi, W. →, *Egypt* 75 F2
Abu Fatma, Ras, *Sudan* 80 C4
Abu Gabra, *Sudan* 81 E2
Abu Ga'da, W. →, *Egypt* 75 F1
Abu Gelba, *Sudan* 81 E3
Abu Gubeiha, *Sudan* 81 E3
Abu Habl, Khawr →, *Sudan* 81 E3
Abū Ḩadrīyah, *Si. Arabia* 71 E6
Abu Hamed, *Sudan* 80 D3
Abu Haraz, *An Nîl el Azraq, Sudan* 80 D3
Abu Haraz, *El Gezira, Sudan* 81 E3
Abu Haraz, *Esh Shamâliya, Sudan* 80 D3
Abu Higar, *Sudan* 81 E3
Abū Kamāl, *Syria* 70 C4
Abu Kuleiwat, *Sudan* 81 E2
Abū Madd, Ra's, *Si. Arabia* 70 E3
Abu Matariq, *Sudan* 81 E2
Abu Mendi, *Ethiopia* 81 E4
Abū Mūsā, *U.A.E.* 71 E7
Abū Qaşr, *Si. Arabia* 70 D3
Abu Qir, *Egypt* 80 H7
Abu Qireiya, *Egypt* 80 C4
Abu Qurqâs, *Egypt* 80 B3
Abu Şafāt, W. →, *Jordan* 75 E5
Abu Shagara, Ras, *Sudan* 80 C4
Abu Shanab, *Sudan* 81 E2
Abu Simbel, *Egypt* 80 C3
Abū Şukhayr, *Iraq* 70 D5
Abu Sultân, *Egypt* 80 H8
Abu Tabari, *Sudan* 80 D2
Abu Tig, *Egypt* 80 B3
Abu Tiga, *Sudan* 81 E3
Abu Tineitin, *Sudan* 81 E3
Abu Uruq, *Sudan* 81 D3
Abu Zabad, *Sudan* 81 E2
Abū Zāby, *U.A.E.* 71 E7
Abū Zeydābād, *Iran* 71 C6
Abuja, *Nigeria* 83 D6
Abukuma-Gawa →, *Japan* 54 E10
Abukuma-Sammyaku, *Japan* 54 F10
Abunã, *Brazil* 124 E5
Abunã →, *Brazil* 124 E5
Abune Yosef, *Ethiopia* 81 E4
Aburo, *Dem. Rep. of the Congo* 86 B3
Abut Hd., *N.Z.* 91 K3
Abuye Meda, *Ethiopia* 81 E4
Abwong, *Sudan* 81 F3
Åby, *Sweden* 11 F10
Aby, Lagune, *Ivory C.* 82 D4
Abyad, *Sudan* 81 E2
Åbybro, *Denmark* 11 G3
Acadia National Park, *U.S.A.* 109 C11
Açailândia, *Brazil* 125 D9
Acajutla, *El Salv.* 120 D2
Acámbaro, *Mexico* 118 D4
Acanthus, *Greece* 40 F7
Acaponeta, *Mexico* 118 C3
Acapulco, *Mexico* 119 D5
Acarai, Serra, *Brazil* 124 C7
Acarigua, *Venezuela* 124 B5
Acatlán, *Mexico* 119 D5
Acayucan, *Mexico* 119 D6
Accéglio, *Italy* 28 D4
Accomac, *U.S.A.* 108 G8
Accous, *France* 20 E3
Accra, *Ghana* 83 D4
Accrington, *U.K.* 12 D5
Acebal, *Argentina* 126 C3
Aceh □, *Indonesia* 62 D1
Acerra, *Italy* 31 B7
Aceuchal, *Spain* 35 G4
Achalpur, *India* 66 J10
Acheng, *China* 57 B14
Achenkirch, *Austria* 26 D4
Achensee, *Austria* 26 D4
Acher, *India* 68 H5
Achern, *Germany* 25 G4
Achill Hd., *Ireland* 15 C1
Achill I., *Ireland* 15 C1
Achim, *Germany* 24 B5
Achinsk, *Russia* 51 D10
Acıgöl, *Turkey* 39 D11
Acıpayam, *Turkey* 39 D11
Acireale, *Italy* 31 E8
Ackerman, *U.S.A.* 113 J10
Acklins I., *Bahamas* 121 B5
Acme, *Canada* 104 C6
Acme, *U.S.A.* 110 F5
Aconcagua, Cerro, *Argentina* 126 C2
Aconquija, Mt., *Argentina* 126 B2
Açores, Is. dos = Azores, *Atl. Oc.* 78 A1
Acornhoek, *S. Africa* 89 C5
Acquapendente, *Italy* 29 F8
Acquasanta Terme, *Italy* 29 F10
Acquasparta, *Italy* 29 F9
Acquaviva delle Fonti, *Italy* 31 B9
Ácqui Terme, *Italy* 28 D5
Acraman, L., *Australia* 95 E2
Acre = 'Akko, *Israel* 75 C4
Acre □, *Brazil* 124 E4
Acre →, *Brazil* 124 E5
Acri, *Italy* 31 C9
Acs, *Hungary* 42 C3
Actium, *Greece* 38 C2
Acton, *Canada* 110 C4
Acuña, *Mexico* 118 B4
Ad Dammām, *Si. Arabia* 71 E6
Ad Dāmūr, *Lebanon* 75 B4
Ad Dawādimī, *Si. Arabia* 70 E5
Ad Dawḩah, *Qatar* 71 E6
Ad Dawr, *Iraq* 70 C4
Ad Dir'īyah, *Si. Arabia* 70 E5
Ad Dīwānīyah, *Iraq* 70 D5
Ad Dujayl, *Iraq* 70 C5
Ad Duwayd, *Si. Arabia* 70 D4
Ada, *Ghana* 83 D5
Ada, *Serbia, Yug.* 42 E5
Ada, *Minn., U.S.A.* 112 B6
Ada, *Okla., U.S.A.* 113 H6
Adabiya, *Egypt* 75 F1
Adair, C., *Canada* 101 A12
Adaja →, *Spain* 34 D6
Adak I., *U.S.A.* 100 C2
Adamaoua, Massif de l', *Cameroon* 83 D7
Adamawa □, *Nigeria* 83 D7
Adamawa Highlands = Adamaoua, Massif de l', *Cameroon* 83 D7
Adamello, Mte., *Italy* 28 B7
Adami Tulu, *Ethiopia* 81 F4
Adaminaby, *Australia* 95 F4
Adams, *Mass., U.S.A.* 111 D11
Adams, *N.Y., U.S.A.* 111 C8
Adams, *Wis., U.S.A.* 112 D10
Adam's Bridge, *Sri Lanka* 66 Q11
Adams L., *Canada* 104 C5
Adams Mt., *U.S.A.* 116 D5
Adam's Peak, *Sri Lanka* 66 R12
Adamuz, *Spain* 35 G6
Adana, *Turkey* 70 B2
Adanero, *Spain* 34 E6
Adapazarı = Sakarya, *Turkey* 72 B4
Adar Gwagwa, J., *Sudan* 80 C4
Adarama, *Sudan* 81 D3
Adare, C., *Antarctica* 5 D11
Adarte, *Eritrea* 81 E5
Adaut, *Indonesia* 63 F8
Adavale, *Australia* 95 D3
Adda →, *Italy* 28 C6
Addis Ababa = Addis Abeba, *Ethiopia* 81 F4
Addis Abeba, *Ethiopia* 81 F4
Addis Alem, *Ethiopia* 81 F4
Addis Zemen, *Ethiopia* 81 E4
Addison, *U.S.A.* 110 D7
Addo, *S. Africa* 88 E4
Adebour, *Niger* 83 C7
Ādeh, *Iran* 70 B5
Adel, *U.S.A.* 109 K4
Adelaide, *Australia* 95 E2
Adelaide, *Bahamas* 120 A4
Adelaide, *S. Africa* 88 E4
Adelaide I., *Antarctica* 5 C17
Adelaide Pen., *Canada* 100 B10
Adelaide River, *Australia* 92 B5
Adelanto, *U.S.A.* 117 L9
Adele I., *Australia* 92 C3
Adélie, Terre, *Antarctica* 5 C10
Adélie Land = Adélie, Terre, *Antarctica* 5 C10
Ademuz, *Spain* 32 E3
Aden = Al 'Adan, *Yemen* 74 E4
Aden, G. of, *Asia* 74 E4
Adendorp, *S. Africa* 88 E3
Aderbissinat, *Niger* 83 B6
Adh Dhayd, *U.A.E.* 71 E7
Adhoi, *India* 68 H4
Adi, *Indonesia* 63 E8
Adi Arkai, *Ethiopia* 81 E4
Adi Daro, *Ethiopia* 81 E4
Adi Keyih, *Eritrea* 81 E4
Adi Kwala, *Eritrea* 81 E4
Adi Ugri, *Eritrea* 81 E4
Adieu, C., *Australia* 93 F5
Adieu Pt., *Australia* 92 C3
Adigala, *Ethiopia* 81 E5
Adige →, *Italy* 29 C9
Adigrat, *Ethiopia* 81 E4
Adıgüzel Barajı, *Turkey* 39 C11
Adilabad, *India* 66 K11
Adilcevaz, *Turkey* 73 C10
Adirondack Mts., *U.S.A.* 111 C10
Adıyaman, *Turkey* 73 D8
Adjohon, *Benin* 83 D5
Adjud, *Romania* 43 D12
Adjumani, *Uganda* 86 B3
Adlavik Is., *Canada* 103 A8
Adler, *Russia* 49 J4
Admer, *Algeria* 83 A6
Admiralty G., *Australia* 92 B4
Admiralty I., *U.S.A.* 104 B2
Admiralty Is., *Papua N. G.* 96 H6
Ado, *Nigeria* 83 D5
Ado-Ekiti, *Nigeria* 83 D6
Adok, *Sudan* 81 F3
Adola, *Ethiopia* 81 E5
Adonara, *Indonesia* 63 F6
Adoni, *India* 66 M10
Adony, *Hungary* 42 C3
Adour →, *France* 20 E2
Adra, *India* 69 H12
Adra, *Spain* 35 J7
Adrano, *Italy* 31 E7
Adrar, *Mauritania* 78 D3
Adrar des Iforas, *Algeria* 78 C5
Ádria, *Italy* 29 C9
Adrian, *Mich., U.S.A.* 108 E3
Adrian, *Tex., U.S.A.* 113 H3
Adriatic Sea, *Medit. S.* 6 G9
Adua, *Indonesia* 63 E7
Adwa, *Ethiopia* 81 E4
Adygea □, *Russia* 49 H5
Adzhar Republic = Ajaria □, *Georgia* 49 K6
Adzopé, *Ivory C.* 82 D4
Ægean Sea, *Medit. S.* 39 C7
Aerhtai Shan, *Mongolia* 60 B4
Ærø, *Denmark* 11 K4
Ærøskøbing, *Denmark* 11 K4
Aëtós, *Greece* 38 D3
'Afak, *Iraq* 70 C5
Afándou, *Greece* 36 C10
Afghanistan ■, *Asia* 66 C4
Afikpo, *Nigeria* 83 D6
Aflou, *Algeria* 78 B6
Afragóla, *Italy* 31 B7
Afram →, *Ghana* 83 D4
Afrera, *Ethiopia* 81 E5
Africa 76 E6
'Afrīn, *Syria* 70 B3
Afşin, *Turkey* 72 C7
Afton, *N.Y., U.S.A.* 111 D9
Afton, *Wyo., U.S.A.* 114 E8
Afuá, *Brazil* 125 D8
'Afula, *Israel* 75 C4
Afyon, *Turkey* 39 C12
Afyon □, *Turkey* 39 C12
Afyonkarahisar = Afyon, *Turkey* 39 C12
Aga, *Egypt* 80 H7
Agadès = Agadez, *Niger* 83 B6
Agadez, *Niger* 83 B6
Agadir, *Morocco* 78 B4
Agaete, *Canary Is.* 37 F4
Agaie, *Nigeria* 83 D6
Again, *Sudan* 81 F2
Ağapınar, *Turkey* 39 B12
Agar, *India* 68 H7
Agaro, *Ethiopia* 81 F4
Agartala, *India* 67 H17
Agăş, *Romania* 43 D11
Agassiz, *Canada* 104 D4
Agats, *Indonesia* 63 F9
Agawam, *U.S.A.* 111 D12
Agbélouvé, *Togo* 83 D5
Agboville, *Ivory C.* 82 D4
Ağcabädi, *Azerbaijan* 49 K8
Ağdam, *Azerbaijan* 49 L8
Ağdaş, *Azerbaijan* 49 K8
Agde, *France* 20 E7
Agde, C. d', *France* 20 E7
Agdzhabedi = Ağcabädi, *Azerbaijan* 49 K8
Agen, *France* 20 D4
Agerbæk, *Denmark* 11 J2
Agersø, *Denmark* 11 J5
Ageyevo, *Russia* 46 E9
Āgh Kand, *Iran* 71 B6
Aghireşu, *Romania* 43 D8
Aginskoye, *Russia* 51 D12
Ağlasun, *Turkey* 39 D12
Agly →, *France* 20 F7
Agnew, *Australia* 93 E3
Agnibilékrou, *Ivory C.* 82 D4
Agnita, *Romania* 43 E9
Agnone, *Italy* 29 G11
Agofie, *Ghana* 83 D5
Agogna →, *Italy* 28 C5
Agogo, *Sudan* 81 F2
Agön, *Sweden* 10 C11
Agon Coutainville, *France* 18 C5
Ágordo, *Italy* 29 B9
Agori, *India* 69 G10
Agouna, *Benin* 83 D5
Agout →, *France* 20 E5
Agra, *India* 68 F7
Agrakhanskiy Poluostrov, *Russia* 49 J8
Agramunt, *Spain* 32 D6
Agreda, *Spain* 32 D3
Ağri, *Turkey* 73 C10
Agri →, *Italy* 31 B9
Ağrı Dağı, *Turkey* 70 B5
Ağri Karakose = Ağri, *Turkey* 73 C10
Agriá, *Greece* 38 B5
Agrigento, *Italy* 30 E6
Agrínion, *Greece* 38 C3
Agrópoli, *Italy* 31 B7
Ağstafa, *Azerbaijan* 49 K7
Agua Caliente, *Baja Calif., Mexico* 117 N10
Agua Caliente, *Sinaloa, Mexico* 118 B3
Agua Caliente Springs, *U.S.A.* 117 N10
Água Clara, *Brazil* 125 H8
Agua Hechicero, *Mexico* 117 N10
Agua Prieta, *Mexico* 118 A3
Aguadilla, *Puerto Rico* 121 C6
Aguadulce, *Panama* 120 E3
Aguanga, *U.S.A.* 117 M10
Aguanish, *Canada* 103 B7
Aguanus →, *Canada* 103 B7
Aguapey →, *Argentina* 126 B4
Aguaray Guazú →, *Paraguay* 126 A4
Aguarico →, *Ecuador* 124 D3
Aguas →, *Spain* 32 D4
Aguas Blancas, *Chile* 126 A2
Aguas Calientes, Sierra de, *Argentina* 126 B2
Aguascalientes, *Mexico* 118 C4
Aguascalientes □, *Mexico* 118 C4
Agudo, *Spain* 35 G6
Águeda, *Portugal* 34 E2
Agueda →, *Spain* 34 D4
Aguelhok, *Mali* 83 B5
Aguié, *Niger* 83 C6
Aguilafuente, *Spain* 34 D6
Aguilar, *Spain* 35 H6
Aguilar de Campóo, *Spain* 34 C6
Aguilares, *Argentina* 126 B2
Aguilas, *Spain* 33 H3
Agüimes, *Canary Is.* 37 G4
Aguja, C. de la, *Colombia* 122 B3
Agulaa, *Ethiopia* 81 E4
Agulhas, C., *S. Africa* 88 E3
Agulo, *Canary Is.* 37 F2
Agung, *Indonesia* 62 F5
Agur, *Uganda* 86 B3
Agusan →, *Phil.* 61 G6
Ağva, *Turkey* 41 E13
Agvali, *Russia* 49 J8
Aha Mts., *Botswana* 88 B3
Ahaggar, *Algeria* 78 D7
Ahamansu, *Ghana* 83 D5
Ahar, *Iran* 70 B5
Ahat, *Turkey* 39 C11
Ahaus, *Germany* 24 C2
Ahipara B., *N.Z.* 91 F4
Ahir Dağı, *Turkey* 39 C12
Ahiri, *India* 66 K12
Ahlat, *Turkey* 73 C10
Ahlen, *Germany* 24 D3
Ahmad Wal, *Pakistan* 68 E1
Ahmadabad, *India* 68 H5
Aḩmadābād, *Khorāsān, Iran* 71 C9
Aḩmadābād, *Khorāsān, Iran* 71 C8
Aḩmadī, *Iran* 71 E8
Ahmadnagar, *India* 66 K9
Ahmadpur, *Pakistan* 68 E4
Ahmadpur Lamma, *Pakistan* 68 E4
Ahmar, *Ethiopia* 81 F5
Ahmedabad = Ahmadabad, *India* 68 H5
Ahmednagar = Ahmadnagar, *India* 66 K9
Ahmetbey, *Turkey* 41 E11
Ahmetler, *Turkey* 39 C11
Ahmetli, *Turkey* 39 C9
Ahoada, *Nigeria* 83 D6
Ahome, *Mexico* 118 B3
Ahoskie, *U.S.A.* 109 G7
Ahr →, *Germany* 24 E3
Ahram, *Iran* 71 D6
Ahrax Pt., *Malta* 36 D1
Ahrensbök, *Germany* 24 A6
Ahrensburg, *Germany* 24 B6
Āhū, *Iran* 71 C6
Ahuachapán, *El Salv.* 120 D2
Ahun, *France* 19 F9
Åhus, *Sweden* 11 J8
Ahvāz, *Iran* 71 D6
Ahvenanmaa = Åland, *Finland* 9 F19
Aḩwar, *Yemen* 74 E4
Ahzar →, *Mali* 83 B5
Ai →, *India* 69 F14
Ai-Ais, *Namibia* 88 D2
Aichach, *Germany* 25 G7
Aichi □, *Japan* 55 G8
Aigle, *Switz.* 25 J2
Aignay-le-Duc, *France* 19 E11
Aigoual, Mt., *France* 20 D7
Aigre, *France* 20 C4
Aigua, *Uruguay* 127 C5
Aigueperse, *France* 19 F10
Aigues →, *France* 21 D8
Aigues-Mortes, *France* 21 E8
Aigues-Mortes, G. d', *France* 21 E8
Aiguilles, *France* 21 D10
Aiguillon, *France* 20 D4
Aigurande, *France* 19 F8
Aihui, *China* 60 A7
Aija, *Peru* 124 E3
Aikawa, *Japan* 54 E9
Aiken, *U.S.A.* 109 J5
Ailao Shan, *China* 58 F3
Aileron, *Australia* 94 C1
Aillant-sur-Tholon, *France* 19 E10
Aillik, *Canada* 103 A8
Ailsa Craig, *U.K.* 14 F3
'Ailūn, *Jordan* 75 C4
Aim, *Russia* 51 D14

Aimere, *Indonesia* 63 F6
Aimogasta, *Argentina* 126 B2
Ain □, *France* 19 F12
Ain ➤, *France* 21 C9
Aïn Ben Tili, *Mauritania* 78 C4
Ain Dalla, *Egypt* 80 B2
Ain el Mafki, *Egypt* 80 B2
Ain Girba, *Egypt* 80 B2
Ain Murr, *Sudan* 80 C2
Ain Qeiqab, *Egypt* 80 B1
Aïn Sefra, *Algeria* 78 B5
Aïn Sheikh Murzûk, *Egypt* 80 B2
Ain Sudr, *Egypt* 75 F2
Ain Sukhna, *Egypt* 80 J8
Ain Zeitûn, *Egypt* 80 B2
Ainaži, *Latvia* 9 H21
Aínos Óros, *Greece* 38 C2
Ainsworth, *U.S.A.* 112 D5
Aiquile, *Bolivia* 124 G5
Aïr, *Niger* 83 B6
Air Force I., *Canada* 101 B12
Air Hitam, *Malaysia* 65 M4
Airaines, *France* 19 C8
Airdrie, *Canada* 104 C6
Airdrie, *U.K.* 14 F5
Aire ➤, *France* 19 C11
Aire ➤, *U.K.* 12 D7
Aire, I. de l', *Spain* 37 B11
Aire-sur-la-Lys, *France* 19 B9
Aire-sur-l'Adour, *France* 20 E3
Airlie Beach, *Australia* 94 C4
Airvault, *France* 18 F6
Aisch ➤, *Germany* 25 F6
Aisne □, *France* 19 C10
Aisne ➤, *France* 19 C9
Ait, *India* 69 G8
Aitana, Sierra de, *Spain* 33 G4
Aitkin, *U.S.A.* 112 B8
Aitolía Kai Akarnanía □, *Greece* 38 C3
Aitolikón, *Greece* 38 C3
Aiud, *Romania* 43 D8
Aix-en-Provence, *France* 21 E9
Aix-la-Chapelle = Aachen, *Germany* 24 E2
Aix-les-Bains, *France* 21 C9
Aixe-sur-Vienne, *France* 20 C5
Áïyina, *Greece* 38 D5
Aiyínion, *Greece* 40 F6
Aíyion, *Greece* 38 C4
Aizawl, *India* 67 H18
Aizenay, *France* 18 F5
Aizkraukle, *Latvia* 9 H21
Aizpute, *Latvia* 9 H19
Aizuwakamatsu, *Japan* 54 F9
Ajaccio, *France* 21 G12
Ajaccio, G. d', *France* 21 G12
Ajaigarh, *India* 69 G9
Ajalpan, *Mexico* 119 D5
Ajanta Ra., *India* 66 J9
Ajari Rep. = Ajaria □, *Georgia* 49 K6
Ajaria □, *Georgia* 49 K6
Ajax, *Canada* 110 C5
Ajdâbiyâ, *Libya* 79 B10
Ajdovščina, *Slovenia* 29 C10
Ajibar, *Ethiopia* 81 E4
Ajka, *Hungary* 42 C2
'Ajmān, *U.A.E.* 71 E7
Ajmer, *India* 68 F6
Ajnala, *India* 68 D6
Ajo, *U.S.A.* 115 K7
Ajo, C. de, *Spain* 34 B7
Ajok, *Sudan* 81 F2
Ajuy, *Phil.* 61 F5
Ak Dağ, *Turkey* 39 E11
Ak Dağları, *Muğla, Turkey* 39 E11
Ak Dağları, *Sivas, Turkey* 72 C7
Akaba, *Togo* 83 D5
Akabira, *Japan* 54 C11
Akaki Beseka, *Ethiopia* 81 F4
Akala, *Sudan* 81 E3
Akamas □, *Cyprus* 36 D11
Akanthou, *Cyprus* 36 D12
Akarca, *Turkey* 39 C11
Akaroa, *N.Z.* 91 K4
Akasha, *Sudan* 80 C3
Akashi, *Japan* 55 G7
Akbarpur, *India* 69 G10
Akbarpur, *Ut. P., India* 69 F10
Akçaabat, *Turkey* 73 B8
Akçadağ, *Turkey* 72 C7
Akçakale, *Turkey* 73 D8
Akçakoca, *Turkey* 72 B4
Akçaova, *Turkey* 41 E13
Akçay, *Turkey* 39 E11
Akçay ➤, *Turkey* 39 D10
Akdağ, *Turkey* 39 C8
Akdağmadeni, *Turkey* 72 C6
Akelamo, *Indonesia* 63 D7
Åkers styckebruk, *Sweden* 10 E11
Åkersberga, *Sweden* 10 E12
Aketi, *Dem. Rep. of the Congo* 84 D4
Akhaïa □, *Greece* 38 C3
Akhalkalaki, *Georgia* 49 K6
Akhaltsikhe, *Georgia* 49 K6
Akharnaí, *Greece* 38 C5
Akhelóös ➤, *Greece* 38 C3
Akhendriá, *Greece* 39 G7
Akhisar, *Turkey* 39 C9
Akhladhókambos, *Greece* 38 D4
Akhmîm, *Egypt* 80 B3
Akhnur, *India* 69 C6
Akhtopol, *Bulgaria* 41 D11
Akhtuba ➤, *Russia* 49 G8
Akhtubinsk, *Russia* 49 F8
Akhty, *Russia* 49 K8
Akhtyrka = Okhtyrka, *Ukraine* 47 G8
Aki, *Japan* 55 H6

Akimiski I., *Canada* 102 B3
Akimovka, *Ukraine* 47 J8
Åkirkeby, *Denmark* 11 J8
Akita, *Japan* 54 E10
Akita □, *Japan* 54 E10
Akjoujt, *Mauritania* 82 B2
Akka, *Mali* 82 B4
Akkaya Tepesi, *Turkey* 39 D11
Akkeshi, *Japan* 54 C12
'Akko, *Israel* 75 C4
Akköy, *Turkey* 39 D9
Aklampa, *Benin* 83 D5
Aklavik, *Canada* 100 B6
Aklera, *India* 68 G7
Akmenė, *Lithuania* 44 B9
Akmenrags, *Latvia* 44 B8
Akmolinsk = Astana, *Kazakstan* 50 D8
Akmonte = Almonte, *Spain* 35 H4
Akô, *Japan* 55 G7
Ako, *Nigeria* 83 C7
Akôbô, *Sudan* 81 F3
Akobo ➤, *Ethiopia* 81 F3
Akola, *India* 66 J10
Akonolinga, *Cameroon* 83 E7
Akor, *Mali* 82 C4
Akordat, *Eritrea* 81 D4
Akosombo Dam, *Ghana* 83 D5
Akot, *Sudan* 81 F3
Akoupé, *Ivory C.* 82 D4
Akpatok I., *Canada* 101 B13
Åkrahamn, *Norway* 9 G11
Akranes, *Iceland* 8 D2
Akreïjit, *Mauritania* 82 B3
Akrítas Venétiko, Ákra, *Greece* 38 E3
Akron, *Colo., U.S.A.* 112 E3
Akron, *Ohio, U.S.A.* 110 E3
Akrotíri, *Cyprus* 36 E11
Akrotíri, Ákra, *Greece* 41 F9
Akrotiri Bay, *Cyprus* 36 E12
Aksai Chin, *India* 69 B8
Aksaray, *Turkey* 72 C2
Aksay, *Kazakstan* 50 D6
Akşehir, *Turkey* 72 C4
Akşehir Gölü, *Turkey* 72 C4
Aksu, *China* 60 B3
Aksu ➤, *Turkey* 72 D4
Aksum, *Ethiopia* 81 E4
Aktash, *Russia* 48 C11
Aktogay, *Kazakstan* 50 E8
Aktsyabrski, *Belarus* 47 F5
Aktyubinsk = Aqtöbe, *Kazakstan* 50 D6
Aku, *Nigeria* 83 D6
Akure, *Nigeria* 83 D6
Akureyri, *Iceland* 8 D4
Akuseki-Shima, *Japan* 55 K4
Akusha, *Russia* 49 J8
Akwa-Ibom □, *Nigeria* 83 E6
Akyab = Sittwe, *Burma* 67 J18
Akyazı, *Turkey* 72 B4
Al 'Adan, *Yemen* 74 E4
Al Aḥsā = Hasa □, *Si. Arabia* 71 E6
Al Ajfar, *Si. Arabia* 70 E4
Al Amādīyah, *Iraq* 70 B4
Al 'Amārah, *Iraq* 70 D5
Al 'Aqabah, *Jordan* 75 F4
Al Arak, *Syria* 70 C3
Al 'Aramah, *Si. Arabia* 70 E5
Al Arṭāwīyah, *Si. Arabia* 70 E5
Al 'Āsimah = 'Ammān □, *Jordan* 75 D5
Al 'Assāfīyah, *Si. Arabia* 70 D3
Al 'Ayn, *Oman* 71 E7
Al 'Ayn, *Si. Arabia* 70 E3
Al 'Azamīyah, *Iraq* 70 C5
Al 'Azīzīyah, *Iraq* 70 C5
Al Bāb, *Syria* 70 B3
Al Bad', *Si. Arabia* 70 D2
Al Bādī, *Iraq* 70 C4
Al Bahrah, *Kuwait* 70 D5
Al Bahral Mayyit = Dead Sea, *Asia* 75 D4
Al Balqā' □, *Jordan* 75 C4
Al Bārūk, J., *Lebanon* 75 B4
Al Baṣrah, *Iraq* 70 D5
Al Baṭḥā, *Iraq* 70 D5
Al Batrūn, *Lebanon* 75 A4
Al Baydā, *Libya* 79 B10
Al Biqā, *Lebanon* 75 A5
Al Bi'r, *Si. Arabia* 70 D3
Al Burayj, *Syria* 75 A5
Al Faḍilī, *Si. Arabia* 71 E6
Al Fallūjah, *Iraq* 70 C4
Al Fāw, *Iraq* 71 D6
Al Fujayrah, *U.A.E.* 71 E8
Al Ghadaf, W. ➤, *Jordan* 75 D5
Al Ghammās, *Iraq* 70 D5
Al Ghazālah, *Si. Arabia* 70 E4
Al Ḥadīthah, *Iraq* 70 C4
Al Ḥadīthah, *Si. Arabia* 75 D6
Al Ḥaḍr, *Iraq* 70 C4
Al Ḥājānah, *Syria* 75 B5
Al Hajar al Gharbi, *Oman* 71 E8
Al Ḥāmad, *Si. Arabia* 70 D3
Al Ḥamdānīyah, *Syria* 70 C3
Al Ḥamīdīyah, *Syria* 75 A4
Al Ḥammār, *Iraq* 70 D5
Al Ḥamrā', *Si. Arabia* 70 E4
Al Ḥanākīyah, *Si. Arabia* 70 E4
Al Ḥarīr, W. ➤, *Syria* 75 C4
Al Ḥasā, W. ➤, *Jordan* 75 D4
Al Ḥasakah, *Syria* 70 B4
Al Ḥayy, *Iraq* 70 C5
Al Ḥaydān, W. ➤, *Jordan* 75 D4
Al Ḥijarah, *Asia* 70 D4
Al Ḥillah, *Iraq* 70 C5

Al Ḥillah, *Si. Arabia* 74 B4
Al Hindīyah, *Iraq* 70 C5
Al Hirmil, *Lebanon* 75 A5
Al Hoceïma, *Morocco* 78 A5
Al Ḥudaydah, *Yemen* 74 E3
Al Hufūf, *Si. Arabia* 71 E6
Al Ḥumayḍah, *Si. Arabia* 70 D2
Al Ḥunayy, *Si. Arabia* 71 E6
Al Īsāwīyah, *Si. Arabia* 70 D3
Al Jafr, *Jordan* 75 E5
Al Jāfūrah, *Si. Arabia* 71 E7
Al Jaghbūb, *Libya* 79 C10
Al Jahrah, *Kuwait* 70 D5
Al Jalāmīd, *Si. Arabia* 70 D3
Al Jamalīyah, *Qatar* 71 E6
Al Janūb □, *Lebanon* 75 B4
Al Jawf, *Libya* 79 D10
Al Jawf, *Si. Arabia* 70 D3
Al Jazirah, *Iraq* 70 C5
Al Jithāmīyah, *Si. Arabia* 70 E4
Al Jubayl, *Si. Arabia* 71 E6
Al Jubaylah, *Si. Arabia* 70 E5
Al Jubb, *Si. Arabia* 70 E4
Al Junaynah, *Sudan* 79 F10
Al Kabā'ish, *Iraq* 70 D5
Al Karak, *Jordan* 75 D4
Al Karak □, *Jordan* 75 E5
Al Kāzim Tyah, *Iraq* 70 C5
Al Khābūra, *Oman* 71 F8
Al Khafji, *Si. Arabia* 71 E6
Al Khalīl, *West Bank* 75 D4
Al Khāliṣ, *Iraq* 70 C5
Al Kharsānīyah, *Si. Arabia* 71 E6
Al Khaṣab, *Oman* 71 E8
Al Khawr, *Qatar* 71 E6
Al Khiḍr, *Iraq* 70 D5
Al Khiyām, *Lebanon* 75 B4
Al Kiswah, *Syria* 75 B5
Al Kūfah, *Iraq* 70 C5
Al Kufrah, *Libya* 79 D10
Al Kuhayfiyah, *Si. Arabia* 70 E4
Al Kūt, *Iraq* 70 C5
Al Kuwayt, *Kuwait* 70 D5
Al Labwah, *Lebanon* 75 A5
Al Lādhiqīyah, *Syria* 70 C2
Al Līth, *Si. Arabia* 74 C3
Al Liwā', *Oman* 71 E8
Al Luḥayyah, *Yemen* 74 D3
Al Madīnah, *Iraq* 70 D5
Al Madīnah, *Si. Arabia* 70 E3
Al Mafraq, *Jordan* 75 C5
Al Maḥmūdīyah, *Iraq* 70 C5
Al Majma'ah, *Si. Arabia* 70 E5
Al Makhruq, W. ➤, *Jordan* 75 D6
Al Makḥūl, *Si. Arabia* 70 E4
Al Manāmah, *Bahrain* 71 E6
Al Maqwa', *Kuwait* 70 D5
Al Marj, *Libya* 79 B10
Al Maṭlā, *Kuwait* 70 D5
Al Mawjib, W. ➤, *Jordan* 75 D4
Al Mawṣil, *Iraq* 70 B4
Al Mayādin, *Syria* 70 C4
Al Mazār, *Jordan* 75 D4
Al Midhnab, *Si. Arabia* 70 E5
Al Minā', *Lebanon* 75 A4
Al Miqdādīyah, *Iraq* 70 C5
Al Mubarraz, *Si. Arabia* 71 E6
Al Mudawwarah, *Jordan* 75 F5
Al Mughayrā', *U.A.E.* 71 E7
Al Muḥarraq, *Bahrain* 71 E6
Al Mukallā, *Yemen* 74 E4
Al Mukhā, *Yemen* 74 E3
Al Musayjid, *Si. Arabia* 70 E3
Al Musayyib, *Iraq* 70 C5
Al Muwayh, *Si. Arabia* 80 C5
Al Muwaylih, *Si. Arabia* 70 E2
Al Owuho = Otukpa, *Nigeria* 83 D6
Al Qā'im, *Iraq* 70 C4
Al Qalībah, *Si. Arabia* 70 D3
Al Qāmishlī, *Syria* 70 B4
Al Qaryatayn, *Syria* 75 A6
Al Qaṣīm, *Si. Arabia* 70 E4
Al Qaṭ'ā, *Syria* 70 C4
Al Qaṭīf, *Si. Arabia* 71 E6
Al Qatrānah, *Jordan* 75 D5
Al Qaṭrūn, *Libya* 79 D9
Al Qayṣūmah, *Si. Arabia* 70 D5
Al Quds = Jerusalem, *Israel* 75 D4
Al Qunayṭirah, *Syria* 75 C4
Al Qunfudhah, *Si. Arabia* 80 D5
Al Qurnah, *Iraq* 70 D5
Al Quṣayr, *Iraq* 70 D5
Al Quṣayr, *Syria* 75 A5
Al Qutayfah, *Syria* 75 B5
Al 'Ubaylah, *Si. Arabia* 74 C5
Al 'Uḍaylīyah, *Si. Arabia* 71 E6
Al 'Ulā, *Si. Arabia* 70 E3
Al 'Uqayr, *Si. Arabia* 71 E6
Al 'Uwaynid, *Si. Arabia* 70 E5
Al 'Uwayqīlah, *Si. Arabia* 70 D4
Al 'Uyūn, *Ḥijāz, Si. Arabia* 70 E3
Al 'Uyūn, *Najd, Si. Arabia* 70 E4
Al 'Uzayr, *Iraq* 70 D5
Al Wajh, *Si. Arabia* 70 E3
Al Wakrah, *Qatar* 71 E6
Al Waqbah, *Si. Arabia* 70 D5
Al Wari'ah, *Si. Arabia* 70 E5

Alaçatı, *Turkey* 39 C8
Alachua, *U.S.A.* 109 L4
Alaejos, *Spain* 34 D5
Alaérma, *Greece* 36 C9
Alagir, *Russia* 49 J7
Alagna Valsésia, *Italy* 28 C4
Alagoa Grande, *Brazil* 125 E11
Alagoas □, *Brazil* 125 E11
Alagoinhas, *Brazil* 125 F11
Alagón, *Spain* 32 D3
Alagón ➤, *Spain* 34 F4
Alaior, *Spain* 37 B11
Alajero, *Canary Is.* 37 F2
Alajuela, *Costa Rica* 120 D3
Alakamisy, *Madag.* 89 C8
Alaknanda ➤, *India* 69 D8
Alakol, Ozero, *Kazakstan* 60 B3
Alamarvdasht, *Iran* 71 E7
Alamata, *Ethiopia* 81 E4
Alameda, *Calif., U.S.A.* 116 H4
Alameda, *N. Mex., U.S.A.* 115 J10
Alaminos, *Phil.* 61 C3
Alamo, *U.S.A.* 117 J11
Alamo Crossing, *U.S.A.* 117 L13
Alamogordo, *U.S.A.* 115 K11
Alamos, *Mexico* 118 B3
Alamosa, *U.S.A.* 115 H11
Åland, *Finland* 9 F19
Alandroal, *Portugal* 35 G3
Ålands hav, *Sweden* 9 F18
Alange, Presa de, *Spain* 35 G4
Alania = North Ossetia □, *Russia* 49 J7
Alanís, *Spain* 35 G5
Alanya, *Turkey* 70 B1
Alaotra, Farihin', *Madag.* 89 B8
Alapayevsk, *Russia* 50 D7
Alappuzha = Alleppey, *India* 66 Q10
Alar del Rey, *Spain* 34 C6
Alaraz, *Spain* 34 E5
Alarcón, Embalse de, *Spain* 32 F2
Alarobia-Vohiposa, *Madag.* 89 C8
Alaşehir, *Turkey* 39 C10
Alaska □, *U.S.A.* 100 B5
Alaska, G. of, *Pac. Oc.* 100 C5
Alaska Peninsula, *U.S.A.* 100 C4
Alaska Range, *U.S.A.* 100 B4
Alássio, *Italy* 28 E5
Ålät, *Azerbaijan* 49 L9
Alatri, *Italy* 29 G10
Alatyr, *Russia* 48 C8
Alatyr ➤, *Russia* 48 C8
Alausi, *Ecuador* 124 D3
Álava □, *Spain* 32 C2
Alava, C., *U.S.A.* 114 B1
Alaverdi, *Armenia* 49 K7
Alavus, *Finland* 9 E20
Alawoona, *Australia* 95 E3
'Alayh, *Lebanon* 75 B4
Alazani ➤, *Azerbaijan* 49 K8
Alba, *Italy* 28 D5
Alba □, *Romania* 43 D8
Alba Adriática, *Italy* 29 F10
Alba de Tormes, *Spain* 34 E5
Alba-Iulia, *Romania* 43 D8
Albac, *Romania* 43 D7
Albacete, *Spain* 33 G3
Albacete □, *Spain* 33 G3
Albacutya, L., *Australia* 95 F3
Ålbæk, *Denmark* 11 G4
Ålbæk Bugt, *Denmark* 11 G4
Albaida, *Spain* 33 G4
Albalate de las Nogueras, *Spain* 32 E2
Albalate del Arzobispo, *Spain* 32 D4
Alban, *France* 20 E6
Albanel, L., *Canada* 102 B5
Albania ■, *Europe* 40 E4
Albano Laziale, *Italy* 29 G9
Albany, *Australia* 93 G2
Albany, *Ga., U.S.A.* 109 K3
Albany, *N.Y., U.S.A.* 111 D11
Albany, *Oreg., U.S.A.* 114 D2
Albany, *Tex., U.S.A.* 113 J5
Albany ➤, *Canada* 102 B3
Albardón, *Argentina* 126 C2
Albarracín, *Spain* 32 E3
Albarracín, Sierra de, *Spain* 32 E3
Albatera, *Spain* 33 G4
Albatross B., *Australia* 94 A3
Albegna ➤, *Italy* 29 F8
Albemarle, *U.S.A.* 109 H5
Albemarle Sd., *U.S.A.* 109 H7
Albenga, *Italy* 28 D5
Alberche ➤, *Spain* 34 F6
Alberdi, *Paraguay* 126 B4
Alberes, Mts., *France* 20 F6
Ålberga, *Sweden* 11 F10
Albersdorf, *Germany* 24 A5
Albert, *France* 19 C9
Albert, L., *Africa* 86 B3
Albert, L., *Australia* 95 F2
Albert Edward Ra., *Australia* 92 C4
Albert Lea, *U.S.A.* 112 D8
Albert Nile ➤, *Uganda* 86 B3
Albert Town, *Bahamas* 121 B5
Alberta □, *Canada* 104 C6
Alberti, *Argentina* 126 D3
Albertinia, *S. Africa* 88 E3
Albertirsa, *Hungary* 42 C4
Alberton, *Canada* 103 C7
Albertville = Kalemie, *Dem. Rep. of the Congo* 86 D2
Albertville, *France* 21 C10
Albertville, *U.S.A.* 109 H2
Albi, *France* 20 E6
Albia, *U.S.A.* 112 E8
Albina, *Surinam* 125 B8

Albina, Ponta, *Angola* 88 B1
Albino, *Italy* 28 C6
Albion, *Mich., U.S.A.* 108 D3
Albion, *Nebr., U.S.A.* 112 E6
Albion, *Pa., U.S.A.* 110 E4
Albocácer, *Spain* 32 E5
Albolote, *Spain* 35 H7
Alborán, *Medit. S.* 35 K7
Alborea, *Spain* 33 F3
Ålborg, *Denmark* 11 G3
Ålborg Bugt, *Denmark* 11 H4
Alborz, Reshteh-ye Kūhhā-ye, *Iran* 71 C7
Albox, *Spain* 33 H2
Albufeira, *Portugal* 35 H2
Albula ➤, *Switz.* 25 J5
Albuñol, *Spain* 35 J7
Albuquerque, *U.S.A.* 115 J10
Albuquerque, Cayos de, *Caribbean* 120 D3
Alburg, *U.S.A.* 111 B11
Alburquerque, *Spain* 35 F4
Albury = Albury-Wodonga, *Australia* 95 F4
Albury-Wodonga, *Australia* 95 F4
Alcácer do Sal, *Portugal* 35 G2
Alcáçovas, *Portugal* 35 G2
Alcalá de Chivert, *Spain* 32 E5
Alcalá de Guadaira, *Spain* 35 H5
Alcalá de Henares, *Spain* 34 E7
Alcalá de los Gazules, *Spain* 35 J5
Alcalá del Júcar, *Spain* 33 F3
Alcalá del Río, *Spain* 35 H5
Alcalá del Valle, *Spain* 35 J5
Alcalá la Real, *Spain* 35 H7
Álcamo, *Italy* 30 E5
Alcanadre, *Spain* 32 C2
Alcanadre ➤, *Spain* 32 D4
Alcanar, *Spain* 32 E5
Alcanede, *Portugal* 35 F2
Alcanena, *Portugal* 35 F2
Alcañices, *Spain* 34 D4
Alcañiz, *Spain* 32 D4
Alcântara, *Brazil* 125 D10
Alcántara, *Spain* 34 F4
Alcántara, Embalse de, *Spain* 34 F4
Alcantarilla, *Spain* 33 H3
Alcaracejos, *Spain* 35 G6
Alcaraz, *Spain* 33 G2
Alcaraz, Sierra de, *Spain* 33 G2
Alcaudete, *Spain* 35 H6
Alcázar de San Juan, *Spain* 35 F7
Alchevsk, *Ukraine* 47 H10
Alcira = Alzira, *Spain* 33 F4
Alcoa, *U.S.A.* 109 H4
Alcobaça, *Portugal* 35 F2
Alcobendas, *Spain* 34 E7
Alcoi = Alcoy, *Spain* 33 G4
Alcora, *Spain* 32 E4
Alcorcón, *Spain* 34 E7
Alcoutim, *Portugal* 35 H3
Alcova, *U.S.A.* 114 E10
Alcoy, *Spain* 33 G4
Alcubierre, Sierra de, *Spain* 32 D4
Alcublas, *Spain* 32 F4
Alcúdia, *Spain* 37 B10
Alcúdia, B. d', *Spain* 37 B10
Alcudia, Sierra de la, *Spain* 35 G6
Aldabra Is., *Seychelles* 77 G8
Aldama, *Mexico* 119 C5
Aldan, *Russia* 51 D13
Aldan ➤, *Russia* 51 C13
Aldea, Pta. de la, *Canary Is.* 37 G4
Aldeburgh, *U.K.* 13 E9
Alder Pk., *U.S.A.* 116 K5
Alderney, *U.K.* 13 H5
Aldershot, *U.K.* 13 F7
Åled, *Sweden* 11 H6
Aledo, *U.S.A.* 112 E9
Alefa, *Ethiopia* 81 E4
Aleg, *Mauritania* 82 B2
Alegranza, *Canary Is.* 37 E6
Alegranza, I., *Canary Is.* 37 E6
Alegre, *Brazil* 127 A7
Alegrete, *Brazil* 127 B4
Aleisk, *Russia* 50 D9
Aleksandriya = Oleksandriya, *Kirovohrad, Ukraine* 47 H7
Aleksandriya = Oleksandriya, *Rivne, Ukraine* 47 G4
Aleksandrov, *Russia* 49 J8
Aleksandrov Gay, *Russia* 48 E9
Aleksandrovac, *Serbia, Yug.* 40 C5
Aleksandrovac, *Serbia, Yug.* 40 B5
Aleksandrovka = Oleksandrovka, *Ukraine* 47 H7
Aleksandrovo, *Bulgaria* 41 C8
Aleksandrovsk-Sakhalinskiy, *Russia* 51 D15
Aleksandrów Kujawski, *Poland* 45 F5
Aleksandrów Łódzki, *Poland* 45 G6
Alekseyevka, *Samara, Russia* 48 D10
Alekseyevka, *Voronezh, Russia* 47 G10
Aleksin, *Russia* 46 E9
Aleksinac, *Serbia, Yug.* 40 C5
Além Paraíba, *Brazil* 127 A7
Alemania, *Argentina* 126 B2
Alemania, *Chile* 126 B2
Alençon, *France* 18 D7
Alenquer, *Brazil* 125 D8
Alenuihaha Channel, *U.S.A.* 106 H17
Alépé, *Ivory C.* 82 D4
Aleppo = Halab, *Syria* 70 B3
Aléria, *France* 21 F13
Alès, *France* 21 D8
Aleşd, *Romania* 42 C7

Alessándria

Alessándria, *Italy* 28 D5
Ålestrup, *Denmark* 11 H3
Ålesund, *Norway* 9 E12
Alet-les-Bains, *France* 20 F6
Aletschhorn, *Switz.* 25 J4
Aleutian Is., *Pac. Oc.* 100 C2
Aleutian Trench, *Pac. Oc.* 96 C10
Alexander, *U.S.A.* 112 B3
Alexander, Mt., *Australia* 93 E3
Alexander Arch., *U.S.A.* 100 C6
Alexander Bay, *S. Africa* 88 D2
Alexander City, *U.S.A.* 109 J3
Alexander I., *Antarctica* 5 C17
Alexandra, *Australia* 95 F4
Alexandra, *N.Z.* 91 L2
Alexandra Falls, *Canada* 104 A5
Alexandria = El Iskandarîya, *Egypt* 80 H7
Alexandria, *B.C., Canada* 104 C4
Alexandria, *Ont., Canada* 102 C5
Alexandria, *Romania* 43 G10
Alexandria, *S. Africa* 88 E4
Alexandria, *U.K.* 14 F4
Alexandria, *La., U.S.A.* 113 K8
Alexandria, *Minn., U.S.A.* 112 C7
Alexandria, *S. Dak., U.S.A.* 112 D6
Alexandria, *Va., U.S.A.* 108 F7
Alexandria Bay, *U.S.A.* 111 B9
Alexandrina, L., *Australia* 95 F2
Alexandroúpolis, *Greece* 41 F9
Alexis ➤, *Canada* 103 B8
Alexis Creek, *Canada* 104 C4
Alfabia, *Spain* 37 B9
Alfambra, *Spain* 32 E3
Alfândega da Fé, *Portugal* 34 D4
Alfaro, *Spain* 32 C3
Alfatar, *Bulgaria* 41 C11
Alfaz del Pi, *Spain* 33 G4
Alfeld, *Germany* 24 D5
Alfenas, *Brazil* 127 A6
Alfiós ➤, *Greece* 38 D3
Alföld, *Hungary* 42 D5
Alfonsine, *Italy* 29 D9
Alford, *Aberds., U.K.* 14 D6
Alford, *Lincs., U.K.* 12 D8
Alfred, *Maine, U.S.A.* 111 C14
Alfred, *N.Y., U.S.A.* 110 D7
Alfreton, *U.K.* 12 D6
Alfta, *Sweden* 10 C10
Alga, *Kazakhstan* 50 E6
Algaida, *Spain* 37 B9
Algar, *Spain* 35 J5
Ålgård, *Norway* 9 G11
Algarinejo, *Spain* 35 H6
Algarve, *Portugal* 35 J2
Algeciras, *Spain* 35 J5
Algemesí, *Spain* 33 F4
Alger, *Algeria* 78 A6
Algeria ■, *Africa* 78 C6
Alghero, *Italy* 30 B1
Älghult, *Sweden* 11 G9
Algiers = Alger, *Algeria* 78 A6
Algoa B., *S. Africa* 88 E4
Algodonales, *Spain* 35 J5
Algodor ➤, *Spain* 34 F7
Algoma, *U.S.A.* 108 C2
Algona, *U.S.A.* 112 D7
Algonac, *U.S.A.* 110 D2
Algonquin Prov. Park, *Canada* 102 C4
Algorta, *Uruguay* 128 C5
Alhama de Almería, *Spain* 35 J8
Alhama de Aragón, *Spain* 32 D3
Alhama de Granada, *Spain* 35 H7
Alhama de Murcia, *Spain* 33 H3
Alhambra, *U.S.A.* 117 L8
Alhaurín el Grande, *Spain* 35 J6
Alhucemas = Al Hoceïma, *Morocco* 78 A5
'Alī al Gharbī, *Iraq* 70 C5
'Alī ash Sharqī, *Iraq* 70 C5
'Alī Bayramlı, *Azerbaijan* 49 L9
'Alī Khēl, *Afghan.* 68 C3
Ali Sahîh, *Djibouti* 81 E5
Alī Shāh, *Iran* 70 B5
Ália, *Italy* 30 E6
'Alīābād, *Khorāsān, Iran* 71 C8
'Alīābād, *Kordestān, Iran* 70 C5
'Alīābād, *Yazd, Iran* 71 D7
Aliaga, *Spain* 32 E4
Aliağa, *Turkey* 39 C8
Aliákmon ➤, *Greece* 40 F6
Alibo, *Ethiopia* 81 F4
Alibori ➤, *Benin* 83 C5
Alibunar, *Serbia, Yug.* 42 E5
Alicante, *Spain* 33 G4
Alicante □, *Spain* 33 G4
Alice, *S. Africa* 88 E4
Alice, *U.S.A.* 113 M5
Alice ➤, *Queens., Australia* 94 C3
Alice ➤, *Queens., Australia* 94 B3
Alice, Punta, *Italy* 31 C10
Alice Arm, *Canada* 104 B3
Alice Springs, *Australia* 94 C1
Alicedale, *S. Africa* 88 E4
Aliceville, *U.S.A.* 109 J1
Alicudi, *Italy* 31 D7
Aliganj, *India* 69 F8
Aligarh, *Raj., India* 68 G7
Aligarh, *Ut. P., India* 68 F8
Alīgūdarz, *Iran* 71 C6
Alijó, *Portugal* 34 D3
Alimnía, *Greece* 36 C9
Alingsås, *Sweden* 11 G6
Alipur, *Pakistan* 68 E4
Alipur Duar, *India* 67 F16
Aliquippa, *U.S.A.* 110 F4
Alishan, *Taiwan* 59 F13

Aliste ➤, *Spain* 34 D5
Alitus = Alytus, *Lithuania* 9 J21
Alivérion, *Greece* 38 C6
Aliwal North, *S. Africa* 88 E4
Alix, *Canada* 104 C6
Aljezur, *Portugal* 35 H2
Aljustrel, *Portugal* 35 H2
Alkamari, *Niger* 83 C7
Alkmaar, *Neths.* 17 B4
All American Canal, *U.S.A.* 115 K6
Allada, *Benin* 83 D5
Allagash ➤, *U.S.A.* 109 B11
Allah Dad, *Pakistan* 68 G2
Allahabad, *India* 69 G9
Allan, *Canada* 105 C7
Allanche, *France* 20 C6
Allanridge, *S. Africa* 88 D4
Allaqi, Wadi ➤, *Egypt* 80 C3
Allariz, *Spain* 34 C3
Allassac, *France* 20 C5
Ålleberg, *Sweden* 11 F7
Allegany, *U.S.A.* 110 D6
Allegheny ➤, *U.S.A.* 110 F5
Allegheny Mts., *U.S.A.* 108 G6
Allegheny Reservoir, *U.S.A.* 110 E6
Allègre, *France* 20 C7
Allen, Bog of, *Ireland* 15 C5
Allen, L., *Ireland* 15 B3
Allendale, *U.S.A.* 109 J5
Allentsteig, *Austria* 26 C8
Alleppey, *India* 66 Q10
Allepuz, *Spain* 32 E4
Aller ➤, *Germany* 24 C5
Alliance, *Nebr., U.S.A.* 112 D3
Alliance, *Ohio, U.S.A.* 110 F3
Allier □, *France* 19 F9
Allier ➤, *France* 19 F10
Alliford Bay, *Canada* 104 C2
Allinge, *Denmark* 11 J8
Alliston, *Canada* 102 D4
Alloa, *U.K.* 14 E5
Allones, *France* 18 D8
Allora, *Australia* 95 D5
Allos, *France* 21 D10
Alluitsup Paa, *Greenland* 4 C5
Alma, *Canada* 103 C5
Alma, *Ga., U.S.A.* 109 K4
Alma, *Kans., U.S.A.* 112 F6
Alma, *Mich., U.S.A.* 108 D3
Alma, *Nebr., U.S.A.* 112 E5
Alma Ata = Almaty, *Kazakhstan* 50 E8
Almacelles, *Spain* 32 D5
Almada, *Portugal* 35 G1
Almaden, *Australia* 94 B3
Almadén, *Spain* 35 G6
Almanor, L., *U.S.A.* 114 F3
Almansa, *Spain* 33 G3
Almanza, *Spain* 34 C5
Almanzor, Pico, *Spain* 34 E5
Almanzora ➤, *Spain* 33 H3
Almaş, Munţii, *Romania* 42 F7
Almassora, *Spain* 32 F4
Almaty, *Kazakhstan* 50 E8
Almazán, *Spain* 32 D2
Almeirim, *Brazil* 125 D8
Almeirim, *Portugal* 35 F2
Almelo, *Neths.* 17 B6
Almenar de Soria, *Spain* 32 D2
Almenara, *Spain* 32 F4
Almenara, Sierra de la, *Spain* 33 H3
Almendra, Embalse de, *Spain* 34 D4
Almendralejo, *Spain* 35 G4
Almere-Stad, *Neths.* 17 B5
Almería, *Spain* 35 J8
Almería □, *Spain* 33 H2
Almería, G. de, *Spain* 33 J2
Almetyevsk, *Russia* 48 C11
Älmhult, *Sweden* 11 H8
Almirante, *Panama* 120 E3
Almiropótamos, *Greece* 38 C6
Almirós, *Greece* 38 B4
Almiroú, Kólpos, *Greece* 36 D6
Almodôvar, *Portugal* 35 H2
Almodóvar del Campo, *Spain* 35 G6
Almodóvar del Río, *Spain* 35 H5
Almond, *U.S.A.* 110 D7
Almont, *U.S.A.* 110 D1
Almonte, *Canada* 111 A8
Almonte, *Spain* 35 H4
Almora, *India* 69 E8
Almoradí, *Spain* 33 G4
Almorox, *Spain* 34 E6
Almoustarat, *Mali* 83 B5
Älmsta, *Sweden* 10 E12
Almudévar, *Spain* 32 C4
Almuñécar, *Spain* 35 J7
Almunge, *Sweden* 10 E12
Almuradiel, *Spain* 35 G7
Alness, *U.K.* 14 D4
Alnmouth, *U.K.* 12 B6
Alnwick, *U.K.* 12 B6
Aloi, *Uganda* 86 B3
Alon, *Burma* 67 H19
Alor, *Indonesia* 63 F6
Alor Setar, *Malaysia* 65 J3
Álora, *Spain* 35 J6
Alosno, *Spain* 35 H3
Alot, *India* 68 H6
Aloysius, Mt., *Australia* 93 E4
Alpaugh, *U.S.A.* 116 K7
Alpedrinha, *Portugal* 34 E3
Alpena, *U.S.A.* 108 C4
Alpes-de-Haute-Provence □, *France* 21 D10
Alpes-Maritimes □, *France* 21 E11

Alpha, *Australia* 94 C4
Alphen aan den Rijn, *Neths.* 17 B4
Alpiarça, *Portugal* 35 F2
Alpine, *Ariz., U.S.A.* 115 K9
Alpine, *Calif., U.S.A.* 117 N10
Alpine, *Tex., U.S.A.* 113 K3
Alps, *Europe* 6 F7
Alpu, *Turkey* 72 C4
Alqueta, Barragem do, *Portugal* 35 G3
Alrø, *Denmark* 11 J4
Als, *Denmark* 11 K3
Alsace, *France* 19 D14
Alsask, *Canada* 105 C7
Alsasua, *Spain* 32 C2
Alsek ➤, *U.S.A.* 104 B1
Alsfeld, *Germany* 24 E5
Alsten, *Norway* 8 D15
Alstermo, *Sweden* 11 H9
Alston, *U.K.* 12 C5
Alta, *Norway* 8 B20
Alta, Sierra, *Spain* 32 E3
Alta Gracia, *Argentina* 126 C3
Alta Sierra, *U.S.A.* 117 K8
Altaelva ➤, *Norway* 8 B20
Altafjorden, *Norway* 8 A20
Altai = Aerhtai Shan, *Mongolia* 60 B4
Altamaha ➤, *U.S.A.* 109 K5
Altamira, *Brazil* 125 D8
Altamira, *Chile* 126 B2
Altamira, *Mexico* 119 C5
Altamira, Cuevas de, *Spain* 34 B6
Altamont, *U.S.A.* 111 D10
Altamura, *Italy* 31 B9
Altanbulag, *Mongolia* 60 A5
Altar, *Mexico* 118 A2
Altar, Desierto de, *Mexico* 118 B2
Altata, *Mexico* 118 C3
Altavista, *U.S.A.* 108 G6
Altay, *China* 60 B3
Altdorf, *Switz.* 25 J4
Alte Mellum, *Germany* 24 B4
Altea, *Spain* 33 G4
Altenberg, *Germany* 24 E9
Altenbruch, *Germany* 24 B4
Altenburg, *Germany* 24 E8
Altenkirchen, *Mecklenburg-Vorpommern, Germany* 24 A9
Altenkirchen, *Rhld.-Pfz., Germany* 24 E3
Altenmarkt, *Austria* 26 D7
Alter do Chão, *Portugal* 35 F3
Altınoluk, *Turkey* 39 B8
Altınova, *Turkey* 39 B8
Altıntaş, *Turkey* 39 B12
Altınyaka, *Turkey* 39 E12
Altınyayla, *Turkey* 39 D11
Altiplano = Bolivian Plateau, *S. Amer.* 122 E4
Altkirch, *France* 19 E14
Altmark, *Germany* 24 C7
Altmühl ➤, *Germany* 25 G7
Altmunster, *Austria* 26 D6
Alto Adige = Trentino-Alto Adige □, *Italy* 29 B8
Alto Araguaia, *Brazil* 125 G8
Alto Cuchumatanes = Cuchumatanes, Sierra de los, *Guatemala* 120 C1
Alto del Carmen, *Chile* 126 B1
Alto del Inca, *Chile* 126 A2
Alto Ligonha, *Mozam.* 87 F4
Alto Molocue, *Mozam.* 87 F4
Alto Paraguay □, *Paraguay* 126 A4
Alto Paraná □, *Paraguay* 127 B5
Alton, *Canada* 110 C4
Alton, *U.K.* 13 F7
Alton, *Ill., U.S.A.* 112 F9
Alton, *N.H., U.S.A.* 111 C13
Altoona, *U.S.A.* 110 F6
Altötting, *Germany* 25 G8
Altstätten, *Switz.* 25 H5
Altūn Küprī, *Iraq* 70 C5
Altun Shan, *China* 60 C3
Alturas, *U.S.A.* 114 F3
Altus, *U.S.A.* 113 H5
Alubijid, *Phil.* 61 G6
Aluk ➤, *Sudan* 81 F2
Alūksne, *Latvia* 9 H22
Alunda, *Sweden* 10 D12
Alunite, *U.S.A.* 117 K12
Aluoro ➤, *Ethiopia* 81 F3
Alupka, *Ukraine* 47 K8
Alushta, *Ukraine* 47 K8
Alusi, *Indonesia* 63 F8
Alustante, *Spain* 32 E3
Alva, *U.S.A.* 113 G5
Alvaiázere, *Portugal* 34 F2
Älvängen, *Sweden* 11 G6
Alvarado, *Mexico* 119 D5
Alvarado, *U.S.A.* 113 J6
Alvaro Obregón, Presa, *Mexico* 118 B3
Alvdalen, *Sweden* 10 C8
Alvear, *Argentina* 126 B4
Alvesta, *Sweden* 11 H8
Alvin, *U.S.A.* 113 L7
Alvinston, *Canada* 110 D3
Alvito, *Portugal* 35 G3
Älvros, *Sweden* 10 B8
Älvsbyn, *Sweden* 8 D19
Alwar, *India* 68 F7
Alxa Zuoqi, *China* 56 E3

Alyata = Älät, *Azerbaijan* 49 L9
Alyth, *U.K.* 14 E5
Alytus, *Lithuania* 9 J21
Alzada, *U.S.A.* 112 C2
Alzey, *Germany* 25 F4
Alzira, *Spain* 33 F4
Am Timan, *Chad* 79 F10
Amadeus, L., *Australia* 93 D5
Amadi, *Dem. Rep. of the Congo* 86 B2
Amâdi, *Sudan* 81 F3
Amadjuak L., *Canada* 101 B12
Amadora, *Portugal* 35 G1
Amagansett, *U.S.A.* 111 F12
Amagasaki, *Japan* 55 G7
Amager, *Denmark* 11 J6
Amagunze, *Nigeria* 83 D6
Amahai, *Indonesia* 63 E7
Amakusa-Shotō, *Japan* 55 H5
Åmål, *Sweden* 10 E6
Amalfi, *Italy* 31 B7
Amaliás, *Greece* 38 D3
Amalner, *India* 66 J9
Amamapare, *Indonesia* 63 E9
Amambaí, *Brazil* 127 A4
Amambaí ➤, *Brazil* 127 A5
Amambay □, *Paraguay* 127 A4
Amambay, Cordillera de, *S. Amer.* 127 A4
Amami-Guntō, *Japan* 55 L4
Amami-Ō-Shima, *Japan* 55 L4
Amaná, L., *Brazil* 124 D6
Amanat ➤, *India* 69 G11
Amanda Park, *U.S.A.* 116 C3
Amangeldy, *Kazakhstan* 50 D7
Amantea, *Italy* 31 C9
Amapá, *Brazil* 125 C8
Amapá □, *Brazil* 125 C8
Amara, *Sudan* 81 E3
Amarante, *Brazil* 125 E10
Amarante, *Portugal* 34 D2
Amaranth, *Canada* 105 C9
Amareleja, *Portugal* 35 G3
Amargosa ➤, *U.S.A.* 117 J10
Amargosa Range, *U.S.A.* 117 J10
Amári, *Greece* 36 D6
Amarillo, *U.S.A.* 113 H4
Amarkantak, *India* 69 H9
Amaro, Mte., *Italy* 29 F11
Amarpur, *India* 69 G12
Amarti, *Eritrea* 81 E5
Amarwara, *India* 69 H8
Amasra, *Turkey* 72 B5
Amassama, *Nigeria* 83 D6
Amasya, *Turkey* 72 B6
Amata, *Australia* 93 E5
Amatikulu, *S. Africa* 89 D5
Amatitlán, *Guatemala* 120 D1
Amatrice, *Italy* 29 F10
Amay, *Belgium* 17 D5
Amazon = Amazonas ➤, *S. Amer.* 122 D5
Amazonas □, *Brazil* 124 E6
Amazonas ➤, *S. Amer.* 122 D5
Ambah, *India* 68 F8
Ambahakily, *Madag.* 89 C7
Ambahita, *Madag.* 89 C8
Ambala, *India* 68 D7
Ambalavao, *Madag.* 89 C8
Ambanja, *Madag.* 89 A8
Ambararata, *Madag.* 89 B8
Ambarchik, *Russia* 51 C17
Ambarijeby, *Madag.* 89 A8
Ambaro, Helodran', *Madag.* 89 A8
Ambato, *Ecuador* 124 D3
Ambato, *Madag.* 89 A8
Ambato, Sierra de, *Argentina* 126 B2
Ambato Boeny, *Madag.* 89 B8
Ambatofinandrahana, *Madag.* 89 C8
Ambatolampy, *Madag.* 89 B8
Ambatomainty, *Madag.* 89 B8
Ambatomanoina, *Madag.* 89 B8
Ambatondrazaka, *Madag.* 89 B8
Ambatosoratra, *Madag.* 89 B8
Ambelón, *Greece* 38 B4
Ambenja, *Madag.* 89 B8
Amberg, *Germany* 25 F7
Ambergris Cay, *Belize* 119 D7
Ambérieu-en-Bugey, *France* 21 C9
Amberley, *N.Z.* 91 K4
Ambert, *France* 20 C7
Ambidédi, *Mali* 82 C2
Ambikapur, *India* 69 H10
Ambikol, *Sudan* 80 C3
Ambilobé, *Madag.* 89 A8
Ambinanindrano, *Madag.* 89 C8
Ambinanitelo, *Madag.* 89 B8
Ambinda, *Madag.* 89 B8
Amble, *U.K.* 12 B6
Ambleside, *U.K.* 12 C5
Ambo, *Peru* 124 F3
Ambohimahasoa, *Madag.* 89 C8
Ambohimanga, *Madag.* 89 C8
Ambohimitombo, *Madag.* 89 C8
Ambohitra, *Madag.* 89 A8
Amboise, *France* 18 E8
Ambon, *Indonesia* 63 E7
Ambondro, *Madag.* 89 D8
Amboseli, L., *Kenya* 86 C4

Ambositra, *Madag.* 89 C8
Ambovombe, *Madag.* 89 D8
Amboy, *U.S.A.* 117 L11
Amboyna Cay, *S. China Sea* 62 C4
Ambridge, *U.S.A.* 110 F4
Ambriz, *Angola* 84 F2
Amchitka I., *U.S.A.* 100 C1
Amderma, *Russia* 50 C7
Amdhi, *India* 69 H9
Ameca, *Mexico* 118 C4
Ameca ➤, *Mexico* 118 C3
Amecameca, *Mexico* 119 D5
Ameland, *Neths.* 17 A5
Amélia, *Italy* 29 F9
Amendolara, *Italy* 31 C9
Amenia, *U.S.A.* 111 E11
American Falls, *U.S.A.* 114 E7
American Falls Reservoir, *U.S.A.* 114 E7
American Fork, *U.S.A.* 114 F8
American Highland, *Antarctica* 5 D6
American Samoa ■, *Pac. Oc.* 91 B13
Americana, *Brazil* 127 A6
Americus, *U.S.A.* 109 K3
Amersfoort, *Neths.* 17 B5
Amersfoort, *S. Africa* 89 D4
Amery Ice Shelf, *Antarctica* 5 C6
Ames, *Spain* 34 C2
Ames, *U.S.A.* 112 E8
Amesbury, *U.S.A.* 111 D14
Amet, *India* 68 G5
Amfíklia, *Greece* 38 C4
Amfilokhía, *Greece* 38 C3
Ámfissa, *Greece* 38 C4
Amga, *Russia* 51 C14
Amga ➤, *Russia* 51 C14
Amgu, *Russia* 51 E14
Amgun ➤, *Russia* 51 D14
Amherst, *Canada* 103 C7
Amherst, *Mass., U.S.A.* 111 D12
Amherst, *N.Y., U.S.A.* 110 D6
Amherst, *Ohio, U.S.A.* 110 E2
Amherst I., *Canada* 111 B8
Amherstburg, *Canada* 102 D3
Amiata, Mte., *Italy* 29 F8
Amidon, *U.S.A.* 112 B3
Amiens, *France* 19 C9
Amindaion, *Greece* 40 F5
Åminne, *Sweden* 11 G7
Amino, *Ethiopia* 81 G5
Aminuis, *Namibia* 88 C2
Amīrābād, *Iran* 70 C5
Amirante Is., *Seychelles* 52 K9
Amisk L., *Canada* 105 C8
Amistad, Presa de la, *Mexico* 118 B4
Amite, *U.S.A.* 113 K9
Amla, *India* 68 J8
Amlia I., *U.S.A.* 100 C2
Amlwch, *U.K.* 12 D3
Amm Adam, *Sudan* 81 D4
'Ammān, *Jordan* 75 D4
'Ammān □, *Jordan* 75 D5
Ammanford, *U.K.* 13 F4
Ammassalik = Tasiilaq, *Greenland* 4 C6
Ammerån ➤, *Sweden* 10 A10
Ammersee, *Germany* 25 G7
Ammon, *U.S.A.* 114 E8
Amnat Charoen, *Thailand* 64 E5
Amnura, *Bangla.* 69 G13
Amo Jiang ➤, *China* 58 F3
Åmol, *Iran* 71 B7
Amorgós, *Greece* 39 E7
Amory, *U.S.A.* 109 J1
Amos, *Canada* 102 C4
Åmot, *Norway* 9 G13
Åmotfors, *Sweden* 10 E6
Amoy = Xiamen, *China* 59 E12
Ampanavoana, *Madag.* 89 B9
Ampang, *Malaysia* 65 L3
Ampanihy, *Madag.* 89 C7
Amparafaravola, *Madag.* 89 B8
Ampasinambo, *Madag.* 89 C8
Ampasindava, Helodranon', *Madag.* 89 A8
Ampasindava, Saikanosy, *Madag.* 89 A8
Ampenan, *Indonesia* 62 F5
Amper, *Nigeria* 83 D6
Amper ➤, *Germany* 25 G7
Ampezzo, *Italy* 29 B9
Ampitsikinana, *Réunion* 89 A8
Ampombiantambo, *Madag.* 89 A8
Amposta, *Spain* 32 E5
Ampotaka, *Madag.* 89 D7
Ampoza, *Madag.* 89 C7
Amqui, *Canada* 103 C6
Amravati, *India* 66 J10
Amreli, *India* 68 J4
Amritsar, *India* 68 D6
Amroha, *India* 69 E8
Amrum, *Germany* 24 A4
Amsterdam, *Neths.* 17 B4
Amsterdam, *U.S.A.* 111 D10
Amsterdam, I. = Nouvelle-Amsterdam, I., *Ind. Oc.* 3 F13
Amstetten, *Austria* 26 C7
Amudarya ➤, *Uzbekistan* 50 E6
Amundsen Gulf, *Canada* 100 A7
Amundsen Sea, *Antarctica* 5 D15
Amungen, *Sweden* 10 C9
Amuntai, *Indonesia* 62 E5
Amur ➤, *Russia* 51 D15
Amur, W. ➤, *Sudan* 80 D3

Amurang, *Indonesia* 63 D6
Amurrio, *Spain* 32 B1
Amursk, *Russia* 51 D14
Amusco, *Spain* 34 C6
Amvrakikós Kólpos, *Greece* .. 38 C2
Amvrosiyivka, *Ukraine* 47 J10
Amyderya = Amudarya ➟,
   Uzbekistan 50 E6
An Bien, *Vietnam* 65 H5
An Hoa, *Vietnam* 64 E7
An Nabatīyah at Tahta,
   Lebanon 75 B4
An Nabk, *Si. Arabia* 70 D3
An Nabk, *Syria* 75 A5
An Nafūd, *Si. Arabia* 70 D4
An Najaf, *Iraq* 70 C5
An Nāşirīyah, *Iraq* 70 D5
An Nhon, *Vietnam* 64 F7
An Nîl □, *Sudan* 80 D3
An Nîl el Abyad □, *Sudan* .. 81 E3
An Nîl el Azraq □, *Sudan* .. 81 E3
An Nu'ayrīyah, *Si. Arabia* .. 71 E6
An Nu'mānīyah, *Iraq* 73 F11
An Nuwayb'ī, W. ➟, *Si. Arabia* 75 F3
An Thoi, Dao, *Vietnam* 65 H4
An Uaimh, *Ireland* 15 C5
Anabar ➟, *Russia* 51 B12
'Anabtā, *West Bank* 75 C4
Anaconda, *U.S.A.* 114 C7
Anacortes, *U.S.A.* 116 B4
Anacuao, Mt., *Phil.* 61 C4
Anadarko, *U.S.A.* 113 H5
Anadia, *Portugal* 34 E2
Anadolu, *Turkey* 72 C5
Anadyr, *Russia* 51 C18
Anadyr ➟, *Russia* 51 C18
Anadyrskiy Zaliv, *Russia* .. 51 C19
Anáfi, *Greece* 39 E7
Anafópoulo, *Greece* 39 E7
Anaga, Pta. de, *Canary Is.* .. 37 F3
Anagni, *Italy* 29 G10
'Ānah, *Iraq* 70 C4
Anaheim, *U.S.A.* 117 M9
Anahim Lake, *Canada* 104 C3
Anáhuac, *Mexico* 118 B4
Anakapalle, *India* 67 L13
Anakie, *Australia* 94 C4
Anaklia, *Georgia* 49 J5
Analalava, *Madag.* 89 A8
Analavoka, *Madag.* 89 C8
Análipsis, *Greece* 36 A3
Anambar ➟, *Pakistan* 68 D3
Anambas, Kepulauan, *Indonesia* 65 L6
Anambas Is. = Anambas,
   Kepulauan, *Indonesia* 65 L6
Anamosa, *U.S.A.* 112 D9
Anambra □, *Nigeria* 83 D6
Anamur, *Turkey* 70 B2
Anamur Burnu, *Turkey* 72 D5
Anan, *Japan* 55 H7
Anand, *India* 68 H5
Anánes, *Greece* 38 E6
Anantnag, *India* 69 C6
Ananyiv, *Ukraine* 47 J5
Anapa, *Russia* 47 K9
Anapodháris ➟, *Greece* 36 E7
Anápolis, *Brazil* 125 G9
Anapu ➟, *Brazil* 125 D8
Anār, *Iran* 71 D7
Anārak, *Iran* 71 C7
Anarisfjällen, *Sweden* 10 A7
Anas ➟, *India* 68 H5
Anatolia = Anadolu, *Turkey* .. 72 C5
Anatsogno, *Madag.* 89 C7
Añatuya, *Argentina* 126 B3
Anaunethad L., *Canada* 105 A8
Anbyŏn, *N. Korea* 57 E14
Ancares, Sierra de, *Spain* .. 34 C4
Ancaster, *Canada* 110 C5
Ancenis, *France* 18 E5
Anchor Bay, *U.S.A.* 116 G3
Anchorage, *U.S.A.* 100 B5
Anci, *China* 56 E9
Ancohuma, Nevada, *Bolivia* .. 122 E4
Ancona, *Italy* 29 E10
Ancud, *Chile* 128 E2
Ancud, G. de, *Chile* 128 E2
Ancy-le-Franc, *France* 19 E11
Andacollo, *Argentina* 126 D1
Andacollo, *Chile* 126 C1
Andaingo, *Madag.* 89 B8
Andalgalá, *Argentina* 126 B2
Åndalsnes, *Norway* 9 E12
Andalucía □, *Spain* 35 H6
Andalusia = Andalucía □, *Spain* 35 H6
Andalusia, *U.S.A.* 109 K2
Andaman Is., *Ind. Oc.* 52 H13
Andaman Sea, *Ind. Oc.* 62 B1
Andamooka Opal Fields,
   Australia 95 E2
Andapa, *Madag.* 89 A8
Andara, *Namibia* 88 B3
Andelot-Blancheville, *France* 19 D12
Andenes, *Norway* 8 B17
Andenne, *Belgium* 17 D5
Andéranboukane, *Mali* 83 B5
Andermatt, *Switz.* 25 J4
Andernach, *Germany* 24 E3
Andernos-les-Bains, *France* .. 20 D2
Anderslöv, *Sweden* 11 J7
Anderson, *Alaska*, *U.S.A.* .. 100 B5
Anderson, *Calif.*, *U.S.A.* .. 114 F2
Anderson, *Ind.*, *U.S.A.* ... 108 E3
Anderson, *Mo.*, *U.S.A.* 113 G7
Anderson, *S.C.*, *U.S.A.* ... 109 H4
Anderson ➟, *Canada* 100 B7

Anderstorp, *Sweden* 11 G7
Andes, *U.S.A.* 111 D10
Andes, Cord. de los, *S. Amer.* .. 122 F4
Andfjorden, *Norway* 8 B17
Andhra Pradesh □, *India* 66 L11
Andijon, *Uzbekistan* 50 E8
Andikíthira, *Greece* 38 F5
Andilamena, *Madag.* 89 B8
Andímilos, *Greece* 38 E6
Andíparos, *Greece* 39 D7
Andípaxoi, *Greece* 38 B2
Andípsara, *Greece* 39 C7
Andírrion, *Greece* 38 C3
Andizhan = Andijon, *Uzbekistan* 50 E8
Andoain, *Spain* 32 B2
Andoany, *Madag.* 89 A8
Andong, *S. Korea* 57 F15
Andongwei, *China* 57 G10
Andoom, *Australia* 94 A3
Andorra, *Spain* 32 E4
Andorra ■, *Europe* 20 F5
Andorra La Vella, *Andorra* .. 20 F5
Andover, *U.K.* 13 F6
Andover, *Maine*, *U.S.A.* .. 111 B14
Andover, *Mass.*, *U.S.A.* .. 111 D13
Andover, *N.J.*, *U.S.A.* ... 111 F10
Andover, *N.Y.*, *U.S.A.* ... 110 D7
Andover, *Ohio*, *U.S.A.* ... 110 E4
Andøya, *Norway* 8 B16
Andradina, *Brazil* 125 H8
Andrahary, Mt., *Madag.* 89 A8
Andramasina, *Madag.* 89 B8
Andranopasy, *Madag.* 89 C7
Andranovory, *Madag.* 89 C7
Andratx, *Spain* 37 B9
Andreanof Is., *U.S.A.* 100 C2
Andreapol, *Russia* 46 D7
Andrews, *S.C.*, *U.S.A.* ... 109 J6
Andrews, *Tex.*, *U.S.A.* ... 113 J3
Andreyevka, *Russia* 48 D10
Ándria, *Italy* 31 A9
Andriamena, *Madag.* 89 B8
Andriandampy, *Madag.* 89 C8
Andriba, *Madag.* 89 B8
Andrijevica, *Montenegro, Yug.* .. 40 D3
Andrítsaina, *Greece* 38 D3
Androka, *Madag.* 89 C7
Andropov = Rybinsk, *Russia* .. 46 C10
Ándros, *Greece* 38 D6
Andros I., *Bahamas* 120 B4
Andros Town, *Bahamas* 120 B4
Androscoggin ➟, *U.S.A.* 111 C14
Andrychów, *Poland* 45 J6
Andselv, *Norway* 8 B18
Andújar, *Spain* 35 G6
Andulo, *Angola* 84 G3
Aneby, *Sweden* 11 G8
Anegada I., *U.S. Virgin Is.* .. 121 C7
Anegada Passage, *W. Indies* .. 121 C7
Aného, *Togo* 83 D5
Anenni-Noi, *Moldova* 43 D14
Aneto, Pico de, *Spain* 32 C5
Anfu, *China* 59 D10
Ang Thong, *Thailand* 64 E3
Angamos, Punta, *Chile* 126 A1
Angara ➟, *Russia* 51 D10
Angara-Débou, *Benin* 83 C5
Angarab, *Ethiopia* 81 E4
Angarbaka, *Sudan* 81 F1
Angarsk, *Russia* 51 D11
Angas Hills, *Australia* 92 D4
Angaston, *Australia* 95 E2
Angaur I., *Pac. Oc.* 63 C8
Ånge, *Sweden* 10 B9
Ángel, Salto = Angel Falls,
   Venezuela 124 B6
Ángel de la Guarda, I., *Mexico* 118 B2
Angel Falls, *Venezuela* 124 B6
Angeles, *Phil.* 61 D4
Ängelholm, *Sweden* 11 H6
Angels Camp, *U.S.A.* 116 G6
Anger ➟, *Ethiopia* 81 F4
Angereb ➟, *Ethiopia* 81 E4
Ängermanälven ➟, *Sweden* ... 10 B11
Ångermanland, *Sweden* 8 E18
Angermünde, *Germany* 24 B9
Angers, *Canada* 111 A9
Angers, *France* 18 E6
Angerville, *France* 19 D9
Ängesån ➟, *Sweden* 8 C20
Angikuni L., *Canada* 105 A9
Angkor, *Cambodia* 64 F4
Anglès, *Spain* 32 D7
Anglesey, Isle of □, *U.K.* .. 12 D3
Anglet, *France* 20 E2
Angleton, *U.S.A.* 113 L7
Anglin ➟, *France* 20 B4
Anglisidhes, *Cyprus* 36 E12
Anglure, *France* 19 D10
Angmagssalik = Tasiilaq,
   Greenland 4 C6
Ango, *Dem. Rep. of the Congo* .. 86 B2
Angoche, *Mozam.* 87 F4
Angoche, I., *Mozam.* 87 F4
Angol, *Chile* 126 D1
Angola, *Ind.*, *U.S.A.* 108 E3
Angola, *N.Y.*, *U.S.A.* 110 D5
Angola ■, *Africa* 85 G3
Angoulême, *France* 20 C4
Angoumois, *France* 20 C4
Angra dos Reis, *Brazil* 127 A7
Angren, *Uzbekistan* 50 E8
Angtassom, *Cambodia* 65 G5
Angu, *Dem. Rep. of the Congo* .. 86 B1
Anguang, *China* 57 B12

Anguilla ■, *W. Indies* 121 C7
Anguo, *China* 56 E8
Angurugu, *Australia* 94 A2
Angus □, *U.K.* 14 E6
Angwa ➟, *Zimbabwe* 89 B5
Anhanduí ➟, *Brazil* 127 A5
Anholt, *Denmark* 11 H5
Anhua, *China* 59 C8
Anhui □, *China* 59 B11
Anhwei = Anhui □, *China* ... 59 B11
Anichab, *Namibia* 88 C1
Ánidhros, *Greece* 39 E7
Anié, *Togo* 83 D5
Animas ➟, *U.S.A.* 115 H9
Anina, *Romania* 42 E6
Aninoasa, *Romania* 43 F9
Anivorano, *Madag.* 89 B8
Anjalankoski, *Finland* 9 F22
Anjar, *India* 68 H4
Anji, *China* 59 B12
Anjou, *France* 18 E6
Anjozorobe, *Madag.* 89 B8
Anju, *N. Korea* 57 E13
Anka, *Nigeria* 83 C6
Ankaboa, Tanjona, *Madag.* .. 89 C7
Ankang, *China* 56 H5
Ankara, *Turkey* 72 C5
Ankaramena, *Madag.* 89 C8
Ankaratra, *Madag.* 85 H9
Ankarsrum, *Sweden* 11 G10
Ankasakasa, *Madag.* 89 B7
Ankavandra, *Madag.* 89 B8
Ankazoabo, *Madag.* 89 C7
Ankazobe, *Madag.* 89 B8
Ankeny, *U.S.A.* 112 E8
Ankilimalinika, *Madag.* 89 C7
Ankilizato, *Madag.* 89 C8
Ankisabe, *Madag.* 89 B8
Anklam, *Germany* 24 B9
Ankober, *Ethiopia* 81 F4
Ankoro, *Dem. Rep. of the Congo* 86 D2
Ankororoka, *Madag.* 89 D8
Anlong, *China* 58 E5
Anlu, *China* 59 B9
Anmyŏn-do, *S. Korea* 57 F14
Änn, *Sweden* 10 A6
Ann, C., *U.S.A.* 111 D14
Ann Arbor, *U.S.A.* 108 D4
Anna, *Russia* 48 E5
Anna, *U.S.A.* 113 G10
Annaba, *Algeria* 78 A7
Annaberg-Buchholz, *Germany* .. 24 E9
Annalee ➟, *Ireland* 15 B4
Annam, *Vietnam* 64 E7
Annamitique, Chaîne, *Asia* .. 64 D6
Annan, *U.K.* 14 G5
Annan ➟, *U.K.* 14 G5
Annapolis, *U.S.A.* 108 F7
Annapolis Royal, *Canada* ... 103 D6
Annapurna, *Nepal* 69 E10
Annean, L., *Australia* 93 E2
Anneberg, *Sweden* 11 G8
Annecy, *France* 21 C10
Annecy, Lac d', *France* 21 C10
Annemasse, *France* 19 F13
Annenskiy Most, *Russia* 46 B9
Anning, *China* 58 E4
Anniston, *U.S.A.* 109 J3
Annobón, *Atl. Oc.* 77 G4
Annonay, *France* 21 C8
Annot, *France* 21 E10
Annotto Bay, *Jamaica* 120 C4
Ånnsjön, *Sweden* 10 A6
Annville, *U.S.A.* 111 F8
Annweiler, *Germany* 25 F3
Áno Arkhánai, *Greece* 39 F7
Áno Porróia, *Greece* 40 E7
Áno Síros, *Greece* 38 D6
Áno Viánnos, *Greece* 36 D7
Anorotsangana, *Madag.* 89 A8
Anosibe, *Madag.* 89 B8
Anou Mellene, *Mali* 83 B5
Anóyia, *Greece* 36 D6
Anping, *Hebei, China* 56 E8
Anping, *Liaoning, China* ... 57 D12
Anpu Gang, *China* 58 G7
Anqing, *China* 59 B11
Anqiu, *China* 57 F10
Anren, *China* 59 D9
Ansager, *Denmark* 11 J2
Ansai, *China* 56 F5
Ansbach, *Germany* 25 F6
Anseba ➟, *Eritrea* 81 D4
Ansfelden, *Austria* 26 C7
Anshan, *China* 57 D12
Anshun, *China* 58 D5
Ansião, *Portugal* 34 F2
Ansley, *U.S.A.* 112 E5
Ansó, *Spain* 32 C4
Ansoain, *Spain* 32 C3
Anson B., *Australia* 92 B5
Ansongo, *Mali* 83 B5
Ansonia, *U.S.A.* 111 E11
Anstruther, *U.K.* 14 E6
Ansudu, *Indonesia* 63 E9
Antabamba, *Peru* 124 F4
Antakya, *Turkey* 70 B3
Antalaha, *Madag.* 89 A9
Antalya, *Turkey* 72 D4
Antalya □, *Turkey* 39 E12
Antalya Körfezi, *Turkey* ... 72 D4
Antambohobe, *Madag.* 89 C8
Antananambao-Manampotsy,
   Madag. 89 B8
Antananarivo, *Madag.* 89 B8
Antanambao, *Madag.* 89 B8

Antananarivo, *Madag.* 89 B8
Antananarivo □, *Madag.* 89 B8
Antanifotsy, *Madag.* 89 B8
Antanimbaribe, *Madag.* 89 C7
Antanimora, *Madag.* 89 C8
Antarctic Pen., *Antarctica* .. 5 C18
Antarctica 5 E3
Antelope, *Zimbabwe* 87 G2
Antequera, *Paraguay* 126 A4
Antequera, *Spain* 35 H6
Antero, Mt., *U.S.A.* 115 G10
Antevamena, *Madag.* 89 C7
Anthemoús, *Greece* 40 F7
Anthony, *Kans.*, *U.S.A.* .. 113 G5
Anthony, *N. Mex.*, *U.S.A.* .. 115 K10
Anti Atlas, *Morocco* 78 C4
Anti-Lebanon = Ash Sharqi, Al
   Jabal, *Lebanon* 75 B5
Antibes, *France* 21 E11
Antibes, C. d', *France* 21 E11
Anticosti, Î. d', *Canada* .. 103 C7
Antifer, C. d', *France* 18 C7
Antigo, *U.S.A.* 112 C10
Antigonish, *Canada* 103 C7
Antigua, *Canary Is.* 37 F5
Antigua, *W. Indies* 121 C7
Antigua & Barbuda ■, *W. Indies* 121 C7
Antigua Guatemala, *Guatemala* 120 D1
Antilla, *Cuba* 120 B4
Antilles = West Indies,
   Cent. Amer. 121 D7
Antioch, *U.S.A.* 116 G5
Antioche, Pertuis d', *France* .. 20 B2
Antioquia, *Colombia* 124 B3
Antipodes Is., *Pac. Oc.* ... 96 M9
Antlers, *U.S.A.* 113 H7
Antoetra, *Madag.* 89 C8
Antofagasta, *Chile* 126 A1
Antofagasta □, *Chile* 126 A2
Antofagasta de la Sierra,
   Argentina 126 B2
Antofalla, *Argentina* 126 B2
Antofalla, Salar de, *Argentina* .. 126 B2
Anton, *U.S.A.* 113 J3
Antongila, Helodrano, *Madag.* .. 89 B8
Antonibé, *Madag.* 89 B8
Antonibé, Presqu'île d', *Madag.* 89 A8
Antonina, *Brazil* 127 B6
Antrain, *France* 18 D5
Antrim, *U.K.* 15 B5
Antrim, *U.S.A.* 110 F3
Antrim □, *U.K.* 15 B5
Antrim, Mts. of, *U.K.* 15 A5
Antrim Plateau, *Australia* .. 92 C4
Antrodoco, *Italy* 29 F10
Antropovo, *Russia* 48 A6
Antsakabary, *Madag.* 89 B8
Antsalova, *Madag.* 89 B7
Antsenavolo, *Madag.* 89 C8
Antsiafabositra, *Madag.* ... 89 B8
Antsirabe, *Antananarivo,
   Madag.* 89 B8
Antsirabe, *Antsiranana, Madag.* 89 A8
Antsirabe, *Mahajanga, Madag.* .. 89 B8
Antsiranana, *Madag.* 89 A8
Antsiranana □, *Madag.* 89 A8
Antsohihy, *Madag.* 89 A8
Antsohimbondrona Seranana,
   Madag. 89 A8
Antu, *China* 57 C15
Antwerp = Antwerpen, *Belgium* 17 C4
Antwerp, *U.S.A.* 111 B9
Antwerpen, *Belgium* 17 C4
Antwerpen □, *Belgium* 17 C4
Anupgarh, *India* 68 E5
Anuppur, *India* 69 H9
Anuradhapura, *Sri Lanka* ... 66 Q12
Anveh, *Iran* 71 E7
Anvers = Antwerpen, *Belgium* .. 17 C4
Anvers I., *Antarctica* 5 C17
Anwen, *China* 59 C13
Anxi, *Fujian, China* 59 E12
Anxi, *Gansu, China* 60 B4
Anxian, *China* 58 B5
Anxiang, *China* 59 C9
Anxious B., *Australia* 95 E1
Anyama, *Ivory C.* 82 D4
Anyang, *China* 56 F8
Anyer-Kidul, *Indonesia* 63 G11
Anyi, *Jiangxi, China* 59 C10
Anyi, *Shanxi, China* 56 G6
Anyuan, *China* 59 E10
Anyue, *China* 58 B5
Anza, *U.S.A.* 117 M10
Anze, *China* 56 F7
Ánzio, *Italy* 30 A5
Aoga-Shima, *Japan* 55 H9
Aoiz, *Spain* 32 C3
Aomen = Macau □, *China* 59 F9
Aomori, *Japan* 54 D10
Aomori □, *Japan* 54 D10
Aonla, *India* 69 E8
Aoraki Mount Cook, *N.Z.* ... 91 K3
Aosta, *Italy* 28 C4
Aoudéras, *Niger* 83 B6
Aoukâr, *Mauritania* 82 B3
Apa ➟, *S. Amer.* 126 A4
Apache, *U.S.A.* 113 H5
Apache Junction, *U.S.A.* ... 115 K8
Apalache B., *U.S.A.* 109 L4
Apalachicola, *U.S.A.* 109 L3
Apalachicola ➟, *U.S.A.* 109 L3
Apam, *Ghana* 83 D4
Apapa, *Nigeria* 83 D5
Apaporis ➟, *Colombia* 124 D5
Aparri, *Phil.* 61 B4

Apateu, *Romania* 42 D6
Apatin, *Serbia, Yug.* 42 E4
Apatity, *Russia* 50 C4
Apatzingán, *Mexico* 118 D4
Apeldoorn, *Neths.* 17 B5
Apen, *Germany* 24 B3
Apennines = Appennini, *Italy* 28 E7
Aphrodisias, *Turkey* 39 D10
Apia, *Samoa* 91 A13
Apiacás, Serra dos, *Brazil* .. 124 E7
Apies ➟, *S. Africa* 89 D4
Apizaco, *Mexico* 119 D5
Aplao, *Peru* 124 G4
Apo, Mt., *Phil.* 63 C7
Apolakkiá, *Greece* 36 C9
Apolakkiá, Órmos, *Greece* .. 36 C9
Apolda, *Germany* 24 D7
Apollonia, *Greece* 38 E6
Apolo, *Bolivia* 124 F5
Aporé ➟, *Brazil* 125 G8
Apóstoles, *Argentina* 127 B4
Apóstolos Andreas, C., *Cyprus* 36 D13
Apostolovo, *Ukraine* 47 J7
Apoteri, *Guyana* 124 C7
Appalachian Mts., *U.S.A.* .. 108 G6
Äppelbo, *Sweden* 10 D8
Appennini, *Italy* 28 E7
Appennino Ligure, *Italy* ... 28 D6
Appenzell-Ausser Rhoden □,
   Switz. 25 H5
Appenzell-Inner Rhoden □,
   Switz. 25 H5
Appiano, *Italy* 29 B8
Apple Hill, *Canada* 111 A10
Apple Valley, *U.S.A.* 117 L9
Appleby-in-Westmorland, *U.K.* 12 C5
Appleton, *U.S.A.* 108 C1
Approuague ➟, *Fr. Guiana* .. 125 C8
Apricena, *Italy* 29 G12
Aprília, *Italy* 30 A5
Apsheronsk, *Russia* 49 H4
Apsley, *Canada* 110 B6
Apt, *France* 21 E9
Apuane, Alpi, *Italy* 28 D7
Apucarana, *Brazil* 127 A5
Apulia = Púglia □, *Italy* .. 31 A9
Apure ➟, *Venezuela* 124 B5
Apurímac ➟, *Peru* 124 F4
Apuseni, Munţii, *Romania* .. 42 D7
Āqā Jari, *Iran* 71 D6
Aqaba = Al 'Aqabah, *Jordan* .. 75 F4
'Aqabah, Khalīj al = Aqaba, G.
   of, *Red Sea* 70 D2
'Aqdā, *Iran* 71 C7
Aqiq, *Sudan* 80 D4
Aqiq, Khalig, *Sudan* 80 D4
Aqmola = Astana, *Kazakstan* .. 50 D8
'Aqrah, *Iraq* 70 B4
Aqtaū, *Kazakstan* 50 E6
Aqtöbe, *Kazakstan* 50 D6
Aquidauana, *Brazil* 125 H7
Aquiles Serdán, *Mexico* 118 B3
Aquin, *Haiti* 121 C5
Aquitaine □, *France* 20 D3
Aqviligjuaq = Pelly Bay, *Canada* 101 B11
Ar Rachidiya = Er Rachidia,
   Morocco 78 B5
Ar Rafid, *Syria* 75 C4
Ar Raḥḥālīyah, *Iraq* 70 C4
Ar Ramādī, *Iraq* 70 C4
Ar Ramthā, *Jordan* 75 C5
Ar Raqqah, *Syria* 70 C3
Ar Rass, *Si. Arabia* 70 E4
Ar Rawshān, *Si. Arabia* 80 C5
Ar Rifā'ī, *Iraq* 70 D5
Ar Riyād, *Si. Arabia* 70 E5
Ar Ru'ays, *Qatar* 71 E6
Ar Rukhaymīyah, *Iraq* 70 D5
Ar Ruşāfah, *Syria* 70 C3
Ar Ruţbah, *Iraq* 70 C4
Ara, *India* 69 G11
Ara Goro, *Ethiopia* 81 F5
Ara Tera, *Ethiopia* 81 F5
'Arab, Bahr el ➟, *Sudan* ... 81 F2
Arab, Khalīg el, *Egypt* 80 A2
Arab, Shatt al ➟, *Asia* 71 D6
'Araba, W. ➟, *Egypt* 80 J8
'Arabābād, *Iran* 71 C8
Araban, *Turkey* 72 D7
Arabatskaya Strelka, *Ukraine* 47 K8
Arabba, *Italy* 29 B8
Arabia, *Asia* 52 G8
Arabian Desert = Es Sahrâ' Esh
   Sharqîya, *Egypt* 80 B3
Arabian Gulf = The Gulf, *Asia* 71 E6
Arabian Sea, *Ind. Oc.* 52 H10
Araç, *Turkey* 72 B5
Aracaju, *Brazil* 125 F11
Araçatuba, *Brazil* 127 A5
Aracena, *Spain* 35 H4
Aracena, Sierra de, *Spain* .. 35 H4
Aračinovo, *Macedonia* 40 D5
Araçuaí, *Brazil* 125 G10
'Arad, *Israel* 75 D4
Arad, *Romania* 42 D6
Arādān, *Iran* 71 C7
Aradhippou, *Cyprus* 36 E12
Arafura Sea, *E. Indies* 52 K17
Aragats, *Armenia* 49 K7
Aragón □, *Spain* 32 D4
Aragón ➟, *Spain* 32 C3
Aragona, *Italy* 30 E6

Araguacema, *Brazil* 125 E9
Araguaia ➤, *Brazil* 122 D6
Araguaína, *Brazil* 125 E9
Araguari, *Brazil* 125 G9
Araguari ➤, *Brazil* 125 C9
Arain, *India* 68 F6
Arak, *Algeria* 78 C6
Arāk, *Iran* 71 C6
Araka, *Sudan* 81 G3
Arakan Coast, *Burma* 67 K19
Arakan Yoma, *Burma* 67 K19
Arákhova, *Greece* 38 C4
Arakli, *Turkey* 73 B8
Araks = Aras, Rūd-e ➤, *Asia* . 49 K9
Aral, *Kazakstan* 50 E7
Aral Sea, *Asia* 50 E7
Aral Tengizi = Aral Sea, *Asia* . 50 E7
Aralsk = Aral, *Kazakstan* ... 50 E7
Aralskoye More = Aral Sea,
  Asia 50 E7
Aralsor, Ozero, *Kazakstan* .. 49 F9
Aramac, *Australia* 94 C4
Aran I., *Ireland* 15 A3
Aran Is., *Ireland* 15 C2
Aranda de Duero, *Spain* 34 D7
Arandān, *Iran* 70 C5
Arandelovac, *Serbia, Yug.* .. 40 B4
Aranjuez, *Spain* 34 E7
Aranos, *Namibia* 88 C2
Aransas Pass, *U.S.A.* 113 M6
Aranyaprathet, *Thailand* 64 F4
Araouane, *Mali* 82 B4
Arapahoe, *U.S.A.* 112 E5
Arapey Grande ➤, *Uruguay* .. 126 C4
Arapgir, *Turkey* 70 B3
Arapiraca, *Brazil* 125 E11
Arapongas, *Brazil* 127 A5
Ar'ar, *Si. Arabia* 70 D4
Araranguá, *Brazil* 127 B6
Araraquara, *Brazil* 125 H9
Ararás, Serra das, *Brazil* .. 127 B5
Ararat, *Armenia* 73 C11
Ararat, *Australia* 95 C3
Ararat, Mt. = Ağrı Dağı, *Turkey* . 70 B5
Araria, *India* 69 F12
Araripe, Chapada do, *Brazil* . 125 E11
Araruama, L. de, *Brazil* 127 A7
Aras, Rūd-e ➤, *Asia* 49 K9
Aratāne, *Mauritania* 82 B3
Arauca, *Colombia* 124 B4
Arauca ➤, *Venezuela* 124 B5
Arauco, *Chile* 126 D1
Arawa, *Ethiopia* 81 F5
Araxá, *Brazil* 125 G9
Araya, Pen. de, *Venezuela* .. 124 A4
Arba Gugu, *Ethiopia* 81 F5
Arba Minch, *Ethiopia* 81 F4
Arbat, *Iraq* 70 C5
Árbatax, *Italy* 30 C2
Arbi, *Ethiopia* 81 F4
Arbīl, *Iraq* 70 B5
Arboga, *Sweden* 10 E9
Arbois, *France* 19 F12
Arbore, *Ethiopia* 81 F4
Arboréa, *Italy* 30 C1
Arborfield, *Canada* 105 C8
Arborg, *Canada* 105 C9
Arbre du Ténéré, *Niger* 83 B7
Arbroath, *U.K.* 14 E6
Arbuckle, *U.S.A.* 116 F4
Arbus, *Italy* 30 C1
Arc ➤, *France* 21 C10
Arc-lès-Gray, *France* 19 E12
Arcachon, *France* 20 D2
Arcachon, Bassin d', *France* . 20 D2
Arcade, *Calif., U.S.A.* 117 L8
Arcade, *N.Y., U.S.A.* 110 D6
Arcadia, *Fla., U.S.A.* 109 M5
Arcadia, *La., U.S.A.* 113 J8
Arcadia, *Pa., U.S.A.* 110 F6
Arcata, *U.S.A.* 114 F1
Arcévia, *Italy* 29 E9
Archangel = Arkhangelsk,
  Russia 50 C5
Archar, *Bulgaria* 40 C6
Archbald, *U.S.A.* 111 E9
Archena, *Spain* 33 G3
Archer ➤, *Australia* 94 A3
Archer B., *Australia* 94 A3
Archers Post, *Kenya* 86 B4
Arches National Park, *U.S.A.* . 115 G9
Archidona, *Spain* 35 H6
Arci, Mte., *Italy* 30 C1
Arcidosso, *Italy* 29 F8
Arcis-sur-Aube, *France* 19 D11
Arckaringa Cr. ➤, *Australia* . 95 D2
Arco, *Italy* 28 C7
Arco, *U.S.A.* 114 E7
Arcos = Arcos de Jalón, *Spain* . 32 D2
Arcos de Jalón, *Spain* 32 D2
Arcos de la Frontera, *Spain* . 35 J5
Arcos de Valdevez, *Portugal* . 34 D2
Arcot, *India* 66 N11
Arcozelo, *Portugal* 34 E3
Arctic Bay, *Canada* 101 A11
Arctic Ocean, *Arctic* 4 B18
Arctic Red River = Tsiigehtchic,
  Canada 100 B6
Arda ➤, *Bulgaria* 41 E10
Ardabīl, *Iran* 71 B6
Ardahan, *Turkey* 73 B10
Ardakān = Sepīdān, *Iran* ... 71 D7
Ardakān, *Iran* 71 C7
Ardala, *Sweden* 11 F7
Ardales, *Spain* 35 J6
Ardèche □, *France* 21 D8

Ardèche ➤, *France* 21 D8
Ardee, *Ireland* 15 C5
Arden, *Canada* 110 B8
Arden, *Denmark* 11 H3
Arden, *Calif., U.S.A.* 116 G5
Arden, *Nev., U.S.A.* 117 J11
Ardenne, *Belgium* 6 F7
Ardennes = Ardenne, *Belgium* . 6 F7
Ardennes □, *France* 19 C11
Ardentes, *France* 19 F8
Arderin, *Ireland* 15 C4
Ardeşen, *Turkey* 73 B9
Ardeştān, *Iran* 71 C7
Árdhas ➤, *Greece* 41 E10
Ardhéa, *Greece* 40 F6
Ardila ➤, *Portugal* 35 G3
Ardino, *Bulgaria* 41 E9
Ardivachar Pt., *U.K.* 14 D1
Ardlethan, *Australia* 95 E4
Ardmore, *Okla., U.S.A.* 113 H6
Ardmore, *Pa., U.S.A.* 111 G9
Ardnamurchan, Pt. of, *U.K.* . 14 E2
Ardnave Pt., *U.K.* 14 F2
Ardon, *Russia* 49 J7
Ardore, *Italy* 31 D9
Ardres, *France* 19 B8
Ardrossan, *Australia* 95 E2
Ardrossan, *U.K.* 14 F4
Ards Pen., *U.K.* 15 B6
Arduan, *Sudan* 80 D3
Ardud, *Romania* 42 C7
Åre, *Sweden* 10 A7
Arecibo, *Puerto Rico* 121 C6
Areia Branca, *Brazil* 125 E11
Arena, Pt., *U.S.A.* 116 G3
Arenal, *Honduras* 120 C2
Arenas = Las Arenas, *Spain* . 34 B6
Arenas de San Pedro, *Spain* . 34 E5
Arendal, *Norway* 9 G13
Arendsee, *Germany* 24 C7
Arenys de Mar, *Spain* 32 D7
Arenzano, *Italy* 28 D5
Areópolis, *Greece* 38 E4
Arequipa, *Peru* 124 G4
Arero, *Ethiopia* 81 G4
Arès, *France* 20 D2
Arévalo, *Spain* 34 D6
Arezzo, *Italy* 29 E8
Arga, *Turkey* 70 B3
Arga ➤, *Spain* 32 C3
Argalastí, *Greece* 38 B5
Argamasilla de Alba, *Spain* . 35 F7
Argamasilla de Calatrava, *Spain* . 35 G6
Arganda, *Spain* 34 E7
Arganil, *Portugal* 34 E2
Argedeb, *Ethiopia* 81 F5
Argelès-Gazost, *France* 20 E3
Argelès-sur-Mer, *France* ... 20 F7
Argens ➤, *France* 21 E10
Argent-sur-Sauldre, *France* . 19 E9
Argenta, *Canada* 104 C5
Argenta, *Italy* 29 D8
Argentan, *France* 18 D6
Argentário, Mte., *Italy* ... 29 F8
Argentat, *France* 20 C5
Argentera, *Italy* 28 D4
Argenteuil, *France* 19 D9
Argentia, *Canada* 103 C9
Argentiera, C. dell', *Italy* . 30 B1
Argentina ■, *S. Amer.* 128 D3
Argentina Is., *Antarctica* .. 5 C17
Argentino, L., *Argentina* ... 128 G2
Argenton-Château, *France* ... 18 F6
Argenton-sur-Creuse, *France* . 19 F8
Argeş □, *Romania* 43 F9
Argeş ➤, *Romania* 43 F11
Arghandab ➤, *Afghan.* 68 D1
Argheile, *Ethiopia* 81 F5
Argo, *Sudan* 80 D3
Argolikós Kólpos, *Greece* .. 38 D4
Argolís □, *Greece* 38 D4
Argonne, *France* 19 C12
Árgos, *Greece* 38 D4
Árgos Orestikón, *Greece* ... 40 F5
Argostólion, *Greece* 38 C2
Arguedas, *Spain* 32 C3
Arguello, Pt., *U.S.A.* 117 L6
Arguineguín, *Canary Is.* ... 37 G4
Argun, *Russia* 49 J7
Argun ➤, *Russia* 51 D13
Argungu, *Nigeria* 83 C5
Argus Pk., *U.S.A.* 117 K9
Argyle, L., *U.S.A.* 92 C4
Argyle, L., *Australia* 92 C4
Argyll & Bute □, *U.K.* 14 E3
Arhavi, *Turkey* 73 B9
Århus, *Denmark* 11 H4
Århus Amtskommune □,
  Denmark 11 H4
Ariadnoye, *Russia* 54 B7
Ariamsvlei, *Namibia* 88 D2
Ariano Irpino, *Italy* 31 A8
Aribinda, *Burkina Faso* 83 C4
Arica, *Chile* 124 G4
Arica, *Colombia* 124 D4
Arico, *Canary Is.* 37 F3
Arid, C., *Australia* 93 F3
Arida, *Japan* 55 G7
Ariège □, *France* 20 F5
Ariège ➤, *France* 20 E5
Arieş ➤, *Romania* 43 D8
Arīhā, *Israel* 80 A4
Arilje, *Serbia, Yug.* 40 C4
Arílla, Ákra, *Greece* 36 A3
Arima, *Trin. & Tob.* 121 D7
Arinos ➤, *Brazil* 122 E5
Ario de Rosales, *Mexico* ... 118 D4
Ariogala, *Lithuania* 44 C10

Aripuanã, *Brazil* 124 E6
Aripuanã ➤, *Brazil* 122 D4
Ariquemes, *Brazil* 124 E6
Arisaig, *U.K.* 14 E3
Arîsh, W. el ➤, *Egypt* 80 A3
Arissa, *Ethiopia* 81 E5
Aristazabal I., *Canada* 104 C3
Arivonimamo, *Madag.* 89 B8
Ariza, *Spain* 32 D2
Arizaro, Salar de, *Argentina* . 126 A2
Arizona, *Argentina* 126 D2
Arizona □, *U.S.A.* 115 J8
Arizpe, *Mexico* 118 A2
Arjäng, *Sweden* 10 E6
Arjeplog, *Sweden* 8 D18
Arjona, *Colombia* 124 A3
Arjona, *Spain* 35 H6
Arjuna, *Indonesia* 63 G15
Arka, *Russia* 51 C15
Arkadak, *Russia* 48 E6
Arkadelphia, *U.S.A.* 113 H8
Arkadhía □, *Greece* 38 D4
Arkaig, L., *U.K.* 14 E3
Arkalyk = Arqalyk, *Kazakstan* . 50 D7
Arkansas □, *U.S.A.* 113 H8
Arkansas ➤, *U.S.A.* 113 J9
Arkansas City, *U.S.A.* 113 G6
Arkaroola, *Australia* 95 E2
Árkathos ➤, *Greece* 38 B3
Arkhángelos, *Greece* 36 C10
Arkhangelsk, *Russia* 50 C5
Arkhangelskoye, *Russia* 48 E5
Arki, *India* 68 D7
Arkiko, *Eritrea* 81 D4
Arklow, *Ireland* 15 D5
Árkoi, *Greece* 38 D9
Arkona, Kap, *Germany* 24 A9
Arkösund, *Sweden* 11 F10
Arkoúdhi, *Greece* 38 C2
Arkport, *U.S.A.* 110 D7
Arkticheskiy, Mys, *Russia* . 51 A10
Arkul, *Russia* 48 B10
Arkville, *U.S.A.* 111 D10
Årla, *Sweden* 10 E10
Arlanza ➤, *Spain* 34 C6
Arlanzón ➤, *Spain* 34 C6
Arlbergpass, *Austria* 26 D3
Arles, *France* 21 E8
Arlington, *S. Africa* 89 D4
Arlington, *N.Y., U.S.A.* ... 111 E11
Arlington, *Oreg., U.S.A.* .. 114 D3
Arlington, *S. Dak., U.S.A.* . 112 C6
Arlington, *Tex., U.S.A.* ... 113 J6
Arlington, *Va., U.S.A.* 108 F7
Arlington, *Vt., U.S.A.* 111 C11
Arlington, *Wash., U.S.A.* .. 116 B4
Arlington Heights, *U.S.A.* . 108 D2
Arlit, *Niger* 78 E7
Arlon, *Belgium* 17 E5
Arltunga, *Australia* 94 C1
Arly, *Burkina Faso* 83 C5
Armagh, *U.K.* 15 B5
Armagh □, *U.K.* 15 B5
Armagnac, *France* 20 E4
Armançon ➤, *France* 19 E10
Armavir, *Russia* 49 H5
Armenia, *Colombia* 124 C3
Armenia ■, *Asia* 49 K7
Armeniş, *Romania* 42 E7
Armenistís, Ákra, *Greece* .. 36 C9
Armentières, *France* 19 B9
Armidale, *Australia* 95 E5
Armilla, *Spain* 35 H7
Armour, *U.S.A.* 112 D5
Armstrong, *B.C., Canada* ... 104 C5
Armstrong, *Ont., Canada* ... 102 B2
Armutlu, *Bursa, Turkey* 41 F12
Armutlu, *Izmir, Turkey* 39 C9
Arnaía, *Greece* 40 F7
Arno ➤, *Italy* 28 E7
Arno Bay, *Australia* 95 E2
Arnold, *U.K.* 12 D6
Arnold, *U.S.A.* 116 G6
Arnoldstein, *Austria* 26 E6
Arnon ➤, *France* 19 E9
Arnot, *Canada* 105 B9
Arnøy, *Norway* 8 A19
Arnprior, *Canada* 102 C4
Arnsberg, *Germany* 24 D4
Arnstadt, *Germany* 24 E6
Aroab, *Namibia* 88 D2
Aroánia Óri, *Greece* 38 D4
Arochuku, *Nigeria* 83 D6
Arolsen, *Germany* 24 D5
Aron, *India* 68 G6
Aron ➤, *France* 19 F10
Arona, *Italy* 28 C5
Aroroy, *Phil.* 61 E5
Arosa, Ría de, *Spain* 34 C2
Arpajon, *France* 19 D9
Arpajon-sur-Cère, *France* .. 20 D6
Arpaşu de Jos, *Romania* 43 F9
Arqalyk, *Kazakstan* 50 D7
Arrah = Ara, *India* 69 G11

Arrah, *Ivory C.* 82 D4
Arraiolos, *Portugal* 35 G3
Arran, *U.K.* 14 F3
Arras, *France* 19 B9
Arrasate, *Spain* 32 B2
Arreau, *France* 20 F4
Arrecife, *Canary Is.* 37 F6
Arrecifes, *Argentina* 126 C3
Arrée, Mts. d', *France* 18 D3
Arresø, *Denmark* 11 J6
Arriaga, *Chiapas, Mexico* .. 119 D6
Arriaga, *San Luis Potosí, Mexico* 118 C4
Arrilalah, *Australia* 94 C3
Arrino, *Australia* 93 E2
Arriondas, *Spain* 34 B5
Arromanches-les-Bains, *France* . 18 C6
Arronches, *Portugal* 35 F3
Arros ➤, *France* 20 E3
Arrow, L., *Ireland* 15 B3
Arrowhead, L., *U.S.A.* 117 L9
Arrowtown, *N.Z.* 91 L2
Arroyo de la Luz, *Spain* ... 35 F4
Arroyo Grande, *U.S.A.* 117 K6
Ärs, *Denmark* 11 H3
Ars, *France* 70 B5
Ars-sur-Moselle, *France* ... 19 C13
Arsenault L., *Canada* 105 B7
Arseniev, *Russia* 54 B6
Arsi □, *Ethiopia* 81 F4
Arsiero, *Italy* 29 C8
Arsin, *Turkey* 73 B8
Arsk, *Russia* 48 B9
Årsunda, *Sweden* 10 D10
Árta, *Greece* 38 B3
Artà, *Spain* 37 B10
Árta □, *Greece* 38 B3
Arteaga, *Mexico* 118 D4
Arteche, *Phil.* 61 E6
Arteijo = Arteixo, *Spain* .. 34 B2
Arteixo, *Spain* 34 B2
Artem = Artyom, *Azerbaijan* . 49 K10
Artem, *Russia* 54 C6
Artemovsk, *Russia* 51 D10
Artemovsk, *Ukraine* 47 H9
Artemovskiy, *Russia* 49 G5
Artenay, *France* 19 D8
Artern, *Germany* 24 D7
Artesa de Segre, *Spain* 32 D6
Artesia = Mosomane, *Botswana* . 88 C4
Artesia, *U.S.A.* 113 J2
Arthington, *Liberia* 82 D2
Arthur, *Canada* 110 C4
Arthur ➤, *Australia* 94 G3
Arthur Cr. ➤, *Australia* ... 94 C2
Arthur Pt., *Australia* 94 C5
Arthur River, *Australia* ... 93 F2
Arthur's Pass, *N.Z.* 91 K3
Arthur's Town, *Bahamas* 121 B4
Artigas, *Uruguay* 126 C4
Artik, *Armenia* 49 K6
Artillery L., *Canada* 105 A7
Artois, *France* 19 B9
Artotína, *Greece* 38 C4
Artrutx, C. de, *Spain* 37 B10
Artsyz, *Ukraine* 47 J5
Artvin, *Turkey* 73 B9
Artyom, *Azerbaijan* 49 K10
Aru, Kepulauan, *Indonesia* . 63 F8
Aru Is. = Aru, Kepulauan,
  Indonesia 63 F8
Arua, *Uganda* 86 B3
Aruanã, *Brazil* 125 F8
Aruba ■, *W. Indies* 121 D6
Arucas, *Canary Is.* 37 F4
Arudy, *France* 20 E3
Arun ➤, *Nepal* 69 F12
Arun ➤, *U.K.* 13 G7
Arunachal Pradesh □, *India* . 67 F19
Arusha, *Tanzania* 86 C4
Arusha □, *Tanzania* 86 C4
Arusha Chini, *Tanzania* 86 C4
Aruwimi ➤, *Dem. Rep. of
  the Congo* 86 B1
Arvada, *Colo., U.S.A.* 112 F2
Arvada, *Wyo., U.S.A.* 114 D10
Arve ➤, *France* 19 F13
Árvi, *Greece* 36 E7
Arviat, *Canada* 105 A10
Arvidsjaur, *Sweden* 8 D18
Arvika, *Sweden* 10 E6
Arvin, *U.S.A.* 117 K8
Arwal, *India* 69 G11
Arxan, *China* 60 B6
Åryd, *Sweden* 11 H8
Aryirádhes, *Greece* 36 B3
Ariyiroúpolis, *Greece* 36 D6
Arys, *Kazakstan* 50 E7
Arzachena, *Italy* 30 A2
Arzamas, *Russia* 48 C6
Arzgir, *Russia* 49 H7
Arzignano, *Italy* 29 C8
Arzúa, *Spain* 34 C2
Aš, *Czech Rep.* 26 A5
Ås, *Sweden* 10 A8
As Pontes de García Rodríguez,
  Spain 34 B3
Aş Şafā, *Syria* 75 B6
As Saffānīyah, *Si. Arabia* . 71 E6
As Safīrah, *Syria* 70 B3
Aş Şahm, *Oman* 71 E8
As Sājir, *Si. Arabia* 70 E5
As Salamīyah, *Syria* 70 C3
As Salmān, *Iraq* 70 D5
As Salṭ, *Jordan* 75 C4
As Salw'a, *Qatar* 71 E6
As Samāwah, *Iraq* 70 D5

As Sanamayn, *Syria* 75 B5
As Sohar = Şuḩār, *Oman* 71 E8
As Sukhnah, *Syria* 70 C3
As Sulaymānīyah, *Iraq* 70 C5
As Sulaymī, *Si. Arabia* 70 E4
As Sulayyil, *Si. Arabia* ... 74 C4
As Summān, *Si. Arabia* 70 E5
As Suwaydā', *Syria* 75 C5
As Suwaydā' □, *Syria* 75 C5
As Şuwayrah, *Iraq* 70 C5
Åsa, *Sweden* 11 G6
Asab, *Namibia* 88 D2
Asaba, *Nigeria* 83 D6
Asad, Buḩayrat al, *Syria* .. 70 C3
Asafo, *Ghana* 82 D4
Asahi-Gawa ➤, *Japan* 55 G6
Asahigawa, *Japan* 54 C11
Asale, L., *Ethiopia* 81 E5
Asamankese, *Ghana* 83 D4
Asan ➤, *India* 69 F8
Asansol, *India* 69 H12
Åsarna, *Sweden* 10 B8
Asayita, *Ethiopia* 81 E5
Asbe Teferi, *Ethiopia* 81 F5
Asbesberge, *S. Africa* 88 D3
Asbestos, *Canada* 103 C5
Asbury Park, *U.S.A.* 111 F10
Ascea, *Italy* 31 B8
Ascensión, *Mexico* 118 A3
Ascensión, B. de la, *Mexico* . 119 D7
Ascension I., *Atl. Oc.* 77 G2
Aschach an der Donau, *Austria* . 26 C7
Aschaffenburg, *Germany* 25 F5
Aschendorf, *Germany* 24 B3
Aschersleben, *Germany* 24 D7
Asciano, *Italy* 29 E8
Áscoli Piceno, *Italy* 29 F10
Áscoli Satriano, *Italy* 31 A8
Ascope, *Peru* 124 E3
Ascotán, *Chile* 126 A2
Aseb, *Eritrea* 81 E5
Åseda, *Sweden* 11 G9
Asela, *Ethiopia* 81 F4
Åsen, *Sweden* 10 C7
Asenovgrad, *Bulgaria* 41 D8
Aserradero, *Mexico* 118 C3
Asfeld, *France* 19 C11
Asfûn el Matâ'na, *Egypt* ... 80 B3
Asgata, *Cyprus* 36 E12
Ash Fork, *U.S.A.* 115 J7
Ash Grove, *U.S.A.* 113 G8
Ash Shabakah, *Iraq* 70 D4
Ash Shamāl □, *Lebanon* 75 A5
Ash Shāmīyah, *Iraq* 70 D5
Ash Shāriqah, *U.A.E.* 71 E7
Ash Sharmah, *Si. Arabia* ... 70 D2
Ash Sharqāt, *Iraq* 70 C4
Ash Sharqi, Al Jabal, *Lebanon* . 75 B5
Ash Shaṭrah, *Iraq* 70 D5
Ash Shawbak, *Jordan* 75 D4
Ash Shawmari, J., *Jordan* .. 75 E6
Ash Shināfīyah, *Iraq* 70 D5
Ash Shu'bah, *Si. Arabia* ... 70 D5
Ash Shumlūl, *Si. Arabia* ... 70 E5
Ash Shur'a, *Iraq* 70 C4
Ash Shurayf, *Si. Arabia* ... 70 E4
Ash Shuwayfāt, *Lebanon* 75 B4
Ashanti □, *Ghana* 83 D4
Ashau, *Vietnam* 64 D6
Ashbourne, *U.K.* 12 D6
Ashburn, *U.S.A.* 109 K4
Ashburton, *N.Z.* 91 K3
Ashburton ➤, *Australia* 92 D1
Ashcroft, *Canada* 104 C4
Ashdod, *Israel* 75 D3
Ashdown, *U.S.A.* 113 J7
Asheboro, *U.S.A.* 109 H6
Ashern, *Canada* 105 C9
Asherton, *U.S.A.* 113 L5
Asheville, *U.S.A.* 109 H4
Ashewat, *Pakistan* 68 D3
Asheweig ➤, *Canada* 102 B2
Ashford, *Australia* 95 D5
Ashford, *U.K.* 13 F8
Ashgabat, *Turkmenistan* 50 F6
Ashibetsu, *Japan* 54 C11
Ashikaga, *Japan* 55 F9
Ashizuri-Zaki, *Japan* 55 H6
Ashkarkot, *Afghan.* 68 C2
Ashkhabad = Ashgabat,
  Turkmenistan 50 F6
Äshkhāneh, *Iran* 71 B8
Ashland, *Kans., U.S.A.* 113 G5
Ashland, *Ky., U.S.A.* 108 F4
Ashland, *Mont., U.S.A.* 114 D10
Ashland, *Ohio, U.S.A.* 110 F2
Ashland, *Oreg., U.S.A.* 114 E2
Ashland, *Pa., U.S.A.* 111 F8
Ashland, *Va., U.S.A.* 108 G7
Ashland, *Wis., U.S.A.* 112 B9
Ashley, *N. Dak., U.S.A.* ... 112 B5
Ashley, *Pa., U.S.A.* 111 E9
Ashmore Reef, *Australia* ... 92 B3
Ashmûn, *Egypt* 80 H7
Ashmyany, *Belarus* 9 J21
Ashokan Reservoir, *U.S.A.* . 111 E10
Ashqelon, *Israel* 75 D3
Ashta, *India* 68 H7
Ashtabula, *U.S.A.* 110 E4
Ashton, *S. Africa* 88 E3
Ashṭon, *U.S.A.* 114 D8
Ashuanipi, L., *Canada* 103 B6
Ashville, *U.S.A.* 110 F6
'Āşi ➤, *Asia* 72 D6

Băbeni

Asia 52 E11
Asia, Kepulauan, *Indonesia* 63 D8
Āsīā Bak, *Iran* 71 C6
Asiago, *Italy* 29 C8
Asifabad, *India* 66 K11
Asinara, *Italy* 30 A1
Asinara, G. dell', *Italy* 30 A1
Asino, *Russia* 50 D9
Asipovichy, *Belarus* 46 F5
'Asīr □, *Si. Arabia* 74 D3
Asir, Ras, *Somali Rep.* 74 E5
Aşkale, *Turkey* 73 C9
Askersund, *Sweden* 11 F8
Askham, *S. Africa* 88 D3
Askim, *Norway* 9 G14
Askja, *Iceland* 8 D5
Askøy, *Norway* 9 F11
Asl, *Egypt* 80 B3
Aslan Burnu, *Turkey* 39 C8
Aslanapa, *Turkey* 39 B11
Asmara = Asmera, *Eritrea* 81 D4
Asmera, *Eritrea* 81 D4
Asnæs, *Denmark* 11 J4
Åsnen, *Sweden* 11 H8
Ásola, *Italy* 28 C7
Asosa, *Ethiopia* 81 E3
Asoteriba, Jebel, *Sudan* 80 C4
Aspe, *Spain* 33 G4
Aspen, *U.S.A.* 115 G10
Aspendos, *Turkey* 72 D4
Aspermont, *U.S.A.* 113 J4
Aspet, *France* 20 E4
Aspiring, Mt., *N.Z.* 91 L2
Aspres-sur-Buëch, *France* 21 D9
Asprókavos, Ákra, *Greece* 36 B4
Aspromonte, *Italy* 31 D9
Aspur, *India* 68 H6
Asquith, *Canada* 105 C7
Assâba, Massif de l', *Mauritania* 82 B2
Assaikio, *Nigeria* 83 D6
Assal, L., *Djibouti* 81 E5
Assam □, *India* 67 G18
Assamakka, *Niger* 83 B6
Asse, *Belgium* 17 D4
Assémini, *Italy* 30 C1
Assen, *Neths.* 17 A6
Assens, *Denmark* 11 J3
Assini, *Ivory C.* 82 D4
Assiniboia, *Canada* 105 D7
Assiniboine →, *Canada* 105 D9
Assiniboine, Mt., *Canada* 104 C5
Assis, *Brazil* 127 A5
Assisi, *Italy* 29 E9
Ássos, *Greece* 38 C2
Assynt, L., *U.K.* 14 C3
Astaffort, *France* 20 D4
Astakidha, *Greece* 39 F8
Astakós, *Greece* 38 C3
Astana, *Kazakstan* 50 D8
Āstāneh, *Iran* 71 B6
Astara, *Azerbaijan* 71 B6
Āstārā, *Iran* 73 C13
Asteroúsia, *Greece* 36 E7
Asti, *Italy* 28 D5
Astipálaia, *Greece* 39 E8
Astorga, *Spain* 34 C4
Astoria, *U.S.A.* 116 D3
Åstorp, *Sweden* 11 H6
Astrakhan, *Russia* 49 G9
Astudillo, *Spain* 34 C6
Asturias □, *Spain* 34 B5
Asunción, *Paraguay* 126 B4
Asunción Nochixtlán, *Mexico* 119 D5
Åsunden, *Sweden* 11 F9
Asutri, *Sudan* 81 D4
Aswa →, *Uganda* 86 B3
Aswad, Ra's al, *Si. Arabia* 80 C4
Aswân, *Egypt* 80 C3
Aswân High Dam = Sadd el Aali, *Egypt* 80 C3
Asyût, *Egypt* 80 B3
Asyûti, Wadi →, *Egypt* 80 B3
Aszód, *Hungary* 42 C4
At Ţafīlah, *Jordan* 75 E4
Aţ Ţā'if, *Si. Arabia* 74 C3
Aţ Ţirāq, *Si. Arabia* 70 E5
Aţ Ţubayq, *Si. Arabia* 70 D3
Atabey, *Turkey* 39 D12
Atacama □, *Chile* 126 B2
Atacama, Desierto de, *Chile* 126 A2
Atacama, Salar de, *Chile* 126 A2
Atakpamé, *Togo* 83 D5
Atalándi, *Greece* 38 C4
Atalaya, *Peru* 124 F4
Atalaya de Femes, *Canary Is.* 37 F6
Atami, *Japan* 55 G9
Atapupu, *Indonesia* 63 F6
Atâr, *Mauritania* 78 D3
Atarfe, *Spain* 35 H7
Atari, *Pakistan* 68 D6
Atascadero, *U.S.A.* 116 K6
Atasu, *Kazakstan* 50 E8
Atatürk Barajı, *Turkey* 73 D8
Atauro, *Indonesia* 63 F7
'Atbara, *Sudan* 80 D3
'Atbara, Nahr →, *Sudan* 80 D3
Atbasar, *Kazakstan* 50 D7
Atça, *Turkey* 39 D10
Atchafalaya B., *U.S.A.* 113 L9
Atchison, *U.S.A.* 112 F7
Atebubu, *Ghana* 83 D4
Ateca, *Spain* 32 D3
Aterno →, *Italy* 29 F10
Āteshān, *Iran* 71 C7
Atesine, Alpi, *Italy* 29 B8
Atessa, *Italy* 29 F11
Atfih, *Egypt* 80 J7
Ath, *Belgium* 17 D3
Athabasca, *Canada* 104 C6
Athabasca →, *Canada* 105 B6
Athabasca, L., *Canada* 105 B7
Athboy, *Ireland* 15 C5
Athenry, *Ireland* 15 C3
Athens = Athínai, *Greece* 38 D5
Athens, *Ala., U.S.A.* 109 H2
Athens, *Ga., U.S.A.* 109 J4
Athens, *N.Y., U.S.A.* 111 D11
Athens, *Ohio, U.S.A.* 108 F4
Athens, *Pa., U.S.A.* 111 E8
Athens, *Tenn., U.S.A.* 109 H3
Athens, *Tex., U.S.A.* 113 J7
Atherley, *Canada* 110 B5
Atherton, *Australia* 94 B4
Athiéme, *Benin* 83 D5
Athienou, *Cyprus* 36 D12
Athínai, *Greece* 38 D5
Athlone, *Ireland* 15 C4
Athna, *Cyprus* 36 D12
Athol, *U.S.A.* 111 D12
Atholl, Forest of, *U.K.* 14 E5
Atholville, *Canada* 103 C6
Áthos, *Greece* 41 F8
Athy, *Ireland* 15 C5
Ati, *Chad* 79 F9
Ati, *Sudan* 81 E2
Atiak, *Uganda* 86 B3
Atienza, *Spain* 32 D2
Atiit, *Sudan* 81 F3
Atik L., *Canada* 105 B9
Atikameg →, *Canada* 102 B3
Atikokan, *Canada* 102 C1
Atikonak L., *Canada* 103 B7
Atimonan, *Phil.* 61 E4
Atka, *Russia* 51 C16
Atka I., *U.S.A.* 100 C2
Atkarsk, *Russia* 48 E7
Atkinson, *U.S.A.* 112 D5
Atlanta, *Ga., U.S.A.* 109 J3
Atlanta, *Tex., U.S.A.* 113 J7
Atlantic, *U.S.A.* 112 E7
Atlantic City, *U.S.A.* 108 F8
Atlantic Ocean 2 E9
Atlas Mts. = Haut Atlas, *Morocco* 78 B4
Atlin, *Canada* 104 B2
Atlin, L., *Canada* 104 B2
Atlin Prov. Park, *Canada* 104 B2
Atmore, *U.S.A.* 109 K2
Atoka, *U.S.A.* 113 H6
Átokos, *Greece* 38 C2
Atolia, *U.S.A.* 117 K9
Atrai →, *Bangla.* 69 G13
Atrak = Atrek →, *Turkmenistan* 71 B8
Ätran, *Sweden* 11 G6
Ätran →, *Sweden* 11 H6
Atrauli, *India* 68 E8
Atrek →, *Turkmenistan* 71 B8
Atri, *Italy* 29 F10
Atsikí, *Greece* 39 B7
Atsoum, Mts., *Cameroon* 83 D7
Atsuta, *Japan* 54 C10
Attalla, *U.S.A.* 109 H2
Attapu, *Laos* 64 E6
Attáviros, *Greece* 36 C9
Attawapiskat, *Canada* 102 B3
Attawapiskat →, *Canada* 102 B3
Attawapiskat L., *Canada* 102 B2
Attersee, *Austria* 26 D6
Attica, *Ind., U.S.A.* 108 E2
Attica, *Ohio, U.S.A.* 110 E2
Attichy, *France* 19 C10
Attigny, *France* 19 C11
Attika = Attikí □, *Greece* 38 D5
Attikamagen L., *Canada* 103 B6
Attikí □, *Greece* 38 D5
Attleboro, *U.S.A.* 111 E13
Attock, *Pakistan* 68 C5
Attopeu = Attapu, *Laos* 64 E6
Attu I., *U.S.A.* 100 C1
Attur, *India* 66 P11
Atuel →, *Argentina* 126 D2
Åtvidaberg, *Sweden* 11 F10
Atwater, *U.S.A.* 116 H6
Atwood, *Canada* 110 C3
Atwood, *U.S.A.* 112 F4
Atyraū, *Kazakstan* 50 E6
Au Sable, *U.S.A.* 110 B1
Au Sable →, *U.S.A.* 108 C4
Au Sable Forks, *U.S.A.* 111 B11
Au Sable Pt., *U.S.A.* 110 B1
Aubagne, *France* 21 E9
Aubarca, C. d', *Spain* 37 B7
Aube □, *France* 19 D11
Aube →, *France* 19 D10
Aubenas, *France* 21 D8
Aubenton, *France* 19 C11
Auberry, *U.S.A.* 116 H7
Aubigny-sur-Nère, *France* 19 E9
Aubin, *France* 20 D6
Aubrac, Mts. d', *France* 20 D7
Auburn, *Ala., U.S.A.* 109 J3
Auburn, *Calif., U.S.A.* 116 G5
Auburn, *Ind., U.S.A.* 108 E3
Auburn, *Maine, U.S.A.* 109 C10
Auburn, *N.Y., U.S.A.* 111 D8
Auburn, *Nebr., U.S.A.* 112 E7
Auburn, *Pa., U.S.A.* 111 F8
Auburn, *Wash., U.S.A.* 116 C4
Auburn Ra., *Australia* 95 D5
Auburndale, *U.S.A.* 109 L5
Aubusson, *France* 20 C6
Auce, *Latvia* 44 B9
Auch, *France* 20 E4
Auchi, *Nigeria* 83 D6
Auckland, *N.Z.* 91 G5
Auckland Is., *Pac. Oc.* 96 N8
Aude □, *France* 20 E6
Aude →, *France* 20 E7
Auden, *Canada* 102 B2
Auderville, *France* 18 C5
Audierne, *France* 18 D2
Audincourt, *France* 19 E13
Audo, *Ethiopia* 81 F5
Audubon, *U.S.A.* 112 E7
Aue, *Germany* 24 E8
Auerbach, *Germany* 24 E8
Augathella, *Australia* 95 D4
Aughnacloy, *U.K.* 15 B5
Augrabies Falls, *S. Africa* 88 D3
Augsburg, *Germany* 25 G6
Augusta, *Australia* 93 F2
Augusta, *Italy* 31 E8
Augusta, *Ark., U.S.A.* 113 H9
Augusta, *Ga., U.S.A.* 109 J5
Augusta, *Kans., U.S.A.* 113 G6
Augusta, *Maine, U.S.A.* 101 D13
Augusta, *Mont., U.S.A.* 114 C7
Augustenborg, *Denmark* 11 K3
Augustów, *Poland* 44 E9
Augustus, Mt., *Australia* 93 D2
Augustus I., *Australia* 92 C3
Aukan, *Eritrea* 81 D5
Aukum, *U.S.A.* 116 G6
Auld, L., *Australia* 92 D3
Aulla, *Italy* 28 D6
Aulnay, *France* 20 B3
Aulne →, *France* 18 D2
Aulnoye-Aymeries, *France* 19 B10
Ault, *France* 18 B8
Ault, *U.S.A.* 112 E2
Aulus-les-Bains, *France* 20 F5
Aumale, *France* 19 C8
Aumont-Aubrac, *France* 20 D7
Auna, *Nigeria* 83 C5
Auning, *Denmark* 11 H4
Aunis, *France* 20 B3
Auponhia, *Indonesia* 63 E7
Aups, *France* 21 E10
Aur, Pulau, *Malaysia* 65 L5
Auraiya, *India* 69 F8
Aurangabad, *Bihar, India* 69 G11
Aurangabad, *Maharashtra, India* 66 K9
Auray, *France* 18 E4
Aurich, *Germany* 24 B3
Aurillac, *France* 20 D6
Auronzo di Cadore, *Italy* 29 B9
Aurora, *Canada* 110 C5
Aurora, *S. Africa* 88 E2
Aurora, *Colo., U.S.A.* 112 F2
Aurora, *Ill., U.S.A.* 108 E1
Aurora, *Mo., U.S.A.* 113 G8
Aurora, *N.Y., U.S.A.* 111 D8
Aurora, *Nebr., U.S.A.* 112 E6
Aurora, *Ohio, U.S.A.* 110 E3
Aurukun, *Australia* 94 A3
Aus, *Namibia* 88 D2
Ausable →, *Canada* 110 C3
Auschwitz = Oświęcim, *Poland* 45 H6
Austerlitz = Slavkov u Brna, *Czech Rep.* 27 B9
Austin, *Minn., U.S.A.* 112 D8
Austin, *Nev., U.S.A.* 114 G5
Austin, *Pa., U.S.A.* 110 E6
Austin, *Tex., U.S.A.* 113 K6
Austin, L., *Australia* 93 E2
Austin I., *Canada* 105 A10
Austra, *Norway* 8 D14
Austral Is. = Tubuai Is., *Pac. Oc.* 97 K13
Austral Seamount Chain, *Pac. Oc.* 97 K13
Australia ■, *Oceania* 96 K5
Australian Capital Territory □, *Australia* 95 F4
Australind, *Australia* 93 F2
Austria ■, *Europe* 26 E7
Austvågøy, *Norway* 8 B16
Auterive, *France* 20 E5
Authie →, *France* 19 B8
Authon-du-Perche, *France* 18 D7
Autlán, *Mexico* 118 D4
Autun, *France* 19 F11
Auvergne, *France* 20 C7
Auvergne, Mts. d', *France* 20 C6
Auvézère →, *France* 20 C4
Auxerre, *France* 19 E10
Auxi-le-Château, *France* 19 B9
Auxonne, *France* 19 E12
Auzances, *France* 19 F9
Ava, *U.S.A.* 113 G8
Avallon, *France* 19 E10
Avalon, *U.S.A.* 117 M8
Avalon Pen., *Canada* 103 C9
Avanos, *Turkey* 70 B2
Avaré, *Brazil* 127 A6
Ávas, *Greece* 41 F9
Avawatz Mts., *U.S.A.* 117 K10
Avdan Dağı, *Turkey* 41 F13
Aveiro, *Brazil* 125 D7
Aveiro, *Portugal* 34 E2
Aveiro □, *Portugal* 34 E2
Āvej, *Iran* 71 C6
Avellaneda, *Argentina* 126 C4
Avellino, *Italy* 31 B7
Avenal, *U.S.A.* 116 K6
Aversa, *Italy* 31 B7
Avery, *U.S.A.* 114 C6
Aves, Is. las, *Venezuela* 121 D6
Avesnes-sur-Helpe, *France* 19 B10
Avesta, *Sweden* 10 D10
Aveyron □, *France* 20 D6
Aveyron →, *France* 20 D5
Avezzano, *Italy* 29 F10
Avgó, *Greece* 39 F7
Aviá Terai, *Argentina* 126 B3
Aviano, *Italy* 29 B9
Aviemore, *U.K.* 14 D5
Avigliana, *Italy* 28 C4
Avigliano, *Italy* 31 B8
Avignon, *France* 21 E8
Ávila, *Spain* 34 E6
Ávila □, *Spain* 34 E6
Ávila, Sierra de, *Spain* 34 E5
Avila Beach, *U.S.A.* 117 K6
Avilés, *Spain* 34 B5
Avintes, *Portugal* 34 D2
Avionárion, *Greece* 38 C6
Avis, *Portugal* 35 F3
Avis, *U.S.A.* 110 E7
Avísio →, *Italy* 28 B8
Aviz = Avis, *Portugal* 35 F3
Avize, *France* 19 D11
Avlum, *Denmark* 11 H2
Avoca, *U.S.A.* 110 D7
Avoca →, *Australia* 95 F3
Avoca →, *Ireland* 15 D5
Avola, *Canada* 104 C5
Avola, *Italy* 31 F8
Avon, *U.S.A.* 110 D7
Avon →, *Australia* 93 F2
Avon →, *Bristol, U.K.* 13 F5
Avon →, *Dorset, U.K.* 13 G6
Avon →, *Warks., U.K.* 13 E5
Avon Park, *U.S.A.* 109 M5
Avondale, *Zimbabwe* 87 F3
Avonlea, *Canada* 105 D8
Avonmore, *Canada* 111 A10
Avramov, *Bulgaria* 41 D10
Avranches, *France* 18 D5
Avre →, *France* 18 D8
Avrig, *Romania* 43 E9
Avrillé, *France* 18 E6
Avtovac, *Bos.-H.* 40 C2
Awag el Baqar, *Sudan* 81 E3
A'waj →, *Syria* 75 B5
Awaji-Shima, *Japan* 55 G7
'Awālī, *Bahrain* 71 E6
Awantipur, *India* 69 C6
Awasa, *Ethiopia* 81 F4
Awasa, L., *Ethiopia* 81 F4
Awash, *Ethiopia* 81 F5
Awash →, *Ethiopia* 81 E5
Awaso, *Ghana* 82 D4
Awatere →, *N.Z.* 91 J5
Awbārī, *Libya* 79 C8
Awe, L., *U.K.* 14 E3
Aweil, *Sudan* 81 F2
Awgu, *Nigeria* 83 D6
Awjilah, *Libya* 79 C10
Awka, *Nigeria* 83 D6
Ax-les-Thermes, *France* 20 F5
Axat, *France* 20 F6
Axe →, *U.K.* 13 F5
Axel Heiberg I., *Canada* 4 B3
Axim, *Ghana* 82 E4
Axintele, *Romania* 43 F11
Axiós →, *Greece* 40 F6
Axminster, *U.K.* 13 G4
Axvall, *Sweden* 11 F7
Ay, *France* 19 C11
Ayabaca, *Peru* 124 D3
Ayabe, *Japan* 55 G7
Ayacucho, *Argentina* 126 D4
Ayacucho, *Peru* 124 F4
Ayaguz, *Kazakstan* 50 E9
Ayamé, *Ivory C.* 82 D4
Ayamonte, *Spain* 35 H3
Ayan, *Russia* 51 D14
Ayancık, *Turkey* 72 B6
Ayas, *Turkey* 72 B5
Ayaviri, *Peru* 124 F4
Aybastı, *Turkey* 72 B7
Aydın, *Turkey* 72 D2
Aydin □, *Turkey* 39 D9
Aydin Dağları, *Turkey* 39 D10
Ayelu, *Ethiopia* 81 E5
Ayenngré, *Togo* 83 D5
Ayer, *U.S.A.* 111 D13
Ayerbe, *Spain* 32 C4
Ayer's Cliff, *Canada* 111 A12
Ayers Rock, *Australia* 93 E5
Ayiá, *Greece* 38 B4
Ayia Aikateríni, Ákra, *Greece* 36 A3
Ayía Ánna, *Greece* 38 C5
Ayia Dhéka, *Greece* 36 D6
Ayia Gálini, *Greece* 36 D6
Ayía Marína, *Kásos, Greece* 39 F8
Ayía Marína, *Léros, Greece* 39 D8
Áyia Napa, *Cyprus* 36 E13
Ayía Paraskeví, *Greece* 39 B8
Áyia Phyla, *Cyprus* 36 E12
Ayia Rouméli, *Greece* 38 F5
Ayia Varvára, *Greece* 36 D7
Ayiássos, *Greece* 39 B8
Ayioi Theódhoroi, *Greece* 38 D5
Áyion Óros □, *Greece* 41 F8
Áyios Amvrósios, *Cyprus* 36 D12
Áyios Andréas, *Greece* 38 D4
Áyios Evstrátios, *Greece* 38 B6
Áyios Ioánnis, Ákra, *Greece* 36 D7
Áyios Isidhoros, *Greece* 36 C9
Áyios Kiríkos, *Greece* 39 D8
Áyios Matthaíos, *Greece* 36 B3
Áyios Mírono, *Greece* 39 F7
Áyios Nikólaos, *Greece* 36 D7
Áyios Pétros, *Greece* 38 C2
Áyios Seryios, *Cyprus* 36 D12
Áyios Theodhoros, *Cyprus* 36 D13
Áyios Yeóryios, *Greece* 38 D5
Aykathonisi, *Greece* 39 D8
Aykirikçi, *Turkey* 39 B12
Aylesbury, *U.K.* 13 F7
Aylmer, *Canada* 110 D4
Aylmer, L., *Canada* 100 B8
'Ayn, Wādī al, *Oman* 71 F7
Ayn Dār, *Si. Arabia* 71 E7
Ayn Zālah, *Iraq* 70 B4
Ayna, *Spain* 33 G2
Ayod, *Sudan* 81 F3
Ayolas, *Paraguay* 126 B4
Ayom, *Sudan* 81 F2
Ayon, Ostrov, *Russia* 51 C17
Ayora, *Spain* 33 F3
Ayorou, *Niger* 83 C5
'Ayoûn el 'Atroûs, *Mauritania* 82 B3
Ayr, *Australia* 94 B4
Ayr, *Canada* 110 C4
Ayr, *U.K.* 14 F4
Ayr →, *U.K.* 14 F4
Ayrancı, *Turkey* 72 D5
Ayrancılar, *Turkey* 39 C9
Ayre, Pt. of, *U.K.* 12 C3
Aysha, *Ethiopia* 81 E5
Ayton, *Australia* 94 B4
Aytos, *Bulgaria* 41 D11
Aytoska Planina, *Bulgaria* 41 D11
Ayu, Kepulauan, *Indonesia* 63 D8
Ayutla, *Guatemala* 120 D1
Ayutla, *Mexico* 119 D5
Ayvacık, *Turkey* 72 C2
Ayvalık, *Turkey* 39 B8
Az Zabadānī, *Syria* 75 B5
Az Zāhirīyah, *West Bank* 75 D3
Az Zahrān, *Si. Arabia* 71 E6
Az Zarqā, *Jordan* 75 C5
Az Zarqā', *U.A.E.* 71 E7
Az Zībār, *Iraq* 70 B5
Az Zilfī, *Si. Arabia* 70 E5
Az Zubayr, *Iraq* 70 D5
Az Zuqur, *Yemen* 81 E5
Azambuja, *Portugal* 35 F2
Azamgarh, *India* 69 F10
Azangaro, *Peru* 124 F4
Azaoua, *Niger* 83 B5
Azaouad, *Mali* 82 B4
Azaouak, Vallée de l', *Mali* 83 B5
Āzār Shahr, *Iran* 70 B5
Azara, *Nigeria* 83 D6
Azarān, *Iran* 70 B5
Azärbayjan = Azerbaijan ■, *Asia* 49 K9
Āzarbāyjān-e Gharbī □, *Iran* 70 B5
Āzarbāyjān-e Sharqī □, *Iran* 70 B5
Azare, *Nigeria* 83 C7
Azay-le-Rideau, *France* 18 E7
A'zāz, *Syria* 70 B3
Azbine = Aïr, *Niger* 83 B6
Azerbaijan ■, *Asia* 49 K9
Azerbaijchan = Azerbaijan ■, *Asia* 49 K9
Azezo, *Ethiopia* 81 E4
Azimganj, *India* 69 G13
Aznalcóllar, *Spain* 35 H4
Azogues, *Ecuador* 124 D3
Azores, *Atl. Oc.* 78 A1
Azov, *Russia* 49 G4
Azov, Sea of, *Europe* 47 J9
Azovskoye More = Azov, Sea of, *Europe* 47 J9
Azpeitia, *Spain* 32 B2
Azraq ash Shīshān, *Jordan* 75 D5
Aztec, *U.S.A.* 115 H10
Azúa de Compostela, *Dom. Rep.* 121 C5
Azuaga, *Spain* 35 G5
Azuara, *Spain* 32 D4
Azuer →, *Spain* 35 F7
Azuero, Pen. de, *Panama* 120 E3
Azuga, *Romania* 43 E10
Azul, *Argentina* 126 D4
Azusa, *U.S.A.* 117 L9
Azzano Décimo, *Italy* 29 C9

B

Ba Don, *Vietnam* 64 D6
Ba Dong, *Vietnam* 65 H6
Ba Ngoi = Cam Lam, *Vietnam* 65 G7
Ba Tri, *Vietnam* 65 G6
Ba Xian = Bazhou, *China* 56 E9
Baa, *Indonesia* 63 F6
Baamonde, *Spain* 34 B3
Baarle-Nassau, *Belgium* 17 C4
Bab el Mandeb, *Red Sea* 74 E3
Baba, *Bulgaria* 40 D7
Bābā, Koh-i-, *Afghan.* 66 B5
Baba Burnu, *Turkey* 39 B8
Baba dag, *Azerbaijan* 49 K9
Bābā Kalū, *Iran* 71 D6
Babadag, *Romania* 43 F13
Babadağ, *Turkey* 39 D10
Babadayhan, *Turkmenistan* 50 F7
Babaeski, *Turkey* 41 E11
Babahoyo, *Ecuador* 124 D3
Babai = Sarju →, *India* 69 F9
Babana, *Nigeria* 83 C5
Babanusa, *Sudan* 81 E2
Babar, *Indonesia* 63 F7
Babar, *Pakistan* 68 D3
Babarkach, *Pakistan* 68 E3
Babayevo, *Russia* 46 C8
Babb, *U.S.A.* 114 B7
Babelthuap, *Pac. Oc.* 63 C8
Babenhausen, *Germany* 25 F4
Băbeni, *Romania* 43 F9

Baberu, *India* ... 69 G9
Babi Besar, Pulau, *Malaysia* ... 65 L4
Babia Gora, *Europe* ... 45 J6
Babian Jiang →, *China* ... 58 F3
Babile, *Ethiopia* ... 81 F5
Babimost, *Poland* ... 45 F2
Babinda, *Australia* ... 94 B4
Babine, *Canada* ... 104 B3
Babine →, *Canada* ... 104 B3
Babine L., *Canada* ... 104 C3
Babo, *Indonesia* ... 63 E8
Babócsa, *Hungary* ... 42 D2
Bābol, *Iran* ... 71 B7
Bābol Sar, *Iran* ... 71 B7
Baborów, *Poland* ... 45 H5
Babruysk, *Belarus* ... 47 F5
Babuhri, *India* ... 68 F3
Babuna, *Macedonia* ... 40 E5
Babura, *Nigeria* ... 83 C6
Babusar Pass, *Pakistan* ... 69 B5
Babushkin, *Russia* ... 60 A5
Babušnica, *Serbia, Yug.* ... 40 C6
Babuyan Chan., *Phil.* ... 61 B4
Babylon, *Iraq* ... 70 C5
Bač, *Serbia, Yug.* ... 42 E4
Bac →, *Moldova* ... 43 D14
Bac Can, *Vietnam* ... 58 F5
Bac Giang, *Vietnam* ... 58 G6
Bac Lieu, *Vietnam* ... 65 H5
Bac Ninh, *Vietnam* ... 58 G6
Bac Phan, *Vietnam* ... 64 B5
Bac Quang, *Vietnam* ... 58 F5
Bacabal, *Brazil* ... 125 D10
Bacalar, *Mexico* ... 119 D7
Bacan, Kepulauan, *Indonesia* ... 63 E7
Bacarra, *Phil.* ... 61 B4
Bacău, *Romania* ... 43 D11
Bacău □, *Romania* ... 43 D11
Baccarat, *France* ... 19 D13
Bacerac, *Mexico* ... 118 A3
Băcești, *Romania* ... 43 D12
Bach Long Vi, Dao, *Vietnam* ... 64 B6
Bacharach, *Germany* ... 25 E3
Bachelina, *Russia* ... 50 D7
Bachhwara, *India* ... 69 G11
Bachuma, *Ethiopia* ... 81 F4
Bačina, *Serbia, Yug.* ... 40 C5
Back →, *Canada* ... 100 B9
Bačka Palanka, *Serbia, Yug.* ... 42 E4
Bačka Topola, *Serbia, Yug.* ... 42 E4
Bäckebo, *Sweden* ... 11 H10
Bäckefors, *Sweden* ... 11 F6
Bäckhammar, *Sweden* ... 10 E8
Bački Petrovac, *Serbia, Yug.* ... 42 E4
Backnang, *Germany* ... 25 G5
Baco, Mt., *Phil.* ... 61 E4
Bacolod, *Phil.* ... 61 F5
Bacqueville-en-Caux, *France* ... 18 C8
Bács-Kiskun □, *Hungary* ... 42 D4
Bácsalmás, *Hungary* ... 42 D4
Bacuag = Placer, *Phil.* ... 61 G6
Bacuk, *Malaysia* ... 65 J4
Bād, *Iran* ... 71 C7
Bad →, *U.S.A.* ... 112 C4
Bad Aussee, *Austria* ... 26 D6
Bad Axe, *U.S.A.* ... 110 C2
Bad Bergzabern, *Germany* ... 25 F3
Bad Berleburg, *Germany* ... 24 D4
Bad Bevensen, *Germany* ... 24 B6
Bad Bramstedt, *Germany* ... 24 B5
Bad Brückenau, *Germany* ... 25 E5
Bad Doberan, *Germany* ... 24 A7
Bad Driburg, *Germany* ... 24 D5
Bad Ems, *Germany* ... 25 E3
Bad Frankenhausen, *Germany* ... 24 D7
Bad Freienwalde, *Germany* ... 24 C10
Bad Goisern, *Austria* ... 26 D6
Bad Harzburg, *Germany* ... 24 D6
Bad Hersfeld, *Germany* ... 24 E5
Bad Hofgastein, *Austria* ... 26 D6
Bad Homburg, *Germany* ... 25 E4
Bad Honnef, *Germany* ... 24 E3
Bad Iburg, *Germany* ... 24 C4
Bad Ischl, *Austria* ... 26 D6
Bad Kissingen, *Germany* ... 25 E6
Bad Königshofen, *Germany* ... 25 E6
Bad Kreuznach, *Germany* ... 25 F3
Bad Krozingen, *Germany* ... 25 H3
Bad Laasphe, *Germany* ... 24 E4
Bad Lands, *U.S.A.* ... 112 D3
Bad Langensalza, *Germany* ... 24 D6
Bad Lauterberg, *Germany* ... 24 D6
Bad Leonfelden, *Austria* ... 26 C7
Bad Liebenwerda, *Germany* ... 24 D9
Bad Mergentheim, *Germany* ... 25 F5
Bad Münstereifel, *Germany* ... 24 E2
Bad Nauheim, *Germany* ... 25 E4
Bad Neuenahr-Ahrweiler, *Germany* ... 24 E3
Bad Neustadt, *Germany* ... 25 E6
Bad Oeynhausen, *Germany* ... 24 C4
Bad Oldesloe, *Germany* ... 24 B6
Bad Orb, *Germany* ... 25 E5
Bad Pyrmont, *Germany* ... 24 D5
Bad Reichenhall, *Germany* ... 25 H8
Bad Säckingen, *Germany* ... 25 H3
Bad Salzuflen, *Germany* ... 24 C4
Bad Salzungen, *Germany* ... 24 E6
Bad Schwartau, *Germany* ... 24 B6
Bad Segeberg, *Germany* ... 24 B6
Bad St. Leonhard, *Austria* ... 26 E7
Bad Tölz, *Germany* ... 25 H7
Bad Urach, *Germany* ... 25 G5
Bad Vöslau, *Austria* ... 27 D9
Bad Waldsee, *Germany* ... 25 H5
Bad Wildungen, *Germany* ... 24 D5
Bad Wimpfen, *Germany* ... 25 F5

Bad Windsheim, *Germany* ... 25 F6
Bad Zwischenahn, *Germany* ... 24 B4
Bada Barabil, *India* ... 69 H11
Badagara, *India* ... 66 P9
Badagri, *Nigeria* ... 83 D5
Badajós, L., *Brazil* ... 124 D6
Badajoz, *Spain* ... 35 G4
Badajoz □, *Spain* ... 35 G4
Badakhshān □, *Afghan.* ... 66 A7
Badalona, *Spain* ... 32 D7
Badalzai, *Afghan.* ... 68 E1
Badampahar, *India* ... 67 H15
Badanah, *Si. Arabia* ... 70 D4
Badarinath, *India* ... 69 D8
Badas, Kepulauan, *Indonesia* ... 62 D3
Baddo →, *Pakistan* ... 66 F4
Bade, *Indonesia* ... 63 F9
Badeggi, *Nigeria* ... 83 D6
Badéguichéri, *Niger* ... 83 C6
Baden, *Austria* ... 27 C9
Baden, *Switz.* ... 25 H4
Baden, *U.S.A.* ... 110 F4
Baden-Baden, *Germany* ... 25 G4
Baden-Württemberg □, *Germany* ... 25 G4
Badgastein, *Austria* ... 26 D6
Badger, *Canada* ... 103 C8
Badger, *U.S.A.* ... 116 J7
Bādghīs □, *Afghan.* ... 66 B3
Badgom, *India* ... 69 B6
Badia Polésine, *Italy* ... 29 C8
Badin, *Pakistan* ... 68 G3
Badlands National Park, *U.S.A.* ... 112 D3
Badogo, *Mali* ... 82 C3
Badoumbé, *Mali* ... 82 C2
Badrah, *Iraq* ... 70 C5
Badrinath, *India* ... 69 D8
Badulla, *Sri Lanka* ... 66 R12
Baena, *Spain* ... 35 H6
Baeza, *Spain* ... 35 H7
Bafang, *Cameroon* ... 83 D7
Baffin B., *Canada* ... 101 A13
Baffin I., *Canada* ... 101 B12
Bafia, *Cameroon* ... 83 E7
Bafilo, *Togo* ... 83 D5
Bafing →, *Mali* ... 82 C2
Bafliyūn, *Syria* ... 70 B3
Bafoulabé, *Mali* ... 82 C2
Bafoussam, *Cameroon* ... 83 D7
Bāfq, *Iran* ... 71 D7
Bafra, *Turkey* ... 72 B6
Bafra Burnu, *Turkey* ... 72 B7
Bāft, *Iran* ... 71 D8
Bafut, *Cameroon* ... 83 D7
Bafwasende, *Dem. Rep. of the Congo* ... 86 B2
Bagam, *Niger* ... 83 B6
Bagamoyo, *Tanzania* ... 86 D4
Bagan Datoh, *Malaysia* ... 65 L3
Bagan Serai, *Malaysia* ... 65 K3
Baganga, *Phil.* ... 61 H7
Bagani, *Namibia* ... 88 B3
Bagansiapiapi, *Indonesia* ... 62 D2
Bagasra, *India* ... 68 J4
Bagaud, *India* ... 68 H6
Bagawi, *Sudan* ... 81 E3
Bagbag, *Sudan* ... 81 D3
Bagdad, *U.S.A.* ... 117 L11
Bagdarin, *Russia* ... 51 D12
Bagé, *Brazil* ... 127 C5
Bagenalstown = Muine Bheag, *Ireland* ... 15 D5
Baggs, *U.S.A.* ... 114 F10
Bagh, *Pakistan* ... 69 C5
Baghain →, *India* ... 69 G9
Baghdād, *Iraq* ... 70 C5
Bagheria, *Italy* ... 30 D6
Baghlān, *Afghan.* ... 66 A6
Baghlān □, *Afghan.* ... 66 B6
Bagley, *U.S.A.* ... 112 B7
Bagnara Cálabra, *Italy* ... 31 D8
Bagnasco, *Italy* ... 28 D5
Bagnères-de-Bigorre, *France* ... 20 E4
Bagnères-de-Luchon, *France* ... 20 F4
Bagni di Lucca, *Italy* ... 28 D7
Bagno di Romagna, *Italy* ... 29 E8
Bagnoles-de-l'Orne, *France* ... 18 D6
Bagnols-sur-Cèze, *France* ... 21 D8
Bagnorégio, *Italy* ... 29 F9
Bago = Pegu, *Burma* ... 67 L20
Bagodar, *India* ... 69 G11
Bagrationovsk, *Russia* ... 9 J19
Bagrdan, *Serbia, Yug.* ... 40 B5
Baguio, *Phil.* ... 61 C4
Bağyurdu, *Turkey* ... 39 C9
Bagzane, Monts, *Niger* ... 83 B6
Bah, *India* ... 69 F8
Bahabón de Esgueva, *Spain* ... 34 D7
Bahadurganj, *India* ... 69 F12
Bahadurgarh, *India* ... 68 E7
Bahama, Canal Viejo de, *W. Indies* ... 120 B4
Bahamas ■, *N. Amer.* ... 121 B5
Bahār, *Iran* ... 73 E13
Baharampur, *India* ... 69 G13
Baharîya, El Wâhât al, *Egypt* ... 80 B2
Bahawalnagar, *Pakistan* ... 68 E5
Bahawalpur, *Pakistan* ... 68 E4
Bahçe, *Turkey* ... 72 D7
Bahçecik, *Turkey* ... 41 F13
Baheri, *India* ... 69 E8
Bahgi →, *India* ... 69 F8
Bahi, *Tanzania* ... 86 D4
Bahi Swamp, *Tanzania* ... 86 D4
Bahía = Salvador, *Brazil* ... 125 F11
Bahía □, *Brazil* ... 125 F10

Bahía, Is. de la, *Honduras* ... 120 C2
Bahía Blanca, *Argentina* ... 126 D3
Bahía de Caráquez, *Ecuador* ... 124 D2
Bahía Honda, *Cuba* ... 120 B3
Bahía Laura, *Argentina* ... 128 F3
Bahía Negra, *Paraguay* ... 124 H7
Bahir Dar, *Ethiopia* ... 81 E4
Bahmanzād, *Iran* ... 71 D6
Bahr el Ahmar □, *Sudan* ... 80 D4
Bahr el Ghazâl □, *Sudan* ... 81 F2
Bahr el Jabal □, *Sudan* ... 81 G3
Bahr Yûsef →, *Egypt* ... 80 B3
Bahraich, *India* ... 69 F9
Bahrain ■, *Asia* ... 71 E6
Bahror, *India* ... 68 F7
Bāhū Kalāt, *Iran* ... 71 E9
Bai, *Mali* ... 82 C4
Bai Bung, Mui = Ca Mau, Mui, *Vietnam* ... 65 H5
Bai Duc, *Vietnam* ... 64 C5
Bai Thuong, *Vietnam* ... 64 C5
Baia de Aramă, *Romania* ... 42 E7
Baia Mare, *Romania* ... 43 C8
Baia-Sprie, *Romania* ... 43 C8
Baião, *Brazil* ... 125 D9
Baïbokoum, *Chad* ... 79 G9
Baicheng, *China* ... 57 B12
Băicoi, *Romania* ... 43 E10
Baidoa, *Somali Rep.* ... 74 G3
Baie Comeau, *Canada* ... 103 C6
Baie-St-Paul, *Canada* ... 103 C5
Baie Trinité, *Canada* ... 103 C6
Baie Verte, *Canada* ... 103 C8
Baignes-Ste-Radegonde, *France* ... 20 C3
Baigneux-les-Juifs, *France* ... 19 E11
Baihar, *India* ... 69 H9
Baihe, *China* ... 56 H6
Ba'ījī, *Iraq* ... 70 C4
Baijnath, *India* ... 69 E8
Baikal, L. = Baykal, Oz., *Russia* ... 51 D11
Baikunthpur, *India* ... 69 H10
Baile Atha Cliath = Dublin, *Ireland* ... 15 C5
Băile Govora, *Romania* ... 43 E9
Băile Herculane, *Romania* ... 42 F7
Băile Olănești, *Romania* ... 43 E9
Băile Tușnad, *Romania* ... 43 D10
Bailén, *Spain* ... 35 G7
Băilești, *Romania* ... 43 F8
Baima, *China* ... 58 A3
Bain-de-Bretagne, *France* ... 18 E5
Bainbridge, Ga., *U.S.A.* ... 109 K3
Bainbridge, N.Y., *U.S.A.* ... 111 D9
Baing, *Indonesia* ... 63 F6
Bainiu, *China* ... 56 H7
Baiona, *Spain* ... 34 C2
Bā'ir, *Jordan* ... 75 E5
Bairin Youqi, *China* ... 57 C10
Bairin Zuoqi, *China* ... 57 C10
Bairnsdale, *Australia* ... 95 F4
Bais, *Phil.* ... 61 G5
Baisha, *China* ... 56 G7
Baissa, *Nigeria* ... 83 D7
Baitadi, *Nepal* ... 69 E9
Baiyin, *China* ... 56 F3
Baiyü, *China* ... 58 B2
Baiyu Shan, *China* ... 56 F4
Baiyuda, *Sudan* ... 80 D3
Baj Baj, *India* ... 69 H13
Baja, *Hungary* ... 42 D3
Baja, Pta., *Mexico* ... 118 B1
Baja California, *Mexico* ... 118 A1
Baja California □, *Mexico* ... 118 B2
Baja California Sur □, *Mexico* ... 118 B2
Bajag, *India* ... 69 H9
Bajamar, *Canary Is.* ... 37 F3
Bajana, *India* ... 68 H4
Bājgīrān, *Iran* ... 71 B8
Bajimba, Mt., *Australia* ... 95 D5
Bajina Bašta, *Serbia, Yug.* ... 40 C3
Bajmok, *Serbia, Yug.* ... 42 E4
Bajo Nuevo, *Caribbean* ... 120 C4
Bajoga, *Nigeria* ... 83 C7
Bajool, *Australia* ... 94 C5
Bak, *Hungary* ... 42 D1
Bakar, *Croatia* ... 29 C11
Bakel, *Senegal* ... 82 C2
Baker, Calif., *U.S.A.* ... 117 K10
Baker, Mont., *U.S.A.* ... 112 B2
Baker City, *U.S.A.* ... 114 D5
Baker I., *Pac. Oc.* ... 96 G10
Baker I., *U.S.A.* ... 104 B2
Baker L., *Australia* ... 93 E4
Baker Lake, *Canada* ... 100 B10
Baker Mt., *U.S.A.* ... 114 B3
Bakers Creek, *Australia* ... 94 C4
Baker's Dozen Is., *Canada* ... 102 A4
Bakersfield, Calif., *U.S.A.* ... 117 K8
Bakersfield, Vt., *U.S.A.* ... 111 B12
Bakhchysaray, *Ukraine* ... 47 K7
Bākhtarān, *Iran* ... 70 C5
Bākhtarān □, *Iran* ... 70 C5
Bakı, *Azerbaijan* ... 49 K9
Bakırdaği, *Turkey* ... 72 C6
Bakkafjörður, *Iceland* ... 8 C6
Baklan, *Turkey* ... 39 C11
Bako, *Ethiopia* ... 81 F4
Bako, *Ivory C.* ... 82 D3
Bakony, *Hungary* ... 42 C2
Bakony Forest = Bakony, *Hungary* ... 42 C2
Bakori, *Nigeria* ... 83 C6
Bakouma, *C.A.R.* ... 84 C4
Baksan, *Russia* ... 49 J6

Bakswaho, *India* ... 69 G8
Baku = Bakı, *Azerbaijan* ... 49 K9
Bakundi, *Nigeria* ... 83 D7
Bakutis Coast, *Antarctica* ... 5 D15
Baky = Bakı, *Azerbaijan* ... 49 K9
Bala, *Canada* ... 110 A5
Bala, *Senegal* ... 82 C2
Bâlâ, *Turkey* ... 72 C5
Bala, *U.K.* ... 12 E4
Balabac I., *Phil.* ... 62 C5
Balabac Str., *E. Indies* ... 62 C5
Balabagh, *Afghan.* ... 68 B4
Ba'labakk, *Lebanon* ... 75 B5
Balabalangan, Kepulauan, *Indonesia* ... 62 E5
Bălăcița, *Romania* ... 43 F8
Balad, *Iraq* ... 70 C5
Balad Rūz, *Iraq* ... 70 C5
Bālādeh, Fārs, *Iran* ... 71 D6
Bālādeh, Māzandaran, *Iran* ... 71 B6
Balaghat, *India* ... 66 J12
Balaghat Ra., *India* ... 66 K10
Balaguer, *Spain* ... 32 D5
Balakhna, *Russia* ... 48 B6
Balaklava, *Ukraine* ... 47 K7
Balakliya, *Ukraine* ... 47 H9
Balakovo, *Russia* ... 48 D8
Balamau, *India* ... 69 F9
Bālan, *Romania* ... 43 D10
Balancán, *Mexico* ... 119 D6
Balashov, *Russia* ... 48 E6
Balasinor, *India* ... 68 H5
Balasore = Baleshwar, *India* ... 67 J15
Balassagyarmat, *Hungary* ... 42 B4
Balāt, *Egypt* ... 80 B2
Balaton, *Hungary* ... 42 D2
Balatonboglár, *Hungary* ... 42 D2
Balatonfüred, *Hungary* ... 42 D2
Balatonszentgyörgy, *Hungary* ... 42 D2
Balayan, *Phil.* ... 61 E4
Balazote, *Spain* ... 33 G2
Balbieriškis, *Lithuania* ... 44 D10
Balbigny, *France* ... 21 C8
Balbina, Reprêsa de, *Brazil* ... 124 D7
Balboa, *Panama* ... 120 E4
Balbriggan, *Ireland* ... 15 C5
Balcarce, *Argentina* ... 126 D4
Balcarres, *Canada* ... 105 C8
Bălcești, *Romania* ... 43 F8
Balchik, *Bulgaria* ... 41 C12
Balclutha, *N.Z.* ... 91 M2
Balcones Escarpment, *U.S.A.* ... 113 L5
Balçova, *Turkey* ... 39 C9
Bald Hd., *Australia* ... 93 G2
Bald I., *Australia* ... 93 F2
Bald Knob, *U.S.A.* ... 113 H9
Baldock L., *Canada* ... 105 B9
Baldwin, Mich., *U.S.A.* ... 108 D3
Baldwin, Pa., *U.S.A.* ... 110 F5
Baldwinsville, *U.S.A.* ... 111 C8
Baldy Mt., *U.S.A.* ... 114 B9
Baldy Peak, *U.S.A.* ... 115 K9
Bale, *Croatia* ... 29 C10
Bale, *Ethiopia* ... 81 F5
Bale □, *Ethiopia* ... 81 F5
Baleares, Is., *Spain* ... 37 B10
Balearic Is. = Baleares, Is., *Spain* ... 37 B10
Baleine = Whale →, *Canada* ... 103 A6
Băleni, *Romania* ... 43 E12
Baler, *Phil.* ... 61 D4
Baler Bay, *Phil.* ... 61 D4
Baleshare, *U.K.* ... 14 D1
Baleshwar, *India* ... 67 J15
Balezino, *Russia* ... 48 B11
Balfate, *Honduras* ... 120 C2
Bali, *Cameroon* ... 83 D7
Balí, *Greece* ... 36 D6
Bali, *India* ... 68 G5
Bali, *Indonesia* ... 62 F4
Bali □, *Indonesia* ... 62 F5
Bali, Selat, *Indonesia* ... 63 H16
Balia, *S. Leone* ... 82 D2
Baliapal, *India* ... 69 J12
Baligród, *Poland* ... 45 J9
Balıkeşir, *Turkey* ... 39 B9
Balıkeşir □, *Turkey* ... 39 B9
Balıklıçeşme, *Turkey* ... 41 F11
Balikpapan, *Indonesia* ... 62 E5
Balimbing, *Phil.* ... 63 C5
Baling, *Malaysia* ... 65 K3
Balingen, *Germany* ... 25 G4
Balint, *Romania* ... 42 E6
Balintang Channel, *Phil.* ... 61 B4
Balipara, *India* ... 67 F18
Balkan Mts. = Stara Planina, *Bulgaria* ... 40 C7
Balkhash = Balqash, *Kazakstan* ... 50 E8
Balkhash, Ozero = Balqash Köl, *Kazakstan* ... 50 E8
Balla, *Bangla.* ... 67 G17
Ballachulish, *U.K.* ... 14 E3
Balladonia, *Australia* ... 93 F3
Ballaghaderreen, *Ireland* ... 15 C3
Ballarat, *Australia* ... 95 F3
Ballard, L., *Australia* ... 93 E3
Ballater, *U.K.* ... 14 D5
Ballé, *Mali* ... 82 B3
Ballenas, Canal de, *Mexico* ... 118 B2
Balleny Is., *Antarctica* ... 5 C11
Balleroy, *France* ... 18 C6
Ballerup, *Denmark* ... 11 J6
Ballı, *Turkey* ... 41 F11
Ballia, *India* ... 69 G11
Ballina, *Australia* ... 95 D5
Ballina, *Ireland* ... 15 B2
Ballinasloe, *Ireland* ... 15 C3

Ballinger, *U.S.A.* ... 113 K5
Ballinrobe, *Ireland* ... 15 C2
Ballinskelligs B., *Ireland* ... 15 E1
Ballon, *France* ... 18 D7
Ballsh, *Albania* ... 40 F3
Ballston Spa, *U.S.A.* ... 111 D11
Ballycastle, *U.K.* ... 15 A5
Ballyclare, *U.K.* ... 15 B5
Ballyhaunis, *Ireland* ... 15 C3
Ballymena, *U.K.* ... 15 B5
Ballymoney, *U.K.* ... 15 A5
Ballymote, *Ireland* ... 15 B3
Ballynahinch, *U.K.* ... 15 B6
Ballyquintin Pt., *U.K.* ... 15 B6
Ballyshannon, *Ireland* ... 15 B3
Balmaceda, *Chile* ... 128 F2
Balmaseda, *Spain* ... 32 B1
Balmazújváros, *Hungary* ... 42 C6
Balmertown, *Canada* ... 105 C10
Balmoral, *Australia* ... 95 F3
Balmorhea, *U.S.A.* ... 113 K3
Balonne →, *Australia* ... 95 D4
Balotra, *India* ... 68 G5
Balqash, *Kazakstan* ... 50 E8
Balqash Köl, *Kazakstan* ... 50 E8
Balrampur, *India* ... 69 F10
Balranald, *Australia* ... 95 E3
Balş, *Romania* ... 43 F9
Balsas, *Mexico* ... 119 D5
Balsas →, *Brazil* ... 125 E9
Balsas →, *Mexico* ... 118 D4
Bålsta, *Sweden* ... 10 E11
Balston Spa, *U.S.A.* ... 111 D11
Balta, *Romania* ... 42 F7
Balta, *Ukraine* ... 47 H5
Baltanás, *Spain* ... 34 D6
Bălți, *Moldova* ... 43 C12
Baltic Sea, *Europe* ... 9 H18
Baltîm, *Egypt* ... 80 H7
Baltimore, *Ireland* ... 15 E2
Baltimore, Md., *U.S.A.* ... 108 F7
Baltimore, Ohio, *U.S.A.* ... 110 G2
Baltit, *Pakistan* ... 69 A6
Baltiysk, *Russia* ... 9 J18
Baltrum, *Germany* ... 24 B3
Baluchistan □, *Pakistan* ... 66 F4
Balurghat, *India* ... 69 G13
Balvi, *Latvia* ... 9 H22
Balya, *Turkey* ... 39 B9
Bam, *Iran* ... 71 D8
Bama, *China* ... 58 E6
Bama, *Nigeria* ... 83 C7
Bamaga, *Australia* ... 94 A3
Bamaji L., *Canada* ... 102 B1
Bamako, *Mali* ... 82 C3
Bamba, *Mali* ... 83 B4
Bambara Maoundé, *Mali* ... 82 B4
Bambari, *C.A.R.* ... 84 C4
Bambaroo, *Australia* ... 94 B4
Bambaya, *Guinea* ... 82 D2
Bamberg, *Germany* ... 25 F6
Bamberg, *U.S.A.* ... 109 J5
Bambesi, *Ethiopia* ... 81 F3
Bambey, *Senegal* ... 82 C1
Bambili, *Dem. Rep. of the Congo* ... 86 B2
Bamboi, *Ghana* ... 82 D4
Bamenda, *Cameroon* ... 83 D7
Bamfield, *Canada* ... 104 D3
Bāmīān □, *Afghan.* ... 66 B5
Bamiancheng, *China* ... 57 C13
Bamkin, *Cameroon* ... 83 D7
Bampūr, *Iran* ... 71 E9
Ban, *Burkina Faso* ... 82 C4
Ban Ban, *Laos* ... 64 C4
Ban Bang Hin, *Thailand* ... 65 H2
Ban Chiang Klang, *Thailand* ... 64 C3
Ban Chik, *Laos* ... 64 D4
Ban Choho, *Thailand* ... 64 E4
Ban Dan Lan Hoi, *Thailand* ... 64 D2
Ban Don = Surat Thani, *Thailand* ... 65 H2
Ban Don, *Vietnam* ... 64 F6
Ban Don, Ao →, *Thailand* ... 65 H2
Ban Dong, *Thailand* ... 64 C3
Ban Hong, *Thailand* ... 64 C2
Ban Kaeng, *Thailand* ... 64 D3
Ban Kantang, *Thailand* ... 65 J2
Ban Keun, *Laos* ... 64 C4
Ban Khai, *Laos* ... 64 F3
Ban Kheun, *Laos* ... 64 B3
Ban Khlong Kua, *Thailand* ... 65 J3
Ban Khuan Mao, *Thailand* ... 65 J2
Ban Ko Yai Chim, *Thailand* ... 65 G2
Ban Kok, *Thailand* ... 64 D4
Ban Laem, *Thailand* ... 64 F2
Ban Lao Ngam, *Laos* ... 64 E6
Ban Le Kathe, *Thailand* ... 64 E2
Ban Mae Chedi, *Thailand* ... 64 C2
Ban Mae Laeng, *Thailand* ... 64 B2
Ban Mae Sariang, *Thailand* ... 64 C1
Ban Mê Thuột = Buon Ma Thuot, *Vietnam* ... 64 F7
Ban Mi, *Thailand* ... 64 E3
Ban Muong Mo, *Laos* ... 64 C4
Ban Na Mo, *Laos* ... 64 D5
Ban Na San, *Thailand* ... 65 H2
Ban Na Tong, *Laos* ... 64 B3
Ban Nam Bac, *Laos* ... 64 B4
Ban Nam Ma, *Laos* ... 64 A3
Ban Nong Bok, *Laos* ... 64 D5
Ban Nong Boua, *Laos* ... 64 E6
Ban Nong Pling, *Thailand* ... 64 E3
Ban Pak Chan, *Thailand* ... 65 G2
Ban Phai, *Thailand* ... 64 D4
Ban Pong, *Thailand* ... 64 F2
Ban Ron Phibun, *Thailand* ... 65 H2

Batavia

Ban Sanam Chai, *Thailand* 65 J3
Ban Sangkha, *Thailand* 64 E4
Ban Tak, *Thailand* 64 D2
Ban Tako, *Thailand* 64 E4
Ban Tha Dua, *Thailand* 64 D2
Ban Tha Li, *Thailand* 64 D3
Ban Tha Nun, *Thailand* 65 H2
Ban Thahine, *Laos* 64 E5
Ban Xien Kok, *Laos* 64 B3
Ban Yen Nhan, *Vietnam* 64 B6
Banaba, *Kiribati* 96 H8
Banalia, *Dem. Rep. of the Congo* 86 B2
Banam, *Cambodia* 65 G5
Banamba, *Mali* 82 C3
Banana Is., *S. Leone* 82 D2
Bananal, I. do, *Brazil* 125 F8
Banaras = Varanasi, *India* 69 G10
Banas →, *Gujarat, India* 68 H4
Banas →, *Mad. P., India* 69 G9
Bânâs, Ras, *Egypt* 80 C4
Banaz, *Turkey* 39 C11
Banaz →, *Turkey* 39 C11
Banbridge, *U.K.* 15 B5
Banbury, *U.K.* 13 E6
Banchory, *U.K.* 14 D6
Banco, *Ethiopia* 81 F4
Bancroft, *Canada* 102 C4
Band, *Romania* 43 D9
Band Bonī, *Iran* 71 E8
Band Qīr, *Iran* 71 D6
Banda, *Mad. P., India* 69 G8
Banda, *Ut. P., India* 69 G9
Banda, Kepulauan, *Indonesia* 63 E7
Banda Aceh, *Indonesia* 62 C1
Banda Banda, Mt., *Australia* 95 E5
Banda Elat, *Indonesia* 63 F8
Banda Is. = Banda, Kepulauan, *Indonesia* 63 E7
Banda Sea, *Indonesia* 63 F7
Bandai-San, *Japan* 54 F10
Bandama →, *Ivory C.* 82 D3
Bandama Blanc →, *Ivory C.* 82 D3
Bandama Rouge →, *Ivory C.* 82 D4
Bandān, *Iran* 71 D9
Bandanaira, *Indonesia* 63 E7
Bandanwara, *India* 68 F6
Bandar = Machilipatnam, *India* 67 L12
Bandār 'Abbās, *Iran* 71 E8
Bandar-e Anzalī, *Iran* 71 B6
Bandar-e Bushehr = Būshehr, *Iran* 71 D6
Bandar-e Chārak, *Iran* 71 E7
Bandar-e Deylam, *Iran* 71 D6
Bandar-e Khomeynı, *Iran* 71 D6
Bandar-e Lengeh, *Iran* 71 E7
Bandar-e Maqām, *Iran* 71 E7
Bandar-e Ma'shur, *Iran* 71 D6
Bandar-e Rīg, *Iran* 71 D6
Bandar-e Torkeman, *Iran* 71 B7
Bandar Maharani = Muar, *Malaysia* 65 L4
Bandar Penggaram = Batu Pahat, *Malaysia* 65 M4
Bandar Seri Begawan, *Brunei* 62 C4
Bandar Sri Aman, *Malaysia* 62 D4
Bandawe, *Malawi* 87 E3
Bande, *Spain* 34 C3
Bandeira, Pico da, *Brazil* 127 A7
Bandera, *Argentina* 126 B3
Banderas, B. de, *Mexico* 118 C3
Bandhogarh, *India* 69 H9
Bandi →, *India* 68 F6
Bandiagara, *Mali* 82 C4
Bandikui, *India* 68 F7
Bandırma, *Turkey* 41 F11
Bandol, *France* 21 E9
Bandon, *Ireland* 15 E3
Bandon →, *Ireland* 15 E3
Bandula, *Mozam.* 87 F3
Bandundu, *Dem. Rep. of the Congo* 84 E3
Bandung, *Indonesia* 62 F3
Bané, *Burkina Faso* 83 C4
Băneasa, *Romania* 43 E12
Bāneh, *Iran* 70 C5
Bañeres, *Spain* 33 G4
Banes, *Cuba* 121 B4
Banff, *Canada* 104 C5
Banff, *U.K.* 14 D6
Banff Nat. Park, *Canada* 104 C5
Banfora, *Burkina Faso* 82 C4
Bang Fai →, *Laos* 64 D5
Bang Hieng →, *Laos* 64 D5
Bang Krathum, *Thailand* 64 D3
Bang Lamung, *Thailand* 64 F3
Bang Mun Nak, *Thailand* 64 D3
Bang Pa In, *Thailand* 64 E3
Bang Rakam, *Thailand* 64 D3
Bang Saphan, *Thailand* 65 G2
Bangaduni I., *India* 69 J13
Bangala Dam, *Zimbabwe* 87 G3
Bangalore, *India* 66 N10
Banganga →, *India* 68 F6
Bangangté, *Cameroon* 83 D7
Bangaon, *India* 69 H13
Bangassou, *C.A.R.* 84 D4
Banggai, *Indonesia* 63 E6
Banggai, Kepulauan, *Indonesia* 63 E6
Banggai Arch. = Banggai, Kepulauan, *Indonesia* 63 E6
Banggi, *Malaysia* 62 C5
Banghāzī, *Libya* 79 B10
Bangjang, *Sudan* 81 E3
Bangka, *Sulawesi, Indonesia* 63 D7
Bangka, *Sumatera, Indonesia* 62 E3
Bangka, Selat, *Indonesia* 62 E3
Bangkalan, *Indonesia* 63 G15
Bangkinang, *Indonesia* 62 D2
Bangko, *Indonesia* 62 E2
Bangkok, *Thailand* 64 F3
Bangladesh ■, *Asia* 67 H17
Bangolo, *Ivory C.* 82 D3
Bangong Co, *India* 69 B8
Bangor, *Down, U.K.* 15 B6
Bangor, *Gwynedd, U.K.* 12 D3
Bangor, *Maine, U.S.A.* 101 D13
Bangor, *Pa., U.S.A.* 111 F9
Bangued, *Phil.* 61 C4
Bangui, *C.A.R.* 84 D3
Bangui, *Phil.* 61 B4
Banguru, *Dem. Rep. of the Congo* 86 B2
Bangweulu, L., *Zambia* 87 E3
Bangweulu Swamp, *Zambia* 87 E3
Bani, *Dom. Rep.* 121 C5
Bani →, *Mali* 82 C4
Bani Bangou, *Niger* 83 B5
Banī Sa'd, *Iraq* 70 C5
Bania, *Ivory C.* 82 D4
Banihal Pass, *India* 69 C6
Banikoara, *Benin* 83 C5
Bāniyās, *Syria* 70 C3
Banja Luka, *Bos.-H.* 42 F2
Banjar, *India* 68 D7
Banjar →, *India* 69 H9
Banjarmasin, *Indonesia* 62 E4
Banjul, *Gambia* 82 C1
Banka, *India* 69 G12
Bankas, *Mali* 82 C4
Bankeryd, *Sweden* 11 G8
Banket, *Zimbabwe* 87 F3
Bankilaré, *Niger* 83 C5
Bankipore, *India* 67 G14
Banks I., *B.C., Canada* 104 C3
Banks I., *N.W.T., Canada* 100 A7
Banks Pen., *N.Z.* 91 K4
Banks Str., *Australia* 94 G4
Bankura, *India* 69 H12
Bankya, *Bulgaria* 40 D7
Banmankhi, *India* 69 G12
Bann →, *Arm., U.K.* 15 B5
Bann →, *L'derry., U.K.* 15 A5
Bannalec, *France* 18 E3
Bannang Sata, *Thailand* 65 J3
Banning, *U.S.A.* 117 M10
Banningville = Bandundu, *Dem. Rep. of the Congo* 84 E3
Banno, *Ethiopia* 81 G4
Bannockburn, *Canada* 110 B7
Bannockburn, *U.K.* 14 E5
Bannockburn, *Zimbabwe* 87 G2
Bannu, *Pakistan* 66 C7
Bano, *India* 69 H11
Bañolas = Banyoles, *Spain* 32 C7
Banon, *France* 21 D9
Baños de la Encina, *Spain* 35 G7
Baños de Molgas, *Spain* 34 C3
Bánovce nad Bebravou, *Slovak Rep.* 27 C11
Banovići, *Bos.-H.* 42 F3
Bansgaon, *India* 69 F10
Banská Bystrica, *Slovak Rep.* 27 C12
Banská Štiavnica, *Slovak Rep.* 27 C11
Bansko, *Bulgaria* 40 E7
Banskobystrický □, *Slovak Rep.* 27 C12
Banswara, *India* 68 H6
Bantaeng, *Indonesia* 63 F5
Bantaji, *Nigeria* 83 D7
Bantayan, *Phil.* 61 F5
Bantry, *Ireland* 15 E2
Bantry B., *Ireland* 15 E2
Bantul, *Indonesia* 63 G14
Bantva, *India* 68 J4
Banya, *Bulgaria* 41 D8
Banyak, Kepulauan, *Indonesia* 62 D1
Banyalbufar, *Spain* 37 B9
Banyo, *Cameroon* 83 D7
Banyoles, *Spain* 32 C7
Banyuls-sur-Mer, *France* 20 F7
Banyumas, *Indonesia* 63 G13
Banyuwangi, *Indonesia* 63 H16
Banzare Coast, *Antarctica* 5 C9
Banzyville = Mobayi, *Dem. Rep. of the Congo* 84 D4
Bao Ha, *Vietnam* 58 F5
Bao Lac, *Vietnam* 64 A5
Bao Loc, *Vietnam* 65 G6
Bao'an = Shenzhen, *China* 59 F10
Baocheng, *China* 56 H4
Baode, *China* 56 E6
Baodi, *China* 57 E9
Baoding, *China* 56 E8
Baoji, *China* 56 G4
Baojing, *China* 58 C7
Baokang, *China* 59 B8
Baoshan, *Shanghai, China* 59 B13
Baoshan, *Yunnan, China* 58 E2
Baotou, *China* 56 D6
Baoxing, *China* 58 B4
Baoying, *China* 57 H10
Bap, *India* 68 F5
Bapatla, *India* 67 M12
Bapaume, *France* 19 B9
Bāqerābād, *Iran* 71 C6
Ba'qūbah, *Iraq* 70 C5
Baquedano, *Chile* 126 A2
Bar, *Montenegro, Yug.* 40 D3
Bar, *Ukraine* 47 H4
Bar Bigha, *India* 69 G11
Bar Harbor, *U.S.A.* 109 C11
Bar-le-Duc, *France* 19 D12
Bar-sur-Aube, *France* 19 D11
Bar-sur-Seine, *France* 19 D11
Bara, *India* 69 G9
Bâra, *Romania* 43 C12
Bara Banki, *India* 69 F9
Barabai, *Indonesia* 62 E5
Baraboo, *U.S.A.* 112 D10
Baracoa, *Cuba* 121 B5
Baradā →, *Syria* 75 B5
Baradero, *Argentina* 126 C4
Baraga, *U.S.A.* 112 B10
Bărăganul, *Romania* 43 F12
Barah →, *India* 68 F6
Barahona, *Dom. Rep.* 121 C5
Barahona, *Spain* 32 D2
Barail Range, *India* 67 G18
Baraka, *Sudan* 81 E2
Baraka →, *Sudan* 80 D4
Barakaldo, *Spain* 32 B2
Barakar →, *India* 69 G12
Barakhola, *India* 67 G18
Barakot, *India* 69 J11
Barakpur, *India* 69 H13
Baralaba, *Australia* 94 C4
Baralla, *Spain* 34 C3
Baralzon L., *Canada* 105 B9
Barameiya, *Sudan* 80 D4
Baramula, *India* 69 B6
Baran, *India* 68 G7
Baran →, *Pakistan* 68 G3
Barañain, *Spain* 32 C3
Baranavichy, *Belarus* 47 F4
Barani, *Burkina Faso* 82 C4
Baranof, *U.S.A.* 104 B2
Baranof I., *U.S.A.* 100 C6
Baranów Sandomierski, *Poland* 45 H8
Baranya □, *Hungary* 42 E3
Baraolt, *Romania* 43 D10
Barapasi, *Indonesia* 63 E9
Barasat, *India* 69 H13
Barat Daya, Kepulauan, *Indonesia* 63 F7
Barataria B., *U.S.A.* 113 L10
Barauda, *India* 68 H6
Baraut, *India* 68 E7
Barbacena, *Brazil* 127 A7
Barbados ■, *W. Indies* 121 D8
Barban, *Croatia* 29 C11
Barbària, C. de, *Spain* 37 C7
Barbaros, *Turkey* 41 F11
Barbastro, *Spain* 32 C5
Barbate = Barbate de Franco, *Spain* 35 J5
Barbate de Franco, *Spain* 35 J5
Barberino di Mugello, *Italy* 29 E8
Barberton, *S. Africa* 89 D5
Barberton, *U.S.A.* 110 E3
Barbezieux-St-Hilaire, *France* 20 C3
Barbosa, *Colombia* 124 B4
Barbourville, *U.S.A.* 109 G4
Barbuda, *W. Indies* 121 C7
Bârca, *Romania* 43 G8
Barcaldine, *Australia* 94 C4
Barcarrota, *Spain* 35 G4
Barcellona Pozzo di Gotto, *Italy* 31 D8
Barcelona, *Spain* 32 D7
Barcelona, *Venezuela* 124 A6
Barcelona □, *Spain* 32 D7
Barcelonette, *France* 21 D10
Barcelos, *Brazil* 124 D6
Barcin, *Poland* 45 F4
Barclayville, *Liberia* 82 E3
Barcoo →, *Australia* 94 D3
Barcs, *Hungary* 42 E2
Barczewo, *Poland* 44 E7
Bärdä, *Azerbaijan* 49 K8
Bardaï, *Chad* 79 D9
Bardas Blancas, *Argentina* 126 D2
Barddhaman, *India* 69 H12
Bardejov, *Slovak Rep.* 27 B14
Bardera, *Somali Rep.* 74 G3
Bardi, *Italy* 28 D6
Bardīyah, *Libya* 79 B10
Bardolino, *Italy* 28 C7
Bardonécchia, *Italy* 28 C3
Bardsey I., *U.K.* 12 E3
Bardstown, *U.S.A.* 108 G3
Bareilly, *India* 69 E8
Barela, *India* 69 H9
Barentin, *France* 18 C7
Barenton, *France* 18 D6
Barents Sea, *Arctic* 4 B9
Barentu, *Eritrea* 81 D4
Barfleur, *France* 18 C5
Barfleur, Pte. de, *France* 18 C5
Barga, *Italy* 28 D7
Bargara, *Australia* 94 C5
Bargas, *Spain* 34 F6
Bârgăului Bistriţa, *Romania* 43 C9
Barge, *Italy* 28 D4
Bargnop, *Sudan* 81 F2
Bargteheide, *Germany* 24 B6
Barguzin, *Russia* 51 D11
Barh, *India* 69 G11
Barhaj, *India* 69 F10
Barharwa, *India* 69 G12
Barhi, *India* 69 G11
Bari, *India* 68 F7
Bari, *Italy* 31 A9
Bari Doab, *Pakistan* 68 D5
Bari Sadri, *India* 68 G6
Bari Sardo, *Italy* 30 C2
Barīdī, Ra's, *Si. Arabia* 70 E3
Barīm, *Yemen* 76 E8
Barinas, *Venezuela* 124 B4
Baring, C., *Canada* 100 B8
Baringo, *Kenya* 86 B4
Baringo, L., *Kenya* 86 B4
Bârîs, *Egypt* 80 C3
Barisal, *Bangla.* 67 H17
Barisal □, *Bangla.* 67 H17
Barisan, Bukit, *Indonesia* 62 E2
Barito →, *Indonesia* 62 E4
Barjac, *France* 21 D8
Barjols, *France* 21 E10
Bark L., *Canada* 110 A7
Barka = Baraka →, *Sudan* 80 D4
Barkakana, *India* 69 H11
Barkam, *China* 58 B4
Barker, *U.S.A.* 110 C6
Barkley, L., *U.S.A.* 109 G2
Barkley Sound, *Canada* 104 D3
Barkly East, *S. Africa* 88 E4
Barkly Roadhouse, *Australia* 94 B2
Barkly Tableland, *Australia* 94 B2
Barkly West, *S. Africa* 88 D3
Barkol, Wadi →, *Sudan* 80 D3
Barla Dağı, *Turkey* 39 C12
Bârlad, *Romania* 43 D12
Bârlad →, *Romania* 43 E12
Barlee, L., *Australia* 93 E2
Barlee, Mt., *Australia* 93 D4
Barletta, *Italy* 31 A9
Barlinek, *Poland* 45 F2
Barlovento, *Canary Is.* 37 F2
Barlow L., *Canada* 105 A8
Barmedman, *Australia* 95 E4
Barmer, *India* 68 G4
Barmera, *Australia* 95 E3
Barmouth, *U.K.* 12 E3
Barmstedt, *Germany* 24 B5
Barna →, *India* 69 G10
Barnagar, *India* 68 H6
Barnala, *India* 68 D6
Barnard Castle, *U.K.* 12 C6
Barnaul, *Russia* 50 D9
Barnesville, *U.S.A.* 109 J3
Barnet □, *U.K.* 13 F7
Barneveld, *Neths.* 17 B5
Barneveld, *U.S.A.* 111 C9
Barneville-Cartevert, *France* 18 C5
Barnhart, *U.S.A.* 113 K4
Barnsley, *U.K.* 12 D6
Barnstaple, *U.K.* 13 F3
Barnstaple Bay = Bideford Bay, *U.K.* 13 F3
Barnsville, *U.S.A.* 112 B6
Barnwell, *U.S.A.* 109 J5
Baro, *Nigeria* 83 D6
Baro →, *Ethiopia* 81 F3
Baroda = Vadodara, *India* 68 H5
Baroda, *India* 68 G7
Baroe, *S. Africa* 88 E3
Baron Ra., *Australia* 92 D4
Barong, *China* 58 B2
Barotseland, *Zambia* 85 H4
Barouéli, *Mali* 82 C3
Barpeta, *India* 67 F17
Barques, Pt. Aux, *U.S.A.* 110 B2
Barquísimeto, *Venezuela* 124 A5
Barr, Ras el, *Egypt* 80 H7
Barr Smith Range, *Australia* 93 E3
Barra, *Brazil* 125 F10
Barra, *U.K.* 14 E1
Barra, Sd. of, *U.K.* 14 D1
Barra de Navidad, *Mexico* 118 D4
Barra do Corda, *Brazil* 125 E9
Barra do Piraí, *Brazil* 127 A7
Barra Falsa, Pta. da, *Mozam.* 89 C6
Barra Hd., *U.K.* 14 E1
Barra Mansa, *Brazil* 127 A7
Barraba, *Australia* 95 E5
Barrackpur = Barakpur, *India* 69 H13
Barradale Roadhouse, *Australia* 92 D1
Barrafranca, *Italy* 31 E7
Barraigh = Barra, *U.K.* 14 E1
Barranca, *Lima, Peru* 124 F3
Barranca, *Loreto, Peru* 124 D3
Barrancabermeja, *Colombia* 124 B4
Barrancas, *Venezuela* 124 B6
Barrancos, *Portugal* 35 G4
Barranqueras, *Argentina* 126 B4
Barranquilla, *Colombia* 124 A4
Barraute, *Canada* 102 C4
Barre, *Mass., U.S.A.* 111 D12
Barre, *Vt., U.S.A.* 111 B12
Barreal, *Argentina* 126 C2
Barreiras, *Brazil* 125 F10
Barreirinhas, *Brazil* 125 D10
Barreiro, *Portugal* 35 G1
Barrême, *France* 21 E10
Barren, Nosy, *Madag.* 89 B7
Barretos, *Brazil* 125 H9
Barrhead, *Canada* 104 C6
Barrie, *Canada* 102 D4
Barrier Ra., *Australia* 95 E3
Barrière, *Canada* 104 C4
Barrington, *U.S.A.* 111 E13
Barrington L., *Canada* 105 B8
Barrington Tops, *Australia* 95 E5
Barringun, *Australia* 95 D4
Barro do Garças, *Brazil* 125 G8
Barron, *U.S.A.* 112 C9
Barrow, *U.S.A.* 100 A4
Barrow →, *Ireland* 15 D5
Barrow, Pt., *U.S.A.* 98 B4
Barrow Creek, *Australia* 94 C1
Barrow I., *Australia* 92 D2
Barrow-in-Furness, *U.K.* 12 C4
Barrow Pt., *Australia* 94 A3
Barrow Ra., *Australia* 93 E4
Barrow Str., *Canada* 4 B3
Barruecopardo, *Spain* 34 D4
Barruelo de Santullán, *Spain* 34 C6
Barry, *U.K.* 13 F4
Barry's Bay, *Canada* 102 C4
Barsalogho, *Burkina Faso* 83 C4
Barsat, *Pakistan* 69 A5
Barsham, *Syria* 70 C4
Barsi, *India* 66 K9
Barsinghausen, *Germany* 24 C5
Barsoi, *India* 67 G15
Barstow, *U.S.A.* 117 L9
Barth, *Germany* 24 A8
Barthélemy, Col, *Vietnam* 64 C5
Bartica, *Guyana* 124 B7
Bartin, *Turkey* 72 B5
Bartlesville, *U.S.A.* 113 G7
Bartlett, *U.S.A.* 116 J8
Bartlett, L., *Canada* 104 A5
Bartolomeu Dias, *Mozam.* 87 G4
Barton, *U.S.A.* 111 B12
Barton upon Humber, *U.K.* 12 D7
Bartoszyce, *Poland* 44 D7
Bartow, *U.S.A.* 109 M5
Barú, Volcan, *Panama* 120 E3
Barumba, *Dem. Rep. of the Congo* 86 B1
Baruth, *Germany* 24 C9
Baruunsuu, *Mongolia* 56 C3
Barvinkove, *Ukraine* 47 H9
Barwani, *India* 68 H6
Barwice, *Poland* 44 E3
Barycz →, *Poland* 45 G3
Barysaw, *Belarus* 46 E5
Barysh, *Russia* 48 D8
Barzān, *Iraq* 70 B5
Bârzava, *Romania* 42 D6
Bas-Rhin □, *France* 19 D14
Bašaid, *Serbia, Yug.* 42 E5
Bāsa'idū, *Iran* 71 E7
Basal, *Pakistan* 68 C5
Basankusa, *Dem. Rep. of the Congo* 84 D3
Basarabeasca, *Moldova* 43 D13
Basarabi, *Romania* 43 F13
Basauri, *Spain* 32 B2
Basawa, *Afghan.* 68 B4
Bascuñán, C., *Chile* 126 B1
Basel, *Switz.* 25 H3
Basel-Landschaft □, *Switz.* 25 H3
Basento →, *Italy* 31 B9
Bashākerd, Kūhhā-ye, *Iran* 71 E8
Bashaw, *Canada* 104 C6
Bāshī, *Iran* 71 D6
Bashkir Republic = Bashkortostan □, *Russia* 50 D6
Bashkortostan □, *Russia* 50 D6
Basibasy, *Madag.* 89 C7
Basilan I., *Phil.* 61 H5
Basilan Str., *Phil.* 61 H5
Basildon, *U.K.* 13 F8
Basile, *Eq. Guin.* 83 E6
Basilicata □, *Italy* 31 B9
Basim = Washim, *India* 66 J10
Basin, *U.S.A.* 114 D9
Basingstoke, *U.K.* 13 F6
Baška, *Croatia* 29 D11
Başkale, *Turkey* 73 C10
Baskatong, Rés., *Canada* 102 C4
Basle = Basel, *Switz.* 25 H3
Başmakçı, *Turkey* 39 D12
Basoda, *India* 68 H7
Basoka, *Dem. Rep. of the Congo* 86 B1
Basque, Pays, *France* 20 E2
Basque Provinces = País Vasco □, *Spain* 32 C2
Basra = Al Başrah, *Iraq* 70 D5
Bass Str., *Australia* 94 F4
Bassano, *Canada* 104 C6
Bassano del Grappa, *Italy* 29 C8
Bassar, *Togo* 83 D5
Bassas da India, *Ind. Oc.* 85 J7
Basse-Normandie □, *France* 18 D6
Basse Santa-Su, *Gambia* 82 C2
Basse-Terre, *Guadeloupe* 121 C7
Bassein, *Burma* 67 L19
Basseterre, *St. Kitts & Nevis* 121 C7
Bassett, *U.S.A.* 112 D5
Bassi, *India* 68 D7
Bassigny, *France* 19 E12
Bassikounou, *Mauritania* 82 B3
Bassila, *Benin* 83 D5
Bassum, *Germany* 24 C4
Båstad, *Sweden* 11 H6
Bastak, *Iran* 71 E7
Baştām, *Iran* 71 B7
Bastar, *India* 67 K12
Bastelica, *France* 21 F13
Basti, *India* 69 F10
Bastia, *France* 21 F13
Bastogne, *Belgium* 17 D5
Bastrop, *La., U.S.A.* 113 J9
Bastrop, *Tex., U.S.A.* 113 K6
Bat Yam, *Israel* 75 C3
Bata, *Eq. Guin.* 84 D1
Bata, *Romania* 42 D7
Bataan □, *Phil.* 61 D4
Batabanó, *Cuba* 120 B3
Batabanó, G. de, *Cuba* 120 B3
Batac, *Phil.* 61 B4
Batagai, *Russia* 51 C14
Batajnica, *Serbia, Yug.* 40 B4
Batak, *Bulgaria* 41 E8
Batala, *India* 68 D6
Batalha, *Portugal* 34 F2
Batama, *Dem. Rep. of the Congo* 86 B2
Batamay, *Russia* 51 C13
Batang, *China* 58 B2
Batang, *Indonesia* 63 G13
Batangas, *Phil.* 61 E4
Batanta, *Indonesia* 63 E8
Batatais, *Brazil* 127 A6
Batavia, *U.S.A.* 110 D6

Bataysk, *Russia* 47 J10
Batchelor, *Australia* 92 B5
Batdambang, *Cambodia* 64 F4
Batemans B., *Australia* 95 F5
Batemans Bay, *Australia* 95 F5
Bates Ra., *Australia* 93 E3
Batesburg-Leesville, *U.S.A.* . . . 109 J5
Batesville, *Ark., U.S.A.* 113 H9
Batesville, *Miss., U.S.A.* 113 H10
Batesville, *Tex., U.S.A.* 113 L5
Bath, *Canada* 111 B8
Bath, *U.K.* 13 F5
Bath, *Maine, U.S.A.* 109 D11
Bath, *N.Y., U.S.A.* 110 D7
Bath & North East Somerset □,
  U.K. 13 F5
Batheay, *Cambodia* 65 G5
Bathurst = Banjul, *Gambia* . . . 82 C1
Bathurst, *Australia* 95 E4
Bathurst, *Canada* 103 C6
Bathurst, *S. Africa* 88 E4
Bathurst, *C., Canada* 100 A7
Bathurst B., *Australia* 94 A3
Bathurst Harb., *Australia* 94 G4
Bathurst I., *Australia* 92 B5
Bathurst I., *Canada* 4 B2
Bathurst Inlet, *Canada* 100 B9
Bati, *Ethiopia* 81 E5
Batie, *Burkina Faso* 82 D4
Batlow, *Australia* 95 F4
Batman, *Turkey* 70 B4
Baṭn al Ghūl, *Jordan* 75 F4
Batna, *Algeria* 78 A7
Batobato = San Isidro, *Phil.* . . 61 H7
Batočina, *Serbia, Yug.* 40 B5
Batoka, *Zambia* 87 F2
Baton Rouge, *U.S.A.* 113 K9
Batong, Ko, *Thailand* 65 J2
Bátonyterenye, *Hungary* 42 C4
Batopilas, *Mexico* 118 B3
Batouri, *Cameroon* 84 D2
Båtsfjord, *Norway* 8 A23
Battambang = Batdambang,
  Cambodia 64 F4
Batticaloa, *Sri Lanka* 66 R12
Battipáglia, *Italy* 31 B7
Battle, *U.K.* 13 G8
Battle ➜, *Canada* 105 C7
Battle Creek, *U.S.A.* 108 D3
Battle Ground, *U.S.A.* 116 E4
Battle Harbour, *Canada* 103 B8
Battle Lake, *U.S.A.* 112 B7
Battle Mountain, *U.S.A.* 114 F5
Battlefields, *Zimbabwe* 87 F2
Battleford, *Canada* 105 C7
Battonya, *Hungary* 42 D6
Batu, *Ethiopia* 81 F4
Batu, Kepulauan, *Indonesia* . . 62 E1
Batu Caves, *Malaysia* 65 L3
Batu Gajah, *Malaysia* 65 K3
Batu Is. = Batu, Kepulauan,
  Indonesia 62 E1
Batu Pahat, *Malaysia* 65 M4
Batuata, *Indonesia* 63 F6
Batumi, *Georgia* 49 K5
Baturaja, *Indonesia* 62 E2
Baturité, *Brazil* 125 D11
Bau, *Malaysia* 62 D4
Baubau, *Indonesia* 63 F6
Bauchi, *Nigeria* 83 C6
Bauchi □, *Nigeria* 83 C7
Baud, *France* 18 E3
Baudette, *U.S.A.* 112 A7
Bauer, C., *Australia* 95 E1
Bauhinia, *Australia* 94 C4
Baukau, *E. Timor* 63 F7
Bauld, C., *Canada* 101 C14
Baume-les-Dames, *France* . . . 19 E13
Baunatal, *Germany* 24 D5
Baunei, *Italy* 30 B2
Baure, *Nigeria* 83 C6
Bauru, *Brazil* 127 A6
Bausi, *India* 69 G12
Bauska, *Latvia* 9 H21
Bautino, *Kazakhstan* 49 H10
Bautzen, *Germany* 24 D10
Bauya, *S. Leone* 82 D2
Bavānāt, *Iran* 71 D7
Bavanište, *Serbia, Yug.* 42 F5
Bavaria = Bayern □, *Germany* . 25 G7
Båven, *Sweden* 10 E10
Bavispe ➜, *Mexico* 118 B3
Bawdwin, *Burma* 67 H20
Bawean, *Indonesia* 62 F4
Bawku, *Ghana* 83 C4
Bawlake, *Burma* 67 K20
Bawolung, *China* 58 C3
Baxley, *U.S.A.* 109 K4
Baxoi, *China* 58 B1
Baxter, *U.S.A.* 112 B7
Baxter Springs, *U.S.A.* 113 G7
Bay, L. de, *Phil.* 61 D4
Bay City, *Mich., U.S.A.* 108 D4
Bay City, *Tex., U.S.A.* 113 L7
Bay Minette, *U.S.A.* 109 K2
Bay Roberts, *Canada* 103 C9
Bay St. Louis, *U.S.A.* 113 K10
Bay Springs, *U.S.A.* 113 K10
Bay View, *N.Z.* 91 H6
Baya, *Dem. Rep. of the Congo* . 87 E2
Bayamo, *Cuba* 120 B4
Bayamón, *Puerto Rico* 121 C6
Bayan Har Shan, *China* 60 C4
Bayan Hot = Alxa Zuoqi, *China* 56 E3
Bayan Obo, *China* 56 D5
Bayan-Ovoo = Erdenetsogt,
  Mongolia 56 C4

Bayana, *India* 68 F7
Bayanaūyl, *Kazakhstan* 50 D8
Bayandalay, *Mongolia* 56 C2
Bayanhongor, *Mongolia* 60 B5
Bayard, *N. Mex., U.S.A.* 115 K9
Bayard, *Nebr., U.S.A.* 112 E3
Bayawan, *Phil.* 61 G5
Baybay, *Phil.* 61 F6
Bayburt, *Turkey* 73 B9
Bayelsa □, *Nigeria* 83 E6
Bayerische Alpen, *Germany* . . 25 H7
Bayerischer Wald, *Germany* . . 25 G8
Bayern □, *Germany* 25 G7
Bayfield, *Canada* 110 C3
Bayfield, *U.S.A.* 112 B9
Bayındır, *Turkey* 39 C9
Baykal, Oz., *Russia* 51 D11
Baykan, *Turkey* 70 B4
Baykonur = Bayqongyr,
  Kazakhstan 50 E7
Baynes Mts., *Namibia* 88 B1
Bayombong, *Phil.* 61 C4
Bayon, *France* 19 D13
Bayona = Baiona, *Spain* 34 C2
Bayonne, *France* 20 E2
Bayonne, *U.S.A.* 111 F10
Bayovar, *Peru* 124 E2
Bayqongyr, *Kazakhstan* 50 E7
Bayram-Ali = Bayramaly,
  Turkmenistan 50 F7
Bayramaly, *Turkmenistan* 50 F7
Bayramiç, *Turkey* 39 B8
Bayreuth, *Germany* 25 F7
Bayrischzell, *Germany* 25 H8
Bayrūt, *Lebanon* 75 B4
Bays, L. of, *Canada* 110 A5
Baysville, *Canada* 110 A5
Bayt Lahm, *West Bank* 75 D4
Baytown, *U.S.A.* 113 L7
Bayzo, *Niger* 83 C5
Baza, *Spain* 35 H8
Bazar Dyuzi, *Russia* 49 K8
Bazarny Karabulak, *Russia* . . . 48 D8
Bazarnyy Syzgan, *Russia* 48 D8
Bazaruto, I. do, *Mozam.* 89 C6
Bazas, *France* 20 D3
Bazhong, *China* 58 B6
Bazhou, *China* 56 E9
Bazmān, Kūh-e, *Iran* 71 D9
Beach, *U.S.A.* 112 B3
Beach City, *U.S.A.* 110 F3
Beachport, *Australia* 95 F3
Beachy Hd., *U.K.* 13 G8
Beacon, *Australia* 93 F2
Beacon, *U.S.A.* 111 E11
Beaconsfield, *Australia* 94 G4
Beagle, Canal, *S. Amer.* 122 J4
Beagle Bay, *Australia* 92 C3
Bealanana, *Madag.* 89 A8
Beals Cr. ➜, *U.S.A.* 113 J4
Beamsville, *Canada* 110 C5
Bear ➜, *Calif., U.S.A.* 116 G5
Bear ➜, *Utah, U.S.A.* 106 B4
Béar, C., *France* 20 F7
Bear I., *Ireland* 15 E2
Bear L., *Canada* 105 B9
Bear L., *U.S.A.* 114 F8
Beardmore, *Canada* 102 C2
Beardmore Glacier, *Antarctica* . 5 E11
Beardstown, *U.S.A.* 112 F9
Bearma ➜, *India* 69 G8
Béarn, *France* 20 E3
Bearpaw Mts., *U.S.A.* 114 B9
Bearskin Lake, *Canada* 102 B1
Beas ➜, *India* 68 D6
Beas de Segura, *Spain* 35 G8
Beasain, *Spain* 32 B2
Beata, C., *Dom. Rep.* 121 C5
Beata, I., *Dom. Rep.* 121 C5
Beatrice, *U.S.A.* 112 E6
Beatrice, *Zimbabwe* 87 F3
Beatrice, C., *Australia* 94 A2
Beatton ➜, *Canada* 104 B4
Beatton River, *Canada* 104 B4
Beatty, *U.S.A.* 116 J10
Beaucaire, *France* 21 E8
Beauce, Plaine de la, *France* . . 19 D8
Beauceville, *Canada* 103 C5
Beaudesert, *Australia* 95 D5
Beaufort, *France* 21 C10
Beaufort, *Malaysia* 62 C5
Beaufort, *N.C., U.S.A.* 109 H7
Beaufort, *S.C., U.S.A.* 109 J5
Beaufort Sea, *Arctic* 4 B1
Beaufort West, *S. Africa* 88 E3
Beaugency, *France* 19 E8
Beauharnois, *Canada* 111 A11
Beaujeu, *France* 19 F11
Beaujolais, *France* 19 F11
Beaulieu ➜, *Canada* 104 A6
Beaulieu-sur-Dordogne, *France* 20 D5
Beaulieu-sur-Mer, *France* 21 E11
Beauly, *U.K.* 14 D4
Beauly ➜, *U.K.* 14 D4
Beaumaris, *U.K.* 12 D3
Beaumont, *Belgium* 17 D4
Beaumont, *France* 20 D4
Beaumont, *U.S.A.* 113 K7
Beaumont-de-Lomagne, *France* 20 E5
Beaumont-le-Roger, *France* . . 18 C7
Beaumont-sur-Sarthe, *France* . 18 D7
Beaune, *France* 19 E11
Beaune-la-Rolande, *France* . . 19 D9
Beaupré, *Canada* 103 C5

Beaupréau, *France* 18 E6
Beauraing, *Belgium* 17 D4
Beaurepaire, *France* 21 C9
Beauséjour, *Canada* 105 C9
Beauvais, *France* 19 C9
Beauval, *Canada* 105 B7
Beauvoir-sur-Mer, *France* 18 F4
Beauvoir-sur-Niort, *France* . . . 20 B3
Beaver, *Okla., U.S.A.* 113 G4
Beaver, *Pa., U.S.A.* 110 F4
Beaver, *Utah, U.S.A.* 115 G7
Beaver ➜, *B.C., Canada* 104 B4
Beaver ➜, *Ont., Canada* 102 A2
Beaver ➜, *Sask., Canada* . . . 105 B7
Beaver ➜, *U.S.A.* 113 G5
Beaver City, *U.S.A.* 112 E5
Beaver Creek, *U.S.A.* 100 B5
Beaver Dam, *U.S.A.* 112 D10
Beaver Falls, *U.S.A.* 110 F4
Beaver Hill L., *Canada* 105 C10
Beaver I., *U.S.A.* 108 C3
Beaverhill L., *Canada* 104 C6
Beaverlodge, *Canada* 104 B5
Beaverstone ➜, *Canada* 102 B2
Beaverton, *Canada* 110 B5
Beaverton, *U.S.A.* 116 E4
Beawar, *India* 68 F6
Bebedouro, *Brazil* 127 A6
Beboa, *Madag.* 89 B7
Bebra, *Germany* 24 E5
Beccles, *U.K.* 13 E9
Bečej, *Serbia, Yug.* 42 E5
Beceni, *Romania* 43 E11
Becerreá, *Spain* 34 C3
Béchar, *Algeria* 78 B5
Bechyně, *Czech Rep.* 26 B7
Beckley, *U.S.A.* 108 G5
Beckum, *Germany* 24 D4
Beclean, *Romania* 43 C9
Bečov nad Teplou, *Czech Rep.* . 26 A5
Bečva ➜, *Czech Rep.* 27 B10
Bédar, *Spain* 33 H3
Bédarieux, *France* 20 E7
Beddouza, Ras, *Morocco* 78 B4
Bedele, *Ethiopia* 81 F4
Bedford, *S. Africa* 88 E4
Bedford, *U.K.* 13 E7
Bedford, *Ind., U.S.A.* 108 F2
Bedford, *Iowa, U.S.A.* 112 E7
Bedford, *Ohio, U.S.A.* 110 E3
Bedford, *Pa., U.S.A.* 110 F6
Bedford, *Va., U.S.A.* 108 G6
Bedford, C., *Australia* 94 B4
Bedfordshire □, *U.K.* 13 E7
Będków, *Poland* 45 G6
Bednja ➜, *Croatia* 29 B13
Bednodemyanovsk, *Russia* . . . 48 D6
Bedónia, *Italy* 28 D6
Bedourie, *Australia* 94 C2
Bedum, *Neths.* 17 A6
Będzin, *Poland* 45 H6
Beebe Plain, *Canada* 111 A12
Beech Creek, *U.S.A.* 110 E7
Beelitz, *Germany* 24 C8
Beenleigh, *Australia* 95 D5
Be'er Menuḥa, *Israel* 70 D2
Be'er Sheva, *Israel* 75 D3
Beersheba = Be'er Sheva, *Israel* 75 D3
Beeskow, *Germany* 24 C10
Beestekraal, *S. Africa* 89 D4
Beeston, *U.K.* 12 E6
Beetzendorf, *Germany* 24 C7
Beeville, *U.S.A.* 113 L6
Befale, *Dem. Rep. of the Congo* 84 D4
Befandriana, Mahajanga,
  Madag. 89 B8
Befandriana, Toliara, *Madag.* . . 89 C7
Befasy, *Madag.* 89 C7
Befotaka, Antsiranana, *Madag.* 89 A8
Befotaka, Fianarantsoa, *Madag.* 89 C8
Bega, *Australia* 95 F4
Bega, Canalul, *Romania* 42 E5
Bégard, *France* 18 D3
Beğendik, *Turkey* 41 F10
Begoro, *Ghana* 83 D4
Begusarai, *India* 69 G12
Behābād, *Iran* 71 C8
Behala, *India* 69 H13
Behara, *Madag.* 89 C8
Behbehān, *Iran* 71 D6
Behm Canal, *U.S.A.* 104 B2
Behshahr, *Iran* 71 B7
Bei Jiang ➜, *China* 59 F9
Bei'an, *China* 60 B7
Beibei, *China* 58 C6
Beichuan, *China* 58 B5
Beihai, *China* 58 G7
Beijing, *China* 56 E9
Beijing □, *China* 56 E9
Beilen, *Neths.* 17 B6
Beiliu, *China* 59 F8
Beilngries, *Germany* 25 G7
Beilpajah, *Australia* 95 E3
Beilul, *Eritrea* 81 E5
Beinn na Faoghla = Benbecula,
  U.K. 14 D1
Beipan Jiang ➜, *China* 58 E5
Beipiao, *China* 57 D11
Beira, *Mozam.* 87 F3
Beirut = Bayrūt, *Lebanon* 75 B4
Beiseker, *Canada* 104 C6
Beitaolaizhao, *China* 57 B13
Beitbridge, *Zimbabwe* 87 G3
Beiuş, *Romania* 42 D7

Beizhen = Binzhou, *China* 57 F10
Beizhen, *China* 57 D11
Beizhengzhen, *China* 57 B12
Beja, *Portugal* 35 G3
Béja, *Tunisia* 79 A7
Beja □, *Portugal* 35 H3
Bejaïa, *Algeria* 78 A7
Béjar, *Spain* 34 E5
Bejestān, *Iran* 71 C8
Bekçiler, *Turkey* 39 E11
Békés, *Hungary* 42 D6
Békés □, *Hungary* 42 D6
Békéscsaba, *Hungary* 42 D6
Bekilli, *Turkey* 39 C11
Bekily, *Madag.* 89 C8
Bekisopa, *Madag.* 89 C8
Bekitro, *Madag.* 89 C8
Bekodoka, *Madag.* 89 B8
Bekoji, *Ethiopia* 81 F4
Bekok, *Malaysia* 65 L4
Bekopaka, *Madag.* 89 B7
Bekwai, *Ghana* 83 D4
Bela, *India* 69 G10
Bela, *Pakistan* 68 F2
Bela Crkva, *Serbia, Yug.* 42 F6
Bela Palanka, *Serbia, Yug.* . . . 40 C6
Bela Vista, *Brazil* 126 A4
Bela Vista, *Mozam.* 89 D5
Belan ➜, *India* 69 G9
Belanovica, *Serbia, Yug.* 40 B4
Belarus ■, *Europe* 46 F4
Belau = Palau ■, *Pac. Oc.* . . . 52 J17
Belavenona, *Madag.* 89 C8
Belawan, *Indonesia* 62 D1
Belaya, *Ethiopia* 81 E4
Belaya Glina, *Russia* 49 G5
Belaya Kalitva, *Russia* 49 F5
Belaya Tserkov = Bila Tserkva,
  Ukraine 47 H6
Belcești, *Romania* 43 C12
Bełchatów, *Poland* 45 G6
Belcher Is., *Canada* 102 A3
Belchite, *Spain* 32 D4
Belden, *U.S.A.* 116 E5
Belém, *Brazil* 125 D9
Belén, *Argentina* 126 B2
Belén, *Paraguay* 126 A4
Belen, *U.S.A.* 115 J10
Belene, *Bulgaria* 41 C9
Beleni, *Turkey* 72 D7
Bélesta, *France* 20 F5
Belet Uen, *Somali Rep.* 74 G4
Belev, *Russia* 46 F9
Belevi, *Turkey* 39 C9
Belfair, *U.S.A.* 116 C4
Belfast, *S. Africa* 89 D5
Belfast, *U.K.* 15 B6
Belfast, *Maine, U.S.A.* 109 C11
Belfast, *N.Y., U.S.A.* 110 D6
Belfast L., *U.K.* 15 B6
Belfield, *U.S.A.* 112 B3
Belfort, *France* 19 E13
Belfort, Territoire de □, *France* . 19 E13
Belfry, *U.S.A.* 114 D9
Belgaum, *India* 66 M9
Belgioioso, *Italy* 28 C6
Belgium ■, *Europe* 17 D4
Belgodère, *France* 21 F13
Belgorod, *Russia* 47 G9
Belgorod-Dnestrovskiy =
  Bilhorod-Dnistrovskyy,
  Ukraine 47 J6
Belgrade = Beograd,
  Serbia, Yug. 40 B4
Belgrade, *U.S.A.* 114 D8
Belhaven, *U.S.A.* 109 H7
Beli, *Nigeria* 83 D7
Beli Manastir, *Croatia* 42 E3
Beli Timok ➜, *Serbia, Yug.* . . . 40 C6
Bélice ➜, *Italy* 30 E5
Belinskiy, *Russia* 48 D6
Belinyu, *Indonesia* 62 E3
Beliton Is. = Belitung, *Indonesia* 62 E3
Belitung, *Indonesia* 62 E3
Beliu, *Romania* 42 D6
Belize ■, *Cent. Amer.* 119 D7
Belize City, *Belize* 119 D7
Beljakovci, *Macedonia* 40 D5
Beljanica, *Serbia, Yug.* 40 B5
Belkovskiy, Ostrov, *Russia* . . . 51 B14
Bell ➜, *Canada* 102 C4
Bell I., *Canada* 103 B8
Bell-Irving ➜, *Canada* 104 B3
Bell Peninsula, *Canada* 101 B11
Bell Ville, *Argentina* 126 C3
Bella, *Italy* 31 B8
Bella Bella, *Canada* 104 C3
Bella Coola, *Canada* 104 C3
Bella Unión, *Uruguay* 126 C4
Bella Vista, Corrientes,
  Argentina 126 B4
Bella Vista, Tucuman, *Argentina* 126 B2
Bellac, *France* 20 B5
Bellágio, *Italy* 28 C6
Bellaire, *U.S.A.* 110 F4
Bellária, *Italy* 29 D9
Bellary, *India* 66 M10
Bellata, *Australia* 95 D4
Belle-Chasse, *U.S.A.* 113 L10
Belle Fourche, *U.S.A.* 112 C3
Belle Fourche ➜, *U.S.A.* 112 C3
Belle Glade, *U.S.A.* 109 M5
Belle-Île, *France* 18 E3
Belle Isle, *Canada* 103 B8
Belle Isle, Str. of, *Canada* . . . 103 B8

Belle Plaine, *U.S.A.* 112 E8
Belle Yella, *Liberia* 82 D3
Belledonne, *France* 21 C10
Bellefontaine, *U.S.A.* 108 E4
Bellefonte, *U.S.A.* 110 F7
Bellegarde, *France* 19 E9
Bellegarde-en-Marche, *France* . 20 C6
Bellegarde-sur-Valserine, *France* 19 F12
Bellême, *France* 18 D7
Belleoram, *Canada* 103 C8
Belleville, *Canada* 102 D4
Belleville, *France* 19 F11
Belleville, *Ill., U.S.A.* 112 F10
Belleville, *Kans., U.S.A.* 112 F6
Belleville, *N.Y., U.S.A.* 111 C8
Belleville-sur-Vie, *France* 18 F5
Bellevue, *Canada* 104 D6
Bellevue, *Idaho, U.S.A.* 114 E6
Bellevue, *Nebr., U.S.A.* 112 E7
Bellevue, *Ohio, U.S.A.* 110 E2
Bellevue, *Wash., U.S.A.* 116 C4
Belley, *France* 21 C9
Bellin = Kangirsuk, *Canada* . . 101 B13
Bellinge, *Denmark* 11 J4
Bellingen, *Australia* 95 E5
Bellingham, *U.S.A.* 100 D7
Bellingshausen Sea, *Antarctica* . 5 C17
Bellinzona, *Switz.* 25 J5
Bello, *Colombia* 124 B3
Bellows Falls, *U.S.A.* 111 C12
Bellpat, *Pakistan* 68 E3
Bellpuig d'Urgell, *Spain* 32 D6
Belluno, *Italy* 29 B9
Bellwood, *U.S.A.* 110 F6
Bélmez, *Spain* 35 G5
Belmont, *S. Africa* 88 D3
Belmont, *Canada* 110 D6
Belmonte, *Brazil* 125 G11
Belmonte, *Portugal* 34 E3
Belmonte, *Spain* 33 F2
Belmopan, *Belize* 119 D7
Belmullet, *Ireland* 15 B2
Belo Horizonte, *Brazil* 125 G10
Belo-sur-Mer, *Madag.* 89 C7
Belo-Tsiribihina, *Madag.* 89 B7
Belogorsk = Bilohirsk, *Ukraine* 47 K8
Belogorsk, *Russia* 51 D13
Belogradchik, *Bulgaria* 40 C6
Belogradets, *Bulgaria* 41 C11
Beloha, *Madag.* 89 D8
Beloit, *Kans., U.S.A.* 112 F5
Beloit, *Wis., U.S.A.* 112 D10
Belokorovichi, *Ukraine* 47 G5
Belomorsk, *Russia* 50 C4
Belonia, *India* 67 H17
Belopolye = Bilopillya, *Ukraine* 47 G8
Belorechensk, *Russia* 49 H4
Belorussia = Belarus ■, *Europe* 46 F4
Beloslav, *Bulgaria* 41 C11
Belovo, *Bulgaria* 41 D8
Belovo, *Russia* 50 D9
Belovodsk, *Ukraine* 47 H10
Beloye, Ozero, *Russia* 46 B9
Beloye More, *Russia* 50 C4
Belozem, *Bulgaria* 41 D9
Belozersk, *Russia* 46 B9
Belpasso, *Italy* 31 E7
Belpre, *U.S.A.* 108 F5
Belrain, *India* 69 E9
Belt, *U.S.A.* 114 C8
Beltana, *Australia* 95 E2
Belterra, *Brazil* 125 D8
Beltinci, *Slovenia* 29 B13
Belton, *U.S.A.* 113 K6
Belton L., *U.S.A.* 113 K6
Beltsy = Bălți, *Moldova* 43 C12
Belturbet, *Ireland* 15 B4
Belukha, *Russia* 50 E9
Beluran, *Malaysia* 62 C5
Beluša, *Slovak Rep.* 27 B11
Belušić, *Serbia, Yug.* 40 C5
Belvedere Maríttimo, *Italy* 31 C8
Belvès, *France* 20 D5
Belvidere, *Ill., U.S.A.* 112 D10
Belvidere, *N.J., U.S.A.* 111 F9
Belvis de la Jara, *Spain* 34 F6
Belyando ➜, *Australia* 94 C4
Belyy, *Russia* 46 E7
Belyy, Ostrov, *Russia* 50 B8
Belyy Yar, *Russia* 50 D9
Bełżec, *Poland* 45 H10
Belzig, *Germany* 24 C8
Belzoni, *U.S.A.* 113 J9
Bełżyce, *Poland* 45 G9
Bemaraha, Lembalemban' i,
  Madag. 89 B7
Bemarivo, *Madag.* 89 C7
Bemarivo ➜, Antsiranana,
  Madag. 89 A9
Bemarivo ➜, Mahajanga,
  Madag. 89 B8
Bemavo, *Madag.* 89 C8
Bembéréke, *Benin* 83 C5
Bembesi ➜, *Zimbabwe* 87 G2
Bembesi, *Zimbabwe* 87 F2
Bembézar ➜, *Spain* 35 H5
Bembibre, *Spain* 34 C4
Bemetara, *India* 69 J9
Bemidji, *U.S.A.* 112 B7
Bemolanga, *Madag.* 89 B8
Ben, *Iran* 71 C6
Ben Cruachan, *U.K.* 14 E3
Ben Dearg, *U.K.* 14 D4
Ben Hope, *U.K.* 14 C4
Ben Lawers, *U.K.* 14 E4
Ben Lomond, *N.S.W., Australia* 95 E5

Ben Lomond, *Tas., Australia* . .	94	G4
Ben Lomond, *U.K.*	14	E4
Ben Luc, *Vietnam*	65	G6
Ben Macdhui, *U.K.* . .	14	D5
Ben Mhor, *U.K.*	14	D1
Ben More, *Arg. & Bute, U.K.* . .	14	E2
Ben More, *Stirl., U.K.*	14	E4
Ben More Assynt, *U.K.*	14	C4
Ben Nevis, *U.K.*	14	E3
Ben Quang, *Vietnam*	64	D6
Ben Vorlich, *U.K.*	14	E4
Ben Wyvis, *U.K.*	14	D4
Bena, *Nigeria*	83	C6
Benāb, *Iran*	73	D12
Benalla, *Australia*	95	F4
Benalmádena, *Spain*	35	J6
Benares = Varanasi, *India*	69	G10
Bénat, C., *France*	21	E10
Benavente, *Portugal*	35	G2
Benavente, *Spain*	34	C5
Benavides, *U.S.A.*	113	M5
Benavides de Órbigo, *Spain* . .	34	C5
Benbecula, *U.K.*	14	D1
Benbonyathe, *Australia*	95	E2
Bend, *U.S.A.*	114	D3
Bender Beila, *Somali Rep.*	74	F5
Bendery = Tighina, *Moldova* . .	43	D14
Bendigo, *Australia*	95	F3
Bendorf, *Germany*	24	E3
Benē Beraq, *Israel*	75	C3
Bénéna, *Mali*	82	C4
Benenitra, *Madag.*	89	C8
Benešov, *Czech Rep.*	26	B7
Benevento, *Italy*	31	A7
Benfeld, *France*	19	D14
Benga, *Mozam.*	87	F3
Bengal, Bay of, *Ind. Oc.*	67	M17
Bengbis, *Cameroon*	83	E7
Bengbu, *China*	57	H9
Benghazi = Banghāzī, *Libya*	79	B10
Bengkalis, *Indonesia*	62	D2
Bengkulu, *Indonesia*	62	E2
Bengkulu □, *Indonesia*	62	E2
Bengough, *Canada*	105	D7
Bengtsfors, *Sweden*	10	E6
Benguela, *Angola*	85	G2
Benguérua, I., *Mozam.*	89	C6
Benha, *Egypt*	80	H7
Beni, *Dem. Rep. of the Congo* . .	86	B2
Beni ➜, *Bolivia*	124	F5
Beni Mazâr, *Egypt*	80	B3
Beni Mellal, *Morocco*	78	B4
Beni Suef, *Egypt*	80	J7
Beniah L., *Canada*	104	A6
Benicarló, *Spain*	32	E5
Benicàssim, *Spain*	32	E5
Benicia, *U.S.A.*	116	G4
Benidorm, *Spain*	33	G4
Benin ■, *Africa*	83	D5
Benin ➜, *Nigeria*	83	D6
Benin, Bight of, *W. Afr.*	83	E5
Benin City, *Nigeria*	83	D6
Benisa, *Spain*	33	G5
Benitses, *Greece*	36	A3
Benjamin Aceval, *Paraguay* . .	126	A4
Benjamin Constant, *Brazil*	124	D4
Benjamin Hill, *Mexico*	118	A2
Benkelman, *U.S.A.*	112	E4
Benkovac, *Croatia*	29	D12
Bennett, *Canada*	104	B2
Bennett, L., *Australia*	92	D5
Bennetta, Ostrov, *Russia*	51	B15
Bennettsville, *U.S.A.*	109	H6
Bennichchāb, *Mauritania*	82	B1
Bennington, *N.H., U.S.A.*	111	D11
Bennington, *Vt., U.S.A.*	111	D11
Bénodet, *France*	18	E2
Benoni, *S. Africa*	89	D4
Benque Viejo, *Belize*	119	D7
Bensheim, *Germany*	25	F4
Benson, *Ariz., U.S.A.*	115	L8
Benson, *Minn., U.S.A.*	112	C7
Bent, *Iran*	71	E8
Benteng, *Indonesia*	63	F6
Bentiu, *Sudan*	81	F2
Bento Gonçalves, *Brazil*	127	B5
Benton, *Ark., U.S.A.*	113	H8
Benton, *Calif., U.S.A.*	116	H8
Benton, *Ill., U.S.A.*	112	G10
Benton, *Pa., U.S.A.*	111	E8
Benton Harbor, *U.S.A.*	108	D2
Bentonville, *U.S.A.*	113	G7
Bentu Liben, *Ethiopia*	81	F4
Bentung, *Malaysia*	65	L3
Benue □, *Nigeria*	83	D6
Benue ➜, *Nigeria*	83	D6
Benxi, *China*	57	D12
Beo, *Indonesia*	63	D7
Beograd, *Serbia, Yug.*	40	B4
Beoumi, *Ivory C.*	82	D3
Bepan Jiang ➜, *China*	58	E6
Beppu, *Japan*	55	H5
Beqaa Valley = Al Biqâ, *Lebanon*	75	A5
Ber Mota, *India*	68	H3
Berach ➜, *India*	68	G6
Beraketa, *Madag.*	89	C7
Berane, *Montenegro, Yug.*	40	D3
Berat, *Albania*	40	F3
Berau, Teluk, *Indonesia*	63	E8
Beravina, *Madag.*	89	B8
Berber, *Sudan*	80	D3
Berbera, *Somali Rep.*	74	E4
Berbérati, *C.A.R.*	84	D3
Berbice ➜, *Guyana*	124	B7
Berceto, *Italy*	28	D6
Berchidda, *Italy*	30	B2
Berchtesgaden, *Germany*	25	H8
Berck, *France*	19	B8
Berdichev = Berdychiv, *Ukraine*	47	H5
Berdsk, *Russia*	50	D9
Berdyansk, *Ukraine*	47	J9
Berdychiv, *Ukraine*	47	H5
Berea, *U.S.A.*	108	G3
Berebere, *Indonesia*	63	D7
Bereda, *Somali Rep.*	74	E5
Berehove, *Ukraine*	47	H2
Berekum, *Ghana*	82	D4
Berenice, *Egypt*	80	C4
Berens ➜, *Canada*	105	C9
Berens I., *Canada*	105	C9
Berens River, *Canada*	105	C9
Beresford, *U.S.A.*	112	D6
Berestechko, *Ukraine*	47	G3
Bereşti, *Romania*	43	D12
Beretău ➜, *Romania*	42	C6
Berettyó ➜, *Hungary*	42	D6
Berettyóújfalu, *Hungary*	42	C6
Berevo, *Mahajanga, Madag.*	89	B7
Berevo, *Toliara, Madag.*	89	B7
Bereza = Byaroza, *Belarus*	47	F3
Berezhany, *Ukraine*	47	H3
Berezina = Byarezina ➜, *Belarus*	47	F6
Berezivka, *Ukraine*	47	J6
Berezna, *Ukraine*	47	G6
Berezniki, *Russia*	50	C5
Berezniki, *Russia*	50	D6
Berezovo, *Russia*	50	C7
Berga, *Spain*	32	C6
Berga, *Sweden*	11	G10
Bergama, *Turkey*	39	B9
Bérgamo, *Italy*	28	C6
Bergara, *Spain*	32	B2
Bergby, *Sweden*	10	D11
Bergdala, *Sweden*	11	H4
Bergedorf, *Germany*	24	B6
Bergeforsen, *Sweden*	10	B11
Bergen, *Mecklenburg-Vorpommern, Germany*	24	A9
Bergen, *Niedersachsen, Germany*	24	C5
Bergen, *Neths.*	17	B4
Bergen, *Norway*	9	F11
Bergen, *U.S.A.*	110	C7
Bergen op Zoom, *Neths.*	17	C4
Bergerac, *France*	20	D4
Bergheim, *Germany*	24	E2
Bergholz, *U.S.A.*	110	F4
Bergisch Gladbach, *Germany* . .	17	D7
Bergkamen, *Germany*	24	D3
Bergkvara, *Sweden*	11	H10
Bergshamra, *Sweden*	10	E12
Bergsjö, *Sweden*	10	C11
Bergues, *France*	19	B9
Bergviken, *Sweden*	10	C10
Bergville, *S. Africa*	89	D4
Berhala, Selat, *Indonesia*	62	E2
Berhampore = Baharampur, *India*	69	G13
Berhampur = Brahmapur, *India*	67	K14
Berheci ➜, *Romania*	43	E12
Bering Sea, *Pac. Oc.*	100	C1
Bering Strait, *Pac. Oc.*	100	B3
Beringovskiy, *Russia*	51	C18
Berisso, *Argentina*	126	C4
Berja, *Spain*	35	J8
Berkeley, *U.S.A.*	116	H4
Berkner I., *Antarctica*	5	D18
Berkovitsa, *Bulgaria*	40	C7
Berkshire, *U.S.A.*	111	D8
Berkshire Downs, *U.K.*	13	F6
Berlanga, *Spain*	35	G5
Berlenga, I., *Portugal*	35	F1
Berlin, *Germany*	24	C9
Berlin, *Md., U.S.A.*	108	F8
Berlin, *N.H., U.S.A.*	111	B13
Berlin, *N.Y., U.S.A.*	111	D11
Berlin, *Wis., U.S.A.*	108	D1
Berlin □, *Germany*	24	C9
Berlin L., *U.S.A.*	110	E4
Bermeja, Sierra, *Spain*	35	J5
Bermejo ➜, *Formosa, Argentina*	126	B4
Bermejo ➜, *San Juan, Argentina*	126	C2
Bermen, L., *Canada*	103	B6
Bermeo, *Spain*	32	B2
Bermillo de Sayago, *Spain*	34	D4
Bermuda ■, *Atl. Oc.*	98	F13
Bern, *Switz.*	25	J3
Bern □, *Switz.*	25	J3
Bernalda, *Italy*	31	B9
Bernardo de Irigoyen, *Argentina*	127	B5
Bernardo O'Higgins □, *Chile* . .	126	C1
Bernardsville, *U.S.A.*	111	F10
Bernasconi, *Argentina*	126	D3
Bernau, *Bayern, Germany*	25	H8
Bernau, *Brandenburg, Germany*	24	C9
Bernay, *France*	18	C7
Bernburg, *Germany*	24	D7
Berndorf, *Austria*	26	D9
Berne = Bern, *Switz.*	25	J3
Berne = Bern □, *Switz.*	25	J3
Berner Alpen, *Switz.*	25	J3
Berneray, *U.K.*	14	D1
Bernier I., *Australia*	93	D1
Bernina, Piz, *Switz.*	25	J5
Bernkastel-Kues, *Germany*	25	F3
Beroroha, *Madag.*	89	C8
Béroubouay, *Benin*	83	C5
Beroun, *Czech Rep.*	26	B7
Berounka ➜, *Czech Rep.*	26	B7
Berovo, *Macedonia*	40	E6
Berre, Étang de, *France*	21	E9
Berre-l'Étang, *France*	21	E9
Berri, *Australia*	95	E3
Berriane, *Algeria*	78	B6
Berry, *Australia*	95	E5
Berry, *France*	19	F8
Berry Is., *Bahamas*	120	A4
Berryville, *U.S.A.*	113	G8
Berseba, *Namibia*	88	D2
Bersenbrück, *Germany*	24	C3
Bershad, *Ukraine*	47	H5
Berthold, *U.S.A.*	112	A4
Berthoud, *U.S.A.*	112	E2
Bertincourt, *France*	19	B9
Bertoua, *Cameroon*	84	D2
Bertraghboy B., *Ireland*	15	C2
Berwick, *U.S.A.*	111	E8
Berwick-upon-Tweed, *U.K.*	12	B6
Berwyn Mts., *U.K.*	12	E4
Beryslav, *Ukraine*	47	J7
Berzasca, *Romania*	42	F6
Berzence, *Hungary*	42	D2
Besal, *Pakistan*	69	B5
Besalampy, *Madag.*	89	B7
Besançon, *France*	19	E13
Besar, *Indonesia*	62	E5
Beshenkovichi, *Belarus*	46	E5
Beška, *Serbia, Yug.*	42	E5
Beslan, *Russia*	49	J7
Besna Kobila, *Serbia, Yug.*	40	D6
Besni, *Turkey*	70	B3
Besor, N. ➜, *Egypt*	75	D3
Bessarabiya, *Moldova*	47	J5
Bessarabka = Basarabeasca, *Moldova*	43	D13
Bessèges, *France*	21	D8
Bessemer, *Ala., U.S.A.*	109	J2
Bessemer, *Mich., U.S.A.*	112	B9
Bessemer, *Pa., U.S.A.*	110	F4
Bessin, *France*	18	C6
Bessines-sur-Gartempe, *France*	20	B5
Beswick, *Australia*	92	B5
Bet She'an, *Israel*	75	C4
Bet Shemesh, *Israel*	75	D4
Betafo, *Madag.*	89	B8
Betancuria, *Canary Is.*	37	F5
Betanzos, *Spain*	34	B2
Bétaré Oya, *Cameroon*	84	C2
Betatao, *Madag.*	89	B8
Bétera, *Spain*	33	F4
Bétérou, *Benin*	83	D5
Bethal, *S. Africa*	89	D4
Bethanien, *Namibia*	88	D2
Bethany, *Canada*	110	B6
Bethany, *U.S.A.*	112	E7
Bethel, *Alaska, U.S.A.*	100	B3
Bethel, *Conn., U.S.A.*	111	E11
Bethel, *Maine, U.S.A.*	111	B14
Bethel, *Vt., U.S.A.*	111	C12
Béthenville, *France*	19	C11
Bethlehem = Bayt Laḥm, *West Bank*	75	D4
Bethlehem, *S. Africa*	89	D4
Bethlehem, *U.S.A.*	111	F9
Bethulie, *S. Africa*	88	E4
Béthune, *France*	19	B9
Béthune ➜, *France*	18	C8
Betioky, *Madag.*	89	C7
Betong, *Thailand*	65	K3
Betoota, *Australia*	94	D3
Betor, *Ethiopia*	81	E4
Betroka, *Madag.*	89	C8
Betsiamites, *Canada*	103	C6
Betsiamites ➜, *Canada*	103	C6
Betsiboka ➜, *Madag.*	89	B8
Bettendorf, *U.S.A.*	112	E9
Bettiah, *India*	69	F11
Bettna, *Sweden*	11	F10
Béttola, *Italy*	28	D6
Betul, *India*	66	J10
Betung, *Malaysia*	62	D4
Betws-y-Coed, *U.K.*	12	D4
Betxi, *Spain*	32	F4
Betzdorf, *Germany*	24	E3
Beuil, *France*	21	D10
Beulah, *Mich., U.S.A.*	108	C2
Beulah, *N. Dak., U.S.A.*	112	B4
Beuvron ➜, *France*	18	E8
Beveren, *Belgium*	17	C4
Beverley, *Australia*	93	F2
Beverley, *U.K.*	12	D7
Beverley Hills, *U.S.A.*	109	L4
Beverly, *U.S.A.*	111	D14
Beverly Hills, *U.S.A.*	117	L8
Beverungen, *Germany*	24	D5
Bevoalavo, *Madag.*	89	D7
Bewas ➜, *India*	69	H8
Bex, *Switz.*	25	J3
Bexhill, *U.K.*	13	G8
Bey Dağları, *Turkey*	39	E12
Beyānlū, *Iran*	70	C5
Beyçayırı, *Turkey*	41	F10
Beyçayırı, *Turkey*	41	F10
Beydağ, *Turkey*	39	C10
Beyeğaç, *Turkey*	39	D10
Beyin, *Ghana*	82	D4
Beykoz, *Turkey*	41	E13
Beyla, *Guinea*	82	D3
Beynat, *France*	20	C5
Beyneu, *Kazakhstan*	50	E6
Beyoba, *Turkey*	39	C9
Beyoğlu, *Turkey*	41	E12
Beypazarı, *Turkey*	72	B5
Beyşehir, *Turkey*	72	D4
Beyşehir Gölü, *Turkey*	70	B1
Beytüşşebap, *Turkey*	73	D10
Bezdan, *Serbia, Yug.*	42	E3
Bezhetsk, *Russia*	46	D9
Béziers, *France*	20	E7
Bezwada = Vijayawada, *India* .	67	L12
Bhabua, *India*	69	G10
Bhachau, *India*	66	H7
Bhadar ➜, *Gujarat, India*	68	H5
Bhadar ➜, *Gujarat, India*	68	J3
Bhadarwah, *India*	69	C6
Bhadohi, *India*	69	G10
Bhadra, *India*	68	E6
Bhadrakh, *India*	67	J15
Bhadran, *India*	68	H5
Bhadravati, *India*	66	N9
Bhag, *Pakistan*	68	E2
Bhagalpur, *India*	69	G12
Bhagirathi ➜, *Ut. P., India*	69	D8
Bhagirathi ➜, *W. Bengal, India*	69	H13
Bhakkar, *Pakistan*	68	D4
Bhakra Dam, *India*	68	D7
Bhamo, *Burma*	67	G20
Bhandara, *India*	66	J11
Bhanpura, *India*	68	G6
Bhanrer Ra., *India*	69	H8
Bhaptiahi, *India*	69	F12
Bharat = India ■, *Asia*	66	K11
Bharatpur, *Mad. P., India*	69	H9
Bharatpur, *Raj., India*	68	F7
Bharno, *India*	69	H11
Bhatpara, *India*	69	H13
Bhattu, *India*	68	E6
Bhaun, *Pakistan*	68	C5
Bhaunagar = Bhavnagar, *India* .	66	J8
Bhavnagar, *India*	66	J8
Bhawari, *India*	68	G5
Bhayavadar, *India*	68	J4
Bhera, *Pakistan*	68	C5
Bhikangaon, *India*	68	J6
Bhilsa = Vidisha, *India*	68	H7
Bhilwara, *India*	68	G6
Bhima ➜, *India*	66	L10
Bhimbar, *Pakistan*	69	C6
Bhind, *India*	69	F8
Bhinga, *India*	69	F9
Bhinmal, *India*	68	G5
Bhiwandi, *India*	66	K8
Bhiwani, *India*	68	E7
Bhogava ➜, *India*	68	H5
Bhola, *Bangla.*	67	H17
Bholari, *Pakistan*	68	G3
Bhopal, *India*	68	H7
Bhubaneshwar, *India*	67	J14
Bhuj, *India*	68	H3
Bhusaval, *India*	66	J9
Bhutan ■, *Asia*	67	F17
Biafra, B. of = Bonny, Bight of, *Africa*	83	E6
Biak, *Indonesia*	63	E9
Biała, *Poland*	45	H4
Biała ➜, *Poland*	45	H7
Biała Piska, *Poland*	44	E9
Biała Podlaska, *Poland*	45	F10
Biała Rawska, *Poland*	45	G7
Białobrzegi, *Poland*	45	G7
Białogard, *Poland*	44	D2
Białowieża, *Poland*	45	F10
Biały Bór, *Poland*	44	E3
Białystok, *Poland*	45	E10
Biancavilla, *Italy*	31	E7
Bianco, *Italy*	31	D9
Biankouma, *Ivory C.*	82	D3
Biaora, *India*	68	H7
Biārjmand, *Iran*	71	B7
Biaro, *Indonesia*	63	D7
Biarritz, *France*	20	E2
Biasca, *Switz.*	25	J4
Biba, *Egypt*	80	J7
Bibai, *Japan*	54	C10
Bibbiena, *Italy*	29	E8
Bibby I., *Canada*	105	A10
Bibel ➜, *Spain*	34	C3
Biberach, *Germany*	25	G5
Bibiani, *Ghana*	82	D4
Bibungwa, *Dem. Rep. of the Congo*	86	C2
Bic, *Canada*	103	C6
Bicaj, *Albania*	40	E4
Bicaz, *Romania*	43	D11
Bicazu Ardelean, *Romania*	43	D10
Bíccari, *Italy*	31	A8
Bicester, *U.K.*	13	F6
Bichena, *Ethiopia*	81	E4
Bicheno, *Australia*	94	G4
Bichia, *India*	69	H9
Bichvinta, *Georgia*	49	J5
Bickerton I., *Australia*	94	A2
Bicske, *Hungary*	42	C3
Bida, *Nigeria*	83	D6
Bidar, *India*	66	L10
Biddeford, *U.S.A.*	109	D10
Biddwara, *Ethiopia*	81	F4
Bideford, *U.K.*	13	F3
Bideford Bay, *U.K.*	13	F3
Bidhuna, *India*	69	F8
Bidor, *Malaysia*	65	K3
Bie, *Sweden*	10	E10
Bié, Planalto de, *Angola*	85	G3
Bieber, *U.S.A.*	114	F3
Biebrza ➜, *Poland*	45	E9
Biecz, *Poland*	45	J8
Biel, *Switz.*	25	H3
Bielawa, *Poland*	45	H3
Bielefeld, *Germany*	24	C4
Bielersee, *Switz.*	25	H3
Biella, *Italy*	28	C5
Bielsk Podlaski, *Poland*	45	F10
Bielsko-Biała, *Poland*	45	J6
Bien Hoa, *Vietnam*	65	G6
Bienne = Biel, *Switz.*	25	H3
Bienvenida, *Spain*	35	G4
Bienville, L., *Canada*	102	A5
Bierné, *France*	18	E6
Bierun, *Poland*	45	H6
Bierutów, *Poland*	45	G4
Biescas, *Spain*	32	C4
Biese ➜, *Germany*	24	C7
Biesiesfontein, *S. Africa*	88	E2
Bietigheim-Bissingen, *Germany*	25	G5
Bieżuń, *Poland*	45	F6
Biferno ➜, *Italy*	29	G12
Big ➜, *Canada*	103	B8
Big B., *Canada*	103	A7
Big Bear City, *U.S.A.*	117	L10
Big Bear Lake, *U.S.A.*	117	L10
Big Belt Mts., *U.S.A.*	114	C8
Big Bend, *Swaziland*	89	D5
Big Bend National Park, *U.S.A.*	113	L3
Big Black ➜, *U.S.A.*	113	K9
Big Blue ➜, *U.S.A.*	112	F6
Big Creek, *U.S.A.*	116	H7
Big Cypress National Preserve, *U.S.A.*	109	M5
Big Cypress Swamp, *U.S.A.*	109	M5
Big Falls, *U.S.A.*	112	A8
Big Fork ➜, *U.S.A.*	112	A8
Big Horn Mts. = Bighorn Mts., *U.S.A.*	114	D10
Big I., *Canada*	104	A5
Big Lake, *U.S.A.*	113	K4
Big Moose, *U.S.A.*	111	C10
Big Muddy Cr. ➜, *U.S.A.*	112	A2
Big Pine, *U.S.A.*	116	H8
Big Piney, *U.S.A.*	114	E8
Big Rapids, *U.S.A.*	108	D3
Big Rideau L., *Canada*	111	B8
Big River, *Canada*	105	C7
Big Run, *U.S.A.*	110	F6
Big Sable Pt., *U.S.A.*	108	C2
Big Salmon ➜, *Canada*	104	A2
Big Sand L., *Canada*	105	B9
Big Sandy, *U.S.A.*	114	B8
Big Sandy ➜, *U.S.A.*	108	F4
Big Sandy Cr. ➜, *U.S.A.*	112	F3
Big Sioux ➜, *U.S.A.*	112	D6
Big Spring, *U.S.A.*	113	J4
Big Stone City, *U.S.A.*	112	C6
Big Stone Gap, *U.S.A.*	109	G4
Big Stone L., *U.S.A.*	112	C6
Big Sur, *U.S.A.*	116	J5
Big Timber, *U.S.A.*	114	D9
Big Trout L., *Canada*	102	B2
Big Trout Lake, *Canada*	102	B2
Biğa, *Turkey*	41	F11
Biga ➜, *Turkey*	41	F11
Bigadiç, *Turkey*	39	B10
Biganos, *France*	20	D3
Biggar, *Canada*	105	C7
Biggar, *U.K.*	14	F5
Bigge I., *Australia*	92	B4
Biggenden, *Australia*	95	D5
Biggleswade, *U.K.*	13	E7
Biggs, *U.S.A.*	116	F5
Bighorn, *U.S.A.*	114	C10
Bighorn ➜, *U.S.A.*	114	C10
Bighorn L., *U.S.A.*	114	D9
Bighorn Mts., *U.S.A.*	114	D10
Bignona, *Senegal*	82	C1
Bigorre, *France*	20	E4
Bigstone L., *Canada*	105	C9
Biguglia, Étang de, *France*	21	F13
Bigwa, *Tanzania*	86	D4
Bihać, *Bos.-H.*	29	D12
Bihar, *India*	69	G11
Bihar □, *India*	69	G12
Biharamulo, *Tanzania*	86	C3
Bihariganj, *India*	69	G12
Biharkeresztes, *Hungary*	42	C6
Bihor □, *Romania*	42	D7
Bihor, Munții, *Romania*	42	D7
Bijagós, Arquipélago dos, *Guinea-Biss.*	82	C1
Bijaipur, *India*	68	F7
Bijapur, *Karnataka, India*	66	L9
Bijapur, *Mad. P., India*	67	K12
Bijār, *Iran*	70	C5
Bijawar, *India*	69	G8
Bijeljina, *Bos.-H.*	42	F3
Bijelo Polje, *Montenegro, Yug.*	40	C3
Bijie, *China*	58	D5
Bijnor, *India*	68	E8
Bikaner, *India*	68	E5
Bikapur, *India*	69	F10
Bikeqi, *China*	56	D6
Bikfayyā, *Lebanon*	75	B4
Bikin, *Russia*	51	E14
Bikin ➜, *Russia*	54	A7
Bikini Atoll, *Marshall Is.*	96	F8
Bikita, *Zimbabwe*	89	C5
Bikoué, *Cameroon*	83	C4
Bila Tserkva, *Ukraine*	47	H6
Bilanga, *Burkina Faso*	83	C4
Bilara, *India*	68	F5
Bilaspur, *Mad. P., India*	69	H10
Bilaspur, *Punjab, India*	68	D7
Bīlāsuvar, *Azerbaijan*	73	C13
Bilauk Taungdan, *Thailand*	64	F2
Bilbao, *Spain*	32	B2
Bilbeis, *Egypt*	80	H7
Bilbo = Bilbao, *Spain*	32	B2
Bilbor, *Romania*	43	C10
Bilciureşti, *Romania*	43	F10

Bíldudalur

Bíldudalur, Iceland ... 8 D2
Bílé Karpaty, Europe ... 27 B11
Bileća, Bos.-H. ... 40 D2
Bilecik, Turkey ... 72 B4
Bilgoraj, Poland ... 45 H9
Bilgram, India ... 69 F9
Bilhaur, India ... 69 F9
Bilhorod-Dnistrovskyy, Ukraine ... 47 J6
Bilibino, Russia ... 51 C17
Bilibiza, Mozam. ... 87 E5
Bilisht, Albania ... 40 F5
Billabalong Roadhouse, Australia ... 93 E2
Billdal, Sweden ... 11 G5
Billiluna, Australia ... 92 C4
Billings, U.S.A. ... 114 D9
Billiton Is. = Belitung, Indonesia ... 62 E3
Billsta, Sweden ... 10 A12
Billund, Denmark ... 11 J3
Bilma, Niger ... 79 E8
Bilo Gora, Croatia ... 42 E2
Biloela, Australia ... 94 C5
Bilohirsk, Ukraine ... 47 K8
Bilopillya, Ukraine ... 47 G8
Biloxi, U.S.A. ... 113 K10
Bilpa Morea Claypan, Australia ... 94 D3
Biltine, Chad ... 79 F10
Bilyarsk, Russia ... 48 C10
Bima, Indonesia ... 63 F5
Bimban, Egypt ... 80 C3
Bimbila, Ghana ... 83 D5
Bimini Is., Bahamas ... 120 A4
Bin Xian, Heilongjiang, China ... 57 B14
Bin Xian, Shaanxi, China ... 56 G5
Bin Yauri, Nigeria ... 83 C5
Bina-Etawah, India ... 68 G8
Bināb, Iran ... 71 B6
Binalbagan, Phil. ... 61 F5
Binalong, Australia ... 95 E4
Bīnālūd, Kūh-e, Iran ... 71 B8
Binatang = Bintangor, Malaysia ... 62 D4
Binche, Belgium ... 17 D4
Binchuan, China ... 58 E3
Binder, Chad ... 83 D7
Bindki, India ... 69 F9
Bindslev, Denmark ... 11 G4
Bindura, Zimbabwe ... 87 F3
Binefar, Spain ... 32 D5
Bingara, Australia ... 95 D5
Bingen, Germany ... 25 F3
Bingerville, Ivory C. ... 82 D4
Bingham, U.S.A. ... 109 C11
Binghamton, U.S.A. ... 111 D9
Bingöl, Turkey ... 70 B4
Bingöl Dağları, Turkey ... 73 C9
Bingsjö, Sweden ... 10 C9
Binh Dinh = An Nhon, Vietnam ... 64 F7
Binh Khe, Vietnam ... 64 F7
Binh Son, Vietnam ... 64 E7
Binhai, China ... 57 G10
Binic, France ... 18 D4
Binisatua, Spain ... 37 B11
Binjai, Indonesia ... 62 D3
Binji, Nigeria ... 83 C5
Binnaway, Australia ... 95 E4
Binongko, Indonesia ... 63 F6
Binscarth, Canada ... 105 C8
Bint Goda, Sudan ... 81 E3
Bintan, Indonesia ... 62 D2
Bintangor, Malaysia ... 62 D4
Bintulu, Malaysia ... 62 D4
Bintuni, Indonesia ... 63 E8
Binyang, China ... 58 F7
Binz, Germany ... 24 A9
Binzert = Bizerte, Tunisia ... 79 A7
Binzhou, China ... 57 F10
Bío Bío □, Chile ... 126 D1
Biograd na Moru, Croatia ... 29 E12
Bioko, Eq. Guin. ... 83 E6
Biokovo, Croatia ... 29 E14
Bipindi, Cameroon ... 83 E7
Bir, India ... 66 K9
Bir, Ras, Djibouti ... 81 E5
Bîr Abu Hashim, Egypt ... 80 C3
Bîr Abu Minqar, Egypt ... 80 B2
Bîr Abu Muḥammad, Egypt ... 75 F3
Bi'r ad Dabbāghāt, Jordan ... 75 E4
Bi'r Adal Deib, Sudan ... 80 C4
Bi'r al Butayyihāt, Jordan ... 75 F4
Bi'r al Mārī, Jordan ... 75 F4
Bi'r al Qattār, Jordan ... 75 F4
Bîr 'Asal, Egypt ... 80 B3
Bîr Atrun, Sudan ... 80 D2
Bîr Beiḍa, Egypt ... 75 E3
Bîr Diqnash, Egypt ... 80 A2
Bîr el 'Abd, Egypt ... 75 D2
Bîr el Basur, Egypt ... 80 B2
Bîr el Biarât, Egypt ... 75 F3
Bîr el Duweidar, Egypt ... 75 E1
Bîr el Garârât, Egypt ... 75 D2
Bîr el Gellaz, Egypt ... 80 A2
Bîr el Heisi, Egypt ... 75 F3
Bîr el Jafir, Egypt ... 75 E1
Bîr el Mâlḥi, Egypt ... 75 E2
Bîr el Shaqqa, Egypt ... 80 A2
Bîr el Thamâda, Egypt ... 75 E2
Bîr Fuad, Egypt ... 80 A2
Bîr Gebeil Ḥişn, Egypt ... 75 E2
Bi'r Ghadir, Syria ... 75 A6
Bîr Ḥaimur, Egypt ... 80 C3
Bîr Ḥasana, Egypt ... 75 E2
Bîr Hōoker, Egypt ... 80 H7
Bîr Kanayis, Egypt ... 80 C3
Bîr Kerawein, Egypt ... 80 B2
Bîr Lahfân, Egypt ... 75 E2
Bîr Madkûr, Egypt ... 75 E1

Bîr Maql, Egypt ... 80 C3
Bir Mîneiga, Sudan ... 80 C4
Bîr Misaha, Egypt ... 80 C2
Bîr Mogreïn, Mauritania ... 78 C3
Bîr Murr, Egypt ... 80 C3
Bi'r Muṭribah, Kuwait ... 70 D5
Bîr Nakheila, Egypt ... 80 C3
Bîr Qaṭia, Egypt ... 75 E1
Bîr Qatrani, Egypt ... 80 A2
Bîr Ranga, Egypt ... 80 C4
Bîr Sahara, Egypt ... 80 C2
Bîr Seiyâla, Egypt ... 80 B3
Bîr Shalatein, Egypt ... 80 C4
Bîr Shebb, Egypt ... 80 C2
Bîr Shût, Egypt ... 80 C4
Bîr Terfawi, Egypt ... 80 C2
Bîr Umm Qubûr, Egypt ... 80 C3
Bîr Ungât, Egypt ... 80 C3
Bîr Za'fârâna, Egypt ... 80 J8
Bîr Zeidûn, Egypt ... 80 B3
Biramféro, Guinea ... 82 C3
Biratnagar, Nepal ... 69 F12
Birawa, Dem. Rep. of the Congo ... 86 C2
Birch ➤, Canada ... 104 B6
Birch Hills, Canada ... 105 C7
Birch I., Canada ... 105 C9
Birch L., N.W.T., Canada ... 104 A5
Birch L., Ont., Canada ... 102 B1
Birch Mts., Canada ... 104 B6
Birch River, Canada ... 105 C8
Birchip, Australia ... 95 F3
Birchiş, Romania ... 42 E7
Bird, Canada ... 105 B10
Bird I. = Las Aves, Is., W. Indies ... 121 C7
Birdsville, Australia ... 94 D2
Birdum Cr. ➤, Australia ... 92 C5
Birecik, Turkey ... 70 B3
Birein, Israel ... 75 E3
Bireuen, Indonesia ... 62 C1
Biri ➤, Sudan ... 81 F2
Birifo, Gambia ... 82 C2
Birigui, Brazil ... 127 A5
Birjand, Iran ... 71 C8
Birkenfeld, Germany ... 25 F3
Birkenhead, U.K. ... 12 D4
Birkerød, Denmark ... 11 J6
Birket Qârûn, Egypt ... 80 J7
Birkfeld, Austria ... 26 D8
Bîrlad = Bârlad, Romania ... 43 D12
Birmingham, U.K. ... 13 E6
Birmingham, U.S.A. ... 109 J2
Birmitrapur, India ... 67 H14
Birni Ngaouré, Niger ... 83 C5
Birni Nkonni, Niger ... 83 C6
Birnin Gwari, Nigeria ... 83 C6
Birnin Kebbi, Nigeria ... 83 C5
Birnin Kudu, Nigeria ... 83 C6
Birobidzhan, Russia ... 51 E14
Birr, Ireland ... 15 C4
Birrie ➤, Australia ... 95 D4
Birsilpur, India ... 68 E5
Birsk, Russia ... 50 D6
Birštonas, Lithuania ... 44 D11
Birtle, Canada ... 105 C8
Birur, India ... 66 N9
Biryuchiy, Ukraine ... 47 J8
Biržai, Lithuania ... 9 H21
Birzebbugga, Malta ... 36 D2
Bisa, Indonesia ... 63 E7
Bisáccia, Italy ... 31 A8
Bisacquino, Italy ... 30 E6
Bisalpur, India ... 69 E8
Bisbee, U.S.A. ... 115 L9
Biscarrosse, France ... 20 D2
Biscarrosse et de Parentis, Étang de, France ... 20 D2
Biscay, B. of, Atl. Oc. ... 6 F5
Biscayne B., U.S.A. ... 109 N5
Biscéglie, Italy ... 31 A9
Bischheim, France ... 19 D14
Bischofshofen, Austria ... 26 D6
Bischofswerda, Germany ... 24 D10
Bischwiller, France ... 19 D14
Biscoe Bay, Antarctica ... 5 D13
Biscoe Is., Antarctica ... 5 C17
Biscostasing, Canada ... 102 C3
Biševo, Croatia ... 29 F13
Bisha, Eritrea ... 81 D4
Bishah, W., Si. Arabia ... 80 C5
Bishan, China ... 58 C6
Bishkek, Kyrgyzstan ... 50 E8
Bishnupur, India ... 69 H12
Bisho, S. Africa ... 89 E4
Bishop, Calif., U.S.A. ... 116 H8
Bishop, Tex., U.S.A. ... 113 M6
Bishop Auckland, U.K. ... 12 C6
Bishop's Falls, Canada ... 103 C8
Bishop's Stortford, U.K. ... 13 F8
Bisignano, Italy ... 31 C9
Bisina, L., Uganda ... 86 B3
Biskra, Algeria ... 78 B7
Biskupiec, Poland ... 44 E7
Bismarck, U.S.A. ... 112 B4
Bismarck Arch., Papua N. G. ... 96 H7
Bismark, Germany ... 24 C7
Bismil, Turkey ... 73 D9
Biso, Uganda ... 86 B3
Bīsotūn, Iran ... 70 C5
Bispgården, Sweden ... 10 A10
Bissagos = Bijagós, Arquipélago dos, Guinea-Biss. ... 82 C1
Bissau, Guinea-Biss. ... 82 C1
Bissaula, Nigeria ... 83 D7
Bissikrima, Guinea ... 82 C2
Bissorã, Guinea-Biss. ... 82 C1
Bistcho L., Canada ... 104 B5

Bistreț, Romania ... 43 G8
Bistrica = Ilirska-Bistrica, Slovenia ... 29 C11
Bistrița, Romania ... 43 C9
Bistrița ➤, Romania ... 43 D11
Bistrița Năsăud □, Romania ... 43 C9
Bistriței, Munții, Romania ... 43 C10
Biswan, India ... 69 F9
Bisztynek, Poland ... 44 D7
Bitburg, Germany ... 25 F2
Bitche, France ... 19 C14
Bithynia, Turkey ... 72 B4
Bitlis, Turkey ... 70 B4
Bitola, Macedonia ... 40 E5
Bitolj = Bitola, Macedonia ... 40 E5
Bitonto, Italy ... 31 A9
Bitter Creek, U.S.A. ... 114 F9
Bitter L. = Buheirat-Murrat-el-Kubra, Egypt ... 80 H8
Bitterfeld, Germany ... 24 D8
Bitterfontein, S. Africa ... 88 E2
Bitterroot ➤, U.S.A. ... 114 C6
Bitterroot Range, U.S.A. ... 114 D6
Bitterwater, U.S.A. ... 116 J6
Bitti, Italy ... 30 B2
Bittou, Burkina Faso ... 83 C4
Biu, Nigeria ... 83 C7
Bivolari, Romania ... 43 C12
Bivolu, Vf., Romania ... 43 C10
Biwa-Ko, Japan ... 55 G8
Biwabik, U.S.A. ... 112 B8
Bixad, Romania ... 43 C8
Bixby, U.S.A. ... 113 H7
Biyang, China ... 56 H7
Biysk, Russia ... 50 D9
Bizana, S. Africa ... 89 E4
Bizen, Japan ... 55 G7
Bizerte, Tunisia ... 79 A7
Bjargtangar, Iceland ... 8 D1
Bjärnum, Sweden ... 11 H7
Bjästa, Sweden ... 10 A12
Bjelasica, Montenegro, Yug. ... 40 D3
Bjelašnica, Bos.-H. ... 42 G3
Bjelovar, Croatia ... 29 C13
Bjerringbro, Denmark ... 11 H3
Björbo, Sweden ... 10 D8
Björklinge, Sweden ... 10 D11
Björneborg, Sweden ... 10 E8
Björnevatn, Norway ... 8 B23
Bjørnøya, Arctic ... 4 B8
Bjursås, Sweden ... 10 D8
Bjuv, Sweden ... 11 H6
Bla, Mali ... 82 C3
Blace, Serbia, Yug. ... 40 C5
Blachownia, Poland ... 45 H5
Black = Da ➤, Vietnam ... 58 G5
Black ➤, Canada ... 110 B5
Black ➤, Ariz., U.S.A. ... 115 K8
Black ➤, Ark., U.S.A. ... 113 H9
Black ➤, Mich., U.S.A. ... 110 D2
Black ➤, N.Y., U.S.A. ... 111 C8
Black ➤, Wis., U.S.A. ... 112 D9
Black Bay Pen., Canada ... 102 C2
Black Birch L., Canada ... 105 B7
Black Diamond, Canada ... 104 C6
Black Duck ➤, Canada ... 102 A2
Black Forest = Schwarzwald, Germany ... 25 G4
Black Forest, U.S.A. ... 112 F2
Black Hd., Ireland ... 15 C2
Black Hills, U.S.A. ... 112 D3
Black I., Canada ... 105 C9
Black L., Canada ... 105 B7
Black L., Mich., U.S.A. ... 108 C3
Black L., N.Y., U.S.A. ... 111 B9
Black Lake, Canada ... 105 B7
Black Mesa, U.S.A. ... 113 G3
Black Mt. = Mynydd Du, U.K. ... 13 F4
Black Mts., U.K. ... 13 F4
Black Range, U.S.A. ... 115 K10
Black River, Jamaica ... 120 C4
Black River Falls, U.S.A. ... 112 C9
Black Sea, Eurasia ... 6 G12
Black Tickle, Canada ... 103 B8
Black Volta ➤, Africa ... 82 D4
Black Warrior ➤, U.S.A. ... 109 J2
Blackall, Australia ... 94 C4
Blackball, N.Z. ... 91 K3
Blackbull, Australia ... 94 B3
Blackburn, U.K. ... 12 D5
Blackburn with Darwen □, U.K. ... 12 D5
Blackfoot, U.S.A. ... 114 E7
Blackfoot ➤, U.S.A. ... 114 C7
Blackfoot River Reservoir, U.S.A. ... 114 E8
Blackpool, U.K. ... 12 D4
Blackpool □, U.K. ... 12 D4
Blackriver, U.S.A. ... 110 B1
Blacks Harbour, Canada ... 103 C6
Blacksburg, U.S.A. ... 108 G5
Blacksod B., Ireland ... 15 B1
Blackstone, U.S.A. ... 108 G6
Blackstone Ra., Australia ... 93 E4
Blackwater, Australia ... 94 C4
Blackwater ➤, Meath, Ireland ... 15 C4
Blackwater ➤, Waterford, Ireland ... 15 D4
Blackwater ➤, U.K. ... 15 B5
Blackwell, U.S.A. ... 113 G6
Blackwells Corner, U.S.A. ... 117 K7
Blaenau Ffestiniog, U.K. ... 12 E4
Blaenau Gwent □, U.K. ... 13 F4
Blagnac, France ... 20 E5
Blagodarnoye = Blagodarnyy, Russia ... 49 H6
Blagodarnyy, Russia ... 49 H6

Blagoevgrad, Bulgaria ... 40 D7
Blagoveshchensk, Russia ... 51 D13
Blain, France ... 18 E5
Blain, U.S.A. ... 110 F7
Blaine, Minn., U.S.A. ... 112 C8
Blaine, Wash., U.S.A. ... 116 B4
Blaine Lake, Canada ... 105 C7
Blair, U.S.A. ... 112 E6
Blair Athol, Australia ... 94 C4
Blair Atholl, U.K. ... 14 E5
Blairgowrie, U.K. ... 14 E5
Blairsden, U.S.A. ... 116 F6
Blairsville, U.S.A. ... 110 F5
Blaj, Romania ... 43 D8
Blake Pt., U.S.A. ... 112 A10
Blakely, Ga., U.S.A. ... 109 K3
Blakely, Pa., U.S.A. ... 111 E9
Blâmont, France ... 19 D13
Blanc, C., Spain ... 37 B9
Blanc, Mont, Alps ... 21 C10
Blanc-Sablon, Canada ... 103 B8
Blanca, B., Argentina ... 122 G4
Blanca Peak, U.S.A. ... 115 H11
Blanche, C., Australia ... 95 E1
Blanche, L., S. Austral., Australia ... 95 D2
Blanche, L., W. Austral., Australia ... 92 D3
Blanco, S. Africa ... 88 E3
Blanco, U.S.A. ... 113 K5
Blanco ➤, Argentina ... 126 C2
Blanco, C., Costa Rica ... 120 E2
Blanco, C., U.S.A. ... 114 E1
Blanda ➤, Iceland ... 8 D3
Blandford Forum, U.K. ... 13 G5
Blanding, U.S.A. ... 115 H9
Blanes, Spain ... 32 D7
Blangy-sur-Bresle, France ... 19 C8
Blanice ➤, Czech Rep. ... 26 B7
Blankaholm, Sweden ... 11 G10
Blankenberge, Belgium ... 17 C3
Blankenburg, Germany ... 24 D6
Blanquefort, France ... 20 D3
Blanquilla, I., Venezuela ... 121 D7
Blanquillo, Uruguay ... 127 C4
Blansko, Czech Rep. ... 27 B9
Blantyre, Malawi ... 87 F4
Blarney, Ireland ... 15 E3
Blasdell, U.S.A. ... 110 D6
Blato, Croatia ... 29 F13
Blaubeuren, Germany ... 25 G5
Blaustein, Germany ... 25 G5
Blåvands Huk, Denmark ... 11 J2
Blaydon, U.K. ... 12 C6
Blaye, France ... 20 C3
Blaye-les-Mines, France ... 20 D6
Blayney, Australia ... 95 E4
Blaze, Pt., Australia ... 92 B5
Błażowa, Poland ... 45 J9
Bleckede, Germany ... 24 B6
Bled, Slovenia ... 29 B11
Bleiburg, Austria ... 26 E7
Blejești, Romania ... 43 F10
Blekinge, Sweden ... 9 H16
Blekinge län □, Sweden ... 11 H9
Blenheim, Canada ... 110 D3
Blenheim, N.Z. ... 91 J4
Bléone ➤, France ... 21 D10
Blérancourt, France ... 19 C10
Bletchley, U.K. ... 13 F7
Blida, Algeria ... 78 A6
Blidö, Sweden ... 10 E12
Blidsberg, Sweden ... 11 G7
Blieskastel, Germany ... 25 F3
Bligh Sound, N.Z. ... 91 L1
Blind River, Canada ... 102 C3
Blinisht, Albania ... 40 E3
Bliss, Idaho, U.S.A. ... 114 E6
Bliss, N.Y., U.S.A. ... 110 D6
Blissfield, U.S.A. ... 110 F8
Blitar, Indonesia ... 63 H15
Blitta, Togo ... 83 D5
Block I., U.S.A. ... 111 E13
Block Island Sd., U.S.A. ... 111 E13
Blodgett Iceberg Tongue, Antarctica ... 5 C9
Bloemfontein, S. Africa ... 88 D4
Bloemhof, S. Africa ... 88 D4
Blois, France ... 18 E8
Blomskog, Sweden ... 10 E6
Blomstermåla, Sweden ... 11 H10
Blönduós, Iceland ... 8 D3
Bloodvein ➤, Canada ... 105 C9
Bloody Foreland, Ireland ... 15 A3
Bloomer, U.S.A. ... 112 C9
Bloomfield, Canada ... 110 C7
Bloomfield, Iowa, U.S.A. ... 112 E8
Bloomfield, N. Mex., U.S.A. ... 115 H10
Bloomfield, Nebr., U.S.A. ... 112 D6
Bloomington, Ill., U.S.A. ... 112 E10
Bloomington, Ind., U.S.A. ... 108 F2
Bloomington, Minn., U.S.A. ... 112 C8
Bloomsburg, U.S.A. ... 111 F8
Blora, Indonesia ... 63 G14
Blossburg, U.S.A. ... 110 E7
Blouberg, S. Africa ... 89 C4
Blountstown, U.S.A. ... 109 K3
Bludenz, Austria ... 26 D2
Blue Earth, U.S.A. ... 112 D8
Blue Mesa Reservoir, U.S.A. ... 115 G10
Blue Mts., Maine, U.S.A. ... 111 B14
Blue Mts., Oreg., U.S.A. ... 114 D4
Blue Mts., Pa., U.S.A. ... 111 F8

Blue Mud B., Australia ... 94 A2
Blue Nile = Nîl el Azraq ➤, Sudan ... 81 D3
Blue Rapids, U.S.A. ... 112 F6
Blue Ridge Mts., U.S.A. ... 109 G5
Blue River, Canada ... 104 C5
Bluefield, U.S.A. ... 108 G5
Bluefields, Nic. ... 120 D3
Bluff, Australia ... 94 C4
Bluff, N.Z. ... 91 M2
Bluff, U.S.A. ... 115 H9
Bluff Knoll, Australia ... 93 F2
Bluff Pt., Australia ... 93 E1
Blufftown, U.S.A. ... 108 E3
Blumenau, Brazil ... 127 B6
Blunt, U.S.A. ... 112 C4
Bly, U.S.A. ... 114 E3
Blyth, Canada ... 110 C3
Blyth, U.K. ... 12 B6
Blythe, U.S.A. ... 117 M12
Blytheville, U.S.A. ... 113 H10
Bo, S. Leone ... 82 D2
Bo Duc, Vietnam ... 65 G6
Bo Hai, China ... 57 E10
Bo Xian = Bozhou, China ... 56 H8
Boa Vista, Brazil ... 124 C6
Boac, Phil. ... 61 E4
Boaco, Nic. ... 120 D2
Bo'ai, China ... 56 G7
Boal, Spain ... 34 B4
Boalsburg, U.S.A. ... 110 F7
Boane, Mozam. ... 89 D5
Boardman, U.S.A. ... 110 E4
Bobadah, Australia ... 95 E4
Bobai, China ... 58 F7
Bobbili, India ... 67 K13
Bóbbio, Italy ... 28 D6
Bobcaygeon, Canada ... 102 D4
Böblingen, Germany ... 25 G5
Bobo-Dioulasso, Burkina Faso ... 82 C4
Bobolice, Poland ... 44 E3
Boboshevo, Bulgaria ... 40 D7
Bobov Dol, Bulgaria ... 40 D6
Bobraomby, Tanjon' i, Madag. ... 89 A8
Bobrinets, Ukraine ... 47 H7
Bobrov, Russia ... 48 E5
Bobrovitsa, Ukraine ... 47 G6
Bobruysk = Babruysk, Belarus ... 47 F5
Boby, Pic, Madag. ... 85 J9
Bôca do Acre, Brazil ... 124 E5
Boca Raton, U.S.A. ... 109 M5
Bocanda, Ivory C. ... 82 D4
Bocas del Toro, Panama ... 120 E3
Boceguillas, Spain ... 34 D7
Bochnia, Poland ... 45 J7
Bocholt, Germany ... 24 D2
Bochum, Germany ... 24 D3
Bockenem, Germany ... 24 C6
Boćki, Poland ... 45 F10
Bocognano, France ... 21 F13
Bocoyna, Mexico ... 118 B3
Bocşa, Romania ... 42 E6
Boda, Dalarnas, Sweden ... 10 C9
Böda, Kalmar, Sweden ... 11 G11
Boda, Västernorrland, Sweden ... 10 B10
Bodafors, Sweden ... 11 G8
Bodaybo, Russia ... 51 D12
Boddam, U.K. ... 14 B7
Boddington, Australia ... 93 F2
Bode Sadu, Nigeria ... 83 D5
Bodega Bay, U.S.A. ... 116 G3
Boden, Sweden ... 8 D19
Bodensee, Europe ... 25 H5
Bodenteich, Germany ... 24 C6
Bodhan, India ... 66 K10
Bodinga, Nigeria ... 83 C6
Bodmin, U.K. ... 13 G3
Bodmin Moor, U.K. ... 13 G3
Bodø, Norway ... 8 C16
Bodrog ➤, Hungary ... 42 B6
Bodrum, Turkey ... 39 D9
Bódva ➤, Hungary ... 42 B5
Boën, France ... 21 C8
Boende, Dem. Rep. of the Congo ... 84 E4
Boerne, U.S.A. ... 113 L5
Boesmans ➤, S. Africa ... 88 E4
Boffa, Guinea ... 82 C2
Bogalusa, U.S.A. ... 113 K10
Bogan ➤, Australia ... 95 E4
Bogan Gate, Australia ... 95 E4
Bogandé, Burkina Faso ... 83 C4
Bogantungan, Australia ... 94 C4
Bogata, U.S.A. ... 113 J7
Bogatić, Serbia, Yug. ... 40 B3
Boğazkale, Turkey ... 72 B6
Boğazlıyan, Turkey ... 72 C6
Bogen, Sweden ... 10 D6
Boggeragh Mts., Ireland ... 15 D3
Boggabilla, Australia ... 95 D5
Boggabri, Australia ... 95 E5
Boglan = Solhan, Turkey ... 70 B4
Bognes, Phil. ... 61 F6
Bognor Regis, U.K. ... 13 G7
Bogodukhov = Bohodukhiv, Ukraine ... 47 G8
Bogol Manya, Ethiopia ... 81 G5
Bogong, Mt., Australia ... 95 F4
Bogor, Indonesia ... 62 F3
Bogoroditsk, Russia ... 46 F10
Bogorodsk, Russia ... 48 B6
Bogoso, Ghana ... 82 D4
Bogotá, Colombia ... 124 C4
Bogotol, Russia ... 50 D9
Bogou, Togo ... 83 C5

Bogra, *Bangla.* 67 G16
Boguchany, *Russia* 51 D10
Boguchar, *Russia* 48 F5
Bogué, *Mauritania* 82 B2
Boguslav, *Ukraine* 47 H6
Boguszów-Gorce, *Poland* ... 45 H3
Bohain-en-Vermandois, *France* 19 C10
Bohemian Forest =
Böhmerwald, *Germany* 25 F9
Bohinjska Bistrica, *Slovenia* ... 29 B11
Böhmerwald, *Germany* 25 F9
Bohmte, *Germany* 24 C4
Bohodukhiv, *Ukraine* 47 G8
Bohol □, *Phil.* 61 G6
Bohol Sea, *Phil.* 63 C6
Bohongou, *Burkina Faso* 83 C5
Böhönye, *Hungary* 42 D2
Bohuslän, *Sweden* 11 F5
Boi, *Nigeria* 83 D6
Boi, Pta. de, *Brazil* 127 A6
Boiaçu, *Brazil* 124 D6
Boileau, C., *Australia* 92 C3
Boing'o, *Sudan* 81 F3
Boiro, *Spain* 34 C2
Boise, *U.S.A.* 114 E5
Boise City, *U.S.A.* 113 G3
Boissevain, *Canada* 105 D8
Bóite →, *Italy* 29 B9
Boitzenburg, *Germany* 24 B9
Boizenburg, *Germany* 24 B6
Bojador C., *W. Sahara* 78 C3
Bojana →, *Albania* 40 E3
Bojano, *Italy* 31 A7
Bojanowo, *Poland* 45 G3
Bøjden, *Denmark* 11 J4
Bojnürd, *Iran* 71 B8
Bojonegoro, *Indonesia* 63 G14
Boju, *Nigeria* 83 D6
Boka, *Serbia, Yug.* 42 E5
Boka Kotorska,
Montenegro, Yug. 40 D2
Bokala, *Ivory C.* 82 D4
Bokani, *Nigeria* 83 D6
Bokaro, *India* 69 H11
Boké, *Guinea* 82 C2
Bokhara →, *Australia* 95 D4
Bokkos, *Nigeria* 83 D6
Boknafjorden, *Norway* 9 G11
Bokoro, *Chad* 79 F9
Bokpyin, *Burma* 65 G2
Boksitogorsk, *Russia* 46 C7
Bol, *Croatia* 29 E13
Bolama, *Guinea-Biss.* 82 C1
Bolan →, *Pakistan* 68 E2
Bolan Pass, *Pakistan* 66 E5
Bolaños →, *Mexico* 118 C4
Bolaños de Calatrava, *Spain* ... 35 G7
Bolayır, *Turkey* 41 F10
Bolbec, *France* 18 C7
Boldāji, *Iran* 71 D6
Boldeşti-Scăeni, *Romania* ... 43 E11
Bole, *China* 60 B3
Bole, *Ethiopia* 81 F4
Bole, *Ghana* 82 D4
Bolekhiv, *Ukraine* 47 H2
Bolesławiec, *Poland* 45 G2
Bolgatanga, *Ghana* 83 C4
Bolgrad = Bolhrad, *Ukraine* ... 47 K5
Bolhrad, *Ukraine* 47 K5
Bolinao, *Phil.* 61 C3
Bolintin-Vale, *Romania* 43 F10
Bolívar, *Argentina* 126 D3
Bolívar, *Mo., U.S.A.* 113 G8
Bolivar, *N.Y., U.S.A.* 110 D6
Bolivar, *Tenn., U.S.A.* 113 H10
Bolivia ■, *S. Amer.* 124 G6
Bolivian Plateau, *S. Amer.* ... 122 E4
Boljevac, *Serbia, Yug.* 40 C5
Bolkhov, *Russia* 46 F9
Bolków, *Poland* 45 H3
Bollebygd, *Sweden* 11 G6
Bollène, *France* 21 D8
Bollnäs, *Sweden* 10 C10
Bollon, *Australia* 95 D4
Bollstabruk, *Sweden* 10 B11
Bolmen, *Sweden* 11 H7
Bolobo, *Dem. Rep. of the Congo* 84 E3
Bologna, *Italy* 29 D8
Bologoye, *Russia* 46 D8
Bolon, *Ozero, Russia* 60 B8
Bolonchenticul, *Mexico* 119 D7
Bolótana, *Italy* 30 B1
Boloven, Cao Nguyen, *Laos* ... 64 E6
Bolpur, *India* 69 H12
Bolsena, *Italy* 29 F8
Bolsena, L. di, *Italy* 29 F8
Bolshaya Chernigovka, *Russia* ... 48 D10
Bolshaya Glushitsa, *Russia* ... 48 D10
Bolshaya Martynovka, *Russia* ... 49 G5
Bolshaya Vradiyevka, *Ukraine* ... 47 J6
Bolshevik, Ostrov, *Russia* 51 B11
Bolshoi Kavkas = Caucasus
Mountains, *Eurasia* 49 J7
Bolshoy Anyuy →, *Russia* ... 51 C17
Bolshoy Begichev, Ostrov,
Russia 51 B12
Bolshoy Lyakhovskiy, Ostrov,
Russia 51 B15
Bolshoy Tokmak = Tokmak,
Ukraine 47 J8
Bolshoy Tyuters, Ostrov, *Russia* 9 G22
Bolsward, *Neths.* 17 A5
Bolt Head, *U.K.* 13 G4
Boltaña, *Spain* 32 C5
Boltigen, *Switz.* 25 J3
Bolton, *Canada* 110 C5
Bolton, *U.K.* 12 D5

Bolton Landing, *U.S.A.* 111 C11
Bolu, *Turkey* 72 B4
Bolungavík, *Iceland* 8 C2
Boluo, *China* 59 F10
Bolvadin, *Turkey* 70 B1
Bolzano, *Italy* 29 B8
Bom Jesus da Lapa, *Brazil* ... 125 F10
Boma, *Dem. Rep. of the Congo* 84 F2
Bombala, *Australia* 95 F4
Bombarral, *Portugal* 35 F1
Bombay = Mumbai, *India* ... 66 K8
Bomboma, *Dem. Rep. of
the Congo* 84 D3
Bombombwa, *Dem. Rep. of
the Congo* 86 B2
Bomi Hills, *Liberia* 82 D2
Bomili, *Dem. Rep. of the Congo* 86 B2
Bømlo, *Norway* 9 G11
Bomokandi →, *Dem. Rep. of
the Congo* 86 B2
Bomu →, *C.A.R.* 84 D4
Bon, C., *Tunisia* 76 C5
Bon Sar Pa, *Vietnam* 64 F6
Bonaigarh, *India* 69 J11
Bonaire, *Neth. Ant.* 121 D6
Bonang, *Australia* 95 F4
Bonanza, *Nic.* 120 D3
Bonaparte Arch., *Australia* ... 92 B3
Boñar, *Spain* 34 C5
Bonaventure, *Canada* 103 C6
Bonavista, *Canada* 103 C9
Bonavista, C., *Canada* 103 C9
Bonavista B., *Canada* 103 C9
Bondeno, *Italy* 29 D8
Bondo, *Dem. Rep. of the Congo* 86 B1
Bondoukou, *Ivory C.* 82 D4
Bondowoso, *Indonesia* 63 G15
Bone, Teluk, *Indonesia* 63 E6
Bonerate, *Indonesia* 63 F6
Bonerate, Kepulauan, *Indonesia* 63 F6
Bo'ness, *U.K.* 14 E5
Bonete, Cerro, *Argentina* ... 126 B2
Bong Son = Hoai Nhon, *Vietnam* 64 E7
Bonga, *Ethiopia* 81 F4
Bongabong, *Phil.* 61 E4
Bongor, *Chad* 79 F9
Bongouanou, *Ivory C.* 82 D4
Bonham, *U.S.A.* 113 J6
Boni, *Mali* 82 B4
Bonifacio, *France* 21 G13
Bonifacio, Bouches de, *Medit. S.* 30 A2
Bonin Is. = Ogasawara Gunto,
Pac. Oc. 52 G18
Bonke, *Ethiopia* 81 F4
Bonkoukou, *Niger* 83 C5
Bonn, *Germany* 24 E3
Bonnat, *France* 19 F8
Bonne Terre, *U.S.A.* 113 G9
Bonners Ferry, *U.S.A.* 114 B5
Bonnétable, *France* 18 D7
Bonneval, *Eure-et-Loir, France* 18 D8
Bonneval, *Savoie, France* ... 21 C11
Bonneville, *France* 19 F13
Bonney, L., *Australia* 95 F3
Bonnie Rock, *Australia* 93 F2
Bonny, *Nigeria* 83 E6
Bonny →, *Nigeria* 83 E6
Bonny, Bight of, *Africa* 83 E6
Bonny-sur-Loire, *France* ... 19 E9
Bonnyrigg, *U.K.* 14 F5
Bonnyville, *Canada* 105 C6
Bono, *Italy* 30 B2
Bonoi, *Indonesia* 63 E9
Bonorva, *Italy* 30 B1
Bonsall, *U.S.A.* 117 M9
Bontang, *Indonesia* 62 D5
Bonthe, *S. Leone* 82 D2
Bontoc, *Phil.* 61 C4
Bonyeri, *Ghana* 82 D4
Bonyhád, *Hungary* 42 D3
Bonython Ra., *Australia* 92 D4
Bookabie, *Australia* 93 F5
Booker, *U.S.A.* 113 G4
Boola, *Guinea* 82 D3
Boolaboolka L., *Australia* ... 95 E3
Booligal, *Australia* 95 E3
Boonah, *Australia* 95 D5
Boone, *Iowa, U.S.A.* 112 D8
Boone, *N.C., U.S.A.* 109 G5
Booneville, *Ark., U.S.A.* ... 113 H8
Booneville, *Miss., U.S.A.* ... 109 H1
Boonville, *Calif., U.S.A.* ... 116 F3
Boonville, *Ind., U.S.A.* 108 F2
Boonville, *Mo., U.S.A.* 112 F8
Boonville, *N.Y., U.S.A.* 111 C9
Boorindal, *Australia* 95 E4
Boorowa, *Australia* 95 E4
Boothia, Gulf of, *Canada* ... 101 A11
Boothia Pen., *Canada* 100 A10
Bootle, *U.K.* 12 D4
Booué, *Gabon* 84 E2
Boppard, *Germany* 25 E3
Boquete, *Panama* 120 E3
Boquilla, Presa de la, *Mexico* ... 118 B3
Boquillas del Carmen, *Mexico* ... 118 B4
Bor, *Czech Rep.* 26 B5
Bor, *Russia* 48 B7
Bor, *Serbia, Yug.* 40 B6
Bôr, *Sudan* 81 F3
Bor, *Sweden* 11 G8
Bor, *Turkey* 72 D6
Bor Mashash, *Israel* 75 D3
Borah Peak, *U.S.A.* 114 D7
Borang, *Sudan* 81 G3
Borås, *Sweden* 11 G6
Borāzjān, *Iran* 71 D6
Borba, *Brazil* 124 D7

Borba, *Portugal* 35 G3
Borborema, Planalto da, *Brazil* 122 D7
Borcea, *Romania* 43 F12
Borçka, *Turkey* 73 B9
Bord Khūn-e Now, *Iran* 71 D6
Borda, C., *Australia* 95 F2
Bordeaux, *France* 20 D3
Borden, *Australia* 93 F2
Borden, *Canada* 103 C7
Borden I., *Canada* 4 B2
Borden Pen., *Canada* 101 A11
Borders = Scottish Borders □,
U.K. 14 F6
Bordertown, *Australia* 95 F3
Borðeyri, *Iceland* 8 D3
Bordighera, *Italy* 28 E4
Bordj Fly Ste. Marie, *Algeria* ... 78 C5
Bordj-in-Eker, *Algeria* 78 D7
Bordj Omar Driss, *Algeria* ... 78 C7
Bore, *Ethiopia* 81 G4
Borehamwood, *U.K.* 13 F7
Borek Wielkopolski, *Poland* ... 45 G4
Borensberg, *Sweden* 11 F9
Borgå = Porvoo, *Finland* ... 9 F21
Borgarfjörður, *Iceland* 8 D7
Borgarnes, *Iceland* 8 D3
Børgefjellet, *Norway* 8 D15
Borger, *Neths.* 17 B6
Borger, *U.S.A.* 113 H4
Borgholm, *Sweden* 11 H10
Bórgia, *Italy* 31 D9
Borgo San Dalmazzo, *Italy* ... 28 D4
Borgo San Lorenzo, *Italy* ... 29 E8
Borgo Val di Taro, *Italy* 28 D6
Borgo Valsugana, *Italy* 29 B8
Borgomanero, *Italy* 28 C5
Borgorose, *Italy* 29 F10
Borgosésia, *Italy* 28 C5
Borhoyn Tal, *Mongolia* 56 C6
Bori, *India* 66 E3
Borikhane, *Laos* 64 C4
Borisoglebsk, *Russia* 48 E6
Borisov = Barysaw, *Belarus* ... 46 E5
Borisovka, *Russia* 47 G9
Borja, *Peru* 124 D3
Borja, *Spain* 32 D3
Borjas Blancas = Les Borges
Blanques, *Spain* 32 D5
Borjomi, *Georgia* 49 K6
Børkop, *Denmark* 11 J3
Borkou, *Chad* 79 E9
Borkum, *Germany* 24 B2
Borlänge, *Sweden* 10 D9
Borley, C., *Antarctica* 5 C5
Borlu, *Turkey* 39 C10
Bormida →, *Italy* 28 D5
Bórmio, *Italy* 28 B7
Borna, *Germany* 24 D8
Borne Sulinowo, *Poland* 44 E3
Borneo, *E. Indies* 62 D5
Bornholm, *Denmark* 11 J8
Bornholms Amtskommune □,
Denmark 11 J8
Bornholmsgattet, *Europe* ... 11 J8
Borno □, *Nigeria* 83 C7
Bornos, *Spain* 35 J5
Bornova, *Turkey* 39 C9
Bornu Yassa, *Nigeria* 83 C7
Boro →, *Sudan* 81 F2
Borodino, *Russia* 46 E8
Borogontsy, *Russia* 51 C14
Boromo, *Burkina Faso* 82 C4
Boron, *U.S.A.* 117 L9
Borongan, *Phil.* 61 F6
Borotangba Mts., *C.A.R.* ... 81 F2
Borotou, *Ivory C.* 82 D3
Borovan, *Bulgaria* 40 C7
Borovichi, *Russia* 46 C8
Borovsk, *Russia* 46 E9
Borrby, *Sweden* 11 J8
Borrego Springs, *U.S.A.* ... 117 M10
Borriol, *Spain* 32 E4
Borroloola, *Australia* 94 B2
Borşa, *Cluj, Romania* 43 D8
Borşa, *Maramureş, Romania* ... 43 C9
Borsad, *India* 68 H5
Borsec, *Romania* 43 D10
Borsod-Abaúj-Zemplén □,
Hungary 42 B6
Bort-les-Orgues, *France* 20 C6
Borth, *U.K.* 13 E3
Börtnan, *Sweden* 10 B7
Borūjerd, *Iran* 71 C6
Boryslav, *Ukraine* 47 H2
Boryspil, *Ukraine* 47 G6
Borzhomi = Borjomi, *Georgia* ... 49 K6
Borzna, *Ukraine* 47 G6
Borzya, *Russia* 51 D12
Bosa, *Italy* 30 B1
Bosanska Dubica, *Bos.-H.* ... 29 C13
Bosanska Gradiška, *Bos.-H.* ... 42 E2
Bosanska Kostajnica, *Bos.-H.* ... 29 C13
Bosanska Krupa, *Bos.-H.* ... 29 D13
Bosanski Brod, *Bos.-H.* 42 E2
Bosanski Novi, *Bos.-H.* 29 C13
Bosanski Petrovac, *Bos.-H.* ... 29 D13
Bosanski Šamac, *Bos.-H.* ... 42 E3
Bosansko Grahovo, *Bos.-H.* ... 29 D13
Bosaso, *Somali Rep.* 74 E4
Boscastle, *U.K.* 13 G3
Bose, *China* 58 F6
Boshan, *China* 57 F9
Boshof, *S. Africa* 88 D4
Boshrūyeh, *Iran* 71 C8
Bosilegrad, *Serbia, Yug.* ... 40 D6
Boskovice, *Czech Rep.* 27 B9
Bosna →, *Bos.-H.* 42 E3

Bosna i Hercegovina = Bosnia-
Herzegovina ■, *Europe* ... 42 G2
Bosnia-Herzegovina ■, *Europe* 42 G2
Bosnik, *Indonesia* 63 E9
Bosobolo, *Dem. Rep. of
the Congo* 84 D3
Bosporus = Istanbul Boğazı,
Turkey 41 E13
Bosque Farms, *U.S.A.* 115 J10
Bossangoa, *C.A.R.* 84 C3
Bossé Bangou, *Niger* 83 C5
Bossier City, *U.S.A.* 113 J8
Bosso, *Niger* 83 C7
Bosso, Dallol →, *Niger* 83 C5
Bostan, *Pakistan* 68 D2
Bostānābād, *Iran* 70 B5
Bosten Hu, *China* 60 B3
Boston, *U.K.* 12 E7
Boston, *U.S.A.* 111 D10
Boston Bar, *Canada* 104 D4
Boston Mts., *U.S.A.* 113 H8
Bosut →, *Croatia* 42 E3
Boswell, *Canada* 104 D5
Boswell, *U.S.A.* 110 F5
Botad, *India* 68 H4
Botan →, *Turkey* 73 D10
Botene, *Laos* 64 D3
Botev, *Bulgaria* 41 D8
Botevgrad, *Bulgaria* 40 D7
Bothaville, *S. Africa* 88 D4
Bothnia, G. of, *Europe* 8 E19
Bothwell, *Australia* 94 G4
Bothwell, *Canada* 110 D3
Boticas, *Portugal* 34 D3
Botletle →, *Botswana* 88 C3
Botlikh, *Russia* 49 J8
Botna →, *Moldova* 43 D14
Botoroaga, *Romania* 43 F10
Botoşani, *Romania* 43 C11
Botoşani □, *Romania* 43 C11
Botou, *Burkina Faso* 83 C5
Botro, *Ivory C.* 82 D3
Botswana ■, *Africa* 88 C3
Bottineau, *U.S.A.* 112 A4
Bottnaryd, *Sweden* 11 G7
Bottrop, *Germany* 24 D2
Botucatu, *Brazil* 127 A6
Botwood, *Canada* 103 C8
Bou Djébéha, *Mali* 82 B4
Boû Rjeïmât, *Mauritania* ... 82 B1
Bouaflé, *Ivory C.* 82 D3
Bouaké, *Ivory C.* 82 D3
Bouar, *C.A.R.* 84 C3
Bouârfa, *Morocco* 78 B5
Boucaut B., *Australia* 94 A1
Bouches-du-Rhône □, *France* ... 21 E9
Bougainville, C., *Australia* ... 92 B4
Bougainville I., *Papua N. G.* ... 96 H7
Bougainville Reef, *Australia* ... 94 B4
Bougie = Bejaïa, *Algeria* ... 78 A7
Bougouni, *Mali* 82 C3
Bouillon, *Belgium* 17 E5
Boukombé, *Benin* 83 C5
Boulal, *Mali* 82 B3
Boulazac, *France* 20 C4
Boulder, *Colo., U.S.A.* 112 E2
Boulder, *Mont., U.S.A.* 114 C7
Boulder City, *U.S.A.* 117 K12
Boulder Creek, *U.S.A.* 116 H4
Boulder Dam = Hoover Dam,
U.S.A. 117 K12
Bouli, *Mauritania* 82 B2
Boulia, *Australia* 94 C2
Bouligny, *France* 19 C12
Boulogne →, *France* 18 E5
Boulogne-sur-Gesse, *France* ... 20 E4
Boulogne-sur-Mer, *France* ... 19 B8
Bouloire, *France* 18 E7
Boulouli, *Mali* 82 B3
Boulsa, *Burkina Faso* 83 C4
Boultoum, *Niger* 83 C7
Boûmdeïd, *Mauritania* 82 B2
Boun Neua, *Laos* 64 B3
Boun Tai, *Laos* 64 B3
Bouna, *Ivory C.* 82 D4
Boundary Peak, *U.S.A.* 116 H8
Boundiali, *Ivory C.* 82 D3
Bountiful, *U.S.A.* 114 F8
Bounty Is., *Pac. Oc.* 96 M9
Boura, *Mali* 82 C4
Bourbon-Lancy, *France* 19 F10
Bourbon-l'Archambault, *France* 19 F10
Bourbonnais, *France* 19 F10
Bourbonne-les-Bains, *France* ... 19 E12
Bourbourg, *France* 19 B9
Bourdel L., *Canada* 102 A5
Bourem, *Mali* 83 B4
Bourg, *France* 20 C3
Bourg-Argental, *France* 21 C9
Bourg-de-Péage, *France* 21 C9
Bourg-en-Bresse, *France* ... 19 F12
Bourg-Lastic, *France* 20 C6
Bourg-Madame, *France* 20 F5
Bourg-St-Andéol, *France* ... 21 D8
Bourg-St-Maurice, *France* ... 21 C10
Bourganeuf, *France* 20 C5
Bourges, *France* 19 E9
Bourget, *Canada* 111 A9
Bourget, Lac du, *France* ... 21 C9
Bourgneuf, B. de, *France* ... 18 E4
Bourgneuf-en-Retz, *France* ... 18 E5
Bourgogne, *France* 19 F11
Bourgoin-Jallieu, *France* ... 21 C9
Bourgueil, *France* 18 E7

Bournemouth, *U.K.* 13 G6
Bournemouth □, *U.K.* 13 G6
Bouroum, *Burkina Faso* 83 C4
Bouse, *U.S.A.* 117 M13
Boussac, *France* 19 F9
Boussé, *Burkina Faso* 83 C4
Boussouma, *Burkina Faso* ... 83 C4
Boutilimit, *Mauritania* 82 B2
Boutonne →, *France* 20 C3
Bouvet I. = Bouvetøya,
Antarctica 3 G10
Bouvetøya, *Antarctica* 3 G10
Bouxwiller, *France* 19 D14
Bouza, *Niger* 83 C6
Bouzonville, *France* 19 C13
Bova Marina, *Italy* 31 E8
Bovalino Marina, *Italy* 31 D9
Bovill, *U.S.A.* 114 C5
Bovino, *Italy* 31 A8
Bovril, *Argentina* 126 C4
Bow →, *Canada* 104 C6
Bow Island, *Canada* 104 D6
Bowbells, *U.S.A.* 112 A3
Bowdle, *U.S.A.* 112 C5
Bowelling, *Australia* 93 F2
Bowen, *Argentina* 126 D2
Bowen, *Australia* 94 C4
Bowen Mts., *Australia* 95 F4
Bowie, *Ariz., U.S.A.* 115 K9
Bowie, *Tex., U.S.A.* 113 J6
Bowkān, *Iran* 70 B5
Bowland, Forest of, *U.K.* ... 12 D5
Bowling Green, *Ky., U.S.A.* ... 108 G2
Bowling Green, *Ohio, U.S.A.* ... 108 E4
Bowling Green, C., *Australia* ... 94 B4
Bowman, *U.S.A.* 112 B3
Bowman I., *Antarctica* 5 C8
Bowmanville, *Canada* 110 C6
Bowmore, *U.K.* 14 F2
Bowral, *Australia* 95 E5
Bowraville, *Australia* 95 E5
Bowron →, *Canada* 104 C4
Bowron Lake Prov. Park,
Canada 104 C4
Bowser L., *Canada* 104 B3
Bowsman, *Canada* 105 C8
Bowwood, *Zambia* 87 F2
Box Cr. →, *Australia* 95 E3
Boxholm, *Sweden* 11 F9
Boxmeer, *Neths.* 17 C5
Boxtel, *Neths.* 17 C5
Boyabat, *Turkey* 72 B6
Boyalıca, *Turkey* 41 F13
Boyang, *China* 59 C10
Boyce, *U.S.A.* 113 K8
Boyd L., *Canada* 102 B4
Boyle, *Canada* 104 C6
Boyle, *Ireland* 15 C3
Boyne →, *Ireland* 15 C5
Boyne City, *U.S.A.* 108 C3
Boynitsa, *Bulgaria* 40 C6
Boynton Beach, *U.S.A.* 109 M5
Boyolali, *Indonesia* 63 G14
Boyoma, Chutes, *Dem. Rep. of
the Congo* 86 B2
Boysen Reservoir, *U.S.A.* ... 114 E9
Boyuibe, *Bolivia* 124 G6
Boyup Brook, *Australia* 93 F2
Boz Burun, *Turkey* 41 F12
Boz Dağ, *Turkey* 39 D11
Boz Dağları, *Turkey* 39 C10
Bozburun, *Turkey* 39 E10
Bozcaada, *Turkey* 72 C2
Bozdoğan, *Turkey* 39 D10
Bozeman, *U.S.A.* 114 D8
Bozen = Bolzano, *Italy* 29 B8
Boževac, *Serbia, Yug.* 40 B5
Bozhou, *China* 56 H8
Bozkır, *Turkey* 72 D5
Bozkurt, *Turkey* 39 D11
Bozouls, *France* 20 D6
Bozoum, *C.A.R.* 84 C3
Bozova, *Antalya, Turkey* ... 39 D12
Bozova, *Şanlıurfa, Turkey* ... 73 D8
Bozovici, *Romania* 42 F7
Bozüyük, *Turkey* 39 B12
Bra, *Italy* 28 D4
Braås, *Sweden* 11 G9
Brabant □, *Belgium* 17 D4
Brabant L., *Canada* 105 B8
Brabrand, *Denmark* 11 H4
Brač, *Croatia* 29 E13
Bracadale, L., *U.K.* 14 D2
Bracciano, *Italy* 29 F9
Bracciano, L. di, *Italy* 29 F9
Bracebridge, *Canada* 102 C4
Brach, *Libya* 79 C8
Bracieux, *France* 18 E8
Bräcke, *Sweden* 10 B9
Brackettville, *U.S.A.* 113 L4
Brački Kanal, *Croatia* 29 E13
Bracknell, *U.K.* 13 F7
Bracknell Forest □, *U.K.* ... 13 F7
Brad, *Romania* 42 D7
Brádano →, *Italy* 31 B9
Bradenton, *U.S.A.* 109 M4
Bradford, *Canada* 110 B5
Bradford, *U.K.* 12 D6
Bradford, *Pa., U.S.A.* 110 E6
Bradford, *Vt., U.S.A.* 111 C12
Bradley, *Ark., U.S.A.* 113 J8
Bradley, *Calif., U.S.A.* 116 K6
Bradley Institute, *Zimbabwe* ... 87 F3
Brady, *U.S.A.* 113 K5
Brædstrup, *Denmark* 11 J3
Braeside, *Canada* 111 A8

Braga, Portugal 34 D2
Braga □, Portugal 34 D2
Bragadiru, Romania 43 G10
Bragado, Argentina 126 D3
Bragança, Brazil 125 D9
Bragança, Portugal 34 D4
Bragança □, Portugal 34 D4
Bragança Paulista, Brazil 127 A6
Brahmanbaria, Bangla. 67 H17
Brahmani →, India 67 J15
Brahmapur, India 67 K14
Brahmaputra →, India 69 H13
Braich-y-pwll, U.K. 12 E3
Braidwood, Australia 95 F4
Brăila, Romania 43 E12
Brăila □, Romania 43 E12
Brainerd, U.S.A. 112 B7
Braintree, U.K. 13 F8
Braintree, U.S.A. 111 D14
Brak →, S. Africa 88 D3
Brake, Germany 24 B4
Brakel, Germany 24 D5
Bräkne-Hoby, Sweden 11 H9
Brakwater, Namibia 88 C2
Brålanda, Sweden 11 F6
Bramberg, Germany 25 E6
Bramdrupdam, Denmark 11 J3
Bramming, Denmark 11 J2
Brämön, Sweden 10 B11
Brampton, Canada 102 D4
Brampton, U.K. 12 C5
Bramsche, Germany 24 C3
Branco →, Brazil 122 D4
Brandberg, Namibia 88 B2
Brande, Denmark 11 J3
Brandenburg =
Neubrandenburg, Germany 24 B9
Brandenburg, Germany 24 C8
Brandenburg □, Germany 24 C9
Brandfort, S. Africa 88 D4
Brando, France 21 F13
Brandon, Canada 105 D9
Brandon, U.S.A. 111 C11
Brandon B., Ireland 15 D1
Brandon Mt., Ireland 15 D1
Brandsen, Argentina 126 D4
Brandvlei, S. Africa 88 E3
Brandýs nad Labem, Czech Rep. 26 A7
Brănești, Romania 43 F11
Branford, U.S.A. 111 E12
Braniewo, Poland 44 D6
Bransfield Str., Antarctica 5 C18
Brańsk, Poland 45 F9
Branson, U.S.A. 113 G8
Brantford, Canada 102 D3
Brantôme, France 20 C4
Branzi, Italy 28 B6
Bras d'Or L., Canada 103 C7
Brasher Falls, U.S.A. 111 B10
Brasil, Planalto, Brazil 122 E6
Brasiléia, Brazil 124 F5
Brasília, Brazil 125 G9
Brasília Legal, Brazil 125 D7
Braslaw, Belarus 9 J22
Braslovče, Slovenia 29 B12
Brașov, Romania 43 E10
Brașov □, Romania 43 E10
Brass, Nigeria 83 E6
Brass →, Nigeria 83 E6
Brassac-les-Mines, France 20 C7
Brasschaat, Belgium 17 C4
Brassey, Banjaran, Malaysia 62 D5
Brassey Ra., Australia 93 E3
Brasstown Bald, U.S.A. 109 H4
Brastad, Sweden 11 F5
Brastavățu, Romania 43 G9
Bratan = Morozov, Bulgaria 41 D9
Brateș, Romania 43 E11
Bratislava, Slovak Rep. 27 C10
Bratislavský □, Slovak Rep. 27 C10
Bratsigovo, Bulgaria 41 D8
Bratsk, Russia 51 D11
Brattleboro, U.S.A. 111 D12
Bratunac, Bos.-H. 42 F4
Braunau, Austria 26 C6
Braunschweig, Germany 24 C6
Braunton, U.K. 13 F3
Bravicea, Moldova 43 C13
Bråviken, Sweden 11 F10
Bravo del Norte, Rio = Grande,
Rio →, U.S.A. 113 N6
Brawley, U.S.A. 117 N11
Bray, Ireland 15 C5
Bray, Mt., Australia 94 A1
Bray-sur-Seine, France 19 D10
Brazeau →, Canada 104 C5
Brazil, U.S.A. 108 F2
Brazil ■, S. Amer. 125 F9
Brazilian Highlands = Brasil,
Planalto, Brazil 122 E6
Brazo Sur →, S. Amer. 126 B4
Brazos →, U.S.A. 113 L7
Brazzaville, Congo 84 E3
Brčko, Bos.-H. 42 F3
Brda →, Poland 45 E5
Brdy, Czech Rep. 26 B6
Breaden, L., Australia 93 E4
Breaksea Sd., N.Z. 91 L1
Bream B., N.Z. 91 F5
Bream Hd., N.Z. 91 F5
Breas, Chile 126 B1
Breaza, Romania 43 E10
Brebes, Indonesia 63 G13
Brechin, Canada 110 B5
Brechin, U.K. 14 E6
Brecht, Belgium 17 C4
Breckenridge, Colo., U.S.A. 114 G10

Breckenridge, Minn., U.S.A. 112 B6
Breckenridge, Tex., U.S.A. 113 J5
Breckland, U.K. 13 E8
Břeclav, Czech Rep. 27 C9
Brecon, U.K. 13 F4
Brecon Beacons, U.K. 13 F4
Breda, Neths. 17 C4
Bredaryd, Sweden 11 G7
Bredasdorp, S. Africa 88 E3
Bredebro, Denmark 11 J2
Bredstedt, Germany 24 A4
Bree, Belgium 17 C5
Bregalnica →, Macedonia 40 E6
Bregenz, Austria 26 D2
Bregovo, Bulgaria 40 B6
Bréhal, France 18 D5
Bréhat, Î. de, France 18 D4
Breiðafjörður, Iceland 8 D2
Breil-sur-Roya, France 21 E11
Brejo, Brazil 125 D10
Bremen, Germany 24 B4
Bremen □, Germany 24 B4
Bremer Bay, Australia 93 F2
Bremer I., Australia 94 A2
Bremerhaven, Germany 24 B4
Bremerton, U.S.A. 116 C4
Bremervörde, Germany 24 B5
Brenes, Spain 35 H5
Brenham, U.S.A. 113 K6
Brenne, France 20 B5
Brennerpass, Austria 26 D4
Breno, Italy 28 C7
Brent, U.S.A. 109 J2
Brenta →, Italy 29 C9
Brentwood, U.K. 13 F8
Brentwood, Calif., U.S.A. 116 H5
Brentwood, N.Y., U.S.A. 111 F11
Bréscia, Italy 28 C7
Breskens, Neths. 17 C3
Breslau = Wrocław, Poland 45 G4
Bresle →, France 18 B8
Bressanone, Italy 29 B8
Bressay, U.K. 14 A7
Bresse, France 19 F12
Bressuire, France 18 F6
Brest, Belarus 47 F2
Brest, France 18 D2
Brest-Litovsk = Brest, Belarus 47 F2
Bretagne, France 18 D3
Bretcu, Romania 43 D11
Bretenoux, France 20 D5
Breteuil, Eure, France 18 D7
Breteuil, Oise, France 19 C9
Breton, Canada 104 C6
Breton, Pertuis, France 20 B2
Breton Sd., U.S.A. 113 L10
Brett, C., N.Z. 91 F5
Bretten, Germany 25 F4
Breuil-Cervínia, Italy 28 C4
Brevard, U.S.A. 109 H4
Breves, Brazil 125 D8
Brewarrina, Australia 95 E4
Brewer, U.S.A. 109 C11
Brewer, Mt., U.S.A. 116 J8
Brewerville, Liberia 82 D2
Brewster, N.Y., U.S.A. 111 E11
Brewster, Ohio, U.S.A. 110 F3
Brewster, Wash., U.S.A. 114 B4
Brewster, Kap = Kangikajik,
Greenland 4 B6
Brewton, U.S.A. 109 K2
Breyten, S. Africa 89 D5
Breza, Bos.-H. 42 F3
Brezhnev = Naberezhnyye
Chelny, Russia 48 C11
Brežice, Slovenia 29 C12
Březnice, Czech Rep. 26 B6
Breznik, Bulgaria 40 D6
Brezno, Slovak Rep. 27 C12
Brezoi, Romania 43 E9
Brezovica, Kosovo, Yug. 40 D5
Brezovo, Bulgaria 41 D9
Briançon, France 21 D10
Briare, France 19 E9
Briático, Italy 31 D9
Bribie I., Australia 95 D5
Bribri, Costa Rica 120 E3
Briceni, Moldova 43 B12
Bricquebec, France 18 C5
Bridgehampton, U.S.A. 111 F12
Bridgend, U.K. 13 F4
Bridgend □, U.K. 13 F4
Bridgeport, Calif., U.S.A. 116 G7
Bridgeport, Conn., U.S.A. 111 E11
Bridgeport, Nebr., U.S.A. 112 E3
Bridgeport, Tex., U.S.A. 113 J6
Bridger, U.S.A. 114 D9
Bridgeton, U.S.A. 108 F8
Bridgetown, Australia 93 F2
Bridgetown, Barbados 121 D8
Bridgetown, Canada 103 D6
Bridgewater, Canada 103 D7
Bridgewater, Mass., U.S.A. 111 E14
Bridgewater, N.Y., U.S.A. 111 D9
Bridgewater, C., Australia 95 F3
Bridgewater-Gagebrook,
Australia 94 G4
Bridgnorth, U.K. 13 E5
Bridgton, U.S.A. 111 B14
Bridgwater, U.K. 13 F5
Bridgwater B., U.K. 13 F4
Bridlington, U.K. 12 C7
Bridlington B., U.K. 12 C7
Bridport, Australia 94 G4
Bridport, U.K. 13 G5
Briec, France 18 D2

Brienne-le-Château, France 19 D11
Brienon-sur-Armançon, France 19 E10
Brienz, Switz. 25 J4
Brienzersee, Switz. 25 J3
Brig, Switz. 25 J3
Brigg, U.K. 12 D7
Brigham City, U.S.A. 114 F7
Bright, Australia 95 F4
Brighton, Australia 95 F2
Brighton, Canada 110 B7
Brighton, U.K. 13 G7
Brighton, Colo., U.S.A. 112 F2
Brighton, N.Y., U.S.A. 110 C7
Brignogan-Plage, France 18 D2
Brignoles, France 21 E10
Brihuega, Spain 32 E2
Brikama, Gambia 82 C1
Brilliant, U.S.A. 110 F4
Brilon, Germany 24 D4
Bríndisi, Italy 31 B10
Brinje, Croatia 29 D12
Brinkley, U.S.A. 113 H9
Brinnon, U.S.A. 116 C4
Brion, I., Canada 103 C7
Brionne, France 18 C7
Brionski, Croatia 29 D10
Brioude, France 20 C7
Briouze, France 18 D6
Brisbane, Australia 95 D5
Brisbane →, Australia 95 D5
Brisighella, Italy 29 D8
Bristol, U.K. 13 F5
Bristol, Conn., U.S.A. 111 E12
Bristol, Pa., U.S.A. 111 F10
Bristol, R.I., U.S.A. 111 E13
Bristol, Tenn., U.S.A. 109 G4
Bristol, City of □, U.K. 13 F5
Bristol B., U.S.A. 100 C4
Bristol Channel, U.K. 13 F3
Bristol I., Antarctica 5 B1
Bristol L., U.S.A. 115 J5
Bristow, U.S.A. 113 H6
Britain = Great Britain, Europe 6 E5
British Columbia □, Canada 104 C3
British Indian Ocean Terr. =
Chagos Arch., Ind. Oc. 52 K11
British Isles, Europe 6 E5
Brits, S. Africa 89 D4
Britstown, S. Africa 88 E3
Britt, Canada 102 C3
Britton, U.S.A. 112 C6
Brive-la-Gaillarde, France 20 C5
Briviesca, Spain 34 C7
Brixen = Bressanone, Italy 29 B8
Brixham, U.K. 13 G4
Brnaze, Croatia 29 E13
Brnenský □, Czech Rep. 27 B9
Brno, Czech Rep. 27 B9
Broad →, U.S.A. 109 J5
Broad Arrow, Australia 93 F3
Broad B., U.K. 14 C2
Broad Haven, Ireland 15 B2
Broad Law, U.K. 14 F5
Broad Sd., Australia 94 C4
Broadalbin, U.S.A. 111 C10
Broadback →, Canada 102 B4
Broadhurst Ra., Australia 92 D3
Broads, The, U.K. 12 E9
Broadus, U.S.A. 112 C2
Broager, Denmark 11 K3
Broby, Sweden 11 H8
Broceni, Latvia 44 B9
Brochet, Canada 105 B8
Brochet, L., Canada 105 B8
Brocken, Germany 24 D6
Brockport, U.S.A. 110 C7
Brockton, U.S.A. 111 D13
Brockville, Canada 102 D4
Brockway, Mont., U.S.A. 112 B2
Brockway, Pa., U.S.A. 110 E6
Brocton, U.S.A. 110 D5
Brod, Macedonia 40 E5
Brodarevo, Serbia, Yug. 40 C3
Brodeur Pen., Canada 101 A11
Brodick, U.K. 14 F3
Brodnica, Poland 45 E6
Brody, Ukraine 47 G3
Brogan, U.S.A. 114 D5
Broglie, France 18 C7
Brok, Poland 45 F8
Broken Arrow, U.S.A. 113 G7
Broken Bow, Nebr., U.S.A. 112 E5
Broken Bow, Okla., U.S.A. 113 H7
Broken Bow Lake, U.S.A. 113 H7
Broken Hill = Kabwe, Zambia 87 E2
Broken Hill, Australia 95 E3
Brokind, Sweden 11 F9
Bromley □, U.K. 13 F8
Bromölla, Sweden 11 H8
Bromsgrove, U.K. 13 E5
Brønderslev, Denmark 11 G3
Brong-Ahafo □, Ghana 82 D4
Broni, Italy 28 C6
Bronkhorstspruit, S. Africa 89 D4
Brønnøysund, Norway 8 D15
Bronte, Italy 31 E7
Brook Park, U.S.A. 110 E4
Brookhaven, U.S.A. 113 K9
Brookings, Oreg., U.S.A. 114 E1
Brookings, S. Dak., U.S.A. 112 C6
Brooklin, Canada 110 C6
Brooklyn Park, U.S.A. 112 C8
Brooks, Canada 104 C6
Brooks Range, U.S.A. 100 B5
Brooksville, U.S.A. 109 L4

Brookton, Australia 93 F2
Brookville, U.S.A. 110 E5
Broom, L., U.K. 14 D3
Broome, Australia 92 C3
Broons, France 18 D4
Brora, U.K. 14 C5
Brora →, U.K. 14 C5
Brørup, Denmark 11 J2
Brösarp, Sweden 11 J8
Brosna →, Ireland 15 C4
Broșteni, Mehedinți, Romania 42 F7
Broșteni, Suceava, Romania 43 C10
Brothers, U.S.A. 114 E3
Brou, France 18 D8
Brouage, France 20 C2
Broughton Island =
Qikiqtarjuaq, Canada 101 B13
Broumov, Czech Rep. 27 A9
Brovary, Ukraine 47 G6
Brovst, Denmark 11 G3
Brown, L., Australia 93 F2
Brown, Pt., Australia 95 E1
Brown City, U.S.A. 110 C2
Brown Willy, U.K. 13 G3
Brownfield, U.S.A. 113 J3
Browning, U.S.A. 114 B7
Brownsville, Oreg., U.S.A. 114 D2
Brownsville, Pa., U.S.A. 110 F5
Brownsville, Tenn., U.S.A. 113 H10
Brownsville, Tex., U.S.A. 113 N6
Brownville, U.S.A. 111 C9
Brownwood, U.S.A. 113 K5
Browse I., Australia 92 B3
Bruas, Malaysia 65 K3
Bruay-la-Buissière, France 19 B9
Bruce, Mt., Australia 92 D2
Bruce Pen., Canada 110 B3
Bruce Rock, Australia 93 F2
Bruche →, France 19 D14
Bruchsal, Germany 25 F4
Bruck an der Leitha, Austria 27 C9
Bruck an der Mur, Austria 26 D8
Brue →, U.K. 13 F5
Bruges = Brugge, Belgium 17 C3
Brugg, Switz. 25 H4
Brugge, Belgium 17 C3
Bruin, U.S.A. 110 E5
Brûlé, Canada 104 C5
Brûlon, France 18 E6
Brumado, Brazil 125 F10
Brumath, France 19 D14
Brumunddal, Norway 9 F14
Bruneau, U.S.A. 114 E6
Bruneau →, U.S.A. 114 E6
Bruneck = Brunico, Italy 29 B8
Brunei = Bandar Seri Begawan,
Brunei 62 C4
Brunei ■, Asia 62 D4
Brunflo, Sweden 10 A8
Brunico, Italy 29 B8
Brunna, Sweden 10 E11
Brunnen, Switz. 25 J4
Brunner, L., N.Z. 91 K3
Brunsbüttel, Germany 24 B5
Brunssum, Neths. 17 D5
Brunswick = Braunschweig,
Germany 24 C6
Brunswick, Ga., U.S.A. 109 K5
Brunswick, Maine, U.S.A. 109 D11
Brunswick, Md., U.S.A. 108 F7
Brunswick, Mo., U.S.A. 112 F8
Brunswick, Ohio, U.S.A. 110 E3
Brunswick, Pen. de, Chile 128 G2
Brunswick B., Australia 92 C3
Brunswick Junction, Australia 93 F2
Bruntál, Czech Rep. 27 B10
Bruny I., Australia 94 G4
Brus Laguna, Honduras 120 C3
Brusartsi, Bulgaria 40 C7
Brush, U.S.A. 112 E3
Brushton, U.S.A. 111 B10
Brusio, Switz. 25 J6
Brusque, Brazil 127 B6
Brussel, Belgium 17 D4
Brussels = Brussel, Belgium 17 D4
Brussels, Canada 110 C3
Brusy, Poland 44 E4
Bruthen, Australia 95 F4
Bruxelles = Brussel, Belgium 17 D4
Bruyères, France 19 D13
Bruz, France 18 D5
Brwinów, Poland 45 F7
Bryagovo, Bulgaria 41 E9
Bryan, Ohio, U.S.A. 108 E3
Bryan, Tex., U.S.A. 113 K6
Bryan, Mt., Australia 95 E2
Bryanka, Ukraine 47 H10
Bryansk, Bryansk, Russia 47 F8
Bryansk, Dagestan, Russia 49 J8
Bryansk = Bryansk, Russia 47 F8
Bryce Canyon National Park,
U.S.A. 115 H7
Bryne, Norway 9 G11
Bryson City, U.S.A. 109 H4
Bryukhovetskaya, Russia 47 K10
Brza Palanka, Serbia, Yug. 40 B6
Brzeg, Poland 45 H4
Brzeg Dolny, Poland 45 G3
Brześć Kujawski, Poland 45 F5
Brzesko, Poland 45 J7
Brzeziny, Poland 45 G6
Brzozów, Poland 45 J9

Bū Ḥasā, U.A.E. 71 F7
Bua, Sweden 11 G6
Bua Yai, Thailand 64 E4
Buapinang, Indonesia 63 E6
Buba, Guinea-Biss. 82 C2
Bubanza, Burundi 86 C2
Bubaque, Guinea-Biss. 82 C1
Bube, Ethiopia 81 F4
Būbiyān, Kuwait 71 D6
Buca, Turkey 39 C9
Bucak, Turkey 39 D12
Bucaramanga, Colombia 124 B4
Bucas Grande I., Phil. 61 G6
Bucasia, Australia 94 C4
Buccaneer Arch., Australia 92 C3
Buccino, Italy 31 B8
Bucecea, Romania 43 C11
Buchach, Ukraine 47 H3
Buchan, U.K. 14 D6
Buchan Ness, U.K. 14 D7
Buchanan, Canada 105 C8
Buchanan, Liberia 82 D2
Buchanan, L., Queens., Australia 94 C4
Buchanan, L., W. Austral.,
Australia 93 E3
Buchanan, U.S.A. 113 K5
Buchanan Cr. →, Australia 94 B2
Buchans, Canada 103 C8
Bucharest = București, Romania 43 F11
Buchen, Germany 25 F5
Buchholz, Germany 24 B5
Buchloe, Germany 25 G6
Buchon, Pt., U.S.A. 116 K6
Buciumi, Romania 42 C8
Buck Hill Falls, U.S.A. 111 E9
Bückeburg, Germany 24 C5
Buckeye, U.S.A. 115 K7
Buckeye Lake, U.S.A. 110 G2
Buckhannon, U.S.A. 108 F5
Buckhaven, U.K. 14 E5
Buckhorn L., Canada 110 B6
Buckie, U.K. 14 D6
Buckingham, Canada 102 C4
Buckingham, U.K. 13 F7
Buckingham B., Australia 94 A2
Buckinghamshire □, U.K. 13 F7
Buckle Hd., Australia 92 B4
Buckleboo, Australia 95 E2
Buckley, U.K. 12 D4
Buckley →, Australia 94 C2
Bucklin, U.S.A. 113 G5
Bucks L., U.S.A. 116 F5
Bucquoy, France 19 B9
Buctouche, Canada 103 C7
București, Romania 43 F11
Bucyrus, U.S.A. 108 E4
Budacu, Vf., Romania 43 C10
Budalin, Burma 67 H19
Budaörs, Hungary 42 C3
Budapest, Hungary 42 C4
Budapest □, Hungary 42 C4
Budaun, India 69 E8
Budd Coast, Antarctica 5 C8
Buddusò, Italy 30 B2
Bude, U.K. 13 G3
Budennovsk, Russia 49 H7
Budești, Romania 43 F11
Budge Budge = Baj Baj, India 69 H13
Budgewoi, Australia 95 E5
Budia, Spain 32 E2
Büdingen, Germany 25 E5
Budjala, Dem. Rep. of the Congo 84 D3
Budoni, Italy 30 B2
Búdrio, Italy 29 D8
Budva, Montenegro, Yug. 40 D2
Budzyń, Poland 45 F3
Buea, Cameroon 83 E6
Buellton, U.S.A. 117 L6
Buena Esperanza, Argentina 126 C2
Buena Park, U.S.A. 117 M9
Buena Vista, Colo., U.S.A. 115 G10
Buena Vista, Va., U.S.A. 108 G6
Buena Vista Lake Bed, U.S.A. 117 K7
Buenaventura, Colombia 124 C3
Buenaventura, Mexico 118 B3
Buendía, Embalse de, Spain 32 E2
Buenos Aires, Argentina 126 C4
Buenos Aires, Costa Rica 120 E3
Buenos Aires □, Argentina 126 D4
Buenos Aires, L., Chile 128 F2
Buffalo, Mo., U.S.A. 113 G8
Buffalo, N.Y., U.S.A. 110 D6
Buffalo, Okla., U.S.A. 113 G5
Buffalo, S. Dak., U.S.A. 112 C3
Buffalo, Wyo., U.S.A. 114 D10
Buffalo →, Canada 104 A5
Buffalo →, S. Africa 89 D5
Buffalo Head Hills, Canada 104 B5
Buffalo L., Alta., Canada 104 C6
Buffalo L., N.W.T., Canada 104 A5
Buffalo Narrows, Canada 105 B7
Buffels →, S. Africa 88 D2
Buford, U.S.A. 109 H4
Bug →, Poland 45 F8
Buga, Colombia 124 C3
Buganda, Uganda 86 C3
Buganga, Uganda 86 C3
Bugasong, Phil. 61 F5
Bugeat, France 20 C5
Bugel, Tanjung, Indonesia 63 G14
Bugibba, Malta 36 D1
Bugsuk, Phil. 62 C5
Buguma, Nigeria 83 E6
Bugun Shara, Mongolia 60 B5
Buguruslan, Russia 50 D6

Calauag

Buh →, *Ukraine* 47 J6
Buharkent, *Turkey* 39 D10
Buheirat-Murrat-el-Kubra, *Egypt* 80 H8
Buhera, *Zimbabwe* 89 B5
Bühl, *Germany* 25 G4
Buhl, *U.S.A.* 114 E6
Buhuşi, *Romania* 43 D11
Builth Wells, *U.K.* 13 E4
Buinsk, *Russia* 48 C9
Buir Nur, *Mongolia* 60 B6
Buis-les-Baronnies, *France* 21 D9
Buitrago = Buitrago del Lozoya, *Spain* 34 E7
Buitrago del Lozoya, *Spain* 34 E7
Bujalance, *Spain* 35 H6
Bujanovac, *Serbia, Yug.* 40 D5
Bujaraloz, *Spain* 32 D4
Buje, *Croatia* 29 C10
Bujumbura, *Burundi* 86 C2
Bük, *Hungary* 42 C1
Buk, *Poland* 45 F3
Bukachacha, *Russia* 51 D12
Bukama, *Dem. Rep. of the Congo* 87 D2
Bukavu, *Dem. Rep. of the Congo* 86 C2
Bukene, *Tanzania* 86 C3
Bukhara = Bukhoro, *Uzbekistan* 50 F7
Bukhoro, *Uzbekistan* 50 F7
Bukima, *Tanzania* 86 C3
Bukit Mertajam, *Malaysia* 65 K3
Bukittinggi, *Indonesia* 62 E2
Bükk, *Hungary* 42 B5
Bukoba, *Tanzania* 86 C3
Bukuru, *Nigeria* 83 D6
Bukuya, *Uganda* 86 B3
Būl, Kuh-e, *Iran* 71 D7
Bula, *Guinea-Biss.* 82 C1
Bula, *Indonesia* 63 E8
Bülach, *Switz.* 25 H4
Bulahdelah, *Australia* 95 E5
Bulan, *Phil.* 61 E5
Bulancak, *Turkey* 73 B8
Bulandshahr, *India* 68 E7
Bulanık, *Turkey* 73 C10
Bûlâq, *Egypt* 80 B3
Bulawayo, *Zimbabwe* 87 G2
Buldan, *Turkey* 39 C10
Bulgar, *Russia* 48 C9
Bulgaria ■, *Europe* 41 D9
Bulgheria, Monte, *Italy* 31 B8
Bulgurca, *Turkey* 39 C9
Buli, Teluk, *Indonesia* 63 D7
Buliluyan, C., *Phil.* 61 G2
Bulki, *Ethiopia* 81 F4
Bulkley →, *Canada* 104 B3
Bull Shoals L., *U.S.A.* 113 G8
Bullaque →, *Spain* 35 G6
Bullas, *Spain* 33 G3
Bulle, *Switz.* 25 J3
Bullhead City, *U.S.A.* 117 K12
Büllingen, *Belgium* 17 D6
Bullock Creek, *Australia* 94 B3
Bulloo →, *Australia* 95 D3
Bulloo L., *Australia* 95 D3
Bulls, *N.Z.* 91 J5
Bully-les-Mines, *France* 19 B9
Bulnes, *Chile* 126 D1
Bulqizë, *Albania* 40 E4
Bulsar = Valsad, *India* 66 J8
Bultfontein, *S. Africa* 88 D4
Bulukumba, *Indonesia* 63 F6
Bulun, *Russia* 51 B13
Bumba, *Dem. Rep. of the Congo* 84 D4
Bumbeşti-Jiu, *Romania* 43 E8
Bumbiri I., *Tanzania* 86 C3
Bumbuna, *S. Leone* 82 D2
Bumhpa Bum, *Burma* 67 F20
Bumi →, *Zimbabwe* 87 F2
Buna, *Kenya* 86 B4
Bunawan, *Phil.* 61 G6
Bunazi, *Tanzania* 86 C3
Bunbury, *Australia* 93 F2
Bunclody, *Ireland* 15 D5
Buncrana, *Ireland* 15 A4
Bundaberg, *Australia* 95 C5
Bünde, *Germany* 24 C4
Bundey →, *Australia* 94 C2
Bundi, *India* 68 G6
Bundoran, *Ireland* 15 B3
Bundukia, *Sudan* 81 F3
Bung Kan, *Thailand* 64 C4
Bunga →, *Nigeria* 83 C6
Bungay, *U.K.* 13 E9
Bungil Cr. →, *Australia* 95 D4
Bungo-Suidō, *Japan* 55 H6
Bungoma, *Kenya* 86 B3
Bungotakada, *Japan* 55 H5
Bungu, *Tanzania* 86 D4
Bunia, *Dem. Rep. of the Congo* 86 B3
Bunji, *Pakistan* 69 B6
Bunkie, *U.S.A.* 113 K8
Bunnell, *U.S.A.* 109 L5
Buñol, *Spain* 33 F4
Bunsuru, *Nigeria* 83 C5
Buntok, *Indonesia* 62 E4
Bununu Dass, *Nigeria* 83 C6
Bununu Kasa, *Nigeria* 83 D6
Bünyan, *Turkey* 72 C6
Bunyu, *Indonesia* 62 D5
Bunza, *Nigeria* 83 C5
Buol, *Indonesia* 63 D6
Buon Brieng, *Vietnam* 64 F7
Buon Ma Thuot, *Vietnam* 64 F7
Buong Long, *Cambodia* 64 F6
Buorkhaya, Mys, *Russia* 51 B14
Buqayq, *Si. Arabia* 71 E6
Buqbuq, *Egypt* 80 A2
Bur Acaba, *Somali Rep.* 74 G3
Bûr Fuad, *Egypt* 80 H8
Bûr Safâga, *Egypt* 70 E2
Bûr Sa'îd, *Egypt* 80 H8
Bûr Sûdân, *Sudan* 80 D4
Bûr Taufiq, *Egypt* 80 J8
Bura, *Kenya* 86 C4
Burakin, *Australia* 93 F2
Buram, *Sudan* 81 E2
Burao, *Somali Rep.* 74 F4
Burāq, *Syria* 75 B5
Buraydah, *Si. Arabia* 70 E4
Burbank, *U.S.A.* 117 L8
Burda, *India* 68 G6
Burdekin →, *Australia* 94 B4
Burdur, *Turkey* 39 D12
Burdur □, *Turkey* 39 D12
Burdur Gölü, *Turkey* 39 D12
Burdwan = Barddhaman, *India* 69 H12
Bure, *Gojam, Ethiopia* 81 E4
Bure, *Ilubabor, Ethiopia* 81 F4
Bure →, *U.K.* 12 E9
Büren, *Germany* 24 D4
Bureya →, *Russia* 51 E13
Burford, *Canada* 110 C4
Burg, *Germany* 24 C7
Burg auf Fehmarn, *Germany* 24 A7
Burg el Arab, *Egypt* 80 H6
Burg et Tuyur, *Sudan* 80 C2
Burg Stargard, *Germany* 24 B9
Burgas, *Bulgaria* 41 D11
Burgas □, *Bulgaria* 41 D10
Burgaski Zaliv, *Bulgaria* 41 D11
Burgdorf, *Germany* 24 C6
Burgdorf, *Switz.* 25 H3
Burgenland □, *Austria* 27 D9
Burgeo, *Canada* 103 C8
Burgersdorp, *S. Africa* 88 E4
Burges, Mt., *Australia* 93 F3
Burghausen, *Germany* 25 G8
Búrgio, *Italy* 30 E6
Burglengenfeld, *Germany* 25 F8
Burgohondo, *Spain* 34 E6
Burgos, *Spain* 34 C7
Burgos □, *Spain* 34 C7
Burgstädt, *Germany* 24 E8
Burgsvik, *Sweden* 11 G12
Burguillos del Cerro, *Spain* 35 G4
Burgundy = Bourgogne, *France* 19 F11
Burhaniye, *Turkey* 39 B8
Burhanpur, *India* 66 J10
Burhi Gandak →, *India* 69 G12
Burhner →, *India* 69 H9
Buri Pen., *Eritrea* 81 D4
Burias I., *Phil.* 61 E5
Burica, Pta., *Costa Rica* 120 E3
Burien, *U.S.A.* 116 C4
Burigi, L., *Tanzania* 86 C3
Burin, *Canada* 103 C8
Buriram, *Thailand* 64 E4
Burj Sāfitā, *Syria* 70 C3
Burji, *Ethiopia* 81 F4
Burkburnett, *U.S.A.* 113 H5
Burke →, *Australia* 94 C2
Burke Chan., *Canada* 104 C3
Burketown, *Australia* 94 B2
Burkina Faso ■, *Africa* 82 C4
Burk's Falls, *Canada* 102 C4
Burlada, *Spain* 32 C3
Burleigh Falls, *Canada* 110 B6
Burley, *U.S.A.* 114 E7
Burlingame, *U.S.A.* 116 H4
Burlington, *Canada* 102 D4
Burlington, *Colo., U.S.A.* 112 F3
Burlington, *Iowa, U.S.A.* 112 E9
Burlington, *Kans., U.S.A.* 112 F7
Burlington, *N.C., U.S.A.* 109 G6
Burlington, *N.J., U.S.A.* 111 F10
Burlington, *Vt., U.S.A.* 111 B11
Burlington, *Wash., U.S.A.* 116 B4
Burlington, *Wis., U.S.A.* 108 D1
Burlyu-Tyube, *Kazakstan* 50 E8
Burma ■, *Asia* 67 J20
Burnaby I., *Canada* 104 C2
Burnet, *U.S.A.* 113 K5
Burney, *U.S.A.* 114 F3
Burnham, *U.S.A.* 110 F7
Burnham-on-Sea, *U.K.* 13 F5
Burnie, *Australia* 94 G4
Burnley, *U.K.* 12 D5
Burns, *U.S.A.* 114 E4
Burns Lake, *Canada* 104 C3
Burnside →, *Canada* 100 B9
Burnside, L., *Australia* 93 E3
Burnsville, *U.S.A.* 112 C8
Burnt L., *Canada* 103 B7
Burnt River, *Canada* 110 B6
Burntwood →, *Canada* 105 B9
Burntwood L., *Canada* 105 B8
Burqān, *Kuwait* 70 D5
Burra, *Australia* 95 E2
Burra, *Nigeria* 83 C6
Burray, *U.K.* 14 C6
Burrel, *Albania* 40 E4
Burren Junction, *Australia* 95 E4
Burriana, *Spain* 32 F4
Burrinjuck Res., *Australia* 95 F4
Burro, Serranías del, *Mexico* 118 B4
Burrow Hd., *U.K.* 14 G4
Burruyacú, *Argentina* 126 B3
Burry Port, *U.K.* 13 F3
Bursa, *Turkey* 41 F13
Burseryd, *Sweden* 11 G7
Burstall, *Canada* 105 C7
Burton, *Ohio, U.S.A.* 110 E3
Burton, *S.C., U.S.A.* 109 J5
Burton, L., *Canada* 102 B4
Burton upon Trent, *U.K.* 12 E6
Buru, *Indonesia* 63 E7
Burullus, Bahra el, *Egypt* 80 H7
Burûn, Râs, *Egypt* 75 D2
Burundi ■, *Africa* 86 C3
Bururi, *Burundi* 86 C2
Burutu, *Nigeria* 83 D6
Burwell, *U.S.A.* 112 E5
Burwick, *U.K.* 14 C5
Bury, *U.K.* 12 D5
Bury St. Edmunds, *U.K.* 13 E8
Buryatia □, *Russia* 51 D11
Buryn, *Ukraine* 47 G7
Burzenin, *Poland* 45 G5
Busalla, *Italy* 28 D5
Busango Swamp, *Zambia* 87 E2
Buşayrah, *Syria* 70 C4
Busca, *Italy* 28 D4
Bushat, *Albania* 40 E3
Büshehr, *Iran* 71 D6
Büshehr □, *Iran* 71 D6
Bushell, *Canada* 105 B7
Bushenyi, *Uganda* 86 C3
Bushire = Büshehr, *Iran* 71 D6
Busie, *Ghana* 82 C4
Businga, *Dem. Rep. of the Congo* 84 D4
Busko-Zdrój, *Poland* 45 H7
Busovača, *Bos.-H.* 42 F2
Buşra ash Shām, *Syria* 75 C5
Busselton, *Australia* 93 F2
Busseri →, *Sudan* 81 F2
Busseto, *Italy* 28 D7
Bussière-Badil, *France* 20 C4
Bussolengo, *Italy* 28 C7
Bussum, *Neths.* 17 B5
Buşteni, *Romania* 43 E10
Busto, C., *Spain* 34 B4
Busto Arsízio, *Italy* 28 C5
Busu-Djanoa, *Dem. Rep. of the Congo* 84 D4
Busuanga I., *Phil.* 61 E3
Büsum, *Germany* 24 A4
Buta, *Dem. Rep. of the Congo* 86 B1
Butare, *Rwanda* 86 C2
Butaritari, *Kiribati* 96 G9
Bute, *U.K.* 14 F3
Bute Inlet, *Canada* 104 C4
Butemba, *Uganda* 86 B3
Butembo, *Dem. Rep. of the Congo* 86 B2
Buteni, *Romania* 42 D7
Butera, *Italy* 31 E7
Butha Qi, *China* 60 B7
Butiaba, *Uganda* 86 B3
Butler, *Mo., U.S.A.* 112 F7
Butler, *Pa., U.S.A.* 110 F5
Buton, *Indonesia* 63 E6
Butte, *Mont., U.S.A.* 114 C7
Butte, *Nebr., U.S.A.* 112 D5
Butte Creek →, *U.S.A.* 116 F5
Butterworth = Gcuwa, *S. Africa* 89 E4
Butterworth, *Malaysia* 65 K3
Buttevant, *Ireland* 15 D3
Buttfield, Mt., *Australia* 93 D4
Button B., *Canada* 105 B10
Buttonwillow, *U.S.A.* 117 K7
Butty Hd., *Australia* 93 F3
Butuan, *Phil.* 61 G6
Butuku-Luba, *Eq. Guin.* 83 E6
Butung = Buton, *Indonesia* 63 E6
Buturlinovka, *Russia* 48 E5
Butzbach, *Germany* 25 E4
Bützow, *Germany* 24 B7
Buxa Duar, *India* 69 F13
Buxar, *India* 69 G10
Buxtehude, *Germany* 24 B5
Buxton, *U.K.* 12 D6
Buxy, *France* 19 F11
Buy, *Russia* 48 A5
Buynaksk, *Russia* 49 J8
Buyo, *Ivory C.* 82 D3
Buyo, L. de, *Ivory C.* 82 D3
Büyük Menderes →, *Turkey* 39 D9
Büyükçekmece, *Turkey* 41 E12
Büyükkariştiran, *Turkey* 41 E11
Büyükkemikli Burnu, *Turkey* 41 F10
Büyükorhan, *Turkey* 39 B10
Büyükyoncalı, *Turkey* 41 E11
Buzançais, *France* 18 F8
Buzău, *Romania* 43 E11
Buzău □, *Romania* 43 E11
Buzău →, *Romania* 43 E12
Buzău, Pasul, *Romania* 43 E11
Buzen, *Japan* 55 H5
Buzet, *Croatia* 29 C10
Buzi →, *Mozam.* 87 F3
Buziaş, *Romania* 42 E6
Buzuluk, *Russia* 50 D6
Buzuluk →, *Russia* 48 E6
Buzzards B., *U.S.A.* 111 E14
Buzzards Bay, *U.S.A.* 111 E14
Bwana Mkubwe, *Dem. Rep. of the Congo* 87 E2
Byala, *Ruse, Bulgaria* 41 C9
Byala, *Varna, Bulgaria* 41 D11
Byala Slatina, *Bulgaria* 40 C7
Byarezina →, *Belarus* 47 F6
Byaroza, *Belarus* 47 F3
Bychawa, *Poland* 45 G9
Byczyna, *Poland* 45 G5
Bydgoszcz, *Poland* 45 E5
Byelarus = Belarus ■, *Europe* 46 F4
Byelorussia = Belarus ■, *Europe* 46 F4
Byers, *U.S.A.* 112 F2
Byesville, *U.S.A.* 110 G3
Byford, *Australia* 93 F2
Bykhaw, *Belarus* 46 F6
Bykhov = Bykhaw, *Belarus* 46 F6
Bykovo, *Russia* 48 F7
Bylas, *U.S.A.* 115 K8
Bylot, *Canada* 105 B10
Bylot I., *Canada* 101 A12
Byrd, C., *Antarctica* 5 C17
Byrock, *Australia* 95 E4
Byron Bay, *Australia* 95 D5
Byrranga, Gory, *Russia* 51 B11
Byrranga Mts. = Byrranga, Gory, *Russia* 51 B11
Byrum, *Denmark* 11 G5
Byske, *Sweden* 8 D19
Byske älv →, *Sweden* 8 D19
Bystrzyca →, *Dolnośląskie, Poland* 45 G3
Bystrzyca →, *Lubelskie, Poland* 45 G9
Bystrzyca Kłodzka, *Poland* 45 H3
Bytča, *Slovak Rep.* 27 B11
Bytom, *Poland* 45 H5
Bytom Odrzański, *Poland* 45 G2
Bytów, *Poland* 44 D4
Byumba, *Rwanda* 86 C3
Bzenec, *Czech Rep.* 27 C10
Bzura →, *Poland* 45 F7

C

Ca →, *Vietnam* 64 C5
Ca Mau, *Vietnam* 65 H5
Ca Mau, Mui, *Vietnam* 65 H5
Ca Na, *Vietnam* 65 G7
Caacupé, *Paraguay* 126 B4
Caála, *Angola* 85 G3
Caamano Sd., *Canada* 104 C3
Caazapá, *Paraguay* 126 B4
Caazapá □, *Paraguay* 127 B4
Cabadbaran, *Phil.* 61 G6
Cabalian = San Juan, *Phil.* 61 F6
Cabana, *Spain* 34 B2
Cabañaquinta, *Spain* 34 B5
Cabanatuan, *Phil.* 61 D4
Cabanes, *Spain* 32 E5
Cabano, *Canada* 103 C6
Čabar, *Croatia* 29 C11
Cabazon, *U.S.A.* 117 M10
Cabedelo, *Brazil* 125 E12
Cabeza del Buey, *Spain* 35 G5
Cabezón de la Sal, *Spain* 34 B6
Cabildo, *Chile* 126 C1
Cabimas, *Venezuela* 124 A4
Cabinda, *Angola* 84 F2
Cabinda □, *Angola* 84 F2
Cabinet Mts., *U.S.A.* 114 C6
Cabo Blanco, *Argentina* 128 F3
Cabo Frio, *Brazil* 127 A7
Cabo Pantoja, *Peru* 124 D3
Cabonga, Réservoir, *Canada* 102 C4
Cabool, *U.S.A.* 113 G8
Caboolture, *Australia* 95 D5
Cabora Bassa Dam = Cahora Bassa, Represa de, *Mozam.* 87 F3
Caborca, *Mexico* 118 A2
Cabot, Mt., *U.S.A.* 111 B13
Cabot Hd., *Canada* 110 A3
Cabot Str., *Canada* 103 C8
Cabra, *Spain* 35 H6
Cabra del Santo Cristo, *Spain* 35 H7
Cábras, *Italy* 30 C1
Cabrera, *Spain* 37 B9
Cabrera, Sierra, *Spain* 34 C4
Cabri, *Canada* 105 C7
Cabriel →, *Spain* 33 F3
Cabugao, *Phil.* 61 C4
Cacabelos, *Spain* 34 C4
Caçador, *Brazil* 127 B5
Čačak, *Serbia, Yug.* 40 C4
Caçapava do Sul, *Brazil* 127 C5
Cáccamo, *Italy* 30 E6
Cacém, *Portugal* 35 G1
Cáceres, *Brazil* 124 G7
Cáceres, *Spain* 35 F4
Cáceres □, *Spain* 34 F5
Cache Bay, *Canada* 102 C4
Cache Cr. →, *U.S.A.* 116 G5
Cache Creek, *Canada* 104 C4
Cacheu, *Guinea-Biss.* 82 C1
Cachi, *Argentina* 126 B2
Cachimbo, Serra do, *Brazil* 125 E7
Cachinal de la Sierra, *Chile* 126 A2
Cachoeira, *Brazil* 125 F11
Cachoeira do Sul, *Brazil* 127 C5
Cachoeiro de Itapemirim, *Brazil* 127 A7
Cachopo, *Portugal* 35 H3
Cacine, *Guinea-Biss.* 82 C1
Cacoal, *Brazil* 124 F6
Cacólo, *Angola* 84 G3
Caconda, *Angola* 85 G3
Čadca, *Slovak Rep.* 27 B11
Caddo, *U.S.A.* 113 H6
Cader Idris, *U.K.* 13 E4
Cadereyta, *Mexico* 118 B5
Cadí, Sierra del, *Spain* 32 C6
Cadibarrawirracanna, L., *Australia* 95 D2
Cadillac, *France* 20 D3
Cadillac, *U.S.A.* 108 C3
Cadiz, *Phil.* 61 F5
Cádiz, *Spain* 35 J4
Cadiz, *Calif., U.S.A.* 117 L11
Cadiz, *Ohio, U.S.A.* 110 F4
Cádiz □, *Spain* 35 J5
Cádiz, G. de, *Spain* 35 J3
Cadiz L., *U.S.A.* 115 J6
Cadney Park, *Australia* 95 D1
Cadomin, *Canada* 104 C5
Cadotte Lake, *Canada* 104 B5
Cadours, *France* 20 E5
Cadoux, *Australia* 93 F2
Caen, *France* 18 C6
Caernarfon, *U.K.* 12 D3
Caernarfon B., *U.K.* 12 D3
Caernarvon = Caernarfon, *U.K.* 12 D3
Caerphilly, *U.K.* 13 F4
Caerphilly □, *U.K.* 13 F4
Caesarea, *Israel* 75 C3
Caetité, *Brazil* 125 F10
Cafayate, *Argentina* 126 B2
Cafu, *Angola* 88 B2
Cagayan →, *Phil.* 61 B4
Cagayan de Oro, *Phil.* 61 G6
Cagayan Is., *Phil.* 61 G4
Cagayan Sulu I., *Phil.* 61 H3
Cagli, *Italy* 29 E9
Cágliari, *Italy* 30 C2
Cágliari, G. di, *Italy* 30 C2
Cagnano Varano, *Italy* 29 G12
Cagnes-sur-Mer, *France* 21 E11
Caguán →, *Colombia* 124 D4
Caguas, *Puerto Rico* 121 C6
Caha Mts., *Ireland* 15 E2
Cahama, *Angola* 88 B1
Caher, *Ireland* 15 D4
Caherciveen, *Ireland* 15 E1
Cahora Bassa, Represa de, *Mozam.* 87 F3
Cahore Pt., *Ireland* 15 D5
Cahors, *France* 20 D5
Cahul, *Moldova* 43 E13
Cai Bau, Dao, *Vietnam* 58 G6
Cai Nuoc, *Vietnam* 65 H5
Caia, *Mozam.* 87 F4
Caianda, *Angola* 87 E1
Caibarién, *Cuba* 120 B4
Caibiran, *Phil.* 61 F6
Caicara, *Venezuela* 124 B5
Caicó, *Brazil* 125 E11
Caicos Is., *Turks & Caicos* 121 B5
Caicos Passage, *W. Indies* 121 B5
Caidian, *China* 59 B10
Căinari, *Moldova* 43 D14
Caird Coast, *Antarctica* 5 D1
Cairn Gorm, *U.K.* 14 D5
Cairngorm Mts., *U.K.* 14 D5
Cairnryan, *U.K.* 14 G3
Cairns, *Australia* 94 B4
Cairns L., *Canada* 105 C10
Cairo = El Qâhira, *Egypt* 80 H7
Cairo, *Ga., U.S.A.* 109 K3
Cairo, *Ill., U.S.A.* 113 G10
Cairo, *N.Y., U.S.A.* 111 D11
Cairo Montenotte, *Italy* 28 D5
Caithness, Ord of, *U.K.* 14 C5
Cajamarca, *Peru* 124 E3
Cajarc, *France* 20 D5
Cajàzeiras, *Brazil* 125 E11
Čajetina, *Serbia, Yug.* 40 C3
Çakirgol, *Turkey* 73 B8
Çakırlar, *Turkey* 39 E12
Čakovec, *Croatia* 29 B13
Çal, *Turkey* 39 C11
Cala, *Spain* 35 H4
Cala →, *Spain* 35 H4
Cala Cadolar, Punta de = Rotja, Pta., *Spain* 33 G6
Cala d'Or, *Spain* 37 B10
Cala en Porter, *Spain* 37 B11
Cala Figuera, C. de, *Spain* 37 B9
Cala Forcat, *Spain* 37 B10
Cala Major, *Spain* 37 B9
Cala Mezquida = Sa Mesquida, *Spain* 37 B11
Cala Millor, *Spain* 37 B10
Cala Ratjada, *Spain* 37 B10
Cala Santa Galdana, *Spain* 37 B10
Calabanga, *Phil.* 61 E5
Calabar, *Nigeria* 83 E6
Calabogie, *Canada* 111 A8
Calabozo, *Venezuela* 124 B5
Calábria □, *Italy* 31 C9
Calaburras, Pta. de, *Spain* 35 J6
Calaceite, *Spain* 32 D5
Calacuccia, *France* 21 F13
Calafat, *Romania* 42 G7
Calafate, *Argentina* 128 G2
Calafell, *Spain* 32 D6
Calahorra, *Spain* 32 C3
Calais, *France* 19 B8
Calais, *U.S.A.* 109 C12
Calalaste, Cord. de, *Argentina* 126 B2
Calama, *Brazil* 124 E6
Calama, *Chile* 126 A2
Calamar, *Colombia* 124 A4
Calamian Group, *Phil.* 61 F3
Calamocha, *Spain* 32 E3
Calamonte, *Spain* 35 G4
Călan, *Romania* 42 E7
Calañas, *Spain* 35 H4
Calanda, *Spain* 32 E4
Calang, *Indonesia* 62 D1
Calangiánus, *Italy* 30 B2
Calapan, *Phil.* 61 E4
Călărasi, *Moldova* 43 C13
Călăraşi, *Romania* 43 F12
Călăraşi □, *Romania* 43 F12
Calasparra, *Spain* 33 G3
Calatafimi, *Italy* 30 E5
Calatayud, *Spain* 32 D3
Călăţele, *Romania* 42 D8
Calato = Kálathos, *Greece* 39 E10
Calauag, *Phil.* 61 E5

Calavà, C., *Italy*	31	D7
Calavite, C., *Phil.*	61	E4
Calayan, *Phil.*	61	B4
Calbayog, *Phil.*	61	E6
Calca, *Peru*	124	F4
Calcasieu L., *U.S.A.*	113	L8
Calcutta = Kolkata, *India*	69	H13
Calcutta, *U.S.A.*	110	F4
Caldaro, *Italy*	29	B8
Caldas da Rainha, *Portugal*	35	F1
Caldas de Reis, *Spain*	34	C2
Calder ➤, *U.K.*	12	D6
Caldera, *Chile*	126	B1
Caldwell, *Idaho, U.S.A.*	114	E5
Caldwell, *Kans., U.S.A.*	113	G6
Caldwell, *Tex., U.S.A.*	113	K6
Caledon, *S. Africa*	88	E2
Caledon ➤, *S. Africa*	88	E4
Caledon B., *Australia*	94	A2
Caledonia, *Canada*	110	C5
Caledonia, *U.S.A.*	110	D7
Calella, *Spain*	32	D7
Calemba, *Angola*	88	B2
Calen, *Australia*	94	C4
Calenzana, *France*	21	F12
Caletones, *Chile*	126	C1
Calexico, *U.S.A.*	117	N11
Calf of Man, *U.K.*	12	C3
Calgary, *Canada*	104	C6
Calheta, *Madeira*	37	D2
Calhoun, *U.S.A.*	109	H3
Cali, *Colombia*	124	C3
Calicut, *India*	66	P9
Caliente, *U.S.A.*	115	H6
California, *Mo., U.S.A.*	112	F8
California, *Pa., U.S.A.*	110	F5
California □, *U.S.A.*	116	H7
California, Baja, *Mexico*	118	A1
California, Baja, T.N. = Baja California □, *Mexico*	118	B2
California, Baja, T.S. = Baja California Sur □, *Mexico*	118	B2
California, G. de, *Mexico*	118	B2
California City, *U.S.A.*	117	K9
California Hot Springs, *U.S.A.*	117	K8
Călimăneşti, *Romania*	43	E9
Călimani, Munţii, *Romania*	43	C10
Calingasta, *Argentina*	126	C2
Calipatria, *U.S.A.*	117	M11
Calistoga, *U.S.A.*	116	G4
Calitri, *Italy*	31	B8
Calitzdorp, *S. Africa*	88	E3
Callabonna, L., *Australia*	95	D3
Callac, *France*	18	D3
Callan, *Ireland*	15	D4
Callander, *U.K.*	14	E4
Callao, *Peru*	124	F3
Calles, *Mexico*	119	C5
Callicoon, *U.S.A.*	111	E9
Calling Lake, *Canada*	104	B6
Calliope, *Australia*	94	C5
Callosa de Ensarriá, *Spain*	33	G4
Callosa de Segura, *Spain*	33	G4
Calne, *U.K.*	13	F6
Calola, *Angola*	88	B2
Calolbon = San Andres, *Phil.*	61	E6
Calonge, *Spain*	32	D8
Caloocan, *Phil.*	61	D4
Calore ➤, *Italy*	31	A7
Caloundra, *Australia*	95	D5
Calpe, *Spain*	33	G5
Calpella, *U.S.A.*	116	F3
Calpine, *U.S.A.*	116	F6
Calstock, *Canada*	102	C3
Caltabellotta, *Italy*	30	E6
Caltagirone, *Italy*	31	E7
Caltanissetta, *Italy*	31	E7
Çaltılıbük, *Turkey*	41	G12
Caluire-et-Cuire, *France*	19	G11
Calulo, *Angola*	84	G2
Caluso, *Italy*	28	C4
Calvados □, *France*	18	C6
Calvert ➤, *Australia*	94	B2
Calvert I., *Canada*	104	C3
Calvert Ra., *Australia*	92	D3
Calvi, *France*	21	F12
Calviá, *Spain*	33	F7
Calvillo, *Mexico*	118	C4
Calvinia, *S. Africa*	88	E2
Calvo = Calvo, Mte., *Italy*	29	G12
Calvo, Mte., *Italy*	29	G12
Calwa, *U.S.A.*	116	J7
Calzada Almuradiel = Almuradiel, *Spain*	35	G7
Calzada de Calatrava, *Spain*	35	G7
Cam ➤, *U.K.*	13	E8
Cam Lam, *Vietnam*	65	G7
Cam Pha, *Vietnam*	58	G6
Cam Ranh, *Vietnam*	65	G7
Cam Xuyen, *Vietnam*	64	C6
Camabatela, *Angola*	84	F3
Camacha, *Madeira*	37	D3
Camacho, *Mexico*	118	C4
Camacupa, *Angola*	85	G3
Camagüey, *Cuba*	120	B4
Camaiore, *Italy*	28	E7
Camaná, *Peru*	124	G4
Camanche Reservoir, *U.S.A.*	116	G6
Camaquã, *Brazil*	127	C5
Camaquã ➤, *Brazil*	127	C5
Câmara de Lobos, *Madeira*	37	D3
Camarat, C., *France*	21	E10
Camarès, *France*	20	E6
Camaret-sur-Mer, *France*	18	D2
Camargo, *Mexico*	119	B5
Camargue, *France*	21	E8
Camarillo, *U.S.A.*	117	L7
Camariñas, *Spain*	34	B1
Camarón, C., *Honduras*	120	C2
Camarones, *Argentina*	128	E3
Camas, *Spain*	35	H4
Camas, *U.S.A.*	116	E4
Camas Valley, *U.S.A.*	114	E2
Camballin, *Australia*	92	C3
Cambará, *Brazil*	127	A5
Cambay = Khambhat, *India*	68	H5
Cambay, G. of = Khambhat, G. of, *India*	66	J8
Cambil, *Spain*	35	H7
Cambo-les-Bains, *France*	20	E2
Cambodia ■, *Asia*	64	F5
Camborne, *U.K.*	13	G2
Cambrai, *France*	19	B10
Cambre, *Spain*	34	B2
Cambria, *U.S.A.*	116	K5
Cambrian Mts., *U.K.*	13	E4
Cambridge, *Canada*	102	D3
Cambridge, *Jamaica*	120	C4
Cambridge, *N.Z.*	91	G5
Cambridge, *U.K.*	13	E8
Cambridge, *Mass., U.S.A.*	111	D13
Cambridge, *Minn., U.S.A.*	112	C8
Cambridge, *N.Y., U.S.A.*	111	C11
Cambridge, *Ohio, U.S.A.*	110	F3
Cambridge Bay = Ikaluktutiak, *Canada*	100	B9
Cambridge G., *Australia*	92	B4
Cambridge Springs, *U.S.A.*	110	E4
Cambridgeshire □, *U.K.*	13	E7
Cambrils, *Spain*	32	D6
Cambuci, *Brazil*	127	A7
Cambundi-Catembo, *Angola*	84	G3
Camden, *Ala., U.S.A.*	109	K2
Camden, *Ark., U.S.A.*	113	J8
Camden, *Maine, U.S.A.*	109	C11
Camden, *N.J., U.S.A.*	111	G9
Camden, *N.Y., U.S.A.*	111	C9
Camden, *S.C., U.S.A.*	109	H5
Camden Sd., *Australia*	92	C3
Camdenton, *U.S.A.*	113	F8
Cameli, *Turkey*	39	D11
Camenca, *Moldova*	43	B13
Camerino, *Italy*	29	E10
Cameron, *Ariz., U.S.A.*	115	J8
Cameron, *La., U.S.A.*	113	L8
Cameron, *Mo., U.S.A.*	112	F7
Cameron, *Tex., U.S.A.*	113	K6
Cameron Highlands, *Malaysia*	65	K3
Cameron Hills, *Canada*	104	B5
Cameroon ■, *Africa*	84	C2
Cameroun ➤, *Cameroon*	83	E6
Cameroun, Mt., *Cameroon*	83	E6
Cametá, *Brazil*	125	D9
Çamiçi Gölü, *Turkey*	39	D9
Camiguin □, *Phil.*	61	G6
Camiguin I., *Phil.*	61	B4
Camiling, *Phil.*	61	D4
Camilla, *U.S.A.*	109	K3
Caminha, *Portugal*	34	D2
Camino, *U.S.A.*	116	G6
Camira Creek, *Australia*	95	D5
Cammal, *U.S.A.*	110	E7
Cammarata, *Italy*	30	E6
Camocim, *Brazil*	125	D10
Camooweal, *Australia*	94	B2
Camopi, *Fr. Guiana*	125	C8
Camotes Is., *Phil.*	61	F6
Camotes Sea, *Phil.*	61	F6
Camp Borden, *Canada*	110	B5
Camp Hill, *U.S.A.*	110	F8
Camp Nelson, *U.S.A.*	117	J8
Camp Pendleton, *U.S.A.*	117	M9
Camp Verde, *U.S.A.*	115	J8
Camp Wood, *U.S.A.*	113	L5
Campagna, *Italy*	31	B8
Campana, *Argentina*	126	C4
Campana, I., *Chile*	128	F1
Campanário, *Madeira*	37	D2
Campanario, *Spain*	35	G5
Campánia □, *Italy*	31	B7
Campbell, *S. Africa*	88	D3
Campbell, *Calif., U.S.A.*	116	H5
Campbell, *Ohio, U.S.A.*	110	E4
Campbell I., *Pac. Oc.*	96	N8
Campbell L., *Canada*	105	A7
Campbell River, *Canada*	104	C3
Campbell Town, *Australia*	94	G4
Campbellford, *Canada*	110	B7
Campbellpur, *Pakistan*	68	C5
Campbellsville, *U.S.A.*	108	G3
Campbellton, *Canada*	103	C6
Campbelltown, *Australia*	95	E5
Campbeltown, *U.K.*	14	F3
Campeche, *Mexico*	119	D6
Campeche □, *Mexico*	119	D6
Campeche, Golfo de, *Mexico*	119	D6
Campello, *Spain*	33	G4
Câmpeni, *Romania*	42	D8
Camperdown, *Australia*	95	F3
Camperville, *Canada*	105	C8
Campi Salentina, *Italy*	31	B11
Câmpia Turzii, *Romania*	43	D8
Campidano, *Italy*	30	C1
Campíglia Maríttima, *Italy*	28	E7
Campillo de Altobuey, *Spain*	33	F3
Campillos, *Spain*	35	H6
Câmpina, *Romania*	43	E10
Campina Grande, *Brazil*	125	E11
Campinas, *Brazil*	127	A6
Campli, *Italy*	29	F10
Campo, *Spain*	32	C5
Campo de Criptana, *Spain*	35	F7
Campo de Gibraltar, *Spain*	35	J5
Campo Grande, *Brazil*	125	H8
Campo Maíor, *Brazil*	125	D10
Campo Maior, *Portugal*	35	F3
Campo Mourão, *Brazil*	127	A5
Campo Túres, *Italy*	29	B8
Campobasso, *Italy*	31	A7
Campobello di Licata, *Italy*	30	E6
Campobello di Mazara, *Italy*	30	E5
Campofelice di Roccella, *Italy*	30	E6
Campomarino, *Italy*	29	G12
Camporeale, *Italy*	30	E6
Camporrobles, *Spain*	32	F3
Campos, *Brazil*	127	A7
Campos Belos, *Brazil*	125	F9
Campos del Puerto, *Spain*	37	B10
Campos Novos, *Brazil*	127	B5
Camprodón, *Spain*	32	C7
Camptonville, *U.S.A.*	116	F5
Camptown, *U.S.A.*	111	E8
Câmpulung, *Argeş, Romania*	43	E10
Câmpulung, *Suceava, Romania*	43	C10
Câmpuri, *Romania*	43	D11
Camrose, *Canada*	104	C6
Camsell Portage, *Canada*	105	B7
Çamyuva, *Turkey*	39	E12
Çan, *Turkey*	41	F11
Can Clavo, *Spain*	37	C7
Can Creu, *Spain*	37	C7
Can Gio, *Vietnam*	65	G6
Can Tho, *Vietnam*	65	G5
Canaan, *U.S.A.*	111	D11
Canada ■, *N. Amer.*	100	C10
Cañada de Gómez, *Argentina*	126	C3
Canadian, *U.S.A.*	113	H4
Canadian ➤, *U.S.A.*	113	H7
Canajoharie, *U.S.A.*	111	D10
Çanakkale, *Turkey*	41	F10
Çanakkale □, *Turkey*	41	F10
Çanakkale Boğazı, *Turkey*	41	F10
Canal Flats, *Canada*	104	C5
Canalejas, *Argentina*	126	D2
Canals, *Argentina*	126	C3
Canals, *Spain*	33	G4
Canandaigua, *U.S.A.*	110	D7
Canandaigua L., *U.S.A.*	110	D7
Cananea, *Mexico*	118	A2
Canarias, Is., *Atl. Oc.*	37	F4
Canarreos, Arch. de los, *Cuba*	120	B3
Canary Is. = Canarias, Is., *Atl. Oc.*	37	F4
Canaseraga, *U.S.A.*	110	D7
Canatlán, *Mexico*	118	C4
Canaveral, C., *U.S.A.*	109	L5
Cañaveruelas, *Spain*	32	E2
Canavieiras, *Brazil*	125	G11
Canberra, *Australia*	95	F4
Canby, *Calif., U.S.A.*	114	F3
Canby, *Minn., U.S.A.*	112	C6
Canby, *Oreg., U.S.A.*	116	E4
Cancale, *France*	18	D5
Canche ➤, *France*	19	B8
Cancún, *Mexico*	119	C7
Candanchu, *Spain*	32	C4
Çandarlı, *Turkey*	39	C8
Çandarlı Körfezi, *Turkey*	39	C8
Candas, *Spain*	34	B5
Candé, *France*	18	E5
Candela, *Italy*	31	A8
Candelaria, *Argentina*	127	B4
Candelaria, *Canary Is.*	37	F3
Candeleda, *Spain*	34	E5
Candelo, *Australia*	95	F4
Candia = Iráklion, *Greece*	36	D7
Candia, Sea of = Crete, Sea of, *Greece*	39	E7
Candle L., *Canada*	105	C7
Candlemas I., *Antarctica*	5	B1
Cando, *U.S.A.*	112	A5
Candon, *Phil.*	61	C4
Canea = Khaniá, *Greece*	36	D6
Canelli, *Italy*	28	D5
Canelones, *Uruguay*	127	C4
Canet-Plage, *France*	20	F7
Cañete, *Chile*	126	D1
Cañete, *Spain*	32	E3
Cañete de las Torres, *Spain*	35	H6
Cangas, *Spain*	34	C2
Cangas de Narcea, *Spain*	34	B4
Cangas de Onís, *Spain*	34	B5
Cangnan, *China*	59	D13
Canguaretama, *Brazil*	125	E11
Canguçu, *Brazil*	127	C5
Canguçu, Serra do, *Brazil*	127	C5
Cangwu, *China*	59	F8
Cangxi, *China*	58	B5
Cangyuan, *China*	58	F2
Cangzhou, *China*	56	E9
Caniapiscau ➤, *Canada*	103	A6
Caniapiscau, Rés. de, *Canada*	103	B6
Canicattì, *Italy*	30	E6
Canicattini Bagni, *Italy*	31	E8
Caniles, *Spain*	35	H8
Canim Lake, *Canada*	104	C4
Canindeyu □, *Paraguay*	127	A5
Canino, *Italy*	29	F8
Canisteo, *U.S.A.*	110	D7
Canisteo ➤, *U.S.A.*	110	D7
Cañitas, *Mexico*	118	C4
Cañizal, *Spain*	34	D5
Canjáyar, *Spain*	35	H8
Çankırı, *Turkey*	72	B5
Cankuzo, *Burundi*	86	C3
Canmore, *Canada*	104	C5
Cann River, *Australia*	95	F4
Canna, *U.K.*	14	D2
Cannanore, *India*	66	P9
Cannes, *France*	21	E11
Canning Town = Port Canning, *India*	69	H13
Cannington, *Canada*	110	B5
Cannóbio, *Italy*	28	B5
Cannock, *U.K.*	13	E5
Cannon Ball ➤, *U.S.A.*	112	B4
Cannondale Mt., *Australia*	94	D4
Cannonsville Reservoir, *U.S.A.*	111	D9
Cannonvale, *Australia*	94	C4
Canoas, *Brazil*	127	B5
Canoe L., *Canada*	105	B7
Canon City, *U.S.A.*	112	F2
Canora, *Canada*	105	C8
Canosa di Púglia, *Italy*	31	A9
Canowindra, *Australia*	95	E4
Canso, *Canada*	103	C7
Cantabria □, *Spain*	34	B7
Cantabria, Sierra de, *Spain*	32	C2
Cantabrian Mts. = Cantábrica, Cordillera, *Spain*	34	C5
Cantábrica, Cordillera, *Spain*	34	C5
Cantal □, *France*	20	C6
Cantal, Plomb du, *France*	20	C6
Cantanhede, *Portugal*	34	E2
Cantavieja, *Spain*	32	E4
Çantavir, *Serbia, Yug.*	42	E4
Cantemir, *Moldova*	43	D13
Canterbury, *Australia*	94	D3
Canterbury, *U.K.*	13	F9
Canterbury Bight, *N.Z.*	91	L3
Canterbury Plains, *N.Z.*	91	K3
Cantil, *U.S.A.*	117	K9
Cantillana, *Spain*	35	H5
Canton = Guangzhou, *China*	59	F9
Canton, *Ga., U.S.A.*	109	H3
Canton, *Ill., U.S.A.*	112	E9
Canton, *Miss., U.S.A.*	113	J9
Canton, *Mo., U.S.A.*	112	E9
Canton, *N.Y., U.S.A.*	111	B9
Canton, *Ohio, U.S.A.*	110	F3
Canton, *Pa., U.S.A.*	110	E8
Canton, *S. Dak., U.S.A.*	112	D6
Canton L., *U.S.A.*	113	G5
Cantù, *Italy*	28	C6
Canudos, *Brazil*	124	E7
Canumã ➤, *Brazil*	124	D7
Canutama, *Brazil*	124	E6
Canutillo, *U.S.A.*	115	L10
Canvey, *U.K.*	13	F8
Canyon, *U.S.A.*	113	H4
Canyonlands National Park, *U.S.A.*	115	G9
Canyonville, *U.S.A.*	114	E2
Cao Bang, *Vietnam*	58	F6
Cao He ➤, *China*	57	D13
Cao Lanh, *Vietnam*	65	G5
Cao Xian, *China*	56	G8
Cáorle, *Italy*	29	C9
Cap-aux-Meules, *Canada*	103	C7
Cap-Chat, *Canada*	103	C6
Cap-de-la-Madeleine, *Canada*	102	C5
Cap-Haïtien, *Haiti*	121	C5
Capac, *U.S.A.*	110	C2
Capácci, *Italy*	31	B8
Capánnori, *Italy*	28	E7
Capbreton, *France*	20	E2
Capdenac, *France*	20	D6
Capdepera, *Spain*	32	F8
Cape ➤, *Australia*	94	C4
Cape Barren I., *Australia*	94	G4
Cape Breton Highlands Nat. Park, *Canada*	103	C7
Cape Breton I., *Canada*	103	C7
Cape Charles, *U.S.A.*	108	G8
Cape Coast, *Ghana*	83	D4
Cape Coral, *U.S.A.*	109	M5
Cape Dorset, *Canada*	101	B12
Cape Fear ➤, *U.S.A.*	109	H6
Cape Girardeau, *U.S.A.*	113	G10
Cape May, *U.S.A.*	108	F8
Cape May Point, *U.S.A.*	108	F8
Cape Province, *S. Africa*	85	L3
Cape Tormentine, *Canada*	103	C7
Cape Town, *S. Africa*	88	E2
Cape Verde Is. ■, *Atl. Oc.*	77	E1
Cape Vincent, *U.S.A.*	111	B8
Cape York Peninsula, *Australia*	94	A3
Capela, *Brazil*	125	F11
Capella, *Australia*	94	C4
Capendu, *France*	20	E6
Capestang, *France*	20	E7
Capim ➤, *Brazil*	125	D9
Capistrello, *Italy*	29	G10
Capitan, *U.S.A.*	115	K11
Capitol Reef National Park, *U.S.A.*	115	G8
Capitola, *U.S.A.*	116	J5
Capizzi, *Italy*	31	E7
Capoche ➤, *Mozam.*	87	F3
Capoterra, *Italy*	30	C1
Cappadocia, *Turkey*	72	C6
Capraia, *Italy*	28	E6
Caprara, Pta., *Italy*	30	A1
Caprarola, *Italy*	29	F9
Capreol, *Canada*	102	C3
Caprera, *Italy*	30	A2
Capri, *Italy*	31	B7
Capricorn Group, *Australia*	94	C5
Capricorn Ra., *Australia*	92	D2
Caprino Veronese, *Italy*	28	C7
Caprivi Strip, *Namibia*	88	B3
Captain's Flat, *Australia*	95	F4
Captieux, *France*	20	D3
Caquetá ➤, *Colombia*	122	D4
Caracal, *Romania*	43	F9
Caracas, *Venezuela*	124	A5
Caracol, *Mato Grosso do Sul, Brazil*	126	A4
Caracol, *Piauí, Brazil*	125	E10
Caráglio, *Italy*	28	D4
Carajas, *Brazil*	125	E8
Carajás, Serra dos, *Brazil*	125	E8
Carangola, *Brazil*	127	A7
Caransebeş, *Romania*	42	E7
Carantec, *France*	18	D3
Caraquet, *Canada*	103	C6
Caras, *Peru*	124	E3
Caraş Severin □, *Romania*	42	E7
Caraşova, *Romania*	42	E6
Caratasca, L., *Honduras*	120	C3
Caratinga, *Brazil*	125	G10
Caraúbas, *Brazil*	125	E11
Caravaca = Caravaca de la Cruz, *Spain*	33	G3
Caravaca de la Cruz, *Spain*	33	G3
Caravággio, *Italy*	28	C6
Caravela, *Guinea-Biss.*	82	C1
Caravelas, *Brazil*	125	G11
Caraveli, *Peru*	124	G4
Caràzinho, *Brazil*	127	B5
Carballino = O Carballiño, *Spain*	34	C2
Carballo, *Spain*	34	B2
Carberry, *Canada*	105	D9
Carbó, *Mexico*	118	B2
Carbonara, C., *Italy*	30	C2
Carbondale, *Colo., U.S.A.*	114	G10
Carbondale, *Ill., U.S.A.*	113	G10
Carbondale, *Pa., U.S.A.*	111	E9
Carbonear, *Canada*	103	C9
Carboneras, *Spain*	33	J3
Carboneras de Guadazaón, *Spain*	32	F3
Carbónia, *Italy*	30	C1
Carcabuey, *Spain*	35	H6
Carcagente = Carcaixent, *Spain*	33	F4
Carcaixent, *Spain*	33	F4
Carcajou, *Canada*	104	B5
Carcar, *Phil.*	61	F5
Carcarana ➤, *Argentina*	126	C3
Carcasse, C., *Haiti*	121	C5
Carcassonne, *France*	20	E6
Carcross, *Canada*	104	A2
Çardak, *Çanakkale, Turkey*	41	F10
Çardak, *Denizli, Turkey*	39	D11
Cardamon Hills, *India*	66	Q10
Cardeña, *Spain*	35	G6
Cárdenas, *Cuba*	120	B3
Cárdenas, *San Luis Potosí, Mexico*	119	C5
Cárdenas, *Tabasco, Mexico*	119	D6
Cardenete, *Spain*	32	F3
Cardiff, *U.K.*	13	F4
Cardiff □, *U.K.*	13	F4
Cardiff-by-the-Sea, *U.S.A.*	117	M9
Cardigan, *U.K.*	13	E3
Cardigan B., *U.K.*	13	E3
Cardinal, *Canada*	111	B9
Cardona, *Spain*	32	D6
Cardona, *Uruguay*	126	C4
Cardoner ➤, *Spain*	32	D6
Cardoso, Ilha do, *Brazil*	127	B5
Cardston, *Canada*	104	D6
Cardwell, *Australia*	94	B4
Careen L., *Canada*	105	B7
Carei, *Romania*	42	C7
Careme = Ciremai, *Indonesia*	63	G13
Carentan, *France*	18	C5
Carey, *U.S.A.*	114	E7
Carey, L., *Australia*	93	E3
Carey L., *Canada*	105	A8
Careysburg, *Liberia*	82	D2
Cargèse, *France*	21	F12
Carhaix-Plouguer, *France*	18	D3
Carhué, *Argentina*	126	D3
Caria, *Turkey*	39	D10
Cariacica, *Brazil*	125	H10
Cariati, *Italy*	31	C9
Caribbean Sea, *W. Indies*	121	D5
Cariboo Mts., *Canada*	104	C4
Caribou, *U.S.A.*	109	B12
Caribou ➤, *Man., Canada*	105	B10
Caribou ➤, *N.W.T., Canada*	104	A3
Caribou I., *Canada*	102	C2
Caribou Is., *Canada*	104	A6
Caribou L., *Man., Canada*	105	B9
Caribou L., *Ont., Canada*	102	B2
Caribou Mts., *Canada*	104	B5
Carichic, *Mexico*	118	B3
Carigara, *Phil.*	61	F6
Carignan, *France*	19	C12
Carignano, *Italy*	28	D4
Carillo, *Mexico*	118	B4
Carinda, *Australia*	95	E4
Cariñena, *Spain*	32	D3
Carinhanha, *Brazil*	125	F10
Carinhanha ➤, *Brazil*	125	F10
Carini, *Italy*	30	D6
Cariño, *Spain*	34	B3
Carínola, *Italy*	30	A6
Carinthia = Kärnten □, *Austria*	26	E6
Caripito, *Venezuela*	124	A6
Carlbrod = Dimitrovgrad, *Serbia, Yug.*	40	C6
Carlet, *Spain*	33	F4
Carleton Place, *Canada*	102	C4
Carletonville, *S. Africa*	88	D4
Cârlibaba, *Romania*	43	C10
Carlin, *U.S.A.*	114	F5
Carlingford L., *U.K.*	15	B5

Český Brod

Carlinville, *U.S.A.* 112 **F10**
Carlisle, *U.K.* 12 **C5**
Carlisle, *U.S.A.* 110 **F7**
Carlit, Pic, *France* 20 **F5**
Carloforte, *Italy* 30 **C1**
Carlos Casares, *Argentina* 126 **D3**
Carlos Tejedor, *Argentina* 126 **D3**
Carlow, *Ireland* 15 **D5**
Carlow □, *Ireland* 15 **D5**
Carlsbad, *Calif., U.S.A.* 117 **M9**
Carlsbad, *N. Mex., U.S.A.* 113 **J2**
Carlsbad Caverns National Park, *U.S.A.* 113 **J2**
Carluke, *U.K.* 14 **F5**
Carlyle, *Canada* 105 **D8**
Carmacks, *Canada* 100 **B6**
Carmagnola, *Italy* 28 **D4**
Carman, *Canada* 105 **D9**
Carmarthen, *U.K.* 13 **F3**
Carmarthen B., *U.K.* 13 **F3**
Carmarthenshire □, *U.K.* 13 **F3**
Carmaux, *France* 20 **D6**
Carmel, *U.S.A.* 111 **E11**
Carmel-by-the-Sea, *U.S.A.* 116 **J5**
Carmel Valley, *U.S.A.* 116 **J5**
Carmelo, *Uruguay* 126 **C4**
Carmen, *Colombia* 124 **B3**
Carmen, *Paraguay* 127 **B4**
Carmen →, *Mexico* 118 **A3**
Carmen, I., *Mexico* 118 **B2**
Carmen de Patagones, *Argentina* 128 **E4**
Cármenes, *Spain* 34 **C5**
Carmensa, *Argentina* 126 **D2**
Carmi, *Canada* 104 **D5**
Carmi, *U.S.A.* 108 **F1**
Carmichael, *U.S.A.* 116 **G5**
Carmila, *Australia* 94 **C4**
Carmona, *Costa Rica* 120 **E2**
Carmona, *Spain* 35 **H5**
Carn Ban, *U.K.* 14 **D4**
Carn Eige, *U.K.* 14 **D3**
Carnamah, *Australia* 93 **E2**
Carnarvon, *Australia* 93 **D1**
Carnarvon, *S. Africa* 88 **E3**
Carnarvon Ra., *Queens., Australia* 94 **D4**
Carnarvon Ra., *W. Austral., Australia* 93 **E3**
Carnation, *U.S.A.* 116 **C5**
Carndonagh, *Ireland* 15 **A4**
Carnduff, *Canada* 105 **D8**
Carnegie, *U.S.A.* 110 **F4**
Carnegie, L., *Australia* 93 **E3**
Carnic Alps = Karnische Alpen, *Europe* 26 **E6**
Carniche Alpi = Karnische Alpen, *Europe* 26 **E6**
Carnot, *C.A.R.* 84 **D3**
Carnot, C., *Australia* 95 **E2**
Carnot B., *Australia* 92 **C3**
Carnoustie, *U.K.* 14 **E6**
Carnsore Pt., *Ireland* 15 **D5**
Caro, *U.S.A.* 108 **D4**
Carol City, *U.S.A.* 109 **N5**
Carolina, *Brazil* 125 **E9**
Carolina, *Puerto Rico* 121 **C6**
Carolina, *S. Africa* 89 **D5**
Caroline I., *Kiribati* 97 **H12**
Caroline Is., *Micronesia* 52 **J17**
Caroni →, *Venezuela* 124 **B6**
Caroníe = Nébrodi, Monti, *Italy* 31 **E7**
Caroona, *Australia* 95 **E5**
Carpathians, *Europe* 6 **F10**
Carpaţii Meridionali, *Romania* 43 **E9**
Carpentaria, G. of, *Australia* 94 **A2**
Carpentras, *France* 21 **D9**
Carpi, *Italy* 28 **D7**
Cărpineni, *Moldova* 43 **D13**
Carpinteria, *U.S.A.* 117 **L7**
Carpio, *Spain* 34 **D5**
Carr Boyd Ra., *Australia* 92 **C4**
Carrabelle, *U.S.A.* 109 **L3**
Carral, *Spain* 34 **B2**
Carranza, Presa V., *Mexico* 118 **B4**
Carrara, *Italy* 28 **D7**
Carrascal, *Phil.* 61 **G6**
Carrascosa del Campo, *Spain* 32 **E2**
Carrauntoohill, *Ireland* 15 **D2**
Carrick-on-Shannon, *Ireland* 15 **C3**
Carrick-on-Suir, *Ireland* 15 **D4**
Carrickfergus, *U.K.* 15 **B6**
Carrickmacross, *Ireland* 15 **C5**
Carrieton, *Australia* 95 **E2**
Carrington, *U.S.A.* 112 **B5**
Carrión →, *Spain* 34 **D6**
Carrión de los Condes, *Spain* 34 **C6**
Carrizal Bajo, *Chile* 126 **B1**
Carrizalillo, *Chile* 126 **B1**
Carrizo Cr. →, *U.S.A.* 113 **G3**
Carrizo Springs, *U.S.A.* 113 **L5**
Carrizozo, *U.S.A.* 115 **K11**
Carroll, *U.S.A.* 112 **D7**
Carrollton, *Ga., U.S.A.* 109 **J3**
Carrollton, *Ill., U.S.A.* 112 **F9**
Carrollton, *Ky., U.S.A.* 108 **F3**
Carrollton, *Mo., U.S.A.* 112 **F8**
Carrollton, *Ohio, U.S.A.* 110 **F3**
Carron →, *U.K.* 14 **D4**
Carron, L., *U.K.* 14 **D3**
Carrot →, *Canada* 105 **C8**
Carrot River, *Canada* 105 **C8**
Carrouges, *France* 18 **D6**
Carrù, *Italy* 28 **D4**
Carruthers, *Canada* 105 **C7**
Carsa Dek, *Ethiopia* 81 **F4**
Çarşamba, *Turkey* 72 **B7**
Carsóli, *Italy* 29 **F10**
Carson, *Calif., U.S.A.* 117 **M8**
Carson, *N. Dak., U.S.A.* 112 **B4**
Carson →, *U.S.A.* 116 **F8**
Carson City, *U.S.A.* 116 **F7**
Carson Sink, *U.S.A.* 114 **G4**
Cartagena, *Colombia* 124 **A3**
Cartagena, *Spain* 33 **H4**
Cartago, *Colombia* 124 **C3**
Cartago, *Costa Rica* 120 **E3**
Cártama, *Spain* 35 **J6**
Cartaxo, *Portugal* 35 **F2**
Cartaya, *Spain* 35 **H3**
Cartersville, *U.S.A.* 109 **H3**
Carterton, *N.Z.* 91 **J5**
Carthage, *Tunisia* 30 **F3**
Carthage, *Ill., U.S.A.* 112 **E9**
Carthage, *Mo., U.S.A.* 113 **G7**
Carthage, *N.Y., U.S.A.* 108 **D8**
Carthage, *Tex., U.S.A.* 113 **J7**
Cartier I., *Australia* 92 **B3**
Cartwright, *Canada* 103 **B8**
Caruaru, *Brazil* 125 **E11**
Carúpano, *Venezuela* 124 **A6**
Caruthersville, *U.S.A.* 113 **G10**
Carvin, *France* 19 **B9**
Carvoeiro, *Brazil* 124 **D6**
Carvoeiro, C., *Portugal* 35 **F1**
Cary, *U.S.A.* 109 **H6**
Casa Branca, *Portugal* 35 **G2**
Casa Grande, *U.S.A.* 115 **K8**
Casablanca, *Chile* 126 **C1**
Casablanca, *Morocco* 78 **B4**
Casacalenda, *Italy* 29 **G11**
Casalbordino, *Italy* 29 **F11**
Casale Monferrato, *Italy* 28 **C5**
Casalmaggiore, *Italy* 28 **D7**
Casalpusterlengo, *Italy* 28 **C6**
Casamance →, *Senegal* 82 **C1**
Casarano, *Italy* 31 **B11**
Casares, *Spain* 35 **J5**
Casas Ibáñez, *Spain* 33 **F3**
Casasimarro, *Spain* 33 **F2**
Casatejada, *Spain* 34 **F5**
Casavieja, *Spain* 34 **E6**
Cascade, *Idaho, U.S.A.* 114 **D5**
Cascade, *Mont., U.S.A.* 114 **C8**
Cascade Locks, *U.S.A.* 116 **E5**
Cascade Ra., *U.S.A.* 116 **D5**
Cascade Reservoir, *U.S.A.* 114 **D5**
Cascais, *Portugal* 35 **G1**
Cascavel, *Brazil* 127 **A5**
Cáscina, *Italy* 28 **E7**
Casco B., *U.S.A.* 109 **D10**
Caselle Torinese, *Italy* 28 **C4**
Caserta, *Italy* 31 **A7**
Cashel, *Ireland* 15 **D4**
Casiguran, *Phil.* 61 **C5**
Casilda, *Argentina* 126 **C3**
Casimcea, *Romania* 43 **F13**
Casino, *Australia* 95 **D5**
Casiquiare →, *Venezuela* 124 **C5**
Čáslav, *Czech Rep.* 26 **B8**
Casma, *Peru* 124 **E3**
Casmalia, *U.S.A.* 117 **L6**
Cásola Valsénio, *Italy* 29 **D8**
Cásoli, *Italy* 29 **F11**
Caspe, *Spain* 32 **D4**
Casper, *U.S.A.* 114 **E10**
Caspian Depression, *Eurasia* 49 **G9**
Caspian Sea, *Eurasia* 50 **E6**
Cass Lake, *U.S.A.* 112 **B7**
Cassà de la Selva, *Spain* 32 **D7**
Cassadaga, *U.S.A.* 110 **D5**
Cassano allo Iónio, *Italy* 31 **C9**
Casse, Grande, *France* 21 **C10**
Cassel, *France* 19 **B9**
Casselman, *Canada* 111 **A9**
Casselton, *U.S.A.* 112 **B6**
Cassiar, *Canada* 104 **B3**
Cassiar Mts., *Canada* 104 **B2**
Cassino, *Italy* 30 **A6**
Cassis, *France* 21 **E9**
Cassville, *U.S.A.* 113 **G8**
Castagneto Carducci, *Italy* 28 **E7**
Castaic, *U.S.A.* 117 **L8**
Castalia, *U.S.A.* 110 **E2**
Castanhal, *Brazil* 125 **D9**
Castéggio, *Italy* 28 **C6**
Castejón de Monegros, *Spain* 32 **D4**
Castèl di Sangro, *Italy* 29 **G11**
Castèl San Giovanni, *Italy* 28 **C6**
Castèl San Pietro Terme, *Italy* 29 **D8**
Castelbuono, *Italy* 31 **E7**
Castelfidardo, *Italy* 29 **E10**
Castelfiorentino, *Italy* 28 **E7**
Castelfranco Emília, *Italy* 28 **D8**
Castelfranco Véneto, *Italy* 29 **C8**
Casteljaloux, *France* 20 **D4**
Castellabate, *Italy* 31 **B7**
Castellammare, G. di, *Italy* 30 **D5**
Castellammare del Golfo, *Italy* 30 **D5**
Castellammare di Stábia, *Italy* 31 **B7**
Castellamonte, *Italy* 28 **C4**
Castellane, *France* 21 **E10**
Castellaneta, *Italy* 31 **B9**
Castelli, *Argentina* 126 **D4**
Castelló de la Plana, *Spain* 32 **F4**
Castellón de la Plana □, *Spain* 32 **E4**
Castellote, *Spain* 32 **E4**
Castelmáuro, *Italy* 29 **G11**
Castelnau-de-Médoc, *France* 20 **C3**
Castelnau-Magnoac, *France* 20 **E4**
Castelnaudary, *France* 20 **E5**
Castelnovo ne' Monti, *Italy* 28 **D7**
Castelnuovo di Val di Cécina, *Italy* 28 **E7**
Castelo, *Brazil* 127 **A7**
Castelo Branco, *Portugal* 34 **F3**
Castelo Branco □, *Portugal* 34 **F3**
Castelo de Paiva, *Portugal* 34 **D2**
Castelo de Vide, *Portugal* 35 **F3**
Castelsardo, *Italy* 30 **B1**
Castelsarrasin, *France* 20 **D5**
Casteltérmini, *Italy* 30 **E6**
Castelvetrano, *Italy* 30 **E5**
Casterton, *Australia* 95 **F3**
Castets, *France* 20 **E2**
Castiglion Fiorentino, *Italy* 29 **E8**
Castiglione del Lago, *Italy* 29 **E9**
Castiglione della Pescáia, *Italy* 28 **F7**
Castiglione delle Stiviere, *Italy* 28 **C7**
Castilblanco, *Spain* 35 **F5**
Castile, *U.S.A.* 110 **D6**
Castilla, Playa de, *Spain* 35 **J4**
Castilla-La Mancha □, *Spain* 6 **H5**
Castilla y Leon □, *Spain* 34 **D6**
Castillo de Locubín, *Spain* 35 **H7**
Castillon-en-Couserans, *France* 20 **F5**
Castillonès, *France* 20 **D4**
Castillos, *Uruguay* 127 **C5**
Castle Dale, *U.S.A.* 114 **G8**
Castle Douglas, *U.K.* 14 **G5**
Castle Rock, *Colo., U.S.A.* 112 **F2**
Castle Rock, *Wash., U.S.A.* 116 **D4**
Castlebar, *Ireland* 15 **C2**
Castleblaney, *Ireland* 15 **B5**
Castlederg, *U.K.* 15 **B4**
Castleford, *U.K.* 12 **D6**
Castlegar, *Canada* 104 **D5**
Castlemaine, *Australia* 95 **F3**
Castlepollard, *Ireland* 15 **C4**
Castlerea, *Ireland* 15 **C3**
Castlereagh →, *Australia* 95 **E4**
Castlereagh B., *Australia* 94 **A2**
Castleton, *U.S.A.* 111 **C11**
Castletown, *U.K.* 12 **C3**
Castletown Bearhaven, *Ireland* 15 **E2**
Castor, *Canada* 104 **C6**
Castor →, *Canada* 102 **B4**
Castorland, *U.S.A.* 111 **C9**
Castres, *France* 20 **E6**
Castricum, *Neths.* 17 **B4**
Castries, *St. Lucia* 121 **D7**
Castril, *Spain* 35 **H8**
Castro, *Brazil* 127 **A6**
Castro, *Chile* 128 **E2**
Castro Alves, *Brazil* 125 **F11**
Castro del Río, *Spain* 35 **H6**
Castro-Urdiales, *Spain* 34 **B7**
Castro Verde, *Portugal* 35 **H2**
Castrojeriz, *Spain* 34 **C6**
Castropol, *Spain* 34 **B4**
Castroreale, *Italy* 31 **D8**
Castrovíllari, *Italy* 31 **C9**
Castroville, *U.S.A.* 116 **J5**
Castuera, *Spain* 35 **G5**
Çat, *Turkey* 73 **C9**
Cat Ba, Dao, *Vietnam* 64 **B6**
Cat I., *Bahamas* 121 **B4**
Cat L., *Canada* 102 **B1**
Cat Lake, *Canada* 102 **B1**
Čata, *Slovak Rep.* 27 **D11**
Catacamas, *Honduras* 120 **D2**
Cataguases, *Brazil* 127 **A7**
Çatak, *Turkey* 73 **C10**
Catalão, *Brazil* 125 **G9**
Çatalca, *Turkey* 41 **E12**
Catalina, *Canada* 103 **C9**
Catalina, *Chile* 126 **B2**
Catalina, *U.S.A.* 115 **K8**
Catalonia = Cataluña □, *Spain* 32 **D6**
Cataluña □, *Spain* 32 **D6**
Çatalzeytin, *Turkey* 72 **B6**
Catamarca, *Argentina* 126 **B2**
Catamarca □, *Argentina* 126 **B2**
Catanauan, *Phil.* 61 **E5**
Catanduanes □, *Phil.* 61 **E6**
Catanduva, *Brazil* 127 **A6**
Catánia, *Italy* 31 **E8**
Catánia, G. di, *Italy* 31 **E8**
Catanzaro, *Italy* 31 **D9**
Catarman, *Phil.* 61 **E6**
Catbalogan, *Phil.* 61 **F6**
Cateel, *Phil.* 61 **H7**
Catembe, *Mozam.* 89 **D5**
Caterham, *U.K.* 13 **F7**
Cathcart, *S. Africa* 88 **E4**
Cathlamet, *U.S.A.* 116 **D3**
Catio, *Guinea-Biss.* 82 **C1**
Catlettsburg, *U.S.A.* 108 **F4**
Çatma Dağı, *Turkey* 39 **C11**
Catoche, C., *Mexico* 119 **C7**
Cátria, Mte., *Italy* 29 **E9**
Catriló, *Argentina* 126 **D3**
Catrimani, *Brazil* 124 **C6**
Catrimani →, *Brazil* 124 **C6**
Catskill, *U.S.A.* 111 **D11**
Catskill Mts., *U.S.A.* 111 **D10**
Catt, Mt., *Australia* 94 **A1**
Cattaraugus, *U.S.A.* 110 **D6**
Cattólica, *Italy* 29 **E9**
Cattólica Eraclea, *Italy* 30 **E6**
Catuala, *Angola* 88 **B2**
Catuane, *Mozam.* 89 **D5**
Catur, *Mozam.* 87 **E4**
Catwick Is., *Vietnam* 65 **G7**
Cauca →, *Colombia* 124 **B4**
Caucaia, *Brazil* 125 **D11**
Caucasus Mountains, *Eurasia* 49 **J7**
Caudete, *Spain* 33 **G3**
Caudry, *France* 19 **B10**
Caulnes, *France* 18 **D4**
Caulónia, *Italy* 31 **D9**
Caungula, *Angola* 84 **F3**
Cauquenes, *Chile* 126 **D1**
Caura →, *Venezuela* 124 **B6**
Cauresi →, *Mozam.* 87 **F3**
Căuşani, *Moldova* 43 **D14**
Causapscal, *Canada* 103 **C6**
Caussade, *France* 20 **D5**
Causse-Méjean, *France* 20 **D7**
Cauterets, *France* 20 **F3**
Cauvery →, *India* 66 **P11**
Caux, Pays de, *France* 18 **C7**
Cava de' Tirreni, *Italy* 31 **B7**
Cávado →, *Portugal* 34 **D2**
Cavaillon, *France* 21 **E9**
Cavalaire-sur-Mer, *France* 21 **E10**
Cavalese, *Italy* 29 **B8**
Cavalier, *U.S.A.* 112 **A6**
Cavalla = Cavally →, *Africa* 82 **E3**
Cavalleria, C. de, *Spain* 37 **A11**
Cavallo, I. de, *France* 21 **G13**
Cavally →, *Africa* 82 **E3**
Cavan, *Ireland* 15 **B4**
Cavan □, *Ireland* 15 **C4**
Cavárzere, *Italy* 29 **C9**
Çavdarhisar, *Turkey* 39 **B11**
Çavdır, *Turkey* 39 **D11**
Cave Creek, *U.S.A.* 115 **K7**
Cavenagh Ra., *Australia* 93 **E4**
Cavendish, *Australia* 95 **F3**
Caviana, I., *Brazil* 125 **C8**
Cavite, *Phil.* 61 **D4**
Cavnic, *Romania* 43 **C8**
Cavour, *Italy* 28 **D4**
Cavtat, *Croatia* 40 **D2**
Cawndilla L., *Australia* 95 **E3**
Cawnpore = Kanpur, *India* 69 **F9**
Caxias, *Brazil* 125 **D10**
Caxias do Sul, *Brazil* 127 **B5**
Çay, *Turkey* 72 **C4**
Cay Sal Bank, *Bahamas* 120 **B4**
Cayambe, *Ecuador* 124 **C3**
Çaycuma, *Turkey* 72 **B5**
Çayeli, *Turkey* 73 **B9**
Cayenne, *Fr. Guiana* 125 **B8**
Caygören Barajı, *Turkey* 39 **B10**
Cayiralan, *Turkey* 72 **C6**
Caylus, *France* 20 **D5**
Cayman Brac, *Cayman Is.* 120 **C4**
Cayman Is. ■, *W. Indies* 120 **C3**
Cayo Romano, *Cuba* 120 **B4**
Cayres, *France* 20 **D7**
Cayuga, *Canada* 110 **D5**
Cayuga, *U.S.A.* 111 **D8**
Cayuga L., *U.S.A.* 111 **D8**
Cazalla de la Sierra, *Spain* 35 **H5**
Căzăneşti, *Romania* 43 **F12**
Cazaubon, *France* 20 **E3**
Cazaux et de Sanguinet, Étang de, *France* 20 **D2**
Cazenovia, *U.S.A.* 111 **D9**
Cazères, *France* 20 **E5**
Cazin, *Bos.-H.* 29 **D12**
Čazma, *Croatia* 29 **C13**
Cazombo, *Angola* 85 **G4**
Cazorla, *Spain* 35 **H7**
Cazorla, Sierra de, *Spain* 35 **G8**
Cea →, *Spain* 34 **C5**
Ceamurlia de Jos, *Romania* 43 **F13**
Ceanannus Mor, *Ireland* 15 **C5**
Ceará = Fortaleza, *Brazil* 125 **D11**
Ceará □, *Brazil* 125 **E11**
Ceará Mirim, *Brazil* 125 **E11**
Ceauru, L., *Romania* 43 **F8**
Cebaco, I. de, *Panama* 120 **E3**
Cebollar, *Argentina* 126 **B2**
Cebollera, Sierra de, *Spain* 32 **D2**
Cebreros, *Spain* 34 **E6**
Cebu, *Phil.* 61 **F5**
Čečava, *Bos.-H.* 42 **F2**
Ceccano, *Italy* 30 **A6**
Cece, *Hungary* 42 **D3**
Cechi, *Ivory C.* 82 **D4**
Cecil Plains, *Australia* 95 **D5**
Cécina, *Italy* 28 **E7**
Cécina →, *Italy* 28 **E7**
Ceclavín, *Spain* 34 **F4**
Cedar →, *U.S.A.* 112 **E9**
Cedar City, *U.S.A.* 115 **H7**
Cedar Creek Reservoir, *U.S.A.* 113 **J6**
Cedar Falls, *Iowa, U.S.A.* 112 **D8**
Cedar Falls, *Wash., U.S.A.* 116 **C5**
Cedar Key, *U.S.A.* 109 **L4**
Cedar L., *Canada* 105 **C9**
Cedar Rapids, *U.S.A.* 112 **E9**
Cedartown, *U.S.A.* 109 **H3**
Cedarvale, *Canada* 104 **B3**
Cedarville, *S. Africa* 89 **E4**
Cedeira, *Spain* 34 **B2**
Cedral, *Mexico* 118 **C4**
Cedrino →, *Italy* 30 **B2**
Cedro, *Brazil* 125 **E11**
Cedros, I. de, *Mexico* 118 **B1**
Ceduna, *Australia* 95 **E1**
Cedynia, *Poland* 45 **F1**
Cée, *Spain* 34 **C1**
Cefalù, *Italy* 31 **D7**
Cega →, *Spain* 34 **D6**
Cegléd, *Hungary* 42 **C4**
Céglie Messápico, *Italy* 31 **B10**
Cehegín, *Spain* 33 **G3**
Ceheng, *China* 58 **E5**
Cehu-Silvaniei, *Romania* 43 **C8**
Ceica, *Romania* 42 **D7**
Ceira →, *Portugal* 34 **E2**
Čelákovice, *Czech Rep.* 26 **A7**
Celano, *Italy* 29 **F10**
Celanova, *Spain* 34 **C3**
Celaya, *Mexico* 118 **C4**
Celebes Sea, *Indonesia* 63 **D6**
Čelić, *Bos.-H.* 42 **F3**
Celina, *U.S.A.* 108 **E3**
Celinac, *Bos.-H.* 42 **F2**
Celje, *Slovenia* 29 **B12**
Celldömölk, *Hungary* 42 **C2**
Celle, *Germany* 24 **C6**
Celorico da Beira, *Portugal* 34 **E3**
Çeltikçi, *Turkey* 39 **D12**
Çemişgezek, *Turkey* 73 **C8**
Cenderwasih, Teluk, *Indonesia* 63 **E9**
Cengong, *China* 58 **D7**
Ceno →, *Italy* 28 **D7**
Centallo, *Italy* 28 **D4**
Centelles, *Spain* 32 **D7**
Center, *N. Dak., U.S.A.* 112 **B4**
Center, *Tex., U.S.A.* 113 **K7**
Centerburg, *U.S.A.* 110 **F2**
Centerville, *Calif., U.S.A.* 116 **J7**
Centerville, *Iowa, U.S.A.* 112 **E8**
Centerville, *Pa., U.S.A.* 110 **F5**
Centerville, *Tenn., U.S.A.* 109 **H2**
Centerville, *Tex., U.S.A.* 113 **K7**
Cento, *Italy* 29 **D8**
Central □, *Ghana* 83 **D4**
Central □, *Kenya* 86 **C4**
Central □, *Malawi* 87 **E3**
Central □, *Zambia* 87 **E2**
Central, Cordillera, *Colombia* 122 **C3**
Central, Cordillera, *Costa Rica* 120 **D3**
Central, Cordillera, *Dom. Rep.* 121 **C5**
Central, Cordillera, *Phil.* 61 **C4**
Central African Rep. ■, *Africa* 84 **C4**
Central America, *America* 98 **H11**
Central Butte, *Canada* 105 **C7**
Central City, *Colo., U.S.A.* 114 **G11**
Central City, *Ky., U.S.A.* 108 **G2**
Central City, *Nebr., U.S.A.* 112 **E6**
Central I., *Kenya* 86 **B4**
Central Makran Range, *Pakistan* 66 **F4**
Central Patricia, *Canada* 102 **B1**
Central Point, *U.S.A.* 114 **E2**
Central Russian Uplands, *Europe* 6 **E13**
Central Siberian Plateau, *Russia* 52 **C14**
Central Square, *U.S.A.* 111 **C8**
Centralia, *Ill., U.S.A.* 112 **F10**
Centralia, *Mo., U.S.A.* 112 **F8**
Centralia, *Wash., U.S.A.* 116 **D4**
Cenxi, *China* 59 **F8**
Ceotina →, *Bos.-H.* 40 **C2**
Cephalonia = Kefallinía, *Greece* 38 **C2**
Čepin, *Croatia* 42 **E3**
Ceprano, *Italy* 30 **A6**
Ceptura, *Romania* 43 **E11**
Cepu, *Indonesia* 63 **G14**
Ceram = Seram, *Indonesia* 63 **E7**
Ceram Sea = Seram Sea, *Indonesia* 63 **E7**
Cerbère, *France* 20 **F7**
Cerbicales, Is., *France* 21 **G13**
Cercal, *Portugal* 35 **H2**
Cerdaña, *Spain* 32 **C6**
Cère →, *France* 20 **D5**
Cerea, *Italy* 29 **C8**
Ceredigion □, *U.K.* 13 **E3**
Ceres, *Argentina* 126 **B3**
Ceres, *S. Africa* 88 **E2**
Ceres, *U.S.A.* 116 **H6**
Céret, *France* 20 **F6**
Cergy, *France* 19 **C9**
Cerignola, *Italy* 31 **A8**
Cerigo = Kíthira, *Greece* 38 **E5**
Cérilly, *France* 19 **F9**
Cerisiers, *France* 19 **D10**
Cerizay, *France* 18 **F6**
Çerkeş, *Turkey* 72 **B5**
Çerkezköy, *Turkey* 41 **E12**
Cerknica, *Slovenia* 29 **C11**
Cerkovica, *Bulgaria* 41 **C8**
Cermerno, *Serbia, Yug.* 40 **C4**
Çermik, *Turkey* 73 **C8**
Cerna, *Romania* 43 **E13**
Cerna →, *Romania* 43 **F8**
Cernavodă, *Romania* 43 **F13**
Cernay, *France* 19 **E14**
Cernik, *Croatia* 42 **E2**
Cerralvo, I., *Mexico* 118 **C3**
Cërrik, *Albania* 40 **E3**
Cerritos, *Mexico* 118 **C4**
Cerro Chato, *Uruguay* 127 **C4**
Certaldo, *Italy* 28 **E8**
Cervaro →, *Italy* 31 **A8**
Cervati, Monte, *Italy* 31 **B8**
Cerventes, *Australia* 93 **F2**
Cervera, *Spain* 32 **D6**
Cervera de Pisuerga, *Spain* 34 **C6**
Cervera del Río Alhama, *Spain* 32 **C3**
Cervéteri, *Italy* 29 **F9**
Cérvia, *Italy* 29 **D9**
Cervignano del Friuli, *Italy* 29 **C10**
Cervinara, *Italy* 31 **A7**
Cervione, *France* 21 **F13**
Cervo, *Spain* 34 **B3**
Cesarò, *Italy* 31 **E7**
Cesena, *Italy* 29 **D9**
Cesenático, *Italy* 29 **D9**
Cēsis, *Latvia* 9 **H21**
Česká Lípa, *Czech Rep.* 26 **A7**
Česká Třebová, *Czech Rep.* 27 **B9**
České Budějovice, *Czech Rep.* 26 **C7**
České Velenice, *Czech Rep.* 26 **C7**
Českobudějovický □, *Czech Rep.* 26 **B7**
Českomoravská Vrchovina, *Czech Rep.* 26 **B8**
Český Brod, *Czech Rep.* 26 **A7**

Český Krumlov, Czech Rep. ... 26 C7
Český Těšín, Czech Rep. 27 B11
Česma →, Croatia 29 C13
Çeşme, Turkey 39 C8
Cessnock, Australia 95 E5
Cesson-Sévigné, France 18 D5
Cestas, France 20 D3
Cestos →, Liberia 82 D3
Cetate, Romania 42 F8
Cetin Grad, Croatia 29 C12
Cetina →, Croatia 29 E13
Cetinje, Montenegro, Yug. 40 D2
Cetraro, Italy 31 C8
Ceuta, N. Afr. 78 A4
Ceva, Italy 28 D5
Cévennes, France 20 D7
Ceyhan, Turkey 70 B2
Ceyhan →, Turkey 72 D6
Ceylânpınar, Turkey 73 D9
Ceylon = Sri Lanka ■, Asia .. 66 R12
Cēze →, France 21 D8
Cha-am, Thailand 64 F2
Cha Pa, Vietnam 64 A4
Chabanais, France 20 C4
Chabeuil, France 21 D9
Chablais, France 19 F13
Chablis, France 19 E10
Chacabuco, Argentina 126 C3
Chachoengsao, Thailand 64 F3
Chachapoyas, Peru 124 E3
Chachran, Pakistan 66 E7
Chachro, Pakistan 68 G4
Chaco □, Argentina 126 B3
Chaco □, Paraguay 126 B4
Chaco →, U.S.A. 115 H9
Chaco Austral, S. Amer. 128 B4
Chaco Boreal, S. Amer. 124 H6
Chaco Central, S. Amer. 128 A4
Chacon, C., U.S.A. 104 C2
Chad ■, Africa 79 F8
Chad, L. = Tchad, L., Chad .. 79 F8
Chadan, Russia 51 D10
Chadileuvú →, Argentina .. 126 D2
Chadiza, Zambia 87 E3
Chadron, U.S.A. 112 D3
Chadyr-Lunga = Ciadâr-Lunga, Moldova 43 D13
Chae Hom, Thailand 64 C2
Chaem →, Thailand 64 C2
Chaeryŏng, N. Korea 57 E13
Chagai Hills = Chāh Gay, Afghan. 66 E3
Chagda, Russia 51 D14
Chaghcharān, Afghan. 66 B4
Chagny, France 19 F11
Chagoda, Russia 46 C8
Chagos Arch., Ind. Oc. 52 K11
Chagrin Falls, U.S.A. 110 E3
Chāh Ākhvor, Iran 71 C8
Chāh Bahar, Iran 71 E9
Chāh-e Kavīr, Iran 71 C8
Chāh Gay, Afghan. 66 E3
Chahar Burjak, Afghan. 66 D3
Chahār Mahāll va Bakhtīarī □, Iran 71 C6
Chaibasa, India 67 H14
Chaillé-les-Marais, France .. 20 B2
Chainat, Thailand 64 E3
Chaiya, Thailand 65 H2
Chaj Doab, Pakistan 68 C5
Chajari, Argentina 126 C4
Chak Amru, Pakistan 68 C6
Chaka, Sudan 81 G3
Chakar →, Pakistan 68 E3
Chakari, Zimbabwe 89 B4
Chake Chake, Tanzania 86 D4
Chakhānsūr, Afghan. 66 D3
Chakonipau, L., Canada 103 A6
Chakradharpur, India 69 H11
Chakrata, India 68 D7
Chakwal, Pakistan 68 C5
Chala, Peru 124 G4
Chalais, France 20 C4
Chalchihuites, Mexico 118 C4
Chalcis = Khalkís, Greece .. 38 C5
Châlette-sur-Loing, France .. 19 D9
Chaleur B., Canada 103 C6
Chalfant, U.S.A. 116 H8
Chalhuanca, Peru 124 F4
Chalindrey, France 19 E12
Chaling, China 59 D9
Chalisgaon, India 66 J9
Chalk River, Canada 102 C4
Chalky Inlet, N.Z. 91 M1
Challans, France 18 F5
Challapata, Bolivia 124 G5
Challis, U.S.A. 114 D6
Chalmette, U.S.A. 113 L10
Chalon-sur-Saône, France .. 19 F11
Chalonnes-sur-Loire, France . 18 E6
Châlons-en-Champagne, France 19 D11
Châlus, France 20 C4
Chalyaphum, Thailand 64 E4
Cham, Germany 25 F8
Cham, Cu Lao, Vietnam 64 E7
Chama, U.S.A. 115 H10
Chamaicó, Argentina 126 D3
Chaman, Pakistan 66 D5
Chamba, India 68 C7
Chamba, Tanzania 87 E4
Chambal →, India 69 F8
Chamberlain, U.S.A. 112 D5
Chamberlain →, Australia .. 92 C4
Chamberlain L., U.S.A. 109 B11
Chambers, U.S.A. 115 J9
Chambersburg, U.S.A. 108 F7
Chambéry, France 21 C9

Chambeshi →, Zambia 84 G6
Chambly, Canada 111 A11
Chambord, Canada 103 C5
Chamboulive, France 20 C5
Chamchamal, Iraq 70 C5
Chamela, Mexico 118 D3
Chamkar Luong, Cambodia .. 65 G4
Chamoli, India 69 D8
Chamonix-Mont Blanc, France 21 C10
Chamouchouane →, Canada . 102 C5
Champa, India 69 H10
Champagne, Canada 104 A1
Champagne, France 19 D11
Champagnole, France 19 F12
Champaign, U.S.A. 108 E1
Champassak, Laos 64 E5
Champaubert, France 19 D10
Champawat, India 69 E9
Champdeniers-St-Denis, France 20 B3
Champdoré, L., Canada 103 A6
Champeix, France 20 C7
Champion, U.S.A. 110 E4
Champlain, U.S.A. 111 B11
Champlain, L., U.S.A. 111 B11
Champlitte, France 19 E12
Champotón, Mexico 119 D6
Champua, India 69 H11
Chamusca, Portugal 35 F2
Chana, Thailand 65 J3
Chañaral, Chile 126 B1
Chanārān, Iran 71 B8
Chanasma, India 68 H5
Chanco, Chile 126 D1
Chand, India 69 J8
Chandan, India 69 G12
Chandan Chauki, India 69 E9
Chandannagar, India 69 H13
Chandausi, India 69 E8
Chandeleur Is., U.S.A. 113 L10
Chandeleur Sd., U.S.A. 113 L10
Chandigarh, India 68 D7
Chandil, India 69 H12
Chandler, Australia 95 D1
Chandler, Canada 103 C7
Chandler, Ariz., U.S.A. .. 115 K8
Chandler, Okla., U.S.A. .. 113 H6
Chandod, India 68 J5
Chandpur, Bangla. 67 H17
Chandrapur, India 66 K11
Chānf, Iran 71 E9
Chang, Pakistan 68 F3
Chang, Ko, Thailand 65 F4
Ch'ang Chiang = Chang Jiang →, China 59 B13
Chang Jiang →, China 59 B13
Changa, India 69 C7
Changanacheri, India 66 Q10
Changane →, Mozam. 89 C5
Changbai, China 57 D15
Changbai Shan, China 57 C15
Changchiak'ou = Zhangjiakou, China 56 D8
Ch'angchou = Changzhou, China 59 B12
Changchun, China 57 C13
Changchunling, China 57 B13
Changde, China 59 C8
Changdo-ri, N. Korea 57 E14
Changfeng, China 59 A11
Changhai = Shanghai, China 59 B13
Changhua, China 59 B12
Changhua, Taiwan 59 E13
Changhŭng, S. Korea 57 G14
Changhŭngni, N. Korea .. 57 D15
Changjiang, China 64 C7
Changjin, N. Korea 57 D14
Changjin-chŏsuji, N. Korea .. 57 D14
Changle, China 59 E12
Changli, China 57 E10
Changling, China 57 B12
Changlun, Malaysia 65 J3
Changning, Hunan, China .. 59 D9
Changning, Sichuan, China .. 58 C5
Changning, Yunnan, China .. 58 E2
Changping, China 56 D9
Changsha, China 59 C9
Changshan, China 59 C12
Changshu, China 59 B13
Changshun, China 58 D6
Changtai, China 59 E11
Changting, China 59 E11
Changwu, China 56 G4
Changxing, China 59 B12
Changyang, China 59 B8
Changyi, China 57 F10
Changyŏn, N. Korea 57 E13
Changyuan, China 56 G8
Changzhi, China 56 F7
Changzhou, China 59 B12
Chanhanga, Angola 88 B1
Chanlar = Xanlar, Azerbaijan 49 K8
Channapatna, India 66 N10
Channel Is., U.K. 13 H5
Channel Is., U.S.A. 117 M10
Channel Islands National Park, U.S.A. 117 M8
Channel-Port aux Basques, Canada 103 C8
Channel Tunnel, Europe .. 13 F9
Channing, U.S.A. 113 H3
Chantada, Spain 34 C3
Chanthaburi, Thailand 64 F4
Chantilly, France 19 C9
Chantonnay, France 18 F5
Chantrey Inlet, Canada 100 B10
Chanute, U.S.A. 113 G7
Chanza →, Spain 35 H3

Chao Hu, China 59 B11
Chao Phraya →, Thailand .. 64 F3
Chao Phraya Lowlands, Thailand 64 E3
Chaohu, China 59 B11
Chaoyang, Guangdong, China 59 F11
Chaoyang, Liaoning, China .. 57 D11
Chaozhou, China 59 F11
Chapais, Canada 102 C5
Chapala, Mozam. 87 F4
Chapala, L. de, Mexico 118 C4
Chapayev, Kazakstan 48 E10
Chapayevsk, Russia 48 D9
Chapecó, Brazil 127 B5
Chapel Hill, U.S.A. 109 H6
Chapleau, Canada 102 C3
Chaplin, Canada 105 C7
Chaplin L., Canada 105 C7
Chaplino, Ukraine 47 H9
Chaplygin, Russia 46 F11
Chappell, U.S.A. 112 E3
Chapra = Chhapra, India .. 69 G11
Chara, Russia 51 D12
Charadai, Argentina 126 B4
Charagua, Bolivia 124 G6
Charambirá, Punta, Colombia 124 C3
Charaña, Bolivia 124 G5
Charantsavan, Armenia 49 K7
Charanwala, India 68 F5
Charata, Argentina 126 B3
Charcas, Mexico 118 C4
Chard, U.K. 13 G5
Chardon, U.S.A. 110 E3
Chardzhou = Chärjew, Turkmenistan 50 F7
Charente □, France 20 C4
Charente →, France 20 C2
Charente-Maritime □, France . 20 C3
Charenton-du-Cher, France . 19 F9
Chari →, Chad 79 F8
Chārīkār, Afghan. 66 B6
Chariton →, U.S.A. 112 F8
Chärjew, Turkmenistan 50 F7
Charkhari, India 69 G8
Charkhi Dadri, India 68 E7
Charleroi, Belgium 17 D4
Charleroi, U.S.A. 110 F5
Charles, C., U.S.A. 108 G8
Charles City, U.S.A. 112 D8
Charles L., Canada 105 B6
Charles Town, U.S.A. 108 F7
Charleston, Ill., U.S.A. 108 F1
Charleston, Miss., U.S.A. .. 113 H9
Charleston, Mo., U.S.A. .. 113 G10
Charleston, S.C., U.S.A. .. 109 J6
Charleston, W. Va., U.S.A. . 108 F5
Charleston L., Canada 111 B9
Charleston Peak, U.S.A. .. 117 J11
Charlestown, Ireland 15 C3
Charlestown, S. Africa 89 D4
Charlestown, Ind., U.S.A. .. 108 F3
Charlestown, N.H., U.S.A. . 111 C12
Charleville = Rath Luirc, Ireland 15 D3
Charleville, Australia 95 D4
Charleville-Mézières, France . 19 C11
Charlevoix, U.S.A. 108 C3
Charlieu, France 19 F11
Charlotte, Mich., U.S.A. .. 108 D3
Charlotte, N.C., U.S.A. .. 109 H5
Charlotte, Vt., U.S.A. 111 B11
Charlotte Amalie, U.S. Virgin Is. 121 C7
Charlotte Harbor, U.S.A. .. 109 M4
Charlotte L., Canada 104 C3
Charlottenberg, Sweden .. 10 E6
Charlottesville, U.S.A. 108 F6
Charlottetown, Nfld., Canada .. 103 B8
Charlottetown, P.E.I., Canada 103 C7
Charlton, Australia 95 F3
Charlton, U.S.A. 112 E8
Charlton I., Canada 102 B4
Charmes, France 19 D13
Charny, Canada 103 C5
Charolles, France 19 F11
Chârost, France 19 F9
Charre, Mozam. 87 F4
Charroux, France 20 B4
Charsadda, Pakistan 68 B4
Charters Towers, Australia .. 94 C4
Chartres, France 18 D8
Chascomús, Argentina 126 D4
Chasefu, Zambia 87 E3
Chashma Barrage, Pakistan .. 68 C4
Chasseneuil-sur-Bonnieure, France 20 C4
Chât, Iran 71 B7
Chatal Balkan = Udvoy Balkan, Bulgaria 41 D10
Château-Arnoux, France .. 21 D10
Château-Chinon, France .. 19 E10
Château-d'Olonne, France . 20 B2
Château-du-Loir, France .. 18 E7
Château-Gontier, France .. 18 E6
Château-la-Vallière, France . 18 E7
Château-Landon, France .. 19 D9
Château-Renault, France .. 18 E7
Château-Salins, France .. 19 D13
Château-Thierry, France .. 19 C10
Châteaubourg, France 18 D5
Châteaubriant, France 18 E5
Châteaudun, France 18 D8
Chateaugay, U.S.A. 111 B10
Châteaugiron, France 18 D5
Châteauguay, L., Canada .. 103 A5
Châteaulin, France 18 D2
Châteaumeillant, France .. 19 F9
Châteauneuf-du-Faou, France . 18 D3

Châteauneuf-sur-Charente, France 20 C3
Châteauneuf-sur-Cher, France . 19 F9
Châteauneuf-sur-Loire, France 19 E9
Châteaurenard, Bouches-du-Rhône, France .. 21 E8
Châteaurenard, Loiret, France . 19 E9
Châteauroux, France 19 F8
Châteauvillain, France 19 D11
Châtelaillon-Plage, France .. 20 B2
Châtelguyon, France 20 C7
Châtellerault, France 18 F7
Châtelus-Malvaleix, France . 19 F9
Chatham = Miramichi, Canada 103 C6
Chatham, Canada 102 D3
Chatham, U.K. 13 F8
Chatham, U.S.A. 111 D11
Chatham Is., Pac. Oc. 96 M10
Châtillon, Italy 28 C4
Châtillon-Coligny, France .. 19 E9
Châtillon-en-Diois, France .. 21 D9
Châtillon-sur-Indre, France .. 18 F8
Châtillon-sur-Loire, France .. 19 E9
Châtillon-sur-Seine, France . 19 E11
Chatmohar, Bangla. 69 G13
Chatra, India 69 G11
Chatrapur, India 67 K14
Chats, L. des, Canada 111 A8
Chatsu, India 68 F6
Chatsworth, Canada 110 B4
Chatsworth, Zimbabwe 87 F3
Chattahoochee, U.S.A. 109 K3
Chattahoochee →, U.S.A. .. 109 K3
Chattanooga, U.S.A. 109 H3
Chatteris, U.K. 13 E8
Chaturat, Thailand 64 E3
Chau Doc, Vietnam 65 G5
Chaudes-Aigues, France .. 20 D7
Chauffailles, France 19 F11
Chaukan Pass, Burma 67 F20
Chaumont, France 19 D12
Chaumont, U.S.A. 111 B8
Chaumont-en-Vexin, France . 19 C8
Chaumont-sur-Loire, France . 18 E8
Chaunay, France 20 B4
Chauny, France 19 C10
Chausey, Îs., France 18 D5
Chaussin, France 19 F12
Chautauqua L., U.S.A. .. 110 D5
Chauvin, Canada 105 C6
Chavanges, France 19 D11
Chaves, Brazil 125 D9
Chaves, Portugal 34 D3
Chazelles-sur-Lyon, France . 21 C8
Chazy, U.S.A. 111 B11
Cheb, Czech Rep. 26 A5
Cheboksarskoye Vdkhr., Russia 48 B8
Cheboksary, Russia 48 B8
Cheboygan, U.S.A. 108 C3
Chebsara, Russia 46 C10
Chech, Erg, Africa 78 D5
Chechenia □, Russia 49 J7
Checheno-Ingush Republic = Chechenia □, Russia 49 J7
Chechnya = Chechenia □, Russia 49 J7
Chech'ŏn, S. Korea 57 F15
Chęciny, Poland 45 H7
Checotah, U.S.A. 113 H7
Chedabucto B., Canada .. 103 C7
Cheduba I., Burma 67 K18
Cheepie, Australia 95 D4
Chef-Boutonne, France .. 20 B3
Chegdomyn, Russia 51 D14
Chegga, Mauritania 78 C4
Chegutu, Zimbabwe 87 F3
Chehalis, U.S.A. 116 D4
Chehalis →, U.S.A. 116 D3
Cheiron, Mt., France 21 E10
Cheju, do, S. Korea 57 H14
Chekalin, Russia 46 E9
Chekiang = Zhejiang □, China 59 C13
Chel = Kuru, Bahr el →, Sudan 81 F2
Chela, Sa. da, Angola 88 B1
Chelan, U.S.A. 114 C4
Chelan, L., U.S.A. 114 B3
Cheleken, Turkmenistan .. 50 F6
Cheleken Yarymadasy, Turkmenistan 71 B7
Chelforó, Argentina 128 D3
Chelkar = Shalqar, Kazakstan . 50 E6
Chelkar Tengiz, Solonchak, Kazakstan 50 E7
Chella, Ethiopia 81 F4
Chelles, France 19 D9
Chełm, Poland 45 G10
Chełmno, Poland 45 E5
Chełmża, Poland 45 E5
Chelsea, U.S.A. 111 C12
Cheltenham, U.K. 13 F5
Chelva, Spain 32 F4
Chelyabinsk, Russia 50 D7
Chelyuskin, C., Russia 52 B14
Chemainus, Canada 116 B3
Chemba, Mozam. 85 H6
Chembar = Belinskiy, Russia 48 D6
Chemillé, France 18 E6
Chemnitz, Germany 24 E8
Chemult, U.S.A. 114 E3
Chen, Gora, Russia 51 C15
Chenab →, Pakistan 68 D4
Chenango Forks, U.S.A. .. 111 D9
Chencha, Ethiopia 81 F4

Chenchiang = Zhenjiang, China 59 A12
Cheney, U.S.A. 114 C5
Cheng Xian, China 56 H3
Chengbu, China 59 D8
Chengcheng, China 56 G5
Chengchou = Zhengzhou, China 56 G7
Chengde, China 57 D9
Chengdong Hu, China 59 A11
Chengdu, China 58 B5
Chenggong, China 58 E4
Chenggu, China 56 H4
Chenghai, China 59 F11
Chengjiang, China 58 E4
Chengkou, China 58 B7
Ch'engmai, China 64 C7
Ch'engtu = Chengdu, China .. 58 B5
Chengwu, China 56 G8
Chengxi Hu, China 59 A11
Chengyang, China 57 F11
Chenjiagang, China 57 G10
Chenkán, Mexico 119 D6
Chennai, India 66 N12
Chenôve, France 19 E12
Chenxi, China 59 C8
Chenzhou, China 59 E9
Cheo Reo, Vietnam 62 B3
Cheom Ksan, Cambodia .. 64 E5
Chepelare, Bulgaria 41 E8
Chepén, Peru 124 E3
Chepes, Argentina 126 C2
Chepo, Panama 120 E4
Chepstow, U.K. 13 F5
Cheptulil, Mt., Kenya 86 B4
Chequamegon B., U.S.A. .. 112 B9
Cher □, France 19 E9
Cher →, France 18 E7
Chéradi, Italy 31 B10
Cherasco, Italy 28 D4
Cheraw, U.S.A. 109 H6
Cherbourg, France 18 C5
Cherdakly, Russia 48 C9
Cherdyn, Russia 50 C6
Cheremkhovo, Russia 51 D11
Cherepanovo, Russia 50 D9
Cherepovets, Russia 46 C9
Chergui, Chott ech, Algeria ... 78 B6
Cherikov = Cherykaw, Belarus . 46 F6
Cherkasy, Ukraine 47 H7
Cherkessk, Russia 49 H6
Cherlak, Russia 50 D8
Chernaya, Russia 51 B9
Cherni, Bulgaria 40 D7
Chernigov = Chernihiv, Ukraine 47 G6
Chernihiv, Ukraine 47 G6
Chernivtsi, Ukraine 47 H3
Chernobyl = Chornobyl, Ukraine 47 G6
Chernogorsk, Russia 51 D10
Chernomorskoye = Chornomorske, Ukraine .. 47 K7
Chernovtsy = Chernivtsi, Ukraine 47 H3
Chernyakhovsk, Russia .. 9 J19
Chernyanka, Russia 47 G9
Chernysheyskiy, Russia .. 51 C12
Chernyye Zemli, Russia .. 49 H8
Cherokee, Iowa, U.S.A. .. 112 D7
Cherokee, Okla., U.S.A. .. 113 G5
Cherokee Village, U.S.A. .. 113 G9
Cherokees, Grand Lake O' The, U.S.A. 113 G7
Cherrapunji, India 67 G17
Cherry Valley, Calif., U.S.A. .. 117 M10
Cherry Valley, N.Y., U.S.A. .. 111 D10
Cherskiy, Russia 51 C17
Cherskogo Khrebet, Russia . 51 C15
Chertkovo, Russia 47 H11
Cherven, Belarus 46 F5
Cherven-Bryag, Bulgaria .. 41 C8
Chervonohrad, Ukraine .. 47 G3
Cherwell →, U.K. 13 F6
Cherykaw, Belarus 46 F6
Chesapeake, U.S.A. 108 G7
Chesapeake B., U.S.A. 108 G7
Cheshire □, U.K. 12 D5
Cheshskaya Guba, Russia .. 50 C5
Cheshunt, U.K. 13 F7
Chesil Beach, U.K. 13 G5
Chesley, Canada 110 B3
Cheste, Spain 33 F4
Chester, U.K. 12 D5
Chester, Calif., U.S.A. .. 114 F3
Chester, Ill., U.S.A. 113 G10
Chester, Mont., U.S.A. .. 114 B8
Chester, Pa., U.S.A. 108 F8
Chester, S.C., U.S.A. 109 H5
Chester, Vt., U.S.A. 111 C12
Chester, W. Va., U.S.A. .. 110 F4
Chester-le-Street, U.K. .. 12 C6
Chesterfield, U.K. 12 D6
Chesterfield, Is., N. Cal. .. 96 J7
Chesterfield Inlet, Canada .. 100 B10
Chesterton Ra., Australia .. 95 D4
Chestertown, U.S.A. 111 C11
Chesterville, Canada 111 A9
Chestnut Ridge, U.S.A. .. 110 F5
Chesuncook L., U.S.A. .. 109 C11
Chéticamp, Canada 103 C7
Chetrosu, Moldova 43 B12
Chetumal, Mexico 119 D7
Chetumal, B. de, Mexico .. 119 D7
Chetwynd, Canada 104 B4
Chevanceaux, France 20 C3
Cheviot, The, U.K. 12 B5
Cheviot Hills, U.K. 12 B5
Cheviot Ra., Australia 94 D3
Chew Bahir, Ethiopia 81 G4
Chewelah, U.S.A. 114 B5

Cheyenne, Okla., U.S.A. 113 H5
Cheyenne, Wyo., U.S.A. 112 E2
Cheyenne →, U.S.A. 112 C4
Cheyne B., Australia 93 F2
Chhabra, India 68 G7
Chhaktala, India 68 H6
Chhapra, India 69 G11
Chhata, India 68 F7
Chhatarpur, Bihar, India 69 G11
Chhatarpur, Mad. P., India 69 G8
Chhattisgarh □, India 69 J10
Chhep, Cambodia 64 F5
Chhindwara, Mad. P., India 69 H8
Chhindwara, Mad. P., India 69 H8
Chhlong, Cambodia 65 F5
Chhota Tawa →, India 68 H7
Chhoti Kali Sindh →, India 68 G6
Chhuikhadan, India 69 J9
Chhuk, Cambodia 65 G5
Chi →, Thailand 64 E5
Chiai, Taiwan 59 F13
Chiali, Taiwan 59 F13
Chiamboni, Somali Rep. 84 E8
Chiamussu = Jiamusi, China 60 B8
Chianciano Terme, Italy 29 E8
Chiang Dao, Thailand 64 C2
Chiang Kham, Thailand 64 C3
Chiang Khan, Thailand 64 D3
Chiang Khong, Thailand 58 G3
Chiang Mai, Thailand 64 C2
Chiang Rai, Thailand 58 H2
Chiang Saen, Thailand 58 G3
Chiapa →, Mexico 119 D6
Chiapa de Corzo, Mexico 119 D6
Chiapas □, Mexico 119 D6
Chiaramonte Gulfi, Italy 31 E7
Chiaravalle, Italy 29 E10
Chiaravalle Centrale, Italy 31 D9
Chiari, Italy 28 C6
Chiatura, Georgia 49 J6
Chiautla, Mexico 119 D5
Chiávari, Italy 28 D6
Chiavenna, Italy 28 B6
Chiba, Japan 55 G10
Chiba □, Japan 55 G10
Chibabava, Mozam. 89 C5
Chibemba, Cunene, Angola 85 H2
Chibemba, Huíla, Angola 88 B2
Chibi, Zimbabwe 89 C5
Chibia, Angola 85 H2
Chibougamau, Canada 102 C5
Chibougamau, L., Canada 102 C5
Chibuk, Nigeria 83 C7
Chibuto, Mozam. 89 C5
Chic-Chocs, Mts., Canada 103 C6
Chicacole = Srikakulam, India 67 K13
Chicago, U.S.A. 108 E2
Chicago Heights, U.S.A. 108 E2
Chichagof I., U.S.A. 100 C6
Chichén-Itzá, Mexico 119 C7
Chicheng, China 56 D8
Chichester, U.K. 13 G7
Chichester Ra., Australia 92 D2
Chichibu, Japan 55 F9
Ch'ich'iaerh = Qiqihar, China 51 E13
Chicholi, India 68 H8
Chickasha, U.S.A. 113 H6
Chiclana de la Frontera, Spain 35 J4
Chiclayo, Peru 124 E3
Chico, U.S.A. 116 F5
Chico →, Chubut, Argentina 128 E3
Chico →, Santa Cruz, Argentina 128 G3
Chicomo, Mozam. 89 C5
Chicontepec, Mexico 119 C5
Chicopee, U.S.A. 111 D12
Chicoutimi, Canada 103 C5
Chicualacuala, Mozam. 89 C5
Chidambaram, India 66 P11
Chidenguele, Mozam. 89 C5
Chidley, C., Canada 101 B13
Chiducuane, Mozam. 89 C5
Chiede, Angola 88 B2
Chiefs Pt., Canada 110 B3
Chiem Hoa, Vietnam 64 A5
Chiemsee, Germany 25 H8
Chiengi, Zambia 87 D2
Chiengmai = Chiang Mai, Thailand 64 C2
Chienti →, Italy 29 E10
Chieri, Italy 28 C4
Chiers →, France 19 C11
Chiesa in Valmalenco, Italy 28 B6
Chiese →, Italy 28 C7
Chieti, Italy 29 F11
Chifeng, China 57 C10
Chigirin, Ukraine 47 H7
Chignecto B., Canada 103 C7
Chiguana, Bolivia 126 A2
Chigwell, U.K. 13 F8
Chiha-ri, N. Korea 57 E14
Chihli, G. of = Bo Hai, China 57 E10
Chihuahua, Mexico 118 B3
Chihuahua □, Mexico 118 B3
Chiili = Shīeli, Kazakstan 50 E7
Chik Bollapur, India 66 N10
Chikmagalur, India 66 N9
Chikwawa, Malawi 87 F3
Chilac, Mexico 119 D5
Chilam Chavki, Pakistan 69 B6
Chilanga, Zambia 87 F2
Chilapa, Mexico 119 D5
Chilas, Pakistan 69 B6
Chilaw, Sri Lanka 66 R11
Chilcotin →, Canada 104 C4
Childers, Australia 95 D5
Childress, U.S.A. 113 H4

Chile ■, S. Amer. 128 D2
Chile Rise, Pac. Oc. 97 L18
Chilecito, Argentina 126 B2
Chilete, Peru 124 E3
Chilia, Brațul →, Romania 43 E14
Chililabombwe, Zambia 87 E2
Chilin = Jilin, China 57 C14
Chilka L., India 67 K14
Chilko →, Canada 104 C4
Chilko L., Canada 104 C4
Chillagoe, Australia 94 B3
Chillán, Chile 126 D1
Chillicothe, Ill., U.S.A. 112 E10
Chillicothe, Mo., U.S.A. 112 F8
Chillicothe, Ohio, U.S.A. 108 F4
Chilliwack, Canada 104 D4
Chilo, India 68 F5
Chiloane, I., Mozam. 89 C5
Chiloé, I. de, Chile 122 H3
Chilpancingo, Mexico 119 D5
Chiltern Hills, U.K. 13 F7
Chilton, U.S.A. 108 C1
Chilubi, Zambia 87 E2
Chilubula, Zambia 87 E3
Chilumba, Malawi 87 E3
Chilung, Taiwan 59 E13
Chilwa, L., Malawi 87 F4
Chimaltitán, Mexico 118 C4
Chimán, Panama 120 E4
Chimanimani, Zimbabwe 89 B5
Chimay, Belgium 17 D4
Chimayo, U.S.A. 115 H11
Chimbay, Uzbekistan 50 E6
Chimborazo, Ecuador 122 D3
Chimbote, Peru 124 E3
Chimkent = Shymkent, Kazakstan 50 E7
Chimoio, Mozam. 87 F3
Chimpembe, Zambia 87 D2
Chin □, Burma 67 J18
Chin Ling Shan = Qinling Shandi, China 56 H5
Chinan = Jinan, China 56 F9
Chinandega, Nic. 120 D2
Chinati Peak, U.S.A. 113 L2
Chincha Alta, Peru 122 E3
Chinchaga →, Canada 104 B5
Chinchilla, Australia 95 D5
Chinchilla de Monte Aragón, Spain 33 G3
Chinchorro, Banco, Mexico 119 D7
Chinchou = Jinzhou, China 57 D11
Chincoteague, U.S.A. 108 G8
Chinde, Mozam. 87 F4
Chindo, S. Korea 57 G14
Chindwin →, Burma 67 J19
Chineni, India 69 C6
Chinga, Mozam. 87 F4
Chingola, Zambia 87 E2
Chingole, Malawi 87 E3
Ch'ingtao = Qingdao, China 57 F11
Chinguetti, Mauritania 78 D3
Chingune, Mozam. 89 C5
Chinhae, S. Korea 57 G15
Chinhanguanine, Mozam. 89 D5
Chinhoyi, Zimbabwe 87 F3
Chini, India 68 D8
Chiniot, Pakistan 68 D5
Chínipas, Mexico 118 B3
Chinji, Pakistan 68 C5
Chinju, S. Korea 57 G15
Chinle, U.S.A. 115 H9
Chinmen, Taiwan 59 E13
Chinmen Tao, Taiwan 59 E12
Chinnampo = Namp'o, N. Korea 57 E13
Chino, Japan 55 G9
Chino, U.S.A. 117 L9
Chino Valley, U.S.A. 115 J7
Chinon, France 18 E7
Chinook, U.S.A. 114 B9
Chinsali, Zambia 87 E3
Chióggia, Italy 29 C9
Chíos = Khíos, Greece 39 C8
Chipata, Zambia 87 E3
Chiperceni, Moldova 43 C13
Chipinge, Zimbabwe 87 G3
Chipiona, Spain 35 J4
Chipley, U.S.A. 109 K3
Chipman, Canada 103 C6
Chipoka, Malawi 87 E3
Chippenham, U.K. 13 F5
Chippewa →, U.S.A. 112 C8
Chippewa Falls, U.S.A. 112 C9
Chipping Norton, U.K. 13 F6
Chiprovtsi, Bulgaria 40 C7
Chiquián, Peru 124 F3
Chiquimula, Guatemala 120 D2
Chiquinquira, Colombia 124 B4
Chirala, India 66 M12
Chiramba, Mozam. 87 F3
Chirawa, India 68 E6
Chirchiq, Uzbekistan 50 E7
Chiredzi, Zimbabwe 89 C5
Chiricahua Peak, U.S.A. 115 L9
Chiriquí, G. de, Panama 120 E3
Chiriquí, L. de, Panama 120 E3
Chirivira Falls, Zimbabwe 87 G3
Chirmiri, India 67 H13
Chirnogi, Romania 43 F11
Chirpan, Bulgaria 41 D9
Chirripó Grande, Cerro, Costa Rica 120 E3

Chirundu, Zimbabwe 89 B4
Chisamba, Zambia 87 E2
Chisapani Garhi, Nepal 67 F14
Chisasibi, Canada 102 B4
Chisholm, Canada 104 C6
Chisholm, U.S.A. 112 B8
Chishtian Mandi, Pakistan 68 E5
Chishui, China 58 C5
Chishui He →, China 58 C5
Chisimaio, Somali Rep. 77 G8
Chisimba Falls, Zambia 87 E3
Chișinău, Moldova 43 C13
Chișineu Criș, Romania 42 D6
Chisone →, Italy 28 D4
Chisos Mts., U.S.A. 113 L3
Chistopol, Russia 48 C10
Chita, Russia 51 D12
Chitipa, Malawi 87 D3
Chitose, Japan 54 C10
Chitral, Pakistan 66 B7
Chitré, Panama 120 E3
Chittagong, Bangla. 67 H17
Chittagong □, Bangla. 67 G17
Chittaurgarh, India 68 G6
Chittoor, India 66 N11
Chitungwiza, Zimbabwe 87 F3
Chiusi, Italy 29 E8
Chiva, Spain 33 F4
Chivasso, Italy 28 C4
Chivhu, Zimbabwe 87 F3
Chivilcoy, Argentina 126 C4
Chiwanda, Tanzania 87 E3
Chixi, China 59 G9
Chizera, Zambia 87 E2
Chkalov = Orenburg, Russia 50 D6
Chkolovsk, Russia 48 B6
Chloride, U.S.A. 117 K12
Chlumec nad Cidlinou, Czech Rep. 26 A8
Chmielnik, Poland 45 H7
Cho Bo, Vietnam 58 G5
Cho-do, N. Korea 57 E13
Cho Phuoc Hai, Vietnam 65 G6
Choba, Kenya 86 B4
Chobe National Park, Botswana 88 B3
Choch'iwon, S. Korea 57 F14
Chocianów, Poland 45 G2
Chociwel, Poland 44 E2
Chocolate Mts., U.S.A. 117 M11
Choctawhatchee →, U.S.A. 109 K3
Chodecz, Poland 45 F6
Chodov, Czech Rep. 26 A5
Chodziez, Poland 45 F3
Choele Choel, Argentina 128 D3
Choix, Mexico 118 B3
Chojna, Poland 45 F1
Chojnice, Poland 44 E4
Chojnów, Poland 45 G2
Chōkai-San, Japan 54 E10
Choke, Ethiopia 81 E4
Choke Canyon L., U.S.A. 113 L5
Chokurdakh, Russia 51 B15
Cholame, U.S.A. 116 K6
Cholet, France 18 E6
Cholguan, Chile 126 D1
Choluteca, Honduras 120 D2
Choluteca →, Honduras 120 D2
Chom Bung, Thailand 64 F2
Chom Thong, Thailand 64 C2
Choma, Zambia 87 F2
Chomen Swamp, Ethiopia 81 F4
Chomun, India 68 F6
Chomutov, Czech Rep. 26 A6
Chon Buri, Thailand 64 F3
Chon Thanh, Vietnam 65 G6
Ch'onan, S. Korea 57 F14
Chone, Ecuador 124 D3
Chong Kai, Cambodia 64 F4
Chong Mek, Thailand 64 E5
Chongde, China 59 B13
Chongdo, S. Korea 57 G15
Chŏngha, S. Korea 57 F15
Chŏngjin, N. Korea 57 D15
Chŏngju, N. Korea 57 E13
Chŏngju, S. Korea 57 F14
Chongli, China 56 D8
Chongming, China 59 B13
Chongming Dao, China 59 B13
Chongqing, Chongqing, China 58 C6
Chongqing, Sichuan, China 58 B4
Chongqing Shi □, China 58 C6
Chongren, China 59 D11
Chonguene, Mozam. 89 C5
Chŏngup, S. Korea 57 G14
Chongyi, China 59 E10
Chongzuo, China 58 F6
Chŏnju, S. Korea 57 G14
Chonos, Arch. de los, Chile 122 H3
Chop, Ukraine 47 H2
Chopim →, Brazil 127 B5
Chopim, Brazil 127 B5
Chor, Pakistan 68 G3
Chorbat La, India 69 B7
Chorley, U.K. 12 D5
Chornobyl, Ukraine 47 G6
Chornomorske, Ukraine 47 K7
Chorolque, Cerro, Bolivia 126 A2
Choroszcz, Poland 45 E9
Chorregon, Australia 94 C3
Chortkiv, Ukraine 47 H3
Ch'orwon, S. Korea 57 E14
Chorzele, Poland 45 E7
Chorzów, Poland 45 H6
Chos-Malal, Argentina 126 D1
Ch'osan, N. Korea 57 D13
Choszczno, Poland 45 E2
Choteau, U.S.A. 114 C7

Chotěboř, Czech Rep. 26 B8
Chotila, India 68 H4
Chotta Udepur, India 68 H6
Chowchilla, U.S.A. 116 H6
Choybalsan, Mongolia 60 B6
Christchurch, N.Z. 91 K4
Christchurch, U.K. 13 G6
Christian I., Canada 110 B4
Christiana, S. Africa 88 D4
Christiansfeld, Denmark 11 J3
Christiansted, U.S. Virgin Is. 121 C7
Christie B., Canada 105 A6
Christina →, Canada 105 B6
Christmas Cr. →, Australia 92 C4
Christmas I. = Kiritimati, Kiribati 97 G12
Christmas I., Ind. Oc. 96 J2
Christopher L., Australia 93 D4
Chrudim, Czech Rep. 26 B8
Chrzanów, Poland 45 H6
Chtimba, Malawi 87 E3
Chu = Shū, Kazakstan 50 E8
Chu →, Vietnam 64 C5
Chu Lai, Vietnam 64 E7
Ch'uanchou = Quanzhou, China 59 E12
Chuankou, China 56 G6
Chubbuck, U.S.A. 114 E7
Chūbu □, Japan 55 F8
Chubut →, Argentina 122 H4
Chuchi L., Canada 104 B4
Chuda, India 68 H4
Chudovo, Russia 46 C6
Chudskoye, Ozero, Russia 9 G22
Chūgoku □, Japan 55 G6
Chūgoku-Sanchi, Japan 55 G6
Chuguyev = Chuhuyiv, Ukraine 47 H9
Chugwater, U.S.A. 112 E2
Chuhuyiv, Ukraine 47 H9
Chukchi Sea, Russia 51 C19
Chukotskoye Nagorye, Russia 51 C18
Chula Vista, U.S.A. 117 N9
Chulman, Russia 51 D13
Chulucanas, Peru 124 E2
Chulym →, Russia 50 D9
Chum Phae, Thailand 64 D4
Chum Saeng, Thailand 64 E3
Chumar, India 69 C8
Chumbicha, Argentina 126 B2
Chumerna, Bulgaria 41 D9
Chumikan, Russia 51 D14
Chumphon, Thailand 65 G2
Chumuare, Mozam. 87 E3
Chumunjin, S. Korea 57 F15
Chuna →, Russia 51 D10
Chun'an, China 59 C12
Chunchura, India 69 H13
Chunga, Zambia 87 F2
Chunggang-ŭp, N. Korea 57 D14
Chunghwa, N. Korea 57 E13
Ch'ungju, S. Korea 57 F14
Chungking = Chongqing, China 58 C6
Chungli, Taiwan 59 E13
Chungt'iaoshan = Zhongtiao Shan, China 56 G6
Chungyang Shanmo, Taiwan 59 F13
Chunian, Pakistan 68 D6
Chunya, Tanzania 87 D3
Chunyang, China 57 C15
Chuquibamba, Peru 124 G4
Chuquicamata, Chile 126 A2
Chur, Switz. 25 J5
Churachandpur, India 67 G18
Churchill, Canada 105 B10
Churchill →, Man., Canada 105 B10
Churchill →, Nfld., Canada 103 B7
Churchill, C., Canada 105 B10
Churchill Falls, Canada 103 B7
Churchill L., Canada 105 B7
Churchill Pk., Canada 104 B3
Churki, India 69 H10
Churu, India 68 E6
Churún Merú = Angel Falls, Venezuela 124 B6
Chushal, India 69 C8
Chuska Mts., U.S.A. 115 H9
Chusovoy, Russia 50 D6
Chute-aux-Outardes, Canada 103 C6
Chuuronjang, N. Korea 57 D15
Chuvash Republic = Chuvashia □, Russia 48 C8
Chuvashia □, Russia 48 C8
Chuwārtah, Iraq 70 C5
Chuxiong, China 58 E3
Chūy = Shū →, Kazakstan 52 E10
Chuy, Uruguay 127 C5
Chuzhou, China 59 A12
Ci Xian, China 56 F8
Ciacova, Romania 42 E6
Ciadâr-Lunga, Moldova 43 D13
Ciamis, Indonesia 63 G13
Cianjur, Indonesia 63 G12
Cianorte, Brazil 127 A5
Cibadak, Indonesia 63 G12
Cibola, U.S.A. 117 M12
Cibuk Burnu, Turkey 72 B7
Cicero, U.S.A. 108 E2
Cide, Turkey 72 B5
Cidacos →, Spain 32 C3
Ciechanów, Poland 45 F7
Ciechanowiec, Poland 45 F9
Ciechocinek, Poland 45 F5
Ciego de Avila, Cuba 120 B4
Ciénaga, Colombia 124 A4
Cienfuegos, Cuba 120 B3
Cierp, France 20 F4
Cíes, Is., Spain 34 C2
Cieszanów, Poland 45 H10
Cieszyn, Poland 45 J5

Cieza, Spain 33 G3
Çifteler, Turkey 72 C4
Cifuentes, Spain 32 E2
Cihanbeyli, Turkey 72 C5
Cihuatlán, Mexico 118 D4
Cijara, Embalse de, Spain 35 F5
Cijulang, Indonesia 63 G13
Cilacap, Indonesia 63 G13
Cıldır, Turkey 73 B10
Çıldır Gölü, Turkey 73 B10
Cili, China 59 C8
Cilibia, Romania 43 E12
Cilicia, Turkey 72 D5
Cill Chainnigh = Kilkenny, Ireland 15 D4
Cilo Dağı, Turkey 73 D10
Cima, U.S.A. 117 K11
Cimarron, Kans., U.S.A. 113 G4
Cimarron, N. Mex., U.S.A. 113 G2
Cimarron →, U.S.A. 113 G6
Cimişlia, Moldova 43 D13
Cimone, Mte., Italy 28 D7
Çınar, Turkey 73 D9
Çınarcık, Turkey 41 F13
Cinca →, Spain 32 D5
Cincar, Bos.-H. 42 G2
Cincinnati, U.S.A. 108 F3
Cincinnatus, U.S.A. 111 D9
Çine, Turkey 39 D10
Ciney, Belgium 17 D5
Cíngoli, Italy 29 E10
Cinigiano, Italy 29 F8
Cinto, Mte., France 21 F12
Cintruénigo, Spain 32 C3
Ciocile, Romania 43 F12
Ciolănești din Deal, Romania 43 F10
Ciorani, Romania 43 F11
Ciovo, Croatia 29 E13
Circeo, Mte., Italy 30 A6
Çirçir, Turkey 72 C7
Circle, Alaska, U.S.A. 100 B5
Circle, Mont., U.S.A. 112 B2
Circleville, U.S.A. 108 F4
Cirebon, Indonesia 62 F3
Ciremai, Indonesia 63 G13
Cirencester, U.K. 13 F6
Cireșu, Romania 42 F7
Cirey-sur-Vezouze, France 19 D13
Ciriè, Italy 28 C4
Cirium, Cyprus 36 E11
Cirò, Italy 31 C10
Cirò Marina, Italy 31 C10
Ciron →, France 20 D3
Cisco, U.S.A. 113 J5
Cislău, Romania 43 E11
Cisna, Poland 45 J9
Cisnădie, Romania 43 E9
Cisterna di Latina, Italy 30 A5
Cisternino, Italy 31 B10
Cistierna, Spain 34 C5
Citeli-Ckaro = Tsiteli-Tsqaro, Georgia 49 K8
Citlaltépetl, Mexico 119 D5
Citrus Heights, U.S.A. 116 G5
Citrusdal, S. Africa 88 E2
Città della Pieve, Italy 29 F9
Città di Castello, Italy 29 E9
Città Sant' Angelo, Italy 29 F11
Cittadella, Italy 29 C8
Cittaducale, Italy 29 F9
Cittanova, Italy 31 D9
Ciuc, Munții, Romania 43 D11
Ciucaș, Vf., Romania 43 E10
Ciucea, Romania 42 D7
Ciuciuleni, Moldova 43 C12
Ciucurova, Romania 43 F13
Ciudad Altamirano, Mexico 118 D4
Ciudad Bolívar, Venezuela 124 B6
Ciudad Camargo, Mexico 118 B3
Ciudad de Valles, Mexico 119 C5
Ciudad del Carmen, Mexico 119 D6
Ciudad del Este, Paraguay 127 B5
Ciudad Delicias = Delicias, Mexico 118 B3
Ciudad Guayana, Venezuela 124 B6
Ciudad Guerrero, Mexico 118 B3
Ciudad Guzmán, Mexico 118 D4
Ciudad Juárez, Mexico 118 A3
Ciudad Madero, Mexico 119 C5
Ciudad Mante, Mexico 119 C5
Ciudad Obregón, Mexico 118 B3
Ciudad Real, Spain 35 G7
Ciudad Real □, Spain 35 G7
Ciudad Rodrigo, Spain 34 E4
Ciudad Trujillo = Santo Domingo, Dom. Rep. 121 C6
Ciudad Victoria, Mexico 119 C5
Ciudadela, Spain 37 B10
Ciulnița, Romania 43 F12
Ciumeghiu, Romania 42 D6
Ciuperceni, Romania 43 F9
Civa Burnu, Turkey 72 B7
Cividale del Friuli, Italy 29 B10
Civita Castellana, Italy 29 F9
Civitanova Marche, Italy 29 E10
Civitavécchia, Italy 29 F8
Civray, France 20 B4
Çivril, Turkey 39 C11
Cixerri →, Italy 30 C1
Cixi, China 59 B13
Cizre, Turkey 70 B4
Cizur Mayor, Spain 32 C3
Clackmannanshire □, U.K. 14 E5
Clacton-on-Sea, U.K. 13 F9
Clain →, France 18 F7
Claire, L., Canada 104 B6
Clairton, U.S.A. 110 F5

Clairvaux-les-Lacs, France 19 F12
Claise ➝, France 20 B5
Clallam Bay, U.S.A. 116 B2
Clamecy, France 19 E10
Clanton, U.S.A. 109 J2
Clanwilliam, S. Africa 88 E2
Clara, Ireland 15 C4
Claraville, U.S.A. 117 K8
Clare, Australia 95 E2
Clare, U.S.A. 108 D3
Clare □, Ireland 15 D3
Clare ➝, Ireland 15 C2
Clare I., Ireland 15 C1
Claremont, Calif., U.S.A. .. 117 L9
Claremont, N.H., U.S.A. .. 111 C12
Claremont Pt., Australia 94 A3
Claremore, U.S.A. 113 G7
Claremorris, Ireland 15 C3
Clarence ➝, Australia 95 D5
Clarence ➝, N.Z. 91 K4
Clarence, I., Chile 128 G2
Clarence I., Antarctica 5 C18
Clarence Str., Australia 92 B5
Clarence Town, Bahamas .. 121 B5
Clarendon, Pa., U.S.A. 110 E5
Clarendon, Tex., U.S.A. .. 113 H4
Clarenville, Canada 103 C9
Claresholm, Canada 104 D6
Clarie Coast, Antarctica 5 C9
Clarinda, U.S.A. 112 E7
Clarion, Iowa, U.S.A. 112 D8
Clarion, Pa., U.S.A. 110 E5
Clarion ➝, U.S.A. 110 E5
Clark, U.S.A. 112 C6
Clark, Pt., Canada 110 B3
Clark Fork, U.S.A. 114 B5
Clark Fork ➝, U.S.A. 114 B5
Clarkdale, U.S.A. 115 J7
Clarke City, Canada 103 B6
Clarke I., Australia 94 G4
Clarke Ra., Australia 94 C4
Clark's Fork ➝, U.S.A. 114 D9
Clarks Harbour, Canada .. 103 D6
Clarks Hill L., U.S.A. 109 J4
Clarks Summit, U.S.A. 111 E9
Clarksburg, U.S.A. 108 F5
Clarksdale, U.S.A. 113 H9
Clarksville, Ark., U.S.A. .. 113 H8
Clarksville, Tenn., U.S.A. . 109 G2
Clarksville, Tex., U.S.A. .. 113 J7
Clatskanie, U.S.A. 116 D3
Claude, U.S.A. 113 H4
Claveria, Phil. 61 B4
Clay, U.S.A. 116 G5
Clay Center, U.S.A. 112 F6
Claypool, U.S.A. 115 K8
Claysburg, U.S.A. 110 F6
Claysville, U.S.A. 110 F4
Clayton, N. Mex., U.S.A. .. 113 G3
Clayton, N.Y., U.S.A. 111 B8
Clear, C., Ireland 15 E2
Clear, L., Canada 110 A7
Clear Hills, Canada 104 B5
Clear I., Ireland 15 E2
Clear L., U.S.A. 116 F4
Clear Lake, Iowa, U.S.A. .. 112 D8
Clear Lake, S. Dak., U.S.A. 112 C6
Clear Lake Reservoir, U.S.A. 114 F3
Clearfield, Pa., U.S.A. 110 E6
Clearfield, Utah, U.S.A. .. 114 F8
Clearlake, U.S.A. 114 G2
Clearlake Highlands, U.S.A. 116 G4
Clearwater, Canada 104 C4
Clearwater, U.S.A. 109 M4
Clearwater ➝, Alta., Canada 104 C6
Clearwater ➝, Alta., Canada 105 B6
Clearwater L., Canada 105 C9
Clearwater Mts., U.S.A. .. 114 C6
Clearwater Prov. Park, Canada 105 C8
Clearwater River Prov. Park,
   Canada 105 B7
Cleburne, U.S.A. 113 J6
Clee Hills, U.K. 13 E5
Cleethorpes, U.K. 12 D7
Cleeve Cloud, U.K. 13 F6
Clelles, France 21 D9
Clemson, U.S.A. 109 H4
Clerke Reef, Australia 92 C2
Clermont, Australia 94 C4
Clermont, France 19 C9
Clermont, U.S.A. 109 L5
Clermont-en-Argonne, France . 19 C12
Clermont-Ferrand, France .. 20 C7
Clermont-l'Hérault, France .. 20 E7
Clerval, France 19 E13
Clervaux, Lux. 17 D6
Cles, Italy 28 B8
Clevedon, U.K. 13 F5
Cleveland, Miss., U.S.A. .. 113 J9
Cleveland, Ohio, U.S.A. .. 110 E3
Cleveland, Okla., U.S.A. .. 113 G6
Cleveland, Tenn., U.S.A. .. 109 H3
Cleveland, Tex., U.S.A. .. 113 K7
Cleveland, C., Australia 94 B4
Cleveland, Mt., U.S.A. 114 B7
Cleveland Heights, U.S.A. . 110 E3
Clevelândia, Brazil 127 B5
Clew B., Ireland 15 C2
Clewiston, U.S.A. 109 M5
Clifden, Ireland 15 C1
Clifden, N.Z. 91 M1
Cliffdell, U.S.A. 116 D5
Cliffy Hd., Australia 93 G2
Clifton, Australia 95 D5
Clifton, Ariz., U.S.A. 115 K9
Clifton, Colo., U.S.A. 115 G9
Clifton, Tex., U.S.A. 113 K6

Clifton Beach, Australia 94 B4
Climax, Canada 105 D7
Clinch ➝, U.S.A. 109 H3
Clingmans Dome, U.S.A. .. 109 H4
Clint, U.S.A. 115 L10
Clinton, B.C., Canada 104 C4
Clinton, Ont., Canada 102 D3
Clinton, N.Z. 91 M2
Clinton, Ark., U.S.A. 113 H8
Clinton, Conn., U.S.A. .. 111 E12
Clinton, Ill., U.S.A. 112 E10
Clinton, Ind., U.S.A. 108 F2
Clinton, Iowa, U.S.A. 112 E9
Clinton, Mass., U.S.A. .. 111 D13
Clinton, Mo., U.S.A. 112 F8
Clinton, N.C., U.S.A. 109 H6
Clinton, Okla., U.S.A. 113 H5
Clinton, S.C., U.S.A. 109 H5
Clinton, Tenn., U.S.A. 109 G3
Clinton, Wash., U.S.A. .. 116 C4
Clinton C., Australia 94 C5
Clinton Colden L., Canada 100 B9
Clintonville, U.S.A. 112 C10
Clipperton, I., Pac. Oc. .. 97 F17
Clisham, U.K. 14 D2
Clisson, France 18 E5
Clitheroe, U.K. 12 D5
Clo-oose, Canada 116 B2
Cloates, Pt., Australia 92 D1
Clocolan, S. Africa 89 D4
Clodomira, Argentina 126 B3
Clogher Hd., Ireland 15 C5
Clonakilty, Ireland 15 E3
Clonakilty B., Ireland 15 E3
Cloncurry, Australia 94 C3
Cloncurry ➝, Australia 94 B3
Clondalkin, Ireland 15 C5
Clones, Ireland 15 B4
Clonmel, Ireland 15 D4
Cloppenburg, Germany 24 C4
Cloquet, U.S.A. 112 B8
Clorinda, Argentina 126 B4
Cloud Bay, Canada 102 C2
Cloud Peak, U.S.A. 114 D10
Cloudcroft, U.S.A. 115 K11
Cloverdale, U.S.A. 116 G4
Clovis, Calif., U.S.A. 116 J7
Clovis, N. Mex., U.S.A. .. 113 H3
Cloyes-sur-le-Loir, France .. 18 E8
Cloyne, Canada 110 B7
Cluj □, Romania 43 D8
Cluj-Napoca, Romania 43 D8
Clunes, Australia 95 F3
Cluny, France 19 F11
Cluses, France 19 F13
Clusone, Italy 28 C6
Clutha ➝, N.Z. 91 M2
Clwyd □, U.K. 12 D4
Clwyd ➝, U.K. 12 D4
Clyde, Canada 104 C6
Clyde, N.Z. 91 L2
Clyde, U.S.A. 110 C8
Clyde ➝, U.K. 14 F4
Clyde, Firth of, U.K. 14 F3
Clyde River, Canada 101 A13
Clydebank, U.K. 14 F4
Clymer, N.Y., U.S.A. 110 D5
Clymer, Pa., U.S.A. 110 D5
Ćmielów, Poland 45 H8
Côa ➝, Portugal 34 D3
Coachella, U.S.A. 117 M10
Coachella Canal, U.S.A. .. 117 N12
Coahoma, U.S.A. 113 J4
Coahuayana ➝, Mexico .. 118 D4
Coahuila □, Mexico 118 B4
Coal ➝, Canada 104 B3
Coalane, Mozam. 87 F4
Coalcomán, Mexico 118 D4
Coaldale, Canada 104 D6
Coalgate, U.S.A. 113 H6
Coalinga, U.S.A. 116 J6
Coalisland, U.K. 15 B5
Coalville, U.K. 12 E6
Coalville, U.S.A. 114 F8
Coari, Brazil 124 D6
Coast □, Kenya 86 C4
Coast Mts., Canada 104 C3
Coast Ranges, U.S.A. 116 G4
Coatbridge, U.K. 14 F4
Coatepec, Mexico 119 D5
Coatepeque, Guatemala .. 120 D1
Coatesville, U.S.A. 108 F8
Coaticook, Canada 103 C5
Coats I., Canada 101 B11
Coats Land, Antarctica 5 D1
Coatzacoalcos, Mexico .. 119 D6
Cobadin, Romania 43 F13
Cobalt, Canada 102 C4
Cobán, Guatemala 120 C1
Cobar, Australia 95 E4
Cóbh, Ireland 15 E3
Cobija, Bolivia 124 F5
Cobleskill, U.S.A. 111 D10
Coboconk, Canada 110 B6
Cobourg, Canada 102 D4
Cobourg Pen., Australia .. 92 B5
Cobram, Australia 95 F4
Cóbué, Mozam. 87 E3
Coburg, Germany 25 E6
Coca, Spain 34 D6
Cocanada = Kakinada, India 67 L13
Cocentaina, Spain 33 G4
Cochabamba, Bolivia 124 G5
Cochem, Germany 25 E3
Cochemane, Mozam. 87 F3
Cochin, India 66 Q10

Cochin China = Nam-Phan,
   Vietnam 65 G6
Cochran, U.S.A. 109 J4
Cochrane, Alta., Canada .. 104 C6
Cochrane, Ont., Canada .. 102 C3
Cochrane, Chile 128 F2
Cochrane ➝, Canada 105 B8
Cochrane, L., Chile 128 F2
Cochranton, U.S.A. 110 E4
Cockburn, Australia 95 E3
Cockburn, Canal, Chile .. 122 J3
Cockburn I., Canada 102 C3
Cockburn Ra., Australia .. 92 C4
Cockermouth, U.K. 12 C4
Cocklebiddy, Australia 93 F4
Coco ➝, Cent. Amer. 120 D3
Coco, I. del, Pac. Oc. 97 G19
Cocoa, U.S.A. 109 L5
Cocobeach, Gabon 84 D1
Cocora, Romania 43 F12
Cocos Is., Ind. Oc. 96 J1
Cod, C., U.S.A. 108 D10
Codajás, Brazil 124 D6
Codigoro, Italy 29 D9
Codlea, Romania 43 E10
Codó, Brazil 125 D10
Codogno, Italy 28 C6
Codróipo, Italy 29 C10
Codru, Munţii, Romania .. 42 D7
Cody, U.S.A. 114 D9
Coe Hill, Canada 110 B7
Coelemu, Chile 126 D1
Coen, Australia 94 A3
Coesfeld, Germany 24 D3
Cœur d'Alene, U.S.A. 114 C5
Cœur d'Alene L., U.S.A. .. 114 C5
Coevorden, Neths. 17 B6
Cofete, Canary Is. 37 F5
Coffeyville, U.S.A. 113 G7
Coffin B., Australia 95 E2
Coffin Bay, Australia 95 E2
Coffin Bay Peninsula, Australia 95 E2
Coffs Harbour, Australia .. 95 E5
Cofrentes, Spain 33 F3
Cogalnic ➝, Moldova 43 E14
Cogealac, Romania 43 F13
Coghinas ➝, Italy 30 B1
Coghinas, L. del, Italy 30 B2
Cognac, France 20 C3
Cogne, Italy 28 C4
Cogolin, France 21 E10
Cogolludo, Spain 32 E1
Cohocton ➝, U.S.A. 110 D7
Cohoctorn ➝, U.S.A. 110 D7
Cohoes, U.S.A. 111 D11
Cohuna, Australia 95 F3
Coiba, I., Panama 120 E3
Coig ➝, Argentina 128 G3
Coigeach, Rubha, U.K. .. 14 C3
Coihaique, Chile 128 F2
Coimbatore, India 66 P10
Coimbra, Brazil 124 G7
Coimbra, Portugal 34 E2
Coimbra □, Portugal 34 E2
Coín, Spain 35 J6
Coipasa, Salar de, Bolivia .. 124 G5
Cojimies, Ecuador 124 C3
Cojocna, Romania 43 D8
Cojutepequé, El Salv. 120 D2
Cokeville, U.S.A. 114 E8
Colac, Australia 95 F3
Colatina, Brazil 125 G10
Colbeck, C., Antarctica .. 5 D13
Colborne, Canada 110 C7
Colby, U.S.A. 112 F4
Colchester, U.K. 13 F8
Cold L., Canada 105 C7
Coldstream, Canada 104 C5
Coldstream, U.K. 14 F6
Coldwater, Canada 110 B5
Coldwater, Kans., U.S.A. .. 113 G5
Coldwater, Mich., U.S.A. . 108 E3
Colebrook, U.S.A. 111 B13
Coleman, U.S.A. 113 K5
Coleman ➝, Australia 94 B3
Colenso, S. Africa 89 D4
Coleraine, Australia 95 F3
Coleraine, U.K. 15 A5
Coleridge, L., N.Z. 91 K3
Colesberg, S. Africa 88 E4
Coleville, U.S.A. 116 G7
Colfax, Calif., U.S.A. 116 F6
Colfax, La., U.S.A. 113 K8
Colfax, Wash., U.S.A. .. 114 C5
Colhué Huapi, L., Argentina 128 F3
Colibaşi, Moldova 43 E13
Colibaşi, Romania 43 F9
Cólico, Italy 28 B6
Coligny, France 19 F12
Coligny, S. Africa 89 D4
Colima, Mexico 118 D4
Colima □, Mexico 118 D4
Colima, Nevado de, Mexico 118 D4
Colina, Chile 126 C1
Colina do Norte, Guinea-Biss. 82 C2
Colinas, Brazil 125 E10
Colindres, Spain 34 B7
Coll, U.K. 14 E2
Collaguasi, Chile 126 A2
Collarada, Peña, Spain .. 32 C4
Collarenebri, Australia .. 95 D4
Colle di Val d'Elsa, Italy .. 28 E8
Collécchio, Italy 28 D7
Colleen Bawn, Zimbabwe .. 87 G2
College Park, U.S.A. 109 J3
College Station, U.S.A. .. 113 K6

Collesalvetti, Italy 28 E7
Collie, Australia 93 F2
Collier B., Australia 92 C3
Collier Ra., Australia 93 D2
Collina, Passo di, Italy .. 28 D7
Collingwood, Canada 102 D3
Collingwood, N.Z. 91 J4
Collins, Canada 102 B2
Collinsville, Australia 94 C4
Collipulli, Chile 126 D1
Colliptown, Ireland 15 B3
Colmar, France 19 D14
Colmars, France 21 D10
Colmenar, Spain 35 J6
Colmenar de Oreja, Spain .. 34 E7
Colmenar Viejo, Spain .. 34 E7
Colo ➝, Australia 95 E5
Cologne = Köln, Germany .. 24 E4
Colom, I. d'en, Spain 37 B11
Coloma, U.S.A. 116 G6
Colomb-Béchar = Béchar,
   Algeria 78 B5
Colombey-les-Belles, France 19 D12
Colombey-les-Deux-Églises,
   France 19 D11
Colombia ■, S. Amer. 124 C4
Colombian Basin, S. Amer. .. 98 H12
Colombo, Sri Lanka 66 R11
Colomiers, France 20 E5
Colón, Buenos Aires, Argentina 126 C3
Colón, Entre Ríos, Argentina 126 C4
Colón, Cuba 120 B3
Colón, Panama 120 E4
Colonia de Sant Jordi, Spain 37 B9
Colonia del Sacramento,
   Uruguay 126 C4
Colonia Dora, Argentina .. 126 B3
Colonial Beach, U.S.A. .. 108 F7
Colonie, U.S.A. 111 D11
Colonna, C., Italy 31 C10
Colonsay, Canada 105 C7
Colonsay, U.K. 14 E2
Colorado □, U.S.A. 115 G10
Colorado ➝, Argentina .. 128 D4
Colorado ➝, N. Amer. .. 115 L6
Colorado ➝, U.S.A. 113 L7
Colorado City, U.S.A. 113 J4
Colorado Plateau, U.S.A. . 115 H8
Colorado River Aqueduct,
   U.S.A. 117 L12
Colorado Springs, U.S.A. .. 112 F2
Colorno, Italy 28 D7
Colotlán, Mexico 118 C4
Colstrip, U.S.A. 114 D10
Colton, U.S.A. 111 B10
Columbia, Ky., U.S.A. .. 108 G3
Columbia, La., U.S.A. .. 113 J8
Columbia, Miss., U.S.A. .. 113 K10
Columbia, Mo., U.S.A. .. 112 F8
Columbia, Pa., U.S.A. .. 111 F8
Columbia, S.C., U.S.A. .. 109 J5
Columbia, Tenn., U.S.A. .. 109 H2
Columbia ➝, N. Amer. .. 116 D2
Columbia, C., Canada 4 A4
Columbia, District of □, U.S.A. 108 F7
Columbia, Mt., Canada .. 104 C5
Columbia Basin, U.S.A. .. 114 C4
Columbia Falls, U.S.A. .. 114 B6
Columbia Mts., U.S.A. .. 104 C5
Columbia Plateau, U.S.A. .. 114 D4
Columbiana, U.S.A. 110 F4
Columbretes, Is., Spain .. 32 F5
Columbus, Ga., U.S.A. .. 109 J3
Columbus, Ind., U.S.A. .. 108 F3
Columbus, Kans., U.S.A. .. 113 G7
Columbus, Miss., U.S.A. .. 109 J1
Columbus, Mont., U.S.A. .. 114 D9
Columbus, N. Mex., U.S.A. 115 L10
Columbus, Nebr., U.S.A. .. 112 E6
Columbus, Ohio, U.S.A. .. 108 F4
Columbus, Tex., U.S.A. .. 113 L6
Colunga, Spain 34 B5
Colusa, U.S.A. 116 F4
Colville, U.S.A. 114 B5
Colville ➝, U.S.A. 100 A4
Colville, C., N.Z. 91 G5
Colwood, Canada 116 B3
Colwyn Bay, U.K. 12 D4
Coma, Ethiopia 81 F4
Comácchio, Italy 29 D9
Comalcalco, Mexico 119 D6
Comallo, Argentina 128 E2
Comana, Romania 43 F11
Comanche, U.S.A. 113 K5
Comănești, Romania 43 D11
Comarnic, Romania 43 E10
Comayagua, Honduras .. 120 D2
Combahee ➝, U.S.A. 109 J5
Combarbalá, Chile 126 C1
Combeaufontaine, France 19 E12
Comber, Canada 110 D2
Comber, U.K. 15 B6
Combermere, Canada 110 A7
Comblain-au-Pont, Belgium 17 D5
Combourg, France 18 D5
Combronde, France 20 C7
Combrailles, France 19 F9
Comeragh Mts., Ireland .. 15 D4
Comet, Australia 94 C4
Comilla, Bangla. 67 H17
Comino, Malta 36 C1
Comino, C., Italy 30 B2
Cómiso, Italy 31 F7
Comitán, Mexico 119 D6
Commentry, France 19 F9
Commerce, Ga., U.S.A. .. 109 H4
Commerce, Tex., U.S.A. .. 113 J7

Commercy, France 19 D12
Committee B., Canada .. 101 B11
Commonwealth B., Antarctica 5 C10
Commoron Cr. ➝, Australia .. 95 D5
Communism Pk. =
   Kommunizma, Pik, Tajikistan 50 F8
Como, Italy 28 C6
Como, Lago di, Italy 28 B6
Comodoro Rivadavia, Argentina 128 F3
Comorâşte, Romania 42 E6
Comorin, C., India 66 Q10
Comoro Is. = Comoros ■,
   Ind. Oc. 77 H8
Comoros ■, Ind. Oc. 77 H8
Comox, Canada 104 D4
Compiègne, France 19 C9
Comporta, Portugal 35 G2
Compostela, Mexico 118 C4
Comprida, I., Brazil 127 A6
Compton, Canada 111 A13
Compton, U.S.A. 117 M8
Comrat, Moldova 43 D13
Con Cuong, Vietnam 64 C5
Con Son, Vietnam 65 H6
Conakry, Guinea 82 D2
Conara, Australia 94 G4
Concarneau, France 18 E3
Conceição, Mozam. 87 F4
Conceição da Barra, Brazil 125 G11
Conceição do Araguaia, Brazil 125 E9
Concepción, Argentina .. 126 B2
Concepción, Bolivia 124 G6
Concepción, Chile 126 D1
Concepción, Mexico 119 D6
Concepción, Paraguay .. 126 A4
Concepción □, Chile 126 D1
Concepción ➝, Mexico .. 118 A2
Concepción, Est. de, Chile 128 G2
Concepción, L., Bolivia .. 124 G6
Concepción, Punta, Mexico 118 B2
Concepción del Oro, Mexico 118 C4
Concepción del Uruguay,
   Argentina 126 C4
Conception, Pt., U.S.A. .. 117 L6
Conception B., Canada .. 103 C9
Conception B., Namibia .. 88 C1
Conception I., Bahamas .. 121 B4
Concession, Zimbabwe .. 87 F3
Conchas Dam, U.S.A. .. 113 H2
Conches-en-Ouche, France 18 D7
Concho, U.S.A. 115 J9
Concho ➝, U.S.A. 113 K5
Conchos ➝, Chihuahua, Mexico 118 B3
Conchos ➝, Tamaulipas,
   Mexico 119 B5
Concord, Calif., U.S.A. .. 116 H4
Concord, N.C., U.S.A. .. 109 H5
Concord, N.H., U.S.A. .. 111 C13
Concordia, Argentina 126 C4
Concórdia, Brazil 124 D5
Concordia, Mexico 118 C3
Concordia, U.S.A. 112 F6
Concrete, U.S.A. 114 B3
Condamine, Australia 95 D5
Condat, France 20 C6
Conde, U.S.A. 112 C5
Condé-sur-Noireau, France 18 D6
Condeúba, Brazil 125 F10
Condobolin, Australia 95 E4
Condom, France 20 E4
Condon, U.S.A. 114 D3
Conegliano, Italy 29 C9
Conejera, I. = Conills, I. des,
   Spain 37 B9
Conejos, Mexico 118 B4
Confolens, France 20 B4
Confuso ➝, Paraguay 126 B4
Congaz, Moldova 43 D13
Conghua, China 59 F9
Congjiang, China 58 E7
Congleton, U.K. 12 D5
Congo (Kinshasa) = Congo,
   Dem. Rep. of the ■, Africa 84 E4
Congo ■, Africa 84 E3
Congo ➝, Africa 84 F2
Congo, Dem. Rep. of the ■,
   Africa 84 E4
Congo Basin, Africa 84 E4
Congonhas, Brazil 127 A7
Congress, U.S.A. 115 J7
Conil = Conil de la Frontera,
   Spain 35 J4
Conil de la Frontera, Spain 35 J4
Conills, I. des, Spain 37 B9
Coniston, Canada 102 C3
Conjeeveram = Kanchipuram,
   India 66 N11
Conklin, Canada 105 B6
Conklin, U.S.A. 111 D9
Conn, L., Ireland 15 B2
Connacht □, Ireland 15 C2
Conneaut, U.S.A. 110 E4
Connecticut □, U.S.A. .. 111 E12
Connecticut ➝, U.S.A. .. 111 E12
Connell, U.S.A. 114 C4
Connellsville, U.S.A. 110 F5
Connemara □, Ireland .. 15 C2
Connemaugh ➝, U.S.A. .. 110 F5
Connerré, France 18 D7
Connersville, U.S.A. 108 F3
Connors Ra., Australia .. 94 C4
Conques, France 20 D6
Conquest, Canada 105 C7
Conrad, U.S.A. 114 B8
Conran, C., Australia .. 95 F4
Conroe, U.S.A. 113 K7
Consecon, Canada 110 C7

Conselheiro Lafaiete, *Brazil* . . . 127 A7
Conselve, *Italy* 29 C8
Consett, *U.K.* 12 C6
Consort, *Canada* 105 C6
Constance = Konstanz, *Germany* 25 H5
Constance, L. = Bodensee,
  Europe 25 H5
Constanța, *Romania* 43 F13
Constanța □, *Romania* 43 F13
Constantia, *U.S.A.* 111 C8
Constantina, *Spain* 35 H5
Constantine, *Algeria* 78 A7
Constitución, *Chile* 126 D1
Constitución, *Uruguay* 126 C4
Consuegra, *Spain* 35 F7
Consul, *Canada* 105 D7
Contact, *U.S.A.* 114 F6
Contai, *India* 69 J12
Contamana, *Peru* 124 E4
Contarina, *Italy* 29 C9
Contas ➤, *Brazil* 125 F11
Contes, *France* 21 E11
Contoocook, *U.S.A.* 111 C13
Contra Costa, *Mozam.* 89 D5
Contres, *France* 18 E8
Contrexéville, *France* 19 D12
Contwoyto L., *Canada* 100 B8
Conversano, *Italy* 31 B10
Conway = Conwy, *U.K.* 12 D4
Conway = Conwy ➤, *U.K.* . . . 12 D4
Conway, *Ark., U.S.A.* 113 H8
Conway, *N.H., U.S.A.* 111 C13
Conway, *S.C., U.S.A.* 109 J6
Conway, L., *Australia* 95 D2
Conwy, *U.K.* 12 D4
Conwy □, *U.K.* 12 D4
Conwy ➤, *U.K.* 12 D4
Coober Pedy, *Australia* 95 D1
Cooch Behar = Koch Bihar,
  India 67 F16
Cooinda, *Australia* 92 B5
Cook, *Australia* 93 F5
Cook, *U.S.A.* 112 B8
Cook, B., *Chile* 128 H3
Cook, C., *Canada* 104 C3
Cook, Mt. = Aoraki Mount
  Cook, *N.Z.* 91 K3
Cook Inlet, *U.S.A.* 100 C4
Cook Is., *Pac. Oc.* 97 J12
Cook Strait, *N.Z.* 91 J5
Cookeville, *U.S.A.* 109 G3
Cookhouse, *S. Africa* 88 E4
Cookshire, *Canada* 111 A13
Cookstown, *U.K.* 15 B5
Cooksville, *Canada* 110 C5
Cooktown, *Australia* 94 B4
Coolabah, *Australia* 95 E4
Cooladdi, *Australia* 95 D4
Coolah, *Australia* 95 E4
Coolamon, *Australia* 95 E4
Coolgardie, *Australia* 93 F3
Coolidge, *U.S.A.* 115 K8
Coolidge Dam, *U.S.A.* 115 K8
Cooma, *Australia* 95 F4
Coon Rapids, *U.S.A.* 112 C8
Coonabarabran, *Australia* . . . 95 E4
Coonamble, *Australia* 95 E4
Coonana, *Australia* 93 F3
Coondapoor, *India* 66 N9
Cooninie, L., *Australia* 95 D2
Cooper, *U.S.A.* 113 J7
Cooper Cr. ➤, *Australia* 95 D2
Cooperstown, *N. Dak., U.S.A.* . 112 B5
Cooperstown, *N.Y., U.S.A.* . . 111 D10
Coorabie, *Australia* 93 F5
Coorong, The, *Australia* 95 F2
Coorow, *Australia* 93 E2
Cooroy, *Australia* 95 D5
Coos Bay, *U.S.A.* 114 E1
Coosa ➤, *U.S.A.* 109 J2
Cootamundra, *Australia* 95 E4
Cootehill, *Ireland* 15 B4
Copahue Paso, *Argentina* . . . 126 D1
Copainalá, *Mexico* 119 D6
Copake Falls, *U.S.A.* 111 D11
Copalnic Mănăştur, *Romania* . 43 C8
Copán, *Honduras* 120 D2
Cope, *U.S.A.* 112 F3
Cope, C., *Spain* 33 H3
Copenhagen = København,
  Denmark 11 J6
Copenhagen, *U.S.A.* 111 C9
Copertino, *Italy* 31 B11
Copiapó, *Chile* 126 B1
Copiapó ➤, *Chile* 126 B1
Coplay, *U.S.A.* 111 F9
Copp L., *Canada* 104 A6
Copparo, *Italy* 29 D8
Coppename ➤, *Surinam* 125 B7
Copper Harbor, *U.S.A.* 108 B2
Copper Queen, *Zimbabwe* . . . 87 F2
Copperbelt □, *Zambia* 87 E2
Coppermine = Kugluktuk,
  Canada 100 B8
Coppermine ➤, *Canada* 100 B8
Copperopolis, *U.S.A.* 116 H6
Copşa Mică, *Romania* 43 D9
Coquet ➤, *U.K.* 12 B6
Coquille, *U.S.A.* 114 E1
Coquimbo, *Chile* 126 C1
Coquimbo □, *Chile* 126 C1
Corabia, *Romania* 43 G9
Coracora, *Peru* 124 G4
Coraki, *Australia* 95 D5
Coral, *U.S.A.* 110 F5
Coral Gables, *U.S.A.* 109 N5

Coral Harbour = Salliq, *Canada* 101 B11
Coral Sea, *Pac. Oc.* 96 J7
Coral Springs, *U.S.A.* 109 M5
Corato, *Italy* 31 A9
Corbeil-Essonnes, *France* . . . 19 D9
Corbie, *France* 19 C9
Corbières, *France* 20 F6
Corbigny, *France* 19 E10
Corbin, *U.S.A.* 108 G3
Corbones ➤, *Spain* 35 H5
Corbu, *Romania* 43 F13
Corby, *U.K.* 13 E7
Corcaigh = Cork, *Ireland* . . . 15 E3
Corcoran, *U.S.A.* 116 J7
Corcubión, *Spain* 34 C1
Cordele, *U.S.A.* 109 K4
Cordell, *U.S.A.* 113 H5
Cordenòns, *Italy* 29 C9
Cordes, *France* 20 D5
Córdoba, *Argentina* 126 C3
Córdoba, *Mexico* 119 D5
Córdoba, *Spain* 35 H6
Córdoba □, *Argentina* 126 C3
Córdoba □, *Spain* 35 G6
Córdoba, Sierra de, *Argentina* . 126 C3
Cordon, *Phil.* 61 C4
Cordova, *U.S.A.* 100 B5
Corella, *Spain* 32 C3
Corella ➤, *Australia* 94 B3
Corfield, *Australia* 94 C3
Corfu = Kérkira, *Greece* 36 A3
Corfu, Str. of, *Greece* 36 A4
Corgo = O Corgo, *Spain* 34 C3
Cori, *Italy* 30 A5
Coria, *Spain* 34 F4
Coria del Río, *Spain* 35 H4
Corigliano Cálabro, *Italy* 31 C9
Coringa Is., *Australia* 94 B4
Corinth = Kórinthos, *Greece* . 38 D4
Corinth, *Miss., U.S.A.* 109 H1
Corinth, *N.Y., U.S.A.* 111 C11
Corinth, G. of = Korinthiakós
  Kólpos, *Greece* 38 C4
Corinth Canal, *Greece* 38 D4
Corinto, *Brazil* 125 G10
Corinto, *Nic.* 120 D2
Cork, *Ireland* 15 E3
Cork □, *Ireland* 15 E3
Cork Harbour, *Ireland* 15 E3
Corlay, *France* 18 D3
Corleone, *Italy* 30 E6
Corleto Perticara, *Italy* 31 B9
Çorlu, *Turkey* 41 E11
Cormack L., *Canada* 104 A4
Cormòns, *Italy* 29 C10
Cormorant, *Canada* 105 C8
Cormorant L., *Canada* 105 C8
Corn Is. = Maiz, Is. del, *Nic.* . 120 D3
Cornélio Procópio, *Brazil* 127 A5
Corner Brook, *Canada* 103 C8
Corneşti, *Moldova* 43 C13
Corníglio, *Italy* 28 D7
Corning, *Ark., U.S.A.* 113 G9
Corning, *Calif., U.S.A.* 114 G2
Corning, *Iowa, U.S.A.* 112 E7
Corning, *N.Y., U.S.A.* 110 D7
Corno Grande, *Italy* 29 F10
Cornwall, *Canada* 102 C5
Cornwall, *U.S.A.* 111 F8
Cornwall □, *U.K.* 13 G3
Corny Pt., *Australia* 95 E2
Coro, *Venezuela* 124 A5
Coroatá, *Brazil* 125 D10
Corocoro, *Bolivia* 124 G5
Coroico, *Bolivia* 124 G5
Coromandel, *N.Z.* 91 G5
Coromandel Coast, *India* . . . 66 N12
Corona, *Calif., U.S.A.* 117 M9
Corona, *N. Mex., U.S.A.* 115 J11
Coronach, *Canada* 105 D7
Coronado, *U.S.A.* 117 N9
Coronado, B. de, *Costa Rica* . 120 E3
Coronados, Is. los, *U.S.A.* . . . 117 N9
Coronation, *Canada* 104 C6
Coronation I., *Antarctica* . . . 5 C18
Coronation Is., *Australia* 92 B3
Coronda, *Argentina* 126 C3
Coronel, *Chile* 126 D1
Coronel Bogado, *Paraguay* . . 126 B4
Coronel Dorrego, *Argentina* . . 126 D3
Coronel Oviedo, *Paraguay* . . 126 B4
Coronel Pringles, *Argentina* . . 126 D3
Coronel Suárez, *Argentina* . . 126 D3
Coronel Vidal, *Argentina* 126 D4
Coropuna, Nevado, *Peru* 124 G4
Çorovodë, *Albania* 40 F4
Corowa, *Australia* 95 F4
Corozal, *Belize* 119 D7
Corps, *France* 21 D9
Corpus, *Argentina* 127 B4
Corpus Christi, *U.S.A.* 113 M6
Corpus Christi, L., *U.S.A.* . . . 113 L6
Corral de Almaguer, *Spain* . . 34 F7
Corralejo, *Canary Is.* 37 F6
Corraun Pen., *Ireland* 15 C2
Corréggio, *Italy* 28 D7
Corrente ➤, *C. Amer., Mozam.* 89 C6
Corrèze □, *France* 20 C5
Corrèze ➤, *France* 20 C5
Corrib, L., *Ireland* 15 C2
Corridónia, *Italy* 29 E10
Corrientes, *Argentina* 126 B4
Corrientes □, *Argentina* 126 B4
Corrientes ➤, *Argentina* 126 C4
Corrientes ➤, *Peru* 124 D4
Corrientes, C., *Colombia* 124 B3

Corrientes, C., *Cuba* 120 B3
Corrientes, C., *Mexico* 118 C3
Corrigan, *U.S.A.* 113 K7
Corrigin, *Australia* 93 F2
Corry, *U.S.A.* 110 E5
Corse, *France* 21 G13
Corse, C., *France* 21 E13
Corse-du-Sud □, *France* 21 G13
Corsica = Corse, *France* 21 G13
Corsicana, *U.S.A.* 113 J6
Corte, *France* 21 F13
Corte Pinto, *Portugal* 35 H3
Cortegana, *Spain* 35 H4
Cortez, *U.S.A.* 115 H9
Cortina d'Ampezzo, *Italy* . . . 29 B9
Cortland, *N.Y., U.S.A.* 111 D8
Cortland, *Ohio, U.S.A.* 110 E4
Cortona, *Italy* 29 E8
Corubal ➤, *Guinea-Biss.* 82 C2
Coruche, *Portugal* 35 G2
Çoruh ➤, *Turkey* 49 K5
Çorum, *Turkey* 72 B6
Corumbá, *Brazil* 124 G7
Corund, *Romania* 43 D10
Corunna = A Coruña, *Spain* . 34 B2
Corvallis, *U.S.A.* 114 D2
Corvette, L. de la, *Canada* . . 102 B5
Corydon, *U.S.A.* 112 E8
Cosalá, *Mexico* 118 C3
Cosamaloapan, *Mexico* 119 D5
Cosenza, *Italy* 31 C9
Coşereni, *Romania* 43 F11
Coshocton, *U.S.A.* 110 F3
Cosmo Newberry, *Australia* . . 93 E3
Cosne-Cours-sur-Loire, *France* 19 E9
Coso Junction, *U.S.A.* 117 J9
Coso Pk., *U.S.A.* 117 J9
Cospeito, *Spain* 34 B3
Cosquín, *Argentina* 126 C3
Cossato, *Italy* 28 C5
Cossé-le-Vivien, *France* 18 E6
Cosson ➤, *France* 18 E8
Costa Blanca, *Spain* 33 G4
Costa Brava, *Spain* 32 D8
Costa del Sol, *Spain* 35 J6
Costa Dorada, *Spain* 32 D6
Costa Mesa, *U.S.A.* 117 M9
Costa Rica ■, *Cent. Amer.* . . 120 E3
Costa Smeralda, *Italy* 30 A2
Costeşti, *Romania* 43 F9
Costigliole d'Asti, *Italy* 28 D5
Cosumnes ➤, *U.S.A.* 116 G5
Coswig, Sachsen, *Germany* . . 24 D9
Coswig, Sachsen-Anhalt,
  Germany 24 D8
Cotabato, *Phil.* 61 H6
Cotagaita, *Bolivia* 126 A2
Côte d'Azur, *France* 21 E11
Côte-d'Ivoire = Ivory Coast ■,
  Africa 82 D4
Côte d'Or, *France* 19 E11
Côte-d'Or □, *France* 19 E11
Coteau des Prairies, *U.S.A.* . . 112 C6
Coteau du Missouri, *U.S.A.* . . 112 B4
Coteau Landing, *Canada* 111 A10
Cotentin, *France* 18 C5
Côtes-d'Armor □, *France* . . . 18 D4
Côtes de Meuse, *France* 19 C12
Côtes-du-Nord = Côtes-
  d'Armor □, *France* 18 D4
Cotiella, *Spain* 32 C5
Cotillo, *Canary Is.* 37 F5
Cotiujeni, *Moldova* 43 C13
Cotonou, *Benin* 83 D5
Cotopaxi, *Ecuador* 122 D3
Cotronei, *Italy* 31 C9
Cotswold Hills, *U.K.* 13 F5
Cottage Grove, *U.S.A.* 114 E2
Cottbus, *Germany* 24 D10
Cottonwood, *U.S.A.* 115 J7
Cotulla, *U.S.A.* 113 L5
Coubre, Pte. de la, *France* . . 20 C2
Couches, *France* 19 F11
Couço, *Portugal* 35 G2
Coudersport, *U.S.A.* 110 E6
Couedic, C. du, *Australia* . . . 95 F2
Couëron, *France* 18 E5
Couesnon ➤, *France* 18 D5
Couhé, *France* 20 B4
Coulanges-sur-Yonne, *France* . 19 E10
Coulee City, *U.S.A.* 114 C4
Coulman I., *Antarctica* 5 D11
Coulommiers, *France* 19 D10
Coulon ➤, *France* 21 E9
Coulonge ➤, *Canada* 102 C4
Coulonges-sur-l'Autize, *France* 20 B3
Coulounieix-Chamiers, *France* . 20 C4
Coulterville, *U.S.A.* 116 H6
Council, *U.S.A.* 114 D5
Council Bluffs, *U.S.A.* 112 E7
Council Grove, *U.S.A.* 112 F6
Coupeville, *U.S.A.* 116 B4
Courantyne ➤, *S. Amer.* 122 C5
Courcelles, *Belgium* 17 D4
Courçon, *France* 20 B3
Courmayeur, *Italy* 28 C3
Couronne, C., *France* 21 E9
Cours-la-Ville, *France* 19 F11
Coursan, *France* 20 E7
Courseulles-sur-Mer, *France* . 18 C6
Courtenay, *Canada* 104 D4
Courtland, *France* 19 D10
Courtland, *U.S.A.* 116 G5
Courtrai = Kortrijk, *Belgium* . 17 D3
Courtright, *Canada* 110 D2
Coushatta, *U.S.A.* 113 J8
Coutances, *France* 18 C5

Coutras, *France* 20 C3
Coutts Crossing, *Australia* . . . 95 D5
Couvin, *Belgium* 17 D4
Covarrubias, *Spain* 34 C7
Covasna, *Romania* 43 E11
Covasna □, *Romania* 43 E10
Cove I., *Canada* 110 A3
Coventry, *U.K.* 13 E6
Covilhã, *Portugal* 34 E3
Covington, *Ga., U.S.A.* 109 J4
Covington, *Ky., U.S.A.* 108 F3
Covington, *Okla., U.S.A.* 113 G6
Covington, *Tenn., U.S.A.* . . . 113 H10
Covington, *Va., U.S.A.* 108 G5
Cowal, L., *Australia* 95 E4
Cowan, L., *Australia* 93 F3
Cowan L., *Canada* 105 C7
Cowangie, *Australia* 95 F3
Cowansville, *Canada* 102 C5
Coward Springs, *Australia* . . . 95 D2
Cowcowing Lakes, *Australia* . . 93 F2
Cowdenbeath, *U.K.* 14 E5
Cowell, *Australia* 95 E2
Cowes, *U.K.* 13 G6
Cowichan L., *Canada* 116 B2
Cowlitz ➤, *U.S.A.* 116 D4
Cowra, *Australia* 95 E4
Cox, *Spain* 33 G4
Coxilha Grande, *Brazil* 127 B5
Coxim, *Brazil* 125 G8
Cox's Bazar, *Bangla.* 67 J17
Coyote Wells, *U.S.A.* 117 N11
Coyuca de Benítez, *Mexico* . . 119 D4
Coyuca de Catalan, *Mexico* . . 118 D4
Cozad, *U.S.A.* 112 E5
Cozes, *France* 20 C3
Cozumel, *Mexico* 119 C7
Cozumel, Isla, *Mexico* 119 C7
Cracow = Kraków, *Poland* . . 45 H6
Cracow, *Australia* 95 D5
Cradock, *Australia* 95 E2
Cradock, *S. Africa* 88 E4
Craig, *U.S.A.* 114 F10
Craigavon, *U.K.* 15 B5
Craigmore, *Zimbabwe* 87 G3
Craik, *Canada* 105 C7
Crailsheim, *Germany* 25 F6
Craiova, *Romania* 43 F8
Cramsie, *Australia* 94 C3
Cranberry L., *U.S.A.* 111 B10
Cranberry Portage, *Canada* . . 105 C8
Cranbrook, *Australia* 93 F2
Cranbrook, *Canada* 104 D5
Crandon, *U.S.A.* 112 C10
Crane, *Oreg., U.S.A.* 114 E4
Crane, *Tex., U.S.A.* 113 K3
Cranston, *U.S.A.* 111 E13
Craon, *France* 18 E6
Craonne, *France* 19 C10
Craponne-sur-Arzon, *France* . 20 C7
Crasna, *Romania* 43 D12
Crasna ➤, *Romania* 42 C7
Crasnei, Munţii, *Romania* . . . 43 C8
Crater L., *U.S.A.* 114 E2
Crater Lake National Park,
  U.S.A. 114 E2
Crateús, *Brazil* 125 E10
Crati ➤, *Italy* 31 C9
Crato, *Brazil* 125 E11
Crato, *Portugal* 35 F3
Craven, L., *Canada* 102 B4
Crawford, *U.S.A.* 112 D3
Crawfordsville, *U.S.A.* 108 E2
Crawley, *U.K.* 13 F7
Crazy Mts., *U.S.A.* 114 C8
Crean L., *Canada* 105 C7
Crécy-en-Ponthieu, *France* . . 19 B8
Crediton, *Canada* 110 C3
Cree ➤, *Canada* 105 B7
Cree ➤, *U.K.* 14 G4
Cree L., *Canada* 105 B7
Creede, *U.S.A.* 115 H10
Creel, *Mexico* 118 B3
Creemore, *Canada* 110 B4
Creighton, *Canada* 105 C8
Creighton, *U.S.A.* 112 D6
Creil, *France* 19 C9
Crema, *Italy* 28 C6
Cremona, *Italy* 28 C7
Crepaja, *Serbia, Yug.* 42 E5
Crépy, *France* 19 C10
Crépy-en-Valois, *France* 19 C9
Cres, *Croatia* 29 D11
Crescent City, *U.S.A.* 114 F1
Crescentino, *Italy* 28 C5
Crespino, *Italy* 29 D8
Crespo, *Argentina* 126 C3
Cresson, *U.S.A.* 110 F6
Crest, *France* 21 D9
Cresta, Mt., *Phil.* 61 C5
Crestline, *Calif., U.S.A.* 117 L9
Crestline, *Ohio, U.S.A.* 110 F2
Creston, *Canada* 104 D5
Creston, *Calif., U.S.A.* 116 K6
Creston, *Iowa, U.S.A.* 112 E7
Crestview, *Calif., U.S.A.* 116 H8
Crestview, *Fla., U.S.A.* 109 K2
Crêt de la Neige, *France* 19 F12
Crete = Kríti, *Greece* 36 D7
Crete, *U.S.A.* 112 E6
Crete, Sea of, *Greece* 39 E7
Créteil, *France* 19 D9
Creus, C. de, *Spain* 32 C8
Creuse □, *France* 19 F9
Creuse ➤, *France* 20 B4
Creutzwald, *France* 19 C13
Creuzburg, *Germany* 24 D6

Crèvecœur-le-Grand, *France* . . 19 C9
Crevillente, *Spain* 33 G4
Crewe, *U.K.* 12 D5
Crewkerne, *U.K.* 13 G5
Criciúma, *Brazil* 127 B6
Cricova, *Moldova* 43 C13
Crieff, *U.K.* 14 E5
Crikvenica, *Croatia* 29 C11
Crimea □, *Ukraine* 47 K8
Crimean Pen. = Krymskyy
  Pivostriv, *Ukraine* 47 K8
Crimmitschau, *Germany* 24 E8
Cristuru Secuiesc, *Romania* . . 43 D10
Crişul Alb ➤, *Romania* 42 D6
Crişul Negru ➤, *Romania* . . . 42 D6
Crişul Repede ➤, *Romania* . . 42 D5
Criuleni, *Moldova* 43 C14
Crivitz, *Germany* 24 B7
Crna ➤, *Macedonia* 40 E5
Crna Gora = Montenegro □,
  Yugoslavia 40 D3
Crna Gora, *Macedonia* 40 D5
Crna Reka = Crna ➤,
  Macedonia 40 E5
Crna Trava, *Serbia, Yug.* . . . 40 D6
Crni Drim ➤, *Macedonia* 40 E4
Crni Timok ➤, *Serbia, Yug.* . . 40 C6
Crnoljeva Planina, *Kosovo, Yug.* 40 D5
Črnomelj, *Slovenia* 29 C12
Croagh Patrick, *Ireland* 15 C2
Croatia ■, *Europe* 29 C13
Crocker, Banjaran, *Malaysia* . . 62 C5
Crockett, *U.S.A.* 113 K7
Crocodile = Krokodil ➤,
  Mozam. 89 D5
Crocodile Is., *Australia* 94 A1
Crocq, *France* 20 C6
Crodo, *Italy* 28 B5
Crohy Hd., *Ireland* 15 B3
Croisette, C., *France* 21 E9
Croisic, Pte. du, *France* 18 E4
Croix, L. La, *Canada* 102 C1
Croker, C., *Australia* 92 B5
Croker, C., *Canada* 110 B4
Croker I., *Australia* 92 B5
Cromarty, *U.K.* 14 D4
Cromer, *U.K.* 12 E9
Cromwell, *N.Z.* 91 L2
Cromwell, *U.S.A.* 111 E12
Cronat, *France* 19 F10
Crook, *U.K.* 12 C6
Crooked ➤, *Canada* 104 C4
Crooked ➤, *U.S.A.* 114 D3
Crooked I., *Bahamas* 121 B5
Crooked Island Passage,
  Bahamas 121 B5
Crookston, *Minn., U.S.A.* 112 B6
Crookston, *Nebr., U.S.A.* . . . 112 D4
Crookwell, *Australia* 95 E4
Crosby, *U.K.* 12 D4
Crosby, *N. Dak., U.S.A.* 112 A3
Crosby, *Pa., U.S.A.* 110 E6
Crosbyton, *U.S.A.* 113 J4
Crosía, *Italy* 31 C9
Cross ➤, *Nigeria* 83 D6
Cross City, *U.S.A.* 109 L4
Cross Fell, *U.K.* 12 C5
Cross L., *Canada* 105 C9
Cross Lake, *Canada* 105 C9
Cross River □, *Nigeria* 83 D6
Cross Sound, *U.S.A.* 100 C6
Crossett, *U.S.A.* 113 J9
Crosshaven, *Ireland* 15 E3
Crossville, *U.S.A.* 109 G3
Croswell, *U.S.A.* 110 C2
Croton-on-Hudson, *U.S.A.* . . . 111 E11
Crotone, *Italy* 31 C10
Crow ➤, *Canada* 104 B4
Crow Agency, *U.S.A.* 114 D10
Crow Hd., *Ireland* 15 E1
Crowell, *U.S.A.* 113 J5
Crowley, *U.S.A.* 113 K8
Crowley, L., *U.S.A.* 116 H8
Crown Point, *Ind., U.S.A.* . . . 108 E2
Crown Point, *N.Y., U.S.A.* . . . 111 C11
Crownpoint, *U.S.A.* 115 J9
Crows Landing, *U.S.A.* 116 H5
Crows Nest, *Australia* 95 D5
Crowsnest Pass, *Canada* 104 D6
Croydon, *Australia* 94 B3
Croydon □, *U.K.* 13 F7
Crozet, Is., *Ind. Oc.* 3 G12
Crozon, *France* 18 D2
Cruz, C., *Cuba* 120 C4
Cruz Alta, *Brazil* 127 B5
Cruz del Eje, *Argentina* 126 C3
Cruzeiro, *Brazil* 127 A7
Cruzeiro do Oeste, *Brazil* . . . 127 A5
Cruzeiro do Sul, *Brazil* 124 E4
Cry L., *Canada* 104 B3
Crystal Bay, *U.S.A.* 116 F7
Crystal Brook, *Australia* 95 E2
Crystal City, *U.S.A.* 113 L5
Crystal Falls, *U.S.A.* 108 B1
Crystal River, *U.S.A.* 109 L4
Crystal Springs, *U.S.A.* 113 K9
Csenger, *Hungary* 42 C7
Csongrád, *Hungary* 42 D5
Csongrád □, *Hungary* 42 D5
Csorna, *Hungary* 42 C2
Csurgo, *Hungary* 42 D2
Cua Rao, *Vietnam* 64 C5
Cuácua ➤, *Mozam.* 87 F4
Cuamato, *Angola* 88 B2
Cuamba, *Mozam.* 87 E4

149

Cuando ➤, *Angola* 85 H4
Cuando Cubango □, *Angola* 88 B3
Cuangar, *Angola* 88 B2
Cuango = Kwango ➤,
　Dem. Rep. of the Congo 84 C4
Cuanza ➤, *Angola* 84 F2
Cuarto ➤, *Argentina* 126 C3
Cuatrociénegas, *Mexico* 118 B4
Cuauhtémoc, *Mexico* 118 B3
Cuba, *Portugal* 35 G3
Cuba, *N. Mex., U.S.A.* 115 J10
Cuba, *N.Y., U.S.A.* 110 D6
Cuba ■, *W. Indies* 120 B4
Cubango ➤, *Africa* 88 B3
Çubuk, *Turkey* 72 B5
Cuchumatanes, Sierra de los,
　Guatemala 120 C1
Cuckfield, *U.K.* 13 F7
Cucuí, *Brazil* 124 C5
Cucurpe, *Mexico* 118 A2
Cúcuta, *Colombia* 124 B4
Cudalbi, *Romania* 43 E12
Cuddalore, *India* 66 P11
Cuddapah, *India* 66 M11
Cuddapan, L., *Australia* 94 D3
Cudillero, *Spain* 34 B4
Cue, *Australia* 93 E2
Cuéllar, *Spain* 34 D6
Cuenca, *Ecuador* 124 D3
Cuenca, *Spain* 32 E2
Cuenca □, *Spain* 32 F3
Cuenca, Serranía de, *Spain* 32 F2
Cuerdo del Pozo, Embalse de la,
　Spain 32 D2
Cuernavaca, *Mexico* 119 D5
Cuero, *U.S.A.* 113 L6
Cuers, *France* 21 E10
Cuevas del Almanzora, *Spain* .. 33 H3
Cuevo, *Bolivia* 124 H6
Cugir, *Romania* 43 E8
Cugnaux, *France* 20 E5
Cuhai-Bakony ➤, *Hungary* .. 42 C2
Cuiabá, *Brazil* 125 G7
Cuiabá ➤, *Brazil* 125 G7
Cuijk, *Neths.* 17 C5
Cuilco, *Guatemala* 120 C1
Cuillin Hills, *U.K.* 14 D2
Cuillin Sd., *U.K.* 14 D2
Cuiseaux, *France* 19 F12
Cuito ➤, *Angola* 88 B3
Cuitzeo, L. de, *Mexico* 118 D4
Cujmir, *Romania* 42 F7
Cukai, *Malaysia* 65 K4
Culbertson, *U.S.A.* 112 A2
Culcairn, *Australia* 95 F4
Culebra, Sierra de la, *Spain* .. 34 D4
Culfa, *Azerbaijan* 73 C11
Culgoa ➤, *Australia* 95 D4
Culiacán, *Mexico* 118 C3
Culiacán ➤, *Mexico* 118 C3
Culion, *Phil.* 61 F4
Cúllar, *Spain* 35 H8
Cullarin Ra., *Australia* 95 E4
Cullen, *Australia* 14 D6
Cullen Pt., *Australia* 94 A3
Cullera, *Spain* 33 F4
Cullman, *U.S.A.* 109 H2
Culoz, *France* 21 C9
Culpeper, *U.S.A.* 108 F7
Culuene ➤, *Brazil* 125 F8
Culver, Pt., *Australia* 93 F3
Culverden, *N.Z.* 91 K4
Cumaná, *Venezuela* 124 A6
Cumaovası, *Turkey* 39 C9
Cumberland, *B.C., Canada* 104 D4
Cumberland, *Ont., Canada* ... 111 A9
Cumberland, *U.S.A.* 108 F6
Cumberland ➤, *U.S.A.* 109 G2
Cumberland, L., *U.S.A.* 109 G3
Cumberland I., *U.S.A.* 109 K5
Cumberland Is., *Australia* 94 C4
Cumberland L., *Canada* 105 C8
Cumberland Pen., *Canada* 101 B13
Cumberland Plateau, *U.S.A.* .. 109 H3
Cumberland Sd., *Canada* 101 B13
Cumbernauld, *U.K.* 14 F5
Cumborah, *Australia* 95 D4
Cumbres Mayores, *Spain* 35 G4
Cumbria □, *U.K.* 12 C5
Cumbrian Mts., *U.K.* 12 C5
Cumbum, *India* 66 M11
Cuminá ➤, *Brazil* 125 D7
Cummings Mt., *U.S.A.* 117 K8
Cummins, *Australia* 95 E2
Cumnock, *Australia* 95 E4
Cumnock, *U.K.* 14 F4
Cumpas, *Mexico* 118 B3
Cumplida, Pta., *Canary Is.* ... 37 F2
Çumra, *Turkey* 72 D5
Cunco, *Chile* 128 D2
Cuncumén, *Chile* 126 C1
Cunderdin, *Australia* 93 F2
Cunene ➤, *Angola* 88 B1
Cúneo, *Italy* 28 D4
Çüngüş, *Turkey* 70 B3
Cunillera, I. = Sa Conillera,
　Spain 37 C7
Cunlhat, *France* 20 C7
Cunnamulla, *Australia* 95 D4
Cuorgnè, *Italy* 28 C4
Cupar, *Canada* 105 C8
Cupar, *U.K.* 14 E5
Cupcini, *Moldova* 43 B12
Cupica, G. de, *Colombia* 124 B3
Ćuprija, *Serbia, Yug.* 40 C5
Curaçao, *Neth. Ant.* 121 D6
Curanilahue, *Chile* 126 D1

Curaray ➤, *Peru* 124 D4
Cure ➤, *France* 19 E10
Curepto, *Chile* 126 D1
Curiapo, *Venezuela* 124 B6
Curicó, *Chile* 126 C1
Curinga, *Italy* 31 D9
Curitiba, *Brazil* 127 B6
Curitibanos, *Brazil* 127 B5
Currabubula, *Australia* 95 E5
Currais Novos, *Brazil* 125 E11
Curralinho, *Brazil* 125 D9
Currant, *U.S.A.* 114 G6
Current ➤, *U.S.A.* 113 G9
Currie, *Australia* 94 F3
Currie, *U.S.A.* 114 F6
Curtea de Argeş, *Romania* ... 43 E9
Curtici, *Romania* 42 D6
Curtis, *U.S.A.* 112 E4
Curtis Group, *Australia* 94 F4
Curtis I., *Australia* 94 C5
Curuápanema ➤, *Brazil* 125 D7
Curuçá, *Brazil* 125 D9
Curuguaty, *Paraguay* 127 A4
Curup, *Indonesia* 62 E2
Cururupu, *Brazil* 125 D10
Curuzú Cuatiá, *Argentina* ... 126 B4
Curvelo, *Brazil* 125 G10
Cushing, *U.S.A.* 113 H6
Cushing, Mt., *Canada* 104 B3
Cusihuiriáchic, *Mexico* 118 B3
Cusna, Mte., *Italy* 28 D7
Cusset, *France* 19 F10
Custer, *U.S.A.* 112 D3
Cut Bank, *U.S.A.* 114 B7
Cutchogue, *U.S.A.* 111 E12
Cuthbert, *U.S.A.* 109 K3
Cutler, *U.S.A.* 116 J7
Cutro, *Italy* 31 C9
Cuttaburra ➤, *Australia* 95 D3
Cuttack, *India* 67 J14
Cuvier, C., *Australia* 93 D1
Cuvier I., *N.Z.* 91 G5
Cuxhaven, *Germany* 24 B4
Cuyahoga Falls, *U.S.A.* 110 E3
Cuyapo, *Phil.* 61 D4
Cuyo, *Phil.* 61 F4
Cuyo East Pass, *Phil.* 61 F4
Cuyo West Pass, *Phil.* 61 F4
Cuyuni ➤, *Guyana* 124 B7
Cuzco, *Bolivia* 124 H5
Cuzco, *Peru* 124 F4
Čvrsnica, *Bos.-H.* 42 G2
Cwmbran, *U.K.* 13 F4
Cyangugu, *Rwanda* 86 C2
Cybinka, *Poland* 45 F1
Cyclades = Kikládhes, *Greece* . 38 E6
Cygnet, *Australia* 94 G4
Cynthiana, *U.S.A.* 108 F3
Cypress Hills, *Canada* 105 D7
Cypress Hills Prov. Park,
　Canada 105 D7
Cyprus ■, *Asia* 36 E12
Cyrenaica, *Libya* 79 C10
Czaplinek, *Poland* 44 E3
Czar, *Canada* 105 C6
Czarna ➤, *Łódzkie, Poland* .. 45 G6
Czarna ➤, *Świętokrzyskie,*
　Poland 45 H8
Czarna Białostocka, *Poland* .. 45 E10
Czarna Woda, *Poland* 44 E5
Czarne, *Poland* 44 E3
Czarnków, *Poland* 45 F3
Czech Rep. ■, *Europe* 26 B8
Czechowice-Dziedzice, *Poland* . 45 J5
Czempiń, *Poland* 45 F3
Czeremcha, *Poland* 45 F10
Czerniejewo, *Poland* 45 F4
Czersk, *Poland* 44 E4
Czerwieńsk, *Poland* 45 F2
Czerwionka-Leszczyny, *Poland* . 45 H5
Częstochowa, *Poland* 45 H6
Człopa, *Poland* 45 E3
Człuchów, *Poland* 44 E4
Czyżew-Osada, *Poland* 45 F9

D

Da ➤, *Vietnam* 58 G5
Da Hinggan Ling, *China* 60 B7
Da Lat, *Vietnam* 65 G7
Da Nang, *Vietnam* 64 D7
Da Qaidam, *China* 60 C4
Da Yunhe ➤, *China* 57 G11
Da'an, *China* 57 B13
Dab'a, Ras el, *Egypt* 80 H6
Daba Shan, *China* 58 B7
Dabai, *Nigeria* 83 C6
Dabakala, *Ivory C.* 82 D4
Dabas, *Hungary* 42 C4
Dabat, *Ethiopia* 81 E4
Dabbagh, Jabal, *Si. Arabia* ... 70 E2
Dabhoi, *India* 68 H5
Dąbie, *Poland* 45 F5
Dabie Shan, *China* 59 B10
Dabilda, *Cameroon* 83 C7
Dabnou = Pasirkuning, *Indonesia* . 62 E2
Dabo = Pasirkuning, *Indonesia* . 62 E2
Dabola, *Guinea* 82 C2
Dabou, *Ivory C.* 82 D4
Daboya, *Ghana* 83 D4
Dąbrowa Białostocka, *Poland* . 44 E10
Dąbrowa Górnicza, *Poland* ... 45 H6
Dąbrowa Tarnowska, *Poland* . 45 H7
Dabu, *China* 59 E11
Dabung, *Malaysia* 65 K4

Dabus ➤, *Ethiopia* 81 E4
Dacato ➤, *Ethiopia* 81 F5
Dacca = Dhaka, *Bangla.* 69 H14
Dacca = Dhaka □, *Bangla.* .. 69 G14
Dachau, *Germany* 25 G7
Dachstein, Hoher, *Austria* ... 26 D6
Dačice, *Czech Rep.* 26 B8
Dadanawa, *Guyana* 124 C7
Daday, *Turkey* 72 B5
Dade City, *U.S.A.* 109 L4
Dadhar, *Pakistan* 68 E2
Dadiya, *Nigeria* 83 D7
Dadra & Nagar Haveli □, *India* . 66 J8
Dadri = Charkhi Dadri, *India* . 68 E7
Dadu, *Pakistan* 68 F2
Dadu He ➤, *China* 58 C5
Daet, *Phil.* 61 D5
Dafang, *China* 58 D5
Dagana, *Senegal* 82 B1
Dagash, *Sudan* 80 D3
Dagestan □, *Russia* 49 J8
Dagestanskiye Ogni, *Russia* .. 49 J9
Daghfeli, *Sudan* 80 D3
Dağlıq Qarabağ = Nagorno-
　Karabakh, *Azerbaijan* 70 B5
Dagö = Hiiumaa, *Estonia* 9 G20
Dagu, *China* 57 E9
Daguan, *China* 58 D4
Dagupan, *Phil.* 61 C4
Daguragu, *Australia* 92 C5
Dahab, *Egypt* 80 B3
Dahlak Kebir, *Eritrea* 81 D5
Dahlenburg, *Germany* 24 B6
Dahlonega, *U.S.A.* 109 H4
Dahme, *Germany* 24 D9
Dahod, *India* 68 H6
Dahong Shan, *China* 59 B9
Dahra, *Senegal* 82 B1
Dahshûr, *Egypt* 80 J7
Dahūk, *Iraq* 70 B3
Dai Hao, *Vietnam* 64 C6
Dai-Sen, *Japan* 55 G6
Dai Xian, *China* 56 B9
Dai Xian, *China* 56 E7
Daicheng, *China* 56 E9
Daimiel, *Spain* 35 F7
Daingean, *Ireland* 15 C4
Dainkog, *China* 58 A1
Daintree, *Australia* 94 B4
Daiō-Misaki, *Japan* 55 G8
Dair, J. ed, *Sudan* 81 E3
Dairût, *Egypt* 80 B3
Daisetsu-Zan, *Japan* 54 C11
Dajarra, *Australia* 94 C2
Dajin Chuan ➤, *China* 58 B3
Dak Dam, *Cambodia* 64 F6
Dak Nhe, *Vietnam* 64 E6
Dak Pek, *Vietnam* 64 E6
Dak Song, *Vietnam* 65 F6
Dak Sui, *Vietnam* 64 E6
Dakar, *Senegal* 82 C1
Dakhla, *W. Sahara* 78 D2
Dakhla, El Wâhât el-, *Egypt* .. 80 B2
Dakingari, *Nigeria* 83 C5
Dakor, *India* 68 H5
Dakoro, *Niger* 83 C6
Dakota City, *U.S.A.* 112 D6
Ðakovica, *Kosovo, Yug.* 40 D4
Ðakovo, *Croatia* 42 E3
Dalaba, *Guinea* 82 C2
Dalachi, *China* 56 F3
Dalai Nur, *China* 56 C9
Dālakī, *Iran* 71 D6
Dalälven ➤, *Sweden* 10 D10
Dalaman, *Turkey* 39 E10
Dalaman ➤, *Turkey* 39 E10
Dalandzadgad, *Mongolia* 56 C3
Dalap-Uliga-Darrit, *Marshall Is.* . 96 G9
Dalarna, *Sweden* 10 D8
Dalarnas län □, *Sweden* 10 C8
Dālbandīn, *Pakistan* 66 E4
Dalbeattie, *U.K.* 14 G5
Dalbeg, *Australia* 94 C4
Dalbosjön, *Sweden* 11 F6
Dalby, *Australia* 95 D5
Dalby, *Sweden* 11 J7
Dale City, *U.S.A.* 108 F7
Dale Hollow L., *U.S.A.* 109 G3
Dalga, *Egypt* 80 B3
Dalgān, *Iran* 71 E8
Dalhart, *U.S.A.* 113 G3
Dalhousie, *Canada* 103 C6
Dalhousie, *India* 68 C6
Dali, *Shaanxi, China* 56 G5
Dali, *Yunnan, China* 58 E3
Dalian, *China* 57 E11
Daliang Shan, *China* 58 D4
Daling He ➤, *China* 57 D11
Dāliyat el Karmel, *Israel* 75 C4
Dalj, *Croatia* 42 E3
Dalkeith, *U.K.* 14 F5
Dalkey, *Ireland* 15 C5
Dallas, *Oreg., U.S.A.* 114 D2
Dallas, *Tex., U.S.A.* 113 J6
Dallol, *Ethiopia* 81 E5
Dalmā, *U.A.E.* 71 E7
Dalmacija, *Croatia* 29 E13
Dalmas, L., *Canada* 103 B5
Dalmatia = Dalmacija, *Croatia* . 29 E13
Dalmau, *India* 69 F9
Dalmellington, *U.K.* 14 F4
Dalnegorsk, *Russia* 51 E14
Dalnerechensk, *Russia* 51 E14

Daloa, *Ivory C.* 82 D3
Dalou Shan, *China* 58 C6
Dalry, *U.K.* 14 F4
Dalrymple, L., *Australia* 94 C4
Dals Långed, *Sweden* 11 F6
Dalsjöfors, *Sweden* 11 G7
Dalsland, *Sweden* 11 F6
Daltenganj, *India* 69 H11
Dalton, *Ga., U.S.A.* 109 H3
Dalton, *Mass., U.S.A.* 111 D11
Dalton, *Nebr., U.S.A.* 112 E3
Dalton Iceberg Tongue,
　Antarctica 5 C9
Dalton-in-Furness, *U.K.* 12 C4
Dalupiri I., *Phil.* 61 B4
Dalvík, *Iceland* 8 D4
Dalwallinu, *Australia* 93 F2
Daly ➤, *Australia* 92 B5
Daly City, *U.S.A.* 116 H4
Daly L., *Canada* 105 B7
Daly River, *Australia* 92 B5
Daly Waters, *Australia* 94 B1
Dalyan, *Turkey* 39 E10
Dam Doi, *Vietnam* 65 H5
Dam Ha, *Vietnam* 64 B6
Daman, *India* 66 J8
Dāmaneh, *Iran* 71 C6
Damanhûr, *Egypt* 80 H7
Damant L., *Canada* 105 A7
Damanzhuang, *China* 56 E9
Damar, *Indonesia* 63 F7
Damaraland, *Namibia* 88 C2
Damascus = Dimashq, *Syria* .. 75 B5
Damaturu, *Nigeria* 83 C7
Damāvand, *Iran* 71 C7
Damāvand, Qolleh-ye, *Iran* .. 71 C7
Damba, *Angola* 84 F3
Dame Marie, *Haiti* 121 C5
Dāmghān, *Iran* 71 B7
Dāmienesti, *Romania* 43 D11
Daming, *China* 56 F8
Damir Qābū, *Syria* 70 B4
Dammam = Ad Dammām,
　Si. Arabia 71 E6
Dammarie-les-Lys, *France* ... 19 D9
Dammartin-en-Goële, *France* . 19 C9
Damme, *Germany* 24 C4
Damodar ➤, *India* 69 H12
Damoh, *India* 69 H8
Dampier, *Australia* 92 D2
Dampier, Selat, *Indonesia* ... 63 E8
Dampier Arch., *Australia* 92 D2
Damrei, Chuor Phnum,
　Cambodia 65 G4
Damvillers, *France* 19 C12
Dan-Gulbi, *Nigeria* 83 C6
Dan Xian, *China* 64 C7
Dana, *Indonesia* 63 F6
Dana, L., *Canada* 102 B4
Dana, Mt., *U.S.A.* 116 H7
Danakil Desert, *Ethiopia* 81 E5
Danané, *Ivory C.* 82 D3
Danao, *Phil.* 61 F6
Danau Poso, *Indonesia* 63 E6
Danba, *China* 58 B3
Danbury, *U.S.A.* 111 E11
Danby L., *U.S.A.* 115 J6
Dand, *Afghan.* 68 D1
Dandeldhura, *Nepal* 69 E9
Dandeli, *India* 66 M9
Dandenong, *Australia* 95 F4
Dandīl, *Egypt* 80 J7
Dandong, *China* 57 D13
Danfeng, *China* 56 H6
Dangan Liedao, *China* 59 F10
Dangé-St-Romain, *France* ... 20 B4
Ðangeni, *Romania* 43 C11
Danger Is. = Pukapuka, *Cook Is.* . 97 J11
Danger Pt., *S. Africa* 88 E2
Dangla, *Ethiopia* 81 E4
Dangla Shan = Tanggula Shan,
　China 60 C4
Dangora, *Nigeria* 83 C6
Dangouadougou, *Burkina Faso* . 82 D4
Dangrek, Phnom, *Thailand* .. 64 E5
Dangriga, *Belize* 119 D7
Dangshan, *China* 56 G9
Dangtu, *China* 59 B12
Dangyang, *China* 59 B8
Dani, *Burkina Faso* 83 C4
Daniel, *U.S.A.* 114 E8
Daniel's Harbour, *Canada* ... 103 B8
Danielskuil, *S. Africa* 88 D3
Danielson, *U.S.A.* 111 E13
Danilov, *Russia* 46 C11
Danilovgrad, *Montenegro, Yug.* . 40 D3
Danilovka, *Russia* 48 E7
Daning, *China* 56 F6
Danissa, *Kenya* 86 B5
Danja, *Nigeria* 83 C6
Danjiangkou, *China* 59 A8
Danjiangkou Shuiku, *China* .. 59 A8
Dank, *Oman* 71 F8
Dankalwa, *Nigeria* 83 C7
Dankama, *Nigeria* 83 C6
Dankhar Gompa, *India* 68 C11
Dankov, *Russia* 46 F10
Danleng, *China* 58 B4
Danlí, *Honduras* 120 D2
Dannemora, *U.S.A.* 111 B11
Dannenberg, *Germany* 24 B7
Dannevirke, *N.Z.* 91 J6
Dannhauser, *S. Africa* 89 D5

Dansville, *U.S.A.* 110 D7
Danta, *India* 68 G5
Dantan, *India* 69 J12
Dante, *Somali Rep.* 74 E5
Danube = Dunărea ➤, *Europe* . 43 E14
Danvers, *U.S.A.* 111 D14
Danville, *Ill., U.S.A.* 108 E2
Danville, *Ky., U.S.A.* 108 G3
Danville, *Pa., U.S.A.* 111 F8
Danville, *Va., U.S.A.* 109 G6
Danville, *Vt., U.S.A.* 111 B12
Danyang, *China* 59 B12
Danzhai, *China* 58 D6
Danzig = Gdańsk, *Poland* ... 44 D5
Dão ➤, *Portugal* 34 E2
Daocheng, *China* 58 C3
Daoukro, *Ivory C.* 82 D4
Dapaong, *Togo* 83 C5
Dapchi, *Nigeria* 83 C7
Dapitan, *Phil.* 61 G5
Daqing Shan, *China* 56 D6
Daqu Shan, *China* 59 B14
Dar Banda, *Africa* 76 F6
Dar el Beida = Casablanca,
　Morocco 78 B4
Dar es Salaam, *Tanzania* 86 D4
Dar Mazār, *Iran* 71 D8
Dar'ā, *Syria* 75 C5
Dar'ā □, *Syria* 75 C5
Dārāb, *Iran* 71 D7
Daraban, *Pakistan* 68 D4
Darabani, *Romania* 43 B11
Daraina, *Madag.* 89 A8
Daraj, *Libya* 79 B8
Dārān, *Iran* 71 C6
Daravica, *Kosovo, Yug.* 40 D4
Daraw, *Egypt* 80 C3
Dārayyā, *Syria* 75 B5
Darazo, *Nigeria* 83 C7
Darband, *Pakistan* 68 B5
Darband, Kūh-e, *Iran* 71 D8
Darbhanga, *India* 69 F11
D'Arcy, *Canada* 104 C4
Darda, *Croatia* 42 E3
Dardanelle, *Ark., U.S.A.* 113 H8
Dardanelle, *Calif., U.S.A.* ... 116 G7
Dardanelles = Çanakkale
　Boğazı, *Turkey* 41 F10
Dare ➤, *Ethiopia* 81 F5
Darende, *Turkey* 72 C7
Dārestān, *Iran* 71 D8
Darfo, *Italy* 28 C7
Dârfûr, *Sudan* 79 F10
Dargai, *Pakistan* 68 B4
Dargan Ata, *Turkmenistan* .. 50 E7
Dargaville, *N.Z.* 91 F4
Dargol, *Niger* 83 C5
Darhan Mumingan Lianheqi,
　China 56 D6
Dari, *Sudan* 81 F3
Darıca, *Turkey* 72 B3
Darién, G. del, *Colombia* 122 C3
Dariganga = Ovoot, *Mongolia* . 56 B7
Darinskoye, *Kazakstan* 48 E10
Darjeeling = Darjiling, *India* .. 69 F13
Darjiling, *India* 69 F13
Darkan, *Australia* 93 F2
Darkhana, *Pakistan* 68 D5
Darkhazīneh, *Iran* 71 D6
Darkot Pass, *Pakistan* 69 A5
Darling ➤, *Australia* 95 E3
Darling Downs, *Australia* 95 D5
Darling Ra., *Australia* 93 F2
Darlington, *U.K.* 12 C6
Darlington, *U.S.A.* 109 H6
Darlington □, *U.K.* 12 C6
Darlington, L., *S. Africa* 88 E4
Darlot, L., *Australia* 93 E3
Darłowo, *Poland* 44 D3
Dărmăneşti, *Bacău, Romania* . 43 D11
Dărmăneşti, *Suceava, Romania* . 43 C11
Darmstadt, *Germany* 25 F9
Darnah, *Libya* 79 B10
Darnall, *S. Africa* 89 D5
Darney, *France* 19 D13
Darnley, C., *Antarctica* 5 C6
Darnley B., *Canada* 100 B7
Daroca, *Spain* 32 D3
Darou-Mousti, *Senegal* 82 C1
Darr ➤, *Australia* 94 C3
Darra Pezu, *Pakistan* 68 C4
Darrequeira, *Argentina* 126 D3
Darrington, *U.S.A.* 114 B3
Darsser Ort, *Germany* 24 A8
Dart ➤, *U.K.* 13 G4
Dart, C., *Antarctica* 5 D14
Dartford, *U.K.* 13 F8
Dartmoor, *U.K.* 13 G4
Dartmouth, *Canada* 103 D7
Dartmouth, *U.K.* 13 G4
Dartmouth, L., *Australia* 95 D4
Dartmouth Res., *Australia* ... 95 D4
Dartuch, C. = Artrutx, C. de,
　Spain 37 B10
Daruvar, *Croatia* 42 E2
Darvaza, *Turkmenistan* 50 E6
Darvel, Teluk = Lahad Datu,
　Teluk, *Malaysia* 63 D5
Darwen, *U.K.* 12 D5
Darwendale, *Zimbabwe* 89 B5
Darwha, *India* 66 J10
Darwin, *Australia* 92 B5
Darwin, *U.S.A.* 117 J9
Darya Khan, *Pakistan* 68 D4
Daryā Amu = Amudarya ➤,
　Uzbekistan 50 E6
Dās, *U.A.E.* 71 E7

Dashen, Ras, *Ethiopia*	81	E4
Dashetai, *China*	56	D5
Dashhowuz, *Turkmenistan*	50	E6
Dashkesan = Daşkäsän, *Azerbaijan*	49	K7
Dashköpri, *Turkmenistan*	71	B9
Dasht, *Iran*	71	B8
Dasht →, *Pakistan*	66	G2
Daska, *Pakistan*	68	C6
Daşkäsän, *Azerbaijan*	49	K7
Dassa, *Benin*	83	D5
Dasuya, *India*	68	D6
Datça, *Turkey*	39	E9
Datia, *India*	69	G8
Datian, *China*	59	E11
Datong, *Anhui, China*	59	B11
Datong, *Shanxi, China*	56	D7
Dattakhel, *Pakistan*	68	C3
Datteln, *Germany*	24	D3
Datu, Tanjung, *Indonesia*	62	D3
Datu Piang, *Phil.*	61	H6
Datuk, Tanjung = Datu, Tanjung, *Indonesia*	62	D3
Daud Khel, *Pakistan*	68	C4
Daudnagar, *India*	69	G11
Daugava →, *Latvia*	9	H21
Daugavpils, *Latvia*	9	J22
Daulpur, *India*	68	F7
Daun, *Germany*	25	E2
Dauphin, *Canada*	105	C8
Dauphin, *U.S.A.*	110	F8
Dauphin L., *Canada*	105	C9
Dauphiné, *France*	21	C9
Daura, *Borno, Nigeria*	83	C7
Daura, *Katsina, Nigeria*	83	C6
Dausa, *India*	68	F7
Däväçi, *Azerbaijan*	49	K9
Davangere, *India*	66	M9
Davao, *Phil.*	61	H6
Davao G., *Phil.*	61	H6
Dävar Panāh, *Iran*	71	E9
Davenport, *Calif., U.S.A.*	116	H4
Davenport, *Iowa, U.S.A.*	112	E9
Davenport, *Wash., U.S.A.*	114	C4
Davenport Ra., *Australia*	94	C1
Daventry, *U.K.*	13	E6
David, *Panama*	120	E3
David City, *U.S.A.*	112	E6
David Gorodok = Davyd Haradok, *Belarus*	47	F4
Davidson, *Canada*	105	C7
Davis, *U.S.A.*	116	G5
Davis Dam, *U.S.A.*	117	K12
Davis Inlet, *Canada*	103	A7
Davis Mts., *U.S.A.*	113	K2
Davis Sea, *Antarctica*	5	C7
Davis Str., *N. Amer.*	101	B14
Davo →, *Ivory C.*	82	D3
Davos, *Switz.*	25	J5
Davutlar, *Turkey*	39	D9
Davy L., *Canada*	105	B7
Davyd Haradok, *Belarus*	47	F4
Dawa →, *Ethiopia*	81	G5
Dawaki, *Bauchi, Nigeria*	83	D6
Dawaki, *Kano, Nigeria*	83	C6
Dawei, *Burma*	64	E2
Dawes Ra., *Australia*	94	C5
Dawlish, *U.K.*	13	G4
Dawna Ra., *Burma*	64	D2
Dawros Hd., *Ireland*	15	B3
Dawson, *Canada*	100	B6
Dawson, *U.S.A.*	109	K3
Dawson, I., *Chile*	128	G2
Dawson B., *Canada*	105	C8
Dawson Creek, *Canada*	104	B4
Dawson Inlet, *Canada*	105	A10
Dawson Ra., *Australia*	94	C4
Dawu, *Hubei, China*	59	B9
Dawu, *Sichuan, China*	58	B3
Dax, *France*	20	E2
Daxian, *China*	58	B6
Daxin, *China*	58	F6
Daxindian, *China*	57	F11
Daxinggou, *China*	57	C15
Daxue Shan, *Sichuan, China*	58	B3
Daxue Shan, *Yunnan, China*	58	F2
Dayao, *China*	58	E3
Daye, *China*	59	B10
Dayet en Naharat, *Mali*	82	B4
Dayi, *China*	58	B4
Daylesford, *Australia*	95	F3
Dayong, *China*	59	C8
Dayr az Zawr, *Syria*	70	C4
Daysland, *Canada*	104	C6
Dayton, *Nev., U.S.A.*	116	F7
Dayton, *Ohio, U.S.A.*	108	F3
Dayton, *Pa., U.S.A.*	110	F5
Dayton, *Tenn., U.S.A.*	109	H3
Dayton, *Wash., U.S.A.*	114	C4
Dayton, *Wyo., U.S.A.*	114	D10
Daytona Beach, *U.S.A.*	109	L5
Dayu, *China*	59	E10
Dayville, *U.S.A.*	114	D4
Dazhu, *China*	58	B6
Dazkırı, *Turkey*	39	D11
Dazu, *China*	58	C5
De Aar, *S. Africa*	88	E3
De Funiak Springs, *U.S.A.*	109	K2
De Grey →, *Australia*	92	D2
De Haan, *Belgium*	17	C3
De Kalb, *U.S.A.*	112	E10
De Land, *U.S.A.*	109	L5
De Leon, *U.S.A.*	113	J5
De Panne, *Belgium*	17	C2
De Pere, *U.S.A.*	108	C1
De Queen, *U.S.A.*	113	H7
De Quincy, *U.S.A.*	113	K8
De Ridder, *U.S.A.*	113	K8
De Smet, *U.S.A.*	112	C6
De Soto, *U.S.A.*	112	F9
De Tour Village, *U.S.A.*	108	C4
De Witt, *U.S.A.*	113	H9
Dead Sea, *Asia*	75	D4
Deadwood, *U.S.A.*	112	C3
Deadwood L., *Canada*	104	B3
Deal, *U.K.*	13	F9
Deal I., *Australia*	94	F4
Dealesville, *S. Africa*	88	D4
De'an, *China*	59	C10
Dean →, *Canada*	104	C3
Dean, Forest of, *U.K.*	13	F5
Dean Chan., *Canada*	104	C3
Deán Funes, *Argentina*	126	C3
Dease →, *Canada*	104	B3
Dease L., *Canada*	104	B2
Dease Lake, *Canada*	104	B2
Death Valley, *U.S.A.*	117	J10
Death Valley Junction, *U.S.A.*	117	J10
Death Valley National Park, *U.S.A.*	117	J10
Deauville, *France*	18	C7
Deba, *Spain*	32	B2
Deba Habe, *Nigeria*	83	C7
Debaltsevo, *Ukraine*	47	H10
Debao, *China*	58	F6
Debar, *Macedonia*	40	E4
Debden, *Canada*	105	C7
Dębica, *Poland*	45	H8
Dęblin, *Poland*	45	G8
Dębno, *Poland*	45	F1
Débo, L., *Mali*	82	B4
Debolt, *Canada*	104	B5
Deborah East, L., *Australia*	93	F2
Deborah West, L., *Australia*	93	F2
Debrc, *Serbia, Yug.*	40	B3
Debre Birhan, *Ethiopia*	81	F4
Debre Markos, *Ethiopia*	81	E4
Debre May, *Ethiopia*	81	E4
Debre Sina, *Ethiopia*	81	F4
Debre Tabor, *Ethiopia*	81	E4
Debre Zevit, *Ethiopia*	81	F4
Debre Zeyit, *Ethiopia*	81	F4
Debrecen, *Hungary*	42	C6
Debrzno, *Poland*	44	E4
Dečani, *Kosovo, Yug.*	40	D4
Decatur, *Ala., U.S.A.*	109	H2
Decatur, *Ga., U.S.A.*	109	J3
Decatur, *Ill., U.S.A.*	112	F10
Decatur, *Ind., U.S.A.*	108	E3
Decatur, *Tex., U.S.A.*	113	J6
Decazeville, *France*	20	D6
Deccan, *India*	66	L11
Deception Bay, *Australia*	95	D5
Deception L., *Canada*	105	B8
Dechang, *China*	58	D4
Dechhu, *India*	68	F5
Děčín, *Czech Rep.*	26	A7
Decize, *France*	19	F10
Deckerville, *U.S.A.*	110	C2
Decollatura, *Italy*	31	C9
Decorah, *U.S.A.*	112	D9
Deda, *Romania*	43	D9
Dedéagach = Alexandroúpolis, *Greece*	41	F9
Deder, *Ethiopia*	81	F5
Dedham, *U.S.A.*	111	D13
Dédougou, *Burkina Faso*	82	C4
Dedovichi, *Russia*	46	D5
Dedza, *Malawi*	87	E3
Dee →, *Aberds., U.K.*	14	D6
Dee →, *Dumf. & Gall., U.K.*	14	G4
Dee →, *Wales, U.K.*	12	D4
Deep B., *Canada*	104	A5
Deepwater, *Australia*	95	D5
Deer →, *Canada*	105	B10
Deer L., *Canada*	105	C10
Deer Lake, *Nfld., Canada*	103	C8
Deer Lake, *Ont., Canada*	105	C10
Deer Lodge, *U.S.A.*	114	C7
Deer Park, *U.S.A.*	114	C5
Deer River, *U.S.A.*	112	B8
Deeragun, *Australia*	94	B4
Deerdepoort, *S. Africa*	88	C4
Deferiet, *U.S.A.*	111	B9
Defiance, *U.S.A.*	108	E3
Degana, *India*	68	F6
Dêgê, *China*	58	B2
Degebe →, *Portugal*	35	G3
Degeberga, *Sweden*	11	J8
Dégelis, *Canada*	103	C6
Degema, *Nigeria*	83	E6
Degerfors, *Sweden*	10	E8
Degerhamn, *Sweden*	11	H10
Deggendorf, *Germany*	25	G8
Degh →, *Pakistan*	68	D5
Değirmendere, *Turkey*	41	F13
Deh Bīd, *Iran*	71	D7
Deh-e Shīr, *Iran*	71	D7
Dehaj, *Iran*	71	D7
Dehak, *Iran*	71	E9
Dehdez, *Iran*	71	D6
Dehej, *India*	68	J5
Dehestān, *Iran*	71	D7
Dehgolān, *Iran*	70	C5
Dehibat, *Tunisia*	79	B8
Dehlorān, *Iran*	70	C5
Dehnow-e Kühestān, *Iran*	71	E8
Dehra Dun, *India*	68	D8
Dehri, *India*	69	G11
Dehua, *China*	59	E12
Dehui, *China*	57	B13
Deim Zubeir, *Sudan*	81	F2
Deinze, *Belgium*	17	D3
Dej, *Romania*	43	C8
Deje, *Sweden*	10	E7
Dejiang, *China*	58	C7
Deka →, *Zimbabwe*	88	B4
Dekemhare, *Eritrea*	81	D4
Dekese, *Dem. Rep. of the Congo*	84	E4
Del Mar, *U.S.A.*	117	N9
Del Norte, *U.S.A.*	115	H10
Del Rio, *U.S.A.*	113	L4
Delai, *Sudan*	80	D4
Delambre I., *Australia*	92	D2
Delami, *Sudan*	81	E3
Delano, *U.S.A.*	117	K7
Delano Peak, *U.S.A.*	115	G7
Delareyville, *S. Africa*	88	D4
Delaronde L., *Canada*	105	C7
Delavan, *U.S.A.*	112	D10
Delaware, *U.S.A.*	108	E4
Delaware □, *U.S.A.*	108	F8
Delaware →, *U.S.A.*	111	G9
Delaware B., *U.S.A.*	108	F8
Delay →, *Canada*	103	A5
Delbrück, *Germany*	24	D4
Delčevo, *Macedonia*	40	E6
Delegate, *Australia*	95	F4
Delémont, *Switz.*	25	H3
Delevan, *U.S.A.*	110	D6
Delft, *Neths.*	17	B4
Delfzijl, *Neths.*	17	A6
Delgado, C., *Mozam.*	87	E5
Delgerhet, *Mongolia*	56	B6
Delgo, *Sudan*	80	C3
Delhi, *Canada*	110	D4
Delhi, *India*	68	E7
Delhi, *La., U.S.A.*	113	J9
Delhi, *N.Y., U.S.A.*	111	D10
Deli Jovan, *Serbia, Yug.*	40	B6
Delia, *Canada*	104	C6
Delice, *Turkey*	72	C6
Delicias, *Mexico*	118	B3
Delījān, *Iran*	71	C6
Déline, *Canada*	100	B7
Delisle, *Canada*	105	C7
Delitzsch, *Germany*	24	D8
Dell City, *U.S.A.*	115	L11
Dell Rapids, *U.S.A.*	112	D6
Delle, *France*	19	E14
Delmar, *U.S.A.*	111	D11
Delmenhorst, *Germany*	24	B4
Delnice, *Croatia*	29	C11
Delonga, Ostrova, *Russia*	51	B15
Deloraine, *Australia*	94	G4
Deloraine, *Canada*	105	D8
Delphi, *Greece*	38	C4
Delphi, *U.S.A.*	108	E2
Delphos, *U.S.A.*	108	E3
Delportshoop, *S. Africa*	88	D3
Delray Beach, *U.S.A.*	109	M5
Delsbo, *Sweden*	10	C10
Delta, *Colo., U.S.A.*	115	G9
Delta, *Utah, U.S.A.*	114	G7
Delta □, *Nigeria*	83	D6
Delta Junction, *U.S.A.*	100	B5
Deltona, *U.S.A.*	109	L5
Delungra, *Australia*	95	D5
Delvada, *India*	68	J4
Delvinákion, *Greece*	38	B2
Delvinë, *Albania*	40	G4
Demak, *Indonesia*	63	G14
Demanda, Sierra de la, *Spain*	32	C2
Demavand = Damāvand, *Iran*	71	C7
Dembecha, *Ethiopia*	81	E4
Dembi, *Ethiopia*	81	F4
Dembia, *Dem. Rep. of the Congo*	86	B2
Dembidolo, *Ethiopia*	81	F3
Demchok, *India*	69	C8
Demer →, *Belgium*	17	D4
Demetrias, *Greece*	38	B5
Demidov, *Russia*	46	E6
Deming, *N. Mex., U.S.A.*	115	K10
Deming, *Wash., U.S.A.*	116	B4
Demini →, *Brazil*	124	D6
Demirci, *Turkey*	39	B10
Demirköprü Barajı, *Turkey*	39	C10
Demirköy, *Turkey*	41	E11
Demmin, *Germany*	24	B9
Demonte, *Italy*	28	D4
Demopolis, *U.S.A.*	109	J2
Dempo, *Indonesia*	62	E2
Demyansk, *Russia*	46	D7
Den Burg, *Neths.*	17	A4
Den Chai, *Thailand*	64	D3
Den Haag = 's-Gravenhage, *Neths.*	17	B4
Den Helder, *Neths.*	17	B4
Den Oever, *Neths.*	17	B5
Denain, *France*	19	B10
Denair, *U.S.A.*	116	H6
Denau, *Uzbekistan*	50	F7
Denbigh, *Canada*	110	A7
Denbigh, *U.K.*	12	D4
Denbighshire □, *U.K.*	12	D4
Dendang, *Indonesia*	62	E3
Dendermonde, *Belgium*	17	C4
Deneba, *Ethiopia*	81	F4
Dengchuan, *China*	58	E3
Denge, *Nigeria*	83	C6
Dengi, *Nigeria*	83	D6
Dengkou, *China*	56	D4
Dengzhou, *China*	59	A9
Denham, *Australia*	93	E1
Denham Ra., *Australia*	94	C4
Denham Sd., *Australia*	93	E1
Denholm, *Canada*	105	C7
Denia, *Spain*	33	G5
Denial B., *Australia*	95	E1
Deniliquin, *Australia*	95	F3
Denison, *Iowa, U.S.A.*	112	E7
Denison, *Tex., U.S.A.*	113	J6
Denison Plains, *Australia*	92	C4
Denizli, *Turkey*	39	D11
Denizli □, *Turkey*	39	D11
Denman Glacier, *Antarctica*	5	C7
Denmark, *Australia*	93	F2
Denmark ■, *Europe*	11	J3
Denmark Str., *Atl. Oc.*	4	C6
Dennison, *U.S.A.*	110	F3
Denny, *U.K.*	14	E5
Denpasar, *Indonesia*	62	F5
Denton, *Mont., U.S.A.*	114	C9
Denton, *Tex., U.S.A.*	113	J6
D'Entrecasteaux, Pt., *Australia*	93	F2
Denu, *Ghana*	83	D5
Denver, *Colo., U.S.A.*	112	F2
Denver, *Pa., U.S.A.*	111	F8
Denver City, *U.S.A.*	113	J3
Deoband, *India*	68	E7
Deogarh, *India*	68	G5
Deoghar, *India*	69	G12
Deolali, *India*	66	K8
Deoli, = Devli, *India*	68	G6
Déols, *France*	19	F8
Deora, *India*	68	F4
Deori, *India*	69	H8
Deoria, *India*	69	F10
Deosai Mts., *Pakistan*	69	B6
Deosri, *India*	69	F14
Depalpur, *India*	68	H6
Deping, *China*	57	F9
Deposit, *U.S.A.*	111	D9
Depuch I., *Australia*	92	D2
Deputatskiy, *Russia*	51	C14
Dêqên, *China*	58	C2
Deqing, *China*	59	F8
Dera Ghazi Khan, *Pakistan*	68	D4
Dera Ismail Khan, *Pakistan*	68	D4
Derabugti, *Pakistan*	68	E3
Derawar Fort, *Pakistan*	68	E4
Derbent, *Russia*	49	J9
Derbent, *Turkey*	39	C10
Derby, *Australia*	92	C3
Derby, *U.K.*	12	E6
Derby, *Conn., U.S.A.*	111	E11
Derby, *Kans., U.S.A.*	113	G6
Derby, *N.Y., U.S.A.*	110	D6
Derby City □, *U.K.*	12	E6
Derby Line, *U.S.A.*	111	B12
Derbyshire □, *U.K.*	12	D6
Derecske, *Hungary*	42	C6
Dereköy, *Turkey*	41	E11
Dereli, *Turkey*	73	B8
Derg →, *Ireland*	15	B4
Derg, L., *Ireland*	15	D3
Dergachi = Derhaci, *Ukraine*	47	G9
Dergaon, *India*	67	F19
Derhaci, *Ukraine*	47	G9
Derik, *Turkey*	73	D9
Derinkuyu, *Turkey*	72	C6
Dermantsi, *Bulgaria*	41	C8
Dermott, *U.S.A.*	113	J9
Derry = Londonderry, *U.K.*	15	B4
Derry = Londonderry □, *U.K.*	15	B4
Derry, *N.H., U.S.A.*	111	D13
Derry, *Pa., U.S.A.*	110	F5
Derryveagh Mts., *Ireland*	15	B3
Derudub, *Sudan*	80	D4
Derval, *France*	18	E5
Derveni, *Greece*	38	C4
Derventa, *Bos.-H.*	42	F2
Derwent →, *Cumb., U.K.*	12	C4
Derwent →, *Derby, U.K.*	12	E6
Derwent →, *N. Yorks., U.K.*	12	D7
Des Moines, *Iowa, U.S.A.*	112	E8
Des Moines, *N. Mex., U.S.A.*	113	G3
Des Moines →, *U.S.A.*	112	E9
Desa, *Romania*	42	G7
Desaguadero →, *Argentina*	126	C2
Desaguadero →, *Bolivia*	124	G5
Descanso, Pta., *Mexico*	117	N9
Descartes, *France*	20	B4
Deschaillons, *Canada*	103	C5
Deschambault L., *Canada*	105	C8
Deschutes →, *U.S.A.*	114	D3
Dese, *Ethiopia*	81	E4
Deseado →, *Argentina*	128	F3
Desenzano del Garda, *Italy*	28	C7
Desert Center, *U.S.A.*	117	M11
Desert Hot Springs, *U.S.A.*	117	M10
Deshnok, *India*	68	F5
Desna →, *Ukraine*	47	G6
Desnățui →, *Romania*	43	G8
Desolación, I., *Chile*	128	G2
Despeñaperros, Paso, *Spain*	35	G7
Despotovac, *Serbia, Yug.*	40	B5
Dessau, *Germany*	24	D8
Dessye = Dese, *Ethiopia*	81	E4
D'Estrees B., *Australia*	95	F2
Desuri, *India*	68	G5
Desvres, *France*	19	B8
Det Udom, *Thailand*	64	E5
Deta, *Romania*	42	F6
Dete, *Zimbabwe*	88	B4
Đetinja →, *Serbia, Yug.*	40	C4
Detmold, *Germany*	24	D4
Detour, Pt., *U.S.A.*	108	C2
Detroit, *U.S.A.*	110	D1
Detroit Lakes, *U.S.A.*	112	B7
Detva, *Slovak Rep.*	27	C12
Deurne, *Neths.*	17	C5
Deutsche Bucht, *Germany*	24	A4
Deutschlandsberg, *Austria*	26	E8
Deux-Sèvres □, *France*	18	F6
Deva, *Romania*	42	E7
Devakottai, *India*	66	Q11
Devaprayag, *India*	69	D8
Dévaványa, *Hungary*	42	C5
Deveci Dağları, *Turkey*	72	B7
Devecikonağı, *Turkey*	41	G12
Devecser, *Hungary*	42	C2
Develi, *Turkey*	72	C6
Deventer, *Neths.*	17	B6
Deveron →, *U.K.*	14	D6
Devesel, *Romania*	42	F7
Devgadh Bariya, *India*	68	H5
Devikot, *India*	68	F4
Devils Den, *U.S.A.*	116	K7
Devils Lake, *U.S.A.*	112	A5
Devils Paw, *Canada*	104	B2
Devils Tower Junction, *U.S.A.*	112	C2
Devin, *Bulgaria*	41	E8
Devine, *U.S.A.*	113	L5
Devizes, *U.K.*	13	F6
Devli, *India*	68	G6
Devnya, *Bulgaria*	41	C11
Devoll →, *Albania*	40	F4
Devon, *Canada*	104	C6
Devon □, *U.K.*	13	G4
Devon I., *Canada*	4	B3
Devonport, *Australia*	94	G4
Devonport, *N.Z.*	91	G5
Devrek, *Turkey*	72	B4
Devrekâni, *Turkey*	72	B5
Devrez →, *Turkey*	72	B6
Dewas, *India*	68	H7
Dewetsdorp, *S. Africa*	88	D4
Dexing, *China*	59	C11
Dexter, *Maine, U.S.A.*	109	C11
Dexter, *Mo., U.S.A.*	113	G10
Dexter, *N. Mex., U.S.A.*	113	J2
Dey-Dey, L., *Australia*	93	E5
Deyang, *China*	58	B5
Deyhūk, *Iran*	71	C8
Deyyer, *Iran*	71	E6
Dezadeash L., *Canada*	104	A1
Dezfūl, *Iran*	71	C6
Dezhneva, Mys, *Russia*	51	C19
Dezhou, *China*	56	F9
Dhadhar →, *India*	69	G11
Dhāfni, *Kríti, Greece*	36	D7
Dhāfni, *Pelópónnisos, Greece*	38	D4
Dhahabān, *Si. Arabia*	80	C4
Dhahiriya = Aẓ Ẓāhirīyah, *West Bank*	75	D3
Dhahran = Aẓ Ẓahrān, *Si. Arabia*	71	E6
Dhak, *Pakistan*	68	C5
Dhaka, *Bangla.*	69	H14
Dhaka □, *Bangla.*	69	G14
Dhali, *Cyprus*	36	D12
Dhamási, *Greece*	38	B4
Dhampur, *India*	69	E8
Dhamtari, *India*	67	J12
Dhanbad, *India*	69	H12
Dhangarhi, *Nepal*	67	E12
Dhankuta, *Nepal*	69	F12
Dhar, *India*	68	H6
Dharampur, *India*	68	H6
Dharamsala = Dharmsala, *India*	68	C7
Dhariwal, *India*	68	D6
Dharla →, *Bangla.*	69	G13
Dharmapuri, *India*	66	N11
Dharmjaygarh, *India*	69	H10
Dharmsala, *India*	68	C7
Dharni, *India*	68	J7
Dharwad, *India*	66	M9
Dhasan →, *India*	69	G8
Dhaulagiri, *Nepal*	69	E10
Dhebar, L., *India*	68	G6
Dheftera, *Cyprus*	36	D12
Dhenkanal, *India*	67	J14
Dhenoúsa, *Greece*	39	D7
Dherinia, *Cyprus*	36	D12
Dheskáti, *Greece*	38	B3
Dhespotikó, *Greece*	38	E6
Dhestina, *Greece*	38	C4
Dhiarrizos →, *Cyprus*	36	E11
Dhībān, *Jordan*	75	D4
Dhidhimótikhon, *Greece*	41	E10
Dhíkti Óros, *Greece*	36	D7
Dhilianáta, *Greece*	38	C2
Dhílos, *Greece*	39	D7
Dhilwan, *India*	68	D6
Dhimarkhera, *India*	69	H9
Dhimitsána, *Greece*	38	D4
Dhírfis Óros, *Greece*	38	C5
Dhodhekánisos □, *Greece*	39	E8
Dhokós, *Greece*	38	D5
Dholiana, *Greece*	38	B2
Dholka, *India*	68	H5
Dhomokós, *Greece*	38	B4
Dhoraji, *India*	68	J4
Dhoxáton, *Greece*	41	E8
Dhragonísi, *Greece*	39	D7
Dhráhstis, Ákra, *Greece*	36	A3
Dhrangadhra, *India*	68	H4
Dhrápanon, Ákra, *Greece*	36	D6
Dhriopís, *Greece*	38	D6
Dhrol, *India*	68	H4
Dhuburi, *India*	67	F16
Dhule, *India*	66	J9
Di-ib, W., *Sudan*	80	C4
Di Linh, *Vietnam*	65	G7
Di Linh, Cao Nguyen, *Vietnam*	65	G7
Día, *Greece*	36	D7
Diabakania, *Guinea*	82	C2
Diablo, Mt., *U.S.A.*	116	H5
Diablo Range, *U.S.A.*	116	J5
Diafarabé, *Mali*	82	C4

Diala, *Mali* 82 C3
Dialakoro, *Mali* 82 C3
Dialakoto, *Senegal* 82 C2
Diallassagou, *Mali* 82 C4
Diamante, *Argentina* 126 C3
Diamante, *Italy* 31 C8
Diamante ➤, *Argentina* 126 C2
Diamantina, *Brazil* 125 G10
Diamantina ➤, *Australia* 95 D2
Diamantino, *Brazil* 125 F7
Diamond Bar, *U.S.A.* 117 L9
Diamond Harbour, *India* 69 H13
Diamond Is., *Australia* 94 B5
Diamond Mts., *U.S.A.* 114 G6
Diamond Springs, *U.S.A.* 116 G6
Dian Chi, *China* 58 E4
Dianalund, *Denmark* 11 J5
Dianbai, *China* 59 G8
Diancheng, *China* 59 G8
Dianjiang, *China* 58 B6
Diano Marina, *Italy* 28 E5
Dianra, *Ivory C.* 82 D3
Diapaga, *Burkina Faso* 83 C5
Diapangou, *Burkina Faso* 83 C5
Diariguila, *Guinea* 82 C2
Dībā, *Oman* 71 E8
Dibai, *India* 68 E8
Dibaya-Lubue, *Dem. Rep. of
    the Congo* 84 E3
Dibete, *Botswana* 88 C4
Dibrugarh, *India* 67 F19
Dickens, *U.S.A.* 113 J4
Dickinson, *U.S.A.* 112 B3
Dickson = Dikson, *Russia* 50 B9
Dickson, *U.S.A.* 109 G2
Dickson City, *U.S.A.* 111 E9
Dicle Nehri ➤, *Turkey* 73 D9
Dicomano, *Italy* 29 E8
Didesa, W. ➤, *Ethiopia* 81 E4
Didi, *Sudan* 81 F3
Didiéni, *Mali* 82 C3
Didsbury, *Canada* 104 C6
Didwana, *India* 68 F6
Die, *France* 21 D9
Diébougou, *Burkina Faso* 82 C4
Diecke, *Guinea* 82 D3
Diefenbaker, L., *Canada* 105 C7
Diego de Almagro, *Chile* 126 B1
Diego Garcia, *Ind. Oc.* 3 E13
Diekirch, *Lux.* 17 E6
Diéma, *Mali* 82 C3
Diembéring, *Senegal* 82 C1
Dien Ban, *Vietnam* 64 E7
Dien Bien, *Vietnam* 58 G4
Dien Khanh, *Vietnam* 65 F7
Diepholz, *Germany* 24 C4
Dieppe, *France* 18 C8
Dierks, *U.S.A.* 113 H8
Diest, *Belgium* 17 D5
Dietikon, *Switz.* 25 H4
Dieulefit, *France* 21 D9
Dieuze, *France* 19 D13
Dif, *Somali Rep.* 74 G3
Differdange, *Lux.* 17 E5
Dig, *India* 68 F7
Digba, *Dem. Rep. of the Congo* 86 B2
Digby, *Canada* 103 D6
Diggi, *India* 68 F6
Dighinala, *Bangla.* 67 H18
Dighton, *U.S.A.* 112 F4
Digna, *Mali* 82 C3
Digne-les-Bains, *France* 21 D10
Digoin, *France* 19 F11
Digor, *Turkey* 73 B10
Digos, *Phil.* 61 H6
Digranes, *Iceland* 8 C6
Digul ➤, *Indonesia* 63 F9
Dihang ➤, *India* 67 F19
Dijlah, Nahr ➤, *Asia* 70 D5
Dijon, *France* 19 E12
Dikhil, *Djibouti* 81 E5
Dikili, *Turkey* 39 B8
Dikirnis, *Egypt* 80 H7
Dikkil = Dikhil, *Djibouti* ... 81 E5
Dikodougou, *Ivory C.* 82 D3
Diksmuide, *Belgium* 17 C2
Dikson, *Russia* 50 B9
Dikwa, *Nigeria* 83 C7
Dila, *Ethiopia* 81 F4
Dili, *E. Timor* 63 F7
Dilijan, *Armenia* 49 K7
Dilizhan = Dilijan, *Armenia* . 49 K7
Dilj, *Croatia* 42 E3
Dillenburg, *Germany* 24 E4
Dilley, *U.S.A.* 113 L5
Dilling, *Sudan* 81 E2
Dillingen, *Bayern, Germany* .. 25 G6
Dillingen, *Saarland, Germany* 25 F2
Dillingham, *U.S.A.* 100 C4
Dillon, *Canada* 105 B7
Dillon, *Mont., U.S.A.* 114 D7
Dillon, *S.C., U.S.A.* 109 H6
Dillon ➤, *Canada* 105 B7
Dillsburg, *U.S.A.* 110 F7
Dilly, *Mali* 82 C3
Dilolo, *Dem. Rep. of the Congo* 84 G4
Dimas, *Mexico* 118 C3
Dimashq, *Syria* 75 B5
Dimashq □, *Syria* 75 B5
Dimbaza, *S. Africa* 89 E4
Dimbokro, *Ivory C.* 82 D4
Dimboola, *Australia* 95 F3
Dîmbovița = Dâmbovița ➤,
    Romania 43 F11
Dimbulah, *Australia* 94 B4
Dimitrovgrad, *Bulgaria* 41 D9
Dimitrovgrad, *Russia* 48 C9

Dimitrovgrad, *Serbia, Yug.* .. 40 C6
Dimitrovo = Pernik, *Bulgaria* 40 D7
Dimmitt, *U.S.A.* 113 H3
Dimo, *Sudan* 81 F2
Dimona, *Israel* 75 D4
Dimovo, *Bulgaria* 40 C6
Dinagat, *Phil.* 61 F6
Dinajpur, *Bangla.* 67 G16
Dinan, *France* 18 D4
Dīnān Āb, *Iran* 71 C8
Dinant, *Belgium* 17 D4
Dinapur, *India* 69 G11
Dinar, *Turkey* 39 C12
Dīnār, Kūh-e, *Iran* 71 D6
Dinara Planina, *Croatia* 29 D13
Dinard, *France* 18 D4
Dinaric Alps = Dinara Planina,
    Croatia 29 D13
Dindanko, *Mali* 82 C3
Dinder, Nahr ed ➤, *Sudan* 81 E3
Dindigul, *India* 66 P11
Dindori, *India* 69 H9
Ding Xian = Dingzhou, *China* . 56 E8
Dinga, *Pakistan* 68 G2
Dingalan, *Phil.* 61 D4
Dingbian, *China* 56 F4
Dingelstädt, *Germany* 24 D6
Dingle, *Ireland* 15 D1
Dingle, *Sweden* 11 F5
Dingle B., *Ireland* 15 D1
Dingmans Ferry, *U.S.A.* 111 E10
Dingnan, *China* 59 E10
Dingo, *Australia* 94 C4
Dingolfing, *Germany* 25 G8
Dingtao, *China* 56 G8
Dinguira, *Mali* 82 C2
Dinguiraye, *Guinea* 82 C2
Dingwall, *U.K.* 14 D4
Dingxi, *China* 56 G3
Dingxiang, *China* 56 E7
Dingyuan, *China* 59 A11
Dingzhou, *China* 56 E8
Dinh, Mui, *Vietnam* 65 G7
Dinh Lap, *Vietnam* 58 G6
Dinokwe, *Botswana* 88 C4
Dinorwic, *Canada* 105 D10
Dinosaur National Monument,
    U.S.A. 114 F9
Dinosaur Prov. Park, *Canada* . 104 C6
Dinuba, *U.S.A.* 116 J7
Diö, *Sweden* 11 H8
Dioïla, *Mali* 82 C3
Dioka, *Mali* 82 C2
Diongoï, *Mali* 82 C3
Diósgyőr, *Hungary* 42 B5
Diosig, *Romania* 42 C7
Diougani, *Mali* 82 C4
Diouloulou, *Senegal* 82 C1
Dioura, *Mali* 82 C3
Diourbel, *Senegal* 82 C1
Dipalpur, *Pakistan* 68 D5
Diplo, *Pakistan* 68 G3
Dipolog, *Phil.* 61 G5
Dir, *Pakistan* 66 B7
Diré, *Mali* 82 B4
Dire Dawa, *Ethiopia* 81 F5
Diriamba, *Nic.* 120 D2
Dirk Hartog I., *Australia* ... 93 E1
Dirranbandi, *Australia* 95 D4
Disa, *India* 68 G5
Disa, *Sudan* 81 E3
Disappointment, C., *U.S.A.* .. 114 C2
Disappointment, L., *Australia* 92 D3
Disaster B., *Australia* 95 F4
Discovery B., *Australia* 95 F3
Dishna, *Egypt* 80 B3
Disina, *Nigeria* 83 C6
Disko = Qeqertarsuaq,
    Greenland 101 B5
Disko Bugt, *Greenland* 4 C5
Disna = Dzisna ➤, *Belarus* ... 46 E5
Diss, *U.K.* 13 E9
Disteghil Sar, *Pakistan* 69 A6
Distrito Federal □, *Brazil* .. 125 G9
Distrito Federal □, *Mexico* .. 119 D5
Disûq, *Egypt* 80 H7
Diu, *India* 68 J4
Dīvāndarreh, *Iran* 70 C5
Dives ➤, *France* 18 C6
Dives-sur-Mer, *France* 18 C6
Divichi = Dəvəçi, *Azerbaijan* 49 K9
Divide, *U.S.A.* 114 D7
Dividing Ra., *Australia* 93 E2
Divinópolis, *Brazil* 125 H10
Divjake, *Albania* 40 F3
Divnoye, *Russia* 49 H6
Divo, *Ivory C.* 82 D3
Divriği, *Turkey* 73 C8
Dixie Mt., *U.S.A.* 116 F6
Dixon, *Calif., U.S.A.* 116 G5
Dixon, *Ill., U.S.A.* 112 E10
Dixon Entrance, *U.S.A.* 100 C6
Dixville, *Canada* 111 A13
Diyadin, *Turkey* 73 C10
Diyālā □, *Iraq* 70 C5
Diyarbakır, *Turkey* 70 B4
Diyodar, *India* 68 G4
Djakarta = Jakarta, *Indonesia* 62 F3
Djamba, *Angola* 88 B1
Djambala, *Congo* 84 E2
Djanet, *Algeria* 78 D7
Djawa = Jawa, *Indonesia* 62 F3
Djelfa, *Algeria* 78 B6
Djema, *C.A.R.* 86 A2
Djenné, *Mali* 82 C4

Djerba, I. de, *Tunisia* 79 B8
Djerid, Chott, *Tunisia* 78 B7
Djibo, *Burkina Faso* 83 C4
Djibouti, *Djibouti* 81 E5
Djibouti ■, *Africa* 81 E5
Djolu, *Dem. Rep. of the Congo* 84 D4
Djougou, *Benin* 83 D5
Djoum, *Cameroon* 84 D2
Djourab, Erg du, *Chad* 79 E9
Djugu, *Dem. Rep. of the Congo* 86 B3
Djúpivogur, *Iceland* 8 D6
Djurås, *Sweden* 10 D9
Djursland, *Denmark* 11 H4
Dmitriya Lapteva, Proliv, *Russia* 51 B15
Dmitriyevskiy, *Russia* 47 H8
Dmitrov, *Russia* 46 D9
Dmitrovsk-Orlovskiy, *Russia* . 47 F8
Dnepr ➤ = Dnipro ➤, *Ukraine* . 47 J7
Dneprodzerzhinsk =
    Dniprodzerzhynsk, *Ukraine* 47 H8
Dneprodzerzhinskoye Vdkhr. =
    Dniprodzerzhynske Vdskh.,
    Ukraine 47 H8
Dnepropetrovsk =
    Dnipropetrovsk, *Ukraine* . 47 H8
Dneprorudnoye = Dniprorudne,
    Ukraine 47 J8
Dnestr ➤ = Dnister ➤, *Europe* 47 J6
Dnestrovski = Belgorod, *Russia* 47 G9
Dnieper = Dnipro ➤, *Ukraine* . 47 J7
Dniester = Dnister ➤, *Europe* 47 J6
Dnipro ➤, *Ukraine* 47 J7
Dniprodzerzhynsk, *Ukraine* ... 47 H8
Dniprodzerzhynske Vdskh.,
    Ukraine 47 H8
Dnipropetrovsk, *Ukraine* 47 H8
Dniprorudne, *Ukraine* 47 J8
Dnister ➤, *Europe* 47 J6
Dnistrovskyy Lyman, *Ukraine* . 47 J6
Dno, *Russia* 46 D5
Dnyapro = Dnipro ➤, *Ukraine* . 47 J7
Doaktown, *Canada* 103 C6
Doan Hung, *Vietnam* 58 G5
Doany, *Madag.* 89 A8
Doba, *Chad* 79 G9
Dobandi, *Pakistan* 68 D2
Dobbiaco, *Italy* 29 B9
Dobbyn, *Australia* 94 B3
Dobczyce, *Poland* 45 J7
Dobele, *Latvia* 9 H20
Dobele □, *Latvia* 44 B10
Döbeln, *Germany* 24 D9
Doberai, Jazirah, *Indonesia* . 63 E8
Doblas, *Argentina* 126 D3
Dobo, *Indonesia* 63 F8
Doboj, *Bos.-H.* 42 F3
Dobra, *Wielkopolskie, Poland* 45 G5
Dobra, *Zachodnio-Pomorskie,
    Poland* 44 E2
Dobra, *Dîmbovita, Romania* ... 43 F10
Dobra, *Hunedoara, Romania* ... 42 E7
Dobre Miasto, *Poland* 44 E7
Dobrești, *Romania* 42 D7
Dobrich, *Bulgaria* 41 C11
Dobrinishta, *Bulgaria* 40 E7
Dobříš, *Czech Rep.* 26 B7
Dobrodzień, *Poland* 45 H5
Dobropole, *Ukraine* 47 H9
Dobruja, *Europe* 43 F13
Dobrush, *Belarus* 47 F6
Dobrzany, *Poland* 44 E2
Dobrzyń nad Wisłą, *Poland* ... 45 F6
Doc, Mui, *Vietnam* 64 D6
Docker River, *Australia* 93 D4
Docksta, *Sweden* 10 A12
Doctor Arroyo, *Mexico* 118 C4
Doda, *India* 69 C6
Doda, L., *Canada* 102 C4
Dodecanese = Dhodhekánisos,
    Greece 39 E8
Dodge City, *U.S.A.* 113 G5
Dodge L., *Canada* 105 B7
Dodgeville, *U.S.A.* 112 D9
Dodo, *Cameroon* 83 D7
Dodo, *Sudan* 81 F2
Dodola, *Ethiopia* 81 F4
Dodoma, *Tanzania* 86 D4
Dodoma □, *Tanzania* 86 D4
Dodona, *Greece* 38 B2
Dodsland, *Canada* 105 C7
Dodson, *U.S.A.* 114 B9
Dodurga, *Turkey* 39 B11
Doesburg, *Neths.* 17 B6
Doetinchem, *Neths.* 17 C6
Dog Creek, *Canada* 104 C4
Dog L., *Man., Canada* 105 C9
Dog L., *Ont., Canada* 102 C2
Doğanşehir, *Turkey* 72 C7
Dogliani, *Italy* 28 D4
Dogondoutchi, *Niger* 83 C5
Dogran, *Pakistan* 68 D5
Doğubayazıt, *Turkey* 70 B5
Doguéraoua, *Niger* 83 C6
Doha = Ad Dawḩah, *Qatar* 71 E6
Dohazari, *Bangla.* 67 H18
Dohrighat, *India* 69 F10
Doi, *Indonesia* 63 D7
Doi Luang, *Thailand* 64 C3
Doi Saket, *Thailand* 64 C2
Dois Irmãos, Sa., *Brazil* 125 E10
Dojransko Jezero, *Macedonia* . 40 E6
Dokkum, *Neths.* 17 A5
Dokri, *Pakistan* 68 F3
Dokuchayevsk, *Ukraine* 47 J9
Dol-de-Bretagne, *France* 18 D5
Dolac, *Kosovo, Yug.* 40 D4

Dolak, Pulau, *Indonesia* 63 F9
Dolbeau, *Canada* 103 C5
Dole, *France* 19 E12
Doleib, Wadi ➤, *Sudan* 81 E3
Dolenji Logatec, *Slovenia* ... 29 C11
Dolgellau, *U.K.* 12 E4
Dolgelley = Dolgellau, *U.K.* . 12 E4
Dolhasca, *Romania* 43 C11
Dolianova, *Italy* 30 C2
Dolinskaya = Dolynska, *Ukraine* 47 H7
Dolj □, *Romania* 43 F8
Dollard, *Neths.* 17 A7
Dolna Banya, *Bulgaria* 40 D7
Dolni Chiflik, *Bulgaria* 41 D11
Dolni Dŭbnik, *Bulgaria* 41 C8
Dolnośląskie □, *Poland* 45 G3
Dolný Kubín, *Slovak Rep.* 27 B12
Dolo, *Ethiopia* 81 G5
Dolo, *Italy* 29 C9
Dolomites = Dolomiti, *Italy* . 29 B8
Dolomiti, *Italy* 29 B8
Dolores, *Argentina* 126 D4
Dolores, *Uruguay* 126 C4
Dolores, *U.S.A.* 115 H9
Dolores ➤, *U.S.A.* 115 G9
Dolovo, *Serbia, Yug.* 42 F5
Dolphin, C., *Falk. Is.* 128 G5
Dolphin and Union Str., *Canada* 100 B8
Dolsk, *Poland* 45 G4
Dolynska, *Ukraine* 47 H7
Dolzhanskaya, *Russia* 47 J9
Dom Pedrito, *Brazil* 127 C5
Doma, *Nigeria* 83 D6
Domaniç, *Turkey* 39 B11
Domariaganj ➤, *India* 69 F10
Domasi, *Malawi* 87 F4
Domažlice, *Czech Rep.* 26 B5
Dombarovskiy, *Russia* 50 D6
Dombås, *Norway* 9 E13
Dombes, *France* 21 C9
Dombóvár, *Hungary* 42 D3
Dombrád, *Hungary* 42 B6
Domel I. = Letsôk-aw Kyun,
    Burma 65 G2
Domérat, *France* 19 F9
Domeyko, *Chile* 126 B1
Domeyko, Cordillera, *Chile* .. 126 A2
Domfront, *France* 18 D6
Dominador, *Chile* 126 A2
Dominica ■, *W. Indies* 121 C7
Dominica Passage, *W. Indies* . 121 C7
Dominican Rep. ■, *W. Indies* . 121 C5
Dömitz, *Germany* 24 B7
Domme, *France* 20 D5
Domneşti, *Romania* 43 E9
Domodóssola, *Italy* 28 B5
Dompaire, *France* 19 D13
Dompierre-sur-Besbre, *France* 19 F10
Dompim, *Ghana* 82 D4
Domrémy-la-Pucelle, *France* .. 19 D12
Domville, Mt., *Australia* 95 D5
Domvraína, *Greece* 38 C4
Domžale, *Slovenia* 29 B11
Don ➤, *Russia* 47 J10
Don ➤, *Aberds., U.K.* 14 D6
Don ➤, *S. Yorks., U.K.* 12 D7
Don, C., *Australia* 92 B5
Don Benito, *Spain* 35 G5
Dona Ana = Nhamaabué,
    Mozam. 87 F4
Doña Mencía, *Spain* 35 H6
Donaghadee, *U.K.* 15 B6
Donald, *Australia* 95 F3
Donaldsonville, *U.S.A.* 113 K9
Donalsonville, *U.S.A.* 109 K3
Donau = Dunărea ➤, *Europe* ... 43 E14
Donau ➤, *Austria* 17 D3
Donaueschingen, *Germany* 25 H4
Donauwörth, *Germany* 25 G6
Doncaster, *U.K.* 12 D6
Dondo, *Mozam.* 87 F3
Dondo, Teluk, *Indonesia* 63 D6
Dondra Head, *Sri Lanka* 66 S12
Donduşeni, *Moldova* 43 B12
Donegal, *Ireland* 15 B3
Donegal □, *Ireland* 15 B4
Donegal B., *Ireland* 15 B3
Donets ➤, *Russia* 49 G5
Donetsk, *Ukraine* 47 J9
Dong Ba Thin, *Vietnam* 65 F7
Dong Dang, *Vietnam* 58 G6
Dong Giam, *Vietnam* 64 C5
Dong Ha, *Vietnam* 64 D6
Dong Hene, *Laos* 64 D5
Dong Hoi, *Vietnam* 64 D6
Dong Jiang ➤, *China* 59 F10
Dong Khe, *Vietnam* 64 A6
Dong Ujimqin Qi, *China* 56 B9
Dong Van, *Vietnam* 58 A5
Dong Xoai, *Vietnam* 65 G6
Donga, *Nigeria* 83 D7
Donga ➤, *Nigeria* 83 D7
Dong'an, *China* 59 D8
Dongara, *Australia* 93 E1
Dongbei, *China* 57 D13
Dongchuan, *China* 58 D4
Donges, *France* 18 E4
Dongfang, *China* 64 C7
Dongfeng, *China* 57 C13
Donggala, *Indonesia* 63 E5
Donggou, *China* 57 E13
Dongguan, *China* 59 F9
Dongguang, *China* 56 F9
Donghai Dao, *China* 59 G8
Dongjingcheng, *China* 57 B15

Dongkou, *China* 59 D8
Donglan, *China* 58 E6
Dongliu, *China* 59 B11
Dongmen, *China* 58 F6
Dongning, *China* 57 B16
Dongnyi, *China* 58 C3
Dongola, *Sudan* 80 D3
Dongping, *China* 56 G9
Dongshan, *China* 59 F11
Dongsheng, *China* 56 E6
Dongtai, *China* 57 H11
Dongting Hu, *China* 59 C9
Dongtou, *China* 59 D13
Dongxiang, *China* 59 C11
Dongxing, *China* 58 G7
Dongyang, *China* 59 C13
Dongzhi, *China* 59 B11
Donington, C., *Australia* 95 E2
Doniphan, *U.S.A.* 113 G9
Donja Stubica, *Croatia* 29 C12
Donji Dušnik, *Serbia, Yug.* .. 40 C6
Donji Miholjac, *Croatia* 42 E3
Donji Milanovac, *Serbia, Yug.* 40 B6
Donji Vakuf, *Bos.-H.* 42 F2
Dønna, *Norway* 8 C15
Donna, *U.S.A.* 113 M5
Donnaconna, *Canada* 103 C5
Donnelly's Crossing, *N.Z.* ... 91 F4
Donnybrook, *Australia* 93 F2
Donnybrook, *S. Africa* 89 D4
Donora, *U.S.A.* 110 F5
Donostia = Donostia-San
    Sebastián, *Spain* 32 B3
Donostia-San Sebastián, *Spain* 32 B3
Donskoy, *Russia* 46 F10
Donsol, *Phil.* 61 E5
Donzère, *France* 21 D8
Donzy, *France* 19 E10
Doon ➤, *U.K.* 14 F4
Dora, L., *Australia* 92 D3
Dora Báltea ➤, *Italy* 28 C5
Dora Ripária ➤, *Italy* 28 C4
Doran L., *Canada* 105 A7
Dorchester, *U.K.* 13 G5
Dorchester, C., *Canada* 101 B12
Dordabis, *Namibia* 88 C2
Dordogne □, *France* 20 C4
Dordogne ➤, *France* 20 C3
Dordrecht, *Neths.* 17 C4
Dordrecht, *S. Africa* 88 E4
Dore ➤, *France* 20 C7
Dore, Mts., *France* 20 C6
Doré L., *Canada* 105 C7
Doré Lake, *Canada* 105 C7
Dorfen, *Germany* 25 G8
Dorgali, *Italy* 30 B2
Dori, *Burkina Faso* 83 C4
Doring ➤, *S. Africa* 88 E2
Doringbos, *S. Africa* 88 E2
Dorion, *Canada* 111 A10
Dormaa-Ahenkro, *Ghana* 82 D4
Dormans, *France* 19 C10
Dormo, Ras, *Eritrea* 81 E5
Dornbirn, *Austria* 26 D2
Dornes, *France* 19 F10
Dornești, *Romania* 43 C11
Dornie, *U.K.* 14 D3
Dornoch, *U.K.* 14 D4
Dornoch Firth, *U.K.* 14 D4
Dornogovĭ □, *Mongolia* 56 C6
Doro, *Mali* 83 B4
Doro, *Hungary* 42 C3
Dorogobuzh, *Russia* 46 E7
Dorohoi, *Romania* 43 C11
Döröö Nuur, *Mongolia* 60 B4
Dorr, *Iran* 71 C6
Dorre I., *Australia* 93 E1
Dorrigo, *Australia* 95 E5
Dorris, *U.S.A.* 114 F3
Dorset, *Canada* 110 A6
Dorset, *U.S.A.* 110 E4
Dorset □, *U.K.* 13 G5
Dorsten, *Germany* 24 D2
Dortmund, *Germany* 24 D3
Dortmund-Ems-Kanal ➤,
    Germany 24 D3
Dörtyol, *Turkey* 72 D7
Dorum, *Germany* 24 B4
Doruma, *Dem. Rep. of
    the Congo* 86 B2
Dorūneh, *Iran* 71 C8
Dos Bahías, C., *Argentina* ... 128 E3
Dos Hermanas, *Spain* 35 H5
Dos Palos, *U.S.A.* 116 J6
Döşemealtı, *Turkey* 39 D12
Dosso, *Niger* 83 C5
Dothan, *U.S.A.* 109 K3
Doty, *U.S.A.* 116 D3
Douai, *France* 19 B10
Douako, *Guinea* 82 D2
Douala, *Cameroon* 83 E6
Douarnenez, *France* 18 D2
Doubabougou, *Mali* 82 C3
Double Island Pt., *Australia* 95 D5
Double Mountain Fork ➤,
    U.S.A. 113 J4
Doubrava ➤, *Czech Rep.* 26 A8
Doubs □, *France* 19 E13
Doubs ➤, *France* 19 F12
Doubtful Sd., *N.Z.* 91 L1
Doubtless B., *N.Z.* 91 F4
Doudeville, *France* 18 C7
Doué-la-Fontaine, *France* 18 E6
Douentza, *Mali* 82 C4
Douglas, *S. Africa* 88 D3
Douglas, *U.K.* 12 C3
Douglas, *Ariz., U.S.A.* 115 L9

Douglas, *Ga., U.S.A.* 109 K4
Douglas, *Wyo., U.S.A.* 112 D2
Douglas Chan., *Canada* 104 C3
Douglas Pt., *Canada* 110 B3
Douglasville, *U.S.A.* 109 J3
Doukáton, Ákra, *Greece* 38 C2
Doulevant-le-Château, *France* . 19 D11
Doullens, *France* 19 B9
Doumen, *China* 59 F9
Douna, *Mali* 82 C3
Douna, *Mali* 83 C4
Dounreay, *U.K.* 14 C5
Dourada, Serra, *Brazil* 125 F9
Dourados, *Brazil* 127 A5
Dourados →, *Brazil* 127 A5
Dourados, Serra dos, *Brazil* .. 127 A5
Dourdan, *France* 19 D9
Douro →, *Europe* 34 D2
Douvaine, *France* 19 F13
Douvres-la-Délivrande, *France* . 18 C6
Douze →, *France* 20 E3
Dove →, *U.K.* 12 E6
Dove Creek, *U.S.A.* 115 H9
Dover, *Australia* 94 G4
Dover, *U.K.* 13 F9
Dover, *Del., U.S.A.* 108 F8
Dover, *N.H., U.S.A.* 111 C14
Dover, *N.J., U.S.A.* 111 F10
Dover, *Ohio, U.S.A.* 110 F3
Dover, Pt., *Australia* 93 F4
Dover, Str. of, *Europe* 13 G9
Dover-Foxcroft, *U.S.A.* 109 C11
Dover Plains, *U.S.A.* 111 E11
Dovey = Dyfi →, *U.K.* 13 E3
Dovrefjell, *Norway* 9 E13
Dow Rūd, *Iran* 71 C6
Dowa, *Malawi* 87 E3
Dowagiac, *U.S.A.* 108 E2
Dowerin, *Australia* 93 F2
Dowgha'i, *Iran* 71 B8
Dowlatābād, *Iran* 71 D8
Down □, *U.K.* 15 B5
Downey, *Calif., U.S.A.* 117 M8
Downey, *Idaho, U.S.A.* 114 E7
Downham Market, *U.K.* 13 E8
Downieville, *U.S.A.* 116 F6
Downpatrick, *U.K.* 15 B6
Downpatrick Hd., *Ireland* ... 15 B2
Downsville, *U.S.A.* 111 D10
Downton, Mt., *Canada* 104 C4
Dowsari, *Iran* 71 D8
Doyle, *U.S.A.* 116 E6
Doylestown, *U.S.A.* 111 F9
Dozois, Rés., *Canada* 102 C4
Dra Khel, *Pakistan* 68 F2
Drac →, *France* 21 C9
Dračevo, *Macedonia* 40 E5
Drachten, *Neths.* 17 A6
Drăgănești, *Moldova* 43 C13
Drăgănești-Olt, *Romania* 43 F9
Drăgănești-Vlașca, *Romania* .. 43 F10
Dragaš, *Kosovo, Yug.* 40 D4
Drăgășani, *Romania* 43 F9
Dragichyn, *Belarus* 47 F3
Dragocvet, *Serbia, Yug.* 40 C5
Dragovishtitsa, *Bulgaria* 40 D6
Draguignan, *France* 21 E10
Drain, *U.S.A.* 114 E2
Drake, *U.S.A.* 112 B4
Drake Passage, *S. Ocean* 5 B17
Drakensberg, *S. Africa* 89 D4
Dráma, *Greece* 41 E8
Dráma □, *Greece* 41 E8
Drammen, *Norway* 9 G14
Drangajökull, *Iceland* 8 C2
Dranov, Ostrov, *Romania* 43 F14
Dras, *India* 69 B6
Drau = Drava →, *Croatia* 42 E3
Drava →, *Croatia* 42 E3
Dravograd, *Slovenia* 29 B12
Drawa →, *Poland* 45 F2
Drawno, *Poland* 45 E2
Drawsko Pomorskie, *Poland* .. 44 E2
Drayton Valley, *Canada* 104 C6
Dreieich, *Germany* 25 E4
Dren, *Kosovo, Yug.* 40 C4
Drenthe □, *Neths.* 17 B6
Drepanum, C., *Cyprus* 36 E11
Dresden, *Canada* 110 D2
Dresden, *Germany* 24 D9
Dreux, *France* 18 D8
Drezdenko, *Poland* 45 F2
Driffield, *U.K.* 12 C7
Driftwood, *U.S.A.* 110 E6
Driggs, *U.S.A.* 114 E8
Drin →, *Albania* 40 D3
Drin i Zi →, *Albania* 40 E4
Drina →, *Bos.-H.* 40 B3
Drincea →, *Romania* 42 F7
Drinjača →, *Bos.-H.* 42 F4
Drissa = Vyerkhnyadzvinsk,
  Belarus 46 E4
Drniš, *Croatia* 29 E13
Drøbak, *Norway* 9 G14
Drobeta-Turnu Severin,
  Romania 42 F7
Drobin, *Poland* 45 F6
Drochia, *Moldova* 43 B12
Drogheda, *Ireland* 15 C5
Drogichin = Dragichyn, *Belarus* 47 F3
Drogobych = Drohobych,
  Ukraine 47 H2
Drohiczyn, *Poland* 45 F9
Drohobych, *Ukraine* 47 H2
Droichead Atha = Drogheda,
  Ireland 15 C5
Droichead Nua, *Ireland* 15 C5

Droitwich, *U.K.* 13 E5
Drôme □, *France* 21 D9
Drôme →, *France* 21 D8
Dromedary, C., *Australia* 95 F5
Dromore, *U.K.* 15 B4
Dromore West, *Ireland* 15 B3
Dronero, *Italy* 28 D4
Dronfield, *U.K.* 12 D6
Dronne →, *France* 20 C3
Dronninglund, *Denmark* 11 G4
Dronten, *Neths.* 17 B5
Dropt →, *France* 20 D3
Drosendorf, *Austria* 26 C8
Droué, *France* 18 D8
Drumbo, *Canada* 110 C4
Drumheller, *Canada* 104 C6
Drummond, *U.S.A.* 114 C7
Drummond I., *U.S.A.* 108 C4
Drummond Pt., *Australia* 95 E2
Drummond Ra., *Australia* 94 C4
Drummondville, *Canada* 102 C5
Drumright, *U.S.A.* 113 H6
Druskininkai, *Lithuania* 9 J20
Drut →, *Belarus* 47 F6
Druya, *Belarus* 46 E4
Družba, *Bulgaria* 41 C12
Druzhina, *Russia* 51 C15
Drvar, *Bos.-H.* 29 D13
Drvenik, *Croatia* 29 E13
Drwęca →, *Poland* 45 E5
Dry Tortugas, *U.S.A.* 120 B3
Dryanovo, *Bulgaria* 41 D9
Dryden, *Canada* 105 D10
Dryden, *U.S.A.* 111 D8
Drygalski I., *Antarctica* 5 C7
Drysdale →, *Australia* 92 B4
Drysdale I., *Australia* 94 A2
Drzewica, *Poland* 45 G7
Drzewiczka →, *Poland* 45 G7
Dschang, *Cameroon* 83 D7
Du Bois, *U.S.A.* 110 E6
Du Gué →, *Canada* 102 A5
Du He, *China* 59 A8
Du Quoin, *U.S.A.* 112 G10
Duanesburg, *U.S.A.* 111 D10
Duaringa, *Australia* 94 C4
Dubā, *Si. Arabia* 70 E2
Dubai = Dubayy, *U.A.E.* 71 E7
Dubăsari, *Moldova* 43 C14
Dubăsari Vdkhr., *Moldova* ... 43 C13
Dubawnt →, *Canada* 105 A8
Dubawnt, L., *Canada* 105 A8
Dubayy, *U.A.E.* 71 E7
Dubbo, *Australia* 95 E4
Dubele, *Dem. Rep. of the Congo* 86 B2
Dübendorf, *Switz.* 25 H4
Dubica, *Croatia* 29 C13
Dublin, *Ireland* 15 C5
Dublin, *Ga., U.S.A.* 109 J4
Dublin, *Tex., U.S.A.* 113 J5
Dublin □, *Ireland* 15 C5
Dubna, *Russia* 46 D9
Dubnica nad Váhom,
  Slovak Rep. 27 C11
Dubno, *Ukraine* 47 G3
Dubois, *U.S.A.* 114 D7
Dubossary = Dubăsari, *Moldova* 43 C14
Dubossary Vdkhr. = Dubăsari
  Vdkhr., *Moldova* 43 C13
Dubovka, *Russia* 49 F7
Dubovskoye, *Russia* 49 G6
Dubrajpur, *India* 69 H12
Dubréka, *Guinea* 82 D2
Dubrovitsa = Dubrovytsya,
  Ukraine 47 G4
Dubrovnik, *Croatia* 40 D7
Dubrovytsya, *Ukraine* 47 G4
Dubuque, *U.S.A.* 112 D9
Dubysa →, *Lithuania* 44 C10
Duchang, *China* 59 C11
Duchesne, *U.S.A.* 114 F8
Duchess, *Australia* 94 C2
Ducie I., *Pac. Oc.* 97 K15
Duck →, *U.S.A.* 109 G2
Duck Cr. →, *Australia* 92 D2
Duck Lake, *Canada* 105 C7
Duck Mountain Prov. Park,
  Canada 105 C8
Duckwall, Mt., *U.S.A.* 116 H6
Duderstadt, *Germany* 24 D6
Dudhi, *India* 67 G13
Dudinka, *Russia* 51 C9
Dudley, *U.K.* 13 E5
Dudwa, *India* 69 E9
Duékoué, *Ivory C.* 82 D3
Dueñas, *Spain* 34 D6
Duero = Douro →, *Europe* 34 D2
Dufftown, *U.K.* 14 D5
Dufourspitz, *Switz.* 25 K3
Dūghī Kalā, *Afghan.* 66 C3
Dugi Otok, *Croatia* 29 D11
Dugo Selo, *Croatia* 29 C13
Duifken Pt., *Australia* 94 A3
Duisburg, *Germany* 24 D2
Duiwelskloof, *S. Africa* 89 C5
Dujiangyan, *China* 58 B4
Duk Fadiat, *Sudan* 81 F3
Duk Faiwil, *Sudan* 81 F3
Dukat, *Albania* 40 F3
Dūkdamīn, *Iran* 71 C8
Dukelský Průsmyk, *Slovak Rep.* 27 B14
Dukhān, *Qatar* 71 E6
Dukhovshchina, *Russia* 46 E7
Duki, *Pakistan* 66 D6
Dukla, *Poland* 45 J8
Duku, *Bauchi, Nigeria* 83 C7

Duku, *Sokoto, Nigeria* 83 C5
Dulag, *Phil.* 61 F6
Dulce →, *U.S.A.* 115 H10
Dulce →, *Argentina* 126 C3
Dulce, G., *Costa Rica* 120 E3
Dulf, *Iraq* 70 C5
Dülgopol, *Bulgaria* 41 C11
Dulit, Banjaran, *Malaysia* ... 62 D4
Duliu, *China* 56 E9
Dullewala, *Pakistan* 68 D4
Dullstroom, *S. Africa* 89 D5
Dülmen, *Germany* 24 D3
Dulovo, *Bulgaria* 41 C11
Dulq Maghār, *Syria* 70 B3
Duluth, *U.S.A.* 112 B8
Dum Dum, *India* 69 H13
Dum Duma, *India* 67 F19
Dūmā, *Syria* 75 B5
Dumaguete, *Phil.* 61 G5
Dumai, *Indonesia* 62 D2
Dumaran, *Phil.* 61 F3
Dumas, *Ark., U.S.A.* 113 J9
Dumas, *Tex., U.S.A.* 113 H4
Ḑumayr, *Syria* 75 B5
Dumbarton, *U.K.* 14 F4
Ḑumbier, *Slovak Rep.* 27 C12
Dumbleyung, *Australia* 93 F2
Dumboa, *Nigeria* 83 C7
Dumbrăveni, *Romania* 43 D9
Dumbrava →, *India* 69 G11
Dumfries, *U.K.* 14 F5
Dumfries & Galloway □, *U.K.* . 14 F5
Dumitrești, *Romania* 43 E11
Dumka, *India* 69 G12
Dumlupınar, *Turkey* 39 C12
Dümmer, *Germany* 24 C4
Dumoine →, *Canada* 102 C4
Dumoine, L., *Canada* 102 C4
Dumraon, *India* 69 G11
Dumyât, *Egypt* 80 H7
Dumyât, Masabb, *Egypt* 80 H7
Dún Dealgan = Dundalk,
  Ireland 15 B5
Dún Laoghaire, *Ireland* 15 C5
Dun-le-Palestel, *France* 19 F8
Dun-sur-Auron, *France* 19 F9
Dun-sur-Meuse, *France* 19 C12
Duna = Dunărea →, *Europe* ... 43 E14
Duna →, *Hungary* 42 E3
Duna-völgy-főcsatorna,
  Hungary 42 D4
Dunaföldvár, *Hungary* 42 D3
Dunagiri, *India* 69 D8
Dunaj = Dunărea →, *Europe* .. 43 E14
Dunaj →, *Slovak Rep.* 27 D11
Dunajec →, *Poland* 45 H7
Dunajská Streda, *Slovak Rep.* 27 C10
Dunakeszi, *Hungary* 42 C4
Dunapataj, *Hungary* 42 D4
Dunărea →, *Europe* 43 E14
Dunaszekcső, *Hungary* 42 D3
Dunaújváros, *Hungary* 42 D3
Dunav = Dunărea →, *Europe* .. 43 E14
Dunavăţu de Jos, *Romania* ... 43 F14
Dunavtsi, *Bulgaria* 40 C6
Dunay, *Russia* 54 C6
Dunback, *N.Z.* 91 L3
Dunbar, *U.K.* 14 E6
Dunblane, *U.K.* 14 E5
Duncan, *Canada* 104 D4
Duncan, *Ariz., U.S.A.* 115 K9
Duncan, *Okla., U.S.A.* 113 H6
Duncan, L., *Canada* 102 B4
Duncan L., *Canada* 104 A6
Duncan Town, *Bahamas* 120 B4
Duncannon, *U.S.A.* 110 F7
Duncansby Head, *U.K.* 14 C5
Duncansville, *U.S.A.* 110 F6
Dundalk, *Canada* 110 B4
Dundalk, *Ireland* 15 B5
Dundalk, *U.S.A.* 108 F7
Dundalk Bay, *Ireland* 15 C5
Dundas, *Canada* 110 C5
Dundas, L., *Australia* 93 F3
Dundas I., *Canada* 104 C2
Dundas Str., *Australia* 92 B5
Dundee, *S. Africa* 89 D5
Dundee, *U.K.* 14 E6
Dundee, *U.S.A.* 110 D8
Dundee City □, *U.K.* 14 E6
Dundgovĭ □, *Mongolia* 56 B4
Dundrum, *U.K.* 15 B6
Dundrum B., *U.K.* 15 B6
Dunedin, *N.Z.* 91 L3
Dunedin, *U.S.A.* 109 L4
Dunfermline, *U.K.* 14 E5
Dungannon, *Canada* 110 C3
Dungannon, *U.K.* 15 B5
Dungarpur, *India* 68 H5
Dungarvan, *Ireland* 15 D4
Dungarvan Harbour, *Ireland* . 15 D4
Dungeness, *U.K.* 13 G8
Dungo, L. do, *Angola* 88 B2
Dungog, *Australia* 95 E5
Dungu, *Dem. Rep. of the Congo* 86 B2
Dungun, *Malaysia* 65 K4
Dungunâb, *Sudan* 80 C4
Dungunâb, Khalij, *Sudan* 80 C4
Dunhua, *China* 57 C15
Dunhuang, *China* 60 B4
Dunk I., *Australia* 94 B4
Dunkassa, *Benin* 83 C5
Dunkeld, *U.K.* 14 E5
Dunkerque, *France* 19 A9
Dunkery Beacon, *U.K.* 13 F4
Dunkirk = Dunkerque, *France* . 19 A9

Dunkirk, *U.S.A.* 110 D5
Dunkuj, *Sudan* 81 E3
Dunkwa, *Central, Ghana* 82 D4
Dunkwa, *Central, Ghana* 83 D4
Dúnleary = Dun Laoghaire,
  Ireland 15 C5
Dunleer, *Ireland* 15 C5
Dunmanus B., *Ireland* 15 E2
Dunmanway, *Ireland* 15 E2
Dunmara, *Australia* 94 B1
Dunmore, *U.S.A.* 111 E9
Dunmore Hd., *Ireland* 15 D1
Dunmore Town, *Bahamas* 120 A4
Dunn, *U.S.A.* 109 H6
Dunnellon, *U.S.A.* 109 L4
Dunnet Hd., *U.K.* 14 C5
Dunning, *U.S.A.* 112 E4
Dunnville, *Canada* 110 D5
Dunolly, *Australia* 95 F3
Dunoon, *U.K.* 14 F4
Dunphy, *U.S.A.* 114 F5
Dunqul, *Egypt* 80 C3
Duns, *U.K.* 14 F6
Dunseith, *U.S.A.* 112 A4
Dunsmuir, *U.S.A.* 114 F2
Dunstable, *U.K.* 13 F7
Dunstan Mts., *N.Z.* 91 L2
Dunster, *Canada* 104 C5
Dunvegan L., *Canada* 105 A7
Duolun, *China* 56 C9
Duong Dong, *Vietnam* 65 G4
Dupree, *U.S.A.* 112 C4
Dupuyer, *U.S.A.* 114 B7
Duque de Caxias, *Brazil* 127 A7
Durack →, *Australia* 92 C4
Durack Ra., *Australia* 92 C4
Durağan, *Turkey* 72 B6
Durak, *Turkey* 39 B10
Đurakovac, *Kosovo, Yug.* 40 D4
Durance →, *France* 21 E8
Durand, *U.S.A.* 112 C9
Durango, *Mexico* 118 C4
Durango, *U.S.A.* 115 H10
Durango □, *Mexico* 118 C4
Durankulak, *Bulgaria* 41 C12
Durant, *Miss., U.S.A.* 113 J10
Durant, *Okla., U.S.A.* 113 J6
Duratón →, *Spain* 34 D6
Durazno, *Uruguay* 126 C4
Durazzo = Durrës, *Albania* .. 40 E3
Durban, *France* 20 F6
Durban, *S. Africa* 89 D5
Durbuy, *Belgium* 17 D5
Dúrcal, *Spain* 35 J7
Đurđevica, *Croatia* 42 D2
Düren, *Germany* 24 E2
Durg, *India* 67 J12
Durgapur, *India* 69 H12
Durham, *Canada* 102 D3
Durham, *U.K.* 12 C6
Durham, *Calif., U.S.A.* 116 F5
Durham, *N.C., U.S.A.* 109 H6
Durham, *N.H., U.S.A.* 111 C14
Durham □, *U.K.* 12 C6
Durham Downs, *Australia* 43 C13
Durmā, *Si. Arabia* 70 E5
Durmitor, *Montenegro, Yug.* . 40 C2
Durness, *U.K.* 14 C4
Durrës, *Albania* 40 E3
Durrow, *Ireland* 15 D4
Dursey I., *Ireland* 15 E1
Dursunbey, *Turkey* 39 B10
Durtal, *France* 18 E6
Duru, *Dem. Rep. of the Congo* 86 B2
Duru Gölü, *Turkey* 41 E12
Durusu, *Turkey* 41 E12
Durūz, Jabal ad, *Jordan* 75 C5
D'Urville, Tanjung, *Indonesia* 63 E9
D'Urville I., *N.Z.* 91 J4
Duryea, *U.S.A.* 111 E9
Dūsh, *Egypt* 80 C3
Dushak, *Turkmenistan* 50 F7
Dushan, *China* 58 E6
Dushanbe, *Tajikistan* 50 F7
Dushore, *U.S.A.* 111 E8
Dusky Sd., *N.Z.* 91 L1
Dussejour, C., *Australia* 92 B4
Düsseldorf, *Germany* 24 D2
Duszniki-Zdrój, *Poland* 45 H3
Dutch Harbor, *U.S.A.* 100 C3
Dutlwe, *Botswana* 88 C3
Dutsan Wai, *Nigeria* 83 C6
Dutton, *Canada* 110 D3
Dutton →, *Australia* 94 C3
Duved, *Sweden* 10 A6
Düvertepe, *Turkey* 39 B10
Duwayhin, Khawr, *U.A.E.* 71 E6
Duyun, *China* 58 D6
Düzağaç, *Turkey* 39 C12
Düzce, *Turkey* 72 B4
Düzdab = Zāhedān, *Iran* 71 D9
Dve Mogili, *Bulgaria* 41 C9
Dvina, Severnaya →, *Russia* . 50 C5
Dvinsk = Daugavpils, *Latvia* . 9 J22
Dvor, *Croatia* 29 C13
Dvůr Králové nad Labem,
  Czech Rep. 26 A8
Dwarka, *India* 68 H3
Dwellingup, *Australia* 93 F2
Dwight, *Canada* 110 A5
Dwight, *U.S.A.* 108 E1
Dyatkovo, *Russia* 46 F8
Dyatlovo = Dzyatlava, *Belarus* 46 F3
Dyce, *U.K.* 14 D6
Dyer, C., *Canada* 101 B13
Dyer Bay, *Canada* 110 A3

Dyer Plateau, *Antarctica* ... 5 D17
Dyersburg, *U.S.A.* 113 G10
Dyfi →, *U.K.* 13 E3
Dyje →, *Czech Rep.* 27 C9
Dymer, *Ukraine* 47 G6
Dynów, *Poland* 45 J9
Dysart, *Australia* 94 C4
Dzamin Üüd = Borhoyn Tal,
  Mongolia 56 C6
Dzerzhinsk, *Russia* 48 B6
Dzhalinda, *Russia* 51 D13
Dzhambul = Taraz, *Kazakstan* . 50 E8
Dzhankoy, *Ukraine* 47 K8
Dzhanybek, *Kazakstan* 48 F8
Dzharylhach, Ostriv, *Ukraine* 47 J7
Dzhezkazgan = Zhezqazghan,
  Kazakstan 50 E7
Dzhizak = Jizzakh, *Uzbekistan* 50 E7
Dzhugdzur, Khrebet, *Russia* .. 51 D14
Dzhvari = Jvari, *Georgia* 49 J6
Działdowo, *Poland* 45 E7
Działoszyce, *Poland* 45 H7
Działoszyn, *Poland* 45 G5
Dzibilchaltun, *Mexico* 119 C7
Dzierzgoń, *Poland* 44 E6
Dzierżoniów, *Poland* 45 H3
Dzilam de Bravo, *Mexico* 119 C7
Dzisna, *Belarus* 46 E5
Dzisna →, *Belarus* 46 E5
Dziwnów, *Poland* 44 D1
Dzungaria = Junggar Pendi,
  China 60 B3
Dzuumod, *Mongolia* 60 B5
Dzyarzhynsk, *Belarus* 46 F4
Dzyatlava, *Belarus* 46 F3

E

Eabamet L., *Canada* 102 B2
Eads, *U.S.A.* 112 F3
Eagar, *U.S.A.* 115 J9
Eagle, *Alaska, U.S.A.* 100 B5
Eagle, *Colo., U.S.A.* 114 G10
Eagle →, *Canada* 103 B8
Eagle Butte, *U.S.A.* 112 C4
Eagle Grove, *U.S.A.* 112 D8
Eagle L., *Canada* 105 D10
Eagle L., *Calif., U.S.A.* ... 114 F3
Eagle L., *Maine, U.S.A.* 109 B11
Eagle Lake, *Canada* 110 A6
Eagle Lake, *Maine, U.S.A.* .. 109 B11
Eagle Lake, *Tex., U.S.A.* ... 113 L6
Eagle Mountain, *U.S.A.* 117 M11
Eagle Nest, *U.S.A.* 115 H11
Eagle Pass, *U.S.A.* 113 L4
Eagle Pk., *U.S.A.* 116 G7
Eagle Pt., *Australia* 92 C3
Eagle River, *Mich., U.S.A.* . 108 B1
Eagle River, *Wis., U.S.A.* .. 112 C10
Eaglehawk, *Australia* 95 F3
Eagles Mere, *U.S.A.* 111 E8
Ealing □, *U.K.* 13 F7
Ear Falls, *Canada* 105 C10
Earle, *U.S.A.* 113 H9
Earlimart, *U.S.A.* 117 K7
Earn →, *U.K.* 14 E5
Earn, L., *U.K.* 14 E4
Earnslaw, Mt., *N.Z.* 91 L2
Earth, *U.S.A.* 113 H3
Easley, *U.S.A.* 109 H4
East Anglia, *U.K.* 12 E9
East Angus, *Canada* 103 C5
East Aurora, *U.S.A.* 110 D6
East Ayrshire □, *U.K.* 14 F4
East Beskids = Vychodné
  Beskydy, *Europe* 27 B15
East Brady, *U.S.A.* 110 F5
East C., *N.Z.* 91 G7
East Chicago, *U.S.A.* 108 E2
East China Sea, *Asia* 60 C7
East Coulee, *Canada* 104 C6
East Dereham, *U.K.* 13 E8
East Dunbartonshire □, *U.K.* . 14 F4
East Falkland, *Falk. Is.* ... 122 J5
East Grand Forks, *U.S.A.* ... 112 B6
East Greenwich, *U.S.A.* 111 E13
East Grinstead, *U.K.* 13 F8
East Hartford, *U.S.A.* 111 E12
East Helena, *U.S.A.* 114 C8
East Indies, *Asia* 52 K15
East Kilbride, *U.K.* 14 F4
East Lansing, *U.S.A.* 108 D3
East Liverpool, *U.S.A.* 110 F4
East London, *S. Africa* 89 E4
East Lothian □, *U.K.* 14 F6
East Main = Eastmain, *Canada* 102 B4
East Northport, *U.S.A.* 111 F11
East Orange, *U.S.A.* 111 F10
East Pacific Ridge, *Pac. Oc.* 97 J17
East Palestine, *U.S.A.* 110 F4
East Pine, *Canada* 104 B4
East Point, *U.S.A.* 109 J3
East Providence, *U.S.A.* 111 E13
East Pt., *Canada* 103 C7
East Retford = Retford, *U.K.* 12 D7
East Riding of Yorkshire □,
  U.K. 12 D7
East Rochester, *U.S.A.* 110 C7
East St. Louis, *U.S.A.* 112 F9
East Schelde =
  Oosterschelde →, *Neths.* .. 17 C4
East Sea = Japan, Sea of, *Asia* 54 E7
East Siberian Sea, *Russia* .. 51 B17

East Stroudsburg

East Stroudsburg, U.S.A. 111 E9
East Sussex □, U.K. 13 G8
East Tawas, U.S.A. 108 C4
East Timor ■, Asia 63 F7
East Toorale, Australia 95 E4
East Walker →, U.S.A. 116 G7
East Windsor, U.S.A. 111 F10
Eastbourne, N.Z. 91 J5
Eastbourne, U.K. 13 G8
Eastend, Canada 105 D7
Easter I. = Pascua, I. de, Pac. Oc. 97 K17
Eastern □, Ghana 83 D4
Eastern □, Kenya 86 C4
Eastern Cape □, S. Africa 88 E4
Eastern Cr. →, Australia 94 C3
Eastern Ghats, India 66 N11
Eastern Group = Lau Group, Fiji 91 C9
Eastern Group, Australia 93 F3
Eastern Province □, S. Leone 82 D2
Eastern Transvaal = Mpumalanga □, S. Africa 89 B5
Easterville, Canada 105 C9
Easthampton, U.S.A. 111 D12
Eastlake, U.S.A. 110 E3
Eastland, U.S.A. 113 J5
Eastleigh, U.K. 13 G6
Eastmain, Canada 102 B4
Eastmain →, Canada 102 B4
Eastman, Canada 111 A12
Eastman, U.S.A. 109 J4
Easton, Md., U.S.A. 108 F7
Easton, Pa., U.S.A. 111 F9
Easton, Wash., U.S.A. 116 C5
Eastpointe, U.S.A. 110 D2
Eastport, U.S.A. 109 C12
Eastsound, U.S.A. 116 B4
Eaton, U.S.A. 112 E2
Eatonia, Canada 105 C7
Eatonton, U.S.A. 109 J4
Eatontown, U.S.A. 111 F10
Eatonville, U.S.A. 116 D4
Eau Claire, U.S.A. 112 C9
Eau Claire, L. à l', Canada 102 A5
Eauze, France 20 E4
Eban, Nigeria 83 D5
Ebbw Vale, U.K. 13 F4
Ebeltoft, Denmark 11 H4
Ebeltoft Vig, Denmark 11 H4
Ebensburg, U.S.A. 110 F6
Ebensee, Austria 26 D6
Eber Gölü, Turkey 72 C4
Eberbach, Germany 25 F4
Eberswalde-Finow, Germany 24 C9
Ebetsu, Japan 54 C10
Ebian, China 58 C4
Ebingen, Germany 25 G5
Éboli, Italy 31 B8
Ebolowa, Cameroon 83 E7
Ebonyi □, Nigeria 83 D6
Ebrach, Germany 25 F6
Ébrié, Lagune, Ivory C. 82 D4
Ebro →, Spain 32 E5
Ebro, Embalse del, Spain 34 C7
Ebstorf, Germany 24 B6
Eceabat, Turkey 41 F10
Ech Cheliff, Algeria 78 A6
Echigo-Sammyaku, Japan 55 F9
Échirolles, France 21 C9
Echizen-Misaki, Japan 55 G7
Echmiadzin = Yejmiadzin, Armenia 49 K7
Echo Bay, N.W.T., Canada 100 B8
Echo Bay, Ont., Canada 102 C3
Echoing →, Canada 102 B1
Echternach, Lux. 17 E6
Echuca, Australia 95 F3
Ecija, Spain 35 H5
Eckental, Germany 25 F7
Eckernförde, Germany 24 A5
Eclipse Is., Australia 92 B4
Eclipse Sd., Canada 101 A11
Écommoy, France 18 E7
Écouché, France 18 D6
Ecuador ■, S. Amer. 124 D3
Écueillé, France 18 E8
Ed, Sweden 11 F5
Ed Dabbura, Sudan 80 D3
Ed Da'ein, Sudan 81 E2
Ed Damazin, Sudan 79 F12
Ed Dâmer, Sudan 80 D3
Ed Debba, Sudan 80 D3
Ed-Déffa, Egypt 80 A2
Ed Deim, Sudan 81 E2
Ed Dueim, Sudan 81 E3
Edam, Canada 105 C7
Edam, Neths. 17 B5
Edane, Sweden 10 E6
Eday, U.K. 14 B6
Edd, Eritrea 81 E5
Eddrachillis B., U.K. 14 C3
Eddystone Pt., Australia 94 G4
Ede, Neths. 17 B5
Ede, Nigeria 83 D5
Edéa, Cameroon 83 E7
Edebäck, Sweden 10 D7
Edehon L., Canada 105 A9
Edelény, Hungary 42 B5
Eden, Australia 95 F4
Eden, N.C., U.S.A. 109 G6
Eden, N.Y., U.S.A. 110 D6
Eden, Tex., U.S.A. 113 K5
Eden →, U.K. 12 C4
Edenburg, S. Africa 88 D4
Edendale, S. Africa 89 D5
Edenderry, Ireland 15 C4
Edenton, U.S.A. 109 G7
Edenville, S. Africa 89 D4
Eder →, Germany 24 D5
Eder-Stausee, Germany 24 D4
Edewecht, Germany 24 B3
Edgar, U.S.A. 112 E6
Edgartown, U.S.A. 111 E14
Edge Hill, U.K. 13 E6
Edgefield, U.S.A. 109 J5
Edgeley, U.S.A. 112 B5
Edgemont, U.S.A. 112 D3
Edgeøya, Svalbard 4 B9
Édhessa, Greece 40 F6
Edievale, N.Z. 91 L2
Edina, Liberia 82 D2
Edina, U.S.A. 112 E8
Edinboro, U.S.A. 110 E4
Edinburg, U.S.A. 113 M5
Edinburgh, U.K. 14 F5
Edinburgh, City of □, U.K. 14 F5
Edineţ, Moldova 43 B12
Edirne, Turkey 41 E10
Edirne □, Turkey 41 E10
Edison, U.S.A. 116 B4
Edithburgh, Australia 95 F2
Edmeston, U.S.A. 111 D9
Edmond, U.S.A. 113 H6
Edmonds, U.S.A. 116 C4
Edmonton, Australia 94 B4
Edmonton, Canada 104 C6
Edmund L., Canada 102 B1
Edmundston, Canada 103 C6
Edna, U.S.A. 113 L6
Edo □, Nigeria 83 D6
Edolo, Italy 28 B7
Edremit, Turkey 39 B9
Edremit Körfezi, Turkey 39 B8
Edsbro, Sweden 10 E12
Edsbyn, Sweden 10 C9
Edson, Canada 104 C5
Eduardo Castex, Argentina 126 D3
Edward →, Australia 95 F3
Edward, L., Africa 86 C2
Edward River, Australia 94 A3
Edward VII Land, Antarctica 5 E13
Edwards, Calif., U.S.A. 117 L9
Edwards, N.Y., U.S.A. 111 B9
Edwards Air Force Base, U.S.A. 117 L9
Edwards Plateau, U.S.A. 113 K4
Edwardsville, U.S.A. 111 E9
Edzo, Canada 104 A5
Eeklo, Belgium 17 C3
Eferding, Austria 26 C7
Effingham, U.S.A. 108 F1
Eforie, Romania 43 F13
Ega →, Spain 32 C3
Égadi, Ísole, Italy 30 E5
Egan Range, U.S.A. 114 G6
Eganville, Canada 102 C4
Eger = Cheb, Czech Rep. 26 A5
Eger, Hungary 42 C5
Eger →, Hungary 42 C5
Egersund, Norway 9 G12
Egg L., Canada 105 B7
Eggenburg, Austria 26 C8
Eggenfelden, Germany 25 G8
Éghezée, Belgium 17 D4
Égletons, France 20 C6
Egmont, Canada 104 D4
Egmont, C., N.Z. 91 H4
Egmont, Mt. = Taranaki, Mt., N.Z. 91 H5
Egra, India 69 J12
Eğridir, Turkey 72 D4
Eğridir Gölü, Turkey 70 B1
Egtved, Denmark 11 J3
Egume, Nigeria 83 D6
Éguzon-Chantôme, France 19 F8
Egvekinot, Russia 51 C19
Egyek, Hungary 42 C5
Egypt ■, Africa 80 B3
Eha Amufu, Nigeria 83 D6
Ehime □, Japan 55 H6
Ehingen, Germany 25 G5
Ehrenberg, U.S.A. 117 M12
Ehrwald, Austria 26 D3
Eibar, Spain 32 B2
Eichstätt, Germany 25 G7
Eider →, Germany 24 A4
Eidsvold, Australia 95 D5
Eidsvoll, Norway 9 F14
Eifel, Germany 25 E2
Eiffel Flats, Zimbabwe 87 F3
Eiger, Switz. 28 B5
Eigg, U.K. 14 E2
Eighty Mile Beach, Australia 92 C3
Eil, Somali Rep. 74 F4
Eil, L., U.K. 14 E3
Eildon, L., Australia 95 F4
Eilenburg, Germany 24 D8
Ein el Luweiqa, Sudan 81 E3
Einasleigh, Australia 94 B3
Einasleigh →, Australia 94 B3
Einbeck, Germany 24 D5
Eindhoven, Neths. 17 C5
Einsiedeln, Switz. 25 H4
Eire = Ireland ■, Europe 15 C4
Eiríksjökull, Iceland 8 D3
Eirunepé, Brazil 124 E5
Eiseb →, Namibia 88 C2
Eisenach, Germany 24 E6
Eisenberg, Germany 24 E7
Eisenerz, Austria 26 D7
Eisenhüttenstadt, Germany 24 C10
Eisenkappel, Austria 26 E7
Eisenstadt, Austria 27 D9
Eisfeld, Germany 25 E6
Eisleben, Germany 24 D7
Eislingen, Germany 25 G5
Eivissa, Spain 37 C7
Eixe, Serra do, Spain 34 C4
Ejea de los Caballeros, Spain 32 C3
Ejeda, Madag. 89 C7
Ejura, Ghana 83 D4
Ejutla, Mexico 119 D5
Ekalaka, U.S.A. 112 C2
Ekenässjön, Sweden 11 G9
Ekerö, Sweden 10 E11
Eket, Nigeria 83 E6
Eketahuna, N.Z. 91 J5
Ekhínos, Greece 41 E9
Ekibastuz, Kazakstan 50 D8
Ekiti □, Nigeria 83 D6
Ekoli, Dem. Rep. of the Congo 86 C1
Ekoln, Sweden 10 E11
Ekshärad, Sweden 10 D7
Eksjö, Sweden 11 G8
Ekuma →, Namibia 88 B2
Ekwan →, Canada 102 B3
Ekwan Pt., Canada 102 B3
El Aaiún, W. Sahara 78 C3
El Abanico, Chile 126 D1
El Abbasiya, Sudan 81 E3
El 'Agrûd, Egypt 75 E3
El Ait, Sudan 81 E2
El 'Aiyat, Egypt 80 J7
El Alamein, Egypt 80 A2
El 'Aqaba, W. →, Egypt 75 E2
El 'Arag, Egypt 80 B2
El Arahal, Spain 35 H5
El Arīḥā, West Bank 75 D4
El 'Arîsh, Egypt 75 D2
El 'Arîsh, W. →, Egypt 75 D2
El Asnam = Ech Cheliff, Algeria 78 A6
El Astillero, Spain 34 B7
El Badâri, Egypt 80 B3
El Bahrein, Egypt 80 B2
El Ballâs, Egypt 80 B3
El Balyana, Egypt 80 B3
El Baqeir, Sudan 80 D3
El Barco de Ávila, Spain 34 E5
El Barco de Valdeorras = O Barco, Spain 34 C4
El Bauga, Sudan 80 D3
El Bawiti, Egypt 80 B2
El Bayadh, Algeria 78 B6
El Bierzo, Spain 34 C4
El Bluff, Nic. 120 D3
El Bonillo, Spain 33 G2
El Brûk, W. →, Egypt 75 E2
El Buheirat □, Sudan 81 F3
El Burgo de Osma, Spain 32 D1
El Cajon, U.S.A. 117 N10
El Campo, U.S.A. 113 L6
El Centro, U.S.A. 117 N11
El Cerro, Bolivia 124 G6
El Cerro de Andévalo, Spain 35 H4
El Compadre, Mexico 117 N10
El Coronil, Spain 35 H5
El Cuy, Argentina 128 D3
El Cuyo, Mexico 119 C7
El Dab'a, Egypt 80 H6
El Daheir, Egypt 75 D3
El Dátil, Mexico 118 B2
El Deir, Egypt 80 B3
El Dere, Somali Rep. 74 G4
El Descanso, Mexico 117 N10
El Desemboque, Mexico 118 A2
El Dilingat, Egypt 80 H7
El Diviso, Colombia 124 C3
El Djouf, Mauritania 78 D4
El Dorado, Ark., U.S.A. 113 J8
El Dorado, Kans., U.S.A. 113 G6
El Dorado, Venezuela 124 B6
El 'Ein, Sudan 81 D2
El Ejido, Spain 35 J8
El Escorial, Spain 34 E6
El Espinar, Spain 34 D6
El Faiyûm, Egypt 80 J7
El Fâsher, Sudan 81 E2
El Fashn, Egypt 80 J7
El Ferrol = Ferrol, Spain 34 B2
El Fifi, Sudan 81 E2
El Fuerte, Mexico 118 B3
El Ga'a, Sudan 81 E2
El Gal, Somali Rep. 74 E5
El Garef, Sudan 81 E3
El Gebir, Sudan 81 E2
El Gedida, Egypt 80 B2
El Geneina = Al Junaynah, Sudan 79 F10
El Geteina, Sudan 81 E3
El Gezira □, Sudan 81 E3
El Gir, Sudan 80 D2
El Gîza, Egypt 80 J7
El Goléa, Algeria 78 B6
El Grau, Spain 33 G4
El Hagiz, Sudan 81 D4
El Hâi, Egypt 80 J7
El Hammam, Egypt 80 A2
El Hawata, Sudan 81 E3
El Heiz, Egypt 80 B2
El Hideib, Sudan 81 D3
El Hilla, Sudan 81 E2
El 'Idisât, Egypt 80 B3
El Iskandarîya, Egypt 80 H7
El Istiwa'iya, Sudan 79 G11
El Jadida, Morocco 78 B4
El Jardal, Honduras 120 D2
El Jebelein, Sudan 81 E3
El Kab, Sudan 80 D3
El Kabrît, G., Egypt 75 F2
El Kafr el Sharqi, Egypt 80 H7
El Kamlin, Sudan 81 D3
El Karaba, Sudan 80 D3
El Kere, Ethiopia 81 F5
El Khandaq, Sudan 80 D3
El Khârga, Egypt 80 B3
El Khartûm, Sudan 81 D3
El Khartûm □, Sudan 81 D3
El Khartûm Bahrî, Sudan 81 D3
El Kuntilla, Egypt 75 E3
El Laqâwa, Sudan 81 E2
El Laqeita, Egypt 80 B3
El Leh, Ethiopia 81 G4
El Leiya, Sudan 81 D4
El Maestrazgo, Spain 32 E4
El Mafâza, Sudan 81 E3
El Maghra, Egypt 80 A2
El Mahalla el Kubra, Egypt 80 H7
El Mahârîq, Egypt 80 B3
El Maîmûn, Egypt 80 J7
El Maks el Bahari, Egypt 80 C3
El Manshâh, Egypt 80 B3
El Mansûra, Egypt 80 H7
El Manzala, Egypt 80 H7
El Marâgha, Egypt 80 B3
El Masid, Sudan 81 D3
El Masnou, Spain 32 D7
El Matariya, Egypt 80 H8
El Meda, Ethiopia 81 F5
El Medano, Canary Is. 37 F3
El Metemma, Sudan 81 D3
El Milagro, Argentina 126 C2
El Minyâ, Egypt 80 B3
El Monte, U.S.A. 117 L8
El Montseny, Spain 32 D7
El Mreyye, Mauritania 82 B3
El Niybo, Ethiopia 81 G4
El Obeid, Sudan 81 E3
El Odaiya, Sudan 81 E2
El Oro, Mexico 119 D4
El Oued, Algeria 78 B7
El Palmito, Presa, Mexico 118 B3
El Paso, U.S.A. 115 L10
El Paso Robles, U.S.A. 116 K6
El Pedernoso, Spain 33 F2
El Pedroso, Spain 35 H5
El Pobo de Dueñas, Spain 32 E3
El Portal, U.S.A. 116 H7
El Porvenir, Mexico 118 A3
El Prat de Llobregat, Spain 32 D7
El Progreso, Honduras 120 C2
El Pueblito, Mexico 118 B3
El Pueblo, Canary Is. 37 F2
El Puente del Arzobispo, Spain 34 F5
El Puerto de Santa María, Spain 35 J4
El Qâhira, Egypt 80 H7
El Qantara, Egypt 75 E1
El Qasr, Egypt 80 B2
El Qubâbât, Egypt 80 J7
El Quseima, Egypt 75 E3
El Qusîya, Egypt 80 B3
El Râshda, Egypt 80 B2
El Real, Panama 124 B3
El Reno, U.S.A. 113 H6
El Ridisiya, Egypt 80 C3
El Rio, U.S.A. 117 L7
El Ronquillo, Spain 35 H4
El Roque, Pta., Canary Is. 37 F4
El Rosarito, Mexico 118 B2
El Rubio, Spain 35 H5
El Saff, Egypt 80 J7
El Saheira, W. →, Egypt 75 E2
El Salto, Mexico 118 C3
El Salvador ■, Cent. Amer. 120 D2
El Sauce, Nic. 120 D2
El Saucejo, Spain 35 H5
El Shallal, Egypt 80 C3
El Simbillawein, Egypt 80 H7
El Sueco, Mexico 118 B3
El Suweis, Egypt 80 J8
El Tabbîn, Egypt 80 J7
El Tamarâni, W. →, Egypt 75 E3
El Thamad, Egypt 75 F3
El Tigre, Venezuela 124 B6
El Tîh, Gebal, Egypt 75 F2
El Tîna, Egypt 80 H8
El Tîna, Khalîg, Egypt 75 D1
El Tofo, Chile 126 B1
El Tránsito, Chile 126 B1
El Tûr, Egypt 70 D2
El Turbio, Argentina 128 G2
El Uqsur, Egypt 80 B3
El Venado, Mexico 118 C4
El Vendrell, Spain 32 D6
El Vergel, Mexico 118 B3
El Vigía, Venezuela 124 B4
El Viso del Alcor, Spain 35 H5
El Wabeira, Egypt 75 F2
El Wak, Kenya 86 B5
El Waqf, Egypt 80 B3
El Weguet, Ethiopia 81 F5
El Wuz, Sudan 81 D3
Elafónisos, Greece 38 E4
Élancourt, France 19 D8
Élassa, Greece 39 F8
Elassón, Greece 38 B4
Elat, Israel 75 F3
Eláthia, Greece 38 C4
Elâzığ, Turkey 70 B3
Elba, Italy 28 F7
Elba, U.S.A. 109 K2
Elbasan, Albania 40 E4
Elbe, U.S.A. 116 D4
Elbe →, Europe 24 B4
Elbe-Seitenkanal, Germany 24 C6
Elbert, Mt., U.S.A. 115 G10
Elberton, U.S.A. 109 H4
Elbeuf, France 18 C8
Elbidtan, Turkey 70 B3
Elbing = Elbląg, Poland 44 D6
Elbistan, Turkey 72 C7
Elbląg, Poland 44 D6
Elbow, Canada 105 C7
Elbrus, Asia 49 J6
Elburz Mts. = Alborz, Reshteh-ye Kūhhā-ye, Iran 71 C7
Elche, Spain 33 G4
Elche de la Sierra, Spain 33 G2
Elcho I., Australia 94 A2
Elda, Spain 33 G4
Elde →, Germany 24 B7
Eldon, Mo., U.S.A. 112 F8
Eldon, Wash., U.S.A. 116 C3
Eldora, U.S.A. 112 D8
Eldorado, Argentina 127 B5
Eldorado, Canada 110 B7
Eldorado, Mexico 118 C3
Eldorado, Ill., U.S.A. 108 G1
Eldorado, Tex., U.S.A. 113 K4
Eldorado Springs, U.S.A. 113 G8
Eldoret, Kenya 86 B4
Eldred, U.S.A. 110 E6
Elea, C., Cyprus 36 D13
Eleanora, Pk., Australia 93 F3
Elefantes →, Mozam. 89 C5
Elektrogorsk, Russia 46 E10
Elektrostal, Russia 46 E10
Elele, Nigeria 83 D6
Elena, Bulgaria 41 D9
Elephant Butte Reservoir, U.S.A. 115 K10
Elephant I., Antarctica 5 C18
Eleshnitsa, Bulgaria 40 E7
Eleşkirt, Turkey 73 C10
Eleuthera, Bahamas 120 B4
Elevsís, Greece 38 C5
Elevtheroúpolis, Greece 41 F8
Elgin, Canada 111 B8
Elgin, U.K. 14 D5
Elgin, Ill., U.S.A. 108 D1
Elgin, N. Dak., U.S.A. 112 B4
Elgin, Oreg., U.S.A. 114 D5
Elgin, Tex., U.S.A. 113 K6
Elgoibar, Spain 32 B2
Elgon, Mt., Africa 86 B3
Eliase, Indonesia 63 F8
Elikón, Greece 38 C4
Elim, Namibia 88 B2
Elim, S. Africa 88 E2
Elin Pelin, Bulgaria 40 D7
Elista, Russia 49 G7
Elizabeth, Australia 95 E2
Elizabeth, N.J., U.S.A. 111 F10
Elizabeth, N.J., U.S.A. 111 F10
Elizabeth City, U.S.A. 109 G7
Elizabethton, U.S.A. 109 G4
Elizabethtown, Ky., U.S.A. 108 G3
Elizabethtown, N.Y., U.S.A. 111 B11
Elizabethtown, Pa., U.S.A. 111 F8
Elizondo, Spain 32 B3
Ełk, Poland 44 E9
Elk →, Canada 104 C5
Ełk →, Poland 44 E9
Elk →, U.S.A. 109 H2
Elk City, U.S.A. 113 H5
Elk Creek, U.S.A. 116 F4
Elk Grove, U.S.A. 116 G5
Elk Island Nat. Park, Canada 104 C6
Elk Lake, Canada 102 C3
Elk Point, Canada 105 C6
Elk River, Idaho, U.S.A. 114 C5
Elk River, Minn., U.S.A. 112 C8
Elkedra →, Australia 94 C2
Elkhart, Ind., U.S.A. 108 E3
Elkhart, Kans., U.S.A. 113 G4
Elkhorn, Canada 105 D8
Elkhorn →, U.S.A. 112 E6
Elkhovo, Bulgaria 41 D10
Elkin, U.S.A. 109 G5
Elkins, U.S.A. 108 F6
Elkland, U.S.A. 110 E7
Elko, Canada 104 D5
Elko, U.S.A. 114 F6
Elkton, U.S.A. 110 C1
Ell, L., Australia 93 E4
Ellef Ringnes I., Canada 4 B2
Ellen, Mt., U.S.A. 111 B12
Ellenburg, U.S.A. 111 B11
Ellendale, U.S.A. 112 B5
Ellensburg, U.S.A. 114 C3
Ellenville, U.S.A. 111 E10
Ellery, Mt., Australia 95 F4
Ellesmere, L., N.Z. 91 M4
Ellesmere I., Canada 4 B4
Ellesmere Port, U.K. 12 D5
Ellice Is. = Tuvalu ■, Pac. Oc. 96 H9
Ellicottville, U.S.A. 110 D6
Elliot, Australia 94 B1
Elliot, S. Africa 89 E4
Elliot Lake, Canada 102 C3
Elliotdale = Xhora, S. Africa 89 E4
Ellis, U.S.A. 112 F5
Elliston, Australia 95 E1
Ellisville, U.S.A. 113 K10
Ellon, U.K. 14 D6
Ellore = Eluru, India 67 L12
Ellsworth, Kans., U.S.A. 112 F5
Ellsworth, Maine, U.S.A. 109 C11
Ellsworth Land, Antarctica 5 D16
Ellsworth Mts., Antarctica 5 D16
Ellwangen, Germany 25 G6
Ellwood City, U.S.A. 110 F4
Elm, Switz. 25 J5
Elma, Canada 105 D9
Elma, U.S.A. 116 D3
Elmadağ, Turkey 72 C5

Elmalı, Turkey 39 E11
Elmhurst, U.S.A. 108 E2
Elmina, Ghana 83 D4
Elmira, Canada 110 C4
Elmira, U.S.A. 110 D8
Elmira Heights, U.S.A. .. 110 D8
Elmore, Australia 95 F3
Elmore, U.S.A. 117 M11
Elmshorn, Germany 24 B5
Elmvale, Canada 110 B5
Elne, France 20 F6
Elora, Canada 110 C4
Elos, Greece 38 E4
Eloúnda, Greece 36 D7
Eloy, U.S.A. 115 K8
Éloyes, France 19 D13
Elrose, Canada 105 C7
Elsdorf, Germany 24 E2
Elsie, U.S.A. 116 E3
Elsinore = Helsingør, Denmark .. 11 H6
Elster ➤, Germany 24 D7
Elsterwerda, Germany 24 D9
Eltham, N.Z. 91 H5
Elton, Russia 49 F8
Elton, Ozero, Russia 49 F8
Eltville, Germany 25 E4
Eluru, India 67 L12
Elvas, Portugal 35 G3
Elven, France 18 E4
Elverum, Norway 9 F14
Elvire ➤, Australia 92 C4
Elvire, Mt., Australia 93 E2
Elvo ➤, Italy 28 C5
Elwell, L., U.S.A. 114 B8
Elwood, Ind., U.S.A. 108 E3
Elwood, Nebr., U.S.A. ... 112 E5
Elx = Elche, Spain 33 G4
Ely, U.K. 13 E8
Ely, Minn., U.S.A. 112 B9
Ely, Nev., U.S.A. 114 G6
Elyria, U.S.A. 110 E2
Elyrus, Greece 38 F5
Elz ➤, Germany 25 G3
Emådalen, Sweden 10 C8
Emāmrūd, Iran 71 B7
Emån ➤, Sweden 11 G10
Emba, Kazakstan 50 E6
Emba ➤, Kazakstan 50 E6
Embarcación, Argentina .. 126 A3
Embarras Portage, Canada . 105 B6
Embetsu, Japan 54 B10
Embi = Emba, Kazakstan ... 50 E6
Embi = Emba ➤, Kazakstan . 50 E6
Embóna, Greece 36 C9
Embrun, France 21 D10
Embu, Kenya 86 C4
Emden, Germany 24 B3
Emecik, Turkey 39 E9
Emerald, Australia 94 C4
Emerson, Canada 105 D9
Emet, Turkey 39 B11
Emi Koussi, Chad 79 E9
Emília-Romagna □, Italy .. 28 D8
Emilius, Mte., Italy 28 C4
Eminabad, Pakistan 68 C6
Emine, Nos, Bulgaria 41 D11
Emirdağ, Turkey 72 C4
Emlenton, U.S.A. 110 E5
Emlichheim, Germany 24 C2
Emmaboda, Sweden 11 H9
Emmaus, S. Africa 88 D4
Emmaus, U.S.A. 111 F9
Emme ➤, Switz. 25 H3
Emmeloord, Neths. 17 B5
Emmen, Neths. 17 B6
Emmen, Switz. 25 H4
Emmendingen, Germany 25 G3
Emmental, Switz. 25 J3
Emmerich, Germany 24 D2
Emmet, Australia 94 C3
Emmetsburg, U.S.A. 112 D7
Emmett, Idaho, U.S.A. ... 114 E5
Emmett, Mich., U.S.A. ... 110 D2
Emmonak, U.S.A. 100 B3
Emo, Canada 105 D10
Emőd, Hungary 42 C5
Emona, Bulgaria 41 D11
Empalme, Mexico 118 B2
Empangeni, S. Africa 89 D5
Empedrado, Argentina ... 126 B4
Emperor Seamount Chain,
    Pac. Oc. 96 D9
Empoli, Italy 28 E7
Emporia, Kans., U.S.A. .. 112 F6
Emporia, Va., U.S.A. ... 109 G7
Emporium, U.S.A. 110 E6
Empress, Canada 105 C7
Empty Quarter = Rub' al Khālī,
    Si. Arabia 74 D4
Ems ➤, Germany 24 B3
Emsdale, Canada 110 A5
Emsdetten, Germany 24 C3
Emu, China 57 C15
Emu Park, Australia 94 C5
En 'Avrona, Israel 75 F4
En Nahud, Sudan 81 E2
En Nofalab, Sudan 81 D3
Ena, Japan 55 G8
Enana, Namibia 88 B2
Enånger, Sweden 10 C11
Enard B., U.K. 14 C3
Enare = Inarijärvi, Finland . 8 B22
Enarotali, Indonesia 63 E9
Encampment, U.S.A. 114 F10
Encantadas, Serra, Brazil . 127 C5
Encarnación, Paraguay ... 127 B4
Encarnación de Diaz, Mexico . 118 C4

Enchi, Ghana 82 D4
Encinitas, U.S.A. 117 M9
Encino, U.S.A. 115 J11
Encounter B., Australia .. 95 F2
Encs, Hungary 42 B6
Endako, Canada 104 C3
Ende, Indonesia 63 F6
Endeavour Str., Australia . 94 A3
Endelave, Denmark 11 J4
Enderbury I., Kiribati .. 96 H10
Enderby, Canada 104 C5
Enderby I., Australia 92 D2
Enderby Land, Antarctica .. 5 C5
Enderlin, U.S.A. 112 B6
Endicott, U.S.A. 111 D8
Endwell, U.S.A. 111 D8
Endyalgout I., Australia . 92 B5
Eneabba, Australia 93 E2
Enewetak Atoll, Marshall Is. . 96 F8
Enez, Turkey 41 F10
Enfield, Canada 103 D7
Enfield, Conn., U.S.A. .. 111 E12
Enfield, N.H., U.S.A. .. 111 C12
Engadin, Switz. 25 J6
Engaño, C., Dom. Rep. .. 121 C6
Engaño, C., Phil. 63 A6
Engaru, Japan 54 B11
Engcobo, S. Africa 89 E4
Engelberg, Switz. 25 J4
Engels, Russia 48 E8
Engemann L., Canada 105 B7
Engershatu, Eritrea 81 D4
Enggano, Indonesia 62 F2
England □, U.K. 12 D7
Englee, Canada 103 B8
Englehart, Canada 102 C4
Englewood, U.S.A. 112 F2
English ➤, Canada 105 C10
English Bazar = Ingraj Bazar,
    India 69 G13
English Channel, Europe .. 13 G6
English River, Canada ... 102 C1
Engures ezers, Latvia ... 44 A10
Enguri ➤, Georgia 49 J5
Enid, U.S.A. 113 G6
Enipévs ➤, Greece 38 B4
Enkhuizen, Neths. 17 B5
Enköping, Sweden 10 E11
Enle, China 58 F3
Enna, Italy 31 E7
Ennadai, Canada 105 A8
Ennadai L., Canada 105 A8
Ennedi, Chad 79 E10
Enngonia, Australia 95 D4
Ennigerloh, Germany 24 D4
Ennis, Ireland 15 D3
Ennis, Mont., U.S.A. ... 114 D8
Ennis, Tex., U.S.A. 113 J6
Enniscorthy, Ireland 15 D5
Enniskillen, U.K. 15 B4
Ennistimon, Ireland 15 D2
Enns, Austria 26 C7
Enns ➤, Austria 26 C7
Enontekiö, Finland 8 B20
Enosburg Falls, U.S.A. .. 111 B12
Enping, China 59 F9
Enriquillo, L., Dom. Rep. . 121 C5
Enschede, Neths. 17 B6
Ensenada, Argentina 126 C4
Ensenada, Mexico 118 A1
Ensenada de los Muertos,
    Mexico 118 C2
Enshi, China 58 B7
Ensiola, Pta. de n', Spain . 37 B9
Ensisheim, France 19 E14
Entebbe, Uganda 86 B3
Enterprise, Canada 104 A5
Enterprise, Ala., U.S.A. . 109 K3
Enterprise, Oreg., U.S.A. . 114 D5
Entraygues-sur-Truyère, France . 20 D6
Entre Ríos, Bolivia 126 A3
Entre Ríos □, Argentina . 126 C4
Entrepeñas, Embalse de, Spain . 32 E2
Entroncamento, Portugal .. 35 F2
Enugu, Nigeria 83 D6
Enugu □, Nigeria 83 D6
Enugu Ezike, Nigeria 83 D6
Enumclaw, U.S.A. 116 C5
Envermeu, France 18 C8
Enviken, Sweden 10 D9
Enying, Hungary 42 D3
Enza ➤, Italy 28 D7
Eólie, Ís., Italy 31 D7
Epanomí, Greece 40 F6
Epe, Neths. 17 B5
Epe, Nigeria 83 D5
Épernay, France 19 C10
Épernon, France 19 D8
Ephesus, Turkey 39 D9
Ephraim, U.S.A. 114 G8
Ephrata, Pa., U.S.A. ... 111 F8
Ephrata, Wash., U.S.A. . 114 C4
Epidaurus Limera, Greece . 38 E5
Épila, Spain 32 D3
Épinac, France 19 F11
Épinal, France 19 D13
Episkopi, Cyprus 36 E11
Episkopí, Greece 36 D6
Episkopi Bay, Cyprus 36 E11
Epitálion, Greece 38 D3
Eppan = Appiano, Italy ... 29 B8
Eppingen, Germany 25 F4
Epsom, U.K. 13 F7
Epukiro, Namibia 88 C2
Equatorial Guinea ■, Africa . 84 D1
Er Hai, China 58 E3

Er Rachidia, Morocco 78 B5
Er Rahad, Sudan 81 E3
Er Rif, Morocco 78 A5
Er Rogel, Sudan 80 D4
Er Roseires, Sudan 81 E3
Er Rua'at, Sudan 81 E3
Eraclea, Italy 29 C9
Erāwadī Myit = Irrawaddy ➤,
    Burma 67 M19
Erāwadī Myitwanya =
    Irrawaddy, Mouths of the,
    Burma 67 M19
Erba, Italy 28 C6
Erba, Sudan 80 D4
Erba, J., Sudan 80 C4
Erbaa, Turkey 72 B7
Erbeskopf, Germany 25 F3
Erbil = Arbīl, Iraq 70 B5
Erbu, Ethiopia 81 E3
Erçek, Turkey 70 B4
Erçiş, Turkey 73 C10
Erciyaş Dağı, Turkey 70 B2
Érd, Hungary 42 C3
Erdao Jiang ➤, China 57 C14
Erdek, Turkey 41 F11
Erdemli, Turkey 72 D6
Erdene = Ulaan-Uul, Mongolia . 56 B6
Erdenetsogt, Mongolia 56 C4
Erding, Germany 25 G7
Erdre ➤, France 18 E5
Erebus, Mt., Antarctica .. 5 D11
Erechim, Brazil 127 B5
Ereğli, Konya, Turkey 70 B2
Ereğli, Zonguldak, Turkey . 72 B4
Erei, Monti, Italy 31 E7
Erenhot, China 56 C7
Eresma ➤, Spain 34 D6
Eressós, Greece 39 B7
Erfenisdam, S. Africa 88 D4
Erfstadt, Germany 24 E2
Erft ➤, Germany 24 D2
Erfurt, Germany 24 E7
Erg Iguidi, Africa 78 C4
Ergani, Turkey 70 B3
Ergel, Mongolia 56 C5
Ergene ➤, Turkey 41 E10
Ergeni Vozvyshennost, Russia . 49 G7
Érgli, Latvia 9 H21
Erhlin, Taiwan 59 F13
Eria ➤, Spain 34 C5
Eriba, Sudan 81 D4
Eriboll, L., U.K. 14 C4
Érice, Italy 30 D5
Erie, U.S.A. 110 D4
Erie, L., N. Amer. 110 D4
Erie Canal, U.S.A. 110 C7
Erieau, Canada 110 D3
Erigavo, Somali Rep. 74 E4
Erikoúsa, Greece 36 A3
Eriksdale, Canada 105 C9
Erímanthos, Greece 38 D3
Erimo-misaki, Japan 54 D11
Erinpura, India 68 G5
Eriskay, U.K. 14 D1
Erithraí, Greece 38 C5
Eritrea ■, Africa 81 E4
Erjas ➤, Portugal 34 F3
Erkelenz, Germany 24 D2
Erkner, Germany 24 C9
Erlangen, Germany 25 F6
Erldunda, Australia 94 D1
Ermelo, Neths. 17 B5
Ermelo, S. Africa 89 D4
Ermenek, Turkey 70 B2
Ermil, Sudan 81 E2
Ermióni, Greece 38 D5
Ermones, Greece 36 A3
Ermoúpolis = Síros, Greece . 38 D6
Ernakulam = Cochin, India . 66 Q10
Erne ➤, Ireland 15 B3
Erne, Lower L., U.K. 15 B4
Erne, Upper L., U.K. 15 B4
Ernée, France 18 D6
Ernest Giles Ra., Australia . 93 E3
Ernstberg, Germany 25 E2
Erode, India 66 P10
Eromanga, Australia 95 D3
Erongo, Namibia 88 C2
Erquy, France 18 D4
Erramala Hills, India ... 66 M11
Errer ➤, Ethiopia 81 F5
Errigal, Ireland 15 A3
Erris Hd., Ireland 15 B1
Erseke, Albania 40 F4
Erskine, U.S.A. 112 B7
Erstein, France 19 D14
Ertholmene, Denmark 11 J9
Ertil, Russia 48 E5
Ertis = Irtysh ➤, Russia . 50 C7
Eruh, Turkey 73 D10
Eruwa, Nigeria 83 D5
Ervy-le-Châtel, France .. 19 D10
Erwin, U.S.A. 109 G4
Eryuan, China 58 D2
Erzgebirge, Germany 24 E9
Erzin, Russia 51 D10
Erzincan, Turkey 70 B3
Erzurum, Turkey 70 B4
Es Caló, Spain 37 C8
Es Canar, Spain 37 B8
Es Mercadal, Spain 37 B11
Es Migjorn Gran, Spain ... 37 B11
Es Safiya, Sudan 81 D3
Es Sahrâ' Esh Sharqîya, Egypt . 80 B3
Es Sînâ', Egypt 75 F3
Es Sûkî, Sudan 81 E3
Es Vedrà, Spain 37 C7

Esambo, Dem. Rep. of
    the Congo 86 C1
Esan-Misaki, Japan 54 D10
Esashi, Hokkaidō, Japan .. 54 B11
Esashi, Hokkaidō, Japan .. 54 D10
Esbjerg, Denmark 11 J2
Escalante, U.S.A. 115 H8
Escalante ➤, U.S.A. 115 H8
Escalón, Mexico 118 B4
Escambia ➤, U.S.A. 109 K2
Escanaba, U.S.A. 108 C2
Esch-sur-Alzette, Lux. ... 17 E6
Eschede, Germany 24 C6
Eschwege, Germany 24 D6
Eschweiler, Germany 24 E2
Escondido, U.S.A. 117 M9
Escravos ➤, Nigeria 83 D6
Escuinapa, Mexico 118 C3
Escuintla, Guatemala ... 120 D1
Eséka, Cameroon 83 E7
Eşen ➤, Turkey 39 E11
Esenguly, Turkmenistan ... 50 F6
Esens, Germany 24 B3
Esenyurt, Turkey 41 E12
Esera ➤, Spain 32 C5
Esfahān, Iran 71 C6
Esfahān □, Iran 71 C6
Esfarāyen, Iran 71 B8
Esfīdeh, Iran 71 C8
Esgueva ➤, Spain 34 D6
Esh Sham = Dimashq, Syria . 75 B5
Esh Shamâlîya □, Sudan ... 80 D2
Esha Ness, U.K. 14 A7
Eshan, China 58 E4
Esher, U.K. 13 F7
Eshowe, S. Africa 89 D5
Esiama, Ghana 82 E4
Esigodini, Zimbabwe 89 C4
Esil = Ishim ➤, Russia ... 50 D8
Esino ➤, Italy 29 E10
Esira, Madag. 89 C8
Esk ➤, Cumb., U.K. 14 G5
Esk ➤, N. Yorks., U.K. ... 12 C7
Eskān, Iran 71 E9
Esker, Canada 103 B6
Eskifjörður, Iceland 8 D7
Eskilsäter, Sweden 11 F7
Eskilstuna, Sweden 10 E10
Eskimalatya, Turkey 73 C8
Eskimo Pt., Canada 100 B10
Eskişehir, Turkey 39 B12
Eskişehir □, Turkey 39 B12
Esla ➤, Spain 34 D4
Eslāmābād-e Gharb, Iran .. 70 C5
Eslāmshahr, Iran 71 C6
Eslöv, Sweden 11 J7
Eşme, Turkey 39 C10
Esmeraldas, Ecuador 124 C3
Esnagi L., Canada 102 C3
Espalion, France 20 D6
Espanola, Canada 102 C3
Espanola, U.S.A. 115 H10
Esparreguera, Spain 32 D6
Esparta, Costa Rica 120 E3
Espelkamp, Germany 24 C4
Esperance, Australia 93 F3
Esperance B., Australia .. 93 F3
Esperanza, Argentina ... 126 C3
Esperanza, Phil. 61 G6
Espéraza, France 20 F6
Espichel, C., Portugal ... 35 G1
Espiel, Spain 35 G5
Espigão, Serra do, Brazil . 127 B5
Espinazo, Sierra del =
    Espinhaço, Serra do, Brazil . 125 G10
Espinhaço, Serra do, Brazil . 125 G10
Espinho, Portugal 34 D2
Espinilho, Serra do, Brazil . 127 B5
Espinosa de los Monteros, Spain . 34 B7
Espírito Santo □, Brazil . 125 H10
Espíritu Santo, Vanuatu .. 96 J8
Espíritu Santo, B. del, Mexico . 119 D7
Espíritu Santo, I., Mexico . 118 C2
Espita, Mexico 119 C7
Espiye, Turkey 73 B8
Espluga de Francolí, Spain . 32 D6
Espoo, Finland 9 F21
Espuña, Sierra de, Spain . 33 H3
Espungabera, Mozam. 89 C5
Esquel, Argentina 128 E2
Esquimalt, Canada 104 D4
Esquina, Argentina 126 C4
Essaouira, Morocco 78 B4
Essebie, Dem. Rep. of the Congo . 86 B3
Essen, Belgium 17 C4
Essen, Germany 24 D3
Essendon, Mt., Australia . 93 E3
Essequibo ➤, Guyana 122 C5
Essex, Canada 110 D2
Essex, Calif., U.S.A. .. 117 L11
Essex, N.Y., U.S.A. 111 B11
Essex □, U.K. 13 F8
Essex Junction, U.S.A. . 111 B11
Esslingen, Germany 25 G5
Essonne □, France 19 D9
Estaca de Bares, C. de, Spain . 34 B3
Estadilla, Spain 32 C5
Estados, I. de Los, Argentina . 122 J4
Estagel, France 20 F6
Eştahbānāt, Iran 71 D7
Estância, Brazil 125 F11
Estancia, U.S.A. 115 J10
Estārm, Iran 71 D8
Estarreja, Portugal 34 E2
Estats, Pic d', Spain 32 C6
Estcourt, S. Africa 89 D4
Este, Italy 29 C8

Estelí, Nic. 120 D2
Estella, Spain 32 C2
Estellencs, Spain 37 B9
Estena ➤, Spain 35 F6
Estepa, Spain 35 H6
Estepona, Spain 35 J5
Esterhazy, Canada 105 C8
Esternay, France 19 D10
Esterri d'Aneu, Spain 32 C6
Estevan, Canada 105 D8
Estevan Group, Canada .. 104 C3
Estherville, U.S.A. 112 D7
Estissac, France 19 D10
Eston, Canada 105 C7
Estonia ■, Europe 9 G21
Estoril, Portugal 35 G1
Estouk, Mali 83 B5
Estreito, Brazil 125 E9
Estrela, Serra da, Portugal . 34 E3
Estrella, Spain 35 G7
Estremoz, Portugal 35 G3
Estrondo, Serra do, Brazil . 125 E9
Esztergom, Hungary 42 C3
Et Tîdra, Mauritania 82 B1
Etah, India 69 F8
Étain, France 19 C12
Étampes, France 19 D9
Etanga, Namibia 88 B1
Étaples, France 19 B8
Etawah, India 69 F8
Etawney L., Canada 105 B9
Ete, Nigeria 83 D6
Ethel, U.S.A. 116 D4
Ethelbert, Canada 105 C8
Ethiopia ■, Africa 74 F3
Ethiopian Highlands, Ethiopia . 41 G10
Etili, Turkey 39 B8
Etive, L., U.K. 14 E3
Etna, Italy 31 E7
Etoile, Dem. Rep. of the Congo . 87 E2
Etosha Nat. Park, Namibia . 88 B2
Etosha Pan, Namibia 88 B2
Etowah, U.S.A. 109 H3
Étréchy, France 19 D9
Étrépagny, France 19 C8
Étretat, France 18 C7
Etropole, Bulgaria 41 D8
Ettelbruck, Lux. 17 E6
Ettlingen, Germany 25 G4
Ettrick Water ➤, U.K. ... 14 F6
Etuku, Dem. Rep. of the Congo . 86 C2
Etulia, Moldova 43 E13
Etzatlán, Mexico 118 C4
Etzná, Mexico 119 D6
Eu, France 18 B8
Euboea = Évvoia, Greece .. 38 C6
Eucla, Australia 93 F4
Euclid, U.S.A. 110 E3
Eucumbene, L., Australia . 95 F4
Eudora, U.S.A. 113 J9
Eufaula, Ala., U.S.A. .. 109 K3
Eufaula, Okla., U.S.A. . 113 H7
Eufaula L., U.S.A. 113 H7
Eugene, U.S.A. 114 E2
Eugowra, Australia 95 E4
Eulo, Australia 95 D4
Eunice, La., U.S.A. 113 K8
Eunice, N. Mex., U.S.A. . 113 J3
Eupen, Belgium 17 D6
Euphrates = Furāt, Nahr al ➤,
    Asia 70 D5
Eure □, France 18 C8
Eure ➤, France 18 C8
Eure-et-Loir □, France ... 18 D8
Eureka, Canada 4 B3
Eureka, Calif., U.S.A. . 114 F1
Eureka, Kans., U.S.A. .. 113 G6
Eureka, Mont., U.S.A. .. 114 B6
Eureka, Nev., U.S.A. ... 114 G5
Eureka, S. Dak., U.S.A. . 112 C5
Eureka, Mt., Australia ... 93 E3
Euroa, Australia 95 F4
Europa, Île, Ind. Oc. 85 J8
Europa, Picos de, Spain .. 34 B6
Europa, Pta. de, Gib. 35 J5
Europe 6 E10
Europoort, Neths. 17 C4
Euskirchen, Germany 24 E2
Eustis, U.S.A. 109 L5
Eutin, Germany 24 A6
Eutsuk L., Canada 104 C3
Evale, Angola 88 B2
Evans, L., Canada 102 B4
Evans, L., Canada 110 F4
Evans City, U.S.A. 110 F4
Evans Head, Australia 95 D5
Evans Mills, U.S.A. 111 B9
Evansburg, Canada 104 C5
Evanston, Ill., U.S.A. . 108 E2
Evanston, Wyo., U.S.A. . 114 F8
Evansville, U.S.A. 108 G2
Évaux-les-Bains, France . 19 F9
Evaz, Iran 71 E7
Evciler, Afyon, Turkey .. 39 C11
Evciler, Çanakkale, Turkey . 39 B8
Eveleth, U.S.A. 112 B8
Evensk, Russia 51 C16
Everard, L., Australia ... 95 E1
Everard Ranges, Australia . 93 E5
Everest, Mt., Nepal 69 E12
Everett, Pa., U.S.A. ... 110 F6
Everett, Wash., U.S.A. . 116 C4
Everglades, The, U.S.A. . 109 N5
Everglades City, U.S.A. . 109 N5
Everglades National Park,
    U.S.A. 109 N5
Evergreen, Ala., U.S.A. . 109 K2

Evergreen, Mont., U.S.A. 114 B6
Everöd, Sweden 11 J8
Evertsberg, Sweden 10 C7
Evesham, U.K. 13 E6
Évian-les-Bains, France 19 F13
Évinos →, Greece 38 C3
Évisa, France 21 F12
Evje, Norway 9 G12
Évora, Portugal 35 G3
Évora □, Portugal 35 G3
Evowghlī, Iran 70 B5
Évreux, France 18 C8
Evritanía □, Greece 38 B3
Évron, France 18 D6
Évros □, Greece 41 E10
Évros →, Greece 72 B2
Evrótas →, Greece 38 E4
Évry, France 19 D9
Évvoia, Greece 38 C6
Évvoia □, Greece 38 C5
Exaltación, Bolivia 124 F5
Excelsior Springs, U.S.A. 112 F7
Excideuil, France 20 C5
Exe →, U.K. 13 G4
Exeter, Canada 110 C3
Exeter, U.K. 13 G4
Exeter, Calif., U.S.A. 116 J7
Exeter, N.H., U.S.A. 111 D14
Exmoor, U.K. 13 F4
Exmouth, Australia 92 D1
Exmouth, U.K. 13 G4
Exmouth G., Australia 92 D1
Expedition Ra., Australia 94 C4
Extremadura □, Spain 35 F4
Exuma Sound, Bahamas 120 B4
Eyasi, L., Tanzania 86 C4
Eye Pen., U.K. 14 C2
Eyemouth, U.K. 14 F6
Eygurande, France 19 G9
Eyjafjörður, Iceland 8 C4
Eymet, France 20 D4
Eymoutiers, France 20 C5
Eynesil, Turkey 73 B8
Eyre (North), L., Australia ... 95 D2
Eyre (South), L., Australia ... 95 D2
Eyre Mts., N.Z. 91 L2
Eyre Pen., Australia 95 E2
Eysturoy, Færoe Is. 8 E9
Eyvānki, Iran 71 C6
Ez Zeidab, Sudan 80 D3
Ezcaray, Spain 32 C1
Ežerėlis, Lithuania 44 D10
Ezhou, China 59 B10
Ezine, Turkey 39 B8
Ezouza →, Cyprus 36 E11

F

F.Y.R.O.M. = Macedonia ■,
  Europe 40 E5
Fabala, Guinea 82 D3
Fabens, U.S.A. 115 L10
Fabero, Spain 34 C4
Fåborg, Denmark 11 J4
Fabriano, Italy 29 E9
Fācāeni, Romania 43 F12
Fachi, Niger 79 E8
Fada, Chad 79 E10
Fada-n-Gourma, Burkina Faso . 83 C5
Fadd, Hungary 42 D3
Faddeyevskiy, Ostrov, Russia .. 51 B15
Faddor, Sudan 81 F3
Fadghāmī, Syria 70 C4
Fadlab, Sudan 80 D3
Faenza, Italy 29 D8
Færoe Is. = Føroyar, Atl. Oc. .. 8 F9
Fafa, Mali 83 B5
Fafe, Portugal 34 D2
Fagam, Nigeria 83 C7
Făgăras, Romania 43 E9
Făgăras, Munţii, Romania 43 E9
Fågelmara, Sweden 11 H9
Fagerhult, Sweden 11 G9
Fagersta, Sweden 10 D9
Fåget, Romania 42 E7
Făget, Munţii, Romania 43 C8
Fagnano, L., Argentina 128 G3
Fagnières, France 19 D11
Faguibine, L., Mali 82 B4
Fahliān, Iran 71 D6
Fahraj, Kermān, Iran 71 D8
Fahraj, Yazd, Iran 71 D7
Fai Tsi Long Archipelago,
  Vietnam 58 G6
Faial, Madeira 37 D3
Fair Haven, U.S.A. 108 D9
Fair Hd., U.K. 15 A5
Fair Oaks, U.S.A. 116 G5
Fairbanks, U.S.A. 100 B5
Fairbury, U.S.A. 112 E6
Fairfax, U.S.A. 111 B11
Fairfield, Ala., U.S.A. 109 J2
Fairfield, Calif., U.S.A. 116 G4
Fairfield, Conn., U.S.A. 111 E11
Fairfield, Idaho, U.S.A. 114 E6
Fairfield, Ill., U.S.A. 108 F1
Fairfield, Iowa, U.S.A. 112 E9
Fairfield, Tex., U.S.A. 113 K7
Fairford, Canada 105 C9
Fairhope, U.S.A. 109 K2
Fairlie, N.Z. 91 L3

Fairmead, U.S.A. 116 H6
Fairmont, Minn., U.S.A. 112 D7
Fairmont, W. Va., U.S.A. 108 F5
Fairmount, Calif., U.S.A. 117 L8
Fairmount, N.Y., U.S.A. 111 C8
Fairplay, U.S.A. 115 G11
Fairport, U.S.A. 110 C7
Fairport Harbor, U.S.A. 110 E3
Fairview, Canada 104 B5
Fairview, Mont., U.S.A. 112 B2
Fairview, Okla., U.S.A. 113 G5
Fairweather, Mt., U.S.A. 104 B1
Faisalabad, Pakistan 68 D5
Faith, U.S.A. 112 C3
Faizabad, India 69 F10
Fajardo, Puerto Rico 121 C6
Fajr, W. →, Si. Arabia 70 D3
Fakenham, U.K. 12 E8
Fåker, Sweden 10 A8
Fakfak, Indonesia 63 E8
Fakiya, Bulgaria 41 D11
Fakobli, Ivory C. 82 D3
Fakse, Denmark 11 J6
Fakse Bugt, Denmark 11 J6
Fakse Ladeplads, Denmark ... 11 J6
Faku, China 57 C12
Falaba, S. Leone 82 D2
Falaise, France 18 D6
Falaise, Mui, Vietnam 64 C5
Falakrón Óros, Greece 40 E7
Falam, Burma 67 H18
Falces, Spain 32 C3
Fălciu, Romania 43 D13
Falcó, C. des, Spain 37 C7
Falcón, Presa, Mexico 119 B5
Falcon Lake, Canada 105 D9
Falcon Reservoir, U.S.A. 113 M5
Falconara Maríttima, Italy ... 29 E10
Falcone, C. del, Italy 30 B1
Falconer, U.S.A. 110 D5
Faléa, Mali 82 C2
Falémé →, Senegal 82 C2
Falerum, Sweden 11 F10
Faleshty = Fălesti, Moldova .. 43 C12
Fălesti, Moldova 43 C12
Falfurrias, U.S.A. 113 M5
Falher, Canada 104 B5
Falirakí, Greece 36 C10
Falkenberg, Germany 24 D9
Falkenberg, Sweden 11 H6
Falkensee, Germany 24 C9
Falkirk, U.K. 14 F5
Falkirk □, U.K. 14 F5
Falkland, U.K. 14 E5
Falkland Is. □, Atl. Oc. 128 G5
Falkland Sd., Falk. Is. 128 G5
Falkonéra, Greece 38 E5
Falköping, Sweden 11 F7
Fall River, U.S.A. 111 E13
Fallbrook, U.S.A. 117 M9
Fallon, U.S.A. 114 G4
Falls City, U.S.A. 112 E7
Falls Creek, U.S.A. 110 E6
Falmouth, Jamaica 120 C4
Falmouth, U.S.A. 13 G2
Falmouth, U.S.A. 111 E14
Falsa, Pta., Mexico 118 B1
False B., S. Africa 88 E2
False, C., Honduras 120 C3
Falster, Denmark 11 K5
Falsterbo, Sweden 9 J15
Fălticeni, Romania 43 C11
Falun, Sweden 10 D9
Famagusta, Cyprus 36 D12
Famagusta Bay, Cyprus 36 D13
Famalé, Niger 78 N4
Famatina, Sierra de, Argentina . 126 B2
Family L., Canada 105 C9
Famoso, U.S.A. 117 K7
Fan Xian, China 56 G8
Fana, Mali 82 C3
Fanad Hd., Ireland 15 A4
Fanárion, Greece 38 B3
Fandriana, Madag. 89 C8
Fang, Thailand 58 H2
Fang Xian, China 59 A8
Fangaga, Sudan 80 D4
Fangak, Sudan 81 F3
Fangchang, China 59 B12
Fangcheng, China 56 H7
Fangchenggang, China 58 G7
Fangliao, Taiwan 59 F13
Fangshan, China 56 E6
Fangzi, China 57 F10
Fani i Madh →, Albania 40 E4
Fanjakana, Madag. 89 C8
Fanjiatun, China 57 C13
Fannich, L., U.K. 14 D4
Fannūj, Iran 71 E8
Fanø, Denmark 11 J2
Fano, Italy 29 E10
Fanshi, China 56 E7
Fao = Al Fāw, Iraq 71 D6
Faqirwali, Pakistan 68 E5
Fâqûs, Egypt 80 H7
Far in Sabina, Italy 29 F9
Faradje, Dem. Rep. of the Congo . 86 B2
Faradofay, Madag. 89 C8
Farafangana, Madag. 89 C8
Farāfra, El Wâhât el-, Egypt .. 80 B2
Farah, Afghan. 66 C3
Farah □, Afghan. 66 C3
Farahalana, Madag. 89 A9
Faraid, Gebel, Egypt 80 C4
Farako, Ivory C. 82 D4
Faramana, Burkina Faso 82 C4
Faranah, Guinea 82 C2
Farasān, Jazā'ir, Si. Arabia ... 74 D3

Farasan Is. = Farasān, Jazā'ir,
  Si. Arabia 74 D3
Faratsiho, Madag. 89 B8
Fardes →, Spain 35 H7
Fareham, U.K. 13 G6
Farewell, C., N.Z. 91 J4
Farewell C. = Nunap Isua,
  Greenland 101 C15
Färgelanda, Sweden 11 F5
Farghona, Uzbekistan 50 E8
Fargo, U.S.A. 112 B6
Fār'iah, W. al →, West Bank .. 75 C4
Faribault, U.S.A. 112 C8
Faridabad, India 68 E6
Faridkot, India 68 D6
Faridpur, Bangla. 69 H13
Faridpur, India 69 E8
Färila, Sweden 10 C9
Farim, Guinea-Biss. 82 C1
Farīmān, Iran 71 C8
Farina, Australia 95 E2
Fariones, Pta., Canary Is. 37 E6
Fâriskûr, Egypt 80 H7
Färjestaden, Sweden 11 H10
Farkadhón, Greece 38 B4
Farmakonísi, Greece 39 D9
Farmerville, U.S.A. 113 J8
Farmingdale, U.S.A. 111 F10
Farmington, Canada 104 B4
Farmington, Calif., U.S.A. ... 116 H6
Farmington, Maine, U.S.A. ... 109 C10
Farmington, Mo., U.S.A. 113 G9
Farmington, N.H., U.S.A. ... 111 C13
Farmington, N. Mex., U.S.A. .. 115 H9
Farmington, Utah, U.S.A. ... 114 F8
Farmington →, U.S.A. 111 E12
Farmville, U.S.A. 108 G6
Farne Is., U.K. 12 B6
Farnham, Canada 111 A12
Farnham, Mt., Canada 104 C5
Faro, Brazil 125 D7
Faro, Canada 100 B6
Faro, Portugal 35 H3
Fårö, Sweden 9 H18
Faro □, Portugal 35 H2
Fårösund, Sweden 11 G13
Farquhar, C., Australia 93 D1
Farrars Cr. →, Australia 94 D3
Farrāshband, Iran 71 D7
Farrell, U.S.A. 110 E4
Farrokhī, Iran 71 C8
Farruch, C. = Ferrutx, C., Spain 37 B10
Fārs □, Iran 71 D7
Fársala, Greece 38 B4
Farsø, Denmark 11 H3
Farson, U.S.A. 114 E9
Farsund, Norway 9 G12
Fartak, Râs, Si. Arabia 70 D2
Fartak, Ra's, Yemen 74 D5
Fârtăţesti, Romania 43 E12
Fartura, Serra da, Brazil 127 B5
Faru, Nigeria 83 C6
Fārūj, Iran 71 B8
Fårup, Denmark 11 H3
Farvel, Kap = Nunap Isua,
  Greenland 101 C15
Farwell, U.S.A. 113 H3
Fāryāb □, Afghan. 66 B4
Fasā, Iran 71 D7
Fasano, Italy 31 B10
Fashoda, Sudan 81 F3
Fassa, Mali 82 C3
Fastiv, Ukraine 47 G5
Fastov = Fastiv, Ukraine 47 G5
Fatagar, Tanjung, Indonesia .. 63 E8
Fatehabad, Haryana, India 68 E6
Fatehabad, Ut. P., India 68 F8
Fatehgarh, India 69 F8
Fatehpur, Bihar, India 69 G11
Fatehpur, Raj., India 68 F6
Fatehpur, Ut. P., India 69 G9
Fatehpur, Ut. P., India 69 F9
Fatehpur Sikri, India 68 F6
Fatesh, Russia 47 F8
Fathai, Sudan 81 F3
Fatick, Senegal 82 C1
Fátima, Canada 103 C7
Fátima, Portugal 35 F2
Fatoya, Guinea 82 C3
Fatsa, Turkey 72 B7
Faucille, Col de la, France ... 19 F13
Faulkton, U.S.A. 112 C5
Faulquemont, France 19 C13
Faure I., Australia 93 E1
Făurei, Romania 43 E12
Fauresmith, S. Africa 88 D4
Fauske, Norway 8 C16
Favara, Italy 30 E6
Favaritx, C. de, Spain 37 B11
Faverges, France 21 C10
Favignana, Italy 30 E5
Favignana, I., Italy 30 E5
Fawcett, Pt., Australia 92 B5
Fawn →, Canada 102 A2
Fawnskin, U.S.A. 117 L10
Faxaflói, Iceland 8 D2
Faxälven →, Sweden 10 A10
Faya-Largeau, Chad 79 E9
Fayd, Si. Arabia 70 E4
Fayence, France 21 E10
Fayette, Ala., U.S.A. 109 J2
Fayette, Mo., U.S.A. 112 F8
Fayetteville, Ark., U.S.A. ... 113 G7
Fayetteville, N.C., U.S.A. ... 109 H6
Fayetteville, Tenn., U.S.A. ... 109 H2
Fayied, Egypt 80 H8

Fayón, Spain 32 D5
Fazilka, India 68 D6
Fazilpur, Pakistan 68 E4
Fdérik, Mauritania 78 D3
Feale →, Ireland 15 D2
Fear, C., U.S.A. 109 J7
Feather →, U.S.A. 114 G3
Feather Falls, U.S.A. 116 F5
Featherston, N.Z. 91 J5
Featherstone, Zimbabwe 87 F3
Fécamp, France 18 C7
Fedala = Mohammedia,
  Morocco 78 B4
Federación, Argentina 126 C4
Féderal, Argentina 128 C5
Federal Capital Terr. □, Nigeria 83 D6
Federal Way, U.S.A. 116 C4
Fedeshkūh, Iran 71 D7
Fehérgyarmat, Hungary 42 C7
Fehmarn, Germany 24 A7
Fehmarn Bælt, Europe 11 K5
Fehmarn Belt = Fehmarn Bælt,
  Europe 11 K5
Fei Xian, China 57 G9
Feijó, Brazil 124 E4
Feilding, N.Z. 91 J5
Feira de Santana, Brazil 125 F11
Feixi, China 59 B11
Feixiang, China 56 F8
Fejér □, Hungary 42 C3
Fejø, Denmark 11 K5
Fekete →, Hungary 42 E3
Felanitx, Spain 37 B10
Feldbach, Austria 26 E8
Feldberg, Baden-W., Germany . 25 H3
Feldberg,
  Mecklenburg-Vorpommern,
  Germany 24 B9
Feldkirch, Austria 26 D2
Feldkirchen, Austria 26 E7
Felipe Carrillo Puerto, Mexico 119 D7
Felixburg, Zimbabwe 89 B5
Felixstowe, U.K. 13 F9
Felletin, France 20 C6
Fellingsbro, Sweden 10 E9
Felton, U.S.A. 116 H4
Feltre, Italy 29 B8
Femer Bælt = Fehmarn Bælt,
  Europe 11 K5
Femø, Denmark 11 K5
Femunden, Norway 9 E14
Fen He →, China 56 G6
Fene, Spain 34 B2
Fenelon Falls, Canada 110 B6
Fener Burnu, Turkey 39 E9
Feneroa, Ethiopia 81 E4
Feng Xian, Jiangsu, China ... 56 G9
Feng Xian, Shaanxi, China .. 56 H4
Fengári, Greece 41 F9
Fengcheng, Jiangxi, China .. 59 C10
Fengcheng, Liaoning, China .. 57 D13
Fengfeng, China 56 F8
Fenggang, China 58 D6
Fenghua, China 59 C13
Fenghuang, China 58 D7
Fengkai, China 59 F8
Fengkang, Taiwan 59 F13
Fengle, Taiwan 59 B9
Fenglin, Taiwan 59 F13
Fengning, China 56 D9
Fengqing, China 58 E2
Fengqiu, China 56 G8
Fengrun, China 57 E10
Fengshan, Guangxi Zhuangzu,
  China 58 E7
Fengshan, Guangxi Zhuangzu,
  China 58 E6
Fengshan, Taiwan 59 F13
Fengshun, China 59 F11
Fengtai, Anhui, China 59 A11
Fengtai, Beijing, China 56 E9
Fengxian, China 59 B13
Fengxiang, China 56 G4
Fengxin, China 59 C10
Fengyang, China 57 H9
Fengyi, China 58 E3
Fengyüan, Taiwan 59 E13
Fengzhen, China 56 D7
Feno, C. de, France 21 G12
Fenoarivo, Fianarantsoa, Madag. 89 C8
Fenoarivo, Fianarantsoa, Madag. 89 C8
Fenoarivo Afovoany, Madag. .. 89 B8
Fenoarivo Atsinanana, Madag. 89 B8
Fens, The, U.K. 12 E7
Fensmark, Denmark 11 J5
Fenton, U.S.A. 108 D4
Fenxi, China 56 F6
Fenyang, China 56 F6
Fenyi, China 59 D10

Fermoselle, Spain 34 D4
Fermoy, Ireland 15 D3
Fernán Núñez, Spain 35 H6
Fernández, Argentina 126 B3
Fernandina Beach, U.S.A. ... 109 K5
Fernando de Noronha, Brazil .. 125 D12
Fernando Póo = Bioko,
  Eq. Guin. 83 E6
Ferndale, U.S.A. 116 B4
Fernie, Canada 104 D5
Fernlees, Australia 94 C4
Fernley, U.S.A. 114 G4
Ferozepore = Firozpur, India .. 68 D6
Férrai, Greece 41 F10
Ferrandina, Italy 31 B9
Ferrara, Italy 29 D8
Ferrato, C., Italy 30 C2
Ferreira do Alentejo, Portugal . 35 G2
Ferreñafe, Peru 124 E3
Ferrerías, Spain 37 B11
Ferret, C., France 20 D2
Ferrette, France 19 E14
Ferriday, U.S.A. 113 K9
Ferriere, Italy 28 D6
Ferrières, France 19 C9
Ferro, Capo, Italy 30 A2
Ferrol, Spain 34 B2
Ferron, U.S.A. 115 G8
Ferrutx, C., Spain 37 B10
Ferryland, Canada 103 C9
Fertile, U.S.A. 112 B6
Fertőszentmiklós, Hungary ... 42 C1
Fès, Morocco 78 B5
Fessenden, U.S.A. 112 B5
Festus, U.S.A. 112 F9
Feté Bowé, Senegal 82 C2
Fetesti, Romania 43 F12
Fethiye, Turkey 39 E11
Fethiye Körfezi, Turkey 39 E10
Fetlar, U.K. 14 A8
Feuilles →, Canada 101 C12
Feurs, France 21 C8
Fez = Fès, Morocco 78 B5
Fezzan, Libya 79 C8
Fiambalá, Argentina 126 B2
Fianarantsoa, Madag. 89 C8
Fianarantsoa □, Madag. 89 B8
Fiche, Ethiopia 81 F4
Fichtelgebirge, Germany 25 E7
Ficksburg, S. Africa 89 D4
Fidenza, Italy 28 D7
Fiditi, Nigeria 83 D5
Field →, Australia 94 C2
Field I., Australia 92 B5
Fieni, Romania 43 E10
Fier, France 40 F3
Fierzë, Albania 40 D4
Fife □, U.K. 14 E5
Fife Ness, U.K. 14 E6
Fifth Cataract, Sudan 80 D3
Figari, France 21 G13
Figeac, France 20 D6
Figeholm, Sweden 11 G10
Figtree, Zimbabwe 87 G2
Figueira Castelo Rodrigo,
  Portugal 34 E4
Figueira da Foz, Portugal ... 34 E2
Figueiró dos Vinhos, Portugal . 34 F2
Figueres, Spain 32 C7
Figuig, Morocco 78 B5
Fihaonana, Madag. 89 B8
Fiherenana, Madag. 89 B8
Fiherenana →, Madag. 89 C7
Fiji ■, Pac. Oc. 91 C8
Fik, Ethiopia 81 F5
Fika, Nigeria 83 C7
Filabres, Sierra de los, Spain .. 35 H8
Filabusi, Zimbabwe 89 C4
Filadélfia, Italy 31 D9
Fil'akovo, Slovak Rep. 27 C12
Filey, U.K. 12 C7
Filey B., U.K. 12 C7
Filfla, Malta 36 D1
Filiasi, Romania 43 F8
Filiátes, Greece 38 B2
Filiatrá, Greece 38 D3
Filicudi, Italy 31 D7
Filingué, Niger 83 C5
Filiourí →, Greece 41 E9
Filipstad, Sweden 10 E8
Filisur, Switz. 25 J5
Fillmore, Calif., U.S.A. 117 L8
Fillmore, Utah, U.S.A. 115 G7
Filótion, Greece 39 D7
Filottrano, Italy 29 E10
Filtu, Ethiopia 81 F5
Finale Emília, Italy 29 D8
Finale Lígure, Italy 28 D5
Fiñana, Spain 35 H8
Finch, Canada 111 A9
Findhorn →, U.K. 14 D5
Findlay, U.S.A. 108 E4
Finger L., Canada 102 B1
Finger Lakes, U.S.A. 111 D8
Fíngoè, Mozam. 87 E3
Finike, Turkey 39 E12
Finike Körfezi, Turkey 39 E12
Finiq, Albania 40 G4
Finistère □, France 18 D3
Finisterre = Fisterra, Spain .. 34 C1
Finisterre, C. = Fisterra, C.,
  Spain 34 C1
Finke, Australia 94 D1
Finland ■, Europe 8 E22
Finland, G. of, Europe 9 G21
Finlay →, Canada 104 B3

Fremantle

Finley, *Australia* 95 F4
Finley, *U.S.A.* 112 B6
Finn →, *Ireland* 15 B4
Finnerödja, *Sweden* 11 F8
Finnigan, Mt., *Australia* 94 B4
Finniss, C., *Australia* 95 E1
Finnmark, *Norway* 8 B20
Finnsnes, *Norway* 8 B18
Finspång, *Sweden* 11 F9
Finsteraarhorn, *Switz.* 25 J4
Finsterwalde, *Germany* 24 D9
Fiora →, *Italy* 29 F8
Fiorenzuola d'Arda, *Italy* 28 D6
Fiq, *Syria* 75 C4
Firat = Furāt, Nahr al →, *Asia* 70 D5
Firebag →, *Canada* 105 B6
Firebaugh, *U.S.A.* 116 J6
Firedrake L., *Canada* 105 A8
Firenze, *Italy* 29 E8
Firenzuola, *Italy* 29 D8
Firk →, *Iraq* 70 D5
Firmi, *France* 20 D6
Firminy, *France* 21 C8
Firozabad, *India* 69 F8
Firozpur, *India* 68 D6
Firozpur-Jhirka, *India* 68 F7
Fīrūzābād, *Iran* 71 D7
Fīrūzkūh, *Iran* 71 C7
Firvale, *Canada* 104 C3
Fish →, *Namibia* 88 D2
Fish →, *S. Africa* 88 E3
Fish River Canyon, *Namibia* 88 D2
Fisher, *Australia* 93 F5
Fisher B., *Canada* 105 C9
Fishers I., *U.S.A.* 111 E13
Fishguard, *U.K.* 13 E3
Fishing L., *Canada* 105 C9
Fishkill, *U.S.A.* 111 E11
Fismes, *France* 19 C10
Fisterra, *Spain* 34 C1
Fisterra, C., *Spain* 34 C1
Fitchburg, *U.S.A.* 111 D13
Fitz Roy, *Argentina* 128 F3
Fitzgerald, *Canada* 104 B6
Fitzgerald, *U.S.A.* 109 K4
Fitzmaurice →, *Australia* 92 B5
Fitzroy →, *Queens., Australia* 94 C5
Fitzroy →, *W. Austral., Australia* 92 C3
Fitzroy, Mte., *Argentina* 128 F2
Fitzroy Crossing, *Australia* 92 C4
Fitzwilliam I., *Canada* 110 A3
Fiuggi, *Italy* 29 G10
Fiume = Rijeka, *Croatia* 29 C11
Five Points, *U.S.A.* 116 J6
Fivizzano, *Italy* 28 D7
Fizi, *Dem. Rep. of the Congo* 86 C2
Fjällbacka, *Sweden* 11 F5
Fjärdhundra, *Sweden* 10 E10
Fjellerup, *Denmark* 11 H4
Fjerritslev, *Denmark* 11 G3
Fjugesta, *Sweden* 10 E8
Flagstaff, *U.S.A.* 115 J8
Flagstaff L., *U.S.A.* 109 C10
Flaherty I., *Canada* 102 A4
Flåm, *Norway* 9 F12
Flambeau →, *U.S.A.* 112 C9
Flamborough Hd., *U.K.* 12 C7
Fläming, *Germany* 24 C8
Flaming Gorge Reservoir, *U.S.A.* 114 F9
Flamingo, Teluk, *Indonesia* 63 F9
Flanders = Flandre, *Europe* 19 B9
Flandre, *Europe* 19 B9
Flandre Occidentale = West-Vlaanderen □, *Belgium* 17 D2
Flandre Orientale = Oost-Vlaanderen □, *Belgium* 17 C3
Flandreau, *U.S.A.* 112 C6
Flanigan, *U.S.A.* 116 E7
Flannan Is., *U.K.* 14 C1
Flåsjön, *Sweden* 8 D16
Flat →, *Canada* 104 A3
Flathead L., *U.S.A.* 114 C7
Flattery, C., *Australia* 94 A4
Flattery, C., *U.S.A.* 116 B2
Flatwoods, *U.S.A.* 108 F4
Fleetwood, *U.K.* 12 D4
Fleetwood, *U.S.A.* 111 F9
Flekkefjord, *Norway* 9 G12
Flemington, *U.S.A.* 110 E7
Flen, *Sweden* 10 E10
Flensburg, *Germany* 24 A5
Flers, *France* 18 D6
Flesherton, *Canada* 110 B4
Flesko, Tanjung, *Indonesia* 63 D6
Fleurance, *France* 20 E4
Fleurier, *Switz.* 25 J2
Fleurieu Pen., *Australia* 95 F2
Flevoland □, *Neths.* 17 B5
Flin Flon, *Canada* 105 C8
Flinders →, *Australia* 94 B3
Flinders B., *Australia* 93 F2
Flinders Group, *Australia* 94 A3
Flinders I., *S. Austral., Australia* 95 E1
Flinders I., *Tas., Australia* 94 G4
Flinders Ranges, *Australia* 95 E2
Flinders Reefs, *Australia* 94 B4
Flint, *U.K.* 12 D4
Flint, *U.S.A.* 108 D4
Flint →, *U.S.A.* 109 K3
Flint I., *Kiribati* 97 J12
Flintshire □, *U.K.* 12 D4
Fliseryd, *Sweden* 11 G10
Flix, *Spain* 32 D5
Flixecourt, *France* 19 B9
Floby, *Sweden* 11 F7
Floda, *Sweden* 11 G6
Flodden, *U.K.* 12 B5
Flogny-la-Chapelle, *France* 19 E10
Floodwood, *U.S.A.* 112 B8
Flora, *U.S.A.* 108 F1
Florac, *France* 20 D7
Florala, *U.S.A.* 109 K2
Florence = Firenze, *Italy* 29 E8
Florence, *Ala., U.S.A.* 109 H2
Florence, *Ariz., U.S.A.* 115 K8
Florence, *Colo., U.S.A.* 112 F2
Florence, *Oreg., U.S.A.* 114 E1
Florence, *S.C., U.S.A.* 109 H6
Florence, L., *Australia* 95 D2
Florencia, *Colombia* 124 C3
Florennes, *Belgium* 17 D4
Florensac, *France* 20 E7
Florenville, *Belgium* 17 E5
Flores, *Guatemala* 120 C2
Flores, *Indonesia* 63 F6
Flores I., *Canada* 104 D3
Flores Sea, *Indonesia* 63 F6
Floreşti, *Moldova* 43 C13
Floresville, *U.S.A.* 113 L5
Floriano, *Brazil* 125 E10
Florianópolis, *Brazil* 127 B6
Florida, *Cuba* 120 B4
Florida, *Uruguay* 127 C4
Florida □, *U.S.A.* 109 L5
Florida, Straits of, *U.S.A.* 120 B4
Florida B., *U.S.A.* 120 B3
Florida Keys, *U.S.A.* 109 N5
Florídia, *Italy* 31 E8
Flórina, *Greece* 40 F5
Flórina □, *Greece* 40 F5
Florø, *Norway* 9 F11
Flower Station, *Canada* 111 A8
Flowerpot I., *Canada* 110 A3
Floydada, *U.S.A.* 113 J4
Fluk, *Indonesia* 63 E7
Flúmen →, *Spain* 32 D4
Flumendosa →, *Italy* 30 C2
Fluminimaggiore, *Italy* 30 C1
Flushing = Vlissingen, *Neths.* 17 C3
Fluviá →, *Spain* 32 C8
Flying Fish, C., *Antarctica* 5 D15
Foam Lake, *Canada* 105 C8
Foča, *Bos.-H.* 40 C2
Foça, *Turkey* 39 C8
Focşani, *Romania* 43 E12
Fodécontéa, *Guinea* 82 C2
Fogang, *China* 59 F9
Fóggia, *Italy* 31 A8
Foggo, *Nigeria* 83 C6
Foglia →, *Italy* 29 E9
Fogo, *Canada* 103 C9
Fogo I., *Canada* 103 C9
Fohnsdorf, *Austria* 26 D7
Föhr, *Germany* 24 A4
Foia, *Portugal* 35 H2
Foix, *France* 20 E5
Fojnica, *Bos.-H.* 42 G2
Fokino, *Russia* 46 F8
Fokís □, *Greece* 38 C4
Fokku, *Nigeria* 83 C5
Folda, *Nord-Trøndelag, Norway* 8 D14
Folda, *Nordland, Norway* 8 C16
Földeák, *Hungary* 42 D5
Folégandros, *Greece* 38 E6
Foley, *Botswana* 88 C4
Foley, *U.S.A.* 109 K2
Foleyet, *Canada* 102 C3
Folgefonni, *Norway* 9 F12
Foligno, *Italy* 29 F9
Folkestone, *U.K.* 13 F9
Folkston, *U.S.A.* 109 K5
Follansbee, *U.S.A.* 110 F4
Follónica, *Italy* 28 F7
Follónica, G. di, *Italy* 28 F7
Folsom L., *U.S.A.* 116 G5
Folteşti, *Romania* 43 E13
Fond-du-Lac, *Canada* 105 B7
Fond du Lac, *U.S.A.* 112 D10
Fond-du-Lac →, *Canada* 105 B7
Fonda, *U.S.A.* 111 D10
Fondi, *Italy* 30 A6
Fonfría, *Spain* 34 D4
Fongafale, *Tuvalu* 96 H9
Fonni, *Italy* 30 B2
Fonsagrada = A Fonsagrada, *Spain* 34 B3
Fonseca, G. de, *Cent. Amer.* 120 D2
Font-Romeu, *France* 20 F5
Fontaine-Française, *France* 19 E12
Fontainebleau, *France* 19 D9
Fontana, *U.S.A.* 117 L9
Fontas →, *Canada* 104 B4
Fonte Boa, *Brazil* 124 D5
Fontem, *Cameroon* 83 D6
Fontenay-le-Comte, *France* 20 B3
Fontenelle Reservoir, *U.S.A.* 114 E8
Fontur, *Iceland* 8 C6
Fonyód, *Hungary* 42 D2
Foochow = Fuzhou, *China* 59 D12
Foping, *China* 56 H5
Forbach, *France* 19 C13
Forbes, *Australia* 95 E4
Forbesganj, *India* 69 F12
Forcados, *Nigeria* 83 D6
Forcados →, *Nigeria* 83 D6
Forcalquier, *France* 21 E9
Forchheim, *Germany* 25 F7
Ford City, *Calif., U.S.A.* 117 K7
Ford City, *Pa., U.S.A.* 110 F5
Førde, *Norway* 9 F11
Ford's Bridge, *Australia* 95 D4
Fordyce, *U.S.A.* 113 J8
Forécariah, *Guinea* 82 D2
Forel, Mt., *Greenland* 4 C6
Foremost, *Canada* 104 D6
Forest, *Canada* 110 C3
Forest, *U.S.A.* 113 J10
Forest City, *Iowa, U.S.A.* 112 D8
Forest City, *N.C., U.S.A.* 109 H5
Forest City, *Pa., U.S.A.* 111 E9
Forest Grove, *U.S.A.* 116 E3
Forestburg, *Canada* 104 C6
Foresthill, *U.S.A.* 116 F6
Forestier Pen., *Australia* 94 G4
Forestville, *Canada* 103 C6
Forestville, *Calif., U.S.A.* 116 G4
Forestville, *N.Y., U.S.A.* 110 D5
Forez, Mts. du, *France* 20 C7
Forfar, *U.K.* 14 E6
Forks, *U.S.A.* 116 C2
Forksville, *U.S.A.* 111 E8
Forlì, *Italy* 29 D9
Forman, *U.S.A.* 112 B6
Formazza, *Italy* 28 B5
Formby Pt., *U.K.* 12 D4
Formentera, *Spain* 37 C7
Formentor, C. de, *Spain* 37 B10
Former Yugoslav Republic of Macedonia = Macedonia ■, *Europe* 40 E5
Fórmia, *Italy* 30 A6
Formígine, *Italy* 28 D7
Formosa = Taiwan ■, *Asia* 59 F13
Formosa, *Argentina* 126 B4
Formosa, *Brazil* 125 G9
Formosa □, *Argentina* 126 B4
Formosa, Serra, *Brazil* 125 F8
Formosa Bay, *Kenya* 86 C5
Formosa Strait = Taiwan Strait, *Asia* 59 E12
Fornells, *Spain* 37 A11
Fornos de Algodres, *Portugal* 34 E3
Fornovo di Taro, *Italy* 28 D7
Føroyar, *Atl. Oc.* 8 F9
Forres, *U.K.* 14 D5
Forrest, *Australia* 93 F4
Forrest, Mt., *Australia* 93 D4
Forrest City, *U.S.A.* 113 H9
Fors, *Sweden* 10 D10
Forsayth, *Australia* 94 B3
Forshaga, *Sweden* 10 E7
Förslöv, *Sweden* 11 H6
Forsmo, *Sweden* 10 A11
Forssa, *Finland* 9 F20
Forst, *Germany* 24 D10
Forsvik, *Sweden* 11 F8
Forsyth, *U.S.A.* 114 C10
Fort Abbas, *Pakistan* 68 E5
Fort Albany, *Canada* 102 B3
Fort Ann, *U.S.A.* 111 C11
Fort Assiniboine, *Canada* 104 C6
Fort Augustus, *U.K.* 14 D4
Fort Beaufort, *S. Africa* 88 E4
Fort Benton, *U.S.A.* 114 C8
Fort Bragg, *U.S.A.* 114 G2
Fort Bridger, *U.S.A.* 114 F8
Fort Chipewyan, *Canada* 105 B6
Fort Collins, *U.S.A.* 112 E2
Fort-Coulonge, *Canada* 102 C4
Fort Covington, *U.S.A.* 111 B10
Fort Davis, *U.S.A.* 113 K3
Fort-de-France, *Martinique* 121 D7
Fort Defiance, *U.S.A.* 115 J9
Fort Dodge, *U.S.A.* 112 D7
Fort Edward, *U.S.A.* 111 C11
Fort Erie, *Canada* 110 D6
Fort Fairfield, *U.S.A.* 109 B12
Fort Frances, *Canada* 105 D10
Fort Garland, *U.S.A.* 115 H11
Fort George = Chisasibi, *Canada* 102 B4
Fort Good-Hope, *Canada* 100 B7
Fort Hancock, *U.S.A.* 115 L11
Fort Hertz = Putao, *Burma* 67 F20
Fort Hope, *Canada* 102 B2
Fort Irwin, *U.S.A.* 117 K10
Fort Kent, *U.S.A.* 109 B11
Fort Klamath, *U.S.A.* 114 E3
Fort Laramie, *U.S.A.* 112 D2
Fort Lauderdale, *U.S.A.* 109 M5
Fort Liard, *Canada* 104 A4
Fort Liberté, *Haiti* 121 C5
Fort Lupton, *U.S.A.* 112 E2
Fort Mackay, *Canada* 104 B6
Fort Macleod, *Canada* 104 D6
Fort McMurray, *Canada* 104 B6
Fort McPherson, *Canada* 100 B6
Fort Madison, *U.S.A.* 112 E9
Fort Meade, *U.S.A.* 109 M5
Fort Morgan, *U.S.A.* 112 E3
Fort Myers, *U.S.A.* 109 M5
Fort Nelson, *Canada* 104 B4
Fort Nelson →, *Canada* 104 B4
Fort Norman = Tulita, *Canada* 100 B7
Fort Payne, *U.S.A.* 109 H3
Fort Peck, *U.S.A.* 114 B10
Fort Peck Dam, *U.S.A.* 114 C10
Fort Peck L., *U.S.A.* 114 C10
Fort Pierce, *U.S.A.* 109 M5
Fort Pierre, *U.S.A.* 112 C4
Fort Pierre Bordes = Ti-n-Zaouatene, *Algeria* 83 B5
Fort Plain, *U.S.A.* 111 D10
Fort Portal, *Uganda* 86 B3
Fort Providence, *Canada* 104 A5
Fort Qu'Appelle, *Canada* 105 C8
Fort Resolution, *Canada* 104 A6
Fort Rixon, *Zimbabwe* 87 G2
Fort Ross, *U.S.A.* 116 G3
Fort Rupert = Waskaganish, *Canada* 102 B4
Fort St. James, *Canada* 104 C4
Fort St. John, *Canada* 104 B4
Fort Saskatchewan, *Canada* 104 C6
Fort Scott, *U.S.A.* 113 G7
Fort Severn, *Canada* 102 A2
Fort Shevchenko, *Kazakstan* 49 H10
Fort Simpson, *Canada* 104 A4
Fort Smith, *Canada* 104 B6
Fort Smith, *U.S.A.* 113 H7
Fort Stockton, *U.S.A.* 113 K3
Fort Sumner, *U.S.A.* 113 H2
Fort Thompson, *U.S.A.* 112 C5
Fort Valley, *U.S.A.* 109 J4
Fort Vermilion, *Canada* 104 B5
Fort Walton Beach, *U.S.A.* 109 K2
Fort Wayne, *U.S.A.* 108 E3
Fort William, *U.K.* 14 E3
Fort Worth, *U.S.A.* 113 J6
Fort Yates, *U.S.A.* 112 B4
Fort Yukon, *U.S.A.* 100 B5
Fortaleza, *Brazil* 125 D11
Forteau, *Canada* 103 B8
Fortescue →, *Australia* 92 D2
Forth →, *U.K.* 14 E5
Forth, Firth of, *U.K.* 14 E6
Fortore →, *Italy* 29 G12
Fortrose, *U.K.* 14 D4
Fortuna, *Spain* 33 G3
Fortuna, *Calif., U.S.A.* 114 F1
Fortuna, *N. Dak., U.S.A.* 112 A3
Fortune, *Canada* 103 C8
Fortune B., *Canada* 103 C8
Forūr, *Iran* 71 E7
Fos-sur-Mer, *France* 21 E8
Foshan, *China* 59 F9
Fosna, *Norway* 8 E14
Fosnavåg, *Norway* 9 E11
Foso, *Ghana* 83 D4
Fossano, *Italy* 28 D4
Fossil, *U.S.A.* 114 D3
Fossombrone, *Italy* 29 E9
Foster, *Canada* 111 A12
Foster →, *Canada* 105 B7
Fosters Ra., *Australia* 94 C1
Fostoria, *U.S.A.* 108 E4
Fotadrevo, *Madag.* 89 C8
Fouesnant, *France* 18 E2
Fougères, *France* 18 D5
Foul Pt., *Sri Lanka* 66 Q12
Foula, *U.K.* 14 A6
Foulalaba, *Mali* 82 C3
Foulness I., *U.K.* 13 F8
Foulpointe, *Madag.* 89 B8
Foulweather, C., *U.S.A.* 106 B2
Foumban, *Cameroon* 83 D7
Foumbot, *Cameroon* 83 D7
Foundiougne, *Senegal* 82 C1
Fountain, *U.S.A.* 112 F2
Fountain Springs, *U.S.A.* 117 K8
Fourchambault, *France* 19 E10
Fouriesburg, *S. Africa* 88 D4
Fourmies, *France* 19 B11
Fournás, *Greece* 38 B3
Foúrnoi, *Greece* 39 D8
Fours, *France* 19 F10
Fourth Cataract, *Sudan* 80 D3
Fouta Djalon, *Guinea* 82 C2
Foux, Cap-à-, *Haiti* 121 C5
Foveaux Str., *N.Z.* 91 M2
Fowey, *U.K.* 13 G3
Fowler, *Calif., U.S.A.* 116 J7
Fowler, *Colo., U.S.A.* 112 F3
Fowlers B., *Australia* 93 F5
Fowman, *Iran* 71 B6
Fox →, *Canada* 105 B10
Fox Creek, *Canada* 104 C5
Fox Lake, *Canada* 104 B6
Fox Valley, *Canada* 105 C7
Foxboro, *U.S.A.* 111 D13
Foxe Basin, *Canada* 101 B12
Foxe Chan., *Canada* 101 B11
Foxe Pen., *Canada* 101 B12
Foxen, *Sweden* 10 E5
Foxton, *N.Z.* 91 J5
Foyle, Lough, *U.K.* 15 A4
Foynes, *Ireland* 15 D2
Foz, *Spain* 34 B3
Foz do Cunene, *Angola* 88 B1
Foz do Iguaçu, *Brazil* 127 B5
Frackville, *U.S.A.* 111 F8
Fraga, *Spain* 32 D5
Fraile Muerto, *Uruguay* 127 C5
Framingham, *U.S.A.* 111 D13
Frampol, *Poland* 45 H9
Franca, *Brazil* 125 H9
Francavilla al Mare, *Italy* 29 F11
Francavilla Fontana, *Italy* 31 B10
France ■, *Europe* 7 F6
Frances, *Australia* 95 F3
Frances →, *Canada* 104 A3
Frances L., *Canada* 104 A3
Franceville, *Gabon* 84 E2
Franche-Comté, *France* 19 F12
Francis Case, L., *U.S.A.* 112 D5
Francisco Beltrão, *Brazil* 127 B5
Francisco I. Madero, *Coahuila, Mexico* 118 B4
Francisco I. Madero, *Durango, Mexico* 118 C4
Francistown, *Botswana* 89 C4
Francofonte, *Italy* 31 E7
François, *Canada* 103 C8
François L., *Canada* 104 C3
Franeker, *Neths.* 17 A5
Frankado, *Djibouti* 81 E5
Frankenberg, *Germany* 24 D4
Frankenwald, *Germany* 25 E7
Frankford, *Canada* 110 B7
Frankfort, *S. Africa* 89 D4
Frankfort, *Ind., U.S.A.* 108 E2
Frankfort, *Kans., U.S.A.* 112 F6
Frankfort, *Ky., U.S.A.* 108 F3
Frankfort, *N.Y., U.S.A.* 111 C9
Frankfurt, *Brandenburg, Germany* 24 C10
Frankfurt, *Hessen, Germany* 25 E4
Fränkische Alb, *Germany* 25 F7
Fränkische Rezat →, *Germany* 25 F7
Fränkische Saale →, *Germany* 25 E5
Fränkische Schweiz, *Germany* 25 F7
Frankland →, *Australia* 93 G2
Franklin, *Ky., U.S.A.* 109 G2
Franklin, *La., U.S.A.* 113 L9
Franklin, *Mass., U.S.A.* 111 D13
Franklin, *N.H., U.S.A.* 111 C13
Franklin, *Nebr., U.S.A.* 112 E5
Franklin, *Pa., U.S.A.* 110 E5
Franklin, *Va., U.S.A.* 109 G7
Franklin, *W. Va., U.S.A.* 108 F6
Franklin B., *Canada* 100 B7
Franklin D. Roosevelt L., *U.S.A.* 114 B4
Franklin I., *Antarctica* 5 D11
Franklin L., *U.S.A.* 114 F6
Franklin Mts., *Canada* 100 B7
Franklin Str., *Canada* 100 A10
Franklinton, *U.S.A.* 113 K9
Franklinville, *U.S.A.* 110 D6
Franks Pk., *U.S.A.* 114 E9
Frankston, *Australia* 95 F4
Frånö, *Sweden* 10 B11
Fransfontein, *Namibia* 88 C2
Fränsta, *Sweden* 10 B10
Frantsa Iosifa, Zemlya, *Russia* 50 A6
Franz, *Canada* 102 C3
Franz Josef Land = Frantsa Iosifa, Zemlya, *Russia* 50 A6
Franzburg, *Germany* 24 A8
Frascati, *Italy* 29 G9
Fraser, *U.S.A.* 110 D2
Fraser →, *B.C., Canada* 104 D4
Fraser →, *Nfld., Canada* 103 A7
Fraser, Mt., *Australia* 93 E2
Fraser I., *Australia* 95 D5
Fraser Lake, *Canada* 104 C4
Fraserburg, *S. Africa* 88 E3
Fraserburgh, *U.K.* 14 D6
Fraserdale, *Canada* 102 C3
Frashër, *Albania* 40 F4
Frasne, *France* 19 F13
Frăteşti, *Romania* 43 G10
Frauenfeld, *Switz.* 25 H4
Fray Bentos, *Uruguay* 126 C4
Frechilla, *Spain* 34 C6
Fredericia, *Denmark* 11 J3
Frederick, *Md., U.S.A.* 108 F7
Frederick, *Okla., U.S.A.* 113 H5
Frederick, *S. Dak., U.S.A.* 112 C5
Fredericksburg, *Pa., U.S.A.* 111 F8
Fredericksburg, *Tex., U.S.A.* 113 K5
Fredericksburg, *Va., U.S.A.* 108 F7
Fredericktown, *Mo., U.S.A.* 113 G9
Fredericktown, *Ohio, U.S.A.* 110 F2
Frederico I. Madero, Presa, *Mexico* 118 B3
Frederico Westphalen, *Brazil* 127 B5
Fredericton, *Canada* 103 C6
Fredericton Junction, *Canada* 103 C6
Frederiksborg Amtskommune □, *Denmark* 11 J6
Frederikshåb = Paamiut, *Greenland* 4 C5
Frederikshavn, *Denmark* 11 G4
Frederikssund, *Denmark* 11 J6
Frederiksted, *U.S. Virgin Is.* 121 C7
Frederiksværk, *Denmark* 11 J6
Fredonia, *Ariz., U.S.A.* 115 H7
Fredonia, *Kans., U.S.A.* 113 G7
Fredonia, *N.Y., U.S.A.* 110 D5
Fredriksberg, *Sweden* 10 D8
Fredrikstad, *Norway* 9 G14
Free State □, *S. Africa* 88 D4
Freehold, *U.S.A.* 111 F10
Freel Peak, *U.S.A.* 116 G7
Freeland, *U.S.A.* 111 E9
Freels, C., *Canada* 103 C9
Freeman, *Calif., U.S.A.* 117 K9
Freeman, *S. Dak., U.S.A.* 112 D6
Freeport, *Bahamas* 120 A4
Freeport, *Ill., U.S.A.* 112 D10
Freeport, *N.Y., U.S.A.* 111 F11
Freeport, *Ohio, U.S.A.* 110 F3
Freeport, *Pa., U.S.A.* 110 F5
Freeport, *Tex., U.S.A.* 113 L7
Freetown, *S. Leone* 82 D2
Frégate, L., *Canada* 102 B5
Fregenal de la Sierra, *Spain* 35 G4
Fregene, *Italy* 29 G9
Fréhel, C., *France* 18 D4
Freiberg, *Germany* 24 E9
Freibourg = Fribourg, *Switz.* 25 J3
Freiburg, *Baden-W., Germany* 25 H3
Freiburg, *Niedersachsen, Germany* 24 B5
Freilassing, *Germany* 25 H8
Freire, *Chile* 128 D2
Freirina, *Chile* 126 B1
Freising, *Germany* 25 G7
Freistadt, *Austria* 26 C7
Freital, *Germany* 24 D9
Fréjus, *France* 21 E10
Fremantle, *Australia* 93 F2

Fremont, *Calif., U.S.A.* 116 H4
Fremont, *Mich., U.S.A.* 108 D3
Fremont, *Nebr., U.S.A.* 112 E6
Fremont, *Ohio, U.S.A.* 108 E4
Fremont ➤, *U.S.A.* 115 G8
French Camp, *U.S.A.* 116 H5
French Creek ➤, *U.S.A.* 110 E5
French Guiana ■, *S. Amer.* 125 C8
French Polynesia ■, *Pac. Oc.* .. 97 K13
Frenchman Cr. ➤, *N. Amer.* 114 B10
Frenchman Cr. ➤, *U.S.A.* 112 E4
Frenštát pod Radhoštěm,
  Czech Rep. 27 B11
Fresco, *Ivory C.* 82 D3
Fresco ➤, *Brazil* 125 E8
Freshfield, C., *Antarctica* 5 C10
Fresnay-sur-Sarthe, *France* 18 D7
Fresnillo, *Mexico* 118 C4
Fresno, *U.S.A.* 116 J7
Fresno Alhandiga, *Spain* 34 E5
Fresno Reservoir, *U.S.A.* 114 B9
Freudenstadt, *Germany* 25 G4
Frévent, *France* 19 B9
Frew ➤, *Australia* 94 C2
Frewsburg, *U.S.A.* 110 D5
Freycinet Pen., *Australia* 94 G4
Freyming-Merlebach, *France* .. 19 C13
Freyung, *Germany* 25 G9
Fria, *Guinea* 82 C2
Fria, C., *Namibia* 88 B1
Friant, *U.S.A.* 116 J7
Frías, *Argentina* 126 B2
Fribourg, *Switz.* 25 J3
Fribourg □, *Switz.* 25 J3
Fridafors, *Sweden* 11 H8
Friday Harbor, *U.S.A.* 116 B3
Friedberg, *Bayern, Germany* .. 25 G6
Friedberg, *Hessen, Germany* .. 25 E4
Friedens, *U.S.A.* 110 F6
Friedland, *Germany* 24 B9
Friedrichshafen, *Germany* 25 H5
Friedrichskoog, *Germany* 24 A4
Friedrichstadt, *Germany* 24 A5
Friendly Is. = Tonga ■, *Pac. Oc.* 91 D11
Friendship, *U.S.A.* 110 D6
Friesach, *Austria* 26 E7
Friesack, *Germany* 24 C8
Friesland □, *Neths.* 17 A5
Friesoythe, *Germany* 24 B3
Friggesund, *Sweden* 10 C10
Frillesås, *Sweden* 11 G6
Frinnaryd, *Sweden* 11 G8
Frio ➤, *U.S.A.* 113 L5
Frio, C., *Brazil* 122 F6
Friol, *Spain* 34 B3
Friona, *U.S.A.* 113 H3
Fristad, *Sweden* 11 G6
Fritch, *U.S.A.* 113 H4
Fritsla, *Sweden* 11 G6
Fritzlar, *Germany* 24 D5
Friuli-Venézia Giulia □, *Italy* .. 29 B9
Frobisher B., *Canada* 101 B13
Frobisher Bay = Iqaluit, *Canada* 101 B13
Frobisher L., *Canada* 105 B7
Frohavet, *Norway* 8 E13
Frohnleiten, *Austria* 26 D8
Frolovo, *Russia* 48 F6
Frombork, *Poland* 44 D6
Frome, *U.K.* 13 F5
Frome ➤, *U.K.* 13 G5
Frome, L., *Australia* 95 E2
Frómista, *Spain* 34 C6
Front Range, *U.S.A.* 106 C5
Front Royal, *U.S.A.* 108 F6
Fronteira, *Portugal* 35 F3
Frontera, *Canary Is.* 37 G2
Frontera, *Mexico* 119 D6
Fronteras, *Mexico* 118 A3
Frontignan, *France* 20 E7
Frosinone, *Italy* 30 A6
Frostburg, *U.S.A.* 108 F6
Frostisen, *Norway* 8 B17
Frouard, *France* 19 D13
Frövi, *Sweden* 10 E9
Frøya, *Norway* 8 E13
Frumoasa, *Romania* 43 D10
Frunze = Bishkek, *Kyrgyzstan* .. 50 E8
Fruška Gora, *Serbia, Yug.* 42 E4
Frutal, *Brazil* 125 H9
Frutigen, *Switz.* 25 J3
Frýdek-Místek, *Czech Rep.* 27 B11
Frýdlant, *Czech Rep.* 26 A8
Fryeburg, *U.S.A.* 111 B14
Fryvaldov = Jeseník, *Czech Rep.* 27 A10
Fthiótis □, *Greece* 38 C4
Fu Jiang ➤, *China* 58 C6
Fu Xian = Wafangdian, *China* .. 57 E11
Fu Xian, *China* 56 G5
Fu'an, *China* 59 D12
Fubian, *China* 58 B4
Fucécchio, *Italy* 28 E7
Fucheng, *China* 56 F9
Fuchou = Fuzhou, *China* 59 D12
Fuchū, *Japan* 55 G6
Fuchuan, *China* 59 E8
Fuchun Jiang ➤, *China* 59 B13
Fúcino, Piana del, *Italy* 29 F10
Fuding, *China* 59 D13
Fuencaliente, *Canary Is.* 37 F2
Fuencaliente, *Spain* 35 G6
Fuencaliente, Pta., *Canary Is.* .. 37 F2
Fuengirola, *Spain* 35 J6
Fuenlabrada, *Spain* 34 E7
Fuensalida, *Spain* 34 E6
Fuente-Álamo, *Spain* 33 G3
Fuente-Álamo de Murcia, *Spain* 33 H3
Fuente de Cantos, *Spain* 35 G4

Fuente del Maestre, *Spain* 35 G4
Fuente el Fresno, *Spain* 35 F7
Fuente Obejuna, *Spain* 35 G5
Fuente Palmera, *Spain* 35 H5
Fuentes de Andalucía, *Spain* .. 35 H5
Fuentes de Ebro, *Spain* 32 D4
Fuentes de León, *Spain* 35 G4
Fuentes de Oñoro, *Spain* 34 E4
Fuentesaúco, *Spain* 34 D5
Fuerte ➤, *Mexico* 118 B3
Fuerte Olimpo, *Paraguay* 126 A4
Fuerteventura, *Canary Is.* 37 F6
Fufeng, *China* 56 G5
Fuga I., *Phil.* 61 B4
Fugong, *China* 58 D2
Fugou, *China* 56 G8
Fugu, *China* 56 E6
Fuhai, *China* 60 B3
Fuḥaymī, *Iraq* 70 C4
Fuji, *Japan* 55 G9
Fuji-San, *Japan* 55 G9
Fuji-Yoshida, *Japan* 55 G9
Fujian □, *China* 59 E12
Fujinomiya, *Japan* 55 G9
Fujisawa, *Japan* 55 G9
Fujiyama, Mt. = Fuji-San, *Japan* 55 G9
Fukien = Fujian □, *China* 59 E12
Fukuchiyama, *Japan* 55 G7
Fukue-Shima, *Japan* 55 H4
Fukui, *Japan* 55 F8
Fukui □, *Japan* 55 G8
Fukuoka, *Japan* 55 H5
Fukuoka □, *Japan* 55 H5
Fukushima, *Japan* 54 F10
Fukushima □, *Japan* 54 F10
Fukuyama, *Japan* 55 G6
Fulacunda, *Guinea-Biss.* 82 C1
Fulda, *Germany* 24 E5
Fulda ➤, *Germany* 24 D5
Fulford Harbour, *Canada* 116 B3
Fuliang, *China* 59 C11
Fullerton, *Calif., U.S.A.* 117 M9
Fullerton, *Nebr., U.S.A.* 112 E6
Fulongquan, *China* 57 B13
Fülöpszállás, *Hungary* 42 D4
Fulton, *Mo., U.S.A.* 112 F9
Fulton, *N.Y., U.S.A.* 111 C8
Fuluälven ➤, *Sweden* 10 C7
Fulufjället, *Sweden* 10 C6
Fumay, *France* 19 C11
Fumel, *France* 20 D4
Fumin, *China* 58 E4
Funabashi, *Japan* 55 G10
Funafuti = Fongafale, *Tuvalu* .. 96 H9
Funäsdalen, *Sweden* 10 B6
Funchal, *Madeira* 37 D3
Fundación, *Colombia* 124 A4
Fundão, *Portugal* 34 E3
Fundu Moldovei, *Romania* ... 43 C10
Fundulea, *Romania* 43 F11
Fundy, B. of, *Canada* 103 D6
Funhalouro, *Mozam.* 89 C5
Funing, *Hebei, China* 57 E10
Funing, *Jiangsu, China* 57 H10
Funing, *Yunnan, China* 58 F5
Funiu Shan, *China* 56 H7
Funsi, *Ghana* 82 C4
Funtua, *Nigeria* 83 C6
Fuping, *Hebei, China* 56 E8
Fuping, *Shaanxi, China* 56 G5
Fuqing, *China* 59 E12
Fuquan, *China* 58 D6
Furano, *Japan* 54 C11
Furāt, Nahr al ➤, *Asia* 70 D5
Fürg, *Iran* 71 D7
Furmanov, *Russia* 48 B5
Furmanovo, *Kazakstan* 48 F9
Furnás, *Spain* 37 B8
Furnas, Reprêsa de, *Brazil* ... 127 A6
Furneaux Group, *Australia* ... 94 G4
Furqlus, *Syria* 75 A6
Fürstenau, *Germany* 24 C3
Fürstenberg, *Germany* 24 B9
Fürstenfeld, *Austria* 26 D9
Fürstenfeldbruck, *Germany* .. 25 G7
Fürstenwalde, *Germany* 24 C10
Fürth, *Germany* 25 F6
Furth im Wald, *Germany* 25 F8
Furtwangen, *Germany* 25 G4
Furudal, *Sweden* 10 C9
Furukawa, *Japan* 54 E10
Furulund, *Sweden* 11 J7
Fury and Hecla Str., *Canada* .. 101 B11
Fusagasuga, *Colombia* 124 C4
Fuscaldo, *Italy* 31 C9
Fushan, *Shandong, China* ... 57 F11
Fushan, *Shanxi, China* 56 G6
Fushë Arrëz, *Albania* 40 D4
Fushë-Krujë, *Albania* 40 E3
Fushun, *Liaoning, China* 57 D12
Fushun, *Sichuan, China* 58 C5
Fusong, *China* 57 C14
Füssen, *Germany* 25 H6
Fusui, *China* 58 F6
Futog, *Yugoslavia* 42 E4
Futuna, *Wall. & F. Is.* 91 B8
Fuwa, *Egypt* 80 H7
Fuxian Hu, *China* 58 E4
Fuxin, *China* 57 C11
Fuyang, *Anhui, China* 56 H8
Fuyang, *Zhejiang, China* 59 B12
Fuyang He ➤, *China* 56 E9
Fuying Dao, *China* 59 D13
Fuyu, *China* 57 B13
Fuyuan, *China* 58 E5
Füzesgyarmat, *Hungary* 42 C6

Fuzhou, *China* 59 D12
Fylde, *U.K.* 12 D5
Fyn, *Denmark* 11 J4
Fyne, L., *U.K.* 14 F3
Fyns Amtskommune □,
  Denmark 11 J4
Fynshav, *Denmark* 11 K3

G

Ga, *Ghana* 82 D4
Gaanda, *Nigeria* 83 C7
Gabarin, *Nigeria* 83 C7
Gabas ➤, *France* 20 E3
Gabela, *Angola* 84 G2
Gabès, *Tunisia* 79 B8
Gabès, G. de, *Tunisia* 79 B8
Gabgaba, W. ➤, *Egypt* 80 C3
Gąbin, *Poland* 45 F6
Gabon ■, *Africa* 84 E2
Gaborone, *Botswana* 88 C4
Gabriels, *U.S.A.* 111 B10
Gābrīk, *Iran* 71 E8
Gabrovo, *Bulgaria* 41 D9
Gacé, *France* 18 D7
Gāch Sār, *Iran* 71 B6
Gachsārān, *Iran* 71 D6
Gacko, *Bos.-H.* 40 C2
Gadag, *India* 66 M9
Gadamai, *Sudan* 81 D4
Gadap, *Pakistan* 68 G2
Gadarwara, *India* 69 H8
Gadebusch, *Germany* 24 B7
Gadein, *Sudan* 81 F2
Gadhada, *India* 68 J4
Gádor, Sierra de, *Spain* 35 J8
Gadra, *Pakistan* 68 G4
Gadsden, *U.S.A.* 109 H3
Gadwal, *India* 66 L10
Gadyach = Hadyach, *Ukraine* .. 47 G8
Găeşti, *Romania* 43 F10
Gaeta, *Italy* 30 A6
Gaeta, G. di, *Italy* 30 A6
Gaffney, *U.S.A.* 109 H5
Gafsa, *Tunisia* 78 B7
Gagarawa, *Nigeria* 83 C6
Gagaria, *India* 68 G4
Gagarin, *Russia* 46 E8
Gaggenau, *Germany* 25 G4
Gaghamni, *Sudan* 81 E2
Gagino, *Russia* 48 C7
Gagliano del Capo, *Italy* 31 C11
Gagnef, *Sweden* 10 D9
Gagnoa, *Ivory C.* 82 D3
Gagnon, *Canada* 103 B6
Gagnon, L., *Canada* 105 A6
Gagra, *Georgia* 49 J5
Gahini, *Rwanda* 86 C3
Gahmar, *India* 69 G10
Gai Xian = Gaizhou, *China* 57 D12
Gaïdhouronísi, *Greece* 36 E7
Gail, *U.S.A.* 113 J4
Gail ➤, *Austria* 26 E6
Gaillac, *France* 20 E5
Gaillimh = Galway, *Ireland* ... 15 C2
Gaillon, *France* 18 C8
Gaines, *U.S.A.* 110 E7
Gainesville, *Fla., U.S.A.* 109 L4
Gainesville, *Ga., U.S.A.* 109 H4
Gainesville, *Mo., U.S.A.* 113 G8
Gainesville, *Tex., U.S.A.* 113 J6
Gainsborough, *U.K.* 12 D7
Gairdner, L., *Australia* 95 E2
Gairloch, L., *U.K.* 14 D3
Gaizhou, *China* 57 D12
Gaj, *Croatia* 42 E2
Gaj ➤, *Pakistan* 68 F2
Gakuch, *Pakistan* 69 A5
Galala, Gebel el, *Egypt* 80 J8
Galán, Cerro, *Argentina* 126 B2
Galana ➤, *Kenya* 86 C5
Galanta, *Slovak Rep.* 27 C10
Galapagar, *Spain* 34 E7
Galápagos, *Pac. Oc.* 122 D1
Galashiels, *U.K.* 14 F6
Galatás, *Greece* 38 D5
Galați, *Romania* 43 E13
Galați □, *Romania* 43 E12
Galatia, *Turkey* 72 C5
Galatina, *Italy* 31 B11
Galátone, *Italy* 31 B11
Galax, *U.S.A.* 109 G5
Galaxídhion, *Greece* 38 C4
Galcaio, *Somali Rep.* 74 F4
Galdhøpiggen, *Norway* 9 F12
Galeana, *Chihuahua, Mexico* .. 118 A3
Galeana, *Nuevo León, Mexico* 118 A3
Galegu, *Sudan* 81 E4
Galela, *Indonesia* 63 D7
Galena, *U.S.A.* 100 B4
Galera, *Spain* 33 H2
Galera Pt., *Trin. & Tob.* 121 D7
Galesburg, *U.S.A.* 112 E9
Galeton, *U.S.A.* 110 E7
Galga, *Ethiopia* 81 F4
Gali, *Georgia* 49 J5
Galicea Mare, *Romania* 43 F8
Galich, *Russia* 48 A6
Galiche, *Bulgaria* 40 C7
Galicia □, *Spain* 34 C3
Galilee = Hagalil, *Israel* 75 C4
Galilee, L., *Australia* 94 C4
Galilee, Sea of = Yam Kinneret,
  Israel 75 C4
Galim, *Cameroon* 83 D7

Galinoporni, *Cyprus* 36 D13
Galion, *U.S.A.* 110 F2
Galiuro Mts., *U.S.A.* 115 K8
Galiwinku, *Australia* 94 A2
Gallabat, *Sudan* 81 E4
Gallan Hd., *U.K.* 14 C1
Gallarate, *Italy* 28 C5
Gallatin, *U.S.A.* 109 G2
Galle, *Sri Lanka* 66 R12
Gállego ➤, *Spain* 32 D4
Gallegos ➤, *Argentina* 128 G3
Galletti ➤, *Ethiopia* 81 F5
Galley Hd., *Ireland* 15 E3
Galliate, *Italy* 28 C5
Gallinas, Pta., *Colombia* 124 A4
Gallipoli = Gelibolu, *Turkey* .. 41 F10
Gallípoli, *Italy* 31 B10
Gallipolis, *U.S.A.* 108 F4
Gällivare, *Sweden* 8 C19
Gallneukirchen, *Austria* 26 C7
Gällö, *Sweden* 10 B9
Gallo, C., *Italy* 30 D6
Gallocanta, L. de, *Spain* 32 E3
Galloo I., *U.S.A.* 111 C8
Galloway, *U.K.* 14 F4
Galloway, Mull of, *U.K.* 14 G4
Gallup, *U.S.A.* 115 J9
Gallur, *Spain* 32 D3
Galoya, *Sri Lanka* 66 Q12
Galt, *U.S.A.* 116 G5
Galten, *Denmark* 11 H3
Galtür, *Austria* 26 E3
Galty Mts., *Ireland* 15 D3
Galtymore, *Ireland* 15 D3
Galva, *U.S.A.* 112 E9
Galve de Sorbe, *Spain* 32 D1
Galveston, *U.S.A.* 113 L7
Galveston B., *U.S.A.* 113 L7
Gálvez, *Argentina* 126 C3
Galway, *Ireland* 15 C2
Galway □, *Ireland* 15 C2
Galway B., *Ireland* 15 C2
Gam ➤, *Vietnam* 64 B5
Gamagōri, *Japan* 55 G8
Gamari L., *Ethiopia* 81 E5
Gamawa, *Nigeria* 83 C7
Gamay, *Phil.* 61 E6
Gambaga, *Ghana* 83 C4
Gambat, *Pakistan* 68 F3
Gambela, *Ethiopia* 81 F3
Gambhir ➤, *India* 68 F6
Gambia ■, *W. Afr.* 82 C1
Gambia ➤, *W. Afr.* 82 C1
Gambier, *U.S.A.* 110 F2
Gambier, C., *Australia* 92 B5
Gambier Is., *Australia* 95 F2
Gambo, *Canada* 103 C9
Gamboli, *Pakistan* 68 E3
Gamboma, *Congo* 84 E3
Gamka ➤, *S. Africa* 88 E3
Gamkab ➤, *Namibia* 88 D2
Gamla Uppsala, *Sweden* 10 E11
Gamlakarleby = Kokkola,
  Finland 8 E20
Gamleby, *Sweden* 11 G10
Gammon ➤, *Canada* 105 C9
Gamo-Gofa □, *Ethiopia* 81 F4
Gamou, *Niger* 83 C6
Gamtoos ➤, *S. Africa* 88 E4
Gan, *France* 20 E3
Gan Goriama, Mts., *Cameroon* 83 D7
Gan Jiang ➤, *China* 59 C11
Ganado, *U.S.A.* 115 J9
Gananita, *Sudan* 80 D3
Gananoque, *Canada* 102 D4
Ganāveh, *Iran* 71 D6
Gäncä, *Azerbaijan* 49 K8
Gancheng, *China* 64 C7
Gand = Gent, *Belgium* 17 C3
Ganda, *Angola* 85 G2
Gandajika, Dem. Rep. of
  the Congo 84 F4
Gandak ➤, *India* 69 G11
Gandava, *Pakistan* 68 E2
Gander, *Canada* 103 C9
Gander L., *Canada* 103 C9
Ganderkesee, *Germany* 24 B4
Ganderowe Falls, *Zimbabwe* .. 87 F2
Gandesa, *Spain* 32 D5
Gandhi Sagar, *India* 68 G6
Gandhinagar, *India* 68 H5
Gandi, *Nigeria* 83 C6
Gandía, *Spain* 33 G4
Gandino, *Italy* 28 C6
Gando, Pta., *Canary Is.* 37 G4
Gandole, *Nigeria* 83 D7
Gâneb, *Mauritania* 82 B2
Ganedidalem = Gani, *Indonesia* 63 E7
Ganetti, *Sudan* 80 D3
Ganga ➤, *India* 69 H14
Ganga Sagar, *India* 69 J13
Gangafani, *Mali* 82 C4
Gangan ➤, *India* 69 E8
Ganganagar, *India* 68 E5
Gangapur, *India* 68 F7
Gangara, *Niger* 83 C6
Gangaw, *Burma* 67 H19
Gangdisê Shan, *China* 67 D12
Ganges = Ganga ➤, *India* 69 H14
Ganges, *Canada* 104 D4
Ganges, *France* 20 E7
Ganges, Mouths of the, *India* .. 69 J14
Gânghester, *Sweden* 11 G7
Gângiova, *Romania* 43 G8
Gangi, *Italy* 31 E7
Gangoh, *India* 68 E7
Gangroti, *India* 69 D8

Gangtok, *India* 67 F16
Gangu, *China* 56 G3
Gangyao, *China* 57 B14
Gani, *Indonesia* 63 E7
Ganj, *India* 69 F8
Ganluc, *China* 58 C4
Gannat, *France* 19 F10
Gannett Peak, *U.S.A.* 114 E9
Ganquan, *China* 56 F5
Gänserdorf, *Austria* 27 C9
Ganshui, *China* 58 C6
Gansu □, *China* 56 G3
Ganta, *Liberia* 82 D3
Gantheaume, C., *Australia* ... 95 F2
Gantheaume B., *Australia* 93 E1
Gantsevichi = Hantsavichy,
  Belarus 47 F4
Ganye, *Nigeria* 83 D7
Ganyem = Genyem, *Indonesia* . 63 E10
Ganyu, *China* 57 G10
Ganyushkino, *Kazakstan* 49 G9
Ganzhou, *China* 59 E10
Gao, *Mali* 83 B4
Gao Xian, *China* 58 C5
Gao'an, *China* 59 C10
Gaochun, *China* 59 B12
Gaohe, *China* 59 F9
Gaohebu, *China* 59 B11
Gaokeng, *China* 59 D9
Gaolan Dao, *China* 59 G9
Gaoligong Shan, *China* 58 E2
Gaomi, *China* 57 F10
Gaoming, *China* 59 F9
Gaoping, *China* 56 G7
Gaotang, *China* 56 F9
Gaoua, *Burkina Faso* 82 C4
Gaoual, *Guinea* 82 C2
Gaoxiong = Kaohsiung, *Taiwan* 59 F13
Gaoyao, *China* 59 F9
Gaoyou, *China* 59 A12
Gaoyou Hu, *China* 57 H10
Gaoyuan, *China* 57 F9
Gaozhou, *China* 59 G8
Gap, *France* 21 D10
Gapan, *Phil.* 61 D4
Gapat ➤, *India* 69 G10
Gapuwiyak, *Australia* 94 A2
Gar, *China* 60 C2
Garabogazköl Aylagy,
  Turkmenistan 50 E6
Garachico, *Canary Is.* 37 F3
Garachiné, *Panama* 120 E4
Garafia, *Canary Is.* 37 F2
Garah, *Australia* 95 D4
Garajonay, *Canary Is.* 37 F2
Garango, *Burkina Faso* 83 C4
Garanhuns, *Brazil* 125 E11
Garautha, *India* 69 G8
Garawe, *Liberia* 82 E3
Garba Tula, *Kenya* 86 B4
Garberville, *U.S.A.* 114 F2
Garbsen, *Germany* 24 C5
Gard □, *France* 21 E8
Gard ➤, *France* 21 E8
Garda, L. di, *Italy* 28 C7
Gardanne, *France* 21 E9
Gårdby, *Sweden* 11 H10
Garde L., *Canada* 105 A7
Gardelegen, *Germany* 24 C7
Garden City, *Ga., U.S.A.* 109 J5
Garden City, *Kans., U.S.A.* .. 113 G4
Garden City, *Tex., U.S.A.* ... 113 K4
Garden Grove, *U.S.A.* 117 M9
Gardez, *Afghan.* 68 C3
Gardhíki, *Greece* 38 C3
Gardiner, *Maine, U.S.A.* 109 C11
Gardiner, *Mont., U.S.A.* 114 D8
Gardiners I., *U.S.A.* 111 E12
Gardner, *U.S.A.* 111 D13
Gardner Canal, *Canada* 104 C3
Gardnerville, *U.S.A.* 116 G7
Gardno, Jezioro, *Poland* 44 D4
Gardo, *Somali Rep.* 74 F4
Gardone Val Trómpia, *Italy* ... 28 C7
Gárdony, *Hungary* 42 C3
Garešnica, *Croatia* 29 C13
Garéssio, *Italy* 28 D5
Garey, *U.S.A.* 117 L6
Garfield, *U.S.A.* 114 C5
Garforth, *U.K.* 12 D6
Gargaliánoi, *Greece* 38 D3
Gargan, Mt., *France* 20 C5
Gargouna, *Mali* 83 B5
Gargždai, *Lithuania* 44 B8
Garhshankar, *India* ....
Garibaldi Prov. Park, *Canada* . 104 D4
Gariep, L., *S. Africa* 88 E4
Garies, *S. Africa* 88 E2
Garigliano ➤, *Italy* 30 A6
Garissa, *Kenya* 86 C4
Garkida, *Nigeria* 83 C7
Garko, *Nigeria* 83 C6
Garland, *Tex., U.S.A.* 113 J6
Garland, *Utah, U.S.A.* 114 F7
Garlasco, *Italy* 28 C5
Garliava, *Lithuania* 44 D10
Garlin, *France* 20 E3
Garm, *Tajikistan* 50 F8
Garmāb, *Iran* 71 C8
Garmisch-Partenkirchen,
  Germany 25 H7
Garmo, Qullai = Kommunizma,
  Pik, *Tajikistan* 50 F8
Garmsār, *Iran* 71 C7
Garner, *U.S.A.* 112 D8
Garnett, *U.S.A.* 112 F7

Garo Hills, *India* 69 G14
Garoe, *Somali Rep.* 74 F4
Garonne ➤, *France* 20 C3
Garonne, Canal Latéral à la,
 France 20 D4
Garot, *India* 68 G6
Garoua, *Cameroon* 83 D7
Garpenberg, *Sweden* 10 D10
Garphyttan, *Sweden* 10 E8
Garrauli, *India* 69 G8
Garrel, *Germany* 24 C4
Garrigue = Garrigues, *France* . . 20 E7
Garrigues, *France* 20 E7
Garrison, Mont., *U.S.A.* 114 C7
Garrison, N. Dak., *U.S.A.* 112 B4
Garrison Res. = Sakakawea, L.,
 U.S.A. 112 B4
Garron Pt., *U.K.* 15 A6
Garrovillas, *Spain* 35 F4
Garrucha, *Spain* 33 H3
Garry ➤, *U.K.* 14 E5
Garry, L., *Canada* 100 B9
Garsen, *Kenya* 86 C5
Gärsnäs, *Sweden* 11 J8
Garson L., *Canada* 105 B6
Gartempe ➤, *France* 20 B4
Gartz, *Germany* 24 B10
Garu, *Ghana* 83 C4
Garu, *India* 69 H11
Garub, *Namibia* 88 D2
Garut, *Indonesia* 63 G12
Garvão, *Portugal* 35 H2
Garvie Mts., *N.Z.* 91 L2
Garwa = Garoua, *Cameroon* . . 83 D7
Garwa, *India* 69 G10
Garwolin, *Poland* 45 G8
Gary, *U.S.A.* 108 E2
Garz, *Germany* 24 A9
Garzê, *China* 58 B3
Garzón, *Colombia* 124 C3
Gas-San, *Japan* 54 E10
Gasan Kuli = Esenguly,
 Turkmenistan 50 F6
Gascogne, *France* 20 E4
Gascogne, G. de, *Europe* 20 E2
Gascony = Gascogne, *France* . . 20 E4
Gascoyne ➤, *Australia* 93 D1
Gascoyne Junction, *Australia* . . 93 E2
Gascueña, *Spain* 32 E2
Gash, Wadi ➤, *Ethiopia* 81 D4
Gashagar, *Nigeria* 83 C7
Gashaka, *Nigeria* 83 D7
Gasherbrum, *Pakistan* 69 B7
Gashua, *Nigeria* 83 C7
Gaspé, *Canada* 103 C7
Gaspé, C. de, *Canada* 103 C7
Gaspé, Pén. de, *Canada* 103 C6
Gaspésie, Parc de Conservation
 de la, *Canada* 103 C6
Gassan, *Burkina Faso* 82 C4
Gassol, *Nigeria* 83 D7
Gastonia, *U.S.A.* 109 H5
Gastoúni, *Greece* 38 D3
Gastoúri, *Greece* 38 B1
Gastre, *Argentina* 128 E3
Gästrikland, *Sweden* 10 D10
Gata, C., *Cyprus* 36 E12
Gata, C. de, *Spain* 33 J2
Gata, Sierra de, *Spain* 34 E4
Gataga ➤, *Canada* 104 B3
Gătaia, *Romania* 42 E6
Gatchina, *Russia* 46 C6
Gatehouse of Fleet, *U.K.* 14 G4
Gates, *U.S.A.* 110 C7
Gateshead, *U.K.* 12 C6
Gatesville, *U.S.A.* 113 K6
Gaths, *Zimbabwe* 87 G3
Gatico, *Chile* 126 A1
Gâtinais, *France* 19 D9
Gâtine, Hauteurs de, *France* . . 20 B3
Gatineau ➤, *Canada* 111 A9
Gatineau, *Canada* 102 C4
Gatineau, Parc Nat. de la,
 Canada 102 C4
Gattaran, *Phil.* 61 B4
Gattinara, *Italy* 28 C5
Gatton, *Australia* 95 D5
Gatun, L., *Panama* 120 E4
Gatyana, *S. Africa* 89 E4
Gau, *Fiji* 91 D8
Gaucín, *Spain* 35 J5
Gauer L., *Canada* 105 B9
Gauhati, *India* 67 F17
Gauja ➤, *Latvia* 9 H21
Gaula ➤, *Norway* 8 E14
Gauri Phanta, *India* 69 E9
Gausta, *Norway* 9 G13
Gauteng □, *S. Africa* 89 D4
Gāv Koshī, *Iran* 71 D8
Gāvakān, *Iran* 71 D7
Gavarnie, *France* 20 F3
Gāvāter, *Iran* 71 E9
Gāvbandī, *Iran* 71 E7
Gavdhopoúla, *Greece* 36 E6
Gávdhos, *Greece* 36 E6
Gavi, *Italy* 28 D5
Gavião, *Portugal* 35 F3
Gaviota, *U.S.A.* 117 L6
Gävkhūnī, Baţlāq-e, *Iran* 71 C7
Gävle, *Sweden* 10 D11
Gävleborgs län □, *Sweden* . . . 10 C10
Gävlebukten, *Sweden* 10 D11
Gavorrano, *Italy* 28 F7
Gavray, *France* 18 D5
Gavrilov Yam, *Russia* 46 D10
Gávrion, *Greece* 38 D6

Gawachab, *Namibia* 88 D2
Gawilgarh Hills, *India* 66 J10
Gawler, *Australia* 95 E2
Gawu, *Nigeria* 83 D6
Gaxun Nur, *China* 60 B5
Gaya, *India* 69 G11
Gaya, *Niger* 83 C5
Gaya, *Nigeria* 83 C6
Gayéri, *Burkina Faso* 83 C5
Gaylord, *U.S.A.* 108 C3
Gayndah, *Australia* 95 D5
Gaysin = Haysyn, *Ukraine* 47 H5
Gayvoron = Hayvoron, *Ukraine* . . 47 H5
Gaza, *Gaza Strip* 75 D3
Gaza □, *Mozam.* 89 C5
Gaza Strip □, *Asia* 75 D3
Gazanjyk, *Turkmenistan* 71 B7
Gazaoua, *Niger* 83 C6
Gāzbor, *Iran* 71 D8
Gazi, *Dem. Rep. of the Congo* . . 86 B1
Gaziantep, *Turkey* 70 B3
Gazipaşa, *Turkey* 72 D5
Gbekebo, *Nigeria* 83 D5
Gboko, *Nigeria* 83 D6
Gbongan, *Nigeria* 83 D5
Gcoverega, *Botswana* 88 B3
Gcuwa, *S. Africa* 89 E4
Gdańsk, *Poland* 44 D5
Gdańska, Zatoka, *Poland* 44 D6
Gdov, *Russia* 9 G22
Gdynia, *Poland* 44 D5
Geba ➤, *Guinea-Biss.* 82 C1
Gebe, *Indonesia* 63 D7
Gebeciler, *Turkey* 39 C12
Gebeit Mine, *Sudan* 80 C4
Gebel Abyad, *Sudan* 80 D2
Gebel Iweibid, *Egypt* 80 H8
Gebze, *Turkey* 41 F13
Gecha, *Ethiopia* 81 F4
Gedaref, *Sudan* 81 E4
Gedaref □, *Sudan* 81 E4
Gediz, *Turkey* 39 B11
Gediz ➤, *Turkey* 39 C8
Gedo, *Ethiopia* 81 F4
Gèdre, *France* 20 F4
Gedser, *Denmark* 11 K5
Geegully Cr. ➤, *Australia* 92 C3
Geel, *Belgium* 17 C4
Geelong, *Australia* 95 F3
Geelvink B. = Cenderwasih,
 Teluk, *Indonesia* 63 E9
Geelvink Chan., *Australia* 93 E1
Geesthacht, *Germany* 24 B6
Geidam, *Nigeria* 83 C7
Geikie ➤, *Canada* 105 B8
Geilenkirchen, *Germany* 24 E2
Geili, *Sudan* 81 D3
Geisingen, *Germany* 25 H4
Geislingen, *Germany* 25 G5
Geistown, *U.S.A.* 110 F6
Geita, *Tanzania* 86 C3
Gejiu, *China* 58 F4
Gel ➤, *Sudan* 81 F2
Gel, Meydān-e, *Iran* 71 D7
Gel River, *Sudan* 81 F2
Gela, *Italy* 31 E7
Gela, G. di, *Italy* 31 F7
Gelahun, *Liberia* 82 D2
Gelderland □, *Neths.* 17 B6
Geldern, *Germany* 24 D2
Geldrop, *Neths.* 17 C5
Geleen, *Neths.* 17 D5
Gelehun, *S. Leone* 82 D2
Gelembe, *Turkey* 39 B9
Gelemso, *Ethiopia* 81 F5
Gelendost, *Turkey* 72 C4
Gelendzhik, *Russia* 47 K10
Gelibolu, *Turkey* 41 F10
Gelibolu Yarımadası, *Turkey* . . 41 F10
Gelidonya Burnu, *Turkey* 72 D4
Gelnhausen, *Germany* 25 E5
Gelnica, *Slovak Rep.* 27 C13
Gelsenkirchen, *Germany* 24 D3
Gelting, *Germany* 24 A5
Gemas, *Malaysia* 65 L4
Gembloux, *Belgium* 17 D4
Gembu, *Nigeria* 83 D7
Gemena, *Dem. Rep. of
 the Congo* 84 D3
Gemerek, *Turkey* 70 B3
Gemla, *Sweden* 11 H8
Gemlik, *Turkey* 41 F13
Gemlik Körfezi, *Turkey* 41 F12
Gemona del Friuli, *Italy* 29 B10
Gemsa, *Egypt* 80 B3
Gemünden, *Germany* 25 E5
Genale ➤, *Ethiopia* 81 F4
Genç, *Turkey* 73 C9
Gençay, *France* 20 B4
Geneina, Gebel, *Egypt* 80 B3
General Acha, *Argentina* 126 D3
General Alvear, *Buenos Aires,
 Argentina* 126 D4
General Alvear, *Mendoza,
 Argentina* 126 D2
General Artigas, *Paraguay* 126 B4
General Belgrano, *Argentina* . . 126 D4
General Cabrera, *Argentina* . . . 126 C3
General Cepeda, *Mexico* 118 B4
General Guido, *Argentina* 126 D4
General Juan Madariaga,
 Argentina 126 D4
General La Madrid, *Argentina* . . 126 D3
General MacArthur, *Phil.* 61 F6
General Martin Miguel de
 Güemes, *Argentina* 126 A3

General Paz, *Argentina* 126 B4
General Pico, *Argentina* 126 D3
General Pinedo, *Argentina* 126 B3
General Pinto, *Argentina* 126 C3
General Roca, *Argentina* 128 D3
General Santos, *Phil.* 61 H6
General Toshevo, *Bulgaria* 41 C12
General Trevino, *Mexico* 119 B5
General Trías, *Mexico* 118 B3
General Viamonte, *Argentina* . . 126 D3
General Villegas, *Argentina* . . . 126 D3
Genesee, *Idaho, U.S.A.* 114 C5
Genesee, *Pa., U.S.A.* 110 E7
Genesee ➤, *U.S.A.* 110 C7
Geneseo, *Ill., U.S.A.* 112 E9
Geneseo, *N.Y., U.S.A.* 110 D7
Geneva = Genève, *Switz.* 25 J2
Geneva, *Ala., U.S.A.* 109 K3
Geneva, *Nebr., U.S.A.* 112 E6
Geneva, *N.Y., U.S.A.* 110 D8
Geneva, *Ohio, U.S.A.* 110 E4
Geneva, L. = Léman, L., *Europe* . . 19 F13
Geneva, L., *U.S.A.* 108 D1
Genève, *Switz.* 25 J2
Gengenbach, *Germany* 25 G4
Gengma, *China* 58 F2
Genichesk = Henichesk, *Ukraine* . . 47 J8
Genil ➤, *Spain* 35 H5
Genk, *Belgium* 17 D5
Genlis, *France* 19 E12
Gennargentu, Mti. del, *Italy* . . . 30 B2
Gennes, *France* 18 E6
Genoa = Génova, *Italy* 28 D5
Genoa, *Australia* 95 F4
Genoa, *N.Y., U.S.A.* 111 D8
Genoa, *Nebr., U.S.A.* 112 E6
Genoa, *Nev., U.S.A.* 116 F7
Génova, *Italy* 28 D5
Génova, G. di, *Italy* 28 D5
Genriyetty, Ostrov, *Russia* 51 B16
Gent, *Belgium* 17 C3
Genteng, *Indonesia* 63 G12
Genthin, *Germany* 24 C8
Genyem, *Indonesia* 63 E10
Genzano di Lucánia, *Italy* 31 B9
Genzano di Roma, *Italy* 29 G9
Geoagiu, *Romania* 43 E8
Geographe B., *Australia* 93 F2
Geographe Chan., *Australia* . . 93 D1
Geokchay = Göyçay, *Azerbaijan* . . 49 K8
Georga, Zemlya, *Russia* 50 A5
George, *S. Africa* 88 E3
George ➤, *Canada* 103 A6
George, L., *N.S.W., Australia* . . 95 F4
George, L., *S. Austral., Australia* . . 95 F3
George, L., *W. Austral.,
 Australia* 92 D3
George, L., *Uganda* 86 B3
George, L., *Fla., U.S.A.* 109 L5
George, L., *N.Y., U.S.A.* 111 C11
George Gill Ra., *Australia* 92 D5
George River =
 Kangiqsualujjuaq, *Canada* . . 101 C13
George Sound, *N.Z.* 91 L1
George Town, *Australia* 94 G4
George Town, *Bahamas* 120 B4
George Town, *Cayman Is.* 120 C3
George Town, *Malaysia* 65 K3
George V Land, *Antarctica* 5 C10
George VI Sound, *Antarctica* . . 5 D17
George West, *U.S.A.* 113 L5
Georgetown, *Ont., Canada* . . . 102 D4
Georgetown, *P.E.I., Canada* . . . 103 C7
Georgetown, *Gambia* 82 C2
Georgetown, *Guyana* 124 B7
Georgetown, *Calif., U.S.A.* . . . 116 G6
Georgetown, *Colo., U.S.A.* . . . 114 G11
Georgetown, *Ky., U.S.A.* 108 F3
Georgetown, *N.Y., U.S.A.* 111 D9
Georgetown, *Ohio, U.S.A.* 108 F4
Georgetown, *S.C., U.S.A.* 109 J6
Georgetown, *Tex., U.S.A.* 113 K6
Georgia □, *U.S.A.* 109 K5
Georgia ■, *Asia* 49 J6
Georgia, Str. of, *Canada* 104 D4
Georgian B., *Canada* 102 C3
Georgina ➤, *Australia* 94 C2
Georgina I., *Canada* 110 B5
Georgiu-Dezh = Liski, *Russia* . . 47 G10
Georgiyevsk, *Russia* 49 H6
Georgsmarienhütte, *Germany* . . 24 C4
Gera, *Germany* 24 E8
Geraardsbergen, *Belgium* 17 D3
Geral, Serra, *Brazil* 127 B6
Geral de Goiás, Serra, *Brazil* . . 125 F9
Geraldine, *U.S.A.* 114 C8
Geraldton, *Australia* 93 E1
Geraldton, *Canada* 102 C2
Gérardmer, *France* 19 D13
Gercüş, *Turkey* 73 D9
Gerede, *Turkey* 72 B5
Gerês, Sierra do, *Portugal* 34 D3
Gereshk, *Afghan.* 66 D4
Gerik, *Malaysia* 65 K3
Gering, *U.S.A.* 112 E3
Gerlach, *U.S.A.* 114 F4
Gerlachovský štít, *Slovak Rep.* . . 27 B13
German Planina, *Macedonia* . . 40 D6
Germansen Landing, *Canada* . . 104 B4
Germantown, *U.S.A.* 113 M10
Germany ■, *Europe* 24 E6
Germencik, *Turkey* 39 D9
Germering, *Germany* 25 G7
Germersheim, *Germany* 25 F4

Germī, *Iran* 71 B6
Germiston, *S. Africa* 89 D4
Gernika-Lumo, *Spain* 32 B2
Gernsheim, *Germany* 25 F4
Gero, *Japan* 55 G8
Gerolzhofen, *Germany* 25 F6
Gerona = Girona, *Spain* 32 D7
Gerrard, *Canada* 104 C5
Gers □, *France* 20 E4
Gers ➤, *France* 20 D4
Gersfeld, *Germany* 24 E5
Gersthofen, *Germany* 25 G6
Gerzat, *France* 20 C7
Gerze, *Turkey* 72 B6
Geseke, *Germany* 24 D4
Geser, *Indonesia* 63 E8
Gesso ➤, *Italy* 28 D4
Gestro, Wabi ➤, *Ethiopia* 81 G5
Getafe, *Spain* 34 E7
Getinge, *Sweden* 11 H6
Gettysburg, Pa., *U.S.A.* 108 F7
Gettysburg, S. Dak., *U.S.A.* . . . 112 C5
Getxo, *Spain* 32 B2
Getz Ice Shelf, *Antarctica* 5 D14
Gevaş, *Turkey* 73 C10
Gévaudan, *France* 20 D7
Gevgelija, *Macedonia* 40 E6
Gévora ➤, *Spain* 35 G4
Gewani, *Ethiopia* 81 E5
Gex, *France* 19 F13
Geyikli, *Turkey* 39 B8
Geyser, *U.S.A.* 114 C8
Geyserville, *U.S.A.* 116 G4
Geyve, *Turkey* 72 B4
Ghâbat el Arab = Wang Kai,
 Sudan 81 F2
Ghabeish, *Sudan* 81 E2
Ghaggar ➤, *India* 68 E6
Ghaghara ➤, *India* 69 G11
Ghaghat ➤, *Bangla.* 69 G13
Ghagra, *India* 69 H11
Ghagra ➤, *India* 69 F9
Ghalla, Wadi el ➤, *Sudan* 81 E2
Ghana ■, *W. Afr.* 83 D4
Ghansor, *India* 69 H9
Ghanzi, *Botswana* 88 C3
Gharb el Istiwa'iya □, *Sudan* . . 81 G3
Gharb Kordofân, *Sudan* 81 E2
Gharbîya, Es Sahrâ el, *Egypt* . . 80 B2
Ghardaïa, *Algeria* 78 B6
Ghârib, G., *Egypt* 80 B3
Gharig, *Sudan* 81 E2
Gharyān, *Libya* 79 B8
Ghat, *Libya* 79 D8
Ghatal, *India* 69 H12
Ghatampur, *India* 69 F9
Ghatsila, *India* 69 H12
Ghaţţī, *Si. Arabia* 70 D3
Ghawdex = Gozo, *Malta* 36 C1
Ghazal, Bahr el ➤, *Chad* 79 F9
Ghazâl, Bahr el ➤, *Sudan* 81 F3
Ghaziabad, *India* 68 E7
Ghazipur, *India* 69 G10
Ghaznī, *Afghan.* 66 C3
Ghaznī □, *Afghan.* 66 C6
Ghedi, *Italy* 28 C7
Ghelari, *Romania* 42 E7
Ghent = Gent, *Belgium* 17 C3
Gheorghe Gheorghiu-Dej =
 Oneşti, *Romania* 43 D11
Gheorgheni, *Romania* 43 D10
Gherla, *Romania* 43 D8
Ghidigeni, *Romania* 43 D12
Ghilarza, *Italy* 30 B1
Ghimeş-Făget, *Romania* 43 D11
Ghīnah, Wādī al ➤, *Si. Arabia* . . 70 D3
Ghisonaccia, *France* 21 F13
Ghisoni, *France* 21 F13
Ghizao, *Afghan.* 68 C1
Ghizar ➤, *Pakistan* 69 A5
Ghot Ogrein, *Egypt* 80 A2
Ghotaru, *India* 68 F4
Ghotki, *Pakistan* 68 E3
Ghowr □, *Afghan.* 66 C4
Ghudaf, W. al ➤, *Iraq* 70 C4
Ghudāmis, *Libya* 77 C4
Ghughri, *India* 69 H9
Ghugus, *India* 66 K11
Ghulam Mohammad Barrage,
 Pakistan 68 G3
Ghūrīan, *Afghan.* 66 B2
Gia Dinh, *Vietnam* 65 G6
Gia Lai = Plei Ku, *Vietnam* . . . 64 F7
Gia Nghia, *Vietnam* 65 G6
Gia Ngoc, *Vietnam* 64 E7
Gia Vuc, *Vietnam* 64 E7
Giannutri, *Italy* 28 F8
Giant Forest, *U.S.A.* 116 J8
Giant Mts. = Krkonoše,
 Czech Rep. 26 A8
Giants Causeway, *U.K.* 15 A5
Giarabub = Al Jaghbûb, *Libya* . . 79 C10
Giarre, *Italy* 31 E8
Giaveno, *Italy* 28 C4
Gibara, *Cuba* 120 B4
Gibb River, *Australia* 92 C4
Gibbon, *U.S.A.* 112 E5
Gibe ➤, *Ethiopia* 81 F4
Gibellina Nuova, *Italy* 30 E5
Gibeon, *Namibia* 88 D2
Gibraleón, *Spain* 35 H4
Gibraltar ■, *Europe* 35 J5
Gibraltar, Str. of, *Medit. S.* . . . 35 K5
Gibson Desert, *Australia* 92 D4
Gibsons, *Canada* 104 D4
Gibsonville, *U.S.A.* 116 F6
Giddings, *U.S.A.* 113 K6

Gidole, *Ethiopia* 81 F4
Giebnegáisi = Kebnekaise,
 Sweden 8 C18
Gien, *France* 19 E9
Giengen, *Germany* 25 G6
Giessen, *Germany* 24 E4
Gīfān, *Iran* 71 B8
Gifatin, Geziret, *Egypt* 80 B3
Gifhorn, *Germany* 24 C6
Gift Lake, *Canada* 104 B5
Gifu, *Japan* 55 G8
Gifu □, *Japan* 55 G8
Gigant, *Russia* 49 G5
Giganta, Sa. de la, *Mexico* . . . 118 B2
Gigen, *Bulgaria* 41 C8
Gigha, *U.K.* 14 F3
Gíglio, *Italy* 28 F7
Gignac, *France* 20 E7
Gigüela ➤, *Spain* 35 F7
Gijón, *Spain* 34 B5
Gil I., *Canada* 104 C3
Gila ➤, *U.S.A.* 115 K6
Gila Bend, *U.S.A.* 115 K7
Gila Bend Mts., *U.S.A.* 115 K7
Gīlān □, *Iran* 71 B6
Gilău, *Romania* 43 D8
Gilbert ➤, *Australia* 94 B3
Gilbert Is., *Kiribati* 96 G9
Gilbert River, *Australia* 94 B3
Gilead, *U.S.A.* 111 B14
Gilf el Kebîr, Hadabat el, *Egypt* . . 80 C2
Gilford I., *Canada* 104 C3
Gilgandra, *Australia* 95 E4
Gilgil, *Kenya* 86 C4
Gilgit, *India* 69 B6
Gilgit ➤, *Pakistan* 69 B6
Giljeva Planina, *Serbia, Yug.* . . 40 C3
Gillam, *Canada* 105 B10
Gilleleje, *Denmark* 11 H6
Gillen, L., *Australia* 93 E3
Gilles, L., *Australia* 95 E2
Gillette, *U.S.A.* 112 C2
Gilliat, *Australia* 94 C3
Gillingham, *U.K.* 13 F8
Gilmer, *U.S.A.* 113 J7
Gilmore, L., *Australia* 93 F3
Gilo ➤, *Ethiopia* 81 F3
Gilort ➤, *Romania* 43 F8
Gilroy, *U.S.A.* 116 H5
Gimbi, *Ethiopia* 81 F4
Gimli, *Canada* 105 C9
Gimo, *Sweden* 10 D12
Gimone ➤, *France* 20 E5
Gimont, *France* 20 E4
Gin Gin, *Australia* 95 D5
Gīnāh, *Egypt* 80 B3
Gineifa, *Egypt* 80 H8
Gingin, *Australia* 93 F2
Gingindlovu, *S. Africa* 89 D5
Ginir, *Ethiopia* 81 F5
Ginosa, *Italy* 31 B9
Ginzo de Limia = Xinzo de
 Limia, *Spain* 34 C3
Gióia, G. di, *Italy* 31 D8
Gióia del Colle, *Italy* 31 B9
Gióia Táuro, *Italy* 31 D8
Gioiosa Iónica, *Italy* 31 D9
Gioiosa Marea, *Italy* 31 D7
Gióna, Óros, *Greece* 38 C4
Giovi, Passo dei, *Italy* 28 D5
Giovinazzo, *Italy* 31 A9
Gir Hills, *India* 68 J4
Girab, *India* 68 F4
Girâfi, W. ➤, *Egypt* 75 F3
Giraltovce, *Slovak Rep.* 27 B14
Girard, Kans., *U.S.A.* 113 G7
Girard, Ohio, *U.S.A.* 110 E4
Girard, Pa., *U.S.A.* 110 E4
Girdle Ness, *U.K.* 14 D6
Giresun, *Turkey* 73 B8
Girga, *Egypt* 80 B3
Giri ➤, *India* 68 D7
Giridih, *India* 69 G12
Girifalco, *Italy* 31 D9
Girne = Kyrenia, *Cyprus* 36 D12
Giro, *Nigeria* 83 C5
Giromagny, *France* 19 E13
Girona, *Spain* 32 D7
Girona □, *Spain* 32 C7
Gironde □, *France* 20 D3
Gironde ➤, *France* 20 C2
Gironella, *Spain* 32 C6
Giru, *Australia* 94 B4
Girvan, *U.K.* 14 F4
Gisborne, *N.Z.* 91 H7
Gisenyi, *Rwanda* 86 C2
Gislaved, *Sweden* 11 G7
Gisors, *France* 19 C8
Gitega, *Burundi* 86 C2
Giuba ➤, *Somali Rep.* 74 G3
Giugliano in Campania, *Italy* . . 31 B7
Giulianova, *Italy* 29 F10
Giurgeni, *Romania* 43 F12
Giurgiu, *Romania* 43 G10
Giurgiu □, *Romania* 43 F10
Giurgiuleşti, *Moldova* 43 E13
Give, *Denmark* 11 J3
Givet, *France* 19 B11
Givors, *France* 21 C8
Givry, *France* 19 F11
Giyon, *Ethiopia* 81 F4
Giza = El Gîza, *Egypt* 80 J7
Gizhiga, *Russia* 51 C17
Gizhiginskaya Guba, *Russia* . . 51 C16
Giżycko, *Poland* 44 D8
Gizzeria, *Italy* 31 D9
Gjalicë e Lumës, Mal., *Albania* . . 40 D4

Gjegjan, *Albania* 40 E4
Gjirokastër, *Albania* 40 F4
Gjoa Haven, *Canada* 100 B10
Gjøvik, *Norway* 9 F14
Gjuhës, Kep i, *Albania* 40 F3
Glace Bay, *Canada* 103 C8
Glacier Bay National Park and
  Preserve, *U.S.A.* 104 B1
Glacier National Park, *Canada* . 104 C5
Glacier National Park, *U.S.A.* . 114 B7
Glacier Peak, *U.S.A.* 114 B3
Gladewater, *U.S.A.* 113 J7
Gladstone, *Queens., Australia* . 94 C5
Gladstone, *S. Austral., Australia* 95 E2
Gladstone, *Canada* 105 C9
Gladstone, *U.S.A.* 108 C2
Gladwin, *U.S.A.* 108 D3
Glafsfjorden, *Sweden* 10 E6
Głogów Małopolski, *Poland* .. 45 H8
Glåma = Glomma →, *Norway* . 9 G14
Gláma, *Iceland* 8 D2
Glamis, *U.S.A.* 117 N11
Glamoč, *Bos.-H.* 29 D13
Glamsbjerg, *Denmark* 11 J4
Glarus, *Switz.* 25 H5
Glarus □, *Switz.* 25 J5
Glasco, *Kans., U.S.A.* 112 F6
Glasco, *N.Y., U.S.A.* 111 D11
Glasgow, *U.K.* 14 F4
Glasgow, *Ky., U.S.A.* 108 G3
Glasgow, *Mont., U.S.A.* 114 B10
Glasgow, City of □, *U.K.* ... 14 F4
Glaslyn, *Canada* 105 C7
Glastonbury, *U.K.* 13 F5
Glastonbury, *U.S.A.* 111 E12
Glauchau, *Germany* 24 E8
Glava, *Sweden* 10 E6
Glavice, *Croatia* 29 E13
Glazov, *Russia* 48 A11
Gleichen, *Canada* 104 C6
Gleisdorf, *Austria* 26 D8
Gleiwitz = Gliwice, *Poland* .. 45 H5
Glen, *U.S.A.* 111 B13
Glen Affric, *U.K.* 14 D3
Glen Canyon, *U.S.A.* 115 H8
Glen Canyon Dam, *U.S.A.* ... 115 H8
Glen Canyon National
  Recreation Area, *U.S.A.* ... 115 H8
Glen Coe, *U.K.* 14 E3
Glen Cove, *U.S.A.* 111 F11
Glen Garry, *U.K.* 14 D3
Glen Innes, *Australia* 95 D5
Glen Lyon, *U.S.A.* 111 E8
Glen Mor, *U.K.* 14 D4
Glen Moriston, *U.K.* 14 D4
Glen Robertson, *Canada* 111 A10
Glen Spean, *U.K.* 14 E4
Glen Ullin, *U.S.A.* 112 B4
Glénan, Îs. de, *France* 18 E3
Glencoe, *Canada* 110 D3
Glencoe, *S. Africa* 89 D5
Glencoe, *U.S.A.* 112 C7
Glendale, *Ariz., U.S.A.* 115 K7
Glendale, *Calif., U.S.A.* 117 L8
Glendale, *Zimbabwe* 87 F3
Glendive, *U.S.A.* 112 B2
Glendo, *U.S.A.* 112 D2
Glenelg →, *Australia* 95 F3
Glenfield, *U.S.A.* 111 C9
Glengarriff, *Ireland* 15 E2
Glenmont, *U.S.A.* 110 F2
Glenmorgan, *Australia* 95 D4
Glenn, *U.S.A.* 116 F4
Glennallen, *U.S.A.* 100 B5
Glennamaddy, *Ireland* 15 C3
Glenns Ferry, *U.S.A.* 114 E6
Glenore, *Australia* 94 B3
Glenreagh, *Australia* 95 E5
Glenrock, *U.S.A.* 114 E11
Glenrothes, *U.K.* 14 E5
Glens Falls, *U.S.A.* 111 C11
Glenside, *U.S.A.* 111 F9
Glenties, *Ireland* 15 B3
Glenville, *U.S.A.* 108 F5
Glenwood, *Canada* 103 C9
Glenwood, *Ark., U.S.A.* 113 H8
Glenwood, *Iowa, U.S.A.* ... 112 E7
Glenwood, *Minn., U.S.A.* ... 112 C7
Glenwood, *Wash., U.S.A.* ... 116 D5
Glenwood Springs, *U.S.A.* .. 114 G10
Glettinganes, *Iceland* 8 D7
Glifádha, *Greece* 38 D5
Glimåkra, *Sweden* 11 H8
Glina, *Croatia* 29 C13
Glinojeck, *Poland* 45 F7
Gliwice, *Poland* 45 H5
Globe, *U.S.A.* 115 K8
Glodeanu Siliştea, *Romania* . 43 F11
Glodeni, *Moldova* 43 C12
Glödnitz, *Austria* 26 E7
Gloggnitz, *Austria* 26 D8
Głogów, *Poland* 45 G3
Głogówek, *Poland* 45 H4
Glomma →, *Norway* 9 G14
Glorieuses, Is., *Ind. Oc.* 89 A8
Glóssa, *Greece* 38 B5
Glossop, *U.K.* 12 D6
Gloucester, *Australia* 95 E5
Gloucester, *U.K.* 13 F5
Gloucester, *U.S.A.* 111 D14
Gloucester I., *Australia* 94 C4
Gloucester Point, *U.S.A.* ... 108 G7
Gloucestershire □, *U.K.* 13 F5
Głowno, *Poland* 45 G6
Głubczyce, *Poland* 45 H4

Glubokiy, *Russia* 49 F5
Glubokoye = Hlybokaye,
  Belarus 46 E4
Głuchołazy, *Poland* 45 H4
Glücksburg, *Germany* 24 A5
Glückstadt, *Germany* 24 B5
Glukhov = Hlukhiv, *Ukraine* . 47 G7
Glusk, *Belarus* 47 F5
Głuszyca, *Poland* 45 H3
Glyngøre, *Denmark* 11 H2
Gmünd, *Kärnten, Austria* ... 26 E6
Gmünd, *Niederösterreich,*
  Austria 26 C8
Gmunden, *Austria* 26 D6
Gnarp, *Sweden* 10 B11
Gnesta, *Sweden* 10 E11
Gniew, *Poland* 44 E5
Gniewkowo, *Poland* 45 F5
Gniezno, *Poland* 45 F4
Gnjilane, *Kosovo, Yug.* 40 D5
Gnoien, *Germany* 24 B8
Gnosjö, *Sweden* 11 G7
Gnowangerup, *Australia* 93 F2
Go Cong, *Vietnam* 65 G6
Gō-no-ura, *Japan* 55 H4
Goa, *India* 66 M8
Goa □, *India* 66 M8
Goalen Hd., *Australia* 95 F5
Goalpara, *India* 67 F17
Goaltor, *India* 69 H12
Goalundo Ghat, *Bangla.* 69 H13
Goaso, *Ghana* 82 D4
Goat Fell, *U.K.* 14 F3
Goba, *Ethiopia* 81 F4
Goba, *Mozam.* 89 D5
Gobabis, *Namibia* 88 C2
Göbel, *Turkey* 41 F12
Gobi, *Asia* 56 C6
Gobō, *Japan* 55 H7
Gobö, *Sudan* 81 F3
Göçbeyli, *Turkey* 39 B9
Goch, *Germany* 24 D2
Gochas, *Namibia* 88 C2
Godavari →, *India* 67 L13
Godavari Pt., *India* 67 L13
Godbout, *Canada* 103 C6
Godda, *India* 69 G12
Godech, *Bulgaria* 40 C7
Goderich, *Canada* 102 D3
Goderville, *France* 18 C7
Godfrey Ra., *Australia* 93 D2
Godhavn = Qeqertarsuaq,
  Greenland 4 C5
Godhra, *India* 68 H5
Gödöllő, *Hungary* 42 C4
Godoy Cruz, *Argentina* 126 C2
Gods →, *Canada* 102 A1
Gods L., *Canada* 102 B1
Gods River, *Canada* 105 C10
Godthåb = Nuuk, *Greenland* . 101 B14
Godwin Austen = K2, *Pakistan* 69 B7
Goeie Hoop, Kaap die = Good
  Hope, C. of, *S. Africa* 88 E2
Goéland, L. au, *Canada* 102 C4
Goeree, *Neths.* 17 C3
Goes, *Neths.* 17 C3
Goffstown, *U.S.A.* 111 C13
Gogama, *Canada* 102 C3
Gogebic, L., *U.S.A.* 112 B10
Goggetti, *Ethiopia* 81 F4
Gogolin, *Poland* 45 H5
Gogonou, *Benin* 83 C5
Gogra = Ghaghara →, *India* . 69 G11
Gogriâl, *Sudan* 81 F2
Gogti, *Ethiopia* 81 E5
Gohana, *India* 68 E7
Goharganj, *India* 68 H7
Goi →, *India* 68 H6
Goiânia, *Brazil* 125 G9
Goiás, *Brazil* 125 G8
Goiás □, *Brazil* 125 F9
Goio-Erê, *Brazil* 127 A5
Góis, *Portugal* 34 E2
Gojam □, *Ethiopia* 81 E4
Gojeb, Wabi →, *Ethiopia* ... 81 F4
Gojō, *Japan* 55 G7
Gojra, *Pakistan* 68 D5
Gökçeada, *Turkey* 41 F9
Gökçedağ, *Turkey* 39 B10
Gökçen, *Turkey* 39 C9
Gökçeören, *Turkey* 39 C10
Gökçeyazı, *Turkey* 39 B9
Gökırmak →, *Turkey* 72 B6
Gökova, *Turkey* 39 D10
Gökova Körfezi, *Turkey* 39 E9
Göksu →, *Turkey* 72 D6
Göksun, *Turkey* 72 C7
Gokteik, *Burma* 67 H20
Göktepe, *Turkey* 39 D10
Gokurt, *Pakistan* 68 E2
Gola, *India* 69 E9
Golakganj, *India* 69 F13
Golan Heights = Hagolan, *Syria* 75 C4
Gołańcz, *Poland* 45 F4
Goläshkerd, *Iran* 71 E8
Golaya Pristen = Hola Pristan,
  Ukraine 47 J7
Gölbaşı, *Adıyaman, Turkey* .. 72 D7
Gölbaşı, *Ankara, Turkey* 72 C5
Golchikha, *Russia* 4 B12
Golconda, *U.S.A.* 114 F5
Gölcük, *Kocaeli, Turkey* 41 F13
Gölcük, *Niğde, Turkey* 72 C6
Gold, *U.S.A.* 110 E7
Gold Beach, *U.S.A.* 114 E1
Gold Coast, *W. Afr.* 83 E4

Gold Hill, *U.S.A.* 114 E2
Gold River, *Canada* 104 D3
Gołdap, *Poland* 44 D9
Goldberg, *Germany* 24 B8
Golden, *Canada* 104 C5
Golden B., *N.Z.* 91 J4
Golden Gate, *U.S.A.* 114 H2
Golden Hinde, *Canada* 104 D3
Golden Lake, *Canada* 110 A7
Golden Vale, *Ireland* 15 D3
Goldendale, *U.S.A.* 114 D3
Goldfield, *U.S.A.* 115 H5
Goldsand L., *Canada* 105 B8
Goldsboro, *U.S.A.* 109 H7
Goldsmith, *U.S.A.* 113 K3
Goldsworthy, *Australia* 92 D2
Goldthwaite, *U.S.A.* 113 K5
Golegã, *Portugal* 35 F2
Goleniów, *Poland* 44 E1
Golestānak, *Iran* 71 D7
Goleta, *U.S.A.* 117 L7
Golfito, *Costa Rica* 120 E3
Golfo Aranci, *Italy* 30 B2
Gölgeli Dağları, *Turkey* 39 D10
Gölhisar, *Turkey* 39 D11
Goliad, *U.S.A.* 113 L6
Golija, *Montenegro, Yug.* ... 40 C2
Golija, *Serbia, Yug.* 40 C4
Golina, *Poland* 45 F5
Gölköy, *Turkey* 73 B8
Golra, *Pakistan* 68 C5
Golspie, *U.K.* 14 D5
Golub-Dobrzyń, *Poland* 45 E6
Golubac, *Serbia, Yug.* 40 B5
Golyam Perelik, *Bulgaria* ... 41 E8
Golyama Kamchiya →, *Bulgaria* 41 C11
Goma, *Dem. Rep. of the Congo* 86 C2
Gomal Pass, *Pakistan* 68 D3
Gomati →, *India* 69 G10
Gombari, *Dem. Rep. of*
  the Congo 86 B2
Gombe, *Nigeria* 83 C7
Gombe, *Turkey* 39 E11
Gombe □, *Nigeria* 83 C7
Gombe →, *Tanzania* 86 C3
Gombi, *Nigeria* 83 C7
Gomel = Homyel, *Belarus* ... 47 F6
Gomera, *Canary Is.* 37 F2
Gómez Palacio, *Mexico* 118 B4
Gomīshān, *Iran* 71 B7
Gommern, *Germany* 24 C7
Gomogomo, *Indonesia* 63 F8
Gomoh, *India* 67 H15
Gomotartsi, *Bulgaria* 40 B6
Gompa = Ganta, *Liberia* 82 D3
Gomphi, *Greece* 38 B3
Gonābād, *Iran* 71 C8
Gonaïves, *Haiti* 121 C5
Gonâve, G. de la, *Haiti* 121 C5
Gonâve, I. de la, *Haiti* 121 C5
Gonbad-e Kāvūs, *Iran* 71 B7
Gönc, *Hungary* 42 B6
Gonda, *India* 69 F9
Gondal, *India* 68 J4
Gonder, *Ethiopia* 81 E4
Gonder □, *Ethiopia* 81 E4
Gondia, *India* 66 J12
Gondola, *Mozam.* 87 F3
Gondomar, *Portugal* 34 D2
Gondrecourt-le-Château, *France* 19 D12
Gönen, *Balıkesir, Turkey* ... 41 F11
Gönen, *Isparta, Turkey* 39 D12
Gönen →, *Turkey* 41 F11
Gong Xian, *China* 58 C5
Gong'an, *China* 59 B9
Gongcheng, *China* 59 E8
Gongga Shan, *China* 58 C3
Gongguan, *China* 58 G7
Gonghe, *China* 60 C5
Gongola →, *Nigeria* 83 D7
Gongolgon, *Australia* 95 E4
Gongshan, *China* 58 D2
Gongtan, *China* 58 C7
Gongzhuling, *China* 57 C13
Goniadz, *Poland* 44 E9
Goniri, *Nigeria* 83 C7
Gonjo, *China* 58 B2
Gonnesa, *Italy* 30 C1
Gónnos, *Greece* 38 B4
Gonnosfanàdiga, *Italy* 30 C1
Gonzaga, *Phil.* 61 B5
Gonzales, *Calif., U.S.A.* 116 J5
Gonzales, *Tex., U.S.A.* 113 L6
González Chaves, *Argentina* . 126 D3
Good Hope, C. of, *S. Africa* . 88 E2
Gooderham, *Canada* 110 B6
Goodhouse, *S. Africa* 88 D2
Gooding, *U.S.A.* 114 E6
Goodland, *U.S.A.* 112 F4
Goodlow, *Canada* 104 B4
Goodooga, *Australia* 95 D4
Goodsprings, *U.S.A.* 117 K11
Goolgowi, *Australia* 95 E4
Goomalling, *Australia* 93 F2
Goomeri, *Australia* 95 D5
Goonda, *Mozam.* 87 F3
Goondiwindi, *Australia* 95 D5
Goongarrie, L., *Australia* ... 93 F3
Goonyella, *Australia* 94 C4
Goose →, *Canada* 103 B7

Goose Creek, *U.S.A.* 109 J5
Goose L., *U.S.A.* 114 F3
Gop, *India* 66 H6
Gopalganj, *India* 69 F11
Göppingen, *Germany* 25 G5
Gor, *Spain* 35 H8
Góra, *Dolnośląskie, Poland* .. 45 G3
Góra, *Mazowieckie, Poland* . 45 F7
Góra Kalwaria, *Poland* 45 G8
Gorakhpur, *India* 69 F10
Goražde, *Bos.-H.* 42 G3
Gorbatov, *Russia* 48 B6
Gorbea, Peña, *Spain* 32 B2
Gorda, *U.S.A.* 116 K5
Gorda, Pta., *Canary Is.* 37 F2
Gorda, Pta., *Nic.* 120 D3
Gordan B., *Australia* 92 B5
Gördes, *Turkey* 39 C10
Gordon, *U.S.A.* 112 D3
Gordon →, *Australia* 94 G4
Gordon L., *Alta., Canada* ... 105 B6
Gordon L., *N.W.T., Canada* .. 104 A6
Gordonvale, *Australia* 94 B4
Gore, *Ethiopia* 81 F4
Gore, *N.Z.* 91 M2
Gore Bay, *Canada* 102 C3
Görele, *Turkey* 73 B8
Goreme, *Turkey* 72 C6
Gorey, *Ireland* 15 D5
Gorg, *Iran* 71 D8
Gorgān, *Iran* 71 B7
Gorgona, *Italy* 28 E6
Gorgona, I., *Colombia* 124 C3
Gorgora, *Ethiopia* 81 E4
Gorgoram, *Nigeria* 83 C7
Gorham, *U.S.A.* 111 B13
Gori, *Georgia* 49 J7
Goriganga →, *India* 69 E9
Gorinchem, *Neths.* 17 C4
Goris, *Armenia* 73 C12
Goritsy, *Russia* 46 D9
Gorízia, *Italy* 29 C10
Gorj □, *Romania* 43 E8
Gorki = Horki, *Belarus* 46 E6
Gorki = Nizhniy Novgorod,
  Russia 48 B7
Gorkiy = Nizhniy Novgorod,
  Russia 48 B7
Gorkovskoye Vdkhr., *Russia* . 48 B6
Gorlice, *Poland* 45 J8
Görlitz, *Germany* 24 D10
Gorlovka = Horlivka, *Ukraine* . 47 H10
Gorman, *U.S.A.* 117 L8
Gorna Dzhumayo =
  Blagoevgrad, *Bulgaria* 40 D7
Gorna Oryahovitsa, *Bulgaria* . 41 C9
Gornja Radgona, *Slovenia* ... 29 B13
Gornja Tuzla, *Bos.-H.* 42 F3
Gornji Grad, *Slovenia* 29 B11
Gornji Milanovac, *Serbia, Yug.* 40 B4
Gornji Vakuf, *Bos.-H.* 42 G2
Gorno Ablanovo, *Bulgaria* .. 41 C9
Gorno-Altaysk, *Russia* 50 D9
Gorno-Altaysk, *Russia* 50 D9
Gornyatskiy, *Russia* 49 F5
Gornyy, *Saratov, Russia* 48 E9
Gornyy, *Sib., Russia* 54 B6
Gorodenka = Horodenka,
  Ukraine 47 H3
Gorodets, *Russia* 48 B6
Gorodishche = Horodyshche,
  Ukraine 47 H6
Gorodishche, *Russia* 48 D8
Gorodnitsa = Horodnytsya,
  Ukraine 47 G4
Gorodnya = Horodnya, *Ukraine* 47 G6
Gorodok = Haradok, *Belarus* . 46 E5
Gorodok = Horodok, *Ukraine* . 47 H2
Gorodovikovsk, *Russia* 49 G5
Gorokhov = Horokhiv, *Ukraine* 47 G3
Gorokhovets, *Russia* 48 B6
Gorom Gorom, *Burkina Faso* . 83 C4
Goromonzi, *Zimbabwe* 87 F3
Gorong, Kepulauan, *Indonesia* 63 E8
Gorongose →, *Mozam.* 89 C5
Gorongoza, *Mozam.* 87 F3
Gorongoza, Sa. da, *Mozam.* . 87 F3
Gorontalo, *Indonesia* 63 D6
Goronyo, *Nigeria* 83 C6
Górowo Iławeckie, *Poland* .. 44 D7
Gorron, *France* 18 D6
Gorshechnoye, *Russia* 47 G10
Gort, *Ireland* 15 C3
Gortis, *Greece* 36 D6
Góry Bystrzyckie, *Poland* ... 45 H3
Goryachiy Klyuch, *Russia* .. 49 H4
Gorzkowice, *Poland* 45 G6
Gorzów Śląski, *Poland* 45 G5
Gorzów Wielkopolski, *Poland* . 45 F2
Gosford, *Australia* 95 E5
Goshen, *Calif., U.S.A.* 116 J7
Goshen, *Ind., U.S.A.* 108 E3
Goshen, *N.Y., U.S.A.* 111 E10
Goshogawara, *Japan* 54 D10
Goslar, *Germany* 24 D6
Gospič, *Croatia* 29 D12
Gosport, *U.K.* 13 G6
Gossas, *Senegal* 82 C1
Gosse →, *Australia* 94 B1
Gossi, *Mali* 83 B4
Gossinga, *Sudan* 81 F2
Gostivar, *Macedonia* 40 E4
Gostyń, *Poland* 45 G4
Gostynin, *Poland* 45 F6
Göta älv →, *Sweden* 11 G5
Göta kanal, *Sweden* 11 F9
Götaland, *Sweden* 11 G8
Göteborg, *Sweden* 11 G5

Götene, *Sweden* 11 F7
Goteşti, *Moldova* 43 D13
Gotha, *Germany* 24 E6
Gothenburg = Göteborg,
  Sweden 11 G5
Gothenburg, *U.S.A.* 112 E4
Gothèye, *Niger* 83 C5
Gotland, *Sweden* 11 G12
Gotlands län □, *Sweden* 11 G12
Gotō-Rettō, *Japan* 55 H4
Gotse Delchev, *Bulgaria* 40 E7
Gotska Sandön, *Sweden* ... 9 G18
Götsu, *Japan* 55 G6
Gott Pk., *Canada* 104 C4
Göttero, Monte, *Italy* 28 D6
Göttingen, *Germany* 24 D5
Gottwald = Zmiyev, *Ukraine* . 47 H9
Gottwaldov = Zlín, *Czech Rep.* . 27 B10
Goubangzi, *China* 57 D11
Gouda, *Neths.* 17 B4
Goúdhoura, Ákra, *Greece* ... 36 E8
Goudiry, *Senegal* 82 C2
Goudoumaria, *Niger* 83 C7
Gouéké, *Guinea* 82 D3
Gough I., *Atl. Oc.* 2 G9
Gouin, Rés., *Canada* 102 C5
Gouitafla, *Ivory C.* 82 D3
Goulburn, *Australia* 95 E4
Goulburn Is., *Australia* 94 A1
Goulia, *Ivory C.* 82 C3
Goulimine, *Morocco* 78 C3
Goumbou, *Mali* 82 B3
Gouménissa, *Greece* 40 F6
Goundam, *Mali* 82 B4
Goúra, *Greece* 38 D4
Gourbassi, *Mali* 82 C2
Gourdon, *France* 20 D5
Gouré, *Niger* 83 C7
Gourits →, *S. Africa* 88 E3
Gourma-Rharous, *Mali* 83 B4
Goúrnais, *Greece* 36 D7
Gournay-en-Bray, *France* ... 19 C8
Goursi, *Burkina Faso* 82 C4
Gouverneur, *U.S.A.* 111 B9
Gouviá, *Greece* 36 A3
Gouzon, *France* 19 F9
Governador Valadares, *Brazil* . 125 G10
Governor's Harbour, *Bahamas* . 120 A4
Govindgarh, *India* 69 G9
Gowan Ra., *Australia* 94 D4
Gowanda, *U.S.A.* 110 D6
Gower, *U.K.* 13 F3
Gowna, L., *Ireland* 15 C4
Goya, *Argentina* 126 B4
Göyçay, *Azerbaijan* 49 K8
Goyder Lagoon, *Australia* .. 95 D2
Goyllarisquisga, *Peru* 124 F3
Göynük, *Antalya, Turkey* ... 39 E12
Göynük, *Bolu, Turkey* 72 B4
Goz Beïda, *Chad* 79 F10
Goz Regeb, *Sudan* 81 D4
Gozdnica, *Poland* 45 G2
Gozo, *Malta* 36 C1
Graaff-Reinet, *S. Africa* 88 E3
Grabo, *Ivory C.* 82 D3
Grabow, *Germany* 24 B7
Grabów nad Prosną, *Poland* . 45 G5
Gračac, *Croatia* 29 D12
Gračanica, *Bos.-H.* 42 F3
Graçay, *France* 19 E8
Gracias a Dios, C., *Honduras* . 120 D3
Graciosa, I., *Canary Is.* 37 E6
Grad Sofiya □, *Bulgaria* 40 D7
Gradac, *Montenegro, Yug.* .. 40 D3
Gradačac, *Bos.-H.* 42 F3
Gradeška Planina, *Macedonia* . 40 E6
Gradets, *Bulgaria* 41 D10
Gradišče, *Slovenia* 29 B12
Grădiştea de Munte, *Romania* . 43 E8
Grado, *Italy* 29 C10
Grado, *Spain* 34 B4
Grady, *U.S.A.* 113 H3
Graeca, Lacul, *Romania* 43 F11
Grafenau, *Germany* 25 G9
Gräfenberg, *Germany* 25 F7
Grafham Water, *U.K.* 13 E7
Grafton, *Australia* 95 D5
Grafton, *N. Dak., U.S.A.* ... 112 A6
Grafton, *W. Va., U.S.A.* 108 F5
Graham, *Canada* 102 C1
Graham, *U.S.A.* 113 J5
Graham, Mt., *U.S.A.* 115 K9
Graham Bell, Ostrov = Greem-
  Bell, Ostrov, *Russia* 50 A7
Graham I., *Canada* 104 C2
Graham Land, *Antarctica* ... 5 C17
Grahamstown, *S. Africa* 88 E4
Grahamsville, *U.S.A.* 111 E10
Grahovo, *Montenegro, Yug.* . 40 D2
Graie, Alpi, *Europe* 21 C11
Grain Coast, *W. Afr.* 82 E3
Grajaú, *Brazil* 125 E9
Grajaú →, *Brazil* 125 D10
Grajewo, *Poland* 44 E9
Gramada, *Bulgaria* 40 C6
Gramat, *France* 20 D5
Grammichele, *Italy* 31 E7
Grámmos, Óros, *Greece* 40 F4
Grampian, *U.S.A.* 110 F6
Grampian Highlands =
  Grampian Mts., *U.K.* 14 E5
Grampian Mts., *U.K.* 14 E5
Grampians, The, *Australia* .. 95 F3
Gramsh, *Albania* 40 F4
Gran Canaria, *Canary Is.* 37 G4
Gran Chaco, *S. Amer.* 126 B3

P

Pa, Burkina Faso — 82 C4
Pa-an, Burma — 67 L20
Pa Mong Dam, Thailand — 64 D4
Pa Sak →, Thailand — 62 B2
Paamiut, Greenland — 4 C5
Paar →, Germany — 25 G7
Paarl, S. Africa — 88 E2
Pab Hills, Pakistan — 68 F2
Pabbay, U.K. — 14 D1
Pabianice, Poland — 45 G6
Pabna, Bangla. — 67 G16
Pabo, Uganda — 86 B3
Pacaja →, Brazil — 125 D8
Pacaraima, Sa., S. Amer. — 122 C4
Pacasmayo, Peru — 124 E3
Paceco, Italy — 30 E5
Pachhar, India — 68 G7
Pachino, Italy — 31 F8
Pachitea →, Peru — 124 E4
Pachmarhi, India — 69 H8
Pachpadra, India — 66 G8
Pachuca, Mexico — 119 C5
Pacific, Canada — 104 C3
Pacific-Antarctic Ridge, Pac. Oc. — 97 M16
Pacific Grove, U.S.A. — 116 J5
Pacific Ocean, Pac. Oc. — 97 G14
Pacific Rim Nat. Park, Canada — 116 B2
Pacifica, U.S.A. — 116 H4
Pacitan, Indonesia — 63 H14
Packwood, U.S.A. — 116 D5
Pacov, Czech Rep. — 26 B8
Pacy-sur-Eure, France — 18 C8
Padaido, Kepulauan, Indonesia — 63 E9
Padang, Indonesia — 62 E2
Padang Endau, Malaysia — 65 L4
Padangpanjang, Indonesia — 62 E2
Padangsidempuan, Indonesia — 62 D1
Padborg, Denmark — 11 K3
Paddle Prairie, Canada — 104 B5
Paddockwood, Canada — 105 C7
Paderborn, Germany — 24 D4
Padeş, Vf., Romania — 42 E7
Padina, Romania — 43 F12
Padma, India — 69 G11
Pádova, Italy — 29 C8
Padra, India — 68 H5
Padrauna, India — 69 F10
Padre I., U.S.A. — 113 M6
Padrón, Spain — 34 C2
Padstow, U.K. — 13 G3
Padua = Pádova, Italy — 29 C8
Paducah, Ky., U.S.A. — 108 G1
Paducah, Tex., U.S.A. — 113 H4
Padul, Spain — 35 H7
Paengnyŏng-do, S. Korea — 57 F13
Paeroa, N.Z. — 91 G5
Paesana, Italy — 28 D4
Pafúri, Mozam. — 89 C5
Pag, Croatia — 29 D12
Paga, Ghana — 83 C4
Pagadian, Phil. — 61 H5
Pagai Selatan, Pulau, Indonesia — 62 E2
Pagai Utara, Pulau, Indonesia — 62 E2
Pagalu = Annobón, Atl. Oc. — 77 G4
Pagara, India — 69 G9
Pagastikós Kólpos, Greece — 38 B5
Pagatan, Indonesia — 62 E5
Page, U.S.A. — 115 H8
Pagégiai, Lithuania — 44 C8
Pago Pago, Amer. Samoa — 91 B13
Pagosa Springs, U.S.A. — 115 H10
Pagwa River, Canada — 102 B2
Pahala, U.S.A. — 106 J17
Pahang →, Malaysia — 65 L4
Pahiatua, N.Z. — 91 J5
Pahokee, U.S.A. — 109 M5
Pahrump, U.S.A. — 117 J11
Pahute Mesa, U.S.A. — 116 H10
Pai, Thailand — 64 C2
Paicines, U.S.A. — 116 J5
Paide, Estonia — 9 G21
Paignton, U.K. — 13 G4
Paiho, Taiwan — 59 F13
Päijänne, Finland — 9 F21
Pailani, India — 69 G9
Pailin, Cambodia — 64 F4
Paimpol, France — 18 D3
Painan, Indonesia — 62 E2
Painesville, U.S.A. — 110 E3
Paint Hills = Wemindji, Canada — 102 B4
Paint L., Canada — 105 B9
Painted Desert, U.S.A. — 115 J8
Paintsville, U.S.A. — 108 G4
País Vasco □, Spain — 32 C2
Paisley, Canada — 110 B3
Paisley, U.K. — 14 F4
Paisley, U.S.A. — 114 E3
Paita, Peru — 124 E2
Paiva →, Portugal — 34 D2
Paizhou, China — 59 B9
Pajares, Spain — 34 B5
Pajares, Puerto de, Spain — 34 C5
Pajęczno, Poland — 45 G5
Pak Lay, Laos — 64 C3
Pak Phanang, Thailand — 65 H3
Pak Sane, Laos — 64 C4
Pak Song, Laos — 64 E6
Pak Suong, Laos — 58 H4
Pakaur, India — 69 G12
Pakenham, Canada — 111 A8
Pákhnes, Greece — 36 D6
Pakhuis, S. Africa — 88 E2
Pakistan ■, Asia — 68 E4
Pakkading, Laos — 64 C4

Pakokku, Burma — 67 J19
Pakość, Poland — 45 F5
Pakowki L., Canada — 105 D6
Pakpattan, Pakistan — 68 D5
Pakrac, Croatia — 42 E2
Pakruojis, Lithuania — 44 C10
Paks, Hungary — 42 D3
Paktīā □, Afghan. — 66 C6
Paktīkā □, Afghan. — 66 C6
Pakwach, Uganda — 86 B3
Pakxe, Laos — 64 E5
Pal Lahara, India — 69 J11
Pala, Chad — 79 G9
Pala, Dem. Rep. of the Congo — 86 D2
Pala, U.S.A. — 117 M9
Palabek, Uganda — 86 B3
Palacios, U.S.A. — 113 L6
Palafrugell, Spain — 32 D8
Palagiano, Italy — 31 B10
Palagonía, Italy — 31 E7
Palagruža, Croatia — 29 F13
Palaiókastron, Greece — 36 D8
Palaiokhóra, Greece — 36 D5
Pálairos, Greece — 38 C2
Palaiseau, France — 19 D9
Palam, India — 66 K10
Palamás, Greece — 38 B4
Palamòs, Spain — 32 D8
Palampur, India — 68 C7
Palamut, Turkey — 39 C9
Palana, Australia — 94 F4
Palana, Russia — 51 D16
Palanan, Phil. — 61 C5
Palanan Pt., Phil. — 61 C5
Palandri, Pakistan — 69 C5
Palanga, Lithuania — 9 J19
Palangkaraya, Indonesia — 62 E4
Palani Hills, India — 66 P10
Palanpur, India — 68 G5
Palapye, Botswana — 88 C4
Palas, Pakistan — 69 B5
Palas de Rei, Spain — 34 C3
Palashi, India — 69 H13
Palasponga, India — 69 J11
Palatka, Russia — 51 C16
Palatka, U.S.A. — 109 L5
Palau, Italy — 30 A2
Palau ■, Pac. Oc. — 52 J17
Palauk, Burma — 64 F2
Palawan, Phil. — 61 G3
Palayankottai, India — 66 Q10
Palazzo, Pte., France — 21 F12
Palazzo San Gervásio, Italy — 31 B8
Palazzolo Acréide, Italy — 31 E7
Paldiski, Estonia — 9 G21
Pale, Bos.-H. — 42 G3
Paleleh, Indonesia — 63 D6
Palembang, Indonesia — 62 E2
Palencia, Spain — 34 C6
Palencia □, Spain — 34 C6
Palenque, Mexico — 119 D6
Paleokastrítsa, Greece — 36 A3
Paleometokho, Cyprus — 36 D12
Palermo, Italy — 30 D6
Palermo, U.S.A. — 114 G3
Palestina, Chile — 128 A3
Palestine, Asia — 75 D4
Palestine, U.S.A. — 113 K7
Palestrina, Italy — 29 G9
Paletwa, Burma — 67 J18
Palghat, India — 66 P10
Palgrave, Mt., Australia — 92 D2
Pali, India — 68 G5
Palikir, Micronesia — 96 G7
Palinuro, Italy — 31 B8
Palinuro, C., Italy — 31 B8
Palioúrion, Ákra, Greece — 40 G7
Palisades Reservoir, U.S.A. — 114 E8
Paliseul, Belgium — 17 E5
Palitana, India — 68 J4
Palizada, Mexico — 119 D6
Palk Bay, Asia — 66 Q11
Palk Strait, Asia — 66 Q11
Palkānah, Iraq — 70 C5
Palkot, India — 69 H11
Palla Road = Dinokwe, Botswana — 88 C4
Pallanza = Verbánia, Italy — 28 C5
Pallarenda, Australia — 94 B4
Pallasovka, Russia — 48 E8
Pallës, Bishti i, Albania — 40 E3
Pallinup →, Australia — 93 F2
Pallisa, Uganda — 86 B3
Pallu, India — 68 E6
Palm Bay, U.S.A. — 109 L5
Palm Beach, U.S.A. — 109 M6
Palm Coast, U.S.A. — 109 L5
Palm Desert, U.S.A. — 117 M10
Palm Is., Australia — 94 B4
Palm Springs, U.S.A. — 117 M10
Palma, Mozam. — 87 E5
Palma, B. de, Spain — 37 B9
Palma de Mallorca, Spain — 37 B9
Palma del Río, Spain — 35 H5
Palma di Montechiaro, Italy — 31 F7
Palma Soriano, Cuba — 120 B4
Palmares, Brazil — 125 E11
Palmarola, Italy — 30 B5
Palmas, Brazil — 127 B5
Palmas, C., Liberia — 82 E3
Pálmas, G. di, Italy — 30 D1
Palmdale, U.S.A. — 117 L8
Palmeira das Missões, Brazil — 127 B5
Palmeira dos Índios, Brazil — 125 E11
Palmela, Portugal — 35 G2
Palmer, U.S.A. — 100 B5
Palmer →, Australia — 94 B3

Palmer Arch., Antarctica — 5 C17
Palmer Lake, U.S.A. — 112 F2
Palmer Land, Antarctica — 5 D18
Palmerston, Canada — 110 C4
Palmerston, N.Z. — 91 L3
Palmerston North, N.Z. — 91 J5
Palmerton, U.S.A. — 111 F9
Palmetto, U.S.A. — 109 M4
Palmi, Italy — 31 D8
Palmira, Argentina — 126 C2
Palmira, Colombia — 124 C3
Palmyra = Tudmur, Syria — 70 C3
Palmyra, Mo., U.S.A. — 112 F9
Palmyra, N.J., U.S.A. — 111 F9
Palmyra, N.Y., U.S.A. — 110 C7
Palmyra, Pa., U.S.A. — 111 F8
Palmyra Is., Pac. Oc. — 97 G11
Palo Alto, U.S.A. — 116 H4
Palo Verde, U.S.A. — 117 M12
Paloich, Sudan — 81 E3
Palompon, Phil. — 61 F6
Palopo, Indonesia — 63 E6
Palos, C. de, Spain — 33 H4
Palos de la Frontera, Spain — 35 H4
Palos Verdes, U.S.A. — 117 M8
Palos Verdes, Pt., U.S.A. — 117 M8
Pålsboda, Sweden — 10 E9
Palu, Indonesia — 63 E5
Palu, Turkey — 70 B3
Paluke, Liberia — 82 D3
Paluzza, Italy — 29 B10
Palwal, India — 68 E7
Pama, Burkina Faso — 83 C5
Pamanukan, Indonesia — 63 G12
Pamiers, France — 20 E5
Pamir, Tajikistan — 50 F8
Pamlico →, U.S.A. — 109 H7
Pamlico Sd., U.S.A. — 109 H8
Pampa, U.S.A. — 113 H4
Pampa de las Salinas, Argentina — 126 C2
Pampanua, Indonesia — 63 E6
Pampas, Argentina — 126 D3
Pampas, Peru — 124 F4
Pamphylia, Turkey — 72 D4
Pamplona, Colombia — 124 B4
Pamplona, Spain — 32 C3
Pampoenpoort, S. Africa — 88 E3
Pamukçu, Turkey — 39 B9
Pamukkale, Turkey — 39 D11
Pan Xian, China — 58 E5
Pana, U.S.A. — 112 F10
Panabo, Phil. — 61 H6
Panaca, U.S.A. — 115 H6
Panagyurishte, Bulgaria — 41 D8
Panaitan, Indonesia — 63 G11
Panaji, India — 66 M8
Panamá, Panama — 120 E4
Panama ■, Cent. Amer. — 120 E4
Panamá, G. de, Panama — 120 E4
Panama Canal, Panama — 120 E4
Panama City, U.S.A. — 109 K3
Panamint Range, U.S.A. — 117 J9
Panamint Springs, U.S.A. — 117 J9
Panão, Peru — 124 E3
Panaon I., Phil. — 61 F6
Panare, Thailand — 65 J3
Panarea, Italy — 31 D8
Panaro →, Italy — 29 D8
Panay, Phil. — 61 F5
Panay, G., Phil. — 63 B6
Pančevo, Serbia, Yug. — 42 F5
Panch'iao, Taiwan — 59 E13
Panciu, Romania — 43 E12
Pancorbo, Desfiladero, Spain — 34 C7
Pâncota, Romania — 42 D6
Panda, U.S.A. — 89 C5
Pandan, Antique, Phil. — 61 F5
Pandan, Catanduanes, Phil. — 61 D6
Pandegelang, Indonesia — 63 G12
Pandhana, India — 68 J7
Pandharpur, India — 66 L9
Pando, Uruguay — 127 C4
Pando, L. = Hope, L., Australia — 95 D2
Pandokrátor, Greece — 36 A3
Pandora, Costa Rica — 120 E3
Pandrup, Denmark — 11 G3
Panevėžys, Lithuania — 9 J21
Panfilov, Kazakhstan — 50 E8
Panfilovo, Russia — 48 E6
Pang-Long, Burma — 67 H21
Pang-Yang, Burma — 67 H21
Pangah, Tanjung, Indonesia — 63 G15
Pangkajene, Indonesia — 63 E5
Pangkalanbrandan, Indonesia — 62 D1
Pangkalanbuun, Indonesia — 62 E4
Pangkalpinang, Indonesia — 62 E3
Pangnirtung, Canada — 101 B13
Pangong Tso, India — 68 B8
Panguitch, U.S.A. — 115 H7
Pangutaran Group, Phil. — 61 H4
Panhandle, U.S.A. — 113 H4
Pani Mines, India — 68 H5
Pania-Mutombo, Dem. Rep. of the Congo — 86 D1
Panikota I., India — 68 J4
Panipat, India — 68 E7
Panjal Range, India — 68 C7
Panjang, Hon, Vietnam — 65 H4

Panjgur, Pakistan — 66 F4
Panjim = Panaji, India — 66 M8
Panjin, China — 57 D12
Panjinad Barrage, Pakistan — 66 E7
Panjnad →, Pakistan — 68 E4
Panjwai, Afghan. — 68 D1
Pankshin, Nigeria — 83 D6
Panmunjŏm, N. Korea — 57 F14
Panna, India — 69 G9
Panna Hills, India — 69 G9
Pannawonica, Australia — 92 D2
Pano Akil, Pakistan — 68 F3
Pano Lefkara, Cyprus — 36 E12
Pano Panayia, Cyprus — 36 E11
Panorama, Brazil — 127 A5
Pánormon, Greece — 36 D6
Pansemal, India — 68 J6
Panshan = Panjin, China — 57 D12
Panshi, China — 57 C14
Pantanal, Brazil — 124 H7
Pantar, Indonesia — 63 F6
Pante Macassar, E. Timor — 63 F6
Pante Makasar = Pante Macassar, E. Timor — 63 F6
Pantelleria, Italy — 30 F4
Pantón, Spain — 34 C3
Pánuco, Mexico — 119 C5
Panyam, Nigeria — 83 D6
Panyu, China — 59 F9
Panzhihua, China — 58 D3
Páola, Italy — 31 C9
Paola, Malta — 36 D2
Paola, U.S.A. — 112 F7
Paonia, U.S.A. — 115 G10
Paoting = Baoding, China — 56 E8
Paot'ou = Baotou, China — 56 D6
Paoua, C.A.R. — 84 C3
Pápa, Hungary — 42 C2
Papa Stour, U.K. — 14 A7
Papa Westray, U.K. — 14 B6
Papagayo →, Mexico — 119 D5
Papagayo, G. de, Costa Rica — 120 D2
Papakura, N.Z. — 91 G5
Papantla, Mexico — 119 C5
Papar, Malaysia — 62 C5
Pápas, Ákra, Greece — 38 C3
Papeete, Tahiti — 97 J13
Papenburg, Germany — 24 B3
Paphlagonia, Turkey — 72 B5
Paphos, Cyprus — 36 E11
Papien Chiang = Da →, Vietnam — 58 G5
Papigochic →, Mexico — 118 B3
Paposo, Chile — 126 B1
Papoutsa, Cyprus — 36 E12
Papua New Guinea ■, Oceania — 96 H6
Papudo, Chile — 126 C1
Papuk, Croatia — 42 E2
Papun, Burma — 67 K20
Papunya, Australia — 92 D5
Pará = Belém, Brazil — 125 D9
Pará □, Brazil — 125 D8
Paraburdoo, Australia — 92 D2
Paracale, Phil. — 61 D5
Paracatu, Brazil — 125 G9
Paracel Is., S. China Sea — 62 A4
Parachilna, Australia — 95 E2
Parachinar, Pakistan — 68 C4
Paraćin, Serbia, Yug. — 40 C5
Paradas, Spain — 35 H5
Paradela, Spain — 34 C3
Paradhísi, Greece — 36 C10
Paradip, India — 67 J15
Paradise, Calif., U.S.A. — 116 F5
Paradise, Nev., U.S.A. — 117 J11
Paradise →, Canada — 103 B8
Paradise Hill, Canada — 105 C7
Paradise River, Canada — 103 B8
Paradise Valley, U.S.A. — 114 F5
Parado, Indonesia — 63 F5
Paragould, U.S.A. — 113 G9
Paragua →, Venezuela — 124 B6
Paraguaçu →, Brazil — 125 F11
Paraguaçu Paulista, Brazil — 127 A5
Paraguaná, Pen. de, Venezuela — 124 A5
Paraguarí, Paraguay — 126 B4
Paraguarí □, Paraguay — 126 B4
Paraguay ■, S. Amer. — 126 A4
Paraguay →, Paraguay — 126 B4
Paraíba = João Pessoa, Brazil — 125 E12
Paraíba □, Brazil — 125 E11
Paraíba do Sul →, Brazil — 127 A7
Parainen, Finland — 9 F20
Paraíso, Mexico — 119 D6
Parak, Iran — 71 E7
Parakhino Paddubye, Russia — 46 C7
Parakou, Benin — 83 D5
Paralimni, Cyprus — 36 D12
Parálion-Astros, Greece — 38 D4
Paramaribo, Surinam — 125 B7
Paramithiá, Greece — 38 B2
Paramushir, Ostrov, Russia — 51 D16
Paran →, Israel — 75 E4
Paraná, Argentina — 126 C3
Paraná □, Brazil — 127 A5
Paraná →, Argentina — 126 C4
Paranã →, Brazil — 125 F9
Paranaguá, Brazil — 127 B6
Paranaíba, Brazil — 125 G8
Paranaíba →, Brazil — 125 H8
Paranapanema →, Brazil — 127 A5
Paranapiacaba, Serra do, Brazil — 127 A6
Paranas, Phil. — 61 F6
Paranavaí, Brazil — 127 A5
Parang, Maguindanao, Phil. — 63 C6
Parang, Sulu, Phil. — 61 J4

Parângul Mare, Vf., Romania — 43 E8
Paraparaumu, N.Z. — 91 J5
Parapóla, Greece — 38 E5
Paraspóri, Ákra, Greece — 39 F9
Paray-le-Monial, France — 19 F11
Parbati →, Mad. P., India — 68 G7
Parbati →, Raj., India — 68 F7
Parbhani, India — 66 K10
Parchim, Germany — 24 B7
Parczew, Poland — 45 G9
Pardes Hanna-Karkur, Israel — 75 C3
Pardilla, Spain — 34 D7
Pardo →, Bahia, Brazil — 125 G11
Pardo →, Mato Grosso, Brazil — 127 A5
Pardubice, Czech Rep. — 26 A8
Pardubický □, Czech Rep. — 26 B8
Pare, Indonesia — 63 G15
Pare Mts., Tanzania — 86 C4
Parecis, Serra dos, Brazil — 124 F7
Paredes de Nava, Spain — 34 C6
Paren, Russia — 51 C17
Parent, Canada — 102 C5
Parent, L., Canada — 102 C4
Parentis-en-Born, France — 20 D2
Parepare, Indonesia — 63 E5
Parfino, Russia — 46 D6
Párga, Greece — 38 B2
Pargo, Pta. do, Madeira — 37 D2
Pariaguán, Venezuela — 124 B6
Paricutín, Cerro, Mexico — 118 D4
Parigi, Indonesia — 63 E6
Parika, Guyana — 124 B7
Parikkala, Finland — 46 B5
Parima, Serra, Brazil — 124 C6
Parinari, Peru — 124 D4
Pariñas, Pta., S. Amer. — 122 D2
Parincea, Romania — 43 D12
Parintins, Brazil — 125 D7
Pariparit Kyun, Burma — 67 M18
Paris, Canada — 110 C4
Paris, France — 19 D9
Paris, Idaho, U.S.A. — 114 E8
Paris, Ky., U.S.A. — 108 F3
Paris, Tenn., U.S.A. — 109 G1
Paris, Tex., U.S.A. — 113 J7
Paris, Ville de □, France — 19 D9
Parish, U.S.A. — 111 C8
Parishville, U.S.A. — 111 B10
Park, U.S.A. — 116 B4
Park City, U.S.A. — 113 G6
Park Falls, U.S.A. — 112 C9
Park Head, Canada — 110 B3
Park Hills, U.S.A. — 113 G9
Park Range, U.S.A. — 114 G10
Park Rapids, U.S.A. — 112 B7
Park River, U.S.A. — 112 A6
Park Rynie, S. Africa — 89 E5
Parkā Bandar, Iran — 71 E8
Parkano, Finland — 9 E20
Parker, Ariz., U.S.A. — 117 L12
Parker, Pa., U.S.A. — 110 E5
Parker Dam, U.S.A. — 117 L12
Parkersburg, U.S.A. — 108 F5
Parkes, Australia — 95 E4
Parkfield, U.S.A. — 116 K6
Parkhill, Canada — 110 C3
Parkland, U.S.A. — 116 C4
Parkston, U.S.A. — 112 D6
Parksville, Canada — 104 D4
Parla, Spain — 34 E7
Pârliţa, Moldova — 43 C12
Parma, Italy — 28 D7
Parma, Idaho, U.S.A. — 114 E5
Parma, Ohio, U.S.A. — 110 E3
Parma →, Italy — 28 D7
Parnaguá, Brazil — 125 F10
Parnaíba, Brazil — 125 D10
Parnaíba →, Brazil — 122 D6
Parnassós, Greece — 38 C4
Parnis, Greece — 38 C5
Párnon Óros, Greece — 38 D4
Pärnu, Estonia — 9 G21
Paroo →, Australia — 95 E3
Páros, Greece — 39 D7
Parowan, U.S.A. — 115 H7
Parpaillon, France — 21 D10
Parral, Chile — 126 D1
Parras, Mexico — 118 B4
Parrett →, U.K. — 13 F4
Parris I., U.S.A. — 109 J5
Parrsboro, Canada — 103 C7
Parry I., Canada — 110 A4
Parry Is., Canada — 4 B2
Parry Sound, Canada — 102 C4
Parsberg, Germany — 25 F7
Parshall, U.S.A. — 112 B3
Parsnip →, Canada — 104 B4
Parsons, U.S.A. — 113 G7
Parsons Ra., Australia — 94 A2
Partanna, Italy — 30 E5
Parthenay, France — 18 F6
Partinico, Italy — 30 D6
Partizánske, Slovak Rep. — 27 C11
Partridge I., Canada — 102 A2
Paru →, Brazil — 125 D8
Parvān □, Afghan. — 66 B6
Parvatipuram, India — 67 K13
Parvatsar, India — 68 F6
Påryd, Sweden — 11 H9
Parys, S. Africa — 88 D4
Pas, Pta. des, Spain — 37 C7
Pas-de-Calais □, France — 19 B9
Pasada, Spain — 34 B5
Pasadena, Canada — 103 C8
Pasadena, Calif., U.S.A. — 117 L8
Pasadena, Tex., U.S.A. — 113 L7
Pasaje →, Argentina — 126 B3

Paşalimanı, Turkey ... 41 F11
Pasay, Phil. ... 61 D4
Pascagoula, U.S.A. ... 113 K10
Pascagoula →, U.S.A. ... 113 K10
Pașcani, Romania ... 43 C11
Pasco, U.S.A. ... 114 C4
Pasco, Cerro de, Peru ... 124 F3
Pasco I., Australia ... 92 D2
Pascoag, U.S.A. ... 111 E13
Pascua, I. de, Pac. Oc. ... 97 K17
Pasewalk, Germany ... 24 B9
Pasfield L., Canada ... 105 B7
Pasha →, Russia ... 46 B7
Pashmakli = Smolyan, Bulgaria ... 41 E8
Pasinler, Turkey ... 73 C9
Pasir Mas, Malaysia ... 65 J4
Pasir Putih, Malaysia ... 65 K4
Pasirian, Indonesia ... 63 H15
Pasirkuning, Indonesia ... 62 E2
Påskallavik, Sweden ... 11 G10
Paskūh, Iran ... 71 E9
Pasłęk, Poland ... 44 D6
Pasłęka →, Poland ... 44 D6
Pasley, C., Australia ... 93 F3
Pašman, Croatia ... 29 E12
Pasni, Pakistan ... 66 G3
Paso Cantinela, Mexico ... 117 N11
Paso de Indios, Argentina ... 128 E3
Paso de los Libres, Argentina ... 126 B4
Paso de los Toros, Uruguay ... 126 C4
Paso Robles, U.S.A. ... 115 J3
Paspébiac, Canada ... 103 C6
Pasrur, Pakistan ... 68 C6
Passage West, Ireland ... 15 E3
Passaic, U.S.A. ... 111 F10
Passau, Germany ... 25 G9
Passero, C., Italy ... 31 F8
Passo Fundo, Brazil ... 127 B5
Passos, Brazil ... 125 H9
Passow, Germany ... 24 B10
Passy, France ... 21 C10
Pastavy, Belarus ... 9 J22
Pastaza →, Peru ... 124 D3
Pasto, Colombia ... 124 C3
Pastrana, Spain ... 32 E2
Pasuruan, Indonesia ... 63 G15
Pasym, Poland ... 44 E7
Pásztó, Hungary ... 42 C4
Patagonia, Argentina ... 122 H4
Patagonia, Argentina ... 115 L8
Patambar, Iran ... 71 D9
Patan, Gujarat, India ... 66 H8
Patan, Maharashtra, India ... 68 H5
Patani, Indonesia ... 63 D7
Pătârlagele, Romania ... 43 E11
Pataudi, India ... 68 E7
Patchewollock, Australia ... 95 F3
Patchogue, U.S.A. ... 111 F11
Patea, N.Z. ... 91 H5
Pategi, Nigeria ... 83 D6
Patensie, S. Africa ... 88 E3
Paterna, Spain ... 33 F4
Paternion, Austria ... 26 E6
Paternò, Italy ... 31 E7
Pateros, U.S.A. ... 114 B4
Paterson, U.S.A. ... 111 F10
Paterson Ra., Australia ... 92 D3
Pathankot, India ... 68 C6
Pathfinder Reservoir, U.S.A. ... 114 E10
Pathiu, Thailand ... 65 G2
Pathum Thani, Thailand ... 64 E3
Pati, Indonesia ... 63 G14
Patía →, Colombia ... 124 C3
Patiala, Punjab, India ... 68 D7
Patiala, Ut. P., India ... 69 F8
Patine Kouka, Senegal ... 82 C2
Patitírion, Greece ... 38 B5
Patkai Bum, India ... 67 F19
Pátmos, Greece ... 39 D8
Patna, India ... 69 G11
Patnos, Turkey ... 73 C10
Pato Branco, Brazil ... 127 B5
Patonga, Uganda ... 86 B3
Patos, Albania ... 40 F3
Patos, Brazil ... 125 E11
Patos, L. dos, Brazil ... 127 C5
Patos, Brazil ... 125 G9
Patos de Minas, Brazil ... 125 G9
Patos, Río de los →, Argentina ... 126 C2
Patquía, Argentina ... 126 C2
Pátrai, Greece ... 38 C3
Pátraikós Kólpos, Greece ... 38 C3
Patras = Pátrai, Greece ... 38 C3
Patrocínio, Brazil ... 125 G9
Patta, Kenya ... 86 C5
Pattada, Italy ... 30 B2
Pattani, Thailand ... 65 J3
Pattaya, Thailand ... 62 B2
Patten, U.S.A. ... 109 C11
Patterson, Calif., U.S.A. ... 116 H5
Patterson, La., U.S.A. ... 113 L9
Patterson, Mt., U.S.A. ... 116 G7
Patti, Punjab, India ... 68 D6
Patti, Ut. P., India ... 69 G10
Patti, Italy ... 31 D7
Pattoki, Pakistan ... 68 D5
Patton, U.S.A. ... 110 F6
Patuakhali, Bangla. ... 67 H17
Patuanak, Canada ... 105 B7
Patuca →, Honduras ... 120 C3
Patuca, Punta, Honduras ... 120 C3
Pătulele, Romania ... 42 F7
Pátzcuaro, Mexico ... 118 D4
Pau, France ... 20 E3
Pau, Gave de →, France ... 20 E2
Pauillac, France ... 20 C3
Pauk, Burma ... 67 J19
Paul I., Canada ... 103 A7

Paul Smiths, U.S.A. ... 111 B10
Paulatuk, Canada ... 100 B7
Paulhan, France ... 20 E7
Paulis = Isiro, Dem. Rep. of the Congo ... 86 B2
Paulistana, Brazil ... 125 E10
Paulo Afonso, Brazil ... 125 E11
Paulpietersburg, S. Africa ... 89 D5
Pauls Valley, U.S.A. ... 113 H6
Pauma Valley, U.S.A. ... 117 M10
Pauri, India ... 69 D8
Pāveh, Iran ... 70 C5
Pavelets, Russia ... 46 F10
Pavia, Italy ... 28 C6
Pavilion, U.S.A. ... 110 D6
Pavilly, France ... 18 C7
Pāvilosta, Latvia ... 9 H19
Pavlikeni, Bulgaria ... 41 C9
Pavlodar, Kazakhstan ... 50 D8
Pavlograd = Pavlohrad, Ukraine ... 47 H8
Pavlohrad, Ukraine ... 47 H8
Pavlovo, Russia ... 48 C6
Pavlovsk, Russia ... 48 E5
Pavlovskaya, Russia ... 49 G4
Pavlovskiy-Posad, Russia ... 46 E10
Pavullo nel Frignano, Italy ... 28 D7
Pawayan, India ... 69 E9
Pawhuska, U.S.A. ... 113 G6
Pawling, U.S.A. ... 111 E11
Pawnee, U.S.A. ... 113 G6
Pawnee City, U.S.A. ... 112 E6
Pawtucket, U.S.A. ... 111 E13
Paxoi, Greece ... 38 B2
Paximádhia, Greece ... 36 E6
Paxton, Ill., U.S.A. ... 108 E1
Paxton, Nebr., U.S.A. ... 112 E4
Payakumbuh, Indonesia ... 62 E2
Payerne, Switz. ... 25 J2
Payette, U.S.A. ... 114 D5
Paymogo, Spain ... 35 H3
Payne Bay = Kangirsuk, Canada ... 101 B13
Payne L., Canada ... 101 C12
Paynes Find, Australia ... 93 E2
Paynesville, Liberia ... 82 D2
Paynesville, U.S.A. ... 112 C7
Pays de la Loire □, France ... 18 E6
Paysandú, Uruguay ... 126 C4
Payson, U.S.A. ... 115 J8
Paz →, Guatemala ... 120 D1
Paz, B. de la, Mexico ... 118 C2
Pāzanān, Iran ... 71 D6
Pazar, Turkey ... 73 B9
Pazarcık, Turkey ... 72 D7
Pazardzhik, Bulgaria ... 41 D8
Pazarköy, Turkey ... 39 B9
Pazarlar, Turkey ... 39 C11
Pazaryeri, Turkey ... 39 B11
Pazaryolu, Turkey ... 73 B9
Pazin, Croatia ... 29 C10
Pčinja →, Macedonia ... 40 E5
Pe Ell, U.S.A. ... 116 D3
Peabody, U.S.A. ... 111 D14
Peace →, Canada ... 104 B6
Peace Point, Canada ... 104 B6
Peace River, Canada ... 104 B5
Peach Springs, U.S.A. ... 115 J7
Peachland, Canada ... 104 D5
Peachtree City, U.S.A. ... 109 J3
Peak, The = Kinder Scout, U.K. ... 12 D6
Peak District, U.K. ... 12 D6
Peak Hill, N.S.W., Australia ... 95 E4
Peak Hill, W. Austral., Australia ... 93 E2
Peak Ra., Australia ... 94 C4
Peake Cr. →, Australia ... 95 D2
Peal de Becerro, Spain ... 35 H7
Peale, Mt., U.S.A. ... 115 G9
Pearblossom, U.S.A. ... 117 L9
Pearl →, U.S.A. ... 113 K10
Pearl City, U.S.A. ... 106 H16
Pearl Harbor, U.S.A. ... 106 H16
Pearl River, U.S.A. ... 111 E10
Pearsall, U.S.A. ... 113 L5
Peary Land, Greenland ... 4 A6
Pease →, U.S.A. ... 113 H5
Peawanuck, Canada ... 101 C11
Pebane, Mozam. ... 87 F4
Pebas, Peru ... 124 D4
Pebble Beach, U.S.A. ... 116 J5
Peć, Kosovo, Yug. ... 40 D4
Péccioli, Italy ... 28 E7
Pechea, Romania ... 43 E12
Pechenga, Russia ... 50 C4
Pechenizhyn, Ukraine ... 47 H3
Pechiguera, Pta., Canary Is. ... 37 F6
Pechnezhskoye Vdkhr., Ukraine ... 47 G9
Pechora, Russia ... 50 C6
Pechora →, Russia ... 50 C6
Pechorskaya Guba, Russia ... 50 C6
Pecica, Romania ... 42 D6
Pecka, Serbia, Yug. ... 40 B3
Pécora, C., Italy ... 30 C1
Pečory, Russia ... 9 H22
Pecos, U.S.A. ... 113 K3
Pecos →, U.S.A. ... 113 L3
Pécs, Hungary ... 42 D3
Pedder, L., Australia ... 94 G4
Peddie, S. Africa ... 89 E4
Pedernales, Dom. Rep. ... 121 C5
Pedieos →, Cyprus ... 36 D12
Pedirka, Australia ... 95 D2
Pedra Azul, Brazil ... 125 G10
Pedreguer, Spain ... 33 G5
Pedreiras, Brazil ... 125 D10
Pedro Afonso, Brazil ... 125 E9
Pedro Cays, Jamaica ... 120 C4
Pedro de Valdivia, Chile ... 126 A2
Pedro Juan Caballero, Paraguay ... 127 A4

Pedro Muñoz, Spain ... 35 F8
Pedrógão Grande, Portugal ... 34 F2
Pee Dee →, U.S.A. ... 109 J6
Peebinga, Australia ... 95 E3
Peebles, U.K. ... 14 F5
Peekskill, U.S.A. ... 111 E11
Peel, U.K. ... 12 C3
Peel →, Australia ... 95 E5
Peel →, Canada ... 100 B6
Peel Sound, Canada ... 100 A10
Peene →, Germany ... 24 A9
Peera Peera Poolanna L., Australia ... 95 D2
Peerless Lake, Canada ... 104 B6
Peers, Canada ... 104 C5
Pegasus Bay, N.Z. ... 91 K4
Peggau, Austria ... 26 D8
Pegnitz, Germany ... 25 F7
Pegnitz →, Germany ... 25 F6
Pego, Spain ... 33 G4
Pegu, Burma ... 67 L20
Pegu Yoma, Burma ... 67 K20
Pehčevo, Macedonia ... 40 E6
Pehlivanköy, Turkey ... 41 E10
Pehuajó, Argentina ... 126 D3
Pei Xian = Pizhou, China ... 56 G9
Peine, Chile ... 126 A2
Peine, Germany ... 24 C6
Peip'ing = Beijing, China ... 56 E9
Peipus, L. = Chudskoye, Ozero, Russia ... 9 G22
Peissenberg, Germany ... 25 H7
Peitz, Germany ... 24 D10
Peixe, Brazil ... 125 F9
Peixe →, Brazil ... 125 H8
Pek →, Serbia, Yug. ... 40 B5
Pekalongan, Indonesia ... 62 F3
Pekan, Malaysia ... 65 L4
Pekanbaru, Indonesia ... 62 D2
Pekang, Taiwan ... 59 F13
Pekin, U.S.A. ... 112 E10
Peking = Beijing, China ... 56 E9
Péla, Guinea ... 82 D3
Pelabuhan Kelang, Malaysia ... 65 L3
Pelabuhan Ratu, Teluk, Indonesia ... 63 G12
Pelabuhanratu, Indonesia ... 63 G12
Pélagos, Greece ... 38 B6
Pelaihari, Indonesia ... 62 E4
Pelat, Mt., France ... 21 D10
Pełczyce, Poland ... 45 E2
Peleaga, Vf., Romania ... 42 E7
Pelée, Mt., Martinique ... 121 D7
Pelee, Pt., Canada ... 102 D3
Pelee I., Canada ... 102 D3
Pelekech, Kenya ... 86 B4
Peleng, Indonesia ... 63 E6
Pélézi, Ivory C. ... 82 D3
Pelhřimov, Czech Rep. ... 26 B8
Pelican, U.S.A. ... 104 B1
Pelican L., Canada ... 105 C8
Pelican Narrows, Canada ... 105 B8
Peljesac, Croatia ... 29 F14
Pelkosenniemi, Finland ... 8 C22
Pella, Greece ... 40 F6
Pella, S. Africa ... 88 D2
Péla □, Greece ... 40 F6
Pello, Finland ... 8 C21
Pellworm, Germany ... 24 A4
Pelly →, Canada ... 100 B6
Pelly Bay, Canada ... 101 B11
Peloponnese = Pelopónnisos □, Greece ... 38 D4
Pelopónnisos □, Greece ... 38 D4
Peloritani, Monti, Italy ... 31 D8
Pelorus Sd., N.Z. ... 91 J4
Pelotas, Brazil ... 127 C5
Pelotas →, Brazil ... 127 B5
Pelovo, Bulgaria ... 41 C8
Pelplin, Poland ... 44 E5
Pelvoux, Massif du, France ... 21 D10
Pemalang, Indonesia ... 63 G13
Pemanggil, Pulau, Malaysia ... 65 L5
Pematangsiantar, Indonesia ... 62 D1
Pemba, Mozam. ... 87 E5
Pemba, Zambia ... 87 F2
Pemba Channel, Tanzania ... 86 D4
Pemba I., Tanzania ... 86 D4
Pemberton, Australia ... 93 F2
Pemberton, Canada ... 104 C4
Pembina, U.S.A. ... 112 A6
Pembroke, Canada ... 102 C4
Pembroke, U.K. ... 13 F3
Pembrokeshire □, U.K. ... 13 F3
Pen-y-Ghent, U.K. ... 12 C5
Peña, Sierra de la, Spain ... 32 C4
Peña de Francia, Sierra de la, Spain ... 34 E4
Penafiel, Portugal ... 34 D2
Peñafiel, Spain ... 34 D6
Peñaflor, Spain ... 35 H5
Peñalara, Spain ... 34 E7
Penamacôr, Portugal ... 34 E3
Penang = Pinang, Malaysia ... 65 K3
Penápolis, Brazil ... 127 A6
Peñaranda de Bracamonte, Spain ... 34 E5
Peñarroya, Spain ... 32 E4
Peñarroya-Pueblonuevo, Spain ... 35 G5
Penarth, U.K. ... 13 F4
Peñas, C. de, Spain ... 34 B5
Peñas de San Pedro, Spain ... 33 G3
Peñas del Chache, Canary Is. ... 37 E6
Peñasende, Spain ... 34 D5
Pench'i = Benxi, China ... 57 D12

Pend Oreille →, U.S.A. ... 114 B5
Pend Oreille, L., U.S.A. ... 114 C5
Pendálofon, Greece ... 40 F5
Pendembu, Eastern, S. Leone ... 82 D2
Pendembu, Northern, S. Leone ... 82 D2
Pender B., Australia ... 92 C3
Pendik, Turkey ... 41 F13
Pendjari →, Benin ... 83 C5
Pendleton, U.S.A. ... 114 D4
Pendra, India ... 69 H9
Penedo, Brazil ... 125 F11
Penetanguishene, Canada ... 102 D4
Penfield, U.S.A. ... 110 E6
Penge, Kasai-Or., Dem. Rep. of the Congo ... 86 D1
Penge, Sud-Kivu, Dem. Rep. of the Congo ... 86 C2
Penghu, Taiwan ... 59 F12
Penglai, China ... 57 F11
Pengshan, China ... 58 B4
Pengshui, China ... 58 C7
Penguin, Australia ... 94 G4
Pengxi, China ... 58 B5
Pengze, China ... 59 C11
Penhalonga, Zimbabwe ... 87 F3
Peniche, Portugal ... 35 F1
Penicuik, U.K. ... 14 F5
Penida, Indonesia ... 62 F5
Peninnes, Alpes = Pennine, Alpi, Alps ... 25 J3
Peninsular Malaysia □, Malaysia ... 65 L4
Peñíscola, Spain ... 32 E5
Penitente, Serra do, Brazil ... 125 E9
Penkridge, U.K. ... 12 E5
Penmarch, France ... 18 E2
Penmarch, Pte. de, France ... 18 E2
Penn Hills, U.S.A. ... 110 F5
Penn Yan, U.S.A. ... 110 D7
Penna, Punta della, Italy ... 29 F11
Pennant, Canada ... 105 C7
Penne, Italy ... 29 F10
Penner →, India ... 66 M12
Pennine, Alpi, Alps ... 25 J3
Pennines, U.K. ... 12 C5
Pennington, U.S.A. ... 116 F5
Pennington →, Nigeria ... 83 E6
Pennino, Mte., Italy ... 29 E9
Pennsburg, U.S.A. ... 111 F9
Pennsylvania □, U.S.A. ... 108 E7
Penny, Canada ... 104 C4
Peno, Russia ... 46 D7
Penobscot →, U.S.A. ... 109 C11
Penobscot B., U.S.A. ... 109 C11
Penola, Australia ... 95 F3
Penong, Australia ... 93 F5
Penonomé, Panama ... 120 E3
Penrith, Australia ... 95 E5
Penrith, U.K. ... 12 C5
Penryn, U.K. ... 13 G2
Pensacola, U.S.A. ... 109 K2
Pensacola Mts., Antarctica ... 5 E1
Pense, Canada ... 105 C8
Penshurst, Australia ... 95 F3
Penticton, Canada ... 104 D5
Pentland, Australia ... 94 C4
Pentland Firth, U.K. ... 14 C5
Pentland Hills, U.K. ... 14 F5
Penza, Russia ... 48 D7
Penzance, U.K. ... 13 G2
Penzberg, Germany ... 25 H7
Penzhino, Russia ... 51 C17
Penzhinskaya Guba, Russia ... 51 C17
Penzhou, China ... 58 B4
Penzlin, Germany ... 24 B9
Peoria, Ariz., U.S.A. ... 115 K7
Peoria, Ill., U.S.A. ... 112 E10
Pepacton Reservoir, U.S.A. ... 111 D10
Pepani →, S. Africa ... 88 D3
Pepel, S. Leone ... 82 D2
Pera Hd., Australia ... 94 A3
Perabumilih, Indonesia ... 62 E2
Perak □, Malaysia ... 65 K3
Perakhóra, Greece ... 38 C4
Perales de Alfambra, Spain ... 32 E4
Perales del Puerto, Spain ... 34 E4
Pérama, Kérkira, Greece ... 36 A3
Pérama, Kríti, Greece ... 36 D6
Peräpohjola, Finland ... 8 C22
Perast, Montenegro, Yug. ... 40 D2
Percé, Canada ... 103 C7
Perche, France ... 18 D8
Perchtoldsdorf, Austria ... 27 C9
Percival Lakes, Australia ... 92 D4
Percy, France ... 18 D5
Percy Is., Australia ... 94 C5
Perdido, Mte., Spain ... 32 C5
Perdu, Mt. = Perdido, Mte., Spain ... 32 C5
Pereira, Colombia ... 124 C3
Perelazovskiy, Russia ... 49 F6
Perenjori, Australia ... 93 E2
Peresecina, Moldova ... 43 C13
Pereslavl-Zalesskiy, Russia ... 46 D10
Peretu, Romania ... 43 F10
Pereyaslav-Khmelnytskyy, Ukraine ... 47 G6
Pérez, I., Mexico ... 119 C7
Perg, Austria ... 26 C7
Pergamino, Argentina ... 126 C3
Pergau →, Malaysia ... 65 K3
Pérgine Valsugana, Italy ... 29 B8
Pérgola, Italy ... 29 E9
Perham, U.S.A. ... 112 B7
Perhentian, Kepulauan, Malaysia ... 62 C2

Periam, Romania ... 42 D5
Péribonca, Canada ... 103 C5
Péribonca, L., Canada ... 103 B5
Perico, Argentina ... 126 A2
Pericos, Mexico ... 118 B3
Périers, France ... 18 C5
Périgord, France ... 20 D4
Périgueux, France ... 20 C4
Perijá, Sierra de, Colombia ... 124 B4
Peristéra, Greece ... 38 B5
Peristerona →, Cyprus ... 36 D12
Perito Moreno, Argentina ... 128 F2
Perivol = Dragovishtitsa, Bulgaria ... 40 D6
Perkasie, U.S.A. ... 111 F9
Perković, Croatia ... 29 E13
Perlas, Arch. de las, Panama ... 120 E4
Perlas, Punta de, Nic. ... 120 D3
Perleberg, Germany ... 24 B7
Perlez, Serbia, Yug. ... 42 E5
Perm, Russia ... 50 D6
Përmet, Albania ... 40 F4
Pernambuco = Recife, Brazil ... 125 E12
Pernambuco □, Brazil ... 125 E11
Pernatty Lagoon, Australia ... 95 E2
Pernik, Bulgaria ... 40 D7
Peron Is., Australia ... 92 B5
Peron Pen., Australia ... 93 E1
Péronne, France ... 19 C9
Perosa Argentina, Italy ... 28 D4
Perow, Canada ... 104 C3
Perpendicular Pt., Australia ... 95 E5
Perpignan, France ... 20 F6
Perris, U.S.A. ... 117 M9
Perros-Guirec, France ... 18 D3
Perry, Fla., U.S.A. ... 109 K4
Perry, Ga., U.S.A. ... 109 J4
Perry, Iowa, U.S.A. ... 112 E7
Perry, Okla., U.S.A. ... 113 G6
Perryton, U.S.A. ... 113 G4
Perryville, U.S.A. ... 113 G10
Persan, France ... 19 C9
Persberg, Sweden ... 10 E8
Perşembe, Turkey ... 72 B7
Persepolis, Iran ... 71 D7
Pershotravensk, Ukraine ... 47 G4
Persia = Iran ■, Asia ... 71 C7
Persian Gulf = Gulf, The, Asia ... 71 E6
Perstorp, Sweden ... 11 H7
Pertek, Turkey ... 73 C8
Perth, Australia ... 93 F2
Perth, Canada ... 102 D4
Perth, U.K. ... 14 E5
Perth & Kinross □, U.K. ... 14 E5
Perth Amboy, U.S.A. ... 111 F10
Perth-Andover, Canada ... 103 C6
Pertuis, France ... 21 E9
Pertusato, C., France ... 21 G13
Peru, Ind., U.S.A. ... 108 E2
Peru, N.Y., U.S.A. ... 111 B11
Peru ■, S. Amer. ... 124 D4
Peru Basin, Pac. Oc. ... 97 J18
Peru-Chile Trench, Pac. Oc. ... 124 G3
Perúgia, Italy ... 29 E9
Perušić, Croatia ... 29 D12
Pervomaysk, Russia ... 48 C6
Pervomaysk, Ukraine ... 47 H6
Pervouralsk, Russia ... 50 D6
Pésaro, Italy ... 29 E9
Pescadores = Penghu, Taiwan ... 59 F12
Pescara, Italy ... 29 F11
Pescara →, Italy ... 29 F11
Peschanokopskoye, Russia ... 49 G5
Péscia, Italy ... 28 E7
Pescina, Italy ... 29 F10
Peshawar, Pakistan ... 68 B4
Peshkopi, Albania ... 40 E4
Peshtera, Bulgaria ... 41 D8
Peshtigo, U.S.A. ... 108 C2
Peski, Russia ... 48 E6
Pêso da Régua, Portugal ... 34 D3
Pesqueira, Brazil ... 125 E11
Pessac, France ... 20 D3
Pest □, Hungary ... 42 C4
Pestovo, Russia ... 46 C8
Pestravka, Russia ... 48 D9
Péta, Greece ... 38 B3
Petah Tiqwa, Israel ... 75 C3
Petalídhion, Greece ... 38 E3
Petaling Jaya, Malaysia ... 65 L3
Petaloudhes, Greece ... 36 C10
Petaluma, U.S.A. ... 116 G4
Pétange, Lux. ... 17 E5
Petaro, Pakistan ... 68 G3
Petatlán, Mexico ... 118 D4
Petauke, Zambia ... 87 E3
Petawawa, Canada ... 102 C4
Petén Itzá, L., Guatemala ... 120 C2
Peter I.s Øy, Antarctica ... 5 C16
Peter Pond L., Canada ... 105 B7
Peterbell, Canada ... 102 C3
Peterborough, Australia ... 95 E2
Peterborough, Canada ... 102 D4
Peterborough, U.K. ... 13 E7
Peterborough, U.S.A. ... 111 D13
Peterborough □, U.K. ... 13 E7
Peterculter, U.K. ... 14 D6
Peterhead, U.K. ... 14 D7
Peterlee, U.K. ... 12 C6
Petermann Bjerg, Greenland ... 98 B17
Petermann Ranges, Australia ... 92 D4
Petersburg, Alaska, U.S.A. ... 100 C6
Petersburg, Pa., U.S.A. ... 110 F6
Petersburg, Va., U.S.A. ... 108 G7
Petersburg, W. Va., U.S.A. ... 108 F6
Petersfield, U.K. ... 13 F7
Petershagen, Germany ... 24 C4

Petília Policastro, Italy 31 C9
Petit Goâve, Haiti 121 C5
Petit Jardin, Canada 103 C8
Petit Lac Manicouagan, Canada 103 B6
Petit-Mécatina →, Canada 103 B8
Petit-Mécatina, I. du, Canada 103 B8
Petit Saint Bernard, Col du, Italy 21 C10
Petitcodiac, Canada 103 C6
Petite Baleine →, Canada 102 A4
Petite Saguenay, Canada 103 C5
Petitot →, Canada 104 A4
Petitsikapau L., Canada 103 B6
Petlad, India 68 H5
Peto, Mexico 119 C7
Petone, N.Z. 91 J5
Petorca, Chile 126 C1
Petoskey, U.S.A. 108 C3
Petra, Jordan 75 E4
Petra, Spain 37 B10
Petra, Ostrova, Russia 4 B13
Petra Velikogo, Zaliv, Russia .. 54 C6
Petrel = Petrer, Spain 33 G4
Petrella, Monte, Italy 30 A6
Petrer, Spain 33 G4
Petreto-Bicchisano, France .. 21 G12
Petrich, Bulgaria 40 E7
Petrified Forest National Park, U.S.A. 115 J9
Petrijanec, Croatia 29 B13
Petrikov = Pyetrikaw, Belarus . 47 F5
Petrila, Romania 43 E8
Petrinja, Croatia 29 C13
Petrodvorets, Russia 46 C5
Petrograd = Sankt-Peterburg, Russia 46 C6
Petrolândia, Brazil 125 E11
Petrolia, Canada 102 D3
Petrolina, Brazil 125 E10
Petropavl, Kazakstan 50 D7
Petropavlovsk = Petropavl, Kazakstan 50 D7
Petropavlovsk-Kamchatskiy, Russia 51 D16
Petropavlovskiy = Akhtubinsk, Russia 49 F8
Petrópolis, Brazil 127 A7
Petroşani, Romania 43 E8
Petrova Gora, Croatia 29 C12
Petrovac, Montenegro, Yug. .. 40 D2
Petrovac, Serbia, Yug. 40 B5
Petrovaradin, Serbia, Yug. ... 42 E4
Petrovsk, Russia 48 D7
Petrovsk-Zabaykalskiy, Russia . 51 D11
Petrovskaya, Russia 47 K9
Petrovskoye = Svetlograd, Russia 49 H6
Petrozavodsk, Russia 46 B8
Petrus Steyn, S. Africa 89 D4
Petrusburg, S. Africa 88 D4
Petzeck, Austria 26 E5
Peumo, Chile 126 C1
Peureulak, Indonesia 62 D1
Pevek, Russia 51 C18
Peveragno, Italy 28 D4
Peyrehorade, France 20 E2
Peyruis, France 21 D9
Pézenas, France 20 E7
Pezinok, Slovak Rep. 27 C10
Pfaffenhofen, Germany 25 G7
Pfarrkirchen, Germany 25 G8
Pfeffenhausen, Germany 25 G7
Pforzheim, Germany 25 G4
Pfullendorf, Germany 25 H5
Pfungstadt, Germany 25 F4
Phagwara, India 66 D9
Phaistós, Greece 36 D6
Phala, Botswana 88 C4
Phalera = Phulera, India 68 F6
Phalodi, India 68 F5
Phalsbourg, France 19 D14
Phan, Thailand 64 C2
Phan Rang, Vietnam 65 G7
Phan Ri = Hoa Da, Vietnam .. 65 G7
Phan Thiet, Vietnam 65 G7
Phanae, Greece 39 C7
Phanat Nikhom, Thailand 64 F3
Phangan, Ko, Thailand 65 H3
Phangnga, Thailand 65 H2
Phanom Sarakham, Thailand .. 64 F3
Phaphund, India 69 F8
Pharenda, India 69 F10
Pharr, U.S.A. 113 M5
Phatthalung, Thailand 65 J3
Phayao, Thailand 64 C2
Phelps, U.S.A. 110 D7
Phelps L., Canada 105 B8
Phenix City, U.S.A. 109 J3
Phet Buri, Thailand 64 F2
Phetchabun, Thailand 64 D3
Phetchabun, Thiu Khao, Thailand 64 E3
Phetchaburi = Phet Buri, Thailand 64 F2
Phi Phi, Ko, Thailand 65 J2
Phiafay, Laos 64 E6
Phibun Mangsahan, Thailand .. 64 E5
Phichai, Thailand 64 D3
Phichit, Thailand 64 D3
Philadelphia, Miss., U.S.A. ... 113 J10
Philadelphia, N.Y., U.S.A. ... 111 B9
Philadelphia, Pa., U.S.A. ... 111 G9
Philip, U.S.A. 112 C4
Philippeville, Belgium 17 D4
Philippi, Greece 41 E8
Philippi, U.S.A. 108 F5
Philippi L., Australia 94 C2
Philippines ■, Asia 61 F5

Philippolis, S. Africa 88 E4
Philippopolis = Plovdiv, Bulgaria 41 D8
Philipsburg, Canada 111 A11
Philipsburg, Mont., U.S.A. ... 114 C7
Philipsburg, Pa., U.S.A. 110 F6
Philipstown = Daingean, Ireland 15 C4
Philipstown, S. Africa 88 E3
Phillip I., Australia 95 F4
Phillips, U.S.A. 112 C9
Phillipsburg, Kans., U.S.A. ... 112 F5
Phillipsburg, N.J., U.S.A. ... 111 F9
Philmont, U.S.A. 111 D11
Philomath, U.S.A. 114 D2
Phimai, Thailand 64 E4
Phitsanulok, Thailand 64 D3
Phnom Dangrek, Thailand ... 62 B2
Phnom Penh, Cambodia 65 G5
Phnom Penh = Phnom Penh, Cambodia 65 G5
Phoenicia, U.S.A. 111 D10
Phoenix, Ariz., U.S.A. 115 K7
Phoenix, N.Y., U.S.A. 111 C8
Phoenix Is., Kiribati 96 H10
Phoenixville, U.S.A. 111 F9
Phon, Thailand 64 E4
Phon Tiou, Laos 64 D5
Phong →, Thailand 64 D4
Phong Saly, Laos 58 G4
Phong Tho, Vietnam 64 A4
Phonhong, Laos 64 C4
Phonum, Thailand 65 H2
Phosphate Hill, Australia 94 C2
Photharam, Thailand 64 F2
Phra Nakhon Si Ayutthaya, Thailand 64 E3
Phra Thong, Ko, Thailand 65 H2
Phrae, Thailand 64 C3
Phrom Phiram, Thailand 64 D3
Phrygia, Turkey 72 C4
Phu Dien, Vietnam 64 C5
Phu Loi, Laos 64 B4
Phu Ly, Vietnam 58 G5
Phu Quoc, Dao, Vietnam 65 G4
Phu Tho, Vietnam 58 G5
Phuc Yen, Vietnam 58 G5
Phuket, Thailand 65 J2
Phuket, Ko, Thailand 65 J2
Phul, India 68 D6
Phulad, India 68 G5
Phulchari, Bangla. 69 G13
Phulera, India 68 F6
Phulpur, India 69 G10
Phun Phin, Thailand 65 H2
Piacenza, Italy 28 C6
Pian Cr. →, Australia 95 E4
Piana, France 21 F12
Pianella, Italy 29 F11
Pianosa, Puglia, Italy 29 F12
Pianosa, Toscana, Italy 28 F7
Piapot, Canada 105 D7
Pias, Portugal 35 G3
Piaseczno, Poland 45 F8
Piaski, Poland 45 G9
Piastów, Poland 45 F7
Piatra, Romania 43 G10
Piatra Neamţ, Romania 43 D11
Piatra Olt, Romania 43 F9
Piauí □, Brazil 125 E10
Piauí →, Brazil 125 E10
Piave →, Italy 29 C9
Piazza Ármerina, Italy 31 E7
Pibor →, Sudan 81 F3
Pibor Post, Sudan 81 F3
Picardie, France 19 C10
Picardie, Plaine de, France .. 19 C9
Picardy = Picardie, France ... 19 C10
Picayune, U.S.A. 113 K10
Picerno, Italy 31 B8
Pichhor, India 69 G8
Pichilemu, Chile 126 C1
Pichor, India 68 G8
Pickerel L., Canada 102 C1
Pickering, U.K. 12 C7
Pickering, Vale of, U.K. 12 C7
Pickle Lake, Canada 102 B1
Pickwick L., U.S.A. 109 H1
Pico Truncado, Argentina ... 128 F3
Picos, Brazil 125 E10
Picton, Australia 95 E5
Picton, Canada 102 D4
Picton, N.Z. 91 J5
Pictou, Canada 103 C7
Picture Butte, Canada 104 D6
Picún Leufú, Argentina 128 D3
Pidurutalagala, Sri Lanka .. 66 R12
Piechowice, Poland 45 H2
Piedmont, Ala., U.S.A. 109 J3
Piedmont = Piemonte □, Italy .. 28 D5
Piedmont, S.C., U.S.A. 107 D10
Piedmont Matese, Italy 31 A7
Piedra →, Spain 32 D3
Piedrabuena, Spain 35 G6
Piedrahita, Spain 34 E5
Piedralaves, Spain 34 E6
Piedras Blancas, Spain 34 B5
Piedras Negras, Mexico 118 B4
Piekary Śląskie, Poland 45 H5
Pieksämäki, Finland 9 E22
Piemonte □, Italy 28 D5
Pienaarsrivier, S. Africa 89 D4
Pieniężno, Poland 44 D7
Pieńsk, Poland 45 G2
Piercefield, U.S.A. 111 B10
Pierceland, Canada 105 C7
Piería □, Greece 40 F6
Pierpont, U.S.A. 110 E4
Pierre, U.S.A. 112 C4

Pierre-Buffière, France 20 C5
Pierre-de-Bresse, France 19 F12
Pierre E. Trudeau, Mt. = Logan, Mt., Canada 100 B5
Pierrefontaine-les-Varans, France 19 E13
Pierrefort, France 20 D6
Pierrelatte, France 21 D8
Piešťany, Slovak Rep. 27 C10
Piesting →, Austria 27 C9
Pieszyce, Poland 45 H3
Piet Retief, S. Africa 89 D5
Pietarsaari, Finland 8 E20
Pietermaritzburg, S. Africa ... 89 D5
Pietersburg, S. Africa 89 C4
Pietragalla, Italy 31 B8
Pietrasanta, Italy 28 E7
Pietrosul, Vf., Maramureş, Romania 43 C9
Pietrosul, Vf., Suceava, Romania 43 C10
Pieve di Cadore, Italy 29 B9
Pieve di Teco, Italy 28 D4
Pievepélago, Italy 28 D7
Pigadhítsa, Greece 40 G5
Pigeon L., Canada 110 B6
Piggott, U.S.A. 113 G9
Pigna, Italy 28 E4
Pigüe, Argentina 126 D3
Pihani, India 69 F9
Pihlajavesi, Finland 9 F23
Pijijiapan, Mexico 119 D6
Pikalevo, Russia 46 C8
Pikangikum Berens, Canada ... 105 C10
Pikes Peak, U.S.A. 112 F2
Piketberg, S. Africa 88 E2
Pikeville, U.S.A. 108 G4
Pikou, China 57 E12
Pikwitonei, Canada 105 B9
Piła, Poland 45 E3
Pila, Spain 33 G3
Pilaía, Greece 40 F6
Pilani, India 68 E6
Pilar, Paraguay 126 B4
Pilar de la Horadada, Spain ... 33 H4
Pilawa, Poland 45 G8
Pilaya →, Bolivia 124 H6
Pilbara, Australia 92 D2
Pilcomayo →, Paraguay 126 B4
Pilgrim's Rest, S. Africa 89 C5
Pilgrimstad, Sweden 10 B9
Píli, Greece 39 E9
Pilibhit, India 69 E8
Pilica →, Poland 45 G8
Pilion, Greece 38 B5
Pilis, Hungary 42 C4
Pilisvörösvár, Hungary 42 C3
Pilkhawa, India 68 E7
Pilliga, Australia 95 E4
Pílos, Greece 38 E3
Pilot Mound, Canada 105 D9
Pilot Point, U.S.A. 113 J6
Pilot Rock, U.S.A. 114 D4
Pilsen = Plzeň, Czech Rep. ... 26 B6
Pilštanj, Slovenia 29 B12
Piltene, Latvia 44 A8
Pilzno, Poland 45 J8
Pima, U.S.A. 115 K9
Pimba, Australia 95 E2
Pimenta Bueno, Brazil 124 F6
Pimentel, Peru 124 E3
Pina de Ebro, Spain 32 D4
Pinamalayan, Phil. 61 E4
Pinang, Malaysia 65 K3
Pinar, C. des, Spain 37 B10
Pinar del Río, Cuba 120 B3
Pınarbaşı, Çanakkale, Turkey . 39 B8
Pınarbaşı, Kayseri, Turkey ... 72 C7
Pınarhisar, Turkey 41 E11
Pinatubo, Mt., Phil. 61 D3
Pincehely, Hungary 42 D3
Pinchang, China 58 B6
Pincher Creek, Canada 104 D6
Pinchi L., Canada 104 C4
Pinckneyville, U.S.A. 112 F10
Pindar, Australia 93 E2
Pindi Gheb, Pakistan 68 C5
Pindiga, Nigeria 83 D7
Pindos Óros, Greece 38 B3
Pindus Mts. = Pindos Óros, Greece 38 B3
Pine →, B.C., Canada 104 B4
Pine →, Sask., Canada 105 B7
Pine, U.S.A. 103 C9
Pine Bluff, U.S.A. 113 H9
Pine Bluffs, U.S.A. 112 E2
Pine City, U.S.A. 112 C8
Pine Cr. →, U.S.A. 110 E7
Pine Creek, Australia 92 B5
Pine Falls, Canada 105 C9
Pine Flat Res., U.S.A. 116 J7
Pine Grove, U.S.A. 111 F8
Pine Pass, Canada 104 B4
Pine Point, Canada 104 A6
Pine Ridge, U.S.A. 112 D3
Pine River, Canada 105 C8
Pine River, U.S.A. 112 B7
Pine Valley, U.S.A. 117 N10
Pinecrest, U.S.A. 116 G6
Pineda de Mar, Spain 32 D7
Pinedale, Calif., U.S.A. 116 J7
Pinedale, Wyo., U.S.A. 114 E9
Pinega →, Russia 50 C5
Pinehill, Australia 94 C4
Pinehouse L., Canada 105 B7
Pineimuta →, Canada 102 B1

Pinerolo, Italy 28 D4
Pineto, Italy 29 F11
Pinetop, U.S.A. 115 J9
Pinetown, S. Africa 89 D5
Pineville, U.S.A. 113 K8
Ping →, Thailand 64 E3
Pingaring, Australia 93 F2
Pingba, China 58 D6
Pingbian, China 58 F4
Pingchuan, China 58 D3
Pingding, China 56 F7
Pingdingshan, China 56 H7
Pingdong, Taiwan 59 F13
Pingdu, China 57 F10
Pingelly, Australia 93 F2
Pingguo, China 58 F6
Pinghe, China 59 E11
Pinghu, China 59 B13
Pingjiang, China 59 C9
Pingle, China 59 E8
Pingli, China 58 A7
Pingliang, China 56 G4
Pinglu, China 56 E7
Pingluo, China 56 E4
Pingnan, Fujian, China 59 D12
Pingnan, Guangxi Zhuangzu, China 59 F8
Pingquan, China 57 D10
Pingrup, Australia 93 F2
Pingshan, China 58 C5
Pingtan, China 59 E12
Pingtang, China 58 E6
P'ingtung, Taiwan 59 F13
Pingwu, China 56 H3
Pingxiang, Guangxi Zhuangzu, China 58 F6
Pingxiang, Jiangxi, China ... 59 D9
Pingyao, China 56 F7
Pingyi, China 57 G9
Pingyin, China 56 F9
Pingyuan, Guangdong, China .. 59 E10
Pingyuan, Shandong, China ... 56 F9
Pingyuanjie, China 58 F4
Pinhal, Brazil 127 A6
Pinhal Novo, Portugal 35 G2
Pinheiro, Brazil 125 D9
Pinheiro Machado, Brazil ... 127 C5
Pinhel, Portugal 34 E3
Pini, Indonesia 62 D1
Piniós →, Ilía, Greece 38 D3
Piniós →, Tríkkala, Greece .. 38 B4
Pinjarra, Australia 93 F2
Pink Mountain, Canada 104 B4
Pinkafeld, Austria 27 D9
Pinnacles, U.S.A. 116 J5
Pinnaroo, Australia 95 F3
Pinneberg, Germany 24 B5
Pínnes, Ákra, Greece 41 F8
Pinon Hills, U.S.A. 117 L9
Pinos, Mexico 118 C4
Pinos, Mt., U.S.A. 117 L7
Pinos Pt., U.S.A. 115 H3
Pinos Puente, Spain 35 H7
Pinotepa Nacional, Mexico ... 119 D5
Pinrang, Indonesia 63 E5
Pins, Pte. aux, Canada 110 D3
Pinsk, Belarus 47 F4
Pintados, Chile 124 H5
Pinyang, China 59 D13
Pinyug, Russia 50 C5
Pioche, U.S.A. 115 H6
Piombino, Italy 28 F7
Piombino, Canale di, Italy ... 28 F7
Pioner, Ostrov, Russia 51 B10
Pionki, Poland 45 G8
Piorini, L., Brazil 124 D6
Piotrków Trybunalski, Poland . 45 G6
Piove di Sacco, Italy 29 C9
Pīp, Iran 71 E9
Pipar, India 68 F5
Pipar Road, India 68 F5
Piparia, Mad. P., India 68 H8
Piparia, Mad. P., India 68 J7
Pipéri, Greece 38 B6
Pipestone, U.S.A. 112 D6
Pipestone →, Canada 102 B2
Pipestone Cr. →, Canada ... 105 D8
Pipmuacan, Rés., Canada ... 103 C5
Pippingarra, Australia 92 D2
Pipriac, France 18 E5
Piqua, U.S.A. 108 E3
Piquiri →, Brazil 127 A5
Pīr Sohrāb, Iran 71 E9
Pira, Benin 83 D5
Piracicaba, Brazil 127 A6
Piracuruca, Brazil 125 D10
Piræus = Piraiévs, Greece ... 38 D5
Pirajuí, Brazil 127 A6
Piram I., India 68 J5
Piran, Slovenia 29 C10
Pirané, Argentina 126 B4
Pirano = Piran, Slovenia ... 29 C10
Pirapora, Brazil 125 G10
Pirawa, India 68 G7
Pirdop, Bulgaria 41 D8
Pírgos, Ilía, Greece 38 D3
Pírgos, Kríti, Greece 39 F7
Piribebuy, Paraguay 126 B4
Pirimapun, Indonesia 63 F9
Pirin Planina, Bulgaria 40 E7
Pííneos = Pyrénées, Europe .. 20 F4
Piripiri, Brazil 125 D10

Pirmasens, Germany 25 F3
Pirna, Germany 24 E9
Pirot, Serbia, Yug. 40 C6
Piru, Indonesia 63 E7
Piru, U.S.A. 117 L8
Piryatin = Pyryatyn, Ukraine .. 47 G7
Piryí, Greece 39 C7
Pisa, Italy 28 E7
Pisa →, Poland 45 E8
Pisagne, Italy 28 C7
Pisagua, Chile 124 G4
Pisarovina, Croatia 29 C12
Pisco, Peru 124 F3
Piscu, Romania 43 E12
Písek, Czech Rep. 26 B7
Pishan, China 60 C2
Pishin, Iran 71 E9
Pishin, Pakistan 68 D2
Pishin Lora →, Pakistan ... 68 E1
Pisidia, Turkey 72 D4
Pising, Indonesia 63 F6
Pismo Beach, U.S.A. 117 K6
Piso, L., Liberia 82 D2
Pissila, Burkina Faso 83 C4
Pissis, Cerro, Argentina ... 126 B2
Pissos, France 20 D3
Pissouri, Cyprus 36 E11
Pisticci, Italy 31 B9
Pistóia, Italy 28 E7
Pistol B., Canada 105 A10
Pisuerga →, Spain 34 D6
Pisz, Poland 44 E8
Pit →, U.S.A. 114 F2
Pita, Guinea 82 C2
Pitarpunga, L., Australia ... 95 E3
Pitcairn I., Pac. Oc. 97 K14
Pite älv →, Sweden 8 D19
Piteå, Sweden 8 D19
Piterka, Russia 48 E8
Piteşti, Romania 43 F9
Pithapuram, India 67 L13
Pithara, Australia 93 F2
Píthion, Greece 41 E10
Pithiviers, France 19 D9
Pithoragarh, India 69 E9
Pithoro, Pakistan 68 G3
Pitigliano, Italy 29 F8
Pitkyaranta, Russia 46 B6
Pitlochry, U.K. 14 E5
Pitsilia □, Cyprus 36 E12
Pitt I., Canada 104 C3
Pittsburg, Calif., U.S.A. ... 116 G5
Pittsburg, Kans., U.S.A. ... 113 G7
Pittsburg, Tex., U.S.A. ... 113 J7
Pittsburgh, U.S.A. 110 F5
Pittsfield, Ill., U.S.A. ... 112 F9
Pittsfield, Maine, U.S.A. ... 109 C11
Pittsfield, Mass., U.S.A. ... 111 D11
Pittsfield, N.H., U.S.A. ... 111 C13
Pittston, U.S.A. 111 E9
Pittsworth, Australia 95 D5
Pituri →, Australia 94 C2
Piura, Peru 124 E2
Piva →, Montenegro, Yug. ... 40 C2
Piwniczna, Poland 45 J7
Pixley, U.S.A. 116 K7
Piyai, Greece 38 B3
Pizarra, Spain 35 J6
Pizhou, China 56 G9
Pizzo, Italy 31 D9
Placentia, Canada 103 C9
Placentia B., Canada 103 C9
Placer, Masbate, Phil. 61 F5
Placer, Surigao N., Phil. ... 61 G6
Placerville, U.S.A. 116 G6
Placetas, Cuba 120 B4
Plačkovica, Macedonia 40 E6
Plainfield, N.J., U.S.A. ... 111 F10
Plainfield, Ohio, U.S.A. ... 110 F3
Plainfield, Vt., U.S.A. ... 111 B12
Plains, Mont., U.S.A. 114 C6
Plains, Tex., U.S.A. 113 J3
Plainview, Nebr., U.S.A. ... 112 D6
Plainview, Tex., U.S.A. ... 113 H4
Plainwell, U.S.A. 108 D3
Plaisance, France 20 E4
Plaistow, U.S.A. 111 D13
Pláka, Greece 39 B7
Pláka, Ákra, Greece 36 D8
Plakenska Planina, Macedonia . 40 E5
Planá, Czech Rep. 26 B5
Plana Cays, Bahamas 121 B5
Planada, U.S.A. 116 H6
Plancoët, France 18 D4
Plandište, Serbia, Yug. 42 E6
Plano, U.S.A. 113 J6
Plant City, U.S.A. 109 M4
Plaquemine, U.S.A. 113 K9
Plasencia, Spain 34 E4
Plaški, Croatia 29 C12
Plaster City, U.S.A. 117 N11
Plaster Rock, Canada 103 C6
Plastun, Russia 54 B8
Plasy, Czech Rep. 26 B6
Plata, Río de la, S. Amer. ... 126 C4
Plátani →, Italy 30 E6
Plátanos, Greece 36 D5
Plateau □, Nigeria 83 D6
Platí, Ákra, Greece 39 D7
Platte →, U.S.A. 112 D5
Platte, U.S.A. 112 D5
Platte →, Mo., U.S.A. ... 112 F7
Platteville, U.S.A. 112 D9
Plattling, Germany 25 G8
Plattsburgh, U.S.A. 111 B11
Plattsmouth, U.S.A. 112 E7
Plau, Germany 24 B8

Plauen, *Germany*	24	E8
Plauer See, *Germany*	24	B8
Plav, *Montenegro, Yug.*	40	D3
Plavinas, *Latvia*	9	H21
Plavnica, *Montenegro, Yug.*	40	D3
Plavno, *Croatia*	29	D13
Plavsk, *Russia*	46	F9
Playa Blanca, *Canary Is.*	37	F6
Playa Blanca Sur, *Canary Is.*	37	F6
Playa de las Americas, *Canary Is.*	37	F3
Playa de Mogán, *Canary Is.*	37	G4
Playa del Inglés, *Canary Is.*	37	G4
Playa Esmerelda, *Canary Is.*	37	F5
Playgreen L., *Canada*	105	C9
Pleasant Bay, *Canada*	103	C7
Pleasant Hill, *U.S.A.*	116	H4
Pleasant Mount, *U.S.A.*	111	E9
Pleasanton, *Calif., U.S.A.*	116	H5
Pleasanton, *Tex., U.S.A.*	113	L5
Pleasantville, *N.J., U.S.A.*	108	F8
Pleasantville, *Pa., U.S.A.*	110	E5
Pléaux, *France*	20	C6
Plei Ku, *Vietnam*	64	F7
Plélan-le-Grand, *France*	18	D4
Pléneuf-Val-André, *France*	18	D4
Plenița, *Romania*	43	F8
Plenty →, *Australia*	94	C2
Plenty, B. of, *N.Z.*	91	G6
Plentywood, *U.S.A.*	112	A2
Plérin, *France*	18	D4
Plessisville, *Canada*	103	C5
Plestin-les-Grèves, *France*	18	D3
Pleszew, *Poland*	45	G4
Pleternica, *Croatia*	42	E2
Plétipi, L., *Canada*	103	B5
Pleven, *Bulgaria*	41	C8
Plevlja, *Montenegro, Yug.*	40	C3
Plevna, *Canada*	110	B8
Pljesevica, *Croatia*	29	D12
Ploaghe, *Italy*	30	B1
Ploče, *Croatia*	29	E14
Płock, *Poland*	45	F6
Plöckenpass, *Italy*	29	B9
Plöckenstein, *Germany*	25	G9
Ploemeur, *France*	18	E3
Ploërmel, *France*	18	E4
Ploiești, *Romania*	43	F11
Plomárion, *Greece*	39	C8
Plombières-les-Bains, *France*	19	E13
Plomin, *Croatia*	29	C11
Plön, *Germany*	24	A6
Plonge, Lac la, *Canada*	105	B7
Płońsk, *Poland*	45	F7
Plopeni, *Romania*	43	E10
Plopișului, Munții, *Romania*	42	C7
Płoty, *Poland*	44	E2
Plouaret, *France*	18	D3
Plouay, *France*	18	E3
Ploučnice →, *Czech Rep.*	26	A7
Ploudalmézeau, *France*	18	D2
Plouescat, *France*	18	D2
Plougasnou, *France*	18	D3
Plougastel-Daoulas, *France*	18	D2
Plouguerneau, *France*	18	D2
Plouha, *France*	18	D4
Plouhinec, *France*	18	E2
Plovdiv, *Bulgaria*	41	D8
Plovdiv □, *Bulgaria*	41	D8
Plum, *U.S.A.*	110	F5
Plum I., *U.S.A.*	111	E12
Plumas, *U.S.A.*	116	F7
Plummer, *U.S.A.*	114	C5
Plumtree, *Zimbabwe*	87	G2
Plungė, *Lithuania*	9	J19
Pluvigner, *France*	18	E3
Plymouth, *U.K.*	13	G3
Plymouth, *Calif., U.S.A.*	116	G6
Plymouth, *Ind., U.S.A.*	108	E2
Plymouth, *Mass., U.S.A.*	111	E14
Plymouth, *N.C., U.S.A.*	109	H7
Plymouth, *N.H., U.S.A.*	111	C13
Plymouth, *Pa., U.S.A.*	111	E9
Plymouth, *Wis., U.S.A.*	108	D2
Plynlimon = Pumlumon Fawr, *U.K.*	13	E4
Plyusa, *Russia*	46	C5
Plyusa →, *Russia*	46	C5
Plyussa = Plyusa, *Russia*	46	C5
Plyussa →, = Plyusa →, *Russia*	46	C5
Plzeň, *Czech Rep.*	26	B6
Plzeňský □, *Czech Rep.*	26	B6
Pniewy, *Poland*	45	F3
Pô, *Burkina Faso*	83	C4
Po →, *Italy*	29	D9
Po, Foci del, *Italy*	29	D9
Po Hai = Bo Hai, *China*	57	E10
Pobé, *Benin*	83	D5
Pobé, *Burkina Faso*	83	C4
Pobeda, *Russia*	51	C15
Pobedy, Pik, *Kyrgyzstan*	50	E8
Pobiedziska, *Poland*	45	F4
Pobla de Segur, *Spain*	32	C5
Pobladura del Valle, *Spain*	34	C5
Pobra de Trives, *Spain*	34	C3
Pocahontas, *Ark., U.S.A.*	113	G9
Pocahontas, *Iowa, U.S.A.*	112	D7
Pocatello, *U.S.A.*	114	E7
Počátky, *Czech Rep.*	26	B8
Pochep, *Russia*	47	F7
Pochinki, *Russia*	48	C7
Pochinok, *Russia*	46	E7
Pöchlarn, *Austria*	26	C8
Pochutla, *Mexico*	119	D5
Pocito Casas, *Mexico*	118	B2
Pocking, *Germany*	25	G9
Pocomoke City, *U.S.A.*	108	F8

Poços de Caldas, *Brazil*	127	A6
Poddębice, *Poland*	45	G5
Poděbrady, *Czech Rep.*	26	A8
Podensac, *France*	20	D3
Podenzano, *Italy*	28	D6
Podgorač, *Croatia*	42	E3
Podgorica, *Montenegro, Yug.*	40	D3
Podgorie, *Albania*	40	F4
Podilska Vysochyna, *Ukraine*	47	H4
Podkarpackie □, *Poland*	45	H9
Podkova, *Bulgaria*	41	E9
Podlapača, *Croatia*	29	D12
Podlaskie □, *Poland*	45	E10
Podoleni, *Romania*	43	D11
Podolínec, *Slovak Rep.*	27	B13
Podolsk, *Russia*	46	E9
Podor, *Senegal*	82	B1
Podporozhye, *Russia*	46	B8
Podu Iloaiei, *Romania*	43	C12
Podu Turcului, *Romania*	43	D12
Podujevo, *Kosovo, Yug.*	40	D5
Poel, *Germany*	24	B6
Pofadder, *S. Africa*	88	D2
Poggiardo, *Italy*	31	B11
Poggibonsi, *Italy*	28	E8
Póggio Mirteto, *Italy*	29	F9
Pogoanele, *Romania*	43	F12
Pogorzela, *Poland*	45	G4
Pogradec, *Albania*	40	F4
Pogranitšnyi, *Russia*	54	B5
Poh, *Indonesia*	63	E6
P'ohang, *S. Korea*	57	F15
Pohjanmaa, *Finland*	8	E20
Pohnpei, *Micronesia*	96	G7
Pohorelá, *Slovak Rep.*	27	C13
Pohořelice, *Czech Rep.*	27	C9
Pohorje, *Slovenia*	29	B12
Pohri, *India*	68	G6
Poiana Mare, *Romania*	42	G8
Poiana Ruscăi, Munții, *Romania*	42	E7
Poiana Stampei, *Romania*	43	C10
Poinsett, C., *Antarctica*	5	C8
Point Arena, *U.S.A.*	116	G3
Point Baker, *U.S.A.*	104	B2
Point Edward, *Canada*	102	D3
Point Hope, *U.S.A.*	100	B3
Point L., *U.S.A.*	100	B8
Point Pedro, *Sri Lanka*	66	Q12
Point Pleasant, *N.J., U.S.A.*	111	F10
Point Pleasant, *W. Va., U.S.A.*	108	F4
Pointe-à-Pitre, *Guadeloupe*	121	C7
Pointe-Claire, *Canada*	111	A11
Pointe-Gatineau, *Canada*	111	A9
Pointe-Noire, *Congo*	84	E2
Poio, *Spain*	34	C2
Poirino, *Italy*	28	D4
Poisonbush Ra., *Australia*	92	D3
Poissonnier Pt., *Australia*	92	C2
Poitiers, *France*	18	F7
Poitou, *France*	20	B3
Poitou-Charentes □, *France*	20	B4
Poix-de-Picardie, *France*	19	C8
Poix-Terron, *France*	19	C11
Pojoaque, *U.S.A.*	115	J11
Pokaran, *India*	66	F7
Pokataroo, *Australia*	95	D4
Pokhara, *Nepal*	69	E10
Pokhvistnevo, *Russia*	48	D11
Poko, *Dem. Rep. of the Congo*	86	B2
Poko, *Sudan*	81	F3
Pokrov, *Russia*	46	E10
Pokrovsk = Engels, *Russia*	48	E8
Pokrovsk, *Russia*	51	C13
Pokrovskoye, *Russia*	47	J10
Pola = Pula, *Croatia*	29	D10
Pola, *Russia*	46	D7
Pola de Allande, *Spain*	34	B4
Pola de Lena, *Spain*	34	B5
Pola de Siero, *Spain*	34	B5
Pola de Somiedo, *Spain*	34	B4
Polacca, *U.S.A.*	115	J8
Polan, *Iran*	71	E9
Pol'ana, *Slovak Rep.*	27	C12
Poland ■, *Europe*	45	G3
Polanica-Zdrój, *Poland*	45	H3
Połaniec, *Poland*	45	H8
Polanów, *Poland*	44	D3
Polar Bear Prov. Park, *Canada*	102	A2
Polatlı, *Turkey*	72	C5
Polatsk, *Belarus*	46	E5
Polcura, *Chile*	126	D1
Połczyn-Zdrój, *Poland*	44	E3
Polessk, *Russia*	9	J19
Polesye = Pripet Marshes, *Europe*	47	F5
Polgar, *Hungary*	42	C6
Pŏlgyo-ri, *S. Korea*	57	G14
Poli, *Cameroon*	83	C7
Políaigos, *Greece*	38	E6
Policastro, G. di, *Italy*	31	C8
Police, *Poland*	44	E1
Polička, *Czech Rep.*	27	B9
Policoro, *Italy*	31	B9
Polignano a Mare, *Italy*	31	A9
Poligny, *France*	19	F12
Políkhnitos, *Greece*	39	B8
Polillo Is., *Phil.*	61	D4
Polillo Strait, *Phil.*	61	D4
Polis, *Cyprus*	36	D11
Polístena, *Italy*	31	D9
Políyiros, *Greece*	40	F7
Polk, *U.S.A.*	110	E5
Polkowice, *Poland*	45	G3
Polla, *Italy*	31	B8
Pollachi, *India*	66	P10
Pollença, *Spain*	37	B10

Pollença, B. de, *Spain*	37	B10
Póllica, *Italy*	31	B8
Pollino, Mte., *Italy*	31	C9
Polna, *Russia*	46	C5
Polnovat, *Russia*	50	C7
Pology, *Ukraine*	47	J9
Polonne, *Ukraine*	47	G4
Polonnoye = Polonne, *Ukraine*	47	G4
Polski Trŭmbesh, *Bulgaria*	41	C9
Polsko Kosovo, *Bulgaria*	41	C9
Polson, *U.S.A.*	114	C6
Poltár, *Slovak Rep.*	27	C12
Poltava, *Ukraine*	47	H8
Põltsamaa, *Estonia*	9	G21
Polunochnoye, *Russia*	50	C7
Põlva, *Estonia*	9	G22
Polynesia, *Pac. Oc.*	97	J11
Polynésie française = French Polynesia ■, *Pac. Oc.*	97	K13
Pomarance, *Italy*	28	E7
Pomaro, *Mexico*	118	D4
Pombal, *Portugal*	34	F2
Pómbia, *Greece*	36	E6
Pomene, *Mozam.*	89	C6
Pomeroy, *Ohio, U.S.A.*	108	F4
Pomeroy, *Wash., U.S.A.*	114	C5
Pomézia, *Italy*	30	A5
Pomichna, *Ukraine*	47	H6
Pomona, *Australia*	95	D5
Pomona, *U.S.A.*	117	L9
Pomorie, *Bulgaria*	41	D11
Pomorskie □, *Poland*	44	D5
Pomorskie, Pojezierze, *Poland*	44	E3
Pomos, *Cyprus*	36	D11
Pomos, C., *Cyprus*	36	D11
Pompano Beach, *U.S.A.*	109	M5
Pompei, *Italy*	31	B7
Pompey, *France*	19	D13
Pompeys Pillar, *U.S.A.*	114	D10
Pompton Lakes, *U.S.A.*	111	F10
Ponape = Pohnpei, *Micronesia*	96	G7
Ponask L., *Canada*	102	B1
Ponca, *U.S.A.*	112	D6
Ponca City, *U.S.A.*	113	G6
Ponce, *Puerto Rico*	121	C6
Ponchatoula, *U.S.A.*	113	K9
Poncheville, L., *Canada*	102	B4
Pond, *U.S.A.*	117	K7
Pond Inlet, *Canada*	101	A12
Pondicherry, *India*	66	P11
Ponds, I. of, *Canada*	103	B8
Ponferrada, *Spain*	34	C4
Pongo, Wadi →, *Sudan*	81	F2
Poniatowa, *Poland*	45	G9
Poniec, *Poland*	45	G3
Ponikva, *Slovenia*	29	B12
Ponnani, *India*	66	P9
Ponoka, *Canada*	104	C6
Ponorogo, *Indonesia*	63	G14
Pons = Ponts, *Spain*	32	D6
Pons, *France*	20	C3
Ponsul →, *Portugal*	34	F3
Pont-à-Mousson, *France*	19	D13
Pont-Audemer, *France*	18	C7
Pont-Aven, *France*	18	E3
Pont Canavese, *Italy*	28	C4
Pont-de-l'Ain, *France*	19	F12
Pont-de-Roide, *France*	19	E13
Pont-de-Salars, *France*	20	D6
Pont-de-Vaux, *France*	19	F11
Pont-de-Veyle, *France*	19	F11
Pont-du-Château, *France*	19	G10
Pont-l'Abbé, *France*	18	E2
Pont-l'Évêque, *France*	18	C7
Pont-St-Esprit, *France*	21	D8
Pont-St-Martin, *Italy*	28	C4
Pont-Ste-Maxence, *France*	19	C9
Pont-sur-Yonne, *France*	19	D10
Ponta do Sol, *Madeira*	37	D2
Ponta Grossa, *Brazil*	127	B5
Ponta Pora, *Brazil*	127	A4
Pontacq, *France*	20	E3
Pontailler-sur-Saône, *France*	19	E12
Pontarlier, *France*	19	F13
Pontassieve, *Italy*	29	E8
Pontaumur, *France*	20	C6
Pontcharra, *France*	21	C10
Pontchartrain L., *U.S.A.*	113	K10
Pontchâteau, *France*	18	E4
Ponte da Barca, *Portugal*	34	D2
Ponte de Sor, *Portugal*	35	F3
Ponte dell'Olio, *Italy*	28	D6
Ponte di Legno, *Italy*	28	B7
Ponte do Lima, *Portugal*	34	D2
Ponte do Pungué, *Mozam.*	87	F3
Ponte-Leccia, *France*	21	F13
Ponte nelle Alpi, *Italy*	29	B9
Ponte Nova, *Brazil*	127	A7
Ponteareas, *Spain*	34	C2
Pontebba, *Italy*	29	B10
Ponteceso, *Spain*	34	B2
Pontecorvo, *Italy*	30	A6
Pontedeume, *Spain*	34	B2
Ponteix, *Canada*	105	D7
Pontevedra, *Spain*	34	C2
Pontevedra □, *Spain*	34	C2
Pontevedra, R. de →, *Spain*	34	C2
Pontevico, *Italy*	28	C7
Pontiac, *Ill., U.S.A.*	112	E10
Pontiac, *Mich., U.S.A.*	108	D4
Pontian Kecil, *Malaysia*	65	M4
Pontianak, *Indonesia*	62	E3
Pontine Is. = Ponziane, Ísole, *Italy*	30	B5
Pontine Mts. = Kuzey Anadolu Dağları, *Turkey*	72	B7
Pontínia, *Italy*	30	A6

Pontivy, *France*	18	D4
Pontoise, *France*	19	C9
Ponton →, *Canada*	104	B5
Pontorson, *France*	18	D5
Pontrémoli, *Italy*	28	D6
Pontrieux, *France*	18	D3
Ponts, *Spain*	32	D6
Pontypool, *Canada*	110	B6
Pontypool, *U.K.*	13	F4
Ponza, *Italy*	30	B5
Ponziane, Ísole, *Italy*	30	B5
Poochera, *Australia*	95	E1
Poole, *U.K.*	13	G6
Poole □, *U.K.*	13	G6
Poona = Pune, *India*	66	K8
Pooncarie, *Australia*	95	E3
Poopelloe L., *Australia*	95	E3
Poopó, L. de, *Bolivia*	122	E4
Popayán, *Colombia*	124	C3
Poperinge, *Belgium*	17	D2
Popilta L., *Australia*	95	E3
Popina, *Bulgaria*	41	B10
Popio L., *Australia*	95	E3
Poplar, *U.S.A.*	112	A2
Poplar →, *Canada*	105	C9
Poplar Bluff, *U.S.A.*	113	G9
Poplarville, *U.S.A.*	113	K10
Popocatépetl, Volcán, *Mexico*	119	D5
Popokabaka, *Dem. Rep. of the Congo*	84	F3
Pópoli, *Italy*	29	F10
Popovača, *Croatia*	29	C13
Popovo, *Bulgaria*	41	C10
Poppberg, *Germany*	25	F7
Poppi, *Italy*	29	E8
Poprad, *Slovak Rep.*	27	B13
Poprad →, *Slovak Rep.*	27	B13
Porali →, *Pakistan*	68	G2
Porbandar, *India*	66	J6
Porcher I., *Canada*	104	C2
Porcuna, *Spain*	35	H6
Porcupine →, *Canada*	105	B8
Porcupine →, *U.S.A.*	100	B5
Pordenone, *Italy*	29	C9
Pordim, *Bulgaria*	41	C8
Poreč, *Croatia*	29	C10
Poretskoye, *Russia*	48	C8
Pori, *Finland*	9	F19
Porí, *Greece*	38	F5
Porkhov, *Russia*	46	D5
Porlamar, *Venezuela*	124	A6
Porlezza, *Italy*	28	B6
Porma →, *Spain*	34	C5
Pornic, *France*	18	E4
Poronaysk, *Russia*	51	E15
Póros, *Greece*	38	D5
Poroshiri-Dake, *Japan*	54	C11
Poroszló, *Hungary*	42	C5
Poroto Mts., *Tanzania*	87	D3
Porpoise B., *Antarctica*	5	C9
Porquerolles, Î. de, *France*	21	F10
Porrentruy, *Switz.*	25	H3
Porreres, *Spain*	37	B10
Porsangen, *Norway*	8	A21
Porsgrunn, *Norway*	9	G13
Port Alberni, *Canada*	104	D4
Port Alfred, *S. Africa*	88	E4
Port Alice, *Canada*	104	C3
Port Allegany, *U.S.A.*	110	E6
Port Allen, *U.S.A.*	113	K9
Port Alma, *Australia*	94	C5
Port Angeles, *U.S.A.*	116	B3
Port Antonio, *Jamaica*	120	C4
Port Aransas, *U.S.A.*	113	M6
Port Arthur = Lüshun, *China*	57	E11
Port Arthur, *Australia*	94	G4
Port Arthur, *U.S.A.*	113	L8
Port au Choix, *Canada*	103	B8
Port au Port B., *Canada*	103	C8
Port-au-Prince, *Haiti*	121	C5
Port Augusta, *Australia*	95	E2
Port Austin, *U.S.A.*	110	B2
Port Bell, *Uganda*	86	B3
Port Bergé Vaovao, *Madag.*	89	B8
Port Blandford, *Canada*	103	C9
Port-Bouët, *Ivory C.*	82	D4
Port Bradshaw, *Australia*	94	A2
Port Broughton, *Australia*	95	E2
Port Burwell, *Canada*	110	D4
Port Canning, *India*	69	H13
Port-Cartier, *Canada*	103	B6
Port Chalmers, *N.Z.*	91	L3
Port Charlotte, *U.S.A.*	109	M4
Port Chester, *U.S.A.*	111	F11
Port Clements, *Canada*	104	C2
Port Clinton, *U.S.A.*	108	E4
Port Colborne, *Canada*	102	D4
Port Coquitlam, *Canada*	104	D4
Port Credit, *Canada*	110	C5
Port Curtis, *Australia*	94	C5
Port d'Alcúdia, *Spain*	37	B10
Port Dalhousie, *Canada*	110	C5
Port Darwin, *Australia*	92	B5
Port Darwin, *Falk. Is.*	128	G5
Port Davey, *Australia*	94	G4
Port-de-Bouc, *France*	21	E8
Port de Pollença, *Spain*	37	B10
Port de Sóller, *Spain*	37	B9
Port Dickson, *Malaysia*	65	L3
Port Douglas, *Australia*	94	B4
Port Dover, *Canada*	110	D4
Port Edward, *Canada*	104	C2
Port Elgin, *Canada*	102	D3
Port Elizabeth, *S. Africa*	88	E4
Port Ellen, *U.K.*	14	F2
Port-en-Bessin, *France*	18	C6

Port Erin, *U.K.*	12	C3
Port Essington, *Australia*	92	B5
Port Etienne = Nouâdhibou, *Mauritania*	78	D2
Port Ewen, *U.S.A.*	111	E11
Port Fairy, *Australia*	95	F3
Port Fouâd = Bûr Fuad, *Egypt*	80	H8
Port Gamble, *U.S.A.*	116	C4
Port-Gentil, *Gabon*	84	E1
Port Germein, *Australia*	95	E2
Port Gibson, *U.S.A.*	113	K9
Port Glasgow, *U.K.*	14	F4
Port Harcourt, *Nigeria*	83	E6
Port Hardy, *Canada*	104	C3
Port Harrison = Inukjuak, *Canada*	101	C12
Port Hawkesbury, *Canada*	103	C7
Port Hedland, *Australia*	92	D2
Port Henry, *U.S.A.*	111	B11
Port Hood, *Canada*	103	C7
Port Hope, *Canada*	102	D4
Port Hope, *U.S.A.*	110	C2
Port Hope Simpson, *Canada*	103	B8
Port Hueneme, *U.S.A.*	117	L7
Port Huron, *U.S.A.*	110	D2
Port Iliç, *Azerbaijan*	73	C13
Port Jefferson, *U.S.A.*	111	F11
Port Jervis, *U.S.A.*	111	E10
Port-Joinville, *France*	18	F4
Port Katon, *Russia*	47	J10
Port Kelang = Pelabuhan Kelang, *Malaysia*	65	L3
Port Kenny, *Australia*	95	E1
Port-la-Nouvelle, *France*	20	E7
Port Laire = Waterford, *Ireland*	15	D4
Port Laoise, *Ireland*	15	C4
Port Lavaca, *U.S.A.*	113	L6
Port Leyden, *U.S.A.*	111	C9
Port Lincoln, *Australia*	95	E2
Port Loko, *S. Leone*	82	D2
Port Louis, *France*	18	E3
Port Louis, *Mauritius*	77	H9
Port Lyautey = Kenitra, *Morocco*	78	B4
Port MacDonnell, *Australia*	95	F3
Port McNeill, *Canada*	104	C3
Port Macquarie, *Australia*	95	E5
Port Maria, *Jamaica*	120	C4
Port Matilda, *U.S.A.*	110	F6
Port Mellon, *Canada*	104	D4
Port-Menier, *Canada*	103	C7
Port Moody, *Canada*	116	A4
Port Morant, *Jamaica*	120	C4
Port Moresby, *Papua N. G.*	96	H6
Port Musgrave, *Australia*	94	A3
Port-Navalo, *France*	18	E4
Port Neches, *U.S.A.*	113	L8
Port Nolloth, *S. Africa*	88	D2
Port Nouveau-Québec = Kangiqsualujjuaq, *Canada*	101	C13
Port of Spain, *Trin. & Tob.*	121	D7
Port Orange, *U.S.A.*	109	L5
Port Orchard, *U.S.A.*	116	C4
Port Orford, *U.S.A.*	114	E1
Port Pegasus, *N.Z.*	91	M1
Port Perry, *Canada*	102	D4
Port Phillip B., *Australia*	95	F3
Port Pirie, *Australia*	95	E2
Port Radium = Echo Bay, *Canada*	100	B8
Port Renfrew, *Canada*	104	D4
Port Roper, *Australia*	94	A2
Port Rowan, *Canada*	110	D4
Port Safaga = Bûr Safâga, *Egypt*	70	E2
Port Said = Bûr Sa'îd, *Egypt*	80	H8
Port St. Joe, *U.S.A.*	109	L3
Port St. Johns = Umzimvubu, *S. Africa*	89	E4
Port-St-Louis-du-Rhône, *France*	21	E8
Port St. Lucie, *U.S.A.*	109	M5
Port-Ste-Marie, *France*	20	D4
Port Sanilac, *U.S.A.*	110	C2
Port Severn, *Canada*	110	B5
Port Shepstone, *S. Africa*	89	E5
Port Simpson, *Canada*	104	C2
Port Stanley = Stanley, *Falk. Is.*	128	G5
Port Stanley, *Canada*	102	D3
Port Sudan = Bûr Sûdân, *Sudan*	80	D4
Port Sulphur, *U.S.A.*	113	L10
Port-sur-Saône, *France*	19	E13
Port Talbot, *U.K.*	13	F4
Port Taufiq = Bûr Taufiq, *Egypt*	80	J8
Port Townsend, *U.S.A.*	116	B4
Port-Vendres, *France*	20	F7
Port Vila, *Vanuatu*	96	J8
Port Wakefield, *Australia*	95	E2
Port Washington, *U.S.A.*	108	D2
Port Weld = Kuala Sepetang, *Malaysia*	65	K3
Portadown, *U.K.*	15	B5
Portaferry, *U.K.*	15	B6
Portage, *Pa., U.S.A.*	110	F6
Portage, *Wis., U.S.A.*	112	D10
Portage La Prairie, *Canada*	105	D9
Portageville, *U.S.A.*	113	G10
Portalegre, *Portugal*	35	F3
Portalegre □, *Portugal*	35	F3
Portales, *U.S.A.*	113	H3
Portarlington, *Ireland*	15	C4
Portbou, *Spain*	32	C8
Portel, *Portugal*	35	G3
Porter L., *N.W.T., Canada*	105	A7
Porter L., *Sask., Canada*	105	B7
Porterville, *S. Africa*	88	E2
Porterville, *U.S.A.*	116	J8
Portes-lès-Valence, *France*	21	D8
Porthcawl, *U.K.*	13	F4

Porthill, U.S.A. 114 B5
Porthmadog, U.K. 12 E3
Portile de Fier, Europe 42 F7
Portimão, Portugal 35 H2
Portishead, U.K. 13 F5
Portiţei, Gura, Romania 43 F14
Portknockie, U.K. 14 D6
Portland, N.S.W., Australia 95 E5
Portland, Vic., Australia 95 F3
Portland, Canada 111 B8
Portland, Conn., U.S.A. 111 E12
Portland, Maine, U.S.A. 101 D12
Portland, Mich., U.S.A. 108 D3
Portland, Oreg., U.S.A. 116 E4
Portland, Pa., U.S.A. 111 F9
Portland, Tex., U.S.A. 113 M6
Portland, I. of, U.K. 13 G5
Portland, B., Australia 95 F3
Portland Bill, U.K. 13 G5
Portland Canal, U.S.A. 104 B2
Portmadoc = Porthmadog, U.K. 12 E3
Porto, France 21 F12
Porto, Portugal 34 D2
Porto □, Portugal 34 D2
Porto, G. de, France 21 F12
Pôrto Alegre, Brazil 127 C5
Porto Amboim = Gunza, Angola 84 G2
Porto Azzurro, Italy 28 F7
Porto Cristo, Spain 37 B10
Pôrto de Móz, Brazil 125 D8
Porto Empédocle, Italy 30 E6
Pôrto Esperança, Brazil 124 G7
Pôrto Franco, Brazil 125 E9
Pórto Lágos, Greece 41 E9
Porto Mendes, Brazil 127 A5
Porto Moniz, Madeira 37 D2
Pôrto Murtinho, Brazil 124 H7
Pôrto Nacional, Brazil 125 F9
Porto-Novo, Benin 83 D5
Porto Petro, Spain 37 B10
Porto San Giórgio, Italy 29 E10
Porto Sant' Elpídio, Italy 29 E10
Porto Santo, I. de, Madeira 78 B2
Porto Santo Stéfano, Italy 28 F8
Pôrto São José, Brazil 127 A5
Pôrto Seguro, Brazil 125 G11
Porto Tolle, Italy 29 D9
Porto Tórres, Italy 30 B1
Pôrto União, Brazil 127 B5
Pôrto Válter, Brazil 124 E4
Porto-Vecchio, France 21 G13
Pôrto Velho, Brazil 124 E6
Portobelo, Panama 120 E4
Portoferráio, Italy 28 F7
Portogruaro, Italy 29 C9
Portola, U.S.A. 116 F6
Portomaggiore, Italy 29 D8
Portoscuso, Italy 30 C1
Portovénere, Italy 28 D6
Portoviejo, Ecuador 124 D2
Portpatrick, U.K. 14 G3
Portree, U.K. 14 D2
Portrush, U.K. 15 A5
Portsmouth, Domin. 121 C7
Portsmouth, U.K. 13 G6
Portsmouth, N.H., U.S.A. 109 D10
Portsmouth, Ohio, U.S.A. 108 F4
Portsmouth, R.I., U.S.A. 111 E13
Portsmouth, Va., U.S.A. 108 G7
Portsmouth □, U.K. 13 G6
Portsoy, U.K. 14 D6
Portstewart, U.K. 15 A5
Porttipahtan tekojärvi, Finland 8 B22
Portugal ■, Europe 34 F3
Portugalete, Spain 32 B1
Portumna, Ireland 15 C3
Portville, U.S.A. 110 D6
Porvenir, Chile 128 G2
Porvoo, Finland 9 F21
Porzuna, Spain 35 F6
Posada, Italy 30 B2
Posada →, Italy 30 B2
Posadas, Argentina 127 B4
Posadas, Spain 35 H5
Poschiavo, Switz. 25 J6
Posets, Spain 32 C5
Poshan = Boshan, China 57 F9
Posht-e-Badam, Iran 71 C7
Posídhion, Ákra, Greece 40 G7
Posidium, Greece 39 F9
Poso, Indonesia 63 E6
Posong, S. Korea 57 G14
Posse, Brazil 125 F9
Possession I., Antarctica 5 D11
Pössneck, Germany 24 E7
Possum Kingdom L., U.S.A. 113 J5
Post, U.S.A. 113 J4
Post Falls, U.S.A. 114 C5
Postavy = Pastavy, Belarus 9 J22
Poste-de-la-Baleine =
  Kuujjuarapik, Canada 102 A4
Postmasburg, S. Africa 88 D3
Postojna, Slovenia 29 C11
Poston, U.S.A. 117 M12
Postville, Canada 103 B8
Potamós, Andikíthira, Greece 38 F5
Potamós, Kíthira, Greece 38 E4
Potchefstroom, S. Africa 88 D4
Potcoava, Romania 43 F9
Poteau, U.S.A. 113 H7
Poteet, U.S.A. 113 L5
Potenza, Italy 31 B8
Potenza →, Italy 29 E10
Potenza Picena, Italy 29 E10
Poteriteri, L., N.Z. 91 M1
Potgietersrus, S. Africa 89 C4
Poti, Georgia 49 J5

Potiskum, Nigeria 83 C7
Potlogi, Romania 43 F10
Potomac →, U.S.A. 108 G7
Potosí, Bolivia 124 G5
Potosi Mt., U.S.A. 117 K11
Pototan, Phil. 61 F5
Potrerillos, Chile 126 B2
Potsdam, Germany 24 C9
Potsdam, U.S.A. 111 B10
Pottenstein, Germany 25 F7
Pottersville, U.S.A. 111 C11
Pottery Hill = Abu Ballas, Egypt 80 C2
Pottstown, U.S.A. 111 F9
Pottsville, U.S.A. 111 F8
Pottuvil, Sri Lanka 66 R12
Pouancé, France 18 E5
Pouce Coupé, Canada 104 B4
Poughkeepsie, U.S.A. 111 E11
Pouilly-sur-Loire, France 19 E9
Poulaphouca Res., Ireland 15 C5
Poulsbo, U.S.A. 116 C4
Poulton-le-Fylde, U.K. 12 D5
Pouso Alegre, Brazil 127 A6
Pout, Senegal 82 C1
Pouthisat, Cambodia 64 F4
Pouzauges, France 18 F6
Pova de Sta. Iria, Portugal 35 G1
Považská Bystrica, Slovak Rep. 27 B11
Poverty B., N.Z. 91 H7
Povlen, Serbia, Yug. 40 B3
Póvoa de Lanhosa, Portugal 34 D2
Póvoa de Varzim, Portugal 34 D2
Povorino, Russia 48 E6
Povungnituk = Puvirnituq,
  Canada 101 B12
Powassan, Canada 102 C4
Poway, U.S.A. 117 N9
Powder →, U.S.A. 112 B2
Powder River, U.S.A. 114 E10
Powell, U.S.A. 114 D9
Powell, L., U.S.A. 115 H8
Powell River, Canada 104 D4
Powers, U.S.A. 108 C2
Powys □, U.K. 13 E4
Poyang Hu, China 59 C11
Poyarkovo, Russia 51 E13
Poysdorf, Austria 27 C9
Poza de la Sal, Spain 34 C7
Poza Rica, Mexico 119 C5
Pozantı, Turkey 72 D6
Požarevac, Serbia, Yug. 40 B5
Pozazal, Puerto, Spain 34 C6
Požega, Croatia 42 E2
Požega, Serbia, Yug. 40 C4
Poznań, Poland 45 F3
Pozo, U.S.A. 117 K6
Pozo Alcón, Spain 35 H8
Pozo Almonte, Chile 124 H5
Pozo Colorado, Paraguay 126 A4
Pozoblanco, Spain 35 G6
Pozzallo, Italy 31 F7
Pozzomaggiore, Italy 30 B1
Pozzuoli, Italy 31 B7
Pra →, Ghana 83 D4
Prabuty, Poland 44 E6
Prača, Bos.-H. 42 G3
Prachatice, Czech Rep. 26 B6
Prachin Buri, Thailand 64 E3
Prachuap Khiri Khan, Thailand 65 G2
Pradelles, France 20 D7
Prades, France 20 F6
Prado, Brazil 125 G11
Prado del Rey, Spain 35 J5
Præstø, Denmark 11 J6
Pragersko, Slovenia 29 B12
Prague = Praha, Czech Rep. 26 A7
Praha, Czech Rep. 26 A7
Prahecq, France 20 B3
Prahova □, Romania 43 E10
Prahova →, Romania 43 F10
Prahovo, Serbia, Yug. 40 B6
Praia, C. Verde Is. 77 E1
Práia a Mare, Italy 31 C8
Praid, Romania 43 D10
Prainha, Amazonas, Brazil 124 E6
Prainha, Pará, Brazil 125 D8
Prairie, Australia 94 C3
Prairie City, U.S.A. 114 D4
Prairie Dog Town Fork →,
  U.S.A. 113 H5
Prairie du Chien, U.S.A. 112 D9
Prairies, L. of the, Canada 105 C8
Pramánda, Greece 38 B3
Prampram, Ghana 83 D5
Pran Buri, Thailand 64 F2
Prang, Ghana 83 D4
Prapat, Indonesia 62 D1
Prasonísi, Ákra, Greece 36 D9
Prästmon, Sweden 10 A11
Praszka, Poland 45 G5
Prata, Brazil 125 G9
Pratabpur, India 69 H10
Pratapgarh, Raj., India 68 G6
Pratapgarh, Ut. P., India 69 G9
Prato, Italy 28 E8
Prátola Peligna, Italy 29 F10
Prats-de-Mollo-la-Preste, France 20 F6
Pratt, U.S.A. 113 G5
Prattville, U.S.A. 109 J2
Pravdinsk, Russia 48 B6
Pravets, Bulgaria 40 D7
Pravia, Spain 34 B4
Praya, Indonesia 62 F5
Pré-en-Pail, France 18 D6
Precordillera, Argentina 126 C2

Predáppio, Italy 29 D8
Predazzo, Italy 29 B8
Predeal, Romania 43 E10
Predejane, Serbia, Yug. 40 D6
Preeceville, Canada 105 C8
Preetz, Germany 24 A6
Pregrada, Croatia 29 B12
Preiļi, Latvia 9 H22
Preko, Croatia 29 D12
Prelog, Croatia 29 B13
Prémery, France 19 E10
Premià de Mar, Spain 32 D7
Premont, U.S.A. 113 M5
Premuda, Croatia 29 D11
Prentice, U.S.A. 112 C9
Prenzlau, Germany 24 B9
Preobrazheniye, Russia 54 C6
Preparis North Channel,
  Ind. Oc. 67 M18
Preparis South Channel, Ind. Oc. 67 M18
Přerov, Czech Rep. 27 B10
Prescott, Canada 102 D4
Prescott, Ariz., U.S.A. 115 J7
Prescott, Ark., U.S.A. 113 J8
Prescott Valley, U.S.A. 115 J7
Preservation Inlet, N.Z. 91 M1
Preševo, Serbia, Yug. 40 D5
Presho, U.S.A. 112 D4
Presicce, Italy 31 C11
Presidencia de la Plaza,
  Argentina 126 B4
Presidencia Roque Saenz Peña,
  Argentina 126 B3
Presidente Epitácio, Brazil 127 A5
Presidente Hayes □, Paraguay 126 A4
Presidente Prudente, Brazil 127 A5
Presidio, Mexico 118 B4
Presidio, U.S.A. 113 L2
Preslav, Bulgaria 41 C10
Preslavska Planina, Bulgaria 41 C10
Prešov, Slovak Rep. 27 B14
Prešovský □, Slovak Rep. 27 B13
Prespa, Bulgaria 41 E8
Prespa = Prespansko Jezero,
  Macedonia 40 F5
Prespansko Jezero, Macedonia 40 F5
Presque I., U.S.A. 110 D4
Presque Isle, U.S.A. 109 B12
Prestatyn, U.K. 12 D4
Prestea, Ghana 82 D4
Presteigne, U.K. 13 E5
Přeštice, Czech Rep. 26 B6
Preston, Canada 110 C4
Preston, U.K. 12 D5
Preston, Idaho, U.S.A. 114 E8
Preston, Minn., U.S.A. 112 D8
Preston, C., Australia 92 D2
Prestonburg, U.S.A. 108 G4
Prestwick, U.K. 14 F4
Pretoria, S. Africa 89 D4
Preuilly-sur-Claise, France 18 F7
Préveza, Greece 38 C2
Préveza □, Greece 38 B2
Prey Veng, Cambodia 65 G5
Priazovskoye, Ukraine 47 J8
Pribilof Is., U.S.A. 100 C2
Priboj, Serbia, Yug. 40 C3
Příbram, Czech Rep. 26 B7
Price, U.S.A. 114 G8
Price I., Canada 104 C3
Prichard, U.S.A. 109 K1
Priego, Spain 32 E2
Priego de Córdoba, Spain 35 H6
Priekule, Latvia 9 H19
Priekulė, Lithuania 9 J20
Prien, Germany 25 H8
Priest L., U.S.A. 114 B5
Priest River, U.S.A. 114 B5
Priest Valley, U.S.A. 116 J6
Prievidza, Slovak Rep. 27 C11
Prijedor, Bos.-H. 29 D13
Prijepolje, Serbia, Yug. 40 C3
Prikaspiyskaya Nizmennost =
  Caspian Depression, Eurasia 49 G9
Prikro, Ivory C. 82 D4
Prikubanskaya Nizmennost,
  Russia 49 H4
Prilep, Macedonia 40 E5
Priluki = Pryluky, Ukraine 47 G7
Prime Seal I., Australia 94 G4
Primorsk, Russia 46 B5
Primorsko, Bulgaria 41 D11
Primorsko-Akhtarsk, Russia 47 J10
Primorskoye, Ukraine 47 J9
Primrose L., Canada 105 C7
Prince Albert, Canada 105 C7
Prince Albert, S. Africa 88 E3
Prince Albert Mts., Antarctica 5 D11
Prince Albert Nat. Park, Canada 105 C7
Prince Albert Pen., Canada 100 A8
Prince Albert Sd., Canada 100 A8
Prince Alfred, C., Canada 4 B1
Prince Charles I., Canada 101 B12
Prince Charles Mts., Antarctica 5 D6
Prince Edward I. □, Canada 103 C7
Prince Edward Is., Ind. Oc. 3 G11
Prince Edward Pt., Canada 110 C8
Prince George, Canada 104 C4
Prince of Wales, C., U.S.A. 98 C3
Prince of Wales I., Australia 94 A3
Prince of Wales I., Canada 100 A10
Prince of Wales I., U.S.A. 100 C6
Prince Patrick I., Canada 4 B2
Prince Regent Inlet, Canada 4 B3
Prince Rupert, Canada 104 C2

Princess Charlotte B., Australia 94 A3
Princess May Ranges, Australia 92 C4
Princess Royal I., Canada 104 C3
Princeton, Canada 104 D4
Princeton, Calif., U.S.A. 116 F4
Princeton, Ill., U.S.A. 112 E10
Princeton, Ind., U.S.A. 108 F2
Princeton, Ky., U.S.A. 108 G2
Princeton, Mo., U.S.A. 112 E8
Princeton, N.J., U.S.A. 111 F10
Princeton, W. Va., U.S.A. 108 G5
Principe, I. de, Atl. Oc. 76 F4
Principe da Beira, Brazil 124 F6
Prineville, U.S.A. 114 D3
Prins Harald Kyst, Antarctica 5 D4
Prinsesse Astrid Kyst, Antarctica 5 D3
Prinsesse Ragnhild Kyst,
  Antarctica 5 D4
Prinzapolca, Nic. 120 D3
Prior, C., Spain 34 B2
Priozersk, Russia 46 B6
Pripet = Prypyat →, Europe 47 G6
Pripet Marshes, Europe 47 F5
Pripyat Marshes = Pripet
  Marshes, Europe 47 F5
Pripyats = Prypyat →, Europe 47 G6
Prislop, Pasul, Romania 43 C9
Pristen, Russia 47 G9
Priština, Kosovo, Yug. 40 D5
Pritzwalk, Germany 24 B8
Privas, France 21 D8
Priverno, Italy 30 A6
Privolzhsk, Russia 48 B5
Privolzhskaya Vozvyshennost,
  Russia 48 E7
Privolzhskiy, Russia 48 E8
Privolzhye, Russia 48 D9
Priyutnoye, Russia 49 G6
Prizren, Kosovo, Yug. 40 D4
Prizzi, Italy 30 E6
Prnjavor, Bos.-H. 42 F2
Probolinggo, Indonesia 63 G15
Prochowice, Poland 45 G3
Proctor, U.S.A. 111 C11
Proddatur, India 66 M11
Prodhromos, Cyprus 36 E11
Proença-a-Nova, Portugal 34 F3
Profítis Ilías, Greece 36 C9
Profondeville, Belgium 17 D4
Progreso, Coahuila, Mexico 118 B4
Progreso, Yucatán, Mexico 119 C7
Prokhladnyy, Russia 49 J7
Prokletije, Albania 40 D3
Prokopyevsk, Russia 50 D9
Prokuplje, Serbia, Yug. 40 C5
Proletarskaya = Proletarsk,
  Russia 49 G5
Prome = Pyè, Burma 67 K19
Prophet →, Canada 104 B4
Prophet River, Canada 104 B4
Propriá, Brazil 125 F11
Propriano, France 21 G12
Proserpine, Australia 94 C4
Prosna →, Poland 45 F4
Prospect, U.S.A. 111 C9
Prosser, U.S.A. 114 C4
Prostějov, Czech Rep. 27 B10
Proston, Australia 95 D5
Proszowice, Poland 45 H7
Próti, Greece 38 D3
Provadiya, Bulgaria 41 C11
Provence, France 21 E9
Provence-Alpes-Côte d'Azur □,
  France 21 D10
Providence, Ky., U.S.A. 108 G2
Providence, R.I., U.S.A. 111 E13
Providence Bay, Canada 102 C3
Providence Mts., U.S.A. 117 K11
Providencia, I. de, Colombia 120 D3
Provideniya, Russia 51 C19
Provins, France 19 D10
Provo, U.S.A. 114 F8
Provost, Canada 105 C6
Prozor, Bos.-H. 42 G2
Prudhoe, Australia 94 C4
Prudhoe Bay, U.S.A. 100 A5
Prudhoe I., Australia 94 C4
Prud'homme, Canada 105 C7
Prudnik, Poland 45 H4
Prüm, Germany 25 E2
Prundu, Romania 43 F11
Pruszcz Gdański, Poland 44 D5
Pruszków, Poland 45 F7
Prut →, Romania 43 E13
Pruzhany, Belarus 47 F3
Prvić, Croatia 29 D11
Prydz B., Antarctica 5 C6
Pryluky, Ukraine 47 G7
Pryor, U.S.A. 113 G7
Prypyat →, Europe 47 G6
Przasnysz, Poland 45 E7
Przedecz, Poland 45 F5
Przemyśl, Poland 45 J9
Przeworsk, Poland 45 H9
Przhevalsk = Karakol,
  Kyrgyzstan 50 E8
Przysucha, Poland 45 G7
Psakhná, Greece 38 C5
Psará, Greece 39 C7
Psathoúra, Greece 38 B6
Psel →, Ukraine 47 H7
Pserimos, Greece 39 E9

Psíra, Greece 36 D7
Pskov, Russia 46 D5
Pskovskoye, Ozero, Russia 46 D5
Psunj, Croatia 42 E2
Pteleón, Greece 38 B4
Ptich = Ptsich →, Belarus 47 F5
Ptolemaís, Greece 40 F5
Ptsich →, Belarus 47 F5
Ptuj, Slovenia 29 B12
Ptujska Gora, Slovenia 29 B12
Pu Xian, China 56 F6
Pua, Thailand 64 C3
Pu'an, China 58 E5
Puan, S. Korea 57 G14
Pubei, China 58 F7
Pucallpa, Peru 124 E4
Pucheng, China 59 D12
Pucheni, Romania 43 E10
Puchheim, Germany 25 G7
Púchov, Slovak Rep. 27 B11
Pucioasa, Romania 43 E10
Pučišća, Croatia 29 E13
Puck, Poland 44 D5
Pucka, Zatoka, Poland 44 D5
Puçol, Spain 33 F4
Pudasjärvi, Finland 8 D22
Puding, China 58 D5
Pudozh, Russia 46 B9
Pudukkottai, India 66 P11
Puebla, Mexico 119 D5
Puebla □, Mexico 119 D5
Puebla de Alcocer, Spain 35 G5
Puebla de Don Fadrique, Spain 33 H2
Puebla de Don Rodrigo, Spain 35 H3
Puebla de Guzmán, Spain 35 H3
Puebla de la Calzada, Spain 35 G4
Puebla de Sanabria, Spain 34 C4
Puebla de Trives = Pobra de
  Trives, Spain 34 C3
Pueblo, U.S.A. 112 F2
Pueblo Hundido, Chile 126 B1
Puelches, Argentina 126 D2
Puelén, Argentina 126 D2
Puente Alto, Chile 126 C1
Puente-Genil, Spain 35 H6
Puente la Reina, Spain 32 C3
Puenteareas = Ponteareas, Spain 34 C2
Puentedeume = Pontedeume,
  Spain 34 B2
Puentes de García Rodríguez =
  As Pontes de García
  Rodríguez, Spain 34 B3
Pu'er, China 58 F3
Puerco →, U.S.A. 115 J10
Puerto, Canary Is. 37 F2
Puerto Aisén, Chile 128 F2
Puerto Ángel, Mexico 119 D5
Puerto Arista, Mexico 119 D6
Puerto Armuelles, Panama 120 E3
Puerto Ayacucho, Venezuela 124 B5
Puerto Barrios, Guatemala 120 C2
Puerto Bermejo, Argentina 126 B4
Puerto Bermúdez, Peru 124 F4
Puerto Bolívar, Ecuador 124 D3
Puerto Cabello, Venezuela 124 A5
Puerto Cabezas, Nic. 120 D3
Puerto Cabo Gracias á Dios,
  Nic. 120 D3
Puerto Carreño, Colombia 124 B5
Puerto Castilla, Honduras 120 C2
Puerto Chicama, Peru 124 E3
Puerto Coig, Argentina 128 G3
Puerto Cortés, Costa Rica 120 E3
Puerto Cortés, Honduras 120 C2
Puerto Cumarebo, Venezuela 124 A5
Puerto de Alcudia = Port
  d'Alcúdia, Spain 37 B10
Puerto de Andraitx, Spain 37 B9
Puerto de Cabrera, Spain 37 B9
Puerto de Gran Tarajal,
  Canary Is. 37 F6
Puerto de la Cruz, Canary Is. 37 F3
Puerto de Mazarrón, Spain 33 H3
Puerto de Pozo Negro,
  Canary Is. 37 F6
Puerto de Sóller = Port de
  Sóller, Spain 37 B9
Puerto de Somosierra, Spain 34 D7
Puerto del Carmen, Canary Is. 37 F6
Puerto del Rosario, Canary Is. 37 F6
Puerto Deseado, Argentina 128 F3
Puerto Escondido, Mexico 119 D5
Puerto Heath, Bolivia 124 F5
Puerto Inírida, Colombia 124 C5
Puerto Juárez, Mexico 119 C7
Puerto La Cruz, Venezuela 124 A6
Puerto Leguízamo, Colombia 124 D4
Puerto Limón, Colombia 124 C4
Puerto Lobos, Argentina 128 E3
Puerto Lumbreras, Spain 33 H3
Puerto Madryn, Argentina 128 E3
Puerto Maldonado, Peru 124 F5
Puerto Manotí, Cuba 120 B4
Puerto Mazarrón = Puerto de
  Mazarrón, Spain 33 H3
Puerto Montt, Chile 128 E2
Puerto Morazán, Nic. 120 D2
Puerto Morelos, Mexico 119 C7
Puerto Natales, Chile 128 G2
Puerto Padre, Cuba 120 B4
Puerto Páez, Venezuela 124 B5
Puerto Peñasco, Mexico 118 A2
Puerto Pinasco, Paraguay 126 A4
Puerto Plata, Dom. Rep. 121 C5
Puerto Pollensa = Port de
  Pollença, Spain 37 B10

Puerto Princesa, *Phil.* ... 61 G3
Puerto Quepos, *Costa Rica* ... 120 E3
Puerto Real, *Spain* ... 35 J4
Puerto Rico, *Canary Is.* ... 37 G4
Puerto Rico ■, *W. Indies* ... 121 C6
Puerto Rico Trench, *Atl. Oc.* ... 121 C6
Puerto San Julián, *Argentina* ... 128 F3
Puerto Sastre, *Paraguay* ... 126 A4
Puerto Serrano, *Spain* ... 35 J5
Puerto Suárez, *Bolivia* ... 124 G7
Puerto Vallarta, *Mexico* ... 118 C3
Puerto Wilches, *Colombia* ... 124 B4
Puertollano, *Spain* ... 35 G6
Pueyrredón, L., *Argentina* ... 128 F2
Puffin I., *Ireland* ... 15 E1
Pugachev, *Russia* ... 48 D9
Pugal, *India* ... 68 E5
Puge, *China* ... 58 D4
Puge, *Tanzania* ... 86 C3
Puget Sound, *U.S.A.* ... 114 C2
Puget-Théniers, *France* ... 21 E10
Púglia □, *Italy* ... 31 A9
Pugŏdong, *N. Korea* ... 57 C16
Pugu, *Tanzania* ... 86 D4
Pūgūnzī, *Iran* ... 71 E8
Pui, *Romania* ... 42 E8
Puieşti, *Romania* ... 43 D12
Puig Major, *Spain* ... 37 B9
Puigcerdà, *Spain* ... 32 C6
Puigmal, *Spain* ... 32 C7
Puigpunyent, *Spain* ... 37 B9
Puijiang, *China* ... 58 B4
Puisaye, Collines de la, *France* ... 19 E10
Puiseaux, *France* ... 19 D9
Pujehun, *S. Leone* ... 82 D2
Pujiang, *China* ... 59 C12
Pujols, *France* ... 20 D3
Pujon-chŏsuji, *N. Korea* ... 57 D14
Pukaki L., *N.Z.* ... 91 L3
Pukapuka, *Cook Is.* ... 97 J11
Pukaskwa Nat. Park, *Canada* ... 102 C2
Pukatawagan, *Canada* ... 105 B8
Pukchin, *N. Korea* ... 57 D13
Pukch'ŏng, *N. Korea* ... 57 D15
Pukë, *Albania* ... 40 D3
Pukekohe, *N.Z.* ... 91 G5
Pukhrayan, *India* ... 69 F8
Pukou, *China* ... 59 A12
Pula, *Croatia* ... 29 D10
Pula, *Italy* ... 30 C1
Pulacayo, *Bolivia* ... 124 H5
Pulandian, *China* ... 57 E11
Pularumpi, *Australia* ... 92 B5
Pulaski, *N.Y., U.S.A.* ... 111 C8
Pulaski, *Tenn., U.S.A.* ... 109 H2
Pulaski, *Va., U.S.A.* ... 108 G5
Pulau ➤, *Indonesia* ... 63 F9
Puławy, *Poland* ... 45 G8
Pulga, *Russia* ... 116 F5
Pulicat L., *India* ... 66 N12
Pullman, *U.S.A.* ... 114 C5
Pulo-Anna, *Pac. Oc.* ... 63 D8
Pulog, Mt., *Phil.* ... 61 C4
Pultusk, *Poland* ... 45 F8
Pülümür, *Turkey* ... 73 C8
Pumlumon Fawr, *U.K.* ... 13 E4
Puná, I., *Ecuador* ... 124 D2
Punakha, *Bhutan* ... 67 F16
Punasar, *India* ... 68 F5
Punata, *Bolivia* ... 124 G5
Punch, *India* ... 69 C6
Punch ➤, *Pakistan* ... 68 C5
Punda Maria, *S. Africa* ... 89 C5
Pune, *India* ... 66 K8
P'ungsan, *N. Korea* ... 57 D15
Pungue, Ponte de, *Mozam.* ... 87 F3
Puning, *China* ... 59 F11
Punjab □, *India* ... 68 D7
Punjab □, *Pakistan* ... 68 E6
Puno, *Peru* ... 124 G4
Punpun ➤, *India* ... 69 G11
Punta Alta, *Argentina* ... 128 D4
Punta Arenas, *Chile* ... 128 G2
Punta de Díaz, *Chile* ... 126 B1
Punta Gorda, *Belize* ... 119 D7
Punta Gorda, *U.S.A.* ... 109 M5
Punta Prieta, *Mexico* ... 118 B2
Punta Prima, *Spain* ... 37 B11
Puntarenas, *Costa Rica* ... 120 E3
Punta Umbria, *Spain* ... 35 H4
Punto Fijo, *Venezuela* ... 124 A4
Punxsatawney, *U.S.A.* ... 110 F6
Puqi, *China* ... 59 C9
Puquio, *Peru* ... 124 F4
Pur ➤, *Russia* ... 50 C8
Purace, Vol., *Colombia* ... 124 C3
Puračić, *Bos.-H.* ... 42 F3
Puralia = Puruliya, *India* ... 69 H12
Puranpur, *India* ... 69 E9
Purbeck, Isle of, *U.K.* ... 13 G6
Purcell, *U.S.A.* ... 113 H6
Purcell Mts., *Canada* ... 104 D5
Puri, *India* ... 67 K14
Purmerend, *Neths.* ... 17 B4
Purnia, *India* ... 69 G12
Pursat = Pouthisat, *Cambodia* ... 64 F4
Purukcahu, *Indonesia* ... 62 E4
Puruliya, *India* ... 69 H12
Purus ➤, *Brazil* ... 122 D4
Puruvesi, *Finland* ... 46 B5
Purvis, *U.S.A.* ... 113 K10
Pŭrvomay, *Bulgaria* ... 41 D9
Purwa, *India* ... 69 F9
Purwakarta, *Indonesia* ... 63 G12
Purwodadi, *Indonesia* ... 63 G14
Purwokerto, *Indonesia* ... 63 G13
Puryŏng, *N. Korea* ... 57 C15

Pusa, *India* ... 69 G11
Pusan, *S. Korea* ... 57 G15
Pushkin, *Russia* ... 46 C6
Pushkino, *Moskva, Russia* ... 46 D9
Pushkino, *Saratov, Russia* ... 48 E8
Püspökladány, *Hungary* ... 42 C6
Pustoshka, *Russia* ... 46 D5
Puszczykowo, *Poland* ... 45 F3
Putahow L., *Canada* ... 105 B8
Putao, *Burma* ... 67 F20
Putaruru, *N.Z.* ... 91 H5
Putbus, *Germany* ... 24 A9
Putian, *China* ... 59 E12
Putignano, *Italy* ... 31 B10
Puting, Tanjung, *Indonesia* ... 62 E4
Putlitz, *Germany* ... 24 B8
Putna, *Romania* ... 43 C10
Putna ➤, *Romania* ... 43 E12
Putnam, *U.S.A.* ... 111 E13
Putnok, *Hungary* ... 42 B5
Putorana, Gory, *Russia* ... 51 C10
Puttalam, *Sri Lanka* ... 66 Q11
Puttgarden, *Germany* ... 24 A7
Püttlingen, *Germany* ... 25 F2
Putumayo ➤, *S. Amer.* ... 122 D4
Putuo, *China* ... 59 C14
Putussibau, *Indonesia* ... 62 D4
Puvirnituq, *Canada* ... 101 B12
Puy-de-Dôme, *France* ... 20 C6
Puy-de-Dôme □, *France* ... 20 C7
Puy-l'Évêque, *France* ... 20 D5
Puyallup, *U.S.A.* ... 116 C4
Puyang, *China* ... 56 G8
Puylaurens, *France* ... 20 E6
Pūzeh Rīg, *Iran* ... 71 E8
Pwani □, *Tanzania* ... 86 D4
Pweto, *Dem. Rep. of the Congo* ... 87 D2
Pwllheli, *U.K.* ... 12 E3
Pyana ➤, *Russia* ... 48 C8
Pyapon, *Burma* ... 67 L19
Pyasina ➤, *Russia* ... 51 B9
Pyatigorsk, *Russia* ... 49 H6
Pyatykhatky, *Ukraine* ... 47 H7
Pydna, *Greece* ... 40 F6
Pyè, *Burma* ... 67 K19
Pyetrikaw, *Belarus* ... 47 F5
Pyhäjoki, *Finland* ... 8 D21
Pyinmana, *Burma* ... 67 K20
Pyla, C., *Cyprus* ... 36 E12
Pymatuning Reservoir, *U.S.A.* ... 110 E4
Pyŏktong, *N. Korea* ... 57 D13
Pyŏnggang, *N. Korea* ... 57 E14
P'yŏngt'aek, *S. Korea* ... 57 F14
P'yŏngyang, *N. Korea* ... 57 E13
Pyote, *U.S.A.* ... 113 K3
Pyramid L., *U.S.A.* ... 114 G4
Pyramid Pk., *U.S.A.* ... 117 J10
Pyramids, *Egypt* ... 80 J7
Pyrénées, *Europe* ... 20 F4
Pyrénées-Atlantiques □, *France* ... 20 E3
Pyrénées-Orientales □, *France* ... 20 F6
Pyryatyn, *Ukraine* ... 47 G7
Pyrzyce, *Poland* ... 45 E1
Pyskowice, *Poland* ... 45 H5
Pytalovo, *Russia* ... 46 D4
Pyu, *Burma* ... 67 K20
Pyzdry, *Poland* ... 45 F4

Q

Qaanaaq, *Greenland* ... 4 B4
Qabirri ➤, *Azerbaijan* ... 49 K8
Qachasnek, *S. Africa* ... 89 E4
Qa'el Jafr, *Jordan* ... 75 E5
Qa'emābād, *Iran* ... 71 D9
Qā'emshahr, *Iran* ... 71 B7
Qagan Nur, *China* ... 56 C8
Qahar Youyi Zhongqi, *China* ... 56 D7
Qahremānshahr = Bākhtarān, *Iran* ... 70 C5
Qaidam Pendi, *China* ... 60 C4
Qajarīyeh, *Iran* ... 71 D6
Qala, Ras il, *Malta* ... 36 C1
Qala-i-Jadid = Spīn Búldak, *Afghan.* ... 68 D2
Qala Viala, *Pakistan* ... 68 D2
Qala Yangi, *Afghan.* ... 68 B2
Qal'at al Akhḍar, *Si. Arabia* ... 70 E3
Qal'at Dīzah, *Iraq* ... 70 B5
Qal'at Şāliḥ, *Iraq* ... 70 D5
Qal'at Sukkar, *Iraq* ... 70 D5
Qalyūb, *Egypt* ... 80 H7
Qamani'tuaq = Baker Lake, *Canada* ... 100 B10
Qamdo, *China* ... 58 B1
Qamruddin Karez, *Pakistan* ... 68 D3
Qandahār, *Afghan.* ... 66 D4
Qandahār □, *Afghan.* ... 66 D4
Qapān, *Iran* ... 71 B7
Qapshaghay, *Kazakstan* ... 50 E8
Qaqortoq, *Greenland* ... 101 B6
Qâra, *Egypt* ... 80 B2
Qara Qash ➤, *India* ... 69 B8
Qarabutaq, *Kazakstan* ... 50 E7
Qaraçala, *Azerbaijan* ... 49 L9
Qaraghandy, *Kazakstan* ... 50 E8
Qārah, *Si. Arabia* ... 70 D4
Qarataū, *Kazakstan* ... 50 E8
Qarataū, *Kazakstan* ... 50 E7
Qareh ➤, *Iran* ... 70 B5
Qareh Tekān, *Iran* ... 71 B6
Qarqan He ➤, *China* ... 60 C3
Qarqaraly, *Kazakstan* ... 50 E8
Qarrasa, *Sudan* ... 81 E3

Qarshi, *Uzbekistan* ... 50 F7
Qartabā, *Lebanon* ... 75 A4
Qaryat al Gharab, *Iraq* ... 70 D5
Qaryat al 'Ulyā, *Si. Arabia* ... 70 E5
Qasr 'Amra, *Jordan* ... 70 D3
Qaşr-e Qand, *Iran* ... 71 E9
Qasr Farâfra, *Egypt* ... 80 B2
Qatanā, *Syria* ... 75 B5
Qatar ■, *Asia* ... 71 E6
Qaţlīsh, *Iran* ... 71 B8
Qattâra, *Egypt* ... 80 A2
Qattâra, Munkhafed el, *Egypt* ... 80 B2
Qattâra Depression = Qattâra, Munkhafed el, *Egypt* ... 80 B2
Qawām al Ḥamzah, *Iraq* ... 70 D5
Qāyen, *Iran* ... 71 C8
Qazaqstan = Kazakstan ■, *Asia* ... 50 E7
Qazimämmäd, *Azerbaijan* ... 49 K9
Qazvin, *Iran* ... 71 B6
Qeissan, *Sudan* ... 81 E3
Qena, *Egypt* ... 80 B3
Qena, W. ➤, *Egypt* ... 80 B3
Qeqertarsuaq, *Greenland* ... 101 B5
Qeqertarsuaq, *Greenland* ... 4 C5
Qeshlāq, *Iran* ... 70 C5
Qeshm, *Iran* ... 71 E8
Qeys, *Iran* ... 71 E7
Qezel Owzen ➤, *Iran* ... 71 B6
Qezi'ot, *Israel* ... 75 E3
Qi Xian, *China* ... 56 G8
Qian Gorlos, *China* ... 57 B13
Qian Xian, *China* ... 56 G5
Qiancheng, *China* ... 58 D7
Qianjiang, *Guangxi Zhuangzu, China* ... 58 F7
Qianjiang, *Hubei, China* ... 59 B9
Qianjiang, *Sichuan, China* ... 58 C7
Qianshan, *China* ... 59 B11
Qianwei, *China* ... 58 C4
Qianxi, *China* ... 58 D6
Qianyang, *Hunan, China* ... 59 D8
Qianyang, *Shaanxi, China* ... 56 G4
Qianyang, *Zhejiang, China* ... 59 B12
Qiaojia, *China* ... 58 D4
Qichun, *China* ... 59 B10
Qidong, *Hunan, China* ... 59 D9
Qidong, *Jiangsu, China* ... 59 B13
Qijiang, *China* ... 58 C6
Qikiqtarjuaq, *Canada* ... 101 B13
Qila Safed, *Pakistan* ... 66 E2
Qila Saifullāh, *Pakistan* ... 68 D3
Qilian Shan, *China* ... 60 C4
Qimen, *China* ... 59 C11
Qin He ➤, *China* ... 56 G7
Qin Jiang ➤, *Guangxi Zhuangzu, China* ... 58 F7
Qin Jiang ➤, *Jiangxi, China* ... 59 D10
Qin Ling = Qinling Shandi, *China* ... 56 H5
Qin'an, *China* ... 56 G3
Qing Xian, *China* ... 56 E9
Qingcheng, *China* ... 57 F9
Qingdao, *China* ... 57 F11
Qingfeng, *China* ... 56 G8
Qinghai □, *China* ... 60 C4
Qinghai Hu, *China* ... 60 C5
Qinghecheng, *China* ... 57 D13
Qinghemen, *China* ... 57 D11
Qingjian, *China* ... 56 F6
Qingjiang = Huaiyin, *China* ... 57 H10
Qingliu, *China* ... 59 D11
Qinglong, *China* ... 58 E5
Qingping, *China* ... 58 D6
Qingpu, *China* ... 59 B13
Qingshui, *China* ... 56 G4
Qingshuihe, *China* ... 56 E6
Qingtian, *China* ... 59 C13
Qingtongxia Shuiku, *China* ... 56 F3
Qingxi, *China* ... 58 D7
Qingxu, *China* ... 56 F7
Qingyang, *Anhui, China* ... 59 B11
Qingyang, *Gansu, China* ... 56 F4
Qingyi Jiang ➤, *China* ... 58 C4
Qingyuan, *Guangdong, China* ... 59 F9
Qingyuan, *Liaoning, China* ... 57 C13
Qingyuan, *Zhejiang, China* ... 59 D12
Qingyun, *China* ... 57 F9
Qingzhen, *China* ... 58 D6
Qinhuangdao, *China* ... 57 E10
Qinling Shandi, *China* ... 56 H5
Qinshui, *China* ... 56 G7
Qinyang = Jiyuan, *China* ... 56 G7
Qinyang, *China* ... 56 F7
Qinzhou, *China* ... 58 G7
Qionghai, *China* ... 64 C8
Qiongjiang ➤, *China* ... 58 B4
Qionglai, *China* ... 58 B4
Qionglai Shan, *China* ... 58 B4
Qiongzhou Haixia, *China* ... 64 B8
Qiqihar, *China* ... 51 E13
Qiraïya, W. ➤, *Egypt* ... 75 E3
Qiryat Ata, *Israel* ... 75 C4
Qiryat Gat, *Israel* ... 75 D3
Qiryat Mal'akhi, *Israel* ... 75 D3
Qiryat Shemona, *Israel* ... 75 B4
Qiryat Yam, *Israel* ... 75 C4
Qishan, *China* ... 56 G4
Qitai, *China* ... 60 B3
Qiubei, *China* ... 58 E5
Qixia, *China* ... 57 F11
Qiyang, *China* ... 59 D8
Qızlağac Körfäzi, *Azerbaijan* ... 71 B6
Qojūr, *Iran* ... 70 B5
Qom, *Iran* ... 71 C6
Qomolangma Feng = Everest, Mt., *Nepal* ... 69 E12
Qomsheh, *Iran* ... 71 D6
Qoraqalpoghistan □, *Uzbekistan* ... 50 E6

Qorveh, *Iran* ... 73 E12
Qostanay, *Kazakstan* ... 50 D7
Qoţūr, *Iran* ... 73 C11
Qu Jiang ➤, *China* ... 58 B6
Qu Xian, *China* ... 58 B6
Quabbin Reservoir, *U.S.A.* ... 111 D12
Quairading, *Australia* ... 93 F2
Quakenbrück, *Germany* ... 24 C3
Quakertown, *U.S.A.* ... 111 F9
Qualicum Beach, *Canada* ... 104 D4
Quambatook, *Australia* ... 95 F3
Quambone, *Australia* ... 95 E4
Quamby, *Australia* ... 94 C3
Quan Long = Ca Mau, *Vietnam* ... 65 H5
Quanah, *U.S.A.* ... 113 H5
Quang Ngai, *Vietnam* ... 64 E7
Quang Tri, *Vietnam* ... 64 D6
Quang Yen, *Vietnam* ... 58 G6
Quannan, *China* ... 59 E10
Quantock Hills, *U.K.* ... 13 F4
Quanzhou, *Fujian, China* ... 59 E12
Quanzhou, *Guangxi Zhuangzu, China* ... 59 E8
Qu'Appelle, *Canada* ... 105 C8
Quaqtaq, *Canada* ... 101 B13
Quaraí, *Brazil* ... 126 C4
Quarré-les-Tombes, *France* ... 19 E11
Quarteira, *Portugal* ... 35 H2
Quartu Sant'Élena, *Italy* ... 30 C2
Quartzsite, *U.S.A.* ... 117 M12
Quatsino Sd., *Canada* ... 104 C3
Quba, *Azerbaijan* ... 49 K9
Qūchān, *Iran* ... 71 B8
Queanbeyan, *Australia* ... 95 F4
Québec, *Canada* ... 103 C5
Québec □, *Canada* ... 103 C6
Quedlinburg, *Germany* ... 24 D7
Queen Alexandra Ra., *Antarctica* ... 5 E11
Queen Charlotte City, *Canada* ... 104 C2
Queen Charlotte Is., *Canada* ... 104 C2
Queen Charlotte Sd., *Canada* ... 104 C3
Queen Charlotte Strait, *Canada* ... 104 C3
Queen Elizabeth Is., *Canada* ... 98 B10
Queen Elizabeth Nat. Park, *Uganda* ... 86 C3
Queen Mary Land, *Antarctica* ... 5 D7
Queen Maud G., *Canada* ... 100 B9
Queen Maud Land, *Antarctica* ... 5 D3
Queen Maud Mts., *Antarctica* ... 5 E13
Queens Chan., *Australia* ... 92 C4
Queenscliff, *Australia* ... 95 F3
Queensland □, *Australia* ... 94 C3
Queenstown, *Australia* ... 94 G4
Queenstown, *N.Z.* ... 91 L2
Queenstown, *S. Africa* ... 88 E4
Queets, *U.S.A.* ... 116 C2
Queguay Grande ➤, *Uruguay* ... 126 C4
Queimadas, *Brazil* ... 125 F11
Quelimane, *Mozam.* ... 87 F4
Quellón, *Chile* ... 128 E2
Quelpart = Cheju do, *S. Korea* ... 57 H14
Queluz, *Portugal* ... 35 G1
Quemado, *N. Mex., U.S.A.* ... 115 J9
Quemado, *Tex., U.S.A.* ... 113 L4
Quemoy = Chinmen, *Taiwan* ... 59 E13
Quemú-Quemú, *Argentina* ... 126 D3
Quequén, *Argentina* ... 126 D4
Querétaro, *Mexico* ... 118 C4
Querétaro □, *Mexico* ... 118 C5
Querfurt, *Germany* ... 24 D7
Quérigut, *France* ... 20 F6
Querqueville, *France* ... 18 C5
Quesada, *Spain* ... 35 H7
Queshan, *China* ... 56 H8
Quesnel, *Canada* ... 104 C4
Quesnel ➤, *Canada* ... 104 C4
Quesnel L., *Canada* ... 104 C4
Questa, *U.S.A.* ... 115 H11
Questembert, *France* ... 18 E4
Quetico Prov. Park, *Canada* ... 102 C1
Quetta, *Pakistan* ... 68 D2
Quezaltenango, *Guatemala* ... 120 D1
Quezon City, *Phil.* ... 61 D4
Qufār, *Si. Arabia* ... 70 E4
Qui Nhon, *Vietnam* ... 64 F7
Quibaxe, *Angola* ... 84 F2
Quibdo, *Colombia* ... 124 B3
Quiberon, *France* ... 18 E3
Quiberon, Presqu'île de, *France* ... 18 E3
Quickborn, *Germany* ... 24 B5
Quiet L., *Canada* ... 104 A2
Quiindy, *Paraguay* ... 126 B4
Quila, *Mexico* ... 118 C3
Quilán, C., *Chile* ... 128 E2
Quilcene, *U.S.A.* ... 116 C4
Quilimarí, *Chile* ... 126 C1
Quilino, *Argentina* ... 126 C3
Quillabamba, *Peru* ... 124 F4
Quillagua, *Chile* ... 126 A2
Quillaicillo, *Chile* ... 126 C1
Quillan, *France* ... 20 F6
Quillota, *Chile* ... 126 C1
Quilmes, *Argentina* ... 126 C4
Quilon, *India* ... 66 Q10
Quilpie, *Australia* ... 95 D3
Quilpué, *Chile* ... 126 C1
Quilua, *Mozam.* ... 87 F4
Quimilí, *Argentina* ... 126 B3
Quimper, *France* ... 18 E2
Quimperlé, *France* ... 18 E3
Quinault ➤, *U.S.A.* ... 116 C2
Quincy, *Fla., U.S.A.* ... 109 K3
Quincy, *Ill., U.S.A.* ... 112 F9
Quincy, *Mass., U.S.A.* ... 111 D14

Quincy, *Wash., U.S.A.* ... 114 C4
Quines, *Argentina* ... 126 C2
Quinga, *Mozam.* ... 87 F5
Quingey, *France* ... 19 E12
Quinns Rocks, *Australia* ... 93 F2
Quintana de la Serena, *Spain* ... 35 G5
Quintana Roo □, *Mexico* ... 119 D7
Quintanar de la Orden, *Spain* ... 35 F7
Quintanar de la Sierra, *Spain* ... 32 D2
Quintanar del Rey, *Spain* ... 33 F3
Quintero, *Chile* ... 126 C1
Quintin, *France* ... 18 D4
Quinto, *Spain* ... 32 D4
Quípar ➤, *Spain* ... 33 G3
Quirihue, *Chile* ... 126 D1
Quirindi, *Australia* ... 95 E5
Quirinópolis, *Brazil* ... 125 G8
Quiroga, *Spain* ... 34 C3
Quissac, *France* ... 21 E8
Quissanga, *Mozam.* ... 87 E5
Quissico, *Mozam.* ... 89 C5
Quitilipi, *Argentina* ... 126 B3
Quitman, *U.S.A.* ... 109 K4
Quito, *Ecuador* ... 124 D3
Quixadá, *Brazil* ... 125 D11
Quixaxe, *Mozam.* ... 87 F5
Qujing, *China* ... 58 E4
Qulan, *Kazakstan* ... 50 E8
Qul'ân, Jazâ'ir, *Egypt* ... 70 E2
Qumbu, *S. Africa* ... 89 E4
Quneitra, *Syria* ... 75 B4
Qunghirot, *Uzbekistan* ... 50 E6
Qu'nyido, *China* ... 58 B2
Quoin I., *Australia* ... 92 B4
Quoin Pt., *S. Africa* ... 88 E2
Quorn, *Australia* ... 95 E2
Qūqon, *Uzbekistan* ... 50 E8
Qurein, *Sudan* ... 81 E3
Qurnat as Sawdā', *Lebanon* ... 75 A5
Qûs, *Egypt* ... 80 B3
Qusar, *Azerbaijan* ... 49 K9
Quşaybā', *Si. Arabia* ... 70 E4
Quşaybah, *Iraq* ... 70 C4
Quseir, *Egypt* ... 70 E2
Qūshchī, *Iran* ... 70 B5
Quthing, *Lesotho* ... 89 E4
Qūṭīābād, *Iran* ... 71 C6
Quwo, *China* ... 56 G6
Quyang, *China* ... 56 E8
Quynh Nhai, *Vietnam* ... 64 B4
Quyon, *Canada* ... 111 A8
Quzhou, *China* ... 59 C12
Quzi, *China* ... 56 F4

R

Ra, Ko, *Thailand* ... 65 H2
Raab, *Austria* ... 26 C6
Raahe, *Finland* ... 8 D21
Raalte, *Neths.* ... 17 B6
Raasay, *U.K.* ... 14 D2
Raasay, Sd. of, *U.K.* ... 14 D2
Rab, *Croatia* ... 29 D11
Raba, *Indonesia* ... 63 F5
Rába ➤, *Hungary* ... 42 C2
Raba ➤, *Poland* ... 45 H7
Rabaçal ➤, *Portugal* ... 34 D3
Rabah, *Nigeria* ... 83 C6
Rabai, *Kenya* ... 86 C4
Rabak, *Sudan* ... 81 E3
Rabastens, *France* ... 20 E5
Rabastens-de-Bigorre, *France* ... 20 E4
Rabat, *Malta* ... 36 D1
Rabat, *Morocco* ... 78 B4
Rabaul, *Papua N. G.* ... 96 H7
Rābigh, *Si. Arabia* ... 74 C2
Rabka, *Poland* ... 45 J6
Rābniţa, *Moldova* ... 43 C14
Rābor, *Iran* ... 71 D8
Rača, *Serbia, Yug.* ... 40 B4
Răcăciuni, *Romania* ... 43 D11
Răcăşdia, *Romania* ... 42 F6
Racconigi, *Italy* ... 28 D4
Race, C., *Canada* ... 103 C9
Rach Gia, *Vietnam* ... 65 G5
Rachid, *Mauritania* ... 82 B2
Raciąż, *Poland* ... 45 F7
Racibórz, *Poland* ... 45 H5
Racine, *U.S.A.* ... 108 D2
Rackerby, *U.S.A.* ... 116 F5
Radama, Nosy, *Madag.* ... 89 A8
Radama, Saikanosy, *Madag.* ... 89 A8
Radan, *Serbia, Yug.* ... 40 D5
Rădăuţi, *Romania* ... 43 C10
Rădăuţi-Prut, *Romania* ... 43 B11
Radbuza ➤, *Czech Rep.* ... 26 B6
Radcliff, *U.S.A.* ... 108 G3
Radeberg, *Germany* ... 24 D9
Radebeul, *Germany* ... 24 D9
Radeče, *Slovenia* ... 29 B12
Radekhiv, *Ukraine* ... 47 G3
Radekhov = Radekhiv, *Ukraine* ... 47 G3
Radenthein, *Austria* ... 26 E6
Radew ➤, *Poland* ... 44 E2
Radford, *U.S.A.* ... 108 G5
Radhanpur, *India* ... 68 H4
Radhwa, Jabal, *Si. Arabia* ... 70 E3
Radika ➤, *Macedonia* ... 40 E4
Radisson, *Qué., Canada* ... 102 B4
Radisson, *Sask., Canada* ... 105 C7
Radium Hot Springs, *Canada* ... 104 C5
Radlje ob Dravi, *Slovenia* ... 29 B12

Radnevo, *Bulgaria* 41 D9
Radnice, *Czech Rep.* 26 B6
Radnor Forest, *U.K.* 13 E4
Radolfzell, *Germany* 25 H4
Radom, *Poland* 45 G8
Radomir, *Bulgaria* 40 D6
Radomka →, *Poland* 45 G8
Radomsko, *Poland* 45 G6
Radomyshl, *Ukraine* 47 G5
Radomyśl Wielki, *Poland* 45 H8
Radoszyce, *Poland* 45 G7
Radoviš, *Macedonia* 40 E6
Radovljica, *Slovenia* 29 B11
Radstadt, *Austria* 26 D6
Radstock, C., *Australia* 95 E1
Răducăneni, *Romania* 43 D12
Raduša, *Macedonia* 40 D5
Radviliškis, *Lithuania* 9 J20
Radville, *Canada* 105 D8
Raḍwá, J., *Si. Arabia* 80 C4
Radymno, *Poland* 45 J9
Radzanów, *Poland* 45 F7
Radziejów, *Poland* 45 F5
Radzyń Chełmiński, *Poland* . . 44 E5
Radzyń Podlaski, *Poland* 45 G9
Rae, *Canada* 104 A5
Rae Bareli, *India* 69 F9
Rae Isthmus, *Canada* 101 B11
Raeren, *Belgium* 17 D6
Raeside, L., *Australia* 93 E3
Raetihi, *N.Z.* 91 H5
Rafaela, *Argentina* 126 C3
Rafah, *Gaza Strip* 75 D3
Rafai, *C.A.R.* 86 B1
Raffadali, *Italy* 30 E6
Raffili, *Sudan* 81 F2
Rafḥā, *Si. Arabia* 70 D4
Rafsanjān, *Iran* 71 D8
Raft Pt., *Australia* 92 C3
Râga, *Sudan* 81 F2
Raga →, *Sudan* 81 F2
Ragachow, *Belarus* 47 F6
Ragag, *Sudan* 81 E1
Ragama, *Sri Lanka* 66 R11
Ragged, Mt., *Australia* 93 F3
Raghunathpalli, *India* 69 H11
Raghunathpur, *India* 69 H12
Raglan, *N.Z.* 91 G5
Ragusa, *Italy* 31 F7
Raha, *Indonesia* 63 E6
Rahad, Nahr ed →, *Sudan* . . . 81 E3
Rahaeng = Tak, *Thailand* 64 D2
Rahatgarh, *India* 69 H8
Rahden, *Germany* 24 C4
Raheita, *Eritrea* 81 E5
Rahimyar Khan, *Pakistan* 68 E4
Rāhjerd, *Iran* 71 C6
Rahon, *India* 68 D7
Raichur, *India* 66 L10
Raiganj, *India* 69 G13
Raigarh, *India* 67 J13
Raijua, *Indonesia* 63 F6
Raikot, *India* 68 D6
Railton, *Australia* 94 G4
Rainbow Lake, *Canada* 104 B5
Rainier, *U.S.A.* 116 D4
Rainier, Mt., *U.S.A.* 116 D5
Rainy L., *Canada* 105 D10
Rainy River, *Canada* 105 D10
Raippaluoto, *Finland* 8 E19
Raipur, *India* 67 J12
Ra'is, *Si. Arabia* 80 C4
Raisen, *India* 68 H8
Raisio, *Finland* 9 F20
Raj Nandgaon, *India* 67 J12
Raj Nilgiri, *India* 69 J12
Raja, Ujung, *Indonesia* 62 D1
Raja Ampat, Kepulauan,
  Indonesia 63 E7
Rajahmundry, *India* 67 L12
Rajang →, *Malaysia* 62 D4
Rajanpur, *Pakistan* 68 E4
Rajapalaiyam, *India* 66 Q10
Rajasthan □, *India* 68 F5
Rajasthan Canal, *India* 68 F5
Rajauri, *India* 69 C6
Rajgarh, Mad. P., *India* 68 G7
Rajgarh, Raj., *India* 68 F7
Rajgarh, Raj., *India* 68 E6
Rajgir, *India* 69 G11
Rajgród, *Poland* 44 E9
Rajkot, *India* 68 H4
Rajmahal Hills, *India* 69 G12
Rajpipla, *India* 66 J8
Rajpur, *India* 68 H6
Rajpura, *India* 68 D7
Rajshahi, *Bangla.* 67 G16
Rajshahi □, *Bangla.* 69 G13
Rajula, *India* 68 J4
Rakaia, *N.Z.* 91 K4
Rakaia →, *N.Z.* 91 K4
Rakan, Ra's, *Qatar* 71 E6
Rakaposhi, *Pakistan* 69 A6
Rakata, Pulau, *Indonesia* 62 F3
Rakhiv, *Ukraine* 47 H3
Rakhni, *Pakistan* 68 D3
Rakhni →, *Pakistan* 68 E3
Rakitnoye, *Russia* 54 B7
Rakitovo, *Bulgaria* 41 E8
Rakiv, *Poland* 45 F3
Rakops, *Botswana* 88 C3
Rakovica, *Croatia* 29 D12
Rakovník, *Czech Rep.* 26 A6
Rakovski, *Bulgaria* 41 D8
Rakvere, *Estonia* 9 G22
Raleigh, *U.S.A.* 109 H6
Ralja, *Serbia, Yug.* 40 B4

Ralls, *U.S.A.* 113 J4
Ralston, *U.S.A.* 110 E8
Ram →, *Canada* 104 A4
Rām Allāh, *West Bank* 75 D4
Rama, *Nic.* 120 D3
Ramacca, *Italy* 31 E7
Ramakona, *India* 69 J8
Ramales de la Victoria, *Spain* . 34 B7
Raman, *Thailand* 65 J3
Ramanathapuram, *India* 66 Q11
Ramanetaka, B. de, *Madag.* . . 89 A8
Ramanujganj, *India* 69 H10
Ramat Gan, *Israel* 75 C3
Ramatlhabama, *S. Africa* 88 D4
Ramban, *India* 69 C6
Rambervillers, *France* 19 D13
Rambipuji, *Indonesia* 63 H15
Rambouillet, *France* 19 D8
Rame Hd., *Australia* 95 F4
Ramechhap, *Nepal* 69 F12
Ramenskoye, *Russia* 46 E10
Ramganga →, *India* 69 F8
Ramgarh, Bihar, *India* 69 H11
Ramgarh, Raj., *India* 68 F6
Ramgarh, Raj., *India* 68 F4
Rāmhormoz, *Iran* 71 D6
Ramīān, *Iran* 71 B7
Ramingining, *Australia* 94 A2
Ramla, *Israel* 75 D3
Ramlu, *Eritrea* 81 E5
Râmna →, *Romania* 43 E12
Ramnad = Ramanathapuram,
  India 66 Q11
Ramnagar, *Jammu & Kashmir,*
  India 69 C6
Ramnagar, Ut. P., *India* 69 E8
Ramnäs, *Sweden* 10 E10
Râmnicu Sărat, *Romania* 43 E12
Râmnicu Vâlcea, *Romania* . . . 43 E9
Ramon, *Russia* 47 G10
Ramona, *U.S.A.* 117 M10
Ramonville-St-Agne, *France* . . 20 E5
Ramore, *Canada* 102 C3
Ramos →, *Nigeria* 83 D6
Ramotswa, *Botswana* 88 C4
Rampur, H.P., *India* 68 D7
Rampur, Mad. P., *India* 68 H5
Rampur, Ut. P., *India* 69 E8
Rampur Hat, *India* 69 G12
Rampura, *India* 68 G6
Ramrama Tola, *India* 69 J8
Ramree I., *Burma* 67 K19
Rāmsar, *Iran* 71 B6
Ramsey, *U.K.* 12 C3
Ramsey, *U.S.A.* 111 E10
Ramsey L., *Canada* 102 C3
Ramsgate, *U.K.* 13 F9
Ramsjö, *Sweden* 10 B9
Ramstein, *Germany* 25 F3
Ramtek, *India* 66 J11
Ramvik, *Sweden* 10 B11
Rana Pratap Sagar Dam, *India* . 68 G6
Ranaghat, *India* 69 H13
Ranahu, *Pakistan* 68 G3
Ranau, *Malaysia* 62 C5
Rancagua, *Chile* 126 C1
Rance →, *France* 18 D5
Rancheria →, *Canada* 104 A3
Ranchester, *U.S.A.* 114 D10
Ranchi, *India* 69 H11
Rancho Cucamonga, *U.S.A.* . . 117 L9
Randalstown, *U.K.* 15 B5
Randan, *France* 19 F10
Randazzo, *Italy* 31 E7
Randers, *Denmark* 11 H4
Randers Fjord, *Denmark* 11 H4
Randfontein, *S. Africa* 89 D4
Randle, *U.S.A.* 116 D5
Randolph, Mass., *U.S.A.* 111 D13
Randolph, N.Y., *U.S.A.* 110 D6
Randolph, Utah, *U.S.A.* 114 F8
Randolph, Vt., *U.S.A.* 111 C12
Randsburg, *U.S.A.* 117 K9
Råne älv →, *Sweden* 8 D20
Rangae, *Thailand* 65 J3
Rangaunu B., *N.Z.* 91 F4
Rangeley, *U.S.A.* 111 B14
Rangeley L., *U.S.A.* 111 B14
Rangely, *U.S.A.* 114 F9
Ranger, *U.S.A.* 113 J5
Rangia, *India* 67 F17
Rangiora, *N.Z.* 91 K4
Rangitaiki →, *N.Z.* 91 G6
Rangitata →, *N.Z.* 91 K3
Rangkasbitung, *Indonesia* . . . 63 G12
Rangon →, *Burma* 67 L20
Rangoon, *Burma* 67 L20
Rangpur, *Bangla.* 67 G16
Rangsit, *Thailand* 64 F3
Ranibennur, *India* 66 M9
Raniganj, Ut. P., *India* 69 F9
Raniganj, W. Bengal, *India* . . . 69 H15
Ranikhet, *India* 69 E8
Raniwara, *India* 66 G8
Ranka, *India* 69 H10
Ranken →, *Australia* 94 C2
Rankin, *U.S.A.* 113 K4
Rankin Inlet, *Canada* 100 B10
Rankins Springs, *Australia* . . 95 E4
Rankweil, *Austria* 26 D2
Rannoch, L., *U.K.* 14 E4
Rannoch Moor, *U.K.* 14 E4
Ranobe, Helodrano' i, *Madag.* . 89 C7
Ranohira, *Madag.* 89 C8
Ranomafana, Toamasina,
  Madag. 89 B8

Ranomafana, Toliara, Madag. . 89 C8
Ranomena, *Madag.* 89 C8
Ranong, *Thailand* 65 H2
Ranotsara Nord, *Madag.* 89 C8
Rânsa, *Iran* 71 C6
Ransiki, *Indonesia* 63 E8
Rantabe, *Madag.* 89 B8
Rantauprapat, *Indonesia* 62 D1
Rantemario, *Indonesia* 63 E5
Rantoul, *U.S.A.* 108 E1
Ranum, *Denmark* 11 H3
Ranyah, W. →, *Si. Arabia* 80 C5
Raon l'Étape, *France* 19 D13
Raoping, *China* 59 F11
Raoyang, *China* 56 E8
Rapa, *Pac. Oc.* 97 K13
Rapallo, *Italy* 28 D6
Rapar, *India* 68 H4
Raper, C., *Canada* 101 B13
Rapid City, *U.S.A.* 112 D3
Rapid River, *U.S.A.* 108 C2
Rapla, *Estonia* 9 G21
Rapti →, *India* 69 F10
Raqaba ez Zarqa →, *Sudan* . . 81 F2
Raquette →, *U.S.A.* 111 B10
Raquette Lake, *U.S.A.* 111 C10
Rarotonga, *Cook Is.* 97 K12
Ra's al 'Ayn, *Syria* 70 B4
Ras al Khaymah, *U.A.E.* 71 E7
Ras Ghārib, *Egypt* 80 B3
Ras Mallap, *Egypt* 80 B3
Rasca, Pta. de la, *Canary Is.* . . 37 G3
Raseiniai, *Lithuania* 9 J20
Rashad, *Sudan* 81 E3
Rashīd, *Egypt* 80 H7
Rashīd, Masabb, *Egypt* 80 H7
Rashmi, *India* 68 G6
Rasht, *Iran* 71 B6
Rasi Salai, *Thailand* 64 E5
Raška, *Serbia, Yug.* 40 C4
Râsnov, *Romania* 43 E10
Rason L., *Australia* 93 E3
Raşova, *Romania* 43 F12
Rasovo, *Bulgaria* 40 C7
Rasra, *India* 69 G10
Rasskazovo, *Russia* 48 D5
Rast, *Romania* 43 G8
Rastatt, *Germany* 25 G4
Rastede, *Germany* 24 B4
Răstoliţa, *Romania* 43 D9
Rasul, *Pakistan* 68 C5
Raszków, *Poland* 45 G4
Rat Buri, *Thailand* 64 F2
Rat Islands, *U.S.A.* 100 C1
Rat L., *Canada* 105 B9
Ratangarh, *India* 68 E6
Rātansbyn, *Sweden* 10 B8
Raţāwī, *Iraq* 70 D5
Rath, *India* 69 G8
Rath Luirc, *Ireland* 15 D3
Rathdrum, *Ireland* 15 D5
Rathenow, *Germany* 24 C8
Rathkeale, *Ireland* 15 D3
Rathlin I., *U.K.* 15 A5
Rathlin O'Birne I., *Ireland* . . . 15 B3
Rathmelton, *Ireland* 15 A4
Ratibor = Racibórz, *Poland* . . 45 H5
Rātikon, *Austria* 26 D2
Ratingen, *Germany* 24 D2
Ratlam, *India* 68 H6
Ratnagiri, *India* 66 L8
Ratodero, *Pakistan* 68 F3
Raton, *U.S.A.* 113 G2
Rattaphum, *Thailand* 65 J3
Ratten, *Austria* 26 D8
Rattray Hd., *U.K.* 14 D7
Rättvik, *Sweden* 10 D9
Ratz, Mt., *Canada* 104 B2
Ratzeburg, *Germany* 24 B6
Raub, *Malaysia* 65 L3
Rauch, *Argentina* 126 D4
Raudales de Malpaso, *Mexico* . 119 D6
Raufarhöfn, *Iceland* 8 C6
Raufoss, *Norway* 9 F14
Raukumara Ra., *N.Z.* 91 H6
Rauma, *Finland* 9 F19
Raurkela, *India* 69 H11
Rausu-Dake, *Japan* 54 B12
Răut →, *Moldova* 43 C14
Rava-Ruska, *Poland* 47 G2
Rava Russkaya = Rava-Ruska,
  Poland 47 G2
Ravalli, *U.S.A.* 114 C6
Ravānsar, *Iran* 70 C5
Ravanusa, *Italy* 30 E6
Rāvar, *Iran* 71 D8
Ravena, *U.S.A.* 111 D11
Ravenna, *Italy* 29 D9
Ravenna, Nebr., *U.S.A.* 112 E5
Ravenna, Ohio, *U.S.A.* 110 E3
Ravensburg, *Germany* 25 H5
Ravenshoe, *Australia* 94 B4
Ravensthorpe, *Australia* 93 F3
Ravenswood, *Australia* 94 C4
Ravenswood, *U.S.A.* 108 F5
Ravi →, *Pakistan* 68 D4
Ravna Gora, *Croatia* 29 C11
Ravna Reka, *Serbia, Yug.* 40 C5
Ravne na Koroškem, *Slovenia* . 29 B11
Rawa Mazowiecka, *Poland* . . . 45 G7
Rawalpindi, *Pakistan* 68 C5
Rawāndūz, *Iraq* 70 B5
Rawang, *Malaysia* 65 L3
Rawene, *N.Z.* 91 F4

Rawicz, *Poland* 45 G3
Rawka →, *Poland* 45 F7
Rawlinna, *Australia* 93 F4
Rawlins, *U.S.A.* 114 F10
Rawlinson Ra., *Australia* 93 D4
Rawson, *Argentina* 128 E3
Raxaul, *India* 69 F11
Ray, *U.S.A.* 112 A3
Ray, C., *Canada* 103 C8
Rayadurg, *India* 66 M10
Rayagada, *India* 67 K13
Raychikhinsk, *Russia* 51 E13
Rāyen, *Iran* 71 D8
Rayleigh, *U.K.* 13 F8
Raymond, *Canada* 104 D6
Raymond, Calif., *U.S.A.* 116 H7
Raymond, N.H., *U.S.A.* 111 C13
Raymond, Wash., *U.S.A.* 116 D3
Raymondville, *U.S.A.* 113 M6
Raymore, *Canada* 105 C8
Rayón, *Mexico* 118 B2
Rayong, *Thailand* 64 F3
Rayville, *U.S.A.* 113 J9
Raz, Pte. du, *France* 18 D2
Razan, *Iran* 71 C6
Razdan, *Armenia* 49 K7
Ražana, *Serbia, Yug.* 40 B3
Ražanj, *Serbia, Yug.* 40 C5
Razdelna, *Bulgaria* 41 C11
Razdel'naya = Rozdilna,
  Ukraine 47 J6
Razdolnoye, *Russia* 54 C5
Razdolnoye, *Ukraine* 47 K7
Razeh, *Iran* 71 C6
Razgrad, *Bulgaria* 41 C10
Razim, Lacul, *Romania* 43 F14
Razlog, *Bulgaria* 40 E7
Razmak, *Pakistan* 68 C3
Ré, Î. de, *France* 20 B2
Reading, *U.K.* 13 F7
Reading, *U.S.A.* 111 F9
Reading □, *U.K.* 13 F7
Realicó, *Argentina* 126 D3
Réalmont, *France* 20 E6
Ream, *Cambodia* 65 G4
Reata, *Mexico* 118 B4
Reay Forest, *U.K.* 14 C4
Rebais, *France* 19 D10
Rebi, *Indonesia* 63 F8
Rebiana, *Libya* 79 D10
Rebun-Tō, *Japan* 54 B10
Recanati, *Italy* 29 E10
Recaş, *Romania* 42 E6
Recco, *Italy* 28 D6
Recherche, Arch. of the,
  Australia 93 F3
Rechna Doab, *Pakistan* 68 D5
Rechytsa, *Belarus* 47 F6
Recife, *Brazil* 125 E12
Recklinghausen, *Germany* . . . 17 C7
Reconquista, *Argentina* 126 B4
Recreo, *Argentina* 126 B2
Recz, *Poland* 45 E2
Red →, La., *U.S.A.* 113 K9
Red →, N. Dak., *U.S.A.* 100 C10
Red Bank, *U.S.A.* 111 F10
Red Bay, *Canada* 103 B8
Red Bluff, *U.S.A.* 114 F2
Red Bluff L., *U.S.A.* 113 K3
Red Cliffs, *Australia* 95 E3
Red Cloud, *U.S.A.* 112 E5
Red Creek, *U.S.A.* 111 C8
Red Deer, *Canada* 104 C6
Red Deer →, Alta., *Canada* . . . 105 C7
Red Deer →, Man., *Canada* . . . 105 C8
Red Deer L., *Canada* 105 C8
Red Hook, *U.S.A.* 111 E11
Red Indian L., *Canada* 103 C8
Red L., *Canada* 105 C10
Red Lake, *Canada* 105 C10
Red Lake Falls, *U.S.A.* 112 B6
Red Lake Road, *Canada* 105 C10
Red Lodge, *U.S.A.* 114 D9
Red Mountain, *U.S.A.* 117 K9
Red Oak, *U.S.A.* 112 E7
Red Rock, *Canada* 102 C2
Red Rock, L., *U.S.A.* 112 E8
Red Rocks Pt., *Australia* 93 F4
Red Sea, *Asia* 74 C2
Red Slate Mt., *U.S.A.* 116 H8
Red Sucker L., *Canada* 102 B1
Red Tower Pass = Turnu Roşu,
  P., *Romania* 43 E9
Red Wing, *U.S.A.* 112 C8
Reda, *Poland* 44 D5
Redang, *Malaysia* 62 C2
Redange, *Lux.* 17 E5
Redcar, *U.K.* 12 C6
Redcar & Cleveland □, *U.K.* . . 12 C7
Redcliff, *Canada* 105 C6
Redcliffe, *Australia* 95 D5
Redcliffe, Mt., *Australia* 93 E3
Reddersburg, *S. Africa* 88 D4
Redding, *U.S.A.* 114 F2
Redditch, *U.K.* 13 E6
Redfield, *U.S.A.* 112 C5
Redford, *U.S.A.* 111 B11
Redkino, *Russia* 46 D9
Redlands, *U.S.A.* 117 M9
Redmond, Oreg., *U.S.A.* 114 D3
Redmond, Wash., *U.S.A.* 116 C4
Redon, *France* 18 E4
Redonda, *Antigua* 121 C7
Redondela, *Spain* 34 C2
Redondo, *Portugal* 35 G3
Redondo Beach, *U.S.A.* 117 M8
Redruth, *U.K.* 13 G2
Redvers, *Canada* 105 D8

Redwater, *Canada* 104 C6
Redwood, *U.S.A.* 111 B9
Redwood City, *U.S.A.* 116 H4
Redwood Falls, *U.S.A.* 112 C7
Redwood National Park, *U.S.A.* 114 F1
Ree, L., *Ireland* 15 C3
Reed, L., *Canada* 105 C8
Reed City, *U.S.A.* 108 D3
Reedley, *U.S.A.* 116 J7
Reedsburg, *U.S.A.* 112 D9
Reedsport, *U.S.A.* 114 E1
Reedsville, *U.S.A.* 110 F7
Reefton, *N.Z.* 91 K3
Rees, *Germany* 24 D2
Reese →, *U.S.A.* 114 F5
Refahiye, *Turkey* 73 C8
Reftele, *Sweden* 11 G7
Refugio, *U.S.A.* 113 L6
Rega →, *Poland* 44 D2
Regalbuto, *Italy* 31 E7
Regen, *Germany* 25 G9
Regen →, *Germany* 25 F8
Regensburg, *Germany* 25 F8
Regenstauf, *Germany* 25 F8
Reggâne = Zaouiet Reggâne,
  Algeria 78 C6
Reggello, *Italy* 29 E8
Réggio di Calábria, *Italy* 31 D8
Réggio nell'Emília, *Italy* 28 D7
Reghin, *Romania* 43 D9
Regina, *Canada* 105 C8
Regina Beach, *Canada* 105 C8
Registro, *Brazil* 127 A6
Reguengos de Monsaraz,
  Portugal 35 G3
Rehar →, *India* 69 H10
Rehli, *India* 69 H8
Rehoboth, *Namibia* 88 C2
Rehovot, *Israel* 75 D3
Reichenbach, *Germany* 24 E8
Reid, *Australia* 93 F4
Reidsville, *U.S.A.* 109 G6
Reigate, *U.K.* 13 F7
Reillo, *Spain* 32 F3
Reims, *France* 19 C11
Reina Adelaida, Arch., *Chile* . . 128 G2
Reinbek, *Germany* 24 B6
Reindeer →, *Canada* 105 B8
Reindeer I., *Canada* 105 C9
Reindeer L., *Canada* 105 B8
Reinga, C., *N.Z.* 91 F4
Reinosa, *Spain* 34 B6
Reitz, *S. Africa* 89 D4
Reivilo, *S. Africa* 88 D3
Rejaf, *Sudan* 81 G3
Rejmyre, *Sweden* 11 F9
Rejowiec Fabryczny, *Poland* . . 45 G10
Reka →, *Slovenia* 29 C11
Rekovac, *Serbia, Yug.* 40 C5
Reliance, *Canada* 105 A7
Rémalard, *France* 18 D7
Remarkable, Mt., *Australia* . . . 95 E2
Rembang, *Indonesia* 63 G14
Remedios, *Panama* 120 E3
Remeshk, *Iran* 71 E8
Remetea, *Romania* 43 D10
Remich, *Lux.* 17 E6
Remiremont, *France* 19 D13
Remo, *Ethiopia* 81 F5
Remontnoye, *Russia* 49 G6
Remoulins, *France* 21 E8
Remscheid, *Germany* 17 C7
Ren Xian, *China* 56 F8
Rende, *Italy* 31 C9
Rendína, *Greece* 38 B3
Rendsburg, *Germany* 24 A5
Renfrew, *Canada* 102 C4
Renfrewshire □, *U.K.* 14 F4
Rengat, *Indonesia* 62 E2
Rengo, *Chile* 126 C1
Renhua, *China* 59 E9
Renhuai, *China* 58 C6
Reni, *Ukraine* 47 K5
Renk, *Sudan* 81 E3
Renmark, *Australia* 95 E3
Rennell Sd., *Canada* 104 C2
Renner Springs, *Australia* . . . 94 B1
Rennes, *France* 18 D5
Rennie L., *Canada* 105 A7
Reno, *U.S.A.* 116 F7
Reno →, *Italy* 29 D9
Renovo, *U.S.A.* 110 E7
Renqiu, *China* 56 E9
Rens, *Denmark* 11 K3
Renshou, *China* 58 C5
Rensselaer, Ind., *U.S.A.* 108 E2
Rensselaer, N.Y., *U.S.A.* 111 D11
Rentería, *Spain* 32 B3
Renton, *U.S.A.* 116 C4
Réo, *Burkina Faso* 82 C4
Reocín, *Spain* 34 B6
Reotipur, *India* 69 G10
Répcelak, *Hungary* 42 C2
Republic, Mo., *U.S.A.* 113 G8
Republic, Wash., *U.S.A.* 114 A4
Republican →, *U.S.A.* 112 F6
Repulse Bay, *Canada* 101 B11
Requena, *Peru* 124 E4
Requena, *Spain* 33 F3
Réquista, *France* 20 D6
Reşadiye = Datça, *Turkey* . . . 39 E9
Reşadiye, *Turkey* 72 B7
Reşadiye Yarımadası, *Turkey* . . 39 E9
Resavica, *Serbia, Yug.* 40 C5
Resen, *Macedonia* 40 E5
Reserve, *U.S.A.* 115 K9
Resht = Rasht, *Iran* 71 B6

199

Resistencia, Argentina 126 B4
Reşiţa, Romania 42 E6
Resko, Poland 44 E2
Resolution I., Canada 101 B13
Resolution I., N.Z. 91 L1
Ressano Garcia, Mozam. 89 D5
Reston, Canada 105 D8
Reszel, Poland 44 D8
Retalhuleu, Guatemala 120 D1
Retenue, L. de, Dem. Rep. of
  the Congo 87 E2
Retezat, Munţii, Romania 42 E8
Retford, U.K. 12 D7
Rethel, France 19 C11
Rethem, Germany 24 C5
Réthímnon, Greece 36 D6
Réthímnon □, Greece 36 D6
Reti, Pakistan 68 E3
Retiche, Alpi, Switz. 25 J6
Retiers, France 18 E5
Retortillo, Spain 34 E4
Retournac, France 21 C8
Rétság, Hungary 42 C4
Réunion ■, Ind. Oc. 77 J9
Reus, Spain 32 D6
Reuterstadt Stavenhagen,
  Germany 24 B8
Reutlingen, Germany 25 G5
Reutte, Austria 26 D3
Reval = Tallinn, Estonia ... 9 G21
Revel, France 20 E6
Revelganj, India 69 G11
Revelstoke, Canada 104 C5
Reventazón, Peru 124 E2
Revigny-sur-Ornain, France . 19 D11
Revin, France 19 C11
Revúca, Slovak Rep. 27 C13
Revue →, Mozam. 87 F3
Rewa, India 69 G9
Rewari, India 68 E7
Rexburg, U.S.A. 114 E8
Rey, Iran 71 C6
Rey, I. del, Panama 120 E4
Rey Malabo, Eq. Guin. 83 E6
Reyðarfjörður, Iceland 8 D6
Reyes, Pt., U.S.A. 116 H3
Reyhanlı, Turkey 72 D7
Reykjahlíð, Iceland 8 D5
Reykjanes, Iceland 8 E2
Reykjavík, Iceland 8 D3
Reynolds Ra., Australia 92 D5
Reynoldsville, U.S.A. 110 E6
Reynosa, Mexico 119 B5
Rēzekne, Latvia 9 H22
Rezina, Moldova 43 C13
Rezovo, Bulgaria 41 D12
Rezvān, Iran 71 E8
Rgotina, Serbia, Yug. 40 B6
Rhamnus, Greece 38 C6
Rhayader, U.K. 13 E4
Rheda-Wiedenbrück, Germany 24 D4
Rhede, Germany 24 D2
Rhein →, Europe 17 C6
Rhein-Main-Donau-Kanal,
  Germany 25 F7
Rheinbach, Germany 24 E2
Rheine, Germany 24 C3
Rheinfelden, Germany 25 H3
Rheinhessen-Pfalz □, Germany 25 F3
Rheinland-Pfalz □, Germany 25 E2
Rheinsberg, Germany 24 B8
Rhin = Rhein →, Europe ... 17 C6
Rhine = Rhein →, Europe .. 17 C6
Rhinebeck, U.S.A. 111 E11
Rhineland-Palatinate =
  Rheinland-Pfalz □, Germany 25 E2
Rhinelander, U.S.A. 112 C10
Rhinns Pt., U.K. 14 F2
Rhino Camp, Uganda 86 B3
Rhir, Cap, Morocco 78 B4
Rho, Italy 28 C6
Rhode Island □, U.S.A. ... 111 E13
Rhodes = Ródhos, Greece .. 36 C10
Rhodesia = Zimbabwe ■, Africa 87 F3
Rhodope Mts. = Rhodopi
  Planina, Bulgaria 41 E8
Rhodopi Planina, Bulgaria .. 41 E8
Rhön, Germany 24 E5
Rhondda, U.K. 13 F4
Rhondda Cynon Taff □, U.K. . 13 F4
Rhône □, France 21 C8
Rhône →, France 21 E8
Rhône-Alpes □, France 21 C9
Rhum, U.K. 14 E2
Rhyl, U.K. 12 D4
Ri-Aba, Eq. Guin. 83 E6
Riachão, Brazil 125 E9
Riangnom, Sudan 81 F3
Riaño, Spain 34 C6
Rians, France 21 E9
Riansáres →, Spain 35 F7
Riasi, India 69 C6
Riau □, Indonesia 62 D2
Riau, Kepulauan, Indonesia . 62 D2
Riau Arch. = Riau, Kepulauan,
  Indonesia 62 D2
Riaza, Spain 34 D7
Riaza →, Spain 34 D7
Riba de Saelices, Spain ... 32 E2
Riba-Roja de Turia, Spain .. 33 F4
Ribadavia, Spain 34 C2
Ribadeo, Spain 34 B3
Ribadesella, Spain 34 B5
Ribado, Nigeria 83 D7
Ribao, Cameroon 83 D7
Ribas = Ribes de Freser, Spain . 32 C7

Ribas do Rio Pardo, Brazil . 125 H8
Ribble →, U.K. 12 D5
Ribe, Denmark 11 J2
Ribe Amtskommune □,
  Denmark 11 J2
Ribeauvillé, France 19 D14
Ribécourt-Dreslincourt, France 19 C9
Ribeira = Santa Uxía, Spain . 34 C2
Ribeira Brava, Madeira ... 37 D2
Ribeirão Prêto, Brazil 127 A6
Ribemont, France 19 C10
Ribera, Italy 30 E6
Ribérac, France 20 C4
Riberalta, Bolivia 124 F5
Ribes de Freser, Spain ... 32 C7
Ribnica, Slovenia 29 C11
Ribnitz-Damgarten, Germany . 24 A8
Ričany, Czech Rep. 26 B7
Riccarton, N.Z. 91 K4
Ríccia, Italy 31 A7
Riccione, Italy 29 E9
Rice, U.S.A. 117 L12
Rice L., Canada 110 B6
Rice Lake, U.S.A. 112 C9
Rich, C., Canada 110 B4
Richard Toll, Senegal 82 B1
Richards Bay, S. Africa ... 89 D5
Richardson →, Canada ... 105 B6
Richardson Lakes, U.S.A. . 108 C10
Richardson Springs, U.S.A. . 116 F5
Riche, C., Australia 93 F2
Richelieu, France 18 E7
Richey, U.S.A. 112 B2
Richfield, U.S.A. 115 G8
Richfield Springs, U.S.A. .. 111 D10
Richford, U.S.A. 111 B12
Richibucto, Canada 103 C7
Richland, Ga., U.S.A. ... 109 J3
Richland, Wash., U.S.A. .. 114 C4
Richland Center, U.S.A. .. 112 D9
Richlands, U.S.A. 108 G5
Richmond, Australia 94 C3
Richmond, N.Z. 91 J4
Richmond, U.K. 12 C6
Richmond, Calif., U.S.A. .. 116 H4
Richmond, Ind., U.S.A. .. 108 F3
Richmond, Ky., U.S.A. .. 108 G3
Richmond, Mich., U.S.A. .. 110 D2
Richmond, Mo., U.S.A. .. 112 F8
Richmond, Tex., U.S.A. .. 113 L7
Richmond, Utah, U.S.A. .. 114 F8
Richmond, Va., U.S.A. ... 108 G7
Richmond, Vt., U.S.A. ... 111 B12
Richmond Hill, Canada ... 110 C5
Richmond Ra., Australia .. 95 D5
Richwood, U.S.A. 108 F5
Ricla, Spain 32 D3
Ridder = Leninogorsk,
  Kazakstan 50 D9
Riddlesburg, U.S.A. 110 F6
Ridgecrest, U.S.A. 117 K9
Ridgefield, Conn., U.S.A. .. 111 E11
Ridgefield, Wash., U.S.A. .. 116 E4
Ridgeland, U.S.A. 109 J5
Ridgetown, Canada 102 D3
Ridgewood, U.S.A. 111 F10
Ridgway, U.S.A. 110 E6
Riding Mountain Nat. Park,
  Canada 105 C9
Ridley, Mt., Australia ... 93 F3
Riebeek-Oos, S. Africa ... 88 E4
Ried, Austria 26 C6
Riedlingen, Germany 25 G5
Riedstadt, Germany 25 F4
Rienza →, Italy 29 B8
Riesa, Germany 24 D9
Riesi, Italy 31 E7
Riet →, S. Africa 88 D3
Rietavas, Lithuania 44 C8
Rietbron, S. Africa 88 E3
Rietfontein, Namibia 88 C3
Rieti, Italy 29 F9
Rieupeyroux, France 20 D6
Riez, France 21 E10
Riffe L., U.S.A. 116 D4
Rifle, U.S.A. 114 G10
Rift Valley □, Kenya 86 B4
Rīga, Latvia 9 H21
Riga, G. of, Latvia 9 H20
Rigacikun, Nigeria 83 C6
Rīgān, Iran 71 D8
Rīgas Jūras Līcis = Riga, G. of,
  Latvia 9 H20
Rigaud, Canada 111 A10
Rigby, U.S.A. 114 E8
Rīgestān, Afghan. 66 D4
Riggins, U.S.A. 114 D5
Rignac, France 20 D6
Rigolet, Canada 103 B8
Rihand Dam, India 69 G10
Riihimäki, Finland 9 F21
Riiser-Larsen-halvøya,
  Antarctica 5 C4
Rijau, Nigeria 83 C6
Rijeka, Croatia 29 C11
Rijeka Crnojevića,
  Montenegro, Yug. 40 D3
Rijssen, Neths. 17 B6
Rike, Ethiopia 81 E4
Rikuzentakada, Japan ... 54 E10
Rila, Bulgaria 40 D7
Rila Planina, Bulgaria ... 40 D7
Riley, U.S.A. 114 E4
Rima →, Nigeria 83 C6
Rimah, Wadi ar →, Si. Arabia . 70 E4
Rimavská Sobota, Slovak Rep. . 27 C13
Rimbey, Canada 104 C6

Rimbo, Sweden 10 E12
Rimersburg, U.S.A. 110 E5
Rimforsa, Sweden 11 F9
Rimi, Nigeria 83 C6
Rímini, Italy 29 D9
Rimouski, Canada 103 C6
Rimrock, U.S.A. 116 D5
Rinca, Indonesia 63 F5
Rincón de la Victoria, Spain . 35 J6
Rincón de Romos, Mexico . 118 C4
Rinconada, Argentina ... 126 A2
Rind →, India 69 G9
Ringarum, Sweden 11 F10
Ringas, India 68 F6
Ringe, Denmark 11 J4
Ringim, Nigeria 83 C6
Ringkøbing, Denmark ... 11 H2
Ringkøbing Amtskommune □,
  Denmark 11 H2
Ringkøbing Fjord, Denmark . 11 H2
Ringsjön, Sweden 11 J7
Ringsted, Denmark 11 J5
Ringvassøy, Norway ... 8 B18
Ringwood, U.S.A. 111 E10
Riní, Greece 39 D7
Rinjani, Indonesia 62 F5
Rinteln, Germany 24 C5
Río, Punta del, Spain ... 33 J2
Rio Branco, Brazil 124 E5
Río Branco, Uruguay ... 127 C5
Río Bravo del Norte →, Mexico . 119 B5
Rio Brilhante, Brazil 127 A5
Rio Claro, Brazil 127 A6
Rio Claro, Trin. & Tob. .. 121 D7
Río Colorado, Argentina .. 128 D4
Río Cuarto, Argentina ... 126 C3
Rio das Pedras, Mozam. .. 89 C6
Rio de Janeiro, Brazil ... 127 A7
Rio de Janeiro □, Brazil .. 127 A7
Rio do Sul, Brazil 127 B6
Río Gallegos, Argentina .. 128 G3
Rio Grande = Grande, Rio →,
  U.S.A. 113 N6
Río Grande, Argentina ... 128 G3
Rio Grande, Brazil 127 C5
Río Grande, Mexico 118 C4
Río Grande, Nic. 120 D3
Rio Grande City, U.S.A. .. 113 M5
Rio Grande de Santiago →,
  Mexico 118 C3
Rio Grande do Norte □, Brazil . 125 E11
Rio Grande do Sul □, Brazil . 127 C5
Río Hato, Panama 120 E3
Rio Lagartos, Mexico ... 119 C7
Rio Largo, Brazil 125 E11
Rio Maior, Portugal 35 F2
Rio Marina, Italy 28 F7
Río Mulatos, Bolivia 124 G5
Río Muni = Mbini □, Eq. Guin. . 84 D2
Rio Negro, Brazil 127 B6
Rio Pardo, Brazil 127 C5
Rio Rancho, U.S.A. 115 J10
Río Segundo, Argentina .. 126 C3
Río Tercero, Argentina ... 126 C3
Rio Tinto, Portugal 34 D2
Rio Verde, Brazil 125 G8
Río Verde, Mexico 119 C5
Rio Vista, U.S.A. 116 G5
Ríobamba, Ecuador 124 D3
Ríohacha, Colombia 124 A4
Riom, France 20 C7
Riom-ès-Montagnes, France . 20 C6
Rion-des-Landes, France .. 20 E3
Rionero in Vúlture, Italy .. 31 B8
Rioni →, Georgia 49 J5
Ríos, Spain 34 D3
Ríosucio, Colombia 124 B3
Riou L., Canada 105 B7
Rioz, France 19 E13
Ripatransone, Italy 29 F10
Ripley, Canada 110 B3
Ripley, Calif., U.S.A. ... 117 M12
Ripley, N.Y., U.S.A. ... 110 D5
Ripley, Tenn., U.S.A. ... 113 H10
Ripley, W. Va., U.S.A. .. 108 F5
Ripoll, Spain 32 C7
Ripon, U.K. 12 C6
Ripon, Calif., U.S.A. ... 116 H5
Ripon, Wis., U.S.A. ... 108 D1
Riposto, Italy 31 E8
Risan, Montenegro, Yug. . 40 D2
Riscle, France 20 E3
Rishã', W. ar →, Si. Arabia . 70 E5
Rishiri-Tō, Japan 54 B10
Rishon le Ziyyon, Israel .. 75 D3
Risle →, France 18 C7
Rison, U.S.A. 113 J8
Risør, Norway 9 G13
Rita Blanca Cr. →, U.S.A. . 113 H3
Riti, Nigeria 83 D6
Ritter, Mt., U.S.A. 116 H7
Rittman, U.S.A. 110 F3
Ritzville, U.S.A. 114 C4
Riva del Garda, Italy ... 28 C7
Riva Lígure, Italy 28 E4
Rivadavia, Buenos Aires,
  Argentina 126 D3
Rivadavia, Mendoza, Argentina . 126 C2
Rivadavia, Salta, Argentina . 126 A3
Rivadavia, Chile 126 B1
Rivarolo Canavese, Italy .. 28 C4
Rivas, Nic. 120 D2
Rive-de-Gier, France ... 21 C8
River Cess, Liberia 82 D3
River Jordan, Canada ... 116 B2
Rivera, Argentina 126 D3
Rivera, Uruguay 127 C4

Riverbank, U.S.A. 116 H6
Riverdale, U.S.A. 116 J7
Riverhead, U.S.A. 111 F12
Riverhurst, Canada ... 105 C7
Rivers, Canada 105 C8
Rivers □, Nigeria 83 E6
Rivers Inlet, Canada ... 104 C3
Riversdale, S. Africa ... 88 E3
Riverside, U.S.A. 117 M9
Riverton, Australia ... 95 E2
Riverton, Canada 105 C9
Riverton, N.Z. 91 M2
Riverton, U.S.A. 114 E9
Riverton Heights, U.S.A. . 116 C4
Rives, France 21 C9
Rivesaltes, France 20 F6
Riviera, U.S.A. 117 K12
Riviera di Levante, Italy .. 28 C6
Riviera di Ponente, Italy .. 28 D5
Rivière-au-Renard, Canada . 103 C7
Rivière-du-Loup, Canada .. 103 C6
Rivière-Pentecôte, Canada . 103 C6
Rivière-Pilote, Martinique . 121 D7
Rivière St. Paul, Canada .. 103 B8
Rivne, Ukraine 47 G4
Rívoli, Italy 28 C4
Rivoli B., Australia ... 95 F3
Rixheim, France 19 E14
Riyadh = Ar Riyāḍ, Si. Arabia . 70 E5
Rize, Turkey 73 B9
Rizhao, China 57 G10
Rizokarpaso, Cyprus ... 36 D13
Rizzuto, C., Italy 31 D10
Rjukan, Norway 9 G13
Ro, Greece 39 E11
Roa, Spain 34 D7
Road Town, Br. Virgin Is. . 121 C7
Roan Plateau, U.S.A. .. 114 G9
Roanne, France 19 F11
Roanoke, Ala., U.S.A. .. 109 J3
Roanoke, Va., U.S.A. .. 108 G6
Roanoke →, U.S.A. ... 109 H7
Roanoke I., U.S.A. ... 109 H8
Roanoke Rapids, U.S.A. . 109 G7
Roatán, Honduras 120 C2
Robāt Sang, Iran 71 C8
Robbins I., Australia ... 94 G4
Róbbio, Italy 28 C5
Robe →, Australia 92 D2
Robe, Ethiopia 81 F4
Röbel, Germany 24 B8
Robert Lee, U.S.A. ... 113 K4
Robertsdale, U.S.A. ... 110 F6
Robertsganj, India 69 G10
Robertson, S. Africa ... 88 E2
Robertson I., Antarctica . 5 C18
Robertson Ra., Australia . 92 D3
Robertsport, Liberia ... 82 D2
Robertstown, Australia .. 95 E2
Roberval, Canada 103 C5
Robeson Chan., Greenland . 4 A4
Robesonia, U.S.A. 111 F8
Robi, Ethiopia 81 F4
Robinson, U.S.A. 108 F2
Robinson →, Australia .. 94 B2
Robinson Ra., Australia .. 93 E2
Robinvale, Australia ... 95 E3
Robledo, Spain 33 G2
Roblin, Canada 105 C8
Roboré, Bolivia 124 G7
Robson, Canada 104 D5
Robson, Mt., Canada ... 104 C5
Robstown, U.S.A. 113 M6
Roca, C. da, Portugal .. 35 G1
Roca Partida, I., Mexico .. 118 D2
Rocamadour, France ... 20 D5
Rocas, I., Brazil 125 D12
Rocca San Casciano, Italy . 29 D8
Roccadáspide, Italy 31 B8
Roccastrada, Italy 29 F8
Roccella Iónica, Italy ... 31 D9
Rocha, Uruguay 127 C5
Rochdale, U.K. 12 D5
Rochechouart, France ... 20 C4
Rochefort, Belgium 17 D5
Rochefort, France 20 C3
Rochefort-en-Terre, France . 18 E4
Rochelle, U.S.A. 112 E10
Rocher River, Canada ... 104 A6
Rochervière, France ... 18 F5
Rochester, U.K. 13 F8
Rochester, Ind., U.S.A. .. 108 E2
Rochester, Minn., U.S.A. . 112 C8
Rochester, N.H., U.S.A. .. 111 C14
Rochester, N.Y., U.S.A. .. 110 C7
Rociu, Romania 43 F10
Rock →, Canada 104 A3
Rock Creek, U.S.A. 110 E4
Rock Falls, U.S.A. 112 E10
Rock Hill, U.S.A. 109 H5
Rock Island, U.S.A. ... 112 E9
Rock Rapids, U.S.A. ... 112 D6
Rock Sound, Bahamas .. 120 B4
Rock Springs, Mont., U.S.A. . 114 C10
Rock Springs, Wyo., U.S.A. . 114 F9
Rock Valley, U.S.A. ... 112 D6
Rockall, Atl. Oc. 6 D3
Rockdale, Tex., U.S.A. .. 113 K6
Rockdale, Wash., U.S.A. . 116 C5
Rockefeller Plateau, Antarctica . 5 E14
Rockford, U.S.A. 112 D10
Rockglen, Canada 105 D7
Rockhampton, Australia . 94 C5
Rockingham, Australia .. 93 F2
Rockingham, U.S.A. ... 109 H6
Rockingham B., Australia . 94 B4
Rocklake, U.S.A. 112 A5
Rockland, Canada 111 A9

Rockland, Idaho, U.S.A. .. 114 E7
Rockland, Maine, U.S.A. .. 109 C11
Rockland, Mich., U.S.A. .. 112 B10
Rocklin, U.S.A. 116 G5
Rockmart, U.S.A. 109 H3
Rockport, Mass., U.S.A. .. 111 D14
Rockport, Mo., U.S.A. .. 112 E7
Rockport, Tex., U.S.A. .. 113 L6
Rocksprings, U.S.A. ... 113 K4
Rockville, Conn., U.S.A. .. 111 E12
Rockville, Md., U.S.A. .. 108 F7
Rockwall, U.S.A. 113 J6
Rockwell City, U.S.A. .. 112 D7
Rockwood, Canada 110 C4
Rockwood, Maine, U.S.A. . 109 C11
Rockwood, Tenn., U.S.A. . 109 H3
Rocky Ford, U.S.A. 112 F3
Rocky Gully, Australia .. 93 F2
Rocky Harbour, Canada .. 103 C8
Rocky Island L., Canada .. 102 C3
Rocky Lane, Canada ... 104 B5
Rocky Mount, U.S.A. ... 109 H7
Rocky Mountain House, Canada . 104 C6
Rocky Mountain National Park,
  U.S.A. 114 F11
Rocky Mts., N. Amer. ... 114 G10
Rocky Point, Namibia ... 88 B2
Rocroi, France 19 C11
Rod, Pakistan 66 E3
Rødby, Denmark 11 K5
Rødbyhavn, Denmark ... 11 K5
Roddickton, Canada ... 103 B8
Rødding, Denmark 11 J3
Rödeby, Sweden 11 H9
Rødekro, Denmark 11 J3
Rodenkirchen, Germany . 24 B4
Rodez, France 20 D6
Rodholívos, Greece ... 40 F7
Rodhópi □, Greece 41 E9
Rodhopoú, Greece 36 D5
Ródhos, Greece 36 C10
Rodi Gargánico, Italy ... 29 G12
Rodna, Romania 43 C9
Rodnei, Munţii, Romania . 43 C9
Rodney, Canada 110 D3
Rodney, C., N.Z. 91 G5
Rodniki, Russia 48 B5
Rodonit, Kepi i, Albania .. 40 E3
Rodriguez, Ind. Oc. ... 3 E13
Roe →, U.K. 15 A5
Roebling, U.S.A. 111 F10
Roebourne, Australia ... 92 D2
Roebuck B., Australia ... 92 C3
Roermond, Neths. 17 C6
Roes Welcome Sd., Canada . 101 B11
Roeselare, Belgium 17 D3
Rogachev = Ragachow, Belarus . 47 F6
Rogagua, L., Bolivia ... 124 F5
Rogaška Slatina, Slovenia . 29 B12
Rogatec, Slovenia 29 B12
Rogatica, Bos.-H. 42 G4
Rogatyn, Ukraine 47 H3
Rogdhia, Greece 36 D7
Rogers, U.S.A. 113 G7
Rogers City, U.S.A. ... 108 C4
Rogersville, Canada ... 103 C6
Roggan →, Canada 102 B4
Roggan L., Canada 102 B4
Roggeveldberge, S. Africa . 88 E3
Roggiano Gravina, Italy .. 31 C9
Rogliano, France 21 F13
Rogliano, Italy 31 C9
Rogoaguado, L., Bolivia .. 124 F5
Rogoźno, Poland 45 F3
Rogue →, U.S.A. 114 E1
Rohan, France 18 D4
Róhda, Greece 36 A3
Rohnert Park, U.S.A. ... 116 G4
Rohri, Pakistan 68 F3
Rohri Canal, Pakistan ... 68 F3
Rohtak, India 68 E7
Roi Et, Thailand 64 D4
Roja, Latvia 9 H20
Rojas, Argentina 126 C3
Rojişte, Romania 43 F8
Rojo, C., Mexico 119 C5
Rokan →, Indonesia ... 62 D2
Rokel →, S. Leone 82 D2
Rokiškis, Lithuania ... 9 J21
Rokitno, Russia 47 G8
Rokycany, Czech Rep. .. 26 B6
Rolândia, Brazil 127 A5
Rolla, U.S.A. 113 G9
Rolleston, Australia ... 94 C4
Rollingstone, Australia .. 94 B4
Rom, Sudan 81 F3
Roma, Australia 95 D4
Roma, Italy 29 G9
Roma, Sweden 11 G12
Roma, U.S.A. 113 M5
Romain C., U.S.A. 109 J6
Romaine →, Canada ... 103 B7
Romaine, Canada 103 B7
Roman, Bulgaria 40 C7
Roman, Romania 43 D11
Roman-Kosh, Gora, Ukraine . 47 K8
Romanche →, France .. 21 C9
Romang, Indonesia ... 63 F7
Români, Egypt 75 E1
Romania ■, Europe ... 43 D10
Romanija, Bos.-H. 42 G3
Romano, Cayo, Cuba ... 120 B4
Romanovka = Basarabeasca,
  Moldova 43 D13
Romans-sur-Isère, France . 21 C9
Romanshorn, Switz. ... 25 H5

Gran Paradiso, Italy 28 C4
Gran Sasso d'Itália, Italy 29 F10
Granada, Nic. 120 D2
Granada, Spain 35 H7
Granada, U.S.A. 113 F3
Granada □, Spain 35 H7
Granadilla de Abona, Canary Is. 37 F3
Granard, Ireland 15 C4
Granbury, U.S.A. 113 J6
Granby, Canada 102 C5
Granby, U.S.A. 114 F11
Grand →, Canada 110 D5
Grand →, Mo., U.S.A. 112 F8
Grand →, S. Dak., U.S.A. 112 C4
Grand Bahama, Bahamas 120 A4
Grand Bank, Canada 103 C8
Grand Bassam, Ivory C. 82 D4
Grand Béréby, Ivory C. 82 E3
Grand-Bourg, Guadeloupe 121 C7
Grand Canal = Yun Ho →,
   China 57 E9
Grand Canyon, U.S.A. 115 H7
Grand Canyon National Park,
   U.S.A. 115 H7
Grand Cayman, Cayman Is. ... 120 C3
Grand Centre, Canada 105 C6
Grand Cess, Liberia 82 E3
Grand Coulee, U.S.A. 114 C4
Grand Coulee Dam, U.S.A. ... 114 C4
Grand Erg Occidental, Algeria . 78 B6
Grand Erg Oriental, Algeria .. 78 B7
Grand Falls, Canada 103 C6
Grand Falls-Windsor, Canada . 103 C8
Grand Forks, Canada 104 D5
Grand Forks, U.S.A. 112 B6
Grand Gorge, U.S.A. 111 D10
Grand Haven, U.S.A. 108 D2
Grand I., Mich., U.S.A. 108 B2
Grand I., N.Y., U.S.A. 110 D6
Grand Island, U.S.A. 112 E5
Grand Isle, La., U.S.A. 113 L9
Grand Isle, Vt., U.S.A. 111 B11
Grand Junction, U.S.A. 115 G9
Grand L., N.B., Canada 103 C6
Grand L., Nfld., Canada 103 C8
Grand L., Nfld., Canada 103 B7
Grand L., U.S.A. 113 L8
Grand Lahou, Ivory C. 82 D3
Grand Lake, U.S.A. 114 F11
Grand-Lieu, L. de, France 18 E5
Grand Manan I., Canada 103 D6
Grand Marais, Canada 112 B9
Grand Marais, U.S.A. 108 B3
Grand-Mère, Canada 102 C5
Grand Popo, Benin 83 D5
Grand Portage, U.S.A. 112 B10
Grand Prairie, U.S.A. 113 J6
Grand Rapids, Canada 105 C9
Grand Rapids, Mich., U.S.A. . 108 D2
Grand Rapids, Minn., U.S.A. . 112 B8
Grand St-Bernard, Col du,
   Europe 25 K3
Grand Teton, U.S.A. 114 E8
Grand Teton National Park,
   U.S.A. 114 D8
Grand Union Canal, U.K. 13 E7
Grand View, Canada 105 C8
Grandas de Salime, Spain 34 B4
Grande →, Jujuy, Argentina . 126 A2
Grande →, Mendoza, Argentina 126 D2
Grande →, Bolivia 124 G6
Grande →, Bahia, Brazil 125 F10
Grande →, Minas Gerais, Brazil 125 H8
Grande, B., Argentina 128 G3
Grande, Rio →, U.S.A. 113 N6
Grande Baleine, R. de la →,
   Canada 102 A4
Grande Cache, Canada 104 C5
Grande-Entrée, Canada 103 C7
Grande Prairie, Canada 104 B5
Grande-Rivière, Canada 103 C7
Grande-Vallée, Canada 103 C6
Grandfalls, U.S.A. 113 K3
Grândola, Portugal 35 G2
Grandpré, France 19 C11
Grandview, U.S.A. 114 C4
Grandvilliers, France 19 C8
Graneros, Chile 126 C1
Grangemouth, U.K. 14 E5
Granger, U.S.A. 114 F9
Grangeville, U.S.A. 114 D5
Grängesberg, Sweden 10 D9
Granite City, U.S.A. 112 F9
Granisle, Canada 104 C3
Granite Falls, U.S.A. 112 C7
Granite L., Canada 103 C8
Granite Mt., U.S.A. 117 M10
Granite Pk., U.S.A. 114 D9
Graniteville, U.S.A. 111 B12
Granitola, C., Italy 30 E5
Granity, N.Z. 91 J3
Granja, Brazil 125 D10
Granja de Moreruela, Spain .. 34 D5
Granja de Torrehermosa, Spain 35 G5
Gränna, Sweden 11 F8
Granollers, Spain 32 D7
Gransee, Germany 24 B9
Grant, U.S.A. 112 E4
Grant, Mt., U.S.A. 114 G4
Grant City, U.S.A. 112 E7
Grant I., Australia 92 B5
Grant Range, U.S.A. 115 G6
Grantham, U.K. 12 E7
Grantown-on-Spey, U.K. 14 D5
Grants, U.S.A. 115 J10
Grants Pass, U.S.A. 114 E2
Grantsville, U.S.A. 114 F7

Granville, France 18 D5
Granville, N. Dak., U.S.A. 112 A4
Granville, N.Y., U.S.A. 111 C11
Granville, Ohio, U.S.A. 110 F2
Granville L., Canada 105 B8
Graskop, S. Africa 89 C5
Gräsö, Sweden 10 D12
Grass →, Canada 105 B9
Grass Range, U.S.A. 114 C9
Grass River Prov. Park, Canada 105 C8
Grass Valley, Calif., U.S.A. ... 116 F6
Grass Valley, Oreg., U.S.A. ... 114 D3
Grassano, Italy 31 B9
Grasse, France 21 E10
Grassflat, U.S.A. 110 F6
Grasslands Nat. Park, Canada . 105 D7
Grassy, Australia 94 G3
Gråsten, Denmark 11 K3
Grästorp, Sweden 11 F6
Gratkorn, Austria 26 D8
Graubünden □, Switz. 25 J5
Graulhet, France 20 E5
Graus, Spain 32 C5
Grave, Pte. de, France 20 C2
Gravelbourg, Canada 105 D7
Gravelines, France 19 A9
's-Gravenhage, Neths. 17 B4
Gravenhurst, Canada 102 D4
Gravesend, Australia 95 D5
Gravesend, U.K. 13 F8
Gravina in Púglia, Italy 31 B9
Gravois, Pointe-à-, Haiti 121 C5
Gravone →, France 21 G12
Gray, France 19 E12
Grayling, U.S.A. 108 C3
Grays Harbor, U.S.A. 114 C1
Grays L., U.S.A. 114 E8
Grays River, U.S.A. 116 D3
Grayvoron, Russia 47 G8
Graz, Austria 26 D8
Grdelica, Serbia, Yug. 40 D6
Greasy L., Canada 104 A4
Great Abaco I., Bahamas 120 A4
Great Artesian Basin, Australia 94 C3
Great Australian Bight,
   Australia 93 F5
Great Bahama Bank, Bahamas 120 B4
Great Barrier I., N.Z. 91 G5
Great Barrier Reef, Australia . 94 B4
Great Barrington, U.S.A. 111 D11
Great Basin, U.S.A. 114 G5
Great Basin Nat. Park, U.S.A. 114 G6
Great Bear →, Canada 100 B7
Great Bear L., Canada 100 B7
Great Belt = Store Bælt,
   Denmark 11 J4
Great Bend, Kans., U.S.A. ... 112 F5
Great Bend, Pa., U.S.A. 111 E9
Great Blasket I., Ireland 15 D1
Great Britain, Europe 6 E5
Great Codroy, Canada 103 C8
Great Dividing Ra., Australia . 94 C4
Great Driffield = Driffield, U.K. 12 C7
Great Exuma I., Bahamas 120 B4
Great Falls, U.S.A. 114 C8
Great Fish = Groot Vis →,
   S. Africa 88 E4
Great Guana Cay, Bahamas .. 120 B4
Great Inagua I., Bahamas 121 B5
Great Indian Desert = Thar
   Desert, India 68 F5
Great Karoo, S. Africa 88 E3
Great Lake, Australia 94 G4
Great Lakes, N. Amer. 98 E11
Great Malvern, U.K. 13 E5
Great Miami →, U.S.A. 108 F3
Great Ormes Head, U.K. 12 D4
Great Ouse →, U.K. 12 E8
Great Palm I., Australia 94 B4
Great Plains, N. Amer. 106 A6
Great Ruaha →, Tanzania .. 86 D4
Great Sacandaga Res., U.S.A. . 111 C10
Great Saint Bernard Pass =
   Grand St-Bernard, Col du,
   Europe 25 K3
Great Salt L., U.S.A. 114 F7
Great Salt Lake Desert, U.S.A. 114 F7
Great Salt Plains L., U.S.A. .. 113 G5
Great Sandy Desert, Australia . 92 D3
Great Sangi = Sangihe, Pulau,
   Indonesia 63 D7
Great Scarcies →, S. Leone .. 82 D2
Great Skellig, Ireland 15 E1
Great Slave L., Canada 104 A5
Great Smoky Mts. Nat. Park,
   U.S.A. 109 H4
Great Snow Mt., Canada 104 B4
Great Stour = Stour →, U.K. . 13 F9
Great Victoria Desert, Australia 93 E4
Great Wall, China 56 E5
Great Whernside, U.K. 12 C6
Great Yarmouth, U.K. 13 E9
Greater Antilles, W. Indies ... 121 C5
Greater London □, U.K. 13 F7
Greater Manchester □, U.K. .. 12 D5
Greater Sunda Is., Indonesia . 62 F4
Grebbestad, Sweden 11 F5
Grebenka = Hrebenka, Ukraine 47 G7
Greco, C., Cyprus 36 E13
Greco, Mte., Italy 29 G10
Gredos, Sierra de, Spain 34 E5
Greece ■, Europe 38 B3
Greeley, Colo., U.S.A. 112 E2
Greeley, Nebr., U.S.A. 112 E5
Greem-Bell, Ostrov, Russia ... 50 A7
Green, U.S.A. 114 E2

Green →, Ky., U.S.A. 108 G2
Green →, Utah, U.S.A. 115 G9
Green B., U.S.A. 108 C2
Green Bay, U.S.A. 108 C2
Green C., Australia 95 F5
Green Cove Springs, U.S.A. .. 109 L5
Green Lake, Canada 105 C7
Green River, Utah, U.S.A. ... 115 G8
Green River, Wyo., U.S.A. ... 114 F9
Green Valley, U.S.A. 115 L8
Greenbank, U.S.A. 116 B4
Greenbush, Mich., U.S.A. ... 110 B1
Greenbush, Minn., U.S.A. ... 112 A6
Greencastle, U.S.A. 108 F2
Greene, U.S.A. 111 D9
Greenfield, Calif., U.S.A. 116 J5
Greenfield, Calif., U.S.A. 117 K6
Greenfield, Ind., U.S.A. 108 F3
Greenfield, Iowa, U.S.A. 112 E7
Greenfield, Mass., U.S.A. ... 111 D12
Greenfield, Mo., U.S.A. 113 G8
Greenfield Park, Canada 111 A11
Greenland ■, N. Amer. 4 C5
Greenland Sea, Arctic 4 B7
Greenock, U.K. 14 F4
Greenore, Ireland 15 B5
Greenore Pt., Ireland 15 D5
Greenough, Australia 93 E1
Greenough →, Australia 93 E1
Greenough Pt., Canada 110 B3
Greenport, U.S.A. 111 E12
Greensboro, Ga., U.S.A. 109 J4
Greensboro, N.C., U.S.A. 109 G6
Greensboro, Vt., U.S.A. 111 B12
Greensburg, Ind., U.S.A. 108 F3
Greensburg, Kans., U.S.A. ... 113 G5
Greensburg, Pa., U.S.A. 110 F5
Greenstone Pt., U.K. 14 D3
Greenvale, Australia 94 B4
Greenville, Liberia 82 D3
Greenville, Ala., U.S.A. 109 K2
Greenville, Calif., U.S.A. 116 E6
Greenville, Maine, U.S.A. 109 C11
Greenville, Mich., U.S.A. 108 D3
Greenville, Miss., U.S.A. 113 J9
Greenville, Mo., U.S.A. 113 G9
Greenville, N.C., U.S.A. 109 H7
Greenville, N.H., U.S.A. 111 D13
Greenville, N.Y., U.S.A. 111 D10
Greenville, Ohio, U.S.A. 108 E3
Greenville, Pa., U.S.A. 110 E4
Greenville, S.C., U.S.A. 109 H4
Greenville, Tenn., U.S.A. 109 G4
Greenville, Tex., U.S.A. 113 J6
Greenwater Lake Prov. Park,
   Canada 105 C8
Greenwich, Conn., U.S.A. ... 111 E11
Greenwich, N.Y., U.S.A. 111 C11
Greenwich, Ohio, U.S.A. 110 E2
Greenwich □, U.K. 13 F8
Greenwood, Canada 104 D5
Greenwood, Ark., U.S.A. 113 H7
Greenwood, Ind., U.S.A. 108 F2
Greenwood, Miss., U.S.A. ... 113 J9
Greenwood, S.C., U.S.A. 109 H4
Greenwood, Mt., Australia ... 92 B5
Gregbe, Ivory C. 82 D3
Gregory, U.S.A. 112 D5
Gregory →, Australia 94 B2
Gregory, L., S. Austral.,
   Australia 95 D2
Gregory, L., W. Austral.,
   Australia 93 E2
Gregory Downs, Australia 94 B2
Gregory L., Australia 92 D4
Gregory Ra., Queens., Australia 94 B3
Gregory Ra., W. Austral.,
   Australia 92 D3
Greiffenberg, Germany 24 B9
Greifswald, Germany 24 A9
Greifswalder Bodden, Germany 24 A9
Grein, Austria 26 C7
Greiz, Germany 24 E8
Gremikha, Russia 50 C4
Grená, Denmark 11 H4
Grenada ■, W. Indies 121 D7
Grenade, France 20 E5
Grenadier I., U.S.A. 111 B8
Grenadines, St. Vincent 121 D7
Grenchen, Switz. 25 H3
Grenen, Denmark 11 G4
Grenfell, Australia 95 E4
Grenfell, Canada 105 C8
Grenoble, France 21 C9
Grenville, C., Australia 94 A3
Grenville Chan., Canada 104 C3
Gréoux-les-Bains, France 21 E9
Gresham, U.S.A. 116 E4
Gresik, Indonesia 63 G15
Gretna, U.K. 14 F5
Greven, Germany 24 C3
Grevená, Greece 40 F5
Grevená □, Greece 40 F5
Grevenbroich, Germany 24 D2
Grevenmacher, Lux. 17 E6
Grevesmühlen, Germany 24 B7
Grevestrand, Denmark 11 J6
Grey →, Canada 103 C8
Grey →, N.Z. 91 K3
Grey, C., Australia 94 A2
Grey Ra., Australia 95 D3
Greybull, U.S.A. 114 D9
Greymouth, N.Z. 91 K3
Greystones, Ireland 15 C5
Greytown, N.Z. 91 J5

Greytown, S. Africa 89 D5
Gribanovskiy, Russia 48 E5
Gribbell I., Canada 104 C3
Gribës, Mal i, Albania 40 F3
Gridley, U.S.A. 116 F5
Griekwastad, S. Africa 88 D3
Griesheim, Germany 25 F4
Grieskirchen, Austria 26 C6
Griffin, U.S.A. 109 J3
Griffith, Australia 95 E4
Griffith, Canada 110 A7
Griffith I., Canada 110 B4
Grignols, France 20 D3
Grigoriopol, Moldova 43 C14
Grimaylov = Hrymayliv, Ukraine 47 H4
Grimes, U.S.A. 116 F5
Grimma, Germany 24 D8
Grimmen, Germany 24 A9
Grimsay, U.K. 14 D1
Grimsby, Canada 110 C5
Grimsby, U.K. 12 D7
Grímsey, Iceland 8 C5
Grimshaw, Canada 104 B5
Grimslöv, Sweden 11 H8
Grimstad, Norway 9 G13
Grindelwald, Switz. 25 J4
Grindsted, Denmark 11 J2
Grindstone I., Canada 111 B8
Grindu, Romania 43 F11
Grinnell, U.S.A. 112 E8
Grintavec, Slovenia 29 B11
Gris-Nez, C., France 19 B8
Grisolles, France 20 E5
Grisons = Graubünden □, Switz. 25 J5
Grisslehamn, Sweden 10 D12
Grmeč Planina, Bos.-H. 29 D13
Groais I., Canada 103 B8
Grobiņa, Latvia 44 B8
Groblersdal, S. Africa 89 D4
Groblershoop, S. Africa 88 D3
Grobming, Austria 26 D6
Grocka, Serbia, Yug. 40 B4
Gródek, Poland 45 E10
Grodków, Poland 45 H4
Grodno = Hrodna, Belarus ... 46 F2
Grodzisk Mazowiecki, Poland . 45 F7
Grodzisk Wielkopolski, Poland 45 F3
Grodzyanka =
   Hrodzyanka, Belarus 46 F5
Groesbeck, U.S.A. 113 K6
Groix, France 18 E3
Groix, Î. de, France 18 E3
Grójec, Poland 45 G7
Gronau, Niedersachsen,
   Germany 24 C5
Gronau, Nordrhein-Westfalen,
   Germany 24 C3
Grong, Norway 8 D15
Grönhögen, Sweden 11 H10
Groningen, Neths. 17 A6
Groningen □, Neths. 17 A6
Groom, U.S.A. 113 H4
Groot →, S. Africa 88 E3
Groot Berg →, S. Africa 88 E2
Groot-Brakrivier, S. Africa ... 88 E3
Groot Karasberge, Namibia ... 88 D2
Groot-Kei →, S. Africa 89 E4
Groot Vis →, S. Africa 88 E4
Grootdrink, S. Africa 88 D3
Groote Eylandt, Australia 94 A2
Grootfontein, Namibia 88 B2
Grootlaagte →, Africa 88 C3
Grootvloer →, S. Africa 88 E3
Gros C., Canada 104 A6
Gros Morne Nat. Park, Canada 103 C8
Grósio, Italy 28 B7
Grosne →, France 19 F11
Grossa, Pta., Spain 37 B8
Grossenbrode, Germany 24 A7
Grossenhain, Germany 24 D9
Grosser Plöner See, Germany . 24 A6
Grosseto, Italy 29 F8
Grossgerungs, Austria 26 C7
Grossglockner, Austria 26 D5
Groswater B., Canada 103 B8
Groton, Conn., U.S.A. 111 E12
Groton, N.Y., U.S.A. 111 D8
Groton, S. Dak., U.S.A. 112 C5
Grottáglie, Italy 31 B10
Grottaminarda, Italy 31 A8
Grottammare, Italy 29 F10
Grouard Mission, Canada 104 B5
Grouin, Pte. du, France 18 D5
Groundhog →, Canada 102 C3
Grouw, Neths. 17 A5
Grove City, U.S.A. 110 E4
Grove Hill, U.S.A. 109 K2
Groveland, U.S.A. 116 H6
Grover City, U.S.A. 117 K6
Groves, U.S.A. 113 L8
Groveton, U.S.A. 111 B13
Grožnjan, Croatia 29 C10
Groznyy, Russia 49 J7
Grubišno Polje, Croatia 42 E2
Grudusk, Poland 45 E7
Grudziądz, Poland 45 E5
Gruinard B., U.K. 14 D3
Gruissan, France 20 E7
Grumo Áppula, Italy 31 A9
Grums, Sweden 10 E7
Grünberg, Germany 24 E4
Gründau, Germany 25 E5
Grundy Center, U.S.A. 112 D8
Grünstadt, Germany 25 F4
Gruvberget, Sweden 10 C10
Gruver, U.S.A. 113 G4

Gruyères, Switz. 25 J3
Gruža, Serbia, Yug. 40 C4
Gryazi, Russia 47 F10
Gryazovets, Russia 46 C11
Grybów, Poland 45 J7
Grycksbo, Sweden 10 D9
Gryfice, Poland 44 E2
Gryfino, Poland 45 E1
Gryfów Śląski, Poland 45 G2
Grythyttan, Sweden 10 E8
Gstaad, Switz. 25 J3
Gua, India 67 H14
Gua Musang, Malaysia 65 K3
Guacanayabo, G. de, Cuba ... 120 B4
Guachípas →, Argentina 126 B2
Guadajoz →, Spain 35 H6
Guadalajara, Mexico 118 C4
Guadalajara, Spain 32 E1
Guadalajara □, Spain 32 E2
Guadalcanal, Solomon Is. 96 H8
Guadalcanal, Spain 35 G5
Guadalén →, Spain 35 G7
Guadales, Argentina 126 C2
Guadalete →, Spain 35 J4
Guadalimar →, Spain 35 G7
Guadalmena →, Spain 35 G8
Guadalmez →, Spain 35 G5
Guadalope →, Spain 32 D4
Guadalquivir →, Spain 35 J4
Guadalupe = Guadeloupe ■,
   W. Indies 121 C7
Guadalupe, Mexico 117 N10
Guadalupe, Spain 35 F5
Guadalupe, U.S.A. 117 L6
Guadalupe, Sierra de, Spain . 35 F5
Guadalupe Bravos, Mexico .. 118 A3
Guadalupe I., Pac. Oc. 98 G8
Guadalupe Mts. Nat. Park,
   U.S.A. 113 K2
Guadalupe Peak, U.S.A. 113 K2
Guadalupe y Calvo, Mexico .. 118 B3
Guadarrama, Sierra de, Spain . 34 E7
Guadauta, Georgia 49 J5
Guadeloupe ■, W. Indies 121 C7
Guadeloupe Passage, W. Indies 121 C7
Guadiamar →, Spain 35 J4
Guadiana →, Portugal 35 H3
Guadiana Menor →, Spain .. 35 H7
Guadiaro →, Spain 35 J5
Guadiato →, Spain 35 H5
Guadiela →, Spain 32 E2
Guadix, Spain 35 H7
Guafo, Boca del, Chile 128 E2
Guainía →, Colombia 124 C5
Guaíra, Brazil 127 A5
Guaíra □, Paraguay 126 B4
Guaitecas, Is., Chile 128 E2
Guajará-Mirim, Brazil 124 F5
Guajira, Pen. de la, Colombia . 124 A4
Gualán, Guatemala 120 C2
Gualdo Tadino, Italy 29 E9
Gualeguay, Argentina 126 C4
Gualeguaychú, Argentina 126 C4
Gualequay →, Argentina 126 C4
Guam ■, Pac. Oc. 96 F6
Guamini, Argentina 126 D3
Guamúchil, Mexico 118 B3
Guanabacoa, Cuba 120 B3
Guanacaste, Cordillera del,
   Costa Rica 120 D2
Guanaceví, Mexico 118 B3
Guanahani = San Salvador I.,
   Bahamas 121 B5
Guanajay, Cuba 120 B3
Guanajuato, Mexico 118 C4
Guanajuato □, Mexico 118 C4
Guandacol, Argentina 126 B2
Guane, Cuba 120 B3
Guang'an, China 58 B6
Guangchang, China 59 D11
Guangde, China 59 B12
Guangdong □, China 59 F9
Guangfeng, China 59 C12
Guanghan, China 58 B5
Guangling, China 56 E8
Guangnan, China 58 E5
Guangning, China 59 F9
Guangrao, China 57 F10
Guangshui, China 59 B9
Guangshun, China 58 D6
Guangwu, China 56 F3
Guangxi Zhuangzu Zizhiqu □,
   China 58 F7
Guangyuan, China 58 A5
Guangze, China 59 D11
Guangzhou, China 59 F9
Guanipa →, Venezuela 124 B6
Guanling, China 58 E5
Guannan, China 57 G10
Guantánamo, Cuba 121 B4
Guantao, China 56 F8
Guanyang, China 59 E8
Guanyun, China 57 G10
Guápiles, Costa Rica 120 D3
Guaporé, Brazil 127 B5
Guaporé →, Brazil 124 F5
Guaqui, Bolivia 124 G5
Guara, Sierra de, Spain 32 C4
Guarabira, Brazil 125 E11
Guaranda, Ecuador 124 D3
Guarapari, Brazil 127 A7
Guarapuava, Brazil 127 B5
Guaratinguetá, Brazil 127 A6
Guaratuba, Brazil 127 B6
Guarda, Portugal 34 E3
Guarda □, Portugal 34 E3
Guardafui, C. = Asir, Ras,

Somali Rep.	74	E5
Guardamar del Segura, *Spain*	33	G4
Guardavalle, *Italy*	31	D9
Guárdia Sanframondi, *Italy*	31	A7
Guardiagrele, *Italy*	29	F11
Guardo, *Spain*	34	C6
Guareña, *Spain*	35	G4
Guareña ➔, *Spain*	34	D5
Guárico □, *Venezuela*	124	B5
Guarujá, *Brazil*	127	A6
Guarus, *Brazil*	127	A7
Guasave, *Mexico*	118	B3
Guasdualito, *Venezuela*	124	B4
Guastalla, *Italy*	28	D7
Guatemala, *Guatemala*	120	D1
Guatemala ■, *Cent. Amer.*	120	C1
Guaviare □, *Colombia*	122	C4
Guaxupé, *Brazil*	127	A6
Guayama, *Puerto Rico*	121	C6
Guayaquil, *Ecuador*	124	D3
Guayaquil, G. de, *Ecuador*	122	D2
Guaymas, *Mexico*	118	B2
Guba, *Dem. Rep. of the Congo*	87	E2
Guba, *Ethiopia*	81	E4
Gûbâl, Madîq, *Egypt*	80	B3
Gubat, *Phil.*	61	E6
Gúbbio, *Italy*	29	E9
Guben, *Germany*	24	D10
Gubin, *Poland*	45	G1
Gubio, *Nigeria*	83	C7
Gubkin, *Russia*	47	G9
Guča, *Serbia, Yug.*	40	C4
Gucheng, *China*	59	A8
Gudata = Guadauta, *Georgia*	49	J5
Gudbrandsdalen, *Norway*	9	F14
Guddu Barrage, *Pakistan*	66	E6
Gudená ➔, *Denmark*	11	H4
Gudermes, *Russia*	49	J8
Gudhjem, *Denmark*	11	J8
Gudur, *India*	66	M11
Guebwiller, *France*	19	E14
Guecho = Getxo, *Spain*	32	B2
Guékédou, *Guinea*	82	D2
Guelph, *Canada*	102	D3
Guémené-Penfao, *France*	18	E5
Guémené-sur-Scorff, *France*	18	D3
Guéné, *Benin*	83	C5
Guer, *France*	18	E4
Guérande, *France*	18	E4
Guéret, *France*	19	F8
Guérigny, *France*	19	E10
Guerneville, *U.S.A.*	116	G4
Guernica = Gernika-Lumo, *Spain*	32	B2
Guernsey, *U.K.*	13	H5
Guernsey, *U.S.A.*	112	D2
Guerrero □, *Mexico*	119	D5
Guessou-Sud, *Benin*	83	C5
Gueugnon, *France*	19	F11
Guéyo, *Ivory C.*	82	D3
Gughe, *Ethiopia*	81	F4
Gûgher, *Iran*	71	D8
Guglionesi, *Italy*	29	G11
Guhakolak, Tanjung, *Indonesia*	63	G11
Gui Jiang ➔, *China*	59	F8
Guia, *Canary Is.*	37	F4
Guia de Isora, *Canary Is.*	37	F3
Guia Lopes da Laguna, *Brazil*	127	A4
Guiana, *S. Amer.*	122	C4
Guibéroua, *Ivory C.*	82	D3
Guichi, *China*	59	B11
Guider, *Cameroon*	83	D7
Guidiguir, *Niger*	83	C6
Guidimouni, *Niger*	83	C6
Guiding, *China*	58	D6
Guidong, *China*	59	D9
Guidónia-Montecélio, *Italy*	29	F9
Guiers, L. de, *Senegal*	82	B1
Guigang, *China*	58	F7
Guiglo, *Ivory C.*	82	D3
Guihulñgan, *Phil.*	61	F5
Guijá, *Mozam.*	89	C5
Guijuelo, *Spain*	34	E5
Guildford, *U.K.*	13	F7
Guilford, *U.S.A.*	111	E12
Guillaume-Delisle L., *Canada*	102	A4
Guillaumes, *France*	21	D10
Guillestre, *France*	21	D10
Guilvinec, *France*	18	E2
Güimar, *Canary Is.*	37	F3
Guimarães, *Portugal*	34	D2
Guimaras □, *Phil.*	61	F5
Guinda, *U.S.A.*	116	G4
Guinea, *Africa*	76	F4
Guinea ■, *W. Afr.*	82	C2
Guinea, Gulf of, *Atl. Oc.*	83	E5
Guinea-Bissau ■, *Africa*	82	C2
Güines, *Cuba*	120	B3
Guingamp, *France*	18	D3
Guinguinéo, *Senegal*	82	C1
Guipavas, *France*	18	D2
Guiping, *China*	59	F8
Guipúzcoa □, *Spain*	32	B2
Guir, *Mali*	82	B4
Guirel, *Mauritania*	82	B3
Güiria, *Venezuela*	124	A6
Guiscard, *France*	19	C10
Guise, *France*	19	C10
Guitiriz, *Spain*	34	B3
Guitri, *Ivory C.*	82	D3
Guiuan, *Phil.*	61	F6
Guixi, *China*	59	C11
Guiyang, *Guizhou, China*	58	D6
Guiyang, *Hunan, China*	59	E9
Guizhou □, *China*	58	D6
Gujan-Mestras, *France*	20	D2
Gujar Khan, *Pakistan*	68	C5
Gujarat □, *India*	68	H4
Gujiang, *China*	59	D10
Gujranwala, *Pakistan*	68	C6
Gujrat, *Pakistan*	68	C6
Gukovo, *Russia*	49	F5
Gulbarga, *India*	66	L10
Gulbene, *Latvia*	9	H22
Gulf, The, *Asia*	71	E6
Gulfport, *U.S.A.*	113	K10
Gulgong, *Australia*	95	E4
Gulin, *China*	58	C5
Gulistan, *Pakistan*	68	D2
Gull Lake, *Canada*	105	C7
Gullbrandstorp, *Sweden*	11	H6
Gullspång, *Sweden*	11	F8
Güllük, *Turkey*	39	D9
Güllük Korfezi, *Turkey*	39	D9
Gulma, *Nigeria*	83	C5
Gulmarg, *India*	69	B6
Gülnar, *Turkey*	72	D5
Gülpınar, *Turkey*	39	B8
Gülşehir, *Turkey*	72	C6
Gulshad, *Kazakhstan*	50	E8
Gulu, *Uganda*	86	B3
Gülübovo, *Bulgaria*	41	D9
Gulud, J., *Sudan*	81	E2
Gulwe, *Tanzania*	86	D4
Gulyaypole = Hulyaypole, *Ukraine*	47	J9
Gumal ➔, *Pakistan*	68	D4
Gumbaz, *Pakistan*	68	D3
Gumel, *Nigeria*	83	C6
Gumiel de Hizán, *Spain*	34	D7
Gumla, *India*	69	H11
Gumlu, *Australia*	94	B4
Gumma □, *Japan*	55	F9
Gummersbach, *Germany*	24	D3
Gummi, *Nigeria*	83	C6
Gümüldür, *Turkey*	39	C9
Gümüşçay, *Turkey*	41	F11
Gümüşhacıköy, *Turkey*	72	B6
Gümüşhane, *Turkey*	73	B8
Gümüşsu, *Turkey*	39	C11
Gumzai, *Indonesia*	63	F8
Guna, *Ethiopia*	81	F4
Guna, *India*	68	G7
Gundelfingen, *Germany*	25	G6
Güney, *Burdur, Turkey*	39	D11
Güney, *Denizli, Turkey*	39	C11
Güneydoğu Toroslar, *Turkey*	73	C9
Gunisao ➔, *Canada*	105	C9
Gunisao L., *Canada*	105	C9
Gunjyal, *Pakistan*	68	C4
Günlüce, *Turkey*	39	E10
Gunnarskog, *Sweden*	10	E6
Gunnbjørn Fjeld, *Greenland*	4	C6
Gunnebo, *Sweden*	11	G10
Gunnedah, *Australia*	95	E5
Gunnewin, *Australia*	95	D4
Gunningbar Cr. ➔, *Australia*	95	E4
Gunnison, *Colo., U.S.A.*	115	G10
Gunnison, *Utah, U.S.A.*	114	G8
Gunnison ➔, *U.S.A.*	115	G9
Gunpowder, *Australia*	94	B2
Guntakal, *India*	66	M10
Guntersville, *U.S.A.*	109	H2
Guntong, *Malaysia*	65	K3
Guntur, *India*	67	L12
Gunungapi, *Indonesia*	63	F7
Gunungsitoli, *Indonesia*	62	D1
Günz ➔, *Germany*	25	G6
Gunza, *Angola*	84	G2
Günzburg, *Germany*	25	G6
Gunzenhausen, *Germany*	25	F6
Guo He ➔, *China*	57	H9
Guoyang, *China*	56	H9
Gupis, *Pakistan*	69	A5
Gura Humorului, *Romania*	43	C10
Gura-Teghii, *Romania*	43	E11
Gurag, *Ethiopia*	81	F4
Gurahonţ, *Romania*	42	D7
Gurdaspur, *India*	68	C6
Gurdon, *U.S.A.*	113	J8
Güre, *Balıkesir, Turkey*	39	B8
Güre, *Uşak, Turkey*	39	C11
Gurgaon, *India*	68	E7
Gürgentepe, *Turkey*	72	B7
Gurghiu, Munţii, *Romania*	43	D10
Gurgueia ➔, *Brazil*	125	E10
Gurha, *India*	68	G4
Guri, Embalse de, *Venezuela*	124	B6
Gurin, *Nigeria*	83	D7
Gurjaani, *Georgia*	49	K7
Gurk ➔, *Austria*	26	E7
Gurkha, *Nepal*	69	E11
Gurley, *Australia*	95	D4
Gurnet Point, *U.S.A.*	111	D14
Gürpınar, *Ist., Turkey*	41	F12
Gürpınar, *Van, Turkey*	73	C10
Gürsu, *Turkey*	41	F13
Gurué, *Mozam.*	87	F4
Gurun, *Malaysia*	65	K3
Gürün, *Turkey*	72	C7
Gurupá, *Brazil*	125	D8
Gurupá, I. Grande de, *Brazil*	125	D8
Gurupí, *Brazil*	125	F9
Gurupi ➔, *Brazil*	125	D9
Guruwe, *Zimbabwe*	89	B5
Guryev = Atyraū, *Kazakstan*	50	E6
Gus-Khrustalnyy, *Russia*	48	C5
Gusev, *Russia*	9	J20
Gushan, *China*	57	E12
Gushi, *China*	59	A10
Gushiago, *Ghana*	83	D4
Gusinje, *Montenegro, Yug.*	40	D3
Gusinoozersk, *Russia*	51	D11
Gúspini, *Italy*	30	C1
Güssing, *Austria*	27	D9
Gustavsberg, *Sweden*	10	E12
Gustavus, *U.S.A.*	104	B1
Gustine, *U.S.A.*	116	H6
Güstrow, *Germany*	24	B8
Gusum, *Sweden*	11	F10
Guta = Kolárovo, *Slovak Rep.*	27	D10
Gütersloh, *Germany*	24	D4
Gutha, *Australia*	93	E2
Guthalungra, *Australia*	94	B4
Guthrie, *Okla., U.S.A.*	113	H6
Guthrie, *Tex., U.S.A.*	113	J4
Gutian, *China*	59	D12
Guttenberg, *U.S.A.*	112	D9
Gutu, *Zimbabwe*	89	B5
Guyana ■, *S. Amer.*	124	C7
Guyane française = French Guiana ■, *S. Amer.*	125	C8
Guyang, *China*	56	D6
Guyenne, *France*	20	D4
Guymon, *U.S.A.*	113	G4
Guyra, *Australia*	95	E5
Guyuan, *Hebei, China*	56	D8
Guyuan, *Ningxia Huizu, China*	56	G4
Güzelbahçe, *Turkey*	39	C8
Guzhang, *China*	58	C7
Guzhen, *China*	57	H9
Guzmán, L. de, *Mexico*	118	A3
Gvardeysk, *Russia*	9	J19
Gvardeyskoye, *Ukraine*	47	K8
Gwa, *Burma*	67	L19
Gwaai, *Zimbabwe*	87	F2
Gwabegar, *Australia*	95	E4
Gwadabawa, *Nigeria*	83	C6
Gwädar, *Pakistan*	66	G3
Gwagwada, *Nigeria*	83	C6
Gwalior, *India*	68	F8
Gwanara, *Nigeria*	83	D5
Gwanda, *Zimbabwe*	87	G2
Gwandu, *Nigeria*	83	C5
Gwane, *Dem. Rep. of the Congo*	86	B2
Gwaram, *Nigeria*	83	C7
Gwarzo, *Nigeria*	83	C6
Gwasero, *Nigeria*	83	D5
Gwda ➔, *Poland*	45	E3
Gweebarra B., *Ireland*	15	B3
Gweedore, *Ireland*	15	A3
Gweru, *Zimbabwe*	87	F2
Gwi, *Nigeria*	83	D6
Gwinn, *U.S.A.*	108	B2
Gwio Kura, *Nigeria*	83	C7
Gwoza, *Nigeria*	83	C7
Gwydir ➔, *Australia*	95	D4
Gwynedd □, *U.K.*	12	E3
Gyandzha = Gäncä, *Azerbaijan*	49	K8
Gyaring Hu, *China*	60	C4
Gydanskiy Poluostrov, *Russia*	50	C8
Gympie, *Australia*	95	D5
Gyomaendrőd, *Hungary*	42	D5
Gyöngyös, *Hungary*	42	C4
Győr, *Hungary*	42	C2
Győr-Moson-Sopron □, *Hungary*	42	C2
Gypsum Pt., *Canada*	104	A6
Gypsumville, *Canada*	105	C9
Gyueshevo, *Bulgaria*	40	D6
Gyula, *Hungary*	42	D6
Gyumri, *Armenia*	49	K6
Gyzylarbat, *Turkmenistan*	50	F6
Gyzyletrek, *Turkmenistan*	71	B7
Gzhatsk = Gagarin, *Russia*	46	E8

H

Ha ʿArava ➔, *Israel*	75	E4
Ha Coi, *Vietnam*	58	G6
Ha Dong, *Vietnam*	58	G5
Ha Giang, *Vietnam*	58	F5
Ha Tien, *Vietnam*	65	G5
Ha Tinh, *Vietnam*	64	C5
Ha Trung, *Vietnam*	64	C5
Haaksbergen, *Neths.*	17	B6
Haapsalu, *Estonia*	9	G20
Haarlem, *Neths.*	17	B4
Haast ➔, *N.Z.*	91	K2
Haast Bluff, *Australia*	92	D5
Hab ➔, *Pakistan*	68	G3
Hab Nadi Chauki, *Pakistan*	68	G2
Habaswein, *Kenya*	86	B4
Habay, *Canada*	104	B5
Ḥabbānīyah, *Iraq*	70	C4
Ḥabbānīyah, Hawr al, *Iraq*	73	F10
Habo, *Sweden*	11	G8
Haboro, *Japan*	54	B10
Ḥabshān, *U.A.E.*	71	F7
Hachenburg, *Germany*	24	E3
Hachijō-Jima, *Japan*	55	H9
Hachinohe, *Japan*	54	D10
Hachiōji, *Japan*	55	G9
Hachŏn, *N. Korea*	57	D15
Hacıbektaş, *Turkey*	72	C6
Hacılar, *Turkey*	72	C6
Hackås, *Sweden*	10	B8
Hackensack, *U.S.A.*	111	F10
Hackettstown, *U.S.A.*	111	F10
Hadali, *Pakistan*	68	C5
Hadarba, Ras, *Sudan*	80	C4
Hadarom □, *Israel*	75	E4
Hadd, Ra's al, *Oman*	74	C6
Hadejia, *Nigeria*	83	C7
Hadejia ➔, *Nigeria*	83	C7
Ḥadera, *Israel*	75	C3
Ḥadera, N. ➔, *Israel*	75	C3
Haderslev, *Denmark*	11	J3
Hadhramaut = Ḥaḍramawt, *Yemen*	74	D4
Hadibu, *Yemen*	74	E5
Hadım, *Turkey*	72	D5
Hadong, *S. Korea*	57	G14
Ḥaḍramawt, *Yemen*	74	D4
Ḥadrānīyah, *Iraq*	70	C4
Hadrian's Wall, *U.K.*	12	B5
Hadsten, *Denmark*	11	H4
Hadsund, *Denmark*	11	H4
Hadyach, *Ukraine*	47	G8
Haeju, *N. Korea*	57	E13
Haenam, *S. Korea*	57	G14
Haenertsburg, *S. Africa*	89	C4
Haerhpin = Harbin, *China*	57	B14
Ḥafar al Bāṭin, *Si. Arabia*	70	D5
Hafik, *Turkey*	72	C7
Ḥafirat al ʿAydā, *Si. Arabia*	70	E3
Ḥafit, *Oman*	71	F7
Hafizabad, *Pakistan*	68	C5
Haflong, *India*	67	G18
Hafnarfjörður, *Iceland*	8	D3
Haft Gel, *Iran*	71	D6
Hafun, Ras, *Somali Rep.*	74	E5
Hagalil, *Israel*	75	C4
Hagby, *Sweden*	11	H10
Hagen, *Germany*	24	D3
Hagenow, *Germany*	24	B7
Hagerman, *U.S.A.*	113	J2
Hagerstown, *U.S.A.*	108	F7
Hagersville, *Canada*	110	D4
Hagetmau, *France*	20	E3
Hagfors, *Sweden*	10	D7
Hagi, *Japan*	55	G5
Hagolan, *Syria*	75	C4
Hagondange, *France*	19	C13
Hags Hd., *Ireland*	15	D2
Hague, C. de la, *France*	18	C5
Hague, The = ʿs-Gravenhage, *Neths.*	17	B4
Haguenau, *France*	19	D14
Hai Duong, *Vietnam*	58	G6
Haiʿan, *Guangdong, China*	59	G8
Haiʿan, *Jiangsu, China*	59	A13
Haicheng, *Fujian, China*	59	E11
Haicheng, *Liaoning, China*	57	D12
Haidar Khel, *Afghan.*	68	C3
Haidargarh, *India*	69	F9
Haifa = Ḥefa, *Israel*	75	C4
Haifeng, *China*	59	F10
Haiger, *Germany*	24	E4
Haikou, *China*	60	D6
Ḥāʿil, *Si. Arabia*	70	E4
Hailar, *China*	60	B6
Hailey, *U.S.A.*	114	E6
Haileybury, *Canada*	102	C4
Hailin, *China*	57	B15
Hailing Dao, *China*	59	G8
Hailong, *China*	57	C13
Hailuoto, *Finland*	8	D21
Haimen, *Guangdong, China*	59	F11
Haimen, *Jiangsu, China*	59	B13
Hainan □, *China*	60	E5
Hainaut □, *Belgium*	17	D4
Hainfeld, *Austria*	26	C8
Haining, *China*	59	B13
Haiphong, *Vietnam*	58	G6
Haitan Dao, *China*	59	E12
Haiti ■, *W. Indies*	121	C5
Haiya, *Sudan*	80	D4
Haiyan, *China*	59	B13
Haiyang, *China*	57	F11
Haiyuan, *Guangxi Zhuangzu, China*	58	F6
Haiyuan, *Ningxia Huizu, China*	56	F3
Haizhou, *China*	57	G10
Haizhou Wan, *China*	57	G10
Hajdú-Bihar □, *Hungary*	42	C6
Hajdúböszörmény, *Hungary*	42	C6
Hajdúdorog, *Hungary*	42	C6
Hajdúhadház, *Hungary*	42	C6
Hajdúnánás, *Hungary*	42	C6
Hajdúszoboszló, *Hungary*	42	C6
Hajipur, *India*	69	G11
Ḥājjī Muḥsin, *Iraq*	70	C5
Ḥājjīābād, *Iran*	71	D7
Ḥājjīābād-e Zarrīn, *Iran*	71	C7
Hajnówka, *Poland*	45	F10
Hakansson, Mts., *Dem. Rep. of the Congo*	87	D2
Hakkâri, *Turkey*	70	B4
Hakkari Dağları, *Turkey*	73	C10
Hakken-Zan, *Japan*	55	G7
Hakodate, *Japan*	54	D10
Hakos, *Namibia*	88	C2
Håksberg, *Sweden*	10	D9
Haku-San, *Japan*	55	F8
Hakui, *Japan*	55	F8
Hala, *Pakistan*	66	G6
Ḥalab, *Syria*	70	B3
Halabjah, *Iraq*	70	C5
Halasa, *Sudan*	81	E3
Ḥalāt ʿAmmār, *Si. Arabia*	70	D3
Halbā, *Lebanon*	75	A5
Halberstadt, *Germany*	24	D7
Halcombe, *N.Z.*	91	J5
Halcon, *Phil.*	63	B6
Halden, *Norway*	9	G14
Haldensleben, *Germany*	24	C7
Haldia, *India*	67	H16
Haldwani, *India*	69	E8
Hale ➔, *Australia*	94	C2
Halesowen, *U.K.*	13	E5
Haleyville, *U.S.A.*	109	H2
Half Assini, *Ghana*	82	D4
Halfmoon Bay, *N.Z.*	91	M2
Halfway ➔, *Canada*	104	B4
Halia, *India*	69	G10
Haliburton, *Canada*	102	C4
Halifax, *Australia*	94	B4
Halifax, *Canada*	103	D7
Halifax, *U.K.*	12	D6
Halifax, *U.S.A.*	110	F8
Halifax B., *Australia*	94	B4
Halifax I., *Namibia*	88	D2
Halīl ➔, *Iran*	71	E8
Halkirk, *U.K.*	14	C5
Hall Beach = Sanirajak, *Canada*	101	B11
Hall in Tirol, *Austria*	26	D4
Hall Pen., *Canada*	101	B13
Hall Pt., *Australia*	92	C3
Hallabro, *Sweden*	11	H9
Halland, *Sweden*	9	H15
Hallands län □, *Sweden*	11	H6
Hallands Väderö, *Sweden*	11	H6
Hallandsås, *Sweden*	11	H7
Hällbybrunn, *Sweden*	10	E10
Halle, *Belgium*	17	D4
Halle, *Nordrhein-Westfalen, Germany*	24	C4
Halle, *Sachsen-Anhalt, Germany*	24	D7
Hällefors, *Sweden*	10	E8
Halleforsnäs, *Sweden*	10	E10
Hallein, *Austria*	26	D6
Hällekis, *Sweden*	11	F7
Hallen, *Sweden*	10	A8
Hallett, *Australia*	95	E2
Hallettsville, *U.S.A.*	113	L6
Hallim, *S. Korea*	57	H14
Hallingdalselvi ➔, *Norway*	9	F13
Hallock, *U.S.A.*	112	A6
Halls Creek, *Australia*	92	C4
Hallsberg, *Sweden*	10	E9
Hallstahammar, *Sweden*	10	E10
Hallstatt, *Austria*	26	D6
Hallstavik, *Sweden*	10	D12
Hallstead, *U.S.A.*	111	E9
Halmahera, *Indonesia*	63	D7
Halmeu, *Romania*	42	C8
Halmstad, *Sweden*	11	H6
Hals, *Denmark*	11	H4
Hälsingborg = Helsingborg, *Sweden*	11	H6
Hälsingland, *Sweden*	10	C10
Halstad, *U.S.A.*	112	B6
Haltern, *Germany*	24	D3
Halti, *Finland*	8	B19
Halton □, *U.K.*	12	D5
Haltwhistle, *U.K.*	12	C5
Ḥalul, *Qatar*	71	E7
Halvad, *India*	68	H4
Ḥalvān, *Iran*	71	C8
Ham, *France*	19	C10
Ham Tan, *Vietnam*	65	G6
Ham Yen, *Vietnam*	64	A5
Hamab, *Namibia*	88	D2
Hamad, *Sudan*	81	D3
Hamada, *Japan*	55	G6
Hamadān, *Iran*	71	C6
Hamadān □, *Iran*	71	C6
Ḥamāh, *Syria*	70	C3
Hamamatsu, *Japan*	55	G8
Hamar, *Norway*	9	F14
Ḥamāta, Gebel, *Egypt*	70	E2
Hambantota, *Sri Lanka*	66	R12
Hamber Prov. Park, *Canada*	104	C5
Hamburg, *Germany*	24	B5
Hamburg, *Ark., U.S.A.*	113	J9
Hamburg, *N.Y., U.S.A.*	110	D6
Hamburg, *Pa., U.S.A.*	111	F9
Hamburg □, *Germany*	24	B5
Ḥamḍ, W. al ➔, *Si. Arabia*	70	E3
Hamden, *U.S.A.*	111	E12
Hamdibey, *Turkey*	39	B9
Häme, *Finland*	9	F20
Hämeenlinna, *Finland*	9	F21
Hamélé, *Ghana*	82	C4
Hamelin Pool, *Australia*	93	E1
Hameln, *Germany*	24	C5
Hamerkaz □, *Israel*	75	C3
Hamersley Ra., *Australia*	92	D2
Hamhung, *N. Korea*	57	E14
Hami, *China*	60	B4
Hamilton, *Australia*	95	F3
Hamilton, *Canada*	102	D4
Hamilton, *N.Z.*	91	G5
Hamilton, *U.K.*	14	F4
Hamilton, *Ala., U.S.A.*	109	H1
Hamilton, *Mont., U.S.A.*	114	C6
Hamilton, *N.Y., U.S.A.*	111	D9
Hamilton, *Ohio, U.S.A.*	108	F3
Hamilton, *Tex., U.S.A.*	113	K5
Hamilton ➔, *Australia*	94	C2
Hamilton City, *U.S.A.*	116	F4
Hamilton Inlet, *Canada*	103	B8
Hamilton Mt., *U.S.A.*	111	C10
Hamina, *Finland*	9	F22
Hamirpur, *H.P., India*	68	D7
Hamirpur, *Ut. P., India*	69	G9
Hamitabat, *Turkey*	41	E11
Hamlet, *U.S.A.*	109	H6
Hamley Bridge, *Australia*	95	E2
Hamlin = Hameln, *Germany*	24	C5

Hamlin, N.Y., U.S.A. 110 C7
Hamlin, Tex., U.S.A. 113 J4
Hamm, Germany 24 D3
Ḥammār, Hawr al, Iraq 70 D5
Hammarstrand, Sweden 10 A10
Hammelburg, Germany 25 E5
Hammeren, Denmark 11 J8
Hammerfest, Norway 8 A20
Hammerum, Denmark 11 H3
Hamminkeln, Germany 24 D2
Hammond, Ind., U.S.A. 108 E2
Hammond, La., U.S.A. 113 K9
Hammond, N.Y., U.S.A. 111 B9
Hammondsport, U.S.A. 110 D7
Hammonton, U.S.A. 108 F8
Hamneda, Sweden 11 H7
Hamoyet, Jebel, Sudan 80 D4
Hampden, N.Z. 91 L3
Hampshire □, U.K. 13 F6
Hampshire Downs, U.K. 13 F6
Hampton, N.B., Canada 103 C6
Hampton, Ont., Canada 110 C6
Hampton, Ark., U.S.A. 113 J8
Hampton, Iowa, U.S.A. 112 D8
Hampton, N.H., U.S.A. 111 D14
Hampton, N.Y., U.S.A. 111 C11
Hampton, S.C., U.S.A. 109 J5
Hampton, Va., U.S.A. 108 G7
Hampton Bays, U.S.A. 111 F12
Hampton Tableland, Australia 93 F4
Hamra, Sweden 10 C8
Hamrat esh Sheykh, Sudan 81 E2
Hamur, Turkey 73 C10
Hamyang, S. Korea 57 G14
Han Jiang ➤, China 59 F11
Han Shui, China 58 A7
Han Shui ➤, China 59 B10
Hanak, Si. Arabia 70 E3
Hanamaki, Japan 54 E10
Hanang, Tanzania 86 C4
Hanau, Germany 25 E4
Hanbogd = Ihbulag, Mongolia . 56 C4
Hançalar, Turkey 39 C11
Hâncești, Moldova 43 D13
Hancheng, China 56 G6
Hanchuan, China 59 B9
Hancock, Mich., U.S.A. 112 B10
Hancock, N.Y., U.S.A. 111 E9
Handa, Japan 55 G8
Handan, China 56 F8
Handeni, Tanzania 86 D4
Handlová, Slovak Rep. 27 C11
Handub, Sudan 80 D4
Handwara, India 69 B6
Hanegev, Israel 75 E4
Hanford, U.S.A. 116 J7
Hang Chat, Thailand 64 C2
Hang Dong, Thailand 64 C2
Hangang ➤, S. Korea 57 F14
Hangayn Nuruu, Mongolia 60 B4
Hangchou = Hangzhou, China . 59 B13
Hanggin Houqi, China 56 D4
Hanggin Qi, China 56 E5
Hangu, China 57 E9
Hangzhou, China 59 B13
Hangzhou Wan, China 59 B13
Hanhongor, Mongolia 56 C3
Ḥanīdh, Si. Arabia 71 E6
Ḥanīsh, Yemen 74 E3
Haniska, Slovak Rep. 27 C14
Hanjiang, China 59 E12
Hankinson, U.S.A. 112 B6
Hanko, Finland 9 G20
Hankou, China 59 B10
Hanksville, U.S.A. 115 G8
Hanle, India 69 C8
Hanmer Springs, N.Z. 91 K4
Hann ➤, Australia 92 C4
Hann, Mt., Australia 92 C4
Hanna, Canada 104 C6
Hanna, U.S.A. 114 F10
Hannah B., Canada 102 B4
Hannibal, Mo., U.S.A. 112 F9
Hannibal, N.Y., U.S.A. 111 C8
Hannik, Sudan 80 D3
Hannover, Germany 24 C5
Hanö, Sweden 11 H8
Hanoi, Vietnam 58 G5
Hanover = Hannover, Germany 24 C5
Hanover, Canada 102 D3
Hanover, S. Africa 88 E3
Hanover, N.H., U.S.A. 111 C12
Hanover, Ohio, U.S.A. 110 F2
Hanover, Pa., U.S.A. 108 F7
Hanover, I., Chile 128 G2
Hansdiha, India 69 G12
Hanshou, China 59 C8
Hansi, India 68 E6
Hanson, L., Australia 95 E2
Hanstholm, Denmark 11 G2
Hantsavichy, Belarus 47 F4
Hanumangarh, India 68 E6
Hanyin, China 58 A7
Hanyuan, China 58 C4
Hanzhong, China 56 H4
Hanzhuang, China 57 G9
Haora, India 69 H13
Haoxue, China 59 B9
Haparanda, Sweden 8 D21
Happy, U.S.A. 113 H4
Happy Camp, U.S.A. 114 F2
Happy Valley-Goose Bay,
 Canada 103 B7
Hapsu, N. Korea 57 D15
Hapur, India 68 E7
Ḥaql, Si. Arabia 75 F3
Har, Indonesia 63 F8

Har-Ayrag, Mongolia 56 B5
Har Hu, China 60 C4
Har Us Nuur, Mongolia 60 B4
Har Yehuda, Israel 75 D3
Ḥaraḍ, Si. Arabia 74 C4
Haradok, Belarus 46 E6
Häradsbäck, Sweden 11 H8
Haranomachi, Japan 54 F10
Harare, Zimbabwe 87 F3
Harat, Eritrea 81 D4
Harbin, China 57 B14
Harbiye, Turkey 72 D7
Harbo, Sweden 10 D11
Harboør, Denmark 11 H2
Harbor Beach, U.S.A. 110 C2
Harbour Breton, Canada 103 C8
Harbour Deep, Canada 103 B8
Harburg, Germany 24 B5
Hårby, Denmark 11 J4
Harda, India 68 H7
Hardangerfjorden, Norway 9 F12
Hardangervidda, Norway 9 F12
Hardap Dam, Namibia 88 C2
Hardenberg, Neths. 17 B6
Harderwijk, Neths. 17 B5
Hardey ➤, Australia 92 D2
Hardin, U.S.A. 114 D10
Harding, S. Africa 89 E4
Harding Ra., Australia 92 C3
Hardisty, Canada 104 C6
Hardoi, India 69 F9
Hardwar = Haridwar, India .. 68 E8
Hardwick, U.S.A. 111 B12
Hardy, Pen., Chile 128 H3
Hare B., Canada 103 B8
Hareid, Norway 9 E12
Haren, Germany 24 C3
Harer, Ethiopia 81 F5
Harerge □, Ethiopia 81 F5
Hareto, Ethiopia 81 F4
Harfleur, France 18 C7
Hargeisa, Somali Rep. 74 F3
Harghita □, Romania 43 D10
Harghita, Munţii, Romania .. 43 D10
Hargshamn, Sweden 10 D12
Hari ➤, Indonesia 62 E2
Haria, Canary Is. 37 E6
Haridwar, India 68 E8
Harim, Jabal al, Oman 71 E8
Haringhata ➤, Bangla. 67 J16
Harīrūd ➤, Asia 66 A2
Härjedalen, Sweden 10 B7
Harlan, Iowa, U.S.A. 112 E7
Harlan, Ky., U.S.A. 109 G4
Hârlău, Romania 43 C11
Harlech, U.K. 12 E3
Harlem, U.S.A. 114 B9
Hårlev, Denmark 11 J6
Harlingen, Neths. 17 A5
Harlingen, U.S.A. 113 M6
Harlow, U.K. 13 F8
Harlowton, U.S.A. 114 C9
Harmancık, Turkey 39 B11
Harmånger, Sweden 10 C11
Harmil, Eritrea 81 D5
Harnai, Pakistan 68 D2
Harney Basin, U.S.A. 114 E4
Harney L., U.S.A. 114 E4
Harney Peak, U.S.A. 112 D3
Härnön, Sweden 10 B12
Härnösand, Sweden 10 B11
Haro, Spain 32 C2
Haroldswick, U.K. 14 A8
Harp L., Canada 103 A7
Harper, Liberia 82 E3
Harplinge, Sweden 11 H6
Harr, Mauritania 82 B2
Harrai, India 69 H8
Harrand, Pakistan 68 E4
Ḥarrat Khaybar, Si. Arabia .. 80 B5
Ḥarrat Nawāṣīf, Si. Arabia .. 80 C5
Harricana ➤, Canada 102 B4
Harrington Harbour, Canada . 103 B8
Harris, U.K. 14 D2
Harris, Sd. of, U.K. 14 D1
Harris L., Australia 95 E2
Harris Pt., Canada 110 C2
Harrisburg, Ill., U.S.A. 113 G10
Harrisburg, Nebr., U.S.A. 112 E3
Harrisburg, Pa., U.S.A. 110 F8
Harrismith, S. Africa 89 D4
Harrison, Ark., U.S.A. 113 G8
Harrison, Maine, U.S.A. 111 B14
Harrison, Nebr., U.S.A. 112 D3
Harrison, C., Canada 103 B8
Harrison, L., Canada 104 D4
Harrisonburg, U.S.A. 108 F6
Harrisonville, U.S.A. 112 F7
Harriston, Canada 110 C4
Harrisville, Mich., U.S.A. 110 B1
Harrisville, N.Y., U.S.A. 111 B9
Harrisville, Pa., U.S.A. 110 E5
Harrodsburg, U.S.A. 108 G3
Harrogate, U.K. 12 C6
Harrow □, U.K. 13 F7
Harrowsmith, Canada 111 B8
Harry S. Truman Reservoir,
 U.S.A. 112 F7
Harsefeld, Germany 24 B5
Harsewinkel, Germany 24 D4
Harsud, India 68 H7
Hârșova, Romania 43 F12
Harstad, Norway 8 B17
Hart, U.S.A. 108 D2
Hart, L., Australia 95 E2

Hartbees ➤, S. Africa 88 D3
Hartberg, Austria 26 D8
Hartford, Conn., U.S.A. 111 E12
Hartford, Ky., U.S.A. 108 G2
Hartford, S. Dak., U.S.A. 112 D6
Hartford, Wis., U.S.A. 112 D10
Hartford City, U.S.A. 108 E3
Hartland, Canada 103 C6
Hartland Pt., U.K. 13 F3
Hartlepool, U.K. 12 C6
Hartlepool □, U.K. 12 C6
Hartley Bay, Canada 104 C3
Hartmannberge, Namibia 88 B1
Hartney, Canada 105 D8
Hârtop, Moldova 43 D13
Harts ➤, S. Africa 88 D3
Hartselle, U.S.A. 109 H2
Hartshorne, U.S.A. 113 H7
Hartstown, U.S.A. 110 E4
Hartsville, U.S.A. 109 H5
Hartswater, S. Africa 88 D3
Hartwell, U.S.A. 109 H4
Harunabad, Pakistan 68 E5
Harvand, Iran 71 D7
Harvey, Australia 93 F2
Harvey, Ill., U.S.A. 108 E2
Harvey, N. Dak., U.S.A. 112 B5
Harwich, U.K. 13 F9
Haryana □, India 68 E7
Haryn ➤, Belarus 47 F4
Harz, Germany 24 D6
Harzgerode, Germany 24 D7
Hasa □, Si. Arabia 71 E6
Hasaheisa, Sudan 81 E3
Ḥasanābād, Iran 71 C7
Hasdo ➤, India 69 J10
Haselünne, Germany 24 C3
Hashimoto, Japan 55 G7
Hashtjerd, Iran 71 C6
Haskell, U.S.A. 113 J5
Hasköy, Turkey 41 E10
Haslach, Germany 25 G4
Hasle, Denmark 11 J8
Haslemere, U.K. 13 F7
Haslev, Denmark 11 J5
Hasparren, France 20 E2
Hassa, Turkey 72 D7
Hassela, Sweden 10 B10
Hasselt, Belgium 17 D5
Hassfurt, Germany 25 E6
Hassi Messaoud, Algeria 78 B7
Hässleholm, Sweden 11 H7
Hassloch, Germany 25 F4
Hästholmen, Sweden 11 F8
Hastings, N.Z. 91 H6
Hastings, U.K. 13 G8
Hastings, Mich., U.S.A. 108 D3
Hastings, Minn., U.S.A. 112 C8
Hastings, Nebr., U.S.A. 112 E5
Hastings Ra., Australia 95 E5
Hästveda, Sweden 11 H7
Hat Yai, Thailand 65 J3
Hatanbulag = Ergel, Mongolia . 56 C5
Hatay = Antalya, Turkey 72 D4
Hatch, U.S.A. 115 K10
Hatchet L., Canada 105 B8
Haţeg, Romania 42 E7
Hateruma-Shima, Japan 55 M1
Hatfield P.O., Australia 95 E3
Hatgal, Mongolia 60 A5
Hathras, India 68 F8
Hatia, Bangla. 67 H17
Hāţibah, Ra's, Si. Arabia 80 C4
Hato Mayor, Dom. Rep. 121 C6
Hatta, India 69 G8
Hattah, Australia 95 E3
Hatteras, C., U.S.A. 109 H8
Hattiesburg, U.S.A. 113 K10
Hatvan, Hungary 42 C4
Hau Bon = Cheo Reo, Vietnam 62 B3
Hau Duc, Vietnam 64 E7
Haugesund, Norway 9 G11
Haukipudas, Finland 8 D21
Haultain ➤, Canada 105 B7
Hauraki G., N.Z. 91 G5
Hausruck, Austria 26 C6
Haut Atlas, Morocco 78 B4
Haut-Rhin □, France 19 E14
Haut-Zaïre = Orientale □,
 Dem. Rep. of the Congo 86 B2
Haute-Corse □, France 21 F13
Haute-Garonne □, France 20 E5
Haute-Loire □, France 20 C7
Haute-Marne □, France 19 D12
Haute-Normandie □, France .. 18 C7
Haute-Saône □, France 19 E13
Haute-Savoie □, France 21 C10
Haute-Vienne □, France 20 C5
Hautes-Alpes □, France 21 D10
Hautes Fagnes = Hohe Venn,
 Belgium 17 D6
Hautes-Pyrénées □, France 20 F4
Hauteville-Lompnès, France .. 21 C9
Hautmont, France 19 B10
Hauts-de-Seine □, France 19 D9
Hauts Plateaux, Algeria 76 C4
Hauzenberg, Germany 25 G9
Havana = La Habana, Cuba .. 120 B3
Havant, U.K. 13 G7
Havârna, Romania 43 B11
Havasu, L., U.S.A. 117 L12
Havdhem, Sweden 11 G12
Havel ➤, Germany 24 C8
Havelian, Pakistan 68 B5
Havelock, Canada 102 D4
Havelock, N.Z. 91 J4

Havelock, U.S.A. 109 H7
Haverfordwest, U.K. 13 F3
Haverhill, U.S.A. 111 D13
Haverstraw, U.S.A. 111 E11
Havirga, Mongolia 56 B7
Havířov, Czech Rep. 27 B11
Havlíčkův Brod, Czech Rep. .. 26 B8
Havneby, Denmark 11 J2
Havran, Turkey 39 B9
Havre, U.S.A. 114 B9
Havre-Aubert, Canada 103 C7
Havre-St.-Pierre, Canada 103 B7
Havsa, Turkey 41 E10
Havza, Turkey 72 B6
Haw ➤, U.S.A. 109 H6
Hawaii □, U.S.A. 106 H16
Hawaii I., Pac. Oc. 106 J17
Hawaiian Is., Pac. Oc. 106 H17
Hawaiian Ridge, Pac. Oc. 97 E11
Hawarden, U.S.A. 112 D6
Hawea, L., N.Z. 91 L2
Hawera, N.Z. 91 H5
Hawick, U.K. 14 F6
Hawk Junction, Canada 102 C3
Hawke B., N.Z. 91 H6
Hawker, Australia 95 E2
Hawkesbury, Canada 102 C5
Hawkesbury I., Canada 104 C3
Hawkesbury Pt., Australia 94 A1
Hawkinsville, U.S.A. 109 J4
Hawley, Minn., U.S.A. 112 B6
Hawley, Pa., U.S.A. 111 E9
Ḥawrān, W. ➤, Iraq 70 C4
Hawsh Mūssá, Lebanon 75 B4
Hawthorne, U.S.A. 114 G4
Hay, Australia 95 E3
Hay ➤, Australia 94 C2
Hay ➤, Canada 104 A5
Hay, C., Australia 92 B4
Hay I., Canada 110 B4
Hay L., Canada 104 B5
Hay-on-Wye, U.K. 13 E4
Hay River, Canada 104 A5
Hay Springs, U.S.A. 112 D3
Haya = Tehoru, Indonesia 63 E7
Hayachine-San, Japan 54 E10
Hayange, France 19 C13
Haydarlı, Turkey 39 C12
Hayden, U.S.A. 114 F10
Haydon, Australia 94 B3
Hayes ➤, Canada 102 A1
Hayes Creek, Australia 92 B5
Hayle, U.K. 13 G2
Hayling I., U.K. 13 G7
Hayman, Turkey 72 C5
Hayrabolu, Turkey 41 E11
Hays, Canada 104 C6
Hays, U.S.A. 112 F5
Haysyn, Ukraine 47 H5
Hayvoron, Ukraine 47 H5
Hayward, Calif., U.S.A. 116 H4
Hayward, Wis., U.S.A. 112 B9
Haywards Heath, U.K. 13 G7
Hazafon □, Israel 75 C4
Hazārān, Kūh-e, Iran 71 D8
Hazard, U.S.A. 108 G4
Hazaribag, India 69 H11
Hazaribag Road, India 69 G11
Hazebrouck, France 19 B9
Hazelton, Canada 104 B3
Hazelton, U.S.A. 112 B4
Hazen, U.S.A. 112 B4
Hazlehurst, Ga., U.S.A. 109 K4
Hazlehurst, Miss., U.S.A. 113 K9
Hazlet, U.S.A. 111 F10
Hazleton, U.S.A. 111 F9
Hazlett, L., Australia 92 D4
Hazro, Turkey 70 B4
He Xian, Anhui, China 59 B12
He Xian, Guangxi Zhuangzu,
 China 59 E8
Head of Bight, Australia 93 F5
Headlands, Zimbabwe 87 F3
Healdsburg, U.S.A. 116 G4
Healdton, U.S.A. 113 H6
Healesville, Australia 95 F4
Heany Junction, Zimbabwe ... 89 C4
Heard I., Ind. Oc. 3 G13
Hearne, U.S.A. 113 K6
Hearst, Canada 102 C3
Heart ➤, U.S.A. 112 B4
Heart's Content, Canada 103 C9
Heath Pt., Canada 103 C7
Heavener, U.S.A. 113 H7
Hebbronville, U.S.A. 113 M5
Hebei □, China 56 E9
Hebel, Australia 95 D4
Heber, U.S.A. 117 N11
Heber City, U.S.A. 114 F8
Heber Springs, U.S.A. 113 H9
Hebert, Canada 105 C7
Hebgen L., U.S.A. 114 D8
Hebi, China 56 G8
Hebrides, U.K. 6 D4
Hebrides, Sea of the, U.K. 14 D2
Hebron = Al Khalīl, West Bank 75 D4
Hebron, Canada 101 C13
Hebron, N. Dak., U.S.A. 112 B3
Hebron, Nebr., U.S.A. 112 E6
Heby, Sweden 10 E10
Hecate Str., Canada 104 C2
Hecete I., U.S.A. 104 B2
Hechi, China 58 E7
Hechingen, Germany 25 G4
Hechuan, China 58 B6

Hecla, U.S.A. 112 C5
Hecla I., Canada 105 C9
Hédé, France 18 D5
Hede, Sweden 10 B7
Hedemora, Sweden 10 D9
Hedensted, Denmark 11 J3
Hedesunda, Sweden 10 D10
Heerde, Neths. 17 B6
Heerenveen, Neths. 17 B5
Heerhugowaard, Neths. 17 B4
Heerlen, Neths. 17 D5
Ḥefa, Israel 75 C4
Ḥefa □, Israel 75 C4
Hefei, China 59 B11
Hefeng, China 59 C8
Hegalig, Sudan 81 E3
Hegang, China 60 B8
Heiban, Sudan 81 E3
Heichengzhen, China 56 F4
Heide, Germany 24 A5
Heidelberg, Germany 25 F4
Heidelberg, S. Africa 88 E3
Heidenau, Germany 24 E9
Heidenheim, Germany 25 G6
Heijing, China 58 E3
Heilbad Heiligenstadt, Germany 24 D6
Heilbron, S. Africa 89 D4
Heilbronn, Germany 25 F5
Heiligenblut, Austria 26 D5
Heiligenhafen, Germany 24 A6
Heilongjiang □, China 60 B7
Heilunkiang = Heilongjiang □,
 China 60 B7
Heimaey, Iceland 8 E3
Heinola, Finland 9 F22
Heinsberg, Germany 24 D2
Heinze Kyun, Burma 64 E1
Heishan, China 57 D12
Heishui, Liaoning, China 57 C10
Heishui, Sichuan, China 58 A4
Hejaz = Ḥijāz □, Si. Arabia ... 70 E3
Hejian, China 56 E9
Hejiang, China 58 C5
Hekimhan, Turkey 70 B3
Hekla, Iceland 8 E4
Hekou, Guangdong, China 59 F9
Hekou, Yunnan, China 58 F4
Hel, Poland 44 D5
Helagsfjället, Sweden 10 B6
Helan Shan, China 56 E3
Helechosa, Spain 35 F6
Helen Atoll, Pac. Oc. 63 D8
Helena, Ark., U.S.A. 113 H9
Helena, Mont., U.S.A. 114 C7
Helendale, U.S.A. 117 L9
Helensburgh, U.K. 14 E4
Helensville, N.Z. 91 G5
Helenvale, Australia 94 B4
Helgasjön, Sweden 11 H8
Helgeland, Norway 8 C15
Helgoland, Germany 24 A3
Heligoland = Helgoland,
 Germany 24 A3
Heligoland B. = Deutsche Bucht,
 Germany 24 A4
Heliopolis, Egypt 80 H7
Hella, Iceland 8 E3
Hellertown, U.S.A. 111 F9
Hellespont = Çanakkale Boğazı,
 Turkey 41 F10
Hellevoetsluis, Neths. 17 C4
Hellín, Spain 33 G3
Helmand □, Afghan. 66 D4
Helmand ➤, Afghan. 66 D2
Helme ➤, Germany 24 D7
Helmeringhausen, Namibia ... 88 D2
Helmond, Neths. 17 C5
Helmsdale, U.K. 14 C5
Helmsdale ➤, U.K. 14 C5
Helmstedt, Germany 24 C7
Helong, China 57 C15
Helper, U.S.A. 114 G8
Helsingborg, Sweden 11 H6
Helsinge, Denmark 11 H6
Helsingfors = Helsinki, Finland 9 F21
Helsingør, Denmark 11 H6
Helsinki, Finland 9 F21
Helska, Mierzeja, Poland 44 D5
Helston, U.K. 13 G2
Helvellyn, U.K. 12 C4
Helwân, Egypt 80 J7
Hemel Hempstead, U.K. 13 F7
Hemet, U.S.A. 117 M10
Hemingford, U.S.A. 112 D3
Hemmingford, Canada 111 A11
Hempstead, U.S.A. 113 K6
Hemse, Sweden 11 G12
Hemsön, Sweden 10 B12
Henån, Sweden 11 F5
Henan □, China 56 H8
Henares ➤, Spain 34 E7
Henashi-Misaki, Japan 54 D9
Hendaye, France 20 E2
Hendek, Turkey 72 B4
Henderson, Argentina 126 D3
Henderson, Ky., U.S.A. 108 G2
Henderson, N.C., U.S.A. 109 G6
Henderson, Nev., U.S.A. 117 J12
Henderson, Tenn., U.S.A. 109 H1
Henderson, Tex., U.S.A. 113 J7
Hendersonville, N.C., U.S.A. .. 109 H4
Hendersonville, Tenn., U.S.A. . 109 G2
Hendorābī, Iran 71 E7
Heng Jiang, China 58 C5
Heng Xian, China 58 F7

Hengcheng, China 56 E4
Hengchun, Taiwan 59 F13
Hengdaohezi, China 57 B15
Hengelo, Neths. 17 B6
Hengfeng, China 59 C10
Hengshan, Hunan, China 59 D9
Hengshan, Shaanxi, China 56 F5
Hengshui, China 56 F8
Hengyang, China 59 D9
Henichesk, Ukraine 47 J8
Hénin-Beaumont, France 19 B9
Henlopen, C., U.S.A. 108 F8
Hennan, China 10 B9
Hennebont, France 18 E3
Hennenman, S. Africa 88 D4
Hennessey, U.S.A. 113 G6
Hennigsdorf, Germany 24 C9
Henrietta, U.S.A. 113 J5
Henrietta, Ostrov = Genriyetty, Ostrov, Russia 51 B16
Henrietta Maria, C., Canada ... 102 A3
Henry, U.S.A. 112 E10
Henryetta, U.S.A. 113 H7
Henryville, Canada 111 A11
Hensall, Canada 110 C3
Henstedt-Ulzburg, Germany 24 B6
Hentiesbaai, Namibia 88 C1
Hentiyn Nuruu, Mongolia 60 B5
Henty, Australia 95 F4
Henzada, Burma 67 L19
Hephaestia, Greece 39 B7
Heping, China 59 E10
Heppner, U.S.A. 114 D4
Hepu, China 58 G7
Hepworth, Canada 110 B3
Heqing, China 58 D3
Hequ, China 56 E6
Héraðsflói, Iceland 8 D6
Héraðsvötn ➔, Iceland 8 D4
Herald Cays, Australia 94 B4
Herāt, Afghan. 66 B3
Herāt □, Afghan. 66 B3
Hérault □, France 20 E7
Hérault ➔, France 20 E7
Herbault, France 18 E8
Herbert ➔, Australia 94 B4
Herberton, Australia 94 B4
Herbertsdale, S. Africa 88 E3
Herbignac, France 18 E4
Herborn, Germany 24 E4
Herby, Poland 45 H5
Herceg-Novi, Montenegro, Yug. 40 D2
Herchmer, Canada 105 B10
Herðubreið, Iceland 8 D5
Hereford, U.K. 13 E5
Hereford, U.S.A. 113 H3
Herefordshire □, U.K. 13 E5
Hereke, Turkey 41 F13
Herencia, Spain 35 F7
Herentals, Belgium 17 C4
Herford, Germany 24 C4
Héricourt, France 19 E13
Herington, U.S.A. 112 F6
Herisau, Switz. 25 H5
Hérisson, France 19 F9
Herkimer, U.S.A. 111 D10
Herlong, U.S.A. 116 E6
Herm, U.K. 13 H5
Hermann, U.S.A. 112 F9
Hermannsburg, Australia 92 D5
Hermannsburg, Germany 24 C6
Hermanus, S. Africa 88 E2
Herment, France 20 C6
Hermidale, Australia 95 E4
Hermiston, U.S.A. 114 D4
Hermite, I., Chile 128 H3
Hermon, U.S.A. 111 B9
Hermon, Mt. = Shaykh, J. ash, Lebanon 75 B4
Hermosillo, Mexico 118 B2
Hernád ➔, Hungary 42 C6
Hernandarias, Paraguay 127 B5
Hernandez, U.S.A. 116 J6
Hernando, Argentina 126 C3
Hernando, U.S.A. 113 H10
Hernani, Spain 32 B3
Herndon, U.S.A. 110 F8
Herne, Germany 17 C7
Herne Bay, U.K. 13 F9
Herning, Denmark 11 H2
Heroica = Caborca, Mexico ... 118 A2
Heroica Nogales = Nogales, Mexico 118 A2
Heron Bay, Canada 102 C2
Herradura, Pta. de la, Canary Is. .. 37 F5
Herreid, U.S.A. 112 C4
Herrenberg, Germany 25 G4
Herrera, Spain 35 H6
Herrera de Alcántara, Spain .. 35 F3
Herrera de Pisuerga, Spain ... 34 C6
Herrera del Duque, Spain 35 F5
Herrestad, Sweden 11 F5
Herrin, U.S.A. 113 G10
Herriot, Canada 105 B8
Herrljunga, Sweden 11 F7
Hersbruck, Germany 25 F7
Hershey, U.S.A. 111 F8
Hersonissos, Greece 36 D7
Herstal, Belgium 17 D5
Hertford, U.K. 13 F7
Hertfordshire □, U.K. 13 F7
's-Hertogenbosch, Neths. 17 C5
Hertzogville, S. Africa 88 D4
Hervás, Spain 34 E5
Hervey B., Australia 94 C5
Herzberg, Brandenburg, Germany 24 D9

Herzberg, Niedersachsen, Germany 24 D6
Herzliyya, Israel 75 C3
Herzogenburg, Austria 26 C8
Heşār, Fārs, Iran 71 D6
Heşār, Markazī, Iran 71 C6
Hesdin, France 19 B9
Heshan, China 58 F7
Heshi, China 56 G5
Heshui, China 56 F7
Hesperia, U.S.A. 117 L9
Hesse = Hessen □, Germany .. 24 E4
Hessen □, Germany 24 E4
Hestra, Sweden 11 G7
Hetch Hetchy Aqueduct, U.S.A. 116 H5
Hettinger, U.S.A. 112 C3
Hettstedt, Germany 24 D7
Heuvelton, U.S.A. 111 B9
Heves, Hungary 42 C5
Heves □, Hungary 42 C5
Hewitt, U.S.A. 113 K6
Hexham, U.K. 12 C5
Hexi, Yunnan, China 58 E4
Hexi, Zhejiang, China 59 D12
Hexigten Qi, China 57 C9
Heydarābād, Iran 71 D7
Heysham, U.K. 12 C5
Heyuan, China 59 F10
Heywood, Australia 95 F3
Heze, China 56 G8
Hezhang, China 58 D5
Hi Vista, U.S.A. 117 L9
Hialeah, U.S.A. 109 N5
Hiawatha, U.S.A. 112 F7
Hibbing, U.S.A. 112 B8
Hibbs B., Australia 94 G4
Hibernia Reef, Australia 92 B3
Hickman, U.S.A. 113 G10
Hickory, U.S.A. 109 H5
Hicks, Pt., Australia 95 F4
Hicks L., Canada 105 A9
Hicksville, U.S.A. 111 F11
Hida, Romania 43 C8
Hida-Gawa ➔, Japan 55 G8
Hida-Sammyaku, Japan 55 F8
Hidaka-Sammyaku, Japan 54 C11
Hidalgo, Mexico 119 C5
Hidalgo □, Mexico 119 C5
Hidalgo, Presa M., Mexico ... 118 B3
Hidalgo, Pta. del, Canary Is. .. 37 F3
Hidalgo del Parral, Mexico ... 118 B3
Hiddensee, Germany 24 A9
Hieflau, Austria 26 D7
Hiendelaencina, Spain 32 D2
Hierro, Canary Is. 37 G1
Higashiajima-San, Japan 54 F10
Higashiōsaka, Japan 55 G7
Higgins, U.S.A. 113 G4
Higgins Corner, U.S.A. 116 F5
High Atlas = Haut Atlas, Morocco 78 B4
High Bridge, U.S.A. 111 F10
High Level, Canada 104 B5
High Point, U.S.A. 109 H6
High Prairie, Canada 104 B5
High River, Canada 104 C6
High Tatra = Tatry, Slovak Rep. 27 B13
High Veld, Africa 76 J6
High Wycombe, U.K. 13 F7
Highland □, U.K. 14 D4
Highland Park, U.S.A. 108 D2
Highmore, U.S.A. 112 C5
Highrock L., Man., Canada ... 105 B8
Highrock L., Sask., Canada ... 105 B7
Higüey, Dom. Rep. 121 C6
Hihya, Egypt 80 H7
Hiiumaa, Estonia 9 G20
Hĳar, Spain 32 D4
Ḥijāz □, Si. Arabia 70 E3
Hĳo = Tagum, Phil. 61 H6
Hikmak, Ras el, Egypt 80 A2
Hiko, U.S.A. 116 H11
Hikone, Japan 55 G8
Hikurangi, N.Z. 91 F5
Hikurangi, Mt., N.Z. 91 H6
Hildburghausen, Germany 24 E6
Hildesheim, Germany 24 C5
Hill ➔, Australia 93 F2
Hill City, Idaho, U.S.A. 114 E6
Hill City, Kans., U.S.A. 112 F5
Hill City, S. Dak., U.S.A. 112 D3
Hill Island L., Canada 105 A7
Hillared, Sweden 11 G7
Hillcrest Center, U.S.A. 117 K8
Hillegom, Neths. 17 B4
Hillerød, Denmark 11 J6
Hillerstorp, Sweden 11 G7
Hillsboro, Kans., U.S.A. 112 F6
Hillsboro, N. Dak., U.S.A. 112 B6
Hillsboro, N.H., U.S.A. 111 C13
Hillsboro, Ohio, U.S.A. 108 F4
Hillsboro, Oreg., U.S.A. 116 E4
Hillsboro, Tex., U.S.A. 113 J6
Hillsborough, Grenada 121 D7
Hillsdale, Mich., U.S.A. 108 E3
Hillsdale, N.Y., U.S.A. 111 D11
Hillston, Australia 95 E4
Hilo, U.S.A. 106 J17
Hilton, U.S.A. 110 C7
Hilton Head Island, U.S.A. ... 109 J5
Hilvan, Turkey 73 D8
Hilversum, Neths. 17 B5
Himachal Pradesh □, India ... 68 D7
Himalaya, Asia 69 E11
Himamaylan, Phil. 61 F5

Himarë, Albania 40 F3
Himatnagar, India 66 H8
Himeji, Japan 55 G7
Himi, Japan 55 F8
Himmerland, Denmark 11 H3
Ḥimş, Syria 75 A5
Ḥimş □, Syria 75 A6
Hinche, Haiti 121 C5
Hinchinbrook I., Australia 94 B4
Hinckley, U.K. 13 E6
Hinckley, U.S.A. 112 B8
Hindaun, India 68 F7
Hindmarsh, L., Australia 95 F3
Hindu Bagh, Pakistan 68 D2
Hindu Kush, Asia 66 B7
Hindubagh, Pakistan 66 D5
Hindupur, India 66 N10
Hines Creek, Canada 104 B5
Hinesville, U.S.A. 109 K5
Hinganghat, India 66 J11
Hingham, U.S.A. 114 B8
Hingir, India 69 J10
Hingoli, India 66 K10
Hinigaran, Phil. 61 F5
Hinis, Turkey 73 C9
Hinna = Imi, Ethiopia 81 F5
Hinna, Nigeria 83 C7
Hinnerup, Denmark 11 H4
Hinnøya, Norway 8 B16
Hinojosa del Duque, Spain ... 35 G5
Hinsdale, U.S.A. 111 D12
Hinterrhein ➔, Switz. 25 J5
Hinton, Canada 104 C5
Hinton, U.S.A. 108 G5
Hınzır Burnu, Turkey 72 D6
Hirado, Japan 55 H4
Hirakud Dam, India 67 J13
Hiran ➔, India 69 H8
Hirapur, India 69 G8
Hiratsuka, Japan 55 G9
Hirfanlı Baraji, Turkey 72 C5
Hiroo, Japan 54 C11
Hirosaki, Japan 54 D10
Hiroshima, Japan 55 G6
Hiroshima □, Japan 55 G6
Hirson, France 19 C11
Hirtshals, Denmark 11 G3
Hisar, India 68 E6
Hisarcık, Turkey 39 B11
Hisaria, Bulgaria 41 D8
Hisb ➔, Iraq 70 D5
Ḥismá, Si. Arabia 70 D3
Hispaniola, W. Indies 121 C5
Ḥīt, Iraq 70 C4
Hita, Japan 55 H5
Hitachi, Japan 55 F10
Hitchin, U.K. 13 F7
Hitoyoshi, Japan 55 H5
Hitra, Norway 8 E13
Hitzacker, Germany 24 B7
Hixon, Canada 104 C4
Ḥiyyon, N. ➔, Israel 75 E4
Hjalmar L., Canada 105 A7
Hjälmaren, Sweden 10 E9
Hjältevad, Sweden 11 G9
Hjo, Sweden 11 F8
Hjørring, Denmark 11 G3
Hjortkvarn, Sweden 11 F9
Hkakabo Razi, Burma 67 E20
Hlinsko, Czech Rep. 26 B8
Hlobane, S. Africa 89 D5
Hlohovec, Slovak Rep. 27 C10
Hlučín, Czech Rep. 27 B11
Hluhluwe, S. Africa 89 D5
Hlukhiv, Ukraine 47 G7
Hlyboka, Ukraine 47 H3
Hlybokaye, Belarus 46 E4
Hnúšťa, Slovak Rep. 27 C12
Ho, Ghana 83 D5
Ho Chi Minh City = Thanh Pho Ho Chi Minh, Vietnam 65 G6
Ho Thuong, Vietnam 64 C5
Hoa Binh, Vietnam 58 G5
Hoa Da, Vietnam 65 G7
Hoa Hiep, Vietnam 65 G5
Hoai Nhon, Vietnam 64 E7
Hoang Lien Son, Vietnam 58 F4
Hoanib ➔, Namibia 88 B2
Hoare B., Canada 101 B13
Hoarusib ➔, Namibia 88 B2
Hobart, Australia 94 G4
Hobart, U.S.A. 113 H5
Hobbs, U.S.A. 113 J3
Hobbs Coast, Antarctica 5 D14
Hobe Sound, U.S.A. 109 M5
Hoboken, U.S.A. 111 F10
Hobro, Denmark 11 H3
Hoburgen, Sweden 11 H12
Hocalar, Turkey 39 C11
Hochfeld, Namibia 88 C2
Hochschwab, Austria 26 D8
Höchstadt, Germany 25 F6
Hodaka-Dake, Japan 55 F8
Hodgeville, Canada 105 C7
Hodgson, Canada 105 C9
Hódmezővásárhely, Hungary .. 42 D5
Hodna, Chott el, Algeria 78 A6
Hodonín, Czech Rep. 27 C10
Hoek van Holland, Neths. 17 C4
Hoengsŏng, S. Korea 57 F14
Hoeryong, N. Korea 57 C15
Hoeyang, N. Korea 57 E14
Hof, Germany 25 E7

Hofgeismar, Germany 24 D5
Hofheim, Germany 25 E4
Hofmeyr, S. Africa 88 E4
Höfn, Iceland 8 D6
Hofors, Sweden 10 D10
Hofsjökull, Iceland 8 D4
Hōfu, Japan 55 G5
Hogan Group, Australia 95 F4
Hogarth, Mt., Australia 94 C2
Hoggar = Ahaggar, Algeria ... 78 D7
Högsäter, Sweden 11 F6
Högsby, Sweden 11 G10
Högsjö, Sweden 10 E9
Hoh ➔, U.S.A. 116 C2
Hohe Acht, Germany 25 E3
Hohe Tauern, Austria 26 D5
Hohe Venn, Belgium 17 D6
Hohenau, Austria 27 C9
Hohenems, Austria 26 D2
Hohenloher Ebene, Germany .. 25 F5
Hohenwald, U.S.A. 109 H2
Hohenwestedt, Germany 24 A5
Hohe Rhön = Rhön, Germany .. 24 E5
Hohhot, China 56 D6
Hóhlakas, Greece 36 D9
Hohoe, Ghana 83 D5
Hoi An, Vietnam 64 E7
Hoi Xuan, Vietnam 58 G5
Hoisington, U.S.A. 112 F5
Højer, Denmark 11 K2
Hōjō, Japan 55 H6
Hok, Sweden 11 G8
Hökensås, Sweden 11 F8
Hökerum, Sweden 11 G7
Hokianga Harbour, N.Z. 91 F4
Hokitika, N.Z. 91 K3
Hokkaidō □, Japan 54 C11
Hol-Hol, Djibouti 81 E5
Hola Pristan, Ukraine 47 J7
Holbæk, Denmark 11 J5
Holbrook, Australia 95 F4
Holbrook, U.S.A. 115 J8
Holden, U.S.A. 114 G7
Holdenville, U.S.A. 113 H6
Holdrege, U.S.A. 112 E5
Holešov, Czech Rep. 27 B10
Holguín, Cuba 120 B4
Holič, Slovak Rep. 27 C10
Holice, Czech Rep. 26 A8
Höljes, Sweden 10 D6
Hollabrunn, Austria 26 C9
Hollams Bird I., Namibia 88 C1
Holland, Mich., U.S.A. 108 D2
Holland, N.Y., U.S.A. 110 D6
Hollandale, U.S.A. 113 J9
Hollandia = Jayapura, Indonesia 63 E10
Holley, U.S.A. 110 C6
Hollfeld, Germany 25 F7
Hollidaysburg, U.S.A. 110 F6
Hollis, U.S.A. 113 H5
Hollister, Calif., U.S.A. 116 J5
Hollister, Idaho, U.S.A. 114 E6
Höllviken = Höllviksnäs, Sweden 11 J6
Höllviksnäs, Sweden 11 J6
Holly Hill, U.S.A. 109 L5
Holly Springs, U.S.A. 113 H10
Hollywood, U.S.A. 109 N5
Holman, Canada 100 A8
Hólmavík, Iceland 8 D3
Holmen, U.S.A. 112 D9
Holmes Reefs, Australia 94 B4
Holmsjö, Sweden 11 H9
Holmsund, Västernorrland, Sweden 10 B10
Holmsjön, Västernorrland, Sweden 10 B9
Holmsland Klit, Denmark 11 J2
Holmsund, Sweden 8 E19
Holod, Romania 42 D7
Holroyd ➔, Australia 94 A3
Holstebro, Denmark 11 H2
Holsworthy, U.K. 13 G3
Holton, Canada 103 B8
Holton, U.S.A. 112 F7
Holtville, U.S.A. 117 N11
Holwerd, Neths. 17 A5
Holy I., Angl., U.K. 12 D3
Holy I., Northumb., U.K. 12 B6
Holyhead, U.K. 12 D3
Holyoke, Colo., U.S.A. 112 E3
Holyoke, Mass., U.S.A. 111 D12
Holyrood, Canada 103 C9
Holzkirchen, Germany 25 H7
Holzminden, Germany 24 D5
Homa Bay, Kenya 86 C3
Homalin, Burma 67 G19
Homand, Iran 71 C8
Homathko ➔, Canada 104 C4
Homberg, Germany 24 D5
Hombori, Mali 83 B4
Homburg, Germany 25 F3
Home B., Canada 101 B13
Home Hill, Australia 94 B4
Homedale, U.S.A. 114 E5
Homer, Alaska, U.S.A. 100 C4
Homer, La., U.S.A. 113 J8
Homer City, U.S.A. 110 F5
Homestead, Australia 94 C4
Homestead, U.S.A. 109 N5
Homewood, U.S.A. 116 F6
Homoine, Mozam. 89 C6
Homoljske Planina, Serbia, Yug. 40 B5
Homorod, Romania 43 D10
Homs = Ḥimş, Syria 75 A5
Homyel, Belarus 47 F6

Hon Chong, Vietnam 65 G5
Hon Me, Vietnam 64 C5
Honan = Henan □, China 56 H8
Honaz, Turkey 39 D11
Honbetsu, Japan 54 C11
Honcut, U.S.A. 116 F5
Honda Bay, Phil. 61 G3
Hondarribia, Spain 32 B3
Hondeklipbaai, S. Africa 88 E2
Hondo, Japan 55 H5
Hondo, U.S.A. 113 L5
Hondo ➔, Belize 119 D7
Honduras ■, Cent. Amer. 120 D2
Honduras, G. de, Caribbean ... 120 C2
Hønefoss, Norway 9 F14
Honesdale, U.S.A. 111 E9
Honey L., U.S.A. 116 E6
Honfleur, France 18 C7
Høng, Denmark 11 J5
Hong ➔, Vietnam 58 F5
Hong Gai, Vietnam 58 G6
Hong He ➔, China 56 H8
Hong Hu, China 59 C9
Hong Kong □, China 59 F10
Hong'an, China 59 B10
Hongch'ŏn, S. Korea 57 F14
Honghai Wan, China 59 F10
Honghe, China 58 F4
Honghu, China 59 C9
Hongjiang, China 58 D7
Hongliu He ➔, China 56 F5
Hongor, Mongolia 56 B7
Hongsa, Laos 64 C3
Hongshui He ➔, China 58 F7
Hongsŏng, S. Korea 57 F14
Hongtong, China 56 F6
Honguedo, Détroit d', Canada .. 103 C7
Hongwon, N. Korea 57 E14
Hongya, China 58 C4
Hongyuan, China 58 A4
Hongze Hu, China 57 H10
Honiara, Solomon Is. 96 H7
Honiton, U.K. 13 G4
Honjō, Japan 54 E10
Honkorâb, Ras, Egypt 80 C4
Honningsvåg, Norway 8 A21
Hönö, Sweden 11 G5
Honolulu, U.S.A. 106 H16
Hontoria del Pinar, Spain 32 D1
Hood, Mt., U.S.A. 114 D3
Hood, Pt., Australia 93 F2
Hood River, U.S.A. 114 D3
Hoodsport, U.S.A. 116 C3
Hooge, Germany 24 A4
Hoogeveen, Neths. 17 B6
Hoogezand-Sappemeer, Neths. 17 A6
Hooghly = Hugli ➔, India 69 J13
Hooghly-Chinsura = Chunchura, India 69 H13
Hook Hd., Ireland 15 D5
Hook I., Australia 94 C4
Hook of Holland = Hoek van Holland, Neths. 17 C4
Hooker, U.S.A. 113 G4
Hooker Creek, Australia 92 C5
Hoonah, U.S.A. 104 B1
Hooper Bay, U.S.A. 100 B3
Hoopeston, U.S.A. 108 E2
Hoopstad, S. Africa 88 D4
Höör, Sweden 11 J7
Hoorn, Neths. 17 B5
Hoover, U.S.A. 109 J2
Hoover Dam, U.S.A. 117 K12
Hooversville, U.S.A. 110 F6
Hop Bottom, U.S.A. 111 E9
Hopa, Turkey 73 B9
Hope, Canada 104 D4
Hope, Ariz., U.S.A. 117 M13
Hope, Ark., U.S.A. 113 J8
Hope, L., S. Austral., Australia .. 95 D2
Hope, L., W. Austral., Australia 93 F3
Hope, I., Canada 110 B4
Hope Town, Bahamas 120 A4
Hopedale, Canada 103 A7
Hopedale, U.S.A. 111 D13
Hopefield, S. Africa 88 E2
Hopei = Hebei □, China 56 E9
Hopelchén, Mexico 119 D7
Hopetoun, Vic., Australia 95 F3
Hopetoun, W. Austral., Australia 93 F3
Hopetown, S. Africa 88 D3
Hopevale, Australia 94 B4
Hopewell, U.S.A. 108 G7
Hopfgarten, Austria 26 D5
Hopkins, L., Australia 92 D4
Hopkinsville, U.S.A. 109 G2
Hopland, U.S.A. 116 G3
Hoquiam, U.S.A. 116 D3
Horasan, Turkey 73 B10
Horaždovice, Czech Rep. 26 B6
Horb, Germany 25 G4
Hörby, Sweden 11 J7
Horcajo de Santiago, Spain ... 32 F1
Horden Hills, Australia 92 D5
Horezu, Romania 43 E8
Horgen, Switz. 25 H4
Horgoš, Serbia, Yug. 42 D4
Hořice, Czech Rep. 26 A8
Horinger, China 56 D6
Horki, Belarus 46 E6
Horlick Mts., Antarctica 5 E11
Horlivka, Ukraine 47 H10
Hormak, Iran 71 D9
Hormoz, Iran 71 E7
Hormoz, Jaz.-ye, Iran 71 E8
Hormozgān □, Iran 71 E8
Hormuz, Kūh-e, Iran 71 E7

Hormuz, Str. of, The Gulf 71 E8
Horn, Austria 26 C8
Horn, Iceland 8 C2
Horn, Sweden 11 G9
Horn →, Canada 104 A5
Horn, Cape = Hornos, C. de,
  Chile 122 J4
Horn Head, Ireland 15 A3
Horn I., Australia 94 A3
Horn Mts., Canada 104 A5
Hornachuelos, Spain 35 H5
Hornavan, Sweden 8 C17
Hornbeck, U.S.A. 113 K8
Hornbrook, U.S.A. 114 F2
Hornburg, Germany 24 C6
Horncastle, U.K. 12 D7
Horndal, Sweden 10 D10
Hornell, U.S.A. 110 D7
Hornell L., Canada 104 A5
Hornepayne, Canada 102 C3
Horní Planá, Czech Rep. ... 26 C7
Hornings Mills, Canada 110 B4
Hornitos, U.S.A. 116 H6
Hornos, C. de, Chile 122 J4
Hornoy-le-Bourg, France ... 19 C8
Hornsea, U.K. 12 D7
Hornslandet, Sweden 10 C11
Hörnum, Germany 24 A4
Horobetsu, Japan 54 C10
Horodenka, Ukraine 47 H3
Horodnya, Ukraine 47 G6
Horodok, Khmelnytskyy,
  Ukraine 47 H4
Horodok, Lviv, Ukraine 47 H2
Horodyshche, Ukraine 47 H6
Horokhiv, Ukraine 47 G3
Horovice, Czech Rep. 26 B6
Horqin Youyi Qianqi, China . 57 A12
Horqueta, Paraguay 126 A4
Horred, Sweden 11 G6
Horse Creek, U.S.A. 112 E3
Horse Is., Canada 103 B8
Horsefly L., Canada 104 C4
Horseheads, U.S.A. 110 D8
Horsens, Denmark 11 J3
Horsham, Australia 95 F3
Horsham, U.K. 13 F7
Horšovský Týn, Czech Rep. . 26 B5
Horten, Norway 9 G14
Hortobágy →, Hungary 42 C6
Horton, U.S.A. 112 F7
Horton →, Canada 100 B7
Horwood L., Canada 102 C3
Hosaina, Ethiopia 81 F4
Hose, Gunung-Gunung,
  Malaysia 62 D4
Ḥoseynābād, Khuzestān, Iran .. 71 C6
Ḥoseynābād, Kordestān, Iran . 70 C5
Hoshangabad, India 68 H7
Hoshiarpur, India 68 D6
Hospet, India 66 M10
Hoste, I., Chile 128 H3
Hostens, France 20 D3
Hot, Thailand 64 C2
Hot Creek Range, U.S.A. .. 114 G6
Hot Springs, Ark., U.S.A. . 113 H8
Hot Springs, S. Dak., U.S.A. . 112 D3
Hotagen, Sweden 8 E16
Hotan, China 60 C2
Hotazel, S. Africa 88 D3
Hotchkiss, U.S.A. 115 G10
Hoting, Sweden 8 D17
Hotolisht, Albania 40 E4
Hotte, Massif de la, Haiti . 121 C5
Hottentotsbaai, Namibia . 88 D1
Houat, Î. de, France 18 E4
Houdan, France 19 D8
Houei Sai, Laos 58 G3
Houeillès, France 20 D4
Houffalize, Belgium 17 D5
Houghton, Mich., U.S.A. . 112 B10
Houghton, N.Y., U.S.A. .. 110 D6
Houghton L., U.S.A. 108 C3
Houhora Heads, N.Z. 91 F4
Houlton, U.S.A. 109 B12
Houma, U.S.A. 113 L9
Houndé, Burkina Faso ... 82 C4
Hourtin, France 20 C2
Hourtin-Carcans, Étang d',
  France 20 C2
Housatonic →, U.S.A. ... 111 E11
Houston, Canada 104 C3
Houston, Mo., U.S.A. 113 G9
Houston, Tex., U.S.A. ... 113 L7
Hout →, S. Africa 89 C4
Houtkraal, S. Africa 88 E3
Houtman Abrolhos, Australia . 93 E1
Hovd, Mongolia 60 B4
Hove, U.K. 13 G7
Hoveyzeh, Iran 71 D6
Hovmantorp, Sweden 11 H9
Hövsgöl, Mongolia 56 C5
Hövsgöl Nuur, Mongolia . 60 A5
Hovsta, Sweden 10 E9
Howakil, Eritrea 81 D5
Howar, Wadi →, Sudan .. 81 D2
Howard, Australia 95 D5
Howard, Pa., U.S.A. 110 F7
Howard, S. Dak., U.S.A. . 112 C6
Howe, U.S.A. 114 E7
Howe, C., Australia 95 F5
Howe I., Canada 111 B8
Howell, U.S.A. 108 D4
Howick, Canada 111 A11
Howick, S. Africa 89 D5
Howick Group, Australia . 94 A4

Howitt, L., Australia 95 D2
Howland I., Pac. Oc. 96 G10
Howrah = Haora, India ... 69 H13
Howth Hd., Ireland 15 C5
Höxter, Germany 24 D5
Hoy, U.K. 14 C5
Hoya, Germany 24 C5
Høyanger, Norway 9 F12
Hoyerswerda, Germany .. 24 D10
Hoylake, U.K. 12 D4
Hoyos, Spain 34 E4
Hpa-an = Pa-an, Burma .. 67 L20
Hpungan Pass, Burma ... 67 F20
Hradec Králové, Czech Rep. . 26 A8
Hrádek, Czech Rep. 27 C9
Hranice, Czech Rep. 27 B10
Hrazdan, Armenia 49 K7
Hrebenka, Ukraine 47 G7
Hrodna, Belarus 46 F2
Hrodzyanka, Belarus ... 46 F5
Hron →, Slovak Rep. ... 27 D11
Hrubieszów, Poland 45 H10
Hrubý Jeseník, Czech Rep. . 27 A10
Hrvatska = Croatia ■, Europe . 29 C13
Hrymayliv, Ukraine 47 H4
Hsenwi, Burma 67 H20
Hsiamen = Xiamen, China . 59 E12
Hsian = Xi'an, China ... 56 G5
Hsinchu, Taiwan 59 E13
Hsinhailien = Lianyungang,
  China 57 G10
Hsinying, Taiwan 59 F13
Hsopket, Burma 58 F2
Hsüchou = Xuzhou, China . 57 G9
Hu Xian, China 56 G5
Hua Hin, Thailand 64 F2
Hua Xian, Henan, China . 56 G8
Hua Xian, Shaanxi, China . 56 G5
Hua'an, China 59 E11
Huab →, Namibia 88 B2
Huacheng, China 59 E10
Huachinera, Mexico 118 A3
Huacho, Peru 124 F3
Huade, China 56 D7
Huadian, China 57 C14
Huadu, China 59 F9
Huai He →, China 59 A12
Huai Yot, Thailand 65 J2
Huai'an, Hebei, China . 56 D8
Huai'an, Jiangsu, China . 57 H10
Huaibei, China 56 G9
Huaibin, China 59 A10
Huaide = Gongzhuling, China . 57 C13
Huaidezhen, China 57 C13
Huaihua, China 58 D7
Huaiji, China 59 F9
Huainan, China 59 A11
Huaining, China 59 B11
Huairen, China 56 E7
Huairou, China 56 D9
Huaiyang, China 56 H8
Huaiyin, China 57 H10
Huaiyuan, Anhui, China . 57 H9
Huaiyuan, Guangxi Zhuangzu,
  China 58 E7
Huajianzi, China 57 D13
Huajuapan de Leon, Mexico . 119 D5
Hualapai Peak, U.S.A. . 115 J7
Hualien, Taiwan 59 E13
Huallaga →, Peru 124 E3
Huambo, Angola 85 G3
Huan Jiang →, China .. 56 G5
Huan Xian, China 56 F4
Huancabamba, Peru ... 124 E3
Huancane, Peru 124 G5
Huancavelica, Peru ... 124 F3
Huancayo, Peru 124 F3
Huanchaca, Bolivia ... 124 H5
Huang Hai = Yellow Sea, China . 57 G12
Huang He →, China ... 57 F10
Huang Xian, China 57 F11
Huangchuan, China ... 59 A10
Huanggang, China 59 B10
Huangguoshu, China .. 58 E5
Huangling, China 56 G5
Huanglong, China 56 G5
Huanglongtan, China .. 59 A8
Huangmei, China 59 B10
Huangpi, China 59 B10
Huangping, China 58 D6
Huangshan, China 59 C12
Huangshi, China 59 B10
Huangsongdian, China . 57 C14
Huangyan, China 59 C13
Huangyangsi, China ... 59 D8
Huaning, China 58 E4
Huanjiang, China 58 E7
Huantai, China 57 F9
Huánuco, Peru 124 E3
Huaping, China 58 D3
Huaraz, Peru 124 E3
Huarmey, Peru 124 F3
Huarong, China 59 C9
Huascarán, Peru 122 D3
Huasco, Chile 126 B1
Huasco →, Chile 126 B1
Huasna, U.S.A. 117 K6
Huatabampo, Mexico .. 118 B3
Huauchinango, Mexico . 119 C5
Huautla de Jiménez, Mexico . 119 D5
Huaxi, China 58 D6
Huay Namota, Mexico . 118 C4
Huayin, China 56 G6
Huayuan, China 58 C7
Huayun, China 58 B6
Huazhou, China 59 G8
Hubbard, Ohio, U.S.A. . 110 E4

Hubbard, Tex., U.S.A. 113 K6
Hubbart Pt., Canada 105 B10
Hubei □, China 59 B9
Huch'ang, N. Korea 57 D14
Hucknall, U.K. 12 D6
Huddersfield, U.K. 12 D6
Hude, Germany 24 B4
Hudi, Sudan 80 D3
Hudiksvall, Sweden 10 C11
Hudson, Canada 102 B1
Hudson, Mass., U.S.A. .. 111 D13
Hudson, N.Y., U.S.A. ... 111 D11
Hudson, Wis., U.S.A. ... 112 C8
Hudson, Wyo., U.S.A. ... 114 E9
Hudson →, U.S.A. 111 F10
Hudson Bay, Nunavut, Canada . 101 C11
Hudson Bay, Sask., Canada ... 105 C8
Hudson Falls, U.S.A. 111 C11
Hudson Mts., Antarctica . 5 D16
Hudson Str., Canada 101 B13
Hudson's Hope, Canada .. 104 B4
Hue, Vietnam 64 D6
Huebra →, Spain 34 D4
Huedin, Romania 42 D8
Huehuetenango, Guatemala . 120 C1
Huejúcar, Mexico 118 C4
Huélamo, Spain 32 E3
Huelgoat, France 18 D3
Huelma, Spain 35 H7
Huelva, Spain 35 H4
Huelva □, Spain 35 H4
Huelva →, Spain 35 H5
Huentelauquén, Chile .. 126 C1
Huércal-Overa, Spain .. 33 H3
Huerta, Sa. de la, Argentina . 126 C2
Huertas, C. de las, Spain .. 33 G4
Huerva →, Spain 32 D4
Huesca, Spain 32 C4
Huesca □, Spain 32 C5
Huéscar, Spain 33 H2
Huetamo, Mexico 118 D4
Huete, Spain 32 E2
Hugh →, Australia ... 94 D1
Hughenden, Australia . 94 C3
Hughes, Australia ... 93 F4
Hughesville, U.S.A. . 111 E8
Hugli →, India 69 J13
Hugo, Colo., U.S.A. . 112 F3
Hugo, Okla., U.S.A. . 113 H7
Hugoton, U.S.A. 113 G4
Hui Xian = Huixian, China . 56 G7
Hui Xian, China 56 H4
Hui'an, China 59 E12
Hui'anbu, China 56 F4
Huichang, China 59 E10
Huichapán, Mexico .. 119 C5
Huidong, Guangdong, China . 59 F10
Huidong, Sichuan, China . 58 D4
Huifa He →, China .. 57 C14
Huila, Nevado del, Colombia . 124 C3
Huilai, China 59 F11
Huili, China 58 D4
Huimin, China 57 F9
Huinan, China 57 C14
Huinca Renancó, Argentina . 126 C3
Huining, China 56 G3
Huinong, China 56 E4
Huisache, Mexico ... 118 C4
Huishui, China 58 D6
Huisne →, France .. 18 E7
Huiting, China 56 G9
Huitong, China 58 D7
Huixian, China 56 G7
Huixtla, Mexico 119 D6
Huize, China 58 D4
Huizhou, China 59 F10
Hukawng Valley, Burma . 67 F20
Hukou, China 59 C11
Hukuntsi, Botswana . 88 C3
Hulayfā', Si. Arabia . 70 E4
Huld = Ulaanjirem, Mongolia . 56 B3
Hulin He →, China .. 57 B12
Hull = Kingston upon Hull, U.K. . 12 D7
Hull, Canada 102 C4
Hull →, U.K. 12 D7
Hulst, Neths. 17 C4
Hultsfred, Sweden .. 11 G9
Hulun Nur, China ... 60 B6
Hulyaypole, Ukraine . 47 J9
Humahuaca, Argentina . 126 A2
Humaitá, Brazil 124 E6
Humaitá, Paraguay .. 126 B4
Humansdorp, S. Africa . 88 E3
Humara, J., Sudan .. 81 D3
Humbe, Angola 88 B1
Humber →, U.K. ... 12 D7
Humboldt, Canada .. 105 C7
Humboldt, Iowa, U.S.A. . 112 D7
Humboldt, Tenn., U.S.A. . 113 H10
Humboldt →, U.S.A. . 114 F4
Humboldt Gletscher, Greenland . 4 B4
Hume, U.S.A. 116 J8
Hume, L., Australia . 95 F4
Humenné, Slovak Rep. . 27 C14
Hummelsta, Sweden . 10 E10
Humphreys, Mt., U.S.A. . 116 H8
Humphreys Peak, U.S.A. . 115 J8
Humpolec, Czech Rep. . 26 B8
Humptulips, U.S.A. . 116 C3
Hūn, Libya 79 C9
Húnaflói, Iceland .. 8 D3
Hunan □, China 59 D9
Hunchun, China 57 C16
Hundested, Denmark . 11 J5
Hundewali, Pakistan . 68 D5
Hundred Mile House, Canada . 104 C4

Hunedoara, Romania 42 E7
Hunedoara □, Romania ... 42 E7
Hünfeld, Germany 24 E5
Hung Yen, Vietnam 58 G6
Hungary ■, Europe 27 D12
Hungary, Plain of, Europe . 6 F10
Hungerford, Australia .. 95 D3
Hŭngnam, N. Korea 57 E14
Huni Valley, Ghana 82 D4
Hunneberg, Sweden 11 F6
Hunnebostrand, Sweden . 11 F5
Hunsberge, Namibia ... 88 D2
Hunsrück, Germany 25 F3
Hunstanton, U.K. 12 E8
Hunte →, Germany 24 B4
Hunter, U.S.A. 111 D10
Hunter I., Australia .. 94 G3
Hunter I., Canada 104 C3
Hunter Ra., Australia . 95 E5
Hunters Road, Zimbabwe . 87 F2
Huntingburg, U.S.A. .. 108 F2
Huntingdon, Canada .. 102 C5
Huntingdon, U.K. 13 E7
Huntingdon, U.S.A. .. 110 F6
Huntington, Ind., U.S.A. . 108 E3
Huntington, Oreg., U.S.A. . 114 D5
Huntington, Utah, U.S.A. . 114 G8
Huntington, W. Va., U.S.A. . 108 F4
Huntington Beach, U.S.A. . 117 M9
Huntington Station, U.S.A. . 111 F11
Huntly, N.Z. 91 G5
Huntly, U.K. 14 D6
Huntsville, Canada ... 102 C4
Huntsville, Ala., U.S.A. . 109 H2
Huntsville, Tex., U.S.A. . 113 K7
Hunyani →, Zimbabwe . 87 F3
Hunyuan, China 56 E7
Hunza →, India 69 B6
Huo Xian = Huozhou, China . 56 F6
Huong Hoa, Vietnam ... 64 D6
Huong Khe, Vietnam ... 64 C5
Huonville, Australia . 94 G4
Huoqiu, China 59 A11
Huoshan, Anhui, China . 59 A12
Huoshan, Anhui, China . 59 B11
Huoshao Dao = Lü-Tao, Taiwan . 59 F13
Huozhou, China 56 F6
Hupeh = Hubei □, China . 59 B9
Ḥūr, Iran 71 D8
Hurbanovo, Slovak Rep. . 27 D11
Hurd, C., Canada 110 A3
Hure Qi, China 57 C11
Hurezani, Romania ... 43 F8
Hurghada, Egypt 80 B3
Hurley, N. Mex., U.S.A. . 115 K9
Hurley, Wis., U.S.A. . 112 B9
Huron, Calif., U.S.A. . 116 J6
Huron, Ohio, U.S.A. . 110 E2
Huron, S. Dak., U.S.A. . 112 C5
Huron, L., U.S.A. 110 B2
Hurricane, U.S.A. ... 115 H7
Hurso, Ethiopia 81 F5
Hurunui →, N.Z. 91 K4
Hurup, Denmark 11 H2
Húsavík, Iceland 8 C5
Huşi, Romania 43 D13
Huskvarna, Sweden .. 11 G8
Hustadvika, Norway . 8 E12
Hustontown, U.S.A. . 110 F6
Hustopeče, Czech Rep. . 27 C9
Husum, Germany 24 A5
Husum, Sweden 10 A13
Hutchinson, Kans., U.S.A. . 113 F6
Hutchinson, Minn., U.S.A. . 112 C7
Hutte Sauvage, L. de la, Canada . 103 A7
Hüttenberg, Austria . 26 E7
Hutton, Mt., Australia . 95 D4
Huwun, Ethiopia 81 G5
Huy, Belgium 17 D5
Huzhou, China 59 B13
Hvalpsund, Denmark . 11 H3
Hvammstangi, Iceland . 8 D3
Hvar, Croatia 29 E13
Hvarski Kanal, Croatia . 29 E13
Hvítá →, Iceland ... 8 D3
Hwachŏn-chŏsuji, S. Korea . 57 E14
Hwang Ho = Huang He →,
  China 57 F10
Hwange, Zimbabwe ... 87 F2
Hwange Nat. Park, Zimbabwe . 88 B4
Hyannis, Mass., U.S.A. . 108 E14
Hyannis, Nebr., U.S.A. . 112 E4
Hyargas Nuur, Mongolia . 60 B4
Hybo, Sweden 10 C10
Hydaburg, U.S.A. ... 104 B2
Hyde Park, U.S.A. .. 111 E11
Hyden, Australia ... 93 F2
Hyder, U.S.A. 104 B2
Hyderabad, India ... 66 L11
Hyderabad, Pakistan . 68 G3
Hyères, France 21 E10
Hyères, Îs. d', France . 21 F10
Hyesan, N. Korea ... 57 D15
Hyland →, Canada .. 104 B3
Hyltebruk, Sweden .. 11 H7
Hymia, India 69 C8
Hyndman Peak, U.S.A. . 114 E6
Hyōgo □, Japan 55 G7
Hyrum, U.S.A. 114 F8
Hysham, U.S.A. 114 C10
Hythe, U.K. 13 F9
Hyūga, Japan 55 H5
Hyvinge = Hyvinkää, Finland . 9 F21
Hyvinkää, Finland .. 9 F21

I

I-n-Gall, Niger 83 B6
I-n-Oudad, Algeria 83 A5
I-n-Ouzzal, Algeria 83 A5
I-n-Tadreft, Niger 83 B6
Iablaniṭa, Romania 42 F7
Iaco →, Brazil 124 E5
Iacobeni, Romania 43 C10
Iakora, Madag. 89 C8
Ialomiṭa □, Romania 43 F12
Ialomiṭa →, Romania 43 F12
Ialoveni, Moldova 43 D13
Ialpug →, Moldova 43 E13
Ianca, Romania 43 E12
Iara, Romania 43 D8
Iardia, Ethiopia 81 E4
Iargara, Moldova 43 D13
Iaşi, Romania 43 C12
Iaşi □, Romania 43 C12
Íasmos, Greece 41 E9
Ib →, India 69 J10
Iba, Phil. 61 D3
Ibadan, Nigeria 83 D5
Ibagué, Colombia 124 C3
Iballë, Albania 40 D4
Ibănești, Botoșani, Romania . 43 B11
Ibănești, Mureș, Romania . 43 D9
Ibar →, Serbia, Yug. 40 C4
Ibaraki □, Japan 55 F10
Ibarra, Ecuador 124 C3
Ibba, Sudan 81 G2
Ibba, Bahr el →, Sudan .. 81 F2
Ibbenbüren, Germany 24 C3
Ibembo, Dem. Rep. of the Congo . 86 B1
Ibera, L., Argentina 126 B4
Iberian Peninsula, Europe . 6 H5
Iberville, Canada 102 C5
Iberville, Lac d', Canada . 102 A5
Ibi, Nigeria 83 D6
Ibi, Spain 33 G4
Ibiá, Brazil 125 G9
Ibiapaba, Sa. da, Brazil . 125 D10
Ibicuí →, Brazil 127 B4
Ibicuy, Argentina 126 C4
Ibiza = Eivissa, Spain .. 37 C7
Íblei, Monti, Italy 31 E7
Ibo, Mozam. 87 E5
Ibonma, Indonesia 63 E8
Ibotirama, Brazil 125 F10
Ibrāhīm →, Lebanon 75 A4
'Ibrī, Oman 71 F8
Ibriktepe, Turkey 41 E10
Ibshawâi, Egypt 80 J7
Ibu, Indonesia 63 D7
Ibusuki, Japan 55 J5
Ica, Peru 124 F3
Ica →, Brazil 124 D5
Içana, Brazil 124 C5
Içana →, Brazil 124 C5
Içel = Mersin, Turkey .. 70 B2
Iceland ■, Europe 8 D4
Ich'ang = Yichang, China . 59 B8
Ichchapuram, India 67 K14
Ichhawar, India 68 H7
Ichihara, Japan 55 G10
Ichikawa, Japan 55 G9
Ichilo →, Bolivia 124 G6
Ichinohe, Japan 54 D10
Ichinomiya, Japan 55 G8
Ichinoseki, Japan 54 E10
Ichnya, Ukraine 47 G7
Icod, Canary Is. 37 F3
Ida Grove, U.S.A. 112 D7
Idabel, U.S.A. 113 J7
Idaga Hamus, Ethiopia . 81 E4
Idah, Nigeria 83 D6
Idaho □, U.S.A. 114 D7
Idaho City, U.S.A. ... 114 E6
Idaho Falls, U.S.A. .. 114 E7
Idanha-a-Nova, Portugal . 34 F3
Idar-Oberstein, Germany . 25 F3
Idfû, Egypt 80 C3
Ídhi Óros, Greece 36 D6
Ídhra, Greece 38 D5
Idi, Indonesia 62 C1
Idiofa, Dem. Rep. of the Congo . 84 E3
Idkerberget, Sweden .. 10 D9
Idku, Bahra el, Egypt . 80 H7
Idlib, Syria 70 C3
Idre, Sweden 10 C6
Idria, U.S.A. 116 J6
Idrija, Slovenia 29 C11
Idritsa, Russia 46 D5
Idutywa, S. Africa ... 89 E4
Ieper, Belgium 17 D2
Ierápetra, Greece ... 36 E7
Ierissós, Greece 40 F7
Ierissoú Kólpos, Greece . 40 F7
Iernut, Romania 43 D9
Iesi, Italy 29 E10
Iésolo, Italy 29 C9
Ifach, Peñón de, Spain . 33 G5
Ifakara, Tanzania ... 84 F7
'Ifāl, W. al →, Si. Arabia . 70 D2
Ifanadiana, Madag. .. 89 C8
Ife, Nigeria 83 D5
Iférouâne, Niger 83 B6
Iffley, Australia ... 94 B3
Ifon, Nigeria 83 D6
Iforas, Adrar des, Africa . 83 B5
Ifould, L., Australia . 93 F5
Iganga, Uganda 86 B3
Igarapava, Brazil ... 125 H9
Igarka, Russia 50 C9
Igatimi, Paraguay ... 127 A4

Igbetti, Nigeria 83 D5
Igbo-Ora, Nigeria 83 D5
Igboho, Nigeria 83 D5
Igbor, Nigeria 83 D6
Iğdır, Turkey 73 C11
Igelfors, Sweden 11 F9
Iggesund, Sweden 10 C11
Iglésias, Italy 30 C1
Igloolik, Canada 101 B11
Iglulignarjuk, Canada 101 B10
Iglulik = Igloolik, Canada 101 B11
'Igma, Gebel el, Egypt 80 B3
Ignace, Canada 102 C1
Iğneada, Turkey 41 E11
Iğneada Burnu, Turkey 41 E12
Igoumenítsa, Greece 38 B2
Igra, Russia 48 B11
Iguaçu →, Brazil 127 B5
Iguaçu, Cat. del, Brazil 127 B5
Iguaçu Falls = Iguaçu, Cat. del, Brazil 127 B5
Iguala, Mexico 119 D5
Igualada, Spain 32 D6
Iguassu = Iguaçu →, Brazil 127 B5
Iguatu, Brazil 125 E11
Iharana, Madag. 89 A9
Ihbulag, Mongolia 56 C4
Iheya-Shima, Japan 55 L3
Ihiala, Nigeria 83 D6
Ihosy, Madag. 89 C8
Ihugh, Nigeria 83 D6
Ii, Finland 8 D21
Ii-Shima, Japan 55 L3
Iida, Japan 55 G8
Iijoki →, Finland 8 D21
Iisalmi, Finland 8 E22
Iiyama, Japan 55 F9
Iizuka, Japan 55 H5
Ijebu-Igbo, Nigeria 83 D5
Ijebu-Ode, Nigeria 83 D5
IJmuiden, Neths. 17 B4
IJssel →, Neths. 17 B5
IJsselmeer, Neths. 17 B5
Ijuí, Brazil 127 B5
Ijuí →, Brazil 127 B5
Ikalamavony, Madag. 89 C8
Ikale, Nigeria 83 D6
Ikaluktutiak, Canada 100 B9
Ikang, Nigeria 83 E6
Ikara, Nigeria 83 C6
Ikare, Nigeria 83 D6
Ikaría, Greece 39 D8
Ikast, Denmark 11 H3
Ikeda, Japan 55 G6
Ikeja, Nigeria 83 D5
Ikela, Dem. Rep. of the Congo 84 E4
Ikerre-Ekiti, Nigeria 83 D6
Ikhtiman, Bulgaria 40 D7
Iki, Japan 55 H4
Ikimba L., Tanzania 86 C3
Ikire, Nigeria 83 D5
Ikizdere, Turkey 73 B9
Ikom, Nigeria 83 D6
Ikongo, Madag. 89 C8
Ikopa →, Madag. 89 B8
Ikot Ekpene, Nigeria 83 D6
Ikungu, Tanzania 86 C3
Ikurun, Nigeria 83 D5
Ila, Nigeria 83 D5
Ilagan, Phil. 61 C4
Ilaka, Madag. 89 B8
Ilām, Iran 70 C5
Ilam, Nepal 69 F12
Ilam □, Iran 70 C5
Ilan, Taiwan 59 E13
Ilanskiy, Russia 51 D10
Ilaro, Nigeria 83 D5
Ilatane, Niger 83 B5
Iława, Poland 44 E6
Ile →, Kazakhstan 50 E8
Ile-à-la-Crosse, Canada 105 B7
Ile-à-la-Crosse, Lac, Canada 105 B7
Île-de-France □, France 19 D9
Ileanda, Romania 43 C8
Ilebo, Dem. Rep. of the Congo 84 E4
Ilek, Russia 50 D6
Ilero, Nigeria 83 D5
Ilesha, Kwara, Nigeria 83 D5
Ilesha, Oyo, Nigeria 83 D5
Ilford, Canada 105 B9
Ilfracombe, Australia 94 C3
Ilfracombe, U.K. 13 F3
Ilgaz, Turkey 72 B5
Ilgaz Dağları, Turkey 72 B5
Ilgın, Turkey 72 C4
Ílhavo, Portugal 34 E2
Ilhéus, Brazil 125 F11
Ili = Ile →, Kazakhstan 50 E8
Ilia, Romania 42 E7
Ilía □, Greece 38 D3
Iliamna L., U.S.A. 100 C4
Iliç, Turkey 73 C8
Ilıca, Turkey 39 B9
Ilichevsk, Azerbaijan 73 C11
Iligan, Phil. 61 G6
Iligan Bay, Phil. 61 G6
Ilíki, L., Greece 38 C5
Ilin I., Phil. 61 E4
Iliodhrómia, Greece 38 B5
Ilion, U.S.A. 111 D9
Ilirska-Bistrica, Slovenia 29 C11
Ilkeston, U.K. 12 E6
Ilkley, U.K. 12 D6
Illampu = Ancohuma, Nevada, Bolivia 122 E4
Illana B., Phil. 61 H5

Illapel, Chile 126 C1
Ille-et-Vilaine □, France 18 D5
Ille-sur-Têt, France 20 F6
Illéla, Niger 83 C6
Iller →, Germany 25 G5
Illertissen, Germany 25 G6
Illescas, Spain 34 E7
Illetas, Spain 37 B9
Illichivsk, Ukraine 47 J6
Illiers-Combray, France 18 D8
Illimani, Nevado, Bolivia 124 G5
Illinois □, U.S.A. 112 E10
Illinois →, U.S.A. 107 C8
Illium = Troy, Turkey 39 B8
Illizi, Algeria 78 C7
Ilkirch-Graffenstaden, France 19 D14
Íllora, Spain 35 H7
Ilm →, Germany 24 D7
Ilmajoki, Finland 9 E20
Ilmen, Ozero, Russia 46 C6
Ilmenau, Germany 24 E6
Ilo, Peru 124 G4
Ilobu, Nigeria 83 D5
Iloilo, Phil. 61 F5
Ilora, Nigeria 83 D5
Ilorin, Nigeria 83 D5
Ilovatka, Russia 48 E7
Ilovlya, Russia 49 F7
Ilovlya →, Russia 49 F7
Iłowa, Poland 45 G2
Ilubabor □, Ethiopia 81 F4
Ilva Mică, Romania 43 C9
Ilwaco, U.S.A. 116 D2
Ilwaki, Indonesia 63 F7
Ilyichevsk = Illichivsk, Ukraine 47 J6
Iłża, Poland 45 G8
Iłżanka →, Poland 45 G8
Imabari, Japan 55 G6
Imaloto →, Madag. 89 C8
Imamoğlu, Turkey 72 D6
Imandra, Ozero, Russia 50 C4
Imanombo, Madag. 89 C8
Imari, Japan 55 H4
Imasa, Sudan 80 D4
Imathía □, Greece 40 F6
Imatra, Finland 46 B5
Imbil, Australia 95 D5
Iménas, Mali 83 B5
imeni 26 Bakinskikh Komissarov = Neftçala, Azerbaijan 71 B6
imeni 26 Bakinskikh Komissarov, Turkmenistan 71 B7
Imeri, Serra, Brazil 124 C5
Imerimandroso, Madag. 89 B8
Imi, Ethiopia 81 F5
Imishly = Imişli, Azerbaijan 49 L9
Imişli, Azerbaijan 49 L9
Imlay, U.S.A. 114 F4
Imlay City, U.S.A. 110 D1
Immaseri, Sudan 81 D2
Immenstadt, Germany 25 H6
Immingham, U.K. 12 D7
Immokalee, U.S.A. 109 M5
Imo □, Nigeria 83 D6
Imo →, Nigeria 83 E6
Ímola, Italy 29 D8
Imotski, Croatia 29 E14
Imperatriz, Brazil 125 E9
Impéria, Italy 28 E5
Imperial, Canada 105 C7
Imperial, Calif., U.S.A. 117 N11
Imperial, Nebr., U.S.A. 112 E4
Imperial Beach, U.S.A. 117 N9
Imperial Dam, U.S.A. 117 N12
Imperial Reservoir, U.S.A. 117 N12
Imperial Valley, U.S.A. 117 N11
Imperieuse Reef, Australia 92 C2
Impfondo, Congo 84 D3
Imphal, India 67 G18
Imphy, France 19 F10
Imranlı, Turkey 73 C8
Imroz = Gökçeada, Turkey 41 F9
Imroz, Turkey 41 F9
Imst, Austria 26 D3
Imuris, Mexico 118 A2
Imuruan B., Phil. 63 B5
In Akhmed, Mali 83 B4
In Aleï, Mali 82 B4
In Delimane, Mali 83 B5
In Guezzam, Algeria 83 B5
In Koufi, Mali 83 B5
In Salah, Algeria 78 C6
In Tallak, Mali 83 B5
In Tebezas, Mali 83 B5
Ina, Japan 55 G8
Inangahua, N.Z. 91 J3
Inanwatan, Indonesia 63 E8
Iñapari, Peru 124 F5
Inari, Finland 8 B22
Inarijärvi, Finland 8 B22
Inawashiro-Ko, Japan 54 F10
Inca, Spain 37 B9
Inca de Oro, Chile 126 B2
Incaguasi, Chile 126 B1
Ince Burun, Turkey 72 A6
Incekum Burnu, Turkey 72 D5
Incesu, Turkey 70 B2
Inch'ŏn, S. Korea 57 F14
Incio = Cruz de Incio, Spain 34 C3
Incline Village, U.S.A. 114 G4
Incomáti →, Mozam. 89 D5
Inda Silase, Ethiopia 81 E4
Indal, Sweden 10 B11
Indalsälven →, Sweden 10 B11
Indaw, Burma 67 G20

Indbir, Ethiopia 81 F4
Independence, Calif., U.S.A. 116 J8
Independence, Iowa, U.S.A. 112 D9
Independence, Kans., U.S.A. 113 G7
Independence, Ky., U.S.A. 108 F3
Independence, Mo., U.S.A. 112 F7
Independence Fjord, Greenland 4 A6
Independence Mts., U.S.A. 114 F5
Independenţa, Romania 43 E12
Index, U.S.A. 116 C5
India ■, Asia 66 K11
Indian →, U.S.A. 109 M5
Indian Cabins, Canada 104 B5
Indian Harbour, Canada 103 B8
Indian Head, Canada 105 C8
Indian Lake, U.S.A. 111 C10
Indian Ocean 52 K11
Indian Springs, U.S.A. 117 J11
Indiana, U.S.A. 110 F5
Indiana □, U.S.A. 108 F3
Indianapolis, U.S.A. 108 F2
Indianola, Iowa, U.S.A. 112 E8
Indianola, Miss., U.S.A. 113 J9
Indigirka →, Russia 51 B15
Indija, Serbia, Yug. 42 E5
Indio, U.S.A. 117 M10
Indo-China, Asia 52 H14
Indonesia ■, Asia 62 F5
Indore, India 68 H6
Indramayu, Indonesia 63 G13
Indravati →, India 67 K12
Indre □, France 19 F8
Indre →, France 18 E7
Indre-et-Loire □, France 18 E7
Indulkana, Australia 95 D1
Indus →, Pakistan 68 G2
Indus, Mouth of the, Pakistan 68 H3
Inebolu, Turkey 72 B5
Inecik, Turkey 41 F11
Inegöl, Turkey 41 F13
Ineu, Romania 42 D6
Infantes = Villanueva de los Infantes, Spain 35 G7
Infiernillo, Presa del, Mexico 118 D4
Infiesto, Spain 34 B5
Ingelstad, Sweden 11 H8
Ingenio, Canary Is. 37 G4
Ingenio Santa Ana, Argentina 126 B2
Ingersoll, Canada 102 D3
Ingham, Australia 94 B4
Ingleborough, U.K. 12 C5
Inglewood, Queens., Australia 95 D5
Inglewood, Vic., Australia 95 F3
Inglewood, N.Z. 91 H5
Inglewood, U.S.A. 117 M8
Ingólfshöfôi, Iceland 8 E5
Ingolstadt, Germany 25 G7
Ingomar, U.S.A. 114 C10
Ingonish, Canada 103 C7
Ingore, Guinea-Biss. 82 C1
Ingraj Bazar, India 69 G13
Ingrid Christensen Coast, Antarctica 5 C6
Ingul → = Inhul →, Ukraine 47 J7
Ingulec = Inhulec, Ukraine 47 J7
Ingulets = Inhulets →, Ukraine 47 J7
Inguri → = Enguri →, Georgia 49 J5
Ingushetia □, Russia 49 J7
Ingwavuma, S. Africa 89 D5
Inhaca, Mozam. 89 D5
Inhafenga, Mozam. 89 C5
Inhambane, Mozam. 89 C6
Inhambane □, Mozam. 89 C5
Inhaminga, Mozam. 87 F4
Inharrime, Mozam. 89 C6
Inharrime →, Mozam. 89 C6
Inhisar, Turkey 39 A12
Inhul →, Ukraine 47 J7
Inhulec, Ukraine 47 J7
Inhulets →, Ukraine 47 J7
Iniesta, Spain 33 F3
Ining = Yining, China 50 E9
Inírida →, Colombia 124 C5
Inishbofin, Ireland 15 C1
Inisheer, Ireland 15 C2
Inishfree B., Ireland 15 A3
Inishkea North, Ireland 15 B1
Inishkea South, Ireland 15 B1
Inishmaan, Ireland 15 C2
Inishmore, Ireland 15 C2
Inishowen Pen., Ireland 15 A4
Inishshark, Ireland 15 C1
Inishturk, Ireland 15 C1
Inishvickillane, Ireland 15 D1
Injibara, Ethiopia 81 E4
Injune, Australia 95 D4
Inklin →, Canada 104 B2
Inland Sea = Setonaikai, Japan 55 G6
Inle L., Burma 67 J20
Inlet, U.S.A. 111 C10
Inn →, Austria 26 C6
Innamincka, Australia 95 D3
Innerkip, Canada 110 C4
Innetalling I., Canada 102 A4
Innisfail, Australia 94 B4
Innisfail, Canada 104 C6
In'noshima, Japan 55 G6
Innsbruck, Austria 26 D4
Innviertel, Austria 26 C6
Inny →, Ireland 15 C4
Inongo, Dem. Rep. of the Congo 84 E3
Inönü, Turkey 39 B12

Inoucdjouac = Inukjuak, Canada 101 C12
Inowrocław, Poland 45 F5
Inpundong, N. Korea 57 D14
Inscription, C., Australia 93 E1
Insein, Burma 67 L20
Insjön, Sweden 10 D9
Ińsko, Poland 44 E2
Însurăţei, Romania 43 F12
Inta, Russia 50 C6
Intendente Alvear, Argentina 126 D3
Intepe, Turkey 39 A8
Interlaken, Switz. 25 J3
Interlaken, U.S.A. 111 D8
International Falls, U.S.A. 112 A8
Intiyaco, Argentina 126 B3
Întorsura Buzăului, Romania 43 E11
Inukjuak, Canada 101 C12
Inútil, B., Chile 128 G2
Inuvik, Canada 100 B6
Inveraray, U.K. 14 E3
Inverbervie, U.K. 14 E6
Invercargill, N.Z. 91 M2
Inverclyde □, U.K. 14 F4
Inverell, Australia 95 D5
Invergordon, U.K. 14 D4
Inverloch, Australia 95 F4
Invermere, Canada 104 C5
Inverness, Canada 103 C7
Inverness, U.K. 14 D4
Inverness, U.S.A. 109 L4
Inverurie, U.K. 14 D6
Investigator Group, Australia 95 E1
Investigator Str., Australia 95 F2
Inya, Russia 50 D9
Inyanga, Zimbabwe 87 F3
Inyangani, Zimbabwe 87 F3
Inyantue, Zimbabwe 88 B4
Inyo Mts., U.S.A. 116 J9
Inyokern, U.S.A. 117 K9
Inza, Russia 48 D8
Inzhavino, Russia 48 D6
Iō-Jima, Japan 55 J5
Ioánnina, Greece 38 B2
Ioánnina □, Greece 38 B2
Iola, U.S.A. 113 G7
Ion Corvin, Romania 43 F12
Iona, U.K. 14 E2
Ione, U.S.A. 116 G6
Ionia, U.S.A. 108 D3
Ionian Is. = Iónioi Nísoi, Greece 38 C2
Ionian Sea, Medit. S. 6 H9
Iónioi Nísoi, Greece 38 C2
Iónioi Nísoi □, Greece 38 C2
Íos, Greece 39 E7
Iowa □, U.S.A. 112 D8
Iowa →, U.S.A. 112 E9
Iowa City, U.S.A. 112 E9
Iowa Falls, U.S.A. 112 D8
Iowa Park, U.S.A. 113 J5
Ipala, Tanzania 86 C3
Ipameri, Brazil 125 G9
Ipáti, Greece 38 C4
Ipatinga, Brazil 125 G10
Ipatovo, Russia 49 H6
Ipel' →, Europe 27 D11
Ipiales, Colombia 124 C3
Ipin = Yibin, China 58 C5
Ipiros □, Greece 38 B2
Ipixuna, Brazil 124 E4
Ipoh, Malaysia 65 K3
Ippy, C.A.R. 84 C4
Ipsala, Turkey 41 F10
Ipsárion, Oros, Greece 41 F8
Ipswich, Australia 95 D5
Ipswich, U.K. 13 E9
Ipswich, Mass., U.S.A. 111 D14
Ipswich, S. Dak., U.S.A. 112 C5
Ipu, Brazil 125 D10
Iqaluit, Canada 101 B13
Iquique, Chile 124 H4
Iquitos, Peru 124 D4
Irabu-Jima, Japan 55 M2
Iracoubo, Fr. Guiana 125 B8
Irafshān, Iran 71 E9
Irahuan, Phil. 61 G3
Iráklia, Kikládhes, Greece 39 E7
Iráklia, Sérrai, Greece 40 E7
Iráklion, Greece 36 D7
Iráklion □, Greece 36 D7
Irala, Paraguay 127 B5
Iran ■, Asia 71 C7
Iran, Gunung-Gunung, Malaysia 62 D4
Iran, Plateau of, Asia 52 F9
Iran Ra. = Iran, Gunung-Gunung, Malaysia 62 D4
Īrānshahr, Iran 71 E9
Irapuato, Mexico 118 C4
Iraq ■, Asia 70 C5
Irati, Brazil 127 B5
Irbes saurums, Latvia 44 A9
Irbid, Jordan 75 C4
Irbid □, Jordan 75 C4
Iregua →, Spain 32 C2
Ireland ■, Europe 15 C4
Irele, Nigeria 83 D6
Irgiz, Bolshaya →, Russia 48 D9
Irhyangdong, N. Korea 57 D15
Iri, S. Korea 57 G14
Irian Jaya □, Indonesia 63 E9
Irié, Guinea 82 D3
Iriga, Phil. 61 E5
Iringa, Tanzania 86 D4
Iringa □, Tanzania 86 D4
Iriomote-Jima, Japan 55 M1
Iriona, Honduras 120 C2
Iriri →, Brazil 125 D8
Irish Republic ■, Europe 15 C3

Irish Sea, U.K. 12 D3
Irkutsk, Russia 51 D11
Irlhanlı, Turkey 39 D11
Irma, Canada 105 C6
Irō-Zaki, Japan 55 G9
Iroise, Mer d', France 18 D2
Iron Baron, Australia 95 E2
Iron Gate = Portile de Fier, Europe 42 F7
Iron Knob, Australia 95 E2
Iron Mountain, U.S.A. 108 C1
Iron River, U.S.A. 112 B10
Irondequoit, U.S.A. 110 C7
Ironton, Mo., U.S.A. 113 G9
Ironton, Ohio, U.S.A. 108 F4
Ironwood, U.S.A. 112 B9
Iroquois, Canada 111 B9
Iroquois Falls, Canada 102 C3
Irosin, Phil. 61 E6
Irpin, Ukraine 47 G6
Irrara Cr. →, Australia 95 D4
Irrawaddy □, Burma 67 L19
Irrawaddy →, Burma 67 M19
Irrawaddy, Mouths of the, Burma 67 M19
Irricana, Canada 104 C6
Irsina, Italy 31 B9
Irtysh →, Russia 50 C7
Irumu, Dem. Rep. of the Congo 86 B2
Irún, Spain 32 B3
Irunea = Pamplona, Spain 32 C3
Irurzun, Spain 32 C3
Irvine, U.K. 14 F4
Irvine, Calif., U.S.A. 117 M9
Irvine, Ky., U.S.A. 108 G4
Irvinestown, U.K. 15 B4
Irving, U.S.A. 113 J6
Irvona, U.S.A. 110 F6
Irwin →, Australia 93 E1
Irymple, Australia 95 E3
Is, Jebel, Sudan 80 C4
Is-sur-Tille, France 19 E12
Isa, Nigeria 83 C6
Isa Khel, Pakistan 68 C4
Isaac →, Australia 94 C4
Isabel, U.S.A. 112 C4
Isabela, Phil. 61 H5
Isabela, I., Mexico 118 C3
Isabela, Cord. Nic. 120 D2
Isabella Ra., Australia 92 D3
Isaccea, Romania 43 E13
Ísafjarðardjúp, Iceland 8 C2
Ísafjörður, Iceland 8 C2
Isagarh, India 68 G7
Isahaya, Japan 55 H5
Isaka, Tanzania 86 C3
Isakly, Russia 48 C10
Işalniţa, Romania 43 F8
Isan →, India 69 F9
Isana = Içana →, Brazil 124 C5
Isanlu Makutu, Nigeria 83 D6
Isar →, Germany 25 G8
Ísarco →, Italy 29 B8
Isari, Greece 38 D3
Íscar, Spain 34 D6
Iscehisar, Turkey 39 C12
Íschia, Italy 30 B6
Isdell →, Australia 92 C3
Ise, Japan 55 G8
Ise-Wan, Japan 55 G8
Isefjord, Denmark 11 J5
Isel →, Austria 26 E5
Iseo, Italy 28 C7
Iseo, L. d', Italy 28 C7
Iseramagazi, Tanzania 86 C3
Isère □, France 21 C9
Isère →, France 21 D8
Iserlohn, Germany 24 D3
Isérnia, Italy 31 A7
Iseyin, Nigeria 83 D5
Isfahan = Eşfahān, Iran 71 C6
Ishëm, Albania 40 E3
Ishigaki-Shima, Japan 55 M2
Ishikari-Gawa →, Japan 54 C10
Ishikari-Sammyaku, Japan 54 C11
Ishikari-Wan, Japan 54 C10
Ishikawa □, Japan 55 F8
Ishim, Russia 50 D7
Ishim →, Russia 50 D8
Ishinomaki, Japan 54 E10
Ishioka, Japan 55 F10
Ishkuman, Pakistan 69 A5
Ishpeming, U.S.A. 108 B2
Isigny-sur-Mer, France 18 C5
Işıklar Dağı, Turkey 41 F11
Isil Kul, Russia 50 D8
Ísili, Italy 30 C2
Isiolo, Kenya 86 B4
Isiro, Dem. Rep. of the Congo 86 B2
Isisford, Australia 94 C3
İskenderun, Turkey 70 B3
İskenderun Körfezi, Turkey 72 D6
İskilip, Turkey 72 B5
Iskŭr →, Bulgaria 41 C8
Iskŭr, Yazovir, Bulgaria 40 D7
Iskut →, Canada 104 B2
Isla →, U.K. 14 E5
Isla Cristina, Spain 35 H3
Isla Vista, U.S.A. 117 L7
Islâhiye, Turkey 72 D7
Islam Headworks, Pakistan 68 E5
Islamabad, Pakistan 68 C5
Islamgarh, Pakistan 68 F4
Islamkot, Pakistan 68 G4
Islampur, India 69 G11
Island L., Canada 105 C10

Island Lagoon, *Australia* 95 E2
Island Pond, *U.S.A.* 111 B13
Islands, B. of, *Canada* 103 C8
Islands, B. of, *N.Z.* 91 F5
Islay, *U.K.* 14 F2
Isle ➤, *France* 20 D3
Isle aux Morts, *Canada* 103 C8
Isle of Wight □, *U.K.* 13 G6
Isle Royale, *U.S.A.* 112 B10
Isle Royale National Park,
  U.S.A. 112 B10
Isleton, *U.S.A.* 116 G5
Ismail = Izmayil, *Ukraine* 47 K5
Ismâ'ilîya, *Egypt* 80 H8
Ismaning, *Germany* 25 G7
Isna, *Egypt* 80 B3
Isoanala, *Madag.* 89 C8
Isogstalo, *India* 69 B8
Ísola del Liri, *Italy* 29 G10
Ísola della Scala, *Italy* 28 C7
Ísola di Capo Rizzuto, *Italy* . . 31 D10
Isparta, *Turkey* 39 D12
Isperikh, *Bulgaria* 41 C10
Íspica, *Italy* 31 F7
Israel ■, *Asia* 75 D3
Isratu, *Eritrea* 81 D4
Issia, *Ivory C.* 82 D3
Issoire, *France* 20 C7
Issoudun, *France* 19 F8
Issyk-Kul, Ozero = Ysyk-Köl,
  Kyrgyzstan 50 E8
Ist, *Croatia* 29 D11
Istállós-kő, *Hungary* 42 B5
Istanbul, *Turkey* 41 E12
Istanbul □, *Turkey* 41 E12
Istanbul Boğazı, *Turkey* 41 E13
Istiaía, *Greece* 38 C5
Istok, *Kosovo, Yug.* 40 D4
Istokpoga, L., *U.S.A.* 109 M5
Istra, *Croatia* 29 C10
Istres, *France* 21 E8
Istria = Istra, *Croatia* 29 C10
Itá, *Paraguay* 126 B4
Itaberaba, *Brazil* 125 F10
Itabira, *Brazil* 125 G10
Itabirito, *Brazil* 127 A7
Itabuna, *Brazil* 125 F11
Itacaunas ➤, *Brazil* 125 E9
Itacoatiara, *Brazil* 124 D7
Itaipú, Reprêsa de, *Brazil* . . . 127 B5
Itaituba, *Brazil* 125 D7
Itajaí, *Brazil* 127 B6
Itajubá, *Brazil* 127 A6
Itaka, *Tanzania* 87 D3
Italy ■, *Europe* 7 G8
Itamaraju, *Brazil* 125 G11
Itampolo, *Madag.* 89 C7
Itandrano, *Madag.* 89 C8
Itapecuru-Mirim, *Brazil* 125 D10
Itaperuna, *Brazil* 127 A7
Itapetininga, *Brazil* 127 A6
Itapeva, *Brazil* 127 A6
Itapicuru ➤, *Bahia, Brazil* . . 125 F11
Itapicuru ➤, *Maranhão, Brazil* 125 D10
Itapipoca, *Brazil* 125 D11
Itapuá □, *Paraguay* 127 B4
Itaquari, *Brazil* 127 A7
Itaquí, *Brazil* 126 B4
Itararé, *Brazil* 127 A6
Itarsi, *India* 68 H7
Itatí, *Argentina* 126 B4
Itbayat, *Phil.* 61 A4
Itchen ➤, *U.K.* 13 G6
Itéa, *Greece* 38 C4
Itezhi Tezhi, L., *Zambia* 87 F2
Ithaca = Itháki, *Greece* 38 C2
Ithaca, *U.S.A.* 111 D8
Itháki, *Greece* 38 C2
Itiquira ➤, *Brazil* 125 G7
Itō, *Japan* 55 G9
Itoigawa, *Japan* 55 F8
Iton ➤, *France* 18 C8
Itonamas ➤, *Bolivia* 124 F6
Itri, *Italy* 30 A6
Itsa, *Egypt* 80 J7
Íttiri, *Italy* 30 B1
Ittoqqortoormiit, *Greenland* . . . 4 B6
Itu, *Brazil* 127 A6
Itu, *Nigeria* 83 D6
Itu Aba I., *S. China Sea* 62 B4
Ituiutaba, *Brazil* 125 G9
Itumbiara, *Brazil* 125 G9
Ituna, *Canada* 105 C8
Itunge Port, *Tanzania* 87 D3
Iturbe, *Argentina* 126 A2
Ituri ➤, *Dem. Rep. of the Congo* 86 B2
Iturup, Ostrov, *Russia* 51 E15
Ituxi ➤, *Brazil* 124 E6
Ituyuro ➤, *Argentina* 126 A3
Itzehoe, *Germany* 24 B5
Ivahona, *Madag.* 89 C8
Ivaí ➤, *Brazil* 127 A5
Ivalo, *Finland* 8 B22
Ivalojoki ➤, *Finland* 8 B22
Ivanava, *Belarus* 47 F3
Ivančice, *Czech Rep.* 27 B9
Ivăneşti, *Romania* 43 D12
Ivangorod, *Russia* 46 C5
Ivanhoe, *Australia* 95 E3
Ivanhoe, *Calif., U.S.A.* 116 J7
Ivanhoe, *Minn., U.S.A.* . . . 112 C6
Ivanić Grad, *Croatia* 29 C13
Ivanjica, *Serbia, Yug.* 40 C4
Ivanjska, *Bos.-H.* 42 F2
Ivankoyskoye Vdkhr., *Russia* . . 46 D9
Ivano-Frankivsk, *Ukraine* 47 H3

Ivano-Frankovsk = Ivano-
  Frankivsk, *Ukraine* 47 H3
Ivanovo = Ivanava, *Belarus* . . 47 F3
Ivanovo, *Russia* 46 D11
Ivanšćica, *Croatia* 29 B13
Ivato, *Madag.* 89 C8
Ivatsevichy, *Belarus* 47 F3
Ivaylovgrad, *Bulgaria* 41 E10
Ivinheima ➤, *Brazil* 127 A5
Ivinhema, *Brazil* 127 A5
Ivohibe, *Madag.* 89 C8
Ivory Coast, *W. Afr.* 82 E4
Ivory Coast ■, *Africa* 82 D4
Ivösjön, *Sweden* 11 H8
Ivrea, *Italy* 28 C4
Ivrindi, *Turkey* 39 B9
Ivujivik, *Canada* 101 B12
Ivybridge, *U.K.* 13 G4
Iwaizumi, *Japan* 54 E10
Iwaki, *Japan* 55 F10
Iwakuni, *Japan* 55 G6
Iwamizawa, *Japan* 54 C10
Iwanai, *Japan* 54 C10
Iwata, *Japan* 55 G8
Iwate □, *Japan* 54 E10
Iwate-San, *Japan* 54 E10
Iwo, *Nigeria* 83 D5
Iwonicz-Zdrój, *Poland* 45 J8
Ixiamas, *Bolivia* 124 F5
Ixopo, *S. Africa* 89 E5
Ixtepec, *Mexico* 119 D5
Ixtlán del Río, *Mexico* 118 C4
Iyal Bakhit, *Sudan* 81 E2
Iyo, *Japan* 55 H6
Izabal, L. de, *Guatemala* . . . 120 C2
Izamal, *Mexico* 119 C7
Izberbash, *Russia* 49 J8
Izbica, *Poland* 45 H10
Izbica Kujawska, *Poland* 45 F5
Izbiceni, *Romania* 43 G9
Izena-Shima, *Japan* 55 L3
Izgrev, *Bulgaria* 41 C10
Izhevsk, *Russia* 50 D6
Izmayil, *Ukraine* 47 K5
Izmir, *Turkey* 39 C9
Izmir □, *Turkey* 39 C9
Izmir Körfezi, *Turkey* 39 C8
Izmit = Kocaeli, *Turkey* 41 F13
Iznájar, *Spain* 35 H6
Iznalloz, *Spain* 35 H7
Iznik, *Turkey* 72 B3
Iznik Gölü, *Turkey* 41 F13
Izobil'nyy, *Russia* 49 H5
Izola, *Slovenia* 29 C10
Izra, *Syria* 75 C5
Iztochni Rodopi, *Bulgaria* . . . 41 E9
Izúcar de Matamoros, *Mexico* . 119 D5
Izumi-Sano, *Japan* 55 G7
Izumo, *Japan* 55 G6
Izyaslav, *Ukraine* 47 G4
Izyum, *Ukraine* 47 H9

J

Jaba, *Ethiopia* 81 F4
Jabal at Ta'ir, *Red Sea* 81 D5
Jabalón ➤, *Spain* 35 G6
Jabalpur, *India* 69 H8
Jabbūl, *Syria* 70 B3
Jabiru, *Australia* 92 B5
Jablah, *Syria* 70 C3
Jablanac, *Croatia* 29 D11
Jablanica, *Bos.-H.* 42 G2
Jablonec nad Nisou, *Czech Rep.* 26 A8
Jabłonowo Pomorskie, *Poland* . 44 E6
Jablonica, *Slovak Rep.* 27 C10
Jablunkov, *Czech Rep.* 27 B11
Jaboatão, *Brazil* 125 E11
Jaboticabal, *Brazil* 127 A6
Jabukovac, *Serbia, Yug.* 40 B6
Jaca, *Spain* 32 C4
Jacareí, *Brazil* 127 A6
Jacarèzinho, *Brazil* 127 A6
Jackman, *U.S.A.* 109 C10
Jacksboro, *U.S.A.* 113 J5
Jackson, *Ala., U.S.A.* 109 K2
Jackson, *Calif., U.S.A.* 116 G6
Jackson, *Ky., U.S.A.* 108 G4
Jackson, *Mich., U.S.A.* 108 D3
Jackson, *Minn., U.S.A.* 112 D7
Jackson, *Miss., U.S.A.* 113 J9
Jackson, *Mo., U.S.A.* 113 G10
Jackson, *N.H., U.S.A.* 111 B13
Jackson, *Ohio, U.S.A.* 108 F4
Jackson, *Tenn., U.S.A.* 109 H1
Jackson, *Wyo., U.S.A.* 114 E8
Jackson B., *N.Z.* 91 K2
Jackson L., *U.S.A.* 114 E8
Jacksons, *N.Z.* 91 K3
Jackson's Arm, *Canada* 103 C8
Jacksonville, *Ala., U.S.A.* . . . 109 J3
Jacksonville, *Ark., U.S.A.* . . . 113 H8
Jacksonville, *Calif., U.S.A.* . . 116 H6
Jacksonville, *Fla., U.S.A.* . . . 109 K5
Jacksonville, *Ill., U.S.A.* . . . 112 F9
Jacksonville, *N.C., U.S.A.* . . 109 H7
Jacksonville, *Tex., U.S.A.* . . 113 K7
Jacksonville Beach, *U.S.A.* . . 109 K5
Jacmel, *Haiti* 121 C5
Jacob Lake, *U.S.A.* 115 H7
Jacobabad, *Pakistan* 68 E3
Jacobina, *Brazil* 125 F10
Jacques Cartier, Dét. de, *Canada* 103 C7
Jacques Cartier, Mt., *Canada* . 103 C6

Jacques Cartier, Parc Prov.,
  Canada 103 C5
Jacqueville, *Ivory C.* 82 D4
Jacuí ➤, *Brazil* 127 C5
Jacumba, *U.S.A.* 117 N10
Jacundá ➤, *Brazil* 125 D8
Jade, *Germany* 24 B4
Jadebusen, *Germany* 24 B4
Jadotville = Likasi, *Dem. Rep. of the Congo* 87 E2
Jadovnik, *Serbia, Yug.* 40 C3
Jadraque, *Spain* 32 E2
Jaén, *Peru* 124 E3
Jaén, *Spain* 35 H7
Jaén □, *Spain* 35 H7
Jafarabad, *India* 68 J4
Jaffa = Tel Aviv-Yafo, *Israel* . . 75 C3
Jaffa, C., *Australia* 95 F2
Jaffna, *Sri Lanka* 66 Q12
Jaffrey, *U.S.A.* 111 D12
Jagadhri, *India* 68 D7
Jagadishpur, *India* 69 G11
Jagdalpur, *India* 67 K13
Jagersfontein, *S. Africa* 88 D4
Jaghīn ➤, *Iran* 71 E8
Jagodina, *Serbia, Yug.* 40 B5
Jagraon, *India* 66 D9
Jagst ➤, *Germany* 25 F5
Jagtial, *India* 66 K11
Jaguariaíva, *Brazil* 127 A6
Jaguaribe ➤, *Brazil* 125 D11
Jagüey Grande, *Cuba* 120 B3
Jahanabad, *India* 69 G11
Jahazpur, *India* 68 G6
Jahrom, *Iran* 71 D7
Jaijon, *India* 68 D7
Jailolo, *Indonesia* 63 D7
Jailolo, Selat, *Indonesia* 63 D7
Jaipur, *India* 68 F6
Jais, *India* 69 F9
Jaisalmer, *India* 68 F4
Jaisinghnagar, *India* 69 H8
Jaitaran, *India* 68 F5
Jaithari, *India* 69 H8
Jājarm, *Iran* 71 B8
Jajce, *Bos.-H.* 42 F2
Jakam ➤, *India* 68 H6
Jakarta, *Indonesia* 62 F3
Jakhal, *India* 68 E6
Jakhau, *India* 68 H3
Jakobstad = Pietarsaari, *Finland* 8 E20
Jakupica, *Macedonia* 40 E5
Jal, *U.S.A.* 113 J3
Jalālābād, *Afghan.* 68 B4
Jalalabad, *India* 69 F8
Jalalpur Jattan, *Pakistan* 68 C6
Jalama, *U.S.A.* 117 L6
Jalapa, *Guatemala* 120 D2
Jalapa Enríquez, *Mexico* . . . 119 D5
Jalasjärvi, *Finland* 9 E20
Jalaun, *India* 69 F8
Jaldhaka ➤, *Bangla.* 69 F13
Jalesar, *India* 68 F8
Jaleswar, *Nepal* 69 F11
Jalgaon, *India* 66 J9
Jalibah, *Iraq* 70 D5
Jalingo, *Nigeria* 83 D7
Jalisco □, *Mexico* 118 D4
Jalkot, *Pakistan* 69 B5
Jallas ➤, *Spain* 34 C1
Jalna, *India* 66 K9
Jalón ➤, *Spain* 32 D3
Jalor, *India* 68 G5
Jalpa, *Mexico* 118 C4
Jalpaiguri, *India* 67 F16
Jalūlā, *Iraq* 70 C5
Jamaari, *Nigeria* 83 C6
Jamaica ■, *W. Indies* 120 C4
Jamalpur, *Bangla.* 67 G16
Jamalpur, *India* 69 G12
Jamalpurganj, *India* 69 H13
Jamanxim ➤, *Brazil* 125 D7
Jambi, *Indonesia* 62 E2
Jambi □, *Indonesia* 62 E2
Jambusar, *India* 68 H5
James ➤, *S. Dak., U.S.A.* . . 112 D6
James ➤, *Va., U.S.A.* 108 G7
James B., *Canada* 102 B3
James Ranges, *Australia* 92 D5
James Ross I., *Antarctica* 5 C18
Jamesabad, *Pakistan* 68 G3
Jamestown, *Australia* 95 E2
Jamestown, *S. Africa* 88 E4
Jamestown, *N. Dak., U.S.A.* . 112 B5
Jamestown, *N.Y., U.S.A.* . . 110 D5
Jamestown, *Pa., U.S.A.* . . . 110 E4
Jamīlābād, *Iran* 71 C6
Jamiltepec, *Mexico* 119 D5
Jamira ➤, *India* 69 J13
Jāmjö, *Sweden* 11 H9
Jamkhandi, *India* 66 L9
Jammerbugt, *Denmark* 11 G3
Jammu, *India* 68 C6
Jammu & Kashmir □, *India* . . 69 B7
Jamnagar, *India* 68 H4
Jamni ➤, *India* 69 G8
Jampur, *Pakistan* 68 E4
Jamrud, *Pakistan* 68 C4
Jämsä, *Finland* 9 F21
Jamshedpur, *India* 69 H12
Jamtara, *India* 69 H12
Jämtland, *Sweden* 8 E15
Jämtlands län □, *Sweden* . . . 10 B7
Jan L., *Canada* 105 C8
Jan Mayen, *Arctic* 4 B7
Janakkala, *Finland* 9 F21

Janaúba, *Brazil* 125 G10
Jand, *Pakistan* 68 C5
Jandaq, *Iran* 71 C7
Jandia, *Canary Is.* 37 F5
Jandia, Pta. de, *Canary Is.* . . 37 F5
Jandola, *Pakistan* 68 C4
Jandowae, *Australia* 95 D5
Jándula ➤, *Spain* 35 G6
Janesville, *U.S.A.* 112 D10
Janga, *Ghana* 83 C4
Jangamo, *Mozam.* 89 C6
Janghai, *India* 69 G10
Janikowo, *Poland* 45 F5
Janīn, *West Bank* 75 C4
Janinà = Ioánnina □, *Greece* . 38 B2
Janja, *Bos.-H.* 42 F4
Janjevo, *Kosovo, Yug.* 40 D5
Janjgir, *India* 69 J10
Janjina, *Croatia* 29 F14
Janjina, *Madag.* 89 C8
Janos, *Mexico* 118 A3
Jánoshalma, *Hungary* 42 D4
Jánosháza, *Hungary* 42 C2
Jánossomorja, *Hungary* 42 C2
Janów, *Poland* 45 H6
Janów Lubelski, *Poland* 45 H9
Janów Podlaski, *Poland* 45 F10
Janowiec Wielkopolski, *Poland* . 45 F4
Januária, *Brazil* 125 G10
Janub Dârfûr □, *Sudan* 81 E2
Janub Kordofân □, *Sudan* . . 81 E3
Janûb Sînî □, *Egypt* 75 F2
Janubio, *Canary Is.* 37 F6
Janville, *France* 19 D8
Janzé, *France* 18 E5
Jaora, *India* 68 H6
Japan ■, *Asia* 55 G8
Japan, Sea of, *Asia* 54 E7
Japan Trench, *Pac. Oc.* 52 F18
Japen = Yapen, *Indonesia* . . . 63 E9
Japla, *India* 69 G11
Japurá ➤, *Brazil* 122 D4
Jaquarão, *Brazil* 127 C5
Jaqué, *Panama* 120 E4
Jarābulus, *Syria* 70 B3
Jaraicejo, *Spain* 35 F5
Jaraíz de la Vera, *Spain* 34 E5
Jarama ➤, *Spain* 34 E7
Jaramānah, *Syria* 72 F7
Jarandilla, *Spain* 34 E5
Jaranwala, *Pakistan* 68 D5
Jarash, *Jordan* 75 C4
Järbo, *Sweden* 10 D10
Jardim, *Brazil* 126 A4
Jardín ➤, *Spain* 33 G2
Jardines de la Reina, Arch. de los, *Cuba* 120 B4
Jargalang, *China* 57 C12
Jargalant = Hovd, *Mongolia* . . 60 B4
Jari ➤, *Brazil* 125 D8
Jarīr, W. al ➤, *Si. Arabia* . . . 70 E4
Järlåsa, *Sweden* 10 E11
Jarmen, *Germany* 24 B9
Järna, *Dalarnas, Sweden* . . . 10 D8
Järna, *Stockholm, Sweden* . . 10 E11
Jarnac, *France* 20 C3
Jarny, *France* 19 C12
Jarocin, *Poland* 45 G4
Jaroměř, *Czech Rep.* 26 A8
Jarosław, *Poland* 45 H9
Järpås, *Sweden* 11 F6
Järpen, *Sweden* 10 A7
Jarrahdale, *Australia* 93 F2
Jarrahi ➤, *Iran* 71 D6
Jarres, Plaine des, *Laos* 64 C4
Jarso, *Ethiopia* 81 F4
Jarud Qi, *China* 57 B11
Jarvenpää, *Finland* 9 F21
Jarvis, *Canada* 110 D4
Jarvis I., *Pac. Oc.* 97 H12
Jarvorník, *Czech Rep.* 27 A10
Järvsö, *Sweden* 10 C10
Jarwa, *India* 69 F10
Jasdan, *India* 68 H4
Jashpurnagar, *India* 69 H11
Jasidih, *India* 69 G12
Jāsin, *Malaysia* 65 L4
Jāsk, *Iran* 71 E8
Jasło, *Poland* 45 J8
Jasmund, *Germany* 24 A9
Jaso, *India* 69 G9
Jasper, *Alta., Canada* 104 C5
Jasper, *Ont., Canada* 111 B9
Jasper, *Ala., U.S.A.* 109 J2
Jasper, *Fla., U.S.A.* 109 K4
Jasper, *Ind., U.S.A.* 108 F2
Jasper, *Tex., U.S.A.* 113 K8
Jasper Nat. Park, *Canada* . . . 104 C5
Jasrasar, *India* 68 F5
Jastarnia, *Poland* 44 D5
Jastrebarsko, *Croatia* 29 C12
Jastrowie, *Poland* 44 E3
Jastrzębie Zdrój, *Poland* 45 J5
Jász-Nagykun-Szolnok □,
  Hungary 42 C5
Jászapáti, *Hungary* 42 C5
Jászárokszállás, *Hungary* . . . 42 C4
Jászberény, *Hungary* 42 C4
Jászkisér, *Hungary* 42 C5
Jászladány, *Hungary* 42 C5
Jataí, *Brazil* 125 G8
Jati, *Pakistan* 68 G3
Jatibarang, *Indonesia* 63 G13

Jatinegara, *Indonesia* 63 G12
Játiva = Xàtiva, *Spain* 33 G4
Jättendal, *Sweden* 10 C11
Jaú, *Brazil* 127 A6
Jauja, *Peru* 124 F3
Jaunpur, *India* 69 G10
Java = Jawa, *Indonesia* 62 F3
Java Barat □, *Indonesia* 63 G12
Java Sea, *Indonesia* 62 E3
Java Tengah □, *Indonesia* . . . 63 G14
Java Timur □, *Indonesia* 63 G15
Java Trench, *Ind. Oc.* 62 F3
Javalambre, Sa. de, *Spain* . . . 32 E4
Jávea, *Spain* 33 G5
Javhlant = Ulyasutay, *Mongolia* 60 B4
Jawa, *Indonesia* 62 F3
Jawad, *India* 68 G6
Jawor, *Poland* 45 G3
Jaworzno, *Poland* 45 H6
Jaworzyna Śląska, *Poland* . . . 45 H3
Jay Peak, *U.S.A.* 111 B12
Jaya, Puncak, *Indonesia* 63 E9
Jayanti, *India* 67 F16
Jayapura, *Indonesia* 63 E10
Jayawijaya, Pegunungan,
  Indonesia 63 E9
Jaynagar, *India* 67 F15
Jayrūd, *Syria* 70 C3
Jayton, *U.S.A.* 113 J4
Jāz Mūrīān, Hāmūn-e, *Iran* . . 71 E8
Jazīreh-ye Shīf, *Iran* 71 D6
Jazminal, *Mexico* 118 C4
Jazzīn, *Lebanon* 75 B4
Jean, *U.S.A.* 117 K11
Jean Marie River, *Canada* . . 104 A4
Jean Rabel, *Haiti* 121 C5
Jeanerette, *U.S.A.* 113 L9
Jeanette, Ostrov = Zhannetty,
  Ostrov, *Russia* 51 B16
Jeannette, *U.S.A.* 110 F5
Jebâl Bârez, Kūh-e, *Iran* . . . 71 D8
Jebba, *Nigeria* 83 D5
Jebel, Bahr el ➤, *Sudan* . . . 81 F3
Jebel Dud, *Sudan* 81 E3
Jebel Qerri, *Sudan* 81 D3
Jedburgh, *U.K.* 14 F6
Jedda = Jiddah, *Si. Arabia* . . 74 C2
Jeddore L., *Canada* 103 C8
Jedlicze, *Poland* 45 J8
Jędrzejów, *Poland* 45 H7
Jedwabne, *Poland* 45 E9
Jeetzel ➤, *Germany* 24 B7
Jefferson, *Iowa, U.S.A.* 112 D7
Jefferson, *Ohio, U.S.A.* 110 E4
Jefferson, *Tex., U.S.A.* 113 J7
Jefferson, *Mt., Nev., U.S.A.* . 114 G5
Jefferson, *Mt., Oreg., U.S.A.* . 114 D3
Jefferson City, *Mo., U.S.A.* . . 112 F8
Jefferson City, *Tenn., U.S.A.* . 109 G4
Jeffersonton, *U.S.A.* 108 F3
Jeffersonville, *U.S.A.* 108 F3
Jeffrey City, *U.S.A.* 114 E10
Jega, *Nigeria* 83 C5
Jēkabpils, *Latvia* 9 H21
Jekyll I., *U.S.A.* 109 K5
Jelcz-Laskowice, *Poland* 45 H4
Jelenia Góra, *Poland* 9 H20
Jelgava, *Latvia* 9 H20
Jelgava □, *Latvia* 44 B10
Jelica, *Serbia, Yug.* 40 C4
Jelli, *Sudan* 81 F3
Jelšava, *Slovak Rep.* 27 C13
Jemaja, *Indonesia* 65 L5
Jemaluang, *Malaysia* 65 L4
Jember, *Indonesia* 63 H15
Jembongan, *Malaysia* 65 G5
Jena, *Germany* 24 E7
Jena, *U.S.A.* 113 K8
Jenbach, *Austria* 26 D4
Jenkins, *U.S.A.* 108 G4
Jenner, *U.S.A.* 116 G3
Jennings, *U.S.A.* 113 K8
Jepara, *Indonesia* 63 G14
Jeparit, *Australia* 95 F3
Jequié, *Brazil* 125 F10
Jequitinhonha, *Brazil* 125 G10
Jequitinhonha ➤, *Brazil* . . . 125 G11
Jerantut, *Malaysia* 65 L4
Jérémie, *Haiti* 121 C5
Jerez, Punta, *Mexico* 119 C5
Jerez de García Salinas, *Mexico* 118 C4
Jerez de la Frontera, *Spain* . . 35 J4
Jerez de los Caballeros, *Spain* . 35 G4
Jericho = El Arīḥā, *West Bank* . 75 D4
Jericho, *Australia* 94 C4
Jerichow, *Germany* 24 C8
Jerid, Chott = Djerid, Chott, *Tunisia* 78 B7
Jerilderie, *Australia* 95 F4
Jermyn, *U.S.A.* 111 E9
Jerome, *U.S.A.* 114 E6
Jerramungup, *Australia* 93 F2
Jersey, *U.K.* 13 H5
Jersey City, *U.S.A.* 111 F10
Jersey Shore, *U.S.A.* 110 E7
Jerseyville, *U.S.A.* 112 F9
Jerusalem, *Israel* 75 D4
Jervis B., *Australia* 95 F5
Jervis Inlet, *Canada* 104 C4
Jerzu, *Italy* 30 C2
Jesenice, *Slovenia* 29 B11
Jeseník, *Czech Rep.* 27 A10
Jesenké, *Slovak Rep.* 27 C13
Jesi = Iesi, *Italy* 29 E10
Jesselton = Kota Kinabalu,
  Malaysia 62 C5
Jessnitz, *Germany* 24 D8

Jessore, *Bangla.* 67 H16
Jesup, *U.S.A.* 109 K5
Jesús Carranza, *Mexico* 119 D5
Jesús María, *Argentina* 126 C3
Jetmore, *U.S.A.* 113 F5
Jetpur, *India* 68 J4
Jeumont, *France* 19 B11
Jevnaker, *Norway* 9 F14
Jewett, *U.S.A.* 110 F3
Jewett City, *U.S.A.* 111 E13
Jeyḥūnābād, *Iran* 71 C6
Jeypore, *India* 67 K13
Jeziorak, Jezioro, *Poland* 44 E6
Jeziorany, *Poland* 44 E7
Jeziorka →, *Poland* 45 F8
Jha Jha, *India* 69 G12
Jhaarkand = Jharkhand □, *India* 69 H11
Jhabua, *India* 68 H6
Jhajjar, *India* 68 E7
Jhal, *Pakistan* 68 E2
Jhal Jhao, *Pakistan* 66 F4
Jhalawar, *India* 68 G7
Jhalida, *India* 69 H11
Jhalrapatan, *India* 68 G7
Jhang Maghiana, *Pakistan* 68 D5
Jhansi, *India* 69 G8
Jhargram, *India* 69 H12
Jharia, *India* 69 H12
Jharkhand □, *India* 69 H11
Jharsuguda, *India* 67 J14
Jhelum, *Pakistan* 68 C5
Jhelum →, *Pakistan* 68 D5
Jhilmilli, *India* 69 H10
Jhudo, *Pakistan* 68 G3
Jhunjhunu, *India* 68 E6
Ji-Paraná, *Brazil* 124 F6
Ji Xian, *Hebei, China* 56 F9
Ji Xian, *Henan, China* 56 G8
Ji Xian, *Shanxi, China* 56 F6
Jia Xian, *Henan, China* 56 H7
Jia Xian, *Shaanxi, China* 56 E6
Jiading, *China* 59 B13
Jiahe, *China* 59 E9
Jialing Jiang →, *China* 58 C6
Jiamusi, *China* 60 B8
Ji'an, *Jiangxi, China* 59 D10
Ji'an, *Jilin, China* 57 D14
Jianchang, *China* 57 D11
Jianchangying, *China* 57 D10
Jianchuan, *China* 58 D2
Jiande, *China* 59 C12
Jiang'an, *China* 58 C5
Jiangbei, *China* 58 C6
Jiangcheng, *China* 58 F3
Jiangdi, *China* 58 D4
Jiangdu, *China* 59 A12
Jiange, *China* 58 A5
Jianghua, *China* 59 E8
Jiangjin, *China* 58 C6
Jiangkou, *China* 58 D7
Jiangle, *China* 59 D11
Jiangling, *China* 59 B9
Jiangmen, *China* 59 F9
Jiangning, *China* 59 B12
Jiangshan, *China* 59 C12
Jiangsu □, *China* 57 H11
Jiangxi □, *China* 59 D11
Jiangyan, *China* 59 A13
Jiangyin, *China* 59 B13
Jiangyong, *China* 59 E8
Jiangyou, *China* 58 B5
Jianhe, *China* 58 D7
Jianli, *China* 59 C9
Jianning, *China* 59 D11
Jian'ou, *China* 59 D12
Jianshi, *China* 58 B7
Jianshui, *China* 58 F4
Jianyang, *Fujian, China* 59 D12
Jianyang, *Sichuan, China* 58 B5
Jiao Xian = Jiaozhou, *China* 57 F11
Jiaohe, *Hebei, China* 56 E9
Jiaohe, *Jilin, China* 57 C14
Jiaojiang, *China* 59 C13
Jiaoling, *China* 59 E11
Jiaozhou, *China* 57 F11
Jiaozhou Wan, *China* 57 F11
Jiaozuo, *China* 56 G7
Jiashan, *China* 59 B13
Jiawang, *China* 57 G9
Jiaxiang, *China* 56 G9
Jiaxing, *China* 59 B13
Jiayi = Chiai, *Taiwan* 59 F13
Jiayu, *China* 59 C9
Jibiya, *Nigeria* 83 C6
Jibou, *Romania* 43 C8
Jibuti = Djibouti ■, *Africa* 81 E5
Jicarón, I., *Panama* 120 E3
Jičín, *Czech Rep.* 26 A8
Jiddah, *Si. Arabia* 74 C2
Jido, *India* 67 E19
Jieshou, *China* 56 H8
Jiexiu, *China* 56 F6
Jieyang, *China* 59 F11
Jigawa □, *Nigeria* 83 C6
Jiggalong, *Australia* 92 D3
Jigni, *India* 69 G8
Jihlava, *Czech Rep.* 26 B8
Jihlava →, *Czech Rep.* 27 C9
Jihlavský □, *Czech Rep.* 26 B8
Jijiga, *Ethiopia* 74 F3
Jikamshi, *Nigeria* 83 C6
Jikau, *Sudan* 81 F3
Jilin, *China* 57 C14
Jilin □, *China* 57 C14
Jiloca →, *Spain* 32 D3
Jilong = Chilung, *Taiwan* 59 E13

Jim Thorpe, *U.S.A.* 111 F9
Jima, *Ethiopia* 81 F4
Jimbolia, *Romania* 42 E5
Jimena de la Frontera, *Spain* 35 J5
Jiménez, *Mexico* 118 B4
Jimo, *China* 57 F11
Jin Jiang →, *China* 59 C10
Jin Xian = Jinzhou, *China* 56 E8
Jin Xian, *China* 57 E11
Jinan, *China* 56 F9
Jincheng, *China* 56 G7
Jinchuan, *China* 58 B4
Jind, *India* 68 E7
Jindabyne, *Australia* 95 F4
Jindřichův Hradec, *Czech Rep.* 26 B8
Jing He →, *China* 56 G5
Jing Shan, *China* 59 B8
Jing Xian, *China* 59 B12
Jing'an, *China* 59 C10
Jingbian, *China* 56 F5
Jingchuan, *China* 56 G4
Jingde, *China* 59 B12
Jingdezhen, *China* 59 C11
Jingdong, *China* 58 E3
Jinggangshan, *China* 59 D10
Jinggu, *China* 58 F3
Jinghai, *China* 56 E9
Jinghong, *China* 58 G3
Jingjiang, *China* 59 A13
Jingle, *China* 56 E6
Jingmen, *China* 59 B9
Jingning, *China* 56 G3
Jingpo Hu, *China* 57 C15
Jingshan, *China* 59 B9
Jingtai, *China* 56 F3
Jingxi, *China* 58 F6
Jingxing, *China* 56 E8
Jingyang, *China* 56 G5
Jingyu, *China* 57 C14
Jingyuan, *China* 56 F3
Jingzhou, *China* 58 D7
Jingziguan, *China* 56 H6
Jinhua, *China* 59 C12
Jining, *Nei Monggol Zizhiqu, China* 56 D7
Jining, *Shandong, China* 56 G9
Jinja, *Uganda* 86 B3
Jinjang, *Malaysia* 65 L3
Jinji, *China* 56 F4
Jinjiang, *Fujian, China* 59 E12
Jinjiang, *Yunnan, China* 58 D3
Jinjini, *Ghana* 82 D4
Jinkou, *China* 59 B10
Jinkouhe, *China* 58 C4
Jinmen Dao, *China* 59 E12
Jinnah Barrage, *Pakistan* 66 C7
Jinning, *China* 58 E4
Jinotega, *Nic.* 120 D2
Jinotepe, *Nic.* 120 D2
Jinping, *Guizhou, China* 58 D7
Jinping, *Yunnan, China* 58 F4
Jinsha, *China* 58 D6
Jinsha Jiang →, *China* 58 C5
Jinshan, *China* 59 B13
Jinshi, *China* 59 C8
Jintan, *China* 59 B12
Jinxi, *Jiangxi, China* 59 D11
Jinxi, *Liaoning, China* 57 D11
Jinxian, *China* 59 C11
Jinxiang, *China* 56 G9
Jinyang, *China* 58 D4
Jinyun, *China* 59 C13
Jinzhai, *China* 59 B10
Jinzhou, *Hebei, China* 56 E8
Jinzhou, *Liaoning, China* 57 D11
Jiparaná →, *Brazil* 124 E6
Jipijapa, *Ecuador* 124 D2
Jiquilpan, *Mexico* 118 D4
Jishan, *China* 56 G6
Jishou, *China* 58 C7
Jishui, *China* 59 D10
Jisr ash Shughūr, *Syria* 70 C3
Jitarning, *Australia* 93 F2
Jitra, *Malaysia* 65 J3
Jiu →, *Romania* 43 G8
Jiudengkou, *China* 56 E4
Jiujiang, *Guangdong, China* 59 F9
Jiujiang, *Jiangxi, China* 59 C10
Jiuling Shan, *China* 59 C10
Jiulong, *China* 58 C3
Jiutai, *China* 57 B13
Jiuxincheng, *China* 56 E8
Jiuyuhang, *China* 59 B12
Jixi, *Anhui, China* 59 B12
Jixi, *Heilongjiang, China* 57 B16
Jiyang, *China* 56 F9
Jiyuan, *China* 56 G7
Jīzān, *Si. Arabia* 74 D3
Jize, *China* 56 F8
Jizera →, *Czech Rep.* 26 A7
Jizl, W. →, *Si. Arabia* 80 B4
Jizl, Wādī al, *Si. Arabia* 70 E3
Jizō-Zaki, *Japan* 55 G6
Jizzakh, *Uzbekistan* 50 E7
Joaçaba, *Brazil* 127 B5
Joal Fadiout, *Senegal* 82 C1
João Pessoa, *Brazil* 125 E12
Joaquín V. González, *Argentina* 126 C3
Jobat, *India* 68 H6
Jobourg, Nez de, *France* 18 C5
Jódar, *Spain* 35 H7
Jodhpur, *India* 68 F5
Jodiya, *India* 68 H4
Jōetsu, *Japan* 55 F9
Jœuf, *France* 19 C12
Jofane, *Mozam.* 89 C5
Jogbani, *India* 69 F12

Jõgeva, *Estonia* 9 G22
Jogjakarta = Yogyakarta, *Indonesia* 62 F4
Johannesburg, *S. Africa* 89 D4
Johannesburg, *U.S.A.* 117 K9
Johansfors, *Sweden* 11 H9
Johilla →, *India* 69 H9
John Day, *U.S.A.* 114 D4
John Day →, *U.S.A.* 114 D3
John D'Or Prairie, *Canada* 104 B5
John H. Kerr Reservoir, *U.S.A.* 109 G6
John o' Groats, *U.K.* 14 C5
Johnnie, *U.S.A.* 117 J10
John's Ra., *Australia* 94 C1
Johnson, *Kans., U.S.A.* 113 G4
Johnson, *Vt., U.S.A.* 111 B12
Johnson City, *N.Y., U.S.A.* 111 D9
Johnson City, *Tenn., U.S.A.* 109 G4
Johnson City, *Tex., U.S.A.* 113 K5
Johnsonburg, *U.S.A.* 110 E6
Johnsondale, *U.S.A.* 117 K8
Johnson's Crossing, *Canada* 104 A2
Johnston, L., *Australia* 93 F3
Johnston Falls = Mambilima Falls, *Zambia* 87 E2
Johnston I., *Pac. Oc.* 97 F11
Johnstone Str., *Canada* 104 C3
Johnstown, *N.Y., U.S.A.* 111 C10
Johnstown, *Ohio, U.S.A.* 110 F2
Johnstown, *Pa., U.S.A.* 110 F6
Johor Baharu, *Malaysia* 65 M4
Jōhvi, *Estonia* 9 G22
Joigny, *France* 19 E10
Joinville, *Brazil* 127 B6
Joinville, *France* 19 D12
Joinville I., *Antarctica* 5 C18
Jojutla, *Mexico* 119 D5
Jokkmokk, *Sweden* 8 C18
Jökulsá á Bru →, *Iceland* 8 D6
Jökulsá á Fjöllum →, *Iceland* 8 C5
Jolfā, *Āzarbājān-e Sharqī, Iran* 70 B5
Jolfā, *Eşfahan, Iran* 71 C6
Joliet, *U.S.A.* 108 E1
Joliette, *Canada* 102 C5
Jolo, *Phil.* 61 J4
Jomalig I., *Phil.* 61 D5
Jombang, *Indonesia* 63 G15
Jomda, *China* 58 B2
Jonava, *Lithuania* 9 J21
Jones Sound, *Canada* 4 B3
Jonesboro, *Ark., U.S.A.* 113 H9
Jonesboro, *La., U.S.A.* 113 J8
Jong →, *S. Leone* 82 D2
Jonglei, *Sudan* 81 F3
Jonglei □, *Sudan* 81 F3
Joniškis, *Lithuania* 9 H20
Jönköping, *Sweden* 11 G8
Jönköpings län □, *Sweden* 11 G8
Jonquière, *Canada* 103 C5
Jonsered, *Sweden* 11 G6
Jonzac, *France* 20 C3
Joplin, *U.S.A.* 113 G7
Jora, *India* 68 F6
Jordan, *Mont., U.S.A.* 114 C10
Jordan, *N.Y., U.S.A.* 111 C8
Jordan ■, *Asia* 75 E5
Jordan →, *Asia* 75 D4
Jordan Valley, *U.S.A.* 114 E5
Jordanów, *Poland* 45 J6
Jorhat, *India* 67 F19
Jörn, *Sweden* 8 D19
Jorong, *Indonesia* 62 E4
Jørpeland, *Norway* 9 G11
Jorquera →, *Chile* 126 B2
Jos, *Nigeria* 83 D6
Jos Plateau, *Nigeria* 83 D6
Jošanička Banja, *Serbia, Yug.* 40 C4
José Batlle y Ordóñez, *Uruguay* 127 C4
Joseni, *Romania* 43 D10
Joseph, L., *Nfld., Canada* 103 B6
Joseph, L., *Ont., Canada* 110 A5
Joseph Bonaparte G., *Australia* 92 B4
Joshinath, *India* 69 D8
Joshua Tree, *U.S.A.* 117 L10
Joshua Tree National Park, *U.S.A.* 117 M10
Josselin, *France* 18 E4
Jostedalsbreen, *Norway* 9 F12
Jotunheimen, *Norway* 9 F13
Joubertberge, *Namibia* 88 B1
Joué-lès-Tours, *France* 18 E7
Jourdanton, *U.S.A.* 113 L5
Joutseno, *Finland* 46 B5
Jovellanos, *Cuba* 120 B3
Joyeuse, *France* 21 D8
Józefów, *Lubelskie, Poland* 45 H10
Józefów, *Mazowieckie, Poland* 45 F10
Ju Xian, *China* 57 F10
Juan Aldama, *Mexico* 118 C4
Juan Bautista Alberdi, *Argentina* 126 C3
Juan de Fuca Str., *Canada* 116 B3
Juan de Nova, *Ind. Oc.* 89 B7
Juan Fernández, Arch. de, *Pac. Oc.* 122 G2
Juan José Castelli, *Argentina* 126 B3
Juan L. Lacaze, *Uruguay* 126 C4
Juárez, *Argentina* 126 D4
Juárez, *Mexico* 117 N11
Juárez, Sierra de, *Mexico* 118 A1
Juàzeiro, *Brazil* 125 E10
Juàzeiro do Norte, *Brazil* 125 E11
Juba, *Sudan* 81 G3
Jubayl, *Lebanon* 75 A4
Jubbah, *Si. Arabia* 70 D4
Jubbal, *India* 68 D7

Jubbulpore = Jabalpur, *India* 69 H8
Jübek, *Germany* 24 A5
Jubga, *Russia* 49 H4
Jubilee L., *Australia* 93 E4
Juby, C., *Morocco* 78 C3
Júcar = Xúquer →, *Spain* 33 F4
Júcaro, *Cuba* 120 B4
Juchitán, *Mexico* 119 D5
Judaea = Har Yehuda, *Israel* 75 D3
Judenburg, *Austria* 26 D7
Judith →, *U.S.A.* 114 C9
Judith, Pt., *U.S.A.* 111 E13
Judith Gap, *U.S.A.* 114 C9
Juelsminde, *Denmark* 11 J4
Jugoslavia = Yugoslavia ■, *Europe* 40 C4
Juigalpa, *Nic.* 120 D2
Juillac, *France* 20 C5
Juist, *Germany* 24 B2
Juiz de Fora, *Brazil* 127 A7
Jujuy □, *Argentina* 126 A2
Julesburg, *U.S.A.* 112 E3
Juli, *Peru* 124 G5
Julia Cr. →, *Australia* 94 C3
Julia Creek, *Australia* 94 C3
Juliaca, *Peru* 124 G4
Julian, *U.S.A.* 117 M10
Julian Alps = Julijske Alpe, *Slovenia* 29 B11
Julian L., *Canada* 102 B4
Julianatop, *Surinam* 125 C7
Julianehåb = Qaqortoq, *Greenland* 101 B6
Jülich, *Germany* 24 E2
Julijske Alpe, *Slovenia* 29 B11
Julimes, *Mexico* 118 B3
Jullundur, *India* 68 D6
Julu, *China* 56 F8
Jumbo, *Zimbabwe* 87 F3
Jumbo Pk., *U.S.A.* 117 J12
Jumentos Cays, *Bahamas* 120 B4
Jumilla, *Spain* 33 G3
Jumla, *Nepal* 69 E10
Jumna = Yamuna →, *India* 69 G9
Junagadh, *India* 68 J4
Junction, *Tex., U.S.A.* 113 K5
Junction, *Utah, U.S.A.* 115 G7
Junction B., *Australia* 94 A1
Junction City, *Kans., U.S.A.* 112 F6
Junction City, *Oreg., U.S.A.* 114 D2
Junction Pt., *Australia* 94 A1
Jundah, *Australia* 94 C3
Jundiaí, *Brazil* 127 A6
Juneau, *U.S.A.* 104 B2
Junee, *Australia* 95 E4
Jungfrau, *Switz.* 25 J3
Junggar Pendi, *China* 60 B3
Jungshahi, *Pakistan* 68 G2
Juniata →, *U.S.A.* 110 F7
Junín, *Argentina* 126 C3
Junín de los Andes, *Argentina* 128 D2
Jūniyah, *Lebanon* 75 B4
Junlian, *China* 58 C5
Juntas, *Chile* 126 B2
Juntura, *U.S.A.* 114 E4
Jur, Nahr el →, *Sudan* 81 F2
Jura = Jura, Mts. du, *Europe* 19 F13
Jura = Schwäbische Alb, *Germany* 25 G5
Jura, *U.K.* 14 F3
Jura □, *France* 19 F12
Jura □, *Switz.* 25 H3
Jūra →, *Lithuania* 44 C9
Jura, Mts. du, *Europe* 19 F13
Jura, Sd. of, *U.K.* 14 F3
Jurbarkas, *Lithuania* 9 J20
Jurien, *Australia* 93 F2
Jurilovca, *Romania* 43 F13
Jūrmala, *Latvia* 9 H20
Jurong, *China* 59 B12
Juruá →, *Brazil* 122 D4
Juruena, *Brazil* 124 F7
Juruena →, *Brazil* 124 E7
Juruti, *Brazil* 125 D7
Jussey, *France* 19 E12
Justo Daract, *Argentina* 126 C2
Jutaí →, *Brazil* 124 D5
Jüterbog, *Germany* 24 D9
Juticalpa, *Honduras* 120 D2
Jutland = Jylland, *Denmark* 11 H3
Juventud, I. de la, *Cuba* 120 B3
Juvigny-sous-Andaine, *France* 18 D6
Jūy Zar, *Iran* 70 C5
Juye, *China* 56 G9
Juzennecourt, *France* 19 D11
Jvari, *Georgia* 49 J6
Jwaneng, *Botswana* 85 J4
Jyderup, *Denmark* 11 J5
Jylland, *Denmark* 11 H3
Jyväskylä, *Finland* 9 E21

K

K2, *Pakistan* 69 B7
Ka →, *Nigeria* 83 C5
Kaap Plateau, *S. Africa* 88 D3
Kaapkruis, *Namibia* 88 C1
Kaapstad = Cape Town, *S. Africa* 88 E2
Kaba, *Guinea* 82 C2
Kabaena, *Indonesia* 63 F6
Kabala, *S. Leone* 82 D2
Kabale, *Uganda* 86 C3
Kabalo, *Dem. Rep. of the Congo* 86 D2

Kabambare, *Dem. Rep. of the Congo* 86 C2
Kabango, *Dem. Rep. of the Congo* 87 D2
Kabankalan, *Phil.* 61 G5
Kabara, *Mali* 82 B4
Kabardinka, *Russia* 47 K10
Kabardino-Balkar Republic = Kabardino-Balkaria □, *Russia* 49 J6
Kabardino-Balkaria □, *Russia* 49 J6
Kabarega Falls = Murchison Falls, *Uganda* 86 B3
Kabasalan, *Phil.* 61 H5
Kabba, *Nigeria* 83 D6
Kabetogama, *U.S.A.* 112 A8
Kabi, *Niger* 83 C7
Kabin Buri, *Thailand* 64 F3
Kabinakagami L., *Canada* 102 C3
Kabinda, *Dem. Rep. of the Congo* 84 F4
Kabna, *Sudan* 80 D3
Kabompo, *Zambia* 87 E1
Kabompo →, *Zambia* 85 G4
Kabondo, *Dem. Rep. of the Congo* 87 D2
Kabongo, *Dem. Rep. of the Congo* 86 D2
Kabou, *Guinea* 82 C2
Kabou, *Togo* 83 D5
Kabr, *Sudan* 81 E2
Kabūd Gonbad, *Iran* 71 B8
Kabugao, *Phil.* 61 B4
Kābul, *Afghan.* 68 B6
Kābul □, *Afghan.* 66 B6
Kābul →, *Pakistan* 68 C5
Kabunga, *Dem. Rep. of the Congo* 86 C2
Kaburuang, *Indonesia* 63 D7
Kabushiya, *Sudan* 81 D3
Kabwe, *Zambia* 87 E2
Kačanik, *Kosovo, Yug.* 40 D5
Kačerginė, *Lithuania* 44 D10
Kachchh, Gulf of, *India* 68 H3
Kachchh, Rann of, *India* 68 H4
Kachchhidhana, *India* 69 J8
Kachebera, *Zambia* 87 E3
Kachia, *Nigeria* 83 D6
Kachikau, *Botswana* 88 B3
Kachin □, *Burma* 58 D1
Kachira, L., *Uganda* 86 C3
Kachiry, *Kazakstan* 50 D8
Kachisi, *Ethiopia* 81 F4
Kachnara, *India* 68 H6
Kachot, *Cambodia* 65 G4
Kaçkar, *Turkey* 73 B9
Kadan, *Czech Rep.* 26 A6
Kadan Kyun, *Burma* 64 F2
Kadanai →, *Afghan.* 68 D1
Kadarkút, *Hungary* 42 D2
Kade, *Ghana* 83 D4
Kadi, *India* 68 H5
Kadina, *Australia* 95 E2
Kadınhanı, *Turkey* 72 C5
Kadiolo, *Mali* 82 C3
Kadipur, *India* 69 F10
Kadirli, *Turkey* 70 B3
Kadiyevka = Stakhanov, *Ukraine* 47 H10
Kadodo, *Sudan* 81 E2
Kadoka, *U.S.A.* 112 D4
Kadoma, *Zimbabwe* 87 F2
Kādugli, *Sudan* 81 E2
Kaduna, *Nigeria* 83 C6
Kaduna □, *Nigeria* 83 C6
Kaduy, *Russia* 46 C9
Kaédi, *Mauritania* 82 B2
Kaélé, *Cameroon* 83 C7
Kaeng Khoï, *Thailand* 64 E3
Kaesŏng, *N. Korea* 57 F14
Kāf, *Si. Arabia* 70 D3
Kafan = Kapan, *Armenia* 70 B5
Kafanchan, *Nigeria* 83 D6
Kafareti, *Nigeria* 83 C7
Kaffrine, *Senegal* 82 C1
Kafia, *Nigeria* 83 D6
Kafin Madaki, *Nigeria* 83 C6
Kafinda, *Zambia* 87 E3
Kafirévs, Ákra, *Greece* 38 C6
Kafr el Battikh, *Egypt* 80 H7
Kafr el Dauwâr, *Egypt* 80 H7
Kafr el Sheikh, *Egypt* 80 H7
Kafue, *Zambia* 87 F2
Kafue →, *Zambia* 87 F2
Kafue Flats, *Zambia* 87 F2
Kafue Nat. Park, *Zambia* 87 F2
Kafulwe, *Zambia* 87 D2
Kaga, *Afghan.* 68 B4
Kaga Bandoro, *C.A.R.* 84 C3
Kagan, *Uzbekistan* 50 F7
Kagarko, *Nigeria* 83 D6
Kagawa □, *Japan* 55 G7
Kagera = Ziwa Magharibi □, *Tanzania* 86 C3
Kagera →, *Uganda* 86 C3
Kağızman, *Turkey* 70 B4
Kagmar, *Sudan* 81 E3
Kagoshima □, *Japan* 55 J5
Kagul = Cahul, *Moldova* 43 E13
Kahak, *Iran* 71 B6
Kahama, *Tanzania* 86 C3
Kahan, *Pakistan* 68 E3
Kahang, *Malaysia* 65 L4
Kahayan →, *Indonesia* 62 E4
Kahe, *Tanzania* 86 C4
Kahnūj, *Iran* 71 E8

Kahoka, U.S.A. ... 112 E9
Kahoolawe, U.S.A. ... 106 H16
Kahramanmaraş, Turkey ... 70 B3
Kâhta, Turkey ... 73 D8
Kahuta, Pakistan ... 68 C5
Kai, Kepulauan, Indonesia ... 63 F8
Kai Besar, Indonesia ... 63 F8
Kai Is. = Kai, Kepulauan, Indonesia ... 63 F8
Kai Kecil, Indonesia ... 63 F8
Kai Xian, China ... 58 B7
Kaiama, Nigeria ... 83 D5
Kaiapoi, N.Z. ... 91 K4
Kaieteur Falls, Guyana ... 124 B7
Kaifeng, China ... 56 G8
Kaihua, China ... 59 C12
Kaijiang, China ... 58 B6
Kaikohe, N.Z. ... 91 F4
Kaikoura, N.Z. ... 91 K4
Kaikoura Ra., N.Z. ... 91 J4
Kailahun, S. Leone ... 82 D2
Kaili, China ... 58 D6
Kailu, China ... 57 C11
Kailua Kona, U.S.A. ... 106 J17
Kaimana, Indonesia ... 63 E8
Kaimanawa Mts., N.Z. ... 91 H5
Kaimganj, India ... 69 F8
Kaimur Hills, India ... 69 G10
Kainab →, Namibia ... 88 D2
Kainji Dam, Nigeria ... 83 D5
Kainji Res., Nigeria ... 83 C5
Kainuu, Finland ... 8 D23
Kaipara Harbour, N.Z. ... 91 G5
Kaiping, China ... 59 F9
Kaipokok B., Canada ... 103 B8
Kaira, India ... 68 H5
Kairana, India ... 68 E7
Kaironi, Indonesia ... 63 E8
Kairouan, Tunisia ... 79 A8
Kaiserslautern, Germany ... 25 F3
Kaiserstuhl, Germany ... 25 G3
Kaitaia, N.Z. ... 91 F4
Kaitangata, N.Z. ... 91 M2
Kaithal, India ... 68 E7
Kaitu →, Pakistan ... 68 C4
Kaiyang, China ... 58 D6
Kaiyuan, Liaoning, China ... 57 C13
Kaiyuan, Yunnan, China ... 58 F4
Kajaani, Finland ... 8 D22
Kajabbi, Australia ... 94 C3
Kajana = Kajaani, Finland ... 8 D22
Kajang, Malaysia ... 65 L3
Kajaran, Armenia ... 73 C12
Kajiado, Kenya ... 86 C4
Kajo Kaji, Sudan ... 81 G3
Kajuru, Nigeria ... 83 C6
Kaka, Sudan ... 81 E3
Kakabeka Falls, Canada ... 102 C2
Kakamas, S. Africa ... 88 D3
Kakamega, Kenya ... 86 B3
Kakanj, Bos.-H. ... 42 F3
Kakanui Mts., N.Z. ... 91 L3
Kakata, Liberia ... 82 D2
Kakdwip, India ... 69 J13
Kake, Japan ... 55 G6
Kake, U.S.A. ... 104 B2
Kakegawa, Japan ... 55 G9
Kakeroma-Jima, Japan ... 55 K4
Kakhib, Russia ... 49 J8
Kakhovka, Ukraine ... 47 J7
Kakhovske Vdskh., Ukraine ... 47 J7
Kakinada, India ... 67 L13
Kakisa →, Canada ... 104 A5
Kakisa L., Canada ... 104 A5
Kakogawa, Japan ... 55 G7
Kakwa →, Canada ... 104 C5
Kāl Gūsheh, Iran ... 71 D8
Kal Safid, Iran ... 70 C5
Kala, Nigeria ... 83 C7
Kalaallit Nunaat = Greenland ■, N. Amer. ... 4 C5
Kalabagh, Pakistan ... 68 C4
Kalabahi, Indonesia ... 63 F6
Kalabáka, Greece ... 38 B3
Kalabana, Mali ... 82 C3
Kalach, Russia ... 48 E5
Kalach na Donu, Russia ... 49 F6
Kaladan →, Burma ... 67 J18
Kaladar, Canada ... 102 D4
Kalahari, Africa ... 88 C3
Kalahari Gemsbok Nat. Park, S. Africa ... 88 D3
Kalajoki, Finland ... 8 D20
Kālak, Iran ... 71 E8
Kalakamati, Botswana ... 89 C4
Kalakan, Russia ... 51 D12
K'alak'unlun Shank'ou = Karakoram Pass, Pakistan ... 69 B7
Kalam, Pakistan ... 69 B5
Kalama, Dem. Rep. of the Congo ... 86 C2
Kalama, U.S.A. ... 116 E4
Kalámai, Greece ... 38 D4
Kalamariá, Greece ... 40 F6
Kalamata = Kalámai, Greece ... 38 D4
Kalamazoo, U.S.A. ... 108 D3
Kalamazoo →, U.S.A. ... 108 D2
Kalambo Falls, Tanzania ... 87 D3
Kálamos, Attikí, Greece ... 38 C5
Kálamos, Iónioi Nísoi, Greece ... 38 C2
Kalannie, Australia ... 93 F2
Kalāntarī, Iran ... 71 C7
Kalao, Indonesia ... 63 F6
Kalaotoa, Indonesia ... 63 F6
Kälarne, Sweden ... 10 B10

Kalasin, Thailand ... 64 D4
Kalat, Pakistan ... 66 E5
Kalāteh, Iran ... 71 B7
Kalāteh-ye Ganj, Iran ... 71 E8
Kálathos, Greece ... 39 E10
Kalaus →, Russia ... 49 H7
Kalávrita, Greece ... 38 C4
Kalbarri, Australia ... 93 E1
Kale, Antalya, Turkey ... 39 E12
Kale, Denizli, Turkey ... 39 D10
Kalecik, Turkey ... 72 B5
Kalegauk Kyun, Burma ... 67 M20
Kalehe, Dem. Rep. of the Congo ... 86 C2
Kalema, Tanzania ... 86 C3
Kalemie, Dem. Rep. of the Congo ... 86 D2
Kalety, Poland ... 45 H5
Kalewa, Burma ... 67 H19
Kaleybar, Iran ... 70 B5
Kalgan = Zhangjiakou, China ... 56 D8
Kalgoorlie-Boulder, Australia ... 93 F3
Kali →, India ... 69 F8
Kali Sindh →, India ... 68 G6
Kaliakra, Nos, Bulgaria ... 41 C12
Kalianda, Indonesia ... 62 F3
Kalibo, Phil. ... 61 F5
Kalima, Dem. Rep. of the Congo ... 86 C2
Kalimantan □, Indonesia ... 62 E4
Kalimantan Barat □, Indonesia ... 62 E4
Kalimantan Selatan □, Indonesia ... 62 E5
Kalimantan Tengah □, Indonesia ... 62 E4
Kalimantan Timur □, Indonesia ... 62 D5
Kálimnos, Greece ... 39 D8
Kalimpong, India ... 69 F13
Kalinin = Tver, Russia ... 46 D8
Kaliningrad, Russia ... 9 J19
Kalininsk, Russia ... 48 E7
Kalinkavichy, Belarus ... 47 F5
Kalinkovichi = Kalinkavichy, Belarus ... 47 F5
Kalinovik, Bos.-H. ... 40 C2
Kalipetrovo, Bulgaria ... 41 B11
Kaliro, Uganda ... 86 B3
Kalirrákhi, Greece ... 41 F8
Kalispell, U.S.A. ... 114 B6
Kalisz, Poland ... 45 G5
Kalisz Pomorski, Poland ... 45 E2
Kaliua, Tanzania ... 86 D3
Kalívia Thorikoú, Greece ... 38 D5
Kalix, Sweden ... 8 D20
Kalix →, Sweden ... 8 D20
Kalka, India ... 68 D7
Kalkan, Turkey ... 39 E11
Kalkarindji, Australia ... 92 C5
Kalkaska, U.S.A. ... 108 C3
Kalkfeld, Namibia ... 88 C2
Kalkfontein, Botswana ... 88 C3
Kalkim, Turkey ... 39 B9
Kalkrand, Namibia ... 88 C2
Kållandsö, Sweden ... 11 F7
Kallavesi, Finland ... 8 E22
Källby, Sweden ... 11 F7
Kållered, Sweden ... 11 G6
Kallimasiá, Greece ... 39 C8
Kallinge, Sweden ... 11 H9
Kallithéa, Greece ... 38 D5
Kallmet, Albania ... 40 E3
Kalloní, Greece ... 39 B8
Kallonís, Kólpos, Greece ... 39 B8
Kallsjön, Sweden ... 8 E15
Kalmalo, Nigeria ... 83 C6
Kalmar, Sweden ... 11 H10
Kalmar län □, Sweden ... 11 G10
Kalmar sund, Sweden ... 11 H10
Kalmyk Republic = Kalmykia □, Russia ... 49 G8
Kalmykia □, Russia ... 49 G8
Kalmykovo, Kazakstan ... 50 E6
Kalna, India ... 69 H13
Kalnai, India ... 69 H10
Kalocsa, Hungary ... 42 D4
Kalofer, Bulgaria ... 41 D8
Kalokhorio, Cyprus ... 36 E12
Kaloko, Dem. Rep. of the Congo ... 86 D2
Kalol, Gujarat, India ... 68 H5
Kalol, Gujarat, India ... 68 H5
Kalolímnos, Greece ... 39 D9
Kalomo, Zambia ... 87 F2
Kalonerón, Greece ... 38 D3
Kalpi, India ... 69 F8
Kaltern = Caldaro, Italy ... 29 B8
Kaltungo, Nigeria ... 83 D7
Kalu, Pakistan ... 68 G2
Kaluga, Russia ... 46 E9
Kalulushi, Zambia ... 87 E2
Kalundborg, Denmark ... 11 J5
Kalush, Ukraine ... 47 H3
Kałuszyn, Poland ... 45 F8
Kalutara, Sri Lanka ... 66 R12
Kalvarija, Lithuania ... 44 D10
Kalyazin, Russia ... 46 D9
Kam, Albania ... 40 D4
Kama →, Nigeria ... 83 D7
Kama, Dem. Rep. of the Congo ... 86 C2
Kama →, Russia ... 50 D6
Kamachumu, Tanzania ... 86 C3
Kamaishi, Japan ... 54 E10
Kamalia, Pakistan ... 68 D5
Kaman, India ... 68 F6
Kaman, Turkey ... 72 C5
Kamanjab, Namibia ... 88 B2
Kamapanda, Zambia ... 87 E1
Kamaran, Yemen ... 74 D3
Kamativi, Zimbabwe ... 88 B4
Kamba, Nigeria ... 83 C5
Kambalda, Australia ... 93 F3

Kambar, Pakistan ... 68 F3
Kambia, S. Leone ... 82 D2
Kambolé, Togo ... 83 D5
Kambolé, Zambia ... 87 D3
Kambos, Cyprus ... 36 D11
Kambove, Dem. Rep. of the Congo ... 87 E2
Kamchatka, Poluostrov, Russia ... 51 D16
Kamchatka Pen. = Kamchatka, Poluostrov, Russia ... 51 D16
Kamchiya →, Bulgaria ... 41 C11
Kamen, Russia ... 50 D9
Kamen-Rybolov, Russia ... 54 B6
Kamenica, Serbia, Yug. ... 40 C6
Kamenica, Serbia, Yug. ... 40 B3
Kamenice nad Lipou, Czech Rep. ... 26 B8
Kamenjak, Rt, Croatia ... 29 D10
Kamenka = Kaminka, Ukraine ... 47 H7
Kamenka, Kazakstan ... 48 E10
Kamenka, Penza, Russia ... 48 D6
Kamenka, Voronezh, Russia ... 47 G10
Kamenka Bugskaya = Kamyanka-Buzka, Ukraine ... 47 G3
Kamenka Dneprovskaya = Kamyanka-Dniprovska, Ukraine ... 47 J8
Kamennomostskiy, Russia ... 49 H5
Kameno, Bulgaria ... 41 D11
Kamenolomini, Russia ... 49 G5
Kamensk-Shakhtinskiy, Russia ... 49 F5
Kamensk Uralskiy, Russia ... 50 D7
Kamenskiy, Russia ... 48 E7
Kamenskoye, Russia ... 51 C17
Kamenyak, Bulgaria ... 41 C10
Kamenz, Germany ... 24 D10
Kameoka, Japan ... 55 G7
Kamiah, U.S.A. ... 114 C5
Kamień Krajeński, Poland ... 44 E4
Kamień Pomorski, Poland ... 44 E1
Kamienna →, Poland ... 45 G8
Kamienna Góra, Poland ... 45 H3
Kamieńsk, Poland ... 45 G6
Kamieskroon, S. Africa ... 88 E2
Kamilukuak, L., Canada ... 105 A8
Kamin-Kashyrskyy, Ukraine ... 47 G3
Kamina, Dem. Rep. of Congo ... 87 D2
Kaminak L., Canada ... 105 A10
Kaministiquia, Canada ... 102 C1
Kaminka, Ukraine ... 47 H7
Kaminoyama, Japan ... 54 E10
Kamiros, Greece ... 36 C9
Kamituga, Dem. Rep. of the Congo ... 86 C2
Kamla →, India ... 69 G12
Kamloops, Canada ... 104 C4
Kamnik, Slovenia ... 29 B11
Kamo, Armenia ... 49 K7
Kamo, Japan ... 54 F9
Kamoke, Pakistan ... 68 C6
Kamp →, Austria ... 26 C8
Kampala, Uganda ... 86 B3
Kampang Chhnang, Cambodia ... 65 F5
Kampar, Malaysia ... 65 K3
Kampar →, Indonesia ... 62 D2
Kampen, Neths. ... 17 B5
Kampene, Dem. Rep. of the Congo ... 84 E5
Kamphaeng Phet, Thailand ... 64 D2
Kampolombo, L., Zambia ... 87 E2
Kampong Saom, Cambodia ... 65 G4
Kampong Saom, Chaak, Cambodia ... 65 G4
Kampong To, Thailand ... 65 J3
Kampot, Cambodia ... 65 G5
Kampti, Burkina Faso ... 82 C4
Kampuchea = Cambodia ■, Asia ... 64 F5
Kampung Air Putih, Malaysia ... 65 K4
Kampung Jerangau, Malaysia ... 65 K4
Kampung Raja, Malaysia ... 65 K4
Kampungbaru = Tolitoli, Indonesia ... 63 D6
Kamrau, Teluk, Indonesia ... 63 E8
Kamsack, Canada ... 105 C8
Kamsai, Guinea ... 82 C2
Kamskoye Ustye, Russia ... 48 C9
Kamuchawie L., Canada ... 105 B8
Kamui-Misaki, Japan ... 54 C10
Kamyanets-Podilskyy, Ukraine ... 47 H4
Kamyanka-Buzka, Ukraine ... 47 G3
Kamyanka-Dniprovska, Ukraine ... 47 J8
Kāmyārān, Iran ... 70 C5
Kamyshin, Russia ... 48 E7
Kamyzyak, Russia ... 49 G9
Kan, Sudan ... 81 F3
Kanaaupscow, Canada ... 102 B4
Kanaaupscow →, Canada ... 101 C12
Kanab, U.S.A. ... 115 H7
Kanab →, U.S.A. ... 115 H7
Kanagi, Japan ... 54 D10
Kanairiktok →, Canada ... 103 A7
Kanália, Greece ... 38 B4
Kananga, Dem. Rep. of the Congo ... 84 F4
Kanash, Russia ... 48 C8
Kanaskat, U.S.A. ... 116 C5
Kanastraíon, Ákra = Palioúrion, Ákra, Greece ... 40 G7
Kanawha →, U.S.A. ... 108 F4
Kanazawa, Japan ... 55 F8
Kanchanaburi, Thailand ... 64 E2
Kanchenjunga, Nepal ... 69 F13
Kanchipuram, India ... 66 N11
Kańczuga, Poland ... 45 J9
Kandaghat, India ... 68 D7
Kandahar = Qandahār, Afghan. ... 66 D4
Kandalaksha, Russia ... 50 C4

Kandangan, Indonesia ... 62 E5
Kandanghaur, Indonesia ... 63 G13
Kandanos, Greece ... 36 D5
Kandava, Latvia ... 44 A9
Kandavu, Fiji ... 91 D8
Kandhíla, Greece ... 38 D4
Kandhkot, Pakistan ... 68 E3
Kandhla, India ... 68 E7
Kandi, Benin ... 83 C5
Kandi, India ... 69 H13
Kandiaro, Pakistan ... 68 F3
Kandra, Turkey ... 72 B4
Kandla, India ... 68 H4
Kandos, Australia ... 95 E4
Kandreho, Madag. ... 89 B8
Kandy, Sri Lanka ... 66 R12
Kane, U.S.A. ... 110 E6
Kane Basin, Greenland ... 4 B4
Kanel, Senegal ... 82 B2
Kaneohe, U.S.A. ... 106 H16
Kanevskaya, Russia ... 49 G4
Kanfanar, Croatia ... 29 C10
Kang, Botswana ... 88 C3
Kangaba, Mali ... 82 C3
Kangal, Turkey ... 72 C7
Kangān, Fārs, Iran ... 71 E7
Kangān, Hormozgān, Iran ... 71 E8
Kangar, Malaysia ... 65 J3
Kangaré, Mali ... 82 C3
Kangaroo I., Australia ... 95 F2
Kangaroo Mts., Australia ... 94 C3
Kangasala, Finland ... 9 F21
Kangāvar, Iran ... 71 C6
Kangding, China ... 58 B3
Kangdong, N. Korea ... 57 E14
Kangean, Kepulauan, Indonesia ... 62 F5
Kangean Is. = Kangean, Kepulauan, Indonesia ... 62 F5
Kangen →, Sudan ... 81 F3
Kanggye, N. Korea ... 57 D14
Kanggyŏng, S. Korea ... 57 F14
Kanghwa, S. Korea ... 57 F14
Kangikajik, Greenland ... 4 B6
Kangiqsliniq = Rankin Inlet, Canada ... 100 B10
Kangiqsualujjuaq, Canada ... 101 C13
Kangiqsujuaq, Canada ... 101 B12
Kangiqtugaapik = Clyde River, Canada ... 101 A13
Kangirsuk, Canada ... 101 B13
Kangnŭng, S. Korea ... 57 F15
Kangping, China ... 57 C12
Kangra, India ... 68 C7
Kangto, India ... 67 F18
Kanhar →, India ... 69 G10
Kani, Ivory C. ... 82 D3
Kaniama, Dem. Rep. of the Congo ... 86 D1
Kaniapiskau = Caniapiscau →, Canada ... 103 A6
Kaniapiskau, Res. = Caniapiscau, Rés. de, Canada ... 103 B6
Kanin, Poluostrov, Russia ... 50 C5
Kanin Nos, Mys, Russia ... 50 C5
Kanin Pen. = Kanin, Poluostrov, Russia ... 50 C5
Kaninë, Albania ... 40 F3
Kaniva, Australia ... 95 F3
Kanjiža, Serbia, Yug. ... 42 D5
Kanjut Sar, Pakistan ... 69 A6
Kankaanpää, Finland ... 9 F20
Kankakee, U.S.A. ... 108 E2
Kankakee →, U.S.A. ... 108 E1
Kankan, Guinea ... 82 C3
Kankendy = Xankändi, Azerbaijan ... 70 B5
Kanker, India ... 67 J12
Kankossa, Mauritania ... 82 B2
Kankroli, India ... 68 G5
Kannapolis, U.S.A. ... 109 H5
Kannauj, India ... 69 F8
Kannod, India ... 66 H10
Kano, Nigeria ... 83 C6
Kano □, Nigeria ... 83 C6
Kan'onji, Japan ... 55 G6
Kanoroba, Ivory C. ... 82 D3
Kanowit, Malaysia ... 62 D4
Kanoya, Japan ... 55 J5
Kanpetlet, Burma ... 67 J18
Kanpur, India ... 69 F9
Kansas □, U.S.A. ... 112 F6
Kansas →, U.S.A. ... 112 F7
Kansas City, Kans., U.S.A. ... 112 F7
Kansas City, Mo., U.S.A. ... 112 F7
Kansenia, Dem. Rep. of the Congo ... 87 E2
Kansk, Russia ... 51 D10
Kansŏng, S. Korea ... 57 E15
Kansu = Gansu □, China ... 56 G3
Kantaphor, India ... 68 H7
Kantchari, Burkina Faso ... 83 C5
Kanté, Togo ... 83 D5
Kantharalak, Thailand ... 64 E5
Kantli →, India ... 68 E6
Kantō □, Japan ... 55 F9
Kantō-Sanchi, Japan ... 55 G9
Kanturk, Ireland ... 15 D3
Kanuma, Japan ... 55 F9
Kanus, Namibia ... 88 D2
Kanye, Botswana ... 88 C4
Kanzenze, Dem. Rep. of the Congo ... 87 E2
Kanzi, Ras, Tanzania ... 86 D4
Kaohsiung, Taiwan ... 59 F13
Kaokoveld, Namibia ... 88 B1

Kaolack, Senegal ... 82 C1
Kaoshan, China ... 57 B13
Kapaa, U.S.A. ... 106 G15
Kapadvanj, India ... 68 H5
Kapaklı, Turkey ... 41 E11
Kapan, Armenia ... 70 B5
Kapanga, Dem. Rep. of the Congo ... 84 F4
Kapchagai = Qapshaghay, Kazakstan ... 50 E8
Kapela = Velika Kapela, Croatia ... 29 C12
Kapéllo, Ákra, Greece ... 38 E5
Kapema, Dem. Rep. of the Congo ... 87 E2
Kapfenberg, Austria ... 26 D8
Kapı Dağı, Turkey ... 41 F11
Kapiri Mposhi, Zambia ... 87 E2
Kāpīsā □, Afghan. ... 66 B6
Kapiskau →, Canada ... 102 B3
Kapit, Malaysia ... 62 D4
Kapiti I., N.Z. ... 91 J5
Kaplan, U.S.A. ... 113 K8
Kaplice, Czech Rep. ... 26 C7
Kapoe, Thailand ... 65 H2
Kapoeta, Sudan ... 81 G3
Kápolnásnyék, Hungary ... 42 C3
Kapos →, Hungary ... 42 D3
Kaposvár, Hungary ... 42 D2
Kapowsin, U.S.A. ... 116 D4
Kappeln, Germany ... 24 A5
Kappelshamn, Sweden ... 11 G12
Kapps, Namibia ... 88 C2
Kaprije, Croatia ... 29 E12
Kapsan, N. Korea ... 57 D15
Kapsukas = Marijampolė, Lithuania ... 9 J20
Kapuas →, Indonesia ... 62 E3
Kapuas Hulu, Pegunungan, Malaysia ... 62 D4
Kapuas Hulu Ra. = Kapuas Hulu, Pegunungan, Malaysia ... 62 D4
Kapulo, Dem. Rep. of the Congo ... 87 D2
Kapunda, Australia ... 95 E2
Kapuni, N.Z. ... 91 H5
Kapurthala, India ... 68 D6
Kapuskasing, Canada ... 102 C3
Kapuskasing →, Canada ... 102 C3
Kapustin Yar, Russia ... 49 F7
Kaputar, Australia ... 95 E5
Kaputir, Kenya ... 86 B4
Kapuvár, Hungary ... 42 C2
Kara, Russia ... 50 C7
Karā, W. →, Si. Arabia ... 80 C5
Kara Ada, Turkey ... 39 E9
Kara Bogaz Gol, Zaliv = Garabogazköl Aylagy, Turkmenistan ... 50 E6
Kara Burun, Turkey ... 39 E9
Kara Kalpak Republic = Qoraqalpoghistan □, Uzbekistan ... 50 E6
Kara Kum, Turkmenistan ... 50 F6
Kara Sea, Russia ... 50 B7
Karaadilli, Turkey ... 41 C12
Karabiğa, Turkey ... 41 F11
Karabük, Turkey ... 72 B5
Karaburun, Albania ... 40 F3
Karaburun, Turkey ... 39 C8
Karabutak = Qarabutaq, Kazakstan ... 50 E7
Karacabey, Turkey ... 41 F12
Karacakılavuz, Turkey ... 41 E11
Karacaköy, Turkey ... 41 E12
Karacasu, Turkey ... 39 D10
Karachala = Qaraçala, Azerbaijan ... 49 L9
Karachayevsk, Russia ... 49 J5
Karachev, Russia ... 47 F8
Karachey-Cherkessia □, Russia ... 49 J5
Karachi, Pakistan ... 68 G2
Karad, India ... 66 L9
Karadirek, Turkey ... 39 C12
Karaga, Ghana ... 83 D4
Karaganda = Qaraghandy, Kazakstan ... 50 E8
Karagayly, Kazakstan ... 50 E8
Karaginskiy, Ostrov, Russia ... 51 D17
Karagola Road, India ... 69 G12
Karagüney Dağları, Turkey ... 72 B6
Karahallı, Turkey ... 39 C11
Karaikal, India ... 66 P11
Karaikkudi, India ... 66 P11
Karaisalı, Turkey ... 72 D6
Karaj, Iran ... 71 C6
Karak, Malaysia ... 65 L4
Karakalpakstan = Qoraqalpoghistan □, Uzbekistan ... 50 E6
Karakelong, Indonesia ... 63 D7
Karakitang, Indonesia ... 63 D7
Karaklis = Vanadzor, Armenia ... 49 K7
Karakoçan, Turkey ... 73 C8
Karakol, Kyrgyzstan ... 50 E8
Karakoram Ra., Pakistan ... 69 B7
Karakoram Pass, Pakistan ... 69 B7
Karakuwisa, Namibia ... 88 B2
Karalon, Russia ... 51 D12
Karaman, Balıkesir, Turkey ... 39 B9
Karaman, Konya, Turkey ... 70 B2
Karaman □, Turkey ... 39 D11
Karamay, China ... 60 B3
Karambu, Indonesia ... 62 E5
Karamea Bight, N.Z. ... 91 J3
Karamnasa →, India ... 69 G10
Karamürsel, Turkey ... 41 F13

Karand, *Iran* 70 C5
Karangana, *Mali* 82 C3
Karanganyar, *Indonesia* 63 G13
Karanjia, *India* 69 J11
Karankasso, *Burkina Faso* 82 C4
Karaova, *Turkey* 39 D9
Karapınar, *Turkey* 72 D5
Karasburg, *Namibia* 88 D2
Karasino, *Russia* 50 C9
Karasjok, *Norway* 8 B21
Karasu, *Turkey* 72 B4
Karasu →, *Turkey* 39 E12
Karasuk, *Russia* 50 D8
Karasuyama, *Japan* 55 F10
Karataş, *Adana, Turkey* 72 D6
Karataş, *Manisa, Turkey* 39 C10
Karataş Burnu, *Turkey* 72 D6
Karatau, Khrebet = Qarataŭ,
  Kazakhstan 50 E7
Karatoprak, *Turkey* 39 D9
Karatsu, *Japan* 55 H5
Karaul, *Russia* 50 B9
Karauli, *India* 68 F7
Karavastasë, L. e, *Albania* .. 40 F3
Karávi, *Greece* 38 E5
Karavostasi, *Cyprus* 36 D11
Karawang, *Indonesia* 63 G12
Karawanken, *Europe* 26 E7
Karayazı, *Turkey* 73 C10
Karazhal, *Kazakhstan* 50 E8
Karbalā', *Iraq* 70 C5
Kårböle, *Sweden* 10 C9
Karcag, *Hungary* 42 C5
Karcha →, *Pakistan* 69 B7
Karchana, *India* 69 G9
Karczew, *Poland* 45 F8
Kardam, *Bulgaria* 41 C12
Kardeljevo = Ploče, *Croatia* .. 29 E14
Kardhámila, *Greece* 39 C8
Kardhítsa, *Greece* 38 B3
Kardhítsa □, *Greece* 38 B3
Kärdla, *Estonia* 9 G20
Kareeberge, *S. Africa* 88 E3
Kareha →, *India* 69 G12
Kareima, *Sudan* 80 D3
Karelia □, *Russia* 50 C4
Karelian Republic = Karelia □,
  Russia 50 C4
Karera, *India* 68 G8
Kārevāndar, *Iran* 71 E9
Kargasok, *Russia* 50 D9
Kargat, *Russia* 50 D9
Kargı, *Turkey* 72 B6
Kargil, *India* 69 B7
Kargopol, *Russia* 46 B10
Kargowa, *Poland* 45 F2
Karguéri, *Niger* 83 C7
Karhal, *India* 69 F8
Kariá, *Greece* 38 C2
Kariaí, *Greece* 41 F8
Karīān, *Iran* 71 E8
Karianga, *Madag.* 89 C8
Kariba, *Zimbabwe* 87 F2
Kariba, L., *Zimbabwe* 87 F2
Kariba Dam, *Zimbabwe* 87 F2
Kariba Gorge, *Zambia* 87 F2
Karibib, *Namibia* 88 C2
Karimata, Kepulauan, *Indonesia* 62 E3
Karimata, Selat, *Indonesia* .. 62 E3
Karimata Is. = Karimata,
  Kepulauan, *Indonesia* 62 E3
Karimnagar, *India* 66 K11
Karimunjawa, Kepulauan,
  Indonesia 62 F4
Karin, *Somali Rep.* 74 E4
Káristos, *Greece* 38 C6
Karīt, *Iran* 71 C8
Kariya, *Japan* 55 G8
Kariyangwe, *Zimbabwe* 89 B4
Karjala, *Finland* 46 A5
Karkaralinsk = Qarqaraly,
  Kazakstan 50 E8
Karkheh →, *Iran* 70 D5
Karkinitska Zatoka, *Ukraine* . 47 K7
Karkinitskiy Zaliv = Karkinitska
  Zatoka, *Ukraine* 47 K7
Karkur Tohl, *Egypt* 80 C2
Karl Liebknecht, *Russia* 47 G8
Karl-Marx-Stadt = Chemnitz,
  Germany 24 E8
Karlholmsbruk, *Sweden* 10 D11
Karlino, *Poland* 44 D2
Karlivka, *Ukraine* 47 H8
Karlobag, *Croatia* 29 D12
Karlovac, *Croatia* 29 C12
Karlovarský □, *Czech Rep.* ... 26 A5
Karlovka = Karlivka, *Ukraine* . 47 H8
Karlovo, *Bulgaria* 41 D8
Karlovy Vary, *Czech Rep.* 26 A5
Karlsbad = Karlovy Vary,
  Czech Rep. 26 A5
Karlsborg, *Sweden* 11 F8
Karlshamn, *Sweden* 11 H8
Karlskoga, *Sweden* 10 E8
Karlskrona, *Sweden* 11 H9
Karlsruhe, *Germany* 25 F4
Karlstad, *Sweden* 10 E7
Karlstad, *U.S.A.* 112 A6
Karlstadt, *Germany* 25 F5
Karma, *Niger* 83 C5
Karmėlava, *Lithuania* 44 D11
Karmi'el, *Israel* 75 C4
Karnak, *Egypt* 79 C12
Karnal, *India* 68 E7
Karnali →, *Nepal* 69 E9
Karnaphuli Res., *Bangla.* 67 H18

Karnaprayag, *India* 69 D8
Karnataka □, *India* 66 N10
Karnes City, *U.S.A.* 113 L6
Karnische Alpen, *Europe* 26 E6
Karnobat, *Bulgaria* 41 D10
Kärnten □, *Austria* 26 E6
Karo, *Mali* 82 C4
Karoi, *Zimbabwe* 87 F2
Karonga, *Malawi* 87 D3
Karoonda, *Australia* 95 F2
Karor, *Pakistan* 68 D4
Karora, *Sudan* 80 D4
Káros, *Greece* 39 E7
Karounga, *Mali* 82 B3
Karousádhes, *Greece* 38 B1
Karpacz, *Poland* 45 H2
Karpasia □, *Cyprus* 36 D13
Kárpathos, *Greece* 39 F9
Kárpathos, Stenón, *Greece* ... 39 F9
Karpenísion, *Greece* 38 C3
Karpuz Burnu = Apostolos
  Andreas, C., *Cyprus* 36 D13
Karpuzlu, *Turkey* 39 D9
Karratha, *Australia* 92 D2
Kars, *Turkey* 73 B10
Karsakpay, *Kazakhstan* 50 E7
Karsha, *Kazakhstan* 48 F10
Karshi = Qarshi, *Uzbekistan* . 50 F7
Karsiyang, *India* 69 F13
Karsog, *India* 68 D7
Karst = Kras, *Croatia* 29 C10
Kartal, *Turkey* 41 F13
Kartál Óros, *Greece* 41 E9
Kartaly, *Russia* 50 D7
Kartapur, *India* 68 D6
Karthaus, *U.S.A.* 110 E6
Kartuzy, *Poland* 44 D5
Karufa, *Indonesia* 63 E8
Karumba, *Australia* 94 B3
Karumo, *Tanzania* 86 C3
Karumwa, *Tanzania* 86 C3
Kārūn →, *Iran* 71 D6
Karungu, *Kenya* 86 C3
Karup, *Denmark* 11 H3
Karviná, *Czech Rep.* 27 B11
Karwan →, *India* 68 F8
Karwar, *India* 66 M9
Karwi, *India* 69 G9
Kaş, *Turkey* 39 E11
Kasaba, *Turkey* 39 E11
Kasache, *Malawi* 87 E3
Kasai →, *Dem. Rep. of
  the Congo* 84 E3
Kasaï-Oriental □, *Dem. Rep. of
  the Congo* 86 D1
Kasaji, *Dem. Rep. of the Congo* 87 E1
Kasama, *Zambia* 87 E3
Kasan-dong, *N. Korea* 57 D14
Kasane, *Namibia* 88 B3
Kasanga, *Tanzania* 87 D3
Kasar, Ras, *Sudan* 80 D4
Kasaragod, *India* 66 N9
Kasba L., *Canada* 105 A8
Kāseh Garān, *Iran* 70 C5
Kasempa, *Zambia* 87 E2
Kasenga, *Dem. Rep. of
  the Congo* 87 E2
Kasese, *Uganda* 86 B3
Kasewa, *Zambia* 87 E2
Kasganj, *India* 69 F8
Kashabowie, *Canada* 102 C1
Kashaf, *Iran* 71 C9
Kāshān, *Iran* 71 C6
Kashechewan, *Canada* 102 B3
Kashgar = Kashi, *China* 60 C2
Kashi, *China* 60 C2
Kashimbo, *Dem. Rep. of
  the Congo* 87 E2
Kashin, *Russia* 46 D9
Kashipur, *India* 69 E8
Kashira, *Russia* 46 E10
Kashiwazaki, *Japan* 55 F9
Kashk-e Kohneh, *Afghan.* 66 B3
Kashkū'īyeh, *Iran* 71 D7
Kāshmar, *Iran* 71 C8
Kashmir, *Asia* 69 C7
Kashmor, *Pakistan* 68 E3
Kashpirovka, *Russia* 48 D9
Kashun Noerh = Gaxun Nur,
  China 60 B5
Kasiari, *India* 69 H12
Kasimov, *Russia* 48 C5
Kasinge, *Dem. Rep. of the Congo* 86 D2
Kasiruta, *Indonesia* 63 E7
Kaskaskia →, *U.S.A.* 112 G10
Kaskattama →, *Canada* 105 B10
Kaskinen, *Finland* 9 E19
Kaslo, *Canada* 104 D5
Kasmere L., *Canada* 105 B8
Kasongo, *Dem. Rep. of
  the Congo* 86 C2
Kasongo Lunda, *Dem. Rep. of
  the Congo* 84 F3
Kásos, *Greece* 39 F8
Kásos, Stenón, *Greece* 39 F8
Kaspi, *Georgia* 49 K7
Kaspichan, *Bulgaria* 41 C11
Kaspiysk, *Russia* 49 J8
Kaspiyskiy, *Russia* 49 H8
Kassab ed Doleib, *Sudan* 81 E3
Kassaba, *Egypt* 80 C2
Kassalâ, *Sudan* 81 D4
Kassalâ □, *Sudan* 81 D4
Kassándra, *Greece* 40 F7
Kassándrinon, *Greece* 40 F7
Kassel, *Germany* 24 D5
Kassinger, *Sudan* 80 D3

Kassiópi, *Greece* 36 A3
Kasson, *U.S.A.* 112 C8
Kastamonu, *Turkey* 72 B5
Kastav, *Croatia* 29 C11
Kastélli, *Greece* 36 D5
Kastéllion, *Greece* 36 D7
Kastellórizon = Megiste, *Greece* 39 E11
Kastéllos, *Greece* 39 E9
Kastellou, Ákra, *Greece* 39 F9
Kasterlee, *Belgium* 17 C4
Kastóri, *Greece* 38 D4
Kastoría, *Greece* 40 F5
Kastoría □, *Greece* 40 F5
Kastorías, Límni, *Greece* 40 F5
Kastornoye, *Russia* 47 G10
Kastrosikiá, *Greece* 38 B2
Kastsyukovichy, *Belarus* 46 F7
Kasulu, *Tanzania* 86 C3
Kasumi, *Japan* 55 G7
Kasumkent, *Russia* 49 K9
Kasungu, *Malawi* 87 E3
Kasur, *Pakistan* 68 D6
Kataba, *Zambia* 87 F2
Katagum, *Nigeria* 83 C7
Katahdin, Mt., *U.S.A.* 109 C11
Katako Kombe, *Dem. Rep. of
  the Congo* 86 C1
Katákolon, *Greece* 38 D3
Katale, *Tanzania* 86 C3
Katanda, Katanga, *Dem. Rep. of
  the Congo* 86 D1
Katanda, Nord-Kivu, *Dem. Rep.
  of the Congo* 86 C2
Katanga □, *Dem. Rep. of
  the Congo* 86 D2
Katangi, *India* 66 J11
Katanning, *Australia* 93 F2
Katastári, *Greece* 38 D2
Katavi Swamp, *Tanzania* 86 D3
Kateríni, *Greece* 40 F6
Katghora, *India* 69 H10
Katha, *Burma* 67 G20
Katherîna, Gebel, *Egypt* 70 D2
Katherine, *Australia* 92 B5
Katherine Gorge, *Australia* .. 92 B5
Kathi, *India* 68 J6
Kathiawar, *India* 68 H4
Kathikas, *Cyprus* 36 E11
Kathua, *India* 68 C6
Kati, *Mali* 82 C3
Katihar, *India* 69 G12
Katima Mulilo, *Zambia* 88 B3
Katimbira, *Malawi* 87 E3
Katingan = Mendawai →,
  Indonesia 62 E4
Katiola, *Ivory C.* 82 D3
Katlanovo, *Macedonia* 40 E5
Katmandu, *Nepal* 69 F11
Katni, *India* 69 H9
Káto Akhaïa, *Greece* 38 C3
Káto Arkhánai, *Greece* 36 D7
Káto Khorió, *Greece* 36 D7
Káto Pyrgos, *Cyprus* 36 D11
Káto Stavros, *Greece* 40 F7
Katokhí, *Greece* 38 C3
Katompe, *Dem. Rep. of
  the Congo* 86 D2
Katonga →, *Uganda* 86 B3
Katoomba, *Australia* 95 E5
Katowice, *Poland* 38 C3
Katowice, *Poland* 45 H6
Katrancı Dağı, *Turkey* 39 D12
Katrine, L., *U.K.* 14 E4
Katrineholm, *Sweden* 11 E10
Katsepe, *Madag.* 89 B8
Katsina, *Nigeria* 83 C6
Katsina □, *Nigeria* 83 C6
Katsina Ala, *Nigeria* 83 D6
Katsina Ala →, *Nigeria* 83 D6
Katsumoto, *Japan* 55 H4
Katsuura, *Japan* 55 G10
Katsuyama, *Japan* 55 F8
Kattaviá, *Greece* 36 D9
Kattegat, *Denmark* 11 H5
Katthammarsvik, *Sweden* 11 G12
Katul, J., *Sudan* 81 E2
Katumba, *Dem. Rep. of
  the Congo* 86 D2
Katungu, *Kenya* 86 C5
Katwa, *India* 69 H13
Katwijk, *Neths.* 17 B4
Kąty Wrocławskie, *Poland* ... 45 G3
Kauai, *U.S.A.* 106 H15
Kauai Channel, *U.S.A.* 106 H15
Kaub, *Germany* 25 E3
Kaufbeuren, *Germany* 25 H6
Kaufman, *U.S.A.* 113 J6
Kauhajoki, *Finland* 9 E20
Kaukauna, *U.S.A.* 108 C1
Kaukauveld, *Namibia* 88 C3
Kaunakakai, *U.S.A.* 106 H16
Kaunas, *Lithuania* 9 J20
Kaunia, *Bangla.* 69 G13
Kaunos, *Turkey* 39 E10
Kaura Namoda, *Nigeria* 83 C6
Kauru, *Nigeria* 83 C6
Kautokeino, *Norway* 8 B20
Kauwapur, *India* 69 F10
Kavacha, *Russia* 51 C17
Kavadarci, *Macedonia* 40 E6
Kavajë, *Albania* 40 E3
Kavak, *Turkey* 72 B7
Kavak Dağı, *Turkey* 39 D10
Kavaklı, *Turkey* 41 E11
Kavaklıdere, *Turkey* 39 D10

Kavalerovo, *Russia* 54 B7
Kavali, *India* 66 M12
Kavála, *Greece* 41 F8
Kavála □, *Greece* 41 E8
Kavála Kólpos, *Greece* 41 F8
Kavār, *Iran* 71 D7
Kavarna, *Bulgaria* 41 C12
Kavi, *India* 68 H5
Kavimba, *Botswana* 88 B3
Kavīr, Dasht-e, *Iran* 71 C7
Kavkaz, *Russia* 47 K9
Kävlinge, *Sweden* 11 J7
Kavos, *Greece* 36 B4
Kavoúsi, *Greece* 39 F7
Kaw, Fr. Guiana 125 C8
Kawa, *Sudan* 81 E3
Kawagama L., *Canada* 110 A6
Kawagoe, *Japan* 55 G9
Kawaguchi, *Japan* 55 G9
Kawambwa, *Zambia* 87 D2
Kawanoe, *Japan* 55 G6
Kawardha, *India* 69 J9
Kawasaki, *Japan* 55 G9
Kawasi, *Indonesia* 63 E7
Kawerau, *N.Z.* 91 H6
Kawhia Harbour, *N.Z.* 91 H5
Kawio, Kepulauan, *Indonesia* . 63 D7
Kawnro, *Burma* 67 H21
Kawthaung, *Burma* 65 H2
Kawthoolei = Kayin □, *Burma* . 67 L20
Kawthule = Kayin □, *Burma* .. 67 L20
Kaxholmen, *Sweden* 11 G8
Kaya, *Burkina Faso* 83 C4
Kayah □, *Burma* 67 K20
Kayalıköy Barajı, *Turkey* ... 41 E11
Kayan →, *Indonesia* 62 D5
Kaycee, *U.S.A.* 114 E10
Kayeli, *Indonesia* 63 E7
Kayenta, *U.S.A.* 115 H8
Kayes, *Mali* 82 C2
Kayı, *Turkey* 39 B12
Kayima, *S. Leone* 82 D2
Kayin □, *Burma* 67 L20
Kaymakçı, *Turkey* 39 C10
Kayoa, *Indonesia* 63 D7
Kayomba, *Zambia* 87 E1
Kaysatskoye, *Russia* 48 F8
Kayseri, *Turkey* 70 B2
Kaysville, *U.S.A.* 114 F8
Kaz Dağı, *Turkey* 39 B8
Kazachye, *Russia* 51 B14
Kazakstan ■, *Asia* 50 E7
Kazan, *Russia* 48 C9
Kazan →, *Canada* 105 A9
Kazan-Rettō, *Pac. Oc.* 96 E6
Kazanlŭk, *Bulgaria* 41 D9
Kazanskaya, *Russia* 48 F5
Kazatin = Kozyatyn, *Ukraine* . 47 H5
Kazaure, *Nigeria* 83 C6
Kazbek, *Russia* 49 J7
Kāzerūn, *Iran* 71 D6
Kazi Magomed = Qazimämmäd,
  Azerbaijan 49 K9
Kazimierz Dolny, *Poland* 45 G8
Kazimierza Wielka, *Poland* .. 45 H7
Kazincbarcika, *Hungary* 42 B5
Kazlu Rūda, *Lithuania* 44 D10
Kaztalovka, *Kazakstan* 48 F9
Kazuno, *Japan* 54 D10
Kazym →, *Russia* 50 C7
Kcynia, *Poland* 45 F4
Ké-Macina, *Mali* 82 C3
Kéa, *Greece* 38 D6
Keady, *U.K.* 15 B5
Kearney, *U.S.A.* 112 E5
Kearny, *U.S.A.* 115 K8
Kearsarge, Mt., *U.S.A.* 111 C13
Keban, *Turkey* 73 C8
Keban Baraji, *Turkey* 70 B3
Kebbi □, *Nigeria* 83 C5
Kébi, *Ivory C.* 82 D3
Kebnekaise, *Sweden* 8 C18
Kebri Dehar, *Ethiopia* 74 F3
Kebumen, *Indonesia* 63 G13
Kecel, *Hungary* 42 D4
Kechika →, *Canada* 104 B3
Keçiborlu, *Turkey* 39 D12
Kecskemét, *Hungary* 42 D4
Kedada, *Ethiopia* 81 F4
Kédainiai, *Lithuania* 9 J21
Kedarnath, *India* 69 D8
Kedgwick, *Canada* 103 C6
Kédhros Óros, *Greece* 36 D6
Kediri, *Indonesia* 62 F4
Kedjebi, *Ghana* 83 D5
Kédougou, *Senegal* 82 C2
Kędzierzyn-Koźle, *Poland* ... 45 H5
Keeler, *U.S.A.* 116 J9
Keeley L., *Canada* 105 C7
Keeling Is. = Cocos Is., *Ind. Oc.* 96 J1
Keelung = Chilung, *Taiwan* .. 59 E13
Keene, *Canada* 110 B6
Keene, Calif., *U.S.A.* 117 K8
Keene, N.H., *U.S.A.* 111 D12
Keene, N.Y., *U.S.A.* 111 B11
Keeper Hill, *Ireland* 15 D3
Keer-Weer, C., *Australia* ... 94 A3
Keeseville, *U.S.A.* 111 B11
Keetmanshoop, *Namibia* 88 D2
Keewatin →, *Canada* 105 D10
Keewatin →, *Canada* 105 B8
Kefa □, *Ethiopia* 81 F4
Kefallinía □, *Greece* 38 C2
Kéfalos, *Greece* 39 E8
Kefamenanu, *Indonesia* 63 F6
Kefar Sava, *Israel* 75 C3

Keffi, *Nigeria* 83 D6
Keffin Hausa, *Nigeria* 83 C6
Keflavík, *Iceland* 8 D2
Keg River, *Canada* 104 B5
Kegaska, *Canada* 103 B7
Keheili, *Sudan* 80 D3
Kehl, *Germany* 25 G3
Keighley, *U.K.* 12 D6
Keila, *Estonia* 9 G21
Keimoes, *S. Africa* 88 D3
Keita, *Niger* 83 C6
Keitele, *Finland* 8 E22
Keith, *Australia* 95 F3
Keith, *U.K.* 14 D6
Keizer, *U.S.A.* 114 D2
Kejimkujik Nat. Park, *Canada* . 103 D6
Kejserr Franz Joseph Fd.,
  Greenland 4 B6
Kekri, *India* 68 G6
Kelam, *Ethiopia* 81 G4
Kelamet, *Eritrea* 81 D4
Kelan, *China* 56 E6
Kelang, *Malaysia* 65 L3
Kelang →, *Malaysia* 65 J4
Këlcyrë, *Albania* 40 F4
Kelekçi, *Turkey* 39 D11
Keles, *Turkey* 41 G13
Keleti-főcsatorna, *Hungary* .. 42 C6
Kelheim, *Germany* 25 G7
Kelkit, *Turkey* 73 B8
Kelkit →, *Turkey* 72 B7
Kellerberrin, *Australia* 93 F2
Kellett, C., *Canada* 4 B1
Kelleys I., *U.S.A.* 110 E2
Kellogg, *U.S.A.* 114 C5
Kells = Ceanannus Mor, *Ireland* 15 C5
Kelmė, *Lithuania* 44 C9
Kelokedhara, *Cyprus* 36 E11
Kelowna, *Canada* 104 D5
Kelseyville, *U.S.A.* 116 G4
Kelso, *N.Z.* 91 L2
Kelso, *U.K.* 14 F6
Kelso, *U.S.A.* 116 D4
Keluang, *Malaysia* 65 L4
Kelvington, *Canada* 105 C8
Kem, *Russia* 50 C4
Kema, *Indonesia* 63 D7
Kemah, *Turkey* 70 B3
Kemaliye, Erzincan, *Turkey* .. 73 C8
Kemaliye, Manisa, *Turkey* ... 39 C10
Kemalpaşa, *Turkey* 39 C9
Kemamman, *Malaysia* 62 D2
Kemano, *Canada* 104 C3
Kemasik, *Malaysia* 65 K4
Kembolcha, *Ethiopia* 81 E4
Kemer, Antalya, *Turkey* 39 E12
Kemer, Burdur, *Turkey* 39 D12
Kemer, Muğla, *Turkey* 39 E11
Kemer Barajı, *Turkey* 39 D10
Kemerovo, *Russia* 50 D9
Kemi, *Finland* 8 D21
Kemi älv = Kemijoki →, *Finland* 8 D21
Kemijärvi, *Finland* 8 C22
Kemijoki →, *Finland* 8 D21
Kemmerer, *U.S.A.* 114 F8
Kemmuna = Comino, *Malta* ... 36 C1
Kemp, L., *U.S.A.* 113 J5
Kemp Land, *Antarctica* 5 C5
Kempsey, *Australia* 95 E5
Kempt, L., *Canada* 102 C5
Kempten, *Germany* 25 H6
Kempton, *Australia* 94 G4
Kemptville, *Canada* 102 D4
Ken →, *India* 69 G9
Kenai, *U.S.A.* 100 B4
Kenamuke Swamp, *Sudan* 81 F3
Kendai, *India* 69 H10
Kendal, *Indonesia* 63 G14
Kendal, *U.K.* 12 C5
Kendall, *Australia* 95 E5
Kendall, *U.S.A.* 109 N5
Kendall →, *Australia* 94 A3
Kendallville, *U.S.A.* 108 E3
Kendari, *Indonesia* 63 E6
Kendawangan, *Indonesia* 62 E4
Kendrapara, *India* 67 J15
Kendrew, *S. Africa* 88 E3
Kene Thao, *Laos* 64 D3
Kenedy, *U.S.A.* 113 L6
Kenema, *S. Leone* 82 D2
Keng Kok, *Laos* 64 D5
Keng Tawng, *Burma* 67 J21
Keng Tung, *Burma* 58 G2
Kengeja, *Tanzania* 86 D4
Kenhardt, *S. Africa* 88 D3
Kéniéba, *Mali* 82 C2
Kenitra, *Morocco* 78 B4
Kenli, *China* 57 F10
Kenmare, *Ireland* 15 E2
Kenmare, *U.S.A.* 112 A3
Kenmare River, *Ireland* 15 E2
Kennebago Lake, *U.S.A.* 111 A14
Kennebec, *U.S.A.* 112 D5
Kennebec →, *U.S.A.* 109 D11
Kennebunk, *U.S.A.* 111 C14
Kennedy, *Zimbabwe* 88 B4
Kennedy Ra., *Australia* 93 D2
Kennedy Taungdeik, *Burma* .. 67 H18
Kennet →, *U.K.* 13 F7
Kenneth Ra., *Australia* 93 D2
Kennett, *U.S.A.* 113 G9
Kennewick, *U.S.A.* 114 C4
Kenogami →, *Canada* 102 B3
Kenora, *Canada* 105 D10

Kenosha, *U.S.A.*	108	D2
Kensington, *Canada*	103	C7
Kent, *Ohio, U.S.A.*	110	E3
Kent, *Tex., U.S.A.*	113	K2
Kent, *Wash., U.S.A.*	116	C4
Kent □, *U.K.*	13	F8
Kent Group, *Australia*	94	F4
Kent Pen., *Canada*	100	B9
Kentaū, *Kazakstan*	50	E7
Kentland, *U.S.A.*	108	E2
Kenton, *U.S.A.*	108	E4
Kentucky □, *U.S.A.*	108	G3
Kentucky ➤, *U.S.A.*	108	F3
Kentucky L., *U.S.A.*	109	G2
Kentville, *Canada*	103	C7
Kentwood, *U.S.A.*	113	K9
Kenya ■, *Africa*	86	B4
Kenya, Mt., *Kenya*	86	C4
Keo Neua, Deo, *Vietnam*	64	C5
Keokuk, *U.S.A.*	112	E9
Keonjhargarh, *India*	69	J11
Kep, *Cambodia*	65	G5
Kep, *Vietnam*	64	B6
Kepez, *Turkey*	41	F10
Kepi, *Indonesia*	63	F9
Kępice, *Poland*	44	D3
Kępno, *Poland*	45	G4
Kepsut, *Turkey*	39	B10
Kerala □, *India*	66	P10
Kerama-Rettō, *Japan*	55	L3
Keran, *Pakistan*	69	B5
Kerang, *Australia*	95	F3
Keranyo, *Ethiopia*	81	F4
Kerao ➤, *Sudan*	81	E3
Keratéa, *Greece*	38	D5
Keraudren, C., *Australia*	92	C2
Kerava, *Finland*	9	F21
Kerch, *Ukraine*	47	K9
Kerchenskiy Proliv, *Black Sea*	47	K9
Kerchoual, *Mali*	83	B5
Kerempe Burnu, *Turkey*	72	A5
Keren, *Eritrea*	81	D4
Kerewan, *Gambia*	82	C1
Kerguelen, *Ind. Oc.*	3	G13
Keri, *Greece*	38	D2
Keri Kera, *Sudan*	81	E3
Kericho, *Kenya*	86	C4
Kerinci, *Indonesia*	62	E2
Kerki, *Turkmenistan*	50	F7
Kerkinítis, Límni, *Greece*	40	E7
Kérkira, *Greece*	36	A3
Kérkira □, *Greece*	38	B1
Kerkrade, *Neths.*	17	D6
Kerma, *Sudan*	80	D3
Kermadec Is., *Pac. Oc.*	96	L10
Kermadec Trench, *Pac. Oc.*	96	L10
Kermān, *Iran*	71	D8
Kerman, *U.S.A.*	116	J6
Kermān □, *Iran*	71	D8
Kermān, Bīābān-e, *Iran*	71	D8
Kermānshāh = Bākhtarān, *Iran*	70	C5
Kermen, *Bulgaria*	41	D10
Kermit, *U.S.A.*	113	K3
Kern ➤, *U.S.A.*	117	K7
Kernhof, *Austria*	26	D8
Kernow = Cornwall □, *U.K.*	13	G3
Kernville, *U.S.A.*	117	K8
Keroh, *Malaysia*	65	K3
Kérou, *Benin*	83	C5
Kérouane, *Guinea*	82	D3
Kerpen, *Germany*	24	E2
Kerrera, *U.K.*	14	E3
Kerrobert, *Canada*	105	C7
Kerrville, *U.S.A.*	113	K5
Kerry □, *Ireland*	15	D2
Kerry Hd., *Ireland*	15	D2
Kersa, *Ethiopia*	81	F5
Kerulen ➤, *Asia*	60	B6
Kerzaz, *Algeria*	78	C5
Kesagami ➤, *Canada*	102	B3
Kesagami L., *Canada*	102	B3
Keşan, *Turkey*	41	F10
Kesennuma, *Japan*	54	E10
Keshit, *Iran*	71	D8
Keşiş Dağ, *Turkey*	73	C8
Keskin, *Turkey*	72	C5
Kestell, *S. Africa*	89	D4
Kestenga, *Russia*	50	C4
Keswick, *U.K.*	12	C4
Keszthely, *Hungary*	42	D2
Ket ➤, *Russia*	50	D9
Keta, *Ghana*	83	D5
Keta Lagoon, *Ghana*	83	D5
Ketapang, *Indonesia*	62	E4
Ketchikan, *U.S.A.*	104	B2
Ketchum, *U.S.A.*	114	E6
Kete Krachi, *Ghana*	83	D4
Ketef, Khalîg Umm el, *Egypt*	70	F2
Keti Bandar, *Pakistan*	68	G2
Kétou, *Benin*	83	D5
Ketri, *India*	68	E6
Kętrzyn, *Poland*	44	D8
Kettering, *U.K.*	13	E7
Kettle ➤, *Canada*	105	B11
Kettle Falls, *U.S.A.*	114	B4
Kettle Pt., *Canada*	110	C2
Kettleman City, *U.S.A.*	116	J7
Kęty, *Poland*	45	J6
Keuka L., *U.S.A.*	110	D7
Keuruu, *Finland*	9	E21
Kevelaer, *Germany*	24	D2
Kewanee, *U.S.A.*	112	E10
Kewaunee, *U.S.A.*	108	C2
Keweenaw B., *U.S.A.*	108	B1
Keweenaw Pen., *U.S.A.*	108	B2
Keweenaw Pt., *U.S.A.*	108	B2
Key Largo, *U.S.A.*	109	N5
Key West, *U.S.A.*	107	F10
Keyala, *Sudan*	81	G3
Keynsham, *U.K.*	13	F5
Keyser, *U.S.A.*	108	F6
Kezhma, *Russia*	51	D11
Kezi, *Zimbabwe*	89	C4
Kežmarok, *Slovak Rep.*	27	B13
Khabarovsk, *Russia*	51	E14
Khabr, *Iran*	71	D8
Khābūr ➤, *Syria*	70	C4
Khachmas = Xaçmaz, *Azerbaijan*	49	K9
Khachrod, *India*	68	H6
Khadari, W. el ➤, *Sudan*	81	E2
Khadro, *Pakistan*	68	F3
Khadyzhensk, *Russia*	49	H4
Khadzhilyangar, *India*	69	B8
Khaga, *India*	69	G9
Khagaria, *India*	69	G12
Khaipur, *Pakistan*	68	E5
Khair, *India*	68	F7
Khairabad, *India*	69	F9
Khairagarh, *India*	69	J9
Khairpur, *Pakistan*	68	F3
Khairpur Nathan Shah, *Pakistan*	68	F2
Khairwara, *India*	68	H5
Khaisor ➤, *Pakistan*	68	D3
Khajuri Kach, *Pakistan*	68	C3
Khakassia □, *Russia*	50	D9
Khakhea, *Botswana*	88	C3
Khalafābād, *Iran*	71	D6
Khalilabad, *India*	69	F10
Khalīlī, *Iran*	71	E7
Khalkhāl, *Iran*	71	B6
Khálki, *Dhodhekánisos, Greece*	39	E9
Khálki, *Thessalía, Greece*	38	B4
Khalkidhikí □, *Greece*	40	F7
Khalkís, *Greece*	38	C5
Khalmer-Sede = Tazovskiy, *Russia*	50	C8
Khalmer Yu, *Russia*	50	C7
Khalūf, *Oman*	74	C6
Kham Keut, *Laos*	64	C5
Khamaria, *India*	69	H9
Khambhaliya, *India*	68	H3
Khambhat, *India*	68	H5
Khambhat, G. of, *India*	66	J8
Khamilonísion, *Greece*	39	F8
Khamīr, *Iran*	71	E7
Khamir, *Yemen*	74	D3
Khamsa, *Egypt*	75	E1
Khan ➤, *Namibia*	88	C2
Khān Abū Shāmat, *Syria*	75	B5
Khān Azād, *Iraq*	70	C5
Khān Mujiddah, *Iraq*	70	C4
Khān Shaykhūn, *Syria*	70	C3
Khān Yūnis, *Gaza Strip*	75	D3
Khanai, *Pakistan*	68	D2
Khānaqīn, *Iraq*	70	C5
Khānbāghī, *Iran*	71	B7
Khandrá, *Greece*	39	F8
Khandwa, *India*	66	J10
Khandyga, *Russia*	51	C14
Khāneh, *Iran*	70	B5
Khanewal, *Pakistan*	68	D4
Khangah Dogran, *Pakistan*	68	D5
Khanh Duong, *Vietnam*	64	F7
Khaniá, *Greece*	36	D6
Khaniá □, *Greece*	36	D6
Khaniadhana, *India*	68	G8
Khaníon, Kólpos, *Greece*	36	D5
Khanka, L., *Asia*	51	E14
Khankendy = Xankändi, *Azerbaijan*	70	B5
Khanna, *India*	68	D7
Khanozai, *Pakistan*	68	D2
Khanpur, *Pakistan*	68	E4
Khanty-Mansiysk, *Russia*	50	C7
Khapalu, *Pakistan*	69	B7
Khapcheranga, *Russia*	51	E12
Kharabali, *Russia*	49	G8
Kharagauli, *Georgia*	49	K6
Kharagpur, *India*	69	H12
Khárakas, *Greece*	36	D7
Kharan Kalat, *Pakistan*	66	E4
Kharānaq, *Iran*	71	C7
Kharda, *India*	66	K9
Khardung La, *India*	69	B7
Khârga, El Wâhât-el, *Egypt*	80	B3
Khargon, *India*	66	J9
Khari ➤, *India*	68	G6
Kharian, *Pakistan*	68	C5
Kharit, Wadi el ➤, *Egypt*	80	C3
Khärk, Jazireh-ye, *Iran*	71	D6
Kharkiv, *Ukraine*	47	H9
Kharkov = Kharkiv, *Ukraine*	47	H9
Kharmanli, *Bulgaria*	41	E9
Kharovsk, *Russia*	46	C11
Kharsawangarh, *India*	69	H11
Kharta, *Turkey*	72	B3
Khartoum = El Khartûm, *Sudan*	81	D3
Khasan, *Russia*	54	C5
Khasavyurt, *Russia*	49	J8
Khāsh, *Iran*	66	E2
Khashm el Girba, *Sudan*	81	E4
Khashum, *Sudan*	81	E2
Khashuri, *Georgia*	49	K6
Khaskovo, *Bulgaria*	41	E9
Khaskovo □, *Bulgaria*	41	E9
Khatanga, *Russia*	51	B11
Khatanga ➤, *Russia*	51	B11
Khatauli, *India*	68	E7
Khatra, *India*	69	H12
Khātūnābād, *Iran*	71	D7
Khatyrka, *Russia*	51	C18
Khavda, *India*	68	H3
Khaybar, Ḥarrat, *Si. Arabia*	70	E4
Khayelitsha, *S. Africa*	85	L3
Khāzimiyah, *Iraq*	70	C4
Khazzân Jabal al Awliyā, *Sudan*	81	D3
Khe Bo, *Vietnam*	64	C5
Khe Long, *Vietnam*	64	B5
Khed Brahma, *India*	66	G8
Khekra, *India*	68	E7
Khemarak Phouminville, *Cambodia*	65	G4
Khemisset, *Morocco*	78	B4
Khemmarat, *Thailand*	64	D5
Khenāman, *Iran*	71	D8
Khenchela, *Algeria*	78	A7
Khersán ➤, *Iran*	71	D6
Khérson, *Greece*	40	E6
Kherson, *Ukraine*	47	J7
Khersónisos Akrotíri, *Greece*	36	D6
Kheta ➤, *Russia*	51	B11
Khewari, *Pakistan*	68	F3
Khilchipur, *India*	68	G7
Khiliomódhion, *Greece*	38	D4
Khilok, *Russia*	51	D12
Khimki, *Russia*	46	E9
Khíos, *Greece*	39	C8
Khíos □, *Greece*	39	C8
Khirsadoh, *India*	69	H8
Khiuma = Hiiumaa, *Estonia*	9	G20
Khiva, *Uzbekistan*	50	E7
Khīyāv, *Iran*	70	B5
Khlong Khlung, *Thailand*	64	D2
Khmelnik, *Ukraine*	47	H4
Khmelnitskiy = Khmelnytskyy, *Ukraine*	47	H4
Khmelnytskyy, *Ukraine*	47	H4
Khmer Rep. = Cambodia ■, *Asia*	64	F5
Khoai, Hon, *Vietnam*	65	H5
Khodoriv, *Ukraine*	47	H3
Khodzent = Khūjand, *Tajikistan*	50	E7
Khojak Pass, *Afghan.*	68	D2
Khok Kloi, *Thailand*	65	H2
Khok Pho, *Thailand*	65	J3
Kholm, *Russia*	46	D6
Kholmsk, *Russia*	51	E15
Khomas Hochland, *Namibia*	88	C2
Khombole, *Senegal*	82	C1
Khomeyn, *Iran*	71	C6
Khomeynī Shahr, *Iran*	71	C6
Khomodino, *Botswana*	88	C3
Khon Kaen, *Thailand*	64	D4
Khong ➤, *Cambodia*	64	F5
Khong Sedone, *Laos*	64	E5
Khonuu, *Russia*	51	C15
Khoper ➤, *Russia*	48	F6
Khor el 'Atash, *Sudan*	81	E3
Khóra, *Greece*	38	D3
Khóra Sfakíon, *Greece*	36	D6
Khorāsān □, *Iran*	71	C8
Khorat = Nakhon Ratchasima, *Thailand*	64	E4
Khorat, Cao Nguyen, *Thailand*	64	E4
Khorixas, *Namibia*	88	C1
Khorol, *Ukraine*	47	H7
Khorramābād, *Khorāsān, Iran*	71	C8
Khorramābād, *Lorestān, Iran*	71	C6
Khorrāmshahr, *Iran*	71	D6
Khorugh, *Tajikistan*	50	F8
Khosravī, *Iran*	71	D6
Khosrowābād, *Khuzestān, Iran*	71	D6
Khosrowābād, *Kordestān, Iran*	70	C5
Khost, *Pakistan*	68	D2
Khosūyeh, *Iran*	71	D7
Khotyn, *Ukraine*	47	H4
Khouribga, *Morocco*	78	B4
Khowst, *Afghan.*	68	C3
Khowst □, *Afghan.*	66	C6
Khoyniki, *Belarus*	47	G5
Khrami ➤, *Georgia*	49	K7
Khrenovoye, *Russia*	48	E5
Khristiná, *Greece*	39	E7
Khrysokhou B., *Cyprus*	36	D11
Khtapodhiá, *Greece*	39	D7
Khu Khan, *Thailand*	64	E5
Khudzhand = Khūjand, *Tajikistan*	50	E7
Khuff, *Si. Arabia*	70	E5
Khūgīānī, *Afghan.*	68	D2
Khuis, *Botswana*	88	D3
Khuiyala, *India*	68	F4
Khujner, *Iran*	68	H7
Khulna, *Bangla.*	67	H16
Khulna □, *Bangla.*	67	H16
Khulo, *Georgia*	49	K6
Khumago, *Botswana*	88	C3
Khūnsorkh, *Iran*	71	E8
Khunti, *India*	69	H11
Khūr, *Iran*	71	C8
Khurai, *India*	68	G8
Khurayş, *Si. Arabia*	71	E6
Khureit, *Sudan*	81	E2
Khurīyā Murīyā, Jazā'ir, *Oman*	74	D6
Khurja, *India*	68	E7
Khurr, Wādī al, *Iraq*	70	C4
Khush, *Afghan.*	66	C3
Khushab, *Pakistan*	68	C5
Khust, *Ukraine*	47	H2
Khuzdar, *Pakistan*	68	F2
Khūzestān □, *Iran*	71	D6
Khvāf, *Iran*	71	C9
Khvājeh, *Iran*	70	B5
Khvalynsk, *Russia*	48	D9
Khvānsār, *Iran*	71	D7
Khvatovka, *Russia*	48	D8
Khvor, *Iran*	71	C7
Khvorgū, *Iran*	71	E8
Khvormūj, *Iran*	71	D6
Khvoy, *Iran*	70	B5
Khvoynaya, *Russia*	46	C8
Khyber Pass, *Afghan.*	68	B4
Kiabukwa, *Dem. Rep. of the Congo*	87	D1
Kiama, *Australia*	95	E5
Kiamba, *Phil.*	61	H6
Kiambi, *Dem. Rep. of the Congo*	86	D2
Kiambu, *Kenya*	86	C4
Kiangara, *Madag.*	89	B8
Kiangsi = Jiangxi □, *China*	59	D11
Kiangsu = Jiangsu □, *China*	57	H11
Kiáton, *Greece*	38	C4
Kibæk, *Denmark*	11	H2
Kibanga Port, *Uganda*	86	B3
Kibara, *Tanzania*	86	C3
Kibare, Mts., *Dem. Rep. of the Congo*	86	D2
Kibombo, *Dem. Rep. of the Congo*	86	C2
Kibondo, *Tanzania*	86	C3
Kibre Mengist, *Ethiopia*	81	F4
Kibumbu, *Burundi*	86	C2
Kibungo, *Rwanda*	86	C3
Kibuye, *Burundi*	86	C2
Kibuye, *Rwanda*	86	C2
Kibwesa, *Tanzania*	86	D2
Kibwezi, *Kenya*	86	C4
Kicasalih, *Turkey*	41	E10
Kičevo, *Macedonia*	40	E4
Kichha, *India*	69	E8
Kichha ➤, *India*	69	E8
Kicking Horse Pass, *Canada*	104	C5
Kidal, *Mali*	83	B5
Kidderminster, *U.K.*	13	E5
Kidete, *Tanzania*	86	D4
Kidira, *Senegal*	82	C2
Kidnappers, C., *N.Z.*	91	H6
Kidsgrove, *U.K.*	12	D5
Kidston, *Australia*	94	B3
Kidugallo, *Tanzania*	86	D4
Kiel, *Germany*	24	A6
Kiel Canal = Nord-Ostsee-Kanal, *Germany*	24	A5
Kielce, *Poland*	45	H7
Kielder Water, *U.K.*	12	B5
Kieler Bucht, *Germany*	24	A6
Kiembara, *Burkina Faso*	82	C4
Kien Binh, *Vietnam*	65	H5
Kien Tan, *Vietnam*	65	G5
Kienge, *Dem. Rep. of the Congo*	87	E2
Kiessé, *Niger*	83	C5
Kiev = Kyyiv, *Ukraine*	47	G6
Kifaya, *Guinea*	82	C2
Kiffa, *Mauritania*	82	B2
Kifisós ➤, *Greece*	38	C5
Kifrī, *Iraq*	70	C5
Kigali, *Rwanda*	86	C3
Kigarama, *Tanzania*	86	C3
Kigelle, *Sudan*	81	F3
Kigoma □, *Tanzania*	86	D3
Kigoma-Ujiji, *Tanzania*	86	C2
Kigomasha, Ras, *Tanzania*	86	C4
Kığı, *Turkey*	70	B4
Kihei, *U.S.A.*	106	H16
Kihnu, *Estonia*	9	G21
Kii-Sanchi, *Japan*	55	G8
Kii-Suidō, *Japan*	55	H7
Kikaiga-Shima, *Japan*	55	K4
Kikinda, *Serbia, Yug.*	42	E5
Kikládhes, *Greece*	38	E6
Kikládhes □, *Greece*	38	D6
Kikwit, *Dem. Rep. of the Congo*	84	E3
Kil, *Sweden*	10	E7
Kilafors, *Sweden*	10	C10
Kilar, *India*	68	C7
Kilauea Crater, *U.S.A.*	106	J17
Kilbrannan Sd., *U.K.*	14	F3
Kilchu, *N. Korea*	57	D15
Kilcoy, *Australia*	95	D5
Kildare, *Ireland*	15	C5
Kildare □, *Ireland*	15	C5
Kileikli, *Sudan*	81	E2
Kilfinnane, *Ireland*	15	D3
Kilgore, *U.S.A.*	113	J7
Kilibo, *Benin*	83	D5
Kilifi, *Kenya*	86	C4
Kilimanjaro □, *Tanzania*	86	C4
Kilimanjaro □, *Tanzania*	86	C4
Kilimli, *Turkey*	72	B4
Kilindini, *Kenya*	86	C4
Kilis, *Turkey*	70	B3
Kiliya, *Ukraine*	47	K5
Kilkee, *Ireland*	15	D2
Kilkeel, *U.K.*	15	B5
Kilkenny, *Ireland*	15	D4
Kilkenny □, *Ireland*	15	D4
Kilkieran B., *Ireland*	15	C2
Kilkís, *Greece*	40	F6
Kilkís □, *Greece*	40	E6
Killala, *Ireland*	15	B2
Killala B., *Ireland*	15	B2
Killaloe Station, *Canada*	110	A7
Killarney, *Australia*	95	D5
Killarney, *Canada*	105	D9
Killarney, *Ireland*	15	D2
Killary Harbour, *Ireland*	15	C2
Killdeer, *Canada*	105	D7
Killdeer, *U.S.A.*	112	B3
Killeberg, *Sweden*	11	H8
Killeen, *U.S.A.*	113	K6
Killin, *U.K.*	14	E4
Killíni, *Ilía, Greece*	38	D3
Killíni, *Korinthía, Greece*	38	D4
Killorglin, *Ireland*	15	D2
Killybegs, *Ireland*	15	B3
Kilmarnock, *U.K.*	14	F4
Kilmez, *Russia*	48	B10
Kilmez ➤, *Russia*	48	B10
Kilmore, *Australia*	95	F3
Kilondo, *Tanzania*	87	D3
Kilosa, *Tanzania*	86	D4
Kilrush, *Ireland*	15	D2
Kilwa Kisiwani, *Tanzania*	87	D4
Kilwa Kivinje, *Tanzania*	87	D4
Kilwa Masoko, *Tanzania*	87	D4
Kilwinning, *U.K.*	14	F4
Kim, *U.S.A.*	113	G3
Kim ➤, *Cameroon*	83	D7
Kimaam, *Indonesia*	63	F9
Kimamba, *Tanzania*	86	D4
Kimba, *Australia*	95	E2
Kimball, *Nebr., U.S.A.*	112	E3
Kimball, *S. Dak., U.S.A.*	112	D5
Kimberley, *Australia*	92	C4
Kimberley, *Canada*	104	D5
Kimberley, *S. Africa*	88	D3
Kimberly, *U.S.A.*	114	E6
Kimch'aek, *N. Korea*	57	D15
Kimch'ŏn, *S. Korea*	57	F15
Kími, *Greece*	38	C6
Kimje, *S. Korea*	57	G14
Kimmirut, *Canada*	101	B13
Kímolos, *Greece*	38	E6
Kimovsk, *Moskva, Russia*	46	E9
Kimovsk, *Tula, Russia*	46	E10
Kimparana, *Mali*	82	C4
Kimpese, *Dem. Rep. of the Congo*	84	F2
Kimry, *Russia*	46	D9
Kimstad, *Sweden*	11	F9
Kinabalu, Gunong, *Malaysia*	62	C5
Kínaros, *Greece*	39	E8
Kinaskan L., *Canada*	104	B2
Kinbasket L., *Canada*	104	C5
Kincardine, *Canada*	102	D3
Kincolith, *Canada*	104	B3
Kinda, *Dem. Rep. of the Congo*	87	D2
Kindberg, *Austria*	26	D8
Kinde, *U.S.A.*	110	C2
Kinder Scout, *U.K.*	12	D6
Kindersley, *Canada*	105	C7
Kindia, *Guinea*	82	D2
Kindu, *Dem. Rep. of the Congo*	86	C2
Kinel, *Russia*	48	D10
Kineshma, *Russia*	48	B6
Kinesi, *Tanzania*	86	C3
King, L., *Australia*	93	F2
King, Mt., *Australia*	94	D4
King City, *U.S.A.*	116	J5
King Cr. ➤, *Australia*	94	C2
King Edward ➤, *Australia*	92	B4
King Frederik VI Land = Kong Frederik VI Kyst, *Greenland*	4	C5
King George B., *Falk. Is.*	128	G4
King George I., *Antarctica*	5	C18
King George Is., *Canada*	101	C11
King I. = Kadan Kyun, *Burma*	64	F2
King I., *Australia*	94	F3
King I., *Canada*	104	C3
King Leopold Ranges, *Australia*	92	C4
King of Prussia, *U.S.A.*	111	F9
King Sd., *Australia*	92	C3
King William I., *Canada*	100	B10
King William's Town, *S. Africa*	88	E4
Kingaok = Bathurst Inlet, *Canada*	100	B9
Kingaroy, *Australia*	95	D5
Kingfisher, *U.S.A.*	113	H6
Kingirbān, *Iraq*	70	C5
Kingisepp = Kuressaare, *Estonia*	9	G20
Kingisepp, *Russia*	46	C5
Kingman, *Ariz., U.S.A.*	117	K12
Kingman, *Kans., U.S.A.*	113	G5
Kingoonya, *Australia*	95	E2
Kingri, *Pakistan*	68	D3
Kings ➤, *U.S.A.*	116	J7
Kings Canyon National Park, *U.S.A.*	116	J8
King's Lynn, *U.K.*	12	E8
Kings Mountain, *U.S.A.*	109	H5
Kings Park, *U.S.A.*	111	F11
King's Peak, *U.S.A.*	114	F8
Kingsbridge, *U.K.*	13	G4
Kingsburg, *U.S.A.*	116	J7
Kingscote, *Australia*	95	F2
Kingscourt, *Ireland*	15	C5
Kingsford, *U.S.A.*	108	C1
Kingsland, *U.S.A.*	109	K5
Kingsley, *U.S.A.*	112	D7
Kingsport, *U.S.A.*	109	G4
Kingston, *Canada*	102	D4
Kingston, *Jamaica*	120	C4
Kingston, *N.Z.*	91	L2
Kingston, *N.H., U.S.A.*	111	D13
Kingston, *N.Y., U.S.A.*	111	E11
Kingston, *Pa., U.S.A.*	111	E9
Kingston, *R.I., U.S.A.*	111	E13
Kingston Pk., *U.S.A.*	117	K11
Kingston South East, *Australia*	95	F2
Kingston upon Hull, *U.K.*	12	D7
Kingston upon Hull □, *U.K.*	12	D7
Kingston upon Thames □, *U.K.*	13	F7
Kingstown, *St. Vincent*	121	D7
Kingstree, *U.S.A.*	109	J6
Kingsville, *Canada*	102	D3
Kingsville, *U.S.A.*	113	M6
Kingussie, *U.K.*	14	D4

Name	Page	Grid
Kingwood, U.S.A.	113	K7
Kınık, Antalya, Turkey	39	E11
Kınık, Izmir, Turkey	39	B9
Kinistino, Canada	105	C7
Kinkala, Congo	84	E2
Kinki □, Japan	55	H8
Kinleith, N.Z.	91	H5
Kinmount, Canada	110	B6
Kinna, Sweden	11	G6
Kinnairds Hd., U.K.	14	D6
Kinnared, Sweden	11	G7
Kinnarodden, Norway	6	A11
Kinnarp, Sweden	11	F7
Kinneviken, Sweden	11	F7
Kinngait = Cape Dorset, Canada	101	B12
Kino, Mexico	118	B2
Kinoje →, Canada	102	B3
Kinomoto, Japan	55	G8
Kinoni, Uganda	86	C3
Kinoosao, Canada	105	B8
Kinross, U.K.	14	E5
Kinsale, Ireland	15	E3
Kinsale, Old Hd. of, Ireland	15	E3
Kinsha = Chang Jiang →, China	59	B13
Kinshasa, Dem. Rep. of the Congo	84	E3
Kinsley, U.S.A.	113	G5
Kinsman, U.S.A.	110	E4
Kinston, U.S.A.	109	H7
Kintampo, Ghana	83	D4
Kintore Ra., Australia	92	D4
Kintyre, U.K.	14	F3
Kintyre, Mull of, U.K.	14	F3
Kinushseo →, Canada	102	A3
Kinuso, Canada	104	B5
Kinyangiri, Tanzania	86	C3
Kinyeti, Sudan	81	G3
Kinzig →, Germany	25	G3
Kinzua, U.S.A.	110	E6
Kinzua Dam, U.S.A.	110	E6
Kióni, Greece	38	C2
Kiosk, Canada	102	C4
Kiowa, Kans., U.S.A.	113	G5
Kiowa, Okla., U.S.A.	113	H7
Kipahigan L., Canada	105	B8
Kipanga, Tanzania	86	D4
Kiparissía, Greece	38	D3
Kiparissiakós Kólpos, Greece	38	D3
Kipawa, L., Canada	102	C4
Kipembawe, Tanzania	86	D3
Kipengere Ra., Tanzania	87	D3
Kipili, Tanzania	86	D3
Kipini, Kenya	86	C5
Kipling, Canada	105	C8
Kippure, Ireland	15	C5
Kipushi, Dem. Rep. of the Congo	87	E2
Kirane, Mali	82	B2
Kiranomena, Madag.	89	B8
Kiraz, Turkey	39	C10
Kirazlı, Turkey	41	F10
Kirchhain, Germany	24	E4
Kirchheim, Germany	25	G5
Kirchheimbolanden, Germany	25	F3
Kirchschlag, Austria	27	D9
Kireç, Turkey	39	B10
Kirensk, Russia	51	D11
Kirghizia = Kyrgyzstan ■, Asia	50	E8
Kirghizstan = Kyrgyzstan ■, Asia	50	E8
Kiribati ■, Pac. Oc.	96	H10
Kırıkhan, Turkey	72	C7
Kırıkkale, Turkey	72	C5
Kirillov, Russia	46	C10
Kirin = Jilin, China	57	C14
Kirishi, Russia	46	C7
Kiritimati, Kiribati	97	G12
Kırka, Turkey	39	B12
Kırkağaç, Turkey	39	B9
Kirkby, U.K.	12	D5
Kirkby Lonsdale, U.K.	12	C5
Kirkcaldy, U.K.	14	E5
Kirkcudbright, U.K.	14	G4
Kirkee, India	66	K8
Kirkenes, Norway	8	B23
Kirkfield, Canada	110	B6
Kirkjubæjarklaustur, Iceland	8	E4
Kirkkonummi, Finland	9	F21
Kirkland Lake, Canada	102	C3
Kırklareli, Turkey	41	E11
Kırklareli □, Turkey	41	E11
Kirksville, U.S.A.	112	E8
Kirkūk, Iraq	70	C5
Kirkwall, U.K.	14	C6
Kirkwood, S. Africa	88	E4
Kirn, Germany	25	F3
Kirov, Kaluga, Russia	46	E8
Kirov, Kirov, Russia	50	D5
Kirovabad = Gäncä, Azerbaijan	49	K8
Kirovakan = Vanadzor, Armenia	49	K7
Kirovograd = Kirovohrad, Ukraine	47	H7
Kirovohrad, Ukraine	47	H7
Kirovsk = Babadayhan, Turkmenistan	50	F7
Kirovskiy, Astrakhan, Russia	49	H9
Kirovskiy, Kamchatka, Russia	51	D16
Kirovskiy, Primorsk, Russia	54	B6
Kirriemuir, U.K.	14	E5
Kirsanov, Russia	48	D6
Kırşehir, Turkey	70	B2
Kirtachi, Niger	83	C5
Kirthar Range, Pakistan	68	F2
Kirtland, U.S.A.	115	H9
Kiruna, Sweden	8	C19
Kirundu, Dem. Rep. of the Congo	86	C2
Kirya, Russia	48	C8
Kiryū, Japan	55	F9
Kisa, Sweden	11	G9
Kisaga, Tanzania	86	C3
Kisalaya, Nic.	120	D3
Kisalföld, Hungary	42	C2
Kisámou, Kólpos, Greece	36	D5
Kisanga, Dem. Rep. of the Congo	86	B2
Kisangani, Dem. Rep. of the Congo	86	B2
Kisar, Indonesia	63	F7
Kisarawe, Tanzania	86	D4
Kisarazu, Japan	55	G9
Kisbér, Hungary	42	C3
Kishanganga →, Pakistan	69	B5
Kishanganj, India	69	F13
Kishangarh, Raj., India	68	F6
Kishangarh, Raj., India	68	F4
Kishi, Nigeria	83	D5
Kishinev = Chişinău, Moldova	43	C13
Kishiwada, Japan	55	G7
Kishtwar, India	69	C6
Kisielice, Poland	44	E6
Kisii, Kenya	86	C3
Kisiju, Tanzania	86	D4
Kisir, Turkey	73	B10
Kisizi, Uganda	86	C2
Kiskomárom = Zalakomár, Hungary	42	D2
Kiskőrei-víztároló, Hungary	42	C5
Kiskőrös, Hungary	42	D4
Kiskundorozsma, Hungary	42	D5
Kiskunfélegyháza, Hungary	42	D4
Kiskunhalas, Hungary	42	D4
Kiskunmajsa, Hungary	42	D4
Kislovodsk, Russia	49	J6
Kismayu = Chisimaio, Somali Rep.	77	G8
Kiso-Gawa →, Japan	55	G8
Kiso-Sammyaku, Japan	55	G8
Kisofukushima, Japan	55	G8
Kisoro, Uganda	86	C2
Kissidougou, Guinea	82	D2
Kissimmee, U.S.A.	109	L5
Kissimmee →, U.S.A.	109	M5
Kississing L., Canada	105	B8
Kissónerga, Cyprus	36	E11
Kissu, J., Sudan	80	C2
Kistanje, Croatia	29	E12
Kisújszállás, Hungary	42	C5
Kisumu, Kenya	86	C3
Kisvárda, Hungary	42	B7
Kiswani, Tanzania	86	C4
Kiswere, Tanzania	87	D4
Kit Carson, U.S.A.	112	F3
Kita, Mali	82	C3
Kitaibaraki, Japan	55	F10
Kitakami, Japan	54	E10
Kitakami-Gawa →, Japan	54	E10
Kitakami-Sammyaku, Japan	54	E10
Kitakata, Japan	54	F9
Kitakyūshū, Japan	55	H5
Kitale, Kenya	86	B4
Kitami, Japan	54	C11
Kitami-Sammyaku, Japan	54	B11
Kitangiri, L., Tanzania	86	C3
Kitaya, Tanzania	87	E5
Kitchener, Canada	102	D3
Kitee, Finland	46	A6
Kitega = Gitega, Burundi	86	C2
Kitengo, Dem. Rep. of the Congo	86	D1
Kitgum, Uganda	86	B3
Kíthira, Greece	38	E5
Kíthnos, Greece	38	D6
Kiti, Cyprus	36	E12
Kiti, C., Cyprus	36	E12
Kitimat, Canada	104	C3
Kitinen →, Finland	8	C22
Kitiyab, Sudan	81	D3
Kítros, Greece	40	F6
Kitsuki, Japan	55	H5
Kittakittaooloo, L., Australia	95	D2
Kittanning, U.S.A.	110	F5
Kittatinny Mts., U.S.A.	111	F10
Kittery, U.S.A.	109	D10
Kittilä, Finland	8	C21
Kitui, Kenya	86	C4
Kitwanga, Canada	104	B3
Kitwe, Zambia	87	E2
Kitzbühel, Austria	26	D5
Kitzbühler Alpen, Austria	26	D5
Kitzingen, Germany	25	F6
Kivarli, India	68	G5
Kivertsi, Ukraine	47	G3
Kividhes, Cyprus	36	E11
Kivik, Sweden	11	J8
Kivotós, Greece	40	F5
Kivu, L., Dem. Rep. of the Congo	86	C2
Kiyev = Kyyiv, Ukraine	47	G6
Kiyevskoye Vdkhr. = Kyyivske Vdskh., Ukraine	47	G6
Kıyıköy, Turkey	41	E12
Kizel Adalar, Turkey	41	F13
Kizil Irmak →, Turkey	72	B6
Kizil Jilga, India	69	B8
Kizil Yurt, Russia	49	J8
Kızılcabölük, Turkey	39	D11
Kızılcadağ, Turkey	39	D11
Kızılcahamam, Turkey	72	B5
Kızılhisar, Turkey	39	D11
Kızılırmak, Turkey	72	B5
Kızıllören, Turkey	39	D12
Kızıltepe, Turkey	70	B4
Kizimkazi, Tanzania	86	D4
Kizlyar, Russia	49	J8
Kizyl-Arvat = Gyzylarbat, Turkmenistan	50	F6
Kjellerup, Denmark	11	H3
Kjölur, Iceland	8	D4
Kladanj, Bos.-H.	42	F3
Kladnica, Serbia, Yug.	40	C4
Kladno, Czech Rep.	26	A7
Kladovo, Serbia, Yug.	40	B6
Klaeng, Thailand	64	F3
Klagenfurt, Austria	26	E7
Klaipėda, Lithuania	9	J19
Klaipėda □, Lithuania	44	C8
Klaksvík, Færoe Is.	8	E9
Klamath →, U.S.A.	114	F1
Klamath Falls, U.S.A.	114	E3
Klamath Mts., U.S.A.	114	F2
Klamono, Indonesia	63	E8
Klanjec, Croatia	29	B12
Klappan →, Canada	104	B3
Klarälven →, Sweden	10	E7
Klässbol, Sweden	10	E6
Klatovy, Czech Rep.	26	B6
Klawer, S. Africa	88	E2
Klazienaveen, Neths.	17	B6
Klé, Mali	82	C3
Kłecko, Poland	45	F4
Kleczew, Poland	45	F5
Kleena Kleene, Canada	104	C4
Klein-Karas, Namibia	88	D2
Klekovaca, Bos.-H.	29	D13
Klenoec, Macedonia	40	E4
Klenovec, Slovak Rep.	27	C12
Klerksdorp, S. Africa	88	D4
Kleszczele, Poland	45	F10
Kletnya, Russia	46	F7
Kletsk = Klyetsk, Belarus	47	F4
Kletskiy, Russia	49	F6
Kleve, Germany	24	D2
Klickitat, U.S.A.	114	D3
Klickitat →, U.S.A.	116	E5
Klidhes, Cyprus	36	D13
Klimovichi, Belarus	46	F6
Klin, Russia	46	D9
Klina, Kosovo, Yug.	40	D4
Klinaklini →, Canada	104	C3
Klintehamn, Sweden	11	G12
Klintsy, Russia	47	F7
Klip →, S. Africa	89	D4
Klipdale, S. Africa	88	E2
Klippan, Sweden	11	H7
Klipplaat, S. Africa	88	E3
Klisura, Bulgaria	41	D8
Kljajićevo, Serbia, Yug.	42	E4
Ključ, Bos.-H.	29	D13
Kłobuck, Poland	45	H5
Klockestrand, Sweden	10	B11
Kłodawa, Poland	45	F5
Kłodzko, Poland	45	H3
Klos, Albania	40	E4
Klosterneuburg, Austria	27	C9
Klosters, Switz.	25	J5
Klötze, Germany	24	C7
Klouto, Togo	83	D5
Kluane L., Canada	100	B6
Kluane Nat. Park, Canada	104	A1
Kluczbork, Poland	45	H5
Klukwan, U.S.A.	104	B1
Klyetsk, Belarus	47	F4
Klyuchevskaya, Gora, Russia	51	D17
Knäred, Sweden	11	H7
Knaresborough, U.K.	12	C6
Knee L., Man., Canada	102	A1
Knee L., Sask., Canada	105	B7
Knezha, Bulgaria	41	C8
Knić, Serbia, Yug.	40	C4
Knight Inlet, Canada	104	C3
Knighton, U.K.	13	E4
Knights Ferry, U.S.A.	116	H6
Knights Landing, U.S.A.	116	G5
Knin, Croatia	29	D13
Knislinge, Sweden	11	H8
Knittelfeld, Austria	26	D7
Knivsta, Sweden	10	E11
Knjazevac, Serbia, Yug.	40	C6
Knob, C., Australia	93	F2
Knock, Ireland	15	C3
Knockmealdown Mts., Ireland	15	D4
Knokke-Heist, Belgium	17	C3
Knossós, Greece	36	D7
Knowlton, Canada	111	A12
Knox, U.S.A.	108	E2
Knox Coast, Antarctica	5	C8
Knoxville, Iowa, U.S.A.	112	E8
Knoxville, Tenn., U.S.A.	109	H4
Knysna, S. Africa	88	E3
Knyszyn, Poland	44	E9
Ko Kha, Thailand	64	C2
Koartac = Quaqtaq, Canada	101	B13
Koba, Indonesia	63	F8
Kobarid, Slovenia	29	B10
Kobayashi, Japan	55	J5
Kobdo = Hovd, Mongolia	60	B4
Kōbe, Japan	55	G7
Kobelyaky, Ukraine	47	H8
Kobenni, Mauritania	82	B3
Kōbi-Sho, Japan	55	M1
Kobo, Ethiopia	81	E4
Kobryn, Belarus	47	F3
Kobylin, Poland	45	G4
Kobyłka, Poland	45	F8
Kobylkino, Russia	48	C6
Koca →, Turkey	41	F11
Kocabaş, Turkey	39	D11
Kocaeli, Turkey	41	F13
Kocaeli □, Turkey	41	F13
Kočane, Serbia, Yug.	40	C5
Kočani, Macedonia	40	E6
Koçarlı, Turkey	39	D9
Koceljevo, Serbia, Yug.	40	B3
Koch Bihar, India	67	F16
Kochas, India	69	G10
Kocher →, Germany	25	F5
Kochi = Cochin, India	66	Q10
Kōchi, Japan	55	H6
Kōchi □, Japan	55	H6
Kochiu = Gejiu, China	58	F4
Kodarma, India	69	G11
Kode, Sweden	11	G5
Kodiak, U.S.A.	100	C4
Kodiak I., U.S.A.	100	C4
Kodinar, India	68	J4
Kodok, Sudan	81	F3
Kodori →, Georgia	49	J5
Koedoesberge, S. Africa	88	E3
Koes, Namibia	88	D2
Kofçaz, Turkey	41	E11
Koffiefontein, S. Africa	88	D4
Kofiau, Indonesia	63	E7
Köflach, Austria	26	D8
Koforidua, Ghana	83	D4
Kōfu, Japan	55	G9
Koga, Japan	55	F9
Kogaluk →, Canada	103	A7
Køge, Denmark	11	J6
Køge Bugt, Denmark	11	J6
Kogi □, Nigeria	83	D6
Kogin Baba, Nigeria	83	D7
Koh-i-Khurd, Afghan.	68	C1
Koh-i-Maran, Pakistan	68	E2
Kohat, Pakistan	68	C4
Kohima, India	67	G19
Kohkīlūyeh va Būyer Aḥmadi □, Iran	71	D6
Kohler Ra., Antarctica	5	D15
Kohlu, Pakistan	68	E3
Kohtla-Järve, Estonia	9	G22
Koillismaa, Finland	8	D23
Koin-dong, N. Korea	57	D14
Koinare, Bulgaria	41	C8
Koindu, S. Leone	82	D2
Kojetín, Czech Rep.	27	B10
Kojŏ, N. Korea	57	E14
Kojonup, Australia	93	F2
Kojūr, Iran	71	B6
Koka, Sudan	80	C3
Kokand = Qŭqon, Uzbekistan	50	E8
Kokas, Indonesia	63	E8
Kokava, Slovak Rep.	27	C12
Kokchetav = Kökshetaū, Kazakstan	50	D7
Kokemäenjoki →, Finland	9	F19
Kokhma, Russia	48	B5
Koki, Senegal	82	B1
Kokkola, Finland	8	E20
Koko, Nigeria	83	C5
Koko Kyunzu, Burma	67	M18
Kokomo, U.S.A.	108	E2
Kokopo, Papua N. G.	96	H7
Kokoro, Niger	83	C5
Koksan, N. Korea	57	E14
Kökshetaū, Kazakstan	50	D7
Koksoak →, Canada	101	C13
Kokstad, S. Africa	89	E4
Kokubu, Japan	55	J5
Kola, Indonesia	63	F8
Kola Pen. = Kolskiy Poluostrov, Russia	50	C4
Kolachi →, Pakistan	68	F2
Kolahoi, India	69	B6
Kolahun, Liberia	82	D2
Kolaka, Indonesia	63	E6
Kolar, India	66	N11
Kolar Gold Fields, India	66	N11
Kolaras, India	68	G6
Kolari, Finland	8	C20
Kolárovo, Slovak Rep.	27	D10
Kolašin, Montenegro, Yug.	40	D3
Kolayat, India	66	F8
Kolbäck, Sweden	10	E10
Kolbäcksån →, Sweden	10	E10
Kolbermoor, Germany	25	H8
Kolbuszowa, Poland	45	H9
Kolchugino = Leninsk-Kuznetskiy, Russia	50	D9
Kolchugino, Russia	46	D10
Kolda, Senegal	82	C2
Koldegi, Sudan	81	E3
Kolding, Denmark	11	J3
Kolepom = Dolak, Pulau, Indonesia	63	F9
Kolguyev, Ostrov, Russia	50	C5
Kolhapur, India	66	L9
Kolia, Ivory C.	82	D3
Kolín, Czech Rep.	26	A8
Kolind, Denmark	11	H4
Kolkas rags, Latvia	9	H20
Kolkata, India	69	H13
Kollam = Quilon, India	66	Q10
Kollum, Neths.	17	A6
Kolmanskop, Namibia	88	D2
Köln, Germany	24	E2
Kolno, Poland	44	E8
Koło, Poland	45	F5
Kołobrzeg, Poland	44	D2
Kolokani, Mali	82	C3
Koloko, Burkina Faso	82	C3
Kololo, Ethiopia	81	F5
Kolomna, Russia	46	E10
Kolomyya, Ukraine	47	H3
Kolondiéba, Mali	82	C3
Kolonodale, Indonesia	63	E6
Kolonowskie, Poland	45	H5
Kolosib, India	67	G18
Kolpashevo, Russia	50	D9
Kolpino, Russia	46	C6
Kolpny, Russia	47	F9
Kolskiy Poluostrov, Russia	50	C4
Kolsva, Sweden	10	E9
Kolubara →, Serbia, Yug.	40	B4
Koluszki, Poland	45	G6
Kolwezi, Dem. Rep. of the Congo	87	E2
Kolyma →, Russia	51	C17
Kolymskoye Nagorye, Russia	51	C16
Kôm Hamâda, Egypt	80	H7
Kôm Ombo, Egypt	80	C3
Komadugu Gana →, Nigeria	83	C7
Komandorskiye Is. = Komandorskiye Ostrova, Russia	51	D17
Komandorskiye Ostrova, Russia	51	D17
Komárno, Slovak Rep.	27	D11
Komárom, Hungary	42	C3
Komárom-Esztergom □, Hungary	42	C3
Komatipoort, S. Africa	89	D5
Komatou Yialou, Cyprus	36	D13
Komatsu, Japan	55	F8
Komatsushima, Japan	55	H7
Kombissiri, Burkina Faso	83	C4
Kombori, Burkina Faso	82	C4
Kombóti, Greece	38	B3
Komen, Slovenia	29	C10
Komenda, Ghana	83	D4
Komi □, Russia	50	C6
Komiža, Croatia	29	E13
Komló, Hungary	42	D3
Kommunarsk = Alchevsk, Ukraine	47	H10
Kommunizma, Pik, Tajikistan	50	F8
Komodo, Indonesia	63	F5
Komoé →, Ivory C.	82	D4
Komoran, Pulau, Indonesia	63	F9
Komoro, Japan	55	F9
Komotini, Greece	41	E9
Komovi, Montenegro, Yug.	40	D3
Kompasberg, S. Africa	88	E3
Kompong Bang, Cambodia	65	F5
Kompong Cham, Cambodia	65	F5
Kompong Chhnang = Kampang Chhnang, Cambodia	65	F5
Kompong Chikreng, Cambodia	64	F5
Kompong Kleang, Cambodia	64	F5
Kompong Luong, Cambodia	65	G5
Kompong Pranak, Cambodia	64	F5
Kompong Som = Kampong Saom, Cambodia	65	G4
Kompong Som, Chhung = Kampong Saom, Chaak, Cambodia	65	G4
Kompong Speu, Cambodia	65	G5
Kompong Sralao, Cambodia	64	E5
Kompong Thom, Cambodia	64	F5
Kompong Trabeck, Cambodia	65	G5
Kompong Trabeck, Cambodia	65	F5
Kompong Trach, Cambodia	65	G5
Kompong Tralach, Cambodia	65	G5
Komrat = Comrat, Moldova	43	D13
Komsberg, S. Africa	88	E3
Komsomolets, Ostrov, Russia	51	A10
Komsomolsk, Amur, Russia	51	D14
Komsomolsk, Ivanovo, Russia	46	D11
Komsomolskiy, Russia	48	C7
Kömür Burnu, Turkey	39	C8
Kon Tum, Vietnam	64	E7
Kon Tum, Plateau du, Vietnam	64	E7
Kona, Mali	82	C4
Konakovo, Russia	46	D9
Konarhā □, Afghan.	66	B7
Konārī, Iran	71	D6
Konch, India	69	G8
Konde, Tanzania	86	C4
Kondiá, Greece	39	B7
Kondinin, Australia	93	F2
Kondoa, Tanzania	86	C4
Kondókali, Greece	36	A3
Kondopaga, Russia	46	A8
Kondratyevo, Russia	51	D10
Kondrovo, Russia	46	E8
Konduga, Nigeria	83	C7
Köneürgench, Turkmenistan	50	E6
Konevo, Russia	46	A10
Kong = Khong →, Cambodia	64	F5
Kong, Ivory C.	82	D4
Kong, Koh, Cambodia	65	G4
Kong Christian IX Land, Greenland	4	C6
Kong Christian X Land, Greenland	4	B6
Kong Frederik IX Land, Greenland	4	C5
Kong Frederik VI Kyst, Greenland	4	C5
Kong Frederik VIII Land, Greenland	4	B6
Kong Oscar Fjord, Greenland	4	B6
Kongeå →, Denmark	11	J2
Kongerslev, Denmark	11	H4
Kongju, S. Korea	57	F14
Konglu, Burma	67	F20
Kongola, Namibia	88	B3

Kongolo, Kasai-Or., Dem. Rep. of the Congo . 86 D1
Kongolo, Katanga, Dem. Rep. of the Congo . 86 D2
Kongor, Sudan . 81 F3
Kongoussi, Burkina Faso . 83 C4
Kongsberg, Norway . 9 G13
Kongsvinger, Norway . 9 F15
Kongwa, Tanzania . 86 D4
Koni, Dem. Rep. of the Congo . 87 E2
Koni, Mts., Dem. Rep. of the Congo . 87 E2
Koniakari, Mali . 82 C2
Koniecpol, Poland . 45 H6
Königs Wusterhausen, Germany . 24 C9
Königsberg = Kaliningrad, Russia . 9 J19
Königsbrunn, Germany . 25 G6
Königslutter, Germany . 24 C6
Konin, Poland . 45 F5
Konispol, Albania . 40 G4
Kónitsa, Greece . 38 A2
Konjic, Bos.-H. . 42 G2
Konkiep, Namibia . 88 D2
Konkouré →, Guinea . 82 D2
Könnern, Germany . 24 D7
Kono, S. Leone . 82 D2
Konongo, Ghana . 83 D4
Konosha, Russia . 46 B11
Kōnosu, Japan . 55 F9
Konotop, Ukraine . 47 G7
Konsankoro, Guinea . 82 D3
Końskie, Poland . 45 G7
Konstancin-Jeziorna, Poland . 45 F8
Konstantinovka = Kostyantynivka, Ukraine . 47 H9
Konstantinovsk, Russia . 49 G5
Konstantynów Łódźki, Poland . 45 G6
Konstanz, Germany . 25 H5
Kont, Iran . 71 E9
Kontagora, Nigeria . 83 C6
Kontcha, Cameroon . 83 D7
Konya, Turkey . 70 B2
Konya Ovası, Turkey . 72 C5
Konz, Germany . 25 F2
Konza, Kenya . 86 C4
Koocanusa, L., Canada . 114 B6
Kookynie, Australia . 93 E3
Koolyanobbing, Australia . 93 F2
Koonibba, Australia . 95 E1
Koorawatha, Australia . 95 E4
Koorda, Australia . 93 F2
Kooskia, U.S.A. . 114 C6
Kootenay →, U.S.A. . 104 D5
Kootenay L., Canada . 104 D5
Kootenay Nat. Park, Canada . 104 C5
Kootjieskolk, S. Africa . 88 E3
Kopanovka, Russia . 49 G8
Kopaonik, Yugoslavia . 40 C4
Kópavogur, Iceland . 8 D3
Koper, Slovenia . 29 C10
Kopervik, Norway . 9 G11
Kopet Dagh, Asia . 71 B8
Kopi, Australia . 95 E2
Köping, Sweden . 10 E10
Köpingsvik, Sweden . 11 H10
Kopište, Croatia . 29 F13
Koplik, Albania . 40 D3
Köpmanholmen, Sweden . 10 A12
Kopparberg, Sweden . 10 E9
Koppeh Dāgh = Kopet Dagh, Asia . 71 B8
Koppies, S. Africa . 89 D4
Koppom, Sweden . 10 E6
Koprivlen, Bulgaria . 40 E7
Koprivnica, Croatia . 29 B13
Kopřivnice, Czech Rep. . 27 B11
Koprivshtitsa, Bulgaria . 41 D8
Köprübaşı, Turkey . 39 C10
Kopychyntsi, Ukraine . 47 H3
Korab, Macedonia . 40 E4
Korakiána, Greece . 36 A3
Koral, India . 68 J5
Korarou, L., Mali . 82 B4
Korba, India . 69 H10
Korbach, Germany . 24 D4
Korbu, G., Malaysia . 65 K3
Korce = Korçë, Albania . 40 F4
Korçë, Albania . 40 F4
Korčula, Croatia . 29 F13
Korčulanski Kanal, Croatia . 29 E13
Kord Kūy, Iran . 71 B7
Kord Sheykh, Iran . 71 D7
Kordestān □, Iran . 70 C5
Kordofân, Sudan . 79 F11
Koré Mayroua, Niger . 83 C5
Korea, North ■, Asia . 57 E14
Korea, South ■, Asia . 57 G15
Korea Bay, Korea . 57 E13
Korea Strait, Asia . 57 H15
Korem, Ethiopia . 81 E4
Korenevo, Russia . 47 G8
Korenovsk, Russia . 49 H4
Korets, Ukraine . 47 G4
Korfantów, Poland . 45 H4
Korgan, Turkey . 72 B7
Korgus, Sudan . 80 D3
Korhogo, Ivory C. . 82 D3
Koribundu, S. Leone . 82 D2
Korienzé, Mali . 82 B4
Korinthía □, Greece . 38 D4
Korinthiakós Kólpos, Greece . 38 C4
Korioumé, Mali . 82 B4
Kórissa, Límni, Greece . 36 B3
Kōriyama, Japan . 54 F10
Korkuteli, Turkey . 39 D12

Kormakiti, C., Cyprus . 36 D11
Körmend, Hungary . 42 C1
Kornat, Croatia . 29 E12
Korneshty = Corneşti, Moldova . 43 C13
Korneuburg, Austria . 27 C9
Kórnik, Poland . 45 F4
Koro, Fiji . 91 C8
Koro, Ivory C. . 82 D3
Koro, Mali . 82 C4
Koro Sea, Fiji . 91 C9
Korocha, Russia . 47 G9
Köroğlu Dağları, Turkey . 72 B5
Korogwe, Tanzania . 86 D4
Koronadal, Phil. . 61 H6
Koróni, Greece . 38 E3
Korónia, Limni, Greece . 40 F7
Koronís, Greece . 39 D7
Koronowo, Poland . 45 E4
Koror, Palau . 63 C8
Körös →, Hungary . 42 D5
Köröstarcsa, Hungary . 42 D6
Korosten, Ukraine . 47 G5
Korostyshev, Ukraine . 47 G5
Korotoyak, Russia . 47 G10
Korraraika, Helodranon' i, Madag. . 89 B7
Korsakov, Russia . 51 E15
Korsberga, Sweden . 11 G9
Korshunovo, Russia . 51 D12
Korsør, Denmark . 11 J5
Korsun Shevchenkovskiy, Ukraine . 47 H6
Korsze, Poland . 44 D8
Korti, Sudan . 80 D3
Kortrijk, Belgium . 17 D3
Korucu, Turkey . 39 B9
Korwai, India . 68 G8
Koryakskoye Nagorye, Russia . 51 C18
Koryŏng, S. Korea . 57 G15
Koryukivka, Ukraine . 47 G7
Kos, Greece . 39 E9
Kosa, Ethiopia . 81 F4
Kosaya Gora, Russia . 46 E9
Kościan, Poland . 45 F3
Kościerzyna, Poland . 44 D4
Kosciusko, U.S.A. . 113 J10
Kosciuszko, Mt., Australia . 95 F4
Kösely →, Hungary . 42 C6
Kosha, Sudan . 80 C3
Koshava, Bulgaria . 40 B7
K'oshih = Kashi, China . 60 C2
Koshiki-Rettō, Japan . 55 J4
Kosi, India . 68 F7
Kosi →, India . 69 E8
Košice, Slovak Rep. . 27 C14
Košický □, Slovak Rep. . 27 C14
Kosjerić, Serbia, Yug. . 40 B3
Köşk, Turkey . 39 D10
Koskhinoú, Greece . 36 C10
Košong, N. Korea . 57 E15
Kosovo □, Yugoslavia . 40 D4
Kosovo Polje, Kosovo, Yug. . 40 D5
Kosovska Kamenica, Kosovo, Yug. . 40 D5
Kosovska Mitrovica, Kosovo, Yug. . 40 D4
Kossou, L. de, Ivory C. . 82 D3
Kosta, Sweden . 11 H9
Kostajnica, Croatia . 29 C13
Kostanjevica, Slovenia . 29 C12
Kostenets, Bulgaria . 40 D7
Koster, S. Africa . 88 D4
Kōstî, Sudan . 81 E3
Kostinbrod, Bulgaria . 40 D7
Kostolac, Serbia, Yug. . 40 B5
Kostopil, Ukraine . 47 G4
Kostroma, Russia . 46 D11
Kostromskoye Vdkhr., Russia . 46 D11
Kostrzyn, Lubuskie, Poland . 45 F1
Kostrzyn, Wielkopolskie, Poland . 45 F4
Kostyantynivka, Ukraine . 47 H9
Kostyukovichi = Kastsyukovichy, Belarus . 46 F7
Koszalin, Poland . 44 D3
Kőszeg, Hungary . 42 C1
Kot Addu, Pakistan . 68 D4
Kot Kapura, India . 68 D6
Kot Moman, Pakistan . 68 C5
Kot Sultan, Pakistan . 68 D4
Kota, India . 68 G6
Kota Baharu, Malaysia . 65 J4
Kota Barrage, India . 68 G6
Kota Belud, Malaysia . 62 C5
Kota Kinabalu, Malaysia . 62 C5
Kota Kubu Baharu, Malaysia . 65 L3
Kota Tinggi, Malaysia . 65 M4
Kotaagung, Indonesia . 62 F2
Kotabaru, Indonesia . 62 E5
Kotabumi, Indonesia . 62 E2
Kotamobagu, Indonesia . 63 D6
Kotcho L., Canada . 104 B4
Kotdwara, India . 69 E8
Kotel, Bulgaria . 41 D10
Kotelnich, Russia . 48 A9
Kotelnikovo, Russia . 49 G6
Kotelny, Ostrov, Russia . 51 B14
Kothari →, India . 68 G6
Köthen, Germany . 24 D7
Kothi, Mad. P., India . 69 H10
Kothi, Mad. P., India . 69 G9
Kotiro, Pakistan . 68 G2
Kotka, Finland . 9 F22
Kotlas, Russia . 50 C5
Kotlenska Planina, Bulgaria . 41 D10
Kotli, Pakistan . 68 C5
Kotma, India . 69 H9

Kotmul, Pakistan . 69 B6
Koton-Karifi, Nigeria . 83 D6
Kotonkoro, Nigeria . 83 C6
Kotor, Montenegro, Yug. . 40 D2
Kotor Varoš, Bos.-H. . 42 F2
Kotoriba, Croatia . 29 B13
Kotovo, Russia . 48 E7
Kotovsk, Russia . 48 D5
Kotovsk, Ukraine . 47 J5
Kotputli, India . 68 F7
Kotri, Pakistan . 68 G3
Kótronas, Greece . 38 E4
Kötschach-Mauthen, Austria . 26 E6
Kotturu, India . 66 M10
Kotuy →, Russia . 51 B11
Kotzebue, U.S.A. . 100 B3
Koudougou, Burkina Faso . 82 C4
Koufonísi, Greece . 36 E8
Koufonísia, Greece . 39 E7
Kougaberge, S. Africa . 88 E3
Kouibli, Ivory C. . 82 D3
Kouilou →, Congo . 84 E2
Koula Moutou, Gabon . 84 E2
Koulen = Kulen, Cambodia . 64 F5
Koulikoro, Mali . 82 C3
Kouloúra, Greece . 36 A3
Koúm-bournoú, Ákra, Greece . 36 C10
Koumala, Australia . 94 C4
Koumankou, Mali . 82 C3
Koumbia, Burkina Faso . 82 C4
Koumbia, Guinea . 82 C2
Koumboum, Guinea . 82 C2
Koumpenntoum, Senegal . 82 C2
Koumra, Chad . 79 G9
Koun-Fao, Ivory C. . 82 D4
Koundara, Guinea . 82 C2
Koundian, Guinea . 82 C2
Koungheul, Senegal . 82 C2
Kounradskiy, Kazakstan . 50 E8
Kountze, U.S.A. . 113 K7
Koupéla, Burkina Faso . 83 C4
Kourémalé, Mali . 82 C3
Kouris →, Cyprus . 36 E11
Kourou, Fr. Guiana . 125 B8
Kouroukoto, Mali . 82 C2
Kouroussa, Guinea . 82 C2
Koussané, Mali . 82 C2
Koussane, Senegal . 82 C2
Kousséri, Cameroon . 79 F8
Koutiala, Mali . 82 C3
Kouto, Ivory C. . 82 D3
Kouvé, Togo . 83 D5
Kouvola, Finland . 9 F22
Kovačica, Serbia, Yug. . 42 E5
Kovel, Ukraine . 47 G3
Kovin, Serbia, Yug. . 42 F5
Kovrov, Russia . 48 B5
Kowal, Poland . 45 F6
Kowalewo Pomorskie, Poland . 45 E5
Kowanyama, Australia . 94 B3
Kowloon, H.K. . 59 F10
Kowŏn, N. Korea . 57 E14
Köyceğiz, Turkey . 39 E10
Köyceğiz Gölü, Turkey . 39 E10
Koyulhisar, Turkey . 72 B7
Koyunyeri, Turkey . 41 F10
Koza, Japan . 55 L3
Kozak, Turkey . 39 B9
Kozan, Turkey . 70 B2
Kozáni, Greece . 40 F5
Kozáni □, Greece . 40 F5
Kozara, Bos.-H. . 29 D14
Kozarac, Bos.-H. . 29 D13
Kozelets, Ukraine . 47 G6
Kozelsk, Russia . 46 E8
Kozhikode = Calicut, India . 66 P9
Koziegłowy, Poland . 45 H6
Kozienice, Poland . 45 G8
Kozje, Slovenia . 29 B12
Kozloduy, Bulgaria . 40 C7
Kozlovets, Bulgaria . 41 C9
Kozlovka, Russia . 48 C9
Kozlu, Turkey . 72 B4
Kozluk, Turkey . 73 C9
Koźmin, Poland . 45 G4
Kozmodemyansk, Russia . 48 B8
Kożuchów, Poland . 45 G2
Kozyatyn, Ukraine . 47 H5
Kpabia, Ghana . 83 D4
Kpalimé, Togo . 83 D5
Kpandae, Ghana . 83 D4
Kpessi, Togo . 83 D5
Kra, Isthmus of = Kra, Kho Khot, Thailand . 65 G2
Kra, Kho Khot, Thailand . 65 G2
Kra Buri, Thailand . 65 G2
Kraai →, S. Africa . 88 E4
Krabi, Thailand . 65 H2
Kracheh, Cambodia . 64 F6
Kragan, Indonesia . 63 G14
Kragerø, Norway . 9 G13
Kragujevac, Serbia, Yug. . 40 B4
Krajenka, Poland . 45 E3
Krajina, Bos.-H. . 29 D13
Krakatau = Rakata, Pulau, Indonesia . 62 F3
Krakatoa = Rakata, Pulau, Indonesia . 62 F3
Krakor, Cambodia . 64 F5
Kraków, Poland . 45 H6
Kralanh, Cambodia . 64 F4
Králíky, Czech Rep. . 27 A9
Kraljevo, Serbia, Yug. . 40 C4

Kralovéhradecký □, Czech Rep. . 26 A8
Královský Chlmec, Slovak Rep. . 27 C14
Kralupy nad Vltavou, Czech Rep. . 26 A7
Kramatorsk, Ukraine . 47 H9
Kramfors, Sweden . 10 B11
Kraniá, Greece . 40 G5
Kranía Elassónas, Greece . 38 B4
Kranídhion, Greece . 38 D5
Kranj, Slovenia . 29 B11
Kranjska Gora, Slovenia . 29 B10
Krankskop, S. Africa . 89 D5
Krapina, Croatia . 29 B12
Krapina →, Croatia . 29 C12
Krapkowice, Poland . 45 H4
Kras, Croatia . 29 C10
Kraskino, Russia . 51 E14
Kråslava, Latvia . 46 E4
Kraslice, Czech Rep. . 26 A5
Krasnaya Gorbatka, Russia . 48 C5
Krasnaya Polyana, Russia . 49 J5
Kraśnik, Poland . 45 H9
Krasnoarmeisk, Ukraine . 47 H9
Krasnoarmeysk, Russia . 48 E7
Krasnoarmeyskiy, Russia . 49 G6
Krasnobród, Poland . 45 H10
Krasnodar, Russia . 49 H4
Krasnodon, Ukraine . 47 H10
Krasnogorskiy, Russia . 48 B9
Krasnograd = Krasnohrad, Ukraine . 47 H8
Krasnogvardeyskoye, Russia . 49 H5
Krasnogvardysk, Ukraine . 47 K8
Krasnohrad, Ukraine . 47 H8
Krasnokutsk, Ukraine . 47 G8
Krasnolesnyy, Russia . 47 G10
Krasnoperekopsk, Ukraine . 47 J7
Krasnorechenskiy, Russia . 54 B7
Krasnoselkup, Russia . 50 C9
Krasnoslobodsk, Mordvinia, Russia . 48 C6
Krasnoslobodsk, Volgograd, Russia . 49 F7
Krasnoturinsk, Russia . 50 D7
Krasnovodsk = Türkmenbashi, Turkmenistan . 50 E6
Krasnoyarsk, Russia . 51 D10
Krasnoye = Krasnyy, Russia . 46 E6
Krasnozavodsk, Russia . 46 D10
Krasny Sulin, Russia . 47 J11
Krasnystaw, Poland . 45 H10
Krasnyy, Russia . 46 E6
Krasnyy Kholm, Russia . 46 C9
Krasnyy Kut, Russia . 48 E8
Krasnyy Liman, Ukraine . 47 H9
Krasnyy Luch, Ukraine . 47 H10
Krasnyy Profintern, Russia . 46 D11
Krasnyy Yar, Astrakhan, Russia . 49 G9
Krasnyy Yar, Samara, Russia . 48 D10
Krasnyy Yar, Volgograd, Russia . 48 E7
Krasnyye Baki, Russia . 48 B7
Krasnyyoskolske Vdskh., Ukraine . 47 H9
Kraszna →, Hungary . 42 B7
Kratie = Kracheh, Cambodia . 64 F6
Kratovo, Macedonia . 40 D6
Krau, Indonesia . 63 E10
Kravanh, Chuor Phnum, Cambodia . 65 G4
Krefeld, Germany . 24 D2
Krémaston, Límni, Greece . 38 C3
Kremen, Croatia . 29 D12
Kremenchug = Kremenchuk, Ukraine . 47 H7
Kremenchuk, Ukraine . 47 H7
Kremenchuksk Vdskh., Ukraine . 47 H7
Kremenets, Ukraine . 47 G3
Kremennaya, Ukraine . 47 H10
Kremges = Svitlovodsk, Ukraine . 47 H7
Kremmen, Germany . 24 C9
Kremmling, U.S.A. . 114 F10
Kremnica, Slovak Rep. . 27 C11
Krems, Austria . 26 C8
Kremsmünster, Austria . 26 C7
Kretinga, Lithuania . 9 J19
Krettsy, Russia . 46 C7
Kreuzberg, Germany . 25 E5
Kreuztal, Germany . 24 E4
Kría Vrísi, Greece . 40 F6
Kribi, Cameroon . 83 E6
Krichem, Bulgaria . 41 D8
Krichev = Krychaw, Belarus . 46 F6
Krim, Slovenia . 29 C11
Kriós, Ákra, Greece . 36 D5
Krishna →, India . 67 M12
Krishnanagar, India . 69 H13
Kristdala, Sweden . 11 G10
Kristiansand, Norway . 9 G13
Kristianstad, Sweden . 11 H8
Kristiansund, Norway . 8 E12
Kristiinankaupunki, Finland . 9 E19
Kristinehamn, Sweden . 10 E8
Kristinestad = Kristiinankaupunki, Finland . 9 E19
Kríti, Greece . 36 D7
Kritsá, Greece . 36 D7
Kriva →, Macedonia . 40 D5
Kriva Palanka, Macedonia . 40 D6
Krivaja →, Bos.-H. . 42 F3
Krivelj, Serbia, Yug. . 40 B6
Krivoy Rog = Kryvyy Rih, Ukraine . 47 J7
Križevci, Croatia . 29 B13
Krk, Croatia . 29 C11
Krka →, Slovenia . 29 C12
Krkonoše, Czech Rep. . 26 A8
Krnov, Czech Rep. . 27 A10

Krobia, Poland . 45 G3
Krokeaí, Greece . 38 E4
Krokek, Sweden . 11 F10
Krokodil →, Mozam. . 89 D5
Krokom, Sweden . 10 A8
Krokowa, Poland . 44 D5
Krolevets, Ukraine . 47 G7
Kroměříž, Czech Rep. . 27 B10
Krompachy, Slovak Rep. . 27 C13
Kromy, Russia . 47 F8
Kronach, Germany . 25 E7
Krong Kaoh Kong, Cambodia . 62 B2
Kronobergs län □, Sweden . 11 H8
Kronprins Olav Kyst, Antarctica . 5 C5
Kronshtadt, Russia . 46 C5
Kroonstad, S. Africa . 88 D4
Kröpelin, Germany . 24 A7
Kropotkin, Russia . 49 H5
Kropp, Germany . 24 A5
Krosna, Lithuania . 44 D10
Krośniewice, Poland . 45 F6
Krosno, Poland . 45 J8
Krosno Odrzańskie, Poland . 45 F2
Krotoszyn, Poland . 45 G4
Krotovka, Russia . 48 D10
Kroussón, Greece . 36 D6
Krrabë, Albania . 40 E3
Krško, Slovenia . 29 C12
Krstača, Serbia, Yug. . 40 D4
Kruger Nat. Park, S. Africa . 89 C5
Krugersdorp, S. Africa . 89 D4
Kruisfontein, S. Africa . 88 E3
Krujë, Albania . 40 E3
Krulevshchina = Krulyewshchyna, Belarus . 46 E4
Krulyewshchyna, Belarus . 46 E4
Krumbach, Germany . 25 G6
Krumë, Albania . 40 D4
Krumovgrad, Bulgaria . 41 E9
Krung Thep = Bangkok, Thailand . 64 F3
Krupanj, Serbia, Yug. . 40 B3
Krupina, Slovak Rep. . 27 C12
Krupinica →, Slovak Rep. . 27 C11
Krupki, Belarus . 46 E5
Kruševac, Serbia, Yug. . 40 C5
Kruševo, Macedonia . 40 E5
Kruszwica, Poland . 45 F5
Krychaw, Belarus . 46 F6
Krymsk, Russia . 47 K10
Krymskiy Poluostrov = Krymskyy Pivostriv, Ukraine . 47 K8
Krymskyy Pivostriv, Ukraine . 47 K8
Krynica, Poland . 45 J7
Krynica Morska, Poland . 44 D6
Krynki, Poland . 45 E10
Kryvyy Rih, Ukraine . 47 J7
Krzepice, Poland . 45 H5
Krzeszów, Poland . 45 H9
Krzna →, Poland . 45 F10
Krzywiń, Poland . 45 G3
Krzyż Wielkopolski, Poland . 45 F2
Ksar el Kebir, Morocco . 78 B4
Ksar es Souk = Er Rachidia, Morocco . 78 B5
Książ Wielkopolski, Poland . 45 F4
Kstovo, Russia . 48 B7
Ku, W. el →, Sudan . 81 E2
Kuala Belait, Malaysia . 62 D4
Kuala Berang, Malaysia . 65 K4
Kuala Dungun = Dungun, Malaysia . 65 K4
Kuala Kangsar, Malaysia . 65 K3
Kuala Kelawang, Malaysia . 65 L4
Kuala Kerai, Malaysia . 65 K4
Kuala Lipis, Malaysia . 65 K4
Kuala Lumpur, Malaysia . 65 L3
Kuala Pilah, Malaysia . 65 L4
Kuala Rompin, Malaysia . 65 L4
Kuala Selangor, Malaysia . 65 L3
Kuala Sepetang, Malaysia . 65 K3
Kuala Terengganu, Malaysia . 65 K4
Kualajelai, Indonesia . 62 E4
Kualakapuas, Indonesia . 62 E4
Kualakurun, Indonesia . 62 E4
Kualapembuang, Indonesia . 62 E4
Kualasimpang, Indonesia . 62 D1
Kuancheng, China . 57 D10
Kuandang, Indonesia . 63 D6
Kuandian, China . 57 D13
Kuangchou = Guangzhou, China . 59 F9
Kuanshan, Taiwan . 59 F13
Kuantan, Malaysia . 65 L4
Kuba = Quba, Azerbaijan . 49 K9
Kuban →, Russia . 47 K9
Kubenskoye, Ozero, Russia . 46 C10
Kubokawa, Japan . 55 H6
Kubrat, Bulgaria . 41 C10
Kučevo, Serbia, Yug. . 40 B5
Kucha Gompa, India . 69 B7
Kuchaman, India . 68 F6
Kuchenspitze, Austria . 26 D3
Kuchinda, India . 69 J11
Kuching = Kuching, Malaysia . 62 D4
Kuchino-eruba-Jima, Japan . 55 J5
Kuchino-Shima, Japan . 55 K4
Kuchinotsu, Japan . 55 H5
Kuchl, Austria . 26 D6
Kucing = Kuching, Malaysia . 62 D4
Kuçovë, Albania . 40 F3
Küçükköy, Turkey . 39 B8
Küçükçekmece, Turkey . 41 E12
Küçükkuyu, Turkey . 39 B8
Küçükmenderes →, Turkey . 39 D9
Kud →, Pakistan . 68 F2
Kuda, India . 66 H7

Kudat, Malaysia ... 62 C5
Kudirkos Naumiestis, Lithuania 44 D9
Kudowa-Zdrój, Poland ... 45 H3
Kudus, Indonesia ... 63 G14
Kudymkar, Russia ... 50 D6
Kueiyang = Guiyang, China ... 58 D6
Kufra Oasis = Al Kufrah, Libya 79 D10
Kufstein, Austria ... 26 D5
Kugluktuk, Canada ... 100 B8
Kugong I., Canada ... 102 A4
Kühak, Iran ... 66 F3
Kuhan, Pakistan ... 68 E2
Kühbonān, Iran ... 71 D8
Kühestak, Iran ... 71 E8
Kuhin, Iran ... 71 B6
Kührī, Iran ... 71 E9
Kuhnsdorf, Austria ... 26 E7
Kühpāyeh, Eṣfahan, Iran ... 71 C7
Kühpāyeh, Kermān, Iran ... 71 D8
Kührān, Küh-e, Iran ... 71 E8
Kui Buri, Thailand ... 65 F2
Kuiseb →, Namibia ... 88 B2
Kuito, Angola ... 85 G3
Kuiu I., U.S.A. ... 104 B2
Kujang, N. Korea ... 57 E14
Kujawsko-Pomorskie □, Poland 44 E5
Kuji, Japan ... 54 D10
Kujū-San, Japan ... 55 H5
Kukavica, Serbia, Yug. ... 40 D5
Kukawa, Nigeria ... 83 C7
Kukës, Albania ... 40 D4
Kukmor, Russia ... 48 B10
Kukup, Malaysia ... 65 M4
Kukvidze, Russia ... 48 E6
Kula, Bulgaria ... 40 C6
Kula, Serbia, Yug. ... 42 E4
Kula, Turkey ... 39 C10
Kulachi, Pakistan ... 68 D4
Kulai, Malaysia ... 65 M4
Kulal, Mt., Kenya ... 86 B4
Kulaly, Ostrov, Kazakstan ... 49 H10
Kulasekarappattinam, India ... 66 Q11
Kulautuva, Lithuania ... 44 D10
Kuldīga, Latvia ... 9 H19
Kuldīga □, Latvia ... 44 B8
Kuldja = Yining, China ... 50 E9
Kuldu, Sudan ... 81 E2
Kulebaki, Russia ... 48 C6
Kulen, Cambodia ... 64 F5
Kulen Vakuf, Bos.-H. ... 29 D13
Kulgam, India ... 69 C6
Kulgera, Australia ... 94 D1
Kulim, Malaysia ... 65 K3
Kulin, Australia ... 93 F2
Kullen, Sweden ... 11 H6
Kulmbach, Germany ... 25 E7
Kŭlob, Tajikistan ... 50 F7
Kulp, Turkey ... 73 C9
Kulpawn →, Ghana ... 83 D4
Kulsary, Kazakstan ... 50 E6
Kulti, India ... 69 H12
Kulu, India ... 68 D7
Kulu, Turkey ... 72 C5
Kulumbura, Australia ... 92 B4
Kulunda, Russia ... 50 D8
Kulungar, Afghan. ... 68 C3
Kūlvand, Iran ... 71 D7
Kulwin, Australia ... 95 F3
Kulyab = Kŭlob, Tajikistan ... 50 F7
Kuma →, Russia ... 49 H8
Kumafşarı, Turkey ... 39 D11
Kumaganum, Nigeria ... 83 C7
Kumagaya, Japan ... 55 F9
Kumai, Indonesia ... 62 E4
Kumalar Dağı, Turkey ... 39 C12
Kumamba, Kepulauan, Indonesia ... 63 E9
Kumamoto, Japan ... 55 H5
Kumamoto □, Japan ... 55 H5
Kumanovo, Macedonia ... 40 D5
Kumara, N.Z. ... 91 K3
Kumarina, Australia ... 93 D2
Kumasi, Ghana ... 82 D4
Kumayri = Gyumri, Armenia ... 49 K6
Kumba, Cameroon ... 83 E6
Kumbağ, Turkey ... 41 F11
Kumbakonam, India ... 66 P11
Kumbarilla, Australia ... 95 D5
Kumbhraj, India ... 68 G7
Kumbia, Australia ... 95 D5
Kumbo, Cameroon ... 83 D7
Kŭmch'ŏn, N. Korea ... 57 E14
Kumdok, India ... 69 C8
Kume-Shima, Japan ... 55 L3
Kumeny, Russia ... 48 A9
Kumharsain, India ... 68 D7
Kŭmhwa, S. Korea ... 57 E14
Kumi, Uganda ... 86 B3
Kumkale, Turkey ... 41 G10
Kumla, Sweden ... 10 E9
Kumluca, Turkey ... 39 E12
Kummerower See, Germany ... 24 B8
Kumo, Nigeria ... 83 C7
Kumon Bum, Burma ... 67 F20
Kumylzhenskaya, Russia ... 48 F6
Kunágota, Hungary ... 42 D6
Kunashir, Ostrov, Russia ... 51 E15
Kunda, Estonia ... 9 G22
Kunda, India ... 69 G9
Kundar →, Pakistan ... 68 D3
Kundian, Pakistan ... 68 C4
Kundla, India ... 68 J4
Kunga →, Bangla. ... 69 J13
Kungälv, Sweden ... 11 G5
Kunghit I., Canada ... 104 C2
Kungrad = Qŭnghirot, Uzbekistan ... 50 E6

Kungsängen, Sweden ... 10 E11
Kungsbacka, Sweden ... 11 G6
Kungsgården, Sweden ... 10 D10
Kungshamn, Sweden ... 11 F5
Kungsör, Sweden ... 10 E10
Kungur, Russia ... 50 D6
Kunhar →, Pakistan ... 69 B5
Kunhegyes, Hungary ... 42 C5
Kuningan, Indonesia ... 63 G13
Kunlong, Burma ... 58 F2
Kunlun Shan, Asia ... 60 C3
Kunmadaras, Hungary ... 42 C5
Kunming, China ... 58 E4
Kunów, Poland ... 45 H8
Kunsan, S. Korea ... 57 G14
Kunshan, China ... 59 B13
Kunszentmárton, Hungary ... 42 D5
Kunszentmiklós, Hungary ... 42 C4
Kuntaur, Senegal ... 82 C2
Kununurra, Australia ... 92 C4
Kunwari →, India ... 69 F8
Kunya-Urgench = Köneürgench, Turkmenistan ... 50 E6
Künzelsau, Germany ... 25 F5
Kuopio, Finland ... 8 E22
Kupa →, Croatia ... 29 C13
Kupang, Indonesia ... 63 F6
Kupreanof I., U.S.A. ... 104 B2
Kupyansk, Ukraine ... 47 H9
Kupyansk-Uzlovoi, Ukraine ... 47 H9
Kuqa, China ... 60 B3
Kür →, Azerbaijan ... 73 C13
Kür Dili, Azerbaijan ... 71 B6
Kura = Kür →, Azerbaijan ... 73 C13
Kuranda, Australia ... 94 B4
Kuranga, India ... 68 H3
Kurashiki, Japan ... 55 G6
Kurayoshi, Japan ... 55 G6
Kürdämir, Azerbaijan ... 49 K9
Kurdistan, Asia ... 73 D10
Kŭrdzhali, Bulgaria ... 41 E9
Kure, Japan ... 55 G6
Küre, Turkey ... 72 B5
Küre Dağları, Turkey ... 72 B6
Kuressaare, Estonia ... 9 G20
Kurgan, Russia ... 50 D7
Kurganinsk, Russia ... 49 H5
Kurgannaya = Kurganinsk, Russia ... 49 H5
Kuri, India ... 68 F4
Kuria Maria Is. = Khurīyā Muriyā, Jazā'ir, Oman ... 74 D6
Kuridala, Australia ... 94 C3
Kurigram, Bangla. ... 67 G16
Kurikka, Finland ... 9 E20
Kuril Is. = Kurilskiye Ostrova, Russia ... 51 E15
Kuril Trench, Pac. Oc. ... 52 E19
Kurilsk, Russia ... 51 E15
Kurilskiye Ostrova, Russia ... 51 E15
Kurino, Japan ... 55 J5
Kurinskaya Kosa = Kür Dili, Azerbaijan ... 71 B6
Kurkur, Egypt ... 80 C3
Kurlovskiy, Russia ... 48 C5
Kurmuk, Sudan ... 81 E3
Kurnool, India ... 66 M11
Kuro-Shima, Kagoshima, Japan 55 J4
Kuro-Shima, Okinawa, Japan .. 55 M2
Kuror, J., Sudan ... 80 C3
Kurow, N.Z. ... 91 L3
Kurów, Poland ... 45 G9
Kurram →, Pakistan ... 68 C4
Kurri Kurri, Australia ... 95 E5
Kurrimine, Australia ... 94 B4
Kursavka, Russia ... 49 H6
Kurshskiy Zaliv, Russia ... 9 J19
Kursk, Russia ... 47 G9
Kuršumlija, Serbia, Yug. ... 40 C5
Kuršumlijska Banja, Serbia, Yug. 40 C5
Kurşunlu, Bursa, Turkey ... 41 F13
Kurşunlu, Çankırı, Turkey ... 72 B5
Kurtalan, Turkey ... 73 D9
Kurtbey, Turkey ... 41 E10
Kuru, Sudan ... 81 F2
Kuru, Bahr el →, Sudan ... 81 F2
Kurucaşile, Turkey ... 72 B5
Kuruçay, Turkey ... 70 B3
Kuruktag, China ... 60 B3
Kuruman, S. Africa ... 88 D3
Kuruman →, S. Africa ... 88 D3
Kurume, Japan ... 55 H5
Kurun →, Sudan ... 81 F3
Kurunegala, Sri Lanka ... 66 R12
Kurya, Russia ... 50 C6
Kus Gölü, Turkey ... 41 F11
Kuşadası, Turkey ... 72 D2
Kuşadası Körfezi, Turkey ... 39 D8
Kusatsu, Japan ... 55 F9
Kusawa L., Canada ... 104 A1
Kusel, Germany ... 25 F3
Kushaka, Nigeria ... 83 C6
Kushalgarh, India ... 68 H6
Kushchevskaya, Russia ... 49 G4
Kusheriki, Nigeria ... 83 C6
Kushikino, Japan ... 55 J5
Kushima, Japan ... 55 J5
Kushimoto, Japan ... 55 H7
Kushiro, Japan ... 54 C12
Kushiro-Gawa →, Japan ... 54 C12
Kūshk, Iran ... 71 D8
Kushka = Gushgy, Turkmenistan 50 F7
Kūshkī, Iran ... 70 C5
Kushol, India ... 69 C7
Kushtia, Bangla. ... 67 H16
Kushum →, Kazakstan ... 48 F10

Kuskokwim B., U.S.A. ... 100 C3
Kusmi, India ... 69 H10
Kussharo-Ko, Japan ... 54 C12
Kustanay = Qostanay, Kazakstan ... 50 D7
Kut, Ko, Thailand ... 65 G4
Kütahya, Turkey ... 39 B12
Kütahya □, Turkey ... 39 B11
Kutaisi, Georgia ... 49 J6
Kutaraja = Banda Aceh, Indonesia ... 62 C1
Kutch, Gulf of = Kachchh, Gulf of, India ... 68 H3
Kutch, Rann of = Kachchh, Rann of, India ... 68 H4
Kutina, Croatia ... 29 C13
Kutiyana, India ... 68 J4
Kutjevo, Croatia ... 42 E2
Kutkashen, Azerbaijan ... 49 K8
Kutná Hora, Czech Rep. ... 26 B8
Kutno, Poland ... 45 F6
Kutse, Botswana ... 88 C3
Kutu, Dem. Rep. of the Congo . 84 E3
Kutum, Sudan ... 81 E1
Kúty, Slovak Rep. ... 27 C10
Kuujjuaq, Canada ... 101 C13
Kuujjuarapik, Canada ... 102 A4
Kuŭp-tong, N. Korea ... 57 D14
Kuusamo, Finland ... 8 D23
Kuusankoski, Finland ... 9 F22
Kuvshinovo, Russia ... 46 D8
Kuwait = Al Kuwayt, Kuwait ... 70 D5
Kuwait ■, Asia ... 70 D5
Kuwana, Japan ... 55 G8
Kuwana →, India ... 69 F10
Kuybyshev = Samara, Russia ... 48 D10
Kuybyshev, Russia ... 50 D8
Kuybyshevo, Ukraine ... 47 J9
Kuybyshevskoye Vdkhr., Russia 48 C9
Kuye He →, China ... 56 E6
Kūyeh, Iran ... 70 B5
Kūysanjaq, Iraq ... 70 B5
Kuyucak, Turkey ... 39 D10
Kuyumba, Russia ... 51 C10
Kuzey Anadolu Dağları, Turkey 72 B7
Kuzmin, Serbia, Yug. ... 42 E4
Kuznetsk, Russia ... 48 D8
Kuzomen, Russia ... 50 C4
Kvænangen, Norway ... 8 A19
Kvaløy, Norway ... 8 B18
Kværndrup, Denmark ... 11 J4
Kvänum, Sweden ... 11 F7
Kvareli = Qvareli, Georgia ... 49 K7
Kvarner, Croatia ... 29 D11
Kvarnerič, Croatia ... 29 D11
Kvicksund, Sweden ... 10 E10
Kvillsfors, Sweden ... 11 G9
Kvissleby, Sweden ... 10 B11
Kwa-Nobuhle, S. Africa ... 85 L5
Kwabhaca, S. Africa ... 89 E4
Kwakhanai, Botswana ... 88 C3
Kwakoegron, Surinam ... 125 B7
Kwale, Kenya ... 86 C4
Kwale, Nigeria ... 83 D6
KwaMashu, S. Africa ... 89 D5
Kwando →, Africa ... 88 B3
Kwangdaeri, N. Korea ... 57 D14
Kwangju, S. Korea ... 57 G14
Kwango →, Dem. Rep. of the Congo ... 84 E3
Kwangsi-Chuang = Guangxi Zhuangzu Zizhiqu □, China . 58 F7
Kwangtung = Guangdong □, China ... 59 F10
Kwara □, Nigeria ... 83 D6
Kwataboahegan →, Canada ... 102 B3
Kwatisore, Indonesia ... 63 E8
Kweichow = Guizhou □, China 58 D6
Kwekwe, Zimbabwe ... 87 F2
Kwidzyn, Poland ... 44 E5
Kwiha, Ethiopia ... 81 E4
Kwinana New Town, Australia .. 93 F2
Kwisa →, Poland ... 45 G2
Kwoka, Indonesia ... 63 E8
Kwolla, Nigeria ... 83 D6
Kyabra Cr. →, Australia ... 95 D3
Kyabram, Australia ... 95 F4
Kyaikto, Burma ... 64 D1
Kyakhta, Russia ... 51 D11
Kyancutta, Australia ... 95 E2
Kyaukpadaung, Burma ... 67 J19
Kyaukpyu, Burma ... 67 K18
Kyaukse, Burma ... 67 J20
Kyburz, U.S.A. ... 116 G6
Kyelang, India ... 68 C7
Kyenjojo, Uganda ... 86 B3
Kyjov, Czech Rep. ... 27 B10
Kyle, Canada ... 105 C7
Kyle Dam, Zimbabwe ... 87 G3
Kyle of Lochalsh, U.K. ... 14 D3
Kyll →, Germany ... 25 E2
Kyllburg, Germany ... 25 E2
Kymijoki →, Finland ... 9 F22
Kyneton, Australia ... 95 F3
Kynuna, Australia ... 94 C3
Kyō-ga-Saki, Japan ... 55 G7
Kyoga, L., Uganda ... 86 B3
Kyogle, Australia ... 95 D5
Kyom →, Sudan ... 81 F2
Kyongju, S. Korea ... 57 G15
Kyongpyaw, Burma ... 67 L19
Kyŏngsŏng, N. Korea ... 57 D15
Kyōto, Japan ... 55 G7
Kyōto □, Japan ... 55 G7

Kyparissovouno, Cyprus ... 36 D12
Kyperounda, Cyprus ... 36 E11
Kyrenia, Cyprus ... 36 D12
Kyrgyzstan ■, Asia ... 50 E8
Kyritz, Germany ... 24 C8
Kyrkhult, Sweden ... 11 H8
Kyrönjoki →, Finland ... 8 E19
Kystatyam, Russia ... 51 C13
Kysucké Nové Mesto, Slovak Rep. ... 27 B11
Kythréa, Cyprus ... 36 D12
Kyunhla, Burma ... 67 H19
Kyuquot Sound, Canada ... 104 D3
Kyurdamir = Kürdämir, Azerbaijan ... 49 K9
Kyūshū, Japan ... 55 H5
Kyūshū □, Japan ... 55 H5
Kyūshū-Sanchi, Japan ... 55 H5
Kyustendil, Bulgaria ... 40 D6
Kyusyur, Russia ... 51 B13
Kyyiv, Ukraine ... 47 G6
Kyyivske Vdskh., Ukraine ... 47 G6
Kyzyl, Russia ... 51 D10
Kyzyl Kum, Uzbekistan ... 50 E7
Kyzyl-Kyya, Kyrgyzstan ... 50 E8
Kzyl-Orda = Qyzylorda, Kazakstan ... 50 E7

L

La Albuera, Spain ... 35 G4
La Alcarria, Spain ... 32 E2
La Almarcha, Spain ... 32 F2
La Almunia de Doña Godina, Spain ... 32 D3
La Asunción, Venezuela ... 124 A6
La Baie, Canada ... 103 C5
La Banda, Argentina ... 126 B3
La Bañeza, Spain ... 34 C5
La Barca, Mexico ... 118 C4
La Barge, U.S.A. ... 114 E8
La Bastide-Puylaurent, France . 20 D7
La Baule-Escoublac, France ... 18 E4
La Belle, U.S.A. ... 109 M5
La Biche →, Canada ... 104 B4
La Biche, L., Canada ... 104 C6
La Bisbal d'Empordà, Spain ... 32 D8
La Bomba, Mexico ... 118 A1
La Brède, France ... 20 D3
La Bresse, France ... 19 D13
La Bureba, Spain ... 34 C7
La Calera, Chile ... 126 C1
La Campiña, Spain ... 35 H6
La Canal = Sa Canal, Spain ... 37 C7
La Canourgue, France ... 20 D7
La Capelle, France ... 19 C10
La Carlota, Argentina ... 126 C3
La Carlota, Phil. ... 61 F5
La Carlota, Spain ... 35 H6
La Carolina, Spain ... 35 G7
La Cavalerie, France ... 20 D7
La Ceiba, Honduras ... 120 C2
La Chaise-Dieu, France ... 20 C7
La Chapelle d'Angillon, France . 19 E9
La Chapelle-sur-Erdre, France . 18 E5
La Charité-sur-Loire, France ... 19 E10
La Chartre-sur-le-Loir, France . 18 E7
La Châtaigneraie, France ... 20 B3
La Châtre, France ... 19 F9
La Chaux-de-Fonds, Switz. ... 25 H2
La Chorrera, Panama ... 120 E4
La Ciotat, France ... 21 E9
La Clayette, France ... 19 F11
La Cocha, Argentina ... 126 B2
La Concepción = Ri-Aba, Eq. Guin. ... 83 E6
La Concepción, Panama ... 120 E3
La Concordia, Mexico ... 119 D6
La Coruña = A Coruña, Spain . 34 B2
La Coruña □, Spain ... 34 B2
La Côte-St-André, France ... 21 C9
La Courtine-le-Trucq, France . 20 C6
La Crau, Bouches-du-Rhône, France ... 21 E8
La Crau, Var, France ... 21 E10
La Crescent, U.S.A. ... 112 D7
La Crete, Canada ... 104 B5
La Crosse, Kans., U.S.A. ... 112 F5
La Crosse, Wis., U.S.A. ... 112 D9
La Cruz, Costa Rica ... 120 D2
La Cruz, Mexico ... 118 C3
La Désirade, Guadeloupe ... 121 C7
La Escondida, Mexico ... 118 C5
La Esmeralda, Paraguay ... 126 A3
La Esperanza, Honduras ... 120 D2
La Estrada = A Estrada, Spain . 34 C2
La Faouët, France ... 18 E3
La Fayette, U.S.A. ... 109 H3
La Fé, Cuba ... 120 B3
La Fère, France ... 19 C10
La Ferté-Gaucher, France ... 19 D10
La Ferté-Macé, France ... 18 D6
La Ferté-St-Aubin, France ... 19 E8
La Ferté-sous-Jouarre, France . 19 D10
La Ferté-Vidame, France ... 18 D7
La Flèche, France ... 18 E6
La Follette, U.S.A. ... 109 G3
La Fuente de San Esteban, Spain ... 34 E4
La Gacilly, France ... 18 E4

La Gineta, Spain ... 33 F2
La Grand-Combe, France ... 21 D8
La Grande, U.S.A. ... 114 D4
La Grande →, Canada ... 102 B5
La Grande Deux, Rés., Canada 102 B4
La Grande-Motte, France ... 21 E8
La Grande Quatre, Rés., Canada 102 B5
La Grande Trois, Rés., Canada 102 B4
La Grange, Calif., U.S.A. ... 116 H6
La Grange, Ga., U.S.A. ... 109 J3
La Grange, Ky., U.S.A. ... 108 F3
La Grange, Tex., U.S.A. ... 113 L6
La Grave, France ... 21 C10
La Guaira, Venezuela ... 124 A5
La Guardia = A Guarda, Spain 34 D2
La Gudiña = A Gudiña, Spain . 34 C3
La Guerche-de-Bretagne, France 18 E5
La Guerche-sur-l'Aubois, France 19 F9
La Habana, Cuba ... 120 B3
La Haye-du-Puits, France ... 18 C5
La Horra, Spain ... 34 D7
La Independencia, Mexico ... 119 D6
La Isabela, Dom. Rep. ... 121 C5
La Jonquera, Spain ... 32 C7
La Junta, U.S.A. ... 113 F3
La Laguna, Canary Is. ... 37 F3
La Libertad, Guatemala ... 120 C1
La Libertad, Mexico ... 118 B2
La Ligua, Chile ... 126 C1
La Línea de la Concepción, Spain ... 35 J5
La Loche, Canada ... 105 B7
La Londe-les-Maures, France .. 21 E10
La Lora, Spain ... 34 C7
La Loupe, France ... 18 D8
La Louvière, Belgium ... 17 D4
La Machine, France ... 19 F10
La Maddalena, Italy ... 30 A2
La Malbaie, Canada ... 103 C5
La Mancha, Spain ... 33 F2
La Mariña, Spain ... 34 B3
La Martre, L., Canada ... 104 A5
La Mesa, U.S.A. ... 117 N9
La Misión, Mexico ... 118 A1
La Mothe-Achard, France ... 18 F5
La Motte, France ... 21 D10
La Motte-Chalançon, France .. 21 D9
La Motte-Servolex, France ... 21 C9
La Moure, U.S.A. ... 112 B5
La Muela, Spain ... 32 D3
La Mure, France ... 21 D9
La Negra, Chile ... 126 A1
La Oliva, Canary Is. ... 37 F6
La Orotava, Canary Is. ... 37 F3
La Oroya, Peru ... 124 F3
La Pacaudière, France ... 19 F10
La Palma, Canary Is. ... 37 F2
La Palma, Panama ... 120 E4
La Palma del Condado, Spain . 35 H4
La Paloma, Chile ... 126 C1
La Pampa □, Argentina ... 126 D2
La Paragua, Venezuela ... 124 B6
La Paz, Entre Ríos, Argentina . 126 C4
La Paz, San Luis, Argentina ... 126 C2
La Paz, Bolivia ... 124 G5
La Paz, Honduras ... 120 D2
La Paz, Mexico ... 118 C2
La Paz, Phil. ... 61 D4
La Paz Centro, Nic. ... 120 D2
La Pedrera, Colombia ... 124 D5
La Pérade, Canada ... 103 C5
La Perouse Str., Asia ... 54 B11
La Pesca, Mexico ... 119 C5
La Piedad, Mexico ... 118 C4
La Pine, U.S.A. ... 114 E3
La Plata, Argentina ... 126 D4
La Pobla de Lillet, Spain ... 32 C6
La Pocatière, Canada ... 103 C5
La Pola de Gordón, Spain ... 34 C5
La Porta, France ... 21 F13
La Porte, Ind., U.S.A. ... 108 E2
La Porte, Tex., U.S.A. ... 113 L7
La Presanella, Italy ... 28 B7
La Puebla = Sa Pobla, Spain ... 32 F8
La Puebla de los Infantes, Spain 35 H5
La Puebla de Montalbán, Spain 34 F6
La Puebla del Río, Spain ... 35 H4
La Puerta de Segura, Spain ... 35 G8
La Purísima, Mexico ... 118 B2
La Push, U.S.A. ... 116 C2
La Quiaca, Argentina ... 126 A2
La Réole, France ... 20 D3
La Restinga, Canary Is. ... 37 G2
La Rioja, Argentina ... 126 B2
La Rioja □, Argentina ... 126 B2
La Rioja □, Spain ... 32 C2
La Robla, Spain ... 34 C5
La Roche-Bernard, France ... 18 E4
La Roche-Canillac, France ... 20 C5
La Roche-en-Ardenne, Belgium 17 D5
La Roche-sur-Foron, France ... 19 F13
La Roche-sur-Yon, France ... 18 F5
La Rochefoucauld, France ... 20 C4
La Rochelle, France ... 20 B2
La Roda, Spain ... 33 F2
La Roda de Andalucía, Spain .. 35 H6
La Romana, Dom. Rep. ... 121 C6
La Ronge, Canada ... 105 B7
La Rumorosa, Mexico ... 117 N10
La Sabina = Sa Savina, Spain . 37 C7
La Sagra, Spain ... 33 H2
La Salle, U.S.A. ... 112 E10
La Sanabria, Spain ... 34 C4
La Santa, Canary Is. ... 37 E6
La Sarre, Canada ... 102 C4
La Scie, Canada ... 103 C8

La Selva, *Spain*	32	C7
La Selva Beach, *U.S.A.*	116	J5
La Selva del Camp, *Spain*	32	D6
La Serena, *Chile*	126	B1
La Serena, *Spain*	35	G5
La Seu d'Urgell, *Spain*	32	C6
La Seyne-sur-Mer, *France*	21	E9
La Sila, *Italy*	31	C9
La Solana, *Spain*	35	G7
La Soufrière, *St. Vincent*	121	D7
La Souterraine, *France*	19	F8
La Spézia, *Italy*	28	D6
La Suze-sur-Sarthe, *France*	18	E7
La Tagua, *Colombia*	124	C4
La Teste, *France*	20	D2
La Tortuga, *Venezuela*	121	D6
La Tour-du-Pin, *France*	21	C9
La Tranche-sur-Mer, *France*	18	F5
La Tremblade, *France*	20	C2
La Tuque, *Canada*	102	C5
La Unión, *Chile*	128	E2
La Unión, *El Salv.*	120	D2
La Unión, *Mexico*	118	D4
La Unión, *Spain*	33	H4
La Urbana, *Venezuela*	124	B5
La Vall d'Uixó, *Spain*	32	F4
La Vecilla de Curveño, *Spain*	34	C5
La Vega, *Dom. Rep.*	121	C5
La Vela de Coro, *Venezuela*	124	A5
La Veleta, *Spain*	35	H7
La Venta, *Mexico*	119	D6
La Ventura, *Mexico*	118	C4
La Voulte-sur-Rhône, *France*	21	D8
Laa an der Thaya, *Austria*	27	C9
Laaber, Grosse ➔, *Germany*	25	G8
Laage, *Germany*	24	B8
Laatzen, *Germany*	24	C5
Laba ➔, *Russia*	49	H4
Labasa, *Fiji*	91	C8
Labason, *Phil.*	61	G5
Labastide-Murat, *France*	20	D5
Labastide-Rouairoux, *France*	20	E6
Labbézenga, *Mali*	83	B5
Labe = Elbe ➔, *Europe*	24	B4
Labé, *Guinea*	82	C2
Laberge, L., *Canada*	104	A1
Labin, *Croatia*	29	C11
Labinsk, *Russia*	49	H5
Labis, *Malaysia*	65	L4
Łabiszyn, *Poland*	45	F4
Labo, *Phil.*	61	D5
Laboe, *Germany*	24	A6
Laborec ➔, *Slovak Rep.*	27	C14
Labouheyre, *France*	20	D3
Laboulaye, *Argentina*	126	C3
Labrador, *Canada*	103	B7
Labrador City, *Canada*	103	B6
Labrador Sea, *Atl. Oc.*	101	C14
Lábrea, *Brazil*	124	E6
Labruguière, *France*	20	E6
Labuan, *Malaysia*	62	C5
Labuan, Pulau, *Malaysia*	62	C5
Labuha, *Indonesia*	63	E7
Labuhan, *Indonesia*	63	G11
Labuhanbajo, *Indonesia*	63	F6
Labuk, Telok, *Malaysia*	62	C5
Labyrinth, L., *Australia*	95	E2
Labytnangi, *Russia*	50	C7
Laç, *Albania*	40	E3
Lac Bouchette, *Canada*	103	C5
Lac Édouard, *Canada*	102	C5
Lac La Biche, *Canada*	104	C6
Lac la Martre = Wha Ti, *Canada*	100	B8
Lac La Ronge Prov. Park, *Canada*	105	B7
Lac-Mégantic, *Canada*	103	C5
Lac Thien, *Vietnam*	64	F7
Lacanau, *France*	20	D2
Lacanau, Étang de, *France*	20	D2
Lacantúm ➔, *Mexico*	119	D6
Lacara ➔, *Spain*	35	G4
Lacaune, *France*	20	E6
Lacaune, Mts. de, *France*	20	E6
Laccadive Is. = Lakshadweep Is., *India*	52	H11
Lacepede B., *Australia*	95	F2
Lacepede Is., *Australia*	92	C3
Lacerdónia, *Mozam.*	87	F4
Lacey, *U.S.A.*	116	C4
Lachhmangarh, *India*	68	F6
Lachi, *Pakistan*	68	C4
Lachine, *Canada*	102	C5
Lachlan ➔, *Australia*	95	E3
Lachute, *Canada*	102	C5
Lackawanna, *U.S.A.*	110	D6
Lackawaxen, *U.S.A.*	111	E10
Lacolle, *Canada*	111	A11
Lacombe, *Canada*	104	C6
Lacona, *U.S.A.*	111	C8
Láconi, *Italy*	30	C2
Laconia, *U.S.A.*	111	C13
Lacq, *France*	20	E3
Ladakh Ra., *India*	69	C8
Ładek-Zdrój, *Poland*	45	H3
Ládhon ➔, *Greece*	38	D3
Ladik, *Turkey*	72	B6
Ladismith, *S. Africa*	88	E3
Ladíspoli, *Italy*	29	G9
Lādīz, *Iran*	71	D9
Ladnun, *India*	68	F6
Ladoga, L. = Ladozhskoye Ozero, *Russia*	46	B6
Ladozhskoye Ozero, *Russia*	46	B6
Lady Elliott I., *Australia*	94	C5
Lady Grey, *S. Africa*	88	E4
Ladybrand, *S. Africa*	88	D4
Ladysmith, *Canada*	104	D4
Ladysmith, *S. Africa*	89	D4
Ladysmith, *U.S.A.*	112	C9
Lae, *Papua N. G.*	96	H6
Laem Ngop, *Thailand*	65	F4
Laem Pho, *Thailand*	65	J3
Læsø, *Denmark*	11	G5
Læsø Rende, *Denmark*	11	G4
Lafayette, *Colo., U.S.A.*	112	F2
Lafayette, *Ind., U.S.A.*	108	E2
Lafayette, *La., U.S.A.*	113	K9
Lafayette, *Tenn., U.S.A.*	109	G2
Laferte ➔, *Canada*	104	A5
Lafia, *Nigeria*	83	D6
Lafiagi, *Nigeria*	83	D6
Laflèche, *Canada*	105	D7
Lafon, *Sudan*	81	F3
Lagan, *Sweden*	11	H7
Lagan ➔, *Sweden*	11	H6
Lagan ➔, *U.K.*	15	B6
Lagarfljót ➔, *Iceland*	8	D6
Lage, *Germany*	24	D4
Lagen ➔, *Oppland, Norway*	9	F14
Lågen ➔, *Vestfold, Norway*	9	G14
Lägerdorf, *Germany*	24	B5
Laghouat, *Algeria*	78	B6
Lagnieu, *France*	21	C9
Lagny-sur-Marne, *France*	19	D9
Lago, *Italy*	31	C9
Lagôa, *Portugal*	35	H2
Lagoa Vermelha, *Brazil*	127	B5
Lagoaça, *Portugal*	34	D4
Lagodekhi, *Georgia*	49	K8
Lagónegro, *Italy*	31	B8
Lagonoy G., *Phil.*	61	E5
Lagos, *Nigeria*	83	D5
Lagos, *Portugal*	35	H2
Lagos □, *Nigeria*	83	D5
Lagos de Moreno, *Mexico*	118	C4
Lagrange, *Australia*	92	C3
Lagrange B., *Australia*	92	C3
Laguardia, *Spain*	32	C2
Laguépie, *France*	20	D5
Laguna, *Brazil*	127	B6
Laguna, *U.S.A.*	115	J10
Laguna Beach, *U.S.A.*	117	M9
Laguna de Duera, *Spain*	34	D6
Laguna Limpia, *Argentina*	126	B4
Lagunas, *Chile*	126	A2
Lagunas, *Peru*	124	E3
Lahad Datu, *Malaysia*	63	C5
Lahad Datu, Teluk, *Malaysia*	63	D5
Lahan Sai, *Thailand*	64	E4
Lahanam, *Laos*	64	D5
Lahar, *India*	69	F8
Laharpur, *India*	69	F9
Lahat, *Indonesia*	62	E2
Lahewa, *Indonesia*	62	D1
Lāhījān, *Iran*	71	B6
Lahn ➔, *Germany*	25	E3
Lahnstein, *Germany*	25	E3
Laholm, *Sweden*	11	H7
Laholmsbukten, *Sweden*	11	H6
Lahore, *Pakistan*	68	D6
Lahr, *Germany*	25	G3
Lahri, *Pakistan*	68	E3
Lahti, *Finland*	9	F21
Lahtis = Lahti, *Finland*	9	F21
Laï, *Chad*	79	G9
Lai Chau, *Vietnam*	58	F4
Lai'an, *China*	59	A12
Laibin, *China*	58	F7
Laifeng, *China*	58	C7
L'Aigle, *France*	18	D7
Laignes, *France*	19	E11
L'Aiguillon-sur-Mer, *France*	20	B2
Laila = Laylá, *Si. Arabia*	74	C4
Laingsburg, *S. Africa*	88	E3
Lainio älv ➔, *Sweden*	8	C20
Lairg, *U.K.*	14	C4
Laishui, *China*	56	E8
Laissac, *France*	20	D6
Láives, *Italy*	29	B8
Laiwu, *China*	57	F9
Laixi, *China*	57	F11
Laiyang, *China*	57	F11
Laiyuan, *China*	56	E8
Laizhou, *China*	57	F10
Laizhou Wan, *China*	57	F10
Laja ➔, *Mexico*	118	C4
Lajere, *Nigeria*	83	C7
Lajes, *Brazil*	127	B5
Lajkovac, *Serbia, Yug.*	40	B4
Lajosmizse, *Hungary*	42	C4
Lak Sao, *Laos*	64	C5
Lakaband, *Pakistan*	68	D3
Lakamané, *Mali*	82	C3
Lake Alpine, *U.S.A.*	116	G7
Lake Andes, *U.S.A.*	112	D5
Lake Arthur, *U.S.A.*	113	K8
Lake Cargelligo, *Australia*	95	E4
Lake Charles, *U.S.A.*	113	K8
Lake City, *Colo., U.S.A.*	115	G10
Lake City, *Fla., U.S.A.*	109	K4
Lake City, *Mich., U.S.A.*	108	C3
Lake City, *Minn., U.S.A.*	112	C8
Lake City, *Pa., U.S.A.*	110	D4
Lake City, *S.C., U.S.A.*	109	J6
Lake Cowichan, *Canada*	104	D4
Lake District, *U.K.*	12	C4
Lake Elsinore, *U.S.A.*	117	M9
Lake George, *U.S.A.*	111	C11
Lake Grace, *Australia*	93	F2
Lake Harbour = Kimmirut, *Canada*	101	B13
Lake Havasu City, *U.S.A.*	117	L12
Lake Hughes, *U.S.A.*	117	L8
Lake Isabella, *U.S.A.*	117	K8
Lake Jackson, *U.S.A.*	113	L7
Lake Junction, *U.S.A.*	114	D8
Lake King, *Australia*	93	F2
Lake Lenore, *Canada*	105	C8
Lake Louise, *Canada*	104	C5
Lake Mead National Recreation Area, *U.S.A.*	117	K12
Lake Mills, *U.S.A.*	112	D8
Lake Placid, *U.S.A.*	111	B11
Lake Pleasant, *U.S.A.*	111	C10
Lake Providence, *U.S.A.*	113	J9
Lake St. Peter, *Canada*	110	A6
Lake Superior Prov. Park, *Canada*	102	C3
Lake Village, *U.S.A.*	113	J9
Lake Wales, *U.S.A.*	109	M5
Lake Worth, *U.S.A.*	109	M5
Lakeba, *Fiji*	91	D9
Lakefield, *Canada*	102	D4
Lakehurst, *U.S.A.*	111	F10
Lakeland, *Australia*	94	B3
Lakeland, *U.S.A.*	109	M5
Lakeport, *Calif., U.S.A.*	116	F4
Lakeport, *Mich., U.S.A.*	110	C2
Lakes Entrance, *Australia*	95	F4
Lakeside, *Ariz., U.S.A.*	115	J9
Lakeside, *Calif., U.S.A.*	117	N10
Lakeside, *Nebr., U.S.A.*	112	D3
Lakeside, *Ohio, U.S.A.*	110	E2
Lakeview, *U.S.A.*	114	E3
Lakeville, *U.S.A.*	112	C8
Lakewood, *Colo., U.S.A.*	112	F2
Lakewood, *N.J., U.S.A.*	111	F10
Lakewood, *N.Y., U.S.A.*	110	D5
Lakewood, *Ohio, U.S.A.*	110	E3
Lakewood, *Wash., U.S.A.*	116	C4
Lakha, *India*	68	F4
Lakhaniá, *Greece*	36	D9
Lakhimpur, *India*	69	F9
Lakhnadon, *India*	69	H8
Lakhonpheng, *Laos*	64	E5
Lakhpat, *India*	68	H3
Läki, *Azerbaijan*	49	K8
Lakin, *U.S.A.*	113	G4
Lakitusaki ➔, *Canada*	102	B3
Lakki, *Pakistan*	68	C4
Lákkoi, *Greece*	36	D5
Lakonía □, *Greece*	38	E4
Lakonikós Kólpos, *Greece*	38	E4
Lakor, *Indonesia*	63	F7
Lakota, *Ivory C.*	82	D3
Lakota, *U.S.A.*	112	A5
Laksar, *India*	68	E8
Laksefjorden, *Norway*	8	A22
Lakselv, *Norway*	8	A21
Lakshadweep Is., *India*	52	H11
Lakshmanpur, *India*	69	H10
Lakshmikantapur, *India*	69	H13
Lala Ghat, *India*	67	G18
Lala Musa, *Pakistan*	68	C5
Lalago, *Tanzania*	86	C3
Lalapanzi, *Zimbabwe*	87	F3
Lalapaşa, *Turkey*	41	E10
Lalbenque, *France*	20	D5
L'Albufera, *Spain*	33	F4
Lalganj, *India*	69	G11
Lalgola, *India*	69	G13
Lālī, *Iran*	71	C6
Lalibela, *Ethiopia*	81	E4
Lalín, *China*	57	B14
Lalín, *Spain*	34	C2
Lalin He ➔, *China*	57	B13
Lalinde, *France*	20	D4
Lalitpur, *India*	69	G8
Lalkua, *India*	69	E8
Lalsot, *India*	68	F7
Lam, *Vietnam*	64	B6
Lam Pao Res., *Thailand*	64	D4
Lama Kara, *Togo*	83	D5
Lamaing, *Burma*	67	M20
Lamar, *Colo., U.S.A.*	112	F3
Lamar, *Mo., U.S.A.*	113	G7
Lamas, *Peru*	124	E3
Lamastre, *France*	21	D8
Lambaréné, *Gabon*	84	E2
Lambay I., *Ireland*	15	C5
Lambert Glacier, *Antarctica*	5	D6
Lambert's Bay, *S. Africa*	88	E2
Lambesc, *France*	21	E9
Lambeth, *Canada*	110	D3
Lámbia, *Greece*	38	D3
Lambomakondro, *Madag.*	89	C7
Lambro ➔, *Italy*	28	C6
Lame, *Nigeria*	83	C6
Lame Deer, *U.S.A.*	114	D10
Lamego, *Portugal*	34	D3
Lamèque, *Canada*	103	C7
Lameroo, *Australia*	95	F3
Lamesa, *U.S.A.*	113	J4
Lamía, *Greece*	38	E4
Lamitan, *Phil.*	61	H5
Lammermuir Hills, *U.K.*	14	F6
Lammhult, *Sweden*	11	G8
Lamoille ➔, *U.S.A.*	111	B11
Lamon B., *Phil.*	61	D5
Lamont, *Canada*	104	C6
Lamont, *Calif., U.S.A.*	117	K8
Lamont, *Wyo., U.S.A.*	114	E10
Lamotte-Beuvron, *France*	19	E9
Lampa, *Peru*	124	G4
Lampang, *Thailand*	64	C2
Lampasas, *U.S.A.*	113	K5
Lampazos de Naranjo, *Mexico*	118	B4
Lampedusa, *Medit. S.*	36	F1
Lampertheim, *Germany*	25	F4
Lampeter, *U.K.*	13	E3
Lampman, *Canada*	105	D8
Lamprechtshausen, *Austria*	26	D5
Lampung □, *Indonesia*	62	F2
Lamta, *India*	69	H9
Lamu, *Kenya*	86	C5
Lamy, *U.S.A.*	115	J11
Lan Xian, *China*	56	E6
Lan Yu = Hungt'ou Hsü, *Taiwan*	59	G13
Lanak La, *India*	69	B8
Lanak'o Shank'ou = Lanak La, *India*	69	B8
Lanao, L., *Phil.*	61	H6
Lanark, *Canada*	111	A8
Lanark, *U.K.*	14	F5
Lanbi Kyun, *Burma*	65	G2
Lancang, *China*	58	F2
Lancang Jiang ➔, *China*	58	G3
Lancashire □, *U.K.*	12	D5
Lancaster, *Canada*	111	A10
Lancaster, *U.K.*	12	C5
Lancaster, *Calif., U.S.A.*	117	L8
Lancaster, *Ky., U.S.A.*	108	G3
Lancaster, *N.H., U.S.A.*	111	B13
Lancaster, *N.Y., U.S.A.*	110	D6
Lancaster, *Ohio, U.S.A.*	108	F4
Lancaster, *Pa., U.S.A.*	111	F8
Lancaster, *S.C., U.S.A.*	109	H5
Lancaster, *Wis., U.S.A.*	112	D9
Lancaster Sd., *Canada*	101	A11
Lancelin, *Australia*	93	F2
Lanchow = Lanzhou, *China*	56	F2
Lanciano, *Italy*	29	F11
Lancun, *China*	57	F11
Landau, *Bayern, Germany*	25	G8
Landau, *Rhld-Pfz., Germany*	25	F4
Landeck, *Austria*	26	D3
Lander, *U.S.A.*	114	E9
Lander ➔, *Australia*	92	D5
Landerneau, *France*	18	D2
Landeryd, *Sweden*	11	G7
Landes, *France*	20	D2
Landes □, *France*	20	E3
Landete, *Spain*	32	F3
Landi Kotal, *Pakistan*	68	B4
Landisburg, *U.S.A.*	110	F7
Landivisiau, *France*	18	D2
Landquart, *Switz.*	25	J5
Landrecies, *France*	19	B10
Land's End, *U.K.*	13	G2
Landsberg, *Germany*	25	G6
Landsborough Cr. ➔, *Australia*	94	C3
Landsbro, *Sweden*	11	G8
Landshut, *Germany*	25	G8
Landskrona, *Sweden*	11	J6
Landstuhl, *Germany*	25	F3
Landvetter, *Sweden*	11	G6
Lanesboro, *U.S.A.*	111	E9
Lanester, *France*	18	E3
Lanett, *U.S.A.*	109	J3
Lang Qua, *Vietnam*	64	A5
Lang Shan, *China*	56	D4
Lang Son, *Vietnam*	58	G6
Lang Suan, *Thailand*	65	H2
Langá, *Denmark*	11	H3
La'nga Co, *China*	67	D12
Lángadhás, *Greece*	40	F7
Langádhia, *Greece*	38	D4
Långan ➔, *Sweden*	10	A8
Langano, L., *Ethiopia*	81	F4
Langar, *Iran*	71	C9
Langara I., *Canada*	104	C2
Långås, *Sweden*	11	H6
Langdai, *China*	58	D5
Langdon, *U.S.A.*	112	A5
Länge Jan = Ölands södra udde, *Sweden*	11	H10
Langeac, *France*	20	C7
Langeais, *France*	18	E7
Langeb Baraka ➔, *Sudan*	80	D4
Langeberg, *S. Africa*	88	E3
Langeberge, *S. Africa*	88	D3
Langeland, *Denmark*	11	K4
Langelands Bælt, *Denmark*	11	K4
Langen, *Hessen, Germany*	25	F4
Langen, *Niedersachsen, Germany*	24	B4
Langenburg, *Canada*	105	C8
Langeneß, *Germany*	24	A4
Langenlois, *Austria*	26	C8
Langeoog, *Germany*	24	B3
Langeskov, *Denmark*	11	J4
Länghem, *Sweden*	11	G7
Langhirano, *Italy*	28	D7
Langholm, *U.K.*	14	F5
Langjökull, *Iceland*	8	D3
Langkawi, Pulau, *Malaysia*	65	J2
Langklip, *S. Africa*	88	D3
Langkon, *Malaysia*	62	C5
Langlade, *St- P. & M.*	103	C8
Langley, *Canada*	116	A4
Langnau, *Switz.*	25	J3
Langogne, *France*	20	D7
Langon, *France*	20	D3
Langøya, *Norway*	8	B16
Langreo, *Spain*	34	B5
Langres, *France*	19	E12
Langres, Plateau de, *France*	19	E12
Langsa, *Indonesia*	62	D1
Långsele, *Sweden*	10	A11
Långshyttan, *Sweden*	10	D10
Langtry, *U.S.A.*	113	L4
Languedoc, *France*	20	E7
Languedoc-Roussillon □, *France*	20	E6
Langxi, *China*	59	B12
Langxiangzhen, *China*	56	E9
Langzhong, *China*	58	B5
Lanigan, *Canada*	105	C7
Lankao, *China*	56	G8
Länkäran, *Azerbaijan*	71	B6
Lanmeur, *France*	18	D3
Lannemezan, *France*	20	E4
Lannilis, *France*	18	D2
Lannion, *France*	18	D3
L'Annonciation, *Canada*	102	C5
Lanouaille, *France*	20	C5
Lanping, *China*	58	D2
Lansdale, *U.S.A.*	111	F9
Lansdowne, *Australia*	95	E5
Lansdowne, *Canada*	111	B8
Lansdowne, *India*	69	E8
Lansdowne House, *Canada*	102	B2
L'Anse, *U.S.A.*	108	B1
L'Anse au Loup, *Canada*	103	B8
L'Anse aux Meadows, *Canada*	103	B8
Lansford, *U.S.A.*	111	F9
Lanshan, *China*	59	E9
Lansing, *U.S.A.*	108	D3
Lanslebourg-Mont-Cenis, *France*	21	C10
Lanta Yai, Ko, *Thailand*	65	J2
Lantewa, *Nigeria*	83	C7
Lantian, *China*	56	G5
Lanus, *Argentina*	126	C4
Lanusei, *Italy*	30	C2
Lanxi, *China*	59	C12
Lanzarote, *Canary Is.*	37	F6
Lanzhou, *China*	56	F2
Lanzo Torinese, *Italy*	28	C4
Lao ➔, *Italy*	31	C8
Lao Bao, *Laos*	64	D6
Lao Cai, *Vietnam*	58	F4
Laoag, *Phil.*	61	B4
Laoang, *Phil.*	61	E6
Laoha He ➔, *China*	57	C11
Laohekou, *China*	59	A8
Laois □, *Ireland*	15	D4
Laon, *France*	19	C10
Laona, *U.S.A.*	108	C1
Laos ■, *Asia*	64	D5
Lapa, *Brazil*	127	B6
Lapai, *Nigeria*	83	D6
Lapalisse, *France*	19	F10
Lapeer, *U.S.A.*	108	D4
Lapeyrade, *France*	20	D3
Lapithos, *Cyprus*	36	D12
Lapland = Lappland, *Europe*	8	B21
Laporte, *U.S.A.*	111	E8
Lapovo, *Serbia, Yug.*	40	B5
Lappeenranta, *Finland*	9	F23
Lappland, *Europe*	8	B21
Laprida, *Argentina*	126	D3
Lapseki, *Turkey*	41	F10
Laptev Sea, *Russia*	51	B13
Lapua, *Finland*	8	E20
Lăpuş ➔, *Romania*	43	C8
Lăpuş, Munţii, *Romania*	43	C8
Lăpuşna, *Moldova*	43	D13
Łapy, *Poland*	45	F9
Laqiya Arba'in, *Sudan*	80	C2
Laqiya Umran, *Sudan*	80	D2
L'Aquila, *Italy*	29	F10
Lār, *Āzarbājān-e Sharqī, Iran*	70	B5
Lār, *Fārs, Iran*	71	E7
Larabanga, *Ghana*	82	D4
Laragne-Montéglin, *France*	21	D9
Laramie, *U.S.A.*	112	E2
Laramie ➔, *U.S.A.*	114	F11
Laramie Mts., *U.S.A.*	112	E2
Laranjeiras do Sul, *Brazil*	127	B5
Larantuka, *Indonesia*	63	F6
Larat, *Indonesia*	63	F8
L'Arbresle, *France*	21	C8
Lärbro, *Sweden*	11	G12
Larde, *Mozam.*	87	F4
Larder Lake, *Canada*	102	C4
Lardhos, Ákra = Líndhos, Ákra, *Greece*	36	C10
Lardhos, Órmos, *Greece*	36	C10
Laredo, *Spain*	34	B7
Laredo, *U.S.A.*	113	M5
Laredo Sd., *Canada*	104	C3
Largentière, *France*	21	D8
L'Argentière-la-Bessée, *France*	21	D10
Largo, *U.S.A.*	109	M4
Largs, *U.K.*	14	F4
Lari, *Italy*	28	E7
Lariang, *Indonesia*	63	E5
Larimore, *U.S.A.*	112	B6
Lārīn, *Iran*	71	C7
Larino, *Italy*	29	G11
Lárisa, *Greece*	38	B4
Lárisa □, *Greece*	38	B4
Larkana, *Pakistan*	68	F3
Larnaca, *Cyprus*	36	E12
Larnaca Bay, *Cyprus*	36	E12
Larne, *U.K.*	15	B6
Larned, *U.S.A.*	112	F5
Laroquebrou, *France*	20	D6
Larose, *U.S.A.*	113	L9
Larrimah, *Australia*	92	C5
Larsen Ice Shelf, *Antarctica*	5	C17
Laruns, *France*	20	E3
Larvik, *Norway*	9	G14
Larzac, Causse du, *France*	20	E7
Las Alpujarras, *Spain*	33	J1
Las Animas, *U.S.A.*	112	F3
Las Anod, *Somali Rep.*	74	F4
Las Arenas, *Spain*	34	B6
Las Aves, Is., *W. Indies*	121	C7
Las Breñas, *Argentina*	126	B3
Las Cabezas de San Juan, *Spain*	35	J5
Las Cejas, *Argentina*	128	B4

Las Chimeneas, *Mexico* 117 N10
Las Cruces, *U.S.A.* 115 K10
Las Flores, *Argentina* 126 D4
Las Heras, *Argentina* 126 C2
Las Lajas, *Argentina* 128 D2
Las Lomitas, *Argentina* 126 A3
Las Marismas, *Spain* 35 H4
Las Minas, *Spain* 33 G3
Las Navas de la Concepción,
  Spain 35 H5
Las Navas del Marqués, *Spain* . 34 E6
Las Palmas, *Argentina* 126 B4
Las Palmas, *Canary Is.* 37 F4
Las Palmas �, *Mexico* 117 N10
Las Pedroñas, *Spain* 33 F2
Las Piedras, *Uruguay* 127 C4
Las Pipinas, *Argentina* 126 D4
Las Plumas, *Argentina* 128 E3
Las Rosas, *Argentina* 126 C3
Las Rozas, *Spain* 34 E7
Las Tablas, *Panama* 120 E4
Las Termas, *Argentina* 126 B3
Las Toscas, *Argentina* 126 B4
Las Truchas, *Mexico* 118 D4
Las Varillas, *Argentina* 126 C3
Las Vegas, *N. Mex., U.S.A.* ... 115 J11
Las Vegas, *Nev., U.S.A.* 117 J11
Lasarte, *Spain* 32 B2
Lascano, *Uruguay* 127 C5
Lash-e Joveyn, *Afghan.* 66 D2
Lashburn, *Canada* 105 C7
Lashio, *Burma* 67 H20
Lashkar, *India* 68 F8
Łasin, *Poland* 44 E6
Lasíthi, *Greece* 36 D7
Lasíthi □, *Greece* 36 D7
Lāsjerd, *Iran* 71 C7
Łask, *Poland* 45 G6
Łaskarzew, *Poland* 45 G8
Laško, *Slovenia* 29 B12
Lassay-les-Châteaux, *France* .. 18 D6
Lassen Pk., *U.S.A.* 114 F3
Lassen Volcanic National Park,
  U.S.A. 114 F3
Last Mountain L., *Canada* 105 C7
Lastchance Cr. �, *U.S.A.* 116 E5
Lastoursville, *Gabon* 84 E2
Lastovo, *Croatia* 29 F13
Lastovski Kanal, *Croatia* 29 F14
Lat Yao, *Thailand* 64 E2
Latacunga, *Ecuador* 124 D3
Latakia = Al Lādhiqīyah, *Syria* . 70 C2
Latchford, *Canada* 102 C4
Latehar, *India* 69 H11
Laterza, *Italy* 31 B9
Latham, *Australia* 93 E2
Lathen, *Germany* 24 C3
Lathi, *India* 68 F4
Lathrop Wells, *U.S.A.* 117 J10
Latiano, *Italy* 31 B10
Latina, *Italy* 30 A5
Latisana, *Italy* 29 C10
Latium = Lazio □, *Italy* 29 F9
Laton, *U.S.A.* 116 J7
Latorytsya ➚, *Slovak Rep.* 27 C14
Latouche Treville, C., *Australia* . 92 C3
Latrobe, *Australia* 94 G4
Latrobe, *U.S.A.* 110 F5
Latrónico, *Italy* 31 B9
Latvia ■, *Europe* 9 H20
Lau, *Nigeria* 83 D7
Lau Group, *Fiji* 91 C9
Lauchhammer, *Germany* 24 D9
Lauda-Königshofen, *Germany* . 25 F5
Lauenburg, *Germany* 24 B6
Lauf, *Germany* 25 F7
Laughlin, *U.S.A.* 115 J6
Laujar de Andarax, *Spain* 33 H2
Laukaa, *Finland* 9 E21
Launceston, *Australia* 94 G4
Launceston, *U.K.* 13 G3
Launglon Bok, *Burma* 64 F1
Laupheim, *Germany* 25 G5
Laura, *Australia* 94 B3
Laureana di Borrello, *Italy* 31 D9
Laurel, *Miss., U.S.A.* 113 K10
Laurel, *Mont., U.S.A.* 114 D9
Laurencekirk, *U.K.* 14 E6
Laurens, *U.S.A.* 109 H4
Laurentian Plateau, *Canada* ... 103 B6
Lauria, *Italy* 31 B8
Laurie L., *Canada* 105 B8
Laurinburg, *U.S.A.* 109 H6
Laurium, *U.S.A.* 108 B1
Lausanne, *Switz.* 25 J2
Laut, *Indonesia* 65 K6
Laut, Pulau, *Indonesia* 62 E5
Laut Kecil, Kepulauan,
  Indonesia 62 E5
Lauterbach, *Germany* 24 E5
Lauterecken, *Germany* 25 F3
Lautoka, *Fiji* 91 C7
Lauzès, *France* 20 D5
Lavagh More, *Ireland* 15 B3
Lavagna, *Italy* 28 D6
Laval, *France* 18 D6
Lavalle, *Argentina* 126 B2
Lavant Station, *Canada* 111 A8
Lāvar Meydān, *Iran* 71 D7
Lávara, *Greece* 41 E10
Lavardac, *France* 20 D4
Lavaur, *France* 20 E5
Lavelanet, *France* 20 F5
Lavello, *Italy* 31 A8
Laverton, *Australia* 93 E3
Lavìs, *Italy* 28 B8

Lávkos, *Greece* 38 B5
Lavos, *Portugal* 34 E2
Lavradio, *Portugal* 35 G1
Lavras, *Brazil* 127 A7
Lavre, *Portugal* 35 G2
Lávrion, *Greece* 38 D6
Lávris, *Greece* 36 D6
Lavumisa, *Swaziland* 89 D5
Lawas, *Malaysia* 62 D5
Lawele, *Indonesia* 63 F6
Lawng Pit, *Burma* 67 G20
Lawqah, *Si. Arabia* 70 D4
Lawra, *Ghana* 82 C4
Lawrence, *N.Z.* 91 L2
Lawrence, *Kans., U.S.A.* 112 F7
Lawrence, *Mass., U.S.A.* 111 D13
Lawrenceburg, *Ind., U.S.A.* ... 108 F3
Lawrenceburg, *Tenn., U.S.A.* .. 109 H2
Lawrenceville, *Ga., U.S.A.* 109 J4
Lawrenceville, *Pa., U.S.A.* 110 E7
Laws, *U.S.A.* 116 H8
Lawton, *U.S.A.* 113 H5
Lawu, *Indonesia* 63 G14
Lawz, J. al, *Si. Arabia* 80 B4
Laxå, *Sweden* 11 F8
Laxford, L., *U.K.* 14 C3
Laxou, *France* 19 D13
Lay ➚, *France* 20 B2
Laylá, *Si. Arabia* 74 C4
Laylān, *Iraq* 70 C5
Layon ➚, *France* 18 E6
Layton, *U.S.A.* 114 F7
Laytonville, *U.S.A.* 114 G2
Lazarevac, *Serbia, Yug.* 40 B4
Lazarevskoye, *Russia* 49 J4
Lazarivo, *Madag.* 89 C8
Lazdijai, *Lithuania* 44 D10
Lazio □, *Italy* 29 F9
Lazo, *Moldova* 43 C13
Lazo, *Russia* 54 C6
Le Beausset, *France* 21 E9
Le Blanc, *France* 20 B5
Le Bleymard, *France* 20 D7
Le Bourgneuf-la-Forêt, *France* . 18 D6
Le Bugue, *France* 20 D4
Le Canourgue = La Canourgue,
  France 20 D7
Le Cateau Cambrésis, *France* .. 19 B10
Le Caylar, *France* 20 E7
Le Chambon-Feugerolles,
  France 21 C8
Le Châtelet, *France* 19 F9
Le Chesne, *France* 19 C11
Le Cheylard, *France* 21 D8
Le Conquet, *France* 18 D2
Le Creusot, *France* 19 F11
Le Croisic, *France* 18 E4
Le Donjon, *France* 19 F10
Le Dorat, *France* 20 B5
Le François, *Martinique* 121 D7
Le Grand-Lucé, *France* 18 E7
Le Grand-Pressigny, *France* ... 18 F7
Le Grand-Quevilly, *France* 18 C8
Le Havre, *France* 18 C7
Le Lavandou, *France* 21 E10
Le Lion-d'Angers, *France* 18 E6
Le Louroux-Béconnais, *France* . 18 E6
Le Luc, *France* 21 E10
Le Lude, *France* 18 E7
Le Mans, *France* 18 E7
Le Mars, *U.S.A.* 112 D6
Le Mayet-de-Montagne, *France* 19 F10
Le Mêle-sur-Sarthe, *France* ... 18 D7
Le Monastier-sur-Gazeille,
  France 20 D7
Le Monêtier-les-Bains, *France* . 21 D10
Le Mont-Dore, *France* 20 C6
Le Mont-St-Michel, *France* 18 D5
Le Moule, *Guadeloupe* 121 C7
Le Muy, *France* 21 E10
Le Palais, *France* 18 E3
Le Perthus, *France* 20 F6
Le Puy-en-Velay, *France* 20 C7
Le Sueur, *U.S.A.* 112 C8
Le Teil, *France* 21 D8
Le Teilleul, *France* 18 D6
Le Theil, *France* 18 D7
Le Thillot, *France* 19 E13
Le Thuy, *Vietnam* 64 D6
Le Touquet-Paris-Plage, *France* 19 B8
Le Tréport, *France* 18 B8
Le Val-d'Ajol, *France* 19 E13
Le Verdon-sur-Mer, *France* ... 20 C2
Le Vigan, *France* 20 E7
Lea ➚, *U.K.* 13 F8
Leach, *Cambodia* 65 F4
Lead, *U.S.A.* 112 C3
Leader, *Canada* 105 C7
Leadhills, *U.K.* 14 F5
Leadville, *U.S.A.* 115 G10
Leaf ➚, *U.S.A.* 113 K10
Leaf Rapids, *Canada* 105 B9
Leamington, *Canada* 102 D3
Leamington, *U.S.A.* 114 G7
Leamington Spa = Royal
  Leamington Spa, *U.K.* 13 E6
Le'an, *China* 59 D10
Leandro Norte Alem, *Argentina* 127 B4
Leane, L., *Ireland* 15 D2
Learmonth, *Australia* 92 D1
Leask, *Canada* 105 C7
Leatherhead, *U.K.* 13 F7
Leavenworth, *Kans., U.S.A.* ... 112 F7
Leavenworth, *Wash., U.S.A.* .. 114 C3
Łeba, *Poland* 44 D4
Łeba ➚, *Poland* 44 D4
Lebach, *Germany* 25 F2
Lebak, *Phil.* 61 H6

Lebam, *U.S.A.* 116 D3
Lebane, *Serbia, Yug.* 40 D5
Lebanon, *Ind., U.S.A.* 108 E2
Lebanon, *Kans., U.S.A.* 112 F5
Lebanon, *Ky., U.S.A.* 108 G3
Lebanon, *Mo., U.S.A.* 113 G8
Lebanon, *N.H., U.S.A.* 111 C12
Lebanon, *Oreg., U.S.A.* 114 D2
Lebanon, *Pa., U.S.A.* 111 F8
Lebanon, *Tenn., U.S.A.* 109 G2
Lebanon ■, *Asia* 75 B5
Lebec, *U.S.A.* 117 L8
Lebedyan, *Russia* 47 F10
Lebedyn, *Ukraine* 47 G8
Lebel-sur-Quévillon, *Canada* .. 102 C4
Lebomboberge, *S. Africa* 89 C5
Lębork, *Poland* 44 D4
Lebrija, *Spain* 35 J4
Łebsko, Jezioro, *Poland* 44 D4
Lebu, *Chile* 126 D1
Leca da Palmeira, *Portugal* ... 34 D2
Lecce, *Italy* 31 B11
Lecco, *Italy* 28 C6
Lecco, L. di, *Italy* 28 C6
Lécera, *Spain* 32 D4
Lech, *Austria* 26 D3
Lech ➚, *Germany* 25 G6
Lechang, *China* 59 E9
Lechtaler Alpen, *Austria* 26 D3
Lecontes Mills, *U.S.A.* 110 E6
Lectoure, *France* 20 E4
Łęczna, *Poland* 45 G9
Łęczyca, *Poland* 45 F6
Ledesma, *Spain* 34 D5
Ledong, *China* 64 C7
Leduc, *Canada* 104 C6
Lee, *U.S.A.* 111 D11
Lee ➚, *Ireland* 15 E3
Lee Vining, *U.S.A.* 116 H7
Leech L., *U.S.A.* 112 B7
Leechburg, *U.S.A.* 110 F5
Leeds, *U.K.* 12 D6
Leeds, *U.S.A.* 109 J2
Leek, *Neths.* 17 A6
Leek, *U.K.* 12 D5
Leeman, *Australia* 93 E1
Leeper, *U.S.A.* 110 E5
Leer, *Germany* 24 B3
Leesburg, *U.S.A.* 109 L5
Leesville, *U.S.A.* 113 K8
Leeton, *Australia* 95 E4
Leetonia, *U.S.A.* 110 F4
Leeu Gamka, *S. Africa* 88 E3
Leeuwarden, *Neths.* 17 A5
Leeuwin, C., *Australia* 93 F2
Leeward Is., *Atl. Oc.* 121 C7
Lefka, *Cyprus* 36 D11
Lefkoniko, *Cyprus* 36 D12
Lefroy, *Canada* 110 B5
Lefroy, L., *Australia* 93 F3
Łeg ➚, *Poland* 45 H8
Leganés, *Spain* 34 E7
Legazpi, *Phil.* 61 E5
Lège-Cap-Ferret, *France* 20 D2
Lege Hida, *Ethiopia* 81 F5
Legendre I., *Australia* 92 D2
Leghorn = Livorno, *Italy* 28 E7
Legionowo, *Poland* 45 F8
Legnago, *Italy* 29 C8
Legnano, *Italy* 28 C5
Legnica, *Poland* 45 G3
Legrad, *Croatia* 29 B13
Leh, *India* 69 B7
Lehigh Acres, *U.S.A.* 109 M5
Lehighton, *U.S.A.* 111 F9
Lehliu, *Romania* 43 F11
Leho, *Sudan* 81 F3
Lehrte, *Germany* 24 C5
Lehututu, *Botswana* 88 C3
Lei Shui ➚, *China* 59 D9
Leiah, *Pakistan* 68 D4
Leibnitz, *Austria* 26 E8
Leibo, *China* 58 C4
Leicester, *U.K.* 13 E6
Leicester City □, *U.K.* 13 E6
Leicestershire □, *U.K.* 13 E6
Leichhardt ➚, *Australia* 94 B2
Leichhardt Ra., *Australia* 94 C4
Leiden, *Neths.* 17 B4
Leie ➚, *Belgium* 17 C3
Leifers = Láives, *Italy* 29 B8
Leimen, *Germany* 25 F4
Leine ➚, *Germany* 24 C5
Leinefelde, *Germany* 24 D6
Leinster, *Australia* 93 E3
Leinster □, *Ireland* 15 C4
Leinster, Mt., *Ireland* 15 D5
Leipalingis, *Lithuania* 44 D10
Leipzig, *Germany* 24 D8
Leiria, *Portugal* 34 F2
Leiria □, *Portugal* 34 F2
Leirvik, *Norway* 9 G11
Leishan, *China* 58 D7
Leisler, Mt., *Australia* 92 D4
Leith, *U.K.* 14 F5
Leith Hill, *U.K.* 13 F7
Leitha ➚, *Europe* 27 D10
Leitrim, *Ireland* 15 B3
Leitrim □, *Ireland* 15 B3
Leitza, *Spain* 32 B3
Leiyang, *China* 59 D9
Leizhou, *China* 59 G8
Leizhou Bandao, *China* 58 G7
Leizhou Wan, *China* 59 G8
Lek ➚, *Neths.* 17 C4
Leka, *Norway* 8 D14
Lekáni, *Greece* 41 E8

Lekbibaj, *Albania* 40 D3
Lekeitio, *Spain* 32 B2
Lekhainá, *Greece* 38 D3
Lekoui, *Burkina Faso* 82 C4
Leksand, *Sweden* 10 D9
Lékva Óros, *Greece* 36 D6
Leland, *Mich., U.S.A.* 108 C3
Leland, *Miss., U.S.A.* 113 J9
Lelång, *Sweden* 10 E6
Leleque, *Argentina* 128 E2
Lelystad, *Neths.* 17 B5
Lem, *Denmark* 11 H2
Lema, *Nigeria* 83 C5
Lema Shilindi, *Ethiopia* 81 G5
Léman, L., *Europe* 19 F13
Lemera, *Dem. Rep. of the Congo* 86 C2
Lemery, *Phil.* 61 E4
Lemhi Ra., *U.S.A.* 114 D7
Lemmer, *Neths.* 17 B5
Lemmon, *U.S.A.* 112 C3
Lemon Grove, *U.S.A.* 117 N9
Lemoore, *U.S.A.* 116 J7
Lempdes, *France* 20 C7
Lemvig, *Denmark* 11 H2
Lena ➚, *Russia* 51 B13
Lenart, *Slovenia* 29 B12
Lenartovce, *Slovak Rep.* 27 C13
Lencloître, *France* 18 F7
Léndas, *Greece* 36 E6
Lendava, *Slovenia* 29 B13
Lendeh, *Iran* 71 D6
Lendinara, *Italy* 29 C8
Lengerich, *Germany* 24 C3
Lenggong, *Malaysia* 65 K3
Lengnau, *U.S.A.* 111 D11
Lenggries, *Germany* 25 H7
Lengshuijiang, *China* 59 D8
Lengshuitan, *China* 59 D8
Lengua de Vaca, Pta., *Chile* ... 126 C1
Lengyeltóti, *Hungary* 42 D2
Lenhovda, *Sweden* 11 G9
Lenina, Kanal ➚, *Russia* 49 J7
Leninabad = Khŭjand, *Tajikistan* 50 D8
Leninakan = Gyumri, *Armenia* . 49 K6
Leningrad = Sankt-Peterburg,
  Russia 46 C6
Leningorsk, *Kazakstan* 50 D9
Leninsk, *Russia* 49 F7
Leninsk-Kuznetskiy, *Russia* ... 50 D9
Leninskoye, *Russia* 48 A8
Lenk, *Switz.* 25 J3
Lenkoran = Länkäran,
  Azerbaijan 71 B6
Lenmalu, *Indonesia* 63 E8
Lenne ➚, *Germany* 24 D3
Lennestadt, *Germany* 24 D4
Lennox, *U.S.A.* 112 D6
Lennoxville, *Canada* 111 A13
Leno, *Italy* 28 C7
Lenoir, *U.S.A.* 109 H5
Lenoir City, *U.S.A.* 109 H3
Lenore L., *Canada* 105 C8
Lenox, *U.S.A.* 111 D11
Lens, *France* 19 B9
Lensahn, *Germany* 24 A6
Lensk, *Russia* 51 C12
Lentekhi, *Georgia* 49 J6
Lenti, *Hungary* 42 D1
Lentini, *Italy* 31 E8
Lenwood, *U.S.A.* 117 L9
Lenya, *Burma* 62 B1
Lenzen, *Germany* 24 B7
Léo, *Burkina Faso* 82 C4
Leoben, *Austria* 26 D8
Leodhas = Lewis, *U.K.* 14 C2
Leola, *U.S.A.* 112 C5
Leominster, *U.K.* 13 E5
Leominster, *U.S.A.* 111 D13
León, *France* 20 E2
León, *Mexico* 118 C4
León, *Nic.* 120 D2
León, *Spain* 34 C5
León, *U.S.A.* 112 E8
León □, *Spain* 34 C5
León, Montes de, *Spain* 34 C4
Leonardtown, *U.S.A.* 108 F7
Leonardville, *Namibia* 88 C2
Leonessa, *Italy* 29 F9
Leonforte, *Italy* 31 E7
Leongatha, *Australia* 95 F4
Leonídhion, *Greece* 38 D4
Leonora, *Australia* 93 E3
Leopoldina, *Brazil* 127 A7
Leopoldsburg, *Belgium* 17 C5
Leoti, *U.S.A.* 112 F4
Leova, *Moldova* 43 D13
Leoville, *Canada* 105 C7
Lepe, *Spain* 35 H3
Lepel = Lyepyel, *Belarus* 46 E5
Lepenoú, *Greece* 38 C3
Leping, *China* 59 C11
Lépo, L. do, *Angola* 88 B5
Lepontine, Alpi, *Italy* 28 B5
Lepsény, *Hungary* 42 D3
Lequeitio = Lekeitio, *Spain* ... 32 B2
Lercara Friddi, *Italy* 30 E6
Lerdo, *Mexico* 118 B4
Léré, *Chad* 83 D7
Léré, *Mali* 82 B4
Lere, *Kaduna, Nigeria* 83 C6
Leribe, *Lesotho* 89 D4
Lérici, *Italy* 28 D6

Lérida = Lleida, *Spain* 32 D5
Lérins, Îs. de, *France* 21 E11
Lerma, *Spain* 34 C7
Léros, *Greece* 39 D8
Lérouville, *France* 19 D12
Lerum, *Sweden* 11 G6
Lerwick, *U.K.* 14 A7
Leş, *Romania* 42 D6
Les, *Romania* 21 C9
Les Abrets, *France* 21 C9
Les Andelys, *France* 18 C8
Les Borges Blanques, *Spain* ... 32 D5
Les Cayes, *Haiti* 121 C5
Les Essarts, *France* 18 F5
Les Herbiers, *France* 18 F5
Les Minquiers, Plateau des,
  Chan. Is. 18 D4
Les Pieux, *France* 18 C5
Les Ponts-de-Cé, *France* 18 E6
Les Riceys, *France* 19 E11
Les Sables-d'Olonne, *France* .. 20 B2
Les Vans, *France* 21 D8
Lesbos = Lésvos, *Greece* 39 B8
L'Escala, *Spain* 32 C8
Leshan, *China* 58 C4
Lésina, *Italy* 29 G12
Lésina, L. di, *Italy* 29 G12
Lesjöfors, *Sweden* 10 E8
Lesko, *Poland* 45 J9
Leskovac, *Serbia, Yug.* 40 C5
Leskovik, *Albania* 40 F4
Leśna, *Poland* 45 H2
Lesneven, *France* 18 D2
Leśnica, *Poland* 45 H5
Lesnica, *Serbia, Yug.* 40 B3
Lesnoye, *Russia* 46 C8
Lesogorsk, *Russia* 54 A7
Lesopilnoye, *Russia* 54 A7
Lesotho ■, *Africa* 89 D4
Lesozavodsk, *Russia* 51 E14
Lesparre-Médoc, *France* 20 C3
Lessay, *France* 18 C5
Lesse ➚, *Belgium* 17 D4
Lessebo, *Sweden* 11 H9
Lesser Antilles, *W. Indies* 121 D7
Lesser Slave L., *Canada* 104 B5
Lesser Sunda Is., *Indonesia* ... 63 F6
Lessines, *Belgium* 17 D3
Lester, *U.S.A.* 116 C5
Lestock, *Canada* 105 C8
Lesuer I., *Australia* 92 B4
Lésvos, *Greece* 39 B8
Leszno, *Poland* 45 G3
Letaba, *S. Africa* 89 C5
Letälven, *Sweden* 10 E8
Létavértes, *Hungary* 42 C6
Letchworth, *U.K.* 13 F7
Letea, Ostrov, *Romania* 43 E14
Lethbridge, *Canada* 104 D6
Leti, Kepulauan, *Indonesia* ... 63 F7
Leti Is. = Leti, Kepulauan,
  Indonesia 63 F7
Letiahau ➚, *Botswana* 88 C3
Leticia, *Colombia* 124 D5
Leting, *China* 57 E10
Letjiesbos, *S. Africa* 88 E3
Letlhakane, *Botswana* 88 C4
Letlhakeng, *Botswana* 88 C4
Letong, *Indonesia* 62 D3
Letpadan, *Burma* 67 L19
Letpan, *Burma* 67 K19
Letsôk-aw Kyun, *Burma* 65 G2
Letterkenny, *Ireland* 15 B4
Leu, *Romania* 43 F9
Leucadia, *U.S.A.* 117 M9
Leucate, *France* 20 F7
Leucate, Étang de, *France* 20 F7
Leuk, *Switz.* 25 J3
Leuşeni, *Moldova* 43 D13
Leuser, G., *Indonesia* 62 D1
Leutkirch, *Germany* 25 H6
Leuven, *Belgium* 17 D4
Leuze-en-Hainaut, *Belgium* ... 17 D3
Lev Tolstoy, *Russia* 46 F10
Levádhia, *Greece* 38 C4
Levan, *Albania* 40 F3
Levanger, *Norway* 8 E14
Levant, Î. du, *France* 21 E10
Lévanto, *Italy* 28 D6
Lévanzo, *Italy* 30 D5
Levelland, *U.S.A.* 113 J3
Leven, *U.K.* 14 E6
Leven, L., *U.K.* 14 E5
Leven, Toraka, *Madag.* 89 A8
Leveque C., *Australia* 92 C3
Leverano, *Italy* 31 B10
Leverkusen, *Germany* 24 D2
Levice, *Slovak Rep.* 27 C11
Lévico Terme, *Italy* 29 B8
Levie, *France* 21 G13
Levier, *France* 19 F13
Levin, *N.Z.* 91 J5
Lévis, *Canada* 103 C5
Levis, L., *Canada* 104 A5
Levítha, *Greece* 39 D8
Levittown, *N.Y., U.S.A.* 111 F11
Levittown, *Pa., U.S.A.* 111 F10
Levka, *Bulgaria* 41 E10
Levkás □, *Greece* 38 C2
Levkímmi, *Greece* 38 B2
Levkímmi, Ákra, *Greece* 36 B4
Levkôsia = Nicosia, *Cyprus* ... 36 D12
Levoča, *Slovak Rep.* 27 B13
Levroux, *France* 19 F8
Levski, *Bulgaria* 41 C9
Levskigrad = Karlovo, *Bulgaria* 41 D8

Levuka, *Fiji* 91 C8
Lewes, *U.K.* 13 G8
Lewes, *U.S.A.* 108 F8
Lewin Brzeski, *Poland* 45 H4
Lewis, *U.K.* 14 C2
Lewis ➡, *U.S.A.* 116 E4
Lewis, Butt of, *U.K.* 14 C2
Lewis Ra., *Australia* 92 D4
Lewis Range, *U.S.A.* 114 C7
Lewis Run, *U.S.A.* 110 E6
Lewisburg, *Pa., U.S.A.* 110 F8
Lewisburg, *Tenn., U.S.A.* 109 H2
Lewisburg, *W. Va., U.S.A.* . . . 108 G5
Lewisporte, *Canada* 103 C8
Lewiston, *Idaho, U.S.A.* 114 C5
Lewiston, *Maine, U.S.A.* 109 C11
Lewiston, *N.Y., U.S.A.* 110 C5
Lewistown, *Mont., U.S.A.* 114 C9
Lewistown, *Pa., U.S.A.* 110 F7
Lexington, *Ill., U.S.A.* 112 E10
Lexington, *Ky., U.S.A.* 108 F3
Lexington, *Mich., U.S.A.* 110 C2
Lexington, *Mo., U.S.A.* 112 F8
Lexington, *N.C., U.S.A.* 109 H5
Lexington, *N.Y., U.S.A.* 111 D10
Lexington, *Nebr., U.S.A.* 112 E5
Lexington, *Ohio, U.S.A.* 110 F2
Lexington, *Tenn., U.S.A.* 109 H1
Lexington, *Va., U.S.A.* 108 G6
Lexington Park, *U.S.A.* 108 F7
Leyburn, *U.K.* 12 C6
Leye, *China* 58 E6
Leyland, *U.K.* 12 D5
Leyre ➡, *France* 20 D2
Leyte □, *Phil.* 61 F6
Leyte Gulf, *Phil.* 61 F6
Leżajsk, *Poland* 45 H9
Lezay, *France* 20 B3
Lezhë, *Albania* 40 E3
Lezhi, *China* 58 B5
Lézignan-Corbières, *France* . . 20 E6
Lezoux, *France* 20 C7
Lgov, *Russia* 47 G8
Lhasa, *China* 60 D4
Lhazê, *China* 60 D3
Lhokkruet, *Indonesia* 62 D1
Lhokseumawe, *Indonesia* 62 C1
L'Hospitalet de Llobregat, *Spain* 32 D7
Li, *Thailand* 64 D2
Li Shui ➡, *China* 59 C9
Li Xian, *Gansu, China* 56 G3
Li Xian, *Hebei, China* 56 E8
Li Xian, *Hunan, China* 59 C8
Liádhoi, *Greece* 39 E8
Liancheng, *China* 59 E11
Lianga, *Phil.* 61 G7
Liangcheng,
  Nei Monggol Zizhiqu, China 56 D7
Liangcheng, *Shandong, China* . 57 G10
Liangdang, *China* 56 H4
Lianghe, *China* 58 E2
Lianghekou, *China* 58 C7
Liangping, *China* 58 B6
Liangpran, *Indonesia* 62 D4
Lianhua, *China* 59 D9
Lianjiang, *Fujian, China* 59 D12
Lianjiang, *Guangdong, China* . 59 G8
Lianping, *China* 59 E10
Lianshan, *China* 59 E9
Lianshanguan, *China* 57 D12
Lianshui, *China* 57 H10
Lianyuan, *China* 59 D8
Lianyungang, *China* 57 G10
Lianzhou, *China* 59 E9
Liao He ➡, *China* 57 D11
Liaocheng, *China* 56 F8
Liaodong Bandao, *China* 57 E12
Liaodong Wan, *China* 57 D11
Liaoning □, *China* 57 D12
Liaoyang, *China* 57 D12
Liaoyuan, *China* 57 C13
Liaozhong, *China* 57 D12
Liapádhes, *Greece* 38 B1
Liard ➡, *Canada* 104 A4
Liard River, *Canada* 104 B3
Liari, *Pakistan* 68 G2
Libau = Liepāja, *Latvia* 9 H19
Libby, *U.S.A.* 114 B6
Libenge, *Dem. Rep. of*
  the Congo 84 D3
Liberal, *U.S.A.* 113 G4
Liberec, *Czech Rep.* 26 A8
Liberecký □, *Czech Rep.* 26 A8
Liberia, *Costa Rica* 120 D2
Liberia ■, *W. Afr.* 82 D3
Liberty, *Mo., U.S.A.* 112 F7
Liberty, *N.Y., U.S.A.* 111 E10
Liberty, *Pa., U.S.A.* 110 E7
Liberty, *Tex., U.S.A.* 113 K7
Libiąż, *Poland* 45 H6
Lîbîya, Sahrâ', *Africa* 79 C10
Libo, *China* 58 E6
Libobo, Tanjung, *Indonesia* . . 63 E7
Libode, *S. Africa* 89 E4
Libohovë, *Albania* 40 F4
Libourne, *France* 20 D3
Libramont, *Belgium* 17 E5
Librazhd, *Albania* 40 E4
Libreville, *Gabon* 84 D1
Libya ■, *N. Afr.* 79 C9
Libyan Desert = Lîbîya, Sahrâ',
  Africa 79 C10
Libyan Plateau = Ed-Déffa,
  Egypt 80 A2
Licantén, *Chile* 126 D1
Licata, *Italy* 30 E6
Lice, *Turkey* 73 C9

Licheng, *China* 56 F7
Lichfield, *U.K.* 13 E6
Lichinga, *Mozam.* 87 E4
Lichtenburg, *S. Africa* 88 D4
Lichtenfels, *Germany* 25 E7
Lichuan, *Hubei, China* 58 B7
Lichuan, *Jiangxi, China* 59 D11
Licking ➡, *U.S.A.* 108 F3
Licosa, Punta, *Italy* 31 B7
Lida, *Belarus* 9 K21
Liden, *Sweden* 10 B10
Lidhoríkion, *Greece* 38 C4
Lidhult, *Sweden* 11 H7
Lidköping, *Sweden* 11 F7
Lido, *Italy* 29 C9
Lido, *Niger* 83 C5
Lido di Roma = Óstia, Lido di,
  Italy 29 G9
Lidzbark, *Poland* 45 E6
Lidzbark Warmiński, *Poland* . . 44 D7
Liebenwalde, *Germany* 24 C9
Lieberose, *Germany* 24 D10
Liebig, Mt., *Australia* 92 D5
Liebling, *Romania* 42 E6
Liechtenstein ■, *Europe* 25 H5
Liège, *Belgium* 17 D5
Liège □, *Belgium* 17 D5
Liegnitz = Legnica, *Poland* . . 45 G3
Lienart, *Dem. Rep. of the Congo* 86 B2
Lienyünchiangshih =
  Lianyungang, *China* 57 G10
Lienz, *Austria* 26 E5
Liepāja, *Latvia* 9 H19
Liepāja □, *Latvia* 44 B8
Liepājas ezers, *Latvia* 44 B8
Lier, *Belgium* 17 C4
Liernais, *France* 19 E11
Lieşti, *Romania* 43 E12
Liévin, *France* 19 B9
Lièvre ➡, *Canada* 102 C4
Liezen, *Austria* 26 D7
Liffey ➡, *Ireland* 15 C5
Lifford, *Ireland* 15 B4
Liffré, *France* 18 D5
Lifudzin, *Russia* 54 B7
Ligao, *Phil.* 61 E5
Lightning Ridge, *Australia* . . . 95 D4
Lignano Sabbiadoro, *Italy* . . . 29 C10
Ligny-en-Barrois, *France* 19 D12
Ligonier, *U.S.A.* 110 F5
Ligoúrion, *Greece* 38 D5
Ligueil, *France* 18 E7
Liguria □, *Italy* 28 D5
Ligurian Sea, *Medit. S.* 6 G7
Lihou Reefs and Cays, *Australia* 94 B5
Lihue, *U.S.A.* 106 H15
Lijiang, *China* 58 D3
Likasi, *Dem. Rep. of the Congo* 87 E2
Likenäs, *Sweden* 10 D8
Likhoslavl, *Russia* 46 D8
Likhovskoy, *Russia* 47 H11
Likoma I., *Malawi* 87 E3
Likumburu, *Tanzania* 87 D4
L'Île-Bouchard, *France* 18 E7
L'Île-Rousse, *France* 21 F12
Liling, *China* 59 D9
Lilla Edet, *Sweden* 11 F6
Lille, *France* 19 B10
Lille Bælt, *Denmark* 11 J3
Lillebonne, *France* 18 C7
Lillehammer, *Norway* 9 F14
Lillesand, *Norway* 9 G13
Lillhärdal, *Sweden* 10 C8
Lillo, *Spain* 34 F7
Lillooet, *Canada* 104 C4
Lillooet ➡, *Canada* 104 D4
Lilongwe, *Malawi* 87 E3
Liloy, *Phil.* 63 C6
Lim ➡, *Bos.-H.* 40 C3
Lima, *Indonesia* 63 E7
Lima, *Peru* 124 F3
Lima, *Mont., U.S.A.* 114 D7
Lima, *Ohio, U.S.A.* 108 E3
Lima ➡, *Portugal* 34 D2
Liman, *Indonesia* 63 G14
Liman, *Russia* 49 H8
Limanowa, *Poland* 45 J7
Limassol, *Cyprus* 36 E12
Limavady, *U.K.* 15 A5
Limay ➡, *Argentina* 128 D3
Limay Mahuida, *Argentina* . . . 126 D2
Limbach-Oberfrohna, *Germany* 24 E8
Limbang, *Brunei* 62 D5
Limbara, Mte., *Italy* 30 B2
Limbaži, *Latvia* 9 H21
Limbdi, *India* 68 H4
Limbe, *Cameroon* 83 E6
Limburg, *Germany* 25 E4
Limburg □, *Belgium* 17 C5
Limburg □, *Neths.* 17 C5
Limedsforsen, *Sweden* 10 D7
Limeira, *Brazil* 127 A6
Limenária, *Greece* 41 F8
Limerick, *Ireland* 15 D3
Limerick □, *Ireland* 15 D3
Limestone, *U.S.A.* 110 D6
Limestone ➡, *Canada* 105 B10
Limfjorden, *Denmark* 11 H3
Limia = Lima ➡, *Portugal* . . . 34 D2
Limín Khersonísou, *Greece* . . 39 F7
Limmared, *Sweden* 11 G7
Limmen, *Norway* 8 D15
Limmen Bight, *Australia* 94 A2
Limmen Bight ➡, *Australia* . . 94 B2
Límni, *Greece* 38 C5

Límnos, *Greece* 39 B7
Limoges, *Canada* 111 A9
Limoges, *France* 20 C5
Limón, *Costa Rica* 120 E3
Limon, *U.S.A.* 112 F3
Limone Piemonte, *Italy* 28 D4
Limousin, *France* 20 C5
Limousin, Plateau du, *France* . 20 C5
Limoux, *France* 20 E6
Limpopo ➡, *Africa* 89 D5
Limuru, *Kenya* 86 C4
Lin Xian, *China* 56 F6
Lin'an, *China* 59 B12
Linapacan I., *Phil.* 61 F3
Linapacan Str., *Phil.* 61 F3
Linares, *Chile* 126 D1
Linares, *Mexico* 119 C5
Linares, *Spain* 35 G7
Linaro, Capo, *Italy* 29 F8
Línas Mte., *Italy* 30 C1
Lincang, *China* 58 F3
Lincheng, *China* 56 F8
Linchuan, *China* 59 D11
Lincoln, *Argentina* 126 C3
Lincoln, *N.Z.* 91 K4
Lincoln, *U.K.* 12 D7
Lincoln, *Calif., U.S.A.* 116 G5
Lincoln, *Ill., U.S.A.* 112 E10
Lincoln, *Kans., U.S.A.* 112 F5
Lincoln, *Maine, U.S.A.* 109 C11
Lincoln, *N.H., U.S.A.* 111 B13
Lincoln, *N. Mex., U.S.A.* 115 K11
Lincoln, *Nebr., U.S.A.* 112 E6
Lincoln City, *U.S.A.* 114 D1
Lincoln Hav = Lincoln Sea,
  Arctic 4 A5
Lincoln Sea, *Arctic* 4 A5
Lincolnshire □, *U.K.* 12 D7
Lincolnshire Wolds, *U.K.* 12 D7
Lincolnton, *U.S.A.* 109 H5
L'Incudine, *France* 21 G13
Lind, *U.S.A.* 114 C4
Linda, *U.S.A.* 116 F5
Lindau, *Germany* 25 H5
Linden, *Guyana* 124 B7
Linden, *Ala., U.S.A.* 109 J2
Linden, *Calif., U.S.A.* 116 G5
Linden, *Tex., U.S.A.* 113 J7
Lindenhurst, *U.S.A.* 111 F11
Lindesberg, *Sweden* 10 E9
Lindesnes, *Norway* 9 H12
Líndhos, *Greece* 36 C10
Líndhos, Ákra, *Greece* 36 C10
Lindi, *Tanzania* 87 D4
Lindi □, *Tanzania* 87 D4
Lindi ➡, *Dem. Rep. of*
  the Congo 86 B2
Lindö, *Sweden* 11 F10
Lindome, *Sweden* 11 G6
Lindoso, *Portugal* 34 D2
Lindow, *Germany* 24 C8
Lindsay, *Canada* 102 D4
Lindsay, *Calif., U.S.A.* 116 J7
Lindsay, *Okla., U.S.A.* 113 H6
Lindsborg, *U.S.A.* 112 F6
Lindsdal, *Sweden* 11 H10
Linesville, *U.S.A.* 110 E4
Linfen, *China* 56 F6
Ling Xian, *Hunan, China* 59 D9
Ling Xian, *Shandong, China* . . 56 F9
Lingao, *China* 64 C7
Lingayen, *Phil.* 63 A6
Lingayen G., *Phil.* 61 C4
Lingbi, *China* 57 H9
Lingbo, *Sweden* 10 C10
Lingchuan, *Guangxi Zhuangzu,*
  China 59 E8
Lingchuan, *Shanxi, China* 56 G7
Lingen, *Germany* 24 C3
Lingga, *Indonesia* 62 E2
Lingga, Kepulauan, *Indonesia* . 62 E2
Lingga Arch. = Lingga,
  Kepulauan, *Indonesia* 62 E2
Linghem, *Sweden* 11 F9
Lingle, *U.S.A.* 112 D2
Lingqiu, *China* 56 E8
Lingshan, *China* 58 F7
Lingshi, *China* 56 F6
Lingshou, *China* 56 E8
Lingtai, *China* 56 G4
Linguère, *Senegal* 82 B1
Lingui, *China* 59 E8
Lingwu, *China* 56 E4
Lingyuan, *China* 57 D10
Linhai, *China* 59 C13
Linhares, *Brazil* 125 G10
Linhe, *China* 56 D4
Linjiang, *China* 57 D14
Linköping, *Sweden* 11 F9
Linkou, *China* 57 B16
Linli, *China* 59 C8
Linnhe, L., *U.K.* 14 E3
Linqi, *China* 56 G7
Linqing, *China* 56 F8
Linqu, *China* 57 F10
Linru, *China* 56 G7
Lins, *Brazil* 127 A6
Linshui, *China* 58 B6
Linta ➡, *Madag.* 89 D7
Linth ➡, *Switz.* 25 H5
Linthal, *Switz.* 25 H5
Linton, *Ind., U.S.A.* 108 F2
Linton, *N. Dak., U.S.A.* 112 B4
Lintong, *China* 56 G5
Linwood, *Canada* 110 C4

Linwu, *China* 59 E9
Linxi, *China* 57 C10
Linxia, *China* 60 C5
Linxiang, *China* 59 C9
Linyanti ➡, *Africa* 88 B4
Linyi, *China* 57 G10
Linz, *Austria* 26 C7
Linz, *Germany* 24 E3
Linzhenzhen, *China* 56 F5
Lion, G. du, *France* 20 E7
Lionárisso, *Cyprus* 36 D13
Lioni, *Italy* 31 B8
Lions, G. of = Lion, G. du,
  France 20 E7
Lion's Den, *Zimbabwe* 87 F3
Lion's Head, *Canada* 110 B3
Liozno = Lyozna, *Belarus* 46 E6
Lipa, *Phil.* 61 E4
Lipali, *Mozam.* 87 F4
Lipany, *Slovak Rep.* 27 B13
Lípari, *Italy* 31 D7
Lípari, I., *Italy* 31 D7
Lípari, Is. = Eólie, Ís., *Italy* . . 31 D7
Lipcani, *Moldova* 43 B11
Lipetsk, *Russia* 47 F10
Lipiany, *Poland* 45 E1
Liping, *China* 58 D7
Lipkany = Lipcani, *Moldova* . . 43 B11
Lipljan, *Kosovo, Yug.* 40 D5
Lipník nad Bečvou, *Czech Rep.* 27 B10
Lipno, *Poland* 45 F6
Lipova, *Romania* 42 D6
Lipovcy Manzovka, *Russia* . . . 54 B6
Lipovets, *Ukraine* 47 H5
Lippe ➡, *Germany* 24 D2
Lippstadt, *Germany* 24 D4
Lipscomb, *U.S.A.* 113 G4
Lipsk, *Poland* 44 E10
Lipsko, *Poland* 45 G8
Lipsói, *Greece* 39 D8
Liptovský Hrádok, *Slovak Rep.* 27 B12
Liptovský Mikuláš, *Slovak Rep.* 27 B12
Liptrap C., *Australia* 95 F4
Lipu, *China* 59 E8
Lira, *Uganda* 86 B3
Liri ➡, *Italy* 30 A6
Liria = Lliria, *Spain* 33 F4
Lisala, *Dem. Rep. of the Congo* 84 D4
Lisboa, *Portugal* 35 G1
Lisboa □, *Portugal* 35 G1
Lisbon = Lisboa, *Portugal* . . . 35 G1
Lisbon, *N. Dak., U.S.A.* 112 B6
Lisbon, *N.H., U.S.A.* 111 B13
Lisbon, *Ohio, U.S.A.* 110 F4
Lisbon Falls, *U.S.A.* 109 D10
Lisburn, *U.K.* 15 B5
Liscannor B., *Ireland* 15 D2
Liscia ➡, *Italy* 30 A2
Lishe Jiang ➡, *China* 58 E3
Lishi, *China* 56 F6
Lishu, *China* 57 C13
Lishui, *Jiangsu, China* 59 B12
Lishui, *Zhejiang, China* 59 C12
Lisianski I., *Pac. Oc.* 96 E10
Lisichansk = Lysychansk,
  Ukraine 47 H10
Lisieux, *France* 18 C7
Liski, *Russia* 47 G10
L'Isle-Jourdain, *Gers, France* . 20 E5
L'Isle-Jourdain, *Vienne, France* 20 B4
L'Isle-sur-la-Sorgue, *France* . . 21 E9
Lisle-sur-Tarn, *France* 20 E5
Lismore, *Australia* 95 D5
Lismore, *Ireland* 15 D4
Lista, *Norway* 9 G12
Lister, Mt., *Antarctica* 5 D11
Liston, *Australia* 95 D5
Listowel, *Canada* 102 D3
Listowel, *Ireland* 15 D2
Lit, *Sweden* 10 A8
Lit-et-Mixe, *France* 20 D2
Litang, *Guangxi Zhuangzu,*
  China 58 F7
Litang, *Sichuan, China* 58 B3
Litang Qu ➡, *China* 58 C3
Litani ➡, *Lebanon* 75 B4
Litchfield, *Calif., U.S.A.* 116 E6
Litchfield, *Conn., U.S.A.* 111 E11
Litchfield, *Ill., U.S.A.* 112 F10
Litchfield, *Minn., U.S.A.* 112 C7
Liteni, *Romania* 43 C11
Lithgow, *Australia* 95 E5
Líthinon, Ákra, *Greece* 36 E6
Lithuania ■, *Europe* 9 J20
Litija, *Slovenia* 29 B11
Lititz, *U.S.A.* 111 F8
Litókhoron, *Greece* 40 F6
Litoměřice, *Czech Rep.* 26 A7
Litomyšl, *Czech Rep.* 27 B9
Litschau, *Austria* 26 C8
Little Abaco I., *Bahamas* 120 A4
Little Barrier I., *N.Z.* 91 G5
Little Belt Mts., *U.S.A.* 114 C8
Little Blue ➡, *U.S.A.* 112 F6
Little Buffalo ➡, *Canada* 104 A6
Little Cayman, *Cayman Is.* . . . 120 C3
Little Churchill ➡, *Canada* . . . 105 B9
Little Colorado ➡, *U.S.A.* 115 H8
Little Current, *Canada* 102 C3
Little Current ➡, *Canada* 102 B3
Little Falls, *Minn., U.S.A.* . . . 112 C7
Little Falls, *N.Y., U.S.A.* 111 C10
Little Fork ➡, *U.S.A.* 112 A8
Little Grand Rapids, *Canada* . . 105 C9
Little Humboldt ➡, *U.S.A.* . . . 114 F5
Little Inagua I., *Bahamas* 121 B5

Little Karoo, *S. Africa* 88 E3
Little Lake, *U.S.A.* 117 K9
Little Laut Is. = Laut Kecil,
  Kepulauan, *Indonesia* 62 E5
Little Mecatina = Petit-
  Mécatina ➡, *Canada* 103 B8
Little Minch, *U.K.* 14 D2
Little Missouri ➡, *U.S.A.* 112 B3
Little Ouse ➡, *U.K.* 13 E9
Little Rann, *India* 68 H4
Little Red ➡, *U.S.A.* 113 H9
Little River, *N.Z.* 91 K4
Little Rock, *U.S.A.* 113 H8
Little Ruaha ➡, *Tanzania* 86 D4
Little Sable Pt., *U.S.A.* 108 D2
Little Scarcies ➡, *S. Leone* . . . 82 D2
Little Sioux ➡, *U.S.A.* 112 E6
Little Smoky ➡, *Canada* 104 C5
Little Snake ➡, *U.S.A.* 114 F9
Little Valley, *U.S.A.* 110 D6
Little Wabash ➡, *U.S.A.* 108 G1
Little White ➡, *U.S.A.* 112 D4
Littlefield, *U.S.A.* 113 J3
Littlehampton, *U.K.* 13 G7
Littleton, *U.S.A.* 111 B13
Litvinov, *Czech Rep.* 26 A6
Liu He ➡, *China* 57 D11
Liu Jiang ➡, *China* 58 F7
Liuba, *China* 56 H4
Liucheng, *China* 58 E7
Liugou, *China* 57 D10
Liuhe, *China* 57 C13
Liuheng Dao, *China* 59 C14
Liujiang, *China* 58 E7
Liukang Tenggaja = Sabalana,
  Kepulauan, *Indonesia* 63 F5
Liuli, *Tanzania* 87 E3
Liuwa Plain, *Zambia* 85 G4
Liuyang, *China* 59 C9
Liuzhou, *China* 58 E7
Liuzhuang, *China* 57 H11
Livada, *Romania* 42 C8
Livadherón, *Greece* 40 F5
Livadhia, *Cyprus* 36 E12
Livádhion, *Greece* 38 A4
Livarot, *France* 18 D7
Live Oak, *Calif., U.S.A.* 116 F5
Live Oak, *Fla., U.S.A.* 109 K4
Liveras, *Cyprus* 36 D11
Livermore, *U.S.A.* 116 H5
Livermore, Mt., *U.S.A.* 113 K2
Livermore Falls, *U.S.A.* 109 C11
Liverpool, *Canada* 103 D7
Liverpool, *U.K.* 12 D4
Liverpool, *U.S.A.* 111 C8
Liverpool Bay, *U.K.* 12 D4
Liverpool Plains, *Australia* . . . 95 E5
Liverpool Ra., *Australia* 95 E5
Livigno, *Italy* 28 B7
Livingston, *Guatemala* 120 C2
Livingston, *U.K.* 14 F5
Livingston, *Ala., U.S.A.* 109 J1
Livingston, *Calif., U.S.A.* 116 H6
Livingston, *Mont., U.S.A.* 114 D8
Livingston, *S.C., U.S.A.* 109 J5
Livingston, *Tenn., U.S.A.* 109 G3
Livingston, *Tex., U.S.A.* 113 K7
Livingston, L., *U.S.A.* 113 K7
Livingston Manor, *U.S.A.* 111 E10
Livingstone, *Zambia* 87 F2
Livingstone Mts., *Tanzania* . . . 87 D3
Livingstonia, *Malawi* 87 E3
Livno, *Bos.-H.* 42 G2
Livny, *Russia* 47 F9
Livonia, *Mich., U.S.A.* 108 D4
Livonia, *N.Y., U.S.A.* 110 D7
Livorno, *Italy* 28 E7
Livramento, *Brazil* 127 C4
Livron-sur-Drôme, *France* . . . 21 D8
Liwale, *Tanzania* 87 D4
Liwiec ➡, *Poland* 45 F8
Lixi, *China* 58 D3
Lixian, *China* 58 B4
Lixoúrion, *Greece* 38 C2
Liyang, *China* 59 B12
Lizard I., *Australia* 94 A4
Lizard Pt., *U.K.* 13 H2
Lizzano, *Italy* 31 B10
Ljig, *Serbia, Yug.* 40 B4
Ljubija, *Bos.-H.* 29 D13
Ljubinje, *Bos.-H.* 40 D2
Ljubljana, *Slovenia* 29 B11
Ljubno, *Slovenia* 29 B11
Ljubovija, *Serbia, Yug.* 40 B3
Ljugarn, *Sweden* 11 G12
Ljung, *Sweden* 11 G7
Ljungan ➡, *Sweden* 10 B11
Ljungaverk, *Sweden* 10 B10
Ljungby, *Sweden* 9 H15
Ljungbyh-olm, *Sweden* 11 H10
Ljungsbro, *Sweden* 11 F9
Ljungskile, *Sweden* 11 F5
Ljusdal, *Sweden* 10 C10
Ljusfallshammar, *Sweden* 11 F9
Ljusnan ➡, *Sweden* 10 C11
Ljusne, *Sweden* 10 C11
Ljutomer, *Slovenia* 29 B13
Llagostera, *Spain* 32 D7
Llancanelo, Salina, *Argentina* . 126 D2
Llandeilo, *U.K.* 13 F4
Llandovery, *U.K.* 13 F4
Llandrindod Wells, *U.K.* 13 E4
Llandudno, *U.K.* 12 D4
Llanelli, *U.K.* 13 F3
Llanes, *Spain* 34 B6
Llangollen, *U.K.* 12 E4

Llanidloes, *U.K.* 13 E4
Llano, *U.S.A.* 113 K5
Llano →, *U.S.A.* 113 K5
Llano Estacado, *U.S.A.* 113 J3
Llanos, *S. Amer.* 122 C3
Llanquihue, L., *Chile* 128 E1
Llanwrtyd Wells, *U.K.* 13 E4
Llebeig, C. des, *Spain* 37 B9
Lleida, *Spain* 32 D5
Lleida □, *Spain* 32 C6
Llentrisca, C., *Spain* 37 C7
Llera, *Mexico* 119 C5
Llerena, *Spain* 35 G5
Lleyn Peninsula, *U.K.* 12 E3
Llico, *Chile* 126 C1
Lliria, *Spain* 33 F4
Llobregat →, *Spain* 32 D7
Llodio, *Spain* 32 B2
Lloret de Mar, *Spain* 32 D7
Lloyd B., *Australia* 94 A3
Lloyd L., *Canada* 105 B7
Lloydminster, *Canada* 105 C7
Llucena del Cid, *Spain* 32 E4
Llucmajor, *Spain* 37 B9
Llullaillaco, Volcán, *S. Amer.* .. 126 A2
Lo →, *Vietnam* 64 B5
Loa, *U.S.A.* 115 G8
Loa →, *Chile* 126 A1
Loaita I., *S. China Sea* 62 B4
Loange →, *Dem. Rep. of
the Congo* 84 E4
Loano, *Italy* 28 D5
Lobatse, *Botswana* 88 D4
Löbau, *Germany* 24 D10
Lobenstein, *Germany* 24 E7
Lobería, *Argentina* 126 D4
Löberöd, *Sweden* 11 J7
Łobez, *Poland* 44 E2
Lobito, *Angola* 85 G2
Lobo →, *Ivory C.* 82 D3
Lobos, *Argentina* 126 D4
Lobos, I., *Mexico* 118 B2
Lobos, I. de, *Canary Is.* 37 F6
Łobżenica, *Poland* 45 E4
Loc Binh, *Vietnam* 64 B6
Loc Ninh, *Vietnam* 65 G6
Locarno, *Switz.* 25 J4
Loch Baghasdail =
Lochboisdale, *U.K.* 14 D1
Loch Garman = Wexford,
Ireland 15 D5
Loch Nam Madadh =
Lochmaddy, *U.K.* 14 D1
Lochaber, *U.K.* 14 E3
Locharbriggs, *U.K.* 14 F5
Lochboisdale, *U.K.* 14 D1
Loche, L. La, *Canada* 105 B7
Lochem, *Neths.* 17 B6
Loches, *France* 18 E7
Lochgilphead, *U.K.* 14 E3
Lochinver, *U.K.* 14 C3
Lochmaddy, *U.K.* 14 D1
Lochnagar, *Australia* 94 C4
Lochnagar, *U.K.* 14 E5
Łochów, *Poland* 45 F8
Lochy, L., *U.K.* 14 E4
Lock, *Australia* 95 E2
Lock Haven, *U.S.A.* 110 E7
Lockeford, *U.S.A.* 116 G5
Lockeport, *Canada* 103 D6
Lockerbie, *U.K.* 14 F5
Lockhart, *U.S.A.* 113 L6
Lockhart, L., *Australia* 93 F2
Lockhart River, *Australia* 94 A3
Lockney, *U.S.A.* 113 H4
Lockport, *U.S.A.* 110 C6
Locminé, *France* 18 E4
Locri, *Italy* 31 D9
Locronan, *France* 18 D2
Locri, *Israel* 75 D3
Lodeinoye Pole, *Russia* 46 B7
Lodève, *France* 20 E7
Lodge Bay, *Canada* 103 B8
Lodge Grass, *U.S.A.* 114 D10
Lodgepole Cr. →, *U.S.A.* 112 E2
Lodhran, *Pakistan* 68 E4
Lodi, *Italy* 28 C6
Lodi, *Calif., U.S.A.* 116 G5
Lodi, *Ohio, U.S.A.* 110 E3
Lodja, *Dem. Rep. of the Congo* . 86 C1
Lodosa, *Spain* 32 C2
Lödöse, *Sweden* 11 F6
Lodwar, *Kenya* 86 B4
Łódź, *Poland* 45 G6
Łódzkie □, *Poland* 45 G6
Loei, *Thailand* 64 D3
Loenga, *Dem. Rep. of the Congo* 86 C2
Loeriesfontein, *S. Africa* 88 E2
Lofa →, *Liberia* 83 D2
Lofer, *Austria* 26 D5
Lofoten, *Norway* 8 B15
Lofsdalen, *Sweden* 10 B7
Lofsen →, *Sweden* 10 B7
Loftahammar, *Sweden* 11 G10
Loga, *Niger* 83 C5
Logan, *Iowa, U.S.A.* 112 E7
Logan, *Ohio, U.S.A.* 108 F4
Logan, *Utah, U.S.A.* 114 F8
Logan, *W. Va., U.S.A.* 108 G5
Logan, Mt., *Canada* 100 B5
Logandale, *U.S.A.* 117 J12
Logansport, *Ind., U.S.A.* 108 E2
Logansport, *La., U.S.A.* 113 K8
Logirim, *Sudan* 81 G3
Logo, *Sudan* 81 F3
Logone →, *Chad* 79 F9
Logroño, *Spain* 32 C2

Logrosán, *Spain* 35 F5
Løgstør, *Denmark* 11 H3
Løgumkloster, *Denmark* 11 J2
Lohals, *Denmark* 11 J4
Lohardaga, *India* 69 H11
Loharia, *India* 68 H6
Loharu, *India* 68 E6
Lohja, *Finland* 9 F21
Löhne, *Germany* 24 C4
Lohr, *Germany* 25 F5
Lohri Wah →, *Pakistan* 68 F2
Loi-kaw, *Burma* 67 K20
Loimaa, *Finland* 9 F20
Loir →, *France* 18 E6
Loir-et-Cher □, *France* 18 E8
Loire □, *France* 21 C8
Loire →, *France* 18 E4
Loire-Atlantique □, *France* ... 18 E5
Loiret □, *France* 19 E9
Loitz, *Germany* 24 B9
Loja, *Ecuador* 124 D3
Loja, *Spain* 35 H6
Loji = Kawasi, *Indonesia* 63 E7
Løjt Kirkeby, *Denmark* 11 J3
Lojung, *China* 58 E7
Loka, *Sudan* 81 G3
Lokandu, *Dem. Rep. of
the Congo* 86 C2
Lokeren, *Belgium* 17 C3
Lokgwabe, *Botswana* 88 C3
Lokhvitsa, *Ukraine* 47 G7
Lokichokio, *Kenya* 86 B3
Lokitaung, *Kenya* 86 B4
Lokkan tekojärvi, *Finland* 8 C22
Løkken, *Denmark* 11 G3
Loknya, *Russia* 46 D6
Loko, *Nigeria* 83 D6
Lokoja, *Nigeria* 83 D6
Lokot, *Russia* 47 F8
Lol →, *Sudan* 81 F2
Lola, *Guinea* 82 D3
Lola, Mt., *U.S.A.* 116 F6
Lolibai, Gebel, *Sudan* 81 G3
Lolimi, *Sudan* 81 G3
Loliondo, *Tanzania* 86 C4
Lolland, *Denmark* 11 K5
Lollar, *Germany* 24 E4
Lolo, *U.S.A.* 114 C6
Lolodorf, *Cameroon* 83 E7
Lom →, *Bulgaria* 40 C7
Lom, *Bulgaria* 40 C7
Lom Kao, *Thailand* 64 D3
Lom Sak, *Thailand* 64 D3
Loma, *U.S.A.* 114 C8
Loma Linda, *U.S.A.* 117 L9
Lomami →, *Dem. Rep. of
the Congo* 86 B1
Lomas de Zamóra, *Argentina* . 126 C4
Lombadina, *Australia* 92 C3
Lombárdia □, *Italy* 28 C6
Lombardy = Lombárdia □, *Italy* 28 C6
Lombez, *France* 20 E4
Lomblen, *Indonesia* 63 F6
Lombok, *Indonesia* 62 F5
Lomé, *Togo* 83 D5
Lomela, *Dem. Rep. of the Congo* 84 E4
Lomela →, *Dem. Rep. of
the Congo* 84 E4
Lomianki, *Poland* 45 F7
Lomma, *Sweden* 11 J7
Lommel, *Belgium* 17 C5
Lomond, *Canada* 104 C6
Lomond, L., *U.K.* 14 E4
Lomphat, *Cambodia* 64 F6
Lompobatang, *Indonesia* 63 F5
Lompoc, *U.S.A.* 117 L6
Łomża, *Poland* 45 E9
Loncoche, *Chile* 128 D2
Londa, *India* 66 M9
Londiani, *Kenya* 86 C4
Londinières, *France* 18 C8
London, *Canada* 102 D3
London, *U.K.* 13 F7
London, *Ky., U.S.A.* 108 G3
London, *Ohio, U.S.A.* 108 F4
London, Greater □, *U.K.* 13 F7
Londonderry, *U.K.* 15 B4
Londonderry □, *U.K.* 15 B4
Londonderry, C., *Australia* ... 92 B4
Londonderry, I., *Chile* 128 H2
Londres, *Argentina* 128 B3
Londrina, *Brazil* 127 A5
Lone Pine, *U.S.A.* 116 J8
Lonely Mine, *Zimbabwe* 89 B4
Long B., *U.S.A.* 109 J6
Long Beach, *Calif., U.S.A.* ... 117 M8
Long Beach, *N.Y., U.S.A.* 111 F11
Long Beach, *Wash., U.S.A.* ... 116 D2
Long Branch, *U.S.A.* 111 F11
Long Creek, *U.S.A.* 114 D4
Long Eaton, *U.K.* 12 E6
Long I., *Australia* 94 C4
Long I., *Bahamas* 121 B4
Long I., *Canada* 102 B4
Long I., *Ireland* 15 E2
Long I., *U.S.A.* 111 F11
Long Island Sd., *U.S.A.* 111 E12
Long L., *Canada* 102 C2
Long Lake, *U.S.A.* 111 C10
Long Point B., *Canada* 110 D4
Long Prairie →, *U.S.A.* 112 C7
Long Pt., *Canada* 110 D4
Long Range Mts., *Canada* 103 C8
Long Reef, *Australia* 92 B4
Long Spruce, *Canada* 105 B10
Long Str. = Longa, Proliv, *Russia* 4 C16
Long Thanh, *Vietnam* 65 G6

Long Xian, *China* 56 G4
Long Xuyen, *Vietnam* 65 G5
Longá, *Greece* 38 E3
Longa, Proliv, *Russia* 4 C16
Long'an, *China* 58 F6
Longarone, *Italy* 29 B9
Longbenton, *U.K.* 12 B6
Longboat Key, *U.S.A.* 109 M4
Longchang, *China* 58 C5
Longchi, *China* 58 C4
Longchuan, *Guangdong, China* 59 E10
Longchuan, *Yunnan, China* .. 58 E1
Longde, *China* 56 G4
Longeau, *France* 19 E12
Longford, *Australia* 94 G4
Longford, *Ireland* 15 C4
Longford □, *Ireland* 15 C4
Longhai, *China* 59 E11
Longhua, *China* 57 D9
Longhui, *China* 59 D8
Longido, *Tanzania* 86 C4
Longiram, *Indonesia* 62 E5
Longkou, *Jiangxi, China* 59 D10
Longkou, *Shandong, China* .. 57 F11
Longlac, *Canada* 102 C2
Longli, *China* 58 D6
Longlin, *China* 58 E5
Longling, *China* 58 E2
Longmeadow, *U.S.A.* 111 D12
Longmen, *China* 59 F10
Longming, *China* 58 F6
Longmont, *U.S.A.* 112 E2
Longnan, *China* 59 E10
Longnawan, *Indonesia* 62 D4
Longobucco, *Italy* 31 C9
Longquan, *China* 59 C12
Longreach, *Australia* 94 C3
Longshan, *China* 58 C7
Longsheng, *China* 59 E8
Longué-Jumelles, *France* 18 E6
Longueau, *France* 19 C9
Longueuil, *Canada* 111 A11
Longuyon, *France* 19 C12
Longvic, *France* 19 E12
Longview, *Tex., U.S.A.* 113 J7
Longview, *Wash., U.S.A.* 116 D4
Longwy, *France* 19 C12
Longxi, *China* 56 G3
Longyan, *China* 59 E11
Longyou, *China* 59 C12
Longzhou, *China* 58 F6
Lonigo, *Italy* 29 C8
Löningen, *Germany* 24 C3
Lonja →, *Croatia* 29 C13
Lonoke, *U.S.A.* 113 H9
Lonquimay, *Chile* 128 D2
Lons-le-Saunier, *France* 19 F12
Lönsboda, *Sweden* 11 H8
Looe, *U.K.* 13 G3
Lookout, C., *Canada* 102 A3
Lookout, C., *U.S.A.* 109 H7
Loolmalasin, *Tanzania* 86 C4
Loon →, *Alta., Canada* 104 B5
Loon →, *Man., Canada* 105 B8
Loon Lake, *Canada* 105 C7
Loongana, *Australia* 93 F4
Loop Hd., *Ireland* 15 D2
Lop Buri, *Thailand* 64 E3
Lop Nor = Lop Nur, *China* ... 60 B4
Lop Nur, *China* 60 B4
Lopare, *Bos.-H.* 42 F3
Lopatin, *Russia* 49 J8
Lopatina, Gora, *Russia* 51 D15
Lopaye, *Sudan* 81 F3
Lopez, *Phil.* 61 E5
Lopez, *U.S.A.* 111 E8
Lopez, C., *Gabon* 84 E1
Lopphavet, *Norway* 8 A19
Lora →, *Afghan.* 66 D4
Lora, Hāmūn-i-, *Pakistan* 66 E4
Lora Cr. →, *Australia* 95 D2
Lora del Río, *Spain* 35 H5
Lorain, *U.S.A.* 110 E2
Loralai, *Pakistan* 68 D3
Lorca, *Spain* 33 H3
Lord Howe I., *Pac. Oc.* 96 L7
Lord Howe Ridge, *Pac. Oc.* .. 96 L8
Lordsburg, *U.S.A.* 115 K9
Lorestan □, *Iran* 71 C6
Loreto, *Brazil* 125 E9
Loreto, *Italy* 29 E10
Loreto, *Mexico* 118 B2
Lorgues, *France* 21 E10
Lorhosso, *Burkina Faso* 82 C4
Lorient, *France* 18 E3
Lőrinci, *Hungary* 42 C4
Lormi, *India* 69 H9
Lorn, *U.K.* 14 E3
Lorn, Firth of, *U.K.* 14 E3
Lorne, *Australia* 95 F3
Loronyo, *Sudan* 81 G3
Lorovouno, *Cyprus* 36 D11
Lörrach, *Germany* 25 H3
Lorraine □, *France* 19 D13
Los, Sweden 10 C9
Los, Îles de, *Guinea* 82 D2
Los Alamos, *Calif., U.S.A.* ... 117 L6
Los Alamos, *N. Mex., U.S.A.* . 115 J10
Los Altos, *U.S.A.* 116 H4
Los Andes, *Chile* 126 C1
Los Angeles, *Chile* 126 D1
Los Angeles, *U.S.A.* 117 M8
Los Angeles, Bahia de, *Mexico* 118 B2
Los Angeles Aqueduct, *U.S.A.* 117 K9
Los Banos, *U.S.A.* 116 H6
Los Barrios, *Spain* 35 J5
Los Blancos, *Argentina* 126 A3

Los Chiles, *Costa Rica* 120 D3
Los Corrales de Buelna, *Spain* . 34 B6
Los Cristianos, *Canary Is.* ... 37 F3
Los Gallardos, *Spain* 33 H3
Los Gatos, *U.S.A.* 116 H5
Los Hermanos Is., *Venezuela* . 121 D7
Los Islotes, *Canary Is.* 37 E6
Los Llanos de Aridane,
Canary Is. 37 F2
Los Loros, *Chile* 126 B1
Los Lunas, *U.S.A.* 115 J10
Los Mochis, *Mexico* 118 B3
Los Monegros, *Spain* 32 D4
Los Nietos, *Spain* 33 H4
Los Olivos, *U.S.A.* 117 L6
Los Palacios, *Cuba* 120 B3
Los Palacios y Villafranca, *Spain* 35 H5
Los Reyes, *Mexico* 118 D4
Los Roques Is., *Venezuela* ... 121 D6
Los Santos de Maimona, *Spain* 35 G4
Los Teques, *Venezuela* 124 A5
Los Testigos, Is., *Venezuela* .. 124 A6
Los Vilos, *Chile* 126 C1
Los Yébenes, *Spain* 35 F7
Łosice, *Poland* 45 F9
Loskop Dam, *S. Africa* 89 D4
Løsning, *Denmark* 11 J3
Lossiemouth, *U.K.* 14 D5
Lostwithiel, *U.K.* 13 G3
Lot □, *France* 20 D5
Lot →, *France* 20 D4
Lot-et-Garonne □, *France* 20 D4
Lota, *Chile* 126 D1
Lotagipi Swamp, *Sudan* 81 G3
Lotfābād, *Iran* 71 B8
Lothair, *S. Africa* 89 D5
Lotorp, *Sweden* 11 F9
Lötschbergtunnel, *Switz.* 25 J3
Löttorp, *Sweden* 11 G11
Lotung, *Taiwan* 59 E13
Loubomo, *Congo* 84 E2
Loudéac, *France* 18 D4
Loudi, *China* 59 D8
Loudonville, *U.S.A.* 110 F2
Loudun, *France* 18 E7
Loue →, *France* 19 E12
Louga, *Senegal* 82 B1
Loughborough, *U.K.* 12 E6
Loughrea, *Ireland* 15 C3
Loughros More B., *Ireland* ... 15 B3
Louhans, *France* 19 F12
Louis Trichardt, *S. Africa* 89 C4
Louis XIV, Pte., *Canada* 102 B4
Louisa, *U.S.A.* 108 F4
Louisbourg, *Canada* 103 C8
Louise I., *Canada* 104 C2
Louiseville, *Canada* 102 C5
Louisiade Arch., *Papua N. G.* . 96 J7
Louisiana, *U.S.A.* 112 F9
Louisiana □, *U.S.A.* 113 K9
Louisville, *Ky., U.S.A.* 108 F3
Louisville, *Miss., U.S.A.* 113 J10
Louisville, *Ohio, U.S.A.* 110 F3
Loulay, *France* 20 B3
Loulé, *Portugal* 35 H3
Louny, *Czech Rep.* 26 A6
Loup City, *U.S.A.* 112 E5
Loups Marins, Lacs des, *Canada* 102 A5
Lourdes, *France* 20 E3
Lourinhã, *Portugal* 35 F1
Lousã, *Portugal* 34 E2
Louta, *Burkina Faso* 82 C4
Louth, *Australia* 95 E4
Louth, *Ireland* 15 C5
Louth, *U.K.* 12 D7
Louth □, *Ireland* 15 C5
Loutrá Aidhipsoú, *Greece* 38 C5
Loutráki, *Greece* 38 D4
Louvain = Leuven, *Belgium* .. 17 D4
Louviers, *France* 18 C8
Louwsburg, *S. Africa* 89 D5
Lovat →, *Russia* 46 C6
Lovćen, *Montenegro, Yug.* ... 40 D2
Lovech, *Bulgaria* 41 C8
Lovech □, *Bulgaria* 41 C8
Loveland, *U.S.A.* 112 E2
Lovell, *U.S.A.* 114 D9
Lovelock, *U.S.A.* 114 F4
Lóvere, *Italy* 28 C7
Lövestad, *Sweden* 11 J7
Loviisa, *Finland* 9 F22
Loving, *U.S.A.* 113 J2
Lovington, *U.S.A.* 113 J3
Lovisa = Loviisa, *Finland* 9 F22
Lovosice, *Czech Rep.* 26 A7
Lovran, *Croatia* 29 C11
Lovrin, *Romania* 42 E5
Lövstabruk, *Sweden* 10 D11
Lövstabukten, *Sweden* 10 D11
Low, L., *U.S.A.* 102 B4
Low Pt., *Australia* 93 F4
Low Tatra = Nízké Tatry,
Slovak Rep. 27 C12
Lowa, *Dem. Rep. of the Congo* . 86 C2
Lowa →, *Dem. Rep. of
the Congo* 86 C2
Lowell, *U.S.A.* 111 D13
Lowellville, *U.S.A.* 110 E4
Löwen →, *Namibia* 88 D2
Lower Alkali L., *U.S.A.* 114 F3
Lower Arrow L., *Canada* 104 D5
Lower Austria =
Niederösterreich □, *Austria* . 26 C8
Lower California = Baja
California, *Mexico* 118 A1
Lower Hutt, *N.Z.* 91 J5
Lower Lake, *U.S.A.* 116 G4

Lower Manitou L., *Canada* ... 105 D10
Lower Post, *Canada* 104 B3
Lower Red L., *U.S.A.* 112 B7
Lower Saxony =
Niedersachsen □, *Germany* . 24 C4
Lower Tunguska = Tunguska,
Nizhnyaya →, *Russia* 51 C9
Lowestoft, *U.K.* 13 E9
Lowgar □, *Afghan.* 66 B6
Łowicz, *Poland* 45 F6
Lowville, *U.S.A.* 111 C9
Loxton, *Australia* 95 E3
Loxton, *S. Africa* 88 E3
Loyalton, *U.S.A.* 116 F6
Loyalty Is. = Loyauté, Is., *N. Cal.* 96 K8
Loyang = Luoyang, *China* 56 G7
Loyauté, Is., *N. Cal.* 96 K8
Loyev = Loyew, *Belarus* 47 G6
Loyew, *Belarus* 47 G6
Loyoro, *Uganda* 86 B3
Lož, *Slovenia* 29 C11
Lozère □, *France* 20 D7
Loznica, *Serbia, Yug.* 40 B3
Lozova, *Ukraine* 47 H9
Lü Shan, *China* 59 C11
Lü-Tao, *Taiwan* 59 F13
Luachimo, *Angola* 84 F4
Luajan →, *India* 69 G11
Lualaba →, *Dem. Rep. of
the Congo* 86 C2
Luampa, *Zambia* 87 F1
Lu'an, *China* 59 B11
Luan Chau, *Vietnam* 58 G4
Luan He →, *China* 57 E10
Luan Xian, *China* 57 E10
Luancheng, *Guangxi Zhuangzu,
China* 58 F7
Luancheng, *Hebei, China* 56 F8
Luanco, *Spain* 34 B5
Luanda, *Angola* 84 F2
Luang, Thale, *Thailand* 65 J3
Luang Prabang, *Laos* 58 H4
Luangwa, *Zambia* 87 F3
Luangwa →, *Zambia* 87 E3
Luangwa Valley, *Zambia* 87 E3
Luanne, *China* 57 D9
Luanping, *China* 57 D9
Luanshya, *Zambia* 87 E2
Luapula □, *Zambia* 87 E2
Luapula →, *Africa* 87 D2
Luarca, *Spain* 34 B4
Luashi, *Dem. Rep. of the Congo* 87 E1
Luau, *Angola* 84 G4
Lubaczów, *Poland* 45 H10
Lubań, *Poland* 45 G2
Lubana, Ozero = Lubānas Ezers,
Latvia 9 H22
Lubānas Ezers, *Latvia* 9 H22
Lubang, *Phil.* 61 E4
Lubang Is., *Phil.* 63 B6
Lubartów, *Poland* 45 G9
Lubawa, *Poland* 44 E6
Lübbecke, *Germany* 24 C4
Lübben, *Germany* 24 D9
Lübbenau, *Germany* 24 D9
Lubbock, *U.S.A.* 113 J4
Lübeck, *Germany* 24 B6
Lübecker Bucht, *Germany* ... 24 A6
Lubefu, *Dem. Rep. of the Congo* 86 C1
Lubefu →, *Dem. Rep. of
the Congo* 86 C1
Lubelskie □, *Poland* 45 G9
Lubero = Luofu, *Dem. Rep. of
the Congo* 86 C2
Lubersac, *France* 20 C5
Lubicon L., *Canada* 104 B5
Lubień Kujawski, *Poland* 45 F6
Lubilash →, *Dem. Rep. of
the Congo* 84 F4
Lubin, *Poland* 45 G3
Lublin, *Poland* 45 G9
Lubliniec, *Poland* 45 H5
Lubnān, Jabal, *Lebanon* 75 B4
Lubniewice, *Poland* 45 F2
Lubny, *Ukraine* 47 G7
Lubomierz, *Poland* 45 G2
Luboń, *Poland* 45 F3
Lubongola, *Dem. Rep. of
the Congo* 86 C2
L'ubotín, *Slovak Rep.* 27 B13
Lubraniec, *Poland* 45 F5
Lubsko, *Poland* 45 G1
Lübtheen, *Germany* 24 B7
Lubuagan, *Phil.* 61 C4
Lubudi, *Dem. Rep. of the Congo* 84 F4
Lubudi →, *Dem. Rep. of
the Congo* 87 D2
Lubuklinggau, *Indonesia* 62 E2
Lubuksikaping, *Indonesia* ... 62 D2
Lubumbashi, *Dem. Rep. of
the Congo* 87 E2
Lubunda, *Dem. Rep. of
the Congo* 86 D2
Lubungu, *Zambia* 87 E2
Lubuskie □, *Poland* 45 F2
Lubutu, *Dem. Rep. of the Congo* 86 C2
Luc An Chau, *Vietnam* 64 A5
Luc-en-Diois, *France* 21 D9
Lucan, *Canada* 110 C3
Lucania, Mt., *Canada* 100 B5
Lucas Channel, *Canada* 110 A3
Lucea, *Phil.* 61 D4
Lucca, *Italy* 28 E7
Lucé, *France* 18 D8
Luce Bay, *U.K.* 14 G4
Lucea, *Jamaica* 120 C4
Lucedale, *U.S.A.* 109 K1

Lucena, *Phil.* 61 E4
Lucena, *Spain* 35 H6
Lučenec, *Slovak Rep.* 27 C12
Lucera, *Italy* 31 A8
Lucerne = Luzern, *Switz.* 25 H4
Lucerne, *U.S.A.* 116 F4
Lucerne Valley, *U.S.A.* 117 L10
Lucero, *Mexico* 118 A3
Luchena →, *Spain* 33 H3
Lucheng, *China* 56 F7
Lucheringo →, *Mozam.* 87 E4
Luchuan, *China* 59 F8
Lucia, *U.S.A.* 116 J5
Lucinda, *Australia* 94 B4
Luckau, *Germany* 24 D9
Luckenwalde, *Germany* 24 C9
Luckhoff, *S. Africa* 88 D3
Lucknow, *Canada* 110 C3
Lucknow, *India* 69 F9
Luçon, *France* 20 B2
Lüda = Dalian, *China* 57 E11
Luda Kamchiya →, *Bulgaria* .. 41 C11
Ludbreg, *Croatia* 29 B13
Lüdenscheid, *Germany* 24 D3
Lüderitz, *Namibia* 88 D2
Lüderitzbaai, *Namibia* 88 D2
Ludhiana, *India* 68 D6
Ludian, *China* 58 D4
Luding Qiao, *China* 58 C4
Lüdinghausen, *Germany* 24 D3
Ludington, *U.S.A.* 108 D2
Ludlow, *U.K.* 13 E5
Ludlow, *Calif., U.S.A.* 117 L10
Ludlow, *Pa., U.S.A.* 110 E6
Ludlow, *Vt., U.S.A.* 111 C12
Ludus, *Romania* 43 D9
Ludvika, *Sweden* 10 D9
Ludwigsburg, *Germany* 25 G5
Ludwigsfelde, *Germany* 24 C9
Ludwigshafen, *Germany* 25 F4
Ludwigslust, *Germany* 24 B7
Ludza, *Latvia* 46 D4
Lueki, *Dem. Rep. of the Congo* 86 C2
Luena, *Dem. Rep. of the Congo* 87 D2
Luena, *Zambia* 87 E3
Lüeyang, *China* 56 H4
Lufeng, *Guangdong, China* ... 59 F10
Lufeng, *Yunnan, China* 58 E4
Lufira →, *Dem. Rep. of the Congo* 87 D2
Lufkin, *U.S.A.* 113 K7
Lufupa, *Dem. Rep. of the Congo* 87 E1
Luga, *Russia* 46 C5
Luga →, *Russia* 46 C5
Lugano, *Switz.* 25 J4
Lugano, L. di, *Switz.* 28 C6
Lugansk = Luhansk, *Ukraine* . 47 H10
Lugard's Falls, *Kenya* 86 C4
Lugela, *Mozam.* 87 F4
Lugenda →, *Mozam.* 87 E4
Lugh Ganana, *Somali Rep.* .. 74 G3
Lugnaquilla, *Ireland* 15 D5
Lugo, *Italy* 29 D8
Lugo, *Spain* 34 B3
Lugo □, *Spain* 34 C3
Lugoj, *Romania* 42 E6
Lugovoy = Qulan, *Kazakstan* . 50 E8
Luhansk, *Ukraine* 47 H10
Luhe →, *China* 59 A12
Luhe →, *Germany* 24 B6
Luhuo, *China* 58 B3
Luiana, *Angola* 88 B3
Luimneach = Limerick, *Ireland* 15 D3
Luing, *U.K.* 14 E3
Luino, *Italy* 28 C5
Luís Correia, *Brazil* 125 D10
Luitpold Coast, *Antarctica* ... 5 D1
Luiza, *Dem. Rep. of the Congo* 84 F4
Luizi, *Dem. Rep. of the Congo* 86 D2
Luján, *Argentina* 126 C4
Lujiang, *China* 59 B11
Lukang, *Taiwan* 59 E13
Lukanga Swamp, *Zambia* 87 E2
Lukavac, *Bos.-H.* 42 F7
Lukenie →, *Dem. Rep. of the Congo* 84 E3
Lukhisaral, *India* 69 G12
Lüki, *Bulgaria* 41 E8
Lukolela, *Dem. Rep. of the Congo* 86 D1
Lukosi, *Zimbabwe* 87 F2
Lukovë, *Albania* 40 G3
Lukovit, *Bulgaria* 41 C8
Łuków, *Poland* 45 G9
Lukoyanov, *Russia* 48 C7
Lule älv →, *Sweden* 8 D19
Luleå, *Sweden* 8 D20
Lüleburgaz, *Turkey* 41 E11
Luliang, *China* 58 E4
Luling, *U.S.A.* 113 L6
Lulong, *China* 57 E10
Lulonga →, *Dem. Rep. of the Congo* 84 D3
Lulua →, *Dem. Rep. of the Congo* 84 E4
Lumajang, *Indonesia* 63 H15
Lumbala N'guimbo, *Angola* .. 85 G4
Lumberton, *U.S.A.* 109 H6
Lumbwa, *Kenya* 86 C4
Lumsden, *Canada* 105 C8
Lumsden, *N.Z.* 91 L2
Lumut, *Malaysia* 65 K3
Lumut, Tanjung, *Indonesia* .. 62 E3
Luna, *India* 68 H3
Lunan, *China* 58 E4
Lunavada, *India* 68 H5

Lunca, *Romania* 43 C10
Lunca Corbului, *Romania* ... 43 F9
Lund, *Sweden* 11 J7
Lundazi, *Zambia* 87 E3
Lunderskov, *Denmark* 11 J3
Lundi →, *Zimbabwe* 87 G3
Lundu, *Malaysia* 62 D3
Lundy, *U.K.* 13 F3
Lune →, *U.K.* 12 C5
Lüneburg, *Germany* 24 B6
Lüneburg Heath = Lüneburger Heide, *Germany* 24 B6
Lüneburger Heide, *Germany* .. 24 B6
Lunel, *France* 21 E8
Lünen, *Germany* 24 D3
Lunenburg, *Canada* 103 D7
Lunéville, *France* 19 D13
Lunga →, *Zambia* 87 E2
Lungi Airport, *S. Leone* 82 D2
Lunglei, *India* 67 H18
Luni, *India* 68 G5
Luni →, *India* 68 G4
Luninets = Luninyets, *Belarus* 47 F4
Luning, *U.S.A.* 114 G4
Lunino, *Russia* 48 D7
Luninyets, *Belarus* 47 F4
Lunkaransar, *India* 68 E5
Lunsemfwa →, *Zambia* 87 E3
Lunsemfwa Falls, *Zambia* ... 87 E2
Luo He →, *China* 56 G6
Luocheng, *China* 58 E7
Luochuan, *China* 56 G5
Luoci, *China* 58 E4
Luodian, *China* 58 E6
Luoding, *China* 59 F8
Luofu, *Dem. Rep. of the Congo* 86 C2
Luohe, *China* 56 H8
Luojiang, *China* 58 B5
Luonan, *China* 56 G6
Luoning, *China* 56 G6
Luoshan, *China* 59 A10
Luotian, *China* 59 B10
Luoxiao Shan, *China* 59 D10
Luoyang, *China* 56 G7
Luoyuan, *China* 59 D12
Luozigou, *China* 57 C16
Lupanshui, *China* 58 D5
Lupeni, *Romania* 43 E8
Lupilichi, *Mozam.* 87 E4
Łupków, *Poland* 45 J9
Luping, *China* 58 E5
Luquan, *China* 58 E4
Luque, *Paraguay* 126 B4
Lúras, *Italy* 30 B2
Luray, *U.S.A.* 108 F6
Lure, *France* 19 E13
Lurgan, *U.K.* 15 B5
Lusaka, *Zambia* 87 F2
Lusambo, *Dem. Rep. of the Congo* 86 C1
Lusangaye, *Dem. Rep. of the Congo* 86 C2
Luseland, *Canada* 105 C7
Lushan, *Henan, China* 56 H7
Lushan, *Sichuan, China* 58 B4
Lushi, *China* 56 G6
Lushnjë, *Albania* 40 F3
Lushoto, *Tanzania* 86 C4
Lushui, *China* 58 E2
Lüshun, *China* 57 E11
Lusignan, *France* 20 B4
Lusigny-sur-Barse, *France* ... 19 D11
Lusk, *U.S.A.* 112 D2
Lussac-les-Châteaux, *France* . 20 B4
Lustenau, *Austria* 26 D2
Lüt, Dasht-e, *Iran* 71 D8
Luta = Dalian, *China* 57 E11
Lutherstadt Wittenberg, *Germany* 24 D8
Luton, *U.K.* 13 F7
Luton □, *U.K.* 13 F7
Lutselke, *Canada* 105 A6
Lutsk, *Ukraine* 47 G3
Lützow Holmbukta, *Antarctica* 5 C4
Lutzputs, *S. Africa* 88 D3
Luverne, *Ala., U.S.A.* 109 K2
Luverne, *Minn., U.S.A.* 112 D6
Luvua, *Dem. Rep. of the Congo* 87 D2
Luvua →, *Dem. Rep. of the Congo* 86 D2
Luvuvhu →, *S. Africa* 89 C5
Luwegu →, *Tanzania* 87 D4
Luwuk, *Indonesia* 63 E6
Luxembourg, *Lux.* 17 E6
Luxembourg □, *Belgium* 17 E5
Luxembourg ■, *Europe* 7 F7
Luxeuil-les-Bains, *France* ... 19 E13
Luxi, *Hunan, China* 59 C8
Luxi, *Yunnan, China* 58 E4
Luxi, *Yunnan, China* 58 E2
Luxor = El Uqsur, *Egypt* 80 B3
Luy →, *France* 20 E2
Luy-de-Béarn →, *France* 20 E3
Luy-de-France →, *France* ... 20 E3
Luyi, *China* 56 H8
Luz-St-Sauveur, *France* 20 F4
Luzern, *Switz.* 25 H4
Luzern □, *Switz.* 25 H3
Luzhai, *China* 58 E7
Luzhou, *China* 58 C5
Luziânia, *Brazil* 125 G9
Luzon, *Phil.* 61 D4
Luzy, *France* 19 F10
Luzzi, *Italy* 31 C9
Lviv, *Ukraine* 47 H3
Lvov = Lviv, *Ukraine* 47 H3

Lwówek, *Poland* 45 F3
Lwówek Śląski, *Poland* 45 G2
Lyakhavichy, *Belarus* 47 F4
Lyakhovskiye, Ostrova, *Russia* 51 B15
Lyaki = Läki, *Azerbaijan* ... 49 K8
Lyal I., *Canada* 110 B3
Lyallpur = Faisalabad, *Pakistan* 68 D5
Lyaskovets, *Bulgaria* 41 C9
Lybster, *U.K.* 14 C5
Lycaonia, *Turkey* 72 D5
Lychen, *Germany* 24 B9
Lychkova, *Russia* 46 D7
Lycia, *Turkey* 39 E11
Lyckeby →, *Sweden* 11 H9
Lycksele, *Sweden* 8 D18
Lycosura, *Greece* 38 D4
Lydda = Lod, *Israel* 75 D3
Lydenburg, *S. Africa* 89 D5
Lydia, *Turkey* 39 C10
Łydynia →, *Poland* 45 F7
Lyell, *N.Z.* 91 J4
Lyell I., *Canada* 104 C2
Lyepyel, *Belarus* 46 E5
Lygnern, *Sweden* 11 G6
Lykens, *U.S.A.* 111 F8
Lyman, *U.S.A.* 114 F8
Lyme B., *U.K.* 13 G4
Lyme Regis, *U.K.* 13 G5
Lymington, *U.K.* 13 G6
Łyna →, *Poland* 9 J19
Lynchburg, *U.S.A.* 108 G6
Lynd →, *Australia* 94 B3
Lynd Ra., *Australia* 95 D4
Lynden, *Canada* 110 C4
Lynden, *U.S.A.* 116 B4
Lyndhurst, *Australia* 95 E2
Lyndon →, *Australia* 93 D1
Lyndonville, *N.Y., U.S.A.* ... 110 C6
Lyndonville, *Vt., U.S.A.* ... 111 B12
Lyngen, *Norway* 8 B19
Lynher Reef, *Australia* 92 C3
Lynn, *U.S.A.* 111 D14
Lynn Lake, *Canada* 105 B8
Lynnwood, *U.S.A.* 116 C4
Lynton, *U.K.* 13 F4
Lyntupy, *Belarus* 9 J22
Lynx L., *Canada* 105 A7
Lyon, *France* 21 C8
Lyonnais, *France* 21 C8
Lyons = Lyon, *France* 21 C8
Lyons, *Ga., U.S.A.* 109 J4
Lyons, *Kans., U.S.A.* 112 F5
Lyons, *N.Y., U.S.A.* 110 C8
Lyons →, *Australia* 93 E2
Lyons Falls, *U.S.A.* 111 C9
Lyozna, *Belarus* 46 E6
Lys = Leie →, *Belgium* 17 C3
Lysá nad Labem, *Czech Rep.* . 26 A7
Lysekil, *Sweden* 11 F5
Lyskovo, *Russia* 48 B7
Lystrup, *Denmark* 11 H4
Lysva, *Russia* 10 D7
Lysychansk, *Ukraine* 47 H10
Lytham St. Anne's, *U.K.* 12 D4
Lyttelton, *N.Z.* 91 K4
Lytton, *Canada* 104 C4
Lyuban, *Russia* 46 C6
Lyubertsy, *Russia* 46 E9
Lyubim, *Russia* 46 C11
Lyubimets, *Bulgaria* 41 E10
Lyuboml, *Ukraine* 47 G3
Lyubotyn, *Ukraine* 47 H8
Lyubytino, *Russia* 46 C7
Lyudinovo, *Russia* 46 F8

M

M.R. Gomez, Presa, *Mexico* .. 119 B5
Ma →, *Vietnam* 58 H5
Ma'adaba, *Jordan* 75 E4
Maamba, *Zambia* 88 B4
Ma'ān, *Jordan* 75 E4
Ma'ān □, *Jordan* 75 F5
Maanselkä, *Finland* 8 C23
Ma'anshan, *China* 59 B12
Maarianhamina, *Finland* 9 F18
Ma'arrat an Nu'mān, *Syria* .. 70 C3
Maas →, *Neths.* 17 C4
Maaseik, *Belgium* 17 C5
Maasin, *Phil.* 63 B6
Maastricht, *Neths.* 17 D5
Maave, *Mozam.* 89 C5
Mababe Depression, *Botswana* 88 B3
Mabalane, *Mozam.* 89 C5
Mabel L., *Canada* 104 C5
Mabenge, *Dem. Rep. of the Congo* 86 B1
Maberly, *Canada* 111 B8
Mabian, *China* 58 C4
Mabil, *Ethiopia* 81 E4
Mablethorpe, *U.K.* 12 D8
Mably, *France* 19 F11
Maboma, *Dem. Rep. of the Congo* 86 B2
Mabonto, *S. Leone* 82 D2
Mabrouk, *Mali* 83 B4
Mac Bac, *Vietnam* 65 H6
Macachín, *Argentina* 126 D3
Macaé, *Brazil* 127 A7
Macael, *Spain* 33 H2
Macaé, *Brazil* 127 A7
Macalester, *U.S.A.* 113 H7
McAllen, *U.S.A.* 113 M5
MacAlpine L., *Canada* 100 B9
Macamic, *Canada* 102 C4
Macao = Macau □, *China* ... 59 F9

Macão, *Portugal* 35 F3
Macapá, *Brazil* 125 C8
McArthur →, *Australia* 94 B2
McArthur, Port, *Australia* ... 94 B2
Macau, *Brazil* 125 E11
Macau □, *China* 59 F9
McBride, *Canada* 104 C4
McCall, *U.S.A.* 114 D5
McCamey, *U.S.A.* 113 K3
McCammon, *U.S.A.* 114 E7
McCauley I., *Canada* 104 C2
McCleary, *U.S.A.* 116 C3
Macclenny, *U.S.A.* 109 K4
Macclesfield, *U.K.* 12 D5
M'Clintock Chan., *Canada* .. 100 A9
McClintock Ra., *Australia* ... 92 C4
McCloud, *U.S.A.* 114 F2
McCluer I., *Australia* 92 B5
McClure, *U.S.A.* 110 F7
McClure, L., *U.S.A.* 116 H6
M'Clure Str., *Canada* 4 B2
McClusky, *U.S.A.* 112 B4
McComb, *U.S.A.* 113 K9
McConaughy, L., *U.S.A.* 112 E4
McCook, *U.S.A.* 112 E4
McCreary, *Canada* 105 C9
McCullough Mt., *U.S.A.* ... 117 K11
McCusker →, *Canada* 105 B7
McDame, *Canada* 104 B3
McDermitt, *U.S.A.* 114 F5
McDonald, *U.S.A.* 110 F4
Macdonald, L., *Australia* ... 92 D4
McDonald Is., *Ind. Oc.* 3 G13
MacDonnell Ranges, *Australia* . 92 D5
McDouall Ra., *Canada* 102 B1
Macduff, *U.K.* 14 D6
Maceda, *Spain* 34 C3
Macedonia, *U.S.A.* 110 E3
Macedonia ■, *Europe* 40 E5
Maceió, *Brazil* 125 E11
Maceira, *Portugal* 34 F2
Macenta, *Guinea* 82 D3
Macerata, *Italy* 29 E10
McFarland, *U.S.A.* 117 K7
McFarlane →, *Canada* 105 B7
Macfarlane, L., *Australia* ... 95 E2
McGehee, *U.S.A.* 113 J9
McGill, *U.S.A.* 114 G6
Macgillycuddy's Reeks, *Ireland* 15 E2
McGraw, *U.S.A.* 111 D8
McGregor, *U.S.A.* 112 D9
McGregor Ra., *Australia* 95 D3
Mach, *Pakistan* 66 E5
Māch Kowr, *Iran* 71 E9
Machado = Jiparaná →, *Brazil* 124 E6
Machagai, *Argentina* 126 B3
Machakos, *Kenya* 86 C4
Machala, *Ecuador* 124 D3
Machanga, *Mozam.* 89 C6
Machattie, L., *Australia* 94 C2
Machault, *France* 19 C11
Machava, *Mozam.* 89 D5
Machece, *Mozam.* 87 F4
Machecoul, *France* 18 F5
Macheke, *Zimbabwe* 89 B5
Macheng, *China* 59 B10
Machero, *Spain* 35 F6
Machhu →, *India* 68 H4
Machias, *Maine, U.S.A.* 109 C12
Machias, *N.Y., U.S.A.* 110 D6
Machichi →, *Canada* 105 B10
Machico, *Madeira* 37 D3
Machilipatnam, *India* 67 L12
Machiques, *Venezuela* 124 A4
Machupicchu, *Peru* 124 F4
Machynlleth, *U.K.* 13 E4
Macia, *Mozam.* 89 D5
Maciejowice, *Poland* 45 G8
McIlwraith Ra., *Australia* ... 94 A3
Măcin, *Romania* 43 E13
Macina, *Mali* 82 C4
McInnes L., *Canada* 105 C10
McIntosh, *U.S.A.* 112 C4
McIntosh L., *Canada* 105 B8
Macintosh Ra., *Australia* ... 93 E4
Macintyre →, *Australia* 95 D5
Macizo Galaico, *Spain* 34 C3
Mackay, *Australia* 94 C4
Mackay, *U.S.A.* 114 E7
MacKay →, *Canada* 104 B6
Mackay, L., *Australia* 92 D4
McKay Ra., *Australia* 92 D3
McKeesport, *U.S.A.* 110 F5
McKellar, *Canada* 110 A5
McKenna, *U.S.A.* 116 D4
Mackenzie, *Canada* 104 B4
McKenzie, *U.S.A.* 109 G1
Mackenzie →, *Australia* 94 C4
Mackenzie →, *Canada* 100 B6
McKenzie →, *U.S.A.* 114 D2
Mackenzie Bay, *Canada* 4 B1
Mackenzie City = Linden, *Guyana* 124 B7
Mackenzie Mts., *Canada* ... 100 B6
Mackinaw City, *U.S.A.* 108 C3
McKinlay, *Australia* 94 C3
McKinlay →, *Australia* 94 C3
McKinley, Mt., *U.S.A.* 100 B4
McKinley Sea, *Arctic* 4 A7
McKinney, *U.S.A.* 113 J6
Mackinnon Road, *Kenya* ... 86 C4
McKittrick, *U.S.A.* 117 K7
Macklin, *Canada* 105 C7
Macksville, *Australia* 95 E5
Maclean, *Australia* 95 D5
McLean, *U.S.A.* 113 H4

McLeansboro, *U.S.A.* 112 F10
Maclear, *S. Africa* 89 E4
Macleay →, *Australia* 95 E5
McLennan, *Canada* 104 B5
McLeod →, *Canada* 104 C5
MacLeod, B., *Canada* 105 A7
McLeod, L., *Australia* 93 D1
MacLeod Lake, *Canada* 104 C4
McLoughlin, Mt., *U.S.A.* ... 114 E2
McMechen, *U.S.A.* 110 G4
McMinnville, *Oreg., U.S.A.* . 114 D2
McMinnville, *Tenn., U.S.A.* . 109 H3
McMurdo Sd., *Antarctica* ... 5 D11
McMurray = Fort McMurray, *Canada* 104 B6
McMurray, *U.S.A.* 116 B4
Macodoene, *Mozam.* 89 C6
Macomb, *U.S.A.* 112 E9
Macomer, *Italy* 30 B1
Mâcon, *France* 19 F11
Macon, *Ga., U.S.A.* 109 J4
Macon, *Miss., U.S.A.* 109 J1
Macon, *Mo., U.S.A.* 112 F8
Macossa, *Mozam.* 87 F3
Macoun L., *Canada* 105 B8
Macovane, *Mozam.* 89 C6
McPherson, *U.S.A.* 112 F6
McPherson Pk., *U.S.A.* 117 L7
McPherson Ra., *Australia* ... 95 D5
Macquarie →, *Australia* 95 E4
Macquarie Harbour, *Australia* . 94 G4
Macquarie Is., *Pac. Oc.* 96 N7
MacRobertson Land, *Antarctica* 5 D6
Macroom, *Ireland* 15 E3
MacTier, *Canada* 110 A5
Macubela, *Mozam.* 87 F4
Macugnaga, *Italy* 28 C4
Macuiza, *Mozam.* 87 F3
Macusani, *Peru* 124 F4
Macuse, *Mozam.* 87 F4
Macuspana, *Mexico* 119 D6
Macusse, *Angola* 88 B3
Mada →, *Nigeria* 83 D6
Madadeni, *S. Africa* 89 D5
Madagali, *Nigeria* 83 C7
Madagascar ■, *Africa* 89 C8
Madā'in Sālih, *Si. Arabia* ... 70 E3
Madama, *Niger* 79 D8
Madame I., *Canada* 103 C7
Madan, *Bulgaria* 41 E8
Madaoua, *Niger* 83 C6
Madara, *Nigeria* 83 C7
Madaripur, *Bangla.* 67 H17
Madauk, *Burma* 67 L20
Madawaska, *Canada* 110 A7
Madawaska →, *Canada* 102 C4
Madaya, *Burma* 67 H20
Madbar, *Sudan* 81 F3
Maddalena, *Italy* 30 A2
Maddaloni, *Italy* 31 A7
Madeira, *Atl. Oc.* 37 D3
Madeira →, *Brazil* 122 D5
Madeleine, Îs. de la, *Canada* . 103 C7
Maden, *Turkey* 73 C8
Madera, *Mexico* 118 B3
Madera, *Calif., U.S.A.* 116 J6
Madera, *Pa., U.S.A.* 110 F6
Madha, *India* 66 L9
Madhavpur, *India* 68 J3
Madhepura, *India* 69 F12
Madhubani, *India* 69 F12
Madhupur, *India* 69 G12
Madhya Pradesh □, *India* ... 68 J8
Madidi →, *Bolivia* 124 F5
Madikeri, *India* 66 N9
Madill, *U.S.A.* 113 H6
Madimba, *Dem. Rep. of the Congo* 84 E3
Ma'din, *Syria* 70 C3
Madina, *Mali* 82 C3
Madinani, *Ivory C.* 82 D3
Madingou, *Congo* 84 E2
Madirovalo, *Madag.* 89 B8
Madison, *Calif., U.S.A.* 116 G5
Madison, *Fla., U.S.A.* 109 K4
Madison, *Ind., U.S.A.* 108 F3
Madison, *Nebr., U.S.A.* 112 E6
Madison, *Ohio, U.S.A.* 110 E3
Madison, *S. Dak., U.S.A.* ... 112 D6
Madison, *Wis., U.S.A.* 112 D10
Madison →, *U.S.A.* 114 D8
Madison Heights, *U.S.A.* ... 108 G6
Madisonville, *Ky., U.S.A.* .. 108 G2
Madisonville, *Tex., U.S.A.* .. 113 K7
Madista, *Botswana* 88 C4
Madiun, *Indonesia* 62 F4
Madoc, *Canada* 110 B7
Madol, *Sudan* 81 F2
Madon →, *France* 19 D13
Madona, *Latvia* 9 H22
Madonie, *Italy* 30 E6
Madonna di Campíglio, *Italy* . 28 B7
Madra Dağı, *Turkey* 39 B9
Madrakah, Ra's al, *Oman* ... 74 D6
Madras = Chennai, *India* ... 66 N12
Madras = Tamil Nadu □, *India* 66 P10
Madras, *U.S.A.* 114 D3
Madre, Laguna, *U.S.A.* 113 M6
Madre, Sierra, *Phil.* 61 C4
Madre de Dios →, *Bolivia* .. 122 E4
Madre de Dios, I., *Chile* 122 H1
Madre del Sur, Sierra, *Mexico* 119 D5
Madre Occidental, Sierra, *Mexico* 118 B3
Madre Oriental, Sierra, *Mexico* 118 C5
Madri, *India* 68 G5
Madrid, *Spain* 34 E7

Madrid, U.S.A. 111 B9
Madrid □, Spain 34 E7
Madridejos, Spain 35 F7
Madrigal de las Altas Torres, Spain 34 D6
Madrona, Sierra, Spain 35 G6
Madroñera, Spain 35 F5
Madu, Sudan 81 E2
Madura, Australia 93 F4
Madura, Indonesia 63 G15
Madura, Selat, Indonesia ... 63 G15
Madurai, India 66 Q11
Madurantakam, India 66 N11
Madzhalis, Russia 49 J8
Mae Chan, Thailand 64 B2
Mae Hong Son, Thailand .. 64 C2
Mae Khlong →, Thailand .. 64 F3
Mae Phrik, Thailand 64 D2
Mae Ramat, Thailand 64 D2
Mae Rim, Thailand 64 C2
Mae Sot, Thailand 64 D2
Mae Suai, Thailand 58 H2
Mae Tha, Thailand 64 C2
Maebashi, Japan 55 F9
Maella, Spain 32 D5
Maestra, Sierra, Cuba 120 B4
Maevatanana, Madag. 89 B8
Mafeking = Mafikeng, S. Africa 88 D4
Mafeking, Canada 105 C8
Maféré, Ivory C. 82 D4
Mafeteng, Lesotho 88 D4
Maffra, Australia 95 F4
Mafia I., Tanzania 86 D4
Mafikeng, S. Africa 88 D4
Mafra, Brazil 127 B6
Mafra, Portugal 35 G1
Mafungabusi Plateau, Zimbabwe 87 F2
Magadan, Russia 51 D16
Magadi, Kenya 86 C4
Magadi, L., Kenya 86 C4
Magaliesburg, S. Africa ... 89 D4
Magallanes, Estrecho de, Chile 122 J3
Magaluf, Spain 33 F7
Magangué, Colombia 124 B4
Magaria, Niger 83 C6
Magburaka, S. Leone 82 D2
Magdalen Is. = Madeleine, Îs. de la, Canada 103 C7
Magdalena, Argentina 126 D4
Magdalena, Bolivia 124 F6
Magdalena, Mexico 118 A2
Magdalena, U.S.A. 115 J10
Magdalena →, Colombia .. 122 B3
Magdalena →, Mexico 118 A2
Magdalena, B., Mexico ... 118 C2
Magdalena, Llano de la, Mexico 118 C2
Magdeburg, Germany 24 C7
Magdelaine Cays, Australia . 94 B5
Magdub, Sudan 81 E2
Magee, U.S.A. 113 K10
Magelang, Indonesia 62 F4
Magellan's Str. = Magallanes, Estrecho de, Chile 122 J3
Magenta, Italy 28 C5
Magenta, L., Australia 93 F2
Magerøya, Norway 8 A21
Maggia →, Switz. 25 J4
Maggiorasca, Mte., Italy ... 28 D6
Maggiore, Lago, Italy 28 C5
Maghâgha, Egypt 80 B3
Maghama, Mauritania 82 B2
Magherafelt, U.K. 15 B5
Maghreb, N. Afr. 78 B5
Magione, Italy 29 E9
Magistralnyy, Russia 51 D11
Maglaj, Bos.-H. 42 F3
Magliano in Toscana, Italy . 29 F8
Máglie, Italy 31 B11
Magnac-Laval, France 20 B5
Magnetic Pole (North) = North Magnetic Pole, Canada 4 B2
Magnetic Pole (South) = South Magnetic Pole, Antarctica 5 C9
Magnísía □, Greece 38 B5
Magnitogorsk, Russia 50 D6
Magnolia, Ark., U.S.A. 113 J8
Magnolia, Miss., U.S.A. ... 113 K9
Magny-en-Vexin, France .. 19 C8
Magog, Canada 103 C5
Magoro, Uganda 86 B3
Magosa = Famagusta, Cyprus 36 D12
Magouládhes, Greece 36 A3
Magoye, Zambia 87 F2
Magozal, Mexico 119 C5
Magpie, L., Canada 103 B7
Magrath, Canada 104 D6
Magre →, Spain 33 F4
Magrur, Sudan 81 E3
Magrur, Wadi →, Sudan ... 81 D2
Magta Lahjar, Mauritania .. 82 B2
Maguan, China 58 F5
Maguarinho, C., Brazil 125 D9
Magude, Mozam. 89 D5
Magude = Famagusta, Cyprus 36 D12
Maguse L., Canada 105 A9
Maguse Pt., Canada 105 A10
Magvana, India 68 H3
Magwe, Burma 67 J19
Magwe, Sudan 81 G3
Maha Sarakham, Thailand .. 64 D4
Mahābād, Iran 70 B5
Mahabharat Lekh, Nepal .. 69 E10
Mahabo, Madag. 89 C7
Mahadeo Hills, India 69 H8
Mahaffey, U.S.A. 110 F6
Mahagi, Dem. Rep. of the Congo 86 B3

Mahajamba →, Madag. 89 B8
Mahajamba, Helodranon' i, Madag. 89 B8
Mahajan, India 68 E5
Mahajanga, Madag. 89 B8
Mahajanga □, Madag. 89 B8
Mahajilo →, Madag. 89 B8
Mahakam →, Indonesia ... 62 E5
Mahalapye, Botswana 88 C4
Mahallāt, Iran 71 C6
Māhān, Iran 71 D8
Mahan →, India 69 H10
Mahanadi →, India 67 J15
Mahananda →, India 69 G12
Mahanoro, Madag. 89 B8
Mahanoy City, U.S.A. 111 F8
Maharashtra □, India 66 J9
Mahari Mts., Tanzania 86 D3
Mahasham, W. →, Egypt .. 75 E3
Mahasoa, Madag. 89 C8
Mahasolo, Madag. 89 B8
Mahattat ash Shīdīyah, Jordan . 75 F4
Mahattat 'Unayzah, Jordan . 75 E4
Mahavavy →, Madag. 89 B8
Mahaxay, Laos 64 D5
Mahbubnagar, India 66 L10
Mahdah, Oman 71 E7
Mahdia, Tunisia 79 A8
Mahdia, Sudan 81 D3
Mahe, India 69 C8
Mahendragarh, India 68 E7
Mahenge, Tanzania 87 D4
Maheno, N.Z. 91 L3
Mahesana, India 68 H5
Maheshwar, India 68 H6
Mahgawan, India 69 F8
Mahi →, India 68 H5
Mahia Pen., N.Z. 91 H6
Mahilyow, Belarus 46 F6
Mahmiya, Sudan 81 D3
Mahmud Kot, Pakistan ... 68 D4
Mahmudia, Romania 43 E14
Mahmudiye, Turkey 39 B12
Mahmutbey, Turkey 41 E12
Mahnomen, U.S.A. 112 B7
Mahoba, India 69 G8
Mahón = Maó, Spain 37 B11
Mahone Bay, Canada 103 D7
Mahopac, U.S.A. 111 E11
Mahuta, Nigeria 83 C5
Mahuva, India 68 J4
Mahya Dağı, Turkey 41 E11
Mai-Ndombe, L., Dem. Rep. of the Congo 84 E3
Mai-Sai, Thailand 58 G2
Maia, Portugal 34 D2
Maia, Spain 32 B3
Maials, Spain 32 D5
Maîche, France 19 E13
Maicurú →, Brazil 125 D8
Máida, Italy 31 D9
Maidan Khula, Afghan. ... 68 C3
Maidenhead, U.K. 13 F7
Maidstone, Canada 105 C7
Maidstone, U.K. 13 F8
Maiduguri, Nigeria 83 C7
Măieruş, Romania 43 E10
Maigatari, Nigeria 83 C6
Maignelay Montigny, France 19 C9
Maigo, Phil. 61 G5
Maigudo, Ethiopia 81 F4
Maihar, India 69 G9
Maijdi, Bangla. 67 H17
Maikala Ra., India 67 J12
Mailani, India 69 E9
Maillezais, France 20 B3
Mailsi, Pakistan 68 E5
Main →, Germany 25 F4
Main →, U.K. 15 B5
Mainburg, Germany 25 G7
Maine, France 18 D6
Maine □, U.S.A. 109 C11
Maine →, Ireland 15 D2
Maine-et-Loire □, France . 18 E6
Maïne-Soroa, Niger 83 C7
Maingkwan, Burma 67 F20
Mainit, L., Phil. 61 G6
Mainland, Orkney, U.K. ... 14 C5
Mainland, Shet., U.K. 14 A7
Mainoru, Australia 94 A1
Mainpuri, India 69 F8
Maintal, Germany 25 E4
Maintenon, France 19 D8
Maintirano, Madag. 89 B7
Mainz, Germany 25 E4
Maipú, Argentina 126 D4
Maiquetía, Venezuela 124 A5
Máira →, Italy 28 D4
Mairabari, India 67 F18
Maisí, Cuba 121 B5
Maisí, Pta. de, Cuba 121 B5
Maitland, N.S.W., Australia . 95 E5
Maitland, S. Austral., Australia . 95 E2
Maitland →, Canada 110 C3
Maiyema, Nigeria 83 C5
Maiyuan, China 59 E11
Maiz, Is. del, Nic. 120 D3
Maizuru, Japan 55 G7
Majalengka, Indonesia ... 63 G13
Majene, Indonesia 63 E5
Majevica, Bos.-H. 42 F3
Maji, Ethiopia 81 F4
Majorca = Mallorca, Spain . 37 B10
Maka, Senegal 82 C2
Makaha, Zimbabwe 89 B5
Makak, Cameroon 83 E7
Makalamabedi, Botswana . 88 C3

Makale, Indonesia 63 E5
Makamba, Burundi 86 C2
Makari, Cameroon 83 C7
Makarikari = Makgadikgadi Salt Pans, Botswana 88 C4
Makarovo, Russia 51 D11
Makarska, Croatia 29 E14
Makaryev, Russia 48 B6
Makasar = Ujung Pandang, Indonesia 63 F5
Makasar, Selat, Indonesia . 63 E5
Makasar, Str. of = Makasar, Selat, Indonesia 63 E5
Makat, Kazakstan 50 E6
Makedonija = Macedonia ■, Europe 40 E5
Makeni, S. Leone 82 D2
Makeyevka = Makiyivka, Ukraine 47 H9
Makgadikgadi Salt Pans, Botswana 88 C4
Makhachkala, Russia 49 J8
Makharadze = Ozurgeti, Georgia 49 K5
Makhmūr, Iraq 70 C4
Makian, Indonesia 63 D7
Makindu, Kenya 86 C4
Makinsk, Kazakstan 50 D8
Makiyivka, Ukraine 47 H9
Makkah, Si. Arabia 74 C2
Makkovik, Canada 103 A8
Makó, Hungary 42 D5
Mako, Senegal 82 C2
Makokou, Gabon 84 D2
Makongo, Dem. Rep. of the Congo 86 B2
Makoro, Dem. Rep. of the Congo 86 B2
Maków Mazowiecki, Poland . 45 F8
Maków Podhalański, Poland . 45 J6
Makrá, Greece 39 E7
Makran Coast Range, Pakistan 66 G4
Makrana, India 68 F6
Mákri, Greece 41 F9
Makriyialos, Greece 36 D7
Mākū, Iran 70 B5
Makunda, Botswana 88 C3
Makung, Taiwan 59 F12
Makurazaki, Japan 55 J5
Makurdi, Nigeria 83 D6
Makūyeh, Iran 71 D7
Makwassie, S. Africa 88 D4
Makwiro, Zimbabwe 89 B5
Mâl, Mauritania 82 B2
Mal B., Ireland 15 D2
Mala, Pta., Panama 120 E3
Mala Belozërka, Ukraine .. 47 J8
Mala Kapela, Croatia 29 D12
Mała Panew →, Poland ... 45 H4
Mala Vyska, Ukraine 47 H6
Malabang, Phil. 61 H6
Malabar Coast, India 66 P9
Malabo = Rey Malabo, Eq. Guin. 83 E6
Malabon, Phil. 61 D4
Malabu, Nigeria 83 D7
Malacca, Str. of, Indonesia . 65 L3
Malacky, Slovak Rep. 27 C10
Malad City, U.S.A. 114 E7
Maladzyechna, Belarus ... 46 E4
Málaga, Spain 35 J6
Málaga □, Spain 35 J6
Malagarasi, Tanzania 86 D3
Malagarasi →, Tanzania .. 86 D2
Malagasy Rep. = Madagascar ■, Africa 89 C8
Malagón, Spain 35 F7
Malagón →, Spain 35 H3
Malahide, Ireland 15 C5
Malaimbandy, Madag. ... 89 C8
Malakâl, Sudan 81 F3
Malakand, Pakistan 68 B4
Malakwal, Pakistan 68 C5
Malamala, Indonesia 63 E6
Malanda, Australia 94 B4
Malang, Indonesia 62 F4
Malangen, Norway 8 B18
Malanje, Angola 84 F3
Mälaren, Sweden 10 E11
Malargüe, Argentina 126 D2
Malartic, Canada 102 C4
Malaryta, Belarus 47 G3
Malatya, Turkey 70 B3
Malawi ■, Africa 87 E3
Malawi, L. = Nyasa, L., Africa 87 E3
Malay Pen., Asia 65 J3
Malaya Belozërka = Mala Belozërka, Ukraine 47 J8
Malaya Vishera, Russia ... 46 C7
Malaya Viska = Mala Vyska, Ukraine 47 H6
Malaybalay, Phil. 61 G6
Malāyer, Iran 71 C6
Malaysia ■, Asia 65 K4
Malazgirt, Turkey 70 B4
Malbaza, Niger 83 C6
Malbon, Australia 94 C3
Malbooma, Australia 95 E1
Malbork, Poland 44 D6
Malcésine, Italy 28 C7
Malchin, Germany 24 B8
Malchow, Germany 24 B8
Malcolm, Australia 93 E3
Malcolm, Pt., Australia ... 93 F3
Malczyce, Poland 45 G3
Maldah, India 69 G13
Maldegem, Belgium 17 C3

Malden, Mass., U.S.A. ... 111 D13
Malden, Mo., U.S.A. 113 G10
Malden I., Kiribati 97 H12
Maldives ■, Ind. Oc. 52 J11
Maldonado, Uruguay 127 C5
Maldonado, Punta, Mexico . 119 D5
Malè, Italy 28 B7
Malé, Maldives 53 J11
Malé Karpaty, Slovak Rep. . 27 C10
Maléa, Ákra, Greece 38 E5
Malegaon, India 66 J9
Malei, Mozam. 87 F4
Malek, Sudan 81 F3
Malek Kandī, Iran 70 B5
Malela, Dem. Rep. of the Congo 86 C2
Máleme, Greece 36 D5
Malema, Mozam. 87 E4
Máleras, Sweden 11 H9
Malerkotla, India 68 D6
Máles, Greece 36 D7
Malesherbes, France 19 D9
Maleshevska Planina, Europe . 40 E7
Malesína, Greece 38 C5
Malestroit, France 18 E4
Malfa, Italy 31 D7
Malgobek, Russia 49 J7
Malgomaj, Sweden 8 D17
Malgrat = Malgrat de Mar, Spain 32 D7
Malgrat de Mar, Spain ... 32 D7
Malha, Sudan 81 D2
Malhargarh, India 68 G6
Malheur →, U.S.A. 114 D5
Malheur L., U.S.A. 114 E4
Mali ■, Guinea 82 C2
Mali →, Africa 82 B4
Mali →, Burma 67 G20
Mali Kanal, Serbia, Yug. .. 42 E4
Mali Kyun, Burma 64 F2
Malibu, U.S.A. 117 L8
Maliku, Indonesia 63 E6
Malili, Indonesia 63 E6
Mälilla, Sweden 11 G9
Malimba, Mts., Dem. Rep. of the Congo 86 D2
Malin Hd., Ireland 15 A4
Malin Pen., Ireland 15 A4
Malindi, Kenya 86 C5
Malines = Mechelen, Belgium . 17 C4
Malino, Indonesia 63 D6
Malinyi, Tanzania 87 D4
Malipo, China 58 F5
Maliq, Albania 40 F4
Maliwun, Burma 62 B1
Maliya, India 68 H4
Maljenik, Serbia, Yug. ... 40 C5
Malkara, Turkey 41 F10
Małkinia Górna, Poland .. 45 F9
Malko Tŭrnovo, Bulgaria . 41 E11
Mallacoota Inlet, Australia . 95 F4
Mallaig, U.K. 14 D3
Mallaoua, Niger 83 C6
Mallawan, India 69 F9
Mallawi, Egypt 80 B3
Mallemort, France 21 E9
Málles Venosta, Italy 28 B7
Mállia, Greece 36 D7
Mallión, Kólpos, Greece .. 36 D7
Mallorca, Spain 37 B10
Mallorytown, Canada ... 111 B9
Mallow, Ireland 15 D3
Malmbäck, Sweden 11 G8
Malmberget, Sweden ... 8 C19
Malmédy, Belgium 17 D6
Malmesbury, S. Africa ... 88 E2
Malmköping, Sweden ... 10 E10
Malmö, Sweden 11 J6
Malmslätt, Sweden 11 F9
Malmyzh, Russia 48 B10
Malnaş, Romania 43 D10
Malo Konare, Bulgaria ... 41 D8
Maloarkhangelsk, Russia . 47 F9
Malolos, Phil. 61 D4
Malombe L., Malawi 87 E4
Małomice, Poland 45 G2
Malomir, Bulgaria 41 D10
Malone, U.S.A. 111 B10
Malong, China 58 E4
Małopolskie □, Poland .. 45 J7
Malorad, Bulgaria 40 C7
Måløy, Norway 9 F11
Maloyaroslovets, Russia . 46 E9
Malpartida, Spain 35 F4
Malpaso, Canary Is. 37 G1
Malpelo, I. de, Colombia . 124 C2
Malpica de Bergantiños, Spain 34 B2
Malpur, India 68 H5
Malpura, India 68 F6
Mals = Málles Venosta, Italy . 28 B7
Malta, Idaho, U.S.A. 114 E7
Malta, Mont., U.S.A. 114 B10
Malta ■, Europe 36 D2
Maltahöhe, Namibia 88 C2
Maltepe, Turkey 41 F13
Malton, Canada 110 C5
Malton, U.K. 12 C7
Maluku, Indonesia 63 E7
Maluku □, Indonesia ... 63 E7
Maluku Sea = Molucca Sea, Indonesia 63 E6
Malumfashi, Nigeria 83 C6
Malung, Sweden 10 D7
Malungsfors, Sweden ... 10 D7
Maluwe, Ghana 82 D4
Malvan, India 66 L8
Malvern, U.S.A. 113 H8

Malvern Hills, U.K. 13 E5
Malvinas, Is. = Falkland Is. □, Atl. Oc. 128 G5
Malý Dunaj →, Slovak Rep. . 27 D11
Malya, Tanzania 86 C3
Malyn, Ukraine 47 G5
Malyy Lyakhovskiy, Ostrov, Russia 51 B15
Mama, Russia 51 D12
Mamadysh, Russia 48 C10
Mamanguape, Brazil ... 125 E11
Mamarr Mitlâ, Egypt ... 75 E1
Mamasa, Indonesia 63 E5
Mambasa, Dem. Rep. of the Congo 86 B2
Mamberamo →, Indonesia . 63 E9
Mambilima Falls, Zambia . 87 E2
Mambirima, Dem. Rep. of the Congo 87 E2
Mambo, Tanzania 86 C4
Mambrui, Kenya 86 C5
Mamburao, Phil. 61 E4
Mameigwess L., Canada . 102 B2
Mamers, France 18 D7
Mamfé, Cameroon 83 D6
Mammoth, U.S.A. 115 K8
Mammoth Cave National Park, U.S.A. 108 G3
Mamoré →, Bolivia 122 E4
Mamou, Guinea 82 C2
Mampatá, Guinea-Biss. . 82 C2
Mampikony, Madag. ... 89 B8
Mampong, Ghana 83 D4
Mamry, Jezioro, Poland . 44 D8
Mamuju, Indonesia 63 E5
Mamuno, Botswana ... 88 C3
Mamuras, Albania 40 E3
Man, Ivory C. 82 D3
Man, I. of, U.K. 12 C3
Man-Bazar, India 69 H12
Man Na, Burma 67 H20
Mana →, Fr. Guiana ... 125 B8
Manaar, G. of = Mannar, G. of, Asia 66 Q11
Manacapuru, Brazil 124 D6
Manacor, Spain 37 B10
Manado, Indonesia 63 D6
Managua, Nic. 120 D2
Managua, L. de, Nic. ... 120 D2
Manakara, Madag. 89 C8
Manali, India 68 C7
Manama = Al Manāmah, Bahrain 71 E6
Manambao →, Madag. .. 89 B7
Manambato, Madag. ... 89 A8
Manambolo →, Madag. .. 89 B7
Manambolosy, Madag. . 89 B8
Mananara, Madag. 89 B8
Manánara →, Madag. ... 89 C8
Mananjary, Madag. 89 C8
Manankoro, Mali 82 C3
Manantenina, Madag. .. 89 C8
Manaos = Manaus, Brazil . 124 D7
Manapire →, Venezuela . 124 B5
Manapouri, N.Z. 91 L1
Manapouri, L., N.Z. ... 91 L1
Manaqil, Sudan 81 E3
Manār, Jabal, Yemen .. 74 E3
Manaravolo, Madag. .. 89 C8
Manas, China 60 B3
Manas →, India 67 F17
Manaslu, Nepal 69 E11
Manasquan, U.S.A. ... 111 F10
Manassa, U.S.A. 115 H11
Manaung, Burma 67 K18
Manaus, Brazil 124 D7
Manavgat, Turkey 72 D4
Manawan L., Canada .. 105 B8
Manay, Phil. 61 H7
Manbij, Syria 70 B3
Mancha Real, Spain ... 35 H7
Manche □, France 18 C5
Manchegorsk, Russia .. 27 C10
Manchester, U.K. 12 D5
Manchester, Calif., U.S.A. . 116 G3
Manchester, Conn., U.S.A. . 111 E12
Manchester, Ga., U.S.A. .. 109 J3
Manchester, Iowa, U.S.A. . 112 D9
Manchester, Ky., U.S.A. .. 108 G4
Manchester, N.H., U.S.A. . 111 D13
Manchester, N.Y., U.S.A. . 110 D7
Manchester, Pa., U.S.A. .. 111 F8
Manchester, Tenn., U.S.A. . 109 H2
Manchester, Vt., U.S.A. .. 111 C11
Manchester L., Canada .. 105 A7
Manchhar L., Pakistan ... 68 F2
Manchuria = Dongbei, China . 57 D13
Manchurian Plain, China . 52 E16
Manciano, Italy 29 F8
Mancifa, Ethiopia 81 F5
Mand →, India 69 J10
Mand →, Iran 71 D7
Manda, Ludewe, Tanzania . 87 E3
Manda, Mbeya, Tanzania . 87 D3
Manda, Mbeya, Tanzania . 87 D3
Mandabé, Madag. 89 C7
Mandaguari, Brazil 127 A5
Mandah = Töhöm, Mongolia . 56 B5
Mandal, Norway 9 G12
Mandala, Puncak, Indonesia . 63 E10
Mandalay, Burma 67 J20
Mandale = Mandalay, Burma . 67 J20
Mandalgarh, India 68 G6
Mandalgovi, Mongolia . 56 B4
Mandalī, Iraq 70 C5
Mandan, U.S.A. 112 B4
Mandaon, Phil. 61 E5

Mandar, Teluk, *Indonesia* 63 E5
Mándas, *Italy* 30 C2
Mandaue, *Phil.* 61 F5
Mandelieu-la-Napoule, *France* . 21 E10
Mandera, *Kenya* 86 B5
Mandi, *India* 68 D7
Mandi Dabwali, *India* 68 E6
Mandiana, *Guinea* 82 C3
Mandimba, *Mozam.* 87 E4
Mandioli, *Indonesia* 63 E7
Mandla, *India* 69 H9
Mandø, *Denmark* 11 J2
Mandorah, *Australia* 92 B5
Mandoto, *Madag.* 89 B8
Mandoúdhion, *Greece* 38 C5
Mándra, *Greece* 38 C5
Mandra, *Pakistan* 68 C5
Mandrákhi, *Greece* 39 E9
Mandrare →, *Madag.* 89 D8
Mandritsara, *Madag.* 89 B8
Mandronarivo, *Madag.* 89 C8
Mandsaur, *India* 68 G6
Mandurah, *Australia* 93 F2
Mandúria, *Italy* 31 B10
Mandvi, *India* 68 H3
Mandya, *India* 66 N10
Mandzai, *Pakistan* 68 D2
Mané, *Burkina Faso* 83 C4
Maneh, *Iran* 71 B8
Manengouba, Mts., *Cameroon* . 83 E6
Manera, *Madag.* 89 C7
Manérbio, *Italy* 28 C7
Maneroo Cr. →, *Australia* ... 94 C3
Manfalût, *Egypt* 80 B3
Manfredónia, *Italy* 29 G12
Manfredónia, G. di, *Italy* ... 29 G13
Manga, *Burkina Faso* 83 C4
Manga, *Niger* 83 C7
Mangabeiras, Chapada das,
  Brazil 125 F9
Mangalia, *Romania* 43 G13
Mangalore, *India* 66 N9
Mangan, *India* 69 F13
Mangaung, *S. Africa* 85 K5
Mangawan, *India* 69 G9
Mangaweka, *N.Z.* 91 H5
Manggar, *Indonesia* 62 E4
Manggawitu, *Indonesia* 63 E8
Mangindrano, *Madag.* 89 A8
Mangkalihat, Tanjung, *Indonesia* 63 D5
Mangla, *Pakistan* 68 C5
Mangla Dam, *Pakistan* 69 C5
Manglaur, *India* 68 E7
Mangnai, *China* 60 C4
Mango, *Togo* 83 C5
Mangoche, *Malawi* 87 E4
Mangoky →, *Madag.* 89 C7
Mangole, *Indonesia* 63 E6
Mangombe, *Dem. Rep. of
  the Congo* 86 C2
Mangonui, *N.Z.* 91 F4
Mangoro →, *Madag.* 89 B8
Mangrol, *Mad. P., India* 68 J4
Mangrol, *Raj., India* 68 G6
Mangualde, *Portugal* 34 E3
Mangueira, L. da, *Brazil* ... 127 C5
Mangum, *U.S.A.* 113 H5
Mangyshlak Poluostrov,
  Kazakstan 50 E6
Manhattan, *U.S.A.* 112 F6
Manhiça, *Mozam.* 89 D5
Mania →, *Madag.* 89 B8
Maniago, *Italy* 29 B9
Manica, *Mozam.* 89 B5
Manica □, *Mozam.* 89 B5
Manicaland □, *Zimbabwe* 87 F3
Manicoré, *Brazil* 124 E6
Manicouagan →, *Canada* 103 C6
Manicouagan, Rés., *Canada* . 103 B6
Maniema □, *Dem. Rep. of
  the Congo* 86 C2
Manifah, *Si. Arabia* 71 E6
Manifold, C., *Australia* 94 C5
Maniganggo, *China* 58 B2
Manigotagan, *Canada* 105 C9
Manigotagan →, *Canada* 105 C9
Manihari, *India* 69 G12
Manihiki, *Cook Is.* 97 J11
Manika, Plateau de la,
  Dem. Rep. of the Congo 87 E2
Manikpur, *India* 69 G9
Manila, *Phil.* 61 D4
Manila, *U.S.A.* 114 F9
Manila B., *Phil.* 61 D4
Manilla, *Australia* 95 E5
Manimpé, *Mali* 82 C3
Maningrida, *Australia* 94 A1
Maninian, *Ivory C.* 82 C3
Manipur □, *India* 67 G19
Manipur →, *Burma* 67 H19
Manisa, *Turkey* 39 C9
Manisa □, *Turkey* 39 C9
Manistee, *U.S.A.* 108 C2
Manistee →, *U.S.A.* 108 C2
Manistique, *U.S.A.* 108 C2
Manito L., *Canada* 105 C7
Manitoba □, *Canada* 105 B9
Manitoba, L., *Canada* 105 C9
Manitou, *Canada* 105 D9
Manitou, L., *Canada* 103 B6
Manitou Is., *U.S.A.* 108 C3
Manitou Springs, *U.S.A.* 112 F2
Manitoulin I., *Canada* 102 C3
Manitouwadge, *Canada* 102 C2
Manitowoc, *U.S.A.* 108 C2
Manizales, *Colombia* 124 B3
Manja, *Madag.* 89 C7

Manjacaze, *Mozam.* 89 C5
Manjakandriana, *Madag.* 89 B8
Manjhand, *Pakistan* 68 G3
Manjil, *Iran* 71 B6
Manjimup, *Australia* 93 F2
Manjra →, *India* 66 K10
Mankato, *Kans., U.S.A.* 112 F5
Mankato, *Minn., U.S.A.* 112 C8
Mankayane, *Swaziland* 89 D5
Mankera, *Pakistan* 68 D4
Mankim, *Cameroon* 83 D7
Mankono, *Ivory C.* 82 D3
Mankota, *Canada* 105 D7
Manlay = Üydzin, *Mongolia* .. 56 B4
Manlleu, *Spain* 32 C7
Manmad, *India* 66 J9
Mann Ranges, *Australia* 93 E5
Manna, *Indonesia* 62 E2
Mannahill, *Australia* 95 E3
Mannar, *Sri Lanka* 66 Q11
Mannar, G. of, *Asia* 66 Q11
Mannar I., *Sri Lanka* 66 Q11
Mannheim, *Germany* 25 F4
Manning, *Canada* 104 B5
Manning, *Oreg., U.S.A.* 116 E3
Manning, *S.C., U.S.A.* 109 J5
Manning Prov. Park, *Canada* . 104 D4
Mannu →, *Italy* 30 C2
Mannu, C., *Italy* 30 B1
Mannum, *Australia* 95 E2
Mano, *S. Leone* 82 D2
Mano →, *Liberia* 82 D2
Mano River, *Liberia* 82 D2
Manoharpur, *India* 69 H11
Manokwari, *Indonesia* 63 E8
Manolás, *Greece* 38 C3
Manombo, *Madag.* 89 C7
Manono, *Dem. Rep. of
  the Congo* 86 D2
Manoppello, *Italy* 29 F11
Manosque, *France* 21 E9
Manotick, *Canada* 111 A9
Manouane →, *Canada* 103 C5
Manouane, L., *Canada* 103 B5
Manp'o, *N. Korea* 57 D14
Manpojin = Manp'o, *N. Korea* . 57 D14
Manpur, *Mad. P., India* 68 H6
Manpur, *Mad. P., India* 69 H10
Manresa, *Spain* 32 D6
Mansa, *Gujarat, India* 68 H5
Mansa, *Punjab, India* 68 E6
Mansa, *Zambia* 87 E2
Mânsåsen, *Sweden* 10 A8
Mansehra, *Pakistan* 68 B5
Mansel I., *Canada* 101 B11
Mansfield, *Australia* 95 F4
Mansfield, *U.K.* 12 D6
Mansfield, *La., U.S.A.* 113 J8
Mansfield, *Mass., U.S.A.* 111 D13
Mansfield, *Ohio, U.S.A.* 110 F2
Mansfield, *Pa., U.S.A.* 110 E7
Mansfield, *Mt., U.S.A.* 111 B12
Mansilla de las Mulas, *Spain* . 34 C5
Mansle, *France* 20 C4
Mansoa, *Guinea-Biss.* 82 C1
Manson Creek, *Canada* 104 B4
Manta, *Ecuador* 124 D2
Mantalingajan, Mt., *Phil.* 61 G2
Mantare, *Tanzania* 86 C3
Manteca, *U.S.A.* 116 H5
Manteo, *U.S.A.* 109 H8
Mantes-la-Jolie, *France* 19 D8
Manthani, *India* 66 K11
Manti, *U.S.A.* 114 G8
Mantiqueira, Serra da, *Brazil* . 127 A7
Manton, *U.S.A.* 108 C3
Mantorp, *Sweden* 11 F9
Mántova, *Italy* 28 C7
Mänttä, *Finland* 9 E21
Mantua = Mántova, *Italy* 28 C7
Manturovo, *Russia* 48 A7
Manu, *Peru* 124 F4
Manu →, *Peru* 124 F4
Manua Is., *Amer. Samoa* 91 B14
Manuel Alves →, *Brazil* 125 F9
Manui, *Indonesia* 63 E6
Manukau, *N.Z.* 91 G5
Manuripi →, *Bolivia* 124 F5
Many, *U.S.A.* 113 K8
Manyara, L., *Tanzania* 86 C4
Manyas, *Turkey* 41 F11
Manych →, *Russia* 49 G5
Manych-Gudilo, Ozero, *Russia* 49 G6
Manyonga →, *Tanzania* 86 C3
Manyoni, *Tanzania* 86 D3
Manzai, *Pakistan* 68 C4
Manzala, Bahra el, *Egypt* 80 H7
Manzanares, *Spain* 35 F7
Manzaneda, *Spain* 34 C3
Manzanillo, *Cuba* 120 B4
Manzanillo, *Mexico* 118 D4
Manzanillo, Pta., *Panama* ... 120 E4
Manzano Mts., *U.S.A.* 115 J10
Manzariyeh, *Iran* 71 C6
Manzhouli, *China* 60 B6
Manzini, *Swaziland* 89 D5
Mao, *Chad* 79 F9
Maó, *Spain* 37 B11
Maoke, Pegunungan, *Indonesia* 63 E9
Maolin, *China* 57 C12
Maoming, *China* 59 G8
Maopi T'ou, *China* 59 G13
Maouri, Dallol →, *Niger* 83 C5
Maoxian, *China* 58 B4
Maoxing, *China* 57 B13
Mapam Yumco, *China* 60 C3
Mapastepec, *Mexico* 119 D6

Mapia, Kepulauan, *Indonesia* .. 63 D8
Mapimí, *Mexico* 118 B4
Mapimí, Bolsón de, *Mexico* .. 118 B4
Maping, *China* 59 B9
Mapinga, *Tanzania* 86 D4
Mapinhane, *Mozam.* 89 C6
Maple Creek, *Canada* 105 D7
Maple Valley, *U.S.A.* 116 C4
Mapleton, *U.S.A.* 114 D2
Mapuera →, *Brazil* 124 D7
Mapulanguene, *Mozam.* 89 C5
Maputo, *Mozam.* 89 D5
Maputo □, *Mozam.* 89 D5
Maputo, B. de, *Mozam.* 89 D5
Maqiaohe, *China* 57 B16
Maqnā, *Si. Arabia* 70 D2
Maqueda, *Spain* 34 E6
Maquela do Zombo, *Angola* .. 84 F3
Maquinchao, *Argentina* 128 E3
Maquoketa, *U.S.A.* 112 D9
Mar, Serra do, *Brazil* 127 B6
Mar Chiquita, L., *Argentina* .. 126 C3
Mar del Plata, *Argentina* 126 D4
Mar Menor, *Spain* 33 H4
Mara, *Tanzania* 86 C3
Mara □, *Tanzania* 86 C3
Maraã, *Brazil* 124 D5
Marabá, *Brazil* 125 E9
Maracá, I. de, *Brazil* 125 C8
Maracaibo, *Venezuela* 124 A4
Maracaibo, L. de, *Venezuela* . 122 C3
Maracaju, *Brazil* 127 A4
Maracay, *Venezuela* 124 A5
Maracena, *Spain* 35 H7
Maradi, *Niger* 83 C6
Marägheh, *Iran* 70 B5
Marāh, *Si. Arabia* 70 E5
Marajó, I. de, *Brazil* 122 D6
Maralal, *Kenya* 86 B4
Maralinga, *Australia* 93 F5
Maramaereğlisi, *Turkey* 41 F11
Marampa, *S. Leone* 82 D2
Maramureş □, *Romania* 43 C9
Maran, *Malaysia* 65 L4
Marana, *U.S.A.* 115 K8
Maranboy, *Australia* 92 B5
Maranchón, *Spain* 32 D2
Marand, *Iran* 70 B5
Marang, *Malaysia* 65 K4
Maranguape, *Brazil* 125 D11
Maranhão = São Luís, *Brazil* . 125 D10
Maranhão □, *Brazil* 125 E9
Marano, L. di, *Italy* 29 C10
Maranoa →, *Australia* 95 D4
Marañón →, *Peru* 122 D3
Marão, *Mozam.* 89 C5
Maraş = Kahramanmaraş,
  Turkey 70 B3
Mărăşeşti, *Romania* 43 E12
Maratea, *Italy* 31 C8
Marateca, *Portugal* 35 G2
Marathasa □, *Cyprus* 36 E11
Marathókambos, *Greece* 39 D8
Marathon, *Australia* 94 C3
Marathon, *Canada* 102 C2
Marathón, *Greece* 38 C5
Marathon, *N.Y., U.S.A.* 111 D8
Marathon, *Tex., U.S.A.* 113 K3
Marathóvouno, *Cyprus* 36 D12
Maratua, *Indonesia* 63 D5
Maravatío, *Mexico* 118 D4
Marawi City, *Phil.* 61 G6
Marāwih, *U.A.E.* 71 E7
Marbella, *Spain* 35 J6
Marble Bar, *Australia* 92 D2
Marble Falls, *U.S.A.* 113 K5
Marblehead, *U.S.A.* 111 D14
Marburg, *Germany* 24 E4
Marcal →, *Hungary* 42 C2
Marcali, *Hungary* 42 D2
Marcaria, *Italy* 28 C7
Mărcăuţi, *Moldova* 43 B12
March, *U.K.* 13 E8
Marche, *France* 20 B5
Marche □, *Italy* 29 E10
Marche-en-Famenne, *Belgium* . 17 D5
Marchena, *Spain* 35 H5
Marches = Marche □, *Italy* .. 29 E10
Marciana Marina, *Italy* 28 F7
Marcianise, *Italy* 31 A7
Marcigny, *France* 19 F11
Marcillat-en-Combraille, *France* 19 F9
Marck, *France* 19 B8
Marckolsheim, *France* 19 D14
Marco, *U.S.A.* 109 N5
Marcos Juárez, *Argentina* ... 126 C3
Mărculeşti, *Moldova* 43 C13
Marcus I. = Minami-Tori-Shima,
  Pac. Oc. 96 E7
Marcus Necker Ridge, *Pac. Oc.* 96 F9
Marcy, Mt., *U.S.A.* 111 B11
Mardan, *Pakistan* 68 B5
Mardin, *Turkey* 70 B4
Mårdsjön, *Sweden* 10 A9
Marécchia →, *Italy* 29 D9
Maree, L., *U.K.* 14 D3
Mareeba, *Australia* 94 B4
Mareetsane, *S. Africa* 88 D4
Maremma, *Italy* 29 F8
Maréna, *Mali* 82 C3
Marengo, *U.S.A.* 112 E8
Marenyi, *Kenya* 86 C4
Marerano, *Madag.* 89 C7
Maréttimo, *Italy* 30 E5

Mareuil, *France* 20 C4
Marfa, *U.S.A.* 113 K2
Marfa Pt., *Malta* 36 D1
Marganets = Marhanets, *Ukraine* 47 J8
Margaret →, *Australia* 92 C4
Margaret Bay, *Canada* 104 C3
Margaret L., *Canada* 104 B5
Margaret River, *Australia* ... 93 F2
Margarita, I. de, *Venezuela* .. 122 B4
Margarítion, *Greece* 38 B2
Margaritovo, *Russia* 54 C7
Margate, *S. Africa* 89 E5
Margate, *U.K.* 13 F9
Margeride, Mts. de la, *France* . 20 D7
Margherita di Savóia, *Italy* .. 31 A9
Marghita, *Romania* 42 C7
Märgow, Dasht-e, *Afghan.* ... 66 D3
Marguerite, *Canada* 104 C4
Marhanets, *Ukraine* 47 J8
Mari El □, *Russia* 48 B8
Mari Indus, *Pakistan* 68 C4
Mari Republic = Mari El □,
  Russia 48 B8
María, Sa. de, *Spain* 33 H2
María Elena, *Chile* 126 A2
María Grande, *Argentina* 126 C4
Maria I., *N. Terr., Australia* .. 94 A2
Maria I., *Tas., Australia* 94 G4
Maria van Diemen, C., *N.Z.* .. 91 F4
Mariager, *Denmark* 11 H3
Mariager Fjord, *Denmark* ... 11 H4
Mariakani, *Kenya* 86 C4
Marian L., *Canada* 104 A5
Mariana Trench, *Pac. Oc.* ... 52 H18
Marianao, *Cuba* 120 B3
Marianna, *Ark., U.S.A.* 113 H9
Marianna, *Fla., U.S.A.* 109 K3
Mariannelund, *Sweden* 11 G9
Mariánské Lázně, *Czech Rep.* . 26 B5
Marias →, *U.S.A.* 114 C8
Mariato, Punta, *Panama* 120 E3
Mariazell, *Austria* 26 D8
Maribo, *Denmark* 11 K5
Maribor, *Slovenia* 29 B12
Marico →, *Africa* 88 C4
Maricopa, *Ariz., U.S.A.* 115 K7
Maricopa, *Calif., U.S.A.* 117 K7
Marīdī, *Sudan* 81 G2
Marīdī, Wadi →, *Sudan* 81 F2
Marié →, *Brazil* 124 D5
Marie Byrd Land, *Antarctica* . 5 D14
Marie-Galante, *Guadeloupe* .. 121 C7
Mariecourt = Kangiqsujuaq,
  Canada 101 B12
Mariefred, *Sweden* 10 E11
Marieholm, *Sweden* 11 J7
Mariembourg, *Belgium* 17 D4
Marienbad = Mariánské Lázně,
  Czech Rep. 26 B5
Marienberg, *Germany* 24 E9
Mariental, *Namibia* 88 C2
Marienville, *U.S.A.* 110 E5
Mariestad, *Sweden* 11 F7
Marietta, *Ga., U.S.A.* 109 J3
Marietta, *Ohio, U.S.A.* 108 F5
Marieville, *Canada* 111 A11
Mariga →, *Nigeria* 83 C6
Marignane, *France* 21 E9
Marihatag, *Phil.* 61 G7
Mariinsk, *Russia* 50 D9
Mariinskiy Posad, *Russia* ... 48 B8
Marijampolė, *Lithuania* 9 J20
Marijampolė □, *Lithuania* ... 44 D10
Marília, *Brazil* 127 A6
Marín, *Spain* 34 C2
Marina, *U.S.A.* 116 J5
Marinduque, *Phil.* 63 B6
Marine City, *U.S.A.* 110 D2
Marineo, *Italy* 30 E6
Marinette, *U.S.A.* 108 C2
Maringá, *Brazil* 127 A5
Marinha Grande, *Portugal* ... 34 F2
Marino, *Italy* 29 G9
Marion, *Ala., U.S.A.* 109 J2
Marion, *Ill., U.S.A.* 113 G10
Marion, *Ind., U.S.A.* 108 E3
Marion, *Iowa, U.S.A.* 112 D9
Marion, *Kans., U.S.A.* 112 F6
Marion, *N.C., U.S.A.* 109 H4
Marion, *Ohio, U.S.A.* 108 E4
Marion, *S.C., U.S.A.* 109 H6
Marion, *Va., U.S.A.* 109 G5
Marion, *L., U.S.A.* 109 J5
Mariposa, *U.S.A.* 116 H7
Mariscal Estigarribia, *Paraguay* 126 A3
Maritime Alps = Maritimes,
  Alpes, *Europe* 21 D11
Maritimes, Alpes, *Europe* ... 21 D11
Maritsa = Évros →, *Greece* .. 72 B2
Maritsá, *Greece* 36 C10
Mariupol, *Ukraine* 47 J9
Marīvān, *Iran* 70 C5
Marj 'Uyūn, *Lebanon* 75 B4
Marka, *Si. Arabia* 80 D5
Markam, *China* 58 C2
Markapur, *India* 66 M11
Markaryd, *Sweden* 11 H7
Markazī □, *Iran* 71 C6
Markdale, *Canada* 110 B4
Marked Tree, *U.S.A.* 113 H9
Markelsdorfer Huk, *Germany* . 24 A7
Market Drayton, *U.K.* 12 E5
Market Harborough, *U.K.* ... 13 E7
Market Rasen, *U.K.* 12 D7

Markham, Mt., *Antarctica* 5 E11
Marki, *Poland* 45 F8
Markkleeberg, *Germany* 24 D8
Markleeville, *U.S.A.* 116 G7
Markoupoulon, *Greece* 38 D5
Markovac, *Serbia, Yug.* 40 B5
Markovo, *Russia* 51 C17
Markoye, *Burkina Faso* 83 C5
Marks, *Russia* 48 E8
Marksville, *U.S.A.* 113 K8
Markt Schwaben, *Germany* ... 25 G7
Marktoberdorf, *Germany* 25 H6
Marktredwitz, *Germany* 25 E8
Marl, *Germany* 24 D3
Marla, *Australia* 95 D1
Marlbank, *Canada* 110 B7
Marlboro, *Mass., U.S.A.* 111 D13
Marlboro, *N.Y., U.S.A.* 111 E11
Marlborough, *Australia* 94 C4
Marlborough, *U.K.* 13 F6
Marlborough Downs, *U.K.* ... 13 F6
Marle, *France* 19 C10
Marlin, *U.S.A.* 113 K6
Marlow, *Germany* 24 A8
Marlow, *U.S.A.* 113 H6
Marmagao, *India* 66 M8
Marmande, *France* 20 D4
Marmara, *Turkey* 41 F11
Marmara, Sea of = Marmara
  Denizi, *Turkey* 41 F12
Marmara Denizi, *Turkey* 41 F12
Marmara Gölü, *Turkey* 39 C10
Marmaris, *Turkey* 39 E10
Marmaris Limani, *Turkey* ... 39 E10
Marmion, Mt., *Australia* 93 E2
Marmion L., *Canada* 102 C1
Marmolada, Mte., *Italy* 29 B8
Marmolejo, *Spain* 35 G6
Marmora, *Canada* 102 D4
Mármora, La, *Italy* 30 C2
Marnay, *France* 19 E12
Marne, *Germany* 24 B5
Marne □, *France* 19 D11
Marne →, *France* 19 D9
Marneuli, *Georgia* 49 K7
Maroala, *Madag.* 89 B8
Maroantsetra, *Madag.* 89 B8
Maroelaboom, *Namibia* 88 B2
Marofandilia, *Madag.* 89 C7
Marolambo, *Madag.* 89 C8
Maromandia, *Madag.* 89 A8
Marondera, *Zimbabwe* 87 F3
Maroni →, *Fr. Guiana* 125 B8
Marónia, *Greece* 41 F9
Maronne →, *France* 20 C5
Maroochydore, *Australia* 95 D5
Maroona, *Australia* 95 F3
Maros →, *Hungary* 42 D5
Marosakoa, *Madag.* 89 B8
Maroseranana, *Madag.* 89 B8
Maróstica, *Italy* 29 C8
Marotandrano, *Madag.* 89 B8
Marotaolano, *Madag.* 89 A8
Maroua, *Cameroon* 83 C7
Marovato, *Madag.* 89 B8
Marovoay, *Madag.* 89 B8
Marquard, *S. Africa* 88 D4
Marquesas Is. = Marquises, Is.,
  Pac. Oc. 97 H14
Marquette, *U.S.A.* 108 B2
Marquise, *France* 19 B8
Marquises, Is., *Pac. Oc.* 97 H14
Marra, Djebel, *Sudan* 79 F10
Marra, Gebel, *Sudan* 81 F2
Marracuene, *Mozam.* 89 D5
Marradi, *Italy* 29 D8
Marrakech, *Morocco* 78 B4
Marratxi, *Spain* 32 F7
Marrawah, *Australia* 94 G3
Marree, *Australia* 95 D2
Marrero, *U.S.A.* 113 L9
Marrimane, *Mozam.* 89 C5
Marromeu, *Mozam.* 89 B6
Marroquí, Punta, *Spain* 35 K5
Marrowie Cr. →, *Australia* ... 95 E4
Marrubane, *Mozam.* 87 F4
Marrúbiu, *Italy* 30 C1
Marrupa, *Mozam.* 87 E4
Mars Hill, *U.S.A.* 109 B12
Marsá 'Alam, *Egypt* 80 B3
Marsá Matrûh, *Egypt* 80 A2
Marsá Sha'b, *Sudan* 80 C4
Marsabit, *Kenya* 86 B4
Marsala, *Italy* 30 E5
Marsalforn, *Malta* 36 C1
Mârşani, *Romania* 43 F9
Marsberg, *Germany* 24 D4
Marsciano, *Italy* 29 F9
Marsden, *Australia* 95 E4
Marseillan, *France* 20 E7
Marseille, *France* 21 E9
Marseilles = Marseille, *France* . 21 E9
Marsh I., *U.S.A.* 113 L9
Marshall, *Liberia* 82 D2
Marshall, *Ark., U.S.A.* 113 H8
Marshall, *Mich., U.S.A.* 108 D3
Marshall, *Minn., U.S.A.* 112 C7
Marshall, *Mo., U.S.A.* 112 F8
Marshall, *Tex., U.S.A.* 113 J7
Marshall →, *Australia* 94 C2
Marshall Is. ■, *Pac. Oc.* 96 G9
Marshalltown, *U.S.A.* 112 D8
Marshbrook, *Zimbabwe* 89 B5
Marshfield, *Mo., U.S.A.* 113 G8
Marshfield, *Vt., U.S.A.* 111 B12
Marshfield, *Wis., U.S.A.* 112 C9
Marshūn, *Iran* 71 B6

Mársico Nuovo

Mársico Nuovo, Italy 31 B8
Märsta, Sweden 10 E11
Marstal, Denmark 11 K4
Marstrand, Sweden 11 G5
Mart, U.S.A. 113 K6
Marta →, Italy 29 F8
Martaban, Burma 67 L20
Martaban, G. of, Burma 67 L20
Martano, Italy 31 B11
Martapura, Kalimantan, Indonesia 62 E4
Martapura, Sumatera, Indonesia 62 E2
Marte, Nigeria 83 C7
Martel, France 20 D5
Martelange, Belgium 17 E5
Martellago, Italy 29 C9
Martés, Sierra, Spain 33 F4
Martfű, Hungary 42 C5
Martha's Vineyard, U.S.A. 111 E14
Martigné-Ferchaud, France 18 E5
Martigny, Switz. 25 J3
Martigues, France 21 E9
Martin, Slovak Rep. 27 B11
Martin, S. Dak., U.S.A. 112 D4
Martin, Tenn., U.S.A. 113 G10
Martín →, Spain 32 D4
Martin, L., U.S.A. 109 J3
Martina Franca, Italy 31 B10
Martinborough, N.Z. 91 J5
Martinez, Calif., U.S.A. 116 G4
Martinez, Ga., U.S.A. 109 J4
Martinique ■, W. Indies 121 D7
Martinique Passage, W. Indies 121 C7
Martínon, Greece 38 C5
Martinópolis, Brazil 127 A5
Martins Ferry, U.S.A. 110 F4
Martinsberg, Austria 26 C8
Martinsburg, Pa., U.S.A. 110 F6
Martinsburg, W. Va., U.S.A. 108 F7
Martinsicuro, Italy 29 F10
Martinsville, Ind., U.S.A. 108 F2
Martinsville, Va., U.S.A. 109 G6
Marton, N.Z. 91 J5
Martorell, Spain 32 D6
Martos, Spain 35 H7
Martuni, Armenia 49 K7
Maru, Nigeria 83 C6
Marudi, Malaysia 62 D4
Maruf, Afghan. 66 D5
Marugame, Japan 55 G6
Marunga, Angola 88 B3
Marungu, Mts., Dem. Rep. of the Congo 86 D3
Marv Dasht, Iran 71 D7
Marvast, Iran 71 D7
Marvejols, France 20 D7
Marvel Loch, Australia 93 F2
Marwar, India 68 G5
Mary, Turkmenistan 50 F7
Maryborough = Port Laoise, Ireland 15 C4
Maryborough, Queens., Australia 95 D5
Maryborough, Vic., Australia 95 F3
Maryfield, Canada 105 D8
Maryland □, U.S.A. 108 F7
Maryland Junction, Zimbabwe 87 F3
Maryport, U.K. 12 C4
Mary's Harbour, Canada 103 B8
Marystown, Canada 103 C8
Marysville, Canada 104 D5
Marysville, Calif., U.S.A. 116 F5
Marysville, Kans., U.S.A. 112 F6
Marysville, Mich., U.S.A. 110 D2
Marysville, Ohio, U.S.A. 108 E4
Marysville, Wash., U.S.A. 116 B4
Maryville, Mo., U.S.A. 112 E7
Maryville, Tenn., U.S.A. 109 H4
Marzūq, Libya 79 C8
Masahunga, Tanzania 86 C3
Masai Steppe, Tanzania 86 C4
Masaka, Uganda 86 C3
Masalembo, Kepulauan, Indonesia 62 F4
Masalima, Kepulauan, Indonesia 62 F5
Masallı, Azerbaijan 73 C13
Masamba, Indonesia 63 E6
Masan, S. Korea 57 G15
Masandam, Ra's, Oman 71 E8
Masasi, Tanzania 87 E4
Masaya, Nic. 120 D2
Masba, Nigeria 83 C7
Masbate, Phil. 61 E5
Máscali, Italy 31 E8
Mascara, Algeria 78 A6
Mascota, Mexico 118 C4
Masela, Indonesia 63 F7
Maseru, Lesotho 88 D4
Mashaba, Zimbabwe 87 G3
Mashābih, Si. Arabia 70 E3
Mashan, China 58 F7
Mashar, Sudan 81 F2
Mashegu, Nigeria 83 D6
Masherbrum, Pakistan 69 B7
Mashhad, Iran 71 B8
Mashi, Nigeria 83 C6
Mashīz, Iran 71 D8
Māshkel, Hāmūn-i-, Pakistan 66 E3
Mashki Chāh, Pakistan 66 E3
Mashonaland, Zimbabwe 85 H6
Mashonaland Central □, Zimbabwe 89 B5
Mashonaland East □, Zimbabwe 89 B5
Mashonaland West □, Zimbabwe 89 B4
Mashrakh, India 69 F11
Mashtaga = Maştağa, Azerbaijan 49 K10
Masindi, Uganda 86 B3
Masindi Port, Uganda 86 B3
Maşīrah, Oman 74 C6
Maşīrah, Khalīj, Oman 74 C6
Masisi, Dem. Rep. of the Congo 86 C2
Masjed Soleyman, Iran 71 D6
Mask, L., Ireland 15 C2
Maskin, Oman 71 F8
Maslen Nos, Bulgaria 41 D11
Maslinica, Croatia 29 E13
Masnou = El Masnou, Spain 32 D7
Masoala, Tanjon' i, Madag. 89 B9
Masoarivo, Madag. 89 B7
Masohi = Amahai, Indonesia 63 E7
Masomeloka, Madag. 89 C8
Mason, Nev., U.S.A. 116 G7
Mason, Tex., U.S.A. 113 K5
Mason City, U.S.A. 112 D8
Maspalomas, Canary Is. 37 G4
Maspalomas, Pta., Canary Is. 37 G4
Masqat, Oman 74 C6
Massa, Italy 28 D7
Massa Maríttima, Italy 28 E7
Massachusetts □, U.S.A. 111 D13
Massachusetts B., U.S.A. 111 D14
Massafra, Italy 31 B10
Massakory, Chad 79 F9
Massanella, Spain 37 B9
Massangena, Mozam. 89 C5
Massango, Angola 84 F3
Massat, France 20 F5
Massawa = Mitsiwa, Eritrea 81 D4
Massena, U.S.A. 111 B10
Massénya, Chad 79 F9
Masset, Canada 104 C2
Masseube, France 20 E4
Massiac, France 20 C7
Massif Central, France 20 D7
Massigui, Mali 82 C3
Massillon, U.S.A. 110 F3
Massinga, Mozam. 89 C6
Massingir, Mozam. 89 C5
Mässlingen, Sweden 10 B6
Masson, Canada 111 A9
Masson I., Antarctica 5 C7
Maştağa, Azerbaijan 49 K10
Mastanli = Momchilgrad, Bulgaria 41 E9
Masterton, N.Z. 91 J5
Mastic, U.S.A. 111 F12
Mástikho, Ákra, Greece 39 C8
Mastuj, Pakistan 69 A5
Mastung, Pakistan 66 E5
Mastūrah, Si. Arabia 80 C4
Masty, Belarus 46 F3
Masuda, Japan 55 G5
Masvingo, Zimbabwe 87 G3
Masvingo □, Zimbabwe 87 G3
Maşyāf, Syria 70 C3
Maszewo, Poland 44 E2
Mat →, Albania 40 E3
Matabeleland, Zimbabwe 85 H5
Matabeleland North □, Zimbabwe 87 F2
Matabeleland South □, Zimbabwe 87 G2
Matachel →, Spain 35 G4
Matachewan, Canada 102 C3
Matadi, Dem. Rep. of the Congo 84 F2
Matagalpa, Nic. 120 D2
Matagami, Canada 102 C4
Matagami, L., Canada 102 C4
Matagorda B., U.S.A. 113 L6
Matagorda I., U.S.A. 113 L6
Matak, Indonesia 65 L6
Mátala, Greece 36 E6
Matam, Senegal 82 B2
Matameye, Niger 83 C6
Matamoros, Campeche, Mexico 119 D6
Matamoros, Coahuila, Mexico 118 B4
Matamoros, Tamaulipas, Mexico 119 B5
Ma'ṭan as Sarra, Libya 79 D10
Matandu →, Tanzania 87 D3
Matane, Canada 103 C6
Matang, China 58 F5
Matankari, Niger 83 C5
Matanomadh, India 68 H3
Matanzas, Cuba 120 B3
Matapa, Botswana 88 C3
Matapan, C. = Taínaron, Ákra, Greece 38 E4
Matapédia, Canada 103 C6
Matara, Sri Lanka 66 S12
Mataram, Indonesia 62 F5
Matarani, Peru 124 G4
Mataranka, Australia 92 B5
Matarma, Râs, Egypt 75 E1
Mataró, Spain 32 D7
Matarraña →, Spain 32 D5
Mataruška Banja, Serbia, Yug. 40 C4
Matatiele, S. Africa 89 E4
Mataura, N.Z. 91 M2
Matehuala, Mexico 118 C4
Mateke Hills, Zimbabwe 87 G3
Matera, Italy 31 B9
Matese, Monti del, Italy 31 A7
Mátészalka, Hungary 42 C7
Matetsi, Zimbabwe 87 F2
Matfors, Sweden 10 B11
Matha, France 20 C3
Mathis, U.S.A. 113 L6
Mathráki, Greece 36 A3
Mathura, India 68 F7
Mati, Phil. 61 H7
Matiakoali, Burkina Faso 83 C5
Matiali, India 69 F13
Matías Romero, Mexico 119 D5
Matibane, Mozam. 87 E5
Matima, Botswana 88 C3
Matiri Ra., N.Z. 91 J4
Matjiesfontein, S. Africa 88 E3
Matla →, India 69 J13
Matlamanyane, Botswana 88 B4
Matli, Pakistan 68 G3
Matlock, U.K. 12 D6
Matna, Sudan 81 E4
Mato Grosso □, Brazil 125 F8
Mato Grosso, Planalto do, Brazil 122 E5
Mato Grosso do Sul □, Brazil 125 G8
Matochkin Shar, Russia 50 B6
Matopo Hills, Zimbabwe 87 G2
Matopos, Zimbabwe 87 G2
Matosinhos, Portugal 34 D2
Matour, France 19 F11
Matroosberg, S. Africa 88 E2
Maṭruḥ, Oman 74 C6
Matsena, Nigeria 83 C7
Matsesta, Russia 49 J4
Matsu Tao, Taiwan 59 E13
Matsue, Japan 55 G6
Matsumae, Japan 54 D10
Matsumoto, Japan 55 F9
Matsusaka, Japan 55 G8
Matsuura, Japan 55 H4
Matsuyama, Japan 55 H6
Mattagami →, Canada 102 B3
Mattancheri, India 66 Q10
Mattawa, Canada 102 C4
Matterhorn, Switz. 25 K3
Mattersburg, Austria 27 D9
Matthew Town, Bahamas 121 B5
Matthew's Ridge, Guyana 124 B6
Mattice, Canada 102 C3
Mattituck, U.S.A. 111 F12
Mattō, Japan 55 F8
Mattoon, U.S.A. 108 F1
Matuba, Mozam. 89 C5
Matucana, Peru 124 F3
Matūn = Khowst, Afghan. 68 C3
Maturín, Venezuela 124 B6
Matveyev Kurgan, Russia 47 J10
Matxitxako, C., Spain 32 B2
Mau, Mad. P., India 69 F8
Mau, Ut. P., India 69 G10
Mau, Ut. P., India 69 G9
Mau Escarpment, Kenya 86 C4
Mau Ranipur, India 69 G8
Maubeuge, France 19 B10
Maubourguet, France 20 E4
Maud, Pt., Australia 92 D1
Maude, Australia 95 E3
Maudin Sun, Burma 67 M19
Maués, Brazil 124 D7
Mauganj, India 67 G12
Maughold Hd., U.K. 12 C3
Mauguio, France 20 E7
Maui, U.S.A. 106 H16
Maulamyaing = Moulmein, Burma 67 L20
Maule □, Chile 126 D1
Mauléon-Licharre, France 20 E3
Maumee, U.S.A. 108 E4
Maumee →, U.S.A. 108 E4
Maumere, Indonesia 63 F6
Maumusson, Pertuis de, France 20 C2
Maun, Botswana 88 C3
Mauna Kea, U.S.A. 106 J17
Mauna Loa, U.S.A. 106 J17
Maungmagan Kyunzu, Burma 64 E1
Maupin, U.S.A. 114 D3
Maure-de-Bretagne, France 18 E5
Maurepas, L., U.S.A. 113 K9
Maures, France 21 E10
Mauriac, France 20 C6
Maurice, L., Australia 93 E5
Mauricie, Parc Nat. de la, Canada 102 C5
Maurienne, France 21 C10
Mauritania ■, Africa 78 E3
Mauritius ■, Ind. Oc. 77 J9
Mauron, France 18 D4
Maurs, France 20 D6
Mauston, U.S.A. 112 D9
Mauterndorf, Austria 26 D6
Mauthen, Austria 26 E6
Mauvezin, France 20 E4
Mauzé-sur-le-Mignon, France 20 B3
Mavli, India 68 G5
Mavrovë, Albania 40 F3
Mavuradonha Mts., Zimbabwe 87 F3
Mawa, Dem. Rep. of the Congo 86 B2
Mawai, India 69 H9
Mawana, India 68 E7
Mawand, Pakistan 68 E3
Mawk Mai, Burma 67 J20
Mawlaik, Burma 67 H19
Mawlamyine = Moulmein, Burma 67 L20
Mawqaq, Si. Arabia 70 E4
Mawson Coast, Antarctica 5 C6
Max, U.S.A. 112 B4
Maxcanú, Mexico 119 C6
Maxesibeni, S. Africa 89 E4
Maxhamish L., Canada 104 B4
Maxixe, Mozam. 89 C6
Maxville, Canada 111 A10
Maxwell, U.S.A. 116 F4
Maxwelton, Australia 94 C3
May, C., U.S.A. 108 F8
May Pen, Jamaica 120 C4
Maya →, Russia 51 D14
Maya Mts., Belize 119 D7
Mayaguana, Bahamas 121 B5
Mayagüez, Puerto Rico 121 C6
Mayahi, Niger 83 C6
Mayals = Maials, Spain 32 D5
Mayāmey, Iran 71 B7
Mayang, China 58 D7
Mayanup, Australia 93 F2
Mayapan, Mexico 119 C7
Mayarí, Cuba 121 B4
Maybell, U.S.A. 114 F9
Maybole, U.K. 14 F4
Maychew, Ethiopia 81 E4
Maydān, Iraq 70 C5
Maydena, Australia 94 G4
Mayen, Germany 25 E3
Mayenne, France 18 D6
Mayenne □, France 18 D6
Mayenne →, France 18 E6
Mayer, U.S.A. 115 J7
Mayerthorpe, Canada 104 C5
Mayfield, Ky., U.S.A. 109 G1
Mayfield, N.Y., U.S.A. 111 C10
Mayhill, U.S.A. 115 K11
Maykop, Russia 49 H5
Maymyo, Burma 64 A1
Maynard, Mass., U.S.A. 111 D13
Maynard, Wash., U.S.A. 116 C4
Maynard Hills, Australia 93 E2
Mayne →, Australia 94 C3
Maynooth, Ireland 15 C5
Mayo, Canada 100 B6
Mayo □, Ireland 15 C2
Mayo Daga, Nigeria 83 D7
Mayo Faran, Nigeria 83 D7
Mayon Volcano, Phil. 61 E5
Mayor I., N.Z. 91 G6
Mayorga, Spain 34 C5
Mayotte, Ind. Oc. 85 G9
Mayraira Pt., Phil. 61 B4
Mayskiy, Russia 49 J7
Maysville, U.S.A. 108 F4
Mayu, Indonesia 63 D7
Mayville, N. Dak., U.S.A. 112 B6
Mayville, N.Y., U.S.A. 110 D5
Mayya, Russia 51 C14
Mazabuka, Zambia 87 F2
Mazagán = El Jadida, Morocco 78 B4
Mazagão, Brazil 125 D8
Mazamet, France 20 E6
Mazán, Peru 124 D4
Māzandarān □, Iran 71 B7
Mazapil, Mexico 118 C4
Mazara del Vallo, Italy 30 E5
Mazarrón, Spain 33 H3
Mazarrón, G. de, Spain 33 H3
Mazaruni →, Guyana 124 B7
Mazatán, Mexico 118 B2
Mazatenango, Guatemala 120 D1
Mazatlán, Mexico 118 C3
Mažeikiai, Lithuania 9 H20
Māzhān, Iran 71 C8
Mazīnān, Iran 71 B8
Mazoe, Mozam. 87 F3
Mazoe →, Mozam. 87 F3
Mazowe, Zimbabwe 87 F3
Mazowieckie □, Poland 45 F8
Mazrûb, Sudan 81 E2
Mazu Dao, China 59 D12
Mazurian Lakes = Mazurski, Pojezierze, Poland 44 E7
Mazurski, Pojezierze, Poland 44 E7
Mazyr, Belarus 47 F5
Mbaba, Senegal 82 C1
Mbabane, Swaziland 89 D5
Mbagne, Mauritania 82 B2
M'bahiakro, Ivory C. 82 D4
Mbaïki, C.A.R. 84 D3
Mbala, Zambia 87 D3
Mbalabala, Zimbabwe 89 C4
Mbale, Uganda 86 B3
Mbalmayo, Cameroon 83 E7
Mbam →, Cameroon 83 E7
Mbamba Bay, Tanzania 87 E3
Mbandaka, Dem. Rep. of the Congo 84 D3
Mbanga, Cameroon 83 E6
Mbanza Congo, Angola 84 F2
Mbanza Ngungu, Dem. Rep. of the Congo 84 F2
Mbarara, Uganda 86 C3
Mbashe →, S. Africa 89 E4
Mbatto, Ivory C. 82 D4
Mbenkuru →, Tanzania 87 D4
Mberengwa, Zimbabwe 87 G2
Mberengwa, Mt., Zimbabwe 87 G2
Mberubu, Nigeria 83 D6
Mbesuma, Zambia 87 E3
Mbeya, Tanzania 87 D3
Mbeya □, Tanzania 86 D3
M'bili, Sudan 81 F2
Mbinga, Tanzania 87 E4
Mbini □, Eq. Guin. 84 D2
Mboki, C.A.R. 81 F2
M'bonge, Cameroon 83 E6
Mboro, Senegal 82 B1
M'boukou Res., Cameroon 83 D7
Mboune, Senegal 82 C2
Mbour, Senegal 82 C1
Mbout, Mauritania 82 B2
Mbuji-Mayi, Dem. Rep. of the Congo 86 D1
Mbulu, Tanzania 86 C4
Mburucuyá, Argentina 126 B4
Mchinja, Tanzania 87 D4
Mchinji, Malawi 87 E3
Mdantsane, S. Africa 85 L5
Mead, L., U.S.A. 117 J12
Meade, U.S.A. 113 G4
Meadow Lake, Canada 105 C7
Meadow Lake Prov. Park, Canada 105 C7
Meadow Valley Wash →, U.S.A. 117 J12
Meadville, U.S.A. 110 E4
Meaford, Canada 102 D3
Mealhada, Portugal 34 E2
Mealy Mts., Canada 103 B8
Meander River, Canada 104 B5
Meares, C., U.S.A. 114 D2
Mearim →, Brazil 125 D10
Meath □, Ireland 15 C5
Meath Park, Canada 105 C7
Meaulne, France 19 F9
Meaux, France 19 D9
Mebechi-Gawa →, Japan 54 D10
Mecanhelas, Mozam. 87 F4
Mecca = Makkah, Si. Arabia 74 C2
Mecca, U.S.A. 117 M10
Mechanicsburg, U.S.A. 110 F8
Mechanicville, U.S.A. 111 D11
Mechara, Ethiopia 81 F5
Mechelen, Belgium 17 C4
Mecheria, Algeria 78 B5
Mechernich, Germany 24 E2
Mechetinskaya, Russia 49 G5
Mecidiye, Turkey 41 F10
Mecitözü, Turkey 72 B6
Mecklenburg-Vorpommern □, Germany 24 B8
Mecklenburger Bucht, Germany 24 A7
Meconta, Mozam. 87 E4
Mecsek, Hungary 42 D3
Meda, Portugal 34 E3
Medan, Indonesia 62 D1
Medanosa, Pta., Argentina 128 F3
Mede, Italy 28 C5
Médéa, Algeria 78 A6
Mededa, Bos.-H. 42 G4
Medellín, Colombia 124 B3
Medelpad, Sweden 10 B10
Medemblik, Neths. 17 B5
Mederdra, Mauritania 82 B1
Medford, Mass., U.S.A. 111 D13
Medford, Oreg., U.S.A. 114 E2
Medford, Wis., U.S.A. 112 C9
Medgidia, Romania 43 F13
Medi, Sudan 81 F3
Media Agua, Argentina 126 C2
Media Luna, Argentina 126 C2
Medianeira, Brazil 127 B5
Mediaş, Romania 43 D9
Medicina, Italy 29 D8
Medicine Bow, U.S.A. 114 F10
Medicine Bow Pk., U.S.A. 114 F10
Medicine Bow Ra., U.S.A. 114 F10
Medicine Hat, Canada 105 D6
Medicine Lake, U.S.A. 112 A2
Medicine Lodge, U.S.A. 113 G5
Medina = Al Madīnah, Si. Arabia 70 E3
Medina, N. Dak., U.S.A. 112 B5
Medina, N.Y., U.S.A. 110 C6
Medina, Ohio, U.S.A. 110 E3
Medina →, U.S.A. 113 L5
Medina de Pomar, Spain 34 C7
Medina de Ríoseco, Spain 34 D5
Medina del Campo, Spain 34 D6
Medina L., U.S.A. 113 L5
Medina Sidonia, Spain 35 J5
Medinaceli, Spain 32 D2
Medinipur, India 69 H12
Mediterranean Sea, Europe 6 H7
Médoc, France 20 C3
Medulin, Croatia 29 D10
Medveđa, Serbia, Yug. 40 D5
Medvedevo, Russia 48 B8
Medveditsa →, Tver, Russia 46 D9
Medveditsa →, Volgograd, Russia 48 F6
Medvedok, Russia 48 B10
Medvezhi, Ostrava, Russia 51 B17
Medvezhyegorsk, Russia 50 C4
Medway □, U.K. 13 F8
Medway →, U.K. 13 F8
Medzev, Slovak Rep. 27 C13
Medzilaborce, Slovak Rep. 27 B14
Medžitlija, Macedonia 40 F5
Meekatharra, Australia 93 E2
Meeker, U.S.A. 114 F10
Meelpaeg Res., Canada 103 C8
Meersburg, Germany 25 H5
Meerut, India 68 E7
Meeteetse, U.S.A. 114 D9
Mega, Ethiopia 81 G4
Megálo Khorío, Greece 39 E9
Megálo Petalí, Greece 38 D6
Megalópolis, Greece 38 D4
Meganísi, Greece 38 C2
Mégara, Greece 38 D5
Megasini, India 69 J12
Megdhova →, Greece 38 B3
Megève, France 21 C10
Meghalaya □, India 67 G17
Meghezez, Ethiopia 81 F4
Mégiscane, L., Canada 102 C4
Megiste, Greece 39 E11
Megra, Russia 46 B9
Mehadia, Romania 42 F7
Meharry, Mt., Australia 92 D2
Mehedeby, Sweden 10 D11
Mehedinţi □, Romania 42 F7
Meheisa, Sudan 80 D3
Mehlville, U.S.A. 112 F9
Mehndawal, India 69 F10
Mehr Jān, Iran 71 C7
Mehrābād, Iran 70 B5
Mehrān, Iran 70 C5

Mehrīz, Iran ... 71 D7
Mehun-sur-Yèvre, France ... 19 E9
Mei Jiang →, China ... 59 E11
Mei Xian, China ... 56 G4
Meicheng, China ... 59 C12
Meichengzhen, China ... 59 C8
Meichuan, China ... 59 B10
Meigu, China ... 58 C4
Meiktila, Burma ... 67 J19
Meinerzhagen, Germany ... 24 D3
Meiningen, Germany ... 24 E6
Meira, Serra de, Spain ... 34 B3
Meiringen, Switz. ... 25 J4
Meishan, China ... 58 B4
Meissen, Germany ... 24 D9
Meissner, Germany ... 24 D5
Meitan, China ... 58 D6
Meizhou, China ... 59 E11
Meja, India ... 69 G10
Mejillones, Chile ... 126 A1
Mekdela, Ethiopia ... 81 E4
Mekele, Ethiopia ... 81 E4
Mekhtar, Pakistan ... 66 D6
Meknès, Morocco ... 78 B4
Meko, Nigeria ... 83 D5
Mekong →, Asia ... 65 H6
Mekongga, Indonesia ... 63 E6
Mekrou →, Benin ... 83 C5
Mekvari = Kür →, Azerbaijan . 73 C13
Mel, Italy ... 29 B9
Melagiri Hills, India ... 66 N10
Melaka, Malaysia ... 65 L4
Melalap, Malaysia ... 62 C5
Mélambes, Greece ... 36 D6
Melanesia, Pac. Oc. ... 96 H7
Melbourne, Australia ... 95 F4
Melbourne, U.S.A. ... 109 L5
Melchor Múzquiz, Mexico ... 118 B4
Melchor Ocampo, Mexico ... 118 C4
Méldola, Italy ... 29 D9
Meldorf, Germany ... 24 A5
Melegnano, Italy ... 28 C6
Melenci, Serbia, Yug. ... 42 E5
Melenki, Russia ... 48 C5
Mélèzes →, Canada ... 102 A5
Melfi, Italy ... 31 B8
Melfort, Canada ... 105 C8
Melfort, Zimbabwe ... 87 F3
Melgaço, Portugal ... 34 C2
Melgar de Fernamental, Spain . 34 C6
Melhus, Norway ... 8 E14
Melide, Spain ... 34 C2
Meligalá, Greece ... 38 D3
Melilla, N. Afr. ... 78 A5
Melilli, Italy ... 31 E8
Melipilla, Chile ... 126 C1
Mélissa, Ákra, Greece ... 36 D6
Mélissa Óros, Greece ... 39 D8
Melita, Canada ... 105 D8
Mélito di Porto Salvo, Italy ... 31 E8
Melitopol, Ukraine ... 47 J8
Melk, Austria ... 26 C8
Mellan Fryken, Sweden ... 10 E7
Mellansel, Sweden ... 8 E18
Mellbystrand, Sweden ... 11 H6
Melle, France ... 20 B3
Melle, Germany ... 24 C4
Mellen, U.S.A. ... 112 B9
Mellerud, Sweden ... 11 F6
Mellette, U.S.A. ... 112 C5
Mellid = Melide, Spain ... 34 C2
Mellieha, Malta ... 36 D1
Mellit, Sudan ... 81 E2
Mellrichstadt, Germany ... 24 E6
Melnik, Bulgaria ... 40 E7
Mělník, Czech Rep. ... 26 A7
Melo, Uruguay ... 127 C5
Melolo, Indonesia ... 63 F6
Melouprey, Cambodia ... 64 F5
Melrose, Australia ... 95 E4
Melrose, U.K. ... 14 F6
Melrose, Minn., U.S.A. ... 112 C7
Melrose, N. Mex., U.S.A. ... 113 H3
Melstone, U.S.A. ... 114 C10
Melsungen, Germany ... 24 D5
Melton Mowbray, U.K. ... 12 E7
Melun, France ... 19 D9
Melut, Sudan ... 81 E3
Melville, Canada ... 105 C8
Melville, C., Australia ... 94 A3
Melville, L., Canada ... 103 B8
Melville, Australia ... 94 A2
Melville I., Australia ... 92 B5
Melville I., Canada ... 4 B2
Melville Pen., Canada ... 101 B11
Mélykút, Hungary ... 42 D4
Memaliaj, Albania ... 40 F3
Memba, Mozam. ... 87 E5
Memboro, Indonesia ... 63 F5
Membrilla, Spain ... 35 G7
Memel = Klaipėda, Lithuania . 9 J19
Memel, S. Africa ... 89 D4
Memmingen, Germany ... 25 H6
Mempawah, Indonesia ... 62 D3
Memphis, Egypt ... 80 J7
Memphis, Mich., U.S.A. ... 110 D2
Memphis, Tenn., U.S.A. ... 113 H10
Memphis, Tex., U.S.A. ... 113 H4
Memphrémagog, L., U.S.A. ... 111 B12
Mena, Ukraine ... 47 G7
Mena, U.S.A. ... 113 H7
Mena →, Ethiopia ... 81 F5
Menai Strait, U.K. ... 12 D3
Ménaka, Mali ... 83 B5
Menan = Chao Phraya →, Thailand ... 64 F3

Menard, U.S.A. ... 113 K5
Menawashei, Sudan ... 81 E1
Mendawai →, Indonesia ... 62 E4
Mende, France ... 20 D7
Mendebo, Ethiopia ... 81 F4
Menden, Germany ... 24 D3
Menderes, Turkey ... 39 C9
Mendez, Mexico ... 119 B5
Mendhar, India ... 69 C6
Mendi, Ethiopia ... 81 F4
Mendip Hills, U.K. ... 13 F5
Mendocino, U.S.A. ... 114 G2
Mendocino, C., U.S.A. ... 114 F1
Mendota, Calif., U.S.A. ... 116 J6
Mendota, Ill., U.S.A. ... 112 E10
Mendoza, Argentina ... 126 C2
Mendoza □, Argentina ... 126 C2
Mene Grande, Venezuela ... 124 B4
Menemen, Turkey ... 39 C9
Menen, Belgium ... 17 D3
Menfi, Italy ... 30 E5
Mengdingjie, China ... 58 F2
Menggala, Indonesia ... 62 E3
Menghai, China ... 58 G3
Mengíbar, Spain ... 35 H7
Mengjin, China ... 56 G7
Mengla, China ... 58 G3
Menglian, China ... 58 F2
Mengshan, China ... 59 E8
Mengyin, China ... 57 G9
Mengzhe, China ... 58 F3
Mengzi, China ... 58 F4
Menihek, Canada ... 103 B6
Menihek L., Canada ... 103 B6
Menin = Menen, Belgium ... 17 D3
Menindee, Australia ... 95 E3
Menindee L., Australia ... 95 E3
Meningie, Australia ... 95 F2
Menlo Park, U.S.A. ... 116 H4
Menominee, U.S.A. ... 108 C2
Menominee →, U.S.A. ... 108 C2
Menomonie, U.S.A. ... 112 C9
Menongue, Angola ... 85 G3
Menorca, Spain ... 37 B11
Mentakab, Malaysia ... 65 L4
Mentawai, Kepulauan, Indonesia 62 E1
Menton, France ... 21 E11
Mentor, U.S.A. ... 110 E3
Menzies, Australia ... 93 E3
Meob B., Namibia ... 88 B2
Me'ona, Israel ... 75 B4
Meoqui, Mexico ... 118 B3
Mepaco, Mozam. ... 87 F3
Meppel, Neths. ... 17 B6
Meppen, Germany ... 24 C3
Mequinenza, Spain ... 32 D5
Mequinenza, Embalse de, Spain 32 D5
Mer, France ... 18 E8
Merabéllou, Kólpos, Greece ... 36 D7
Merak, Indonesia ... 63 F12
Meramangye, L., Australia ... 93 E5
Meran = Merano, Italy ... 29 B8
Merano, Italy ... 29 B8
Merate, Italy ... 28 C6
Merauke, Indonesia ... 63 F10
Merca, Somali Rep. ... 74 G3
Mercato Saraceno, Italy ... 29 E9
Merced, U.S.A. ... 116 H6
Merced →, U.S.A. ... 116 H6
Merced Pk., U.S.A. ... 116 H7
Mercedes, Buenos Aires, Argentina ... 126 C4
Mercedes, Corrientes, Argentina 126 B4
Mercedes, San Luis, Argentina . 126 C2
Mercedes, Uruguay ... 126 C4
Mercedes, U.S.A. ... 113 M6
Merceditas, Chile ... 126 B1
Mercer, N.Z. ... 91 G5
Mercer, U.S.A. ... 110 E4
Mercer Island, U.S.A. ... 116 C4
Mercury, U.S.A. ... 117 J11
Mercy C., Canada ... 101 B13
Merdrignac, France ... 18 D4
Mere, U.K. ... 13 F5
Meredith, C., Falk. Is. ... 128 G4
Meredith, L., U.S.A. ... 113 H4
Merefa, Ukraine ... 47 H9
Merei, Romania ... 43 E11
Merga = Nukheila, Sudan ... 80 D2
Mergui, Burma ... 64 F2
Mergui Arch. = Myeik Kyunzu, Burma ... 65 G1
Meriç, Turkey ... 41 E10
Meriç →, Turkey ... 41 F10
Mérida, Mexico ... 119 C7
Mérida, Spain ... 35 G4
Mérida, Venezuela ... 124 B4
Mérida, Cord. de, Venezuela ... 122 C3
Meriden, U.K. ... 13 E6
Meriden, U.S.A. ... 111 E12
Meridian, Calif., U.S.A. ... 116 F5
Meridian, Idaho, U.S.A. ... 114 E5
Meridian, Miss., U.S.A. ... 109 J1
Mérignac, France ... 20 D3
Mérinaghène, Senegal ... 82 B1
Merinda, Australia ... 94 C4
Meringa, Nigeria ... 83 C7
Merir, Pac. Oc. ... 63 D8
Merirumã, Brazil ... 125 C8
Merkel, U.S.A. ... 113 J5
Mermaid Reef, Australia ... 92 C2
Merowe, Sudan ... 80 D3
Merredin, Australia ... 93 F2
Merrick, U.K. ... 14 F4

Merrickville, Canada ... 111 B9
Merrill, Oreg., U.S.A. ... 114 E3
Merrill, Wis., U.S.A. ... 112 C10
Merrimack →, U.S.A. ... 111 D14
Merriman, U.S.A. ... 112 D4
Merritt, Canada ... 104 C4
Merritt Island, U.S.A. ... 109 L5
Merriwa, Australia ... 95 E5
Merry I., Canada ... 102 A4
Merryville, U.S.A. ... 113 K8
Mersa Fatma, Eritrea ... 81 E5
Mersch, Lux. ... 17 E6
Merse →, Italy ... 29 E8
Mersea I., U.K. ... 13 F8
Merseburg, Germany ... 24 D7
Mersey →, U.K. ... 12 D4
Merseyside □, U.K. ... 12 D4
Mersin, Turkey ... 70 B2
Mersing, Malaysia ... 65 L4
Merta, India ... 68 F6
Merta Road, India ... 68 F5
Merthyr Tydfil, U.K. ... 13 F4
Merthyr Tydfil □, U.K. ... 13 F4
Mértola, Portugal ... 35 H3
Mertzon, U.S.A. ... 113 K4
Méru, France ... 19 C9
Meru, Kenya ... 86 B4
Meru, Tanzania ... 86 C4
Merville, France ... 19 B9
Méry-sur-Seine, France ... 19 D10
Merzifon, Turkey ... 72 B6
Merzig, Germany ... 25 F2
Mesa, U.S.A. ... 115 K8
Mesa Verde National Park, U.S.A. ... 115 H9
Mesanagrós, Greece ... 36 C9
Mesaoría □, Cyprus ... 36 D12
Mesarás, Kólpos, Greece ... 36 D6
Meschede, Germany ... 24 D4
Mesfinto, Ethiopia ... 81 E4
Mesgouez, L., Canada ... 102 B5
Meshchovsk, Russia ... 46 E8
Meshed = Mashhad, Iran ... 71 B8
Meshoppen, U.S.A. ... 111 E8
Meshra er Req, Sudan ... 81 F2
Mesilinka →, Canada ... 104 B4
Mesilla, U.S.A. ... 115 K10
Meslay-du-Maine, France ... 18 E6
Mesocco, Switz. ... 25 J5
Mesolóngion, Greece ... 38 C3
Mesopotamia = Al Jazirah, Iraq 70 C5
Mesopotamia, U.S.A. ... 110 E4
Mesopótamon, Greece ... 38 B2
Mesoraca, Italy ... 31 C9
Mésou Volímais = Volímai, Greece ... 38 D2
Mesquite, U.S.A. ... 115 H6
Messaad, Algeria ... 78 B6
Messac, France ... 18 E5
Messalo →, Mozam. ... 87 E4
Méssaména, Cameroon ... 83 E7
Messeue, Greece ... 38 D3
Messina, Italy ... 31 D8
Messina, S. Africa ... 89 C5
Messina, Str. di, Italy ... 31 D8
Messíni, Greece ... 38 D4
Messíni □, Greece ... 38 D3
Messiniakós Kólpos, Greece ... 38 E4
Messkirch, Germany ... 25 H5
Messonghi, Greece ... 36 B3
Mesta →, Bulgaria ... 40 E7
Mestá, Ákra, Greece ... 39 C7
Mestanza, Spain ... 35 G6
Mestre, Italy ... 29 C9
Mesudiye, Turkey ... 72 B7
Meta □, Colombia ... 124 C4
Meta →, S. Amer. ... 122 C4
Meta Incognita Peninsula, Canada ... 101 B13
Metabetchouan, Canada ... 103 C5
Metairie, U.S.A. ... 113 L9
Metaline Falls, U.S.A. ... 114 B5
Metalici, Munţii, Romania ... 42 D7
Metallifere, Colline, Italy ... 28 E8
Metán, Argentina ... 126 B3
Metangula, Mozam. ... 87 E3
Metauro →, Italy ... 29 E10
Metema, Ethiopia ... 81 E4
Metengobalame, Mozam. ... 87 E3
Méthana, Greece ... 38 D5
Methóni, Greece ... 38 E3
Methven, N.Z. ... 91 K3
Metil, Mozam. ... 87 F4
Metković, Croatia ... 29 E14
Metlakatla, U.S.A. ... 100 C6
Metlaoui, Tunisia ... 78 B7
Metlika, Slovenia ... 29 C12
Metropolis, U.S.A. ... 113 G10
Métsovon, Greece ... 38 B3
Metu, Ethiopia ... 81 F4
Metz, France ... 19 C13
Metzingen, Germany ... 25 G5
Meulaboh, Indonesia ... 62 D1
Meung-sur-Loire, France ... 19 E8
Meureudu, Indonesia ... 62 C1
Meurthe →, France ... 19 D13
Meurthe-et-Moselle □, France . 19 D13
Meuse □, France ... 19 C12
Meuse →, Europe ... 17 D5
Meuselwitz, Germany ... 24 D8
Mexia, U.S.A. ... 113 K6
Mexiana, I., Brazil ... 125 D9
Mexicali, Mexico ... 117 N11
Mexican Plateau, Mexico ... 98 G9
Mexican Water, U.S.A. ... 115 H9
México, Mexico ... 119 D5

Mexico, Maine, U.S.A. ... 111 B14
Mexico, Mo., U.S.A. ... 112 F9
Mexico, N.Y., U.S.A. ... 111 C8
México □, Mexico ... 119 D5
Mexico ■, Cent. Amer. ... 118 C4
Mexico, G. of, Cent. Amer. ... 119 C7
Mexico B., U.S.A. ... 111 C8
Meydān-e Naftūn, Iran ... 71 D6
Meydani, Ra's-e, Iran ... 71 E8
Meyenburg, Germany ... 24 B8
Meymac, France ... 20 C6
Meymaneh, Afghan. ... 66 B4
Meyrueis, France ... 20 D7
Meyssac, France ... 20 C5
Meyzieu, France ... 21 C8
Mezdra, Bulgaria ... 40 C7
Mèze, France ... 20 E7
Mezen, Russia ... 50 C5
Mezen →, Russia ... 50 C5
Mézenc, Mt., France ... 21 D8
Mezeş, Munţii, Romania ... 42 C8
Mezha →, Russia ... 46 E6
Mezhdurechenskiy, Russia ... 50 D7
Mézidon-Canon, France ... 18 C6
Mézières-en-Brenne, France ... 20 B5
Mézilhac, France ... 21 D8
Mézin, France ... 20 D4
Mezőberény, Hungary ... 42 D6
Mezőfalva, Hungary ... 42 D3
Mezőhegyes, Hungary ... 42 D5
Mezőkovácsháza, Hungary ... 42 D5
Mezőkövesd, Hungary ... 42 C5
Mézos, France ... 20 D2
Mezőtúr, Hungary ... 42 C5
Mezquital, Mexico ... 118 C4
Mezzolombardo, Italy ... 28 B8
Mfolozi →, S. Africa ... 89 D5
Mgeta, Tanzania ... 87 D4
Mglin, Russia ... 47 F7
Mhlaba Hills, Zimbabwe ... 87 F3
Mhow, India ... 68 H6
Miajadas, Spain ... 35 F5
Miami, Fla., U.S.A. ... 109 N5
Miami, Okla., U.S.A. ... 113 G7
Miami, Tex., U.S.A. ... 113 H4
Miami Beach, U.S.A. ... 109 N5
Mian Xian, China ... 56 G4
Mianchi, China ... 56 G6
Mīāndarreh, Iran ... 71 C7
Mīāndowāb, Iran ... 70 B5
Miandrivazo, Madag. ... 89 B8
Mīāneh, Iran ... 70 B5
Mianning, China ... 58 C4
Mianwali, Pakistan ... 68 C4
Mianyang, China ... 58 B5
Mianzhu, China ... 58 B5
Miaoli, Taiwan ... 59 E13
Miarinarivo, Antananarivo, Madag. ... 89 B8
Miarinarivo, Toamasina, Madag. 89 B8
Miariravaratra, Madag. ... 89 C8
Miass, Russia ... 50 D7
Miastko, Poland ... 44 E3
Miasteczko Krajeńskie, Poland 45 E4
Mica, S. Africa ... 89 C5
Micăsasa, Romania ... 43 D9
Michalovce, Slovak Rep. ... 27 C14
Michigan □, U.S.A. ... 108 C3
Michigan, L., U.S.A. ... 108 D2
Michigan City, U.S.A. ... 108 E2
Michika, Nigeria ... 83 C7
Michipicoten I., Canada ... 102 C2
Michoacan □, Mexico ... 118 D4
Michurin, Bulgaria ... 41 D11
Michurinsk, Russia ... 48 D5
Mico, Pta., Nic. ... 120 D3
Micronesia, Pac. Oc. ... 96 G7
Micronesia, Federated States of ■, Pac. Oc. ... 96 G7
Midai, Indonesia ... 65 L6
Midale, Canada ... 105 D8
Middelburg, Neths. ... 17 C3
Middelburg, Eastern Cape, S. Africa ... 88 E4
Middelburg, Mpumalanga, S. Africa ... 89 D4
Middelfart, Denmark ... 11 J3
Middelpos, S. Africa ... 88 E3
Middelwit, S. Africa ... 88 C4
Middle Alkali L., U.S.A. ... 114 F3
Middle Bass I., U.S.A. ... 110 E2
Middle East, Asia ... 52 F7
Middle Fork Feather →, U.S.A. 116 F5
Middle I., Australia ... 93 F3
Middle Loup →, U.S.A. ... 112 E5
Middle Sackville, Canada ... 103 D7
Middleboro, U.S.A. ... 111 E14
Middleburg, N.Y., U.S.A. ... 111 D10
Middleburg, Pa., U.S.A. ... 110 F7
Middleburg, Fla., U.S.A. ... 111 D11
Middlemount, Australia ... 94 C4
Middleport, Ohio, U.S.A. ... 108 F4
Middlesboro, U.S.A. ... 109 G4
Middlesbrough, U.K. ... 12 C6
Middlesbrough □, U.K. ... 12 C6
Middlesex, Belize ... 120 C2
Middlesex, N.J., U.S.A. ... 111 F10
Middlesex, N.Y., U.S.A. ... 110 D7
Middleton, Australia ... 94 C3
Middleton, Canada ... 103 D6
Middleton Cr. →, Australia ... 94 C3
Middletown, U.K. ... 15 B5
Middletown, Calif., U.S.A. ... 116 G4
Middletown, Conn., U.S.A. ... 111 E12

Middletown, N.Y., U.S.A. ... 111 E10
Middletown, Ohio, U.S.A. ... 108 F3
Middletown, Pa., U.S.A. ... 111 F8
Midhurst, U.K. ... 13 G7
Mīdī, Yemen ... 81 D5
Midi, Canal du →, France ... 20 E5
Midi d'Ossau, Pic du, France . 20 F3
Midi-Pyrénées □, France ... 20 E5
Midland, Canada ... 102 D4
Midland, Calif., U.S.A. ... 117 M12
Midland, Mich., U.S.A. ... 108 D3
Midland, Pa., U.S.A. ... 110 F4
Midland, Tex., U.S.A. ... 113 K3
Midlands □, Zimbabwe ... 87 F2
Midleton, Ireland ... 15 E3
Midlothian, U.S.A. ... 113 J6
Midlothian □, U.K. ... 14 F5
Midongy, Tangorombohitr' i, Madag. ... 89 C8
Midongy Atsimo, Madag. ... 89 C8
Midou →, France ... 20 E3
Midouze →, France ... 20 E3
Midsayap, Phil. ... 61 H6
Midu, China ... 58 E3
Midway Is., Pac. Oc. ... 96 E10
Midway Wells, U.S.A. ... 117 N11
Midwest, U.S.A. ... 114 E10
Midwest City, U.S.A. ... 113 H6
Midyat, Turkey ... 70 B4
Midzŏr, Bulgaria ... 40 C6
Mie □, Japan ... 55 G8
Miechów, Poland ... 45 H7
Miedwie, Jezioro, Poland ... 44 E1
Międzybórz, Poland ... 45 G4
Międzychód, Poland ... 45 F2
Międzylesie, Poland ... 45 H3
Międzyrzec Podlaski, Poland ... 45 G9
Międzyrzecz, Poland ... 45 F2
Międzyzdroje, Poland ... 44 E1
Miejska Górka, Poland ... 45 G3
Miélan, France ... 20 E4
Mielec, Poland ... 45 H8
Mienga, Angola ... 88 B2
Miercurea-Ciuc, Romania ... 43 D10
Miercurea Sibiului, Romania ... 43 E8
Mieres, Spain ... 34 B5
Mieroszów, Poland ... 45 H3
Mieso, Ethiopia ... 81 F5
Mieszkowice, Poland ... 44 E1
Mifflintown, U.S.A. ... 110 F7
Mifraz Hefa, Israel ... 75 C4
Migennes, France ... 19 E10
Migliarino, Italy ... 29 D8
Miguel Alemán, Presa, Mexico . 119 D5
Miguelturra, Spain ... 35 G7
Mihăileni, Romania ... 43 C11
Mihăilești, Romania ... 43 F10
Mihailovca, Moldova ... 43 C13
Mihalgazi, Turkey ... 39 A12
Mihaliççik, Turkey ... 72 C4
Mihara, Japan ... 55 G6
Miheşu de Cîmpie, Romania ... 43 D9
Mijas, Spain ... 35 J6
Mikese, Tanzania ... 86 D4
Mikha-Tskhakaya = Senaki, Georgia ... 49 J6
Mikhailovka = Mykhaylivka, Ukraine ... 47 J8
Mikhaylov, Russia ... 46 E10
Mikhaylovgrad = Montana, Bulgaria ... 40 C7
Mikhaylovka, Russia ... 48 E6
Mikhnevo, Russia ... 46 E9
Mikínai, Greece ... 38 D4
Mikkeli, Finland ... 9 F22
Mikkwa →, Canada ... 104 B6
Mikniya, Sudan ... 81 D3
Mikołajki, Poland ... 44 E8
Míkonos, Greece ... 39 D7
Mikrí Préspa, Límni, Greece ... 40 F5
Mikrón Dhérion, Greece ... 41 E10
Mikstat, Poland ... 45 G4
Mikulov, Czech Rep. ... 27 C9
Mikumi, Tanzania ... 86 D4
Milaca, U.S.A. ... 112 C8
Milagro, Ecuador ... 124 D3
Milagros, Phil. ... 61 E5
Milan = Milano, Italy ... 28 C6
Milan, Mo., U.S.A. ... 112 E8
Milan, Tenn., U.S.A. ... 109 H1
Milange, Mozam. ... 87 F4
Milano, Italy ... 28 C6
Milanoa, Madag. ... 89 A8
Milâs, Turkey ... 39 D9
Milatos, Greece ... 36 D7
Milazzo, Italy ... 31 D8
Milbank, U.S.A. ... 112 C6
Milbanke Sd., Canada ... 104 C3
Milden, Canada ... 105 C7
Mildenhall, U.K. ... 13 E8
Mildmay, Canada ... 110 B3
Mildura, Australia ... 95 E3
Mile, China ... 58 E4
Miléai, Greece ... 38 B5
Miles, Australia ... 95 D5
Miles City, U.S.A. ... 112 B2
Mileştii Mici, Moldova ... 43 C13
Milestone, Canada ... 105 D8
Mileto, Italy ... 31 D8
Miletto, Mte., Italy ... 31 A7
Miletus, Turkey ... 39 D9
Milevsko, Czech Rep. ... 26 B7
Milford, Calif., U.S.A. ... 116 E6
Milford, Conn., U.S.A. ... 111 E11
Milford, Del., U.S.A. ... 108 F8
Milford, Mass., U.S.A. ... 111 D13
Milford, N.H., U.S.A. ... 111 D13

Milford

Milford, *Pa., U.S.A.* 111 E10
Milford, *Utah, U.S.A.* 115 G7
Milford Haven, *U.K.* 13 F2
Milford Sd., *N.Z.* 91 L1
Milḩ, Baḩr al, *Iraq* 70 C4
Milicz, *Poland* 45 G4
Milikapiti, *Australia* 92 B5
Miling, *Australia* 93 F2
Militello in Val di Catánia, *Italy* 31 E7
Milk →, *U.S.A.* 114 B10
Milk, Wadi el →, *Sudan* 80 D3
Milk River, *Canada* 104 D6
Mill I., *Antarctica* 5 C8
Mill Valley, *U.S.A.* 116 H4
Millárs →, *Spain* 32 F4
Millau, *France* 20 D7
Millbridge, *Canada* 110 B7
Millbrook, *Canada* 110 B6
Millbrook, *U.S.A.* 111 E11
Mille Lacs, L. des, *Canada* 102 C1
Mille Lacs L., *U.S.A.* 112 B8
Milledgeville, *U.S.A.* 109 J4
Millen, *U.S.A.* 109 J5
Millennium I. = Caroline I., *Kiribati* 97 H12
Miller, *U.S.A.* 112 C5
Millerovo, *Russia* 49 F5
Millersburg, *Ohio, U.S.A.* 110 F3
Millersburg, *Pa., U.S.A.* 110 F8
Millerton, *U.S.A.* 111 E11
Millerton L., *U.S.A.* 116 J7
Millevaches, Plateau de, *France* 20 C6
Millheim, *U.S.A.* 110 F7
Millicent, *Australia* 95 F3
Millington, *U.S.A.* 113 H10
Millinocket, *U.S.A.* 109 C11
Millmerran, *Australia* 95 D5
Millom, *U.K.* 12 C4
Mills L., *Canada* 104 A5
Millsboro, *U.S.A.* 110 G5
Milltown Malbay, *Ireland* 15 D2
Millville, *N.J., U.S.A.* 108 F8
Millville, *Pa., U.S.A.* 111 E8
Millwood L., *U.S.A.* 113 J8
Milna, *Croatia* 29 E13
Milne →, *Australia* 94 C2
Milo, *U.S.A.* 109 C11
Mílos, *Greece* 38 E6
Miłosław, *Poland* 45 F4
Milot, *Albania* 40 E3
Milparinka, *Australia* 95 D3
Miltenberg, *Germany* 25 F5
Milton, *N.S., Canada* 103 D7
Milton, *Ont., Canada* 110 C5
Milton, *N.Z.* 91 M2
Milton, *Calif., U.S.A.* 116 G6
Milton, *Fla., U.S.A.* 109 K2
Milton, *Pa., U.S.A.* 110 F8
Milton, *Vt., U.S.A.* 111 B11
Milton-Freewater, *U.S.A.* 114 D4
Milton Keynes, *U.K.* 13 E7
Milton Keynes □, *U.K.* 13 E7
Miluo, *China* 59 C9
Milverton, *Canada* 110 C4
Milwaukee, *U.S.A.* 108 D2
Milwaukee Deep, *Atl. Oc.* 121 C6
Milwaukie, *U.S.A.* 116 E4
Mim, *Ghana* 82 D4
Mimizan, *France* 20 D2
Mimoň, *Czech Rep.* 26 A7
Min Jiang →, *Fujian, China* 59 E12
Min Jiang →, *Sichuan, China* 58 C5
Min Xian, *China* 56 G3
Mina Pirquitas, *Argentina* 126 A2
Mīnā Su'ud, *Si. Arabia* 71 D6
Mīnā'al Aḩmadī, *Kuwait* 71 D6
Minago →, *Canada* 105 C9
Minaki, *Canada* 105 D10
Minamata, *Japan* 55 H5
Minami-Tori-Shima, *Pac. Oc.* 96 E7
Minas, *Uruguay* 127 C4
Minas, Sierra de las, *Guatemala* 120 C2
Minas Basin, *Canada* 103 C7
Minas de Rio Tinto = Minas de Riotinto, *Spain* 35 H4
Minas de Riotinto, *Spain* 35 H4
Minas Gerais □, *Brazil* 125 G9
Minatitlán, *Mexico* 119 D6
Minbu, *Burma* 67 J19
Minchinabad, *Pakistan* 68 D5
Mincio →, *Italy* 28 C7
Minčol, *Slovak Rep.* 27 B13
Mindanao, *Phil.* 61 H6
Mindanao Sea = Bohol Sea, *Phil.* 63 C6
Mindanao Trench, *Pac. Oc.* 61 F7
Mindel →, *Germany* 25 G6
Mindelheim, *Germany* 25 G6
Minden, *Canada* 110 B6
Minden, *Germany* 24 C4
Minden, *La., U.S.A.* 113 J8
Minden, *Nev., U.S.A.* 116 G7
Mindiptana, *Indonesia* 63 F10
Mindoro, *Phil.* 61 E4
Mindoro Str., *Phil.* 61 E4
Mine, *Japan* 55 G5
Minehead, *U.K.* 13 F4
Mineola, *N.Y., U.S.A.* 111 F11
Mineola, *Tex., U.S.A.* 113 J7
Mineral King, *U.S.A.* 116 J8
Mineral Wells, *U.S.A.* 113 J5
Mineralnyye Vody, *Russia* 49 H6
Minersville, *U.S.A.* 111 F8
Minerva, *U.S.A.* 110 F3
Minervino Murge, *Italy* 31 A9
Minetto, *U.S.A.* 111 C8
Mingäçevir, *Azerbaijan* 49 K8
Mingäçevir Su Anbarı, *Azerbaijan* 49 K8
Mingan, *Canada* 103 B7
Mingechaur = Mingäçevir, *Azerbaijan* 49 K8
Mingechaurskoye Vdkhr. = Mingäçevir Su Anbarı, *Azerbaijan* 49 K8
Mingela, *Australia* 94 B4
Mingenew, *Australia* 93 E2
Mingera Cr. →, *Australia* 94 C2
Minggang, *China* 59 A10
Mingguang, *China* 59 A11
Mingin, *Burma* 67 H19
Mingir, *Moldova* 43 D13
Minglanilla, *Spain* 33 F3
Minglun, *China* 58 E7
Mingo Junction, *U.S.A.* 110 F4
Mingorria, *Spain* 34 E6
Mingshan, *China* 58 B4
Mingteke Daban = Mintaka Pass, *Pakistan* 69 A6
Mingxi, *China* 59 D11
Mingyuegue, *China* 57 C15
Minho = Miño →, *Spain* 34 D2
Minhou, *China* 59 E12
Minićevo, *Serbia, Yug.* 42 G7
Minidoka, *U.S.A.* 114 E7
Minigwal, L., *Australia* 93 E3
Minilya →, *Australia* 93 D1
Minilya Roadhouse, *Australia* 93 D1
Minipi L., *Canada* 103 B7
Mink L., *Canada* 104 A5
Minkammen, *Sudan* 81 F3
Minna, *Nigeria* 83 D6
Minneapolis, *Kans., U.S.A.* 112 F6
Minneapolis, *Minn., U.S.A.* 112 C8
Minnedosa, *Canada* 105 C9
Minnesota □, *U.S.A.* 112 B8
Minnesota →, *U.S.A.* 112 C8
Minnewaukan, *U.S.A.* 112 A5
Minnipa, *Australia* 95 E2
Minnitaki L., *Canada* 102 C1
Mino, *Japan* 55 G8
Miño, *Spain* 34 B2
Miño →, *Spain* 34 D2
Minoa, *Greece* 39 F7
Minorca = Menorca, *Spain* 37 B11
Minot, *U.S.A.* 112 A4
Minqin, *China* 56 E2
Minqing, *China* 59 D12
Minsen, *Germany* 24 B3
Minsk, *Belarus* 46 F4
Mińsk Mazowiecki, *Poland* 45 F8
Mintabie, *Australia* 95 D1
Mintaka Pass, *Pakistan* 69 A6
Minto, *Canada* 103 C6
Minto, L., *Canada* 102 A5
Minton, *Canada* 105 D8
Minturn, *U.S.A.* 114 G10
Minturno, *Italy* 30 A6
Minûf, *Egypt* 80 H7
Minusinsk, *Russia* 51 D10
Minutang, *India* 67 E20
Minya el Qamh, *Egypt* 80 H7
Mionica, *Bos.-H.* 42 F3
Mionica, *Serbia, Yug.* 40 B4
Miquelon, *Canada* 102 C4
Miquelon, *St- P. & M.* 103 C8
Mīr, *Niger* 83 C7
Mīr Kūh, *Iran* 71 E8
Mīr Shahdād, *Iran* 71 E8
Mira, *Italy* 29 C9
Mira, *Portugal* 34 E2
Mira →, *Portugal* 35 H2
Mira por vos Cay, *Bahamas* 121 B5
Mirabella Eclano, *Italy* 31 A7
Miraj, *India* 66 L9
Miram Shah, *Pakistan* 68 C4
Miramar, *Argentina* 126 D4
Miramar, *Mozam.* 89 C6
Miramas, *France* 21 E8
Mirambeau, *France* 20 C3
Miramichi, *Canada* 103 C6
Miramichi B., *Canada* 103 C7
Miramont-de-Guyenne, *France* 20 D4
Miranda, *Brazil* 125 H7
Miranda →, *Brazil* 124 G7
Miranda de Ebro, *Spain* 32 C2
Miranda do Corvo, *Portugal* 34 E2
Miranda do Douro, *Portugal* 34 D4
Mirande, *France* 20 E4
Mirandela, *Portugal* 34 D3
Mirándola, *Italy* 28 D8
Mirandópolis, *Brazil* 127 A5
Mirango, *Malawi* 87 E3
Mirano, *Italy* 29 C9
Miras, *Albania* 40 F4
Mirassol, *Brazil* 127 A6
Mirbāţ, *Oman* 74 D5
Mirear, *Egypt* 80 C4
Mirebeau, *Côte-d'Or, France* 19 E12
Mirebeau, *Vienne, France* 18 F7
Mirecourt, *France* 19 D13
Mirgorod = Myrhorod, *Ukraine* 47 H7
Miri, *Malaysia* 62 D4
Miriam Vale, *Australia* 94 C5
Miribel, *France* 19 G11
Mirim, L., *S. Amer.* 127 C5
Mirnyy, *Russia* 51 C12
Miroč, *Serbia, Yug.* 40 B6
Mirokhan, *Pakistan* 68 F3
Mirond L., *Canada* 105 B8
Mirosławiec, *Poland* 44 E3
Mirpur, *Pakistan* 69 C5
Mirpur Batoro, *Pakistan* 68 G3
Mirpur Bibiwari, *Pakistan* 68 E2
Mirpur Khas, *Pakistan* 68 G3
Mirpur Sakro, *Pakistan* 68 G2
Mirria, *Niger* 83 C6
Mirsk, *Poland* 45 H2
Mirtağ, *Turkey* 70 B4
Miryang, *S. Korea* 57 G15
Mirzaani, *Georgia* 49 K8
Mirzapur, *India* 69 G10
Mirzapur-cum-Vindhyachal = Mirzapur, *India* 69 G10
Misantla, *Mexico* 119 D5
Misawa, *Japan* 54 D10
Miscou I., *Canada* 103 C7
Mish'āb, Ra's al, *Si. Arabia* 71 D6
Mishan, *China* 60 B8
Mishawaka, *U.S.A.* 108 E2
Mishbih, Gebel, *Egypt* 80 C3
Mishima, *Japan* 55 G9
Misión, *Mexico* 117 N10
Misiones □, *Argentina* 127 B5
Misiones □, *Paraguay* 126 B4
Miskah, *Si. Arabia* 70 E4
Miskitos, Cayos, *Nic.* 120 D3
Miskolc, *Hungary* 42 B5
Misoke, *Dem. Rep. of the Congo* 86 C2
Misool, *Indonesia* 63 E8
Mişrātah, *Libya* 79 B9
Missanabie, *Canada* 102 C3
Missinaibi →, *Canada* 102 B3
Missinaibi L., *Canada* 102 C3
Mission, *Canada* 104 D4
Mission, *S. Dak., U.S.A.* 112 D4
Mission, *Tex., U.S.A.* 113 M5
Mission Beach, *Australia* 94 B4
Mission Viejo, *U.S.A.* 117 M9
Missirah, *Senegal* 82 C1
Missisa L., *Canada* 102 B2
Missisicabi →, *Canada* 102 B4
Mississagi →, *Canada* 102 C3
Mississauga, *Canada* 110 C5
Mississippi □, *U.S.A.* 113 J10
Mississippi →, *U.S.A.* 113 L10
Mississippi L., *Canada* 111 A8
Mississippi River Delta, *U.S.A.* 113 L9
Mississippi Sd., *U.S.A.* 113 K10
Missoula, *U.S.A.* 114 C7
Missouri □, *U.S.A.* 112 F8
Missouri →, *U.S.A.* 112 F9
Missouri City, *U.S.A.* 113 L7
Missouri Valley, *U.S.A.* 112 E7
Mist, *U.S.A.* 116 E3
Mistassibi →, *Canada* 103 B5
Mistassini, *Canada* 103 C5
Mistassini →, *Canada* 103 C5
Mistassini, L., *Canada* 102 B5
Mistastin L., *Canada* 103 A7
Mistelbach, *Austria* 27 C9
Misterbianco, *Italy* 31 E8
Mistinibi, L., *Canada* 103 A7
Mistretta, *Italy* 31 E7
Misty L., *Canada* 105 B8
Misurata = Mişrātah, *Libya* 79 B9
Mît Ghamr, *Egypt* 80 H7
Mitatib, *Sudan* 81 D4
Mitchell, *Australia* 95 D4
Mitchell, *Canada* 110 C3
Mitchell, *Nebr., U.S.A.* 112 E3
Mitchell, *Oreg., U.S.A.* 114 D3
Mitchell, *S. Dak., U.S.A.* 112 D6
Mitchell →, *Australia* 94 B3
Mitchell, Mt., *U.S.A.* 109 H4
Mitchell Ranges, *Australia* 94 A2
Mitchelstown, *Ireland* 15 D3
Mitha Tiwana, *Pakistan* 68 C5
Mithi, *Pakistan* 68 G3
Míthimna, *Greece* 39 B8
Mithrao, *Pakistan* 68 F3
Mitilíni, *Greece* 39 B8
Mitilinoí, *Greece* 39 D8
Mito, *Japan* 55 F10
Mitrofanovka, *Russia* 47 H10
Mitrovica = Kosovska Mitrovica, *Kosovo, Yug.* 40 D4
Mitsinjo, *Madag.* 89 B8
Mitsiwa, *Eritrea* 81 D4
Mitsiwa Channel, *Eritrea* 81 D5
Mitsukaidō, *Japan* 55 F9
Mittagong, *Australia* 95 E5
Mittelberg, *Austria* 26 D3
Mittelfranken □, *Germany* 25 F6
Mittellandkanal →, *Germany* 24 C4
Mittenwalde, *Germany* 24 C9
Mittersill, *Austria* 26 D5
Mitterteich, *Germany* 25 F8
Mittimatalik = Pond Inlet, *Canada* 101 A12
Mittweida, *Germany* 24 E8
Mitú, *Colombia* 124 C4
Mitumba, *Tanzania* 86 D3
Mitumba, Mts., *Dem. Rep. of the Congo* 86 D2
Mitwaba, *Dem. Rep. of the Congo* 87 D2
Mityana, *Uganda* 86 B3
Mixteco →, *Mexico* 119 D5
Miyagi □, *Japan* 54 E10
Miyāh, W. el →, *Egypt* 80 C3
Miyāh, W. el →, *Syria* 70 C3
Miyake-Jima, *Japan* 55 G9
Miyako, *Japan* 54 E10
Miyako-Jima, *Japan* 55 M2
Miyako-Rettō, *Japan* 55 M2
Miyakonojō, *Japan* 55 J5
Miyani, *India* 68 J3
Miyanoura-Dake, *Japan* 55 J5
Miyazaki, *Japan* 55 J5
Miyazaki □, *Japan* 55 H5
Miyazu, *Japan* 55 G7
Miyet, Bahr el = Dead Sea, *Asia* 75 D4
Miyi, *China* 58 D4
Miyoshi, *Japan* 55 G6
Miyun, *China* 56 D9
Miyun Shuiku, *China* 57 D9
Mizan Teferi, *Ethiopia* 81 F4
Mizdah, *Libya* 79 B8
Mizen Hd., *Cork, Ireland* 15 E2
Mizen Hd., *Wick., Ireland* 15 D5
Mizhi, *China* 56 F6
Mizil, *Romania* 43 F11
Mizoram □, *India* 67 H18
Miẕpe Ramon, *Israel* 75 E3
Mizusawa, *Japan* 54 E10
Mjällby, *Sweden* 11 H8
Mjöbäck, *Sweden* 11 G6
Mjölby, *Sweden* 11 F9
Mjörn, *Sweden* 11 G6
Mjøsa, *Norway* 9 F14
Mkata, *Tanzania* 86 D4
Mkokotoni, *Tanzania* 86 D4
Mkomazi, *Tanzania* 86 C4
Mkomazi →, *S. Africa* 89 E5
Mkulwe, *Tanzania* 87 D3
Mkumbi, Ras, *Tanzania* 86 D4
Mkushi, *Zambia* 87 E2
Mkushi River, *Zambia* 87 E2
Mkuze, *S. Africa* 89 D5
Mladá Boleslav, *Czech Rep.* 26 A7
Mladenovac, *Serbia, Yug.* 40 B4
Mlala Hills, *Tanzania* 86 D3
Mlange = Mulanje, *Malawi* 87 F4
Mlanje, Pic, *Malawi* 85 H7
Mlava →, *Serbia, Yug.* 40 B5
Mława, *Poland* 45 E7
Mlinište, *Bos.-H.* 29 D13
Mljet, *Croatia* 29 F14
Mljetski Kanal, *Croatia* 29 F14
Młynary, *Poland* 44 D6
Mmabatho, *S. Africa* 88 D4
Mme, *Cameroon* 83 D7
Mnichovo Hradiště, *Czech Rep.* 26 A7
Mo i Rana, *Norway* 8 C16
Moa, *Cuba* 121 B4
Moa, *Indonesia* 63 F7
Moa →, *S. Leone* 82 D2
Moab, *U.S.A.* 115 G9
Moala, *Fiji* 91 D8
Moama, *Australia* 95 F3
Moamba, *Mozam.* 89 D5
Moapa, *U.S.A.* 117 J12
Moate, *Ireland* 15 C4
Moba, *Dem. Rep. of the Congo* 86 D2
Mobārakābād, *Iran* 71 D7
Mobaye, *C.A.R.* 84 D4
Mobayi, *Dem. Rep. of the Congo* 84 D4
Moberley Lake, *Canada* 104 B4
Moberly, *U.S.A.* 112 F8
Mobile, *U.S.A.* 109 K1
Mobile B., *U.S.A.* 109 K2
Mobridge, *U.S.A.* 112 C4
Mobutu Sese Seko, L. = Albert, L., *Africa* 86 B3
Moc Chau, *Vietnam* 64 B5
Moc Hoa, *Vietnam* 65 G5
Mocabe Kasari, *Dem. Rep. of the Congo* 87 D2
Moçambique, *Mozam.* 87 F5
Moçâmedes = Namibe, *Angola* 85 H2
Mocanaqua, *U.S.A.* 111 E8
Mochudi, *Botswana* 88 C4
Mocimboa da Praia, *Mozam.* 87 E5
Mociu, *Romania* 43 D9
Möckeln, *Sweden* 11 H8
Mockfjärd, *Sweden* 10 D8
Moclips, *U.S.A.* 116 C2
Mocoa, *Colombia* 124 C3
Mococa, *Brazil* 127 A6
Mocorito, *Mexico* 118 B3
Moctezuma, *Mexico* 118 B3
Moctezuma →, *Mexico* 119 C5
Mocuba, *Mozam.* 87 F4
Mocúzari, Presa, *Mexico* 118 B3
Modane, *France* 21 C10
Modasa, *India* 68 H5
Modder →, *S. Africa* 88 D3
Modderrivier, *S. Africa* 88 D3
Módena, *Italy* 28 D7
Modena, *U.S.A.* 115 H7
Modesto, *U.S.A.* 116 H6
Módica, *Italy* 31 F7
Mödling, *Austria* 27 C9
Modo, *Sudan* 81 F3
Modra, *Slovak Rep.* 27 C10
Modriča, *Bos.-H.* 42 F3
Moe, *Australia* 95 F4
Moebase, *Mozam.* 87 F4
Moëlan-sur-Mer, *France* 18 E3
Moengo, *Surinam* 125 B8
Moffat, *U.K.* 14 F5
Moga, *India* 68 D6
Mogadishu = Muqdisho, *Somali Rep.* 74 G4
Mogador = Essaouira, *Morocco* 78 B4
Mogadouro, *Portugal* 34 D4
Mogalakwena →, *S. Africa* 89 C4
Mogami-Gawa →, *Japan* 54 E10
Mogán, *Canary Is.* 37 G4
Mogaung, *Burma* 67 G20
Mogente = Moixent, *Spain* 33 G4
Mogho, *Ethiopia* 81 G5
Mogi das Cruzes, *Brazil* 127 A6
Mogi-Guaçu →, *Brazil* 127 A6
Mogi-Mirim, *Brazil* 127 A6
Mogielnica, *Poland* 45 G7
Mogige, *Ethiopia* 81 F4
Mogilev = Mahilyow, *Belarus* 46 F6
Mogilev-Podolskiy = Mohyliv-Podilskyy, *Ukraine* 47 H4
Mogilno, *Poland* 45 F4
Mogincual, *Mozam.* 87 F5
Mogliano Véneto, *Italy* 29 C9
Mogocha, *Russia* 51 D12
Mogok, *Burma* 67 H20
Mogollon Rim, *U.S.A.* 115 J8
Mógoro, *Italy* 30 C1
Mograt, *Sudan* 80 D3
Moguer, *Spain* 35 H4
Mogumber, *Australia* 93 F2
Mohács, *Hungary* 42 E3
Mohales Hoek, *Lesotho* 88 E4
Mohall, *U.S.A.* 112 A4
Moḩammadābād, *Iran* 71 B8
Mohammedia, *Morocco* 78 B4
Mohana →, *India* 69 G11
Mohanlalganj, *India* 69 F9
Mohave, L., *U.S.A.* 117 K12
Mohawk →, *U.S.A.* 111 D11
Moheda, *Sweden* 11 G8
Mohenjodaro, *Pakistan* 68 F3
Mohicanville Reservoir, *U.S.A.* 110 F3
Möhne →, *Germany* 24 D3
Mohoro, *Tanzania* 86 D4
Mohyliv-Podilskyy, *Ukraine* 47 H4
Moia, *Sudan* 81 F2
Moidart, L., *U.K.* 14 E3
Moineşti, *Romania* 43 D11
Moira →, *Canada* 110 B7
Moirans, *France* 21 C9
Moirans-en-Montagne, *France* 19 F12
Moíres, *Greece* 36 D6
Moisaküla, *Estonia* 9 G21
Moisie, *Canada* 103 B6
Moisie →, *Canada* 103 B6
Moissac, *France* 20 D5
Moita, *Portugal* 35 G2
Moixent, *Spain* 33 G4
Möja, *Sweden* 10 E12
Mojácar, *Spain* 33 H3
Mojados, *Spain* 34 D6
Mojave, *U.S.A.* 117 K8
Mojave Desert, *U.S.A.* 117 L10
Mojiang, *China* 58 F3
Mojjo →, *Ethiopia* 81 F5
Mojkovac, *Montenegro, Yug.* 40 D3
Mojo, *Bolivia* 126 A2
Mojo, *Ethiopia* 81 F4
Mojokerto, *Indonesia* 63 G15
Mokai, *N.Z.* 91 H5
Mokambo, *Dem. Rep. of the Congo* 87 E2
Mokameh, *India* 69 G11
Mokau, *N.Z.* 91 H5
Mokelumne →, *U.S.A.* 116 G5
Mokelumne Hill, *U.S.A.* 116 G6
Mokhós, *Greece* 36 D7
Mokhotlong, *Lesotho* 89 D4
Möklinta, *Sweden* 10 D10
Mokokchung, *India* 67 F19
Mokolo, *Cameroon* 83 C7
Mokolo →, *S. Africa* 89 C4
Mokp'o, *S. Korea* 57 G14
Mokra Gora, *Yugoslavia* 40 D4
Mokronog, *Slovenia* 29 C12
Moksha →, *Russia* 48 C6
Mokshan, *Russia* 48 D7
Mokwa, *Nigeria* 83 D6
Mol, *Belgium* 17 C5
Mola di Bari, *Italy* 31 A10
Molale, *Ethiopia* 81 E4
Moláoi, *Greece* 38 E4
Molara, *Italy* 30 B2
Molat, *Croatia* 29 D11
Molchanovo, *Russia* 50 D9
Mold, *U.K.* 12 D4
Moldava nad Bodvou, *Slovak Rep.* 27 C14
Moldavia = Moldova ■, *Europe* 43 C13
Moldavia, *Romania* 43 D12
Molde, *Norway* 8 E12
Moldova ■, *Europe* 43 C13
Moldova Nouă, *Romania* 42 F6
Moldoveanu, Vf., *Romania* 43 E9
Moldoviţa, *Romania* 43 C10
Mole →, *U.K.* 13 F7
Mole Creek, *Australia* 94 G4
Molepolole, *Botswana* 88 C4
Molfetta, *Italy* 31 A9
Molina de Aragón, *Spain* 32 E3
Molina de Segura, *Spain* 33 G3
Moline, *U.S.A.* 112 E9
Molinella, *Italy* 29 D8
Molinos, *Argentina* 126 B2
Moliro, *Dem. Rep. of the Congo* 86 D3
Moliterno, *Italy* 31 B8
Molkom, *Sweden* 10 E7
Mölle, *Sweden* 11 H6
Molledo, *Spain* 34 B6
Mollendo, *Peru* 124 G4
Mollerin, L., *Australia* 93 F2
Mollerussa, *Spain* 32 D5
Mollina, *Spain* 35 H6
Mölln, *Germany* 24 B6
Mölltorp, *Sweden* 11 F8
Mölnlycke, *Sweden* 11 G6
Molochansk, *Ukraine* 47 J8
Molochnoye, Ozero, *Ukraine* 47 J8
Molodechno = Maladzyechna, *Belarus* 46 E4
Molokai, *U.S.A.* 106 H16
Molong, *Australia* 95 E4
Molopo →, *Africa* 88 D3
Mólos, *Greece* 38 C4

Moshi

Molotov = Perm, *Russia* 50 D6
Molsheim, *France* 19 D14
Molson L., *Canada* 105 C9
Molteno, *S. Africa* 88 E4
Molu, *Indonesia* 63 F8
Molucca Sea, *Indonesia* 63 E6
Moluccas = Maluku, *Indonesia* 63 E7
Moma, *Dem. Rep. of the Congo* 86 C1
Moma, *Mozam.* 87 F4
Mombasa, *Kenya* 86 C4
Mombetsu, *Japan* 54 B11
Mombuey, *Spain* 34 C4
Momchilgrad, *Bulgaria* 41 E9
Momi, *Dem. Rep. of the Congo* 86 C2
Mompós, *Colombia* 124 B4
Møn, *Denmark* 11 K6
Mon □, *Burma* 67 L20
Mona, Canal de la, *W. Indies* 121 C6
Mona, Isla, *Puerto Rico* 121 C6
Mona, Pta., *Costa Rica* 120 E3
Monaca, *U.S.A.* 110 F4
Monaco ■, *Europe* 21 E11
Monadhliath Mts., *U.K.* 14 D4
Monadnock, Mt., *U.S.A.* 111 D12
Monaghan, *Ireland* 15 B5
Monaghan □, *Ireland* 15 B5
Monahans, *U.S.A.* 113 K3
Monapo, *Mozam.* 87 E5
Monar, L., *U.K.* 14 D3
Monarch Mt., *Canada* 104 C3
Monashee Mts., *Canada* 104 C5
Monasterevin, *Ireland* 15 C4
Monastir = Bitola, *Macedonia* 40 E5
Moncada, *Phil.* 61 D4
Moncalieri, *Italy* 28 D4
Moncalvo, *Italy* 28 C5
Moncão, *Portugal* 34 C2
Moncarapacho, *Portugal* 35 H3
Moncayo, Sierra del, *Spain* 32 D3
Mönchengladbach, *Germany* 24 D2
Monchique, *Portugal* 35 H2
Moncks Corner, *U.S.A.* 109 J5
Monclova, *Mexico* 118 B4
Moncontour, *France* 18 D4
Moncton, *Canada* 103 C7
Mondariz, *Spain* 34 C2
Mondego →, *Portugal* 34 E2
Mondego, C., *Portugal* 34 E2
Mondeodo, *Indonesia* 63 E6
Mondeville, *France* 18 C6
Mondolfo, *Italy* 29 E10
Mondoñedo, *Spain* 34 B3
Mondovì, *Italy* 28 D4
Mondragon, *Phil.* 61 E6
Mondragone, *Italy* 30 A6
Mondrain I., *Australia* 93 F3
Monemvasía, *Greece* 38 E5
Monessen, *U.S.A.* 110 F5
Monesterio, *Spain* 35 G4
Monestier-de-Clermont, *France* 21 D9
Monett, *U.S.A.* 113 G8
Moneymore, *U.K.* 15 B5
Monfalcone, *Italy* 29 C10
Monflanquin, *France* 20 D4
Monforte, *Portugal* 35 F3
Monforte de Lemos, *Spain* 34 C3
Mong Hsu, *Burma* 58 G2
Mong Kung, *Burma* 67 J20
Mong Nai, *Burma* 67 J20
Mong Pawk, *Burma* 67 H21
Mong Ping, *Burma* 58 G2
Mong Ton, *Burma* 67 J21
Mong Wa, *Burma* 67 J22
Mong Yai, *Burma* 67 H21
Mongalla, *Sudan* 81 F3
Mongers, L., *Australia* 93 E2
Monghyr = Munger, *India* 69 G12
Mongibello = Etna, *Italy* 31 E7
Mongo, *Chad* 79 F9
Mongo →, *S. Leone* 82 D2
Mongolia ■, *Asia* 51 E10
Mongonu, *Nigeria* 83 C7
Mongu, *Zambia* 85 H4
Môngua, *Angola* 88 B2
Monifieth, *U.K.* 14 E6
Monistrol-sur-Loire, *France* 21 C8
Monkey Bay, *Malawi* 87 E4
Monkey Mia, *Australia* 93 E1
Monkey River, *Belize* 119 D7
Mońki, *Poland* 44 E9
Monkoto, *Dem. Rep. of the Congo* 84 E4
Monkton, *Canada* 110 C3
Monmouth, *U.K.* 13 F5
Monmouth, *Ill., U.S.A.* 112 E9
Monmouth, *Oreg., U.S.A.* 114 D2
Monmouthshire □, *U.K.* 13 F5
Mono L., *U.S.A.* 116 H7
Monolith, *U.S.A.* 117 K8
Monólithos, *Greece* 36 C9
Monongahela, *U.S.A.* 110 F5
Monópoli, *Italy* 31 B10
Monor, *Hungary* 42 C4
Monóvar, *Spain* 33 G4
Monreal del Campo, *Spain* 32 E3
Monreale, *Italy* 30 D6
Monroe, *Ga., U.S.A.* 109 J4
Monroe, *La., U.S.A.* 113 J8
Monroe, *Mich., U.S.A.* 108 E4
Monroe, *N.C., U.S.A.* 109 H5
Monroe, *N.Y., U.S.A.* 111 E10
Monroe, *Utah, U.S.A.* 115 G7
Monroe, *Wash., U.S.A.* 116 C5
Monroe, *Wis., U.S.A.* 112 D10
Monroe City, *U.S.A.* 112 F9
Monroeton, *U.S.A.* 111 E8
Monroeville, *Ala., U.S.A.* 109 K2
Monroeville, *Pa., U.S.A.* 110 F5
Monrovia, *Liberia* 82 D2
Mons, *Belgium* 17 D3
Møns Klint, *Denmark* 11 K6
Monsaraz, *Portugal* 35 G3
Monse, *Indonesia* 63 E6
Monségur, *France* 20 D4
Monsélice, *Italy* 29 C8
Mönsterås, *Sweden* 11 G10
Mont Cenis, Col du, *France* 21 C10
Mont-de-Marsan, *France* 20 E3
Mont-Joli, *Canada* 103 C6
Mont-Laurier, *Canada* 102 C4
Mont-Louis, *Canada* 103 C6
Mont-roig del Camp, *Spain* 32 D5
Mont-St-Michel, Le = Le Mont-St-Michel, *France* 18 D5
Mont Tremblant, Parc Recr. du, *Canada* 102 C5
Montabaur, *Germany* 24 E3
Montagnac, *France* 20 E7
Montagnana, *Italy* 29 C8
Montagu, *S. Africa* 88 E3
Montagu I., *Antarctica* 5 B1
Montague, *Canada* 103 C7
Montague, I., *Mexico* 118 A2
Montague Ra., *Australia* 93 E2
Montague Sd., *Australia* 92 B4
Montaigu, *France* 18 F5
Montalbán, *Spain* 32 E4
Montalbano Iónico, *Italy* 31 B9
Montalbo, *Spain* 32 F2
Montalcino, *Italy* 29 E8
Montalegre, *Portugal* 34 D3
Montalto, *Italy* 31 D8
Montalto di Castro, *Italy* 29 F8
Montalto Uffugo, *Italy* 31 C9
Montalvo, *U.S.A.* 117 L7
Montamarta, *Spain* 34 D5
Montana, *Bulgaria* 40 C7
Montaña, *Peru* 124 E4
Montana □, *Bulgaria* 40 C7
Montana □, *U.S.A.* 114 C9
Montaña Clara, I., *Canary Is.* 37 E6
Montánchez, *Spain* 35 F4
Montargil, *Portugal* 35 F2
Montargis, *France* 19 E9
Montauban, *France* 20 D5
Montauk, *U.S.A.* 111 E13
Montauk Pt., *U.S.A.* 111 E13
Montbard, *France* 19 E11
Montbarrey, *France* 19 E12
Montbéliard, *France* 19 E13
Montblanc, *Spain* 32 D6
Montbrison, *France* 21 C8
Montcalm, Pic de, *France* 20 F5
Montceau-les-Mines, *France* 19 F11
Montcenis, *France* 21 B8
Montclair, *U.S.A.* 111 F10
Montcornet, *France* 19 C11
Montcuq, *France* 20 D5
Montdidier, *France* 19 C9
Monte Albán, *Mexico* 119 D5
Monte Alegre, *Brazil* 125 D8
Monte Azul, *Brazil* 125 G10
Monte Bello Is., *Australia* 92 D2
Monte-Carlo, *Monaco* 21 E11
Monte Caseros, *Argentina* 126 C4
Monte Comán, *Argentina* 126 C2
Monte Cristi, *Dom. Rep.* 121 C5
Monte Lindo →, *Paraguay* 126 A4
Monte Patria, *Chile* 126 C1
Monte Quemado, *Argentina* 126 B3
Monte Redondo, *Portugal* 34 F2
Monte Rio, *U.S.A.* 116 G4
Monte San Giovanni Campano, *Italy* 30 A6
Monte San Savino, *Italy* 29 E8
Monte Sant' Ángelo, *Italy* 29 G12
Monte Santu, C. di, *Italy* 30 B2
Monte Vista, *U.S.A.* 115 H10
Monteagudo, *Argentina* 127 B5
Montealegre del Castillo, *Spain* 33 G3
Montebello, *Canada* 102 C5
Montebello Iónico, *Italy* 31 E8
Montebelluna, *Italy* 29 C9
Montebourg, *France* 18 C5
Montecastrilli, *Italy* 29 F9
Montecatini Terme, *Italy* 28 E7
Montecito, *U.S.A.* 117 L7
Montecristo, *Italy* 28 F7
Montefalco, *Italy* 29 F9
Montefiascone, *Italy* 29 F9
Montefrío, *Spain* 35 H7
Montegiórgio, *Italy* 29 E10
Montego Bay, *Jamaica* 120 C4
Montehermoso, *Spain* 34 E4
Montejicar, *Spain* 35 H7
Montélimar, *France* 21 D8
Montella, *Italy* 31 B8
Montellano, *Spain* 35 J5
Montello, *U.S.A.* 112 D10
Montemor-o-Novo, *Portugal* 35 G2
Montemor-o-Velho, *Portugal* 34 E2
Montemorelos, *Mexico* 119 B5
Montendre, *France* 20 C3
Montenegro, *Brazil* 127 B5
Montenegro □, *Yugoslavia* 40 D3
Montenero di Bisáccia, *Italy* 29 G11
Montepuez, *Mozam.* 87 E4
Montepuez →, *Mozam.* 87 E5
Montepulciano, *Italy* 29 E8
Montereale, *Italy* 29 F10
Montereau-Faut-Yonne, *France* 19 D9
Monterey, *U.S.A.* 116 J5
Monterey B., *U.S.A.* 116 J5
Montería, *Colombia* 124 B3
Monteros, *Argentina* 126 B2
Monterotondo, *Italy* 29 F9
Monterrey, *Mexico* 118 B4
Montes Claros, *Brazil* 125 G10
Montesano, *U.S.A.* 116 D3
Montesano sulla Marcellana, *Italy* 31 B8
Montesárchio, *Italy* 31 A7
Montescaglioso, *Italy* 31 B9
Montesilvano, *Italy* 29 F11
Montevarchi, *Italy* 29 E8
Montevideo, *Uruguay* 127 C4
Montevideo, *U.S.A.* 112 C7
Montezuma, *U.S.A.* 112 E8
Montfaucon, *France* 18 E5
Montfaucon-d'Argonne, *France* 19 C12
Montfaucon-en-Velay, *France* 21 C8
Montfort, *France* 18 D5
Montfort-le-Gesnois, *France* 18 D7
Montgenèvre, *France* 21 D10
Montgomery = Sahiwal, *Pakistan* 68 D5
Montgomery, *U.K.* 13 E4
Montgomery, *Ala., U.S.A.* 109 J2
Montgomery, *Pa., U.S.A.* 110 E8
Montgomery, *W. Va., U.S.A.* 108 F5
Montgomery City, *U.S.A.* 112 F9
Montguyon, *France* 20 C3
Monthermé, *France* 19 C11
Monthey, *Switz.* 25 J2
Monthois, *France* 19 C11
Monti, *Italy* 30 B2
Monticelli d'Ongina, *Italy* 28 C6
Monticello, *Ark., U.S.A.* 113 J9
Monticello, *Fla., U.S.A.* 109 K4
Monticello, *Ind., U.S.A.* 108 E2
Monticello, *Iowa, U.S.A.* 112 D9
Monticello, *Ky., U.S.A.* 109 G3
Monticello, *Minn., U.S.A.* 112 C8
Monticello, *Miss., U.S.A.* 113 K9
Monticello, *N.Y., U.S.A.* 111 E10
Monticello, *Utah, U.S.A.* 115 H9
Montichiari, *Italy* 28 C7
Montier-en-Der, *France* 19 D11
Montignac, *France* 20 C5
Montigny-les-Metz, *France* 19 C13
Montigny-sur-Aube, *France* 19 E11
Montijo, *Portugal* 35 G2
Montijo, *Spain* 35 G4
Montilla, *Spain* 35 H6
Montivilliers, *France* 18 C7
Montluçon, *France* 19 F9
Montmagny, *Canada* 103 C5
Montmarault, *France* 19 F9
Montmartre, *Canada* 105 C8
Montmédy, *France* 19 C12
Montmélian, *France* 21 C10
Montmirail, *France* 19 D10
Montmoreau-St-Cybard, *France* 20 C4
Montmorillon, *France* 20 B4
Montmort-Lucy, *France* 19 D10
Monto, *Australia* 94 C5
Montoire-sur-le-Loir, *France* 18 E7
Montório al Vomano, *Italy* 29 F10
Montoro, *Spain* 35 G6
Montour Falls, *U.S.A.* 110 D8
Montoursville, *U.S.A.* 110 E8
Montpelier, *Idaho, U.S.A.* 114 E8
Montpelier, *Vt., U.S.A.* 111 B12
Montpellier, *France* 20 E7
Montpezat-de-Quercy, *France* 20 D5
Montpon-Ménestérol, *France* 20 D4
Montréal, *Canada* 102 C5
Montréal, *Aude, France* 20 E6
Montréal, *Gers, France* 20 E4
Montreal →, *Canada* 102 C3
Montreal L., *Canada* 105 C7
Montreal Lake, *Canada* 105 C7
Montredon-Labessonnié, *France* 20 E6
Montrésor, *France* 18 E8
Montret, *France* 19 F12
Montreuil, *Pas-de-Calais, France* 19 B8
Montreuil, *Seine-St-Denis, France* 19 D9
Montreuil-Bellay, *France* 18 E6
Montreux, *Switz.* 25 J2
Montrevel-en-Bresse, *France* 19 F12
Montrichard, *France* 18 E8
Montrose, *U.K.* 14 E6
Montrose, *Colo., U.S.A.* 115 G10
Montrose, *Pa., U.S.A.* 111 E9
Monts, Pte. des, *Canada* 103 C6
Montsalvy, *France* 20 D6
Montsant, Serra de, *Spain* 32 D6
Montsauche-les-Settons, *France* 19 E11
Montsec, Serra del, *Spain* 32 C5
Montserrat, *Spain* 32 D6
Montserrat ■, *W. Indies* 121 C7
Montuenga, *Spain* 34 D6
Montuiri, *Spain* 37 B9
Monywa, *Burma* 67 H19
Monza, *Italy* 28 C6
Monze, *Zambia* 87 F2
Monze, C., *Pakistan* 68 G2
Monzón, *Spain* 32 D5
Mooers, *U.S.A.* 111 B11
Mooi →, *S. Africa* 89 D5
Mooi River, *S. Africa* 89 D4
Moonah →, *Australia* 94 C2
Moonda, L., *Australia* 94 D3
Moonie, *Australia* 95 D5
Moonie →, *Australia* 95 D4
Moonta, *Australia* 95 E2
Moora, *Australia* 93 F2
Moorcroft, *U.S.A.* 112 C2
Moore →, *Australia* 93 F2
Moore, L., *Australia* 93 E2
Moore Park, *Australia* 94 C5
Moore Reefs, *Australia* 94 B4
Moorefield, *U.S.A.* 108 F6
Moores Res., *U.S.A.* 111 B13
Moorfoot Hills, *U.K.* 14 F5
Moorhead, *U.S.A.* 112 B6
Moormerland, *Germany* 24 B3
Moorpark, *U.S.A.* 117 L8
Moorreesburg, *S. Africa* 88 E2
Moosburg, *Germany* 25 G7
Moose →, *Canada* 102 B3
Moose →, *U.S.A.* 111 C9
Moose Creek, *Canada* 111 A10
Moose Factory, *Canada* 102 B3
Moose Jaw, *Canada* 105 C7
Moose Jaw →, *Canada* 105 C7
Moose Lake, *Canada* 105 C8
Moose Lake, *U.S.A.* 112 B8
Moose Mountain Prov. Park, *Canada* 105 D8
Moosehead L., *U.S.A.* 109 C11
Mooselookmeguntic L., *U.S.A.* 109 C10
Moosilauke, Mt., *U.S.A.* 111 B13
Moosomin, *Canada* 105 C8
Moosonee, *Canada* 102 B3
Moosup, *U.S.A.* 111 E13
Mopane, *S. Africa* 89 C4
Mopeia Velha, *Mozam.* 87 F4
Mopipi, *Botswana* 88 C3
Mopoi, *C.A.R.* 86 A2
Mopti, *Mali* 82 C4
Moqatta, *Sudan* 81 E4
Moqor, *Afghan.* 68 C2
Moquegua, *Peru* 124 G4
Mór, *Hungary* 42 C3
Mora, *Cameroon* 83 C7
Móra, *Portugal* 35 G2
Mora, *Spain* 35 F7
Mora, *Sweden* 10 C8
Mora, *Minn., U.S.A.* 112 C8
Mora, *N. Mex., U.S.A.* 115 J11
Mora →, *U.S.A.* 113 H2
Mora de Ebro = Mòra d'Ebre, *Spain* 32 D5
Mora de Rubielos, *Spain* 32 E4
Mòra d'Ebre, *Spain* 32 D5
Mòra la Nova, *Spain* 32 D5
Morača →, *Montenegro, Yug.* 40 D3
Moradabad, *India* 69 E8
Morafenobe, *Madag.* 89 B7
Morąg, *Poland* 44 E6
Moral de Calatrava, *Spain* 35 G7
Moraleja, *Spain* 34 E4
Moramanga, *Madag.* 89 B8
Moran, *Kans., U.S.A.* 113 G7
Moran, *Wyo., U.S.A.* 114 E8
Moranbah, *Australia* 94 C4
Morano Cálabro, *Italy* 31 C9
Morant Cays, *Jamaica* 120 C4
Morant Pt., *Jamaica* 120 C4
Morar, *India* 68 F8
Morar, L., *U.K.* 14 E3
Moratalla, *Spain* 33 G3
Moratuwa, *Sri Lanka* 66 R11
Morava →, *Slovak Rep.* 27 C9
Moravia, *U.S.A.* 111 D8
Moravian Hts. = Českomoravská Vrchovina, *Czech Rep.* 26 B8
Moravica →, *Serbia, Yug.* 40 C4
Moraviţa, *Romania* 42 E6
Moravská Třebová, *Czech Rep.* 27 B9
Moravské Budějovice, *Czech Rep.* 26 B8
Morawa, *Australia* 93 E2
Morawhanna, *Guyana* 124 B7
Moray □, *U.K.* 14 D5
Moray Firth, *U.K.* 14 D5
Morbach, *Germany* 25 F3
Morbegno, *Italy* 28 B6
Morbi, *India* 68 H4
Morbihan □, *France* 18 E4
Mörbylånga, *Sweden* 11 H10
Morcenx, *France* 20 D3
Morcone, *Italy* 31 A7
Mordelles, *France* 18 D5
Morden, *Canada* 105 D9
Mordoğan, *Turkey* 39 C8
Mordovian Republic = Mordvinia □, *Russia* 48 C7
Mordovo, *Russia* 48 D5
Mordvinia □, *Russia* 48 C7
Mordy, *Poland* 45 F9
Morea, *Greece* 6 H10
Moreau →, *U.S.A.* 112 C4
Morecambe, *U.K.* 12 C5
Morecambe B., *U.K.* 12 C5
Moree, *Australia* 95 D4
Morehead, *U.S.A.* 108 F4
Morehead City, *U.S.A.* 109 H7
Morel →, *India* 68 F7
Morelia, *Mexico* 118 D4
Morella, *Australia* 94 C3
Morella, *Spain* 32 E4
Morelos, *Mexico* 118 B3
Morelos □, *Mexico* 119 D5
Morena, *India* 68 F8
Morena, Sierra, *Spain* 35 G7
Moreni, *Romania* 43 F10
Moreno Valley, *U.S.A.* 117 M10
Moresby I., *Canada* 104 C2
Morestel, *France* 21 C9
Moreton I., *Australia* 95 D5
Moreuil, *France* 19 C9
Morey, *Spain* 37 B10
Morez, *France* 19 F13
Morgan, *U.S.A.* 114 F8
Morgan City, *U.S.A.* 113 L9
Morgan Hill, *U.S.A.* 116 H5
Morganfield, *U.S.A.* 108 G2
Morganton, *U.S.A.* 109 H5
Morgantown, *U.S.A.* 108 F6
Morgenzon, *S. Africa* 89 D4
Morges, *Switz.* 25 J2
Morghak, *Iran* 71 D8
Morgongåva, *Sweden* 10 E10
Morhange, *France* 19 D13
Morhar →, *India* 69 G11
Mori, *Italy* 28 C7
Moriarty, *U.S.A.* 115 J10
Moribaya, *Guinea* 82 D3
Morice L., *Canada* 104 C3
Moriki, *Nigeria* 83 C6
Morinville, *Canada* 104 C6
Morioka, *Japan* 54 E10
Moris, *Mexico* 118 B3
Morlaàs, *France* 20 E3
Morlaix, *France* 18 D3
Mörlunda, *Sweden* 11 G9
Mormanno, *Italy* 31 C8
Mormant, *France* 19 D9
Mornington, *Australia* 95 F4
Mornington, I., *Chile* 128 F1
Mornington I., *Australia* 94 B2
Mórnos →, *Greece* 38 C3
Moro, *Pakistan* 68 F2
Moro, *Sudan* 81 E3
Moro →, *Pakistan* 68 E2
Moro G., *Phil.* 61 H5
Morocco ■, *N. Afr.* 78 B4
Morogoro, *Tanzania* 86 D4
Morogoro □, *Tanzania* 86 D4
Moroleón, *Mexico* 118 C4
Morombe, *Madag.* 89 C7
Moron, *Argentina* 126 C4
Morón, *Cuba* 120 B4
Morón de Almazán, *Spain* 32 D2
Morón de la Frontera, *Spain* 35 H5
Morona →, *Peru* 124 D3
Morondava, *Madag.* 89 C7
Morondo, *Ivory C.* 82 D3
Morongo Valley, *U.S.A.* 117 L10
Moroni, *Comoros Is.* 77 H8
Moroni, *U.S.A.* 114 G8
Moronou, *Ivory C.* 82 D4
Morotai, *Indonesia* 63 D7
Moroto, *Uganda* 86 B3
Moroto Summit, *Kenya* 86 B3
Morozov, *Bulgaria* 41 D9
Morozovsk, *Russia* 49 F5
Morpeth, *U.K.* 12 B6
Morphou, *Cyprus* 36 D11
Morphou Bay, *Cyprus* 36 D11
Morrilton, *U.S.A.* 113 H8
Morrinhos, *Brazil* 125 G9
Morrinsville, *N.Z.* 91 G5
Morris, *Canada* 105 D9
Morris, *Ill., U.S.A.* 112 E10
Morris, *Minn., U.S.A.* 112 C7
Morris, *N.Y., U.S.A.* 111 D9
Morris, *Pa., U.S.A.* 110 E7
Morris, Mt., *Australia* 93 E5
Morrisburg, *Canada* 111 B9
Morristown, *Ariz., U.S.A.* 115 K7
Morristown, *N.J., U.S.A.* 111 F10
Morristown, *N.Y., U.S.A.* 111 B9
Morristown, *Tenn., U.S.A.* 109 G4
Morrisville, *N.Y., U.S.A.* 111 D9
Morrisville, *Pa., U.S.A.* 111 F10
Morrisville, *Vt., U.S.A.* 111 B12
Morro, Pta., *Chile* 126 B1
Morro Bay, *U.S.A.* 116 K6
Morro del Jable, *Canary Is.* 37 F5
Morro Jable, Pta. de, *Canary Is.* 37 F5
Morrosquillo, G. de, *Colombia* 120 E4
Mörrum, *Sweden* 11 H8
Morrumbene, *Mozam.* 89 C6
Mörrumsån →, *Sweden* 11 H8
Mors, *Denmark* 11 H2
Morshansk, *Russia* 48 D5
Mörsil, *Sweden* 10 A7
Mortagne →, *France* 19 D13
Mortagne-au-Perche, *France* 18 D7
Mortagne-sur-Gironde, *France* 20 C3
Mortagne-sur-Sèvre, *France* 18 F6
Mortain, *France* 18 D6
Mortara, *Italy* 28 C5
Morteau, *France* 19 E13
Morteros, *Argentina* 126 C3
Mortlach, *Canada* 105 C7
Mortlake, *Australia* 95 F3
Morton, *Tex., U.S.A.* 113 J3
Morton, *Wash., U.S.A.* 116 D4
Morundah, *Australia* 95 E4
Moruya, *Australia* 95 F5
Morvan, *France* 19 E11
Morven, *Australia* 95 D4
Morvern, *U.K.* 14 E3
Morwell, *Australia* 95 F4
Moryń, *Poland* 45 F1
Morzine, *France* 19 F13
Mosalsk, *Russia* 46 E8
Mosbach, *Germany* 25 F5
Mošćenice, *Croatia* 29 C11
Mosciano Sant' Ángelo, *Italy* 29 F10
Moscos Is., *Burma* 64 E1
Moscow = Moskva, *Russia* 46 E9
Moscow, *Idaho, U.S.A.* 114 C5
Moscow, *Pa., U.S.A.* 111 E9
Mosel →, *Europe* 19 B14
Moselle = Mosel →, *Europe* 19 B14
Moselle □, *France* 19 D13
Moses Lake, *U.S.A.* 114 C4
Mosgiel, *N.Z.* 91 L3
Moshaweng →, *S. Africa* 88 D3
Moshi, *Tanzania* 86 C4

Moshupa, *Botswana* 88 C4
Mosina, *Poland* 45 F3
Mosjøen, *Norway* 8 D15
Moskenesøya, *Norway* 8 C15
Moskenstraumen, *Norway* 8 C15
Moskva, *Russia* 46 E9
Moskva →, *Russia* 46 E10
Moslavačka Gora, *Croatia* . . 29 C13
Mosomane, *Botswana* 88 C4
Mosonmagyaróvár, *Hungary* . 42 C2
Mošorin, *Serbia, Yug.* 42 E5
Mospino, *Ukraine* 47 J9
Mosquera, *Colombia* 124 C3
Mosquero, *U.S.A.* 113 H3
Mosqueruela, *Spain* 32 E4
Mosquitia, *Honduras* 120 C3
Mosquito Coast = Mosquitia,
. . *Honduras* 120 C3
Mosquito Creek L., *U.S.A.* . . 110 E4
Mosquito L., *Canada* 105 A8
Mosquitos, G. de los, *Panama* . 120 E3
Moss, *Norway* 9 G14
Moss Vale, *Australia* 95 E5
Mossbank, *Canada* 105 D7
Mossburn, *N.Z.* 91 L2
Mosselbaai, *S. Africa* 88 E3
Mossendjo, *Congo* 84 E2
Mossgiel, *Australia* 95 E3
Mossingen, *Germany* 25 G5
Mossman, *Australia* 94 B4
Mossoró, *Brazil* 125 E11
Mossuril, *Mozam.* 87 E5
Most, *Czech Rep.* 26 A6
Mosta, *Malta* 36 D1
Mostaganem, *Algeria* 78 A6
Mostar, *Bos.-H.* 42 G2
Mostardas, *Brazil* 127 C5
Mostiska = Mostyska, *Ukraine* . 47 H2
Móstoles, *Spain* 34 E7
Mosty = Masty, *Belarus* 46 F3
Mostyska, *Ukraine* 47 H2
Mosul = Al Mawṣil, *Iraq* 70 B4
Mosûlpo, *S. Korea* 57 H14
Mota, *Ethiopia* 81 E4
Mota del Cuervo, *Spain* 33 F2
Mota del Marqués, *Spain* 34 D5
Motagua →, *Guatemala* 120 C2
Motala, *Sweden* 11 F9
Motaze, *Mozam.* 89 C5
Moţca, *Romania* 43 C11
Moth, *India* 69 G8
Motherwell, *U.K.* 14 F5
Motihari, *India* 69 F11
Motilla del Palancar, *Spain* . . 33 F3
Motnik, *Slovenia* 29 B11
Motovun, *Croatia* 29 C10
Motozintla de Mendoza, *Mexico* 119 D6
Motril, *Spain* 35 J7
Motru, *Romania* 42 F7
Motru →, *Romania* 43 F8
Mott, *U.S.A.* 112 B3
Móttola, *Italy* 31 B10
Motueka, *N.Z.* 91 J4
Motueka →, *N.Z.* 91 J4
Motul, *Mexico* 119 C7
Mouchalagane →, *Canada* . . 103 B6
Moúdhros, *Greece* 39 B7
Mouding, *China* 58 E3
Moudjeria, *Mauritania* 82 B2
Moudon, *Switz.* 25 J2
Mouila, *Gabon* 84 E2
Moulamein, *Australia* 95 F3
Mouliana, *Greece* 36 D7
Moulins, *France* 19 F10
Moulmein, *Burma* 67 L20
Moulouya, O. →, *Morocco* . . . 78 B5
Moultrie, *U.S.A.* 109 K4
Moultrie, L., *U.S.A.* 109 J5
Mound City, Mo., *U.S.A.* . . . 112 E7
Mound City, S. Dak., *U.S.A.* . 112 C4
Moúnda, Ákra, *Greece* 38 C2
Moundou, *Chad* 79 G9
Moundsville, *U.S.A.* 110 G4
Moung, *Cambodia* 64 F4
Mount Airy, *U.S.A.* 109 G5
Mount Albert, *Canada* 110 B5
Mount Barker, S. Austral.,
. . *Australia* 95 F2
Mount Barker, W. Austral.,
. . *Australia* 93 F2
Mount Brydges, *Canada* 110 D3
Mount Burr, *Australia* 95 F3
Mount Carmel, Ill., *U.S.A.* . . 108 F2
Mount Carmel, Pa., *U.S.A.* . . 111 F8
Mount Charleston, *U.S.A.* . . . 117 J11
Mount Clemens, *U.S.A.* 110 D2
Mount Coolon, *Australia* 94 C4
Mount Darwin, *Zimbabwe* . . . 87 F3
Mount Desert I., *U.S.A.* 109 C11
Mount Dora, *U.S.A.* 109 L5
Mount Edziza Prov. Park,
. . *Canada* 104 B2
Mount Fletcher, *S. Africa* 89 E4
Mount Forest, *Canada* 102 D3
Mount Gambier, *Australia* . . . 95 F3
Mount Garnet, *Australia* 94 B4
Mount Holly, *U.S.A.* 111 G10
Mount Holly Springs, *U.S.A.* . 110 F7
Mount Hope, N.S.W., *Australia* . 95 E4
Mount Hope, S. Austral.,
. . *Australia* 95 E2
Mount Isa, *Australia* 94 C2
Mount Jewett, *U.S.A.* 110 E6
Mount Kisco, *U.S.A.* 111 E11
Mount Laguna, *U.S.A.* 117 N10
Mount Larcom, *Australia* 94 C5
Mount Lofty Ra., *Australia* . . . 95 E2

Mount Magnet, *Australia* 93 E2
Mount Maunganui, *N.Z.* 91 G6
Mount Molloy, *Australia* 94 B4
Mount Morgan, *Australia* 94 C5
Mount Morris, *U.S.A.* 110 D7
Mount Pearl, *Canada* 103 C9
Mount Penn, *U.S.A.* 111 F9
Mount Perry, *Australia* 95 D5
Mount Pleasant, Iowa, *U.S.A.* . 112 E9
Mount Pleasant, Mich., *U.S.A.* . 108 D3
Mount Pleasant, Pa., *U.S.A.* . . 110 F5
Mount Pleasant, S.C., *U.S.A.* . . 109 J6
Mount Pleasant, Tenn., *U.S.A.* . 109 H2
Mount Pleasant, Tex., *U.S.A.* . 113 J7
Mount Pleasant, Utah, *U.S.A.* . 114 G8
Mount Pocono, *U.S.A.* 111 E9
Mount Rainier Nat. Park, *U.S.A.* 116 D5
Mount Revelstoke Nat. Park,
. . *Canada* 104 C5
Mount Robson Prov. Park,
. . *Canada* 104 C5
Mount Selinda, *Zimbabwe* . . . 89 C5
Mount Shasta, *U.S.A.* 114 F2
Mount Signal, *U.S.A.* 117 N11
Mount Sterling, Ill., *U.S.A.* . . 112 F9
Mount Sterling, Ky., *U.S.A.* . . 108 F4
Mount Surprise, *Australia* 94 B3
Mount Union, *U.S.A.* 110 F7
Mount Upton, *U.S.A.* 111 D9
Mount Vernon, Ill., *U.S.A.* . . . 108 F1
Mount Vernon, Ind., *U.S.A.* . . 112 F10
Mount Vernon, N.Y., *U.S.A.* . . 111 F11
Mount Vernon, Ohio, *U.S.A.* . 110 F2
Mount Vernon, Wash., *U.S.A.* . 116 B4
Mountain Ash, *U.K.* 13 F4
Mountain Center, *U.S.A.* 117 M10
Mountain City, Nev., *U.S.A.* . 114 F6
Mountain City, Tenn., *U.S.A.* . 109 G5
Mountain Dale, *U.S.A.* 111 E10
Mountain Grove, *U.S.A.* 113 G8
Mountain Home, Ark., *U.S.A.* . 113 G8
Mountain Home, Idaho, *U.S.A.* . 114 E6
Mountain Iron, *U.S.A.* 112 B8
Mountain Pass, *U.S.A.* 117 K11
Mountain View, Ark., *U.S.A.* . 113 H8
Mountain View, Calif., *U.S.A.* . 116 H4
Mountain View, Hawaii, *U.S.A.* 106 J17
Mountainair, *U.S.A.* 115 J10
Mountlake Terrace, *U.S.A.* . . 116 C4
Mountmellick, *Ireland* 15 C4
Mountrath, *Ireland* 15 D4
Moura, *Australia* 94 C4
Moura, *Brazil* 124 D6
Moura, *Portugal* 35 G3
Mourão, *Portugal* 35 G3
Mourdi, Dépression du, *Chad* . 79 E10
Mourdiah, *Mali* 82 C3
Mourenx, *France* 20 E3
Mouri, *Ghana* 83 D4
Mourilyan, *Australia* 94 B4
Mourmelon-le-Grand, *France* . 19 C11
Mourne →, *U.K.* 15 B4
Mourne Mts., *U.K.* 15 B5
Mourniaí = Mourniaí, *Greece* . 36 D6
Mournies = Mourniaí, *Greece* . 36 D6
Mouscron, *Belgium* 17 D3
Moussoro, *Chad* 79 F9
Mouthe, *France* 19 F13
Moutier, *Switz.* 25 H3
Moûtiers, *France* 21 C10
Moutong, *Indonesia* 63 D6
Mouy, *France* 19 C9
Mouzáki, *Greece* 38 B3
Mouzon, *France* 19 C12
Movas, *Mexico* 118 B3
Moville, *Ireland* 15 A4
Mowandjum, *Australia* 92 C3
Moy →, *Ireland* 15 B2
Moyale, *Kenya* 81 G4
Moyamba, *S. Leone* 82 D2
Moyen Atlas, *Morocco* 78 B4
Moyne, L. le, *Canada* 103 A6
Moyo, *Indonesia* 62 F5
Moyobamba, *Peru* 124 E3
Moyyero →, *Russia* 51 C11
Moyynty, *Kazakstan* 50 E8
Mozambique = Moçambique,
. . *Mozam.* 87 F5
Mozambique ■, *Africa* 87 F4
Mozambique Chan., *Africa* . . . 89 B7
Mozdok, *Russia* 49 J7
Mozdūrān, *Iran* 71 B9
Mozhaysk, *Russia* 46 E9
Mozhga, *Russia* 48 B11
Mozhnābād, *Iran* 71 C9
Mozirje, *Slovenia* 29 B11
Mozyr = Mazyr, *Belarus* 47 F5
Mpanda, *Tanzania* 86 D3
Mpésoba, *Mali* 82 C3
Mphoengs, *Zimbabwe* 89 C4
Mpika, *Zambia* 87 E3
Mpulungu, *Zambia* 87 D3
Mpumalanga, *S. Africa* 89 D5
Mpumalanga □, *S. Africa* 89 B5
Mpwapwa, *Tanzania* 86 D4
Mqanduli, *S. Africa* 89 E4
Mqinvartsveri = Kazbek, *Russia* 49 J7
Mrągowo, *Poland* 44 E8
Mramor, *Serbia, Yug.* 40 C5
Mrkonjić Grad, *Bos.-H.* 42 F2
Mrkopalj, *Croatia* 29 C11
Mrocza, *Poland* 45 E4
Msambansovu, *Zimbabwe* 87 F3
M'sila, *Algeria* 78 A6
Msoro, *Zambia* 87 E3
Msta →, *Russia* 46 C6
Mstislavl = Mstsislaw, *Belarus* . 46 E6

Mstsislaw, *Belarus* 46 E6
Mszana Dolna, *Poland* 45 J7
Mszczonów, *Poland* 45 G7
Mtama, *Tanzania* 87 E4
Mtamvuna →, *S. Africa* 89 E5
Mtilikwe →, *Zimbabwe* 87 G3
Mtsensk, *Russia* 46 F9
Mtskheta, *Georgia* 49 K7
Mtubatuba, *S. Africa* 89 D5
Mtwalume, *S. Africa* 89 E5
Mtwara-Mikindani, *Tanzania* . 87 E5
Mu Gia, Deo, *Vietnam* 64 D5
Mu Us Shamo, *China* 56 E5
Muang Chiang Rai = Chiang
. . Rai, *Thailand* 58 H2
Muang Khong, *Laos* 64 E5
Muang Lamphun, *Thailand* . . . 64 C2
Muang Pak Beng, *Laos* 58 H3
Muar, *Malaysia* 65 L4
Muarabungo, *Indonesia* 62 E2
Muaraenim, *Indonesia* 62 E2
Muarajuloi, *Indonesia* 62 E4
Muarakaman, *Indonesia* 62 E5
Muaratebo, *Indonesia* 62 E2
Muaratembesi, *Indonesia* 62 E2
Muaratewe, *Indonesia* 62 E4
Mubarakpur, *India* 69 F10
Mubarraz = Al Mubarraz,
. . *Si. Arabia* 71 E6
Mubende, *Uganda* 86 B3
Mubi, *Nigeria* 83 C7
Mubur, Pulau, *Indonesia* 65 L6
Mucajaí →, *Brazil* 124 C6
Muchachos, Roque de los,
. . *Canary Is.* 37 F2
Mücheln, *Germany* 24 D7
Muchinga Mts., *Zambia* 87 E3
Muchkapskiy, *Russia* 48 E6
Muchuan, *China* 58 C5
Muck, *U.K.* 14 E2
Muckadilla, *Australia* 95 D4
Mucur, *Turkey* 72 C6
Mucuri, *Brazil* 125 G11
Mucusso, *Angola* 88 B3
Muda, *Canary Is.* 37 F6
Mudanjiang, *China* 57 B15
Mudanya, *Turkey* 41 F12
Muddy Cr. →, *U.S.A.* 115 H8
Mudgee, *Australia* 95 E4
Mudjatik →, *Canada* 105 B7
Mudurnu, *Turkey* 72 B4
Muecate, *Mozam.* 87 E4
Mueda, *Mozam.* 87 E4
Mueller Ra., *Australia* 92 C4
Muende, *Mozam.* 87 E3
Muerto, Mar, *Mexico* 119 D6
Mufu Shan, *China* 59 C10
Mufulira, *Zambia* 87 E2
Mufumbiro Range, *Africa* 86 C2
Mugardos, *Spain* 34 B2
Muge, *Portugal* 35 F2
Múggia, *Italy* 29 C10
Mughal Sarai, *India* 69 G10
Mughayrā', *Si. Arabia* 70 D3
Mugi, *Japan* 55 H7
Mugia = Muxía, *Spain* 34 B1
Mugila, Mts., *Dem. Rep. of
. . the Congo* 86 D2
Muǧla, *Turkey* 39 D10
Muǧla □, *Turkey* 39 D10
Muglad, *Sudan* 81 E2
Müglizh, *Bulgaria* 41 D9
Mugu, *Nepal* 69 E10
Muhammad, Ras, *Egypt* 70 E2
Muhammad Qol, *Sudan* 80 C4
Muhammadabad, *India* 69 F10
Muhesi →, *Tanzania* 86 D4
Mühlacker, *Germany* 25 G4
Mühldorf, *Germany* 25 G8
Mühlhausen, *Germany* 24 D6
Mühlig Hofmann fjell, *Antarctica* 5 D3
Mühlviertel, *Austria* 26 C7
Muhos, *Finland* 8 D22
Muhu, *Estonia* 9 G20
Muhutwe, *Tanzania* 86 C3
Muine Bheag, *Ireland* 15 D5
Muir, L., *Australia* 93 F2
Mujnak = Muynak, *Uzbekistan* . 50 E6
Mukacheve, *Ukraine* 47 H2
Mukachevo = Mukacheve,
. . *Ukraine* 47 H2
Mukah, *Malaysia* 62 D4
Mukandwara, *India* 68 G6
Mukawwa, Geziret, *Egypt* 80 C4
Mukawwar, *Sudan* 80 C4
Mukdahan, *Thailand* 64 D5
Mukden = Shenyang, *China* . . 57 D12
Mukerian, *India* 68 D6
Mukhtolovo, *Russia* 48 C6
Mukhtuya = Lensk, *Russia* . . . 51 C12
Mukinbudin, *Australia* 93 F2
Mukishi, *Dem. Rep. of
. . the Congo* 87 D1
Mukomuko, *Indonesia* 62 E2
Mukomwenze, *Dem. Rep. of
. . the Congo* 86 D2
Muktsar, *India* 68 D6
Mukur = Moqor, *Afghan.* 68 C2
Mukutawa →, *Canada* 105 C9
Mukwela, *Zambia* 87 F2
Mula, *Spain* 33 G3
Mula →, *Pakistan* 68 F2
Mulange, *Dem. Rep. of
. . the Congo* 86 C2
Mulanje, *Malawi* 87 F4
Mulchén, *Chile* 126 D1
Mulde →, *Germany* 24 D8

Mule Creek Junction, *U.S.A.* . . 112 D2
Muleba, *Tanzania* 86 C3
Mulejé, *Mexico* 118 B2
Muleshoe, *U.S.A.* 113 H3
Muletta, Gara, *Ethiopia* 81 F5
Mulgrave, *Canada* 103 C7
Mulhacén, *Spain* 35 H7
Mülheim, *Germany* 24 D2
Mulhouse, *France* 19 E14
Muli, *China* 58 D3
Muling, *China* 57 B16
Mull, *U.K.* 14 E3
Mull, Sound of, *U.K.* 14 E3
Mullaittivu, *Sri Lanka* 66 Q12
Mullen, *U.S.A.* 112 D4
Mullens, *U.S.A.* 108 G5
Muller, Pegunungan, *Indonesia* . 62 D4
Mullet Pen., *Ireland* 15 B1
Mullewa, *Australia* 93 E2
Müllheim, *Germany* 25 H3
Mulligan →, *Australia* 94 D2
Mullingar, *Ireland* 15 C4
Mullins, *U.S.A.* 109 H6
Mullumbimby, *Australia* 95 D5
Mulobezi, *Zambia* 87 F2
Mulroy B., *Ireland* 15 A4
Multan, *Pakistan* 68 D4
Mulumbe, Mts., *Dem. Rep. of
. . the Congo* 87 D2
Mulungushi Dam, *Zambia* 87 E2
Mulvane, *U.S.A.* 113 G6
Mulwad, *Sudan* 80 D3
Mumbai, *India* 66 K8
Mumbwa, *Zambia* 87 F2
Mumra, *Russia* 49 H8
Mun →, *Thailand* 64 E5
Muna, *Indonesia* 63 F6
Munabao, *India* 68 G4
Munamagi, *Estonia* 9 H22
Münchberg, *Germany* 25 E7
Müncheberg, *Germany* 24 C10
München, *Germany* 25 G7
Munchen-Gladbach =
. . Mönchengladbach, *Germany* . 24 D2
Muncho Lake, *Canada* 104 B3
Munch'ŏn, N. *Korea* 57 E14
Muncie, *U.S.A.* 108 E3
Muncoonie, L., *Australia* 94 D2
Mundabbera, *Australia* 95 D5
Munday, *U.S.A.* 113 J5
Münden, *Germany* 24 D5
Mundiwindi, *Australia* 92 D3
Mundo →, *Spain* 33 G2
Mundo Novo, *Brazil* 125 F10
Mundra, *India* 68 H3
Mundrabilla, *Australia* 93 F4
Munera, *Spain* 33 F2
Mungallala, *Australia* 95 D4
Mungallala Cr. →, *Australia* . . 95 D4
Mungana, *Australia* 94 B3
Mungaoli, *India* 68 G8
Mungari, *Mozam.* 87 F3
Mungbere, *Dem. Rep. of
. . the Congo* 86 B2
Mungeli, *India* 69 H9
Munger, *India* 69 G12
Munich = München, *Germany* . 25 G7
Munising, *U.S.A.* 108 B2
Munka-Ljungby, *Sweden* 11 H6
Munkebo, *Denmark* 11 J4
Munkedal, *Sweden* 11 F5
Munkfors, *Sweden* 10 E7
Munku-Sardyk, *Russia* 51 D11
Münnerstadt, *Germany* 25 E6
Muñoz Gamero, Pen., *Chile* . . 128 G2
Munroe L., *Canada* 105 B9
Munsan, S. *Korea* 57 F14
Munster, *France* 19 D14
Munster, Niedersachsen,
. . *Germany* 24 C6
Münster, Nordrhein-Westfalen,
. . *Germany* 24 D3
Munster □, *Ireland* 15 D3
Muntadgin, *Australia* 93 F2
Muntele Mare, Vf., *Romania* . . 43 D8
Muntok, *Indonesia* 62 E3
Munyama, *Zambia* 87 F2
Munzur Dağları, *Turkey* 73 C8
Muong Beng, *Laos* 58 G3
Muong Boum, *Vietnam* 58 F4
Muong Et, *Laos* 64 B5
Muong Hai, *Laos* 58 G3
Muong Hiem, *Laos* 58 B4
Muong Houn, *Laos* 58 G3
Muong Hung, *Vietnam* 58 G4
Muong Kau, *Laos* 64 E5
Muong Khao, *Laos* 64 C4
Muong Khoua, *Laos* 58 G4
Muong Liep, *Laos* 64 C3
Muong May, *Laos* 64 E6
Muong Ngeun, *Laos* 58 G3
Muong Ngoi, *Laos* 58 G4
Muong Nhie, *Vietnam* 58 F4
Muong Nong, *Laos* 64 D6
Muong Ou Tay, *Laos* 58 F3
Muong Oua, *Laos* 64 C3
Muong Peun, *Laos* 58 G4
Muong Phalane, *Laos* 64 D5
Muong Phieng, *Laos* 64 C3
Muong Phine, *Laos* 64 D6
Muong Sai, *Laos* 58 G3
Muong Saiapoun, *Laos* 64 C3
Muong Sen, *Vietnam* 64 C5
Muong Sing, *Laos* 58 G3
Muong Son, *Laos* 58 G4

Muong Soui, *Laos* 64 C4
Muong Va, *Laos* 58 G4
Muong Xia, *Vietnam* 64 B5
Muonio, *Finland* 8 C20
Muonionjoki →, *Finland* 8 C20
Muping, *China* 57 F11
Mupoi, *Sudan* 81 F2
Muqaddam, Wadi →, *Sudan* . . 80 D3
Muqdisho, *Somali Rep.* 74 G4
Mur →, *Austria* 27 E9
Mur-de-Bretagne, *France* 18 D4
Muradiye, Manisa, *Turkey* 39 C9
Muradiye, Van, *Turkey* 73 C10
Murakami, *Japan* 54 E9
Murallón, Cerro, *Chile* 128 F2
Muranda, *Rwanda* 86 C2
Murang'a, *Kenya* 86 C4
Murashi, *Russia* 50 D5
Murat, *France* 20 C6
Murat →, *Turkey* 73 C9
Murat Dağı, *Turkey* 39 C11
Muratlı, *Turkey* 41 E11
Murato, *France* 21 F13
Murau, *Austria* 26 D7
Muravera, *Italy* 30 C2
Murayama, *Japan* 54 E10
Murça, *Portugal* 34 D3
Murchison →, *Australia* 93 E1
Murchison, Mt., *Antarctica* . . . 5 D11
Murchison Falls, *Uganda* 86 B3
Murchison Ra., *Australia* 94 C1
Murchison Rapids, *Malawi* . . . 87 F3
Murcia, *Spain* 33 G3
Murcia □, *Spain* 33 H3
Murdo, *U.S.A.* 112 D4
Murdoch Pt., *Australia* 94 A3
Mürefte, *Turkey* 41 F11
Mureş □, *Romania* 43 D9
Mureş →, *Romania* 42 D5
Mureşul = Mureş →, *Romania* . 42 D5
Muret, *France* 20 E5
Murewa, *Zimbabwe* 89 B5
Murfreesboro, N.C., *U.S.A.* . . 109 G7
Murfreesboro, Tenn., *U.S.A.* . 109 H2
Murgab = Murghob, *Tajikistan* . 50 F8
Murgab →, *Turkmenistan* . . . 71 B9
Murgenella, *Australia* 92 B5
Murgeni, *Romania* 43 D13
Murgha Kibzai, *Pakistan* 68 D3
Murghob, *Tajikistan* 50 F8
Murgon, *Australia* 95 D5
Muri, *India* 69 H11
Muria, *Indonesia* 63 G14
Muriaé, *Brazil* 127 A7
Murias de Paredes, *Spain* 34 C4
Muriel Mine, *Zimbabwe* 87 F3
Müritz, *Germany* 24 B8
Murka, *Kenya* 86 C4
Murliganj, *India* 69 G12
Murmansk, *Russia* 50 C4
Murnau, *Germany* 25 H7
Muro, *France* 21 F12
Muro, *Spain* 37 B10
Muro, C. de, *France* 21 G12
Muro de Alcoy, *Spain* 33 G4
Muro Lucano, *Italy* 31 B8
Murom, *Russia* 48 C6
Muroran, *Japan* 54 C10
Muros, *Spain* 34 C1
Muros y de Noya, Ría de, *Spain* . 34 C1
Muroto, *Japan* 55 H7
Muroto-Misaki, *Japan* 55 H7
Murowana Goślina, *Poland* . . . 45 F3
Murphy, *U.S.A.* 114 E5
Murphys, *U.S.A.* 116 G6
Murrat, *Sudan* 80 D2
Murrat Wells, *Sudan* 80 C3
Murray, Ky., *U.S.A.* 109 G1
Murray, Utah, *U.S.A.* 114 F8
Murray →, *Australia* 95 F2
Murray, L., *U.S.A.* 109 H5
Murray Bridge, *Australia* 95 F2
Murray Harbour, *Canada* 103 C7
Murraysburg, *S. Africa* 88 E3
Murree, *Pakistan* 68 C5
Murrieta, *U.S.A.* 117 M9
Murro di Porco, Capo, *Italy* . . 31 F8
Murrumbidgee →, *Australia* . . 95 E3
Murrumburrah, *Australia* 95 E4
Murrurundi, *Australia* 95 E5
Murshid, *Sudan* 80 C3
Murshidabad, *India* 69 G13
Murska Sobota, *Slovenia* 29 B13
Murtle L., *Canada* 104 C5
Murtoa, *Australia* 95 F3
Murtosa, *Portugal* 34 E2
Murungu, *Tanzania* 86 C3
Mururoa, *Pac. Oc.* 97 K14
Murwara, *India* 69 H9
Murwillumbah, *Australia* 95 D5
Mürz →, *Austria* 26 D8
Mürzzuschlag, *Austria* 26 D8
Muş, *Turkey* 70 B4
Mûsa, Gebel, *Egypt* 70 D2
Musa Khel, *Pakistan* 68 D3
Mûsa Qal'eh, *Afghan.* 66 C4
Musafirkhana, *India* 69 F9
Musala, *Bulgaria* 40 D7
Musala, *Indonesia* 62 D1
Musan, N. *Korea* 57 C15
Musangu, *Dem. Rep. of
. . the Congo* 87 E1
Musasa, *Tanzania* 86 C3
Musay'īd, *Qatar* 71 E6
Muscat = Masqaṭ, *Oman* 74 C6
Muscat & Oman = Oman ■,
. . *Asia* 74 C6

Muscatine, *U.S.A.* 112 E9
Musgrave Harbour, *Canada* 103 C9
Musgrave Ranges, *Australia* 93 E5
Mushie, *Dem. Rep. of the Congo* 84 E3
Mushin, *Nigeria* 83 D5
Musi ➤, *Indonesia* 62 E2
Muskeg ➤, *Canada* 104 A4
Muskegon, *U.S.A.* 108 D2
Muskegon ➤, *U.S.A.* 108 D2
Muskegon Heights, *U.S.A.* 108 D2
Muskogee, *U.S.A.* 113 H7
Muskoka, L., *Canada* 110 B5
Muskwa ➤, *Canada* 104 B4
Muslīmiyah, *Syria* 70 B3
Musmar, *Sudan* 80 D4
Musofu, *Zambia* 87 E2
Musoma, *Tanzania* 86 C3
Musquaro, L., *Canada* 103 B7
Musquodoboit Harbour, *Canada* 103 D7
Musselburgh, *U.K.* 14 F5
Musselshell ➤, *U.S.A.* 114 C10
Mussidan, *France* 20 C4
Mussomeli, *Italy* 30 E6
Mussoorie, *India* 68 D8
Mussuco, *Angola* 88 B2
Mustafakemalpaşa, *Turkey* 41 F12
Mustang, *Nepal* 69 E10
Musters, L., *Argentina* 128 F3
Musudan, *N. Korea* 57 D15
Muswellbrook, *Australia* 95 E5
Muszyna, *Poland* 45 J7
Mût, *Egypt* 80 B2
Mut, *Turkey* 70 B2
Mutanda, *Mozam.* 89 C5
Mutanda, *Zambia* 87 E2
Mutare, *Zimbabwe* 87 F3
Muting, *Indonesia* 63 F10
Mutoko, *Zimbabwe* 89 B5
Mutoray, *Russia* 51 C11
Mutshatsha, *Dem. Rep. of the Congo* 87 E1
Mutsu, *Japan* 54 D10
Mutsu-Wan, *Japan* 54 D10
Muttaburra, *Australia* 94 C3
Muttalip, *Turkey* 39 B12
Mutton I., *Ireland* 15 D2
Mutuáli, *Mozam.* 87 E4
Mutum Biyu, *Nigeria* 83 D7
Muweilih, *Egypt* 75 E3
Muxía, *Spain* 34 B1
Muy Muy, *Nic.* 120 D2
Muyinga, *Burundi* 86 C3
Muynak, *Uzbekistan* 50 E6
Muzaffarabad, *Pakistan* 69 B5
Muzaffargarh, *Pakistan* 68 D4
Muzaffarnagar, *India* 68 E7
Muzaffarpur, *India* 69 F11
Muzafırpur, *Pakistan* 68 D3
Muzhi, *Russia* 50 C7
Muzillac, *France* 18 E4
Muzūra, *Egypt* 80 J7
Mvôlô, *Sudan* 81 F2
Mvuma, *Zimbabwe* 87 F3
Mvurwi, *Zimbabwe* 87 F3
Mwadui, *Tanzania* 86 C3
Mwambo, *Tanzania* 87 E5
Mwandi, *Zambia* 87 F1
Mwanza, *Dem. Rep. of the Congo* 86 D2
Mwanza, *Tanzania* 86 C3
Mwanza, *Zambia* 87 F1
Mwanza □, *Tanzania* 86 C3
Mwaya, *Tanzania* 87 D3
Mweelrea, *Ireland* 15 C2
Mweka, *Dem. Rep. of the Congo* 84 E4
Mwenezi, *Zimbabwe* 87 G3
Mwenezi ➤, *Mozam.* 87 G3
Mwenga, *Dem. Rep. of the Congo* 86 C2
Mweru, L., *Zambia* 87 D2
Mweza Range, *Zimbabwe* 87 G3
Mwilambwe, *Dem. Rep. of the Congo* 86 D2
Mwimbi, *Tanzania* 87 D3
Mwinilunga, *Zambia* 87 E1
My Tho, *Vietnam* 65 G6
Myajlar, *India* 68 F4
Myanaung, *Burma* 67 K19
Myanmar = Burma ■, *Asia* 67 J20
Myaungmya, *Burma* 67 L19
Myeik Kyunzu, *Burma* 65 G1
Myers Chuck, *U.S.A.* 104 B2
Myerstown, *U.S.A.* 111 F8
Myingyan, *Burma* 67 J19
Myitkyina, *Burma* 67 G20
Myjava, *Slovak Rep.* 27 C10
Mykhaylivka, *Ukraine* 47 J8
Mykines, *Færoe Is.* 8 E9
Mykolayiv, *Ukraine* 47 J7
Mymensingh, *Bangla.* 67 G17
Mynydd Du, *U.K.* 13 F4
Mýrdalsjökull, *Iceland* 8 E4
Myrhorod, *Ukraine* 47 H7
Myrtle Beach, *U.S.A.* 109 J6
Myrtle Creek, *U.S.A.* 114 E2
Myrtle Point, *U.S.A.* 114 E1
Myrtou, *Cyprus* 36 D12
Mysia, *Turkey* 41 G11
Myślenice, *Poland* 45 J6
Myślibórz, *Poland* 45 F1
Mysłowice, *Poland* 45 H6
Mysore = Karnataka □, *India* 66 N10
Mysore, *India* 66 N10
Mystic, *U.S.A.* 111 E13
Myszków, *Poland* 45 H6
Myszyniec, *Poland* 44 E8

Mytishchi, *Russia* 46 E9
Mývatn, *Iceland* 8 D5
Mže ➤, *Czech Rep.* 26 B6
Mzimba, *Malawi* 87 E3
Mzimkulu ➤, *S. Africa* 89 E5
Mzimvubu ➤, *S. Africa* 89 E4
Mzuzu, *Malawi* 87 E3

N

Na Hearadh = Harris, *U.K.* 14 D2
Na Noi, *Thailand* 64 C3
Na Phao, *Laos* 64 D5
Na Sam, *Vietnam* 58 F6
Na San, *Vietnam* 64 B5
Naab ➤, *Germany* 25 F8
Na'am, *Sudan* 81 F2
Na'am ➤, *Sudan* 81 F2
Naantali, *Finland* 9 F19
Naas, *Ireland* 15 C5
Nababeep, *S. Africa* 88 D2
Nabadwip = Navadwip, *India* 69 H13
Nabari, *Japan* 55 G8
Nabawa, *Australia* 93 E1
Nabberu, L., *Australia* 93 E3
Nabburg, *Germany* 25 F8
Naberezhnyye Chelny, *Russia* 48 C11
Nabeul, *Tunisia* 79 A8
Nabha, *India* 68 D7
Nabīd, *Iran* 71 D8
Nabire, *Indonesia* 63 E9
Nabisar, *Pakistan* 68 G3
Nabisipi ➤, *Canada* 103 B7
Nabiswera, *Uganda* 86 B3
Nablus = Nābulus, *West Bank* 75 C4
Naboomspruit, *S. Africa* 89 C4
Nabou, *Burkina Faso* 82 C4
Nabua, *Phil.* 61 E5
Nābulus, *West Bank* 75 C4
Nacala, *Mozam.* 87 E5
Nacala-Velha, *Mozam.* 87 E5
Nacaome, *Honduras* 120 D2
Nacaroa, *Mozam.* 87 E4
Naches, *U.S.A.* 114 C3
Naches ➤, *U.S.A.* 116 D6
Nachicapau, L., *Canada* 103 A6
Nachingwea, *Tanzania* 87 E4
Nachna, *India* 68 F4
Náchod, *Czech Rep.* 26 A9
Nacimiento L., *U.S.A.* 116 K6
Naco, *Mexico* 118 A3
Nacogdoches, *U.S.A.* 113 K7
Nácori Chico, *Mexico* 118 B3
Nacozari, *Mexico* 118 A3
Nadi, *Sudan* 80 D3
Nadiad, *India* 68 H5
Nădlac, *Romania* 42 D5
Nador, *Morocco* 78 B5
Nadur, *Malta* 36 C1
Nadūshan, *Iran* 71 C7
Nadvirna, *Ukraine* 47 H3
Nadvornaya = Nadvirna, *Ukraine* 47 H3
Nadym, *Russia* 50 C8
Nadym ➤, *Russia* 50 C8
Nærbø, *Norway* 9 G11
Næstved, *Denmark* 11 J5
Nafada, *Nigeria* 83 C7
Naft-e Safīd, *Iran* 71 D6
Naftshahr, *Iran* 70 C5
Nafud Desert = An Nafūd, *Si. Arabia* 70 D4
Nag Hammâdi, *Egypt* 80 B3
Naga, *Phil.* 61 E5
Nagahama, *Japan* 55 G8
Nagai, *Japan* 54 E10
Nagaland □, *India* 67 G19
Nagano, *Japan* 55 F9
Nagano □, *Japan* 55 F9
Nagaoka, *Japan* 55 F9
Nagappattinam, *India* 66 P11
Nagar ➤, *Bangla.* 69 G13
Nagar Parkar, *Pakistan* 68 G4
Nagasaki, *Japan* 55 H4
Nagasaki □, *Japan* 55 H4
Nagato, *Japan* 55 G5
Nagaur, *India* 68 F5
Nagda, *India* 68 H6
Nagercoil, *India* 66 Q10
Nagina, *India* 69 E8
Nagīneh, *Iran* 71 C8
Nagir, *Pakistan* 69 A6
Naglarby, *Sweden* 10 D9
Nagod, *India* 69 G9
Nagold, *Germany* 25 G4
Nagold ➤, *Germany* 25 G4
Nagoorin, *Australia* 94 C5
Nagorno-Karabakh, *Azerbaijan* 70 B5
Nagornyy, *Russia* 51 D13
Nagoya, *Japan* 55 G8
Nagpur, *India* 66 J11
Nagua, *Dom. Rep.* 121 C6
Nagyatád, *Hungary* 42 D2
Nagyecsed, *Hungary* 42 C7
Nagykálló, *Hungary* 42 C6
Nagykanizsa, *Hungary* 42 D2
Nagykáta, *Hungary* 42 C4
Nagykőrös, *Hungary* 42 C4
Naha, *Japan* 55 L3
Nahan, *India* 68 D7
Nahanni Butte, *Canada* 104 A4
Nahanni Nat. Park, *Canada* 104 A4
Nahargarh, *Mad. P., India* 68 G6
Nahargarh, *Raj., India* 68 G7
Nahariyya, *Israel* 70 C3

Nahāvand, *Iran* 71 C6
Nahe ➤, *Germany* 25 F3
Nahîya, W. ➤, *Egypt* 80 B3
Naicá, *Mexico* 118 B3
Naicam, *Canada* 105 C8
Naikoon Prov. Park, *Canada* 104 C2
Naila, *Germany* 25 E7
Naimisharanya, *India* 69 F9
Nain, *Canada* 103 A7
Nā'īn, *Iran* 71 C7
Naini Tal, *India* 69 E8
Nainpur, *India* 66 H12
Nairn, *U.K.* 14 D5
Nairobi, *Kenya* 86 C4
Naissaar, *Estonia* 9 G21
Naita, Mt., *Ethiopia* 81 F4
Naivasha, *Kenya* 86 C4
Naivasha, L., *Kenya* 86 C4
Najac, *France* 20 D5
Najafābād, *Iran* 71 C6
Najd, *Si. Arabia* 74 B3
Nájera, *Spain* 32 C2
Najerilla ➤, *Spain* 32 C2
Najibabad, *India* 68 E8
Najin, *N. Korea* 57 C16
Najmah, *Si. Arabia* 71 E6
Naju, *S. Korea* 57 G14
Nakadōri-Shima, *Japan* 55 H4
Nakalagba, *Dem. Rep. of the Congo* 86 B2
Nakaminato, *Japan* 55 F10
Nakamura, *Japan* 55 H6
Nakano, *Japan* 55 F9
Nakano-Shima, *Japan* 55 K4
Nakashibetsu, *Japan* 54 C12
Nakfa, *Eritrea* 81 D4
Nakhfar al Buşayyah, *Iraq* 70 D5
Nakhichevan = Naxçivan, *Azerbaijan* 70 B5
Nakhichevan Republic = Naxçivan □, *Azerbaijan* 50 F5
Nakhl, *Egypt* 75 F2
Nakhl-e Taqī, *Iran* 71 E7
Nakhodka, *Russia* 51 E14
Nakhon Nayok, *Thailand* 64 E3
Nakhon Pathom, *Thailand* 64 F3
Nakhon Phanom, *Thailand* 64 D5
Nakhon Ratchasima, *Thailand* 64 E4
Nakhon Sawan, *Thailand* 64 E3
Nakhon Si Thammarat, *Thailand* 65 H3
Nakhon Thai, *Thailand* 64 D3
Nakhtarana, *India* 68 H3
Nakina, *Canada* 102 B2
Nakło nad Notecią, *Poland* 45 E4
Nako, *Burkina Faso* 82 C4
Nakodar, *India* 68 D6
Nakskov, *Denmark* 11 K5
Naktong ➤, *S. Korea* 57 G15
Nakuru, *Kenya* 86 C4
Nakuru, L., *Kenya* 86 C4
Nakusp, *Canada* 104 C5
Nal, *Pakistan* 68 F2
Nal ➤, *Pakistan* 68 G1
Nalázi, *Mozam.* 89 C5
Nalchik, *Russia* 49 J6
Nałęczów, *Poland* 45 G9
Nalerigu, *Ghana* 83 C4
Nalgonda, *India* 66 L11
Nalhati, *India* 69 G12
Naliya, *India* 68 H3
Nallamalai Hills, *India* 66 M11
Nallıhan, *Turkey* 72 B4
Nalón ➤, *Spain* 34 B4
Nam Can, *Vietnam* 65 H5
Nam-ch'on, *N. Korea* 57 E14
Nam Co, *China* 60 C4
Nam Dinh, *Vietnam* 58 G6
Nam Du, Hon, *Vietnam* 65 H5
Nam Ngum Dam, *Laos* 64 C4
Nam-Phan, *Vietnam* 65 G6
Nam Phong, *Thailand* 64 D4
Nam Tha, *Laos* 58 G3
Nam Tok, *Thailand* 64 E2
Namacunde, *Angola* 88 B2
Namacurra, *Mozam.* 89 B6
Namak, Daryācheh-ye, *Iran* 71 C7
Namak, Kavir-e, *Iran* 71 C8
Namakzār, Daryācheh-ye, *Iran* 71 C9
Namaland, *Namibia* 88 C2
Namangan, *Uzbekistan* 50 E8
Namapa, *Mozam.* 87 E4
Namaqualand, *S. Africa* 88 E2
Namasagali, *Uganda* 86 B3
Namber, *Indonesia* 63 E8
Nambour, *Australia* 95 D5
Nambucca Heads, *Australia* 95 E5
Namche Bazar, *Nepal* 69 F12
Namchonjŏm = Nam-ch'on, *N. Korea* 57 E14
Namecunda, *Mozam.* 87 E4
Nameponda, *Mozam.* 87 F4
Náměšt' nad Oslavou, *Czech Rep.* 27 B9
Námestovo, *Slovak Rep.* 27 B12
Nametil, *Mozam.* 87 F4
Namew L., *Canada* 105 C8
Namgia, *India* 69 D8
Namhkam, *Burma* 58 E1
Namib Desert, *Namibia* 88 C2
Namibe, *Angola* 85 H2
Namibe □, *Angola* 88 B1
Namibia ■, *Africa* 88 C2
Namibwoestyn = Namib Desert, *Namibia* 88 C2

Namīn, *Iran* 73 C13
Namlea, *Indonesia* 63 E7
Namoi ➤, *Australia* 95 E4
Nampa, *U.S.A.* 114 E5
Nampala, *Mali* 82 B3
Namp'o, *N. Korea* 57 E13
Nampō-Shotō, *Japan* 55 J10
Nampula, *Mozam.* 87 F4
Namrole, *Indonesia* 63 E7
Namse Shankou, *China* 67 E13
Namsen ➤, *Norway* 8 D14
Namsos, *Norway* 8 D14
Namtsy, *Russia* 51 C13
Namtu, *Burma* 67 H20
Namtumbo, *Tanzania* 87 E4
Namu, *Canada* 104 C3
Namur, *Belgium* 17 D4
Namur □, *Belgium* 17 D4
Namutoni, *Namibia* 88 B2
Namwala, *Zambia* 87 F2
Namwŏn, *S. Korea* 57 G14
Namysłów, *Poland* 45 G4
Nan, *Thailand* 64 C3
Nan ➤, *Thailand* 64 E3
Nan-ch'ang = Nanchang, *China* 59 C10
Nan Ling, *China* 59 E8
Nan Xian, *China* 59 C9
Nana, *Romania* 43 F11
Nana Kru, *Liberia* 82 E3
Nanaimo, *Canada* 104 D4
Nanam, *N. Korea* 57 D15
Nanan, *China* 59 E12
Nanango, *Australia* 95 D5
Nan'ao, *China* 59 F11
Nanao, *Japan* 55 F8
Nanbu, *China* 58 B6
Nanchang, *Jiangxi, China* 59 C10
Nanchang, *Kiangsi, China* 59 C10
Nancheng, *China* 59 D11
Nanching = Nanjing, *China* 59 A12
Nanchong, *China* 58 B6
Nanchuan, *China* 58 C6
Nancy, *France* 19 D13
Nanda Devi, *India* 69 D8
Nanda Kot, *India* 69 D9
Nandan, *China* 58 E6
Nandan, *Japan* 55 G7
Nanded, *India* 66 K10
Nandewar Ra., *Australia* 95 E5
Nandi, *Fiji* 91 C7
Nandigram, *India* 69 H12
Nandurbar, *India* 66 J9
Nandyal, *India* 66 M11
Nanfeng, *Guangdong, China* 59 F8
Nanfeng, *Jiangxi, China* 59 D11
Nanga-Eboko, *Cameroon* 83 E7
Nanga Parbat, *Pakistan* 69 B6
Nangade, *Mozam.* 87 E4
Nangapinoh, *Indonesia* 62 E4
Nangarhār □, *Afghan.* 66 B7
Nangatayap, *Indonesia* 62 E4
Nangeya Mts., *Uganda* 86 B3
Nangis, *France* 19 D10
Nangong, *China* 56 F8
Nanhua, *China* 58 E3
Nanhuang, *China* 57 F11
Nanhui, *China* 59 B13
Nanjeko, *Zambia* 87 F1
Nanji Shan, *China* 59 D13
Nanjian, *China* 58 E3
Nanjiang, *China* 58 A6
Nanjing, *Fujian, China* 59 E11
Nanjing, *Jiangsu, China* 59 A12
Nanjinji, *Indonesia* 87 D4
Nankana Sahib, *Pakistan* 68 D5
Nankang, *China* 59 E10
Nanking = Nanjing, *China* 59 A12
Nankoku, *Japan* 55 H6
Nanling, *China* 59 B12
Nanning, *China* 58 F7
Nannup, *Australia* 93 F2
Nanpan Jiang ➤, *China* 58 E6
Nanpara, *India* 69 F9
Nanpi, *China* 56 E9
Nanping, *Fujian, China* 59 D12
Nanping, *Henan, China* 59 C9
Nanri Dao, *China* 59 E12
Nanripe, *Mozam.* 87 E4
Nansei-Shotō = Ryūkyū-rettō, *Japan* 55 M3
Nansen Sd., *Canada* 4 A3
Nanshan I., *S. China Sea* 62 B5
Nansio, *Tanzania* 86 C3
Nant, *France* 20 D7
Nanterre, *France* 19 D9
Nantes, *France* 18 E5
Nantiat, *France* 20 D7
Nanticoke, *U.S.A.* 111 E8
Nanton, *Canada* 104 C6
Nantong, *China* 59 A13
Nantou, *Taiwan* 59 F13
Nantua, *France* 19 F12
Nantucket I., *U.S.A.* 108 D10
Nantwich, *U.K.* 12 D5
Nanuque, *Brazil* 125 G10
Nanusa, Kepulauan, *Indonesia* 63 D7
Nanutarra Roadhouse, *Australia* 92 D2
Nanxi, *China* 58 C5
Nanxiong, *China* 59 E10
Nanyang, *China* 56 H7
Nanyi Hu, *China* 59 B12
Nanyuki, *Kenya* 86 B4
Nanzhang, *China* 59 B8
Nao, C. de la, *Spain* 33 G5
Naococane, L., *Canada* 103 B5
Naogaon, *Bangla.* 69 G13

Náousa, *Kikládhes, Greece* 39 D7
Naozhou Dao, *China* 59 G8
Napa, *U.S.A.* 116 G4
Napa ➤, *U.S.A.* 116 G4
Napanee, *Canada* 102 D4
Napanoch, *U.S.A.* 111 E10
Nape, *Laos* 64 C5
Nape Pass = Keo Neua, Deo, *Vietnam* 64 C5
Napier, *N.Z.* 91 H6
Napier Broome B., *Australia* 92 B4
Napier Pen., *Australia* 94 A2
Napierville, *Canada* 111 A11
Naples = Nápoli, *Italy* 31 B7
Naples, *U.S.A.* 109 M5
Napo, *China* 58 F5
Napo ➤, *Peru* 122 D3
Napoleon, *N. Dak., U.S.A.* 112 B5
Napoleon, *Ohio, U.S.A.* 108 E3
Nápoli, *Italy* 31 B7
Nápoli, G. di, *Italy* 31 B7
Napopo, *Dem. Rep. of the Congo* 86 B2
Naqâda, *Egypt* 80 B3
Naqadeh, *Iran* 73 D11
Naqb, Ra's an, *Jordan* 75 F4
Naqqāsh, *Iran* 71 C6
Nara, *Japan* 55 G7
Nara, *Mali* 82 B3
Nara □, *Japan* 55 G8
Nara Canal, *Pakistan* 68 G3
Nara Visa, *U.S.A.* 113 H3
Naracoorte, *Australia* 95 F3
Naradhan, *Australia* 95 E4
Naraini, *India* 69 G9
Narasapur, *India* 67 L12
Narathiwat, *Thailand* 65 J3
Narayanganj, *Bangla.* 67 H17
Narayanpet, *India* 66 L10
Narbonne, *France* 20 E7
Narcea ➤, *Spain* 34 B4
Nardīn, *Iran* 71 B7
Nardò, *Italy* 31 B11
Narembeen, *Australia* 93 F2
Narendranagar, *India* 68 D8
Nares Str., *Arctic* 98 A13
Naretha, *Australia* 93 F3
Narew ➤, *Poland* 45 F7
Nari ➤, *Pakistan* 68 F2
Narin, *Afghan.* 66 A6
Narindra, Helodranon' i, *Madag.* 89 A8
Narita, *Japan* 55 G10
Närke, *Sweden* 10 E8
Narmada ➤, *India* 68 J5
Narman, *Turkey* 73 B9
Narmland, *Sweden* 9 F15
Narnaul, *India* 68 E7
Narni, *Italy* 29 F9
Naro, *Ghana* 82 C4
Naro Fominsk, *Russia* 46 E9
Narodnaya, *Russia* 6 B17
Narok, *Kenya* 86 C4
Narón, *Spain* 34 B2
Narooma, *Australia* 95 F5
Narowal, *Pakistan* 68 C6
Narrabri, *Australia* 95 E4
Narran ➤, *Australia* 95 D4
Narrandera, *Australia* 95 E4
Narrogin, *Australia* 93 F2
Narromine, *Australia* 95 E4
Narrow Hills Prov. Park, *Canada* 105 C8
Narsimhapur, *India* 69 H8
Narsinghgarh, *India* 68 H7
Nartes, L. e, *Albania* 40 F3
Nartkala, *Russia* 49 J6
Naruto, *Japan* 55 G7
Narva, *Estonia* 46 C5
Narva ➤, *Russia* 9 G22
Narva Bay, *Estonia* 9 G19
Narvik, *Norway* 8 B17
Narvskoye Vdkhr., *Russia* 46 C5
Narwana, *India* 68 E7
Naryan-Mar, *Russia* 50 C6
Naryilco, *Australia* 95 D3
Narym, *Russia* 50 D9
Naryn, *Kyrgyzstan* 50 E8
Nasa, *Norway* 8 C16
Nasarawa, *Nigeria* 83 D6
Năsăud, *Romania* 43 C9
Naseby, *N.Z.* 91 L3
Naselle, *U.S.A.* 116 D3
Naser, Buheirat en, *Egypt* 80 C3
Nashua, *Mont., U.S.A.* 114 B10
Nashua, *N.H., U.S.A.* 111 D13
Nashville, *Ark., U.S.A.* 113 J8
Nashville, *Ga., U.S.A.* 109 K4
Nashville, *Tenn., U.S.A.* 109 G2
Našice, *Croatia* 42 E3
Nasielsk, *Poland* 45 F7
Nasik, *India* 66 K8
Nasipit, *Phil.* 61 G6
Nasir, *Sudan* 81 F3
Nasirabad, *India* 68 F6
Nasirabad, *Pakistan* 68 E3
Naskaupi ➤, *Canada* 103 B7
Naso, *Italy* 31 D7
Naşrābād, *Iran* 71 C6
Naşrīān-e Pā'īn, *Iran* 70 C5
Nass ➤, *Canada* 104 C3
Nassau, *Bahamas* 120 A4
Nassau, B., *Chile* 128 H3
Nasser, L. = Naser, Buheirat en, *Egypt* 80 C3
Nasser City = Kôm Ombo, *Egypt* 80 C3
Nassian, *Ivory C.* 82 D4
Nässjö, *Sweden* 11 G8
Nastapoka ➤, *Canada* 102 A4

Nastapoka, Is.

Nastapoka, Is., *Canada* 102 A4
Nasugbu, *Phil.* 61 D4
Näsum, *Sweden* 11 H8
Näsviken, *Sweden* 10 C10
Nata, *Botswana* 88 C4
Nata →, *Botswana* 88 C4
Natal, *Brazil* 125 E11
Natal, *Indonesia* 62 D1
Natal, *S. Africa* 85 K6
Natalinci, *Serbia, Yug.* 42 F5
Naṭanz, *Iran* 71 C6
Natashquan, *Canada* 103 B7
Natashquan →, *Canada* 103 B7
Natchez, *U.S.A.* 113 K9
Natchitoches, *U.S.A.* 113 K8
Nathalia, *Australia* 95 F4
Nathdwara, *India* 68 G5
Nati, Pta., *Spain* 37 A10
Natimuk, *Australia* 95 F3
Nation →, *Canada* 104 B4
National City, *U.S.A.* 117 N9
Natitingou, *Benin* 83 C5
Natividad, I., *Mexico* 118 B1
Natkyizin, *Burma* 64 E1
Natron, L., *Tanzania* 86 C4
Natrona Heights, *U.S.A.* 110 F5
Natrûn, W. el →, *Egypt* 80 H7
Nättraby, *Sweden* 11 H9
Natukanaoka Pan, *Namibia* 88 B2
Natuna Besar, Kepulauan, *Indonesia* 65 L7
Natuna Is. = Natuna Besar, Kepulauan, *Indonesia* 65 L7
Natuna Selatan, Kepulauan, *Indonesia* 65 L7
Natural Bridge, *U.S.A.* 111 B9
Naturaliste, C., *Australia* 94 G4
Nau Qala, *Afghan.* 68 B3
Naucelle, *France* 20 D6
Nauders, *Austria* 26 E3
Nauen, *Germany* 24 C8
Naugatuck, *U.S.A.* 111 E11
Naujaat = Repulse Bay, *Canada* 101 B11
Naujoji Akmenė, *Lithuania* 44 B9
Naumburg, *Germany* 24 D7
Nā'ūr at Tunayb, *Jordan* 75 D4
Nauru ■, *Pac. Oc.* 96 H8
Naushahra = Nowshera, *Pakistan* 66 C8
Naushahro, *Pakistan* 68 F3
Naushon I., *U.S.A.* 111 E14
Nauta, *Peru* 124 D4
Nautanwa, *India* 67 F13
Nautla, *Mexico* 119 C5
Nava, *Mexico* 118 B4
Nava, *Spain* 34 B5
Nava del Rey, *Spain* 34 D5
Navadwip, *India* 69 H13
Navahermosa, *Spain* 35 F6
Navahrudak, *Belarus* 46 F3
Navajo Reservoir, *U.S.A.* 115 H10
Navalcarnero, *Spain* 34 E6
Navalmoral de la Mata, *Spain* 34 F5
Navalvillar de Pela, *Spain* 35 F5
Navan = An Uaimh, *Ireland* 15 C5
Navapolatsk, *Belarus* 46 E5
Navarino, I., *Chile* 128 H3
Navarra □, *Spain* 32 C3
Navarre, *U.S.A.* 110 F3
Navarro →, *U.S.A.* 116 F3
Navas de San Juan, *Spain* 35 G7
Navasota, *U.S.A.* 113 K6
Navassa I., *W. Indies* 121 C5
Nävekvarn, *Sweden* 11 F10
Naver →, *U.K.* 14 C4
Navia, *Spain* 34 B4
Navia →, *Spain* 34 B4
Navia de Suarna, *Spain* 34 C3
Navibandar, *India* 68 J3
Navidad, *Chile* 126 C1
Naviraí, *Brazil* 127 A5
Navlakhi, *India* 68 H4
Navlya, *Russia* 47 F8
Năvodari, *Romania* 43 F13
Navoi = Nawoiy, *Uzbekistan* 50 E7
Navojoa, *Mexico* 118 B3
Navolato, *Mexico* 118 C3
Návpaktos, *Greece* 38 C3
Návplion, *Greece* 38 D4
Navrongo, *Ghana* 83 C4
Navsari, *India* 66 J8
Nawa Kot, *Pakistan* 68 E4
Nawab Khan, *Pakistan* 68 D3
Nawabganj, *Ut. P., India* 69 F9
Nawabganj, *Ut. P., India* 69 E8
Nawabshah, *Pakistan* 68 F3
Nawada, *India* 69 G11
Nawakot, *Nepal* 69 F11
Nawalgarh, *India* 68 F6
Nawanshahr, *India* 69 C6
Nawar, Dasht-i-, *Afghan.* 68 C3
Nawi, *Sudan* 80 D3
Nawoiy, *Uzbekistan* 50 E7
Naxçıvan, *Azerbaijan* 70 B5
Naxçıvan □, *Azerbaijan* 50 F5
Náxos, *Greece* 39 D7
Nay, *France* 20 E3
Nay, Mui, *Vietnam* 62 B3
Nāy Band, *Būshehr, Iran* 71 E7
Nāy Band, *Khorāsān, Iran* 71 C8
Nayakhan, *Russia* 51 C16
Nayarit □, *Mexico* 118 C4
Nayé, *Senegal* 82 C2
Nayong, *China* 58 D5
Nayoro, *Japan* 54 B11
Nayyāl, W. →, *Si. Arabia* 70 D3
Nazaré, *Brazil* 125 F11
Nazaré, *Portugal* 35 F1
Nazareth = Naẕerat, *Israel* 75 C4
Nazareth, *U.S.A.* 111 F9
Nazas, *Mexico* 118 B4
Nazas →, *Mexico* 118 B4
Nazca, *Peru* 124 F4
Naze, The, *U.K.* 13 F9
Naẕerat, *Israel* 75 C4
Nāzīk, *Iran* 70 B5
Nazilli, *Turkey* 39 D10
Nazko, *Canada* 104 C4
Nazko →, *Canada* 104 C4
Nazret, *Ethiopia* 81 F4
Nazwá, *Oman* 74 C6
Nchanga, *Zambia* 87 E2
Ncheu, *Malawi* 87 E3
Ndala, *Tanzania* 86 C3
Ndalatando, *Angola* 84 F2
Ndali, *Benin* 83 D5
Ndareda, *Tanzania* 86 C4
Ndélé, *C.A.R.* 84 C4
Ndikinimeki, *Cameroon* 83 E7
N'Dioum, *Senegal* 82 B2
Ndjamena, *Chad* 79 F8
Ndola, *Zambia* 87 E2
Ndoto Mts., *Kenya* 86 B4
Nduguti, *Tanzania* 86 C3
Néa Alikarnassós, *Greece* 39 F7
Néa Ankhíalos, *Greece* 38 B4
Néa Epídhavros, *Greece* 38 D5
Néa Flippiás, *Greece* 38 B2
Néa Ionía, *Greece* 38 B4
Néa Kallikrátia, *Greece* 40 F7
Néa Mákri, *Greece* 38 C5
Néa Moudhaniá, *Greece* 40 F7
Néa Péramos, *Attikí, Greece* 38 C5
Néa Péramos, *Kavála, Greece* 41 F8
Néa Víssi, *Greece* 41 E10
Néa Zíkhna, *Greece* 40 E7
Neagh, Lough, *U.K.* 15 B5
Neah Bay, *U.S.A.* 116 B2
Neale, L., *Australia* 92 D5
Neamţ □, *Romania* 43 C11
Neápolis, *Kozáni, Greece* 40 F5
Neápolis, *Kríti, Greece* 36 D7
Neápolis, *Lakonía, Greece* 38 E5
Near Is., *U.S.A.* 100 C1
Neath, *U.K.* 13 F4
Neath Port Talbot □, *U.K.* 13 F4
Nebbou, *Burkina Faso* 83 C4
Nebelat el Hagana, *Sudan* 81 E2
Nebine Cr. →, *Australia* 95 D4
Nebitdag, *Turkmenistan* 50 F6
Nebo, *Australia* 94 C4
Nebolchy, *Russia* 46 C7
Nebraska □, *U.S.A.* 112 E5
Nebraska City, *U.S.A.* 112 E7
Nébrodi, Monti, *Italy* 31 E7
Necedah, *U.S.A.* 112 C9
Nechako →, *Canada* 104 C4
Neches →, *U.S.A.* 113 L8
Neckar →, *Germany* 25 F4
Necochea, *Argentina* 126 D4
Neda, *Spain* 34 B2
Nedelino, *Bulgaria* 41 E9
Nedelišće, *Croatia* 29 B13
Nédha →, *Greece* 38 D3
Needles, *Canada* 104 D5
Needles, *U.S.A.* 117 L12
Needles, The, *U.K.* 13 G6
Ñeembucú □, *Paraguay* 126 B4
Neemuch = Nimach, *India* 68 G6
Neenah, *U.S.A.* 108 C1
Neepawa, *Canada* 105 C9
Neftçala, *Azerbaijan* 71 B6
Neftegorsk, *Russia* 49 H4
Neftekumsk, *Russia* 49 H7
Nefyn, *U.K.* 12 E3
Négala, *Mali* 82 C3
Negapatam = Nagappattinam, *India* 66 P11
Negaunee, *U.S.A.* 108 B2
Negele, *Ethiopia* 81 F4
Negev Desert = Hanegev, *Israel* 75 E4
Negoiul, Vf., *Romania* 43 E9
Negombo, *Sri Lanka* 66 R11
Negotin, *Serbia, Yug.* 40 B6
Negotino, *Macedonia* 40 E6
Negra, Peña, *Spain* 34 C4
Negra, Pta., *Peru* 122 D2
Negrais, C. = Maudin Sun, *Burma* 67 M19
Negreşti, *Romania* 43 D12
Negreşti-Oaş, *Romania* 43 C8
Negril, *Jamaica* 120 C4
Negro →, *Argentina* 122 H4
Negro →, *Brazil* 122 D4
Negro →, *Uruguay* 127 C4
Negros, *Phil.* 61 G5
Negru Vodă, *Romania* 43 G13
Neguac, *Canada* 103 C6
Nehalem →, *U.S.A.* 116 E3
Nehāvand, *Iran* 71 C6
Nehbandān, *Iran* 71 D9
Nehoiu, *Romania* 43 E11
Nei Monggol Zizhiqu □, *China* 56 D7
Neijiang, *China* 58 C5
Neillsville, *U.S.A.* 112 C9
Neilton, *U.S.A.* 114 C2
Neiqiu, *China* 56 F8
Neiva, *Colombia* 124 C3
Neixiang, *China* 56 H6
Nejanilini L., *Canada* 105 B9
Nejd = Najd, *Si. Arabia* 74 B3
Nejo, *Ethiopia* 81 F4
Nekā, *Iran* 71 B7
Nekemte, *Ethiopia* 81 F4
Nêkheb, *Egypt* 80 B3
Neksø, *Denmark* 11 J9
Nelas, *Portugal* 34 E3
Nelia, *Australia* 94 C3
Nelidovo, *Russia* 46 D7
Neligh, *U.S.A.* 112 D5
Nelkan, *Russia* 51 D14
Nellore, *India* 66 M11
Nelson, *Canada* 104 D5
Nelson, *N.Z.* 91 J4
Nelson, *U.K.* 12 D5
Nelson, *Ariz., U.S.A.* 115 J7
Nelson, *Nev., U.S.A.* 117 K12
Nelson →, *Canada* 105 C9
Nelson, C., *Australia* 95 F3
Nelson, Estrecho, *Chile* 128 G2
Nelson Forks, *Canada* 104 B4
Nelson House, *Canada* 105 B9
Nelson L., *Canada* 105 B8
Nelspoort, *S. Africa* 88 E3
Nelspruit, *S. Africa* 89 D5
Néma, *Mauritania* 82 B3
Neman, *Russia* 9 J20
Neman →, *Lithuania* 9 J19
Neméa, *Greece* 38 D4
Nemeiben L., *Canada* 105 B7
Nemërçkë, Mal, *Albania* 40 F4
Nemira, Vf., *Romania* 43 D11
Némiscau, *Canada* 102 B4
Némiscau, L., *Canada* 102 B4
Nemours, *France* 19 D9
Nemšová, *Slovak Rep.* 27 C11
Nemunas = Neman →, *Lithuania* 9 J19
Nemuro, *Japan* 54 C12
Nemuro-Kaikyō, *Japan* 54 C12
Nen Jiang →, *China* 57 B13
Nenagh, *Ireland* 15 D3
Nenasi, *Malaysia* 65 L4
Nene →, *U.K.* 13 E8
Nénita, *Greece* 39 C8
Nenjiang, *China* 60 B7
Neno, *Malawi* 87 F3
Neodesha, *U.S.A.* 113 G7
Neokhórion, *Aitolía kai Akarnanía, Greece* 38 C3
Neokhórion, *Árta, Greece* 38 B2
Néon Karlovásion, *Greece* 39 D8
Néon Petrítsi, *Greece* 40 E7
Neosho, *U.S.A.* 113 G7
Neosho →, *U.S.A.* 113 H7
Nepal ■, *Asia* 69 F11
Nepalganj, *Nepal* 69 E9
Nepalganj Road, *India* 69 E9
Nephi, *U.S.A.* 114 G8
Nephin, *Ireland* 15 B2
Nepi, *Italy* 29 F9
Nepomuk, *Czech Rep.* 26 B6
Neptune, *U.S.A.* 111 F10
Nera →, *Italy* 29 F9
Nera →, *Romania* 42 F6
Nérac, *France* 20 D4
Nerang, *Australia* 95 D5
Neratovice, *Czech Rep.* 26 A7
Nerchinsk, *Russia* 51 D12
Nereju, *Romania* 43 E11
Nerekhta, *Russia* 46 D11
Néret, L., *Canada* 103 B5
Neretvanski Kanal, *Croatia* 29 E14
Neringa, *Lithuania* 9 J19
Nerja, *Spain* 35 J7
Nerl →, *Russia* 46 D11
Nerpio, *Spain* 33 G2
Nerva, *Spain* 35 H4
Nervi, *Italy* 28 D6
Neryungri, *Russia* 51 D13
Nescopeck, *U.S.A.* 111 E8
Nesebŭr, *Bulgaria* 41 D11
Ness, L., *U.K.* 14 D4
Ness City, *U.S.A.* 112 F5
Nesterov, *Poland* 47 G2
Nestórion, *Greece* 40 F5
Néstos →, *Greece* 41 E8
Nesvady, *Slovak Rep.* 27 D11
Nesvizh = Nyasvizh, *Belarus* 47 F4
Netanya, *Israel* 75 C3
Netarhat, *India* 69 H11
Nete →, *Belgium* 17 C4
Netherdale, *Australia* 94 C4
Netherlands ■, *Europe* 17 C5
Netherlands Antilles ■, *W. Indies* 124 A5
Neto →, *Italy* 31 C10
Netrang, *India* 68 J5
Nettancourt, *France* 19 D11
Nettetal, *Germany* 24 D2
Nettilling L., *Canada* 101 B12
Nettuno, *Italy* 30 A5
Netzahualcoyotl, Presa, *Mexico* 119 D6
Neu-Isenburg, *Germany* 25 E4
Neu-Ulm, *Germany* 25 G6
Neubrandenburg, *Germany* 24 B9
Neubukow, *Germany* 24 A7
Neuburg, *Germany* 25 G7
Neuchâtel, *Switz.* 25 J2
Neuchâtel □, *Switz.* 25 J2
Neuchâtel, Lac de, *Switz.* 25 J2
Neudau, *Austria* 26 D9
Neuenhagen, *Germany* 24 C9
Neuenhaus, *Germany* 24 C2
Neuf-Brisach, *France* 19 D14
Neufahrn, *Bayern, Germany* 25 G8
Neufahrn, *Bayern, Germany* 25 G7
Neufchâteau, *Belgium* 17 E5
Neufchâteau, *France* 19 D12
Neufchâtel-en-Bray, *France* 18 C8
Neufchâtel-sur-Aisne, *France* 19 C11
Neuhaus, *Germany* 24 B6
Neuillé-Pont-Pierre, *France* 18 E7
Neuilly-St-Front, *France* 19 C10
Neukalen, *Germany* 24 B8
Neumarkt, *Germany* 25 F7
Neumünster, *Germany* 24 A5
Neung-sur-Beuvron, *France* 19 E8
Neunkirchen, *Austria* 26 D9
Neunkirchen, *Germany* 25 F3
Neuquén, *Argentina* 128 D3
Neuquén □, *Argentina* 126 D2
Neuruppin, *Germany* 24 C8
Neusäss, *Germany* 25 G6
Neuse →, *U.S.A.* 109 H7
Neusiedl, *Austria* 27 D9
Neusiedler See, *Austria* 27 D9
Neuss, *Germany* 24 D2
Neussargues-Moissac, *France* 20 C7
Neustadt, *Bayern, Germany* 25 F8
Neustadt, *Bayern, Germany* 25 G7
Neustadt, *Bayern, Germany* 25 F6
Neustadt, *Bayern, Germany* 25 E7
Neustadt, *Brandenburg, Germany* 24 C8
Neustadt, *Hessen, Germany* 24 E5
Neustadt, *Niedersachsen, Germany* 24 C5
Neustadt, *Rhld-Pfz., Germany* 25 F4
Neustadt, *Sachsen, Germany* 24 D10
Neustadt, *Schleswig-Holstein, Germany* 24 A6
Neustadt, *Thüringen, Germany* 24 E7
Neustrelitz, *Germany* 24 B9
Neuvic, *France* 20 C6
Neuville-sur-Saône, *France* 21 C8
Neuvy-le-Roi, *France* 18 E7
Neuvy-St-Sépulchre, *France* 19 F8
Neuvy-sur-Barangeon, *France* 19 E9
Neuwerk, *Germany* 24 B4
Neuwied, *Germany* 24 E3
Neva →, *Russia* 46 C6
Nevada, *Iowa, U.S.A.* 112 D8
Nevada, *Mo., U.S.A.* 113 G7
Nevada □, *U.S.A.* 114 G5
Nevada City, *U.S.A.* 116 F6
Nevado, Cerro, *Argentina* 126 D2
Nevel, *Russia* 46 D5
Nevers, *France* 19 F10
Nevertire, *Australia* 95 E4
Nevesinje, *Bos.-H.* 40 C2
Neville, *Canada* 105 D7
Nevinnomyssk, *Russia* 49 H6
Nevis, *St. Kitts & Nevis* 121 C7
Nevrokop = Gotse Delchev, *Bulgaria* 40 E7
Nevşehir, *Turkey* 70 B2
New →, *U.S.A.* 108 F5
New Aiyansh, *Canada* 104 B3
New Albany, *Ind., U.S.A.* 108 F3
New Albany, *Miss., U.S.A.* 113 H10
New Albany, *Pa., U.S.A.* 111 E8
New Amsterdam, *Guyana* 124 B7
New Angledool, *Australia* 95 D4
New Baltimore, *U.S.A.* 110 D2
New Bedford, *U.S.A.* 111 E14
New Berlin, *N.Y., U.S.A.* 111 D9
New Berlin, *Pa., U.S.A.* 110 F8
New Bern, *U.S.A.* 109 H7
New Bethlehem, *U.S.A.* 110 F5
New Bloomfield, *U.S.A.* 110 F7
New Boston, *U.S.A.* 113 J7
New Braunfels, *U.S.A.* 113 L5
New Brighton, *N.Z.* 91 K4
New Brighton, *U.S.A.* 110 F4
New Britain, *Papua N. G.* 96 H7
New Britain, *U.S.A.* 111 E12
New Brunswick, *U.S.A.* 111 F10
New Brunswick □, *Canada* 103 C6
New Bussa, *Nigeria* 83 D5
New Caledonia ■, *Pac. Oc.* 96 K8
New Castile = Castilla-La Mancha □, *Spain* 6 H5
New Castle, *Ind., U.S.A.* 108 F3
New Castle, *Pa., U.S.A.* 110 F4
New City, *U.S.A.* 111 E11
New Concord, *U.S.A.* 110 G3
New Cumberland, *U.S.A.* 110 F4
New Cuyama, *U.S.A.* 117 L7
New Delhi, *India* 68 E7
New Denver, *Canada* 104 D5
New Don Pedro Reservoir, *U.S.A.* 116 H6
New England, *U.S.A.* 112 B3
New England Ra., *Australia* 95 E5
New Forest, *U.K.* 13 G6
New Galloway, *U.K.* 14 F4
New Glasgow, *Canada* 103 C7
New Guinea, *Oceania* 52 K17
New Hamburg, *Canada* 110 C4
New Hampshire □, *U.S.A.* 111 C13
New Hampton, *U.S.A.* 112 D8
New Hanover, *S. Africa* 89 D5
New Hartford, *U.S.A.* 111 C9
New Haven, *Conn., U.S.A.* 111 E12
New Haven, *Mich., U.S.A.* 110 D2
New Hazelton, *Canada* 104 B3
New Hebrides = Vanuatu ■, *Pac. Oc.* 96 J8
New Holland, *U.S.A.* 111 F8
New Iberia, *U.S.A.* 113 K9
New Ireland, *Papua N. G.* 96 H7
New Jersey □, *U.S.A.* 108 E8
New Kensington, *U.S.A.* 110 F5
New Lexington, *U.S.A.* 108 F4
New Liskeard, *Canada* 102 C4
New London, *Conn., U.S.A.* 111 E12
New London, *Ohio, U.S.A.* 110 E2
New London, *Wis., U.S.A.* 112 C10
New Madrid, *U.S.A.* 113 G10
New Martinsville, *U.S.A.* 108 F5
New Meadows, *U.S.A.* 114 D5
New Melones L., *U.S.A.* 116 H6
New Mexico □, *U.S.A.* 115 J10
New Milford, *Conn., U.S.A.* 111 E11
New Milford, *Pa., U.S.A.* 111 E9
New Norcia, *Australia* 93 F2
New Norfolk, *Australia* 94 G4
New Orleans, *U.S.A.* 113 L9
New Philadelphia, *U.S.A.* 110 F3
New Plymouth, *N.Z.* 91 H5
New Plymouth, *U.S.A.* 114 E5
New Port Richey, *U.S.A.* 109 L4
New Providence, *Bahamas* 120 A4
New Quay, *U.K.* 13 E3
New Radnor, *U.K.* 13 E4
New Richmond, *Canada* 103 C6
New Richmond, *U.S.A.* 112 C8
New Roads, *U.S.A.* 113 K9
New Rochelle, *U.S.A.* 111 F11
New Rockford, *U.S.A.* 112 B5
New Romney, *U.K.* 13 G8
New Ross, *Ireland* 15 D5
New Salem, *U.S.A.* 112 B4
New Scone, *U.K.* 14 E5
New Siberian I. = Novaya Sibir, Ostrov, *Russia* 51 B16
New Siberian Is. = Novosibirskiye Ostrova, *Russia* 51 B15
New Smyrna Beach, *U.S.A.* 109 L5
New South Wales □, *Australia* 95 E4
New Town, *U.S.A.* 112 B3
New Tredegar, *U.K.* 13 F4
New Ulm, *U.S.A.* 112 C7
New Waterford, *Canada* 103 C7
New Westminster, *Canada* 116 A4
New York, *U.S.A.* 111 F11
New York □, *U.S.A.* 111 D9
New York Mts., *U.S.A.* 115 J6
New Zealand ■, *Oceania* 91 J6
Newaj →, *India* 68 G7
Newala, *Tanzania* 87 E4
Newark, *Del., U.S.A.* 108 F8
Newark, *N.J., U.S.A.* 111 F10
Newark, *N.Y., U.S.A.* 110 C7
Newark, *Ohio, U.S.A.* 110 F2
Newark-on-Trent, *U.K.* 12 D7
Newark Valley, *U.S.A.* 111 D8
Newberg, *U.S.A.* 114 D2
Newberry, *Mich., U.S.A.* 108 B3
Newberry, *S.C., U.S.A.* 109 H5
Newberry Springs, *U.S.A.* 117 L10
Newboro L., *Canada* 111 B8
Newbridge = Droichead Nua, *Ireland* 15 C5
Newburgh, *Canada* 110 B8
Newburgh, *U.S.A.* 111 E10
Newbury, *U.K.* 13 F6
Newbury, *N.H., U.S.A.* 111 B12
Newbury, *Vt., U.S.A.* 111 B12
Newburyport, *U.S.A.* 109 D10
Newcastle, *Australia* 95 E5
Newcastle, *N.B., Canada* 103 C6
Newcastle, *Ont., Canada* 102 D4
Newcastle, *S. Africa* 89 D4
Newcastle, *U.K.* 15 B6
Newcastle, *Calif., U.S.A.* 116 G5
Newcastle, *Wyo., U.S.A.* 112 D2
Newcastle Emlyn, *U.K.* 13 E3
Newcastle Ra., *Australia* 92 C5
Newcastle-under-Lyme, *U.K.* 12 D5
Newcastle-upon-Tyne, *U.K.* 12 C6
Newcastle Waters, *Australia* 94 B1
Newcastle West, *Ireland* 15 D2
Newcomb, *U.S.A.* 111 C10
Newcomerstown, *U.S.A.* 110 F3
Newdegate, *Australia* 93 F2
Newell, *Australia* 94 B4
Newell, *U.S.A.* 112 C3
Newfane, *U.S.A.* 110 C6
Newfield, *U.S.A.* 111 D8
Newfound L., *U.S.A.* 111 C13
Newfoundland, *Canada* 98 E14
Newfoundland, *U.S.A.* 111 E9
Newfoundland □, *Canada* 103 B8
Newhall, *U.S.A.* 117 L8
Newhaven, *U.K.* 13 G8
Newkirk, *U.S.A.* 113 G6
Newlyn, *U.K.* 13 G2
Newman, *Australia* 92 D2
Newman, *U.S.A.* 116 H5
Newmarket, *Canada* 110 B5
Newmarket, *Ireland* 15 D2
Newmarket, *U.K.* 13 E8
Newmarket, *U.S.A.* 111 C14
Newnan, *U.S.A.* 109 J3
Newport, *Ireland* 15 C2
Newport, *I. of W., U.K.* 13 G6
Newport, *Newp., U.K.* 13 F5
Newport, *Ark., U.S.A.* 113 H9
Newport, *Ky., U.S.A.* 108 F3
Newport, *N.H., U.S.A.* 111 C12
Newport, *N.Y., U.S.A.* 111 C9
Newport, *Oreg., U.S.A.* 114 D1
Newport, *Pa., U.S.A.* 110 F7
Newport, *R.I., U.S.A.* 111 E13
Newport, *Tenn., U.S.A.* 109 H4
Newport, *Vt., U.S.A.* 111 B12
Newport, *Wash., U.S.A.* 114 B5
Newport □, *U.K.* 13 F4
Newport Beach, *U.S.A.* 117 M9
Newport News, *U.S.A.* 108 G7
Newport Pagnell, *U.K.* 13 E7
Newquay, *U.K.* 13 G2

Newry, *U.K.* 15 B5
Newton, *Ill., U.S.A.* 112 F10
Newton, *Iowa, U.S.A.* 112 E8
Newton, *Kans., U.S.A.* 113 F6
Newton, *Mass., U.S.A.* 111 D13
Newton, *Miss., U.S.A.* 113 J10
Newton, *N.C., U.S.A.* 109 H5
Newton, *N.J., U.S.A.* 111 E10
Newton, *Tex., U.S.A.* 113 K8
Newton Abbot, *U.K.* 13 G4
Newton Aycliffe, *U.K.* 12 C6
Newton Falls, *U.S.A.* 110 E4
Newton Stewart, *U.K.* 14 G4
Newtonmore, *U.K.* 14 D4
Newtown, *U.K.* 13 E4
Newtownabbey, *U.K.* 15 B6
Newtownards, *U.K.* 15 B6
Newtownbarry = Bunclody,
  Ireland 15 D5
Newtownstewart, *U.K.* 15 B4
Newville, *U.S.A.* 110 F7
Nexon, *France* 20 C5
Neya, *Russia* 48 A6
Neyrīz, *Iran* 71 D7
Neyshābūr, *Iran* 71 B8
Nezhin = Nizhyn, *Ukraine* 47 G6
Nezperce, *U.S.A.* 114 C5
Ngabang, *Indonesia* 62 D3
Ngabordamlu, Tanjung,
  Indonesia 63 F8
N'Gage, *Angola* 84 F3
Ngala, *Nigeria* 83 C7
Ngambé, *Cameroon* 83 D7
Ngambé, *Cameroon* 83 E7
Ngami Depression, *Botswana* .. 88 C3
Ngamo, *Zimbabwe* 87 F2
Ngangala, *Sudan* 81 G3
Nganglong Kangri, *China* 67 C12
Ngao, *Thailand* 64 C2
Ngaoundéré, *Cameroon* 84 C2
Ngapara, *N.Z.* 91 L3
Ngara, *Tanzania* 86 C3
Ngawi, *Indonesia* 63 G14
Nghia Lo, *Vietnam* 58 G5
Ngoboli, *Sudan* 81 G3
Ngoma, *Malawi* 87 E3
Ngomahura, *Zimbabwe* 87 G3
Ngomba, *Tanzania* 87 D3
Ngop, *Sudan* 81 F3
Ngoring Hu, *China* 60 C4
Ngorkou, *Mali* 82 B4
Ngorongoro, *Tanzania* 86 C4
Ngozi, *Burundi* 86 C2
Ngudu, *Tanzania* 86 C3
Nguigmi, *Niger* 79 F8
Nguila, *Cameroon* 83 E7
Nguiu, *Australia* 92 B5
Ngukurr, *Australia* 94 A1
Ngulu Atoll, *Pac. Oc.* 63 C9
Ngunga, *Tanzania* 86 C3
Nguru, *Nigeria* 83 C7
Nguru Mts., *Tanzania* 86 D4
Nguyen Binh, *Vietnam* 58 F5
Nha Trang, *Vietnam* 65 F7
Nhacoongo, *Mozam.* 89 C6
Nhamaabué, *Mozam.* 87 F4
Nhamundá →, *Brazil* 125 D7
Nhangulaze, L., *Mozam.* 89 C5
Nhill, *Australia* 95 F3
Nho Quan, *Vietnam* 58 G5
Nhulunbuy, *Australia* 94 A2
Nia-nia, *Dem. Rep. of the Congo* 86 B2
Niafounké, *Mali* 82 B4
Niagara Falls, *Canada* 102 D4
Niagara Falls, *U.S.A.* 110 C6
Niagara-on-the-Lake, *Canada* . 110 C5
Niah, *Malaysia* 62 D4
Niamey, *Niger* 83 C5
Niandan-Koro, *Guinea* 82 C3
Nianforando, *Guinea* 82 D2
Niangara, *Dem. Rep. of
  the Congo* 86 B2
Niangbo, *Ivory C.* 82 D3
Niangoloko, *Burkina Faso* 82 C4
Niantic, *U.S.A.* 111 E12
Niaro, *Sudan* 81 E3
Nias, *Indonesia* 62 D1
Niassa □, *Mozam.* 87 E4
Nibāk, *Si. Arabia* 71 E7
Nibe, *Denmark* 11 H3
Nicaragua ■, *Cent. Amer.* 120 D2
Nicaragua, L. de, *Nic.* 120 D2
Nicastro, *Italy* 31 D9
Nice, *France* 21 E11
Niceville, *U.S.A.* 109 K2
Nichicun, L., *Canada* 103 B5
Nichinan, *Japan* 55 J5
Nicholás, Canal, *W. Indies* 120 B3
Nicholasville, *U.S.A.* 108 G3
Nichols, *U.S.A.* 111 D8
Nicholson, *Australia* 92 C4
Nicholson, *U.S.A.* 111 E9
Nicholson →, *Australia* 94 B2
Nicholson, *Canada* 105 A8
Nicholson Ra., *Australia* 93 E2
Nicholville, *U.S.A.* 111 B10
Nicobar Is., *Ind. Oc.* 52 J13
Nicola, *Canada* 104 C4
Nicolls Town, *Bahamas* 120 A4
Nicopolis, *Greece* 38 B2
Nicosia, *Cyprus* 36 D12
Nicosia, *Italy* 31 E7
Nicótera, *Italy* 31 D8
Nicoya, *Costa Rica* 120 D2
Nicoya, G. de, *Costa Rica* 120 E3
Nicoya, Pen. de, *Costa Rica* 120 E2
Nidd →, *U.K.* 12 D6

Nidda, *Germany* 25 E5
Nidda →, *Germany* 25 E4
Nidwalden □, *Switz.* 25 J4
Nidzica, *Poland* 45 E7
Niebüll, *Germany* 24 A4
Nied →, *Germany* 19 C13
Niederaula, *Germany* 24 E5
Niederbayern □, *Germany* 25 G8
Niederbronn-les-Bains, *France* . 19 D14
Niedere Tauern, *Austria* 26 D7
Niederlausitz, *Germany* 24 D9
Niederösterreich □, *Austria* ... 26 C8
Niedersachsen □, *Germany* 24 C4
Niekerkshoop, *S. Africa* 88 D3
Niellé, *Ivory C.* 82 C3
Niemba, *Dem. Rep. of the Congo* 86 D2
Niemen = Neman →, *Lithuania* . 9 J19
Niemodlin, *Poland* 45 H4
Nienburg, *Germany* 24 C5
Niepołomice, *Poland* 45 H7
Niers →, *Germany* 24 D1
Niesky, *Germany* 24 D10
Nieszawa, *Poland* 45 F5
Nieu Bethesda, *S. Africa* 88 E3
Nieuw Amsterdam, *Surinam* . 125 B7
Nieuw Nickerie, *Surinam* 125 B7
Nieuwoudtville, *S. Africa* 88 E2
Nieuwpoort, *Belgium* 17 C2
Nieves, Pico de las, *Canary Is.* . 37 G4
Nièvre □, *France* 19 E10
Niga, *Mali* 82 C3
Niğde, *Turkey* 70 B2
Nigel, *S. Africa* 89 D4
Niger □, *Nigeria* 83 D6
Niger ■, *W. Afr.* 83 B7
Niger →, *W. Afr.* 51 D6
Niger Delta, *Africa* 83 E6
Nigeria ■, *W. Afr.* 83 D6
Nighasin, *India* 69 E9
Nightcaps, *N.Z.* 91 L2
Nigríta, *Greece* 40 F7
Nii-Jima, *Japan* 55 G9
Niigata, *Japan* 54 F9
Niigata □, *Japan* 55 F9
Niihama, *Japan* 55 H6
Niʻihau, *U.S.A.* 106 H14
Niimi, *Japan* 55 G6
Niitsu, *Japan* 54 F9
Níjar, *Spain* 33 J2
Nijil, *Jordan* 75 E4
Nijkerk, *Neths.* 17 B5
Nijmegen, *Neths.* 17 C5
Nijverdal, *Neths.* 17 B6
Nīk Pey, *Iran* 71 B6
Nike, *Nigeria* 83 D6
Nikiniki, *Indonesia* 63 F6
Nikísiani, *Greece* 41 F8
Nikítas, *Greece* 40 F7
Nikki, *Benin* 83 D5
Nikkō, *Japan* 55 F9
Nikolayev = Mykolayiv, *Ukraine* 47 J7
Nikolayevsk, *Russia* 48 E7
Nikolayevsk-na-Amur, *Russia* . 51 D15
Nikolsk, *Russia* 48 D8
Nikolskoye, *Russia* 51 D17
Nikopol, *Bulgaria* 41 C8
Nikopol, *Ukraine* 47 J8
Niksar, *Turkey* 72 B7
Nīkshahr, *Iran* 71 E9
Nikšić, *Montenegro, Yug.* 40 D2
Nîl, Nahr en →, *Africa* 80 H7
Nîl el Abyad →, *Sudan* 81 D3
Nîl el Azraq →, *Sudan* 81 D3
Nila, *Indonesia* 63 F7
Niland, *U.S.A.* 117 M11
Nile = Nîl, Nahr en →, *Africa* . 80 H7
Niles, *Mich., U.S.A.* 108 E2
Niles, *Ohio, U.S.A.* 110 E4
Nilüfer →, *Turkey* 41 F12
Nim Ka Thana, *India* 68 F6
Nimach, *India* 68 G6
Nimbahera, *India* 68 G6
Nîmes, *France* 21 E8
Nimfaíon, Ákra = Pínnes, Ákra,
  Greece 41 F8
Nimmitabel, *Australia* 95 F4
Nimule, *Sudan* 81 G3
Nin, *Croatia* 29 D12
Nīnawā, *Iraq* 70 B4
Nindigully, *Australia* 95 D4
Nineveh = Nīnawā, *Iraq* 70 B4
Ning Xian, *China* 56 G4
Ning'an, *China* 57 B15
Ningbo, *China* 59 C13
Ningcheng, *China* 57 D10
Ningdu, *China* 59 D10
Ningde, *China* 59 D12
Ninggang, *China* 59 D9
Ningguo, *China* 59 B12
Ninghai, *China* 59 C13
Ninghua, *China* 59 D11
Ningi, *Nigeria* 83 C6
Ningjin, *China* 56 F8
Ningjing Shan, *China* 58 C2
Ninglang, *China* 58 D3
Ningling, *China* 56 G8
Ningming, *China* 58 F6
Ningnan, *China* 58 D4
Ningpo = Ningbo, *China* 59 C13
Ningqiang, *China* 56 H4
Ningshan, *China* 56 H5
Ningsia Hui A.R. = Ningxia
  Huizu Zizhiqu □, *China* 56 F4
Ningwu, *China* 56 E7
Ningxia Huizu Zizhiqu □, *China* 56 F4
Ningxiang, *China* 59 C9
Ningyang, *China* 56 G9

Ningyuan, *China* 59 E8
Ninh Binh, *Vietnam* 58 G5
Ninh Giang, *Vietnam* 64 B6
Ninh Hoa, *Vietnam* 64 F7
Ninh Ma, *Vietnam* 64 F7
Ninove, *Belgium* 17 D4
Nioaque, *Brazil* 127 A4
Niobrara, *U.S.A.* 112 D6
Niobrara →, *U.S.A.* 112 D6
Niono, *Mali* 82 C3
Nioro du Rip, *Senegal* 82 C1
Nioro du Sahel, *Mali* 82 B3
Niort, *France* 20 B3
Nipawin, *Canada* 105 C8
Nipfjället, *Sweden* 10 C6
Nipigon, *Canada* 102 C2
Nipigon, L., *Canada* 102 C2
Nipishish L., *Canada* 103 B7
Nipissing, L., *Canada* 102 C4
Nipomo, *U.S.A.* 117 K6
Nipton, *U.S.A.* 117 K11
Niquelândia, *Brazil* 125 F9
Nīr, *Iran* 70 B5
Nirasaki, *Japan* 55 G9
Nirmal, *India* 66 K11
Nirmali, *India* 69 F12
Niš, *Serbia, Yug.* 40 C5
Nisa, *Portugal* 35 F3
Nisáb, *Si. Arabia* 70 D5
Nisāb, *Yemen* 74 E4
Nišava →, *Serbia, Yug.* 40 C5
Niscemi, *Italy* 31 E7
Nishinomiya, *Japan* 55 G7
Nishino'omote, *Japan* 55 J5
Nishiwaki, *Japan* 55 G7
Nísíros, *Greece* 39 E9
Niška Banja, *Serbia, Yug.* 40 C6
Niskibi →, *Canada* 102 A2
Nisko, *Poland* 45 H9
Nisporeni, *Moldova* 43 C13
Nisqually →, *U.S.A.* 116 C4
Nissáki, *Greece* 36 A3
Nissan →, *Sweden* 11 H6
Nissum Bredning, *Denmark* 11 H2
Nissum Fjord, *Denmark* 11 H2
Nistru = Dnister →, *Europe* 47 J6
Nisutlin →, *Canada* 104 A2
Nitchequon, *Canada* 103 B5
Niterói, *Brazil* 127 A7
Nith →, *Canada* 110 C4
Nith →, *U.K.* 14 F5
Nitra, *Slovak Rep.* 27 C11
Nitra →, *Slovak Rep.* 27 D11
Nitriansky □, *Slovak Rep.* 27 C11
Nittedal, *Norway* 9 F14
Nittenau, *Germany* 25 F8
Niuafo'ou, *Tonga* 91 B11
Niue, *Cook Is.* 97 J11
Niulan Jiang →, *China* 58 D4
Niut, *Indonesia* 62 D4
Niutou Shan, *China* 59 C13
Niuzhuang, *China* 57 D12
Nivala, *Finland* 8 E21
Nivelles, *Belgium* 17 D4
Nivernais, *France* 19 E10
Niwas, *India* 69 H9
Nixon, *U.S.A.* 113 L6
Nizamabad, *India* 66 K11
Nizamghat, *India* 67 E19
Nizhne Kolymsk, *Russia* 51 C17
Nizhnegorskiy = Nyzhnohirskyy,
  Ukraine 47 K8
Nizhnekamsk, *Russia* 48 C10
Nizhneudinsk, *Russia* 51 D10
Nizhnevartovsk, *Russia* 50 C8
Nizhniy Chir, *Russia* 49 F6
Nizhniy Lomov, *Russia* 48 D6
Nizhniy Novgorod, *Russia* 48 B7
Nizhniy Tagil, *Russia* 50 D6
Nizhyn, *Ukraine* 47 G6
Nizina Mazowiecka, *Poland* 45 F8
Nizip, *Turkey* 70 B3
Nízké Tatry, *Slovak Rep.* 27 C12
Nízký Jeseník, *Czech Rep.* 27 B10
Nizza Monferrato, *Italy* 28 D5
Njakwa, *Malawi* 87 E3
Njanji, *Zambia* 87 E3
Njegoš, *Montenegro, Yug.* 40 D2
Njinjo, *Tanzania* 87 D4
Njombe, *Tanzania* 87 D3
Njombe →, *Tanzania* 86 D4
Njurundabommen, *Sweden* 10 B11
Nkambe, *Cameroon* 83 D7
Nkana, *Zambia* 87 E2
Nkandla, *S. Africa* 89 D5
Nkawkaw, *Ghana* 83 D4
Nkhata Bay, *Malawi* 87 E3
Nkhotakota, *Malawi* 87 E3
Nkongsamba, *Cameroon* 83 E6
Nkurenkuru, *Namibia* 88 B2
Nkwanta, *Ghana* 82 D4
Nmai →, *Burma* 58 F2
Noakhali = Maijdi, *Bangla.* 67 H17
Nobel, *Canada* 110 A4
Nobeoka, *Japan* 55 H5
Noblejas, *Spain* 34 F7
Noblesville, *U.S.A.* 108 E3
Noce →, *Italy* 28 B8
Nocera Inferiore, *Italy* 31 B7
Nocera Umbra, *Italy* 29 E9
Noci, *Italy* 31 B10
Nocona, *U.S.A.* 113 J6
Nocrich, *Romania* 43 E9
Noda, *Japan* 55 G9
Nogales, *Mexico* 118 A2
Nogales, *U.S.A.* 115 L8
Nogaro, *France* 20 E3

Nogat →, *Poland* 44 D6
Nōgata, *Japan* 55 H5
Nogent, *France* 19 D12
Nogent-le-Rotrou, *France* 18 D7
Nogent-sur-Seine, *France* 19 D10
Noggerup, *Australia* 93 F2
Noginsk, *Moskva, Russia* 46 E10
Noginsk, *Tunguska, Russia* 51 C10
Nogoa →, *Australia* 94 C4
Nógrád □, *Hungary* 42 C4
Noguera Pallaresa →, *Spain* ... 32 D5
Noguera Ribagorzana →, *Spain* 32 D5
Nohar, *India* 68 E6
Nohfelden, *Germany* 25 F3
Nohta, *India* 69 H8
Noia, *Spain* 34 C2
Noire, Montagne, *France* 20 E6
Noires, Mts., *France* 18 D3
Noirétable, *France* 20 C7
Noirmoutier, Î. de, *France* 18 F4
Noirmoutier-en-l'Île, *France* 18 F4
Nojane, *Botswana* 88 C3
Nojima-Zaki, *Japan* 55 G9
Nok Kundi, *Pakistan* 66 E3
Nok Ta, *India* .... (not listed)
Nokaneng, *Botswana* 88 B3
Nokia, *Finland* 9 F20
Nokomis, *Canada* 105 C8
Nokomis L., *Canada* 105 B8
Nol, *Sweden* 11 G6
Nola, *C.A.R.* 84 D3
Nola, *Italy* 31 B7
Nolay, *France* 19 F11
Noli, C. di, *Italy* 28 D5
Nolinsk, *Russia* 48 B9
Noma Omuramba →, *Namibia* 88 B3
Nomo-Zaki, *Japan* 55 H4
Nonacho L., *Canada* 105 A7
Nonancourt, *France* 18 D8
Nonda, *Australia* 94 C3
None, *Italy* 28 D4
Nong Chang, *Thailand* 64 E2
Nong Het, *Laos* 64 C5
Nong Khai, *Thailand* 64 D4
Nong'an, *China* 57 B13
Nongoma, *S. Africa* 89 D5
Nonoava, *Mexico* 118 B3
Nonoava →, *Mexico* 118 B3
Nonthaburi, *Thailand* 64 F3
Nontron, *France* 20 C4
Nonza, *France* 21 F13
Noonamah, *Australia* 92 B5
Noord Brabant □, *Neths.* 17 C5
Noord Holland □, *Neths.* 17 B4
Noordbeveland, *Neths.* 17 C3
Noordoostpolder, *Neths.* 17 B5
Noordwijk, *Neths.* 17 B4
Nootka I., *Canada* 104 D3
Nopiming Prov. Park, *Canada* ... 105 C9
Nora, *Eritrea* 81 D5
Nora, *Sweden* 10 E9
Noralee, *Canada* 104 C3
Noranda = Rouyn-Noranda,
  Canada 102 C4
Norberg, *Sweden* 10 D9
Nórcia, *Italy* 29 F10
Norco, *U.S.A.* 117 M9
Nord □, *France* 19 B10
Nord-Kivu □, *Dem. Rep. of
  the Congo* 86 C2
Nord-Ostsee-Kanal, *Germany* .. 24 A5
Nord-Pas-de-Calais □, *France* .. 19 B9
Nordaustlandet, *Svalbard* 4 B9
Nordborg, *Denmark* 11 J3
Nordby, *Denmark* 11 J2
Norddeich, *Germany* 24 B3
Nordegg, *Canada* 104 C5
Norden, *Germany* 24 B3
Nordenham, *Germany* 24 B4
Norderney, *Germany* 24 B3
Norderstedt, *Germany* 24 B6
Nordfjord, *Norway* 9 F11
Nordfriesische Inseln, *Germany* 24 A4
Nordhausen, *Germany* 24 D6
Nordhorn, *Germany* 24 C3
Norðoyar, *Færoe Is.* 8 E9
Nordingrå, *Sweden* 10 B12
Nordjyllands Amtskommune □,
  Denmark 11 G4
Nordkapp, *Norway* 8 A21
Nordkapp, *Svalbard* 4 A9
Nordkinn = Kinnarodden,
  Norway 6 A11
Nordkinn-halvøya, *Norway* 8 A22
Nördlingen, *Germany* 25 G6
Nordrhein-Westfalen □,
  Germany 24 D3
Nordstrand, *Germany* 24 A4
Nordvik, *Russia* 51 B12
Nore →, *Ireland* 15 D4
Norfolk, *Nebr., U.S.A.* 112 D6
Norfolk, *Va., U.S.A.* 108 G7
Norfolk □, *U.K.* 13 E8
Norfolk I., *Pac. Oc.* 96 K8
Norfork L., *U.S.A.* 113 G8
Norilsk, *Russia* 51 C9
Norma, Mt., *Australia* 94 C3
Normal, *U.S.A.* 112 E10
Norman, *U.S.A.* 113 H6
Norman →, *Australia* 94 B3
Norman Wells, *Canada* 100 B7
Normanby →, *Australia* 94 A3
Normandin, *Canada* 102 C5
Normanhurst, Mt., *Australia* 93 E3
Normanton, *Australia* 94 B3

Normétal, *Canada* 102 C4
Norquay, *Canada* 105 C8
Norquinco, *Argentina* 128 E2
Norra Dellen, *Sweden* 10 C10
Norra Ulvön, *Sweden* 10 A12
Norrahammar, *Sweden* 11 G8
Norrbotten □, *Sweden* 8 C19
Nørre Åby, *Denmark* 11 J3
Nørre Alslev, *Denmark* 11 K5
Nørresundby, *Denmark* 11 G3
Norrhult, *Sweden* 11 G9
Norris Point, *Canada* 103 C8
Norristown, *U.S.A.* 111 F9
Norrköping, *Sweden* 11 F10
Norrland, *Sweden* 9 E16
Norrsundet, *Sweden* 10 D11
Norrtälje, *Sweden* 10 E12
Norseman, *Australia* 93 F3
Norsk, *Russia* 51 D14
Norte, Pta. del, *Canary Is.* 37 G2
Norte, Serra do, *Brazil* 124 F7
North, C., *Canada* 103 C7
North Adams, *U.S.A.* 111 D11
North Arm, *Canada* 104 A5
North Augusta, *U.S.A.* 109 J5
North Ayrshire □, *U.K.* 14 F4
North Bass I., *U.S.A.* 110 E2
North Battleford, *Canada* 105 C7
North Bay, *Canada* 102 C4
North Belcher Is., *Canada* 102 A4
North Bend, *Oreg., U.S.A.* 114 E1
North Bend, *Pa., U.S.A.* 110 E7
North Bend, *Wash., U.S.A.* 116 C5
North Bennington, *U.S.A.* 111 D11
North Berwick, *U.K.* 14 E6
North Berwick, *U.S.A.* 111 C14
North C., *Canada* 103 C7
North C., *N.Z.* 91 F4
North Canadian →, *U.S.A.* 113 H7
North Canton, *U.S.A.* 110 F3
North Cape = Nordkapp,
  Norway 8 A21
North Cape = Nordkapp,
  Svalbard 4 A9
North Caribou L., *Canada* 102 B1
North Carolina □, *U.S.A.* 109 H6
North Cascades National Park,
  U.S.A. 114 B3
North Channel, *Canada* 102 C3
North Channel, *U.K.* 14 F3
North Charleston, *U.S.A.* 109 J6
North Chicago, *U.S.A.* 108 D2
North Creek, *U.S.A.* 111 C11
North Dakota □, *U.S.A.* 112 B5
North Downs, *U.K.* 13 F8
North East, *U.S.A.* 110 D5
North East Frontier Agency =
  Arunachal Pradesh □, *India* . 67 F19
North East Lincolnshire □, *U.K.* 12 D7
North Eastern □, *Kenya* 86 B5
North Esk →, *U.K.* 14 E6
North European Plain, *Europe* 6 E10
North Foreland, *U.K.* 13 F9
North Fork, *U.S.A.* 116 H7
North Fork American →, *U.S.A.* 116 G5
North Fork Feather →, *U.S.A.* 116 F5
North Fork Grand →, *U.S.A.* 112 C3
North Fork Red →, *U.S.A.* 113 H5
North Frisian Is. =
  Nordfriesische Inseln,
  Germany 24 A4
North Gower, *Canada* 111 A9
North Hd., *Australia* 93 F1
North Henik L., *Canada* 105 A9
North Highlands, *U.S.A.* 116 G5
North Horr, *Kenya* 86 B4
North I., *Kenya* 86 B4
North I., *N.Z.* 91 H5
North Kingsville, *U.S.A.* 110 E4
North Knife →, *Canada* 105 B10
North Koel →, *India* 69 G10
North Korea ■, *Asia* 57 E14
North Lakhimpur, *India* 67 F19
North Lanarkshire □, *U.K.* 14 F5
North Las Vegas, *U.S.A.* 117 J11
North Lincolnshire □, *U.K.* 12 D7
North Little Rock, *U.S.A.* 113 H8
North Loup →, *U.S.A.* 112 E5
North Magnetic Pole, *Canada* . 4 B2
North Minch, *U.K.* 14 C3
North Moose L., *Canada* 105 C8
North Myrtle Beach, *U.S.A.* 109 J6
North Nahanni →, *Canada* 104 A4
North Olmsted, *U.S.A.* 110 E3
North Ossetia □, *Russia* 49 J7
North Pagai, I. = Pagai Utara,
  Pulau, *Indonesia* 62 E2
North Palisade, *U.S.A.* 116 H8
North Platte, *U.S.A.* 112 E4
North Platte →, *U.S.A.* 112 E4
North Pole, *Arctic* .... 4 A
North Portal, *Canada* 105 D8
North Powder, *U.S.A.* 114 D5
North Pt., *U.S.A.* 110 A1
North Rhine Westphalia =
  Nordrhein-Westfalen □,
  Germany 24 D3
North River, *Canada* 103 B8
North Ronaldsay, *U.K.* 14 B6
North Saskatchewan →, *Canada* 105 C7
North Sea, *Europe* 6 D6
North Seal →, *Canada* 105 B9
North Somerset □, *U.K.* 13 F5
North Sporades = Vórial
  Sporádhes, *Greece* 38 B5
North Sydney, *Canada* 103 C7
North Syracuse, *U.S.A.* 111 C8

189

North Taranaki Bight, *N.Z.* ... 91 H5
North Thompson →, *Canada* ... 104 C4
North Tonawanda, *U.S.A.* ... 110 C6
North Troy, *U.S.A.* ... 111 B12
North Truchas Pk., *U.S.A.* ... 115 J11
North Twin I., *Canada* ... 102 B4
North Tyne →, *U.K.* ... 12 B5
North Uist, *U.K.* ... 14 D1
North Vancouver, *Canada* ... 104 D4
North Vernon, *U.S.A.* ... 108 F3
North Wabasca L., *Canada* ... 104 B6
North Walsham, *U.K.* ... 12 E9
North-West □, *S. Africa* ... 88 D4
North West C., *Australia* ... 92 D1
North West Christmas I. Ridge, *Pac. Oc.* ... 97 G11
North West Frontier □, *Pakistan* ... 68 C4
North West Highlands, *U.K.* ... 14 D4
North West River, *Canada* ... 103 B7
North Western □, *Zambia* ... 87 E2
North Wildwood, *U.S.A.* ... 108 F8
North York Moors, *U.K.* ... 12 C7
North Yorkshire □, *U.K.* ... 12 C6
Northallerton, *U.K.* ... 12 C6
Northam, *Australia* ... 93 F2
Northam, *S. Africa* ... 88 C4
Northampton, *Australia* ... 93 E1
Northampton, *U.K.* ... 13 E7
Northampton, *Mass., U.S.A.* ... 111 D12
Northampton, *Pa., U.S.A.* ... 111 F9
Northamptonshire □, *U.K.* ... 13 E7
Northbridge, *U.S.A.* ... 111 D13
Northcliffe, *Australia* ... 93 F2
Northeast Providence Chan., *W. Indies* ... 120 A4
Northeim, *Germany* ... 24 D6
Northern □, *Ghana* ... 83 D4
Northern □, *Malawi* ... 87 E3
Northern □, *Zambia* ... 87 E3
Northern Areas □, *Pakistan* ... 69 A5
Northern Cape □, *S. Africa* ... 88 D3
Northern Circars, *India* ... 67 L13
Northern Indian L., *Canada* ... 105 B9
Northern Ireland □, *U.K.* ... 15 B5
Northern Light L., *Canada* ... 102 C1
Northern Marianas ■, *Pac. Oc.* ... 96 F6
Northern Province □, *S. Leone* ... 82 D2
Northern Province □, *S. Africa* ... 89 C4
Northern Territory □, *Australia* ... 92 D5
Northfield, *Minn., U.S.A.* ... 112 C8
Northfield, *Vt., U.S.A.* ... 111 B12
Northland □, *N.Z.* ... 91 F4
Northome, *U.S.A.* ... 112 B7
Northport, *Ala., U.S.A.* ... 109 J2
Northport, *Wash., U.S.A.* ... 114 B5
Northumberland □, *U.K.* ... 12 B6
Northumberland, C., *Australia* ... 95 F4
Northumberland Is., *Australia* ... 94 C4
Northumberland Str., *Canada* ... 103 C7
Northville, *U.S.A.* ... 111 C10
Northwest Providence Channel, *W. Indies* ... 120 A4
Northwest Territories □, *Canada* ... 100 B9
Northwood, *Iowa, U.S.A.* ... 112 D8
Northwood, *N. Dak., U.S.A.* ... 112 B6
Norton, *U.S.A.* ... 112 F5
Norton, *Zimbabwe* ... 87 F3
Norton Sd., *U.S.A.* ... 100 B3
Nortorf, *Germany* ... 24 A5
Norwalk, *Calif., U.S.A.* ... 117 M8
Norwalk, *Conn., U.S.A.* ... 111 E11
Norwalk, *Iowa, U.S.A.* ... 112 E8
Norwalk, *Ohio, U.S.A.* ... 110 E2
Norway, *Maine, U.S.A.* ... 109 C10
Norway, *Mich., U.S.A.* ... 108 C2
Norway ■, *Europe* ... 8 E14
Norway House, *Canada* ... 105 C9
Norwegian Sea, *Atl. Oc.* ... 4 C8
Norwich, *Canada* ... 110 D4
Norwich, *U.K.* ... 13 E9
Norwich, *Conn., U.S.A.* ... 111 E12
Norwich, *N.Y., U.S.A.* ... 111 D9
Norwood, *Canada* ... 110 B7
Norwood, *U.S.A.* ... 111 B10
Noshiro, *Japan* ... 54 D10
Nosivka, *Ukraine* ... 47 G6
Nosovka = Nosivka, *Ukraine* ... 47 G6
Noṣraṭābād, *Iran* ... 71 D8
Noss Hd., *U.K.* ... 14 C5
Nossebro, *Sweden* ... 11 F6
Nossob →, *S. Africa* ... 88 D3
Nossombougou, *Mali* ... 82 C3
Nosy Barren, *Madag.* ... 85 H8
Nosy Be, *Madag.* ... 85 G9
Nosy Boraha, *Madag.* ... 89 B8
Nosy Lava, *Madag.* ... 89 A8
Nosy Varika, *Madag.* ... 89 C8
Noteć →, *Poland* ... 45 F2
Notikewin →, *Canada* ... 104 B5
Notio Aigaio = Notios Aiyaíon □ ... 39 E7
Notios Aiyaíon □ ... 39 E7
Notios Evvoïkos Kólpos, *Greece* ... 38 C5
Noto, *Italy* ... 31 F8
Noto, G. di, *Italy* ... 31 F8
Notodden, *Norway* ... 9 G13
Notre Dame B., *Canada* ... 103 C8
Notre Dame de Koartac = Quaqtaq, *Canada* ... 101 B13
Notre-Dame-des-Bois, *Canada* ... 111 A13
Notre Dame d'Ivugivic = Ivujivik, *Canada* ... 101 B12
Notre-Dame-du-Nord, *Canada* ... 102 C4
Notsé, *Togo* ... 83 D5
Nottawasaga B., *Canada* ... 110 B4
Nottaway →, *Canada* ... 102 B4
Nottingham, *U.K.* ... 12 E6

Nottingham, City of □, *U.K.* ... 12 E6
Nottingham I., *Canada* ... 101 B12
Nottinghamshire □, *U.K.* ... 12 D6
Nottoway →, *U.S.A.* ... 108 G7
Notwane →, *Botswana* ... 88 C4
Nouâdhibou, *Mauritania* ... 78 D2
Nouâdhibou, Ras, *Mauritania* ... 78 D2
Nouakchott, *Mauritania* ... 82 B1
Nouâmghâr, *Mauritania* ... 82 B1
Nouméa, *N. Cal.* ... 96 K8
Nouna, *Burkina Faso* ... 82 C4
Noupoort, *S. Africa* ... 88 E3
Nouveau Comptoir = Wemindji, *Canada* ... 102 B4
Nouvelle-Amsterdam, I., *Ind. Oc.* ... 3 F13
Nouvelle-Calédonie = New Caledonia ■, *Pac. Oc.* ... 96 K8
Nouzonville, *France* ... 19 C11
Nová Baňa, *Slovak Rep.* ... 27 C11
Nová Bystřice, *Czech Rep.* ... 26 B8
Nova Casa Nova, *Brazil* ... 125 E10
Nova Esperança, *Brazil* ... 127 A5
Nova Friburgo, *Brazil* ... 127 A7
Nova Gaia = Cambundi-Catembo, *Angola* ... 84 G3
Nova Gorica, *Slovenia* ... 29 C10
Nova Gradiška, *Croatia* ... 42 E2
Nova Iguaçu, *Brazil* ... 127 A7
Nova Iorque, *Brazil* ... 125 E10
Nova Kakhovka, *Ukraine* ... 47 J7
Nova Lamego, *Guinea-Biss.* ... 82 C2
Nova Lima, *Brazil* ... 127 A7
Nova Lisboa = Huambo, *Angola* ... 85 G3
Nova Lusitânia, *Mozam.* ... 87 F3
Nova Mambone, *Mozam.* ... 89 C6
Nova Odesa, *Ukraine* ... 47 J6
Nová Paka, *Czech Rep.* ... 26 A8
Nova Pavova, *Serbia, Yug.* ... 42 F5
Nova Scotia □, *Canada* ... 103 C7
Nova Siri, *Italy* ... 31 B9
Nova Sofala, *Mozam.* ... 89 C5
Nova Varoš, *Serbia, Yug.* ... 40 C3
Nova Venécia, *Brazil* ... 125 G10
Nova Zagora, *Bulgaria* ... 41 D10
Novaci, *Macedonia* ... 40 E5
Novaci, *Romania* ... 43 E8
Novaféltria, *Italy* ... 29 E9
Novaleksandrovskaya = Novoaleksandrovsk, *Russia* ... 49 H5
Novannenskiy = Novoannenskiy, *Russia* ... 48 E6
Novar, *Canada* ... 110 A5
Novara, *Italy* ... 28 C5
Novato, *U.S.A.* ... 116 G4
Novaya Kakhovka = Nova Kakhovka, *Ukraine* ... 47 J7
Novaya Kazanka, *Kazakstan* ... 49 F9
Novaya Ladoga, *Russia* ... 46 B7
Novaya Lyalya, *Russia* ... 50 D7
Novaya Sibir, Ostrov, *Russia* ... 51 B16
Novaya Zemlya, *Russia* ... 50 B6
Nové Město, *Slovak Rep.* ... 27 C10
Nové Město na Moravě, *Czech Rep.* ... 26 B9
Nové Město nad Metují, *Czech Rep.* ... 27 A9
Nové Zámky, *Slovak Rep.* ... 27 C11
Novelda, *Spain* ... 33 G4
Novellara, *Italy* ... 28 D7
Noventa Vicentina, *Italy* ... 29 C8
Novgorod, *Russia* ... 46 C6
Novgorod-Severskiy = Novhorod-Siverskyy, *Ukraine* ... 47 G7
Novhorod-Siverskyy, *Ukraine* ... 47 G7
Novi Bečej, *Serbia, Yug.* ... 42 E5
Novi Iskar, *Bulgaria* ... 40 D7
Novi Kneževac, *Serbia, Yug.* ... 42 E5
Novi Lígure, *Italy* ... 28 D5
Novi Pazar, *Bulgaria* ... 41 C11
Novi Pazar, *Serbia, Yug.* ... 40 C4
Novi Sad, *Serbia, Yug.* ... 42 E4
Novi Slankamen, *Serbia, Yug.* ... 42 E5
Novi Vinodolski, *Croatia* ... 29 C11
Novigrad, *Istra, Croatia* ... 29 C10
Novigrad, *Zadar, Croatia* ... 29 D12
Novigradsko More, *Croatia* ... 29 D12
Nôvo Hamburgo, *Brazil* ... 127 B5
Novo Mesto, *Slovenia* ... 29 C12
Novo Miloševo, *Serbia, Yug.* ... 42 E5
Novo Remanso, *Brazil* ... 125 E10
Novoaleksandrovsk, *Russia* ... 49 H5
Novoannenskiy, *Russia* ... 48 E6
Novoataysk, *Russia* ... 50 D9
Novocheboksarsk, *Russia* ... 48 B8
Novocherkassk, *Russia* ... 49 G5
Novodevichye, *Russia* ... 48 D9
Novogrudok = Navahrudak, *Belarus* ... 46 F3
Novohrad-Volynskyy, *Ukraine* ... 47 G4
Novokachalinsk, *Russia* ... 54 B6
Novokazalinsk = Zhangaqazaly, *Kazakstan* ... 50 E7
Novokhopersk, *Russia* ... 48 E5
Novokuybyshevsk, *Russia* ... 48 D9
Novokuznetsk, *Russia* ... 50 D9
Novomirgorod, *Ukraine* ... 47 H6
Novomoskovsk, *Russia* ... 46 E10
Novomoskovsk, *Ukraine* ... 47 H8
Novopolotsk = Navapolatsk, *Belarus* ... 46 E5
Novorossiysk, *Russia* ... 47 K9
Novorybnoye, *Russia* ... 51 B11
Novorzhev, *Russia* ... 46 D5
Novosej, *Albania* ... 40 E4

Novoselytsya, *Ukraine* ... 47 H4
Novoshakhtinsk, *Russia* ... 47 J10
Novosibirsk, *Russia* ... 50 D9
Novosibirskiye Ostrova, *Russia* ... 51 B15
Novosil, *Russia* ... 47 F9
Novosokolniki, *Russia* ... 46 D6
Novotitarovskaya, *Russia* ... 49 H4
Novotroitsk, *Russia* ... 50 D6
Novoukrayinka, *Ukraine* ... 47 H6
Novouljanovsk, *Russia* ... 48 C9
Novovoronezhskiy, *Russia* ... 47 G10
Novozybkov, *Russia* ... 47 F6
Novska, *Croatia* ... 29 C14
Novvy Port, *Russia* ... 50 C8
Novy Urengoy, *Russia* ... 50 C8
Nový Bor, *Czech Rep.* ... 26 A7
Novy Bug = Novyy Buh, *Ukraine* ... 47 J7
Nový Bydžov, *Czech Rep.* ... 26 A8
Nový Dwór Mazowiecki, *Poland* ... 45 F7
Nový Jičín, *Czech Rep.* ... 27 B11
Novyy Afon, *Georgia* ... 49 J5
Novyy Buh, *Ukraine* ... 47 J7
Novyy Oskol, *Russia* ... 47 G9
Novyy Port, *Russia* ... 50 C8
Now Shahr, *Iran* ... 71 B6
Nowa Deba, *Poland* ... 45 H8
Nowa Ruda, *Poland* ... 45 H3
Nowa Sarzyna, *Poland* ... 45 H9
Nowa Sól, *Poland* ... 45 G2
Nowata, *U.S.A.* ... 113 G7
Nowbarān, *Iran* ... 71 C6
Nowe, *Poland* ... 44 E5
Nowe Miasteczko, *Poland* ... 45 G2
Nowe Miasto, *Poland* ... 45 G7
Nowe Miasto Lubawskie, *Poland* ... 44 E6
Nowe Skalmierzyce, *Poland* ... 45 G4
Nowe Warpno, *Poland* ... 44 E1
Nowghāb, *Iran* ... 71 C8
Nowgong, *Assam, India* ... 67 F18
Nowgong, *Mad. P., India* ... 69 G8
Nowogard, *Poland* ... 44 E2
Nowogród, *Poland* ... 44 E8
Nowogród Bobrzanski, *Poland* ... 45 G2
Nowogrodziec, *Poland* ... 45 G2
Nowra, *Australia* ... 95 E5
Nowshera, *Pakistan* ... 66 C8
Nowy Dwór Gdański, *Poland* ... 44 D6
Nowy Sącz, *Poland* ... 45 J7
Nowy Staw, *Poland* ... 44 D6
Nowy Targ, *Poland* ... 45 J7
Nowy Tomyśl, *Poland* ... 45 F3
Nowy Wiśnicz, *Poland* ... 45 J7
Noxen, *U.S.A.* ... 111 E8
Noxon, *U.S.A.* ... 114 C6
Noyabr'sk, *Russia* ... 50 C8
Noyant, *France* ... 18 E7
Noyers, *France* ... 19 E10
Noyon, *France* ... 19 C9
Noyon, *Mongolia* ... 56 C2
Nozay, *France* ... 18 E5
Nqutu, *S. Africa* ... 89 D5
Nsanje, *Malawi* ... 87 F4
Nsomba, *Zambia* ... 87 E2
Nsawam, *Ghana* ... 83 D4
Nsukka, *Nigeria* ... 83 D6
Ntui, *Cameroon* ... 83 E7
Nu Jiang →, *China* ... 58 E2
Nu Shan, *China* ... 58 E2
Nuba Mts. = Nubah, Jibalan, *Sudan* ... 81 E3
Nubah, Jibalan, *Sudan* ... 81 E3
Nubia, *Africa* ... 76 D7
Nubian Desert = Nûbîya, Es Sahrâ en, *Sudan* ... 80 C3
Nûbîya, Es Sahrâ en, *Sudan* ... 80 C3
Nubledo, *Spain* ... 34 B5
Nuboai, *Indonesia* ... 63 E9
Nubra →, *India* ... 69 B7
Nucet, *Romania* ... 42 D7
Nueces →, *U.S.A.* ... 113 M6
Nueltin L., *Canada* ... 105 A9
Nueva Asunción □, *Paraguay* ... 126 A3
Nueva Carteya, *Spain* ... 35 H6
Nueva Gerona, *Cuba* ... 120 B3
Nueva Palmira, *Uruguay* ... 126 C4
Nueva Rosita, *Mexico* ... 118 B4
Nueva San Salvador, *El Salv.* ... 120 D2
Nueva Tabarca, *Spain* ... 33 G4
Nuéve de Julio, *Argentina* ... 126 D3
Nuevitas, *Cuba* ... 120 B4
Nuevo, G., *Argentina* ... 128 E4
Nuevo Casas Grandes, *Mexico* ... 118 A3
Nuevo Guerrero, *Mexico* ... 119 B5
Nuevo Laredo, *Mexico* ... 119 B5
Nuevo León □, *Mexico* ... 118 C5
Nuevo Rocafuerte, *Ecuador* ... 124 D3
Nugget Pt., *N.Z.* ... 91 M2
Nugrus, Gebel, *Egypt* ... 80 C3
Nuhaka, *N.Z.* ... 91 H6
Nuhuyb, *Iraq* ... 70 C4
Nukey Bluff, *Australia* ... 95 E2
Nukheila, *Sudan* ... 80 D2
Nuku'alofa, *Tonga* ... 91 E12
Nukus, *Uzbekistan* ... 50 E6
Nules, *Spain* ... 32 F4
Nullagine, *Australia* ... 92 D3
Nullagine →, *Australia* ... 92 D3
Nullarbor, *Australia* ... 93 F5
Nullarbor Plain, *Australia* ... 93 F4
Numalla, L., *Australia* ... 95 D3
Numan, *Nigeria* ... 83 D7
Numata, *Japan* ... 55 F9
Numatinna →, *Sudan* ... 81 F2
Numazu, *Japan* ... 55 G9

Numbulwar, *Australia* ... 94 A2
Numfoor, *Indonesia* ... 63 E8
Numurkah, *Australia* ... 95 F4
Nunaksaluk I., *Canada* ... 103 A7
Nunap Isua, *Greenland* ... 101 C15
Nunavut □, *Canada* ... 101 B11
Nunda, *U.S.A.* ... 110 D7
Nungarin, *Australia* ... 93 F2
Nungo, *Mozam.* ... 87 E4
Nungwe, *Tanzania* ... 86 C3
Nunivak I., *U.S.A.* ... 100 B3
Nunkun, *India* ... 69 C7
Núoro, *Italy* ... 30 B2
Nūrābād, *Iran* ... 71 E8
Nure →, *Italy* ... 28 C6
Nuremberg = Nürnberg, *Germany* ... 25 F7
Nuri, *Mexico* ... 118 B3
Nuriootpa, *Australia* ... 95 E2
Nuristān □, *Afghan.* ... 66 B7
Nurlat, *Russia* ... 48 C10
Nurmes, *Finland* ... 8 E23
Nürnberg, *Germany* ... 25 F7
Nurpur, *Pakistan* ... 68 D4
Nurran, L. = Terewah, L., *Australia* ... 95 D4
Nurrari Lakes, *Australia* ... 93 E5
Nurri, *Italy* ... 30 C2
Nürtingen, *Germany* ... 25 G5
Nurzec →, *Poland* ... 45 F9
Nus, *Italy* ... 28 C4
Nusa Barung, *Indonesia* ... 63 H15
Nusa Kambangan, *Indonesia* ... 63 G13
Nusa Tenggara Barat □, *Indonesia* ... 62 F5
Nusa Tenggara Timur □, *Indonesia* ... 63 F6
Nusaybin, *Turkey* ... 73 D9
Nushki, *Pakistan* ... 68 E2
Nuuk, *Greenland* ... 101 B14
Nuwakot, *Nepal* ... 69 E10
Nuweiba', *Egypt* ... 70 D2
Nuwerus, *S. Africa* ... 88 E2
Nuweveldberge, *S. Africa* ... 88 E3
Nuyts, C., *Australia* ... 93 F5
Nuyts, Pt., *Australia* ... 93 G2
Nuyts Arch., *Australia* ... 95 E1
Nxau-Nxau, *Botswana* ... 88 B3
Nyaake, *Liberia* ... 82 E3
Nyabing, *Australia* ... 93 F2
Nyack, *U.S.A.* ... 111 E11
Nyahanga, *Tanzania* ... 86 C3
Nyahua, *Tanzania* ... 86 D3
Nyahururu, *Kenya* ... 86 B4
Nyainqentanglha Shan, *China* ... 60 C4
Nyakanazi, *Tanzania* ... 86 C3
Nyakrom, *Ghana* ... 83 D4
Nyâlâ, *Sudan* ... 81 E1
Nyamandhlovu, *Zimbabwe* ... 87 F2
Nyambiti, *Tanzania* ... 86 C3
Nyamlell, *Sudan* ... 81 F2
Nyamwaga, *Tanzania* ... 86 C3
Nyandekwa, *Tanzania* ... 86 C3
Nyanding →, *Sudan* ... 81 F3
Nyandoma, *Russia* ... 46 B11
Nyangana, *Namibia* ... 88 B3
Nyanguge, *Tanzania* ... 86 C3
Nyanza, *Rwanda* ... 86 C2
Nyanza □, *Kenya* ... 86 C3
Nyanza-Lac, *Burundi* ... 86 C2
Nyaponges, *Sudan* ... 81 F3
Nyasa, L., *Africa* ... 87 E3
Nyasvizh, *Belarus* ... 47 F4
Nyazura, *Zimbabwe* ... 87 F3
Nyazwidzi →, *Zimbabwe* ... 87 G3
Nyborg, *Denmark* ... 11 J4
Nybro, *Sweden* ... 11 H9
Nyda, *Russia* ... 50 C8
Nyeri, *Kenya* ... 86 C4
Nyerol, *Sudan* ... 81 F3
Nyhammar, *Sweden* ... 10 D8
Nyinahin, *Ghana* ... 82 D4
Nyíradony, *Hungary* ... 42 C6
Nyírbátor, *Hungary* ... 42 C7
Nyíregyháza, *Hungary* ... 42 C6
Nykøbing, *Storstrøm, Denmark* ... 11 K5
Nykøbing, *Vestsjælland, Denmark* ... 11 J5
Nykøbing, *Viborg, Denmark* ... 11 H2
Nyköping, *Sweden* ... 11 F11
Nykroppa, *Sweden* ... 10 E8
Nykvarn, *Sweden* ... 10 E11
Nyland, *Sweden* ... 10 A11
Nylstroom, *S. Africa* ... 89 C4
Nymagee, *Australia* ... 95 E4
Nymburk, *Czech Rep.* ... 26 A8
Nynäshamn, *Sweden* ... 11 F11
Nyngan, *Australia* ... 95 E4
Nyoma Rap, *India* ... 69 C8
Nyoman = Neman →, *Lithuania* ... 9 J19
Nyon, *Switz.* ... 25 J2
Nyong →, *Cameroon* ... 83 E6
Nyons, *France* ... 21 D9
Nyou, *Burkina Faso* ... 82 C4
Nýrsko, *Czech Rep.* ... 26 B6
Nysa, *Poland* ... 45 H4
Nysa →, *Europe* ... 24 C10
Nysa Kłodzka →, *Poland* ... 45 H4
Nysäter, *Sweden* ... 10 E6
Nyssa, *U.S.A.* ... 114 E5
Nysted, *Denmark* ... 11 K5
Nyunzu, *Dem. Rep. of the Congo* ... 86 D2
Nyurba, *Russia* ... 51 C12
Nyzhnohirskyy, *Ukraine* ... 47 K8

Nzébéla, *Guinea* ... 82 D3
Nzega, *Tanzania* ... 86 C3
Nzérékoré, *Guinea* ... 82 D3
Nzeto, *Angola* ... 84 F2
Nzilo, Chutes de, *Dem. Rep. of the Congo* ... 87 E2
Nzo →, *Ivory C.* ... 82 D3
Nzubuka, *Tanzania* ... 86 C3

O

O Barco, *Spain* ... 34 C4
O Carballiño, *Spain* ... 34 C2
O Corgo, *Spain* ... 34 C3
O Pino, *Spain* ... 34 C2
O Porriño, *Spain* ... 34 C2
O-Shima, *Japan* ... 55 G9
Oa, Mull of, *U.K.* ... 14 F2
Oacoma, *U.S.A.* ... 112 D5
Oahe, L., *U.S.A.* ... 112 C4
Oahe Dam, *U.S.A.* ... 112 C4
Oahu, *U.S.A.* ... 106 H16
Oak Harbor, *U.S.A.* ... 116 B4
Oak Hill, *U.S.A.* ... 108 G5
Oak Ridge, *U.S.A.* ... 109 G3
Oak View, *U.S.A.* ... 117 L7
Oakan-Dake, *Japan* ... 54 C12
Oakdale, *Calif., U.S.A.* ... 116 H6
Oakdale, *La., U.S.A.* ... 113 K8
Oakes, *U.S.A.* ... 112 B5
Oakesdale, *U.S.A.* ... 114 C5
Oakey, *Australia* ... 95 D5
Oakfield, *U.S.A.* ... 110 C6
Oakham, *U.K.* ... 13 E7
Oakhurst, *U.S.A.* ... 116 H7
Oakland, *U.S.A.* ... 116 H4
Oakley, *Idaho, U.S.A.* ... 114 E7
Oakley, *Kans., U.S.A.* ... 112 F4
Oakover →, *Australia* ... 92 D3
Oakridge, *U.S.A.* ... 114 E2
Oakville, *Canada* ... 110 C5
Oakville, *U.S.A.* ... 116 D3
Oamaru, *N.Z.* ... 91 L3
Oancea, *Romania* ... 43 E12
Oasis, *Calif., U.S.A.* ... 117 M10
Oasis, *Nev., U.S.A.* ... 116 H9
Oates Land, *Antarctica* ... 5 C11
Oatlands, *Australia* ... 94 G4
Oatman, *U.S.A.* ... 117 K12
Oaxaca, *Mexico* ... 119 D5
Oaxaca □, *Mexico* ... 119 D5
Ob →, *Russia* ... 50 C7
Ob, *Canada* ... 102 C3
Oba, *Cameroon* ... 83 E7
Obala, *Cameroon* ... 83 E7
Obama, *Japan* ... 55 G7
Oban, *Nigeria* ... 83 D6
Oban, *U.K.* ... 14 E3
Obbia, *Somali Rep.* ... 74 F4
Obera, *Argentina* ... 127 B4
Oberammergau, *Germany* ... 25 H7
Oberasbach, *Germany* ... 25 F6
Oberbayern □, *Germany* ... 25 G7
Oberdrauburg, *Austria* ... 26 E5
Oberfranken □, *Germany* ... 25 E7
Oberhausen, *Germany* ... 24 D2
Oberkirch, *Germany* ... 25 G4
Oberlausitz, *Germany* ... 24 D10
Oberlin, *Kans., U.S.A.* ... 112 F4
Oberlin, *La., U.S.A.* ... 113 K8
Oberlin, *Ohio, U.S.A.* ... 110 E2
Obernai, *France* ... 19 D14
Oberndorf, *Germany* ... 25 G4
Oberon, *Australia* ... 95 E4
Oberösterreich □, *Austria* ... 26 C7
Oberpfalz □, *Germany* ... 25 F8
Oberpfälzer Wald, *Germany* ... 25 F8
Oberstdorf, *Germany* ... 25 H6
Oberursel, *Germany* ... 25 E4
Oberwart, *Austria* ... 27 D9
Obi, Kepulauan, *Indonesia* ... 63 E7
Obi Is. = Obi, Kepulauan, *Indonesia* ... 63 E7
Obiaruku, *Nigeria* ... 83 D6
Óbidos, *Brazil* ... 125 D7
Óbidos, *Portugal* ... 35 F1
Obihiro, *Japan* ... 54 C11
Obilatu, *Indonesia* ... 63 E7
Obilnoye, *Russia* ... 49 G7
Obing, *Germany* ... 25 G8
Objat, *France* ... 20 C5
Obluchye, *Russia* ... 51 E14
Obninsk, *Russia* ... 46 E9
Obo, *C.A.R.* ... 86 A2
Oboa, Mt., *Uganda* ... 86 B3
Obock, *Djibouti* ... 81 E5
Oborniki, *Poland* ... 45 F3
Oborniki Śląskie, *Poland* ... 45 G3
Oboyan, *Russia* ... 47 G9
Obozerskaya = Obozerskiy, *Russia* ... 50 C5
Obozerskiy, *Russia* ... 50 C5
Obrenovac, *Serbia, Yug.* ... 42 F5
Obrovac, *Croatia* ... 29 D12
Obruk, *Turkey* ... 72 C5
Observatory Inlet, *Canada* ... 104 B3
Obshchi Syrt, *Russia* ... 6 E16
Obskaya Guba, *Russia* ... 50 C8
Obuasi, *Ghana* ... 83 D4
Obubra, *Nigeria* ... 83 D6
Obudu, *Nigeria* ... 83 D6
Obzor, *Bulgaria* ... 41 D11
Ocala, *U.S.A.* ... 109 L4
Ocampo, *Chihuahua, Mexico* ... 118 B3

Ocampo, *Tamaulipas, Mexico* . 119 C5
Ocaña, *Spain* 34 F7
Ocanomowoc, *U.S.A.* 112 D10
Occidental, Cordillera,
  Colombia 122 C3
Ocean City, *Md., U.S.A.* 108 F8
Ocean City, *N.J., U.S.A.* 108 F8
Ocean City, *Wash., U.S.A.* . . . 116 C2
Ocean Falls, *Canada* 104 C3
Ocean I. = Banaba, *Kiribati* . . 96 H8
Ocean Park, *U.S.A.* 116 D2
Oceano, *U.S.A.* 117 K6
Oceanport, *U.S.A.* 111 F10
Oceanside, *U.S.A.* 117 M9
Ochagavía, *Spain* 32 C3
Ochakiv, *Ukraine* 47 J6
Ochamchira, *Georgia* 49 J5
Ochil Hills, *U.K.* 14 E5
Ochsenfurt, *Germany* 25 F6
Ochsenhausen, *Germany* 25 G5
Ocilla, *U.S.A.* 109 K4
Ockelbo, *Sweden* 10 D10
Ocmulgee →, *U.S.A.* 109 K4
Ocna Mureș, *Romania* 43 D8
Ocna Sibiului, *Romania* 43 E9
Ocnele Mari, *Romania* 43 E9
Ocnița, *Moldova* 43 B12
Oconee →, *U.S.A.* 109 K4
Oconto, *U.S.A.* 108 C2
Oconto Falls, *U.S.A.* 108 C1
Ocosingo, *Mexico* 119 D6
Ocotal, *Nic.* 120 D2
Ocotlán, *Mexico* 118 C4
Ocotlán de Morelos, *Mexico* . . 119 D5
Ocreza →, *Portugal* 35 F3
Ócsa, *Hungary* 42 C4
Octeville, *France* 18 C5
Oda, *Ghana* 83 D4
Ōda, *Japan* 55 G6
Oda, J., *Sudan* 80 C4
Ódáðahraun, *Iceland* 8 D5
Odåkra, *Sweden* 11 H6
Odate, *Japan* 54 D10
Odawara, *Japan* 55 G9
Odda, *Norway* 9 F12
Odder, *Denmark* 11 J4
Odei →, *Canada* 105 B9
Odemira, *Portugal* 35 H2
Ödemiş, *Turkey* 39 C9
Odendaalsrus, *S. Africa* 88 D4
Odensbacken, *Sweden* 10 E9
Odense, *Denmark* 11 J4
Odenwald, *Germany* 25 F5
Oder →, *Europe* 24 B10
Oder-Havel Kanal, *Germany* . . 24 C10
Oderzo, *Italy* 29 C9
Odesa, *Ukraine* 47 J6
Ödeshög, *Sweden* 11 F8
Odessa = Odesa, *Ukraine* 47 J6
Odessa, *Canada* 111 B8
Odessa, *Tex., U.S.A.* 113 K3
Odessa, *Wash., U.S.A.* 114 C4
Odiakwe, *Botswana* 88 C4
Odiel →, *Spain* 35 H4
Odienné, *Ivory C.* 82 D3
Odintsovo, *Russia* 46 E9
Odiongan, *Phil.* 61 E4
Odobești, *Romania* 43 E12
Odolanów, *Poland* 45 G4
O'Donnell, *U.S.A.* 113 J4
Odorheiu Secuiesc, *Romania* . 43 D10
Odoyevo, *Russia* 46 F9
Odra = Oder →, *Europe* 24 B10
Odra →, *Spain* 34 C6
Odžaci, *Serbia, Yug.* 42 E4
Odžak, *Bos.-H.* 42 E3
Odzi, *Zimbabwe* 89 B5
Odzi →, *Zimbabwe* 89 B5
Oebisfelde, *Germany* 24 C6
Oeiras, *Brazil* 125 E10
Oeiras, *Portugal* 35 G1
Oelrichs, *U.S.A.* 112 D3
Oelsnitz, *Germany* 25 E8
Oelwein, *U.S.A.* 112 D9
Oenpelli, *Australia* 92 B5
Oetz, *Austria* 26 D3
Of, *Turkey* 73 B9
Ofanto →, *Italy* 31 A9
Offa, *Nigeria* 83 D5
Offaly □, *Ireland* 15 C4
Offenbach, *Germany* 25 E4
Offenburg, *Germany* 25 G3
Offida, *Italy* 29 F10
Ofidhoussa, *Greece* 39 E8
Ofotfjorden, *Norway* 8 B17
Ofunato, *Japan* 54 E10
Oga, *Japan* 54 E9
Oga-Hantō, *Japan* 54 E9
Ogaden, *Ethiopia* 74 F3
Ōgaki, *Japan* 55 G8
Ogallala, *U.S.A.* 112 E4
Ogasawara Gunto, *Pac. Oc.* . . . 52 G18
Ogbomosho, *Nigeria* 83 D5
Ogden, *U.S.A.* 114 F7
Ogdensburg, *U.S.A.* 111 B9
Ogeechee →, *U.S.A.* 109 K5
Ogilby, *U.S.A.* 117 N12
Oglio →, *Italy* 28 C7
Ogmore, *Australia* 94 C4
Ognon →, *France* 19 E12
Ogoja, *Nigeria* 83 D6
Ogoki, *Canada* 102 B2
Ogoki →, *Canada* 102 B2
Ogoki L., *Canada* 102 B2
Ogoki Res., *Canada* 102 B2
Ogooué →, *Gabon* 84 E1
Ogosta →, *Bulgaria* 40 C7

Ogowe = Ogooué →, *Gabon* . . 84 E1
Ogr = Sharafa, *Sudan* 81 E2
Ograźden, *Macedonia* 40 E6
Ogre, *Latvia* 9 H21
Ogrein, *Sudan* 80 D3
Ogulin, *Croatia* 29 C12
Ogun □, *Nigeria* 83 D5
Ogurchinskiy, Ostrov,
  Turkmenistan 71 B7
Oguta, *Nigeria* 83 D6
Ogwashi-Uku, *Nigeria* 83 D6
Ogwe, *Nigeria* 83 E6
Ohai, *N.Z.* 91 L2
Ohakune, *N.Z.* 91 H5
Ohata, *Japan* 54 D10
Ohau, L., *N.Z.* 91 L2
Ohio □, *U.S.A.* 110 F2
Ohio →, *U.S.A.* 108 G1
Ohře →, *Czech Rep.* 26 A7
Ohre →, *Germany* 24 C7
Ohrid, *Macedonia* 40 E4
Ohridsko Jezero, *Macedonia* . . 40 E4
Ohrigstad, *S. Africa* 89 C5
Öhringen, *Germany* 25 F5
Oi Qu, *China* 58 C2
Oiapoque, *Brazil* 125
Oikou, *China* 57 E9
Oil City, *U.S.A.* 110 E5
Oil Springs, *Canada* 110 D2
Oildale, *U.S.A.* 117 K7
Oinousa, *Greece* 39 C8
Oise □, *France* 19 C9
Oise →, *France* 19 C9
Ōita, *Japan* 55 H5
Ōita □, *Japan* 55 H5
Oiticica, *Brazil* 125 E10
Ojacaliente, *Mexico* 118 C4
Ojai, *U.S.A.* 117 L7
Ojinaga, *Mexico* 118 B4
Ojiya, *Japan* 55 F9
Ojos del Salado, Cerro,
  Argentina 126 B2
Oka →, *Russia* 48 B7
Okaba, *Indonesia* 63 F9
Okahandja, *Namibia* 88 C2
Okanagan L., *Canada* 104 D5
Okanogan, *U.S.A.* 114 B4
Okanogan →, *U.S.A.* 114 B4
Okány, *Hungary* 42 D6
Okaputa, *Namibia* 88 C2
Okara, *Pakistan* 68 D5
Okaukuejo, *Namibia* 88 B2
Okavango Swamps, *Botswana* . 88 B3
Okaya, *Japan* 55 F9
Okayama, *Japan* 55 G6
Okayama □, *Japan* 55 G6
Okazaki, *Japan* 55 G8
Oke-Iho, *Nigeria* 83 D5
Okeechobee, *U.S.A.* 109 M5
Okeechobee, L., *U.S.A.* 109 M5
Okefenokee Swamp, *U.S.A.* . . . 109 K4
Okehampton, *U.K.* 13 G4
Okene, *Nigeria* 83 D6
Oker →, *Germany* 24 C6
Okha, *India* 68 H3
Okha, *Russia* 51 D15
Ókhi Óros, *Greece* 38 C6
Okhotsk, *Russia* 51 D15
Okhotsk, Sea of, *Asia* 51 D15
Okhotskiy Perevoz, *Russia* . . . 51 C14
Okhtyrka, *Ukraine* 47 G8
Oki-Shotō, *Japan* 55 F6
Okiep, *S. Africa* 88 D2
Okigwi, *Nigeria* 83 D6
Okija, *Nigeria* 83 D6
Okinawa □, *Japan* 55 L4
Okinawa-Guntō, *Japan* 55 L4
Okinawa-Jima, *Japan* 55 L4
Okino-erabu-Shima, *Japan* . . . 55 L4
Okitipupa, *Nigeria* 83 D5
Oklahoma □, *U.S.A.* 113 H6
Oklahoma City, *U.S.A.* 113 H6
Okmulgee, *U.S.A.* 113 H7
Oknitsa = Ocnița, *Moldova* . . 43 B12
Oko, W. →, *Sudan* 80 C4
Okolo, *Uganda* 86 B3
Okolona, *U.S.A.* 113 J10
Okombahe, *Namibia* 88 C2
Okonek, *Poland* 44 E3
Okotoks, *Canada* 104 C6
Okrika, *Nigeria* 83 E6
Oksibil, *Indonesia* 63 E10
Oktabrsk = Oktyabrsk,
  Kazakstan 50 E6
Oktyabrsk, *Kazakstan* 50 E6
Oktyabrsk, *Russia* 48 D9
Oktyabrskiy = Aktsyabrski,
  Belarus 47 F5
Oktyabrskiy, *Russia* 49 G5
Oktyabrskoy Revolyutsii,
  Ostrov, *Russia* 51 B10
Oktyabrskoye = Zhovtneve,
  Ukraine 47 J7
Okulovka, *Russia* 46 C7
Okuru, *N.Z.* 91 K2
Okushiri-Tō, *Japan* 54 C9
Okuta, *Nigeria* 83 D5
Okwa →, *Botswana* 88 C3
Ola, *U.S.A.* 113 H8
Ólafsfjörður, *Iceland* 8 C4
Ólafsvík, *Iceland* 8 D2
Olaine, *Latvia* 44 B10
Olancha, *U.S.A.* 117 J8
Olancha Pk., *U.S.A.* 117 J8
Olanchito, *Honduras* 120 C2
Öland, *Sweden* 11 H10

Ölands norra udde, *Sweden* . . . 11 G11
Ölands södra udde, *Sweden* . . . 11 H10
Olargues, *France* 20 E6
Olary, *Australia* 95 E3
Olascoaga, *Argentina* 126 D3
Olathe, *U.S.A.* 112 F7
Olavarría, *Argentina* 126 D3
Oława, *Poland* 45 H4
Olbernhau, *Germany* 24 E9
Ólbia, *Italy* 30 B2
Ólbia, G. di, *Italy* 30 B2
Olching, *Germany* 25 G7
Olcott, *U.S.A.* 110 C6
Old Bahama Chan. = Bahama,
  Canal Viejo de, *W. Indies* . . . 120 B4
Old Baldy Pk. = San Antonio,
  Mt., *U.S.A.* 117 L9
Old Castile = Castilla y Leon □,
  Spain 34 D6
Old Crow, *Canada* 100 B6
Old Dale, *U.S.A.* 117 L11
Old Dongola, *Sudan* 80 D3
Old Forge, *N.Y., U.S.A.* 111 C10
Old Forge, *Pa., U.S.A.* 111 E9
Old Perlican, *Canada* 103 C9
Old Shinyanga, *Tanzania* 86 C3
Old Speck Mt., *U.S.A.* 111 B14
Old Town, *U.S.A.* 109 C11
Old Washington, *U.S.A.* 110 F3
Old Wives L., *Canada* 105 C7
Oldbury, *U.K.* 13 F5
Oldcastle, *Ireland* 15 C4
Oldeani, *Tanzania* 86 C4
Oldenburg, *Niedersachsen,*
  Germany 24 B4
Oldenburg, *Schleswig-Holstein,*
  Germany 24 A6
Oldenzaal, *Neths.* 17 B6
Oldham, *U.K.* 12 D5
Oldman →, *Canada* 104 D6
Oldmeldrum, *U.K.* 14 D6
Olds, *Canada* 104 C6
Oldziyt, *Mongolia* 56 B5
Olean, *U.S.A.* 110 D6
Olecko, *Poland* 44 D9
Oléggio, *Italy* 28 C5
Oleiros, *Portugal* 34 F3
Oleiros, *Spain* 34 B2
Olekma →, *Russia* 51 C13
Olekminsk, *Russia* 51 C13
Olema, *U.S.A.* 116 G4
Olenek, *Russia* 51 C12
Olenek →, *Russia* 51 B13
Olenino, *Russia* 46 D7
Oléron, Î. d', *France* 20 C2
Oleśnica, *Poland* 45 G4
Olesno, *Poland* 45 H5
Olevsk, *Ukraine* 47 G4
Olga, *Russia* 51 E14
Olga, L., *Canada* 102 C4
Olga, Mt., *Australia* 93 E5
Ølgod, *Denmark* 11 J2
Olhão, *Portugal* 35 H3
Olib, *Croatia* 29 D11
Oliena, *Italy* 30 B2
Oliete, *Spain* 32 D4
Olifants →, *Africa* 89 C5
Olifants →, *Namibia* 88 C2
Olifantshoek, *S. Africa* 88 D3
Ólimbos, *Greece* 39 F9
Ólimbos, Óros, *Greece* 40 F6
Olímpia, *Brazil* 127 A6
Olinda, *Brazil* 125 E12
Olite, *Spain* 32 C3
Oliva, *Argentina* 126 C3
Oliva, *Spain* 33 G4
Oliva, Punta del, *Spain* 34 B5
Oliva de la Frontera, *Spain* . . . 35 G4
Olivares, *Spain* 32 F2
Olivehurst, *U.S.A.* 116 F5
Oliveira de Azeméis, *Portugal* . 34 E2
Oliveira do Douro, *Portugal* . . 34 D2
Olivenza, *Spain* 35 G3
Oliver, *Canada* 104 D5
Oliver L., *Canada* 105 B8
Olivet, *France* 19 E8
Olkhovka, *Russia* 48 F7
Olkusz, *Poland* 45 H6
Ollagüe, *Chile* 126 A2
Olmedo, *Spain* 34 D6
Olmeto, *France* 21 G12
Olney, *Ill., U.S.A.* 108 F1
Olney, *Tex., U.S.A.* 113 J5
Olofström, *Sweden* 11 H8
Oloma, *Cameroon* 83 E7
Olomane →, *Canada* 103 B7
Olomouc, *Czech Rep.* 27 B10
Olomoucký □, *Czech Rep.* . . . 27 B10
Olonets, *Russia* 46 B8
Olongapo, *Phil.* 61 D4
Olonne-sur-Mer, *France* 20 B2
Oloron, Gave d' →, *France* . . . 20 E2
Oloron-Ste-Marie, *France* 20 E3
Olot, *Spain* 32 C7
Olovo, *Bos.-H.* 42 F3
Olovyannaya, *Russia* 51 D12
Oloy →, *Russia* 51 C16
Olsberg, *Germany* 24 D4
Olshammar, *Sweden* 11 F8
Olshanka, *Ukraine* 47 H6
Olshany, *Ukraine* 47 G8
Olsztyn, *Poland* 44 E7

Olsztynek, *Poland* 44 E7
Olt □, *Romania* 43 F9
Olt →, *Romania* 43 G9
Olten, *Switz.* 25 H3
Oltenița, *Romania* 43 F11
Olton, *U.S.A.* 113 H3
Oltu, *Turkey* 73 B9
Oluanpi, *Taiwan* 59 G13
Olula del Rio, *Spain* 33 H2
Olur, *Turkey* 73 B10
Olutanga, *Phil.* 61 H5
Olvega, *Spain* 32 D2
Olvera, *Spain* 35 J5
Olymbos, *Cyprus* 36 D12
Olympia, *Greece* 38 D3
Olympia, *U.S.A.* 116 D4
Olympic Dam, *Australia* 95 E2
Olympic Mts., *U.S.A.* 116 C3
Olympic Nat. Park, *U.S.A.* . . . 116 C3
Olympus, *Cyprus* 36 E11
Olympus, Mt. = Ólimbos, Óros,
  Greece 40 F6
Olympus, Mt. = Uludağ, *Turkey* 41 F13
Olympus, Mt., *U.S.A.* 116 C3
Olyphant, *U.S.A.* 111 E9
Om →, *Russia* 50 D8
Om Hajer, *Eritrea* 81 E4
Om Koi, *Thailand* 64 D2
Ōma, *Japan* 54 D10
Ōmachi, *Japan* 55 F8
Omae-Zaki, *Japan* 55 G9
Ōmagari, *Japan* 54 E10
Omagh, *U.K.* 15 B4
Omagh □, *U.K.* 15 B4
Omaha, *U.S.A.* 112 E7
Omak, *U.S.A.* 114 B4
Omalos, *Greece* 36 D5
Oman ■, *Asia* 74 C6
Oman, G. of, *Asia* 71 E8
Omaruru, *Namibia* 88 C2
Omaruru →, *Namibia* 88 C1
Omate, *Peru* 124 G4
Ombai, Selat, *Indonesia* 63 F6
Omboué, *Gabon* 84 E1
Ombrone →, *Italy* 28 F8
Omdurmân, *Sudan* 81 D3
Omegna, *Italy* 28 C5
Omemee, *Canada* 110 B6
Omeonga, *Dem. Rep. of*
  the Congo 86 C1
Ometepe, I. de, *Nic.* 120 D2
Ometepec, *Mexico* 119 D5
Omineca →, *Canada* 104 B4
Omiš, *Croatia* 29 E13
Omišalj, *Croatia* 29 C11
Omitara, *Namibia* 88 C2
Ōmiya, *Japan* 55 G9
Ommen, *Neths.* 17 B6
Ömnögovĭ □, *Mongolia* 56 C3
Omo →, *Ethiopia* 81 F4
Omodeo, L., *Italy* 30 B1
Omodhos, *Cyprus* 36 E11
Omoko, *Nigeria* 83 D6
Omolon →, *Russia* 51 C16
Omono-Gawa →, *Japan* 54 E10
Omsk, *Russia* 50 D8
Omsukchan, *Russia* 51 C16
Ōmu, *Japan* 54 B11
Omul, Vf., *Romania* 43 E10
Omulew →, *Poland* 45 E8
Ōmura, *Japan* 55 H4
Omuramba Omatako →,
  Namibia 88 B2
Omuramba Ovambo →,
  Namibia 88 B2
Omurtag, *Bulgaria* 41 C10
Ōmuta, *Japan* 55 H5
Oña, *Spain* 34 C7
Onaga, *U.S.A.* 112 F6
Onalaska, *U.S.A.* 112 D9
Onancock, *U.S.A.* 108 G8
Onang, *Indonesia* 63 E5
Onaping L., *Canada* 102 C3
Oñati, *Spain* 32 B2
Onavas, *Mexico* 118 B3
Onawa, *U.S.A.* 112 D6
Oncócua, *Angola* 88 B1
Onda, *Spain* 32 F4
Ondaejin, *N. Korea* 57 D15
Ondangwa, *Namibia* 88 B2
Ondarroa, *Spain* 32 B2
Ondava →, *Slovak Rep.* 27 C14
Ondjiva, *Angola* 88 B2
Ondo, *Nigeria* 83 D5
Ondo □, *Nigeria* 83 D6
Öndörhaan, *Mongolia* 60 B6
Öndörshil, *Mongolia* 56 B5
Önderðarnes, *Iceland* 8 D1
One Tree, *Australia* 95 E3
Onega, *Russia* 50 C4
Onega →, *Russia* 6 C13
Onega, L. = Onezhskoye Ozero,
  Russia 46 B8
Oneida, *U.S.A.* 111 C9
Oneida L., *U.S.A.* 111 C9
O'Neill, *U.S.A.* 112 D5
Onekotan, Ostrov, *Russia* 51 E16
Onema, *Dem. Rep. of the Congo* 86 C1
Oneonta, *U.S.A.* 111 D9
Onești, *Romania* 43 D11
Onezhskoye Ozero, *Russia* . . . 46 B8
Ongarue, *N.Z.* 91 H5
Ongers →, *S. Africa* 88 E3
Ongerup, *Australia* 93 F2
Ongjin, *N. Korea* 57 F13

Ongkharak, *Thailand* 64 E3
Ongniud Qi, *China* 57 C10
Ongoka, *Dem. Rep. of the Congo* 86 C2
Ongole, *India* 66 M12
Ongon = Havirga, *Mongolia* . . 56 B7
Oni, *Georgia* 49 J6
Onida, *U.S.A.* 112 C4
Onilahy →, *Madag.* 89 C7
Onitsha, *Nigeria* 83 D6
Onoda, *Japan* 55 G5
Onpyŏng-ni, *S. Korea* 57 H14
Ons, I. de, *Spain* 34 C2
Onslow, *Australia* 92 D2
Onslow B., *U.S.A.* 109 H7
Ontake-San, *Japan* 55 G8
Ontario, *Calif., U.S.A.* 117 L9
Ontario, *Oreg., U.S.A.* 114 D5
Ontario □, *Canada* 102 B2
Ontario, L., *N. Amer.* 110 C7
Ontinyent, *Spain* 33 G4
Ontonagon, *U.S.A.* 112 B10
Ontur, *Spain* 33 G3
Onyx, *U.S.A.* 117 K8
Oodnadatta, *Australia* 95 D2
Ooldea, *Australia* 93 F5
Oombulgurri, *Australia* 92 C4
Oorindi, *Australia* 94 C3
Oost-Vlaanderen □, *Belgium* . . 17 C3
Oostende, *Belgium* 17 C2
Oosterhout, *Neths.* 17 C4
Oosterschelde →, *Neths.* 17 C4
Oosterwolde, *Neths.* 17 B6
Ootacamund =
  Udagamandalam, *India* 66 P10
Ootsa L., *Canada* 104 C3
Opaka, *Bulgaria* 41 C10
Opala, *Dem. Rep. of the Congo* 86 C1
Opalenica, *Poland* 45 F3
Opan, *Bulgaria* 41 D9
Opanake, *Sri Lanka* 66 R12
Opasatika, *Canada* 102 C3
Opasquia Prov. Park, *Canada* . 102 B1
Opatija, *Croatia* 29 C11
Opatów, *Poland* 45 H8
Opava, *Czech Rep.* 27 B10
Opelika, *U.S.A.* 109 J3
Opelousas, *U.S.A.* 113 K8
Opémisca, L., *Canada* 102 C5
Opheim, *U.S.A.* 114 B10
Ophthalmia Ra., *Australia* 92 D2
Opi, *Nigeria* 83 D6
Opinaca →, *Canada* 102 B4
Opinaca, Rés., *Canada* 102 B4
Opinnagau →, *Canada* 102 B3
Opiscoteo, L., *Canada* 103 B6
Opobo, *Nigeria* 83 E6
Opochka, *Russia* 46 D5
Opoczno, *Poland* 45 G7
Opol, *Phil.* 61 G6
Opole, *Poland* 45 H4
Opole Lubelskie, *Poland* 45 G8
Opolskie □, *Poland* 45 H5
Oponono L., *Namibia* 88 B2
Oporto = Porto, *Portugal* 34 D2
Opotiki, *N.Z.* 91 H6
Opp, *U.S.A.* 109 K2
Oppdal, *Norway* 9 E13
Óppido Mamertina, *Italy* 31 D8
Opportunity, *U.S.A.* 114 C5
Oprișor, *Romania* 42 F8
Oprtalj, *Croatia* 29 C10
Opua, *N.Z.* 91 F5
Opunake, *N.Z.* 91 H4
Opuwo, *Namibia* 88 B1
Opuzen, *Croatia* 29 E14
Ora, *Cyprus* 36 E12
Oracle, *U.S.A.* 115 K8
Oradea, *Romania* 42 C6
Öræfajökull, *Iceland* 8 D5
Orahovac, *Kosovo, Yug.* 40 D4
Orahovica, *Croatia* 42 E2
Orai, *India* 69 G8
Oraison, *France* 21 E9
Oral = Zhayyq →, *Kazakstan* . 50 E6
Oral, *Kazakstan* 48 E10
Oran, *Algeria* 78 A5
Orange, *Australia* 95 E4
Orange, *France* 21 D8
Orange, *Calif., U.S.A.* 117 M9
Orange, *Mass., U.S.A.* 111 D12
Orange, *Tex., U.S.A.* 113 K8
Orange, *Va., U.S.A.* 108 F6
Orange →, *S. Africa* 88 D2
Orange, C., *Brazil* 122 C5
Orange Cove, *U.S.A.* 116 J7
Orange Free State = Free
  State □, *S. Africa* 88 D4
Orange Grove, *U.S.A.* 113 M6
Orange Walk, *Belize* 119 D7
Orangeburg, *U.S.A.* 109 J5
Orangeville, *Canada* 102 D3
Orango, *Guinea-Biss.* 82 C1
Orani, *Italy* 61 D4
Oranienburg, *Germany* 24 C9
Oranje = Orange →, *S. Africa* . 88 D2
Oranje Vrystaat = Free State □,
  S. Africa 88 D4
Oranjemund, *Namibia* 88 D2
Oranjerivier, *S. Africa* 88 D3
Orapa, *Botswana* 85 J5
Orarak, *Sudan* 81 F3
Oras, *Phil.* 61 E6
Orăștie, *Romania* 43 E8
Orașul Stalin = Brașov, *Romania* 43 E10
Orava →, *Slovak Rep.* 27 B12

Orava, Vodna nádriž, Slovak Rep. 27 B12
Oravița, Romania 42 E6
Orb →, France 20 E7
Orba →, Italy 28 D5
Ørbæk, Denmark 11 J4
Orbe, Switz. 25 J2
Orbec, France 18 C7
Orbetello, Italy 29 F8
Órbigo →, Spain 34 C5
Orbisonia, U.S.A. 110 F7
Orbost, Australia 95 F4
Örbyhus, Sweden 10 D11
Orcas I., U.S.A. 116 B4
Orce, Spain 33 H2
Orce →, Spain 33 H2
Orchard City, U.S.A. 115 G10
Orchies, France 19 B10
Orchila, I., Venezuela 121 D6
Órcia →, Italy 29 F8
Orco →, Italy 28 C4
Orcutt, U.S.A. 117 L6
Ord, U.S.A. 112 E5
Ord →, Australia 92 C4
Ord, Mt., Australia 92 C4
Ordenes = Ordes, Spain 34 B2
Orderville, U.S.A. 115 H7
Ordes, Spain 34 B2
Ording = St-Peter-Ording, Germany 24 A4
Ordos = Mu Us Shamo, China 56 E5
Ordu, Turkey 72 B7
Ordubad, Azerbaijan 73 C12
Orduña, Álava, Spain 32 C2
Orduña, Granada, Spain 35 H7
Ordway, U.S.A. 112 F3
Ordzhonikidze = Vladikavkaz, Russia 49 J7
Ordzhonikidze, Ukraine 47 J8
Ore, Dem. Rep. of the Congo 86 B2
Ore Mts. = Erzgebirge, Germany 24 E8
Orebić, Croatia 29 F14
Örebro, Sweden 10 E9
Örebro län □, Sweden 10 E8
Oregon, U.S.A. 112 D10
Oregon □, U.S.A. 114 E3
Oregon City, U.S.A. 116 E4
Öregrund, Sweden 10 D12
Öregrundsgrepen, Sweden 10 D12
Orekhov = Orikhiv, Ukraine 47 J8
Orekhovo-Zuyevo, Russia 46 E10
Orel, Russia 47 F9
Orel →, Ukraine 47 H8
Orellana, Spain 35 F5
Orellana, Canal de, Spain 35 F5
Orellana, Embalse de, Spain 35 F5
Orem, U.S.A. 114 F8
Ören, Turkey 39 D9
Orenburg, Russia 50 D6
Örencik, Turkey 39 B11
Orense = Ourense, Spain 34 C3
Orense □, Spain 34 C3
Orepuki, N.Z. 91 M1
Orestiás, Greece 41 E10
Orestos Pereyra, Mexico 118 B3
Øresund, Europe 11 J6
Orford Ness, U.K. 13 E9
Orgañá = Organyà, Spain 32 C6
Organos, Pta. de los, Canary Is. 37 F2
Organyà, Spain 32 C6
Orgaz, Spain 35 F7
Orgeyev = Orhei, Moldova 43 C13
Orhaneli, Turkey 41 G12
Orhaneli →, Turkey 41 G12
Orhangazi, Turkey 41 F13
Orhei, Moldova 43 C13
Orhon Gol →, Mongolia 60 A5
Óría, Italy 31 B10
Oriental, Cordillera, Colombia 122 C3
Orientale □, Dem. Rep. of the Congo 86 B2
Oriente, Argentina 126 D3
Orihuela, Spain 33 G4
Orihuela del Tremedal, Spain 32 E3
Orikhiv, Ukraine 47 J8
Orikum, Albania 40 F3
Orillia, Canada 102 D4
Orinoco →, Venezuela 122 C4
Orion, Canada 105 D6
Oriskany, U.S.A. 111 C9
Orissa □, India 67 K14
Orissaare, Estonia 9 G20
Oristano, Italy 30 C1
Oristano, G. di, Italy 30 C1
Orizaba, Mexico 119 D5
Orizare, Bulgaria 41 D11
Orjen, Bos.-H. 40 D2
Orjiva, Spain 35 J7
Orkanger, Norway 8 E13
Örkelljunga, Sweden 11 H7
Örken, Sweden 11 G9
Örkény, Hungary 42 C4
Orkla →, Norway 8 E13
Orkney, S. Africa 88 D4
Orkney □, U.K. 14 B5
Orkney Is., U.K. 14 B6
Orland, U.S.A. 116 F4
Orlando, U.S.A. 109 L5
Orléanais, France 19 E9
Orléans, France 19 E8
Orleans, U.S.A. 111 B12
Orléans, Î. d', Canada 103 C5
Orlice →, Czech Rep. 26 A8
Orlov, Slovak Rep. 27 B13
Orlov Gay, Russia 48 E9
Orlová, Czech Rep. 27 B11

Orlovat, Serbia, Yug. 42 E5
Ormara, Pakistan 66 G4
Ormea, Italy 28 D4
Ormília, Greece 40 F7
Ormoc, Phil. 61 F6
Ormond, N.Z. 91 H6
Ormond Beach, U.S.A. 109 L5
Ormož, Slovenia 29 B13
Ormskirk, U.K. 12 D5
Ormstown, Canada 111 A11
Ornans, France 19 E13
Orne □, France 18 D7
Orne →, France 18 C6
Orneta, Poland 44 D7
Örnö, Sweden 10 E12
Örnsköldsvik, Sweden 10 A12
Oro, N. Korea 57 D14
Oro →, Mexico 118 B3
Oro Grande, U.S.A. 117 L9
Oro Valley, U.S.A. 115 K8
Orobie, Alpi, Italy 28 B6
Orocué, Colombia 124 C4
Orodara, Burkina Faso 82 C4
Orodo, Nigeria 83 D6
Orofino, U.S.A. 114 C5
Orol Dengizi = Aral Sea, Asia 50 E7
Oromocto, Canada 103 C6
Oron, Nigeria 83 E6
Orono, Canada 110 C6
Orono, U.S.A. 109 C11
Oronsay, U.K. 14 E2
Oropesa, Spain 34 F5
Oroquieta, Phil. 61 G5
Orosei, Italy 30 B2
Orosei, G. di, Italy 30 B2
Orosháza, Hungary 42 D5
Oroszlány, Hungary 42 C3
Orotukan, Russia 51 C16
Oroville, Calif., U.S.A. 116 F5
Oroville, Wash., U.S.A. 114 B4
Oroville, L., U.S.A. 116 F5
Orrefors, Sweden 11 H9
Orroroo, Australia 95 E2
Orrviken, Sweden 10 A8
Orrville, U.S.A. 110 F3
Orsa, Sweden 10 C8
Orsara di Púglia, Italy 31 A8
Orsasjön, Sweden 10 C8
Orsha, Belarus 46 E6
Örsjö, Sweden 11 H9
Orsk, Russia 50 D6
Orşova, Romania 42 F7
Østavall, Sweden 10 B9
Ørsted, Denmark 11 H4
Örsundsbro, Sweden 10 E11
Orta, L. d', Italy 28 C5
Orta Nova, Italy 31 A8
Ortaca, Turkey 39 E10
Ortakent, Turkey 39 D9
Ortaklar, Turkey 39 D9
Ortaköy, Çorum, Turkey 72 B6
Ortaköy, Niğde, Turkey 72 C6
Orte, Italy 29 F9
Ortegal, C., Spain 34 B3
Orthez, France 20 E3
Ortigueira, Spain 34 B3
Orting, U.S.A. 116 C4
Ortisei, Italy 29 B8
Ortles, Italy 28 B7
Ortón →, Bolivia 124 F5
Ortona, Italy 29 F11
Ortonville, U.S.A. 112 C6
Orūmīyeh, Iran 70 B5
Orūmīyeh, Daryācheh-ye, Iran 70 B5
Orune, Italy 30 B2
Oruro, Bolivia 124 G5
Orust, Sweden 11 F5
Oruzgān □, Afghan. 66 C5
Orvault, France 18 E5
Orvieto, Italy 29 F9
Orwell, N.Y., U.S.A. 111 C9
Orwell, Ohio, U.S.A. 110 E4
Orwell →, U.K. 13 F9
Orwigsburg, U.S.A. 111 F8
Oryakhovo, Bulgaria 40 C7
Orzinuovi, Italy 28 C6
Orzyc →, Poland 45 F8
Orzysz, Poland 44 E8
Osa, Poland 44 E5
Osa, Pen. de, Costa Rica 120 E3
Osage, U.S.A. 112 D8
Osage →, U.S.A. 112 F9
Osage City, U.S.A. 112 F7
Ōsaka, Japan 55 G7
Osan, S. Korea 57 F14
Osawatomie, U.S.A. 112 F7
Osborne, U.S.A. 112 F5
Osby, Sweden 11 H7
Osceola, Ark., U.S.A. 113 H10
Osceola, Iowa, U.S.A. 112 E8
Oschatz, Germany 24 D9
Oschersleben, Germany 24 C7
Óschiri, Italy 30 B2
Oscoda, U.S.A. 110 B1
Ošečina, Serbia, Yug. 40 B3
Osel = Saaremaa, Estonia 9 G20
Osery, Russia 46 E10
Osgoode, Canada 111 A9
Osh, Kyrgyzstan 50 E8
Oshakati, Namibia 85 H3
Oshawa, Canada 102 D4
Oshigambo, Namibia 88 B2
Oshkosh, Nebr., U.S.A. 112 E3
Oshkosh, Wis., U.S.A. 112 C10

Oshwe, Dem. Rep. of the Congo 84 E3
Osi, Nigeria 83 D6
Osieczna, Poland 45 G3
Osijek, Croatia 42 E3
Ósilo, Italy 30 B1
Ósimo, Italy 29 E10
Osintorf, Belarus 46 E6
Osipenko = Berdyansk, Ukraine 47 J9
Osipovichi = Asipovichy, Belarus 46 F5
Osiyan, India 68 F5
Osizweni, S. Africa 89 D5
Oskaloosa, U.S.A. 112 E8
Oskarshamn, Sweden 11 G10
Oskarström, Sweden 11 H6
Oskélanéo, Canada 102 C4
Öskemen, Kazakstan 50 E9
Oskol →, Ukraine 47 H9
Oslo, Norway 9 G14
Oslob, Phil. 61 G5
Oslofjorden, Norway 9 G14
Osmanabad, India 66 K10
Osmancık, Turkey 72 B6
Osmaniye, Turkey 70 B3
Osmanlı, Turkey 41 E10
Ösmo, Sweden 10 F11
Osnabrück, Germany 24 C4
Ośno Lubuskie, Poland 45 F1
Osoblaha, Czech Rep. 27 A10
Osogovska Planina, Macedonia 40 D6
Osor, Italy 29 D11
Osório, Brazil 127 B5
Osorno, Chile 128 E2
Osorno, Spain 34 C6
Osoyoos, Canada 104 D5
Osøyro, Norway 9 F11
Ospika →, Canada 104 B4
Osprey Reef, Australia 94 A4
Oss, Neths. 17 C5
Ossa, Mt., Australia 94 G4
Ossa, Óros, Greece 38 B4
Ossa de Montiel, Spain 33 G2
Ossabaw I., U.S.A. 109 K5
Osse →, France 20 D4
Osse →, Nigeria 83 D6
Ossi, Italy 30 B1
Ossining, U.S.A. 111 E11
Ossipee, U.S.A. 111 C13
Ossokmanuan L., Canada 103 B7
Ossora, Russia 51 D17
Ostashkov, Russia 46 D7
Östavall, Sweden 10 B9
Oste →, Germany 24 B5
Ostend = Oostende, Belgium 17 C2
Oster, Ukraine 47 G6
Osterburg, Germany 24 C7
Osterburg, U.S.A. 110 F6
Osterburken, Germany 25 F5
Österbybruk, Sweden 10 D11
Österbymo, Sweden 11 G9
Österdalälven →, Sweden 10 C7
Österdalen, Norway 9 F14
Österfärnebo, Sweden 10 D10
Österforse, Sweden 10 A11
Östergötlands län □, Sweden 11 F9
Osterholz-Scharmbeck, Germany 24 B4
Østerild, Denmark 11 G2
Osterode, Germany 24 D6
Östersund, Sweden 10 A8
Östervåla, Sweden 10 D11
Ostfriesische Inseln, Germany 24 B3
Ostfriesland, Germany 24 B3
Östhammar, Sweden 10 D12
Óstia, Lido di, Italy 29 G9
Ostíglia, Italy 29 C8
Östmark, Sweden 10 D6
Östra Husby, Sweden 11 F10
Ostrava, Czech Rep. 27 B11
Ostravský □, Czech Rep. 27 B10
Ostróda, Poland 44 E6
Ostrogozhsk, Russia 47 G10
Ostroh, Ukraine 47 G4
Ostrołęka, Poland 45 E8
Ostrov, Bulgaria 41 C8
Ostrov, Czech Rep. 26 A5
Ostrov, Romania 43 F12
Ostrov, Russia 46 D5
Ostrów Lubelski, Poland 45 G9
Ostrów Mazowiecka, Poland 45 F8
Ostrów Wielkopolski, Poland 45 G4
Ostrowiec-Świętokrzyski, Poland 45 H8
Ostrožac, Bos.-H. 42 G2
Ostrzeszów, Poland 45 G4
Ostseebad Kühlungsborn, Germany 24 A7
Osttirol □, Austria 26 E5
Ostuni, Italy 31 B10
Osum →, Albania 40 F4
Ōsŭm →, Bulgaria 41 C8
Ōsumi-Kaikyō, Japan 55 J5
Ōsumi-Shotō, Japan 55 J5
Osun □, Nigeria 83 D5
Osuna, Spain 35 H5
Oswegatchie →, U.S.A. 111 B9
Oswego, U.S.A. 111 C8
Oswego →, U.S.A. 111 C8
Oswestry, U.K. 12 E4
Oświęcim, Poland 45 H6
Otago □, N.Z. 91 L2
Otago Harbour, N.Z. 91 L3
Ōtake, Japan 55 G6
Otaki, N.Z. 91 J5
Otaru, Japan 54 C10

Otaru-Wan = Ishikari-Wan, Japan 54 C10
Otava, Czech Rep. 26 B7
Otavalo, Ecuador 124 C3
Otavi, Namibia 88 B2
Otchinjau, Angola 88 B1
Otelec, Romania 42 E5
Oțelnuk L., Canada 103 A6
Oțelu Roșu, Romania 42 E7
Otero de Rey = Outeiro de Rei, Spain 34 B3
Othello, U.S.A. 114 C4
Othonoí, Greece 38 B1
Óthris, Óros, Greece 38 B4
Otjiwarongo, Namibia 88 C2
Otmuchów, Poland 45 H4
Otočac, Croatia 29 D12
Otoineppu, Japan 54 B11
Otok, Croatia 29 E13
Otorohanga, N.Z. 91 H5
Otoskwin →, Canada 102 B2
Otra →, Norway 9 G13
Otradnyy, Russia 48 D10
Otranto, Italy 31 B11
Otranto, C. d', Italy 31 B11
Otranto, Str. of, Italy 31 B11
Otrokovice, Czech Rep. 27 B10
Otse, S. Africa 88 D4
Ōtsu, Japan 55 G7
Ōtsuki, Japan 55 G9
Ottawa = Outaouais →, Canada 102 C4
Ottawa, Canada 102 C4
Ottawa, Ill., U.S.A. 112 E10
Ottawa, Kans., U.S.A. 112 F7
Ottawa Is., Canada 101 C11
Ottélé, Cameroon 83 E7
Ottensheim, Austria 26 C7
Otter Cr. →, U.S.A. 111 B11
Otter L., Canada 105 B8
Otterndorf, Germany 24 B4
Otterup, Denmark 11 J4
Otterville, Canada 110 D4
Ottery St. Mary, U.K. 13 G4
Otto Beit Bridge, Zimbabwe 87 F2
Ottosdal, S. Africa 88 D4
Ottumwa, U.S.A. 112 E8
Otu, Nigeria 83 D5
Otukpa, Nigeria 83 D6
Oturkpo, Nigeria 83 D6
Otway, B., Chile 128 G2
Otway, C., Australia 95 F3
Otwock, Poland 45 F8
Ötztaler Ache →, Austria 26 D3
Ötztaler Alpen, Austria 26 E3
Ou →, Laos 64 B4
Ou Neua, Laos 58 F3
Ou-Sammyaku, Japan 54 E10
Ouachita →, U.S.A. 113 K9
Ouachita, L., U.S.A. 113 H8
Ouachita Mts., U.S.A. 113 H7
Ouagadougou, Burkina Faso 83 C4
Ouahigouya, Burkina Faso 82 C4
Ouahran = Oran, Algeria 78 A5
Oualâta, Mauritania 82 B3
Ouallam, Niger 83 C5
Ouallene, Algeria 78 D6
Ouargaye, Burkina Faso 83 C5
Ouargla, Algeria 78 B7
Ouarkoye, Burkina Faso 82 C4
Ouarzazate, Morocco 78 B4
Ouassouas, Mali 83 B5
Ouatagouna, Mali 83 B5
Oubangi →, Dem. Rep. of the Congo 84 E3
Ouche →, France 19 E12
Ouddorp, Neths. 17 C3
Oude Rijn →, Neths. 17 B4
Oudeïka, Mali 83 B4
Oudenaarde, Belgium 17 D3
Oudon →, France 18 E6
Oudtshoorn, S. Africa 88 E3
Ouéllé, Ivory C. 82 D4
Ouéme →, Benin 83 D5
Ouessa, Burkina Faso 82 C4
Ouessant, Î. d', France 18 D1
Ouesso, Congo 84 D3
Ouest, Pte. de l', Canada 103 C7
Ouezzane, Morocco 78 B4
Ougarou, Burkina Faso 83 C5
Oughter, L., Ireland 15 B4
Oughterard, Ireland 15 C2
Ouidah, Benin 83 D5
Ouidi, Niger 83 C7
Ouistreham, France 18 C6
Oujda, Morocco 78 B5
Oujeft, Mauritania 82 A2
Oulainen, Finland 8 D21
Ould Yenjé, Mauritania 82 B2
Oullins, France 21 C8
Oulu, Finland 8 D21
Oulujärvi, Finland 8 D22
Oulujoki →, Finland 8 D21
Oulx, Italy 28 C3
Oum Chalouba, Chad 79 E10
Oum Hadjer, Chad 79 F9
Oumé, Ivory C. 82 D3
Ounasjoki →, Finland 8 C21
Ounguati, Namibia 88 C2
Ounianga Sérir, Chad 79 E10
Our →, Lux. 17 E6
Ouray, U.S.A. 115 G10
Ourcq →, France 19 C10
Ourense, Spain 34 C3
Ouricuri, Brazil 125 E10
Ourinhos, Brazil 127 A6
Ourique, Portugal 35 H2

Ouro Fino, Brazil 127 A6
Ouro-Ndia, Mali 82 B4
Ouro Prêto, Brazil 127 A7
Ouro Sogui, Senegal 82 B2
Oursi, Burkina Faso 83 C4
Ourthe →, Belgium 17 D5
Ouse →, E. Susx., U.K. 13 G8
Ouse →, N. Yorks., U.K. 12 D7
Oust, France 20 F5
Oust →, France 18 E4
Outaouais →, Canada 102 C5
Outardes →, Canada 103 C6
Outeiro de Rei, Spain 34 B3
Outer Hebrides, U.K. 14 D1
Outes = Serra de Outes, Spain 34 C2
Outjo, Namibia 88 C2
Outlook, Canada 105 C7
Outokumpu, Finland 8 E23
Outreau, France 19 B8
Ouvèze →, France 21 E8
Ouyen, Australia 95 F3
Ouzouer-le-Marché, France 18 E8
Ovada, Italy 28 D5
Ovalau, Fiji 91 C8
Ovalle, Chile 126 C1
Ovamboland, Namibia 88 B2
Ovar, Portugal 34 E2
Overath, Germany 24 E3
Overflakkee, Neths. 17 C4
Overijssel □, Neths. 17 B6
Overland Park, U.S.A. 112 F7
Overton, U.S.A. 117 J12
Övertorneå, Sweden 8 C20
Överum, Sweden 11 F10
Ovid, U.S.A. 111 D8
Ovidiopol, Ukraine 47 J6
Ovidiu, Romania 43 F13
Oviedo, Spain 34 B5
Oviksfjällen, Sweden 10 A7
Oviši, Latvia 9 H19
Ovoot, Mongolia 56 B7
Övör Hangay □, Mongolia 56 B2
Ovoro, Nigeria 83 D6
Øvre Årdal, Norway 9 F12
Øvre Fryken, Sweden 10 E7
Ovruch, Ukraine 47 G5
Owaka, N.Z. 91 M2
Owambo = Ovamboland, Namibia 88 B2
Owasco L., U.S.A. 111 D8
Owase, Japan 55 G8
Owatonna, U.S.A. 112 C8
Owbeh, Afghan. 66 B3
Owego, U.S.A. 111 D8
Owen Falls Dam, Uganda 86 B3
Owen Sound, Canada 102 D3
Owens →, U.S.A. 116 J9
Owens L., U.S.A. 117 J9
Owensboro, U.S.A. 108 G2
Owerri, Nigeria 83 D6
Owl →, Canada 105 B10
Owo, Nigeria 83 D6
Owosso, U.S.A. 108 D3
Owyhee, U.S.A. 114 F5
Owyhee →, U.S.A. 114 E5
Owyhee, L., U.S.A. 114 E5
Ox Mts. = Slieve Gamph, Ireland 15 B3
Öxarfjörður, Iceland 8 C5
Oxbow, Canada 105 D8
Oxelösund, Sweden 11 F11
Oxford, N.Z. 91 K4
Oxford, U.K. 13 F6
Oxford, Mass., U.S.A. 111 D13
Oxford, Miss., U.S.A. 113 H10
Oxford, N.C., U.S.A. 109 G6
Oxford, N.Y., U.S.A. 111 D9
Oxford, Ohio, U.S.A. 108 F3
Oxford L., Canada 105 C9
Oxfordshire □, U.K. 13 F6
Oxía, Greece 38 C3
Oxie, Sweden 11 J7
Oxílithos, Greece 38 C6
Oxnard, U.S.A. 117 L7
Oxsjövålen, Sweden 10 B7
Oxus = Amudarya →, Uzbekistan 50 E6
Oya, Malaysia 62 D4
Oyama, Japan 55 F9
Oyem, Gabon 84 D2
Oyen, Canada 105 C6
Oykel →, U.K. 14 D4
Oymyakon, Russia 51 C15
Oyo, Nigeria 83 D5
Oyo □, Nigeria 83 D5
Oyonnax, France 19 F12
Oyster Bay, U.S.A. 111 F11
Ōyūbari, Japan 54 C11
Özalp, Turkey 73 C10
Ozamiz, Phil. 61 G5
Ozark, Ala., U.S.A. 109 K3
Ozark, Ark., U.S.A. 113 H8
Ozark, Mo., U.S.A. 113 G8
Ozark Plateau, U.S.A. 113 G9
Ozarks, L. of the, U.S.A. 112 F8
Ozarów, Poland 45 H8
Ózd, Hungary 42 B5
Ozernoye, Russia 48 E10
Ozette L., U.S.A. 116 B2
Ozieri, Italy 30 B2
Ozimek, Poland 45 H5
Ozinki, Russia 48 E9
Ozona, U.S.A. 113 K4
Ozorków, Poland 45 G6
Ozren, Bos.-H. 42 G3
Ozuluama, Mexico 119 C5
Ozun, Romania 43 E10
Ozurgeti, Georgia 49 K5

Rombari, *Sudan* **81 G3**
Romblon, *Phil.* **61 E5**
Rome = Roma, *Italy* **29 G9**
Rome, Ga., *U.S.A.* **109 H3**
Rome, N.Y., *U.S.A.* **111 C9**
Rome, Pa., *U.S.A.* **111 E8**
Rometta, *Italy* **31 D8**
Romilly-sur-Seine, *France* **19 D10**
Romney, *U.S.A.* **108 F6**
Romney Marsh, *U.K.* **13 F8**
Romny, *Ukraine* **47 G7**
Rømø, *Denmark* **11 J2**
Romodan, *Ukraine* **47 G7**
Romodanovo, *Russia* **48 C7**
Romont, *Switz.* **25 J2**
Romorantin-Lanthenay, *France* .. **19 E8**
Romsdalen, *Norway* **9 E12**
Romsey, *U.K.* **13 G6**
Ron, *Vietnam* **64 D6**
Rona, *U.K.* **14 D3**
Ronan, *U.S.A.* **114 C6**
Roncador, Cayos, *Caribbean* .. **120 D3**
Roncador, Serra do, *Brazil* .. **125 F8**
Ronciglione, *Italy* **29 F9**
Ronco ➤, *Italy* **29 D9**
Ronda, *Spain* **35 J5**
Ronda, Serranía de, *Spain* .. **35 J5**
Rondane, *Norway* **9 F13**
Rondônia □, *Brazil* **124 F6**
Rondonópolis, *Brazil* **125 G8**
Rong, Koh, *Cambodia* **65 G4**
Rong Jiang ➤, *China* **58 E7**
Rong Xian, Guangxi Zhuangzu,
  China **59 F8**
Rong Xian, Sichuan, *China* .. **58 C5**
Rong'an, *China* **58 E7**
Rongchang, *China* **58 C5**
Ronge, L. la, *Canada* **105 B7**
Rongjiang, *China* **58 E7**
Rongshui, *China* **58 E7**
Rønne, *Denmark* **11 J8**
Ronne Ice Shelf, *Antarctica* .. **5 D18**
Ronneby, *Sweden* **11 H9**
Ronnebyån ➤, *Sweden* .. **11 H9**
Rönnöfors, *Sweden* **8 D16**
Rönnöshyttan, *Sweden* .. **11 F9**
Ronsard, C., *Australia* **93 D1**
Ronse, *Belgium* **17 D3**
Roodepoort, *S. Africa* **89 D4**
Roof Butte, *U.S.A.* **115 H9**
Rooiboklaagte ➤, *Namibia* ... **88 C3**
Roorkee, *India* **68 E7**
Roosendaal, *Neths.* **17 C4**
Roosevelt, *U.S.A.* **114 F8**
Roosevelt ➤, *Brazil* **122 D4**
Roosevelt, Mt., *Canada* .. **104 B3**
Roosevelt I., *Antarctica* .. **5 D12**
Ropczyce, *Poland* **45 H8**
Roper ➤, *Australia* **94 A2**
Roper Bar, *Australia* **94 A1**
Roque Pérez, *Argentina* .. **126 D4**
Roquefort, *France* **20 D3**
Roquemaure, *France* **21 D8**
Roquetas de Mar, *Spain* .. **33 J2**
Roquetes, *Spain* **32 E5**
Roquevaire, *France* **21 E9**
Roraima □, *Brazil* **124 C6**
Roraima, Mt., *Venezuela* .. **122 C4**
Røros, *Norway* **9 E14**
Rorschach, *Switz.* **25 H5**
Rosa, *Zambia* **87 D3**
Rosa, L., *Bahamas* **121 B5**
Rosa, Monte, *Italy* **28 C4**
Rosal de la Frontera, *Spain* .. **35 H3**
Rosalia, *U.S.A.* **114 C5**
Rosamond, *U.S.A.* **117 L8**
Rosans, *France* **21 D9**
Rosario, *Argentina* **126 C3**
Rosário, *Brazil* **125 D10**
Rosario, Baja Calif., *Mexico* .. **118 B1**
Rosario, Sinaloa, *Mexico* .. **118 C3**
Rosario, *Paraguay* **126 A4**
Rosario de la Frontera,
  Argentina **126 B3**
Rosario de Lerma, *Argentina* .. **126 A2**
Rosario del Tala, *Argentina* .. **126 C4**
Rosário do Sul, *Brazil* .. **127 C5**
Rosarito, *Mexico* **117 N9**
Rosarno, *Italy* **31 D8**
Rosas = Roses, *Spain* **32 C8**
Roscoe, *U.S.A.* **111 E10**
Roscoff, *France* **18 D3**
Roscommon, *Ireland* **15 C3**
Roscommon □, *Ireland* .. **15 C3**
Roscrea, *Ireland* **15 D4**
Rose ➤, *Australia* **94 A2**
Rose Blanche, *Canada* .. **103 C8**
Rose Pt., *Canada* **104 C2**
Rose Valley, *Canada* **105 C8**
Roseau, *Domin.* **121 C7**
Roseau, *U.S.A.* **112 A7**
Rosebery, *Australia* **94 G4**
Rosebud, S. Dak., *U.S.A.* .. **112 D4**
Rosebud, Tex., *U.S.A.* .. **113 K6**
Roseburg, *U.S.A.* **114 E2**
Rosedale, *U.S.A.* **113 J9**
Roseland, *U.S.A.* **116 G4**
Rosemary, *Canada* **104 C6**
Rosenberg, *U.S.A.* **113 L7**
Rosendaël, *France* **19 A9**
Rosenheim, *Germany* **25 H8**
Roses, *Spain* **32 C8**
Roses, G. de, *Spain* **32 C8**
Roseto degli Abruzzi, *Italy* .. **29 F11**
Rosetown, *Canada* **105 C7**
Rosetta = Rashîd, *Egypt* .. **80 H7**
Roseville, Calif., *U.S.A.* .. **116 G5**
Roseville, Mich., *U.S.A.* .. **110 D2**

Rosewood, *Australia* **95 D5**
Roshkhvār, *Iran* **71 C8**
Rosières-en-Santerre, *France* .. **19 C9**
Rosignano Maríttimo, *Italy* .. **28 E7**
Rosignol, *Guyana* **124 B7**
Roşiori de Vede, *Romania* .. **43 F10**
Rositsa, *Bulgaria* **41 C11**
Rositsa ➤, *Bulgaria* **41 C9**
Roskilde, *Denmark* **11 J6**
Roskilde Amtskommune □,
  Denmark **11 J6**
Roskovec, *Albania* **40 F3**
Roslavl, *Russia* **46 F7**
Rosmaninhal, *Portugal* .. **34 F3**
Rosmead, *S. Africa* **88 E4**
Røsnæs, *Denmark* **11 J4**
Rosolini, *Italy* **31 F7**
Rosporden, *France* **18 E3**
Ross, *Australia* **94 G4**
Ross, *N.Z.* **91 K3**
Ross Béthio, *Mauritania* .. **82 B1**
Ross I., *Antarctica* **5 D11**
Ross Ice Shelf, *Antarctica* .. **5 E12**
Ross L., *U.S.A.* **114 B3**
Ross-on-Wye, *U.K.* **13 F5**
Ross River, *Australia* **94 C1**
Ross River, *Canada* **104 A2**
Ross Sea, *Antarctica* **5 D11**
Rossall Pt., *U.K.* **12 D4**
Rossan Pt., *Ireland* **15 B3**
Rossano, *Italy* **31 C9**
Rossburn, *Canada* **105 C8**
Rosseau, *Canada* **110 A5**
Rosseau L., *Canada* **110 A5**
Rossignol, L., *Canada* .. **103 D6**
Rossignol Res., *Canada* .. **103 D6**
Rossland, *Canada* **104 D5**
Rosslare, *Ireland* **15 D5**
Rosslau, *Germany* **24 D8**
Rosso, *Mauritania* **82 B1**
Rosso, C., *France* **21 F12**
Rossosh, *Russia* **47 G10**
Røssvatnet, *Norway* **8 D16**
Røst, *Norway* **8 C15**
Rosthern, *Canada* **105 C7**
Rostock, *Germany* **24 A8**
Rostov, Don, *Russia* **47 J10**
Rostov, Yaroslavl, *Russia* .. **46 D10**
Rostrenen, *France* **18 D3**
Roswell, Ga., *U.S.A.* **109 H3**
Roswell, N. Mex., *U.S.A.* .. **113 J2**
Rota, *Spain* **35 J4**
Rotan, *U.S.A.* **113 J4**
Rotenburg, Hessen, Germany .. **24 E5**
Rotenburg, Niedersachsen,
  Germany **24 B5**
Roth, *Germany* **25 F7**
Rothaargebirge, *Germany* .. **24 D4**
Rothenburg ob der Tauber,
  Germany **25 F6**
Rother ➤, *U.K.* **13 G8**
Rotherham, *U.K.* **12 D6**
Rothes, *U.K.* **14 D5**
Rothesay, *Canada* **103 C6**
Rothesay, *U.K.* **14 F3**
Roti, *Indonesia* **63 F6**
Rotja, Pta., *Spain* **33 G6**
Roto, *Australia* **95 E4**
Rotondo, Mte., *France* .. **21 F13**
Rotoroa, L., *N.Z.* **91 J4**
Rotorua, *N.Z.* **91 H6**
Rotorua, L., *N.Z.* **91 H6**
Rott ➤, *Germany* **25 G9**
Rottenburg, *Germany* **25 G4**
Rottnest I., *Australia* **93 F2**
Rottumeroog, *Neths.* **17 A6**
Rottweil, *Germany* **25 G4**
Roubaix, *France* **19 B10**
Roudnice nad Labem,
  Czech Rep. **26 A7**
Rouen, *France* **18 C8**
Rouergue, *France* **20 D5**
Rouillac, *France* **20 C3**
Rouleau, *Canada* **105 C8**
Round Mountain, *U.S.A.* .. **114 G5**
Round Mt., *Australia* **95 E5**
Round Rock, *U.S.A.* **113 K6**
Roundup, *U.S.A.* **114 C9**
Rousay, *U.K.* **14 B5**
Rouses Point, *U.S.A.* **111 B11**
Rouseville, *U.S.A.* **110 E5**
Roussillon, Isère, *France* .. **21 C8**
Roussillon, Pico, *France* .. **20 F6**
Rouxville, *S. Africa* **88 E4**
Rouyn-Noranda, *Canada* .. **102 C4**
Rovaniemi, *Finland* **8 C21**
Rovato, *Italy* **28 C7**
Rovenki, *Ukraine* **47 H10**
Rovereto, *Italy* **28 C8**
Rovigo, *Italy* **29 C8**
Rovinj, *Croatia* **29 C10**
Rovno = Rivne, *Ukraine* .. **47 G4**
Rovnoye, *Russia* **48 E8**
Rovuma = Ruvuma ➤,
  Tanzania **87 E5**
Row'ān, *Iran* **71 C6**
Rowena, *Australia* **95 D4**
Rowley Shoals, *Australia* .. **92 C2**
Roxa, Guinea-Biss. **82 C1**
Roxas, Capiz, *Phil.* **61 F5**
Roxas, Isabela, *Phil.* **61 C4**

Roxas, Mind. Or., *Phil.* .. **61 E4**
Roxboro, *U.S.A.* **109 G6**
Roxburgh, *N.Z.* **91 L2**
Roxbury, *U.S.A.* **110 F7**
Roy, Mont., *U.S.A.* **114 C9**
Roy, N. Mex., *U.S.A.* **113 H2**
Roy, Utah, *U.S.A.* **114 F7**
Royal Canal, *Ireland* **15 C4**
Royal Leamington Spa, *U.K.* .. **13 E6**
Royal Tunbridge Wells, *U.K.* .. **13 F8**
Royan, *France* **20 C2**
Roye, *France* **19 C9**
Royston, *U.K.* **13 E7**
Rožaj, Montenegro, *Yug.* .. **40 D4**
Rózan, *Poland* **45 F8**
Rozay-en-Brie, *France* .. **19 D9**
Rozdilna, *Ukraine* **47 J6**
Rozhyshche, *Ukraine* **47 G3**
Rožmitál pod Třemšínem,
  Czech Rep. **26 B6**
Rožňava, *Slovak Rep.* **27 C13**
Rozogi, *Poland* **44 E8**
Rozoy-sur-Serre, *France* .. **19 C11**
Rozzano, *Italy* **28 C6**
Rrëshen, *Albania* **40 E3**
Rrogozhine, *Albania* **40 E3**
Rtanj, Serbia, *Yug.* **40 C5**
Rtishchevo, *Russia* **48 D6**
Rúa = A Rúa, *Spain* **34 C3**
Ruacaná, *Namibia* **88 B1**
Ruahine Ra., *N.Z.* **91 H6**
Ruapehu, *N.Z.* **91 H5**
Ruapuke I., *N.Z.* **91 M2**
Ruâq, W. ➤, *Egypt* **75 F2**
Rub' al Khālī, Si. Arabia .. **74 D4**
Rubeho Mts., *Tanzania* .. **86 D4**
Rubezhnoye = Rubizhne,
  Ukraine **47 H10**
Rubh a' Mhail, *U.K.* **14 F2**
Rubha Hunish, *U.K.* **14 D2**
Rubha Robhanais = Lewis, Butt
  of, *U.K.* **14 C2**
Rubi, *Spain* **32 D7**
Rubicon ➤, *U.S.A.* **116 G5**
Rubicone ➤, *Italy* **29 D9**
Rubik, *Albania* **40 E3**
Rubino, Ivory C. **82 D4**
Rubio, *Venezuela* **124 B4**
Rubizhne, *Ukraine* **47 H10**
Rubtsovsk, *Russia* **50 D9**
Ruby L., *U.S.A.* **114 F6**
Ruby Mts., *U.S.A.* **114 F6**
Rubyvale, *Australia* **94 C4**
Rucheng, *China* **59 E9**
Ruciane-Nida, *Poland* .. **44 E8**
Rüd Sar, *Iran* **71 B6**
Ruda, *Sweden* **11 G10**
Ruda Śląska, *Poland* **45 H5**
Rudall, *Australia* **95 E2**
Rudall ➤, *Australia* **92 D3**
Rüdersdorf, *Germany* **24 C9**
Rudewa, *Tanzania* **87 E3**
Rudkøbing, *Denmark* **11 K4**
Rudna, *Poland* **45 G3**
Rudnik, *Bulgaria* **41 D11**
Rudnik, *Poland* **45 H9**
Rudnik, Serbia, *Yug.* **40 B4**
Rudnya, *Russia* **46 E6**
Rudnyy, *Kazakstan* **50 D7**
Rudolfa, Ostrov, *Russia* .. **50 A6**
Rudolstadt, *Germany* **24 E7**
Rudong, *China* **59 A13**
Rudozem, *Bulgaria* **41 E8**
Rudyard, *U.S.A.* **108 B3**
Rue, *France* **19 B8**
Rufa'a, *Sudan* **81 E3**
Rufiji ➤, *Tanzania* **86 D4**
Rufino, *Argentina* **126 C3**
Rufisque, *Senegal* **82 C1**
Rufunsa, *Zambia* **87 F2**
Rugao, *China* **59 A13**
Rugby, *U.K.* **13 E6**
Rugby, *U.S.A.* **112 A5**
Rügen, *Germany* **24 A9**
Rugles, *France* **18 D7**
Ruhengeri, *Rwanda* **86 C2**
Ruhla, *Germany* **24 E6**
Ruhland, *Germany* **24 D9**
Ruhnu, *Estonia* **9 H20**
Ruhr ➤, *Germany* **24 D2**
Ruhuhu ➤, *Tanzania* **87 E3**
Rui'an, *China* **59 D13**
Ruichang, *China* **59 C10**
Ruidoso, *U.S.A.* **115 K11**
Ruijin, *China* **59 E10**
Ruili, *China* **58 E1**
Ruivo, Pico, *Madeira* **37 D3**
Ruj, *Bulgaria* **40 D6**
Rujm Tal'at al Jamā'ah, *Jordan* .. **75 E4**
Ruk, *Pakistan* **68 F3**
Rukhla, *Pakistan* **68 C4**
Ruki ➤, Dem. Rep. of
  the Congo **84 E3**
Rukwa □, *Tanzania* **86 D3**
Rukwa, L., *Tanzania* **86 D3**
Rulhieres, C., *Australia* .. **92 B4**
Rum = Rhum, *U.K.* **14 E2**
Rum Cay, *Bahamas* **121 B5**
Rum Jungle, *Australia* .. **92 B5**
Ruma, Serbia, *Yug.* **42 E4**
Rumāḥ, Si. Arabia **70 E5**
Rumania = Romania ■, *Europe* .. **43 D10**
Rumaylah, *Iraq* **70 D5**
Rumbêk, *Sudan* **81 F2**

Rumburk, *Czech Rep.* **26 A7**
Rumford, *U.S.A.* **109 C10**
Rumia, *Poland* **44 D5**
Rumilly, *France* **21 C9**
Rumoi, *Japan* **54 C10**
Rumonge, *Burundi* **86 C2**
Rumson, *U.S.A.* **111 F11**
Rumuruti, *Kenya* **86 B4**
Runan, *China* **56 H8**
Runanga, *N.Z.* **91 K3**
Runaway, C., *N.Z.* **91 G6**
Runcorn, *U.K.* **12 D5**
Rundu, *Namibia* **88 B2**
Rungwa, *Tanzania* **86 D3**
Rungwa ➤, *Tanzania* **86 D3**
Rungwe, *Tanzania* **87 D3**
Rungwe, Mt., *Tanzania* .. **84 F6**
Runka, *Nigeria* **83 C6**
Runn, *Sweden* **10 D9**
Runton Ra., *Australia* .. **92 D3**
Ruokolahti, *Finland* **46 B5**
Ruoqiang, *China* **60 C3**
Rupa, *India* **67 F18**
Rupar, *India* **68 D7**
Rupat, *Indonesia* **62 D2**
Rupea, *Romania* **43 D10**
Rupen ➤, *India* **68 H4**
Rupert ➤, *Canada* **102 B4**
Rupert, *U.S.A.* **114 E7**
Rupert B., *Canada* **102 B4**
Rupert House = Waskaganish,
  Canada **102 B4**
Rupsa, *India* **69 J12**
Rur ➤, *Germany* **24 D1**
Rurrenabaque, *Bolivia* .. **124 F5**
Rus ➤, *Spain* **33 F2**
Rusambo, *Zimbabwe* **87 F3**
Rusape, *Zimbabwe* **87 F3**
Ruschuk = Ruse, *Bulgaria* .. **41 C9**
Ruse, *Bulgaria* **41 C9**
Ruse □, *Bulgaria* **41 C10**
Ruşeţu, *Romania* **43 F12**
Rush, *Ireland* **15 C5**
Rushan, *China* **57 F11**
Rushden, *U.K.* **13 E7**
Rushmore, Mt., *U.S.A.* .. **112 D3**
Rushville, Ill., *U.S.A.* .. **112 E9**
Rushville, Ind., *U.S.A.* .. **108 F3**
Rushville, Nebr., *U.S.A.* .. **112 D3**
Russas, *Brazil* **125 D11**
Russell, *Canada* **105 C8**
Russell, Kans., *U.S.A.* .. **112 F5**
Russell, N.Y., *U.S.A.* **111 B9**
Russell, Pa., *U.S.A.* **110 E5**
Russell L., Man., *Canada* .. **105 B8**
Russell L., N.W.T., *Canada* .. **104 A5**
Russellkonda, *India* **67 K14**
Russellville, Ala., *U.S.A.* .. **109 H2**
Russellville, Ark., *U.S.A.* .. **113 H8**
Russellville, Ky., *U.S.A.* .. **109 G2**
Rüsselsheim, *Germany* .. **25 F4**
Russi, *Italy* **29 D9**
Russia ■, *Eurasia* **51 C11**
Russian ➤, *U.S.A.* **116 G3**
Russkoye Ustie, *Russia* .. **4 B15**
Rust, *Austria* **27 D9**
Rustam, *Pakistan* **68 B5**
Rustam Shahr, *Pakistan* .. **68 F2**
Rustavi, *Georgia* **49 K7**
Rustenburg, S. Africa **88 D4**
Ruston, *U.S.A.* **113 J8**
Rutana, *Burundi* **86 C3**
Rute, *Spain* **35 H6**
Ruteng, *Indonesia* **63 F6**
Ruth, *U.S.A.* **110 C2**
Rutherford, *U.S.A.* **116 G4**
Rutland, *U.S.A.* **111 C12**
Rutland □, *U.K.* **13 E7**
Rutland Water, *U.K.* **13 E7**
Rutledge ➤, *Canada* **105 A6**
Rutledge L., *Canada* **105 A6**
Rutqa, W. ➤, *Syria* **73 E9**
Rutshuru, Dem. Rep. of
  the Congo **86 C2**
Ruvo di Púglia, *Italy* .. **31 A9**
Ruvu, *Tanzania* **86 D4**
Ruvu ➤, *Tanzania* **86 D4**
Ruvuma □, *Tanzania* **87 E4**
Ruvuma ➤, *Tanzania* **87 E5**
Ruwais, *U.A.E.* **71 E7**
Ruwenzori, *Africa* **86 B2**
Ruya ➤, *Zimbabwe* **89 B5**
Ruyigi, *Burundi* **86 C3**
Ruyuan, *China* **59 E9**
Ruzayevka, *Russia* **48 C7**
Růzhevo Konare, *Bulgaria* .. **41 D8**
Ružomberok, *Slovak Rep.* .. **27 B12**
Rwanda ■, *Africa* **86 C3**
Ryakhovo, *Bulgaria* **41 C10**
Ryan, L., *U.K.* **14 G3**
Ryazan, *Russia* **46 E10**
Ryazhsk, *Russia* **46 F11**
Rybache = Rybachye, *Kazakstan* .. **50 E9**
Rybachye, *Kazakstan* **50 E9**
Rybinsk, *Russia* **46 C10**
Rybinsk Vdkhr., *Russia* .. **46 C10**
Rybnik, *Poland* **45 H5**
Rybnitsa = Râbniţa, *Moldova* .. **43 C14**
Rychnov nad Kněžnou,
  Czech Rep. **27 A9**
Rychwał, *Poland* **45 F5**
Rycroft, *Canada* **104 B5**
Ryd, *Sweden* **11 H8**
Rydaholm, *Sweden* **11 H8**
Ryde, *U.K.* **13 G6**
Ryderwood, *U.S.A.* **116 D3**

Rydzyna, *Poland* **45 G3**
Rye, *U.K.* **13 G8**
Rye ➤, *U.K.* **12 C7**
Rye Bay, *U.K.* **13 G8**
Rye Patch Reservoir, *U.S.A.* .. **114 F4**
Ryegate, *U.S.A.* **114 C9**
Ryki, *Poland* **45 G8**
Ryley, *Canada* **104 C6**
Rylsk, *Russia* **47 G8**
Rylstone, *Australia* **95 E4**
Rymanów, *Poland* **45 J8**
Ryn, *Poland* **44 E8**
Ryn Peski, *Kazakstan* .. **49 G9**
Ryōtsu, *Japan* **54 E9**
Rypin, *Poland* **45 E6**
Ryssby, *Sweden* **11 H8**
Ryūgasaki, *Japan* **55 G10**
Ryūkyū Is. = Ryūkyū-rettō,
  Japan **55 M3**
Ryūkyū-rettō, *Japan* **55 M3**
Rzepin, *Poland* **45 F1**
Rzeszów, *Poland* **45 H8**
Rzhev, *Russia* **46 D8**

S

Sa, *Thailand* **64 C3**
Sa Canal, *Spain* **37 C7**
Sa Conillera, *Spain* **37 C7**
Sa Dec, *Vietnam* **65 G5**
Sa Dragonera, *Spain* .. **37 B9**
Sa Mesquida, *Spain* **37 B11**
Sa Pobla, *Spain* **32 F8**
Sa Savina, *Spain* **37 C7**
Sa'ādatābād, Fārs, *Iran* .. **71 D7**
Sa'ādatābād, Hormozgān, *Iran* .. **71 D7**
Sa'ādatābād, Hormozgān, *Iran* .. **71 D7**
Saale ➤, *Germany* **24 D7**
Saaler Bodden, *Germany* .. **24 A8**
Saalfeld, *Germany* **24 E7**
Saalfelden, *Austria* **26 D5**
Saane ➤, *Switz.* **25 H3**
Saar ➤, *Europe* **17 E6**
Saarbrücken, *Germany* .. **25 F2**
Saarburg, *Germany* **25 F2**
Saaremaa, *Estonia* **9 G20**
Saarijärvi, *Finland* **9 E21**
Saariselkä, *Finland* **8 B23**
Saarland □, *Germany* .. **25 F2**
Saarlouis, *Germany* **25 F2**
Sab 'Ābar, *Syria* **70 C3**
Saba, W. Indies **121 C7**
Šabac, Serbia, *Yug.* **40 B3**
Sabadell, *Spain* **32 D7**
Sabah □, *Malaysia* **62 C5**
Sabak Bernam, *Malaysia* .. **65 L3**
Sabalān, Kūhhā-ye, *Iran* .. **70 B5**
Sabalana, Kepulauan, *Indonesia* .. **63 F5**
Sábana de la Mar, Dom. Rep. .. **121 C6**
Sábanalarga, *Colombia* .. **124 A4**
Sabang, *Indonesia* **62 C1**
Săbăoani, *Romania* **43 C11**
Sabará, *Brazil* **125 G10**
Sabarmati ➤, *India* **68 H5**
Sabattis, *U.S.A.* **111 B10**
Sabáudia, *Italy* **30 A6**
Saberania, *Indonesia* .. **63 E9**
Sabhah, *Libya* **79 C8**
Sabi ➤, *India* **68 E7**
Sabidana, J., *Sudan* **80 D4**
Sabie, S. Africa **89 D5**
Sabinal, *Mexico* **118 A3**
Sabinal, *U.S.A.* **113 L5**
Sabiñánigo, *Spain* **32 C4**
Sabinar, Punta del, *Spain* .. **33 J2**
Sabinas, *Mexico* **118 B4**
Sabinas ➤, *Mexico* **118 B4**
Sabinas Hidalgo, *Mexico* .. **118 B4**
Sabine ➤, *U.S.A.* **113 L8**
Sabine L., *U.S.A.* **113 L8**
Sabine Pass, *U.S.A.* **113 L8**
Sabinov, Slovak Rep. **27 B14**
Sabinsville, *U.S.A.* **110 E7**
Sabirabad, *Azerbaijan* .. **49 K9**
Sabkhet el Bardawîl, *Egypt* .. **75 D2**
Sablayan, *Phil.* **61 E4**
Sable, *Canada* **103 A6**
Sable, C., *Canada* **103 D6**
Sable, C., *U.S.A.* **107 E10**
Sable I., *Canada* **103 D8**
Sablé-sur-Sarthe, *France* .. **18 E6**
Sabonkafi, *Niger* **83 C6**
Sabor ➤, *Portugal* **34 D3**
Sabou, Burkina Faso **82 C4**
Sabres, *France* **20 D3**
Sabrina Coast, *Antarctica* .. **5 C9**
Sabugal, *Portugal* **34 E3**
Sabulubbek, *Indonesia* .. **62 E1**
Sabuncu, *Turkey* **39 B12**
Sabzevār, *Iran* **71 B8**
Sabzvārān, *Iran* **71 D8**
Sac City, *U.S.A.* **112 D7**
Sacedón, *Spain* **32 E2**
Săcele, *Romania* **43 E10**
Sachigo ➤, *Canada* **102 A2**
Sachigo, L., *Canada* **102 B1**
Sachkhere, *Georgia* **49 J6**
Sachsen □, *Germany* .. **24 E9**
Sachsen-Anhalt □, *Germany* .. **24 D7**
Sacile, *Italy* **29 C9**
Sackets Harbor, *U.S.A.* .. **111 C8**
Sackville, *Canada* **103 C7**
Saco, Maine, *U.S.A.* **109 D10**
Saco, Mont., *U.S.A.* **114 B10**
Sacramento, *U.S.A.* **116 G5**

Sacramento

Sacramento →, *U.S.A.* 116 G5
Sacramento Mts., *U.S.A.* 115 K11
Sacramento Valley, *U.S.A.* 116 G5
Sacratif, C., *Spain* 35 J7
Săcueni, *Romania* 42 C7
Sada, *Spain* 34 B2
Sada-Misaki, *Japan* 55 H6
Sádaba, *Spain* 32 C3
Sadabad, *India* 68 F8
Sadani, *Tanzania* 86 D4
Sadao, *Thailand* 65 J3
Sadd el Aali, *Egypt* 80 C3
Saddle Mt., *U.S.A.* 116 E3
Sade, *Nigeria* 83 C7
Sadimi, *Dem. Rep. of the Congo* 87 D1
Sadiola, *Mali* 82 C2
Sa'dīyah, Hawr as, *Iraq* 73 F12
Sado, *Japan* 54 F9
Sado →, *Portugal* 35 G2
Sadon, *Burma* 67 G20
Sadon, *Russia* 49 J6
Sadra, *India* 68 H5
Sadri, *India* 68 G5
Sæby, *Denmark* 11 G4
Saegertown, *U.S.A.* 110 E4
Saelices, *Spain* 32 F2
Safaalan, *Turkey* 41 E12
Safaga, *Egypt* 80 B3
Şafājah, *Si. Arabia* 70 E3
Šafárikovo = Tornaľa, *Slovak Rep.* 27 C13
Säffle, *Sweden* 10 E6
Safford, *U.S.A.* 115 K9
Saffron Walden, *U.K.* 13 E8
Safi, *Morocco* 78 B4
Şafīābād, *Iran* 71 B8
Safīd Dasht, *Iran* 71 C6
Safīd Kūh, *Afghan.* 66 B3
Safīd Rūd →, *Iran* 71 B6
Safipur, *India* 69 F9
Safonovo, *Russia* 46 E7
Safranbolu, *Turkey* 72 B5
Saft Rashîn, *Egypt* 80 J7
Safwān, *Iraq* 70 D5
Sag Harbor, *U.S.A.* 111 F12
Saga, *Japan* 55 H5
Saga □, *Japan* 55 H5
Sagae, *Japan* 54 E10
Sagala, *Mali* 82 C3
Sagamore, *U.S.A.* 110 F5
Sagar, *Karnataka, India* 66 M9
Sagar, *Mad. P., India* 69 H8
Sagara, L., *Tanzania* 86 D3
Sagay, *Phil.* 61 F5
Saginaw, *U.S.A.* 108 D4
Saginaw →, *U.S.A.* 108 D4
Saginaw B., *U.S.A.* 108 D4
Sagleipie, *Liberia* 82 D3
Saglouc = Salluit, *Canada* 101 B12
Sagŏ-ri, *S. Korea* 57 G14
Sagone, *France* 21 F12
Sagone, G. de, *France* 21 F12
Sagres, *Portugal* 35 J2
Sagua la Grande, *Cuba* 120 B3
Saguache, *U.S.A.* 115 G10
Saguaro Nat. Park, *U.S.A.* 115 K8
Saguenay →, *Canada* 103 C5
Sagunt, *Spain* 32 F4
Sagunto = Sagunt, *Spain* 32 F4
Sagwara, *India* 68 H6
Sahaba, *Sudan* 80 D3
Sahagún, *Spain* 34 C5
Saḩam al Jawlān, *Syria* 75 C4
Sahamandrevo, *Madag.* 89 C8
Sahand, Kūh-e, *Iran* 70 B5
Sahara, *Africa* 78 D6
Saharan Atlas = Saharien, Atlas, *Algeria* 78 B6
Saharanpur, *India* 68 E7
Saharien, Atlas, *Algeria* 78 B6
Saharsa, *India* 69 G12
Sahasinaka, *Madag.* 89 C8
Sahaswan, *India* 69 E8
Sahel, *Africa* 78 E5
Sahel, Canal du, *Mali* 82 C3
Sahibganj, *India* 69 G12
Sāḩilīyah, *Iraq* 70 C4
Sahiwal, *Pakistan* 68 D5
Şahneh, *Iran* 70 C5
Sahuaripa, *Mexico* 118 B3
Sahuarita, *U.S.A.* 115 L8
Sahuayo, *Mexico* 118 C4
Šahy, *Slovak Rep.* 27 C11
Sai →, *India* 69 G10
Sai Buri, *Thailand* 65 J3
Sa'id Bundas, *Sudan* 79 G10
Sa'īdābād, *Kermān, Iran* 71 D7
Sa'īdābād, *Semnān, Iran* 71 B7
Sa'īdīyeh, *Iran* 71 B6
Saidpur, *Bangla.* 67 G16
Saidpur, *India* 69 G10
Saidu, *Pakistan* 69 B5
Saignes, *France* 20 C6
Saigon = Thanh Pho Ho Chi Minh, *Vietnam* 65 G6
Saijō, *Japan* 55 H6
Saikanosy Masoala, *Madag.* 89 B9
Saikhoa Ghat, *India* 67 F19
Saiki, *Japan* 55 H5
Sailana, *India* 68 H6
Saillans, *France* 21 D9
Sailolof, *Indonesia* 63 E8
Saimaa, *Finland* 9 F23
Saimbeyli, *Turkey* 72 D7
Şa'in Dezh, *Iran* 70 B5
St. Abb's Head, *U.K.* 14 F6
St-Affrique, *France* 20 E6
St-Agrève, *France* 21 C8
St-Aignan, *France* 18 E8
St. Alban's, *Canada* 103 C8
St. Albans, *U.K.* 13 F7
St. Albans, *Vt., U.S.A.* 111 B11
St. Albans, *W. Va., U.S.A.* 108 F5
St. Alban's Head, *U.K.* 13 G5
St. Albert, *Canada* 104 C6
St-Amand-en-Puisaye, *France* 19 E10
St-Amand-les-Eaux, *France* 19 B10
St-Amand-Montrond, *France* 19 F9
St-Amarin, *France* 19 E14
St-Amour, *France* 19 F12
St-André-de-Cubzac, *France* 20 D3
St-André-les-Alpes, *France* 21 E10
St. Andrew's, *Canada* 103 C8
St. Andrews, *U.K.* 14 E6
St-Anicet, *Canada* 111 A10
St. Ann B., *Canada* 103 C7
St. Ann's Bay, *Jamaica* 120 C4
St. Anthony, *Canada* 103 B8
St. Anthony, *U.S.A.* 114 E8
St. Antoine, *Canada* 103 C7
St-Antonin-Noble-Val, *France* 20 D5
St. Arnaud, *Australia* 95 F3
St-Astier, *France* 20 C4
St-Aubin-du-Cormier, *France* 18 D5
St-Augustin →, *Canada* 103 B8
St-Augustin-Saguenay, *Canada* 103 B8
St. Augustine, *U.S.A.* 109 L5
St-Aulaye, *France* 20 C4
St. Austell, *U.K.* 13 G3
St-Avold, *France* 19 C13
St. Barbe, *Canada* 103 B8
St-Barthélemy, *W. Indies* 121 C7
St-Béat, *France* 20 F4
St. Bees Hd., *U.K.* 12 C4
St-Benoît-du-Sault, *France* 20 B5
St-Bonnet, *France* 21 D10
St-Brévin-les-Pins, *France* 18 E4
St-Brice-en-Coglès, *France* 18 D5
St. Bride's, *Canada* 103 C9
St. Brides B., *U.K.* 13 F2
St-Brieuc, *France* 18 D4
St-Calais, *France* 18 E7
St-Cast-le-Guildo, *France* 18 D4
St. Catharines, *Canada* 102 D4
St. Catherines I., *U.S.A.* 109 K5
St. Catherine's Pt., *U.K.* 13 G6
St-Céré, *France* 20 D5
St-Cergue, *Switz.* 25 J2
St-Cernin, *France* 20 C6
St-Chamond, *France* 21 C8
St. Charles, *Ill., U.S.A.* 108 E1
St. Charles, *Mo., U.S.A.* 112 F9
St. Charles, *Va., U.S.A.* 108 F7
St-Chély-d'Apcher, *France* 20 D7
St-Chinian, *France* 20 E6
St. Christopher-Nevis = St. Kitts & Nevis ■, *W. Indies* 121 C7
St-Ciers-sur-Gironde, *France* 20 C3
St. Clair, *Mich., U.S.A.* 110 D2
St. Clair, *Pa., U.S.A.* 111 F8
St. Clair →, *U.S.A.* 110 D2
St. Clair, L., *Canada* 102 D3
St. Clair, L., *U.S.A.* 110 D2
St. Clairsville, *U.S.A.* 110 F4
St-Claud, *France* 20 C4
St. Claude, *Canada* 105 D9
St-Claude, *France* 19 F12
St-Clet, *Canada* 111 A10
St. Cloud, *Fla., U.S.A.* 109 L5
St. Cloud, *Minn., U.S.A.* 112 C7
St. Cricq, C., *Australia* 93 E1
St. Croix, *U.S. Virgin Is.* 121 C7
St. Croix →, *U.S.A.* 112 C8
St. Croix Falls, *U.S.A.* 112 C8
St-Cyprien, *France* 20 F7
St-Cyr-sur-Mer, *France* 21 E9
St. David's, *Canada* 103 C8
St. David's, *U.K.* 13 F2
St. David's Head, *U.K.* 13 F2
St-Denis, *France* 19 D9
St-Dié, *France* 19 D13
St-Dizier, *France* 19 D11
St-Égrève, *France* 21 C9
St. Elias, Mt., *U.S.A.* 100 B5
St. Elias Mts., *Canada* 104 A1
St. Elias Mts., *U.S.A.* 100 C6
St-Eloy-les-Mines, *France* 19 F9
St-Émilion, *France* 20 D3
St-Étienne, *France* 21 C8
St-Étienne-de-Tinée, *France* 21 D10
St-Étienne-du-Rouvray, *France* 18 C8
St. Eugène, *Canada* 111 A10
St. Eustatius, *W. Indies* 121 C7
St-Fargeau, *France* 19 E10
St-Félicien, *Canada* 102 C5
St-Florent, *France* 21 F13
St-Florent, G. de, *France* 21 F13
St-Florent-sur-Cher, *France* 19 F9
St-Florentin, *France* 19 E10
St-Flour, *France* 20 C7
St. Francis, *U.S.A.* 112 F4
St. Francis →, *U.S.A.* 113 H9
St. Francis, C., *S. Africa* 88 E3
St. Francisville, *U.S.A.* 113 K9
St-François, L., *Canada* 111 A10
St-Fulgent, *France* 18 F5
St-Gabriel, *Canada* 102 C5
St. Gallen = Sankt Gallen, *Switz.* 25 H5
St-Galmier, *France* 19 G11
St-Gaudens, *France* 20 E4
St-Gaultier, *France* 18 F8
St-Gengoux-le-National, *France* 19 F11
St-Geniez-d'Olt, *France* 20 D6
St. George, *Australia* 95 D4
St. George, *Canada* 103 C6
St. George, *S.C., U.S.A.* 109 J5
St. George, *Utah, U.S.A.* 115 H7
St. George, C., *Canada* 103 C8
St. George, C., *U.S.A.* 109 L3
St. George Ra., *Australia* 92 C4
St. George's, *Canada* 103 C8
St-Georges, *Canada* 103 C5
St. George's, *Grenada* 121 D7
St. George's B., *Canada* 103 C8
St. Georges Basin, *N.S.W., Australia* 95 F5
St. Georges Basin, *W. Austral., Australia* 92 C4
St. George's Channel, *Europe* 15 E6
St. Georges Hd., *Australia* 95 F5
St-Georges-lès-Baillargeaux, *France* 20 B4
St-Germain-de-Calberte, *France* 20 D7
St-Germain-en-Laye, *France* 19 D9
St-Germain-Lembron, *France* 20 C7
St-Gervais-d'Auvergne, *France* 19 F9
St-Gervais-les-Bains, *France* 21 C10
St-Gildas, Pte. de, *France* 18 E4
St-Gilles, *France* 21 E8
St-Girons, *Ariège, France* 20 F5
St-Girons, *Landes, France* 20 E2
St. Gotthard P. = San Gottardo, P. del, *Switz.* 25 J4
St. Helena, *U.S.A.* 114 G2
St. Helena ■, *Atl. Oc.* 76 H3
St. Helena, Mt., *U.S.A.* 116 G4
St. Helena B., *S. Africa* 88 E2
St. Helens, *Australia* 94 G4
St. Helens, *U.K.* 12 D5
St. Helens, *U.S.A.* 116 E4
St. Helens, Mt., *U.S.A.* 116 D4
St. Helier, *U.K.* 13 H5
St-Herblain, *France* 18 E5
St-Hilaire-du-Harcouët, *France* 18 D5
St-Hippolyte, *France* 19 E13
St-Hippolyte-du-Fort, *France* 20 E7
St-Honoré-les-Bains, *France* 19 F10
St-Hubert, *Belgium* 17 D5
St-Hyacinthe, *Canada* 102 C5
St. Ignace, *U.S.A.* 108 C3
St. Ignace I., *Canada* 102 C2
St. Ignatius, *U.S.A.* 114 C6
St-Imier, *Switz.* 25 H2
St. Ives, *U.K.* 13 G2
St-James, *France* 18 D5
St. James, *U.S.A.* 112 D7
St-Jean →, *Canada* 103 B7
St-Jean, L., *Canada* 103 C5
St-Jean-d'Angély, *France* 20 C3
St-Jean-de-Braye, *France* 19 E8
St-Jean-de-Luz, *France* 20 E2
St-Jean-de-Maurienne, *France* 21 C10
St-Jean-de-Monts, *France* 18 F4
St-Jean-du-Gard, *France* 20 D7
St-Jean-en-Royans, *France* 21 C9
St-Jean-Pied-de-Port, *France* 20 E2
St-Jean-Port-Joli, *Canada* 103 C5
St-Jean-sur-Richelieu, *Canada* 102 C5
St-Jérôme, *Canada* 102 C5
St. John, *Canada* 103 C6
St. John, *U.S.A.* 113 G5
St. John →, *Liberia* 82 D2
St. John →, *U.S.A.* 109 C12
St. John, C., *Canada* 103 C8
St. John's, *Antigua* 121 C7
St. John's, *Canada* 103 C9
St. Johns, *Ariz., U.S.A.* 115 J9
St. Johns, *Mich., U.S.A.* 108 D3
St. Johns →, *U.S.A.* 109 K5
St. John's Pt., *Ireland* 15 B3
St. Johnsbury, *U.S.A.* 111 B12
St. Johnsville, *U.S.A.* 111 D10
St. Joseph, *La., U.S.A.* 113 K9
St. Joseph, *Mo., U.S.A.* 112 F7
St. Joseph →, *U.S.A.* 108 D2
St. Joseph, I., *Canada* 102 C3
St. Joseph, L., *Canada* 102 B1
St-Jovite, *Canada* 102 C5
St-Juéry, *France* 20 E6
St-Julien-Chapteuil, *France* 21 C8
St-Julien-de-Vouvantes, *France* 18 E5
St-Julien-en-Genevois, *France* 19 F13
St-Junien, *France* 20 C4
St-Just-en-Chaussée, *France* 19 C9
St-Just-en-Chevalet, *France* 20 C7
St. Kitts & Nevis ■, *W. Indies* 121 C7
St. Laurent, *Canada* 105 C9
St-Laurent-de-la-Salanque, *France* 20 F6
St-Laurent-du-Pont, *France* 21 C9
St-Laurent-en-Grandvaux, *France* 19 F12
St-Laurent-Médoc, *France* 20 C3
St. Lawrence, *Australia* 94 C4
St. Lawrence, *Canada* 103 C8
St. Lawrence →, *Canada* 103 C6
St. Lawrence, Gulf of, *Canada* 103 C7
St. Lawrence I., *U.S.A.* 100 B3
St. Leonard, *Canada* 103 C6
St-Léonard-de-Noblat, *France* 20 C5
St. Lewis →, *Canada* 103 B8
St-Lô, *France* 18 C5
St-Louis, *France* 19 E14
St. Louis, *Senegal* 82 B1
St. Louis, *U.S.A.* 112 F9
St. Louis →, *U.S.A.* 112 B8
St-Loup-sur-Semouse, *France* 19 E13
St. Lucia ■, *W. Indies* 121 D7
St. Lucia, L., *S. Africa* 89 D5
St. Lucia Channel, *W. Indies* 121 D7
St. Maarten, *W. Indies* 121 C7
St. Magnus B., *U.K.* 14 A7
St-Maixent-l'École, *France* 20 B3
St-Malo, *France* 18 D4
St-Malo, G. de, *France* 18 D4
St-Mandrier-sur-Mer, *France* 21 E9
St-Marc, *Haiti* 121 C5
St-Marcellin, *France* 21 C9
St-Marcouf, Îs., *France* 18 C5
St. Maries, *U.S.A.* 114 C5
St-Martin, *W. Indies* 121 C7
St. Martin, L., *Canada* 105 C9
St-Martin-de-Crau, *France* 21 E8
St-Martin-de-Ré, *France* 20 B2
St-Martin-d'Hères, *France* 21 C9
St-Martin-Vésubie, *France* 21 D11
St-Martory, *France* 20 E4
St. Mary Pk., *Australia* 95 E2
St. Marys, *Australia* 94 G4
St. Marys, *Canada* 110 C3
St. Mary's, *Corn., U.K.* 13 H1
St. Mary's, *Orkney, U.K.* 14 C6
St. Marys, *Ga., U.S.A.* 109 K5
St. Marys, *Pa., U.S.A.* 110 E6
St. Mary's, C., *Canada* 103 C9
St. Mary's B., *Canada* 103 C9
St. Marys Bay, *Canada* 103 D6
St-Mathieu, Pte., *France* 18 D2
St. Matthew I., *U.S.A.* 100 B2
St. Matthews, I. = Zadetkyi Kyun, *Burma* 65 G1
St-Maurice →, *Canada* 102 C5
St-Maximin-la-Ste-Baume, *France* 21 E9
St-Médard-en-Jalles, *France* 20 D3
St-Méen-le-Grand, *France* 18 D4
St-Mihiel, *France* 19 D12
St. Moritz, *Switz.* 25 J5
St-Nazaire, *France* 18 E4
St. Neots, *U.K.* 13 E7
St-Nicolas-de-Port, *France* 19 D13
St-Niklaas, *Belgium* 17 C4
St-Omer, *France* 19 B9
St-Palais-sur-Mer, *France* 20 C2
St-Pamphile, *Canada* 103 C6
St-Pardoux-la-Rivière, *France* 20 C4
St. Pascal, *Canada* 103 C6
St. Paul, *Canada* 104 C6
St-Paul, *France* 21 D10
St. Paul, *Minn., U.S.A.* 112 C8
St. Paul, *Nebr., U.S.A.* 112 E5
St-Paul →, *Canada* 103 B8
St. Paul →, *Liberia* 82 D2
St. Paul, Î., *Ind. Oc.* 3 F13
St-Paul-de-Fenouillet, *France* 20 F6
St. Paul I., *Canada* 103 C7
St-Paul-lès-Dax, *France* 20 E2
St-Péray, *France* 21 D8
St. Peter, *U.S.A.* 112 C8
St-Peter-Ording, *Germany* 24 A4
St. Peter Port, *U.K.* 13 H5
St. Peters, *N.S., Canada* 103 C7
St. Peters, *P.E.I., Canada* 103 C7
St. Petersburg = Sankt-Peterburg, *Russia* 46 C6
St. Petersburg, *U.S.A.* 109 M4
St-Philbert-de-Grand-Lieu, *France* 18 E5
St-Pie, *Canada* 111 A12
St-Pierre, *St- P. & M.* 103 C8
St-Pierre, L., *Canada* 102 C5
St-Pierre-d'Oléron, *France* 20 C2
St-Pierre-en-Port, *France* 18 C7
St-Pierre et Miquelon □, *St- P. & M.* 103 C8
St-Pierre-le-Moûtier, *France* 19 F10
St-Pierre-sur-Dives, *France* 18 C6
St-Pol-de-Léon, *France* 18 D3
St-Pol-sur-Mer, *France* 19 A9
St-Pol-sur-Ternoise, *France* 19 B9
St-Pons, *France* 20 E6
St-Pourçain-sur-Sioule, *France* 19 F10
St-Priest, *France* 21 C8
St-Quay-Portrieux, *France* 18 D4
St. Quentin, *Canada* 103 C6
St-Quentin, *France* 19 C10
St-Rambert-d'Albon, *France* 21 C8
St-Raphaël, *France* 21 E10
St. Regis, *U.S.A.* 114 C6
St-Renan, *France* 18 D2
St-Saëns, *France* 18 C8
St-Savin, *France* 20 B4
St-Savinien, *France* 20 C3
St. Sebastien, Tanjon' i, *Madag.* 89 A8
St-Seine-l'Abbaye, *France* 19 E11
St-Sernin-sur-Rance, *France* 20 E6
St-Sever, *France* 20 E3
St-Siméon, *Canada* 103 C6
St. Simons I., *U.S.A.* 109 K5
St. Simons Island, *U.S.A.* 109 K5
St. Stephen, *Canada* 103 C6
St-Sulpice, *France* 20 E5
St-Sulpice-Laurière, *France* 20 B5
St-Sulpice-les-Feuilles, *France* 20 B5
St-Syprien = St-Cyprien, *France* 20 F7
St-Thégonnec, *France* 18 D3
St. Thomas, *Canada* 102 D3
St. Thomas I., *U.S. Virgin Is.* 121 C7
St-Tite, *Canada* 102 C5
St-Tropez, *France* 21 E10
St. Troud = St. Truiden, *Belgium* 17 D5
St. Truiden, *Belgium* 17 D5
St-Vaast-la-Hougue, *France* 18 C5
St-Valery-en-Caux, *France* 18 C7
St-Valéry-sur-Somme, *France* 19 B8
St-Vallier, *France* 19 F11
St-Vallier-de-Thiey, *France* 21 E10
St-Varent, *France* 18 F6
St-Vaury, *France* 20 B5
St. Vincent, *Italy* 28 C4
St. Vincent, G., *Australia* 95 F2
St. Vincent & the Grenadines ■, *W. Indies* 121 D7
St-Vincent-de-Tyrosse, *France* 20 E2
St. Vincent Passage, *W. Indies* 121 D7
St-Vith, *Belgium* 17 D6
St-Vivien-de-Médoc, *France* 20 C2
St. Walburg, *Canada* 105 C7
St-Yrieix-la-Perche, *France* 20 C5
Ste-Adresse, *France* 18 C7
Ste-Agathe-des-Monts, *Canada* 102 C5
Ste-Anne, L., *Canada* 103 B6
Ste-Anne-des-Monts, *Canada* 103 C6
Ste-Croix, *Switz.* 25 J2
Ste-Enimie, *France* 20 D7
Ste-Foy-la-Grande, *France* 20 D4
Ste. Genevieve, *U.S.A.* 112 G9
Ste-Hermine, *France* 20 B2
Ste-Livrade-sur-Lot, *France* 20 D4
Ste-Marguerite →, *Canada* 103 B6
Ste-Marie, *Martinique* 121 D7
Ste-Marie-aux-Mines, *France* 19 D14
Ste-Marie de la Madeleine, *Canada* 103 C5
Ste-Maure-de-Touraine, *France* 18 E7
Ste-Maxime, *France* 21 E10
Ste-Menehould, *France* 19 C11
Ste-Mère-Église, *France* 18 C5
Ste-Rose, *Guadeloupe* 121 C7
Ste. Rose du Lac, *Canada* 105 C9
Ste-Savine, *France* 19 D11
Ste-Sigolène, *France* 21 C8
Saintes, *France* 20 C3
Saintes, I. des, *Guadeloupe* 121 C7
Stes-Maries-de-la-Mer, *France* 21 E8
Saintfield, *U.K.* 15 B6
Saintonge, *France* 20 C3
Saipan, *Pac. Oc.* 96 F6
Sairang, *India* 67 H18
Sairecábur, Cerro, *Bolivia* 126 A2
Saitama □, *Japan* 55 F9
Saiteli = Kadınhanı, *Turkey* 72 C5
Saiţi, *Moldova* 43 D14
Saiyid, *Pakistan* 68 C5
Sajama, *Bolivia* 124 G5
Sajan, *Serbia, Yug.* 42 E5
Sajó →, *Hungary* 42 C6
Sajószentpéter, *Hungary* 42 B5
Sajum, *India* 69 C8
Sak →, *S. Africa* 88 E3
Sakaba, *Nigeria* 83 C6
Sakai, *Japan* 55 G7
Sakaide, *Japan* 55 G6
Sakaiminato, *Japan* 55 G6
Sakākah, *Si. Arabia* 70 D4
Sakakawea, L., *U.S.A.* 112 B4
Sakami →, *Canada* 102 B4
Sakami, L., *Canada* 102 B4
Sâkâne, 'Erg i-n, *Mali* 83 A4
Sakania, *Dem. Rep. of the Congo* 87 E2
Sakaraha, *Madag.* 89 C7
Sakarya, *Turkey* 72 B4
Sakarya →, *Turkey* 72 B4
Sakashima-Guntō, *Japan* 55 M2
Sakassou, *Ivory C.* 82 D3
Sakata, *Japan* 54 E9
Sakchu, *N. Korea* 57 D13
Sakeny →, *Madag.* 89 C8
Sakété, *Benin* 83 D5
Sakha □, *Russia* 51 C13
Sakhalin, *Russia* 51 D15
Sakhalinskiy Zaliv, *Russia* 51 D15
Şaki, *Azerbaijan* 49 K8
Šakiai, *Lithuania* 9 J20
Sakon Nakhon, *Thailand* 64 D5
Sakrand, *Pakistan* 68 F3
Sakri, *India* 69 F12
Sakrivier, *S. Africa* 88 E3
Sakskøbing, *Denmark* 11 K5
Sakti, *India* 69 H10
Sakuma, *Japan* 55 G8
Sakurai, *Japan* 55 G7
Saky, *Ukraine* 47 K7
Sal →, *Russia* 49 G5
Sala, *Eritrea* 81 D4
Šal'a, *Slovak Rep.* 27 C10
Sala, *Sweden* 10 E10
Sala →, *Eritrea* 81 D4
Sala Consilina, *Italy* 31 B8
Sala-y-Gómez, *Pac. Oc.* 97 K17
Salaberry-de-Valleyfield, *Canada* 102 C5
Saladas, *Argentina* 126 B4
Saladillo, *Argentina* 126 D4
Salado →, *Buenos Aires, Argentina* 126 D4
Salado →, *La Pampa, Argentina* 128 D3
Salado →, *Santa Fe, Argentina* 126 C3
Salado →, *Mexico* 113 M5
Salaga, *Ghana* 83 D4
Sālah, *Syria* 75 C5
Sălaj □, *Romania* 42 C8
Sálakhos, *Greece* 36 C9
Salala, *Liberia* 82 D2
Salala, *Sudan* 80 C4
Salālah, *Oman* 74 D5
Salamanca, *Chile* 126 C1
Salamanca, *Spain* 34 E5
Salamanca, *U.S.A.* 110 D6
Salamanca □, *Spain* 34 E5
Salamatābād, *Iran* 70 C5
Salamis, *Cyprus* 36 D12
Salamís, *Greece* 38 D5
Salar de Atacama, *Chile* 126 A2
Salar de Uyuni, *Bolivia* 124 H5

Sălard, Romania 42 C7
Salas, Spain 34 B4
Salas de los Infantes, Spain ... 34 C7
Salatiga, Indonesia 63 G14
Salaverry, Peru 124 E3
Salawati, Indonesia 63 E8
Salayar, Indonesia 63 F6
Salazar ➤, Spain 32 C3
Salbris, France 19 E9
Salcia, Romania 43 G9
Sălciua, Romania 43 D8
Salcombe, U.K. 13 G4
Saldaña, Spain 34 C6
Saldanha, S. Africa 88 E2
Saldanha B., S. Africa 88 E2
Saldus, Latvia 9 H20
Saldus □, Latvia 44 B9
Sale, Australia 95 F4
Sale, Italy 28 D5
Salé, Morocco 78 B4
Sale, U.K. 12 D5
Salekhard, Russia 50 C7
Salem, India 66 P11
Salem, Ill., U.S.A. 108 F1
Salem, Ind., U.S.A. 108 F2
Salem, Mass., U.S.A. 111 D14
Salem, Mo., U.S.A. 113 G9
Salem, N.H., U.S.A. 111 D13
Salem, N.J., U.S.A. 108 F8
Salem, N.Y., U.S.A. 111 C11
Salem, Ohio, U.S.A. 110 F4
Salem, Oreg., U.S.A. 114 D2
Salem, S. Dak., U.S.A. 112 D6
Salem, Va., U.S.A. 108 G5
Salemi, Italy 30 E5
Sälen, Sweden 10 C7
Salernes, France 21 E10
Salerno, Italy 31 B7
Salerno, G. di, Italy 31 B7
Salford, U.K. 12 D5
Salgir ➤, Ukraine 47 K8
Salgótarján, Hungary 42 B4
Salgueiro, Brazil 125 E11
Salibabu, Indonesia 63 D7
Salida, U.S.A. 106 C5
Salies-de-Béarn, France 20 E3
Salihli, Turkey 72 C3
Salihorsk, Belarus 47 F4
Salima, Malawi 85 G6
Salina, Italy 31 D7
Salina, Kans., U.S.A. 112 F6
Salina, Utah, U.S.A. 115 G8
Salina Cruz, Mexico 119 D5
Salinas, Brazil 125 G10
Salinas, Chile 126 A2
Salinas, Ecuador 124 D2
Salinas, U.S.A. 116 J5
Salinas ➤, Guatemala 119 D6
Salinas ➤, U.S.A. 116 J5
Salinas, B. de, Nic. 120 D2
Salinas, Pampa de las, Argentina 126 C2
Salinas Ambargasta, Argentina 126 B3
Salinas de Hidalgo, Mexico ... 118 C4
Salinas Grandes, Argentina ... 126 C3
Saline ➤, Ark., U.S.A. 113 J8
Saline ➤, Kans., U.S.A. 112 F6
Salines, Spain 37 B10
Salines, C. de ses, Spain 37 B10
Salinópolis, Brazil 125 D9
Salins-les-Bains, France 19 F12
Salir, Portugal 35 H2
Salisbury = Harare, Zimbabwe . 87 F3
Salisbury, U.K. 13 F6
Salisbury, Md., U.S.A. 108 F8
Salisbury, N.C., U.S.A. 109 H5
Salisbury I., Canada 101 B12
Salisbury Plain, U.K. 13 F6
Salka, Nigeria 83 C5
Sâlişte, Romania 43 E8
Salla, Finland 8 C23
Sallanches, France 21 C10
Sallent, Spain 32 D6
Salles, France 20 D3
Salles-Curan, France 20 D6
Salling, Denmark 11 H2
Salliq, Canada 101 B11
Sallisaw, U.S.A. 113 H7
Sallom Junction, Sudan 80 D4
Salluit, Canada 101 B12
Salmās, Iran 70 B5
Salmerón, Spain 32 E2
Salmo, Canada 104 D5
Salmon, U.S.A. 114 D7
Salmon ➤, Canada 104 C4
Salmon ➤, U.S.A. 114 D5
Salmon Arm, Canada 104 C5
Salmon Gums, Australia 93 F3
Salmon River Mts., U.S.A. ... 114 D6
Salo, Finland 9 F20
Salò, Italy 28 C7
Salobreña, Spain 35 J7
Salome, U.S.A. 117 M13
Salon, India 69 F9
Salon-de-Provence, France ... 21 E9
Salonica = Thessaloníki, Greece 40 F6
Salonta, Romania 42 D6
Salor ➤, Spain 35 F3
Salou, Spain 32 D6
Salou, C. de, Spain 32 D6
Saloum ➤, Senegal 82 C1
Salpausselkä, Finland 9 F22
Salsacate, Argentina 126 C2
Salses, France 20 F6
Salsk, Russia 49 G5
Salso ➤, Italy 30 E6

Salsomaggiore Terme, Italy ... 28 D6
Salt, Spain 32 D7
Salt ➤, Canada 104 B6
Salt ➤, U.S.A. 115 K7
Salt Lake City, U.S.A. 114 F8
Salt Range, Pakistan 68 C5
Salta, Argentina 126 A2
Salta □, Argentina 126 A2
Saltara, Italy 29 E9
Saltash, U.K. 13 G3
Saltburn by the Sea, U.K. 12 C7
Saltcoats, U.K. 14 F4
Saltee Is., Ireland 15 D5
Saltfjellet, Norway 8 C16
Saltfjorden, Norway 8 C16
Saltholm, Denmark 11 J6
Saltillo, Mexico 118 B4
Salto, Argentina 126 C3
Salto, Uruguay 126 C4
Salto del Guaíra, Paraguay ... 127 A5
Salton City, U.S.A. 117 M11
Salton Sea, U.S.A. 117 M11
Saltpond, Ghana 83 D4
Saltsburg, U.S.A. 110 F5
Saltsjöbaden, Sweden 10 E12
Saluda ➤, U.S.A. 109 J5
Salûm, Egypt 80 A2
Salûm, Khâlig el, Egypt 80 A2
Salur, India 67 K13
Saluzzo, Italy 28 D4
Salvador, Brazil 125 F11
Salvador, Canada 105 C7
Salvador, L., U.S.A. 113 L9
Salvaterra de Magos, Portugal . 35 F2
Sálvora, I. de, Spain 34 C2
Salween ➤, Burma 67 L20
Salyan, Azerbaijan 50 F5
Salza ➤, Austria 26 D7
Salzach ➤, Austria 26 C5
Salzburg, Austria 26 D6
Salzburg □, Austria 26 D6
Salzgitter, Germany 24 C6
Salzkotten, Germany 24 D4
Salzwedel, Germany 24 C7
Sam, India 68 F4
Sam Neua, Laos 58 G5
Sam Ngao, Thailand 64 D2
Sam Rayburn Reservoir, U.S.A. 113 K7
Sam Son, Vietnam 64 C5
Sam Teu, Laos 64 C5
Sama de Langreo = Langreo,
  Spain 34 B5
Samagaltay, Russia 51 D10
Samales Group, Phil. 61 J4
Samâlût, Egypt 80 B3
Samana, India 68 D7
Samana Cay, Bahamas 121 B5
Samandağı, Turkey 72 D6
Samandra, Turkey 41 F13
Samanga, Tanzania 87 D4
Samangân □, Afghan. 66 B5
Samangwa, Dem. Rep. of
  the Congo 86 C1
Samani, Japan 54 C11
Samanli Dağları, Turkey 41 F13
Samar, Phil. 61 F6
Samara, Russia 48 D10
Samara ➤, Russia 48 D10
Samara ➤, Ukraine 47 H8
Samaria = Shōmrōn, West Bank 75 C4
Samariá, Greece 36 D5
Samarinda, Indonesia 62 E5
Samarkand = Samarqand,
  Uzbekistan 50 F7
Samarqand, Uzbekistan 50 F7
Sāmarrā, Iraq 70 C4
Samastipur, India 69 G11
Şamaxı, Azerbaijan 49 K9
Samba, Dem. Rep. of the Congo 86 C2
Samba, India 69 C6
Sambalpur, India 67 J14
Sambar, Tanjung, Indonesia .. 62 E4
Sambas, Indonesia 62 D3
Sambava, Madag. 89 A9
Sambawizi, Zimbabwe 87 F2
Sambhal, India 69 E8
Sambhar, India 68 F6
Sambhar L., India 68 F6
Sambiase, Italy 31 D9
Sambir, Ukraine 47 H2
Sambor, Cambodia 64 F6
Samborombón, B., Argentina .. 126 D4
Samch'ŏk, S. Korea 57 F15
Samch'onp'o, S. Korea 57 G15
Same, Tanzania 86 C4
Samer, France 19 B8
Samfya, Zambia 87 E2
Sámi, Greece 38 C2
Şamkir, Azerbaijan 49 K8
Şamlı, Turkey 39 B9
Samnah, Si. Arabia 70 E3
Samo Alto, Chile 126 C1
Samoa ■, Pac. Oc. 91 B13
Samobor, Croatia 29 C12
Samoëns, France 19 F13
Samokov, Bulgaria 40 D7
Šamorín, Slovak Rep. 27 C10
Samorogouan, Burkina Faso .. 82 C4
Sámos, Greece 39 D8
Samoš, Serbia, Yug. 42 E5
Samos, Spain 34 C3
Sámos □, Greece 39 D8
Samothráki = Mathráki, Greece 36 A3
Samothráki, Évros, Greece 41 F9
Samothráki, Évros, Greece 41 F9
Samoylovka, Russia 48 E6

Sampa, Ghana 82 D4
Sampacho, Argentina 126 C3
Sampang, Indonesia 63 G15
Samper de Calanda, Spain ... 32 D4
Sampéyre, Italy 28 D4
Sampit, Indonesia 62 E4
Sampit, Teluk, Indonesia 62 E4
Samrong, Cambodia 64 E4
Samrong, Thailand 64 E3
Samsø, Denmark 11 J4
Samsø Bælt, Denmark 11 J4
Samsun, Turkey 72 B7
Samtredia, Georgia 49 J6
Samu, Ko, Thailand 65 H3
Samur ➤, Russia 49 K9
Samurskiy Khrebet, Russia ... 49 K8
Samusole, Dem. Rep. of
  the Congo 87 E1
Samut Prakan, Thailand 64 F3
Samut Songkhram ➤, Thailand 62 B1
Samwari, Pakistan 68 E2
San, Mali 82 C4
San ➤, Cambodia 64 F5
San ➤, Poland 45 H8
San Adrián, Spain 32 C3
San Adrián, C. de, Spain 34 B2
San Agustin, C., Phil. 61 H7
San Agustín de Valle Fértil,
  Argentina 126 C2
San Ambrosio, Pac. Oc. 122 F3
San Andreas, U.S.A. 116 G6
San Andres, Phil. 61 E6
San Andrés, I. de, Caribbean .. 120 D3
San Andres Mts., U.S.A. 115 K10
San Andrés del Rabanedo, Spain 34 C5
San Andres Tuxtla, Mexico ... 119 D5
San Angelo, U.S.A. 113 K4
San Anselmo, U.S.A. 116 H4
San Antonio, Belize 119 D7
San Antonio, Chile 126 C1
San Antonio, Phil. 61 D4
San Antonio, N. Mex., U.S.A. . 115 K10
San Antonio, Tex., U.S.A. 113 L5
San Antonio ➤, U.S.A. 113 L6
San Antonio, C., Argentina ... 126 D4
San Antonio, C., Cuba 120 B3
San Antonio, C. de, Spain 33 G5
San Antonio, Mt., U.S.A. 117 L9
San Antonio de los Baños, Cuba 120 B3
San Antonio de los Cobres,
  Argentina 126 A2
San Antonio Oeste, Argentina . 128 E4
San Arcángelo, Italy 31 B9
San Ardo, U.S.A. 116 J6
San Augustín, Canary Is. 37 G4
San Augustine, U.S.A. 113 K7
San Bartolomé, Canary Is. ... 37 F6
San Bartolomé de Tirajana,
  Canary Is. 37 G4
San Bartolomeo in Galdo, Italy 31 A8
San Benedetto del Tronto, Italy 29 F10
San Benedetto Po, Italy 28 C7
San Benedicto, I., Mexico 118 D2
San Benito, U.S.A. 113 M6
San Benito ➤, U.S.A. 116 J5
San Benito Mt., U.S.A. 116 J6
San Bernardino, U.S.A. 117 L9
San Bernardino Mts., U.S.A. .. 117 L10
San Bernardino Str., Phil. 61 E6
San Bernardo, Chile 126 C1
San Bernardo, I. de, Colombia . 124 B3
San Blas, Mexico 118 B3
San Blas, Arch. de, Panama ... 120 E4
San Blas, C., U.S.A. 109 L3
San Bonifacio, Italy 29 C8
San Borja, Bolivia 124 F5
San Buenaventura, Mexico ... 118 B4
San Carlos = Butuku-Luba,
  Eq. Guin. 83 E6
San Carlos = Sant Carles, Spain 37 B8
San Carlos, Argentina 126 C2
San Carlos, Chile 126 D1
San Carlos, Baja Calif. S.,
  Mexico 118 C2
San Carlos, Coahuila, Mexico . 118 B4
San Carlos, Nic. 120 D3
San Carlos, Neg. Occ., Phil. .. 61 F5
San Carlos, Pangasinan, Phil. . 61 D4
San Carlos, Uruguay 127 C5
San Carlos, U.S.A. 115 K8
San Carlos, Venezuela 124 B5
San Carlos de Bariloche,
  Argentina 128 E2
San Carlos de Bolívar, Argentina 128 D4
San Carlos de la Rápita = Sant
  Carles de la Ràpita, Spain .. 32 E5
San Carlos del Zulia, Venezuela 124 B4
San Carlos L., U.S.A. 115 K8
San Cataldo, Italy 30 E6
San Celoni = Sant Celoni, Spain 32 D7
San Clemente, Chile 126 D1
San Clemente, Spain 33 F2
San Clemente, U.S.A. 117 M9
San Clemente I., U.S.A. 117 N8
San Cristóbal = Es Migjorn
  Gran, Spain 37 B11
San Cristóbal, Argentina 126 C3
San Cristóbal, Dom. Rep. 121 C5
San Cristóbal, Venezuela 124 B4
San Cristóbal de la Casas,
  Mexico 119 D6
San Damiano d'Asti, Italy 28 D5
San Diego, Calif., U.S.A. 117 N9
San Diego, Tex., U.S.A. 113 M5
San Diego, C., Argentina 128 G3
San Diego de la Unión, Mexico 118 C4

Sampa, Ghana 82 D4
San Dimitri, Ras, Malta 36 C1
San Donà di Piave, Italy 29 C9
San Estanislao, Paraguay 126 A4
San Esteban de Gormaz, Spain 32 D1
San Felice Circeo, Italy 30 A6
San Felice sul Panaro, Italy ... 29 D8
San Felipe, Chile 126 C1
San Felipe, Mexico 118 A2
San Felipe, Venezuela 124 A5
San Felipe ➤, U.S.A. 117 M11
San Felix, Chile 126 B1
San Félix, Pac. Oc. 122 F2
San Fernando = Sant Ferran,
  Spain 37 C7
San Fernando, Chile 126 C1
San Fernando, Baja Calif.,
  Mexico 118 B1
San Fernando, Tamaulipas,
  Mexico 119 C5
San Fernando, La Union, Phil. . 61 C4
San Fernando, Pampanga, Phil. 61 D4
San Fernando, Spain 35 J4
San Fernando, Trin. & Tob. ... 121 D7
San Fernando, U.S.A. 117 L8
San Fernando de Apure,
  Venezuela 124 B5
San Fernando de Atabapo,
  Venezuela 124 C5
San Fernando di Púglia, Italy . 31 A9
San Francisco, Argentina 126 C3
San Francisco ➤, U.S.A. 115 K9
San Francisco, Paso de, S. Amer. 126 B2
San Francisco de Macorís,
  Dom. Rep. 121 C5
San Francisco del Monte de Oro,
  Argentina 126 C2
San Francisco del Oro, Mexico . 118 B3
San Francisco Javier = Sant
  Francesc de Formentera,
  Spain 37 C7
San Francisco Solano, Pta.,
  Colombia 122 C3
San Fratello, Italy 31 D7
San Gabriel, Chile 126 C1
San Gabriel Mts., U.S.A. 117 L9
San Gavino Monreale, Italy .. 30 C1
San Gimignano, Italy 28 E8
San Giórgio di Nogaro, Italy .. 29 C10
San Giórgio Iónico, Italy 31 B10
San Giovanni Bianco, Italy ... 28 C6
San Giovanni in Fiore, Italy .. 31 C9
San Giovanni in Persiceto, Italy 29 D8
San Giovanni Rotondo, Italy .. 29 G12
San Giovanni Valdarno, Italy . 29 E8
San Giuliano Terme, Italy 28 E7
San Gorgonio Mt., U.S.A. 117 L10
San Gottardo, P. del, Switz. .. 25 J4
San Gregorio, Uruguay 127 C4
San Gregorio, U.S.A. 116 H4
San Guiseppe Jato, Italy 30 E6
San Ignacio, Belize 119 D7
San Ignacio, Bolivia 124 G6
San Ignacio, Mexico 118 B2
San Ignacio, Paraguay 120 C2
San Ignacio, L., Mexico 118 B2
San Ildefonso, C., Phil. 61 C5
San Isidro, Argentina 126 C4
San Isidro, Phil. 61 E6
San Jacinto, U.S.A. 117 M10
San Jaime = Sant Jaume, Spain 37 B11
San Javier, Misiones, Argentina 127 B4
San Javier, Santa Fe, Argentina 126 C4
San Javier, Bolivia 124 G6
San Javier, Chile 126 D1
San Javier, Spain 33 H4
San Jeronimo Taviche, Mexico 119 D5
San Joaquin, U.S.A. 116 J6
San Joaquin ➤, U.S.A. 116 G5
San Joaquin Valley, U.S.A. ... 116 J6
San Jon, U.S.A. 113 H3
San Jordi = Sant Jordi, Spain . 37 B9
San Jorge, Argentina 126 C3
San Jorge, Spain 37 C7
San Jorge, B. de, Mexico 118 A2
San Jorge, G. de, Argentina .. 128 F3
San Jorge, G. of, Argentina .. 122 H4
San Jose = San Josep, Spain .. 37 C7
San José, Costa Rica 120 E3
San José, Guatemala 120 D1
San José, Mexico 118 C2
San Jose, Mind. Occ., Phil. ... 61 E4
San Jose, Nueva Ecija, Phil. .. 61 D4
San Jose, U.S.A. 116 H5
San Jose ➤, U.S.A. 115 J10
San Jose de Buenavista, Phil. . 63 B6
San José de Chiquitos, Bolivia . 124 G6
San José de Feliciano, Argentina 126 C4
San José de Jáchal, Argentina . 126 C2
San José de Mayo, Uruguay ... 126 C4
San José del Cabo, Mexico ... 118 C3
San José del Guaviare,
  Colombia 124 C4
San Josep, Spain 37 C7
San Juan, Argentina 126 C2
San Juan, Mexico 118 C4
San Juan, Phil. 61 F6
San Juan, Puerto Rico 121 C6
San Juan □, Argentina 126 C2
San Juan ➤, Argentina 126 C2
San Juan ➤, Nic. 120 D3
San Juan ➤, U.S.A. 115 H8
San Juan Bautista = Sant Joan
  Baptista, Spain 37 B8
San Juan Bautista, Paraguay .. 126 B4
San Juan Bautista, U.S.A. 116 J5

San Juan Bautista Valle
  Nacional, Mexico 119 D5
San Juan Capistrano, U.S.A. .. 117 M9
San Juan Cr. ➤, U.S.A. 116 J5
San Juan de Alicante, Spain .. 33 G4
San Juan de Guadalupe, Mexico 118 C4
San Juan de la Costa, Mexico . 118 C2
San Juan de los Morros,
  Venezuela 124 B5
San Juan del Norte, Nic. 120 D3
San Juan del Norte, B. de, Nic. 120 D3
San Juan del Río, Mexico 119 C5
San Juan del Sur, Nic. 120 D2
San Juan I., U.S.A. 116 B3
San Juan Mts., U.S.A. 115 H10
San Just, Sierra de, Spain 32 E4
San Justo, Argentina 126 C3
San Kamphaeng, Thailand ... 64 C2
San Lázaro, C., Mexico 118 C2
San Lázaro, Sa., Mexico 118 C3
San Leandro, U.S.A. 116 H4
San Leonardo de Yagüe, Spain 32 D1
San Lorenzo = Sant Llorenç des
  Cardassar, Spain 37 B10
San Lorenzo, Argentina 126 C3
San Lorenzo, Ecuador 124 C3
San Lorenzo, Paraguay 126 B4
San Lorenzo ➤, Mexico 118 C3
San Lorenzo, I., Mexico 118 B2
San Lorenzo, Mte., Argentina . 128 F2
San Lorenzo de la Parrilla, Spain 32 F2
San Lorenzo de Morunys = Sant
  Llorenç de Morunys, Spain . 32 C6
San Lucas, Bolivia 124 H5
San Lucas, Baja Calif. S., Mexico 118 C3
San Lucas, Baja Calif. S., Mexico 118 B2
San Lucas, U.S.A. 116 J5
San Lucas, C., Mexico 118 C3
San Lúcido, Italy 31 C9
San Luis, Argentina 126 C2
San Luis, Cuba 120 B3
San Luis, Guatemala 120 C2
San Luis, Ariz., U.S.A. 115 K6
San Luis, Colo., U.S.A. 115 H11
San Luis □, Argentina 126 C2
San Luis, I., Mexico 118 B2
San Luis, Sierra de, Argentina . 126 C2
San Luis de la Paz, Mexico ... 118 C4
San Luis Obispo, U.S.A. 117 K6
San Luis Potosí, Mexico 118 C4
San Luis Potosí □, Mexico ... 118 C4
San Luis Reservoir, U.S.A. ... 116 H5
San Luis Río Colorado, Mexico 118 A2
San Manuel, U.S.A. 115 K8
San Marco, C., Italy 30 C1
San Marco Argentano, Italy .. 31 C9
San Marco in Lámis, Italy 29 G12
San Marcos, Guatemala 120 D1
San Marcos, Mexico 118 B2
San Marcos, Calif., U.S.A. ... 117 M9
San Marcos, Tex., U.S.A. 113 L6
San Marino, San Marino 29 E9
San Marino ■, Europe 29 E9
San Martín, Argentina 126 C2
San Martín ➤, Bolivia 124 F6
San Martín, L., Argentina 128 F2
San Martín de la Vega, Spain . 34 E7
San Martín de los Andes,
  Argentina 128 E2
San Martín de Valdeiglesias,
  Spain 34 E6
San Mateo = Sant Mateu,
  Baleares, Spain 37 B7
San Mateo = Sant Mateu,
  Valencia, Spain 32 E5
San Mateo, Phil. 61 C4
San Mateo, U.S.A. 116 H4
San Matías, Bolivia 124 G7
San Matías, G., Argentina 122 H4
San Miguel = Sant Miquel, Spain 37 B7
San Miguel, El Salv. 120 D2
San Miguel, Panama 120 E4
San Miguel, U.S.A. 116 K6
San Miguel ➤, Bolivia 124 F6
San Miguel de Tucumán,
  Argentina 126 B2
San Miguel del Monte,
  Argentina 126 D4
San Miguel I., U.S.A. 117 L6
San Miniato, Italy 28 E7
San Nicolás, Canary Is. 37 G4
San Nicolas, Phil. 61 B4
San Nicolás de los Arroyos,
  Argentina 126 C3
San Nicolas I., U.S.A. 117 M7
San Onofre, U.S.A. 117 M9
San Pablo, Bolivia 126 A2
San Pablo, Phil. 61 D4
San Pablo, U.S.A. 116 H4
San Páolo di Civitate, Italy ... 29 G12
San Pedro, Buenos Aires,
  Argentina 126 C4
San Pedro, Misiones, Argentina 127 B5
San Pedro, Chile 126 C1
San Pédro, Ivory C. 82 E3
San Pedro, Mexico 126 C2
San Pedro □, Paraguay 126 A4
San Pedro ➤, Chihuahua,
  Mexico 118 B3
San Pedro ➤, Nayarit, Mexico 118 C3
San Pedro ➤, U.S.A. 115 K8
San Pedro, Pta., Chile 126 B1
San Pedro, Sierra de, Spain ... 35 F4
San Pedro Channel, U.S.A. ... 117 M8
San Pedro de Atacama, Chile . 126 A2
San Pedro de Jujuy, Argentina . 126 A3

203

San Pedro de las Colonias

San Pedro de las Colonias,
Mexico **118 B4**
San Pedro de Macorís,
Dom. Rep. **121 C6**
San Pedro del Norte, *Nic.* **120 D3**
San Pedro del Paraná, *Paraguay* **126 B4**
San Pedro del Pinatar, *Spain* . . **33 H4**
San Pedro Mártir, Sierra, *Mexico* **118 A1**
San Pedro Mixtepec, *Mexico* . . . **119 D5**
San Pedro Ocampo = Melchor
Ocampo, *Mexico* **118 C4**
San Pedro Sula, *Honduras* . . . **120 C2**
San Pietro, *Italy* **30 C1**
San Pietro Vernótico, *Italy* . . . **31 B11**
San Quintín, *Mexico* **118 A1**
San Rafael, *Argentina* **126 C2**
San Rafael, *Calif., U.S.A.* **116 H4**
San Rafael, *N. Mex., U.S.A.* . . . **115 J10**
San Rafael Mt., *U.S.A.* **117 L7**
San Rafael Mts., *U.S.A.* **117 L7**
San Ramón de la Nueva Orán,
Argentina **126 A3**
San Remo, *Italy* **28 E4**
San Roque, *Argentina* **126 B4**
San Roque, *Spain* **35 J5**
San Rosendo, *Chile* **126 D1**
San Saba, *U.S.A.* **113 K5**
San Salvador, *El Salv.* **120 D2**
San Salvador, *Spain* **37 B10**
San Salvador de Jujuy, *Argentina* **126 A3**
San Salvador I., *Bahamas* **121 B5**
San Salvo, *Italy* **29 F11**
San Sebastián = Donostia-San
Sebastián, *Spain* **32 B3**
San Sebastián, *Argentina* **128 G3**
San Sebastian de la Gomera,
Canary Is. **37 F2**
San Serra = Son Serra, *Spain* . . **37 B10**
San Serverino Marche, *Italy* . . . **29 E10**
San Severo, *Italy* **29 G12**
San Simeon, *U.S.A.* **116 K5**
San Simon, *U.S.A.* **115 K9**
San Stéfano di Cadore, *Italy* . . . **29 B9**
San Stino di Livenza, *Italy* **29 C9**
San Telmo = Sant Telm, *Spain* . . **37 B9**
San Telmo, *Mexico* **118 A1**
San Tiburcio, *Mexico* **118 C4**
San Valentin, Mte., *Chile* **122 H3**
San Vicente de Alcántara, *Spain* . **35 F3**
San Vicente de la Barquera,
Spain **34 B6**
San Vincente del Raspeig, *Spain* **33 G4**
San Vincenzo, *Italy* **28 E7**
San Vito, *Costa Rica* **120 E3**
San Vito, *Italy* **30 C2**
San Vito, C., *Italy* **30 D5**
San Vito al Tagliamento, *Italy* . . **29 C9**
San Vito Chietino, *Italy* **29 F11**
San Vito dei Normanni, *Italy* . . **31 B10**
Sana', *Yemen* **74 D3**
Sana →, *Bos.-H.* **29 C13**
Sanaba, *Burkina Faso* **82 C4**
Şanâfir, *Si. Arabia* **80 B3**
Sanaga →, *Cameroon* **83 E6**
Sanaloa, Presa, *Mexico* **118 C3**
Sanana, *Indonesia* **63 E7**
Sanand, *India* **68 H5**
Sanandaj, *Iran* **70 C5**
Sanandita, *Bolivia* **126 A3**
Sanary-sur-Mer, *France* **21 E9**
Sanawad, *India* **68 H7**
Sancellas = Sencelles, *Spain* . . . **37 B9**
Sancergues, *France* **19 E9**
Sancerre, *France* **19 E9**
Sancerrois, Collines du, *France* . **19 E9**
Sancha He →, *China* **58 D6**
Sanchahe, *China* **57 B14**
Sánchez, *Dom. Rep.* **121 C6**
Sanchor, *India* **68 G4**
Sancoins, *France* **19 F9**
Sancti Spíritus, *Cuba* **120 B4**
Sancy, Puy de, *France* **20 C6**
Sand →, *S. Africa* **89 C5**
Sand Hills, *U.S.A.* **112 D4**
Sand Springs, *U.S.A.* **113 G6**
Sanda, *Japan* **55 G7**
Sandakan, *Malaysia* **62 C5**
Sandan = Sambor, *Cambodia* . . **64 F6**
Sandanski, *Bulgaria* **40 E7**
Sandaré, *Mali* **82 C2**
Sandared, *Sweden* **11 G6**
Sandarne, *Sweden* **10 C11**
Sanday, *U.K.* **14 B6**
Sandefjord, *Norway* **9 G14**
Sanders, *U.S.A.* **115 J9**
Sanderson, *U.S.A.* **113 K3**
Sandersville, *U.S.A.* **109 J4**
Sandfire Roadhouse, *Australia* . **92 C3**
Sandfly L., *Canada* **105 B7**
Sandfontein, *Namibia* **88 C2**
Sandhammaren, C., *Sweden* . . . **11 J8**
Sandía, *Peru* **124 F5**
Sandıklı, *Turkey* **39 C12**
Sandila, *India* **69 F9**
Sandnes, *Norway* **9 G11**
Sandnessjøen, *Norway* **8 C15**
Sandoa, *Dem. Rep. of the Congo* **84 F4**
Sandomierz, *Poland* **45 H8**
Sândominic, *Romania* **43 D10**
Sandover →, *Australia* **94 C2**
Sandoway, *Burma* **67 K19**
Sandoy, *Færoe Is.* **8 F9**
Sandpoint, *U.S.A.* **114 B5**
Sandray, *U.K.* **14 E1**
Sandringham, *U.K.* **12 E8**
Sandstone, *Australia* **93 E2**
Sandu, *China* **58 E6**

Sandusky, *Mich., U.S.A.* **110 C2**
Sandusky, *Ohio, U.S.A.* **110 E2**
Sandvig, *Sweden* **11 J8**
Sandviken, *Sweden* **10 D10**
Sandwich, C., *Australia* **94 B4**
Sandwich B., *Canada* **103 B8**
Sandwich B., *Namibia* **88 C1**
Sandy, *Oreg., U.S.A.* **116 E4**
Sandy, *Pa., U.S.A.* **110 E6**
Sandy, *Utah, U.S.A.* **114 F8**
Sandy Bay, *Canada* **105 B8**
Sandy Bight, *Australia* **93 F3**
Sandy C., *Queens., Australia* . . **94 C5**
Sandy C., *Tas., Australia* **94 G3**
Sandy Cay, *Bahamas* **121 B4**
Sandy Cr. →, *U.S.A.* **114 F9**
Sandy L., *Canada* **102 B1**
Sandy Lake, *Canada* **102 B1**
Sandy Valley, *U.S.A.* **117 K11**
Sanford, *Fla., U.S.A.* **109 L5**
Sanford, *Maine, U.S.A.* **109 D10**
Sanford, *N.C., U.S.A.* **109 H6**
Sanford →, *Australia* **93 E2**
Sanford, Mt., *U.S.A.* **100 B5**
Sang-i-Masha, *Afghan.* **68 C2**
Sanga, *Mozam.* **87 E4**
Sanga →, *Congo* **84 E3**
Sangamner, *India* **66 K9**
Sangar, *Afghan.* **68 C1**
Sangar, *Russia* **51 C13**
Sangar Sarai, *Afghan.* **68 B4**
Sangareddi, *India* **66 L10**
Sangaredi, *Guinea* **82 C2**
Sangarh →, *Pakistan* **68 D4**
Sangasso, *Mali* **82 C3**
Sangatte, *France* **19 B8**
Sangay, *Ecuador* **124 D3**
Sange, *Dem. Rep. of the Congo* **86 D2**
Sangeang, *Indonesia* **63 F5**
Sângeorz-Băi, *Romania* **43 C9**
Sanger, *U.S.A.* **116 J7**
Sangerhausen, *Germany* **24 D7**
Sanggan He →, *China* **56 E9**
Sanggau, *Indonesia* **62 D4**
Sanghar, *Pakistan* **68 F3**
Sangihe, Kepulauan, *Indonesia* . **63 D7**
Sangihe, Pulau, *Indonesia* **63 D7**
Sangju, *S. Korea* **57 F15**
Sangkapura, *Indonesia* **62 F4**
Sangkhla, *Thailand* **64 E2**
Sangkulirang, *Indonesia* **62 D5**
Sangla, *Pakistan* **68 D5**
Sangli, *India* **66 L9**
Sangmélima, *Cameroon* **83 E7**
Sangod, *India* **68 G7**
Sangro →, *Italy* **29 F11**
Sangrur, *India* **68 D6**
Sangudo, *Canada* **104 C6**
Sangue →, *Brazil* **124 F7**
Sangüesa, *Spain* **32 C3**
Sanguinaires, Îs., *France* **21 G12**
Sangzhi, *China* **59 C8**
Sanhala, *Ivory C.* **82 C3**
Sanibel, *U.S.A.* **109 M4**
Sanirajak, *Canada* **101 B11**
Sanjawi, *Pakistan* **68 D3**
Sanje, *Uganda* **86 C3**
Sanjiang, *China* **58 E7**
Sanjo, *Japan* **54 F9**
Sankh →, *India* **69 H11**
Sankt Andrä, *Austria* **26 E7**
Sankt Augustin, *Germany* **24 E3**
Sankt Blasien, *Germany* **25 H4**
Sankt Gallen, *Switz.* **25 H5**
Sankt Gallen □, *Switz.* **25 H5**
Sankt Goar, *Germany* **25 E3**
Sankt Ingbert, *Germany* **25 F3**
Sankt Johann im Pongau,
Austria **26 D6**
Sankt Johann in Tirol, *Austria* . **26 D5**
Sankt-Peterburg, *Russia* **46 C6**
Sankt Pölten, *Austria* **26 C8**
Sankt Ulrich = Ortisei, *Italy* . . **29 B8**
Sankt Valentin, *Austria* **26 C7**
Sankt Veit an der Glan, *Austria* . **26 E7**
Sankt Wendel, *Germany* **25 F3**
Sankt Wolfgang, *Austria* **26 D6**
Sankuru →, *Dem. Rep. of
the Congo* **84 E4**
Sanliurfa, *Turkey* **70 B3**
Sanlúcar de Barrameda, *Spain* . **35 J4**
Sanluri, *Italy* **30 C1**
Sânmartin, *Romania* **43 D10**
Sanmen, *China* **59 C13**
Sanmenxia, *China* **56 G6**
Sanming, *China* **59 D11**
Sannaspos, *S. Africa* **88 D4**
Sânnicolau Mare, *Romania* . . . **42 D5**
Sannieshof, *S. Africa* **88 D4**
Sannīn, J., *Lebanon* **75 B4**
Sanniquellie, *Liberia* **82 D3**
Sannûr, W. →, *Egypt* **80 B3**
Sanok, *Poland* **45 J9**
Sanquhar, *U.K.* **14 F5**
Sansanding, *Mali* **82 C3**
Sansepolcro, *Italy* **29 E9**
Sansha, *China* **59 D13**
Sanshui, *China* **59 F9**
Sanski Most, *Bos.-H.* **29 D13**
Sansui, *China* **58 D7**
Sant Antoni Abat, *Spain* **37 C7**
Sant Boi de Llobregat, *Spain* . . **32 D7**
Sant Carles, *Spain* **37 B8**
Sant Carles de la Ràpita, *Spain* . **32 E5**
Sant Celoni, *Spain* **32 D7**

Sant Feliu de Guíxols, *Spain* . . . **32 D8**
Sant Feliu de Llobregat, *Spain* . . **32 D7**
Sant Ferran, *Spain* **37 C7**
Sant Francesc de Formentera,
Spain **37 C7**
Sant Jaume, *Spain* **37 B11**
Sant Joan Baptista, *Spain* **37 B8**
Sant Jordi, *Spain* **37 B9**
Sant Jordi, G. de, *Spain* **32 E6**
Sant Llorenç de Morunys, *Spain* **32 C6**
Sant Llorenç des Cardassar,
Spain **37 B10**
Sant Mateu, *Baleares, Spain* . . . **37 B7**
Sant Mateu, *Valencia, Spain* . . . **32 E5**
Sant Miquel, *Spain* **37 B7**
Sant Telm, *Spain* **37 B9**
Sant' Ágata Militello, *Italy* **31 D7**
Santa Agnés, *Spain* **37 B7**
Santa Ana, *Bolivia* **124 F5**
Santa Ana, *El Salv.* **120 D2**
Santa Ana, *Mexico* **118 A2**
Santa Ana, *U.S.A.* **117 M9**
Sant' Ángelo Lodigiano, *Italy* . . **28 C6**
Sant' Antíoco, *Italy* **30 C1**
Santa Barbara, *Chile* **126 D1**
Santa Barbara, *Honduras* **120 D2**
Santa Bárbara, *Mexico* **118 B3**
Santa Bárbara, *Spain* **32 E5**
Santa Bárbara, *U.S.A.* **117 L7**
Santa Bárbara, Mt., *U.S.A.* . . . **33 H2**
Santa Barbara Channel, *U.S.A.* . **117 L7**
Santa Barbara I., *U.S.A.* **117 M7**
Santa Catalina, Gulf of, *U.S.A.* . **117 N9**
Santa Catalina, I., *Mexico* **118 B2**
Santa Catalina I., *U.S.A.* **117 M8**
Santa Catarina □, *Brazil* **127 B6**
Santa Catarina, I. de, *Brazil* . . . **127 B6**
Santa Caterina di Pittinuri, *Italy* **30 B1**
Santa Caterina Villarmosa, *Italy* **31 E7**
Santa Cecília, *Brazil* **127 B5**
Santa Clara, *Cuba* **120 B4**
Santa Clara, *Calif., U.S.A.* . . . **116 H5**
Santa Clara, *Utah, U.S.A.* **115 H7**
Santa Clara, El Golfo de, *Mexico* **118 A2**
Santa Clara de Olimar, *Uruguay* **127 C5**
Santa Clarita, *U.S.A.* **117 L8**
Santa Clotilde, *Peru* **124 D4**
Santa Coloma de Farners, *Spain* **32 D7**
Santa Coloma de Gramenet,
Spain **32 D7**
Santa Comba, *Spain* **34 B2**
Santa Croce Camerina, *Italy* . . . **31 F7**
Santa Croce di Magliano, *Italy* . **29 G11**
Santa Cruz, *Argentina* **128 G3**
Santa Cruz, *Bolivia* **124 G6**
Santa Cruz, *Chile* **126 C1**
Santa Cruz, *Costa Rica* **120 D2**
Santa Cruz, *Madeira* **37 D3**
Santa Cruz, *Phil.* **61 D4**
Santa Cruz, *U.S.A.* **116 J4**
Santa Cruz →, *Argentina* **128 G3**
Santa Cruz de la Palma,
Canary Is. **37 F2**
Santa Cruz de Mudela, *Spain* . . **35 G7**
Santa Cruz de Tenerife,
Canary Is. **37 F3**
Santa Cruz del Norte, *Cuba* . . . **120 B3**
Santa Cruz del Retamar, *Spain* . **34 E6**
Santa Cruz del Sur, *Cuba* **120 B4**
Santa Cruz do Rio Pardo, *Brazil* **127 A6**
Santa Cruz do Sul, *Brazil* **127 B5**
Santa Cruz I., *U.S.A.* **117 M7**
Santa Cruz Is., *Solomon Is.* . . . **96 J8**
Santa Domingo, Cay, *Bahamas* . **120 B4**
Sant' Egídio alla Vibrata, *Italy* . **29 F10**
Santa Elena, *Argentina* **126 C4**
Santa Elena, C., *Costa Rica* . . . **120 D2**
Santa Eufémia, G. di, *Italy* . . . **31 D9**
Santa Eulàlia des Riu, *Spain* . . **37 C8**
Santa Fe, *Argentina* **126 C3**
Santa Fe, *Spain* **35 H7**
Santa Fe, *U.S.A.* **115 J11**
Santa Fe □, *Argentina* **126 C3**
Santa Fé do Sul, *Brazil* **125 H8**
Santa Filomena, *Brazil* **125 E9**
Santa Fiora, *Italy* **29 F8**
Santa Gertrudis, *Spain* **37 C7**
Santa Giustina, *Italy* **29 B9**
Santa Inês, *Brazil* **125 F11**
Santa Inés, *Spain* **35 G5**
Santa Inés, I., *Chile* **122 J3**
Santa Isabel = Rey Malabo,
Eq. Guin. **83 E6**
Santa Isabel, *Argentina* **126 D2**
Santa Isabel, Pico, *Eq. Guin.* . . **83 E6**
Santa Isabel do Morro, *Brazil* . . **125 F8**
Santa Lucía, *Corrientes,
Argentina* **126 B4**
Santa Lucía, *San Juan, Argentina* **126 C2**
Santa Lucía, *Spain* **33 H4**
Santa Lucía, *Uruguay* **126 C4**
Santa Lucia Range, *U.S.A.* **116 K5**
Santa Magdalena, I., *Mexico* . . . **118 C2**
Santa Margarita, *Argentina* . . . **126 D3**
Santa Margarita, *Spain* **37 B10**
Santa Margarita, *U.S.A.* **116 K6**
Santa Margarita →, *U.S.A.* . . . **117 M9**
Santa Margarita, I., *Mexico* . . . **118 C2**
Santa Margherita, *Italy* **30 D1**
Santa Margherita Ligure, *Italy* . **28 D6**
Santa María, *Argentina* **126 B2**
Santa María, *Brazil* **127 B5**
Santa Maria, *Phil.* **61 C4**
Santa María →, *Mexico* **118 A3**
Santa María, B. de, *Mexico* . . . **118 B3**
Santa Maria, C. de, *Portugal* . . **35 J3**

Santa Maria Cápua Vétere, *Italy* **31 A7**
Santa Maria da Feira, *Portugal* . **34 E2**
Santa Maria da Vitória, *Brazil* . **125 F10**
Santa Maria di Camí, *Spain* . . . **37 B9**
Santa Maria di Léuca, C., *Italy* . **31 C11**
Santa María la Real de Nieva,
Spain **34 D6**
Santa Marinella, *Italy* **29 F9**
Santa Marta, *Colombia* **124 A4**
Santa Marta, Sierra Nevada de,
Colombia **122 B3**
Santa Marta de Tormes, *Spain* . **34 E5**
Santa Marta Grande, C., *Brazil* . **127 B6**
Santa Marta Ortigueira, Ría de,
Spain **34 B3**
Santa Maura = Levkás, *Greece* . **38 C2**
Santa Monica, *U.S.A.* **117 M8**
Santa Olalla, *Huelva, Spain* . . . **35 H4**
Santa Olalla, *Toledo, Spain* . . . **34 E6**
Santa Paula, *U.S.A.* **117 L7**
Santa Pola, *Spain* **33 G4**
Santa Ponsa, *Spain* **37 B9**
Santa Rita, *La Pampa,
Argentina* **126 D3**
Santa Rosa, *San Luis, Argentina* **126 C2**
Santa Rosa, *Brazil* **127 B5**
Santa Rosa, *Calif., U.S.A.* **116 G4**
Santa Rosa, *N. Mex., U.S.A.* . . . **113 H2**
Santa Rosa de Copán, *Honduras* **120 D2**
Santa Rosa de Río Primero,
Argentina **126 C3**
Santa Rosa del Sara, *Bolivia* . . **124 G6**
Santa Rosa I., *Calif., U.S.A.* . . . **117 M6**
Santa Rosa I., *Fla., U.S.A.* **109 K2**
Santa Rosa Range, *U.S.A.* **114 F5**
Santa Rosalía, *Mexico* **118 B2**
Santa Sylvina, *Argentina* **126 B3**
Santa Tecla = Nueva San
Salvador, *El Salv.* **120 D2**
Santa Teresa, *Argentina* **126 C3**
Santa Teresa, *Australia* **94 C1**
Santa Teresa, *Mexico* **119 B5**
Santa Teresa di Riva, *Italy* **31 E8**
Santa Teresa Gallura, *Italy* . . . **30 A2**
Santa Uxía, *Spain* **34 C2**
Santa Vitória do Palmar, *Brazil* **127 C5**
Santa Ynez →, *U.S.A.* **117 L6**
Santa Ynez Mts., *U.S.A.* **117 L6**
Santa Ysabel, *U.S.A.* **117 M10**
Santadi, *Italy* **30 C1**
Santaella, *Spain* **35 H6**
Santai, *China* **58 B5**
Sântana, *Romania* **42 D6**
Santana, *Madeira* **37 D3**
Santana, Coxilha de, *Brazil* . . . **127 C4**
Santana do Livramento, *Brazil* . **127 C4**
Santander, *Spain* **34 B7**
Santander Jiménez, *Mexico* . . . **119 C5**
Santanyí, *Spain* **37 B10**
Santaquin, *U.S.A.* **114 G8**
Santarcángelo di Romagna, *Italy* **29 D9**
Santarém, *Brazil* **125 D8**
Santarém, *Portugal* **35 F2**
Santarém □, *Portugal* **35 F2**
Santaren Channel, *W. Indies* . . **120 B4**
Santee, *U.S.A.* **117 N10**
Santee →, *U.S.A.* **109 J6**
Santéramo in Colle, *Italy* **31 B9**
Santerno →, *Italy* **29 D8**
Santhià, *Italy* **28 C5**
Santiago, *Brazil* **127 B5**
Santiago, *Chile* **126 C1**
Santiago, *Panama* **120 E3**
Santiago, *Phil.* **61 C4**
Santiago □, *Chile* **126 C1**
Santiago →, *Mexico* **98 G9**
Santiago →, *Peru* **124 D3**
Santiago, Punta de, *Eq. Guin.* . . **83 E6**
Santiago de Compostela, *Spain* . **34 C2**
Santiago de Cuba, *Cuba* **120 C4**
Santiago de los Cabelleros,
Dom. Rep. **121 C5**
Santiago del Estero, *Argentina* . **126 B3**
Santiago del Estero □, *Argentina* **126 B3**
Santiago del Teide, *Canary Is.* . **37 F3**
Santiago do Cacém, *Portugal* . . **35 G2**
Santiago Ixcuintla, *Mexico* . . . **118 C3**
Santiago Papasquiaro, *Mexico* . **118 C3**
Santiaguillo, L. de, *Mexico* . . . **118 C4**
Santiguila, *Mali* **82 C3**
Santillana, *Spain* **34 B6**
Santisteban del Puerto, *Spain* . . **35 G7**
Santo Amaro, *Brazil* **125 F11**
Santo Anastácio, *Brazil* **127 A5**
Santo André, *Brazil* **127 A6**
Santo Ângelo, *Brazil* **127 B5**
Santo Antônio do Içá, *Brazil* . . **124 D5**
Santo Antônio do Leverger,
Brazil **125 G7**
Santo Domingo, *Dom. Rep.* . . . **121 C6**
Santo Domingo, *Baja Calif.,
Mexico* **118 A1**
Santo Domingo, *Baja Calif. S.,
Mexico* **118 B2**
Santo Domingo, *Nic.* **120 D3**
Santo Domingo de la Calzada,
Spain **32 C2**
Santo Domingo de los
Colorados, *Ecuador* **124 D3**
Santo Domingo Pueblo, *U.S.A.* . **115 J10**
Santo Stéfano di Camastro, *Italy* **31 D7**
Santo Tirso, *Portugal* **34 D2**
Santo Tomás, *Mexico* **118 A1**
Santo Tomás, *Peru* **124 F4**
Santo Tomé, *Argentina* **127 B4**

Santo Tomé de Guayana =
Ciudad Guayana, *Venezuela* . **124 B6**
Santomera, *Spain* **33 G3**
Santoña, *Spain* **34 B7**
Santoríni = Thíra, *Greece* **39 E7**
Santos, *Brazil* **127 A6**
Santos, Sierra de los, *Spain* . . . **35 G5**
Santos Dumont, *Brazil* **127 A7**
Sanwer, *India* **68 H6**
Sanxenxo, *Spain* **34 C2**
Sanyuan, *China* **56 G5**
São Bartolomeu de Messines,
Portugal **35 H2**
São Bernardo do Campo, *Brazil* **127 A6**
São Borja, *Brazil* **127 B4**
São Brás d'Alportel, *Portugal* . . **35 H3**
São Carlos, *Brazil* **127 A6**
São Cristóvão, *Brazil* **125 F11**
São Domingos, *Brazil* **125 F9**
São Domingos, *Guinea-Biss.* . . . **82 C1**
São Francisco, *Brazil* **125 G10**
São Francisco →, *Brazil* **122 E7**
São Francisco do Sul, *Brazil* . . **127 B6**
São Gabriel, *Brazil* **127 C5**
São Gonçalo, *Brazil* **127 A7**
Sao Hill, *Tanzania* **87 D4**
São João, *Guinea-Biss.* **82 C1**
São João da Boa Vista, *Brazil* . . **127 A6**
São João da Madeira, *Portugal* . **34 E2**
São João da Pesqueira, *Portugal* **34 D3**
São João del Rei, *Brazil* **127 A7**
São João do Araguaia, *Brazil* . . **125 E9**
São João do Piauí, *Brazil* **125 E10**
São Joaquim, *Brazil* **127 B6**
São Jorge, Pta. de, *Madeira* . . . **37 D3**
São José, *Brazil* **127 B5**
São José do Norte, *Brazil* **127 C5**
São José do Rio Prêto, *Brazil* . . **127 A6**
São José dos Campos, *Brazil* . . **127 A6**
São Leopoldo, *Brazil* **127 B5**
São Lourenço, *Brazil* **127 A6**
São Lourenço →, *Brazil* **125 G7**
São Lourenço, Pta. de, *Madeira* . **37 D3**
São Lourenço do Sul, *Brazil* . . **127 C5**
São Luís, *Brazil* **125 D10**
São Luís Gonzaga, *Brazil* **127 B5**
São Marcos →, *Brazil* **125 G9**
São Marcos, B. de, *Brazil* **125 D10**
São Martinho da Cortiça,
Portugal **34 E2**
São Mateus, *Brazil* **125 G11**
São Mateus do Sul, *Brazil* **127 B5**
São Miguel do Oeste, *Brazil* . . . **127 B5**
São Paulo, *Brazil* **127 A6**
São Paulo □, *Brazil* **127 A6**
São Paulo, I., *Atl. Oc.* **2 D8**
São Paulo de Olivença, *Brazil* . . **124 D5**
São Pedro do Sul, *Portugal* . . . **34 E2**
São Roque, *Madeira* **37 D3**
São Roque, C. de, *Brazil* **122 D7**
São Sebastião, I. de, *Brazil* **127 A6**
São Sebastião do Paraíso, *Brazil* **127 A6**
São Teotónio, *Portugal* **35 H2**
São Tomé, *Atl. Oc.* **76 F4**
São Tomé, C. de, *Brazil* **127 A7**
São Tomé & Príncipe ■, *Africa* . **77 F4**
São Vicente, *Brazil* **127 A6**
São Vicente, *Madeira* **37 D2**
São Vicente, C. de, *Portugal* . . . **35 H1**
Saona, I., *Dom. Rep.* **121 C6**
Saône →, *France* **19 G11**
Saône-et-Loire □, *France* **19 F11**
Saonek, *Indonesia* **63 E8**
Sápai, *Greece* **41 E9**
Sapanca, *Turkey* **72 B4**
Saparua, *Indonesia* **63 E7**
Sapele, *Nigeria* **83 D6**
Sapelo I., *U.S.A.* **109 K5**
Saphane, *Turkey* **39 B11**
Sapiéntza, *Greece* **38 E3**
Sapone, *Burkina Faso* **83 C4**
Saposoa, *Peru* **124 E3**
Sapouy, *Burkina Faso* **83 C4**
Sapozhok, *Russia* **48 D5**
Sapphire, *Australia* **94 C4**
Sappho, *U.S.A.* **116 B2**
Sapporo, *Japan* **54 C10**
Sapri, *Italy* **31 B8**
Sapulpa, *U.S.A.* **113 H6**
Saqqez, *Iran* **70 B5**
Sar Dasht, *Iran* **71 C6**
Sar-e Pol □, *Afghan.* **66 B4**
Sar Gachineh = Yāsūj, *Iran* . . . **71 D6**
Sar Planina, *Macedonia* **40 E4**
Sara, *Burkina Faso* **82 C4**
Sara, *Phil.* **61 F5**
Sara Buri = Saraburi, *Thailand* . **64 E3**
Sarāb, *Iran* **70 B5**
Sarabadi, *Iraq* **70 C5**
Saraburi, *Thailand* **64 E3**
Saradiya, *India* **68 J4**
Saraféré, *Mali* **82 C4**
Saragossa = Zaragoza, *Spain* . . **32 D4**
Saraguro, *Ecuador* **124 D3**
Sarai Naurang, *Pakistan* **68 C4**
Saraikela, *India* **69 H11**
Saraiu, *Romania* **43 F13**
Sarajevo, *Bos.-H.* **42 G3**
Sarakhs, *Turkmenistan* **71 B9**
Saran, Gunung, *Indonesia* **62 E4**
Saranac L., *U.S.A.* **111 B10**
Saranac Lake, *U.S.A.* **111 B10**
Saranda, *Tanzania* **86 D3**
Sarandë, *Albania* **40 G3**
Sarandí del Yi, *Uruguay* **127 C4**
Sarandí Grande, *Uruguay* **126 C4**
Sarangani B., *Phil.* **61 J6**

Sarangani Is., *Phil.* 61 J6
Sarangarh, *India* 67 J13
Saransk, *Russia* 48 C7
Sarapul, *Russia* 50 D6
Sarasota, *U.S.A.* 109 M4
Saratoga, *Calif., U.S.A.* 116 H4
Saratoga, *Wyo., U.S.A.* 114 F10
Saratoga Springs, *U.S.A.* 111 C11
Saratok, *Malaysia* 62 D4
Saratov, *Russia* 48 E7
Saravane, *Laos* 64 E6
Sarawak □, *Malaysia* 62 D4
Saray, *Tekirdağ, Turkey* 41 E11
Saray, *Van, Turkey* 73 C11
Saraya, *Guinea* 82 C2
Saraya, *Senegal* 82 C2
Sarayçık, *Turkey* 39 B11
Sarayköy, *Turkey* 39 D10
Saraylar, *Turkey* 41 F11
Sarayönü, *Turkey* 72 C5
Sarbāz, *Iran* 71 E9
Sarbīsheh, *Iran* 71 C8
Sárbogárd, *Hungary* 42 D3
Sarca ➤, *Italy* 28 C7
Sarcelles, *France* 19 D9
Sarda ➤, *India* 67 F12
Sardarshahr, *India* 68 E6
Sardegna □, *Italy* 30 B1
Sardhana, *India* 68 E7
Sardina, Pta., *Canary Is.* ... 37 F4
Sardinia = Sardegna □, *Italy* . 30 B1
Sardis, *Turkey* 39 C10
Sārdūīyeh = Dar Mazār, *Iran* . 71 D8
S'Arenal, *Spain* 37 B9
Sarentino, *Italy* 29 B8
Saréyamou, *Mali* 82 B4
Sargasso Sea, *Atl. Oc.* 97 D20
Sargodha, *Pakistan* 68 C5
Sarh, *Chad* 79 G9
Sārī, *Iran* 71 B7
Sari d'Orcino, *France* 21 F12
Sária, *Greece* 39 F9
Saria, *India* 69 J10
Sariab, *Pakistan* 68 D2
Sarıbeyler, *Turkey* 39 B9
Sarıgöl, *Turkey* 72 C3
Sarıkamış, *Turkey* 73 B10
Sarıkaya, *Turkey* 72 C6
Sarikei, *Malaysia* 62 D4
Sarıköy, *Turkey* 41 F11
Sarila, *India* 69 G8
Sarina, *Australia* 94 C4
Sariñena, *Spain* 32 D4
Sarita, *U.S.A.* 113 M6
Sariwŏn, *N. Korea* 57 E13
Sarıyar Barajı, *Turkey* 72 B4
Sarıyer, *Turkey* 41 E13
Sarju ➤, *India* 69 F9
Sark, *U.K.* 13 H5
Sarkad, *Hungary* 42 D6
Sarkari Tala, *India* 68 F4
Şarkışla, *Turkey* 72 C7
Şarköy, *Turkey* 41 F11
Sarlat-la-Canéda, *France* 20 D5
Sărmăşag, *Romania* 42 C7
Sărmaşu, *Romania* 43 D9
Sarmi, *Indonesia* 63 E9
Sarmiento, *Argentina* 128 F3
Sarmizegetusa, *Romania* 42 E7
Särna, *Sweden* 10 C7
Sarnano, *Italy* 29 E10
Sarnen, *Switz.* 25 J4
Sarnia, *Canada* 102 D3
Sarno, *Italy* 31 B7
Sarnthein = Sarentino, *Italy* . 29 B8
Särö, *Sweden* 11 G5
Sarolangun, *Indonesia* 62 E2
Saronikós Kólpos, *Greece* 38 D5
Saronno, *Italy* 28 C6
Saros Körfezi, *Turkey* 41 F10
Sárospatak, *Hungary* 42 B6
Sarpsborg, *Norway* 9 G14
Sarracín, *Spain* 34 C7
Sarralbe, *France* 19 D14
Sarre = Saar ➤, *Europe* 17 E6
Sarre, *Italy* 28 C4
Sarre-Union, *France* 19 D14
Sarrebourg, *France* 19 D14
Sarreguemines, *France* 19 C14
Sarria, *Spain* 34 C3
Sarrión, *Spain* 32 E4
Sarro, *Mali* 82 C3
Sarstedt, *Germany* 24 C5
Sartène, *France* 21 G12
Sarthe □, *France* 18 D7
Sarthe ➤, *France* 18 E6
Sartilly, *France* 18 D5
Saruhanlı, *Turkey* 39 C9
Săruleşti, *Romania* 43 F11
Saruna ➤, *Pakistan* 68 F2
Sárvár, *Hungary* 42 C1
Sarvar, *India* 68 F6
Sarvestān, *Iran* 71 D7
Sarvfjället, *Sweden* 10 B7
Sárviz ➤, *Hungary* 42 D3
Sary-Tash, *Kyrgyzstan* 50 F8
Sarych, Mys, *Ukraine* 47 K7
Saryshagan, *Kazakhstan* 50 E8
Sarzana, *Italy* 28 D6
Sarzeau, *France* 18 E4
Sasan Gir, *India* 68 J4
Sasaram, *India* 69 G11
Sasebo, *Japan* 55 H4
Saser, *India* 69 B7
Saskatchewan □, *Canada* 105 C7
Saskatchewan ➤, *Canada* ... 105 C8

Saskatoon, *Canada* 105 C7
Saskylakh, *Russia* 51 B12
Sasolburg, *S. Africa* 89 D4
Sasovo, *Russia* 48 C5
Sassandra, *Ivory C.* 82 E3
Sassandra ➤, *Ivory C.* 82 E3
Sássari, *Italy* 30 B1
Sassnitz, *Germany* 24 A9
Sasso Marconi, *Italy* 29 D8
Sassocorvaro, *Italy* 29 E9
Sassoferrato, *Italy* 29 E9
Sasstown, *Liberia* 82 E3
Sassuolo, *Italy* 28 D7
Sástago, *Spain* 32 D4
Sasumua Dam, *Kenya* 86 C4
Sasyk, Ozero, *Ukraine* 47 K5
Sata-Misaki, *Japan* 55 J5
Satadougou, *Mali* 82 C2
Satakunta, *Finland* 9 F20
Satama-Soukoura, *Ivory C.* .. 82 D4
Satara, *India* 66 L8
Satara, *S. Africa* 89 C5
Satbarwa, *India* 69 H11
Såtenäs, *Sweden* 11 F6
Säter, *Sweden* 10 D9
Satevó, *Mexico* 118 B3
Satilla ➤, *U.S.A.* 109 K5
Satmala Hills, *India* 66 J9
Satna, *India* 69 G9
Šator, *Bos.-H.* 29 D13
Sátoraljaújhely, *Hungary* 42 B6
Satpura Ra., *India* 66 J10
Satrup, *Germany* 24 A5
Satsuna-Shotō, *Japan* 55 K5
Sattahip, *Thailand* 64 F3
Satu Mare, *Romania* 42 C7
Satu Mare □, *Romania* 42 C8
Satui, *Indonesia* 62 E5
Satun, *Thailand* 65 J3
Saturnina ➤, *Brazil* 124 F7
Sauce, *Argentina* 126 C4
Sauceda, *Mexico* 118 B4
Saucillo, *Mexico* 118 B3
Sauda, *Norway* 9 G12
Sauðarkrókur, *Iceland* 8 D4
Saudi Arabia ■, *Asia* 70 B3
Saugeen ➤, *Canada* 110 B3
Saugerties, *U.S.A.* 111 D11
Saugues, *France* 20 D7
Saugus, *U.S.A.* 117 L8
Saujon, *France* 20 C3
Sauk Centre, *U.S.A.* 112 C7
Sauk Rapids, *U.S.A.* 112 C7
Saulgau, *Germany* 25 G5
Saulieu, *France* 19 E11
Sault, *France* 21 D9
Sault Ste. Marie, *Canada* ... 102 C3
Sault Ste. Marie, *U.S.A.* 101 D11
Saumlaki, *Indonesia* 63 F8
Saumur, *France* 18 E6
Saunders C., *N.Z.* 91 L3
Saunders I., *Antarctica* 5 B1
Saunders Point, *Australia* ... 93 E4
Sauri, *Nigeria* 83 C6
Saurimo, *Angola* 84 F4
Sausalito, *U.S.A.* 116 H4
Sauveterre-de-Béarn, *France* . 20 E3
Sauzé-Vaussais, *France* 20 B4
Savá, *Honduras* 120 C2
Sava, *Italy* 31 B10
Sava ➤, *Serbia, Yug.* 42 F5
Savage, *U.S.A.* 112 B2
Savage I. = Niue, *Cook Is.* .. 97 J11
Savage River, *Australia* 94 G4
Savai'i, *Samoa* 91 A12
Savalou, *Benin* 83 D5
Savane, *Mozam.* 87 F4
Savanna, *U.S.A.* 112 D9
Savanna-la-Mar, *Jamaica* 120 C4
Savannah, *Ga., U.S.A.* 109 J5
Savannah, *Mo., U.S.A.* 112 F7
Savannah, *Tenn., U.S.A.* 109 H1
Savannah ➤, *U.S.A.* 109 J5
Savannakhet, *Laos* 64 D5
Savant L., *Canada* 102 B1
Savant Lake, *Canada* 102 B1
Săvârşin, *Romania* 42 D7
Savaştepe, *Turkey* 39 B9
Savé, *Benin* 83 D5
Save ➤, *France* 20 E5
Save ➤, *Mozam.* 89 C5
Sāveh, *Iran* 71 C6
Savelugu, *Ghana* 83 D4
Savenay, *France* 18 E5
Săveni, *Romania* 43 C11
Saverdun, *France* 20 E5
Saverne, *France* 19 D14
Savigliano, *Italy* 28 D4
Savigny-sur-Braye, *France* ... 18 E7
Sávio ➤, *Italy* 29 D9
Šavnik, *Montenegro, Yug.* ... 40 D3
Savo, *Finland* 8 E22
Savoie □, *France* 21 C10
Savona, *Italy* 28 D5
Savona, *U.S.A.* 110 D7
Savonlinna, *Finland* 46 B5
Savoy = Savoie □, *France* ... 21 C10
Şavşat, *Turkey* 73 B10
Sävsjö, *Sweden* 11 G8
Savur, *Turkey* 70 B4
Sawahlunto, *Indonesia* 62 E2
Sawai, *Indonesia* 63 E7
Sawai Madhopur, *India* 68 G7
Sawang Daen Din, *Thailand* . 64 D4
Sawankhalok, *Thailand* 64 D2
Sawara, *Japan* 55 G10
Sawatch Range, *U.S.A.* 115 G10

Sawel Mt., *U.K.* 15 B4
Sawi, *Thailand* 65 G2
Sawla, *Ghana* 82 D4
Sawmills, *Zimbabwe* 87 F2
Sawtooth Range, *U.S.A.* 114 E6
Sawu, *Indonesia* 63 F6
Sawu Sea, *Indonesia* 63 F6
Saxby ➤, *Australia* 94 B3
Saxmundham, *U.K.* 13 E9
Saxony = Sachsen □, *Germany* 24 E9
Saxony, Lower =
  Niedersachsen □, *Germany* . 24 C4
Saxton, *U.S.A.* 110 F6
Say, *Mali* 82 C4
Say, *Niger* 83 C5
Saya, *Nigeria* 83 D5
Sayabec, *Canada* 103 C6
Sayaboury, *Laos* 64 C3
Sayán, *Peru* 124 F3
Sayan, Vostochnyy, *Russia* ... 51 D10
Sayan, Zapadnyy, *Russia* 51 D10
Saydā, *Lebanon* 75 B4
Sayhandulaan = Oldziyt,
  Mongolia 56 B5
Sayḩūt, *Yemen* 74 D5
Saykhin, *Kazakhstan* 49 F8
Saynshand, *Mongolia* 60 B6
Sayre, *Okla., U.S.A.* 113 H5
Sayre, *Pa., U.S.A.* 111 E8
Sayreville, *U.S.A.* 111 F10
Sayula, *Mexico* 118 D4
Sayward, *Canada* 104 C3
Sazanit, *Albania* 40 F3
Sazin, *Pakistan* 69 B5
Sazlika ➤, *Bulgaria* 41 E9
Scaër, *France* 18 D3
Scafell Pike, *U.K.* 12 C4
Scalea, *Italy* 31 C8
Scalloway, *U.K.* 14 A7
Scalpay, *U.K.* 14 D3
Scandia, *Canada* 104 C6
Scandiano, *Italy* 28 D7
Scandicci, *Italy* 29 E8
Scandinavia, *Europe* 8 E16
Scansano, *Italy* 29 F8
Scapa Flow, *U.K.* 14 C5
Scappoose, *U.S.A.* 116 E4
Scarámia, Capo, *Italy* 31 F7
Scarba, *U.K.* 14 E3
Scarborough, *Trin. & Tob.* .. 121 D7
Scarborough, *U.K.* 12 C7
Scariff I., *Ireland* 15 E1
Scarp, *U.K.* 14 C1
Scebeli, Wabi ➤, *Somali Rep.* . 74 G3
Ŝćedro, *Croatia* 29 E13
Schaal See, *Germany* 24 B6
Schaffhausen, *Switz.* 25 H4
Schagen, *Neths.* 17 B4
Schaghticoke, *U.S.A.* 111 D11
Schärding, *Austria* 26 C6
Scharhörn, *Germany* 24 B4
Scheessel, *Germany* 24 B5
Schefferville, *Canada* 103 B6
Scheibbs, *Austria* 26 C8
Schelde ➤, *Belgium* 17 C4
Schell Creek Ra., *U.S.A.* 114 G6
Schellsburg, *U.S.A.* 110 F6
Schenectady, *U.S.A.* 111 D11
Schenevus, *U.S.A.* 111 D10
Scherfede, *Germany* 24 D5
Schesslitz, *Germany* 25 F7
Schiedam, *Neths.* 17 C4
Schiermonnikoog, *Neths.* 17 A6
Schiltigheim, *France* 19 D14
Schio, *Italy* 29 C8
Schladming, *Austria* 26 D6
Schlanders = Silandro, *Italy* . 28 B7
Schleiden, *Germany* 24 E2
Schleiz, *Germany* 24 E7
Schleswig, *Germany* 24 A5
Schleswig-Holstein □, *Germany* 24 A5
Schlüchtern, *Germany* 25 E5
Schmalkalden, *Germany* 24 E6
Schmölln, *Germany* 24 E8
Schneeberg, *Austria* 26 D8
Schneeberg, *Germany* 24 E8
Schneverdingen, *Germany* ... 24 B5
Schoharie, *U.S.A.* 111 D10
Schoharie ➤, *U.S.A.* 111 D10
Scholls, *U.S.A.* 116 E4
Schönberg,
  Mecklenburg-Vorpommern,
  Germany 24 B6
Schönberg, *Schleswig-Holstein,*
  Germany 24 A6
Schönebeck, *Germany* 24 C7
Schöneck, *Germany* 25 H6
Schöningen, *Germany* 24 C6
Schopfheim, *Germany* 25 H3
Schorndorf, *Germany* 25 G5
Schortens, *Germany* 24 B3
Schouten, *Neths.* 94 G4
Schouten Is. = Supiori, *Indonesia* 63 E9
Schouwen, *Neths.* 17 C3
Schramberg, *Germany* 25 G4
Schrankogel, *Austria* 26 D4
Schreiber, *Canada* 102 C2
Schrems, *Austria* 26 C8
Schrobenhausen, *Germany* ... 25 G7
Schroffenstein, *Namibia* 88 D2
Schroon Lake, *U.S.A.* 111 C11
Schruns, *Austria* 26 D2
Schuler, *Canada* 105 C6
Schumacher, *Canada* 102 C3
Schurz, *U.S.A.* 114 G4

Schuyler, *U.S.A.* 112 E6
Schuylerville, *U.S.A.* 111 C11
Schuylkill ➤, *U.S.A.* 111 G9
Schuylkill Haven, *U.S.A.* 111 F8
Schwabach, *Germany* 25 F7
Schwaben □, *Germany* 25 G6
Schwäbisch Gmünd, *Germany* . 25 G5
Schwäbisch Hall, *Germany* ... 25 F5
Schwäbische Alb, *Germany* ... 25 G5
Schwabmünchen, *Germany* ... 25 G6
Schwalmstadt, *Germany* 24 E5
Schwaner, Pegunungan,
  Indonesia 62 E4
Schwanewede, *Germany* 24 B4
Schwarmstedt, *Germany* 24 C5
Schwarze Elster ➤, *Germany* . 24 D8
Schwarzenberg, *Germany* 24 E8
Schwarzrand, *Namibia* 88 D2
Schwarzwald, *Germany* 25 G4
Schwaz, *Austria* 26 D4
Schwechat, *Austria* 27 C9
Schwedt, *Germany* 24 B10
Schweinfurt, *Germany* 25 E6
Schweizer-Reneke, *S. Africa* .. 88 D4
Schwenningen = Villingen-
  Schwenningen, *Germany* ... 25 G4
Schwerin, *Germany* 24 B7
Schweriner See, *Germany* 24 B7
Schwetzingen, *Germany* 25 F4
Schwyz, *Switz.* 25 H4
Schwyz □, *Switz.* 25 H4
Sciacca, *Italy* 30 E6
Scicli, *Italy* 31 F7
Scilla, *Italy* 31 D8
Scilly, Isles of, *U.K.* 13 H1
Ścinawa, *Poland* 45 G3
Scione, *Greece* 40 G7
Scioto ➤, *U.S.A.* 108 F4
Scituate, *U.S.A.* 111 D14
Scobey, *U.S.A.* 112 A2
Scone, *Australia* 95 E5
Scordia, *Italy* 31 E7
Scoresbysund =
  Ittoqqortoormiit, *Greenland* . 4 B6
Scornicești, *Romania* 43 F9
Scotia, *Calif., U.S.A.* 114 F1
Scotia, *N.Y., U.S.A.* 111 D11
Scotia Sea, *Antarctica* 5 B18
Scotland, *Canada* 110 C4
Scotland □, *U.K.* 14 E5
Scott, C., *Canada* 92 B4
Scott City, *U.S.A.* 112 F4
Scott Glacier, *Antarctica* 5 C8
Scott I., *Antarctica* 5 C11
Scott Is., *Canada* 104 C3
Scott L., *Canada* 105 B7
Scott Reef, *Australia* 92 B3
Scottburgh, *S. Africa* 89 E5
Scottdale, *U.S.A.* 110 F5
Scottsbluff, *U.S.A.* 112 E3
Scottsboro, *U.S.A.* 109 H3
Scottsburg, *U.S.A.* 108 F3
Scottsdale, *Australia* 94 G4
Scottsdale, *U.S.A.* 115 K7
Scottsville, *Ky., U.S.A.* 109 G2
Scottsville, *N.Y., U.S.A.* 110 C7
Scottville, *U.S.A.* 108 D2
Scranton, *U.S.A.* 111 E9
Scugog, L., *Canada* 110 B6
Sculeni, *Moldova* 43 C12
Scunthorpe, *U.K.* 12 D7
Scuol Schuls, *Switz.* 25 J6
Scutari = Üsküdar, *Turkey* ... 41 F13
Seabrook, L., *Australia* 93 F2
Seaford, *U.K.* 13 G8
Seaford, *U.S.A.* 108 F8
Seaforth, *Australia* 94 C4
Seaforth, *Canada* 110 C3
Seaforth, L., *U.K.* 14 D2
Seagraves, *U.S.A.* 113 J3
Seaham, *U.K.* 12 C6
Seal ➤, *Canada* 105 B10
Seal L., *Canada* 103 B7
Sealy, *U.S.A.* 113 L6
Searchlight, *U.S.A.* 117 K12
Searcy, *U.S.A.* 113 H9
Searles L., *U.S.A.* 117 K9
Seascale, *U.K.* 12 C4
Seaside, *Calif., U.S.A.* 116 J5
Seaside, *Oreg., U.S.A.* 116 E3
Seaspray, *Australia* 95 F4
Seattle, *U.S.A.* 116 C4
Seaview Ra., *Australia* 94 B4
Sebago L., *U.S.A.* 111 C14
Sebago L., *U.S.A.* 111 C14
Sebastián Vizcaíno, B., *Mexico* . 118 B2
Sebastopol = Sevastopol,
  Ukraine 47 K7
Sebastopol, *U.S.A.* 116 G4
Sebba, *Burkina Faso* 83 C5
Sebderat, *Eritrea* 81 D4
Sébékoro, *Mali* 82 C3
Sebeş, *Romania* 43 E8
Sebeşului, Munţii, *Romania* .. 43 E8
Sebewaing, *U.S.A.* 108 D4
Sebezh, *Russia* 46 D5
Sebha = Sabhah, *Libya* 79 C8
Ŝébi, *Mali* 82 B4
Şebinkarahisar, *Turkey* 73 B8
Sebiş, *Romania* 42 D7
Sebnitz, *Germany* 24 E10
Sebring, *Fla., U.S.A.* 109 M5
Sebring, *Ohio, U.S.A.* 110 F3
Sebringville, *Canada* 110 C3

Sebta = Ceuta, *N. Afr.* 78 A4
Sebuku, *Indonesia* 62 E5
Sebuku, Teluk, *Malaysia* 62 D5
Sečanj, *Serbia, Yug.* 42 E5
Secchia ➤, *Italy* 28 C8
Sechelt, *Canada* 104 D4
Sechura, Desierto de, *Peru* .. 124 E2
Seclin, *France* 19 B10
Secondigny, *France* 18 F6
Sečovce, *Slovak Rep.* 27 C14
Secretary I., *N.Z.* 91 L1
Secunderabad, *India* 66 L11
Security-Widefield, *U.S.A.* ... 112 F2
Sedalia, *U.S.A.* 112 F8
Sedan, *France* 19 C11
Sedan, *U.S.A.* 113 G6
Sedano, *Spain* 34 C7
Seddon, N.Z. 91 J5
Seddonville, N.Z. 91 J4
Sedé Boqér, *Israel* 75 E3
Sedeh, *Fārs, Iran* 71 D7
Sedeh, *Khorāsān, Iran* 71 C8
Séderon, *France* 21 D9
Sederot, *Israel* 75 D3
Sédhiou, *Senegal* 82 C1
Sedico, *Italy* 29 B9
Sedlčany, *Czech Rep.* 26 B7
Sedley, *Canada* 105 C8
Sedona, *U.S.A.* 115 J8
Sedova, Pik, *Russia* 50 B6
Sedro Woolley, *U.S.A.* 116 B4
Šeduva, *Lithuania* 44 C10
Sędziszów, *Poland* 45 H7
Sędziszów Małopolski, *Poland* . 45 H8
Seebad Ahlbeck, *Germany* ... 24 B10
Seefeld in Tirol, *Austria* 26 D4
Seehausen, *Germany* 24 C7
Seeheim, *Namibia* 88 D2
Seeheim-Jugenheim, *Germany* . 25 F4
Seeis, *Namibia* 88 C2
Seekoei ➤, *S. Africa* 88 E4
Seeley's Bay, *Canada* 111 B8
Seelow, *Germany* 24 C10
Sées, *France* 18 D7
Seesen, *Germany* 24 D6
Seevetal, *Germany* 24 B6
Sefadu, *S. Leone* 82 D2
Seferihisar, *Turkey* 39 C8
Séfeto, *Mali* 82 C3
Sefwi Bekwai, *Ghana* 82 D4
Segamat, *Malaysia* 65 L4
Şegarcea, *Romania* 43 F8
Ségbana, *Benin* 83 C5
Segbwema, S. Leone 82 D2
Seget, *Indonesia* 63 E8
Segonzac, *France* 20 C3
Segorbe, *Spain* 32 F4
Ségou, *Mali* 82 C3
Segovia = Coco ➤, *Cent. Amer.* 120 D3
Segovia, *Spain* 34 E6
Segovia □, *Spain* 34 E6
Segré, *France* 18 E6
Segre ➤, *Spain* 32 D5
Séguéla, *Ivory C.* 82 D3
Séguénéga, *Burkina Faso* 83 C4
Seguin, *U.S.A.* 113 L6
Segundo ➤, *Argentina* 126 C3
Segura ➤, *Spain* 33 G4
Segura, Sierra de, *Spain* 33 G2
Seh Konj, Kūh-e, *Iran* 71 D8
Seh Qal'eh, *Iran* 71 C8
Sehitwa, *Botswana* 88 C3
Sehore, *India* 68 H7
Sehwan, *Pakistan* 68 F2
Șeica Mare, *Romania* 43 D9
Seil, *U.K.* 14 E3
Seiland, *Norway* 8 A20
Seilhac, *France* 20 C5
Seiling, *U.S.A.* 113 G5
Seille ➤, *Moselle, France* 19 C13
Seille ➤, *Saône-et-Loire, France* 19 F11
Sein, Î. de, *France* 18 D2
Seinäjoki, *Finland* 9 E20
Seine ➤, *France* 18 C7
Seine, B. de la, *France* 18 C6
Seine-et-Marne □, *France* ... 19 D10
Seine-Maritime □, *France* ... 18 C7
Seine-St-Denis □, *France* 19 D9
Seini, *Romania* 43 C8
Seirijai, *Lithuania* 44 D10
Seistan = Sīstān, *Asia* 71 D9
Seistan, Daryācheh-ye = Sīstān,
  Daryācheh-ye, *Iran* 71 D9
Sejerø, *Denmark* 11 J5
Sejerø Bugt, *Denmark* 11 J5
Sejny, *Poland* 44 D10
Seka, *Ethiopia* 81 F4
Sekayu, *Indonesia* 62 E2
Seke, *Tanzania* 86 C3
Sekenke, *Tanzania* 86 C3
Seki, *Turkey* 39 E11
Sekondi-Takoradi, *Ghana* 82 E4
Sekota, *Ethiopia* 81 E4
Seksna, *Russia* 46 C10
Sekuma, *Botswana* 88 C3
Selah, *U.S.A.* 114 C3
Selama, *Malaysia* 65 K3
Selárgius, *Italy* 30 C2
Selaru, *Indonesia* 63 F8
Selb, *Germany* 25 E8
Selby, *U.K.* 12 D6
Selby, *U.S.A.* 112 C4
Selca, *Croatia* 29 E13
Selçuk, *Turkey* 39 D9
Selden, *U.S.A.* 112 F4
Sele ➤, *Italy* 31 B7
Selebi-Pikwe, *Botswana* 89 C4

Selemdzha →, Russia 51 D13
Selendi, Manisa, Turkey 39 C10
Selendi, Manisa, Turkey 39 C9
Selenga = Selenge Mörön →, Asia 60 A5
Selenge Mörön →, Asia 60 A5
Selenicë, Albania 40 F3
Selenter See, Germany 24 A6
Sélestat, France 19 D14
Seletan, Tanjung, Indonesia 62 E4
Selevac, Serbia, Yug. 40 B4
Sélibabi, Mauritania 82 B2
Seliger, Ozero, Russia 46 D7
Seligman, U.S.A. 115 J7
Şelim, Turkey 73 B10
Selîma, El Wâhât el, Sudan 80 C2
Selimiye, Turkey 39 D9
Selinda Spillway →, Botswana 88 B3
Selinoús, Greece 38 D3
Selinsgrove, U.S.A. 110 F8
Selizharovo, Russia 46 D7
Selkirk, Canada 105 C9
Selkirk, U.K. 14 F6
Selkirk I., Canada 105 C9
Selkirk Mts., Canada 100 C8
Sellama, Sudan 81 E2
Selliá, Greece 36 D6
Sellières, France 19 F12
Sells, U.S.A. 115 L8
Sellye, Hungary 42 E2
Selma, Ala., U.S.A. 109 J2
Selma, Calif., U.S.A. 116 J7
Selma, N.C., U.S.A. 109 H6
Selmer, U.S.A. 109 H1
Selongey, France 19 E12
Selowandoma Falls, Zimbabwe 87 G3
Selpele, Indonesia 63 E8
Selsey Bill, U.K. 13 G7
Seltso, Russia 46 F8
Seltz, France 19 D15
Selu, Indonesia 63 F8
Sélune →, France 18 D5
Selva = La Selva del Camp, Spain 32 D6
Selva, Argentina 126 B3
Selvas, Brazil 122 D4
Selwyn L., Canada 105 B8
Selwyn Mts., Canada 100 B6
Selwyn Ra., Australia 94 C3
Seman →, Albania 40 F3
Semarang, Indonesia 62 F4
Sembabule, Uganda 86 C3
Şemdinli, Turkey 73 D11
Sémé, Senegal 82 B2
Semeih, Sudan 81 E3
Semenov, Russia 48 B7
Semenovka, Chernihiv, Ukraine 47 F7
Semenovka, Kremenchuk, Ukraine 47 H7
Semeru, Indonesia 63 H15
Semey, Kazakstan 50 D9
Semikarakorskiy, Russia 49 G5
Semiluki, Russia 47 G10
Seminoe Reservoir, U.S.A. 114 F10
Seminole, Okla., U.S.A. 113 H6
Seminole, Tex., U.S.A. 113 J3
Seminole Draw →, U.S.A. 113 J3
Semipalatinsk = Semey, Kazakstan 50 D9
Semirara Is., Phil. 61 F4
Semitau, Indonesia 62 D4
Semiyarka, Kazakstan 50 D8
Semiyarskoye = Semiyarka, Kazakstan 50 D8
Semmering P., Austria 26 D8
Semnān, Iran 71 C7
Semnān □, Iran 71 C7
Semporna, Malaysia 63 D5
Semuda, Indonesia 62 E4
Semur-en-Auxois, France 19 E11
Sen →, Cambodia 62 B3
Sena, Iran 71 D6
Sena, Mozam. 87 F4
Sena Madureira, Brazil 124 E5
Senador Pompeu, Brazil 125 E11
Senaki, Georgia 49 J6
Senanga, Zambia 85 H4
Senatobia, U.S.A. 113 H10
Sencelles, Spain 37 B9
Sendafa, Ethiopia 81 F4
Sendai, Kagoshima, Japan 55 J5
Sendai, Miyagi, Japan 54 E10
Sendai-Wan, Japan 54 E10
Senden, Bayern, Germany 25 G6
Senden, Nordrhein-Westfalen, Germany 24 D3
Sendhwa, India 68 J6
Sene →, Ghana 83 D4
Senec, Slovak Rep. 27 C10
Seneca, U.S.A. 109 H4
Seneca Falls, U.S.A. 111 D8
Seneca L., U.S.A. 110 D8
Senecaville L., U.S.A. 110 G3
Senegal ■, W. Afr. 82 C2
Sénégal →, W. Afr. 82 B1
Senegambia, Africa 76 E2
Senekal, S. Africa 89 D4
Senftenberg, Germany 24 D10
Senga Hill, Zambia 87 D3
Senge Khambab = Indus →, Pakistan 68 G2
Sengiley, Russia 48 D9
Sengua →, Zimbabwe 87 F2
Senhor-do-Bonfim, Brazil 125 F10
Senica, Slovak Rep. 27 C10
Senigállia, Italy 29 E10
Senio →, Italy 29 D9

Senirkent, Turkey 39 C12
Senise, Italy 31 B9
Senj, Croatia 29 D11
Senja, Norway 8 B17
Senkaku-Shotō, Japan 55 L1
Senlis, France 19 C9
Senmonorom, Cambodia 64 F6
Sennâr, Sudan 81 E3
Sennâr □, Sudan 81 E3
Senneterre, Canada 102 C4
Senno, Belarus 46 E5
Sénnori, Italy 30 B1
Seno, Laos 64 D5
Senonches, France 18 D8
Senorbì, Italy 30 C2
Senožeče, Slovenia 29 C11
Sens, France 19 D10
Senta, Serbia, Yug. 42 E5
Sentani, Indonesia 63 E10
Sentery, Dem. Rep. of the Congo 86 D2
Sentinel, U.S.A. 115 K7
Šentjur, Slovenia 29 B12
Senya Beraku, Ghana 83 D4
Seo de Urgel = La Seu d'Urgell, Spain 32 C6
Seohara, India 69 E8
Seonath →, India 69 J10
Seondha, India 69 F8
Seoni, India 69 H8
Seoni Malwa, India 68 H8
Seoul = Sŏul, S. Korea 57 F14
Sepīdān, Iran 71 D7
Sepo-ri, N. Korea 57 E14
Sępólno Krajeńskie, Poland 44 E4
Sepone, Laos 64 D6
Sępopol, Poland 44 D8
Sept-Îles, Canada 103 B6
Septemvri, Bulgaria 41 D8
Sepúlveda, Spain 34 D7
Sequeros, Spain 34 E4
Sequim, U.S.A. 116 B3
Sequoia National Park, U.S.A. 116 J8
Serafimovich, Russia 48 F6
Seraing, Belgium 17 D5
Seraja, Indonesia 65 L7
Serakhis →, Cyprus 36 D11
Seram, Indonesia 63 E7
Seram Sea, Indonesia 63 E7
Seranantsara, Madag. 89 B8
Serang, Indonesia 63 G12
Serasan, Indonesia 65 L7
Seravezza, Italy 28 E7
Şerbettar, Turkey 41 E10
Serbia □, Yugoslavia 40 C5
Şercaia, Romania 43 E10
Serdo, Ethiopia 81 E5
Serdobsk, Russia 48 D7
Sered', Slovak Rep. 27 C10
Seredka, Russia 46 C5
Şereflikoçhisar, Turkey 72 C5
Seregno, Italy 28 C6
Seremban, Malaysia 65 L3
Serengeti Plain, Tanzania 86 C4
Serenje, Zambia 87 E3
Sereth = Siret →, Romania 43 E12
Sergach, Russia 48 C7
Sergen, Turkey 41 E11
Sergino, Russia 50 C7
Sergipe □, Brazil 125 F11
Sergiyev Posad, Russia 46 D10
Seria, Brunei 62 D4
Serian, Malaysia 62 D4
Seriate, Italy 28 C6
Seribu, Kepulauan, Indonesia 62 F3
Sérifontaine, France 19 C8
Sérifos, Greece 38 D6
Sérignan, France 20 E7
Sérigny →, Canada 103 A6
Sérigny, Turkey 72 D4
Serinhisar, Turkey 39 D11
Sermaize-les-Bains, France 19 D11
Sermata, Indonesia 63 F7
Sérmide, Italy 29 D8
Sernovodsk, Russia 48 D10
Sernur, Russia 48 B9
Serock, Poland 45 F8
Serón, Spain 33 H2
Serós, Spain 32 D5
Serov, Russia 50 D7
Serowe, Botswana 88 C4
Serpa, Portugal 35 H3
Serpeddì, Punta, Italy 30 C2
Serpentara, Italy 30 C2
Serpentine Lakes, Australia 93 E4
Serpis →, Spain 33 G4
Serpukhov, Russia 46 E9
Serra de Outes, Spain 34 C2
Serra do Navio, Brazil 125 C8
Serra San Bruno, Italy 31 D9
Serradilla, Spain 34 F4
Sérrai, Greece 40 E7
Sérrai □, Greece 40 E7
Serramanna, Italy 30 C1
Serravalle Scrívia, Italy 28 D5
Serre-Ponçon, L. de, France 21 D10
Serres, France 21 D9
Serrezuela, Argentina 126 C2
Serrinha, Brazil 125 F11
Sertã, Portugal 34 F2
Sertânopolis, Brazil 127 A5
Sêrtar, China 58 A3
Serua, Indonesia 63 F8
Serui, Indonesia 63 E9
Serule, Botswana 88 C4
Sérvia, Greece 40 F6

Serzedelo, Portugal 34 D2
Sese Is., Uganda 86 C3
Sesepe, Indonesia 63 E7
Sesfontein, Namibia 88 B1
Sesheke, Zambia 88 B3
Sésia →, Italy 28 C5
Sesimbra, Portugal 35 G1
S'Espalmador, Spain 37 C7
S'Espardell, Spain 37 C7
Sessa Aurunca, Italy 30 A6
S'Estanyol, Spain 37 B9
Sestao, Spain 32 B2
Sesto Calende, Italy 28 C5
Sesto San Giovanni, Italy 28 C6
Sestri Levante, Italy 28 D6
Sestriere, Italy 28 D3
Sestroretsk, Russia 46 B6
Sestrunj, Croatia 29 D11
Sestu, Italy 30 C2
Setana, Japan 54 C9
Sète, France 20 E7
Sete Lagôas, Brazil 125 G10
Sétif, Algeria 78 A7
Seto, Japan 55 G8
Setonaikai, Japan 55 G6
Settat, Morocco 78 B4
Setting L., Canada 105 C9
Settle, U.K. 12 C5
Settlement Pt., Bahamas 109 M6
Settlers, S. Africa 89 C4
Setúbal, Portugal 35 G2
Setúbal □, Portugal 35 G2
Setúbal, B. de, Portugal 35 G2
Seugne →, France 20 C3
Seul, Lac, Canada 102 B1
Seurre, France 19 F12
Sevan, Armenia 49 K7
Sevan, Ozero = Sevana Lich, Armenia 49 K7
Sevana Lich, Armenia 49 K7
Sevastopol, Ukraine 47 K7
Seven Sisters, Canada 104 C3
Sever →, Spain 35 F3
Sévérac-le-Château, France 20 D7
Severn →, Canada 102 A2
Severn →, U.K. 13 F5
Severn L., Canada 102 B1
Severnaya Zemlya, Russia 51 B10
Severo-Kurilsk, Russia 51 D16
Severo-Yeniseyskiy, Russia 51 C10
Severodonetsk = Syeverodonetsk, Ukraine 47 H10
Severodvinsk, Russia 50 C4
Sevier, U.S.A. 115 G7
Sevier →, U.S.A. 115 G7
Sevier Desert, U.S.A. 114 G7
Sevier L., U.S.A. 114 G7
Sevilla, Spain 35 H5
Sevilla □, Spain 35 H5
Seville = Sevilla, Spain 35 H5
Sevlievo, Bulgaria 41 C9
Sevnica, Slovenia 29 B12
Sèvre-Nantaise →, France 18 E5
Sèvre-Niortaise →, France 20 B3
Sevsk, Russia 47 F8
Sewa →, S. Leone 82 D2
Sewani, India 68 E6
Seward, Alaska, U.S.A. 100 B5
Seward, Nebr., U.S.A. 112 E6
Seward, Pa., U.S.A. 110 F5
Seward Peninsula, U.S.A. 100 B3
Sewell, Chile 126 C1
Sewer, Indonesia 63 F8
Sewickley, U.S.A. 110 F4
Sexsmith, Canada 104 B5
Seychelles ■, Ind. Oc. 52 K9
Seyðisfjörður, Iceland 8 D6
Seydişehir, Turkey 72 D4
Seydvān, Iran 70 B5
Seyhan →, Turkey 70 D6
Seyhan Barajı, Turkey 72 D6
Seyitgazi, Turkey 39 B12
Seyitömer, Turkey 39 B11
Seym →, Ukraine 47 G7
Seymen, Turkey 41 E11
Seymour, Australia 95 F4
Seymour, S. Africa 89 E4
Seymour, Conn., U.S.A. 111 E11
Seymour, Ind., U.S.A. 108 F3
Seymour, Tex., U.S.A. 113 J5
Seyne, France 21 D10
Seyssel, France 21 C9
Sežana, Slovenia 29 C10
Sézanne, France 19 D10
Sezze, Italy 30 A6
Sfântu Gheorghe, Covasna, Romania 43 E10
Sfântu Gheorghe, Tulcea, Romania 43 F14
Sfântu Gheorghe, Brațul →, Romania 43 F14
Sfax, Tunisia 79 B8
Sha Xi →, China 59 D12
Shaanxi □, China 56 G5
Shaba = Katanga □, Dem. Rep. of the Congo 86 D2
Shabla, Bulgaria 41 C12
Shabogamo L., Canada 103 B6
Shabunda, Dem. Rep. of the Congo 86 C2
Shache, China 60 C2
Shackleton Ice Shelf, Antarctica 5 C8
Shackleton Inlet, Antarctica 5 E11
Shādegān, Iran 71 D6
Shadi, China 59 D10

Shadi, India 69 C7
Shadrinsk, Russia 50 D7
Shadyside, U.S.A. 110 G4
Shaffa, Nigeria 83 C7
Shafter, U.S.A. 117 K7
Shaftesbury, U.K. 13 F5
Shagamu, Nigeria 83 D5
Shagram, Pakistan 69 A5
Shah Alizai, Pakistan 68 E2
Shah Bunder, Pakistan 68 G2
Shahabad, Punjab, India 68 D7
Shahabad, Raj., India 68 G7
Shahabad, Ut. P., India 69 F8
Shahadpur, Pakistan 68 G3
Shahba, Syria 75 C5
Shahdād, Iran 71 D8
Shahdād, Namakzār-e, Iran 71 D8
Shahdadkot, Pakistan 68 F2
Shahdol, India 69 H9
Shahe, China 56 F8
Shahganj, India 69 F10
Shahgarh, India 66 F6
Shahjahanpur, India 69 F8
Shahpur, India 68 H7
Shahpur, Baluchistan, Pakistan 68 E3
Shahpur, Punjab, Pakistan 68 C5
Shahpur Chakar, Pakistan 68 G3
Shahpura, Mad. P., India 69 H9
Shahpura, Raj., India 68 G6
Shahr-e Bābak, Iran 71 D7
Shahr-e Kord, Iran 71 C6
Shāhrakht, Iran 71 C9
Shahrig, Pakistan 68 D2
Shahukou, China 56 D7
Shaikhabad, Afghan. 68 B3
Shajapur, India 68 H7
Shakargarh, Pakistan 68 C6
Shakawe, Botswana 88 B3
Shaker Heights, U.S.A. 110 E3
Shakhty, Russia 49 G5
Shakhunya, Russia 48 B8
Shaki, Nigeria 83 D5
Shakir, Egypt 80 B3
Shala, L., Ethiopia 81 F4
Shali, Russia 49 J7
Shallow Lake, Canada 110 B3
Shalqar, Kazakstan 50 E6
Shalskiy, Russia 46 B8
Shaluli Shan, China 58 B2
Shām, Iran 71 E8
Shām, Bādiyat ash, Asia 70 C3
Shamāl Bahr el Ghazal □, Sudan 81 F2
Shamāl Dârfûr □, Sudan 81 E2
Shamāl Kordofân □, Sudan 81 E3
Shamāl Sīnî □, Egypt 75 E2
Shamattawa, Canada 102 A1
Shamattawa →, Canada 102 A2
Shambe, Sudan 81 F3
Shambu, Ethiopia 81 F4
Shamīl, Iran 71 E8
Shamkhor = Şämkir, Azerbaijan 49 K8
Shāmkūh, Iran 71 C8
Shamli, India 68 E7
Shammar, Jabal, Si. Arabia 70 E4
Shamo = Gobi, Asia 56 C6
Shamo, L., Ethiopia 81 F4
Shamokin, U.S.A. 111 F8
Shamrock, U.S.A. 113 H4
Shamva, Zimbabwe 87 F3
Shan □, Burma 67 J21
Shan Xian, China 56 G9
Shanan →, Ethiopia 81 F5
Shanchengzhen, China 57 C13
Shāndak, Iran 71 D9
Shandon, U.S.A. 116 K6
Shandong □, China 57 G10
Shandong Bandao, China 57 F11
Shang Xian = Shangzhou, China 56 H5
Shanga, Nigeria 83 C5
Shangalowe, Dem. Rep. of the Congo 87 E2
Shangani, Zimbabwe 89 B4
Shangani →, Zimbabwe 87 F2
Shangbancheng, China 57 D10
Shangcheng, China 59 B10
Shangchuan Dao, China 59 G9
Shangdu, China 56 D7
Shanggao, China 59 C10
Shanghai, China 59 B13
Shanghai Shi □, China 59 B13
Shanghang, China 59 E11
Shanghe, China 57 F9
Shanglin, China 58 F7
Shangnan, China 56 H6
Shangqiu, China 56 G8
Shangrao, China 59 C11
Shangshui, China 56 H8
Shangsi, China 58 F6
Shangyou, China 59 E10
Shangyu, China 59 B13
Shangzhi, China 57 B14
Shangzhou, China 56 H5
Shanhetun, China 57 B14
Shani, Nigeria 83 C7
Shannon, N.Z. 91 J5
Shannon →, Ireland 15 D2
Shannon, Mouth of the, Ireland 15 D2
Shannon Airport, Ireland 15 D3
Shansi = Shanxi □, China 56 F7
Shantar, Ostrov Bolshoy, Russia 51 D14
Shantipur, India 69 H13
Shantou, China 59 F11
Shantung = Shandong □, China 57 G10
Shanwei, China 59 F10
Shanxi □, China 56 F7
Shanyang, China 56 H5
Shanyin, China 56 E7

Shaodong, China 59 D8
Shaoguan, China 59 E9
Shaoshan, China 59 D9
Shaowu, China 59 D11
Shaoxing, China 59 C13
Shaoyang, Hunan, China 59 D8
Shaoyang, Hunan, China 59 D8
Shap, U.K. 12 C5
Shapinsay, U.K. 14 B6
Shaqq el Gi'eifer →, Sudan 81 D2
Shaqra', Si. Arabia 70 E5
Shaqrā', Yemen 74 E4
Sharafa, Sudan 81 E2
Sharafkhāneh, Iran 70 B5
Sharbot Lake, Canada 111 B8
Shari, Japan 54 C12
Sharjah = Ash Shāriqah, U.A.E. 71 E7
Shark B., Australia 93 E1
Sharm el Sheikh, Egypt 80 B3
Sharon, Mass., U.S.A. 111 D13
Sharon, Pa., U.S.A. 110 E4
Sharon Springs, Kans., U.S.A. 112 F4
Sharon Springs, N.Y., U.S.A. 111 D10
Sharp Pt., Australia 94 A3
Sharpe L., Canada 102 B1
Sharpsville, U.S.A. 110 E4
Sharq el Istiwa'iya □, Sudan 81 G3
Sharya, Russia 48 A7
Shasha, Ethiopia 81 F4
Shashemene, Ethiopia 81 F4
Shashi, Botswana 89 C4
Shashi, China 59 B9
Shashi →, Africa 87 G2
Shasta, Mt., U.S.A. 114 F2
Shasta L., U.S.A. 114 F2
Shatawi, Sudan 81 E3
Shatsk, Russia 48 C5
Shatt al Arab = Arab, Shatt al →, Asia 71 D6
Shatura, Russia 46 E10
Shaumyani = Shulaveri, Georgia 49 K7
Shaunavon, Canada 105 D7
Shaver L., U.S.A. 116 H7
Shaw →, Australia 92 D2
Shaw I., Australia 94 C4
Shawanaga, Canada 110 A4
Shawangunk Mts., U.S.A. 111 E10
Shawano, U.S.A. 108 C1
Shawinigan, Canada 102 C5
Shawnee, U.S.A. 113 H6
Shay Gap, Australia 92 D3
Shayang, China 59 B9
Shaybārā, Si. Arabia 70 E3
Shayib el Banat, Gebel, Egypt 80 B3
Shaykh, J. ash, Lebanon 75 B4
Shaykh Miskīn, Syria 75 C5
Shaykh Sa'īd, Iraq 70 C5
Shchekino, Russia 46 E9
Shcherbakov = Rybinsk, Russia 46 C10
Shchigry, Russia 47 G9
Shchors, Ukraine 47 G6
Shchuchinsk, Kazakstan 50 D8
She Xian, Anhui, China 59 C12
She Xian, Hebei, China 56 F7
Shebekino, Russia 47 G9
Shebele = Scebeli, Wabi →, Somali Rep. 74 G3
Sheboygan, U.S.A. 108 D2
Shebshi Mts., Nigeria 83 D7
Shediac, Canada 103 C7
Sheelin, L., Ireland 15 C4
Sheep Haven, Ireland 15 A4
Sheerness, U.K. 13 F8
Sheet Harbour, Canada 103 D7
Sheffield, U.K. 12 D6
Sheffield, Ala., U.S.A. 109 H2
Sheffield, Mass., U.S.A. 111 D11
Sheffield, Pa., U.S.A. 110 E5
Shelburne, N.S., Canada 103 D6
Shelburne, Ont., Canada 102 D3
Shelburne, U.S.A. 111 B11
Shelburne B., Australia 94 A3
Shelburne Falls, U.S.A. 111 D12
Shelby, Mich., U.S.A. 108 D2
Shelby, Miss., U.S.A. 113 J9
Shelby, Mont., U.S.A. 114 B8
Shelby, N.C., U.S.A. 109 H5
Shelby, Ohio, U.S.A. 110 F2
Shelbyville, Ill., U.S.A. 112 F10
Shelbyville, Ind., U.S.A. 108 F3
Shelbyville, Ky., U.S.A. 108 F3
Shelbyville, Tenn., U.S.A. 109 H2
Sheldon, U.S.A. 112 D7
Sheldrake, Canada 103 B7
Shelengo, Khawr →, Sudan 81 E2
Shelikhova, Zaliv, Russia 51 D16
Shell Lakes, Australia 93 E4
Shellbrook, Canada 105 C7
Shellharbour, Australia 95 E5
Shelon →, Russia 46 C6
Shelter I., U.S.A. 111 E12
Shelton, Conn., U.S.A. 111 E11
Shelton, Wash., U.S.A. 116 C3
Shemakha = Şamaxi, Azerbaijan 49 K9
Shemri, Albania 57 F11
Shemsi, Sudan 80 D2
Shen Xian, China 56 F8
Shenandoah, Iowa, U.S.A. 112 E7
Shenandoah, Pa., U.S.A. 111 F8
Shenandoah, Va., U.S.A. 108 F6

Shenandoah →, U.S.A.	108 F7	Shīndand, Afghan.	66 C3
Shenandoah National Park, U.S.A.	108 F6	Shinglehouse, U.S.A.	110 E6
Shenchi, China	56 E7	Shingū, Japan	55 H7
Shendam, Nigeria	83 D6	Shingwidzi, S. Africa	89 C5
Shendî, Sudan	81 D3	Shinjō, Japan	54 E10
Shenge, S. Leone	82 D2	Shinkafe, Nigeria	83 C6
Shengfang, China	56 E9	Shinshār, Syria	75 A5
Shëngjergj, Albania	40 E4	Shinyanga, Tanzania	86 C3
Shëngjin, Albania	40 E3	Shinyanga □, Tanzania	86 C3
Shengzhou, China	59 C13	Shio-no-Misaki, Japan	55 H7
Shenjingzi, China	57 B13	Shiogama, Japan	54 E10
Shenmu, China	56 E6	Shiojiri, Japan	55 F8
Shennongjia, China	59 B8	Shipchenski Prokhod, Bulgaria	41 D9
Shenqiu, China	56 H8	Shiping, China	58 F4
Shensi = Shaanxi □, China	56 G5	Shippagan, Canada	103 C7
Shenyang, China	57 D12	Shippensburg, U.S.A.	110 F7
Shenzhen, China	59 F10	Shippenville, U.S.A.	110 E5
Sheo, India	68 F4	Shiprock, U.S.A.	115 H9
Sheopur Kalan, India	66 G10	Shiqian, China	58 D7
Shepetivka, Ukraine	47 G4	Shiqma, N. →, Israel	75 D3
Shepetovka = Shepetivka, Ukraine	47 G4	Shiquan, China	56 H5
Shepparton, Australia	95 F4	Shiquan He = Indus →, Pakistan	68 G2
Sheppey, I. of, U.K.	13 F8	Shīr Kūh, Iran	71 D7
Shepton Mallet, U.K.	13 F5	Shiragami-Misaki, Japan	54 D10
Sheqi, China	56 H7	'Shirakawa, Fukushima, Japan	55 F10
Sher Qila, Pakistan	69 A6	Shirakawa, Gifu, Japan	55 F8
Sherab, Sudan	81 E1	Shirane-San, Gumma, Japan	55 F9
Sherborne, U.K.	13 G5	Shirane-San, Yamanashi, Japan	55 G9
Sherbro →, S. Leone	82 D2	Shiraoi, Japan	54 C10
Sherbro I., S. Leone	82 D2	Shīrāz, Iran	71 D7
Sherbrooke, N.S., Canada	103 C7	Shirbīn, Egypt	80 H7
Sherbrooke, Qué., Canada	103 C5	Shire →, Africa	87 F4
Sherburne, U.S.A.	111 D9	Shiretoko-Misaki, Japan	54 B12
Shereik, Sudan	80 D3	Shirinab →, Pakistan	68 D2
Shergarh, India	68 F5	Shiriya-Zaki, Japan	54 D10
Sherghati, India	69 G11	Shiroishi, Japan	54 F10
Sheridan, Ark., U.S.A.	113 H8	Shīrvān, Iran	71 B8
Sheridan, Wyo., U.S.A.	114 D10	Shirwa, L. = Chilwa, L., Malawi	87 F4
Sheringham, U.K.	12 E9	Shishi, China	59 E12
Sherkin I., Ireland	15 E2	Shishou, China	59 C9
Sherkot, India	69 E8	Shitai, China	59 B11
Sherman, U.S.A.	113 J6	Shivpuri, India	68 G7
Sherpur, India	69 G10	Shixian, China	57 C15
Sherridon, Canada	105 B8	Shixing, China	59 E10
Sherwood Forest, U.K.	12 D6	Shiyan, China	59 A8
Sherwood Park, Canada	104 C6	Shiyata, Egypt	80 B2
Sheslay →, Canada	104 B2	Shizhu, China	58 C7
Shethanei L., Canada	105 B9	Shizong, China	58 E5
Shetland □, U.K.	14 A7	Shizuishan, China	56 E4
Shetland Is., U.K.	14 A7	Shizuoka, Japan	55 G9
Shetrunji →, India	68 J5	Shizuoka □, Japan	55 G9
Shewa □, Ethiopia	81 F4	Shklov = Shklow, Belarus	46 E6
Shewa Gimira, Ethiopia	81 F4	Shklow, Belarus	46 E6
Sheyenne →, U.S.A.	112 B6	Shkodër = Shkodër, Albania	40 D3
Shibâm, Yemen	74 D4	Shkodër, Albania	40 D3
Shibata, Japan	54 F9	Shkumbini →, Albania	40 E3
Shibecha, Japan	54 C12	Shmidta, Ostrov, Russia	51 A10
Shibetsu, Japan	54 B11	Shō-Gawa →, Japan	55 F8
Shibîn el Kôm, Egypt	80 H7	Shoal L., Canada	105 D9
Shibîn el Qanâtir, Egypt	80 H7	Shoal Lake, Canada	105 C8
Shibing, China	58 D7	Shōdo-Shima, Japan	55 G7
Shibogama L., Canada	102 B2	Sholapur = Solapur, India	66 L9
Shibushi, Japan	55 J5	Shologontsy, Russia	51 C12
Shicheng, China	59 D11	Shōmrōn, West Bank	75 C4
Shickshinny, U.S.A.	111 E8	Shoreham by Sea, U.K.	13 G7
Shickshock Mts. = Chic-Chocs, Mts., Canada	103 C6	Shori →, Pakistan	68 E3
Shidao, China	57 F12	Shorkot Road, Pakistan	68 D5
Shidian, China	58 E2	Shoshone, Calif., U.S.A.	117 K10
Shido, Japan	55 G7	Shoshone, Idaho, U.S.A.	114 E6
Shiel, L., U.K.	14 E3	Shoshone L., U.S.A.	114 D8
Shield, C., Australia	94 A2	Shoshone Mts., U.S.A.	114 G5
Shieli, Kazakstan	50 E7	Shoshong, Botswana	88 C4
Shifang, China	58 B5	Shoshoni, U.S.A.	114 E9
Shiga □, Japan	55 G8	Shostka, Ukraine	47 G7
Shigu, China	58 D2	Shou Xian, China	59 A11
Shiguaigou, China	56 D6	Shouchang, China	59 C12
Shihchiachuangi = Shijiazhuang, China	56 E8	Shouguang, China	57 F10
Shijak, Albania	40 E3	Shouning, China	59 D12
Shijiazhuang, China	56 E8	Shouyang, China	56 F7
Shijiu Hu, China	59 B12	Show Low, U.S.A.	115 J9
Shikarpur, India	68 E8	Shpola, Ukraine	47 H6
Shikarpur, Pakistan	68 F3	Shreveport, U.S.A.	113 J8
Shikohabad, India	69 F8	Shrewsbury, U.K.	13 E5
Shikoku □, Japan	55 H6	Shri Mohangarh, India	68 F4
Shikoku-Sanchi, Japan	55 H6	Shrirampur, India	69 H13
Shiliguri, India	67 F16	Shropshire □, U.K.	13 E5
Shilka, Russia	51 D12	Shū, Kazakstan	50 E8
Shilka →, Russia	51 D13	Shū →, Kazakstan	52 E10
Shillelagh, Ireland	15 D5	Shuangbai, China	58 E3
Shillington, U.S.A.	111 F9	Shuangcheng, China	57 B14
Shillong, India	67 G17	Shuangfeng, China	59 D9
Shilo, West Bank	75 C4	Shuanggou, China	57 G9
Shilong, China	59 F9	Shuangjiang, China	58 F2
Shilou, China	56 F6	Shuangliao, China	57 C12
Shilovo, Russia	48 C5	Shuangshanzi, China	57 D10
Shimabara, Japan	55 H5	Shuangyang, China	57 C13
Shimada, Japan	55 G9	Shuangyashan, China	60 B8
Shimane □, Japan	55 G6	Shubra Khit, Egypt	80 H7
Shimanovsk, Russia	51 D13	Shucheng, China	59 B11
Shimen, China	59 C8	Shugozero, Russia	46 C8
Shimenjie, China	59 C11	Shuguri Falls, Tanzania	87 D4
Shimian, China	58 C4	Shuiji, China	59 D12
Shimizu, Japan	55 G9	Shuiye, China	56 F8
Shimodate, Japan	55 F9	Shujalpur, India	68 H7
Shimoga, India	66 N9	Shukpa Kunzang, India	69 B8
Shimoni, Kenya	86 C4	Shulan, China	57 B14
Shimonoseki, Japan	55 H5	Shulaveri, Georgia	49 K7
Shimpuru Rapids, Angola	88 B2	Shule, China	60 C2
Shimsk, Russia	46 C6	Shumagin Is., U.S.A.	100 C4
Shin, L., U.K.	14 C4	Shumen, Bulgaria	41 C10
Shinan, China	58 F7	Shumerlya, Russia	48 C8
Shinano-Gawa →, Japan	55 F9	Shumikha, Russia	50 D7
Shināş, Oman	71 E8	Shunchang, China	59 D11
		Shunde, China	59 F9
		Shungay, Kazakstan	49 F8
		Shuo Xian = Shuozhou, China	56 E7
		Shuozhou, China	56 E7

Shūr →, Fārs, Iran	71 D7	Siemiatycze, Poland	45 F9
Shūr →, Kermān, Iran	71 D8	Siemreab, Cambodia	64 F4
Shūr →, Yazd, Iran	71 D7	Siena, Italy	29 E8
Shūr Āb, Iran	71 C6	Sieniawa, Poland	45 H9
Shūr Gaz, Iran	71 D8	Sieradz, Poland	45 G5
Shūrāb, Iran	71 C8	Sieraków, Poland	45 F3
Shūrjestān, Iran	71 D7	Sierck-les-Bains, France	19 C13
Shūsf, Iran	71 D9	Sierning, Austria	26 C7
Shūsh, Iran	73 F13	Sierpc, Poland	45 F6
Shūshtar, Iran	71 D6	Sierra Blanca, U.S.A.	115 L11
Shuswap L., Canada	104 C5	Sierra Blanca Peak, U.S.A.	115 K11
Shuya, Russia	48 B5	Sierra City, U.S.A.	116 F6
Shuyang, China	57 G10	Sierra Colorada, Argentina	128 E3
Shūzū, Iran	71 D7	Sierra de Yeguas, Spain	35 H6
Shwebo, Burma	67 H19	Sierra Gorda, Chile	126 A2
Shwegu, Burma	67 G20	Sierra Leone ■, W. Afr.	82 D2
Shweli →, Burma	67 H20	Sierra Madre, Mexico	119 D6
Shymkent, Kazakstan	50 E7	Sierra Mojada, Mexico	118 B4
Shyok, India	69 B8	Sierra Nevada, Spain	35 H7
Shyok →, Pakistan	69 B6	Sierra Nevada, U.S.A.	116 H8
Si Chon, Thailand	65 H2	Sierra Vista, U.S.A.	115 L8
Si Kiang = Xi Jiang →, China	59 F9	Sierraville, U.S.A.	116 F6
Si-ngan = Xi'an, China	56 G5	Sierre, Switz.	25 J3
Si Prachan, Thailand	64 E3	Sifani, Ethiopia	81 E5
Si Racha, Thailand	64 F3	Sifié, Ivory C.	82 D3
Si Xian, China	57 H9	Sífnos, Greece	38 E6
Siahaf →, Pakistan	68 E3	Sifton, Canada	105 C8
Siahan Range, Pakistan	66 F4	Sifton Pass, Canada	104 B3
Siaksriindrapura, Indonesia	62 D2	Sigean, France	20 E6
Sialkot, Pakistan	68 C6	Sighetu-Marmaţiei, Romania	43 C8
Siam = Thailand ■, Asia	64 E4	Sighişoara, Romania	43 D9
Sian = Xi'an, China	56 G5	Sigli, Indonesia	62 C1
Sianów, Poland	44 D3	Siglufjörður, Iceland	8 C4
Siantan, Indonesia	62 D3	Sigmaringen, Germany	25 G5
Siāreh, Iran	71 D9	Signa, Italy	28 E8
Siargao I., Phil.	61 G7	Signakhi = Tsnori, Georgia	49 K7
Siari, Pakistan	69 B7	Signal, U.S.A.	117 L13
Siasi, Phil.	63 C6	Signal Pk., U.S.A.	117 M12
Siasi I., Phil.	61 J4	Signy-l'Abbaye, France	19 C11
Siátista, Greece	40 F5	Sigsig, Ecuador	124 D3
Siau, Indonesia	63 D7	Sigüenza, Spain	32 D2
Šiauliai, Lithuania	9 J20	Siguiri, Guinea	82 C3
Šiauliai □, Lithuania	44 C10	Sigulda, Latvia	9 H21
Siazan = Siyäzän, Azerbaijan	49 K9	Sihanoukville = Kampong Saom, Cambodia	65 G4
Sībā, Gebel el, Egypt	70 E2	Sihora, India	69 H9
Sibay, L., S. Africa	89 D5	Sihui, China	59 F9
Sibdu, Sudan	81 E2	Siikajoki →, Finland	8 D21
Sibenik, Croatia	29 E12	Siilinjärvi, Finland	8 E22
Siberia, Russia	4 D13	Siirt, Turkey	73 D9
Siberut, Indonesia	62 E1	Sijarira Ra., Zimbabwe	87 F2
Sibi, Pakistan	68 E2	Sika, India	68 H3
Sibil = Oksibil, Indonesia	63 E10	Sikao, Thailand	65 J2
Sibiti, Congo	84 E2	Sikar, India	68 F6
Sibiu, Romania	43 E9	Sikasso, Mali	82 C3
Sibiu □, Romania	43 E9	Sikeston, U.S.A.	113 G10
Sibley, U.S.A.	112 D7	Sikhote Alin, Khrebet, Russia	51 E14
Sibolga, Indonesia	62 D1	Sikhote Alin Ra. = Sikhote Alin, Khrebet, Russia	51 E14
Sibsagar, India	67 F19	Sikiá, Greece	40 F7
Sibu, Malaysia	62 D4	Síkinos, Greece	39 E7
Sibuco, Phil.	61 H5	Sikkani Chief →, Canada	104 B4
Sibuguey B., Phil.	61 H5	Sikkim □, India	67 F16
Sibut, C.A.R.	84 C3	Siklós, Hungary	42 E3
Sibutu, Phil.	63 D5	Sikotu-Ko, Japan	54 C10
Sibutu Group, Phil.	61 J3	Sil →, Spain	34 C3
Sibutu Passage, E. Indies	63 D5	Silacayoapan, Mexico	119 D5
Sibuyan I., Phil.	61 E5	Šilalė, Lithuania	44 C9
Sibuyan Sea, Phil.	61 E5	Silandro, Italy	28 B7
Sic, Romania	43 D8	Silawad, India	68 J6
Sicamous, Canada	104 C5	Silay, Phil.	61 F5
Siccus →, Australia	95 E2	Silba, Croatia	29 D11
Sichuan □, China	58 B5	Silchar, India	67 G18
Sichuan Pendi, China	58 B5	Şile, Turkey	41 E13
Sicilia □, Italy	31 E7	Siler City, U.S.A.	109 H6
Sicilia □, Italy	31 E7	Silgarhi Doti, Nepal	69 E9
Sicily = Sicilia, Italy	31 E7	Silghat, India	67 F18
Sicuani, Peru	124 F4	Sili, Burkina Faso	82 C4
Šid, Serbia, Yug.	42 E4	Silifke, Turkey	70 B2
Sidamo □, Ethiopia	81 G4	Siliguri = Shiliguri, India	67 F16
Sidaouet, Niger	83 B6	Siling Co, China	60 C3
Sidári, Greece	36 A3	Silistea Nouă, Romania	43 F9
Siddhapur, India	68 H5	Silistra, Bulgaria	41 B11
Siddipet, India	66 K11	Silivri, Turkey	41 E12
Sidensjö, Sweden	10 A12	Siljan, Sweden	10 D8
Sidéradougou, Burkina Faso	82 C4	Siljansnäs, Sweden	10 D8
Siderno, Italy	31 D9	Silkeborg, Denmark	11 H3
Sidhauli, India	69 F9	Silkwood, Australia	94 B4
Sídheros, Ákra, Greece	36 D8	Silla, Spain	33 F4
Sidhi, India	69 G9	Sillajhuay, Cordillera, Chile	124 G5
Sidhirókastron, Greece	40 E7	Silleda, Spain	34 C2
Sîdi Abd el Rahmân, Egypt	80 A2	Sillé-le-Guillaume, France	18 D6
Sîdi Barrâni, Egypt	80 A2	Silloth, U.K.	12 C4
Sidi-bel-Abbès, Algeria	78 A5	Sílo, Greece	38 C5
Sidi Haneish, Egypt	80 A2	Siloam Springs, U.S.A.	113 G7
Sidi Ifni, Morocco	78 C3	Silopi, Turkey	73 D10
Sidi Omar, Egypt	80 A1	Silsbee, U.S.A.	113 K7
Sidlaw Hills, U.K.	14 E5	Siluko, Nigeria	83 D6
Sidley, Mt., Antarctica	5 D14	Šilutė, Lithuania	9 J19
Sidmouth, U.K.	13 G4	Silva Porto = Kuito, Angola	85 G3
Sidmouth, C., Australia	94 A3	Silvan, Turkey	73 C9
Sidney, Canada	104 D4	Silvani, India	69 H8
Sidney, Mont., U.S.A.	112 B2	Silver City, U.S.A.	115 K9
Sidney, N.Y., U.S.A.	111 D9	Silver Cr. →, U.S.A.	114 E4
Sidney, Nebr., U.S.A.	112 E3	Silver Creek, U.S.A.	110 D5
Sidney, Ohio, U.S.A.	108 E3	Silver L., U.S.A.	116 G6
Sidney Lanier, L., U.S.A.	109 H4	Silver Lake, Calif., U.S.A.	117 K10
Sido, Mali	82 C3	Silver Lake, Oreg., U.S.A.	114 E3
Sidoarjo, Indonesia	63 G15	Silverdalen, Sweden	11 G9
Sidon = Saydā, Lebanon	75 B4	Silverton, Colo., U.S.A.	115 H10
Sidra, G. of = Surt, Khalīj, Libya	79 B9	Silverton, Tex., U.S.A.	113 H4
Siedlce, Poland	45 F9	Silves, Portugal	35 H2
Sieg →, Germany	24 E4	Silvi Marina, Italy	29 F11
Siegburg, Germany	24 E3	Silvies →, U.S.A.	114 E4
Siegen, Germany	24 E4	Silvretta horn, Switz.	28 B7
Siem Pang, Cambodia	64 E6	Silwa Bahari, Egypt	80 C3
Siem Reap = Siemreab, Cambodia	64 F4		

Silz, Austria	26 D3
Simaltala, India	69 G12
Simanggang = Bandar Sri Aman, Malaysia	62 D4
Simao, China	58 F3
Simard, L., Canada	102 C4
Sīmareh →, Iran	73 F12
Simav, Turkey	39 B10
Simav →, Turkey	41 F12
Simav Dağları, Turkey	39 B10
Simba, Tanzania	86 C4
Simbach, Germany	25 G9
Simbirsk, Russia	48 C9
Simbo, Tanzania	86 C2
Simcoe, Canada	102 D3
Simcoe, L., Canada	102 D4
Simdega, India	69 H11
Simeonovgrad, Bulgaria	41 D9
Simeria, Romania	42 E8
Simeto →, Italy	31 E8
Simeulue, Indonesia	62 D1
Simferopol, Ukraine	47 K8
Sími, Greece	39 E9
Simi Valley, U.S.A.	117 L8
Simikot, Nepal	69 E9
Simitli, Bulgaria	40 E7
Simla, India	68 D7
Simlångsdalen, Sweden	11 H7
Şimleu-Silvaniei, Romania	42 C7
Simmern, Germany	25 F3
Simmie, Canada	105 D7
Simmler, U.S.A.	117 K7
Simnas, Lithuania	44 D10
Simojoki →, Finland	8 D21
Simojovel, Mexico	119 D6
Simonette →, Canada	104 B5
Simonstown, S. Africa	88 E2
Simontornya, Hungary	42 D3
Simplonpass, Switz.	25 J4
Simplontunnel, Switz.	25 J4
Simpson Desert, Australia	94 D2
Simpson Pen., Canada	101 B11
Simpungdong, N. Korea	57 D15
Simrishamn, Sweden	11 J8
Simsbury, U.S.A.	111 E12
Simushir, Ostrov, Russia	51 E16
Sin Cowe I., S. China Sea	62 C4
Sinabang, Indonesia	62 D1
Sinadogo, Somali Rep.	74 F4
Sinai = Es Sînâ', Egypt	75 F3
Sinai, Mt. = Mûsa, Gebel, Egypt	70 D2
Sinai Peninsula, Egypt	75 F3
Sinaia, Romania	43 E10
Sinaloa □, Mexico	118 C3
Sinaloa de Leyva, Mexico	118 B3
Sinalunga, Italy	29 E8
Sinan, China	58 D7
Sînandrei, Romania	42 E6
Sinarádhes, Greece	36 A3
Sincan, Turkey	72 B5
Sincanlı, Turkey	39 C12
Sincelejo, Colombia	124 B3
Sinch'ang, N. Korea	57 D15
Sinchang, N. Korea	57 E14
Sinclair, U.S.A.	114 F10
Sinclair Mills, Canada	104 C4
Sinclair's B., U.K.	14 C5
Sinclairville, U.S.A.	110 D5
Sincorá, Serra do, Brazil	125 F10
Sind, Pakistan	68 G3
Sind □, Pakistan	68 G3
Sind →, Jammu & Kashmir, India	69 B6
Sind →, Mad. P., India	69 F8
Sind Sagar Doab, Pakistan	68 D4
Sindal, Denmark	11 G4
Sindangan, Phil.	61 G5
Sindangbarang, Indonesia	63 G12
Sinde, Zambia	87 F2
Sindelfingen, Germany	25 G4
Sındırgı, Turkey	39 B10
Sindou, Burkina Faso	82 C3
Sindri, India	69 H12
Sine →, Senegal	82 C1
Sinegorskiy, Russia	49 G5
Sinelnikove = Synelnykove, Ukraine	47 H8
Sinendé, Benin	83 C5
Sines, Portugal	35 H2
Sines, C. de, Portugal	35 H2
Sineu, Spain	37 B10
Sinfra, Ivory C.	82 D3
Sing Buri, Thailand	64 E3
Singa, Sudan	81 E3
Singapore ■, Asia	65 M4
Singapore, Straits of, Asia	65 M5
Singaraja, Indonesia	62 F5
Singen, Germany	25 H4
Singida, Tanzania	86 C3
Singida □, Tanzania	86 D3
Singitikós Kólpos, Greece	40 F7
Singkaling Hkamti, Burma	67 G19
Singkang, Indonesia	63 E6
Singkawang, Indonesia	62 D3
Singkep, Indonesia	62 E2
Singleton, Australia	95 E5
Singleton, Mt., N. Terr., Australia	92 D5
Singleton, Mt., W. Austral., Australia	93 E2
Singö, Sweden	10 D12
Singoli, India	68 G6
Singora = Songkhla, Thailand	65 J3
Singosan, N. Korea	57 E14
Sinhung, N. Korea	57 D14
Siniátsikon, Óros, Greece	40 F5

Siniscóla, Italy ... 30 B2
Sinj, Croatia ... 29 E13
Sinjai, Indonesia ... 63 F6
Sinjajevina, Montenegro, Yug. . 40 D3
Sinjär, Iraq ... 70 B4
Sinkat, Sudan ... 80 D4
Sinkiang Uighur = Xinjiang
  Uygur Zizhiqu □, China 60 B3
Sinmak, N. Korea ... 57 E14
Sínnai, Italy ... 30 C2
Sinnamary, Fr. Guiana ... 125 B8
Sinni →, Italy ... 31 B9
Sinnuris, Egypt ... 80 J7
Sinoie, Lacul, Romania ... 43 F13
Sinop, Turkey ... 72 A6
Sinor, India ... 68 J5
Sinp'o, N. Korea ... 57 E15
Sinsheim, Germany ... 25 F4
Sinsk, Russia ... 51 C13
Sintang, Indonesia ... 62 D4
Sinton, U.S.A. ... 113 L6
Sintra, Portugal ... 35 G1
Sinúiju, N. Korea ... 57 D13
Sinyukha →, Ukraine ... 47 H6
Sinzig, Germany ... 24 E3
Sio →, Hungary ... 42 D3
Siocon, Phil. ... 61 H5
Siófok, Hungary ... 42 D3
Sion, Switz. ... 25 J3
Sion Mills, U.K. ... 15 B4
Sioux City, U.S.A. ... 112 D6
Sioux Falls, U.S.A. ... 112 D6
Sioux Lookout, Canada ... 102 B1
Sioux Narrows, Canada ... 105 D10
Sipalay, Phil. ... 61 G5
Šipan, Croatia ... 40 D1
Siping, China ... 57 C13
Sipiwesk L., Canada ... 105 B9
Sipra →, India ... 68 H6
Sipura, Indonesia ... 62 E1
Siquia →, Nic. ... 120 D3
Siquijor, Phil. ... 61 G5
Siquirres, Costa Rica ... 120 D3
Şīr Banī Yās, U.A.E. ... 71 E7
Sir Edward Pellew Group,
  Australia ... 94 B2
Sir Graham Moore Is., Australia 92 B4
Sir James MacBrien, Mt.,
  Canada ... 100 B7
Sira →, Norway ... 9 G12
Siracusa, Italy ... 31 E8
Sirajganj, Bangla. ... 69 G13
Sirakoro, Mali ... 82 C3
Şiran, Turkey ... 73 B8
Sirasso, Ivory C. ... 82 D3
Sirathu, India ... 69 G9
Sīrdān, Iran ... 71 B6
Sirdaryo = Syrdarya →,
  Kazakstan ... 50 E7
Sire, Ethiopia ... 81 F4
Siren, U.S.A. ... 112 C8
Sirer, Spain ... 37 C7
Siret, Romania ... 43 C11
Siret →, Romania ... 43 E12
Sirghāyā, Syria ... 75 B5
Şiria, Romania ... 42 D6
Sirino, Mte., Italy ... 31 B8
Sirmaur, India ... 69 G9
Sírna, Greece ... 39 E8
Şirnak, Turkey ... 73 D10
Sirohi, India ... 68 G5
Sironj, India ... 68 G7
Síros, Greece ... 38 D6
Sirretta Pk., U.S.A. ... 117 K8
Sīrrī, Iran ... 71 E7
Sirsa, India ... 68 E6
Sirsa →, India ... 69 F8
Siruela, Spain ... 35 G5
Sisak, Croatia ... 29 C13
Sisaket, Thailand ... 64 E5
Sisante, Spain ... 33 F2
Sisargas, Is., Spain ... 34 B2
Sishen, S. Africa ... 88 D3
Sishui, Henan, China ... 56 G7
Sishui, Shandong, China ... 57 G9
Sisipuk L., Canada ... 105 B8
Sisophon, Cambodia ... 64 F4
Sisseton, U.S.A. ... 112 C6
Sissonne, France ... 19 C10
Sīstān, Asia ... 71 D9
Sīstān, Daryācheh-ye, Iran ... 71 D9
Sīstān va Balūchestān □, Iran . 71 E9
Sisteron, France ... 21 D9
Sisters, U.S.A. ... 114 D3
Siswa Bazar, India ... 69 F10
Sitakili, Mali ... 82 C2
Sitamarhi, India ... 69 F11
Sitampiky, Madag. ... 89 B8
Sitapur, India ... 69 F9
Siteki, Swaziland ... 89 D5
Sitges, Spain ... 32 D6
Sithoniá, Greece ... 40 F7
Sitía, Greece ... 36 D8
Sitka, U.S.A. ... 104 B1
Sitoti, Botswana ... 88 C3
Sitra, Egypt ... 80 B2
Sittang Myit →, Burma ... 67 L20
Sittard, Neths. ... 17 C5
Sittensen, Germany ... 24 B5
Sittingbourne, U.K. ... 13 F8
Sittona, Eritrea ... 81 E4
Sittoung = Sittang Myit →,
  Burma ... 67 L20
Sittwe, Burma ... 67 J18
Situbondo, Indonesia ... 63 G16
Siuna, Nic. ... 120 D3

Siuri, India ... 69 H12
Siutghiol, Lacul, Romania ... 43 F13
Sīvand, Iran ... 71 D7
Sivas, Turkey ... 70 B3
Sivashi, Turkey ... 39 C11
Siverek, Turkey ... 70 B3
Sivrihisar, Turkey ... 72 C4
Sîwa, Egypt ... 80 B2
Sîwa, El Wâhât es, Egypt ... 80 B2
Siwa Oasis = Sîwa, El Wâhât es,
  Egypt ... 80 B2
Siwalik Range, Nepal ... 69 F10
Siwan, India ... 69 F11
Siwana, India ... 68 G5
Sixmilebridge, Ireland ... 15 D3
Sixth Cataract, Sudan ... 81 D3
Siyāl, Jazā'ir, Egypt ... 80 C4
Siyäzän, Azerbaijan ... 49 K9
Siziwang Qi, China ... 56 D6
Sjælland, Denmark ... 11 J5
Sjællands Odde, Denmark ... 11 J5
Sjenica, Serbia, Yug. ... 40 C3
Sjöbo, Sweden ... 11 J7
Sjötofta, Sweden ... 11 G7
Sjötorp, Sweden ... 11 F8
Sjumen = Shumen, Bulgaria ... 41 C10
Sjuntorp, Sweden ... 11 F6
Skadarsko Jezero,
  Montenegro, Yug. ... 40 D3
Skadovsk, Ukraine ... 47 J7
Skælskør, Denmark ... 11 J5
Skærbæk, Denmark ... 11 J2
Skaftafell, Iceland ... 8 D5
Skagafjörður, Iceland ... 8 D4
Skagastølstindane, Norway ... 9 F12
Skagaströnd, Iceland ... 8 D3
Skagen, Denmark ... 11 G4
Skagern, Sweden ... 10 F8
Skagerrak, Denmark ... 11 G2
Skagit →, U.S.A. ... 116 B4
Skagway, U.S.A. ... 100 C6
Skala-Podilska, Ukraine ... 47 H4
Skala Podolskaya = Skala-
  Podilska, Ukraine ... 47 H4
Skalat, Ukraine ... 47 H3
Skalbmierz, Poland ... 45 H7
Skålderviken, Denmark ... 11 H6
Skalica, Slovak Rep. ... 27 C10
Skallingen, Denmark ... 11 J2
Skalni Dol = Kamenyak,
  Bulgaria ... 41 C10
Skanderborg, Denmark ... 11 H3
Skåne, Sweden ... 11 J7
Skåne län □, Sweden ... 11 H7
Skaneateles, U.S.A. ... 111 D8
Skaneateles L., U.S.A. ... 111 D8
Skänninge, Sweden ... 11 F9
Skanör med Falsterbo, Sweden . 11 J6
Skantzoúra, Greece ... 38 B6
Skara, Sweden ... 11 F7
Skärblacka, Sweden ... 11 F9
Skardu, Pakistan ... 69 B6
Skåre, Sweden ... 10 E7
Skärhamn, Sweden ... 11 G5
Skarszewy, Poland ... 44 D5
Skaryszew, Poland ... 45 G8
Skarżysko-Kamienna, Poland . 45 G7
Skattkärr, Sweden ... 10 E7
Skattungbyn, Sweden ... 10 C8
Skawina, Poland ... 45 J6
Skebobruk, Sweden ... 10 E12
Skeena →, Canada ... 104 C2
Skeena Mts., Canada ... 104 B3
Skegness, U.K. ... 12 D8
Skeldon, Guyana ... 124 B7
Skeleton Coast Park, Namibia . 88 C1
Skellefte älv →, Sweden ... 8 D19
Skellefteå, Sweden ... 8 D19
Skelleftehamn, Sweden ... 8 D19
Skender Vakuf, Bos.-H. ... 42 F2
Skerries, The, U.K. ... 12 D3
Skhíza, Greece ... 38 E3
Skhoinoúsa, Greece ... 39 E7
Ski, Norway ... 9 G14
Skíathos, Greece ... 38 B5
Skibbereen, Ireland ... 15 E2
Skiddaw, U.K. ... 12 C4
Skidegate, Canada ... 104 C2
Skídhra, Greece ... 40 F6
Skien, Norway ... 9 G13
Skierniewice, Poland ... 45 G7
Skikda, Algeria ... 78 A7
Skillingaryd, Sweden ... 11 G8
Skillinge, Sweden ... 11 J8
Skilloura, Cyprus ... 36 D12
Skinári, Ákra, Greece ... 38 D2
Skinnskatteberg, Sweden ... 10 E9
Skipton, U.K. ... 12 D5
Skirmish Pt., Australia ... 94 A1
Skiropoúla, Greece ... 38 C6
Skíros, Greece ... 38 C6
Skivarp, Sweden ... 11 J7
Skive, Denmark ... 11 H3
Skjálfandafljót →, Iceland ... 8 D5
Skjálfandi, Iceland ... 8 C5
Skjern, Denmark ... 11 J2
Skoczów, Poland ... 45 J5
Skofja Loka, Slovenia ... 29 B11
Skoghall, Sweden ... 10 E7
Skogstorp, Sweden ... 10 E10
Skoki, Poland ... 45 F4
Skole, Ukraine ... 47 H2
Skópelos, Greece ... 38 B5
Skopí, Greece ... 36 D8
Skopin, Russia ... 46 F10
Skopje, Macedonia ... 40 D5
Skórcz, Poland ... 44 E5

Skørping, Denmark ... 11 H3
Skövde, Sweden ... 11 F7
Skovorodino, Russia ... 51 D13
Skowhegan, U.S.A. ... 109 C11
Skradin, Croatia ... 29 E12
Skrea, Sweden ... 11 H6
Skrunda, Latvia ... 44 B9
Skrwa →, Poland ... 45 F6
Skull, Ireland ... 15 E2
Skultorp, Sweden ... 11 F7
Skultuna, Sweden ... 10 E10
Skunk →, U.S.A. ... 112 E9
Skuodas, Lithuania ... 9 H19
Skurup, Sweden ... 11 J7
Skutskär, Sweden ... 10 D11
Skvyra, Ukraine ... 47 H5
Skwierzyna, Poland ... 45 F2
Skye, U.K. ... 14 D2
Skykomish, U.S.A. ... 114 C3
Skyros = Skíros, Greece ... 38 C6
Skyttorp, Sweden ... 10 D11
Slættaratindur, Færoe Is. ... 8 E9
Slagelse, Denmark ... 11 J5
Slamet, Indonesia ... 63 G13
Slaney →, Ireland ... 15 D5
Slangberge, S. Africa ... 88 E3
Slănic, Romania ... 43 E10
Slano, Croatia ... 40 D1
Slantsy, Russia ... 46 C5
Slaný, Czech Rep. ... 26 A7
Śląskie □, Poland ... 45 H6
Slätbaken, Sweden ... 11 F10
Slate Is., Canada ... 102 C2
Slatina, Croatia ... 42 E2
Slatina, Romania ... 43 F9
Slatina Timiş, Romania ... 42 E7
Slatington, U.S.A. ... 111 F9
Slaton, U.S.A. ... 113 J4
Slave →, Canada ... 104 A6
Slave Coast, W. Afr. ... 83 D5
Slave Lake, Canada ... 104 B6
Slave Pt., Canada ... 104 A5
Slavgorod, Russia ... 50 D8
Slavinja, Serbia, Yug. ... 40 C6
Slavkov u Brna, Czech Rep. ... 27 B9
Slavonija, Europe ... 42 E2
Slavonski Brod, Croatia ... 42 E3
Slavuta, Ukraine ... 47 G4
Slavyanka, Russia ... 54 C5
Slavyanovo, Bulgaria ... 41 C8
Slavyansk = Slovyansk, Ukraine 47 H9
Slavyansk-na-Kubani, Russia . 47 K10
Sława, Poland ... 45 G3
Sławharad, Belarus ... 46 F6
Sławno, Poland ... 44 D3
Sławoborze, Poland ... 44 E2
Sleaford, U.K. ... 12 D7
Sleaford B., Australia ... 95 E2
Sleat, Sd. of, U.K. ... 14 D3
Sleeper Is., Canada ... 101 C11
Sleepy Eye, U.S.A. ... 112 C7
Slemon L., Canada ... 104 A5
Ślesin, Poland ... 45 F5
Slide Mt., U.S.A. ... 111 E10
Slidell, U.S.A. ... 113 K10
Sliema, Malta ... 36 D2
Slieve Aughty, Ireland ... 15 C3
Slieve Bloom, Ireland ... 15 C4
Slieve Donard, U.K. ... 15 B6
Slieve Gamph, Ireland ... 15 B3
Slieve Gullion, U.K. ... 15 B5
Slieve Mish, Ireland ... 15 D2
Slievenamon, Ireland ... 15 D4
Sligeach = Sligo, Ireland ... 15 B3
Sligo, Ireland ... 15 B3
Sligo, U.S.A. ... 110 E5
Sligo □, Ireland ... 15 B3
Sligo B., Ireland ... 15 B3
Slippery Rock, U.S.A. ... 110 E4
Slite, Sweden ... 11 G12
Sliven, Bulgaria ... 41 D10
Slivnitsa, Bulgaria ... 40 D7
Sljeme, Croatia ... 29 C12
Sloan, U.S.A. ... 117 K11
Sloansville, U.S.A. ... 111 D10
Slobozia, Moldova ... 43 D14
Slobozia, Argeş, Romania ... 43 F10
Slobozia, Ialomiţa, Romania . 43 F12
Slocan, Canada ... 104 D5
Słomniki, Poland ... 45 H7
Slonim, Belarus ... 46 F3
Slough, U.K. ... 13 F7
Slough □, U.K. ... 13 F7
Sloughhouse, U.S.A. ... 116 G5
Slovak Rep. ■, Europe ... 27 C13
Slovakia = Slovak Rep. ■,
  Europe ... 27 C13
Slovakian Ore Mts. = Slovenské
  Rudohorie, Slovak Rep. ... 27 C12
Slovenia ■, Europe ... 29 C11
Slovenija = Slovenia ■, Europe 29 C11
Slovenj Gradec, Slovenia ... 29 B12
Slovenska Bistrica, Slovenia . 29 B12
Slovenske Konjice, Slovenia ... 29 B12
Slovenské Rudohorie,
  Slovak Rep. ... 27 C12
Slovyansk, Ukraine ... 47 H9
Słubice, Poland ... 45 F1
Sluch →, Ukraine ... 47 G4
Sluis, Neths. ... 17 C3
Slunchev Bryag, Bulgaria ... 41 D11
Slunj, Croatia ... 29 C12
Słupca, Poland ... 45 F4
Słupia →, Poland ... 44 D3
Słupsk, Poland ... 44 D3
Slurry, S. Africa ... 88 D4
Slutsk, Belarus ... 47 F4

Slyne Hd., Ireland ... 15 C1
Slyudyanka, Russia ... 51 D11
Småland, Sweden ... 11 G9
Smålandsfarvandet, Denmark . 11 J5
Smålandsstenar, Sweden ... 11 G7
Smalltree L., Canada ... 105 A8
Smallwood Res., Canada ... 103 B7
Smarhon, Belarus ... 46 E4
Smarje, Slovenia ... 29 B12
Smartt Syndicate Dam, S. Africa 88 E3
Smartville, U.S.A. ... 116 F5
Smeaton, Canada ... 105 C8
Smedby, Sweden ... 11 H10
Smederevo, Serbia, Yug. ... 40 B4
Smederevska Palanka,
  Serbia, Yug. ... 40 B4
Smedjebacken, Sweden ... 10 D9
Smela = Smila, Ukraine ... 47 H6
Smerwick Harbour, Ireland ... 15 D1
Smethport, U.S.A. ... 110 E6
Smidovich, Russia ... 51 E14
Śmigiel, Poland ... 45 F3
Smila, Ukraine ... 47 H6
Smilyan, Bulgaria ... 41 E8
Smith, Canada ... 104 B6
Smith Center, U.S.A. ... 112 F5
Smith Sund, Greenland ... 4 B4
Smithburne →, Australia ... 94 B3
Smithers, Canada ... 104 C3
Smithfield, S. Africa ... 89 E4
Smithfield, N.C., U.S.A. ... 109 H6
Smithfield, Utah, U.S.A. ... 114 F8
Smiths Falls, Canada ... 102 D4
Smithton, Australia ... 94 G4
Smithville, Canada ... 110 C5
Smithville, U.S.A. ... 113 K6
Smoky →, Canada ... 104 B5
Smoky Bay, Australia ... 95 E1
Smoky Hill →, U.S.A. ... 112 F6
Smoky Hills, U.S.A. ... 112 F5
Smoky Lake, Canada ... 104 C6
Smøla, Norway ... 8 E13
Smolensk, Russia ... 46 E7
Smolikas, Óros, Greece ... 40 F4
Smolník, Slovak Rep. ... 27 C13
Smolyan, Bulgaria ... 41 E8
Smooth Rock Falls, Canada ... 102 C3
Smoothstone L., Canada ... 105 C7
Smorgon = Smarhon, Belarus . 46 E4
Smulţi, Romania ... 43 E12
Smyadovo, Bulgaria ... 41 C11
Smygehamn, Sweden ... 11 J7
Smyrna = İzmir, Turkey ... 39 C9
Smyrna, U.S.A. ... 108 F8
Snæfell, Iceland ... 8 D6
Snaefell, U.K. ... 12 C3
Snæfellsjökull, Iceland ... 8 D2
Snake →, U.S.A. ... 114 C4
Snake I., Australia ... 95 F4
Snake Range, U.S.A. ... 114 G6
Snake River Plain, U.S.A. ... 114 E7
Snasahögarna, Sweden ... 10 A6
Snåsavatnet, Norway ... 8 D14
Snedsted, Denmark ... 11 H2
Sneek, Neths. ... 17 A5
Sneeuberge, S. Africa ... 88 E3
Snejbjerg, Denmark ... 11 H2
Snelling, U.S.A. ... 116 H6
Snezhnoye, Ukraine ... 47 J10
Snežnik, Slovenia ... 29 C11
Śniadowo, Poland ... 45 E8
Śniardwy, Jezioro, Poland ... 44 E8
Śnieżka, Europe ... 26 A8
Snigirevka = Snihurivka,
  Ukraine ... 47 J7
Snihurivka, Ukraine ... 47 J7
Snina, Slovak Rep. ... 27 C15
Snizort, L., U.K. ... 14 D2
Snøhetta, Norway ... 9 E13
Snohomish, U.S.A. ... 116 C4
Snoul, Cambodia ... 65 F6
Snow Hill, U.S.A. ... 108 F8
Snow Lake, Canada ... 105 C8
Snow Mt., Calif., U.S.A. ... 116 F4
Snow Mt., Maine, U.S.A. ... 111 A14
Snow Shoe, U.S.A. ... 110 E7
Snowbird L., Canada ... 105 A8
Snowdon, U.K. ... 12 D3
Snowdrift →, Canada ... 105 A6
Snowflake, U.S.A. ... 115 J8
Snowshoe Pk., U.S.A. ... 114 B6
Snowtown, Australia ... 95 E2
Snowville, U.S.A. ... 114 F7
Snowy →, Australia ... 95 F4
Snowy Mt., U.S.A. ... 111 C10
Snowy Mts., Australia ... 95 F4
Snug Corner, Bahamas ... 121 B5
Snyatyn, Ukraine ... 47 H3
Snyder, Okla., U.S.A. ... 113 H5
Snyder, Tex., U.S.A. ... 113 J4
Soahanina, Madag. ... 89 B7
Soalala, Madag. ... 89 B8
Soaloka, Madag. ... 89 B8
Soamanonga, Madag. ... 89 C7
Soan →, Pakistan ... 68 C5
Soanierana-Ivongo, Madag. ... 89 B8
Soanindrariny, Madag. ... 89 B8
Şoarş, Romania ... 43 E9
Soavina, Madag. ... 89 C8
Soavinandriana, Madag. ... 89 C8
Soba, Nigeria ... 83 C6
Sobat, Nahr →, Sudan ... 81 F3
Sobhapur, India ... 68 H8
Sobinka, Russia ... 46 E11
Sobótka, Poland ... 45 H3
Sobra, Croatia ... 29 F9

Sobradinho, Reprêsa de, Brazil 125 E10
Sobral, Brazil ... 125 D10
Sobrance, Slovak Rep. ... 27 C15
Sobreira Formosa, Portugal ... 34 F3
Soc Giang, Vietnam ... 58 F6
Soc Trang, Vietnam ... 65 H5
Soča →, Europe ... 26 C6
Socastee, U.S.A. ... 109 J6
Sochaczew, Poland ... 45 F7
Soch'e = Shache, China ... 60 C2
Sochi, Russia ... 49 J4
Société, Is. de la, Pac. Oc. ... 97 J12
Society Is. = Société, Is. de la,
  Pac. Oc. ... 97 J12
Socompa, Portezuelo de, Chile . 126 A2
Socorro, N. Mex., U.S.A. ... 115 J10
Socorro, Tex., U.S.A. ... 115 L10
Socorro, I., Mexico ... 118 D2
Socotra, Yemen ... 74 E5
Socovos, Spain ... 33 G3
Socuéllamos, Spain ... 33 F2
Soda L., U.S.A. ... 115 C6
Soda Plains, India ... 69 B8
Soda Springs, U.S.A. ... 114 E8
Sodankylä, Finland ... 8 C22
Soddy-Daisy, U.S.A. ... 109 H3
Söderala, Sweden ... 10 C10
Söderbärke, Sweden ... 10 D9
Söderfors, Sweden ... 10 D11
Söderhamn, Sweden ... 10 C11
Söderköping, Sweden ... 11 F10
Södermanland, Sweden ... 9 G17
Södermanlands län □, Sweden . 10 E11
Södertälje, Sweden ... 10 E11
Sodiri, Sudan ... 81 E2
Sodo, Ethiopia ... 81 F4
Södra Dellen, Sweden ... 10 C10
Södra Finnskoga, Sweden ... 10 D6
Södra Sandby, Sweden ... 11 J7
Södra Ulvön, Sweden ... 10 B12
Södra Vi, Sweden ... 11 G9
Sodražica, Slovenia ... 29 C11
Sodus, U.S.A. ... 110 C7
Soekmekaar, S. Africa ... 89 C4
Soest, Germany ... 24 D4
Soest, Neths. ... 17 B5
Sofádhes, Greece ... 38 B4
Sofala □, Mozam. ... 89 B5
Sofara, Mali ... 82 C4
Sofia = Sofiya, Bulgaria ... 40 D7
Sofia →, Madag. ... 89 B8
Sofievka, Ukraine ... 47 H7
Sofikón, Greece ... 38 D5
Sofiya, Bulgaria ... 40 D7
Sofiya □, Bulgaria ... 40 D7
Sōfu-Gan, Japan ... 55 K10
Sogakofe, Ghana ... 83 D5
Sogamoso, Colombia ... 124 B4
Sogār, Iran ... 71 E8
Sögel, Germany ... 24 C3
Sogndalsfjøra, Norway ... 9 F12
Søgne, Norway ... 9 G12
Sognefjorden, Norway ... 9 F11
Söğüt, Bilecik, Turkey ... 39 A12
Söğüt, Burdur, Turkey ... 39 D11
Söğüt Dağı, Turkey ... 39 D11
Söğütköy, Turkey ... 39 E10
Sögwipo, S. Korea ... 57 H14
Soh, Iran ... 71 C6
Sohâg, Egypt ... 80 B3
Sohagpur, India ... 68 H8
Sŏhori, N. Korea ... 57 D15
Soignies, Belgium ... 17 D4
Soin, Burkina Faso ... 82 C4
Soira, Eritrea ... 81 E4
Soissons, France ... 19 C10
Sōja, Japan ... 55 G6
Sojat, India ... 68 G5
Sok →, Russia ... 48 D10
Sokal, Ukraine ... 47 G3
Söke, Turkey ... 39 D9
Sokelo, Dem. Rep. of the Congo 87 D1
Sokhós, Greece ... 40 F6
Sokhumi, Georgia ... 49 J5
Soko Banja, Serbia, Yug. ... 40 C5
Sokodé, Togo ... 83 D5
Sokol, Russia ... 46 C11
Sokolac, Bos.-H. ... 42 G3
Sokółka, Poland ... 44 E10
Sokolo, Mali ... 82 C3
Sokolo, Mali ... 82 C3
Sokolov, Czech Rep. ... 26 A5
Sokołów Małopolski, Poland ... 45 H9
Sokołów Podlaski, Poland ... 45 F9
Sokoły, Poland ... 45 F9
Sokoto, Nigeria ... 83 C6
Sokoto □, Nigeria ... 83 C6
Sokoto →, Nigeria ... 83 C5
Sol Iletsk, Russia ... 50 D6
Sola →, Poland ... 45 J6
Solai, Kenya ... 86 B4
Solan, India ... 68 D7
Solano, Phil. ... 61 C4
Solapur, India ... 66 L9
Solca, Romania ... 43 C10
Solda Gölü, Turkey ... 39 D11
Soldăneşti, Moldova ... 43 C13
Soldotna, U.S.A. ... 100 B4
Soléa □, Cyprus ... 36 D12
Solec Kujawski, Poland ... 45 E5
Soledad, Colombia ... 124 A4
Soledad, U.S.A. ... 116 J5
Soledad, Venezuela ... 124 B6
Solent, The, U.K. ... 13 G6
Solenzara, France ... 21 G13
Solesmes, France ... 19 B10
Solfonn, Norway ... 9 F12

Solhan, *Turkey* 70 B4
Soligorsk = Salihorsk, *Belarus* 47 F4
Solihull, *U.K.* 13 E6
Solikamsk, *Russia* 50 D6
Solila, *Madag.* 89 C8
Solimões = Amazonas →,
  S. Amer. 122 D5
Solin, *Croatia* 29 E13
Solingen, *Germany* 24 D3
Sollebrunn, *Sweden* 11 F6
Solleftea, *Sweden* 10 A11
Sollentuna, *Sweden* 10 E11
Sóller, *Spain* 37 B9
Sollerön, *Sweden* 10 D8
Solling, *Germany* 24 D5
Solnechnogorsk, *Russia* 46 D9
Solo →, *Indonesia* 63 G15
Solofra, *Italy* 31 B7
Sologne, *France* 19 E8
Solok, *Indonesia* 62 E2
Sololá, *Guatemala* 120 D1
Solomon, N. Fork →, *U.S.A.* 112 F5
Solomon, S. Fork →, *U.S.A.* 112 F5
Solomon Is. ■, *Pac. Oc.* 96 H7
Solon, *China* 60 B7
Solon Springs, *U.S.A.* 112 B9
Solor, *Indonesia* 63 F6
Solotcha, *Russia* 46 E10
Solothurn, *Switz.* 25 H3
Solothurn □, *Switz.* 25 H3
Solsona, *Spain* 32 C6
Solt, *Hungary* 42 D4
Šolta, *Croatia* 29 E13
Solţānābād, *Khorāsān, Iran* 71 C8
Solţānābād, *Khorāsān, Iran* 71 B8
Soltau, *Germany* 24 C5
Soltsy, *Russia* 46 C6
Solunska Glava, *Macedonia* 40 E5
Solvang, *U.S.A.* 117 L6
Solvay, *U.S.A.* 111 C8
Sölvesborg, *Sweden* 11 H8
Solway Firth, *U.K.* 12 C4
Solwezi, *Zambia* 87 E2
Sōma, *Japan* 54 F10
Soma, *Turkey* 39 B9
Somabhula, *Zimbabwe* 89 B4
Somali Pen., *Africa* 76 F8
Somali Rep. ■, *Africa* 74 F4
Somalia = Somali Rep. ■, *Africa* 74 F4
Sombernon, *France* 19 E11
Sombor, *Serbia, Yug.* 42 E4
Sombra, *Canada* 110 D2
Sombrerete, *Mexico* 118 C4
Sombrero, *Anguilla* 121 C7
Şomcuta Mare, *Romania* 43 C8
Somdari, *India* 68 G5
Somers, *U.S.A.* 114 B6
Somerset, *Ky., U.S.A.* 108 G3
Somerset, *Mass., U.S.A.* 111 E13
Somerset, *Pa., U.S.A.* 110 F5
Somerset □, *U.K.* 13 F5
Somerset East, *S. Africa* 88 E4
Somerset I., *Canada* 100 A10
Somerset West, *S. Africa* 88 E2
Somersworth, *U.S.A.* 111 C14
Somerton, *U.S.A.* 115 K6
Somerville, *U.S.A.* 111 F10
Somes →, *Romania* 42 C7
Someşul Mare →, *Romania* 43 C8
Somme □, *France* 19 C9
Somme →, *France* 19 B8
Somme, B. de la, *France* 18 B8
Sommen, *Jönköping, Sweden* 11 F8
Sommen, *Östergötland, Sweden* 11 F9
Sommepy-Tahure, *France* 19 C11
Sömmerda, *Germany* 24 D7
Sommesous, *France* 19 D11
Sommières, *France* 21 E8
Somnath, *India* 68 J4
Somogy □, *Hungary* 42 D2
Somogyszob, *Hungary* 42 D2
Somoto, *Nic.* 120 D2
Sompolno, *Poland* 45 F5
Somport, Puerto de, *Spain* 32 C4
Son →, *India* 69 G11
Son Ha, *Vietnam* 64 E7
Son Hoa, *Vietnam* 64 F7
Son La, *Vietnam* 58 G4
Son Serra, *Spain* 37 B10
Son Servera, *Spain* 32 F8
Son Tay, *Vietnam* 58 G5
Soná, *Panama* 120 E3
Sonamarg, *India* 69 B6
Sonamukhi, *India* 69 H12
Sonar →, *India* 69 G8
Sŏnch'ŏn, *N. Korea* 57 E13
Sondags →, *S. Africa* 88 E4
Sóndalo, *Italy* 28 B7
Sondar, *India* 69 C6
Sønder Felding, *Denmark* 11 J2
Sønder Omme, *Denmark* 11 J2
Sønderborg, *Denmark* 11 K3
Sønderjyllands
  Amtskommune □, *Denmark* 11 J3
Sondershausen, *Germany* 24 D6
Sóndrio, *Italy* 28 B6
Sone, *Mozam.* 87 F3
Sonepur, *India* 67 J13
Song, *Nigeria* 83 D7
Song, *Thailand* 64 C3
Song Cau, *Vietnam* 64 F7
Song Xian, *China* 56 G7
Songch'ŏn, *N. Korea* 57 E14
Songea, *Tanzania* 87 E4
Songeons, *France* 19 C8
Songhua Hu, *China* 57 C14
Songhua Jiang →, *China* 60 B8

Songjiang, *China* 59 B13
Songjin, *N. Korea* 57 D15
Songjŏng-ni, *S. Korea* 57 G14
Songkan, *China* 58 C6
Songkhla, *Thailand* 65 J3
Songming, *China* 58 E4
Songnim, *N. Korea* 57 E13
Songo, *Mozam.* 85 H6
Songo, *Sudan* 79 G10
Songpan, *China* 58 A4
Songtao, *China* 58 C7
Songwe, *Dem. Rep. of the Congo* 86 C2
Songwe →, *Africa* 87 D3
Songxi, *China* 59 D12
Songzi, *China* 59 B8
Sonhat, *India* 69 H10
Sonid Youqi, *China* 56 C7
Sonipat, *India* 68 E7
Sonkach, *India* 68 H7
Sonkovo, *Russia* 46 D9
Sonmiani, *Pakistan* 68 G2
Sonmiani B., *Pakistan* 68 G2
Sonnino, *Italy* 30 A6
Sono →, *Brazil* 125 E9
Sonoma, *U.S.A.* 116 G4
Sonora, *Calif., U.S.A.* 116 H6
Sonora, *Tex., U.S.A.* 113 K4
Sonora □, *Mexico* 118 B2
Sonora →, *Mexico* 118 B2
Sonoran Desert, *U.S.A.* 117 L12
Sonoyta, *Mexico* 118 A2
Sonqor, *Iran* 73 E12
Sŏnsan, *S. Korea* 57 F15
Sonseca, *Spain* 35 F7
Sonsonate, *El Salv.* 120 D2
Sonsorol Is., *Pac. Oc.* 63 C8
Sonstorp, *Sweden* 11 F9
Sonthofen, *Germany* 25 H6
Soochow = Suzhou, *China* 59 B13
Sooke, *Canada* 116 B3
Sop Hao, *Laos* 58 G5
Sop Prap, *Thailand* 64 D2
Sopelana, *Spain* 32 B2
Sopi, *Indonesia* 63 D7
Sopo, Nahr →, *Sudan* 81 F2
Sopot, *Bulgaria* 41 D8
Sopot, *Poland* 44 D5
Sopot, *Serbia, Yug.* 40 B4
Sopotnica, *Macedonia* 40 E5
Sopron, *Hungary* 42 C1
Sopur, *India* 69 B6
Sør-Rondane, *Antarctica* 5 D4
Sora, *Italy* 29 G10
Sorah, *Pakistan* 68 F3
Söråker, *Sweden* 10 B11
Sorano, *Italy* 29 F8
Soraon, *India* 69 G9
Sorbas, *Spain* 33 H2
Sörbygden, *Sweden* 10 B10
Sore, *France* 20 D3
Sorel, *Canada* 102 C5
Soresina, *Italy* 28 C6
Sörforsa, *Sweden* 10 C10
Sórgono, *Italy* 30 B2
Sorgues, *France* 21 D8
Sorgun, *Turkey* 72 C6
Soria, *Spain* 32 D2
Soria □, *Spain* 32 D2
Soriano, *Uruguay* 126 C4
Soriano nel Cimino, *Italy* 29 F9
Sorkh, Kuh-e, *Iran* 71 C8
Sorkheh, *Iran* 71 C7
Sorø, *Denmark* 11 J5
Soro, *Guinea* 82 C3
Soroca, *Moldova* 43 B13
Sorocaba, *Brazil* 127 A6
Soroki = Soroca, *Moldova* 43 B13
Sorol Atoll, *Pac. Oc.* 63 C10
Sorong, *Indonesia* 63 E8
Soroní, *Greece* 36 C10
Soroti, *Uganda* 86 B3
Sørøya, *Norway* 8 A20
Sørøysundet, *Norway* 8 A20
Sorraia →, *Portugal* 35 G2
Sorrell, *Australia* 94 G4
Sorrento, *Italy* 31 B7
Sorsele, *Sweden* 8 D17
Sörsjön, *Sweden* 10 C7
Sorso, *Italy* 30 B1
Sorsogon, *Phil.* 61 E6
Sortavala, *Russia* 46 B6
Sortino, *Italy* 31 E8
Sortland, *Norway* 8 B16
Sorvizhi, *Russia* 48 B9
Sos = Sos del Rey Católico,
  Spain 32 C3
Sos del Rey Católico, *Spain* 32 C3
Sŏsan, *S. Korea* 57 F14
Soscumica, L., *Canada* 102 B4
Sösdala, *Sweden* 11 H7
Sosna →, *Russia* 47 F10
Sosnovka, *Kirov, Russia* 48 B10
Sosnovka, *Tambov, Russia* 48 D5
Sosnovy Bor, *Russia* 46 C5
Sosnowiec, *Poland* 45 H6
Sospel, *France* 21 E11
Sossus Vlei, *Namibia* 88 C2
Šoštanj, *Slovenia* 29 B12
Sŏsura, *N. Korea* 57 C16
Sot →, *India* 69 F8
Sotkamo, *Finland* 8 D23
Soto del Barco, *Spain* 34 B4
Soto la Marina →, *Mexico* 119 C5
Soto y Amío, *Spain* 34 C5
Sotrondio, *Spain* 34 B5
Sotuta, *Mexico* 119 C7
Souanké, *Congo* 84 D2
Soubré, *Ivory C.* 82 D3

Souderton, *U.S.A.* 111 F9
Soúdha, *Greece* 36 D6
Soúdhas, Kólpos, *Greece* 36 D6
Souflíon, *Greece* 41 E10
Soufrière, *St. Lucia* 121 D7
Souillac, *France* 20 D5
Souilly, *France* 19 C12
Soukhouma, *Laos* 64 E5
Sŏul, *S. Korea* 57 F14
Soulac-sur-Mer, *France* 20 C2
Soulougou, *Burkina Faso* 83 C5
Soultz-sous-Forêts, *France* 19 D14
Sound, The = Øresund, *Europe* 11 J6
Sound, The, *U.K.* 13 G3
Soúnion, Ákra, *Greece* 38 D6
Sources, Mt. aux, *Lesotho* 89 D4
Soure, *Brazil* 125 D9
Soure, *Portugal* 34 E2
Souris, *Man., Canada* 105 D8
Souris, *P.E.I., Canada* 103 C7
Souris →, *Canada* 112 A5
Sourou →, *Africa* 82 C4
Soúrpi, *Greece* 38 B4
Sousa, *Brazil* 125 E11
Sousel, *Portugal* 35 G3
Sousse, *Tunisia* 79 A8
Soustons, *France* 20 E2
Sout →, *S. Africa* 88 E2
South Africa ■, *Africa* 88 E3
South America 122 E5
South Atlantic Ocean 122 H7
South Aulatsivik I., *Canada* 103 A7
South Australia □, *Australia* 95 E2
South Ayrshire □, *U.K.* 14 F4
South Baldy, *U.S.A.* 115 J10
South Bass I., *U.S.A.* 110 E2
South Bend, *Ind., U.S.A.* 108 E2
South Bend, *Wash., U.S.A.* 116 D3
South Boston, *U.S.A.* 109 G6
South Branch, *Canada* 103 C8
South Brook, *Canada* 103 C8
South Carolina □, *U.S.A.* 109 J5
South Charleston, *U.S.A.* 108 F5
South China Sea, *Asia* 62 C4
South Dakota □, *U.S.A.* 112 C5
South Deerfield, *U.S.A.* 111 D12
South Downs, *U.K.* 13 G7
South East C., *Australia* 94 G4
South East Is., *Australia* 93 F3
South Esk →, *U.K.* 14 E6
South Foreland, *U.K.* 13 F9
South Fork American →, *U.S.A.* 116 G5
South Fork Feather →, *U.S.A.* 116 F5
South Fork Grand →, *U.S.A.* 112 C3
South Fork Republican →,
  U.S.A. 112 E4
South Georgia, *Antarctica* 122 J7
South Gloucestershire □, *U.K.* 13 F5
South Hadley, *U.S.A.* 111 D12
South Haven, *U.S.A.* 108 D2
South Henik, L., *Canada* 105 A9
South Honshu Ridge, *Pac. Oc.* 96 E6
South Horr, *Kenya* 86 B4
South I., *Kenya* 86 B4
South I., *N.Z.* 91 L3
South Indian Lake, *Canada* 105 B9
South Invercargill, *N.Z.* 91 M2
South Knife →, *Canada* 105 B10
South Koel →, *India* 69 H11
South Korea ■, *Asia* 57 G15
South Lake Tahoe, *U.S.A.* 116 G6
South Lanarkshire □, *U.K.* 14 F5
South Loup →, *U.S.A.* 112 E5
South Magnetic Pole, *Antarctica* 5 C9
South Milwaukee, *U.S.A.* 108 D2
South Molton, *U.K.* 13 F4
South Moose L., *Canada* 105 C8
South Nahanni →, *Canada* 104 A4
South Nation →, *Canada* 111 A9
South Natuna Is. = Natuna
  Selatan, Kepulauan, *Indonesia* 65 L7
South Negril Pt., *Jamaica* 120 C4
South Orkney Is., *Antarctica* 5 C18
South Ossetia □, *Georgia* 49 J7
South Pagai, I. = Pagai Selatan,
  Pulau, *Indonesia* 62 E2
South Paris, *U.S.A.* 111 B14
South Pittsburg, *U.S.A.* 109 H3
South Platte →, *U.S.A.* 112 E4
South Pole, *Antarctica* 5 E
South Porcupine, *Canada* 102 C3
South Portland, *U.S.A.* 109 D10
South Pt., *U.S.A.* 110 B1
South River, *Canada* 102 C4
South River, *U.S.A.* 111 F10
South Ronaldsay, *U.K.* 14 C6
South Sandwich Is., *Antarctica* 5 B1
South Saskatchewan →, *Canada* 105 C7
South Seal →, *Canada* 105 B9
South Shetland Is., *Antarctica* 5 C18
South Shields, *U.K.* 12 C6
South Sioux City, *U.S.A.* 112 D6
South Taranaki Bight, *N.Z.* 91 H5
South Thompson →, *Canada* 104 C4
South Twin I., *Canada* 102 B4
South Tyne →, *U.K.* 12 C5
South Uist, *U.K.* 14 D1
South West Africa = Namibia ■,
  Africa 88 C2
South West C., *Australia* 94 G4
South Williamsport, *U.S.A.* 110 E8
South Yorkshire □, *U.K.* 12 D6
Southampton, *Canada* 102 D3
Southampton, *U.K.* 13 G6
Southampton □, *U.K.* 13 F12
Southampton □, *U.K.* 13 G6
Southampton I., *Canada* 101 B11

Southaven, *U.S.A.* 113 H9
Southbank, *Canada* 104 C3
Southbridge, *N.Z.* 91 K4
Southbridge, *U.S.A.* 111 D12
Southend, *Canada* 105 B8
Southend-on-Sea, *U.K.* 13 F8
Southend-on-Sea □, *U.K.* 13 F8
Southern □, *Malawi* 87 F4
Southern □, *S. Leone* 82 D2
Southern □, *Zambia* 87 F2
Southern Alps, *N.Z.* 91 K3
Southern Cross, *Australia* 93 F2
Southern Indian L., *Canada* 105 B9
Southern Ocean, *Antarctica* 5 C6
Southern Pines, *U.S.A.* 109 H6
Southern Uplands, *U.K.* 14 F5
Southington, *U.S.A.* 111 E12
Southland □, *N.Z.* 91 L1
Southold, *U.S.A.* 111 E12
Southport, *Australia* 95 D5
Southport, *U.K.* 12 D4
Southport, *Fla., U.S.A.* 109 K3
Southport, *N.Y., U.S.A.* 110 D8
Southwest C., *N.Z.* 91 M1
Southwold, *U.K.* 13 E9
Soutpansberg, *S. Africa* 89 C4
Souvigny, *France* 19 F10
Sovata, *Romania* 43 D10
Soverato, *Italy* 31 D9
Sovetsk, *Kaliningd., Russia* 9 J19
Sovetsk, *Kirov, Russia* 48 B9
Sovetskaya Gavan = Vanino,
  Russia 51 E15
Sovicille, *Italy* 29 E8
Soweto, *S. Africa* 89 D4
Sōya-Kaikyō = La Perouse Str.,
  Asia 54 B11
Sōya-Misaki, *Japan* 54 B10
Soyaux, *France* 20 C4
Sozh →, *Belarus* 47 F6
Sozopol, *Bulgaria* 41 D11
Spa, *Belgium* 17 D5
Spain ■, *Europe* 7 H5
Spalding, *Australia* 95 E2
Spalding, *U.K.* 12 E7
Spangler, *U.S.A.* 110 F6
Spanish, *Canada* 102 C3
Spanish Fork, *U.S.A.* 114 F8
Spanish Town, *Jamaica* 120 C4
Sparks, *U.S.A.* 116 F7
Sparreholm, *Sweden* 10 E10
Sparta = Spárti, *Greece* 38 D4
Sparta, *Mich., U.S.A.* 108 D3
Sparta, *N.J., U.S.A.* 111 E10
Sparta, *Wis., U.S.A.* 112 D9
Spartanburg, *U.S.A.* 109 H5
Spartansburg, *U.S.A.* 110 E5
Spárti, *Greece* 38 D4
Spartivento, C., *Calabria, Italy* 31 E9
Spartivento, C., *Sard., Italy* 30 D1
Sparwood, *Canada* 104 D6
Spas-Demensk, *Russia* 46 E7
Spas-Klepiki, *Russia* 46 E11
Spassk Dalniy, *Russia* 51 E14
Spassk-Ryazanskiy, *Russia* 46 E11
Spátha, Ákra, *Greece* 36 D5
Spatsizi →, *Canada* 104 B3
Spatsizi Plateau Wilderness
  Park, *Canada* 104 B3
Spean →, *U.K.* 14 E4
Spearfish, *U.S.A.* 112 C3
Spearman, *U.S.A.* 113 G4
Speculator, *U.S.A.* 111 C10
Speia, *Moldova* 43 D14
Speightstown, *Barbados* 121 D8
Speke Gulf, *Tanzania* 86 C3
Spello, *Italy* 29 F9
Spencer, *Idaho, U.S.A.* 114 D7
Spencer, *Iowa, U.S.A.* 112 D7
Spencer, *N.Y., U.S.A.* 111 D8
Spencer, *Nebr., U.S.A.* 112 D5
Spencer, C., *Australia* 95 F2
Spencer B., *Namibia* 88 D1
Spencer G., *Australia* 95 E2
Spencerville, *Canada* 111 B9
Spences Bridge, *Canada* 104 C4
Spennymoor, *U.K.* 12 C6
Spenser Mts., *N.Z.* 91 K4
Spentrup, *Denmark* 11 H4
Sperkhiós →, *Greece* 38 C4
Sperrin Mts., *U.K.* 15 B5
Spessart, *Germany* 25 F5
Spétsai, *Greece* 38 D5
Spey →, *U.K.* 14 D5
Speyer, *Germany* 25 F4
Spezand, *Pakistan* 68 E2
Spezzano Albanese, *Italy* 31 C9
Spiekeroog, *Germany* 24 B3
Spiez, *Switz.* 25 J3
Spíli, *Greece* 36 D6
Spin Búldak, *Afghan.* 68 D2
Spinalónga, *Greece* 36 D7
Spinazzola, *Italy* 31 B9
Spineni, *Romania* 43 F9
Spirit Lake, *U.S.A.* 116 D4
Spirit River, *Canada* 104 B5
Spiritwood, *Canada* 105 C7
Spišská Nová Ves, *Slovak Rep.* 27 C13
Spišské Podhradie, *Slovak Rep.* 27 B13
Spital, *Austria* 26 D7
Spittal an der Drau, *Austria* 26 E6
Spitzbergen = Svalbard, *Arctic* 4 B8
Spjelkavik, *Norway* 9 E12
Split, *Croatia* 29 E13
Split L., *Canada* 105 B9

Split Lake, *Canada* 105 B9
Splitski Kanal, *Croatia* 29 E13
Splügenpass, *Switz.* 25 J5
Spofford, *U.S.A.* 113 L4
Spokane, *U.S.A.* 114 C5
Spoleto, *Italy* 29 F9
Spooner, *U.S.A.* 112 C9
Sporyy Navolok, Mys, *Russia* 50 B7
Sprague, *U.S.A.* 114 C5
Spratly I., *S. China Sea* 62 C4
Spratly Is., *S. China Sea* 62 C4
Spray, *U.S.A.* 114 D4
Spreča →, *Bos.-H.* 42 F3
Spree →, *Germany* 24 C9
Spreewald, *Germany* 24 D9
Spremberg, *Germany* 24 D10
Sprengisandur, *Iceland* 8 D5
Spring City, *U.S.A.* 111 F9
Spring Creek, *U.S.A.* 114 F6
Spring Garden, *U.S.A.* 116 F6
Spring Hill, *U.S.A.* 109 L4
Spring Mts., *U.S.A.* 115 H6
Spring Valley, *U.S.A.* 117 N10
Springbok, *S. Africa* 88 D2
Springboro, *U.S.A.* 110 E4
Springdale, *Canada* 103 C8
Springdale, *U.S.A.* 113 G7
Springe, *Germany* 24 C5
Springer, *U.S.A.* 113 G2
Springerville, *U.S.A.* 115 J9
Springfield, *Canada* 110 D4
Springfield, *N.Z.* 91 K3
Springfield, *Colo., U.S.A.* 113 G3
Springfield, *Ill., U.S.A.* 112 F10
Springfield, *Mass., U.S.A.* 111 D12
Springfield, *Mo., U.S.A.* 113 G8
Springfield, *Ohio, U.S.A.* 108 F4
Springfield, *Oreg., U.S.A.* 114 D2
Springfield, *Tenn., U.S.A.* 109 G2
Springfield, *Vt., U.S.A.* 111 C12
Springfontein, *S. Africa* 88 E4
Springhill, *Canada* 103 C7
Springhill, *U.S.A.* 113 J8
Springhouse, *Canada* 104 C4
Springs, *S. Africa* 89 D4
Springsure, *Australia* 94 C4
Springvale, *U.S.A.* 111 C14
Springville, *Calif., U.S.A.* 116 J8
Springville, *N.Y., U.S.A.* 110 D6
Springville, *Utah, U.S.A.* 114 F8
Springwater, *U.S.A.* 110 D7
Spruce-Creek, *U.S.A.* 110 F6
Spruce Mt., *U.S.A.* 111 B12
Spur, *U.S.A.* 113 J4
Spurn Hd., *U.K.* 12 D8
Spuž, *Montenegro, Yug.* 40 D3
Spuzzum, *Canada* 104 D4
Squam L., *U.S.A.* 111 C13
Squamish, *Canada* 104 D4
Square Islands, *Canada* 103 B8
Squillace, G. di, *Italy* 31 D9
Squinzano, *Italy* 31 B11
Squires, Mt., *Australia* 93 E4
Srbac, *Bos.-H.* 42 E2
Srbica, *Kosovo, Yug.* 40 D4
Srbija = Serbia □, *Yugoslavia* 40 C5
Srbobran, *Serbia, Yug.* 42 E4
Sre Ambel, *Cambodia* 65 G4
Sre Khtum, *Cambodia* 65 F6
Sre Umbell = Sre Ambel,
  Cambodia 65 G4
Srebrenica, *Bos.-H.* 42 F4
Sredinny Ranges = Sredinnyy
  Khrebet, *Russia* 51 D16
Sredinnyy Khrebet, *Russia* 51 D16
Središče, *Slovenia* 29 B13
Sredna Gora, *Bulgaria* 41 D8
Srednekolymsk, *Russia* 51 C16
Sredni Rodopi, *Bulgaria* 41 E8
Srednogorie, *Bulgaria* 41 D8
Śrem, *Poland* 45 F4
Sremska Mitrovica, *Serbia, Yug.* 42 F4
Sremski Karlovci, *Serbia, Yug.* 42 E4
Srepok →, *Cambodia* 64 F6
Sretensk, *Russia* 51 D12
Sri Lanka ■, *Asia* 66 R12
Srikakulam, *India* 67 K13
Srinagar, *India* 69 B6
Środa Śląska, *Poland* 45 G3
Środa Wielkopolski, *Poland* 45 F4
Srpska Crnja, *Serbia, Yug.* 42 E5
Srpski Itebej, *Serbia, Yug.* 42 E5
Staaten →, *Australia* 94 B3
Staberhuk, *Germany* 24 A7
Stade, *Germany* 24 B5
Stadskanaal, *Neths.* 17 A6
Stadtallendorf, *Germany* 24 E5
Stadthagen, *Germany* 24 C5
Stadtlohn, *Germany* 24 D2
Stadtroda, *Germany* 24 E7
Staffa, *U.K.* 14 E2
Staffanstorp, *Sweden* 11 J7
Stafford, *U.K.* 12 E5
Stafford, *U.S.A.* 113 G5
Stafford Springs, *U.S.A.* 111 E12
Staffordshire □, *U.K.* 12 E5
Stagnone, *Italy* 30 E5
Staines, *U.K.* 13 F7
Stainz, *Austria* 26 E8
Stakhanov, *Ukraine* 47 H10
Stalać, *Serbia, Yug.* 40 C5
Stalingrad = Volgograd, *Russia* 49 F7
Staliniri = Tskhinvali, *Georgia* 49 J7
Stalino = Donetsk, *Ukraine* 47 J9
Stalinogorsk = Novomoskovsk,
  Russia 46 E10
Stalis, *Greece* 36 D7

Stallarholmen, *Sweden*	10	E11
Ställdalen, *Sweden*	10	E8
Stalowa Wola, *Poland*	45	H9
Stalybridge, *U.K.*	12	D5
Stamford, *Australia*	94	C3
Stamford, *U.K.*	13	E7
Stamford, *Conn., U.S.A.*	111	E11
Stamford, *N.Y., U.S.A.*	111	D10
Stamford, *Tex., U.S.A.*	113	J5
Stampriet, *Namibia*	88	C2
Stamps, *U.S.A.*	113	J8
Stančevo = Kalipetrovo, *Bulgaria*	41	B11
Standerton, *S. Africa*	89	D4
Standish, *U.S.A.*	108	D4
Stanford, *S. Africa*	88	E2
Stanford, *U.S.A.*	114	C8
Stånga, *Sweden*	11	G12
Stanger, *S. Africa*	89	D5
Stanišić, *Serbia, Yug.*	42	E4
Stanislaus →, *U.S.A.*	116	H5
Stanislav = Ivano-Frankivsk, *Ukraine*	47	H3
Stanisławów, *Poland*	45	F8
Stanley, *Australia*	94	G4
Stanley, *Canada*	105	B8
Stanley, *Falk. Is.*	128	G5
Stanley, *U.K.*	12	C6
Stanley, *Idaho, U.S.A.*	114	D6
Stanley, *N. Dak., U.S.A.*	112	A3
Stanley, *N.Y., U.S.A.*	110	D7
Stanovoy Khrebet, *Russia*	51	D13
Stanovoy Ra. = Stanovoy Khrebet, *Russia*	51	D13
Stansmore Ra., *Australia*	92	D4
Stanthorpe, *Australia*	95	D5
Stanton, *U.S.A.*	113	J4
Stanwood, *U.S.A.*	116	B4
Staples, *U.S.A.*	112	B7
Stąporków, *Poland*	45	G7
Star City, *Canada*	105	C8
Star Lake, *U.S.A.*	111	B9
Stará L'ubovňa, *Slovak Rep.*	27	B13
Stara Moravica, *Serbia, Yug.*	42	E4
Stara Pazova, *Serbia, Yug.*	42	F5
Stara Planina, *Bulgaria*	40	C7
Stará Turá, *Slovak Rep.*	27	C10
Stara Zagora, *Bulgaria*	41	D9
Starachowice, *Poland*	45	G8
Staraya Russa, *Russia*	46	D6
Starbuck I., *Kiribati*	97	H12
Starchiojd, *Romania*	43	E11
Stargard Szczeciński, *Poland*	44	E2
Stari Bar, *Montenegro, Yug.*	40	D3
Stari Trg, *Slovenia*	29	C12
Staritsa, *Russia*	46	D8
Starke, *U.S.A.*	109	L4
Starnberg, *Germany*	25	H7
Starnberger See, *Germany*	25	H7
Starobilsk, *Ukraine*	47	H10
Starodub, *Russia*	47	F7
Starogard Gdański, *Poland*	44	E5
Starokonstantinov = Starokonstyantyniv, *Ukraine*	47	H4
Starokonstyantyniv, *Ukraine*	47	H4
Starominskaya, *Russia*	47	J10
Staroshcherbinovskaya, *Russia*	47	J10
Start Pt., *U.K.*	13	G4
Stary Sącz, *Poland*	45	J7
Staryy Biryuzyak, *Russia*	49	H8
Staryy Chartoriysk, *Ukraine*	47	G3
Staryy Krym, *Ukraine*	47	K8
Staryy Oskol, *Russia*	47	G9
Stassfurt, *Germany*	24	D7
Staszów, *Poland*	45	H8
State College, *U.S.A.*	110	F7
Stateline, *U.S.A.*	116	G7
Staten, I. = Estados, I. de Los, *Argentina*	122	J4
Staten I., *U.S.A.*	111	F10
Statesboro, *U.S.A.*	109	J5
Statesville, *U.S.A.*	109	H5
Stauffer, *U.S.A.*	117	L7
Staunton, *Ill., U.S.A.*	112	F10
Staunton, *Va., U.S.A.*	108	F6
Stavanger, *Norway*	9	G11
Staveley, *N.Z.*	91	K3
Stavelot, *Belgium*	17	D5
Stavern, *Norway*	9	G14
Stavoren, *Neths.*	17	B5
Stavropol, *Russia*	49	H6
Stavros, *Cyprus*	36	D11
Stavrós, *Greece*	36	D6
Stavrós, Ákra, *Greece*	36	D6
Stavroúpolis, *Greece*	41	E8
Stawell, *Australia*	95	F3
Stawell →, *Australia*	94	C3
Stawiski, *Poland*	44	E9
Stawiszyn, *Poland*	45	G5
Stayner, *Canada*	110	B4
Stayton, *U.S.A.*	114	D2
Steamboat Springs, *U.S.A.*	114	F10
Steblevë, *Albania*	40	E4
Steele, *U.S.A.*	112	B5
Steelton, *U.S.A.*	110	F8
Steen River, *Canada*	104	B5
Steenkool = Bintuni, *Indonesia*	63	E8
Steens Mt., *U.S.A.*	114	E4
Steenwijk, *Neths.*	17	B6
Steep Pt., *Australia*	93	E1
Steep Rock, *Canada*	105	C9
Ştefan Vodă, *Moldova*	43	D14
Ştefăneşti, *Romania*	43	C12
Stefanie L. = Chew Bahir, *Ethiopia*	81	G4
Stefansson Bay, *Antarctica*	5	C5
Stege, *Denmark*	11	K6

Ştei, *Romania*	42	D7
Steiermark □, *Austria*	26	D8
Steigerwald, *Germany*	25	F6
Steilacoom, *U.S.A.*	116	C4
Steilrandberge, *Namibia*	88	B1
Steinbach, *Canada*	105	D9
Steinfurt, *Germany*	24	C3
Steinhausen, *Namibia*	88	C2
Steinheim, *Germany*	24	D5
Steinhuder Meer, *Germany*	24	C5
Steinkjer, *Norway*	8	D14
Steinkopf, *S. Africa*	88	D2
Stellarton, *Canada*	103	C7
Stellenbosch, *S. Africa*	88	E2
Stelvio, Paso dello, *Italy*	28	B7
Stenay, *France*	19	C12
Stendal, *Germany*	24	C7
Stende, *Latvia*	44	A9
Stenhamra, *Sweden*	10	E11
Stenstorp, *Sweden*	11	F7
Stenungsund, *Sweden*	11	F5
Steornabhaigh = Stornoway, *U.K.*	14	C2
Stepanakert = Xankändi, *Azerbaijan*	70	B5
Stepanavan, *Armenia*	49	K7
Stephens Creek, *Australia*	95	E3
Stephens I., *Canada*	104	C2
Stephens L., *Canada*	105	B9
Stephenville, *Canada*	103	C8
Stephenville, *U.S.A.*	113	J5
Stepnica, *Poland*	44	E1
Stepnoi = Elista, *Russia*	49	G7
Steppe, *Asia*	52	D9
Stereá Ellas □, *Greece*	38	C4
Sterkstroom, *S. Africa*	88	E4
Sterling, *Colo., U.S.A.*	112	E3
Sterling, *Ill., U.S.A.*	112	E10
Sterling, *Kans., U.S.A.*	112	F5
Sterling City, *U.S.A.*	113	K4
Sterling Heights, *U.S.A.*	108	D4
Sterling Run, *U.S.A.*	110	E6
Sterlitamak, *Russia*	50	D6
Sternberg, *Germany*	24	B7
Šternberk, *Czech Rep.*	27	B10
Stérnes, *Greece*	36	D6
Sterzing = Vipiteno, *Italy*	29	B8
Stettin = Szczecin, *Poland*	44	E1
Stettiner Haff, *Germany*	24	B10
Stettler, *Canada*	104	C6
Steubenville, *U.S.A.*	110	F4
Stevenage, *U.K.*	13	F7
Stevens Point, *U.S.A.*	112	C10
Stevenson, *U.S.A.*	116	E5
Stevenson L., *Canada*	105	C9
Stevensville, *U.S.A.*	114	C6
Stevns Klint, *Denmark*	11	J6
Stewart, *Canada*	104	B3
Stewart, *U.S.A.*	116	F7
Stewart →, *Canada*	100	B6
Stewart, C., *Australia*	94	A1
Stewart, I., *Chile*	128	G2
Stewart I., *N.Z.*	91	M1
Stewarts Point, *U.S.A.*	116	G3
Stewartville, *U.S.A.*	112	D8
Stewiacke, *Canada*	103	C7
Steynsburg, *S. Africa*	88	E4
Steyr, *Austria*	26	C7
Steyr →, *Austria*	26	C7
Steytlerville, *S. Africa*	88	E3
Stia, *Italy*	29	E8
Stigler, *U.S.A.*	113	H7
Stigliano, *Italy*	31	B9
Stigtomta, *Sweden*	11	F10
Stikine →, *Canada*	104	B2
Stilfontein, *S. Africa*	88	D4
Stilís, *Greece*	38	C4
Stillwater, *N.Z.*	91	K3
Stillwater, *Minn., U.S.A.*	112	C8
Stillwater, *N.Y., U.S.A.*	111	D11
Stillwater, *Okla., U.S.A.*	113	G6
Stillwater Range, *U.S.A.*	114	G4
Stillwater Reservoir, *U.S.A.*	111	C9
Stilo, Pta., *Italy*	31	D9
Stilwell, *U.S.A.*	113	H7
Štip, *Macedonia*	40	E6
Stíra, *Greece*	38	C6
Stirling, *Canada*	110	B7
Stirling, *U.K.*	14	E5
Stirling □, *U.K.*	14	E4
Stirling Ra., *Australia*	93	F2
Stittsville, *Canada*	111	A9
Stjernøya, *Norway*	8	A20
Stjørdalshalsen, *Norway*	8	E14
Stockach, *Germany*	25	H5
Stockaryd, *Sweden*	11	G8
Stockerau, *Austria*	27	C9
Stockholm, *Sweden*	10	E12
Stockholms län □, *Sweden*	10	E12
Stockport, *U.K.*	12	D5
Stocksbridge, *U.K.*	12	D6
Stockton, *Calif., U.S.A.*	116	H5
Stockton, *Kans., U.S.A.*	112	F5
Stockton, *Mo., U.S.A.*	113	G8
Stockton-on-Tees, *U.K.*	12	C6
Stockton-on-Tees □, *U.K.*	12	C6
Stockton Plateau, *U.S.A.*	113	K3
Stoczek Łukowski, *Poland*	45	G8
Stöde, *Sweden*	10	B10
Stoeng Treng, *Cambodia*	64	F5
Stoer, Pt. of, *U.K.*	14	C3
Stogovo, *Macedonia*	40	E4
Stoholm, *Denmark*	11	H3
Stoke-on-Trent, *U.K.*	12	D5
Stoke-on-Trent □, *U.K.*	12	D5
Stokes Pt., *Australia*	94	G3
Stokes Ra., *Australia*	92	C5

Stokksnes, *Iceland*	8	D6
Stokmarknes, *Norway*	8	B16
Stolac, *Bos.-H.*	40	C1
Stolberg, *Germany*	24	E2
Stolbovoy, Ostrov, *Russia*	51	B14
Stolbtsy = Stowbtsy, *Belarus*	46	F4
Stolin, *Belarus*	47	G4
Stöllet, *Sweden*	10	D7
Stolnici, *Romania*	43	F9
Stomíon, *Greece*	36	D5
Ston, *Croatia*	29	F14
Stone, *U.K.*	12	E5
Stoneboro, *U.S.A.*	110	E4
Stonehaven, *U.K.*	14	E6
Stonehenge, *Australia*	94	C3
Stonehenge, *U.K.*	13	F6
Stonewall, *Canada*	105	C9
Stony L., *Man., Canada*	105	B9
Stony L., *Ont., Canada*	110	B6
Stony Point, *U.S.A.*	111	E11
Stony Pt., *U.S.A.*	111	C8
Stony Rapids, *Canada*	105	B7
Stony Tunguska = Tunguska, Podkamennaya →, *Russia*	51	C10
Stonyford, *U.S.A.*	116	F4
Stopnica, *Poland*	45	H7
Storå, *Sweden*	10	E9
Storå →, *Denmark*	11	H2
Stora Gla, *Sweden*	10	E6
Stora Le, *Sweden*	10	E5
Stora Lulevatten, *Sweden*	8	C18
Storavan, *Sweden*	8	D18
Store Bælt, *Denmark*	11	J4
Store Heddinge, *Denmark*	11	J6
Storebro, *Sweden*	11	G9
Storfors, *Sweden*	10	E8
Storlien, *Sweden*	10	A6
Storm B., *Australia*	94	G4
Storm Lake, *U.S.A.*	112	D7
Stormberge, *S. Africa*	88	E4
Stormsrivier, *S. Africa*	88	E3
Stornoway, *U.K.*	14	C2
Storo, *Italy*	28	C7
Storozhinets = Storozhynets, *Ukraine*	47	H3
Storozhynets, *Ukraine*	47	H3
Storrs, *U.S.A.*	111	E12
Storsjön, *Gävleborg, Sweden*	10	D10
Storsjön, *Jämtland, Sweden*	10	B7
Storsjön, *Jämtland, Sweden*	10	A8
Storstrøms Amtskommune □, *Denmark*	11	J5
Storuman, *Sweden*	8	D17
Storuman, sjö, *Sweden*	8	D17
Storvätteshågna, *Sweden*	10	B6
Storvik, *Sweden*	10	D10
Storvreta, *Sweden*	10	E11
Stouffville, *Canada*	110	C5
Stoughton, *Canada*	105	D8
Stour →, *Dorset, U.K.*	13	G6
Stour →, *Kent, U.K.*	13	F9
Stour →, *Suffolk, U.K.*	13	F9
Stourbridge, *U.K.*	13	E5
Stout L., *Canada*	105	C10
Stove Pipe Wells Village, *U.S.A.*	117	J9
Støvring, *Denmark*	11	H3
Stow, *U.S.A.*	110	E3
Stowbtsy, *Belarus*	46	F4
Stowmarket, *U.K.*	13	E9
Strabane, *U.K.*	15	B4
Stracin, *Macedonia*	40	D6
Stradella, *Italy*	28	C6
Strahan, *Australia*	94	G4
Strajitsa, *Bulgaria*	41	C9
Strakonice, *Czech Rep.*	26	B6
Straldzha, *Bulgaria*	41	D10
Stralsund, *Germany*	24	A9
Strand, *S. Africa*	88	E2
Stranda, *Møre og Romsdal, Norway*	9	E12
Stranda, *Nord-Trøndelag, Norway*	8	E14
Strandby, *Denmark*	11	G4
Strangford L., *U.K.*	15	B6
Strängnäs, *Sweden*	10	E11
Stranraer, *U.K.*	14	G3
Strasbourg, *Canada*	105	C8
Strasbourg, *France*	19	D14
Strasburg, *Germany*	24	B9
Strășeni, *Moldova*	43	C13
Strässa, *Sweden*	10	E9
Stratford, *Canada*	102	D3
Stratford, *N.Z.*	91	H5
Stratford, *Calif., U.S.A.*	116	J7
Stratford, *Conn., U.S.A.*	111	E11
Stratford, *Tex., U.S.A.*	113	G3
Stratford-upon-Avon, *U.K.*	13	E6
Strath Spey, *U.K.*	14	D5
Strathalbyn, *Australia*	95	F2
Strathaven, *U.K.*	14	F4
Strathcona Prov. Park, *Canada*	104	D3
Strathmore, *Canada*	104	C6
Strathmore, *U.K.*	14	E5
Strathmore, *U.S.A.*	116	J7
Strathnaver, *Canada*	104	C4
Strathpeffer, *U.K.*	14	D4
Strathroy, *Canada*	102	D3
Strathy Pt., *U.K.*	14	C4
Strattanville, *U.S.A.*	110	E5
Stratton, *U.S.A.*	111	A14
Stratton Mt., *U.S.A.*	111	C12
Straubing, *Germany*	25	G8
Straumnes, *Iceland*	8	C2
Strausberg, *Germany*	24	C9
Strawberry →, *U.S.A.*	114	F8
Strážnice, *Czech Rep.*	27	C10

Streaky B., *Australia*	95	E1
Streaky Bay, *Australia*	95	E1
Streator, *U.S.A.*	112	E10
Streetsboro, *U.S.A.*	110	E3
Streetsville, *Canada*	110	C5
Strehaia, *Romania*	43	F8
Strelcha, *Bulgaria*	41	D8
Strelka, *Russia*	51	D10
Streng →, *Cambodia*	64	F4
Stresa, *Italy*	28	C5
Streymoy, *Færoe Is.*	8	E9
Strezhevoy, *Russia*	50	C8
Stříbro, *Czech Rep.*	26	A6
Strimón →, *Greece*	40	F7
Strimonikós Kólpos, *Greece*	40	F7
Strofádhes, *Greece*	38	D3
Stroma, *U.K.*	14	C5
Strómboli, *Italy*	31	D8
Stromeferry, *U.K.*	14	D3
Stromness, *U.K.*	14	C5
Strömsbruk, *Sweden*	10	C11
Strömsnäsbruk, *Sweden*	11	H7
Strömstad, *Sweden*	11	F5
Strömsund, *Sweden*	8	E16
Strongilí, *Greece*	39	E11
Stróngoli, *Italy*	31	C10
Strongsville, *U.S.A.*	110	E3
Stronie Śląskie, *Poland*	45	H3
Stronsay, *U.K.*	14	B6
Stropkov, *Slovak Rep.*	27	B14
Stroud, *U.K.*	13	F5
Stroud Road, *Australia*	95	E5
Stroudsburg, *U.S.A.*	111	F9
Stroumbi, *Cyprus*	36	E11
Struer, *Denmark*	11	H2
Struga, *Macedonia*	40	E4
Strugi Krasnyye, *Russia*	46	C5
Strumica, *Macedonia*	40	E6
Strumica →, *Europe*	40	E7
Struthers, *Canada*	102	C2
Struthers, *U.S.A.*	110	E4
Stryama, *Bulgaria*	41	D8
Stryker, *U.S.A.*	114	B6
Stryków, *Poland*	45	G6
Stryy, *Ukraine*	47	H2
Strzegom, *Poland*	45	H3
Strzelce Krajeńskie, *Poland*	45	F2
Strzelce Opolskie, *Poland*	45	H5
Strzelecki Cr. →, *Australia*	95	D2
Strzelin, *Poland*	45	H4
Strzelno, *Poland*	45	F5
Strzybnica, *Poland*	45	H5
Strzyżów, *Poland*	45	J8
Stuart, *Fla., U.S.A.*	109	M5
Stuart, *Nebr., U.S.A.*	112	D5
Stuart →, *Canada*	104	C4
Stuart Bluff Ra., *Australia*	92	D5
Stuart L., *Canada*	104	C4
Stuart Ra., *Australia*	95	D1
Stubbekøbing, *Denmark*	11	K6
Studen Kladenets, Yazovir, *Bulgaria*	41	E9
Studenka, *Czech Rep.*	27	B11
Stugun, *Sweden*	10	A9
Stuhr, *Germany*	24	B4
Stull L., *Canada*	102	B1
Stung Treng = Stoeng Treng, *Cambodia*	64	F5
Stupart →, *Canada*	102	A1
Stupava, *Slovak Rep.*	27	C10
Stupino, *Russia*	46	E10
Sturgeon B., *Canada*	105	C9
Sturgeon Bay, *U.S.A.*	108	C2
Sturgeon Falls, *Canada*	102	C4
Sturgeon L., *Alta., Canada*	104	B5
Sturgeon L., *Ont., Canada*	102	C1
Sturgeon L., *Ont., Canada*	110	B6
Sturgis, *Canada*	105	C8
Sturgis, *Mich., U.S.A.*	108	E3
Sturgis, *S. Dak., U.S.A.*	112	C3
Sturkö, *Sweden*	11	H9
Sturt Cr. →, *Australia*	92	C4
Stutterheim, *S. Africa*	88	E4
Stuttgart, *Germany*	25	G5
Stuttgart, *U.S.A.*	113	H9
Stuyvesant, *U.S.A.*	111	D11
Stykkishólmur, *Iceland*	8	D2
Styria = Steiermark □, *Austria*	26	D8
Styrsö, *Sweden*	11	G5
Su Xian = Suzhou, *China*	56	H9
Suakin, *Sudan*	80	D4
Suan, *N. Korea*	57	E14
Suaqui, *Mexico*	118	B3
Suar, *India*	69	E8
Subang, *Indonesia*	63	G12
Subansiri →, *India*	67	F18
Subarnarekha →, *India*	69	H12
Subayhah, *Si. Arabia*	70	D3
Subcetate, *Romania*	42	E8
Subi, *Indonesia*	65	L7
Subiaco, *Italy*	29	G10
Subotica, *Serbia, Yug.*	42	E4
Suca, *Ethiopia*	81	F4
Suceava, *Romania*	43	C10
Suceava →, *Romania*	43	C11
Sucha-Beskidzka, *Poland*	45	J6
Suchań, *Poland*	45	E2
Suchan, *Russia*	54	C6
Suchedniów, *Poland*	45	G7
Suchitoto, *El Salv.*	120	D2
Suchou = Suzhou, *China*	59	B13
Suchowola, *Poland*	44	E10

Suck →, *Ireland*	15	C3
Sucre, *Bolivia*	124	G5
Sućuraj, *Croatia*	29	E14
Sucuriú →, *Brazil*	125	H8
Sud, Pte. du, *Canada*	103	C7
Sud-Kivu □, *Dem. Rep. of the Congo*	86	C2
Sud-Ouest, Pte. du, *Canada*	103	C7
Suda →, *Russia*	46	C9
Sudak, *Ukraine*	47	K8
Sudan, *U.S.A.*	113	H3
Sudan ■, *Africa*	81	E3
Sudbury, *Canada*	102	C3
Sudbury, *U.K.*	13	E8
Sûdd, *Sudan*	81	F3
Süderbrarup, *Germany*	24	A5
Süderoogsand, *Germany*	24	A4
Sudeten Mts. = Sudety, *Europe*	27	A9
Sudety, *Europe*	27	A9
Suðuroy, *Færoe Is.*	8	F9
Sudi, *Tanzania*	87	E4
Sudirman, Pegunungan, *Indonesia*	63	E9
Sudiţi, *Romania*	43	F12
Sudogda, *Russia*	48	C5
Sudr, *Egypt*	80	B3
Sudzha, *Russia*	47	G8
Sue →, *Sudan*	81	F2
Sueca, *Spain*	33	F4
Sŭedinenie, *Bulgaria*	41	D8
Suemez I., *U.S.A.*	104	B2
Suez = El Suweis, *Egypt*	80	J8
Suez, G. of = Suweis, Khalîg el, *Egypt*	80	J8
Suez Canal = Suweis, Qanâ es, *Egypt*	80	H8
Suffield, *Canada*	104	C6
Suffolk, *U.S.A.*	108	G7
Suffolk □, *U.K.*	13	E9
Şugag, *Romania*	43	E8
Sugarcreek, *U.S.A.*	110	E5
Sugarive →, *India*	69	F12
Suğla Gölü, *Turkey*	72	D5
Sugluk = Salluit, *Canada*	101	B12
Sŭhaia, Lacul, *Romania*	43	G10
Şuḩār, *Oman*	71	E8
Sühbaatar □, *Mongolia*	56	B8
Suhl, *Germany*	24	E6
Şuhut, *Turkey*	39	C12
Sui, *Pakistan*	68	E3
Sui Xian, *China*	56	G8
Šuica, *Bos.-H.*	42	G2
Suichang, *China*	59	C12
Suichuan, *China*	59	D10
Suide, *China*	56	F6
Suifenhe, *China*	57	B16
Suihua, *China*	60	B7
Suijiang, *China*	58	C4
Suining, *Hunan, China*	59	D8
Suining, *Jiangsu, China*	57	H9
Suining, *Sichuan, China*	58	B5
Suiping, *China*	56	H7
Suippes, *France*	19	C11
Suir →, *Ireland*	15	D4
Suisun City, *U.S.A.*	116	G4
Suixi, *China*	59	G8
Suiyang, *Guizhou, China*	58	D6
Suiyang, *Heilongjiang, China*	57	B16
Suizhong, *China*	57	D11
Suizhou, *China*	59	B9
Sujangarh, *India*	68	F6
Sukabumi, *Indonesia*	63	G12
Sukadana, *Indonesia*	62	E3
Sukagawa, *Japan*	55	F10
Sukaraja, *Indonesia*	62	E4
Sukarnapura = Jayapura, *Indonesia*	63	E10
Sukch'ŏn, *N. Korea*	57	E13
Sukhindol, *Bulgaria*	41	C9
Sukhinichi, *Russia*	46	E8
Sukhona →, *Russia*	50	D4
Sukhothai, *Thailand*	64	D2
Sukhumi = Sokhumi, *Georgia*	49	J5
Sukkur, *Pakistan*	68	F3
Sukkur Barrage, *Pakistan*	68	F3
Sukovo, *Serbia, Yug.*	40	C6
Sukri →, *India*	68	G4
Sukumo, *Japan*	55	H6
Sukunka →, *Canada*	104	B4
Sula →, *Ukraine*	47	H7
Sula, Kepulauan, *Indonesia*	63	E7
Sulaco →, *Honduras*	120	C2
Sulaiman Range, *Pakistan*	68	D3
Sulak →, *Russia*	49	J8
Sūlār, *Iran*	71	D6
Sulawesi Sea = Celebes Sea, *Indonesia*	63	D6
Sulawesi Selatan □, *Indonesia*	63	E6
Sulawesi Utara □, *Indonesia*	63	D6
Sulechów, *Poland*	45	F2
Sulęcin, *Poland*	45	F2
Sulejów, *Poland*	45	G6
Sulejówek, *Poland*	45	F8
Süleymanlı, *Turkey*	39	C9
Sulima, *S. Leone*	82	D2
Sulina, *Romania*	43	E14
Sulina, Brațul →, *Romania*	43	E14
Sulingen, *Germany*	24	C4
Suliţa, *Romania*	43	C11
Sulitjelma, *Norway*	8	C17
Sułkowice, *Poland*	45	J6
Sullana, *Peru*	124	D2
Süller, *Turkey*	39	C11
Sullivan, *Ill., U.S.A.*	112	F10
Sullivan, *Ind., U.S.A.*	108	F2
Sullivan, *Mo., U.S.A.*	112	F9

Sullivan Bay, *Canada* 104 C3
Sullivan I. = Lanbi Kyun, *Burma* 65 G2
Sully-sur-Loire, *France* 19 E9
Sulmierzyce, *Poland* 45 G4
Sulmona, *Italy* 29 F10
Süloğlu, *Turkey* 41 E10
Sulphur, *La., U.S.A.* 113 K8
Sulphur, *Okla., U.S.A.* 113 H6
Sulphur Pt., *Canada* 104 A6
Sulphur Springs, *U.S.A.* 113 J7
Sultan, *Canada* 102 C3
Sultan, *U.S.A.* 116 C5
Sultan Dağları, *Turkey* 72 C4
Sultanhisar, *Turkey* 39 D10
Sultaniça, *Turkey* 41 F10
Sultaniye, *Turkey* 41 F12
Sultanpur, *Mad. P., India* 68 H8
Sultanpur, *Punjab, India* 68 D6
Sultanpur, *Ut. P., India* 69 F10
Sulu Arch., *Phil.* 61 J4
Sulu Sea, *E. Indies* 61 G4
Sülüklü, *Turkey* 72 C5
Sululta, *Ethiopia* 81 F4
Suluova, *Turkey* 72 B6
Suluq, *Libya* 79 B10
Sulzbach, *Germany* 25 F3
Sulzbach-Rosenberg, *Germany* . 25 F7
Sulzberger Ice Shelf, *Antarctica* 5 D10
Sumalata, *Indonesia* 63 D6
Sumampa, *Argentina* 126 B3
Sumatera □, *Indonesia* 62 D2
Sumatera Barat □, *Indonesia* .. 62 D2
Sumatera Utara □, *Indonesia* .. 62 D1
Sumatra = Sumatera □,
   Indonesia 62 D2
Sumba, *Indonesia* 63 F5
Sumba, Selat, *Indonesia* 63 F5
Sumbawa, *Indonesia* 62 F5
Sumbawa Besar, *Indonesia* 62 F5
Sumbawanga □, *Tanzania* 84 F6
Sumbe, *Angola* 84 G2
Sumburgh Hd., *U.K.* 14 B7
Sumdeo, *India* 69 D8
Sumdo, *India* 69 B8
Sumedang, *Indonesia* 63 G12
Sümeg, *Hungary* 42 D2
Sumeih, *Sudan* 81 F2
Sumen = Shumen, *Bulgaria* ... 41 C10
Sumenep, *Indonesia* 63 G15
Sumgait = Sumqayıt, *Azerbaijan* 49 K9
Summer L., *U.S.A.* 114 E4
Summerland, *Canada* 104 D5
Summerside, *Canada* 103 C7
Summersville, *U.S.A.* 108 F5
Summerville, *Ga., U.S.A.* 109 H3
Summerville, *S.C., U.S.A.* 109 J5
Summit Lake, *Canada* 104 C4
Summit Peak, *U.S.A.* 115 H10
Sumner, *Iowa, U.S.A.* 112 D8
Sumner, *Wash., U.S.A.* 116 C4
Sumoto, *Japan* 55 G7
Šumperk, *Czech Rep.* 27 B9
Sumqayıt, *Azerbaijan* 49 K9
Sumter, *U.S.A.* 109 J5
Sumy, *Ukraine* 47 G8
Sun City, *Ariz., U.S.A.* 115 K7
Sun City, *Calif., U.S.A.* 117 M9
Sun City Center, *U.S.A.* 109 M4
Sun Lakes, *U.S.A.* 115 K8
Sun Valley, *U.S.A.* 114 E6
Sunagawa, *Japan* 54 C10
Sunan, *N. Korea* 57 E13
Sunart, L., *U.K.* 14 E3
Sunburst, *U.S.A.* 114 B8
Sunbury, *Australia* 95 F3
Sunbury, *U.S.A.* 111 F8
Sunchales, *Argentina* 126 C3
Suncho Corral, *Argentina* 126 B3
Sunch'ŏn, *S. Korea* 57 G14
Suncook, *U.S.A.* 111 C13
Sunda, Selat, *Indonesia* 62 F3
Sunda Is., *Indonesia* 52 K14
Sunda Str. = Sunda, Selat,
   Indonesia 62 F3
Sundance, *Canada* 105 B10
Sundance, *U.S.A.* 112 C2
Sundar Nagar, *India* 68 D7
Sundarbans, The, *Asia* 67 J16
Sundargarh, *India* 67 H14
Sundays = Sondags →, *S. Africa* 88 E4
Sunderland, *Canada* 110 B5
Sunderland, *U.K.* 12 C6
Sundre, *Canada* 104 C6
Sunds, *Denmark* 11 H3
Sundsvall, *Sweden* 10 B11
Sundsvallsbukten, *Sweden* 10 B11
Sung Hei, *Vietnam* 65 G6
Sungai Kolok, *Thailand* 65 J3
Sungai Lembing, *Malaysia* 65 L4
Sungai Petani, *Malaysia* 65 K3
Sungaigerong, *Indonesia* 62 E2
Sungailiat, *Indonesia* 62 E3
Sungaipenuh, *Indonesia* 62 E2
Sungari = Songhua Jiang →,
   China 60 B8
Sunghua Chiang = Songhua
   Jiang →, *China* 60 B8
Sungikai, *Sudan* 81 E2
Sungurlu, *Turkey* 72 B6
Sunja, *Croatia* 29 C13
Sunland Park, *U.S.A.* 115 L10
Sunnansjö, *Sweden* 10 D8
Sunne, *Sweden* 10 E7
Sunnemo, *Sweden* 10 E7
Sunndalsøra, *Norway* 9 E13
Sunnyside, *U.S.A.* 114 C3
Sunnyvale, *U.S.A.* 116 H4

Suntar, *Russia* 51 C12
Sunyani, *Ghana* 82 D4
Suomenselkä, *Finland* 8 E21
Suomussalmi, *Finland* 8 D23
Suoyarvi, *Russia* 46 A7
Supai, *U.S.A.* 115 H7
Supaul, *India* 69 F12
Superior, *Ariz., U.S.A.* 115 K8
Superior, *Mont., U.S.A.* 114 C6
Superior, *Nebr., U.S.A.* 112 E5
Superior, *Wis., U.S.A.* 112 B8
Superior, L., *N. Amer.* 102 C2
Supetar, *Croatia* 29 E13
Suphan Buri, *Thailand* 64 E3
Suphan Dağı, *Turkey* 70 B4
Supiori, *Indonesia* 63 E9
Supung Shuiku, *China* 57 D13
Sũq Suwayq, *Si. Arabia* 70 E3
Suqian, *China* 57 H10
Sũr, *Lebanon* 75 B4
Şũr, *Oman* 74 C6
Sur, Pt., *U.S.A.* 116 J5
Sura →, *Russia* 48 C8
Surab, *Pakistan* 68 E2
Surabaja = Surabaya, *Indonesia* 62 F4
Surabaya, *Indonesia* 62 F4
Surahammar, *Sweden* 10 E10
Suraia, *Romania* 43 E12
Surakarta, *Indonesia* 62 F4
Surakhany, *Azerbaijan* 49 K10
Şũrany, *Slovak Rep.* 27 C11
Surat, *Australia* 95 D4
Surat, *India* 66 J8
Surat Thani, *Thailand* 65 H2
Suratgarh, *India* 68 E5
Suraż, *Poland* 45 F9
Surazh, *Belarus* 46 E6
Surazh, *Russia* 47 F7
Surduc, *Romania* 43 C8
Surduc Pasul, *Romania* 43 E8
Surdulica, *Serbia, Yug.* 40 D6
Surendranagar, *India* 68 H4
Surf, *U.S.A.* 117 L6
Surgères, *France* 20 B3
Surgut, *Russia* 50 C8
Sùria, *Spain* 32 D6
Suriapet, *India* 66 L11
Surigao, *Phil.* 61 G6
Surigao Strait, *Phil.* 61 F6
Surin, *Thailand* 64 E4
Surin Nua, Ko, *Thailand* 65 H1
Surinam ■, *S. Amer.* 125 C7
Suriname = Surinam ■, *S. Amer.* 125 C7
Suriname →, *Surinam* 125 B7
Sũrmaq, *Iran* 71 D7
Sürmene, *Turkey* 73 B9
Surovikino, *Russia* 49 F6
Surrey □, *U.K.* 13 F7
Sursand, *India* 69 F11
Sursar →, *India* 69 F12
Sursee, *Switz.* 25 H4
Sursk, *Russia* 48 D7
Surskoye, *Russia* 48 C8
Surt, *Libya* 79 B9
Surt, Khalīj, *Libya* 79 B9
Surtanahu, *Pakistan* 68 F4
Surte, *Sweden* 11 G6
Surtsey, *Iceland* 8 E3
Sürüç, *Turkey* 73 D8
Suruga-Wan, *Japan* 55 G9
Susa, *Italy* 28 C4
Susã →, *Denmark* 11 J5
Sušac, *Croatia* 29 F13
Susak, *Croatia* 29 D11
Susaki, *Japan* 55 H6
Sũsangerd, *Iran* 71 D6
Susanville, *U.S.A.* 114 F3
Susch, *Switz.* 25 J6
Suşehri, *Turkey* 73 B8
Sušice, *Czech Rep.* 26 B6
Susleni, *Moldova* 43 C13
Susner, *India* 68 H7
Susong, *China* 59 B11
Susquehanna, *U.S.A.* 111 E9
Susquehanna →, *U.S.A.* 111 G8
Susques, *Argentina* 126 A2
Sussex, *Canada* 103 C6
Sussex, *U.S.A.* 111 E10
Sussex, E. □, *U.K.* 13 G8
Sussex, W. □, *U.K.* 13 G7
Sustut →, *Canada* 104 B3
Susuman, *Russia* 51 C15
Susunu, *Indonesia* 63 E8
Susurluk, *Turkey* 39 B10
Susuz, *Turkey* 73 B10
Susz, *Poland* 44 E6
Sütçüler, *Turkey* 72 D4
Şuţeşti, *Romania* 43 E12
Sutherland, *S. Africa* 88 E3
Sutherland, *U.S.A.* 112 E4
Sutherland Falls, *N.Z.* 91 L1
Sutherlin, *U.S.A.* 114 E2
Suthri, *India* 68 H3
Sutlej →, *Pakistan* 68 E4
Sutter, *U.S.A.* 116 F5
Sutter Creek, *U.S.A.* 116 G6
Sutton, *Canada* 111 A12
Sutton, *Nebr., U.S.A.* 112 E6
Sutton, *W. Va., U.S.A.* 108 F5
Sutton →, *Canada* 102 A3
Sutton Coldfield, *U.K.* 13 E6
Sutton in Ashfield, *U.K.* 12 D6
Sutton L., *Canada* 102 B3
Suttor →, *Australia* 94 C4
Suttsu, *Japan* 54 C10

Suva, *Fiji* 91 D8
Suva Gora, *Macedonia* 40 E5
Suva Planina, *Serbia, Yug.* ... 40 C6
Suva Reka, *Kosovo, Yug.* 40 D4
Suvorov, *Russia* 46 E9
Suvorov Is. = Suwarrow Is.,
   Cook Is. 97 J11
Suvorovo, *Bulgaria* 41 C11
Suwałki, *Poland* 44 D9
Suwannaphum, *Thailand* 64 E4
Suwannee →, *U.S.A.* 109 L4
Suwanose-Jima, *Japan* 55 K4
Suwarrow Is., *Cook Is.* 97 J11
Suwayq aş Şuqban, *Iraq* 70 D5
Suweis, Khalîg el, *Egypt* 80 J8
Suweis, Qanâ es, *Egypt* 80 H8
Suwŏn, *S. Korea* 57 F14
Suzdal, *Russia* 46 D11
Suzhou, *Anhui, China* 56 H9
Suzhou, *Jiangsu, China* 59 B13
Suzu, *Japan* 55 F8
Suzu-Misaki, *Japan* 55 F8
Suzuka, *Japan* 55 G8
Suzzara, *Italy* 28 D7
Svalbard, *Arctic* 4 B8
Svalöv, *Sweden* 11 J7
Svaneke, *Denmark* 11 J9
Svängsta, *Sweden* 11 H8
Svanskog, *Sweden* 10 E6
Svappavaara, *Sweden* 8 C19
Svärdsjö, *Sweden* 10 D9
Svartå, *Sweden* 10 E8
Svartisen, *Norway* 8 C15
Svartvik, *Sweden* 10 B11
Svatove, *Ukraine* 47 H10
Svatovo = Svatove, *Ukraine* .. 47 H10
Svay Chek, *Cambodia* 64 F4
Svay Rieng, *Cambodia* 65 G5
Svealand □, *Sweden* 10 D9
Svedala, *Sweden* 11 J7
Sveg, *Sweden* 10 B8
Svendborg, *Denmark* 11 J4
Svenljunga, *Sweden* 11 G7
Svenstavik, *Sweden* 10 B8
Svenstrup, *Denmark* 11 H3
Sverdlovsk = Yekaterinburg,
   Russia 50 D7
Sverdlovsk, *Ukraine* 47 H10
Sverdrup Is., *Canada* 4 B3
Svetac, *Croatia* 29 E12
Sveti Nikola, Prokhod, *Europe* . 40 C6
Sveti Nikole, *Macedonia* 40 E5
Sveti Rok, *Croatia* 29 D12
Svetlaya, *Russia* 54 A9
Svetlogorsk = Svyetlahorsk,
   Belarus 47 F6
Svetlograd, *Russia* 49 H6
Svetlovodsk = Svitlovodsk,
   Ukraine 47 H7
Svidník, *Slovak Rep.* 27 B14
Svilaja Planina, *Croatia* 29 E13
Svilajnac, *Serbia, Yug.* 40 B5
Svilengrad, *Bulgaria* 41 E10
Svir →, *Russia* 46 B7
Sviritsa, *Russia* 46 B7
Svishtov, *Bulgaria* 41 C9
Svislach, *Belarus* 47 F3
Svitava →, *Czech Rep.* 27 B9
Svitavy, *Czech Rep.* 27 B9
Svitlovodsk, *Ukraine* 47 H7
Svobodnyy, *Russia* 51 D13
Svoge, *Bulgaria* 40 D7
Svolvær, *Norway* 8 B16
Svratka →, *Czech Rep.* 27 B9
Svrljig, *Serbia, Yug.* 40 C6
Svyetlahorsk, *Belarus* 47 F5
Swabian Alps = Schwäbische
   Alb, *Germany* 25 G5
Swainsboro, *U.S.A.* 109 J4
Swakop →, *Namibia* 88 C2
Swakopmund, *Namibia* 88 C1
Swale →, *U.K.* 12 C6
Swan →, *Australia* 93 F2
Swan →, *Canada* 105 C8
Swan Hill, *Australia* 95 F3
Swan Hills, *Canada* 104 C5
Swan Is. = Santanilla, Is.,
   W. Indies 120 C3
Swan L., *Canada* 105 C8
Swan Peak, *U.S.A.* 114 C7
Swan Ra., *U.S.A.* 114 C7
Swan River, *Canada* 105 C8
Swanage, *U.K.* 13 G6
Swansea, *Australia* 94 G4
Swansea, *Canada* 110 C5
Swansea, *U.K.* 13 F3
Swansea □, *U.K.* 13 F3
Swar →, *Pakistan* 69 B5
Swartberge, *S. Africa* 88 E3
Swartmodder, *S. Africa* 88 D3
Swartnossob →, *Namibia* ... 88 C2
Swartruggens, *S. Africa* 88 D4
Swarzędz, *Poland* 45 F4
Swastika, *Canada* 102 C3
Swatow = Shantou, *China* ... 59 F11
Swaziland ■, *Africa* 89 D5
Sweden ■, *Europe* 9 G16
Swedru, *Ghana* 83 D4
Sweet Home, *U.S.A.* 114 D2
Sweetgrass, *U.S.A.* 114 B8
Sweetwater, *Nev., U.S.A.* ... 116 G7
Sweetwater, *Tenn., U.S.A.* .. 109 H3
Sweetwater, *Tex., U.S.A.* ... 113 J4
Sweetwater →, *U.S.A.* 114 E10
Swellendam, *S. Africa* 88 E3
Świder →, *Poland* 45 F8
Świdnica, *Poland* 45 H3
Świdnik, *Poland* 45 G9

Świdwin, *Poland* 44 E2
Świebodzice, *Poland* 45 H3
Świebodzin, *Poland* 45 F2
Świecie, *Poland* 44 E5
Świerzawa, *Poland* 45 G2
Świętokrzyskie □, *Poland* 45 H7
Świętokrzyskie, Góry, *Poland* . 45 H7
Swift Current, *Canada* 105 C7
Swiftcurrent →, *Canada* 105 C7
Swilly, L., *Ireland* 15 A4
Swindon, *U.K.* 13 F6
Swindon □, *U.K.* 13 F6
Swinemünde = Świnoujście,
   Poland 44 E1
Swinford, *Ireland* 15 C3
Świnoujście, *Poland* 44 E1
Switzerland ■, *Europe* 25 J4
Swords, *Ireland* 15 C5
Swoyerville, *U.S.A.* 111 E9
Syasstroy, *Russia* 46 B7
Sychevka, *Russia* 46 E8
Syców, *Poland* 45 G4
Sydenham →, *Canada* 110 D2
Sydney, *Australia* 95 E5
Sydney, *Canada* 103 C7
Sydney L., *Canada* 105 C10
Sydney Mines, *Canada* 103 C7
Sydprøven = Alluitsup Paa,
   Greenland 4 C5
Sydra, G. of = Surt, Khalīj, *Libya* 79 B9
Syeverodonetsk, *Ukraine* 47 H10
Syke, *Germany* 24 C4
Sykesville, *U.S.A.* 110 E6
Syktyvkar, *Russia* 50 C6
Sylarna, *Sweden* 8 E15
Sylhet, *Bangla.* 67 G17
Sylhet □, *Bangla.* 67 G17
Sylt, *Germany* 24 A4
Sylvan Beach, *U.S.A.* 111 C9
Sylvan Lake, *Canada* 104 C6
Sylvania, *U.S.A.* 109 J5
Sylvester, *U.S.A.* 109 K4
Sym, *Russia* 50 C9
Symón, *Mexico* 118 C4
Synelnykove, *Ukraine* 47 H8
Synnott Ra., *Australia* 92 C4
Syracuse, *Kans., U.S.A.* 113 G4
Syracuse, *N.Y., U.S.A.* 111 C8
Syracuse, *Nebr., U.S.A.* 112 E6
Syrdarya →, *Kazakhstan* 50 E7
Syria ■, *Asia* 70 C3
Syrian Desert = Shâm, Bādiyat
   ash, *Asia* 70 C3
Sysslebäck, *Sweden* 10 D6
Syzran, *Russia* 48 D9
Szabolcs-Szatmár-Bereg □,
   Hungary 42 B6
Szadek, *Poland* 45 G5
Szamocin, *Poland* 45 E4
Szamos →, *Hungary* 42 B7
Szamotuły, *Poland* 45 F3
Száraz →, *Hungary* 42 D6
Szarvas, *Hungary* 42 D5
Százhalombatta, *Hungary* ... 42 C3
Szczawnica, *Poland* 45 J7
Szczebrzeszyn, *Poland* 45 H9
Szczecin, *Poland* 44 E1
Szczecinek, *Poland* 44 E3
Szczeciński, Zalew = Stettiner
   Haff, *Germany* 24 B10
Szczekociny, *Poland* 45 H6
Szczucin, *Poland* 45 H8
Szczuczyn, *Poland* 44 E9
Szczyrk, *Poland* 45 J6
Szczytna, *Poland* 45 H3
Szczytno, *Poland* 44 E7
Szechwan = Sichuan □, *China* 58 B5
Szécsény, *Hungary* 42 B4
Szeghalom, *Hungary* 42 D5
Szeged, *Hungary* 42 D5
Székesfehérvár, *Hungary* 42 C3
Szekszárd, *Hungary* 42 D3
Szendrő, *Hungary* 42 B5
Szentendre, *Hungary* 42 C4
Szentes, *Hungary* 42 D5
Szentgotthárd, *Hungary* 42 D1
Szentlőrinc, *Hungary* 42 D2
Szerencs, *Hungary* 42 B6
Szigetszentmiklós, *Hungary* .. 42 C4
Szigetvár, *Hungary* 42 D2
Szikszó, *Hungary* 42 B5
Szklarska Poreba, *Poland* ... 45 H2
Szkwa →, *Poland* 45 E8
Szlichtyngowa, *Poland* 45 G3
Szob, *Hungary* 42 C3
Szolnok, *Hungary* 42 C5
Szombathely, *Hungary* 42 C1
Szprotawa, *Poland* 45 G2
Sztum, *Poland* 44 E6
Sztutowo, *Poland* 44 E5
Szubin, *Poland* 45 E4
Szydłowiec, *Poland* 45 G7
Szypliszki, *Poland* 44 D10

T

Ta Khli Khok, *Thailand* 64 E3
Ta Lai, *Vietnam* 65 G6
Tab, *Hungary* 42 D3
Tabacal, *Argentina* 126 A3
Tabaco, *Phil.* 61 E5
Tabagné, *Ivory C.* 82 D4
Ţābah, *Si. Arabia* 70 E4

Tabankort, *Niger* 83 B5
Ţabas, *Khorāsān, Iran* 71 C9
Ţabas, *Khorāsān, Iran* 71 C8
Tabasará, Serranía de, *Panama* 120 E3
Tabasco □, *Mexico* 119 D6
Tabāsīn, *Iran* 71 D8
Tabatinga, Serra da, *Brazil* .. 125 F10
Taber, *Canada* 104 D6
Taberg, *Sweden* 11 G8
Taberg, *U.S.A.* 111 C9
Tabla, *Niger* 83 C5
Tablas I., *Phil.* 61 E5
Tablas Strait, *Phil.* 61 E4
Table B. = Tafelbaai, *S. Africa* 88 E2
Table B., *Canada* 103 B8
Table Mt., *S. Africa* 88 E2
Table Rock L., *U.S.A.* 113 G8
Tabletop, Mt., *Australia* 94 C4
Tábor, *Czech Rep.* 26 B7
Tabora, *Tanzania* 86 D3
Tabora □, *Tanzania* 86 D3
Tabou, *Ivory C.* 82 E3
Tabrīz, *Iran* 70 B5
Tabuaeran, *Kiribati* 97 G12
Tabuenca, *Spain* 32 D3
Tabūk, *Si. Arabia* 70 D3
Täby, *Sweden* 10 E12
Tacámbaro de Codallos, *Mexico* 118 D4
Tacheng, *China* 60 B3
Tach'i, *Taiwan* 59 E13
Tachia, *Taiwan* 59 E13
Tach'ing Shan = Daqing Shan,
   China 56 D6
Tachov, *Czech Rep.* 26 B5
Tácina →, *Italy* 31 D9
Tacloban, *Phil.* 61 F6
Tacna, *Peru* 124 G4
Tacoma, *U.S.A.* 116 C4
Tacuarembó, *Uruguay* 127 C4
Tademaït, Plateau du, *Algeria* . 78 C6
Tadio, L., *Ivory C.* 82 D3
Tadjoura, *Djibouti* 81 E5
Tadjoura, Golfe de, *Djibouti* . 81 E5
Tadmor, *N.Z.* 91 J4
Tadoule, L., *Canada* 105 B9
Tadoussac, *Canada* 103 C6
Tadzhikistan = Tajikistan ■,
   Asia 50 F8
Taechŏn-ni, *S. Korea* 57 F14
Taegu, *S. Korea* 57 G15
Taegwan, *N. Korea* 57 D13
Taejŏn, *S. Korea* 57 F14
Tafalla, *Spain* 32 C3
Tafar, *Sudan* 81 F2
Tafelbaai, *S. Africa* 88 E2
Tafermaar, *Indonesia* 63 F8
Taff Viejo, *Argentina* 126 B2
Tafíhān, *Iran* 71 D7
Tafíré, *Ivory C.* 82 D3
Tafo, *Ghana* 83 D4
Tafresh, *Iran* 71 C6
Taft, *Iran* 71 D7
Taft, *Phil.* 61 F6
Taft, *U.S.A.* 117 K7
Taftān, Kūh-e, *Iran* 71 D9
Taga Dzong, *Bhutan* 67 F16
Taganrog, *Russia* 47 J10
Taganrogskiy Zaliv, *Russia* .. 47 J10
Tagânt, *Mauritania* 82 B2
Tagatay, *Phil.* 61 D4
Tagbilaran, *Phil.* 61 G5
Tággia, *Italy* 28 E4
Tagish, *Canada* 104 A2
Tagish L., *Canada* 104 A2
Tagliacozzo, *Italy* 29 F10
Tagliamento →, *Italy* 29 C10
Táglio di Po, *Italy* 29 D9
Tago, *Phil.* 61 G7
Tagomago, *Spain* 37 B8
Tagouráret, *Mauritania* 82 B3
Taguatinga, *Brazil* 125 F10
Tagudin, *Phil.* 61 C4
Tagum, *Phil.* 61 H6
Tagus = Tejo →, *Europe* ... 35 C2
Tahakopa, *N.Z.* 91 M2
Tahan, Gunong, *Malaysia* ... 65 K4
Tahat, *Algeria* 78 D7
Tāherī, *Iran* 71 E7
Tahiti, *Pac. Oc.* 97 J13
Tahlequah, *U.S.A.* 113 H7
Tahoe, L., *U.S.A.* 116 G6
Tahoe City, *U.S.A.* 116 G6
Tahoka, *U.S.A.* 113 J4
Taholah, *U.S.A.* 116 C2
Tahoua, *Niger* 83 C6
Tahrūd, *Iran* 71 D8
Tahsis, *Canada* 104 D3
Tahta, *Egypt* 80 B3
Tahtakőprü, *Turkey* 41 G13
Tahtalı Dağları, *Turkey* 72 C7
Tahulandang, *Indonesia* 63 D7
Tahuna, *Indonesia* 63 D7
Taï, *Ivory C.* 82 D3
Tai Hu, *China* 59 B12
Tai Shan, *China* 57 F9
Tai'an, *China* 57 F9
Taibei = T'aipei, *Taiwan* 59 E13
Taibique, *Canary Is.* 37 G2
Taibus Qi, *China* 56 D8
Taicang, *China* 59 B13
T'aichung, *Taiwan* 59 E13
Taieri →, *N.Z.* 91 M3
Taigu, *China* 56 F7
Taihang Shan, *China* 56 F7
Taihape, *N.Z.* 91 H5
Taihe, *Anhui, China* 56 H8
Taihe, *Jiangxi, China* 59 D10

Taihu

Taihu, *China* 59 B11
Taijiang, *China* 58 D7
Taikang, *China* 56 G8
Tailem Bend, *Australia* 95 F2
Tailfingen, *Germany* 25 G5
Tailuko, *Taiwan* 59 E13
Taimyr Peninsula = Taymyr, Poluostrov, *Russia* 51 B11
Tain, *U.K.* 14 D4
T'ainan, *Taiwan* 59 F13
Taínaron, Ákra, *Greece* 38 E4
Taining, *China* 59 D11
T'aipei, *Taiwan* 59 E13
Taiping, *China* 59 B12
Taiping, *Malaysia* 65 K3
Taipingzhen, *China* 56 H6
Tairbeart = Tarbert, *U.K.* 14 D2
Taishan, *China* 59 F9
Taishun, *China* 59 D12
Taita Hills, *Kenya* 86 C4
Taitao, Pen. de, *Chile* 122 H3
T'aitung, *Taiwan* 59 F13
Taivalkoski, *Finland* 8 D23
Taiwan ■, *Asia* 59 F13
Taiwan Strait, *Asia* 59 E12
Taixing, *China* 59 A13
Taiyara, *Sudan* 81 E3
Taïyetos Óros, *Greece* 38 D4
Taiyiba, *Israel* 75 C4
Taiyuan, *China* 56 F7
Taizhong = T'aichung, *Taiwan* 59 E13
Taizhou, *China* 59 A12
Taizhou Liedao, *China* 59 C13
Ta'izz, *Yemen* 74 E3
Tājābād, *Iran* 71 D7
Tajikistan ■, *Asia* 50 F8
Tajima, *Japan* 55 F9
Tajo = Tejo →, *Europe* 35 F2
Tajrīsh, *Iran* 71 C6
Tak, *Thailand* 64 D2
Takāb, *Iran* 70 B5
Takachiho, *Japan* 55 H5
Takachu, *Botswana* 88 C3
Takada, *Japan* 55 F9
Takahagi, *Japan* 55 F10
Takaka, *N.Z.* 91 J4
Takamatsu, *Japan* 55 G7
Takaoka, *Japan* 55 F8
Takapuna, *N.Z.* 91 G5
Takasaki, *Japan* 55 F9
Takatsuki, *Japan* 55 G7
Takaungu, *Kenya* 86 C4
Takayama, *Japan* 55 F8
Take-Shima, *Japan* 55 J5
Takefu, *Japan* 55 G8
Takengon, *Indonesia* 62 D1
Takeo, *Japan* 55 H5
Tåkern, *Sweden* 11 F8
Tākestān, *Iran* 71 C6
Taketa, *Japan* 55 H5
Takev, *Cambodia* 65 G5
Takh, *India* 69 C7
Takht-Sulaiman, *Pakistan* 68 D3
Takikawa, *Japan* 54 C10
Takla L., *Canada* 104 B3
Takla Landing, *Canada* 104 B3
Takla Makan = Taklamakan Shamo, *China* 60 C3
Taklamakan Shamo, *China* 60 C3
Taku →, *Canada* 104 B2
Takum, *Nigeria* 83 D6
Tal Halāl, *Iran* 71 D7
Tala, *Uruguay* 127 C4
Talachyn, *Belarus* 46 E5
Talacogan, *Phil.* 61 G6
Talagang, *Pakistan* 68 C5
Talagante, *Chile* 126 C1
Talak, *Niger* 83 B6
Talamanca, Cordillera de, *Cent. Amer.* 120 E3
Talant, *France* 19 E11
Talara, *Peru* 124 D2
Talas, *Kyrgyzstan* 50 E8
Talas, *Turkey* 72 C6
Talâta, *Egypt* 75 E1
Talata Mafara, *Nigeria* 83 C6
Talaud, Kepulauan, *Indonesia* 63 D7
Talaud Is. = Talaud, Kepulauan, *Indonesia* 63 D7
Talavera de la Reina, *Spain* 34 F6
Talavera la Real, *Spain* 35 G4
Talayan, *Phil.* 61 H6
Talayuela, *Spain* 34 F5
Talbandh, *India* 69 H12
Talbert, Sillon de, *France* 18 D3
Talbot, C., *Australia* 92 B4
Talbragar →, *Australia* 95 E4
Talca, *Chile* 126 D1
Talcahuano, *Chile* 126 D1
Talcher, *India* 67 J14
Talcho, *Niger* 83 C5
Taldy Kurgan = Taldyqorghan, *Kazakstan* 50 E8
Taldyqorghan, *Kazakstan* 50 E8
Tālesh, *Iran* 71 B6
Tālesh, Kūhhā-ye, *Iran* 71 B6
Talguharai, *Sudan* 80 D4
Tali Post, *Sudan* 81 F3
Taliabu, *Indonesia* 63 E6
Talibon, *Phil.* 63 B6
Talibong, Ko, *Thailand* 65 J2
Talihina, *U.S.A.* 113 H7
Talisayan, *Phil.* 61 G6
Taliwang, *Indonesia* 62 F5
Tall 'Afar, *Iraq* 70 B4
Tall Kalakh, *Syria* 75 A5
Talla, *Egypt* 80 B3
Talladega, *U.S.A.* 109 J2
Tallahassee, *U.S.A.* 109 K3
Tallangatta, *Australia* 95 F4
Tallard, *France* 21 D10
Tällberg, *Sweden* 10 D9
Tallering Pk., *Australia* 93 E2
Talli, *Pakistan* 68 E3
Tallinn, *Estonia* 9 G21
Tallmadge, *U.S.A.* 110 E3
Tallulah, *U.S.A.* 113 J9
Tălmaciu, *Romania* 43 E9
Talmont-St-Hilaire, *France* 20 B2
Talne, *Ukraine* 47 H6
Talnoye = Talne, *Ukraine* 47 H6
Talodi, *Sudan* 81 E3
Talovaya, *Russia* 48 E5
Taloyoak, *Canada* 100 B10
Talpa de Allende, *Mexico* 118 C4
Talsi, *Latvia* 9 H20
Talsi □, *Latvia* 44 A9
Taltal, *Chile* 126 B1
Taltson →, *Canada* 104 A6
Talurqjuak = Taloyoak, *Canada* 100 B10
Talwood, *Australia* 95 D4
Talyawalka Cr. →, *Australia* 95 E3
Tam Chau, *Vietnam* 65 G5
Tam Ky, *Vietnam* 64 E7
Tam Quan, *Vietnam* 64 E7
Tama, *U.S.A.* 112 E8
Tamale, *Ghana* 83 D4
Taman, *Russia* 47 K9
Tamani, *Mali* 82 C3
Tamano, *Japan* 55 G6
Tamanrasset, *Algeria* 78 D7
Tamaqua, *U.S.A.* 111 F9
Tamar →, *U.K.* 13 G3
Tamarinda, *Spain* 37 B10
Tamarite de Litera, *Spain* 32 D5
Tamashima, *Japan* 55 G6
Tamási, *Hungary* 42 D3
Tamaské, *Niger* 83 C6
Tamaulipas □, *Mexico* 119 C5
Tamaulipas, Sierra de, *Mexico* 119 C5
Tamazula, *Mexico* 118 C3
Tamazunchale, *Mexico* 119 C5
Tamba-Dabatou, *Guinea* 82 C2
Tambacounda, *Senegal* 82 C2
Tambelan, Kepulauan, *Indonesia* 62 D3
Tambellup, *Australia* 93 F2
Tambo, *Australia* 94 C4
Tambo de Mora, *Peru* 124 F3
Tambohorano, *Madag.* 89 B7
Tambora, *Indonesia* 62 F5
Tambov, *Russia* 48 D5
Tambre →, *Spain* 34 C2
Tambuku, *Indonesia* 63 G15
Tamburâ, *Sudan* 81 F2
Tâmchekket, *Mauritania* 82 B2
Tâmega →, *Portugal* 34 D2
Tamenglong, *India* 67 G18
Tamgué, Massif du, *Guinea* 82 C2
Tamiahua, L. de, *Mexico* 119 C5
Tamil Nadu □, *India* 66 P10
Tamis →, *Serbia, Yug.* 42 F5
Tamluk, *India* 69 H12
Tammerfors = Tampere, *Finland* 9 F20
Tammisaari, *Finland* 9 F20
Tämnaren, *Sweden* 10 D11
Tamo Abu, Pegunungan, *Malaysia* 62 D5
Tampa, *U.S.A.* 109 M4
Tampa B., *U.S.A.* 109 M4
Tampere, *Finland* 9 F20
Tampico, *Mexico* 119 C5
Tampin, *Malaysia* 65 L4
Tamsweg, *Austria* 26 D6
Tamu, *Burma* 67 G19
Tamuja →, *Spain* 35 F4
Tamworth, *Australia* 95 E5
Tamworth, *Canada* 110 B8
Tamworth, *U.K.* 13 E6
Tamyang, *S. Korea* 57 G14
Tan An, *Vietnam* 65 G6
Tan-Tan, *Morocco* 78 C3
Tana →, *Kenya* 86 C5
Tana →, *Norway* 8 A23
Tana, L., *Ethiopia* 81 E4
Tana River, *Kenya* 86 C4
Tanabe, *Japan* 55 H7
Tanafjorden, *Norway* 8 A23
Tanaga, Pta., *Canary Is.* 37 G1
Tanahbala, *Indonesia* 62 E1
Tanahgrogot, *Indonesia* 62 E5
Tanahjampea, *Indonesia* 63 F6
Tanahmasa, *Indonesia* 62 E1
Tanahmerah, *Indonesia* 63 F10
Tanakpur, *India* 69 E9
Tanakura, *Japan* 55 F10
Tanami, *Australia* 92 C4
Tanami Desert, *Australia* 92 C5
Tanana →, *U.S.A.* 100 B4
Tananarive = Antananarivo, *Madag.* 89 B8
Tánaro →, *Italy* 28 D5
Tancheng, *China* 57 G10
Tanch'ŏn, *N. Korea* 57 D15
Tanda, *Ut. P., India* 69 F10
Tanda, *Ut. P., India* 69 E8
Tanda, *Ivory C.* 82 D4
Tandag, *Phil.* 61 G7
Tandaia, *Tanzania* 87 D3
Tăndărei, *Romania* 43 F12
Tandaué, *Angola* 88 B2
Tandil, *Argentina* 126 D4
Tandil, Sa. del, *Argentina* 126 D4
Tandlianwala, *Pakistan* 68 D5
Tando Adam, *Pakistan* 68 G3
Tando Allahyar, *Pakistan* 68 G3
Tando Bago, *Pakistan* 68 G3
Tando Mohommed Khan, *Pakistan* 68 G3
Tandou L., *Australia* 95 E3
Tandragee, *U.K.* 15 B5
Tandsjöborg, *Sweden* 10 C8
Tane-ga-Shima, *Japan* 55 J5
Taneatua, *N.Z.* 91 H6
Tanen Tong Dan = Dawna Ra., *Burma* 64 D2
Tanew →, *Poland* 45 H9
Tanezrouft, *Algeria* 78 D6
Tang, Koh, *Cambodia* 65 G4
Tang, Ra's-e, *Iran* 71 E8
Tang Krasang, *Cambodia* 64 F5
Tanga, *Tanzania* 86 D4
Tanga □, *Tanzania* 86 D4
Tanganyika, L., *Africa* 86 D3
Tangaza, *Nigeria* 83 C5
Tanger, *Morocco* 78 A4
Tangerang, *Indonesia* 63 G12
Tangerhütte, *Germany* 24 C7
Tangermünde, *Germany* 24 C7
Tanggu, *China* 57 E9
Tanggula Shan, *China* 60 C4
Tanghe, *China* 56 H7
Tangier = Tanger, *Morocco* 78 A4
Tangorin, *Australia* 94 C3
Tangorombohitr'i Makay, *Madag.* 89 C8
Tangshan, *China* 57 E10
Tangtou, *China* 57 G10
Tanguiéta, *Benin* 83 C5
Tangxi, *China* 59 C12
Tangyan He →, *China* 58 C7
Tanimbar, Kepulauan, *Indonesia* 63 F8
Tanimbar Is. = Tanimbar, Kepulauan, *Indonesia* 63 F8
Taninthari = Tenasserim □, *Burma* 64 F2
Tanjay, *Phil.* 61 G5
Tanjong Malim, *Malaysia* 65 L3
Tanjore = Thanjavur, *India* 66 P11
Tanjung, *Indonesia* 62 E5
Tanjungbalai, *Indonesia* 62 D1
Tanjungbatu, *Indonesia* 62 D5
Tanjungkarang Telukbetung, *Indonesia* 62 F3
Tanjungpandan, *Indonesia* 62 E3
Tanjungpinang, *Indonesia* 62 D2
Tanjungredeb, *Indonesia* 62 D5
Tanjungselor, *Indonesia* 62 D5
Tank, *Pakistan* 68 C4
Tankhala, *India* 68 J5
Tännäs, *Sweden* 10 B6
Tannersville, *U.S.A.* 111 E9
Tannis Bugt, *Denmark* 11 G4
Tannu-Ola, *Russia* 51 D10
Tannum Sands, *Australia* 94 C5
Tano →, *Ghana* 82 D4
Tanon Str., *Phil.* 61 F5
Tanout, *Niger* 83 C6
Tanshui, *Taiwan* 59 E13
Tansilla, *Burkina Faso* 82 C4
Tanta, *Egypt* 80 H7
Tantoyuca, *Mexico* 119 C5
Tantung = Dandong, *China* 57 D13
Tanumshede, *Sweden* 11 F5
Tanunda, *Australia* 95 E2
Tanus, *France* 20 D6
Tanzania ■, *Africa* 86 D3
Tanzilla →, *Canada* 104 B2
Tao, Ko, *Thailand* 65 G2
Tao'an = Taonan, *China* 57 B12
Tao'er He →, *China* 57 B13
Taohua Dao, *China* 59 C14
Taolanaro, *Madag.* 89 D8
Taole, *China* 56 E4
Taonan, *China* 57 B12
Taormina, *Italy* 31 E8
Taos, *U.S.A.* 115 H11
Taoudenni, *Mali* 78 D5
Taoyuan, *China* 59 C8
T'aoyüan, *Taiwan* 59 E13
Tapa, *Estonia* 9 G21
Tapa Shan = Daba Shan, *China* 58 B7
Tapachula, *Mexico* 119 E6
Tapah, *Malaysia* 65 K3
Tapajós →, *Brazil* 122 D5
Tapaktuan, *Indonesia* 62 D1
Tapanahoni →, *Surinam* 125 C8
Tapanui, *N.Z.* 91 L2
Tapauá →, *Brazil* 124 E6
Tapes, *Brazil* 127 C5
Tapeta, *Liberia* 82 D3
Taphan Hin, *Thailand* 64 D3
Tapi →, *India* 66 J8
Tapia de Casariego, *Spain* 34 B4
Tapirapecó, Serra, *Venezuela* 124 C6
Tapolca, *Hungary* 42 D2
Tapuaenuku, Mt., *N.Z.* 91 K4
Tapul Group, *Phil.* 61 J4
Tapurucuará, *Brazil* 124 D5
Ţaqţaq, *Iraq* 70 C5
Taquara, *Brazil* 127 B5
Taquari →, *Brazil* 124 G7
Tara, *Australia* 95 D5
Tara, *Canada* 110 B3
Tara, *Russia* 50 D8
Tara, *Zambia* 87 F2
Tara →, *Montenegro, Yug.* 40 C2
Taraba □, *Nigeria* 83 D7
Taraba →, *Nigeria* 83 D7
Tarabagatay, Khrebet, *Kazakstan* 50 E9
Tarābulus, *Lebanon* 75 A4
Tarābulus, *Libya* 79 B8
Taraclia, *Moldova* 43 D14
Taraclia, *Moldova* 43 E13
Taradehi, *India* 69 H8
Tarajalejo, *Canary Is.* 37 F5
Tarakan, *Indonesia* 62 D5
Tarakit, Mt., *Kenya* 86 B4
Tarama-Jima, *Japan* 55 M2
Taran, Mys, *Russia* 9 J18
Taranagar, *India* 68 E6
Taranaki □, *N.Z.* 91 H5
Taranaki, Mt., *N.Z.* 91 H5
Tarancón, *Spain* 32 E1
Taransay, *U.K.* 14 D1
Táranto, *Italy* 31 B10
Táranto, G. di, *Italy* 31 B10
Tarapacá, *Colombia* 124 D5
Tarapacá □, *Chile* 126 A2
Tarapoto, *Peru* 124 E3
Tarare, *France* 21 C8
Tararua Ra., *N.Z.* 91 J5
Tarascon, *France* 21 E8
Tarascon-sur-Ariège, *France* 20 F5
Tarashcha, *Ukraine* 47 H6
Tarauacá, *Brazil* 124 E4
Tarauacá →, *Brazil* 124 E5
Taravo →, *France* 21 G12
Tarawa, *Kiribati* 96 G9
Tarawera, *N.Z.* 91 H6
Tarawera L., *N.Z.* 91 H6
Taraz, *Kazakstan* 50 E8
Tarazona, *Spain* 32 D3
Tarazona de la Mancha, *Spain* 33 F3
Tarbat Ness, *U.K.* 14 D5
Tarbela Dam, *Pakistan* 68 B5
Tarbert, *Arg. & Bute, U.K.* 14 F3
Tarbert, *W. Isles, U.K.* 14 D2
Tarbes, *France* 20 E4
Tarboro, *U.S.A.* 109 H7
Tărcău, Munţii, *Romania* 43 D11
Tarcento, *Italy* 29 B10
Tarcoola, *Australia* 95 E1
Tarcoon, *Australia* 95 E4
Tardets-Sorholus, *France* 20 E3
Tardoire →, *France* 20 C4
Taree, *Australia* 95 E5
Tarfa, W. el →, *Egypt* 80 B3
Tarfaya, *Morocco* 78 C3
Târgovişte, *Romania* 43 F10
Târgu Bujor, *Romania* 43 E12
Târgu Cărbuneşti, *Romania* 43 F8
Târgu Frumos, *Romania* 43 C12
Târgu-Jiu, *Romania* 43 E8
Târgu Lăpuş, *Romania* 43 C8
Târgu Mureş, *Romania* 43 D9
Târgu Neamţ, *Romania* 43 C11
Târgu Ocna, *Romania* 43 D11
Târgu Secuiesc, *Romania* 43 E11
Târguşor, *Romania* 43 F13
Tărhăus, Vf., *Romania* 43 D11
Ţarif, *U.A.E.* 71 E7
Tarifa, *Spain* 35 J5
Tarija, *Bolivia* 126 A3
Tarija □, *Bolivia* 126 A3
Tariku →, *Indonesia* 63 E9
Tarim Basin = Tarim Pendi, *China* 60 C3
Tarim He →, *China* 60 C3
Tarim Pendi, *China* 60 C3
Taritatu →, *Indonesia* 63 E9
Tarka →, *S. Africa* 88 E4
Tarkastad, *S. Africa* 88 E4
Tarkhankut, Mys, *Ukraine* 47 K7
Tarko Sale, *Russia* 50 C8
Tarkwa, *Ghana* 82 D4
Tarlac, *Phil.* 61 D4
Tarm, *Denmark* 11 J2
Tarma, *Peru* 124 F3
Tarn □, *France* 20 E6
Tarn →, *France* 20 D5
Tarn-et-Garonne □, *France* 20 D5
Tarna →, *Hungary* 42 C4
Târnava Mare →, *Romania* 43 D8
Târnava Mică →, *Romania* 43 D8
Târnăveni, *Romania* 43 D9
Tarnica, *Poland* 45 J9
Tarnobrzeg, *Poland* 45 H8
Tarnogród, *Poland* 45 H9
Tarnos, *France* 20 E2
Târnova, *Moldova* 43 B12
Târnova, *Romania* 42 E6
Tarnów, *Poland* 45 H8
Tarnowskie Góry, *Poland* 45 H5
Tärnsjö, *Sweden* 10 D10
Táro →, *Italy* 28 C7
Ţarom, *Iran* 71 D7
Taroom, *Australia* 95 D4
Taroudannt, *Morocco* 78 B4
Tarp, *Germany* 24 A5
Tarpon Springs, *U.S.A.* 109 L4
Tarquínia, *Italy* 29 F8
Tarragona, *Spain* 32 D6
Tarragona □, *Spain* 32 D6
Tarraleah, *Australia* 94 G4
Tarrasa = Terrassa, *Spain* 32 D7
Tàrrega, *Spain* 32 D6
Tarrytown, *U.S.A.* 111 E11
Tårs, *Denmark* 11 G4
Tarshiha = Me'ona, *Israel* 75 B4
Tarso Emissi, *Chad* 79 D9
Tarsus, *Turkey* 70 B2
Tartagal, *Argentina* 126 A3
Tärtär, *Azerbaijan* 49 K8
Tärtär →, *Azerbaijan* 49 K8
Tartas, *France* 20 E3
Tartu, *Estonia* 9 G22
Ţarţūs, *Syria* 70 C2
Tarumizu, *Japan* 55 J5
Tarussa, *Russia* 46 E9
Tarutao, Ko, *Thailand* 65 J2
Tarutung, *Indonesia* 62 D1
Tarvísio, *Italy* 29 B10
Taseko →, *Canada* 104 C4
Tash-Kömür, *Kyrgyzstan* 50 E8
Tash-Kumyr = Tash-Kömür, *Kyrgyzstan* 50 E8
Tashauz = Dashhowuz, *Turkmenistan* 50 E6
Tashi Chho Dzong = Thimphu, *Bhutan* 67 F16
Ţashk, Daryācheh-ye, *Iran* 71 D7
Tashkent = Toshkent, *Uzbekistan* 50 E7
Tashtagol, *Russia* 50 D9
Tasiilaq, *Greenland* 4 C6
Tasikmalaya, *Indonesia* 63 G13
Tåsinge, *Denmark* 11 J4
Tåsjön, *Sweden* 8 D16
Taskan, *Russia* 51 C16
Tasker, *Niger* 83 C7
Taşköprü, *Turkey* 72 B6
Taşlâc, *Moldova* 43 C14
Tasman B., *N.Z.* 91 J4
Tasman Mts., *N.Z.* 91 J4
Tasman Pen., *Australia* 94 G4
Tasman Sea, *Pac. Oc.* 96 L8
Tasmania □, *Australia* 94 G4
Tăşnad, *Romania* 42 C7
Tassili n'Ajjer, *Algeria* 78 C7
Tassili Tin-Rerhoh, *Algeria* 83 A5
Tata, *Hungary* 42 C3
Tatabánya, *Hungary* 42 C3
Tatahouine, *Tunisia* 79 B8
Tatar Republic = Tatarstan □, *Russia* 48 C10
Tatarbunary, *Ukraine* 47 K5
Tatarsk, *Russia* 50 D8
Tatarstan □, *Russia* 48 C10
Tateyama, *Japan* 55 G9
Tathlina L., *Canada* 104 A5
Tathra, *Australia* 95 F4
Tatinnai L., *Canada* 105 A9
Tatla L., *Canada* 104 C4
Tatlısu, *Turkey* 41 F11
Tatnam, C., *Canada* 105 B10
Tatra = Tatry, *Slovak Rep.* 27 B13
Tatry, *Slovak Rep.* 27 B13
Tatshenshini →, *Canada* 104 B1
Tatsuno, *Japan* 55 G7
Tatta, *Pakistan* 68 G2
Tatuī, *Brazil* 127 A6
Tatum, *U.S.A.* 113 J3
Tat'ung = Datong, *China* 56 D7
Tatvan, *Turkey* 70 B4
Taubaté, *Brazil* 127 A6
Tauberbischofsheim, *Germany* 25 F5
Taucha, *Germany* 24 D8
Tauern-tunnel, *Austria* 26 D6
Taufikia, *Sudan* 81 F3
Taulé, *France* 18 D3
Taumarunui, *N.Z.* 91 H5
Taumaturgo, *Brazil* 124 E4
Taung, *S. Africa* 88 D3
Taungdwingyi, *Burma* 67 J19
Taunggyi, *Burma* 67 J20
Taungup, *Burma* 67 K19
Taungup Taunggya, *Burma* 67 K18
Taunsa, *Pakistan* 68 D4
Taunsa Barrage, *Pakistan* 68 D4
Taunton, *U.K.* 13 F4
Taunton, *U.S.A.* 111 E13
Taunus, *Germany* 25 E4
Taupo, *N.Z.* 91 H6
Taupo, L., *N.Z.* 91 H5
Tauragė, *Lithuania* 9 J20
Tauragė □, *Lithuania* 44 C9
Tauranga, *N.Z.* 91 G6
Tauranga Harb., *N.Z.* 91 G6
Taureau, Rés., *Canada* 102 C5
Taurianova, *Italy* 31 D9
Taurus Mts. = Toros Dağları, *Turkey* 70 B2
Tauste, *Spain* 32 D3
Tauz = Tovuz, *Azerbaijan* 49 K7
Tavas, *Turkey* 39 D11
Tavda, *Russia* 50 D7
Tavda →, *Russia* 50 D7
Tavernes de la Valldigna, *Spain* 33 F4
Taveta, *Tanzania* 86 C4
Taveuni, *Fiji* 91 C9
Taviano, *Italy* 31 C11
Tavignano →, *France* 21 F13
Tavira, *Portugal* 35 H3
Tavistock, *Canada* 110 C4
Tavistock, *U.K.* 13 G3
Tavolara, *Italy* 30 B2
Tâvora →, *Portugal* 34 D3
Tavoy = Dawei, *Burma* 64 E2
Tavşanlı, *Turkey* 39 B11
Taw →, *U.K.* 13 F3
Tawa →, *India* 68 H8
Tawas City, *U.S.A.* 108 C4
Tawau, *Malaysia* 62 D5
Taweisha, *Sudan* 81 E2
Tawitawi, *Phil.* 63 B6
Tawu, *Taiwan* 59 F13
Taxco de Alarcón, *Mexico* 119 D5
Taxila, *Pakistan* 68 C5
Tay →, *U.K.* 14 E5
Tay, Firth of, *U.K.* 14 E5
Tay, L., *Australia* 93 F3
Tay, L., *U.K.* 14 E4
Tay Ninh, *Vietnam* 65 G6

Tayabamba, *Peru* 124 E3
Tayabas Bay, *Phil.* 61 E4
Taylakova, *Russia* 50 D8
Taylakovy = Taylakova, *Russia* .. 50 D8
Taylor, *Canada* 104 B4
Taylor, *Nebr., U.S.A.* 112 E5
Taylor, *Pa., U.S.A.* 111 E9
Taylor, *Tex., U.S.A.* 113 K6
Taylor, Mt., *U.S.A.* 115 J10
Taylorville, *U.S.A.* 112 F10
Taymā, *Si. Arabia* 70 E3
Taymyr, Oz., *Russia* 51 B11
Taymyr, Poluostrov, *Russia* ... 51 B11
Tayport, *U.K.* 14 E6
Tayshet, *Russia* 51 D10
Taytay, *Phil.* 61 F3
Taz ➤, *Russia* 50 C8
Taza, *Morocco* 78 B5
Tāzah Khurmātū, *Iraq* 70 C5
Tazawa-Ko, *Japan* 54 E10
Tazin, *Canada* 105 B7
Tazin L., *Canada* 105 B7
Tazovskiy, *Russia* 50 C8
Tbilisi, *Georgia* 49 K7
Tchad = Chad ■, *Africa* 79 F8
Tchad, L., *Chad* 79 F8
Tchaourou, *Benin* 83 D5
Tch'eng-tou = Chengdu, *China* .. 58 B5
Tchentlo L., *Canada* 104 B4
Tchetti, *Benin* 83 D5
Tchibanga, *Gabon* 84 E2
Tchien, *Liberia* 82 D3
Tchin Tabaraden, *Niger* 83 B6
Tch'ong-k'ing = Chongqing, *China* 58 C6
Tczew, *Poland* 44 D5
Te Anau, *N.Z.* 91 L1
Te Anau, L., *N.Z.* 91 L1
Te Aroha, *N.Z.* 91 G5
Te Awamutu, *N.Z.* 91 H5
Te Kuiti, *N.Z.* 91 H5
Te-n-Dghâmcha, Sebkhet, *Mauritania* 82 B1
Te Puke, *N.Z.* 91 G6
Te Waewae B., *N.Z.* 91 M1
Teaca, *Romania* 43 D9
Teague, *U.S.A.* 113 K6
Teano, *Italy* 31 A7
Teapa, *Mexico* 119 D6
Teba, *Spain* 35 J6
Tebakang, *Malaysia* 62 D4
Teberda, *Russia* 49 J5
Tébessa, *Algeria* 78 A7
Tebicuary ➤, *Paraguay* 126 B4
Tebingtinggi, *Indonesia* 62 D1
Tebintingii, *Indonesia* 62 E2
Tebulos, *Georgia* 49 J7
Tecate, *Mexico* 117 N10
Tecer Dağları, *Turkey* 72 C7
Tech ➤, *France* 20 F7
Techiman, *Ghana* 82 D4
Techirghiol, *Romania* 43 F13
Tecka, *Argentina* 128 E2
Tecomán, *Mexico* 118 D4
Tecopa, *U.S.A.* 117 K10
Tecoripa, *Mexico* 118 B3
Tecuala, *Mexico* 118 C3
Tecuci, *Romania* 43 E12
Tecumseh, *Canada* 110 D2
Tecumseh, *Mich., U.S.A.* 108 D4
Tecumseh, *Okla., U.S.A.* 113 H6
Tedzhen = Tejen, *Turkmenistan* 50 F7
Tees ➤, *U.K.* 12 C6
Tees B., *U.K.* 12 C6
Teeswater, *Canada* 110 C3
Tefé, *Brazil* 124 D6
Tefenni, *Turkey* 39 D11
Tegal, *Indonesia* 62 F3
Tegernsee, *Germany* 25 H7
Teggiano, *Italy* 31 B8
Tegid, L. = Bala, L., *U.K.* ... 12 E4
Tegina, *Nigeria* 83 C6
Tegucigalpa, *Honduras* 120 D2
Teguidda i-n-Tessoum, *Niger* . 83 B6
Tehachapi, *U.S.A.* 117 K8
Tehachapi Mts., *U.S.A.* 117 L8
Tehamiyam, *Sudan* 80 D4
Tehilla, *Sudan* 80 D4
Téhini, *Ivory C.* 82 D4
Tehoru, *Indonesia* 63 E7
Tehrān, *Iran* 71 C6
Tehri, *India* 69 D8
Tehuacán, *Mexico* 119 D5
Tehuantepec, *Mexico* 119 D5
Tehuantepec, G. de, *Mexico* . 119 D6
Tehuantepec, Istmo de, *Mexico* 119 D6
Teide, *Canary Is.* 37 F3
Teifi ➤, *U.K.* 13 E3
Teign ➤, *U.K.* 13 G4
Teignmouth, *U.K.* 13 G4
Teiuş, *Romania* 43 D8
Teixeira Pinto, *Guinea-Biss.* . 82 C1
Tejam, *India* 69 E9
Tejen, *Turkmenistan* 50 F7
Tejen ➤, *Turkmenistan* 71 B9
Tejo ➤, *Europe* 35 F2
Tejon Pass, *U.S.A.* 117 L8
Tekamah, *U.S.A.* 112 E6
Tekapo, L., *N.Z.* 91 K3
Tekax, *Mexico* 119 C7
Teke, *Turkey* 41 E13
Tekeli, *Kazakstan* 50 E8
Tekeze ➤, *Ethiopia* 81 E4
Tekija, *Serbia, Yug.* 40 B6
Tekirdağ, *Turkey* 41 F11
Tekirdağ □, *Turkey* 41 E11
Tekirova, *Turkey* 39 E12

Tekkali, *India* 67 K14
Tekke, *Turkey* 72 B7
Tekman, *Turkey* 73 C9
Tekoa, *U.S.A.* 114 C5
Tel Aviv-Yafo, *Israel* 75 C3
Tel Lakhish, *Israel* 75 D3
Tel Megiddo, *Israel* 75 C4
Tela, *Honduras* 120 C2
Telanaipura = Jambi, *Indonesia* 62 E2
Telavi, *Georgia* 49 J7
Telč, *Czech Rep.* 26 B8
Telciu, *Romania* 43 C9
Telde, *Canary Is.* 37 G4
Telegraph Creek, *Canada* 104 B2
Telekhany = Tsyelyakhany, *Belarus* 47 F3
Telemark, *Norway* 9 G12
Telén, *Argentina* 126 D2
Teleneşti, *Moldova* 43 C13
Teleng, *Iran* 71 E9
Teleño, *Spain* 34 C4
Teleorman □, *Romania* 43 G10
Teleorman ➤, *Romania* 43 G10
Teles Pires ➤, *Brazil* 122 D5
Telescope Pk., *U.S.A.* 117 J9
Teletaye, *Mali* 83 B5
Telfer Mine, *Australia* 92 C3
Telford, *U.K.* 13 E5
Telford and Wrekin □, *U.K.* . 12 E5
Telfs, *Austria* 26 D4
Teljo, J., *Sudan* 81 E2
Tell City, *U.S.A.* 108 G2
Tellicherry, *India* 66 P9
Telluride, *U.S.A.* 115 H10
Teloloapán, *Mexico* 119 D5
Telpos Iz, *Russia* 6 C17
Telsen, *Argentina* 128 E3
Telšiai, *Lithuania* 9 H20
Telšiai □, *Lithuania* 44 C9
Teltow, *Germany* 24 C9
Teluk Anson = Teluk Intan, *Malaysia* 65 K3
Teluk Betung = Tanjungkarang Telukbetung, *Indonesia* .. 62 F3
Teluk Intan, *Malaysia* 65 K3
Telukbutun, *Indonesia* 65 K7
Telukdalem, *Indonesia* 62 D1
Tema, *Ghana* 83 D5
Temax, *Mexico* 119 C7
Temba, *S. Africa* 89 D4
Tembagapura, *Indonesia* 63 E9
Tembe, *Dem. Rep. of the Congo* 86 C2
Tembleque, *Spain* 34 F7
Temblor Range, *U.S.A.* 117 K7
Teme ➤, *U.K.* 13 E5
Temecula, *U.S.A.* 117 M9
Temerloh, *Malaysia* 62 D2
Teminabuan, *Indonesia* 63 E8
Temir, *Kazakstan* 50 E6
Temirtau, *Kazakstan* 50 D8
Temirtau, *Russia* 50 D9
Temiscamie ➤, *Canada* 103 B5
Témiscaming, *Canada* 102 C4
Témiscamingue, L., *Canada* . 102 C4
Temnikov, *Russia* 48 C6
Temo ➤, *Italy* 30 B1
Temora, *Australia* 95 E4
Temosachic, *Mexico* 118 B3
Tempe, *U.S.A.* 115 K8
Tempino, *Indonesia* 62 E2
Témpio Pausánia, *Italy* 30 B2
Tempiute, *U.S.A.* 116 H11
Temple, *U.S.A.* 113 K6
Temple B., *Australia* 94 A3
Templemore, *Ireland* 15 D4
Templeton, *U.S.A.* 116 K6
Templeton ➤, *Australia* 94 C2
Templin, *Germany* 24 B9
Tempoal, *Mexico* 119 C5
Temryuk, *Russia* 47 K9
Temska ➤, *Serbia, Yug.* 40 C6
Temuco, *Chile* 128 D2
Temuka, *N.Z.* 91 L3
Tenabo, *Mexico* 119 C6
Tenaha, *U.S.A.* 113 K7
Tenakee Springs, *U.S.A.* 104 B1
Tenali, *India* 67 L12
Tenancingo, *Mexico* 119 D5
Tenango, *Mexico* 119 D5
Tenasserim, *Burma* 65 F2
Tenasserim □, *Burma* 64 F2
Tenby, *U.K.* 13 F3
Tenda, Colle di, *France* 21 D11
Tendaho, *Ethiopia* 81 E5
Tende, *France* 21 D11
Tendelti, *Sudan* 81 E3
Tendrovskaya Kosa, *Ukraine* . 47 J6
Tendukhera, *India* 69 H8
Teneida, *Egypt* 80 B2
Tenenkou, *Mali* 82 C4
Ténéré, *Niger* 83 B7
Tenerife, *Canary Is.* 37 F3
Tenerife, Pico, *Canary Is.* ... 37 G1
Teng Xian, *Guangxi Zhuangzu, China* 59 F8
Teng Xian, *Shandong, China* . 57 G9
Tengah, *Kepulauan, Indonesia* . 62 F5
Tengchong, *China* 58 E2
Tengchowfu = Penglai, *China* . 57 F11
Tenggara □, *Indonesia* 63 E6
Tenggarong, *Indonesia* 62 E5
Tenggol, Pulau, *Malaysia* ... 65 K4
Tengiz, Ozero, *Kazakstan* 50 D7
Tenhult, *Sweden* 11 G8
Tenino, *U.S.A.* 116 D4
Tenkasi, *India* 66 Q10

Tenke, *Katanga, Dem. Rep. of the Congo* 87 E2
Tenke, *Katanga, Dem. Rep. of the Congo* 87 E2
Tenkodogo, *Burkina Faso* 83 C4
Tenna ➤, *Italy* 29 E10
Tennant Creek, *Australia* 94 B1
Tennessee □, *U.S.A.* 109 H2
Tennessee ➤, *U.S.A.* 108 G1
Teno, *Malaysia* 62 C5
Tenom, *Malaysia* 62 C5
Tenosique, *Mexico* 119 D6
Tenryū-Gawa ➤, *Japan* 55 G8
Tenterden, *U.K.* 13 F8
Tenterfield, *Australia* 95 D5
Teo, *Spain* 34 C2
Teófilo Otoni, *Brazil* 125 G10
Tepa, *Indonesia* 63 F7
Tepalcatepec ➤, *Mexico* 118 D4
Tepecik, *Bursa, Turkey* 41 F12
Tepecik, *Kütahya, Turkey* ... 39 B11
Tepehuanes, *Mexico* 118 B3
Tepelenë, *Albania* 40 F4
Tepetongo, *Mexico* 118 C4
Tepic, *Mexico* 118 C4
Teplá, *Czech Rep.* 26 B5
Teplice, *Czech Rep.* 26 A6
Tepoca, C., *Mexico* 118 A2
Tequila, *Mexico* 118 C4
Ter ➤, *Spain* 32 C8
Ter Apel, *Neths.* 17 B7
Téra, *Niger* 83 C5
Tera ➤, *Spain* 34 D5
Teraina, *Kiribati* 97 G11
Terakeka, *Sudan* 81 F3
Téramo, *Italy* 29 F10
Terang, *Australia* 95 F3
Terazit, Massif de, *Niger* ... 83 A6
Tercan, *Turkey* 73 C9
Tercero ➤, *Argentina* 126 C3
Terebovlya, *Ukraine* 47 H3
Teregova, *Romania* 42 E7
Tereida, *Sudan* 81 E3
Terek ➤, *Russia* 49 J8
Tereshka ➤, *Russia* 48 E8
Teresina, *Brazil* 125 E10
Terespol, *Poland* 45 F10
Terewah, L., *Australia* 95 D4
Terges ➤, *Portugal* 35 H3
Tergnier, *France* 19 C10
Teridgerie Cr. ➤, *Australia* .. 95 E4
Terlizzi, *Italy* 31 A9
Terme, *Turkey* 72 B7
Termez = Termiz, *Uzbekistan* . 50 F7
Términi Imerese, *Italy* 30 E6
Términos, L. de, *Mexico* 119 D6
Termiz, *Uzbekistan* 50 F7
Térmoli, *Italy* 29 F12
Ternate, *Indonesia* 63 D7
Terneuzen, *Neths.* 17 C3
Terney, *Russia* 51 E14
Terni, *Italy* 29 F9
Ternitz, *Austria* 26 D9
Ternopil, *Ukraine* 47 H3
Ternopol = Ternopil, *Ukraine* . 47 H3
Terowie, *Australia* 95 E2
Terpní, *Greece* 40 F7
Terra Bella, *U.S.A.* 117 K7
Terra Nova Nat. Park, *Canada* . 103 C9
Terrace, *Canada* 104 C3
Terrace Bay, *Canada* 102 C2
Terracina, *Italy* 30 A6
Terralba, *Italy* 30 C1
Terranova = Ólbia, *Italy* 30 B2
Terrasini, *Italy* 30 D6
Terrassa, *Spain* 32 D7
Terrasson-la-Villedieu, *France* . 20 C5
Terre Haute, *U.S.A.* 108 F2
Terrebonne B., *U.S.A.* 113 L9
Terrell, *U.S.A.* 113 J6
Terrenceville, *Canada* 103 C9
Terry, *U.S.A.* 112 B2
Terryville, *U.S.A.* 111 E11
Terschelling, *Neths.* 17 A5
Tersko-Kumskiy Kanal ➤, *Russia* 49 H7
Tertenía, *Italy* 30 C2
Terter ➤ = Tärtär ➤, *Azerbaijan* 49 K8
Teruel, *Spain* 32 E3
Teruel □, *Spain* 32 E4
Tervel, *Bulgaria* 41 C11
Tervola, *Finland* 8 C21
Teryaweyna L., *Australia* 95 E3
Tešanj, *Bos.-H.* 42 F3
Teseney, *Eritrea* 81 D4
Tesha ➤, *Russia* 48 C6
Teshio, *Japan* 54 B10
Teshio-Gawa ➤, *Japan* 54 B10
Tešica, *Serbia, Yug.* 40 C5
Teslić, *Bos.-H.* 42 F2
Teslin, *Canada* 104 A2
Teslin L., *Canada* 104 A2
Teslin ➤, *Canada* 104 A2
Tessalit, *Mali* 83 A5
Tessaoua, *Niger* 83 C6
Tessin, *Germany* 24 A8
Tessit, *Mali* 83 B5
Test ➤, *U.K.* 13 G6
Testa del Gargano, *Italy* 29 G13
Testigos, Is. Las, *Venezuela* . 121 D7
Tét, *Hungary* 42 C2
Têt ➤, *France* 20 F7
Tetachuck L., *Canada* 104 C3
Tetas, Pta., *Chile* 126 A1
Tete, *Mozam.* 87 F3

Tete □, *Mozam.* 87 F3
Teterev ➤, *Ukraine* 47 G6
Teterow, *Germany* 24 B8
Teteven, *Bulgaria* 41 D8
Tethul ➤, *Canada* 104 A6
Tetiyev, *Ukraine* 47 H5
Teton ➤, *U.S.A.* 114 C8
Tétouan, *Morocco* 78 A4
Tetovo, *Macedonia* 40 D4
Tetyushi, *Russia* 48 C9
Teuco ➤, *Argentina* 126 B3
Teulada, *Italy* 30 D1
Teulon, *Canada* 105 C9
Teun, *Indonesia* 63 F7
Teutoburger Wald, *Germany* . 24 C4
Tevere ➤, *Italy* 29 G9
Teverya, *Israel* 75 C4
Teviot ➤, *U.K.* 14 F6
Tewantin, *Australia* 95 D5
Tewkesbury, *U.K.* 13 F5
Texada I., *Canada* 104 D4
Texarkana, *Ark., U.S.A.* 113 J8
Texarkana, *Tex., U.S.A.* 113 J7
Texas, *Australia* 95 D5
Texas □, *U.S.A.* 113 K5
Texas City, *U.S.A.* 113 L7
Texel, *Neths.* 17 A4
Texline, *U.S.A.* 113 G3
Texoma, L., *U.S.A.* 113 J6
Teykovo, *Russia* 46 D11
Teza ➤, *Russia* 48 B5
Tezin, *Afghan.* 68 B3
Teziutlán, *Mexico* 119 D5
Tezpur, *India* 67 F18
Tha-anne ➤, *Canada* 105 A10
Tha Deua, *Laos* 64 D4
Tha Deua, *Laos* 64 C3
Tha Pla, *Thailand* 64 D3
Tha Rua, *Thailand* 64 E3
Tha Sala, *Thailand* 65 H2
Tha Song Yang, *Thailand* ... 64 D1
Thaba Putsoa, *Lesotho* 89 D4
Thabana Ntlenyana, *Lesotho* . 89 D4
Thabazimbi, *S. Africa* 89 C4
Thādiq, *Si. Arabia* 70 E5
Thai Binh, *Vietnam* 58 G6
Thai Muang, *Thailand* 65 H2
Thai Nguyen, *Vietnam* 58 G5
Thailand ■, *Asia* 64 E4
Thailand, G. of, *Asia* 65 G3
Thakhek, *Laos* 64 D5
Thal, *Pakistan* 68 C4
Thala La = Hkakabo Razi, *Burma* 67 E20
Thalabarivat, *Cambodia* 64 F5
Thallon, *Australia* 95 D4
Thalwil, *Switz.* 25 H4
Thames, *N.Z.* 91 G5
Thames ➤, *Canada* 102 D3
Thames ➤, *U.K.* 13 F8
Thames ➤, *U.S.A.* 111 E12
Thames Estuary, *U.K.* 13 F8
Thamesford, *Canada* 110 C4
Thamesville, *Canada* 110 D3
Than, *India* 68 H4
Than Uyen, *Vietnam* 58 G4
Thana Gazi, *India* 68 F7
Thandla, *India* 68 H6
Thane, *India* 66 K8
Thanesar, *India* 68 D7
Thanet, I. of, *U.K.* 13 F9
Thangool, *Australia* 94 C5
Thanh Hoa, *Vietnam* 64 C5
Thanh Hung, *Vietnam* 65 H5
Thanh Pho Ho Chi Minh, *Vietnam* 65 G6
Thanh Thuy, *Vietnam* 64 A5
Thanjavur, *India* 66 P11
Thann, *France* 19 E14
Thano Bula Khan, *Pakistan* .. 68 G2
Thaolinta L., *Canada* 105 A9
Thaon-les-Vosges, *France* ... 19 D13
Thap Sakae, *Thailand* 65 G2
Thap Than, *Thailand* 64 E2
Thar Desert, *India* 68 F5
Tharad, *India* 68 G4
Thargomindah, *Australia* ... 95 D3
Tharrawaddy, *Burma* 67 L19
Tharthār, Mileh, *Iraq* 70 C4
Tharthār, W. ath ➤, *Iraq* 70 C4
Thasopoúla, *Greece* 41 F8
Thásos, *Greece* 41 F8
That Khe, *Vietnam* 58 F6
Thatcher, *Ariz., U.S.A.* 115 K9
Thatcher, *Colo., U.S.A.* 113 G2
Thaton, *Burma* 67 L20
Thau, Bassin de, *France* 20 E7
Thaungdut, *Burma* 67 G19
Thayer, *U.S.A.* 113 G9
Thayetmyo, *Burma* 67 K19
Thazi, *Burma* 67 J20
The Alberga ➤, *Australia* ... 95 D2
The Bight, *Bahamas* 121 B4
The Dalles, *U.S.A.* 114 D3
The English Company's Is., *Australia* 94 A2
The Frome ➤, *Australia* 95 D2
The Great Divide = Great Dividing Ra., *Australia* ... 94 C4
The Hague = 's-Gravenhage, *Neths.* 17 B4
The Hamilton ➤, *Australia* . 95 D2
The Macumba ➤, *Australia* . 95 D2
The Neales ➤, *Australia* 95 D2
The Officer ➤, *Australia* 93 E5

The Pas, *Canada* 105 C8
The Range, *Zimbabwe* 87 F3
The Rock, *Australia* 95 F4
The Salt L., *Australia* 95 E3
The Sandheads, *India* 69 J13
The Stevenson ➤, *Australia* . 95 D2
The Warburton ➤, *Australia* . 95 D2
The Woodlands, *U.S.A.* 113 K7
Thebes = Thívai, *Greece* 38 C5
Thebes, *Egypt* 80 B3
Thedford, *Canada* 110 C3
Thedford, *U.S.A.* 112 E4
Theebine, *Australia* 95 D5
Thekulthili L., *Canada* 105 A7
Thelon ➤, *Canada* 105 A8
Thénezay, *France* 18 F6
Thenon, *France* 20 C5
Theodore, *Australia* 94 C5
Theodore, *Canada* 105 C8
Theodore, *U.S.A.* 109 K1
Theodore Roosevelt National Memorial Park, *U.S.A.* .. 112 B3
Theodore Roosevelt Res., *U.S.A.* 115 K8
Thepha, *Thailand* 65 J3
Thérain ➤, *France* 19 C9
Theresa, *U.S.A.* 111 B9
Thermaïkós Kólpos, *Greece* . 40 F6
Thermí, *Greece* 39 B8
Thermopolis, *U.S.A.* 114 E9
Thermopylae P., *Greece* 38 C4
Thesprotía □, *Greece* 38 B2
Thessalía □, *Greece* 38 B4
Thessalon, *Canada* 102 C3
Thessaloníki, *Greece* 40 F6
Thessaloníki □, *Greece* 40 F7
Thessaloniki, Gulf of = Thermaïkós Kólpos, *Greece* . 40 F6
Thessaly = Thessalía □, *Greece* 38 B4
Thetford, *U.K.* 13 E8
Thetford Mines, *Canada* 103 C5
Theun ➤, *Laos* 64 C5
Theunissen, *S. Africa* 88 D4
Thevenard, *Australia* 95 E1
Thiámis ➤, *Greece* 38 B2
Thiberville, *France* 18 C7
Thibodaux, *U.S.A.* 113 L9
Thicket Portage, *Canada* 105 B9
Thief River Falls, *U.S.A.* 112 A6
Thiel Mts., *Antarctica* 5 E16
Thiene, *Italy* 29 C8
Thiérache, *France* 19 C10
Thiers, *France* 20 C7
Thiès, *Senegal* 82 C1
Thiesi, *Italy* 30 B1
Thiet, *Sudan* 81 F2
Thika, *Kenya* 86 C4
Thikombia, *Fiji* 91 B9
Thille-Boubacar, *Senegal* ... 82 B1
Thimphu, *Bhutan* 67 F16
Þingvallavatn, *Iceland* 8 D3
Thionville, *France* 19 C13
Thíra, *Greece* 39 E7
Thirasía, *Greece* 39 E7
Third Cataract, *Sudan* 80 D3
Thirsk, *U.K.* 12 C6
Thiruvananthapuram = Trivandrum, *India* 66 Q10
Thisted, *Denmark* 11 H2
Thistle I., *Australia* 95 F2
Thívai, *Greece* 38 C5
Thiviers, *France* 20 C4
Thizy, *France* 19 F11
Þjórsá ➤, *Iceland* 8 D4
Thlewiaza ➤, *Man., Canada* . 105 B8
Thlewiaza ➤, *N.W.T., Canada* . 105 A10
Thmar Puok, *Cambodia* 64 F4
Tho Vinh, *Vietnam* 64 C5
Thoa ➤, *Canada* 105 A7
Thoen, *Thailand* 64 D2
Thoeng, *Thailand* 64 C3
Thohoyandou, *S. Africa* 85 J6
Tholdi, *Pakistan* 69 B7
Thomas, *U.S.A.* 113 H5
Thomas, L., *Australia* 95 D2
Thomaston, *U.S.A.* 109 J3
Thomasville, *Ala., U.S.A.* ... 109 K2
Thomasville, *Ga., U.S.A.* 109 K4
Thomasville, *N.C., U.S.A.* ... 109 H5
Thompson, *Canada* 105 B9
Thompson, *U.S.A.* 111 E9
Thompson ➤, *Canada* 104 C4
Thompson ➤, *U.S.A.* 112 F8
Thompson Falls, *U.S.A.* 114 C6
Thompson Pk., *U.S.A.* 114 F2
Thompson Springs, *U.S.A.* . 115 G9
Thompsontown, *U.S.A.* 110 F7
Thomson, *U.S.A.* 109 J4
Thomson ➤, *Australia* 94 C3
Thomson's Falls = Nyahururu, *Kenya* 86 B4
Thônes, *France* 21 C10
Thonon-les-Bains, *France* ... 19 F13
Thorez, *Ukraine* 47 H10
Þórisvatn, *Iceland* 8 D4
Thornaby on Tees, *U.K.* 12 C6
Thornbury, *Canada* 110 B4
Thorne, *U.K.* 12 D7
Thornhill, *Canada* 104 C3
Thorold, *Canada* 110 C5
Þórshöfn, *Iceland* 8 C6
Thouarcé, *France* 18 E6
Thouars, *France* 18 E6
Thouet, *France* 18 E6
Thouin, C., *Australia* 92 D2
Thousand Oaks, *U.S.A.* 117 L8
Thrace, *Turkey* 41 F10

Thrakikón Pélagos, *Greece* 41 F8
Three Forks, *U.S.A.* 114 D8
Three Gorges Dam, *China* 59 B8
Three Hills, *Canada* 104 C6
Three Hummock I., *Australia* 94 G3
Three Points, C., *Ghana* 82 E4
Three Rivers, *Calif., U.S.A.* 116 J8
Three Rivers, *Tex., U.S.A.* 113 L5
Three Sisters, *U.S.A.* 114 D3
Three Springs, *Australia* 93 E2
Throssell, L., *Australia* 93 E3
Throssell Ra., *Australia* 92 D3
Thuan Hoa, *Vietnam* 65 H5
Thubun Lakes, *Canada* 105 A6
Thueyts, *France* 21 D8
Thuin, *Belgium* 17 D4
Thuir, *France* 20 F6
Thule = Qaanaaq, *Greenland* 4 B4
Thun, *Switz.* 25 J3
Thunder B., *U.S.A.* 110 B1
Thunder Bay, *Canada* 102 C2
Thunersee, *Switz.* 25 J3
Thung Song, *Thailand* 65 H2
Thunkar, *Bhutan* 67 F17
Thuong Tra, *Vietnam* 64 D6
Thur →, *Switz.* 25 H5
Thurgau □, *Switz.* 25 H5
Thüringen □, *Germany* 24 D6
Thüringer Wald, *Germany* 24 E6
Thurles, *Ireland* 15 D4
Thurn P., *Austria* 26 D5
Thurrock □, *U.K.* 13 F8
Thursday I., *Australia* 94 A3
Thurso, *Canada* 102 C4
Thurso, *U.K.* 14 C5
Thurso →, *U.K.* 14 C5
Thurston I., *Antarctica* 5 D16
Thury-Harcourt, *France* 18 D6
Thutade L., *Canada* 104 B3
Thy, *Denmark* 11 H2
Thyborøn, *Denmark* 11 H2
Thyolo, *Malawi* 87 F4
Thysville = Mbanza Ngungu, *Dem. Rep. of the Congo* 84 F2
Ti-n-Amzi →, *Niger* 83 B5
Ti-n-Barraouene, O. →, *Africa* 83 B5
Ti-n-Zaouatene, *Algeria* 83 B5
Ti Tree, *Australia* 94 C1
Tiadiaye, *Senegal* 82 C1
Tian Shan, *Asia* 60 B3
Tianchang, *China* 59 A12
Tiandeng, *China* 58 F6
Tiandong, *China* 58 F6
Tian'e, *China* 58 E6
Tianhe, *China* 58 E7
Tianjin, *China* 57 E9
Tiankoura, *Burkina Faso* 82 C4
Tianlin, *China* 58 E6
Tianmen, *China* 59 B9
Tianquan, *China* 58 B4
Tianshui, *China* 56 G3
Tiantai, *China* 59 C13
Tianyang, *China* 58 F6
Tianzhen, *China* 56 D8
Tianzhu, *China* 58 D7
Tianzhuangtai, *China* 57 D12
Tiaret, *Algeria* 78 A6
Tiassalé, *Ivory C.* 82 D4
Tibagi, *Brazil* 127 A5
Tibagi →, *Brazil* 127 A5
Tibati, *Cameroon* 83 D7
Tibe, *Ethiopia* 81 F4
Tiber = Tevere →, *Italy* 29 G9
Tiberias = Teverya, *Israel* 75 C4
Tiberias, L. = Yam Kinneret, *Israel* 75 C4
Tibesti, *Chad* 79 D9
Tibet = Xizang Zizhiqu □, *China* 60 C3
Tibet, Plateau of, *Asia* 52 F12
Tibiao, *Phil.* 61 F5
Tibiri, *Niger* 83 C6
Tibleș, Vf., *Romania* 43 C9
Tibleșului, Munții, *Romania* 43 C9
Tibnī, *Syria* 70 C3
Tibooburra, *Australia* 95 D3
Tibro, *Sweden* 11 F8
Tiburón, I., *Mexico* 118 B2
Ticao I., *Phil.* 61 E5
Tîchît, *Mauritania* 82 B3
Ticho, *Ethiopia* 81 F4
Ticino □, *Switz.* 25 J4
Ticino →, *Italy* 28 K5
Ticleni, *Romania* 43 F8
Ticonderoga, *U.S.A.* 111 C11
Ticul, *Mexico* 119 C7
Tidaholm, *Sweden* 11 F7
Tidan, *Sweden* 11 F8
Tiddim, *Burma* 67 H18
Tidioute, *U.S.A.* 110 E5
Tidjikja, *Mauritania* 82 B2
Tidore, *Indonesia* 63 D7
Tiébissou, *Ivory C.* 82 D3
Tiel, *Neths.* 17 C5
Tiel, *Senegal* 82 C1
Tieling, *China* 57 C12
Tielt, *Belgium* 17 C3
Tien Shan = Tian Shan, *Asia* 60 B3
Tien-tsin = Tianjin, *China* 57 E9
Tien Yen, *Vietnam* 64 B6
T'ienching = Tianjin, *China* 57 E9
Tienen, *Belgium* 17 D4
Tiénigbé, *Ivory C.* 82 D3
Tieri, *Australia* 94 C4
Tierp, *Sweden* 10 D11
Tierra Amarilla, *Chile* 126 B1
Tierra Amarilla, *U.S.A.* 115 H10

Tierra Colorada, *Mexico* 119 D5
Tierra de Barros, *Spain* 35 G4
Tierra de Campos, *Spain* 34 C6
Tierra del Fuego, I. Gr. de, *Argentina* 122 J4
Tiétar →, *Spain* 34 F4
Tietê →, *Brazil* 127 A5
Tiffin, *U.S.A.* 108 E4
Tiflis = Tbilisi, *Georgia* 49 K7
Tifton, *U.S.A.* 109 K4
Tifu, *Indonesia* 63 E7
Tighina, *Moldova* 43 D14
Tigil, *Russia* 51 D16
Tignish, *Canada* 103 C7
Tigray □, *Ethiopia* 81 E4
Tigre →, *Peru* 124 D4
Tigre →, *Venezuela* 124 B6
Tigris = Dijlah, Nahr →, *Asia* 70 D5
Tigveni, *Romania* 43 E9
Tigyaing, *Burma* 67 H20
Tîh, Gebel el, *Egypt* 80 B3
Tijara, *India* 68 F7
Tijuana, *Mexico* 117 N9
Tikal, *Guatemala* 120 C2
Tikamgarh, *India* 69 G8
Tikaré, *Burkina Faso* 83 C4
Tikhoretsk, *Russia* 49 H5
Tikhvin, *Russia* 46 C7
Tiko, *Cameroon* 83 E6
Tikrīt, *Iraq* 70 C4
Tiksi, *Russia* 51 B13
Tilamuta, *Indonesia* 63 D6
Tilburg, *Neths.* 17 C5
Tilbury, *Canada* 102 D3
Tilbury, *U.K.* 13 F8
Tilcara, *Argentina* 126 A2
Tilden, *U.S.A.* 112 D6
Tilemses, *Niger* 83 B5
Tilemsi, Vallée du, *Mali* 83 B5
Tilhar, *India* 69 F8
Tilichiki, *Russia* 51 C17
Tílissos, *Greece* 36 D7
Till →, *U.K.* 12 B5
Tillabéri, *Niger* 83 C5
Tillamook, *U.S.A.* 114 D2
Tillberga, *Sweden* 10 E10
Tillia, *Niger* 83 B5
Tillsonburg, *Canada* 102 D3
Tillyeria □, *Cyprus* 36 D11
Tilogne, *Senegal* 82 B2
Tílos, *Greece* 39 E9
Tilpa, *Australia* 95 E3
Tilsit = Sovetsk, *Russia* 9 J19
Tilt →, *U.K.* 14 E5
Tilton, *U.S.A.* 111 C13
Tiltonsville, *U.S.A.* 110 F4
Tim, *Denmark* 11 H2
Timagami, L., *Canada* 102 C3
Timaru, *N.Z.* 91 L3
Timashevo, *Russia* 48 D10
Timashevsk, *Russia* 49 H4
Timau, *Kenya* 86 B4
Timbákion, *Greece* 36 D6
Timbedgha, *Mauritania* 82 B3
Timber Creek, *Australia* 92 C5
Timber Lake, *U.S.A.* 112 C4
Timber Mt., *U.S.A.* 116 H10
Timbo, *Guinea* 82 C2
Timbo, *Liberia* 82 D3
Timbuktu = Tombouctou, *Mali* 82 B4
Timeiaouine, *Algeria* 83 A5
Timétrine, Mts., *Mali* 83 B4
Timfi Óros, *Greece* 38 B2
Timfristós, Óros, *Greece* 38 C3
Timi, *Cyprus* 36 E11
Tímia, *Niger* 83 B6
Timimoun, *Algeria* 78 C6
Timirist, Râs, *Mauritania* 82 B1
Timiș →, *Serbia, Yug.* 42 F5
Timiș □, *Romania* 42 E6
Timișoara, *Romania* 42 E6
Timmersdala, *Sweden* 11 F7
Timmins, *Canada* 102 C3
Timok →, *Serbia, Yug.* 40 B6
Timor, *Indonesia* 63 F7
Timor Sea, *Ind. Oc.* 92 B4
Timor Timur = East Timor ■, *Asia* 63 F7
Timrå, *Sweden* 10 B11
Tin Can Bay, *Australia* 95 D5
Tin Ethisane, *Mali* 83 B4
Tin Gornai, *Mali* 83 B4
Tin Mt., *U.S.A.* 116 J9
Tina →, *S. Africa* 89 E4
Tîna, Khalîg el, *Egypt* 80 A3
Tinaca Pt., *Phil.* 61 J6
Tinajo, *Canary Is.* 37 E6
Tinca, *Romania* 42 D6
Tindal, *Australia* 92 B5
Tindouf, *Algeria* 78 C4
Tinée →, *France* 21 E11
Tineo, *Spain* 34 B4
Ting Jiang →, *China* 59 E11
Tinggi, Pulau, *Malaysia* 65 L5
Tinglev, *Denmark* 11 K3
Tingley, *Ivory C.* 82 C3
Tingo Maria, *Peru* 124 E3
Tingrela, *Ivory C.* 82 C3
Tingsryd, *Sweden* 11 H9
Tingstäde, *Sweden* 11 G12
Tinh Bien, *Vietnam* 65 G5
Tinnevelly = Tirunelveli, *India* 66 Q10
Tinogasta, *Argentina* 126 B2
Tínos, *Greece* 39 D7
Tíñoso, C., *Spain* 33 H3
Tinpahar, *India* 69 G12
Tintina, *Argentina* 126 B3
Tintinara, *Australia* 95 F3

Tintioulé, *Guinea* 82 C3
Tinto →, *Spain* 35 H4
Tioga, *N. Dak., U.S.A.* 112 A3
Tioga, *Pa., U.S.A.* 110 E7
Tioman, Pulau, *Malaysia* 65 L5
Tione di Trento, *Italy* 28 B7
Tionesta, *U.S.A.* 110 E5
Tior, *Sudan* 81 F3
Tipongpani, *India* 67 F19
Tipperary, *Ireland* 15 D3
Tipperary □, *Ireland* 15 D4
Tipton, *Calif., U.S.A.* 116 J7
Tipton, *Iowa, U.S.A.* 112 E9
Tipton, *Ind., U.S.A.* 108 E2
Tipton Mt., *U.S.A.* 117 K12
Tiptonville, *U.S.A.* 113 G10
Tīrān, *Iran* 71 C6
Tīrān, *Si. Arabia* 80 B3
Tiranë, *Albania* 40 E3
Tirano, *Italy* 28 B7
Tiraspol, *Moldova* 43 D14
Tirdout, *Mali* 83 B4
Tire, *Turkey* 39 C9
Tirebolu, *Turkey* 73 B8
Tiree, *U.K.* 14 E2
Tiree, Passage of, *U.K.* 14 E2
Tîrgoviște = Târgoviște, *Romania* 43 F10
Tîrgu-Jiu = Târgu-Jiu, *Romania* 43 E8
Tîrgu Mureș = Târgu Mureș, *Romania* 43 D9
Tirich Mir, *Pakistan* 66 A7
Tiriolo, *Italy* 31 D9
Tiriro, *Guinea* 82 C3
Tirodi, *India* 66 J11
Tirol □, *Austria* 26 D3
Tirschenreuth, *Germany* 25 F8
Tirso →, *Italy* 30 C1
Tirstrup, *Denmark* 11 H4
Tiruchchirappalli, *India* 66 P11
Tirunelveli, *India* 66 Q10
Tirupati, *India* 66 N11
Tiruppur, *India* 66 P10
Tiruvannamalai, *India* 66 N11
Tisa, *India* 68 C7
Tisa →, *Serbia, Yug.* 42 E5
Tisdale, *Canada* 105 C8
Tishomingo, *U.S.A.* 113 H6
Tisjön, *Sweden* 10 D7
Tisnaren, *Sweden* 11 F9
Tišnov, *Czech Rep.* 27 B9
Tisovec, *Slovak Rep.* 27 C12
Tisza = Tisa →, *Serbia, Yug.* 42 E5
Tiszaföldvár, *Hungary* 42 D5
Tiszafüred, *Hungary* 42 C5
Tiszalök, *Hungary* 42 B6
Tiszavasvári, *Hungary* 42 C6
Tit-Ary, *Russia* 51 B13
Titaguas, *Spain* 32 F3
Titao, *Burkina Faso* 83 C4
Titel, *Serbia, Yug.* 42 E5
Tithwal, *Pakistan* 69 B5
Titicaca, L., *S. Amer.* 122 E4
Titisee, *Germany* 25 H4
Titiwa, *Nigeria* 83 C7
Tito, *Italy* 31 B8
Titograd = Podgorica, *Montenegro, Yug.* 40 D3
Titova Korenica, *Croatia* 29 D12
Titu, *Romania* 43 F10
Titule, *Dem. Rep. of the Congo* 86 B2
Titusville, *Fla., U.S.A.* 109 L5
Titusville, *Pa., U.S.A.* 110 E5
Tivaouane, *Senegal* 82 C1
Tivat, *Montenegro, Yug.* 40 D2
Tiverton, *U.K.* 13 G4
Tívoli, *Italy* 29 G9
Tiyo, *Eritrea* 81 E5
Tizi-Ouzou, *Algeria* 78 A6
Tizimín, *Mexico* 119 C7
Tjæreborg, *Denmark* 11 J2
Tjällmo, *Sweden* 11 F9
Tjeggelvas, *Sweden* 8 C17
Tjirebon = Cirebon, *Indonesia* 62 F3
Tjörn, *Sweden* 11 F5
Tkibuli = Tqibuli, *Georgia* 49 J6
Tkvarcheli = Tqvarcheli, *Georgia* 49 J5
Tlacotalpan, *Mexico* 119 D5
Tlahualilo, *Mexico* 118 B4
Tlaquepaque, *Mexico* 118 C4
Tlaxcala, *Mexico* 119 D5
Tlaxcala □, *Mexico* 119 D5
Tlaxiaco, *Mexico* 119 D5
Tlemcen, *Algeria* 78 B5
Tłuszcz, *Poland* 45 F8
Tlyarata, *Russia* 49 J8
To Bong, *Vietnam* 64 F7
Toad →, *Canada* 104 B4
Toad River, *Canada* 104 B3
Toamasina, *Madag.* 89 B8
Toamasina □, *Madag.* 89 B8
Toay, *Argentina* 126 D3
Toba, *Japan* 55 G8
Toba, Danau, *Indonesia* 62 D1
Toba Kakar, *Pakistan* 68 D3
Toba Tek Singh, *Pakistan* 68 D5
Tobago, *Trin. & Tob.* 121 D7
Tobarra, *Spain* 33 G3
Tobelo, *Indonesia* 63 D7
Tobermory, *Canada* 102 C3
Tobermory, *U.K.* 14 E2
Tobi, *Pac. Oc.* 63 D8
Tobin, *U.S.A.* 116 F5
Tobin, L., *Australia* 92 D4
Tobin L., *Canada* 105 C8

Toblach = Dobbiaco, *Italy* 29 B9
Toboali, *Indonesia* 62 E3
Tobol →, *Russia* 50 D7
Toboli, *Indonesia* 63 E6
Tobolsk, *Russia* 50 D7
Tobor, *Senegal* 82 C1
Tobruk = Ṭubruq, *Libya* 79 B10
Tobyhanna, *U.S.A.* 111 E9
Tobyl = Tobol →, *Russia* 50 D7
Tocantinópolis, *Brazil* 125 E9
Tocantins □, *Brazil* 125 F9
Tocantins →, *Brazil* 122 D6
Toccoa, *U.S.A.* 109 H4
Toce →, *Italy* 28 C5
Tochi →, *Pakistan* 68 C4
Tochigi, *Japan* 55 F9
Tochigi □, *Japan* 55 F9
Tocina, *Spain* 35 H5
Töcksfors, *Sweden* 10 E5
Toconao, *Chile* 126 A2
Tocopilla, *Chile* 126 A1
Tocumwal, *Australia* 95 F4
Tocuyo →, *Venezuela* 124 A5
Todd →, *Australia* 94 C2
Todeli, *Indonesia* 63 E6
Todenyang, *Kenya* 86 B4
Todgarh, *India* 68 G5
Todi, *Italy* 29 F9
Todos os Santos, B. de, *Brazil* 125 F11
Todos Santos, *Mexico* 118 C2
Todtnau, *Germany* 25 H3
Toe Hd., *U.K.* 14 D1
Toecé, *Burkina Faso* 83 C4
Tofield, *Canada* 104 C6
Tofino, *Canada* 104 D3
Tofua, *Tonga* 91 D11
Tōgane, *Japan* 55 G10
Tōgba, *Mauritania* 82 B2
Togian, Kepulauan, *Indonesia* 63 E6
Togliatti, *Russia* 48 D9
Togo ■, *W. Afr.* 83 D5
Togtoh, *China* 56 D6
Tohma →, *Turkey* 72 C7
Tōhoku □, *Japan* 54 E10
Töhöm, *Mongolia* 56 B5
Toinya, *Sudan* 81 F2
Toiyabe Range, *U.S.A.* 114 G5
Tojikiston = Tajikistan ■, *Asia* 50 F8
Tojo, *Indonesia* 63 E6
Tōjō, *Japan* 55 G6
Tok, *U.S.A.* 100 B5
Tok-do, *Japan* 55 F5
Tokachi-Dake, *Japan* 54 C11
Tokachi-Gawa →, *Japan* 54 C11
Tokaj, *Hungary* 42 B6
Tokala, *Indonesia* 63 E6
Tōkamachi, *Japan* 55 F9
Tokanui, *N.Z.* 91 M2
Tokar, *Sudan* 80 D4
Tokara-Rettō, *Japan* 55 K4
Tokarahi, *N.Z.* 91 L3
Tokashiki-Shima, *Japan* 55 L3
Tokat, *Turkey* 72 B7
Tŏkch'ŏn, *N. Korea* 57 E14
Tokeland, *U.S.A.* 116 D3
Tokelau Is., *Pac. Oc.* 96 H10
Tokmak, *Kyrgyzstan* 50 E8
Tokmak, *Ukraine* 47 J8
Toko Ra., *Australia* 94 C2
Tokoro-Gawa →, *Japan* 54 B12
Tokuno-Shima, *Japan* 55 L4
Tokushima, *Japan* 55 G7
Tokushima □, *Japan* 55 H7
Tokuyama, *Japan* 55 G5
Tōkyō, *Japan* 55 G9
Tolaga Bay, *N.Z.* 91 H7
Tolbukhin = Dobrich, *Bulgaria* 41 C11
Toledo, *Brazil* 127 A5
Toledo, *Spain* 34 F6
Toledo, *Ohio, U.S.A.* 108 E4
Toledo, *Oreg., U.S.A.* 114 D2
Toledo, *Wash., U.S.A.* 114 C2
Toledo, Montes de, *Spain* 35 F6
Toledo Bend Reservoir, *U.S.A.* 113 K8
Tolentino, *Italy* 29 E10
Tolga, *Australia* 94 B4
Toliara, *Madag.* 89 C7
Toliara □, *Madag.* 89 C8
Tolima, *Colombia* 124 C3
Tolitoli, *Indonesia* 63 D6
Tolkmicko, *Poland* 44 D6
Tollarp, *Sweden* 11 J7
Tollensesee, *Germany* 24 B9
Tollhouse, *U.S.A.* 116 H7
Tolmachevo, *Russia* 46 C5
Tolmezzo, *Italy* 29 B10
Tolmin, *Slovenia* 29 B10
Tolna, *Hungary* 42 D3
Tolna □, *Hungary* 42 D3
Tolo, Teluk, *Indonesia* 63 E6
Tolochin = Talachyn, *Belarus* 46 E5
Tolosa, *Spain* 32 B2
Tolox, *Spain* 35 J6
Toluca, *Mexico* 119 D5
Tom Burke, *S. Africa* 89 C4
Tom Price, *Australia* 92 D2
Toma, *Burkina Faso* 82 C4
Tomah, *U.S.A.* 112 D9
Tomahawk, *U.S.A.* 112 C10
Tomai, *Moldova* 43 D13
Tomakomai, *Japan* 54 C10
Tomales, *U.S.A.* 116 G4
Tomales B., *U.S.A.* 116 G3
Tomar, *Portugal* 35 F2
Tómaros, Óros, *Greece* 38 B2
Tomarza, *Turkey* 72 C6

Tomaszów Lubelski, *Poland* 45 H10
Tomaszów Mazowiecki, *Poland* 45 G7
Tomatlán, *Mexico* 118 D3
Tombadonkéa, *Guinea* 82 C2
Tombador, Serra do, *Brazil* 124 F7
Tombe, *Sudan* 81 F3
Tombigbee →, *U.S.A.* 109 K2
Tombouctou, *Mali* 82 B4
Tombstone, *U.S.A.* 115 L8
Tombua, *Angola* 88 B1
Tomé, *Chile* 126 D1
Tomelilla, *Sweden* 11 J7
Tomelloso, *Spain* 35 F7
Tomini, *Indonesia* 63 D6
Tomini, Teluk, *Indonesia* 63 E6
Tominian, *Mali* 82 C4
Tomiño, *Spain* 34 D2
Tomintoul, *U.K.* 14 D5
Tomislavgrad, *Bos.-H.* 42 G2
Tomkinson Ranges, *Australia* 93 E4
Tommot, *Russia* 51 D13
Tomnop Ta Suos, *Cambodia* 65 G5
Tomo →, *Colombia* 124 B5
Toms Place, *U.S.A.* 116 H8
Toms River, *U.S.A.* 111 G10
Tomsk, *Russia* 50 D9
Tomtabacken, *Sweden* 11 G8
Tona, *Spain* 32 D7
Tonalá, *Mexico* 119 D6
Tonale, Passo del, *Italy* 28 B7
Tonantins, *Brazil* 124 D5
Tonasket, *U.S.A.* 114 B4
Tonawanda, *U.S.A.* 110 D6
Tonbridge, *U.K.* 13 F8
Tondano, *Indonesia* 63 D6
Tondela, *Portugal* 34 E2
Tønder, *Denmark* 11 K2
Tondi Kiwindi, *Niger* 83 C5
Tondibi, *Mali* 83 B4
Tondoro, *Namibia* 88 B2
Tone →, *Australia* 93 F2
Tone-Gawa →, *Japan* 55 F9
Tonekābon, *Iran* 71 B6
Tong Xian, *China* 56 E9
Tônghâ, *Sudan* 81 F3
Tonga ■, *Pac. Oc.* 91 D11
Tonga Trench, *Pac. Oc.* 96 J10
Tongaat, *S. Africa* 89 D5
Tong'an, *China* 59 E12
Tongareva, *Cook Is.* 97 H12
Tongatapu Group, *Tonga* 91 E12
Tongbai, *China* 59 A9
Tongcheng, *Anhui, China* 59 B11
Tongcheng, *Hubei, China* 59 C9
Tongchuan, *China* 56 G5
Tongdao, *China* 58 D7
Tongeren, *Belgium* 17 D5
Tonggu, *China* 59 C10
Tongguan, *China* 56 G6
Tonghai, *China* 58 E4
Tonghua, *China* 57 D13
Tongjiang, *China* 58 B6
Tongjosŏn Man, *N. Korea* 57 E14
Tongking, G. of = Tonkin, G. of, *Asia* 60 E5
Tongliang, *China* 58 C6
Tongliao, *China* 57 C12
Tongling, *China* 59 B11
Tonglu, *China* 59 B12
Tongnae = S. Korea 57 G15
Tongobory, *Madag.* 89 C7
Tongoy, *Chile* 126 C1
Tongren, *China* 58 D7
Tongres = Tongeren, *Belgium* 17 D5
Tongsa Dzong, *Bhutan* 67 F17
Tongue, *U.K.* 14 C4
Tongue →, *U.S.A.* 112 B2
Tongwei, *China* 56 G3
Tongxiang, *China* 59 B13
Tongxin, *China* 56 F3
Tongyang, *N. Korea* 57 E14
Tongyu, *China* 57 B12
Tongzi, *China* 58 C6
Tonj, *Sudan* 81 F2
Tonj →, *Sudan* 81 F2
Tonk, *India* 68 F6
Tonkawa, *U.S.A.* 113 G6
Tonkin = Bac Phan, *Vietnam* 64 B5
Tonkin, G. of, *Asia* 60 E5
Tonle Sap, *Cambodia* 64 F4
Tonnay-Charente, *France* 20 D3
Tonneins, *France* 20 D4
Tonnerre, *France* 19 E10
Tönning, *Germany* 24 A4
Tono, *Japan* 54 E10
Tonopah, *U.S.A.* 115 G5
Tonosí, *Panama* 120 E3
Tons →, *Haryana, India* 68 D7
Tons →, *Ut. P., India* 69 F10
Tønsberg, *Norway* 9 G14
Tonya, *Turkey* 73 B8
Toobanna, *Australia* 94 B4
Toodyay, *Australia* 93 F2
Tooele, *U.S.A.* 114 F7
Toompine, *Australia* 95 D3
Toora, *Australia* 95 F4
Toora-Khem, *Russia* 51 D10
Toowoomba, *Australia* 95 D5
Top Springs, *Australia* 92 C5
Topalu, *Romania* 43 F13
Topaz, *U.S.A.* 116 G7
Topeka, *U.S.A.* 112 F7
Topl'a →, *Slovak Rep.* 27 C14
Topley, *Canada* 104 C3
Toplica →, *Serbia, Yug.* 40 C5

Topliţa, Romania 43 D10
Topocalma, Pta., Chile 126 C1
Topock, U.S.A. 117 L12
Topola, Serbia, Yug. 40 B4
Topolčani, Macedonia 40 E5
Topol'čany, Slovak Rep. 27 C11
Topolnitsa ➝, Bulgaria 41 D8
Topolobampo, Mexico 118 B3
Topoloveni, Romania 43 F10
Topolovgrad, Bulgaria 41 D10
Topolvăţu Mare, Romania ... 42 E6
Toppenish, U.S.A. 114 C3
Topraisar, Romania 43 F13
Topusko, Croatia 29 C12
Torà, Spain 32 D6
Tora Kit, Sudan 81 E3
Toraka Vestale, Madag. 89 B7
Torata, Peru 124 G4
Torbalı, Turkey 39 C9
Torbat-e Heydārīyeh, Iran ... 71 C8
Torbat-e Jām, Iran 71 C9
Torbay, Canada 103 C9
Torbay □, U.K. 13 G4
Torbjörntorp, Sweden 11 F7
Tordesillas, Spain 34 D6
Tordoya, Spain .... [not present]
Torekov, Sweden 11 H6
Torellò, Spain 32 C7
Toreno, Spain 34 C4
Torfaen □, U.K. 13 F4
Torgau, Germany 24 D8
Torgelow, Germany 24 B10
Torhamn, Sweden 11 H9
Torhout, Belgium 17 C3
Tori, Ethiopia 81 F3
Tori-Shima, Japan 55 J10
Torigni-sur-Vire, France 18 C6
Torija, Spain 32 E1
Torin, Mexico 118 B2
Torino, Italy 28 C4
Torit, Sudan 81 G3
Torkamān, Iran 70 B5
Torkovichi, Russia 46 C6
Tormac, Romania 42 E6
Tormes ➝, Spain 34 D4
Tornado Mt., Canada 104 D6
Tornal'a, Slovak Rep. 27 C13
Torne älv ➝, Sweden 8 D21
Torneå = Tornio, Finland 8 D21
Torneträsk, Sweden 8 B18
Tornio, Finland 8 D21
Tornionjoki ➝, Finland 8 D21
Tornquist, Argentina 126 D3
Toro, Baleares, Spain 37 B11
Toro, Zamora, Spain 34 D5
Torö, Sweden 11 F11
Toro, Cerro del, Chile 126 B2
Toro Pk., U.S.A. 117 M10
Törökszentmiklós, Hungary .. 42 C5
Toroníios Kólpos, Greece ... 40 F7
Toronto, Canada 102 D4
Toronto, U.S.A. 110 F4
Toropets, Russia 46 D6
Tororo, Uganda 86 B3
Torpa, India 69 H11
Torquay, U.K. 13 G4
Torquemada, Spain 34 C6
Torrance, U.S.A. 117 M8
Torrão, Portugal 35 G2
Torre Annunziata, Italy 31 B7
Torre de Moncorvo, Portugal .. 34 D3
Torre del Campo, Spain 35 H7
Torre del Greco, Italy 31 B7
Torre del Mar, Spain 35 J6
Torre-Pacheco, Spain 33 H4
Torre Péllice, Italy 28 D4
Torreblanca, Spain 32 E5
Torrecampo, Spain 35 G6
Torrecilla en Cameros, Spain .. 32 C2
Torredembarra, Spain 32 D6
Torredonjimeno, Spain 35 H7
Torrejón de Ardoz, Spain ... 34 E7
Torrejoncillo, Spain 34 F4
Torrelaguna, Spain 34 E7
Torrelavega, Spain 34 B6
Torremaggiore, Italy 29 G12
Torremolinos, Spain 35 J6
Torrens, L., Australia 95 E2
Torrens Cr. ➝, Australia 94 C4
Torrens Creek, Australia 94 C4
Torrent, Spain 33 F4
Torrenueva, Spain 35 G7
Torreón, Mexico 118 B4
Torreperogil, Spain 35 G7
Torres, Brazil 127 B5
Torres, Mexico 118 B2
Torres Novas, Portugal 35 F2
Torres Strait, Australia 96 H6
Torres Vedras, Portugal 35 F1
Torrevieja, Spain 33 H4
Torrey, U.S.A. 115 G8
Torridge ➝, U.K. 13 G3
Torridon, L., U.K. 14 D3
Torrijos, Spain 34 F6
Tørring, Denmark 11 J3
Torrington, Conn., U.S.A. ... 111 E11
Torrington, Wyo., U.S.A. ... 112 D2
Torroella de Montgrì, Spain .. 32 C8
Torrox, Spain 35 J7
Torsås, Sweden 11 H9
Torsby, Sweden 10 D6
Torshälla, Sweden 10 E10
Tórshavn, Færoe Is. 8 E9
Torslanda, Sweden 11 G5
Torsö, Sweden 11 F7
Tortola, Br. Virgin Is. 121 C7

Tórtoles de Esgueva, Spain ... 34 D6
Tortolì, Italy 30 C2
Tortona, Italy 28 D5
Tortorici, Italy 31 D7
Tortosa, Spain 32 E5
Tortosa, C., Spain 32 E5
Tortosendo, Portugal 34 E3
Tortue, I. de la, Haiti 121 B5
Tortum, Turkey 73 B9
Ţorūd, Iran 71 C7
Torul, Turkey 73 B8
Toruń, Poland 45 E5
Tory I., Ireland 15 A3
Torysa ➝, Slovak Rep. 27 C14
Torzhok, Russia 46 D8
Torzym, Poland 45 F2
Tosa, Japan 55 H6
Tosa-Shimizu, Japan 55 H6
Tosa-Wan, Japan 55 H6
Toscana □, Italy 28 E8
Toscano, Arcipelago, Italy ... 28 F7
Toshkent, Uzbekistan 50 E7
Tosno, Russia 46 C6
Tossa de Mar, Spain 32 D7
Tösse, Sweden 11 F6
Tostado, Argentina 126 B3
Tostedt, Germany 24 B5
Tostón, Pta. de, Canary Is. ... 37 F5
Tosu, Japan 55 H5
Tosya, Turkey 72 B6
Toszek, Poland 45 H5
Totana, Spain 33 H3
Totebo, Sweden 11 G10
Toteng, Botswana 88 C3
Tôtes, France 18 C8
Tótkomlós, Hungary 42 D5
Totma, Russia 50 C5
Totnes, U.K. 13 G4
Toto, Nigeria 83 D6
Totonicapán, Guatemala ... 120 D1
Totten Glacier, Antarctica ... 5 C8
Tottenham, Australia 95 E4
Tottenham, Canada 110 B5
Tottori, Japan 55 G7
Tottori □, Japan 55 G7
Touaret, Niger 83 A6
Touba, Ivory C. 82 D3
Touba, Senegal 82 C1
Toubkal, Djebel, Morocco ... 78 B4
Toucy, France 19 E10
Tougan, Burkina Faso 82 C4
Touggourt, Algeria 78 B7
Tougouri, Burkina Faso 83 C4
Tougué, Guinea 82 C2
Toukoto, Mali 82 C3
Toul, France 19 D12
Toulepleu, Ivory C. 82 D3
Toulon, France 21 E9
Toulouse, France 20 E5
Toummo, Niger 79 D8
Toumodi, Ivory C. 82 D3
Tounan, Taiwan 59 F13
Toungo, Nigeria 83 D7
Toungoo, Burma 67 K20
Touques ➝, France 18 C7
Touraine, France 18 E7
Tourane = Da Nang, Vietnam .. 64 D7
Tourcoing, France 19 B10
Touriñán, C., Spain 34 B1
Tournai, Belgium 17 D3
Tournay, France 20 E4
Tournon-St-Martin, France .. 18 F7
Tournon-sur-Rhône, France .. 21 C8
Tournus, France 19 F11
Tours, France 18 E7
Toussora, Mt., C.A.R. 84 C4
Touws ➝, S. Africa 88 E3
Touwsrivier, S. Africa 88 E3
Tovarkovskiy, Russia 46 F10
Tovuz, Azerbaijan 49 K7
Towada, Japan 54 D10
Towada-Ko, Japan 54 D10
Towanda, U.S.A. 111 E8
Towang, India 67 F17
Tower, U.S.A. 112 B8
Towerhill Cr. ➝, Australia .. 94 C3
Towner, U.S.A. 112 A4
Townsend, U.S.A. 114 C8
Townshend I., Australia 94 C5
Townsville, Australia 94 B4
Towraghondi, Afghan. 66 B3
Towson, U.S.A. 108 F7
Towuti, Danau, Indonesia ... 63 E6
Toya-Ko, Japan 54 C10
Toyama, Japan 55 F8
Toyama □, Japan 55 F8
Toyama-Wan, Japan 55 F8
Toyohashi, Japan 55 G8
Toyokawa, Japan 55 G8
Toyonaka, Japan 55 G7
Toyooka, Japan 55 G7
Toyota, Japan 55 G8
Tozeur, Tunisia 78 B7
Tqibuli, Georgia 49 J6
Tqvarcheli, Georgia 49 J5
Trá Li = Tralee, Ireland 15 D2
Trabancos ➝, Spain 34 D5
Traben-Trarbach, Germany .. 25 F3
Trabzon, Turkey 73 B8
Tracadie, Canada 103 C7
Tracy, Calif., U.S.A. 116 H5
Tracy, Minn., U.S.A. 112 C7
Tradate, Italy 28 C5
Trade Town, Liberia 82 D3

Trafalgar, C., Spain 35 J4
Traian, Brăila, Romania 43 E12
Traian, Tulcea, Romania 43 E13
Trail, Canada 104 D5
Trainor L., Canada 104 A4
Trákhonas, Cyprus 36 D12
Tralee, Ireland 15 D2
Tralee B., Ireland 15 D2
Tramore, Ireland 15 D4
Tramore B., Ireland 15 D4
Tran Ninh, Cao Nguyen, Laos .. 64 C4
Tranås, Sweden 11 F8
Tranbjerg, Denmark 11 H4
Trancas, Argentina 126 B2
Trancoso, Portugal 34 E3
Tranebjerg, Denmark 11 J4
Tranemo, Sweden 11 G7
Trang, Thailand 65 J2
Trangahy, Madag. 89 B7
Trangan, Indonesia 63 F8
Trangie, Australia 95 E4
Trångsviken, Sweden 10 A7
Trani, Italy 31 A9
Tranoroa, Madag. 89 C8
Tranqueras, Uruguay 127 C4
Transantarctic Mts., Antarctica .. 5 E12
Transilvania, Romania 43 D9
Transilvanian Alps = Carpaţii
  Meridionali, Romania 43 E9
Transtrand, Sweden 10 C7
Transtrandsfjällen, Sweden .. 10 C6
Transvaal, S. Africa 85 K5
Transylvania = Transilvania,
  Romania 43 D9
Trápani, Italy 30 D5
Trapper Pk., U.S.A. 114 D6
Traralgon, Australia 95 F4
Trarza, Mauritania 82 B2
Trasacco, Italy 29 G10
Trăscău, Munţii, Romania ... 43 D8
Trasimeno, L., Italy 29 E9
Träslövsläge, Sweden 11 G6
Trat, Thailand 65 F4
Tratani ➝, Pakistan 68 E3
Traun, Austria 26 C7
Traun ➝, Austria 26 C7
Traunreut, Germany 25 H8
Traunsee, Austria 26 D6
Traunstein, Germany 25 H8
Traveller's L., Australia 95 E3
Travemünde, Germany 24 B6
Travers, Mt., N.Z. 91 K4
Traverse City, U.S.A. 108 C3
Travis, L., U.S.A. 113 K5
Travnik, Bos.-H. 42 F7
Trbovlje, Slovenia 29 B12
Trébbia ➝, Italy 28 C6
Trebel ➝, Germany 24 B9
Trébeurden, France 18 D3
Třebíč, Czech Rep. 26 B8
Trebinje, Bos.-H. 40 D2
Trebisacce, Italy 31 C9
Trebišnjica ➝, Bos.-H. 40 D2
Trebišov, Slovak Rep. 27 C14
Trebižat ➝, Bos.-H. 29 E14
Trebnje, Slovenia 29 C12
Třeboň, Czech Rep. 26 B7
Trebonne, Australia 94 B4
Trebujena, Spain 35 J4
Trecate, Italy 28 C5
Tregaron, U.K. 13 E4
Tregnago, Italy 29 C8
Tregrosse Is., Australia 94 B5
Tréguier, France 18 D3
Trégunc, France 18 E3
Treherne, Canada 105 D9
Tréia, Italy 29 E10
Treignac, France 20 C5
Treinta y Tres, Uruguay 127 C5
Treis-karden, Germany 25 E3
Treklyano, Bulgaria 40 D6
Trelazé, France 18 E6
Trelew, Argentina 128 E3
Trélissac, France 20 C4
Trelleborg, Sweden 11 J7
Tremadog Bay, U.K. 12 E3
Trémiti, Italy 29 F12
Tremonton, U.S.A. 114 F7
Tremp, Spain 32 C5
Trenche ➝, Canada 102 C5
Trenčiansky □, Slovak Rep. .. 27 C11
Trenčín, Slovak Rep. 27 C11
Trenggalek, Indonesia 63 H14
Trenque Lauquen, Argentina .. 126 D3
Trent ➝, Canada 110 B7
Trent ➝, U.K. 12 D7
Trentino-Alto Adige □, Italy .. 29 B8
Trento, Italy 28 B8
Trenton, Canada 102 D4
Trenton, Mo., U.S.A. 112 E8
Trenton, N.J., U.S.A. 111 F10
Trenton, Nebr., U.S.A. 112 E4
Trepassey, Canada 103 C9
Trepuzzi, Italy 31 B11
Três Corações, Brazil 127 A6
Três Lagoas, Brazil 125 H8
Tres Lomas, Argentina 126 D3
Tres Marías, Islas, Mexico ... 118 C3
Tres Montes, C., Chile 128 F1
Tres Pinos, U.S.A. 116 J5
Três Pontas, Brazil 127 A6
Tres Puentes, Chile 126 B1
Tres Puntas, C., Argentina ... 128 F3
Três Rios, Brazil 127 A7

Tres Valles, Mexico 119 D5
Tresco, U.K. 13 H1
Treska ➝, Macedonia 40 E5
Treskavica, Bos.-H. 42 G3
Trespaderne, Spain 34 C7
Trets, France 21 E9
Treuchtlingen, Germany ... 25 G6
Treuenbrietzen, Germany .. 24 C8
Trevi, Italy 29 F9
Trévíglio, Italy 28 C6
Trevínca, Peña, Spain 34 C4
Treviso, Italy 29 C9
Trévoux, France 21 C8
Trgovište, Serbia, Yug. 40 D6
Triabunna, Australia 94 G4
Triánda, Greece 36 C10
Triangle, Zimbabwe 89 C5
Triaucourt-en-Argonne, France .. 19 D12
Tribal Areas □, Pakistan ... 68 C4
Tribsees, Germany 24 A8
Tribulation, C., Australia ... 94 B4
Tribune, U.S.A. 112 F4
Tricárico, Italy 31 B9
Tricase, Italy 31 C11
Trichinopoly =
  Tiruchchirappalli, India ... 66 P11
Trichur, India 66 P10
Trida, Australia 95 E4
Trier, Germany 25 F2
Trieste, Italy 29 C10
Trieste, G. di, Italy 29 C10
Trieux ➝, France 18 D3
Triggiano, Italy 31 A9
Triglav, Slovenia 29 B10
Trigno ➝, Italy 29 F11
Trigueros, Spain 35 H4
Tríkeri, Greece 38 B5
Trikhonis, Límni, Greece ... 38 C3
Tríkkala, Greece 38 B3
Tríkkala □, Greece 38 B3
Trikomo, Cyprus 36 D12
Trikora, Puncak, Indonesia .. 63 E9
Trilj, Croatia 29 E13
Trillo, Spain 32 E2
Trim, Ireland 15 C5
Trincomalee, Sri Lanka 66 Q12
Trindade, Brazil 125 G9
Trindade, I., Atl. Oc. 2 F8
Třinec, Czech Rep. 27 B11
Trinidad, Bolivia 124 F6
Trinidad, Cuba 120 B4
Trinidad, Trin. & Tob. 121 D7
Trinidad, Uruguay 126 C4
Trinidad, U.S.A. 113 G2
Trinidad ➝, Mexico 119 D5
Trinidad & Tobago ■, W. Indies .. 121 D7
Trinitápoli, Italy 31 A9
Trinity, Canada 103 C9
Trinity, U.S.A. 113 K7
Trinity ➝, Calif., U.S.A. 114 F2
Trinity ➝, Tex., U.S.A. 113 L7
Trinity B., Canada 103 C9
Trinity Is., U.S.A. 100 C4
Trinity Range, U.S.A. 114 F4
Trinkitat, Sudan 80 D4
Trino, Italy 28 C5
Trinway, U.S.A. 110 F2
Trionto, C., Italy 31 C9
Triora, Italy 28 D4
Tripoli = Tarābulus, Lebanon .. 75 A4
Tripoli = Tarābulus, Libya ... 79 B8
Trípolis, Greece 38 D4
Tripolitania, N. Afr. 79 B8
Tripura □, India 67 H18
Tripylos, Cyprus 36 E11
Trischen, Germany 24 A4
Tristan da Cunha, Atl. Oc. ... 77 K2
Trisul, India 69 D8
Trivandrum, India 66 Q10
Trivento, Italy 29 G11
Trnava, Slovak Rep. 27 C10
Trnavský □, Slovak Rep. ... 27 C10
Troarn, France 18 C6
Trochu, Canada 104 C6
Trodely I., Canada 102 B4
Troezen, Greece 38 D5
Trogir, Croatia 29 E13
Troglav, Croatia 29 E13
Tróia, Italy 31 A8
Troilus, L., Canada 102 B5
Troina, Italy 31 E7
Trois-Pistoles, Canada 103 C6
Trois-Rivières, Canada 102 C5
Troisdorf, Germany 24 E3
Troitsk, Russia 50 D7
Troitsko Pechorsk, Russia ... 50 C10
Troitskoye, Russia 49 F6
Trölladyngja, Iceland 8 D5
Trollhättan, Sweden 11 F6
Trollheimen, Norway 8 E13
Trombetas ➝, Brazil 125 D7
Tromsø, Norway 8 B18
Trona, U.S.A. 117 K9
Tronador, Mte., Argentina .. 128 E2
Trøndelag, Norway 8 D14
Trondheim, Norway 8 E14
Trondheimsfjorden, Norway .. 8 E14
Trönninge, Sweden 11 H6
Tronto ➝, Italy 29 F10
Troodos, Cyprus 36 E11
Troon, U.K. 14 F4
Tropea, Italy 31 D8
Tropojë, Albania 40 D4
Trosa, Sweden 11 F11
Trostan, U.K. 15 A5
Trostberg, Germany 25 G8
Trostyanets, Ukraine 47 G8

Trout ➝, Canada 104 A5
Trout L., N.W.T., Canada ... 104 A4
Trout L., Ont., Canada 105 C10
Trout Lake, Canada 104 B6
Trout Lake, U.S.A. 116 E5
Trout River, Canada 103 C8
Trout Run, U.S.A. 110 E7
Trouville-sur-Mer, France .. 18 C7
Trowbridge, U.K. 13 F5
Troy, Turkey 39 B8
Troy, Ala., U.S.A. 109 K3
Troy, Kans., U.S.A. 112 F7
Troy, Mo., U.S.A. 112 F9
Troy, Mont., U.S.A. 114 B6
Troy, N.Y., U.S.A. 111 D11
Troy, Ohio, U.S.A. 108 E3
Troy, Pa., U.S.A. 111 E8
Troyan, Bulgaria 41 D8
Troyes, France 19 D11
Trpanj, Croatia 29 E14
Trstenik, Serbia, Yug. 40 C5
Trubchevsk, Russia 47 F7
Truchas Peak, U.S.A. 113 H2
Trucial States = United Arab
  Emirates ■, Asia 71 F7
Truckee, U.S.A. 116 F6
Trudfront, Russia 49 H8
Trudovoye, Russia 54 C6
Trujillo, Honduras 120 C2
Trujillo, Peru 124 E3
Trujillo, Spain 35 F5
Trujillo, U.S.A. 113 H2
Trujillo, Venezuela 124 B4
Truk, Micronesia 96 G7
Trumann, U.S.A. 113 H9
Trumansburg, U.S.A. 111 D8
Trumbull, Mt., U.S.A. 115 H7
Trŭn, Bulgaria 40 D6
Trun, France 18 D7
Trundle, Australia 95 E4
Trung-Phan = Annam, Vietnam .. 64 E7
Truro, Canada 103 C7
Truro, U.K. 13 G2
Truskavets, Ukraine 47 H2
Trŭstenik, Bulgaria 41 C8
Trustrup, Denmark 11 H4
Trutch, Canada 104 B4
Truth or Consequences, U.S.A. .. 115 K10
Trutnov, Czech Rep. 26 A8
Truxton, U.S.A. 111 D8
Truyère ➝, France 20 D6
Tryavna, Bulgaria 41 D9
Tryonville, U.S.A. 110 E5
Trzcianka, Poland 45 E3
Trzciel, Poland 45 F2
Trzcińsko Zdrój, Poland ... 45 F1
Trzebiatów, Poland 44 D2
Trzebiez, Poland 44 E1
Trzebnica, Poland 45 G4
Trzemeszno, Poland 45 F4
Tržič, Slovenia 29 B11
Tsagan Aman, Russia 49 G8
Tsamandás, Greece 38 B2
Tsandi, Namibia 88 B1
Tsaratanana, Madag. 89 B8
Tsaratanana, Mt. de, Madag. .. 89 A8
Tsarevo = Michurin, Bulgaria .. 41 D11
Tsarevo, Bulgaria 41 D9
Tsaritsáni, Greece 38 B4
Tsau, Botswana 88 C3
Tsebrikovo, Ukraine 47 J6
Tselinograd = Astana,
  Kazakstan 50 D8
Tses, Namibia 88 D2
Tsetserleg, Mongolia 60 B5
Tsévié, Togo 83 D5
Tshabong, Botswana 88 D3
Tshane, Botswana 88 C3
Tshela, Dem. Rep. of the Congo .. 84 E2
Tshesebe, Botswana 89 C4
Tshibeke, Dem. Rep. of
  the Congo 86 C2
Tshibinda, Dem. Rep. of
  the Congo 86 C2
Tshikapa, Dem. Rep. of
  the Congo 84 F4
Tshilenge, Dem. Rep. of
  the Congo 86 D1
Tshinsenda, Dem. Rep. of
  the Congo 87 E2
Tshofa, Dem. Rep. of the Congo .. 86 D2
Tshwane, Botswana 88 C3
Tsigara, Botswana 88 C4
Tsihombe, Madag. 89 D8
Tsiigehtchic, Canada 100 B6
Tsimlyansk, Russia 49 G6
Tsimlyansk Res. =
  Tsimlyanskoye Vdkhr., Russia .. 49 F6
Tsimlyanskoye Vdkhr., Russia .. 49 F6
Tsinan = Jinan, China 56 F9
Tsineng, S. Africa 88 D3
Tsinga, Greece 41 E8
Tsinghai = Qinghai □, China .. 60 C4
Tsingtao = Qingdao, China .. 57 F11
Tsinjoarivo, Madag. 89 B8
Tsinjomitondraka, Madag. .. 89 B8
Tsiroanomandidy, Madag. .. 89 B8
Tsiteli-Tsqaro, Georgia 49 K8
Tsitondroina, Madag. 89 C8
Tsivilsk, Russia 48 C8
Tsivory, Madag. 89 C8
Tskhinvali, Georgia 49 J7
Tsna ➝, Russia 48 C6
Tsnori, Russia 49 K7
Tso Moriri, L., India 69 C8
Tsobis, Namibia 88 B2
Tsodilo Hill, Botswana 88 B3

Tsogttsetsiy = Baruunsuu,
  Mongolia 56 C3
Tsolo, *S. Africa* 89 E4
Tsomo, *S. Africa* 89 E4
Tsu, *Japan* 55 G8
Tsu L., *Canada* 104 A6
Tsuchiura, *Japan* 55 F10
Tsuen Wan, *H.K.* 59 F10
Tsugaru-Kaikyō, *Japan* 54 D10
Tsumeb, *Namibia* 88 B2
Tsumis, *Namibia* 88 C2
Tsuruga, *Japan* 55 G8
Tsurugi-San, *Japan* 55 H7
Tsuruoka, *Japan* 54 E9
Tsushima, *Gifu, Japan* 55 G8
Tsushima, *Nagasaki, Japan* . 55 G4
Tsuyama, *Japan* 55 G7
Tsvetkovo, *Ukraine* 47 H6
Tsyelyakhany, *Belarus* 47 F3
Tua →, *Portugal* 34 D3
Tual, *Indonesia* 63 F8
Tuam, *Ireland* 15 C3
Tuamotu Arch. = Tuamotu Is.,
  Pac. Oc. 97 J13
Tuamotu Is., *Pac. Oc.* 97 J13
Tuamotu Ridge, *Pac. Oc.* ... 97 K14
Tuanfeng, *China* 59 B10
Tuanxi, *China* 58 D6
Tuao, *Phil.* 61 C4
Tuapse, *Russia* 49 H4
Tuatapere, *N.Z.* 91 M1
Tuba City, *U.S.A.* 115 H8
Tuban, *Indonesia* 63 G15
Tubani, *Botswana* 88 C3
Tubarão, *Brazil* 127 B6
Tūbās, *West Bank* 75 C4
Tubas →, *Namibia* 88 C2
Tübingen, *Germany* 25 G5
Tubruq, *Libya* 79 B10
Tubuai Is., *Pac. Oc.* 97 K13
Tuc Trung, *Vietnam* 65 G6
Tucacas, *Venezuela* 124 A5
T'uch'ang, *Taiwan* 59 E13
Tuchodi →, *Canada* 104 B4
Tuchola, *Poland* 44 E4
Tuchów, *Poland* 45 J8
Tuckanarra, *Australia* 93 E2
Tucson, *U.S.A.* 115 K8
Tucumán □, *Argentina* 126 B2
Tucumcari, *U.S.A.* 113 H3
Tucupita, *Venezuela* 124 B6
Tucuruí, *Brazil* 125 D9
Tucuruí, Reprêsa de, *Brazil* . 125 D9
Tuczno, *Poland* 45 E3
Tudela, *Spain* 32 C3
Tudmur, *Syria* 70 C3
Tudor, L., *Canada* 103 A6
Tudora, *Romania* 43 C11
Tuella →, *Portugal* 34 D3
Tugela →, *S. Africa* 89 D5
Tuguegarao, *Phil.* 61 C4
Tugur, *Russia* 51 D14
Tui, *Spain* 34 C2
Tuineje, *Canary Is.* 37 F5
Tukangbesi, Kepulauan,
  Indonesia 63 F6
Tukarak I., *Canada* 102 A4
Tukayyid, *Iraq* 70 D5
Tūkh, *Egypt* 80 H7
Tukobo, *Ghana* 82 D4
Tuktoyaktuk, *Canada* 100 B6
Tukums, *Latvia* 9 H20
Tukums □, *Latvia* 44 B10
Tukuyu, *Tanzania* 87 D3
Tula, *Hidalgo, Mexico* 119 C5
Tula, *Tamaulipas, Mexico* .. 119 C5
Tula, *Nigeria* 83 D7
Tula, *Russia* 46 E9
Tulancingo, *Mexico* 119 C5
Tulare, *Serbia, Yug.* 40 D5
Tulare, *U.S.A.* 116 J7
Tulare Lake Bed, *U.S.A.* ... 116 K7
Tularosa, *U.S.A.* 115 K10
Tulbagh, *S. Africa* 88 E2
Tulcán, *Ecuador* 124 C3
Tulcea, *Romania* 43 E13
Tulcea □, *Romania* 43 E13
Tulchyn, *Ukraine* 47 H5
Tüleh, *Iran* 71 C7
Tulemalu L., *Canada* 105 A9
Tulgheş, *Romania* 43 D10
Tuli, *Zimbabwe* 87 G2
Tulia, *U.S.A.* 113 H4
Tuliszków, *Poland* 45 F5
Tulita, *Canada* 100 B7
Ṭulkarm, *West Bank* 75 C4
Tulla, *Ireland* 15 D3
Tullahoma, *U.S.A.* 109 H2
Tullamore, *Australia* 95 E4
Tullamore, *Ireland* 15 C4
Tulle, *France* 20 C5
Tulln, *Austria* 26 C9
Tullow, *Ireland* 15 D5
Tullus, *Sudan* 81 E1
Tully, *Australia* 94 B4
Tully, *U.S.A.* 111 D8
Tulnici, *Romania* 43 E11
Tulovo, *Bulgaria* 41 D9
Tulsa, *U.S.A.* 113 H7
Tulsequah, *Canada* 104 B2
Tulu Milki, *Ethiopia* 81 F4
Tulu Welel, *Ethiopia* 81 F3
Tulua, *Colombia* 124 C3
Tulucesti, *Romania* 43 E13
Tulun, *Russia* 51 D11
Tulungagung, *Indonesia* ... 63 H14
Tuma →, *Russia* 46 E11

Tuma →, *Nic.* 120 D3
Tumaco, *Colombia* 124 C3
Tumatumari, *Guyana* 124 B7
Tumba, *Sweden* 10 E11
Tumba, L., *Dem. Rep. of*
  the Congo 84 E3
Tumbarumba, *Australia* ... 95 F4
Tumbaya, *Argentina* 126 A2
Tumbes, *Peru* 124 D2
Tumbur, *Sudan* 81 G3
Tumbwe, *Dem. Rep. of*
  the Congo 87 E2
Tumby Bay, *Australia* 95 E2
Tumd Youqi, *China* 56 D6
Tumen, *China* 57 C15
Tumen Jiang →, *China* 57 C16
Tumeremo, *Venezuela* 124 B6
Tumkur, *India* 66 N10
Tump, *Pakistan* 66 F3
Tumpat, *Malaysia* 65 J4
Tumu, *Ghana* 82 C4
Tumucumaque, Serra, *Brazil* 122 C15
Tumut, *Australia* 95 F4
Tumwater, *U.S.A.* 116 C4
Tuna, *India* 68 H4
Tunadal, *Sweden* 10 B11
Tunas de Zaza, *Cuba* 120 B4
Tunbridge Wells = Royal
  Tunbridge Wells, *U.K.* ... 13 F8
Tunçbilek, *Turkey* 39 B11
Tunceli, *Turkey* 73 C8
Tuncurry, *Australia* 95 E5
Tundla, *India* 68 F8
Tundubai, *Sudan* 80 D2
Tunduma, *Tanzania* 87 E4
Tundzha →, *Bulgaria* 41 E10
Tungabhadra →, *India* 66 M11
Tungaru, *Sudan* 81 E3
Tungla, *Nic.* 120 D3
Tungsha Tao, *Taiwan* 59 G11
Tungshih, *Taiwan* 59 E13
Tungsten, *Canada* 104 A3
Tunguska, Nizhnyaya →, *Russia* 51 C9
Tunguska, Podkamennaya →,
  Russia 51 C10
Tunica, *U.S.A.* 113 H9
Tunis, *Tunisia* 78 A7
Tunisia ■, *Africa* 78 B6
Tunja, *Colombia* 124 B4
Tunkhannock, *U.S.A.* 111 E9
Tunliu, *China* 56 F7
Tunnsjøen, *Norway* 8 D15
Tunø, *Denmark* 11 J4
Tunungayualok I., *Canada* . 103 A7
Tununirusiq = Arctic Bay,
  Canada 101 A11
Tunuyán, *Argentina* 126 C2
Tunuyán →, *Argentina* ... 126 C2
Tuo Jiang →, *China* 58 C5
Tuolumne, *U.S.A.* 116 H6
Tuolumne →, *U.S.A.* 116 H5
Tūp Āghāj, *Iran* 70 B5
Tupã, *Brazil* 127 A5
Tupelo, *U.S.A.* 109 H1
Tupik, *Russia* 46 E7
Tupinambaranas, *Brazil* ... 124 D7
Tupiza, *Bolivia* 126 A2
Tupižnica, *Serbia, Yug.* ... 40 C6
Tupman, *U.S.A.* 117 K7
Tupper, *Canada* 104 B4
Tupper Lake, *U.S.A.* 111 B10
Tupungato, Cerro, *S. Amer.* . 126 C2
Tuquan, *China* 57 B11
Túquerres, *Colombia* 124 C3
Tura, *Russia* 51 C11
Turabah, *Si. Arabia* 70 D4
Turabah, *Si. Arabia* 80 C5
Tūrān, *Iran* 71 C8
Turan, *Russia* 51 D10
Ţurayf, *Si. Arabia* 70 D3
Turbacz, *Poland* 45 J7
Turbe, *Bos.-H.* 42 F2
Turbo, *Colombia* 124 B3
Turčianske Teplice, *Slovak Rep.* 27 C11
Turcoaia, *Romania* 43 E13
Turda, *Romania* 43 D8
Turek, *Poland* 45 F5
Turen, *Venezuela* 124 B5
Turfan = Turpan, *China* ... 60 B3
Turfan Depression = Turpan
  Hami, *China* 52 E12
Turgeon →, *Canada* 102 C4
Tŭrgovishte, *Bulgaria* 41 C10
Turgut, *Turkey* 39 C9
Turgutlu, *Turkey* 39 C9
Turgwe →, *Zimbabwe* 89 C5
Turhal, *Turkey* 72 B7
Turia →, *Spain* 33 F4
Turiaçu, *Brazil* 125 D9
Turiaçu →, *Brazil* 125 D9
Turiec →, *Slovak Rep.* 27 B11
Turin = Torino, *Italy* 28 C4
Turkana, L., *Africa* 86 B4
Türkeli, *Turkey* 41 F11
Turkestan = Türkistan,
  Kazakstan 50 E7
Türkeve, *Hungary* 42 C5
Turkey ■, *Eurasia* 72 C7
Turkey Creek, *Australia* ... 92 C4
Turki, *Russia* 48 D6
Türkistan, *Kazakstan* 50 E7
Türkmenbashi, *Turkmenistan* 50 E6
Türkmenli, *Turkey* 39 B8
Türkoğlu, *Turkey* 72 D7
Turks & Caicos Is. ■, *W. Indies* 121 B5
Turks Island Passage, *W. Indies* 121 B5
Turku, *Finland* 9 F20

Turkwel →, *Kenya* 86 B4
Turlock, *U.S.A.* 116 H6
Turnagain →, *Canada* 104 B3
Turnagain, C., *N.Z.* 91 J6
Turneffe Is., *Belize* 119 D7
Turner, *U.S.A.* 114 B9
Turner Pt., *Australia* 94 A1
Turner Valley, *Canada* 104 C6
Turners Falls, *U.S.A.* 111 D12
Turnhout, *Belgium* 17 C4
Türnitz, *Austria* 26 D8
Turnor L., *Canada* 105 B7
Turnov, *Czech Rep.* 26 A8
Tŭrnovo = Veliko Tŭrnovo,
  Bulgaria 41 C9
Turnu Măgurele, *Romania* . 43 G9
Turnu Roşu, P., *Romania* .. 43 E9
Turobin, *Poland* 45 H9
Turpan, *China* 60 B3
Turpan Hami, *China* 52 E12
Turrës, Kala e, *Albania* 40 E3
Turriff, *U.K.* 14 D6
Tursāq, *Iraq* 70 C5
Tursi, *Italy* 31 B9
Turtle Head I., *Australia* .. 94 A3
Turtle Is., *S. Leone* 82 D2
Turtle L., *Canada* 105 C7
Turtle Lake, *U.S.A.* 112 B4
Turtleford, *Canada* 105 C7
Turukhansk, *Russia* 51 C9
Turzovka, *Slovak Rep.* 27 B11
Tuscaloosa, *U.S.A.* 109 J2
Tuscánia, *Italy* 29 F8
Tuscany = Toscana □, *Italy* 28 E8
Tuscarawas →, *U.S.A.* 110 F3
Tuscarora Mt., *U.S.A.* 110 F7
Tuscola, *Ill., U.S.A.* 108 F1
Tuscola, *Tex., U.S.A.* 113 J5
Tuscumbia, *U.S.A.* 109 H2
Tuskegee, *U.S.A.* 109 J3
Tustin, *U.S.A.* 117 M9
Tuszyn, *Poland* 45 G6
Tutak, *Turkey* 73 C10
Tutayev, *Russia* 46 D10
Tuticorin, *India* 66 Q11
Tutin, *Serbia, Yug.* 40 D4
Tutóia, *Brazil* 125 D10
Tutong, *Brunei* 62 D4
Tutova →, *Romania* 43 D12
Tutrakan, *Bulgaria* 41 B10
Tuttle Creek L., *U.S.A.* ... 112 F6
Tuttlingen, *Germany* 25 H4
Tutuala, *Indonesia* 63 F7
Tutuila, *Amer. Samoa* 91 B13
Tutume, *Botswana* 85 J5
Tutun, *Egypt* 80 J7
Tututepec, *Mexico* 119 D5
Tuva □, *Russia* 51 D10
Tuvalu ■, *Pac. Oc.* 96 H9
Tuxer Alpen, *Austria* 26 D4
Tuxpan, *Mexico* 119 C5
Tuxtla Gutiérrez, *Mexico* .. 119 D6
Tuy = Tui, *Spain* 34 C2
Tuy An, *Vietnam* 64 F7
Tuy Duc, *Vietnam* 65 F6
Tuy Hoa, *Vietnam* 64 F7
Tuy Phong, *Vietnam* 65 G7
Tuya L., *Canada* 104 B2
Tuyen Hoa, *Vietnam* 64 D6
Tuyen Quang, *Vietnam* ... 58 G5
Tūysarkān, *Iran* 71 C6
Tuz Gölü, *Turkey* 72 C5
Ţūz Khurmātū, *Iraq* 70 C5
Tuzi, *Montenegro, Yug.* ... 40 D3
Tuzla, *Bos.-H.* 42 F3
Tuzlov →, *Russia* 47 J10
Tuzluca, *Turkey* 73 B10
Tvååker, *Sweden* 11 G6
Tvarditsa, *Moldova* 43 D13
Tver, *Russia* 46 D8
Tvrdošin, *Slovak Rep.* 27 B12
Tvrdošovce, *Slovak Rep.* .. 27 C11
Tvŭrditsa, *Bulgaria* 41 D9
Twain, *U.S.A.* 116 E5
Twain Harte, *U.S.A.* 116 G6
Twardogóra, *Poland* 45 G4
Tweed, *Canada* 110 B7
Tweed →, *U.K.* 14 F6
Tweed Heads, *Australia* ... 95 D5
Tweedsmuir Prov. Park, *Canada* 104 C3
Twentynine Palms, *U.S.A.* . 117 L10
Twillingate, *Canada* 103 C9
Twin Bridges, *U.S.A.* 114 D7
Twin Falls, *Canada* 103 B7
Twin Falls, *U.S.A.* 114 E6
Twin Valley, *U.S.A.* 112 B6
Twinsburg, *U.S.A.* 110 E3
Twisp, *U.S.A.* 114 B4
Twistringen, *Germany* 24 C4
Twitchell Reservoir, *U.S.A.* . 117 L6
Two Harbors, *U.S.A.* 112 B9
Two Hills, *Canada* 104 C6
Two Rivers, *U.S.A.* 108 C2
Two Rocks, *Australia* 93 F2
Twofold B., *Australia* 95 F4
Tyachiv, *Ukraine* 47 H2
Tychy, *Poland* 45 H5
Tyczyn, *Poland* 45 J9
Tykocin, *Poland* 45 E9
Tyler, *Minn., U.S.A.* 112 C6
Tyler, *Tex., U.S.A.* 113 J7
Tyligul →, *Ukraine* 47 J6
Tým nad Vltavou, *Czech Rep.* 26 B7
Tynda, *Russia* 51 D13
Tyndall, *U.S.A.* 112 D6
Tyne →, *U.K.* 12 C6
Tyne & Wear □, *U.K.* 12 B6
Týnec nad Sázavou, *Czech Rep.* 26 B7

Tynemouth, *U.K.* 12 B6
Tyre = Sūr, *Lebanon* 75 B4
Tyrifjorden, *Norway* 9 F14
Tyringe, *Sweden* 11 H7
Tyrnyauz, *Russia* 49 J6
Tyrol = Tirol □, *Austria* ... 26 D3
Tyrone, *U.S.A.* 110 F6
Tyrone □, *U.K.* 15 B4
Tyrrell →, *Australia* 95 F3
Tyrrell, L., *Australia* 95 F3
Tyrrell L., *Canada* 105 A7
Tyrrhenian Sea, *Medit. S.* . 6 G8
Tysfjorden, *Norway* 8 B17
Tystberga, *Sweden* 11 F11
Tytuvėnai, *Lithuania* 44 C10
Tyub Karagan, Mys, *Kazakstan* 49 H10
Tyuleni, Ostrova, *Kazakstan* 49 H10
Tyuleniy, *Russia* 49 H8
Tyuleniy, Mys, *Azerbaijan* . 49 K10
Tyumen, *Russia* 50 D7
Tywi →, *U.K.* 13 F3
Tywyn, *U.K.* 13 E3
Tzaneen, *S. Africa* 89 C5
Tzermíadhes, *Greece* 36 D7
Tzoumérka, Óros, *Greece* .. 38 B3
Tzukong = Zigong, *China* .. 58 C5

U

U Taphao, *Thailand* 64 F3
U.S.A. = United States of
  America ■, *N. Amer.* 106 C7
Uatumã →, *Brazil* 124 D7
Uaupés, *Brazil* 124 D5
Uaupés →, *Brazil* 124 C5
Uaxactún, *Guatemala* 120 C2
Ub, *Serbia, Yug.* 40 B4
Ubá, *Brazil* 127 A7
Uba, *Nigeria* 83 C7
Ubaitaba, *Brazil* 125 F11
Ubangi = Oubangi →,
  Dem. Rep. of the Congo .. 84 E3
Ubauro, *Pakistan* 68 E3
Ubaye →, *France* 21 D10
Ubayyiḍ, W. al →, *Iraq* ... 70 C4
Ube, *Japan* 55 H5
Úbeda, *Spain* 35 G7
Uberaba, *Brazil* 125 G9
Uberlândia, *Brazil* 125 G9
Überlingen, *Germany* 25 H5
Ubiaja, *Nigeria* 83 D6
Ubolratna Res., *Thailand* .. 64 D4
Ubombo, *S. Africa* 89 D5
Ubon Ratchathani, *Thailand* 64 E5
Ubondo, *Dem. Rep. of*
  the Congo 86 C2
Ubort →, *Belarus* 47 F5
Ubrique, *Spain* 35 J5
Ubundu, *Dem. Rep. of*
  the Congo 86 C2
Ucayali →, *Peru* 122 D3
Uchab, *Namibia* 88 B2
Uchiura-Wan, *Japan* 54 C10
Uchquduq, *Uzbekistan* ... 50 E7
Uchte, *Germany* 24 C4
Uchur →, *Russia* 51 D14
Ucluelet, *Canada* 104 D3
Uda →, *Russia* 51 D14
Udagamandalam, *India* ... 66 P10
Udainagar, *India* 68 H7
Udaipur, *India* 68 G5
Udaipur Garhi, *Nepal* 69 F12
Udala, *India* 69 J12
Udbina, *Croatia* 29 D12
Uddeholm, *Sweden* 10 D7
Uddevalla, *Sweden* 11 F5
Uddjaur, *Sweden* 8 D17
Uden, *Neths.* 17 C5
Udgir, *India* 66 K10
Udhampur, *India* 69 C6
Údine, *Italy* 29 B10
Udmurtia □, *Russia* 50 D6
Udon Thani, *Thailand* 64 D4
Udupi, *India* 66 N9
Udvoy Balkan, *Bulgaria* ... 41 D10
Udzungwa Range, *Tanzania* 87 D4
Ueckermünde, *Germany* .. 24 B10
Ueda, *Japan* 55 F9
Uedineniya, Os., *Russia* ... 4 B12
Uele →, *Dem. Rep. of*
  the Congo 84 D4
Uelen, *Russia* 51 C19
Uelzen, *Germany* 24 C6
Uetersen, *Germany* 24 B5
Uetze, *Germany* 24 C6
Ufa, *Russia* 50 D6
Uffenheim, *Germany* 25 F6
Ugab →, *Namibia* 88 C1
Ugalla →, *Tanzania* 86 D3
Uganda ■, *Africa* 86 B3
Ugento, *Italy* 31 C11
Ugep, *Nigeria* 83 D6
Ughelli, *Nigeria* 83 D6
Ugie, *S. Africa* 89 E4
Uğijar, *Spain* 35 J7
Ugine, *France* 21 C10
Uglegorsk, *Russia* 51 E15
Uglich, *Russia* 46 D10
Ugljan, *Croatia* 29 D12
Ugljane, *Croatia* 29 E13
Ugra →, *Russia* 46 E9
Uğurchin, *Bulgaria* 41 C8
Uh →, *Slovak Rep.* 27 C15

Uherské Hradiště, *Czech Rep.* 27 B10
Uherský Brod, *Czech Rep.* . 27 B10
Úhlava →, *Czech Rep.* 26 B6
Uhlenhorst, *Namibia* 88 C2
Uhrichsville, *U.S.A.* 110 F3
Uibhist a Deas = South Uist,
  U.K. 14 D1
Uibhist a Tuath = North Uist,
  U.K. 14 D1
Uig, *U.K.* 14 D2
Uíge, *Angola* 84 F2
Uijŏngbu, *S. Korea* 57 F14
Ŭiju, *N. Korea* 57 D13
Uinta Mts., *U.S.A.* 114 F8
Uis, *Namibia* 88 B2
Uitenhage, *S. Africa* 88 E4
Uithuizen, *Neths.* 17 A6
Ujazd, *Poland* 45 H5
Újfehértó, *Hungary* 42 C6
Ujh →, *India* 68 C6
Ujhani, *India* 69 F8
Uji-guntō, *Japan* 55 J4
Ujjain, *India* 68 H6
Ujście, *Poland* 45 E3
Újszász, *Hungary* 42 C5
Ujung Pandang, *Indonesia* . 63 F5
Uka, *Russia* 51 D17
Ukara I., *Tanzania* 86 C3
Uke-Shima, *Japan* 55 K4
Ukerewe I., *Tanzania* 86 C3
Ukholovo, *Russia* 48 D5
Ukhrul, *India* 67 G19
Ukhta, *Russia* 50 C6
Ukiah, *U.S.A.* 116 F3
Ukki Fort, *India* 69 C7
Ukmergė, *Lithuania* 9 J21
Ukraine ■, *Europe* 47 H7
Ukwi, *Botswana* 88 C3
Ulaan-Uul, *Mongolia* 56 B6
Ulaanbaatar, *Mongolia* ... 51 E11
Ulaangom, *Mongolia* 60 A4
Ulaanjirem, *Mongolia* 56 B3
Ulamba, *Dem. Rep. of the Congo* 87 D1
Ulan Bator = Ulaanbaatar,
  Mongolia 51 E11
Ulan Erge, *Russia* 49 G7
Ulan Khol, *Russia* 49 H8
Ulan Ude, *Russia* 51 D11
Ulanów, *Poland* 45 H9
Ulaş, *Sivas, Turkey* 72 C7
Ulaş, *Tekirdağ, Turkey* ... 41 E11
Ulaya, *Morogoro, Tanzania* 86 D4
Ulaya, *Tabora, Tanzania* .. 86 C3
Ulcinj, *Montenegro, Yug.* . 40 E3
Ulco, *S. Africa* 88 D3
Ulefoss, *Norway* 9 G13
Ulëz, *Albania* 40 E3
Ulfborg, *Denmark* 11 H2
Ulhasnagar, *India* 66 K8
Uliastay = Ulyasutay, *Mongolia* 60 B4
Ulithi Atoll, *Pac. Oc.* 63 B9
Uljma, *Serbia, Yug.* 42 E6
Ulla →, *Spain* 34 C2
Ulladulla, *Australia* 95 F5
Ullapool, *U.K.* 14 D3
Ullared, *Sweden* 11 G6
Ulldecona, *Spain* 32 E5
Ullswater, *U.K.* 12 C5
Ullŭng-do, *S. Korea* 55 F5
Ulm, *Germany* 25 G5
Ulmarra, *Australia* 95 D5
Ulmeni, *Buzău, Romania* .. 43 E11
Ulmeni, *Maramureş, Romania* 43 C8
Ulonguè, *Mozam.* 87 E3
Ulricehamn, *Sweden* 11 G7
Ulrika, *Sweden* 11 F9
Ulsan, *S. Korea* 57 G15
Ulsta, *U.K.* 14 A7
Ulster □, *U.K.* 15 B5
Ulstrem, *Bulgaria* 41 D10
Ulubat Gölü, *Turkey* 41 F12
Ulubey, *Turkey* 39 C11
Uluborlu, *Turkey* 39 C12
Uluçinar, *Turkey* 72 D6
Uludağ, *Turkey* 41 F13
Uludere, *Turkey* 73 D10
Uluguru Mts., *Tanzania* ... 86 D4
Ulukışla, *Turkey* 72 D6
Ulungur He →, *China* 60 B3
Uluru = Ayers Rock, *Australia* 93 E5
Uluru Nat. Park, *Australia* . 93 E5
Ulutau, *Kazakstan* 50 E7
Ulva, *U.K.* 14 E2
Ulverston, *U.K.* 12 C4
Ulverstone, *Australia* 94 G4
Ulya, *Russia* 51 D15
Ulyanovsk = Simbirsk, *Russia* 48 C9
Ulyasutay, *Mongolia* 60 B4
Ulysses, *U.S.A.* 113 G4
Umag, *Croatia* 29 C10
Umala, *Bolivia* 124 G5
Uman, *Ukraine* 47 H6
Umaria, *India* 67 H12
Umarkot, *Pakistan* 66 G6
Umarpada, *India* 68 J5
Umatilla, *U.S.A.* 114 D4
Umbagog L., *U.S.A.* 111 B13
Umbakumba, *Australia* ... 94 A2
Umbértide, *Italy* 29 E9
Umbrella Mts., *N.Z.* 91 L2
Ume älv →, *Sweden* 8 E19
Umeå, *Sweden* 8 E19
Umera, *Indonesia* 63 E7
Umfuli →, *Zimbabwe* 87 F2
Umgusa, *Zimbabwe* 87 F2
Umim Urūmah, *Si. Arabia* . 80 B4

Umka, *Serbia, Yug.* 40 B4
Umkomaas, *S. Africa* 89 E5
Umlazi, *S. Africa* 85 L6
Umm ad Daraj, J., *Jordan* 75 C4
Umm al Qaywayn, *U.A.E.* 71 E7
Umm al Qittayn, *Jordan* 75 C5
Umm Arda, *Sudan* 81 D3
Umm Badr, *Sudan* 81 E2
Umm Baiyud, *Sudan* 81 E3
Umm Bel, *Sudan* 81 E2
Umm Birkah, *Si. Arabia* 80 B4
Umm Boim, *Sudan* 81 E2
Umm Dam, *Sudan* 81 E3
Umm Debi, *Sudan* 81 E3
Umm Dubban, *Sudan* 81 D3
Umm el Fahm, *Israel* 75 C4
Umm Gafala, *Sudan* 81 E2
Umm Gimala, *Sudan* 81 E2
Umm Inderaba, *Sudan* 80 D3
Umm Keddada, *Sudan* 81 E2
Umm Koweika, *Sudan* 81 E3
Umm Lajj, *Si. Arabia* 70 E3
Umm Merwa, *Sudan* 80 D3
Umm Qantur, *Sudan* 81 E3
Umm Qurein, *Sudan* 81 F2
Umm Ruwaba, *Sudan* 81 E3
Umm Saiyala, *Sudan* 81 E3
Umm Shanqa, *Sudan* 81 E2
Umm Shutur, *Sudan* 81 F3
Umm Sidr, *Sudan* 81 E2
Umm Zehetir, *Egypt* 80 J8
Umnak I., *U.S.A.* 100 C3
Umniati →, *Zimbabwe* 87 F2
Umpqua →, *U.S.A.* 114 E1
Umreth, *India* 68 H5
Umtata, *S. Africa* 89 E4
Umuahia, *Nigeria* 83 D6
Umuarama, *Brazil* 127 A5
Umurbey, *Turkey* 41 F10
Umvukwe Ra., *Zimbabwe* 87 F3
Umzimvubu, *S. Africa* 89 E4
Umzingwane →, *Zimbabwe* 87 G2
Umzinto, *S. Africa* 89 E5
Una, *India* 68 J4
Una →, *Bos.-H.* 29 D13
Unac →, *Bos.-H.* 29 D13
Unadilla, *U.S.A.* 111 D9
Unalakleet, *U.S.A.* 100 B3
Unalaska, *U.S.A.* 100 C3
Unalaska I., *U.S.A.* 100 C3
'Unayzah, *Si. Arabia* 70 E4
'Unāzah, J., *Asia* 70 C3
Uncastillo, *Spain* 32 C3
Uncía, *Bolivia* 124 G5
Uncompahgre Peak, *U.S.A.* . . 115 G10
Uncompahgre Plateau, *U.S.A.* . . 115 G9
Unden, *Sweden* 11 F8
Underbool, *Australia* 95 F3
Undersaker, *Sweden* 10 A7
Unecha, *Russia* 47 F7
Ungarie, *Australia* 95 E4
Ungarra, *Australia* 95 E2
Ungava, Pén. d', *Canada* 101 C12
Ungava B., *Canada* 101 C13
Ungeny = Ungheni, *Moldova* . . 43 C12
Unggi, *N. Korea* 57 C16
Ungheni, *Moldova* 43 C12
Unguala →, *Ethiopia* 81 F5
Ungwatiri, *Sudan* 81 D4
Uni, *Russia* 48 B10
União da Vitória, *Brazil* 127 B5
Uničov, *Czech Rep.* 27 B10
Uniejów, *Poland* 45 G5
Unije, *Croatia* 29 D11
Unimak I., *U.S.A.* 100 C3
Union →, *Brazil* 127 B5
Union, Miss., *U.S.A.* 113 J10
Union, Mo., *U.S.A.* 112 F9
Union, S.C., *U.S.A.* 109 H5
Union City, Calif., *U.S.A.* 116 H4
Union City, N.J., *U.S.A.* 111 F10
Union City, Pa., *U.S.A.* 110 E5
Union City, Tenn., *U.S.A.* 113 G10
Union Gap, *U.S.A.* 114 C3
Union Springs, *U.S.A.* 109 J3
Uniondale, *S. Africa* 88 E3
Uniontown, *U.S.A.* 108 F6
Unionville, *U.S.A.* 112 E8
Unirea, *Romania* 43 F12
United Arab Emirates ■, *Asia* . 71 F7
United Kingdom ■, *Europe* . . . 7 E5
United States of America ■,
  N. Amer. 106 C7
Unity, *Canada* 105 C7
Universales, Mtes., *Spain* 32 E3
University Park, *U.S.A.* 115 K10
Unjha, *India* 68 H5
Unna, *Germany* 24 D3
Unnao, *India* 69 F9
Uno, Ilha, *Guinea-Biss.* 82 C1
Unst, *U.K.* 14 A8
Unstrut →, *Germany* 24 D7
Unterfranken □, *Germany* . . . 25 F5
Unterschleissheim, *Germany* . . 25 G7
Unuk →, *Canada* 104 B2
Ünye, *Turkey* 72 B7
Unzha, *Russia* 48 A7
Unzha →, *Russia* 48 B6
Uozu, *Japan* 55 F8
Upata, *Venezuela* 124 B6
Upemba, L., *Dem. Rep. of
  the Congo* 87 D2
Upernavik, *Greenland* 4 B5
Upington, *S. Africa* 88 D3
Upleta, *India* 68 J4
Upolu, *Samoa* 91 A13
Upper □, *Ghana* 83 C4

Upper Alkali L., *U.S.A.* 114 F3
Upper Arrow L., *Canada* 104 C5
Upper Austria =
  Oberösterreich □, *Austria* . . 26 C7
Upper Foster L., *Canada* 105 B7
Upper Hutt, *N.Z.* 91 J5
Upper Klamath L., *U.S.A.* . . . 114 E3
Upper Lake, *U.S.A.* 116 F4
Upper Musquodoboit, *Canada* . 103 C7
Upper Red L., *U.S.A.* 112 A7
Upper Sandusky, *U.S.A.* 108 E4
Upper Volta = Burkina Faso ■,
  Africa 82 C4
Upphärad, *Sweden* 11 F6
Uppland, *Sweden* 10 E11
Upplands-Väsby, *Sweden* 10 E11
Uppsala, *Sweden* 10 E11
Uppsala län □, *Sweden* 10 D11
Upshi, *India* 69 C7
Upstart, C., *Australia* 94 B4
Upton, *U.S.A.* 112 C2
Ur, *Iraq* 70 D5
Urad Qianqi, *China* 56 D5
Urakawa, *Japan* 54 C11
Ural = Zhayyq →, *Kazakstan* . 50 E6
Ural, *Australia* 95 E4
Ural Mts. = Uralskie Gory,
  Eurasia 50 D6
Uralla, *Australia* 95 E5
Uralsk = Oral, *Kazakstan* 48 E10
Uralskie Gory, *Eurasia* 50 D6
Urambo, *Tanzania* 86 D3
Urandangi, *Australia* 94 C2
Uranium City, *Canada* 105 B7
Uraricoera →, *Brazil* 124 C6
Urawa, *Japan* 55 G9
Uray, *Russia* 50 C7
'Uray'irah, *Si. Arabia* 71 E6
Urbana, Ill., *U.S.A.* 108 E1
Urbana, Ohio, *U.S.A.* 108 E4
Urbánia, *Italy* 29 E9
Urbel →, *Spain* 34 C7
Urbino, *Italy* 29 E9
Urbión, Picos de, *Spain* 32 C2
Urcos, *Peru* 124 F4
Urdinarrain, *Argentina* 126 C4
Urdos, *France* 20 F3
Urdzhar, *Kazakstan* 50 E9
Ure →, *U.K.* 12 C6
Uren, *Russia* 48 B7
Ures, *Mexico* 118 B2
Urfa = Sanliurfa, *Turkey* 70 B3
Urganch, *Uzbekistan* 50 E7
Urgench = Urganch, *Uzbekistan* 50 E7
Ürgüp, *Turkey* 70 B2
Uri, *India* 69 B6
Uri □, *Switz.* 25 J4
Uribia, *Colombia* 124 A4
Uricani, *Romania* 42 E8
Uriondo, *Bolivia* 126 A3
Urique, *Mexico* 118 B3
Urique →, *Mexico* 118 B3
Urk, *Neths.* 17 B5
Urla, *Turkey* 39 C8
Urlaţi, *Romania* 43 F11
Urmia = Orūmīyeh, *Iran* 70 B5
Urmia, L. = Orūmīyeh,
  Daryācheh-ye, *Iran* 70 B5
Uroševac, *Kosovo, Yug.* 40 D5
Urshult, *Sweden* 11 H8
Uruaçu, *Brazil* 125 F9
Uruapan, *Mexico* 118 D4
Urubamba →, *Peru* 124 F4
Uruçara, *Brazil* 124 D7
Uruçuí, *Brazil* 125 E10
Uruguai →, *Brazil* 127 B5
Uruguaiana, *Brazil* 126 B4
Uruguay ■, *S. Amer.* 126 C4
Uruguay →, *S. Amer.* 126 C4
Urumchi = Ürümqi, *China* . . . 50 E9
Ürümqi, *China* 50 E9
Urup, *Russia* 49 H5
Urup, Ostrov, *Russia* 51 E16
Uryupinsk, *Russia* 48 E5
Urzhum, *Russia* 48 B9
Urziceni, *Romania* 43 F11
Usa →, *Russia* 50 C6
Uşak, *Turkey* 39 C11
Uşak □, *Turkey* 39 C11
Usakos, *Namibia* 88 C2
Ušče, *Serbia, Yug.* 40 C4
Usedom, *Germany* 24 B10
Useless Loop, *Australia* 93 E1
'Usfān, *Si. Arabia* 80 C4
Ush-Tobe, *Kazakstan* 50 E8
Ushakova, Ostrov, *Russia* . . . 4 A12
Ushant = Ouessant, Î. d', *France* 18 D1
Ushashi, *Tanzania* 86 C3
Ushat, *Sudan* 81 F2
'Ushayrah, *Si. Arabia* 80 C5
Ushibuka, *Japan* 55 H5
Ushuaia, *Argentina* 128 G3
Ushumun, *Russia* 51 D13
Usk, *Canada* 104 C3
Usk →, *U.K.* 13 F5
Uska, *India* 69 F10
Üsküdar, *Turkey* 41 F13
Uslar, *Germany* 24 D5
Usman, *Russia* 47 F10
Usoke, *Tanzania* 86 D3
Usolye Sibirskoye, *Russia* . . . 51 D11
Usoro, *Nigeria* 83 D6
Uspallata, P. de, *Argentina* . . . 126 C2
Uspenskiy, *Kazakstan* 50 E8
Ussel, *France* 20 C6
Usson-du-Poitou, *France* 20 B4

Ussuri →, *Asia* 54 A7
Ussuriysk, *Russia* 51 E14
Ussurka, *Russia* 54 B6
Ust-Aldan = Batamay, *Russia* . 51 C13
Ust-Amginskoye = Khandyga,
  Russia 51 C14
Ust-Bolsheretsk, *Russia* 51 D16
Ust-Buzulukskaya, *Russia* . . . 48 E6
Ust-Chaun, *Russia* 51 C18
Ust-Donetskiy, *Russia* 49 G5
Ust-Ilimpeya = Yukta, *Russia* . 51 C11
Ust-Ilimsk, *Russia* 51 D11
Ust-Ishim, *Russia* 50 D8
Ust-Kamchatsk, *Russia* 51 D17
Ust-Kamenogorsk = Öskemen,
  Kazakstan 50 E9
Ust-Khayryuzovo, *Russia* 51 D16
Ust-Kut, *Russia* 51 D11
Ust-Kuyga, *Russia* 51 B14
Ust-Labinsk, *Russia* 49 H4
Ust-Luga, *Russia* 46 C5
Ust-Maya, *Russia* 51 C14
Ust-Mil, *Russia* 51 D14
Ust-Nera, *Russia* 51 C15
Ust-Nyukzha, *Russia* 51 D13
Ust-Olenek, *Russia* 51 B12
Ust-Omchug, *Russia* 51 C15
Ust-Port, *Russia* 50 C9
Ust-Tsilma, *Russia* 50 C6
Ust Urt = Ustyurt Plateau, *Asia* 50 E6
Ustaritz, *France* 20 E2
Uster, *Switz.* 25 H4
Ústí nad Labem, *Czech Rep.* . 26 A7
Ústí nad Orlicí, *Czech Rep.* . . 27 B9
Ústica, *Italy* 30 D6
Ustinov = Izhevsk, *Russia* . . . 50 D6
Ustka, *Poland* 44 D3
Ustroń, *Poland* 45 J5
Ustrzyki Dolne, *Poland* 45 J9
Ustyurt Plateau, *Asia* 50 E6
Ustyuzhna, *Russia* 46 C9
Usu, *China* 60 B3
Usuki, *Japan* 55 H5
Usulután, *El Salv.* 120 D2
Usumacinta →, *Mexico* 119 D6
Usumbura = Bujumbura,
  Burundi 86 C2
Usure, *Tanzania* 86 C3
Usutuo →, *Mozam.* 89 D5
Uta, *Indonesia* 63 E9
Utah □, *U.S.A.* 114 G8
Utah L., *U.S.A.* 114 F8
Utansjö, *Sweden* 10 B11
Utarni, *India* 68 F4
Utatlan, *Guatemala* 120 C1
Ute Creek →, *U.S.A.* 113 H3
Utebo, *Spain* 32 D3
Utena, *Lithuania* 9 J21
Utete, *Tanzania* 86 D4
Uthai Thani, *Thailand* 64 E3
Uthal, *Pakistan* 68 G2
Utiariti, *Brazil* 124 F7
Utica, N.Y., *U.S.A.* 111 C9
Utica, Ohio, *U.S.A.* 110 F2
Utiel, *Spain* 33 F3
Utikuma L., *Canada* 104 B5
Utö, *Sweden* 10 F12
Utopia, *Australia* 94 C1
Utraula, *India* 69 F10
Utrecht, *Neths.* 17 B5
Utrecht, *S. Africa* 89 D5
Utrecht □, *Neths.* 17 B5
Utrera, *Spain* 35 H5
Utsjoki, *Finland* 8 B22
Utsunomiya, *Japan* 55 F9
Uttar Pradesh □, *India* 69 F9
Uttaradit, *Thailand* 64 D3
Uttaranchal □, *India* 69 D8
Uttoxeter, *U.K.* 12 E6
Uummannarsuaq = Nunap Isua,
  Greenland 101 C15
Uusikaarlepyy, *Finland* 8 E20
Uusikaupunki, *Finland* 9 F19
Uva, *Russia* 48 B11
Uvac →, *Serbia, Yug.* 40 C3
Uvalde, *U.S.A.* 113 L5
Uvarovo, *Russia* 48 E6
Uvat, *Russia* 50 D7
Uvinza, *Tanzania* 86 D3
Uvira, *Dem. Rep. of the Congo* . 86 C2
Uvs Nuur, *Mongolia* 60 A4
'Uwairidh, Ḥarrat al, *Si. Arabia* . 70 E3
Uwajima, *Japan* 55 H6
Uweinat, Jebel, *Sudan* 80 C1
Uxbridge, *Canada* 110 B5
Uxin Qi, *China* 56 E5
Uxmal, *Mexico* 119 C7
Üydzin, *Mongolia* 56 B4
Uyo, *Nigeria* 83 D6
Üyüklü Tepe, *Turkey* 39 D9
Uyûn Mûsa, *Egypt* 75 F1
Uyuni, *Bolivia* 124 H5
Uzbekistan ■, *Asia* 50 E7
Uzen, Bolari →, *Kazakstan* . . . 49 F9
Uzen, Mal →, *Kazakstan* 49 F9
Uzerche, *France* 20 C5
Uzès, *France* 21 D8
Uzh →, *Ukraine* 47 G6
Uzhgorod = Uzhhorod, *Ukraine* 47 H2
Uzhhorod, *Ukraine* 47 H2
Užice, *Serbia, Yug.* 40 C3
Uzlovaya, *Russia* 46 D10
Üzümlü, *Turkey* 39 E11
Üzünköprü, *Turkey* 41 E10
Uzunkuyu, *Turkey* 39 C8

V

Vaal →, *S. Africa* 88 D3
Vaal Dam, *S. Africa* 89 D4
Vaalwater, *S. Africa* 89 C4
Vaasa, *Finland* 8 E19
Vác, *Hungary* 42 C4
Vacaria, *Brazil* 127 B5
Vacaville, *U.S.A.* 116 G5
Vaccarès, Étang de, *France* . . 21 E8
Vach →, *Russia* 50 C8
Vache, Î. à, *Haiti* 121 C5
Väckelsång, *Sweden* 11 H8
Väddö, *Sweden* 10 D12
Väderstad, *Sweden* 11 F8
Vadnagar, *India* 68 H5
Vado Lígure, *Italy* 28 D5
Vadodara, *India* 68 H5
Vadsø, *Norway* 8 A23
Vadstena, *Sweden* 11 F8
Vaduz, *Liech.* 25 H5
Værøy, *Norway* 8 C15
Vágar, *Færoe Is.* 8 E9
Vaggeryd, *Sweden* 11 G8
Vagney, *France* 19 D13
Vagnhärad, *Sweden* 11 F11
Vagos, *Portugal* 34 E2
Vågsfjorden, *Norway* 8 B17
Váh →, *Slovak Rep.* 27 D11
Vahsel B., *Antarctica* 5 D1
Vaï, *Greece* 36 D8
Vaigach, *Russia* 50 B6
Vaiges, *France* 18 D6
Vaihingen, *Germany* 25 G4
Vail, *U.S.A.* 106 C5
Vailly-sur-Aisne, *France* 19 C10
Vaisali →, *India* 69 F8
Vaison-la-Romaine, *France* . . 21 D9
Vakarel, *Bulgaria* 40 D7
Vakfikebir, *Turkey* 73 B8
Vakh →, *Russia* 50 C8
Vakhtan, *Russia* 48 B8
Vál, *Hungary* 42 C3
Val-de-Marne □, *France* 19 D9
Val-d'Isère, *France* 21 C10
Val-d'Oise □, *France* 19 C9
Val-d'Or, *Canada* 102 C4
Val Marie, *Canada* 105 D7
Valaam, *Russia* 46 B6
Valadares, *Portugal* 34 D2
Valahia, *Romania* 43 F9
Valais □, *Switz.* 25 J3
Valais, Alpes du, *Switz.* 25 J3
Valandovo, *Macedonia* 40 E6
Valašské Meziříčí, *Czech Rep.* . 27 B10
Valáxa, *Greece* 38 C6
Vålberg, *Sweden* 10 E7
Valbo, *Sweden* 10 D10
Valbondione, *Italy* 28 B7
Vălcani, *Romania* 42 D5
Vâlcea □, *Romania* 43 F9
Valdagno, *Italy* 29 C8
Valdahon, *France* 19 E13
Valday, *Russia* 46 D7
Valdayskaya Vozvyshennost,
  Russia 46 D7
Valdeazogues →, *Spain* 35 G6
Valdecañas, Embalse de, *Spain* . 34 F5
Valdemarsvik, *Sweden* 11 F10
Valdemoro, *Spain* 34 E7
Valdepeñas, *Spain* 35 G7
Valderaduey →, *Spain* 34 D5
Valdéric, *Italy* 30 D5
Valderrobres, *Spain* 32 E5
Valdés, Pen., *Argentina* 122 H4
Valdez, *U.S.A.* 100 B5
Valdivia, *Chile* 128 D2
Valdobbiádene, *Italy* 29 C8
Valdosta, *U.S.A.* 109 K4
Valdoviño, *Spain* 34 B2
Valdres, *Norway* 9 F13
Vale, *Georgia* 49 K6
Vale, *U.S.A.* 114 E5
Vale of Glamorgan □, *U.K.* . . . 13 F4
Valea lui Mihai, *Romania* 42 C7
Valea Mărului, *Romania* 43 E12
Valemount, *Canada* 104 C5
Valença, *Brazil* 125 F11
Valença, *Portugal* 34 C2
Valença do Piauí, *Brazil* 125 E10
Valençay, *France* 19 E8
Valence = Valence d'Agen,
  France 20 D4
Valence, *France* 21 D8
Valence d'Agen, *France* 20 D4
Valencia, *Spain* 33 F4
Valencia, *U.S.A.* 115 J10
Valencia, *Venezuela* 124 A5
Valencia □, *Spain* 33 F4
Valencia, G. de, *Spain* 33 F5
Valencia de Alcántara, *Spain* . 35 F3
Valencia de Don Juan, *Spain* . 34 C5
Valencia I., *Ireland* 15 E1
Valenciennes, *France* 19 B10
Văleni, *Romania* 43 F9
Valeni de Munte, *Romania* . . . 43 E11
Valensole, *France* 21 E9
Valentigney, *France* 19 E13
Valentin, *Russia* 54 C7
Valentine, Nebr., *U.S.A.* 113 K2
Valenza, *Italy* 28 C5
Valera, *Venezuela* 124 B4
Valga, *Estonia* 9 H22

Valguarnera Caropepe, *Italy* . . 31 E7
Valier, *U.S.A.* 114 B7
Valinco, G. de, *France* 21 G12
Valjevo, *Serbia, Yug.* 40 B3
Valka, *Latvia* 9 H21
Valkeakoski, *Finland* 9 F20
Valkenswaard, *Neths.* 17 C5
Vall de Uxó = La Vall d'Uixó,
  Spain 32 F4
Valla, *Sweden* 10 E10
Valladolid, *Mexico* 119 C7
Valladolid, *Spain* 34 D6
Valladolid □, *Spain* 34 D6
Vallata, *Italy* 31 A8
Valldemossa, *Spain* 37 B9
Valle d'Aosta □, *Italy* 28 C4
Valle de Arán, *Spain* 32 C5
Valle de la Pascua, *Venezuela* . 124 B5
Valle de las Palmas, *Mexico* . 117 N10
Valle de Santiago, *Mexico* . . . 118 C4
Valle de Suchil, *Mexico* 118 C4
Valle de Zaragoza, *Mexico* . . 118 B3
Valle Fértil, Sierra del,
  Argentina 126 C2
Valle Hermoso, *Mexico* 119 B5
Valledupar, *Colombia* 124 A4
Vallehermoso, *Canary Is.* 37 F2
Vallejo, *U.S.A.* 116 G4
Vallenar, *Chile* 126 B1
Vallentuna, *Sweden* 10 E12
Valleraugue, *France* 20 D7
Vallet, *France* 18 E5
Valletta, *Malta* 36 D2
Valley Center, *U.S.A.* 117 M9
Valley City, *U.S.A.* 112 B6
Valley Falls, Oreg., *U.S.A.* . . . 114 E3
Valley Falls, R.I., *U.S.A.* 111 E13
Valley Springs, *U.S.A.* 116 G6
Valley View, *U.S.A.* 111 F8
Valley Wells, *U.S.A.* 117 K11
Valleyview, *Canada* 104 B5
Valli di Comácchio, *Italy* 29 D9
Vallimanca, Arroyo, *Argentina* . 126 D4
Vallo della Lucánia, *Italy* 31 B8
Vallon-Pont-d'Arc, *France* . . . 21 D8
Vallorbe, *Switz.* 25 J2
Valls, *Spain* 32 D6
Valmaseda = Balmaseda, *Spain* . 32 B1
Valmiera, *Latvia* 9 H21
Valnera, *Spain* 34 B7
Valognes, *France* 18 C5
Valona = Vlorë, *Albania* 40 F3
Valongo, *Portugal* 34 D2
Valozhyn, *Belarus* 46 E4
Valpaços, *Portugal* 34 D3
Valparaíso, *Chile* 126 C1
Valparaíso, *Mexico* 118 C4
Valparaiso, *U.S.A.* 108 E2
Valparaíso □, *Chile* 126 C1
Valpovo, *Croatia* 42 E3
Valréas, *France* 21 D9
Vals →, *S. Africa* 88 D4
Vals, *Switz.* 25 J5
Vals, Tanjung, *Indonesia* 63 F9
Vals-les-Bains, *France* 21 D8
Valsad, *India* 66 J8
Valtellina, *Italy* 28 B6
Valuyki, *Russia* 47 G10
Valverde, *Canary Is.* 37 G2
Valverde del Camino, *Spain* . . 35 H4
Valverde del Fresno, *Spain* . . 34 E4
Vama, *Romania* 43 C10
Vamdrup, *Denmark* 11 J3
Vâmhus, *Sweden* 10 C8
Vammala, *Finland* 9 F20
Vámos, *Greece* 36 D6
Van, *Turkey* 70 B4
Van, L. = Van Gölü, *Turkey* . . 70 B4
Van Alstyne, *U.S.A.* 113 J6
Van Blommestein Meer,
  Surinam 125 C7
Van Buren, *Canada* 103 C6
Van Buren, Ark., *U.S.A.* 113 H7
Van Buren, Maine, *U.S.A.* . . . 109 B11
Van Buren, Mo., *U.S.A.* 113 G9
Van Canh, *Vietnam* 64 F7
Van Diemen, C., N. Terr.,
  Australia 92 B5
Van Diemen, C., Queens.,
  Australia 94 B2
Van Diemen G., *Australia* . . . 92 B5
Van Gölü, *Turkey* 70 B4
Van Horn, *U.S.A.* 113 K2
Van Ninh, *Vietnam* 64 F7
Van Rees, Pegunungan,
  Indonesia 63 E9
Van Wert, *U.S.A.* 108 E3
Van Yen, *Vietnam* 58 G5
Vanadzor, *Armenia* 49 K7
Vanavara, *Russia* 51 C11
Vancouver, *Canada* 104 D4
Vancouver, *U.S.A.* 116 E4
Vancouver, C., *Australia* 93 G2
Vancouver I., *Canada* 104 D3
Vandalia, Ill., *U.S.A.* 112 F10
Vandalia, Mo., *U.S.A.* 112 F9
Vandenburg, *U.S.A.* 117 L6
Vanderbijlpark, *S. Africa* 89 D4
Vandergrift, *U.S.A.* 110 F5
Vanderhoof, *Canada* 104 C4
Vanderkloof Dam, *S. Africa* . . 88 E3
Vanderlin I., *Australia* 94 B2
Vänern, *Sweden* 11 F7
Vänersborg, *Sweden* 11 F6
Vang Vieng, *Laos* 64 C4
Vanga, *Kenya* 86 C4
Vangaindrano, *Madag.* 89 C8

Vanguard, Canada … 105 D7
Vanino, Russia … 51 E15
Vânju Mare, Romania … 42 F7
Vanna, Norway … 8 A18
Vännäs, Sweden … 8 E18
Vannes, France … 18 E4
Vanoise, France … 21 C10
Vanrhynsdorp, S. Africa … 88 E2
Vansbro, Sweden … 10 D8
Vansittart B., Australia … 92 B4
Vantaa, Finland … 9 F21
Vanua Balavu, Fiji … 91 C9
Vanua Levu, Fiji … 91 C8
Vanuatu ■, Pac. Oc. … 96 J8
Vanwyksvlei, S. Africa … 88 E3
Vanzylsrus, S. Africa … 88 D3
Vapnyarka, Ukraine … 47 H5
Var □, France … 21 E10
Var →, France … 21 E11
Vara, Sweden … 11 F6
Varades, France … 18 E5
Varáita →, Italy … 28 D4
Varallo, Italy … 28 C5
Varanasi, India … 69 G10
Varangerfjorden, Norway … 8 A23
Varangerhalvøya, Norway … 8 A23
Varano, Lago di, Italy … 29 G12
Varaždin, Croatia … 29 B13
Varazze, Italy … 28 D5
Varberg, Sweden … 11 G6
Vardak □, Afghan. … 66 B6
Vardar = Axiós →, Greece … 40 F6
Varde, Denmark … 11 J2
Varde Å →, Denmark … 11 J2
Vardø, Norway … 8 A24
Varel, Germany … 24 B4
Varella, Mui, Vietnam … 64 F7
Varėna, Lithuania … 9 J21
Varennes-sur-Allier, France … 19 F10
Varennes-Vauzelles, France … 19 E10
Vareš, Bos.-H. … 42 F3
Varese, Italy … 28 C5
Vârfurile, Romania … 42 D7
Vårgårda, Sweden … 11 F6
Varginha, Brazil … 127 A6
Vargön, Sweden … 11 F6
Varillas, Chile … 126 A1
Varkaus, Finland … 9 E22
Värmdölandet, Sweden … 10 E12
Värmeln, Sweden … 10 E6
Värmlands Bro, Sweden … 10 E7
Värmlands län □, Sweden … 10 E6
Varna, Bulgaria … 41 C11
Varna □, Bulgaria … 41 C11
Värnamo, Sweden … 11 G8
Varnsdorf, Czech Rep. … 26 A7
Várpalota, Hungary … 42 C3
Vars, Canada … 111 A9
Vars, France … 21 D10
Varto, Turkey … 73 C9
Varvarin, Serbia, Yug. … 40 C5
Varysburg, U.S.A. … 110 D6
Varzaneh, Iran … 71 C7
Varzi, Italy … 28 D6
Varzy, France … 19 E10
Vas □, Hungary … 42 C1
Vasa Barris →, Brazil … 125 F11
Vásárosnamény, Hungary … 42 B7
Vascão →, Portugal … 35 H3
Vaşcău, Romania … 42 D7
Vascongadas = País Vasco □, Spain … 32 C2
Vasht = Khāsh, Iran … 66 E2
Vasilevichi, Belarus … 47 F5
Vasilikón, Greece … 38 C5
Vasilkov = Vasylkiv, Ukraine … 47 G6
Vaslui, Romania … 43 D12
Vaslui □, Romania … 43 D12
Väsman, Sweden … 10 D9
Vassar, Canada … 105 D9
Vassar, U.S.A. … 108 D4
Västerås, Sweden … 10 E10
Västerbotten, Sweden … 8 D18
Västerdalälven →, Sweden … 10 D8
Västergötland, Sweden … 11 F7
Västerhaninge, Sweden … 10 E12
Västervik, Sweden … 11 G10
Västmanland, Sweden … 9 G16
Västmanlands län □, Sweden … 10 E10
Vasto, Italy … 29 F11
Västra Götalands Län □, Sweden … 11 F6
Vasvár, Hungary … 42 C1
Vasylkiv, Ukraine … 47 G6
Vatan, France … 19 E8
Vatersay, U.K. … 14 E1
Váthia, Greece … 38 E4
Vatican City ■, Europe … 29 G9
Vaticano, C., Italy … 31 D8
Vatili, Cyprus … 36 D12
Vatin, Serbia, Yug. … 42 E6
Vatnajökull, Iceland … 8 D5
Vatoa, Fiji … 91 D9
Vatólakkos, Greece … 36 D5
Vatomandry, Madag. … 89 B8
Vatra-Dornei, Romania … 43 C10
Vatrak →, India … 68 H5
Vättern, Sweden … 11 F8
Vaucluse □, France … 21 E9
Vaucouleurs, France … 19 D12
Vaud □, Switz. … 25 J2
Vaughn, Mont., U.S.A. … 114 C8
Vaughn, N. Mex., U.S.A. … 115 J11
Vaujours L., Canada … 102 A5
Vaupés = Uaupés →, Brazil … 124 C5

Vaupes □, Colombia … 124 C4
Vauvert, France … 21 E8
Vauxhall, Canada … 104 C6
Vav, India … 68 G4
Vava'u, Tonga … 91 D12
Vavoua, Ivory C. … 82 D3
Vawkavysk, Belarus … 47 F3
Vaxholm, Sweden … 10 E12
Växjö, Sweden … 11 H8
Växtorp, Sweden … 11 H7
Vaygach, Ostrov, Russia … 50 C6
Váyia, Greece … 38 C5
Váyia, Ákra, Greece … 36 C10
Vechelde, Germany … 24 C6
Vechta, Germany … 24 C4
Vechte →, Neths. … 17 B6
Vecsés, Hungary … 42 C4
Veddige, Sweden … 11 G6
Vedea →, Romania … 43 G10
Vedia, Argentina … 126 C3
Vedum, Sweden … 11 F7
Veendam, Neths. … 17 A6
Veenendaal, Neths. … 17 B5
Vefsna →, Norway … 8 D15
Vega, Norway … 8 D14
Vega, U.S.A. … 113 H3
Vegadeo, Spain … 34 B3
Vegorrítis, Límni, Greece … 40 F5
Vegreville, Canada … 104 C6
Veinge, Sweden … 11 H7
Veisiejai, Lithuania … 44 D10
Vejbystrand, Sweden … 11 H6
Vejen, Denmark … 11 J3
Vejer de la Frontera, Spain … 35 J5
Vejle, Denmark … 11 J3
Vejle Amtskommune □, Denmark … 11 J3
Vejle Fjord, Denmark … 11 J3
Vela Luka, Croatia … 29 F13
Velas, C., Costa Rica … 120 D2
Velasco, Sierra de, Argentina … 126 B2
Velay, Mts. du, France … 20 D7
Velbert, Germany … 24 D3
Velddrif, S. Africa … 88 E2
Velebit Planina, Croatia … 29 D12
Velebitski Kanal, Croatia … 29 D11
Veleka →, Bulgaria … 41 D11
Velencei-tó, Hungary … 42 C3
Velenje, Slovenia … 29 B12
Veles, Macedonia … 40 E5
Velestínon, Greece … 38 B4
Vélez-Málaga, Spain … 35 J6
Vélez Rubio, Spain … 33 H2
Velhas →, Brazil … 125 G10
Velika, Croatia … 29 D14
Velika Gorica, Croatia … 29 C13
Velika Kapela, Croatia … 29 C12
Velika Kladuša, Bos.-H. … 29 C12
Velika Kruša, Kosovo, Yug. … 40 D4
Velika Morava →, Serbia, Yug. … 40 B5
Velika Plana, Serbia, Yug. … 40 B5
Velikaya →, Russia … 46 D5
Velikaya Kema, Russia … 54 B8
Velikaya Lepetikha, Ukraine … 47 J7
Veliké Kapušany, Slovak Rep. … 27 C15
Velike Lašče, Slovenia … 29 C11
Veliki Jastrebac, Serbia, Yug. … 40 C5
Veliki Kanal, Serbia, Yug. … 42 E4
Veliki Popović, Serbia, Yug. … 40 B5
Velikiye Luki, Russia … 46 D6
Veliko Gradište, Serbia, Yug. … 40 B5
Veliko Tŭrnovo, Bulgaria … 41 C9
Velikonda Range, India … 66 M11
Vélingara, Senegal … 82 C2
Vélingara, Senegal … 82 B2
Velingrad, Bulgaria … 40 D7
Velino, Mte., Italy … 29 F10
Velizh, Russia … 46 E6
Velké Karlovice, Czech Rep. … 27 B11
Velké Meziříčí, Czech Rep. … 26 B9
Vel'ký Javorník, Slovak Rep. … 27 B11
Vel'ký Krtíš, Slovak Rep. … 27 C12
Vel'ký Meder, Slovak Rep. … 27 D10
Vel'ký Tribeč, Slovak Rep. … 27 C11
Velletri, Italy … 30 A5
Vellinge, Sweden … 11 J6
Vellmar, Germany … 24 D5
Vellore, India … 66 N11
Velsk, Russia … 46 B11
Velten, Germany … 24 C9
Velva, U.S.A. … 112 A4
Velvendós, Greece … 40 F6
Vemb, Denmark … 11 H2
Vemdalen, Sweden … 10 B7
Ven, Sweden … 11 J6
Venaco, France … 21 F13
Venado Tuerto, Argentina … 126 C3
Venafro, Italy … 31 A7
Venarey-les-Laumes, France … 19 E11
Venaría, Italy … 28 C4
Venčane, Serbia, Yug. … 40 B4
Vence, France … 21 E11
Vendas Novas, Portugal … 35 G2
Vendée □, France … 18 F5
Vendée →, France … 18 F5
Vendéen, Bocage, France … 20 B2
Vendeuvre-sur-Barse, France … 19 D11
Vendôme, France … 18 E8
Vendrell = El Vendrell, Spain … 32 D6
Vendsyssel, Denmark … 11 G4
Venelles, France … 21 E9

Venezuela ■, S. Amer. … 124 B5
Venezuela, G. de, Venezuela … 122 B3
Vengurla, India … 66 M8
Venice = Venézia, Italy … 29 C9
Venice, U.S.A. … 109 M4
Vénissieux, France … 21 C8
Venkataparam, India … 67 K12
Venlo, Neths. … 17 C6
Vennesla, Norway … 9 G12
Venosa, Italy … 31 B8
Venray, Neths. … 17 C6
Venta →, Latvia … 44 A8
Venta de Baños, Spain … 34 D6
Venta de Cardeña = Cardeña, Spain … 35 G6
Ventana, Punta de la, Mexico … 118 C3
Ventana, Sa. de la, Argentina … 126 D3
Ventersburg, S. Africa … 88 D4
Venterstad, S. Africa … 88 E4
Ventimíglia, Italy … 28 E4
Ventnor, U.K. … 13 G6
Ventoténe, Italy … 30 B6
Ventoux, Mt., France … 21 D9
Ventspils, Latvia … 9 H19
Ventspils □, Latvia … 44 A8
Ventuarí →, Venezuela … 124 C5
Ventucopa, U.S.A. … 117 L7
Ventura, U.S.A. … 117 L7
Venus B., Australia … 95 F4
Vera, Argentina … 126 B3
Vera, Spain … 33 H3
Veracruz, Mexico … 119 D5
Veracruz □, Mexico … 119 D5
Veraval, India … 68 J4
Verbánia, Italy … 28 C5
Verbicaro, Italy … 31 C8
Verbier, Switz. … 25 J3
Vercelli, Italy … 28 C5
Verchovchevo, Ukraine … 47 H8
Verdalsøra, Norway … 8 E14
Verde →, Argentina … 128 E3
Verde →, Goiás, Brazil … 125 G8
Verde →, Mato Grosso do Sul, Brazil … 125 H8
Verde →, Chihuahua, Mexico … 118 B3
Verde →, Oaxaca, Mexico … 119 D5
Verde →, Veracruz, Mexico … 118 C4
Verde →, Paraguay … 126 A4
Verde →, U.S.A. … 106 D4
Verde, Cay, Bahamas … 120 B4
Verden, Germany … 24 C5
Verdhikoúsa, Greece … 38 B3
Verdi, U.S.A. … 116 F7
Verdon →, France … 21 E9
Verdun, France … 19 C12
Verdun-sur-le-Doubs, France … 19 F12
Vereeniging, S. Africa … 89 D4
Verga, C., Guinea … 82 C2
Vergara, Uruguay … 127 C5
Vergato, Italy … 28 D8
Vergemont Cr. →, Australia … 94 C3
Vergennes, U.S.A. … 111 B11
Vergt, France … 20 C4
Verín, Spain … 34 D3
Verkhnedvinsk = Vyerkhnyadzvinsk, Belarus … 46 E4
Verkhnevilyuysk, Russia … 51 C13
Verkhniy Baskunchak, Russia … 49 F8
Verkhovye, Russia … 47 F9
Verkhoyansk, Russia … 51 C14
Verkhoyansk Ra. = Verkhoyanskiy Khrebet, Russia … 51 C13
Verkhoyanskiy Khrebet, Russia … 51 C13
Vermenton, France … 19 E10
Vermilion, Canada … 105 C6
Vermilion, U.S.A. … 110 E2
Vermilion →, Alta., Canada … 105 C6
Vermilion →, Qué., Canada … 102 C5
Vermilion, B., U.S.A. … 113 L9
Vermilion Bay, Canada … 105 D10
Vermilion L., U.S.A. … 112 B8
Vermillion, U.S.A. … 112 D6
Vermont □, U.S.A. … 111 C12
Vermosh, Albania … 40 D3
Vernal, U.S.A. … 114 F9
Vernalis, U.S.A. … 116 H5
Vernazza, Italy … 28 D6
Verner, Canada … 102 C3
Verneukpan, S. Africa … 88 E3
Verneuil-sur-Avre, France … 18 D7
Vernier, Switz. … 25 J2
Vernon, Canada … 104 C5
Vernon, France … 18 C8
Vernon, U.S.A. … 113 H5
Vernonia, U.S.A. … 116 E3
Vero Beach, U.S.A. … 109 M5
Véroia, Greece … 40 F6
Véroli, Italy … 30 A6
Verona, Canada … 111 B8
Verona, Italy … 28 C7
Verona, U.S.A. … 112 D10
Verrès, Italy … 28 C4
Versailles, France … 19 D9
Versmold, Germany … 24 C4
Vert, C., Senegal … 82 C1
Vertou, France … 18 E5
Vertus, France … 19 D11
Verulam, S. Africa … 89 D5
Verviers, Belgium … 17 D5
Vervins, France … 19 C10
Veržej, Slovenia … 29 B13

Verzy, France … 19 C11
Vescovato, France … 21 F13
Veselí nad Lužnicí, Czech Rep. … 26 B7
Veselie, Bulgaria … 41 D11
Veselovskoye Vdkhr., Russia … 49 G5
Veshenskaya, Russia … 48 F5
Vesle →, France … 19 C10
Vesoul, France … 19 E13
Vessigebro, Sweden … 11 H6
Vesterålen, Norway … 8 B16
Vestfjorden, Norway … 8 C15
Vestmannaeyjar, Iceland … 8 E3
Vestsjællands Amtskommune □, Denmark … 11 J5
Vestspitsbergen, Svalbard … 4 B8
Vestvågøy, Norway … 8 B15
Vesuvio, Italy … 31 B7
Vesuvius, Mt. = Vesuvio, Italy … 31 B7
Vesyegonsk, Russia … 46 C9
Veszprém, Hungary … 42 C2
Veszprém □, Hungary … 42 C2
Vésztő, Hungary … 42 D6
Vetlanda, Sweden … 11 G9
Vetluga, Russia … 48 B7
Vetlugu →, Russia … 48 B8
Vetluzhskiy, Kostroma, Russia … 48 A7
Vetluzhskiy, Nizhniy Novgorod, Russia … 48 B7
Vetovo, Bulgaria … 41 C10
Vetralla, Italy … 29 F9
Vetren, Bulgaria … 41 D8
Vettore, Mte., Italy … 29 F10
Veurne, Belgium … 17 C2
Veveno →, Sudan … 81 F3
Vevey, Switz. … 25 J2
Vévi, Greece … 40 F5
Veynes, France … 21 D9
Veys, Iran … 71 D6
Vézelay, France … 19 E10
Vézelise, France … 19 D13
Vézère →, France … 20 D4
Vezhen, Bulgaria … 41 D8
Vezirköprü, Turkey … 72 B6
Vezzani, France … 21 F13
Vi Thanh, Vietnam … 65 H5
Viacha, Bolivia … 124 G5
Viadana, Italy … 28 D7
Viamão, Brazil … 127 C5
Viana, Brazil … 125 D10
Viana, Spain … 32 C2
Viana do Alentejo, Portugal … 35 G3
Viana do Bolo, Spain … 34 C3
Viana do Castelo, Portugal … 34 D2
Viana do Castelo □, Portugal … 34 D2
Vianden, Lux. … 17 E6
Viangchan = Vientiane, Laos … 64 D4
Vianópolis, Brazil … 125 G9
Viar →, Spain … 35 H5
Viaréggio, Italy … 28 E7
Viaur →, France … 20 D5
Vibble, Sweden … 11 G12
Vibo Valéntia, Italy … 31 D9
Viborg, Denmark … 11 H3
Viborg Amtskommune □, Denmark … 11 H3
Vibraye, France … 18 D7
Vic, Spain … 32 D7
Vic, Étang de, France … 20 E7
Vic-en-Bigorre, France … 20 E4
Vic-Fézensac, France … 20 E4
Vic-le-Comte, France … 19 G10
Vic-sur-Cère, France … 20 D6
Vícar, Spain … 33 J2
Vicenza, Italy … 29 C8
Vich = Vic, Spain … 32 D7
Vichada →, Colombia … 124 C5
Vichuga, Russia … 48 B5
Vichy, France … 19 F10
Vicksburg, Ariz., U.S.A. … 117 M13
Vicksburg, Miss., U.S.A. … 113 J9
Vico, France … 21 F12
Vico, L. di, Italy … 29 F9
Vico del Gargano, Italy … 29 G12
Vicovu de Sus, Romania … 43 C10
Victor, India … 68 J4
Victor, U.S.A. … 110 D7
Victor Harbor, Australia … 95 F2
Victoria = Labuan, Malaysia … 62 C5
Victoria, Argentina … 126 C3
Victoria, Canada … 104 D4
Victoria, Chile … 128 D2
Victoria, Guinea … 82 C2
Victoria, Malta … 36 C1
Victoria, Phil. … 61 D4
Victoria, Romania … 43 E9
Victoria, Kans., U.S.A. … 112 F5
Victoria, Tex., U.S.A. … 113 L6
Victoria □, Australia … 95 F3
Victoria →, Australia … 92 C4
Victoria, Grand L., Canada … 102 C4
Victoria, L., Africa … 86 C3
Victoria, L., Australia … 95 E3
Victoria, Mt., Burma … 67 J18
Victoria Beach, Canada … 105 C9
Victoria de Durango = Durango, Mexico … 118 C4
Victoria Falls, Zimbabwe … 87 F2
Victoria Harbour, Canada … 110 B5
Victoria I., Canada … 100 A8
Victoria L., Canada … 103 C8
Victoria Ld., Antarctica … 5 D11
Victoria Nile →, Uganda … 86 B3
Victoria River, Australia … 92 C5
Victoria Str., Canada … 100 B9
Victoria West, S. Africa … 88 E3
Victorias, Phil. … 61 F5

Victoriaville, Canada … 103 C5
Victorica, Argentina … 126 D2
Victorville, U.S.A. … 117 L9
Vicuña, Chile … 126 C1
Vicuña Mackenna, Argentina … 126 C3
Vidal, U.S.A. … 117 L12
Vidal Junction, U.S.A. … 117 L12
Vidalia, U.S.A. … 109 J4
Vidauban, France … 21 E10
Videbæk, Denmark … 11 H2
Videle, Romania … 43 F10
Vídho, Greece … 36 A3
Vidigueira, Portugal … 35 G3
Vidin, Bulgaria … 40 C6
Vidio, C., Spain … 34 B4
Vidisha, India … 68 H7
Vidra, Romania … 43 E11
Vidzy, Belarus … 9 J22
Viechtach, Germany … 25 F8
Viedma, Argentina … 128 E4
Viedma, L., Argentina … 128 F2
Vieira do Minho, Portugal … 34 D2
Vielha, Spain … 32 C5
Viella = Vielha, Spain … 32 C5
Vielsalm, Belgium … 17 D5
Vienenburg, Germany … 24 D6
Vieng Pou Kha, Laos … 58 G3
Vienna = Wien, Austria … 27 C9
Vienna, Ill., U.S.A. … 113 G10
Vienna, Mo., U.S.A. … 112 F9
Vienne, France … 21 C8
Vienne □, France … 20 B4
Vienne →, France … 18 E7
Vientiane, Laos … 64 D4
Vientos, Paso de los, Caribbean … 121 C5
Viernheim, Germany … 25 F4
Viersen, Germany … 24 D2
Vierwaldstättersee, Switz. … 25 J4
Vierzon, France … 19 E9
Vieste, Italy … 29 G13
Vietnam ■, Asia … 64 C6
Vieux-Boucau-les-Bains, France … 20 E2
Vif, France … 21 C9
Vigan, Phil. … 61 C4
Vigévano, Italy … 28 C5
Vigia, Brazil … 125 D9
Vigía Chico, Mexico … 119 D7
Víglas, Ákra, Greece … 36 D9
Vignemalle, France … 20 F3
Vigneulles-lès-Hattonchâtel, France … 19 D12
Vignola, Italy … 28 D8
Vigo, Spain … 34 C2
Vigo, Ría de, Spain … 34 C2
Vigsø Bugt, Denmark … 11 G2
Vihiers, France … 18 E6
Vihowa, Pakistan … 68 D4
Vihowa →, Pakistan … 68 D4
Vijayawada, India … 67 L12
Vijosë →, Albania … 40 F3
Vík, Iceland … 8 E4
Vika, Sweden … 10 D8
Vikarbyn, Sweden … 10 D9
Vikeke, E. Timor … 63 F7
Viken, Skåne, Sweden … 11 H6
Viken, Västra Götaland, Sweden … 11 F8
Viking, Canada … 104 C6
Vikmanshyttan, Sweden … 10 D9
Vikna, Norway … 8 D14
Vila da Maganja, Mozam. … 87 F4
Vila de João Belo = Xai-Xai, Mozam. … 89 D5
Vila de Rei, Portugal … 34 F2
Vila do Bispo, Portugal … 35 H2
Vila do Conde, Portugal … 34 D2
Vila Franca de Xira, Portugal … 35 G2
Vila Gamito, Mozam. … 87 E3
Vila Gomes da Costa, Mozam. … 89 C5
Vila Machado, Mozam. … 87 F3
Vila Mouzinho, Mozam. … 87 E3
Vila Nova de Famalicão, Portugal … 34 D2
Vila Nova de Fos Côa, Portugal … 34 D3
Vila Nova de Foscôa = Vila Nova de Fos Côa, Portugal … 34 D3
Vila Nova de Gaia, Portugal … 34 D2
Vila Nova de Ourém, Portugal … 34 F2
Vila Pouca de Aguiar, Portugal … 34 D3
Vila Real, Portugal … 34 D3
Vila Real □, Portugal … 34 D3
Vila-real de los Infantes, Spain … 32 F4
Vila Real de Santo António, Portugal … 35 H3
Vila Vasco da Gama, Mozam. … 87 E3
Vila Velha, Brazil … 127 A7
Vila Viçosa, Portugal … 35 G3
Vilafranca del Maestrat, Spain … 32 E4
Vilafranca del Penedès, Spain … 32 D6
Vilagarcía de Arousa, Spain … 34 C2
Vilaine →, France … 18 E4
Vilanandro, Tanjona, Madag. … 89 B7
Vilanculos, Mozam. … 89 C6
Vilanova de Castelló, Spain … 33 F4
Vilanova i la Geltrú, Spain … 32 D6
Vilar Formoso, Portugal … 34 E4
Vilaseca, Spain … 32 D6
Vilaseca-Salou = Vilaseca, Spain … 32 D6
Vilches, Spain … 35 G7
Vileyka, Belarus … 46 E4
Vilhelmina, Sweden … 8 D17
Vilhena, Brazil … 124 F6
Viliya →, Lithuania … 9 J21
Vília, Russia … 51 C16
Viljandi, Estonia … 9 G21
Vilkaviškis, Lithuania … 44 D10

Wad Hamid

Vilkija, *Lithuania* 44 C10
Vilkitskogo, Proliv, *Russia* 51 B11
Vilkovo = Vylkove, *Ukraine* 47 K5
Villa Abecia, *Bolivia* 126 A2
Villa Ahumada, *Mexico* 118 A3
Villa Ana, *Argentina* 126 B4
Villa Ángela, *Argentina* 126 B3
Villa Bella, *Bolivia* 124 F5
Villa Bens = Tarfaya, *Morocco* 78 C3
Villa Cañás, *Argentina* 126 C3
Villa Cisneros = Dakhla, *W. Sahara* 78 D2
Villa Colón, *Argentina* 126 C2
Villa Constitución, *Argentina* 126 C3
Villa de María, *Argentina* 126 B3
Villa del Rio, *Spain* 35 H6
Villa Dolores, *Argentina* 126 C2
Villa Frontera, *Mexico* 118 B4
Villa Guillermina, *Argentina* 126 B4
Villa Hayes, *Paraguay* 126 B4
Villa Iris, *Argentina* 126 D3
Villa Juárez, *Mexico* 118 B4
Villa María, *Argentina* 126 C3
Villa Mazán, *Argentina* 126 B2
Villa Minozzo, *Italy* 28 D7
Villa Montes, *Bolivia* 126 A3
Villa Ocampo, *Argentina* 126 B4
Villa Ocampo, *Mexico* 118 B3
Villa Ojo de Agua, *Argentina* 126 B3
Villa San Giovanni, *Italy* 31 D8
Villa San José, *Argentina* 126 C4
Villa San Martín, *Argentina* 126 B3
Villa Santina, *Italy* 29 B9
Villa Unión, *Mexico* 118 C3
Villablino, *Spain* 34 C4
Villacarlos, *Spain* 37 B11
Villacarriedo, *Spain* 34 B7
Villacarrillo, *Spain* 35 G7
Villacastín, *Spain* 34 E6
Villach, *Austria* 26 E6
Villacidro, *Italy* 30 C1
Villada, *Spain* 34 C6
Villadiego, *Spain* 34 C6
Villadóssola, *Italy* 28 B5
Villafeliche, *Spain* 32 D3
Villafranca, *Spain* 32 C3
Villafranca de los Barros, *Spain* 35 G4
Villafranca de los Caballeros, *Baleares, Spain* 37 B10
Villafranca de los Caballeros, *Toledo, Spain* 35 F7
Villafranca del Cid = Vilafranca del Maestrat, *Spain* 32 E4
Villafranca del Panadés = Vilafranca del Penedès, *Spain* 32 D6
Villafranca di Verona, *Italy* 28 C7
Villafranca Tirrena, *Italy* 31 D8
Villagrán, *Mexico* 119 C5
Villaguay, *Argentina* 126 C4
Villaharta, *Spain* 35 G6
Villahermosa, *Mexico* 119 D6
Villahermosa, *Spain* 33 G2
Villaines-la-Juhel, *France* 18 D6
Villajoyosa, *Spain* 33 G4
Villalba, *Spain* 34 B3
Villalba de Guardo, *Spain* 34 C6
Villalón de Campos, *Spain* 34 C5
Villalpando, *Spain* 34 D5
Villaluenga, *Spain* 34 E7
Villamanán, *Spain* 34 C5
Villamartín, *Spain* 35 J5
Villamayor de Santiago, *Spain* 32 F2
Villamblard, *France* 20 C4
Villanova Monteleone, *Italy* 30 B1
Villanueva, *U.S.A.* 113 H2
Villanueva de Castellón = Vilanova de Castelló, *Spain* 33 F4
Villanueva de Córdoba, *Spain* 35 G6
Villanueva de la Fuente, *Spain* 33 G2
Villanueva de la Serena, *Spain* 35 G5
Villanueva de la Sierra, *Spain* 34 E4
Villanueva de los Castillejos, *Spain* 35 H3
Villanueva de los Infantes, *Spain* 35 G7
Villanueva del Arzobispo, *Spain* 33 G2
Villanueva del Fresno, *Spain* 35 G3
Villanueva y Geltrú = Vilanova i la Geltrú, *Spain* 32 D6
Villaputzu, *Italy* 30 C2
Villaquilambre, *Spain* 34 C5
Villar del Arzobispo, *Spain* 32 F4
Villar del Rey, *Spain* 35 F4
Villard-de-Lans, *France* 21 C9
Villarramiel, *Spain* 34 C6
Villarreal = Vila-real de los Infantes, *Spain* 32 F4
Villarrica, *Chile* 128 D2
Villarrica, *Paraguay* 126 B4
Villarrobledo, *Spain* 33 F2
Villarroya de la Sierra, *Spain* 32 D3
Villarrubia de los Ojos, *Spain* 35 F7
Villars-les-Dombes, *France* 19 F12
Villasayas, *Spain* 32 D2
Villaseca de los Gamitos = Villaseco de los Gamitos, *Spain* 34 D4
Villaseco de los Gamitos, *Spain* 34 D4
Villasimíus, *Italy* 30 C2
Villastar, *Spain* 32 E3
Villatobas, *Spain* 34 F7
Villavicencio, *Argentina* 126 C2
Villavicencio, *Colombia* 124 C4
Villaviciosa, *Spain* 34 B5
Villazón, *Bolivia* 126 A2
Ville-Marie, *Canada* 102 C4
Ville Platte, *U.S.A.* 113 K8
Villedieu-les-Poêles, *France* 18 D5
Villefort, *France* 20 D7
Villefranche-de-Lauragais, *France* 20 E5
Villefranche-de-Rouergue, *France* 20 D6
Villefranche-du-Périgord, *France* 20 D5
Villefranche-sur-Saône, *France* 21 C8
Villel, *Spain* 32 E3
Villemur-sur-Tarn, *France* 20 E5
Villena, *Spain* 33 G4
Villenauxe-la-Grande, *France* 19 D10
Villenave-d'Ornon, *France* 20 D3
Villeneuve-d'Ascq, *France* 19 B10
Villeneuve-l'Archevêque, *France* 19 D10
Villeneuve-lès-Avignon, *France* 21 E8
Villeneuve-sur-Allier, *France* 19 F10
Villeneuve-sur-Lot, *France* 20 D4
Villeneuve-sur-Yonne, *France* 19 D10
Villeréal, *France* 20 D4
Villers-Bocage, *France* 18 C6
Villers-Cotterêts, *France* 19 C10
Villers-sur-Mer, *France* 18 C6
Villersexel, *France* 19 E13
Villerupt, *France* 19 C12
Villeurbanne, *France* 21 C8
Villiers, *S. Africa* 89 D4
Villingen-Schwenningen, *Germany* 25 G4
Vilna, *Canada* 104 C6
Vilnius, *Lithuania* 9 J21
Vils, *Austria* 26 D3
Vils →, *Bayern, Germany* 25 G9
Vils →, *Bayern, Germany* 25 F7
Vilsbiburg, *Germany* 25 G8
Vilshofen, *Germany* 25 G9
Vilusi, *Montenegro, Yug.* 40 D2
Vilvoorde, *Belgium* 17 D4
Vilyuy →, *Russia* 51 C13
Vilyuysk, *Russia* 51 C13
Vimianzo, *Spain* 34 B1
Vimioso, *Portugal* 34 D4
Vimmerby, *Sweden* 11 G9
Vimoutiers, *France* 18 D7
Vimperk, *Czech Rep.* 26 B6
Viña del Mar, *Chile* 126 C1
Vinarós, *Spain* 32 E5
Vincennes, *U.S.A.* 108 F2
Vincent, *U.S.A.* 117 L8
Vinchina, *Argentina* 126 B2
Vindelälven →, *Sweden* 8 E18
Vindeln, *Sweden* 8 D18
Vinderup, *Denmark* 11 H2
Vindhya Ra., *India* 68 H7
Vineland, *U.S.A.* 108 F8
Vineuil, *France* 18 E8
Vinga, *Romania* 42 D6
Vingåker, *Sweden* 10 E9
Vinh, *Vietnam* 64 C5
Vinh Linh, *Vietnam* 64 D6
Vinh Long, *Vietnam* 65 G5
Vinh Yen, *Vietnam* 58 G5
Vinhais, *Portugal* 34 D3
Vinica, *Croatia* 29 B13
Vinica, *Macedonia* 40 E6
Vinica, *Slovenia* 29 C12
Vinita, *U.S.A.* 113 G7
Vinkovci, *Croatia* 42 E3
Vinnitsa = Vinnytsya, *Ukraine* 47 H5
Vinnytsya, *Ukraine* 47 H5
Vinslöv, *Sweden* 11 H7
Vintjärn, *Sweden* 10 D10
Vinton, *Calif., U.S.A.* 116 F6
Vinton, *Iowa, U.S.A.* 112 D8
Vinton, *La., U.S.A.* 113 K8
Vinţu de Jos, *Romania* 43 D8
Viöl, *Germany* 24 A5
Vipava, *Slovenia* 29 C10
Vipiteno, *Italy* 29 B8
Vir, *Croatia* 29 D12
Virac, *Phil.* 61 E6
Virachei, *Cambodia* 64 F6
Virago Sd., *Canada* 104 C2
Viramgam, *India* 68 H5
Virananşehir, *Turkey* 70 B3
Virawah, *Pakistan* 68 G4
Virbalis, *Lithuania* 44 D9
Virden, *Canada* 105 D8
Vire, *France* 18 D6
Vire →, *France* 18 C5
Vírgenes, C., *Argentina* 128 G3
Virgin →, *U.S.A.* 115 H6
Virgin Gorda, *Br. Virgin Is.* 121 C7
Virgin Is. (British) ■, *W. Indies* 121 C7
Virgin Is. (U.S.) ■, *W. Indies* 121 C7
Virginia, *S. Africa* 88 D4
Virginia, *U.S.A.* 112 B8
Virginia □, *U.S.A.* 108 G7
Virginia Beach, *U.S.A.* 108 G8
Virginia City, *Mont., U.S.A.* 114 D8
Virginia City, *Nev., U.S.A.* 116 F7
Virginia Falls, *Canada* 104 A3
Virginiatown, *Canada* 102 C4
Virje, *Croatia* 29 B13
Viroqua, *U.S.A.* 112 D9
Virovitica, *Croatia* 42 E2
Virpazar, *Montenegro, Yug.* 40 D3
Virpur, *India* 68 J4
Virserum, *Sweden* 11 G9
Virton, *Belgium* 17 E5
Virudunagar, *India* 66 Q10
Vis, *Croatia* 29 E13
Visalia, *U.S.A.* 116 J7
Visayan Sea, *Phil.* 61 F5
Visby, *Sweden* 11 G12
Viscount Melville Sd., *Canada* 4 B2
Visé, *Belgium* 17 D5
Višegrad, *Bos.-H.* 42 G4
Viseu, *Brazil* 125 D9
Viseu, *Portugal* 34 E3
Viseu □, *Portugal* 34 E3
Vişeu de Sus, *Romania* 43 C9
Vishakhapatnam, *India* 67 L13
Vişina, *Romania* 43 G9
Vişineşti, *Moldova* 43 D13
Visingsö, *Sweden* 11 F8
Viskafors, *Sweden* 11 G6
Viskan →, *Sweden* 11 G6
Viški Kanal, *Croatia* 29 E13
Vislanda, *Sweden* 11 H8
Visnagar, *India* 68 H5
Višnja Gora, *Slovenia* 29 C11
Viso, Mte., *Italy* 28 D4
Viso del Marqués, *Spain* 35 G7
Visoko, *Bos.-H.* 42 G3
Visokoi I., *Antarctica* 5 B1
Visp, *Switz.* 25 J3
Vissefjärda, *Sweden* 11 H9
Visselhövede, *Germany* 24 C5
Vissenbjerg, *Denmark* 11 J4
Vista, *U.S.A.* 117 M9
Vistonikos, Ormos = Vistonís, Límni, *Greece* 41 E9
Vistonís, Límni, *Greece* 41 E9
Vistula = Wisła →, *Poland* 44 D5
Vit →, *Bulgaria* 41 C8
Vitanje, *Slovenia* 29 B12
Vitebsk = Vitsyebsk, *Belarus* 46 E6
Viterbo, *Italy* 29 F9
Vitez, *Bos.-H.* 42 F2
Viti Levu, *Fiji* 91 C7
Vitigudino, *Spain* 34 D4
Vitim, *Russia* 51 D12
Vitim →, *Russia* 51 D12
Vitina, *Bos.-H.* 29 E14
Vitína, *Greece* 38 D4
Vítkov, *Czech Rep.* 27 B10
Vitória, *Brazil* 125 H10
Vitória da Conquista, *Brazil* 125 F10
Vitória de São Antão, *Brazil* 125 E11
Vitoria-Gasteiz, *Spain* 32 C2
Vitré, *France* 18 D5
Vitry-le-François, *France* 19 D11
Vitry-sur-Seine, *France* 19 D9
Vitsand, *Sweden* 10 D7
Vitsi, Óros, *Greece* 40 F5
Vitsyebsk, *Belarus* 46 E6
Vittaryd, *Sweden* 11 H7
Vitteaux, *France* 19 E11
Vittel, *France* 19 D12
Vittória, *Italy* 31 F7
Vittório Véneto, *Italy* 29 C9
Vittsjö, *Sweden* 11 H7
Viveiro, *Spain* 34 B3
Vivian, *U.S.A.* 113 J8
Viviers, *France* 21 D8
Vivonne, *France* 20 B4
Vizcaíno, Desierto de, *Mexico* 118 B2
Vizcaíno, Sierra, *Mexico* 118 B2
Vizcaya □, *Spain* 32 B2
Vize, *Turkey* 41 E11
Vizianagaram, *India* 67 K13
Vizille, *France* 21 C9
Viziñada, *Croatia* 29 C10
Viziru, *Romania* 43 E12
Vizzini, *Italy* 31 E7
Vlaardingen, *Neths.* 17 C4
Vlădeasa, Vf., *Romania* 42 D7
Vladičin Han, *Serbia, Yug.* 40 D6
Vladikavkaz, *Russia* 49 J7
Vladimir, *Russia* 46 D11
Vladimir Volynskiy = Volodymyr-Volynskyy, *Ukraine* 47 G3
Vladimirci, *Serbia, Yug.* 40 B3
Vladimirovac, *Serbia, Yug.* 42 E5
Vladimirovka, *Russia* 49 F8
Vladimirovo, *Bulgaria* 40 C7
Vladimorvka, *Kazakstan* 48 E10
Vladislavovka, *Ukraine* 47 K8
Vladivostok, *Russia* 51 E14
Vlăhiţa, *Romania* 43 D10
Vlakhiótis, *Greece* 38 E4
Vlasenica, *Bos.-H.* 42 F3
Vlašić, *Bos.-H.* 42 F2
Vlašim, *Czech Rep.* 26 B7
Vlasinsko Jezero, *Serbia, Yug.* 40 D6
Vlasotince, *Serbia, Yug.* 40 D6
Vlieland, *Neths.* 17 A4
Vlissingen, *Neths.* 17 C3
Vlorë, *Albania* 40 F3
Vlorës, Gjiri i, *Albania* 40 F3
Vltava →, *Czech Rep.* 26 A7
Vo Dat, *Vietnam* 65 G6
Vobarno, *Italy* 28 C7
Voćin, *Croatia* 42 E2
Vöcklabruck, *Austria* 26 C6
Vodice, *Croatia* 29 E12
Vodňany, *Czech Rep.* 26 B7
Vodnjan, *Croatia* 29 D10
Voe, *U.K.* 14 A7
Vogel Pk., *Nigeria* 83 D7
Vogelkop = Doberai, Jazirah, *Indonesia* 63 E8
Vogelsberg, *Germany* 24 E5
Voghera, *Italy* 28 D6
Vohibinany, *Madag.* 89 B8
Vohilava, *Madag.* 89 C8
Vohimarina = Iharana, *Madag.* 89 A9
Vohimena, Tanjon' i, *Madag.* 89 D8
Vohipeno, *Madag.* 89 C8
Voi, *Kenya* 86 C4
Void-Vacon, *France* 19 D12
Voineşti, *Iaşi, Romania* 43 C12
Voineşti, *Prahova, Romania* 43 E10
Voïotía □, *Greece* 38 C5
Voiron, *France* 21 C9
Voisey B., *Canada* 103 A7
Voitsberg, *Austria* 26 D8
Vojens, *Denmark* 11 J3
Vojmsjön, *Sweden* 8 D17
Vojnić, *Croatia* 29 C12
Vojnik, *Italy* 29 B12
Vojvodina □, *Serbia, Yug.* 42 E5
Vokhtoga, *Russia* 46 C11
Volary, *Czech Rep.* 26 C6
Volborg, *U.S.A.* 112 C2
Volcano Is. = Kazan-Rettō, *Pac. Oc.* 96 E6
Volchansk = Vovchansk, *Ukraine* 47 G9
Volchya →, *Ukraine* 47 H8
Volda, *Norway* 9 E12
Volga, *Russia* 46 C10
Volga →, *Russia* 49 G9
Volga Hts. = Privolzhskaya Vozvyshennost, *Russia* 48 E7
Volgo-Baltiyskiy Kanal, *Russia* 46 B9
Volgo-Donskoy Kanal, *Russia* 49 F7
Volgodonsk, *Russia* 49 G6
Volgograd, *Russia* 49 F7
Volgogradskoye Vdkhr., *Russia* 48 E8
Volgorechensk, *Russia* 48 B5
Volímai, *Greece* 38 D2
Volintiri, *Moldova* 43 D14
Volissós, *Greece* 39 C7
Volkach, *Germany* 25 F6
Völkermarkt, *Austria* 26 E7
Volkhov, *Russia* 46 C7
Volkhov →, *Russia* 46 B7
Völklingen, *Germany* 25 F2
Volkovysk = Vawkavysk, *Belarus* 47 F3
Volksrust, *S. Africa* 89 D4
Volnansk, *Ukraine* 47 H8
Volnovakha, *Ukraine* 47 J9
Volochanka, *Russia* 51 B10
Volodarsk, *Russia* 48 B6
Volodymyr-Volynskyy, *Ukraine* 47 G3
Vologda, *Russia* 46 C10
Volokolamsk, *Russia* 46 D8
Volokonovka, *Russia* 47 G9
Vólos, *Greece* 38 B4
Volosovo, *Russia* 46 C5
Volovets, *Ukraine* 47 H2
Volovo, *Russia* 46 F10
Volozhin = Valozhyn, *Belarus* 46 E4
Volsk, *Russia* 48 D8
Volta □, *Ghana* 83 D5
Volta →, *Ghana* 83 D5
Volta, L., *Ghana* 83 D5
Volta Blanche = White Volta →, *Ghana* 83 D4
Volta Redonda, *Brazil* 127 A7
Voltaire, C., *Australia* 92 B4
Volterra, *Italy* 28 E7
Voltri, *Italy* 28 D5
Volturno →, *Italy* 30 A6
Vólvi, L., *Greece* 40 F7
Volyně, *Czech Rep.* 26 B6
Volzhsk, *Russia* 48 C9
Volzhskiy, *Russia* 49 F7
Vondrozo, *Madag.* 89 C8
Vónitsa, *Greece* 38 C2
Vopnafjörður, *Iceland* 8 D6
Vorarlberg □, *Austria* 26 D2
Vóras Óros, *Greece* 40 F5
Vorbasse, *Denmark* 11 J3
Vorchdorf, *Austria* 26 C6
Vorderrhein →, *Switz.* 25 J5
Vordingborg, *Denmark* 11 J5
Vorë, *Albania* 40 E3
Voreio Aigaio = Vórios Aiyaíon □, *Greece* 39 C7
Voreppe, *France* 21 C9
Vóriai Sporádhes, *Greece* 38 B5
Vórios Aiyaíon □, *Greece* 39 C7
Vórios Evvoïkos Kólpos, *Greece* 38 C5
Vorkuta, *Russia* 50 C7
Vormsi, *Estonia* 9 G20
Vorona →, *Russia* 48 E6
Voronezh, *Russia* 47 G10
Voronezh, *Ukraine* 47 G7
Voronezh →, *Russia* 47 G10
Vorontsovo-Aleksandrovskoye = Zelenokumsk, *Russia* 49 H6
Voroshilovgrad = Luhansk, *Ukraine* 47 H10
Voroshilovsk = Alchevsk, *Ukraine* 47 H10
Vórroi, *Greece* 38 F6
Vorskla →, *Ukraine* 47 H8
Vörts Järv, *Estonia* 9 G22
Võru, *Estonia* 9 H22
Vosges, *France* 19 D14
Vosges □, *France* 19 D13
Voskopojë, *Albania* 40 F4
Voskresensk, *Russia* 46 E10
Voskresenskoye, *Russia* 48 B7
Voss, *Norway* 9 F12
Vostok I., *Kiribati* 97 J12
Votice, *Czech Rep.* 26 B7
Votsuri-Shima, *Japan* 55 M1
Vouga →, *Portugal* 34 E2
Vouillé, *France* 18 F7
Voúxa, Ákra, *Greece* 36 D5
Vouzela, *Portugal* 34 E2
Vouziers, *France* 19 C11
Vovchansk, *Ukraine* 47 G9
Vozhe, Ozero, *Russia* 46 B10
Vozhega, *Russia* 46 B11
Voznesensk, *Ukraine* 47 J6
Voznesenye, *Russia* 46 B8
Vrå, *Denmark* 11 G3
Vráble, *Slovak Rep.* 27 C11
Vraćevšnica, *Serbia, Yug.* 40 B4
Vrakhnéïka, *Greece* 38 C3
Vrancea □, *Romania* 43 E11
Vrancei, Munţii, *Romania* 43 E11
Vrangelya, Ostrov, *Russia* 51 B19
Vranica, *Bos.-H.* 42 G2
Vranje, *Serbia, Yug.* 40 D5
Vranjska Banja, *Serbia, Yug.* 40 D6
Vranov nad Topl'ou, *Slovak Rep.* 27 C14
Vransko, *Slovenia* 29 B11
Vransko Jezero, *Croatia* 29 E12
Vrapčište, *Macedonia* 40 E4
Vratsa, *Bulgaria* 40 C7
Vrbas, *Serbia, Yug.* 42 E4
Vrbas →, *Bos.-H.* 42 E2
Vrbnik, *Croatia* 29 C11
Vrbovec, *Croatia* 29 C13
Vrbovsko, *Croatia* 29 C12
Vrchlabí, *Czech Rep.* 26 A8
Vrede, *S. Africa* 89 D4
Vredefort, *S. Africa* 88 D4
Vreden, *Germany* 24 C2
Vredenburg, *S. Africa* 88 E2
Vredendal, *S. Africa* 88 E2
Vretstorp, *Sweden* 10 E8
Vrgorac, *Croatia* 29 E14
Vrhnika, *Slovenia* 29 C11
Vrïdi, *Ivory C.* 82 D4
Vrigstad, *Sweden* 11 G8
Vrindavan, *India* 68 F7
Vrises, *Greece* 36 D6
Vrnograč, *Bos.-H.* 29 C12
Vrondádhes, *Greece* 39 C8
Vrpolje, *Croatia* 42 E3
Vršac, *Serbia, Yug.* 42 E6
Vrsacki Kanal, *Serbia, Yug.* 42 E5
Vrútky, *Slovak Rep.* 27 B11
Vryburg, *S. Africa* 88 D3
Vryheid, *S. Africa* 89 D5
Vsetín, *Czech Rep.* 27 B11
Vu Liet, *Vietnam* 64 C5
Vůcha →, *Bulgaria* 41 D8
Vučitrn, *Kosovo, Yug.* 40 D4
Vukovar, *Croatia* 42 E3
Vulcan, *Canada* 104 C6
Vulcan, *Romania* 43 E8
Vulcaneşti, *Moldova* 43 E13
Vulcano, *Italy* 31 D7
Vŭlchedruma, *Bulgaria* 40 C7
Vulkaneshty = Vulcaneşti, *Moldova* 43 E13
Vunduzi →, *Mozam.* 87 F3
Vung Tau, *Vietnam* 65 G6
Vŭrbitsa, *Bulgaria* 41 D10
Vurshets, *Bulgaria* 40 C7
Vutcani, *Romania* 43 D12
Vuya, *Sudan* 81 F2
Vyartsilya, *Russia* 46 A6
Vyatka = Kirov, *Russia* 50 D5
Vyatka →, *Russia* 48 C10
Vyatskiye Polyany, *Russia* 48 B10
Vyazemskiy, *Russia* 51 E14
Vyazma, *Russia* 46 E8
Vyazniki, *Russia* 48 B6
Vyborg, *Russia* 46 B5
Vychegda →, *Russia* 50 C5
Vychodné Beskydy, *Europe* 27 B15
Vyerkhnyadzvinsk, *Belarus* 46 E4
Vyksa, *Russia* 48 C6
Vylkove, *Ukraine* 47 K5
Vynohradiv, *Ukraine* 47 H2
Vyrnwy, L., *U.K.* 12 E4
Vyshniy Volochek, *Russia* 46 D8
Vyshzha = imeni 26 Bakinskikh Komissarov, *Turkmenistan* 71 B7
Vyškov, *Czech Rep.* 27 B9
Vysoké Mýto, *Czech Rep.* 27 B9
Vysokovsk, *Russia* 46 D9
Vyšší Brod, *Czech Rep.* 26 C7
Vytegra, *Russia* 46 B9

W

W.A.C. Bennett Dam, *Canada* 104 B4
Wa, *Ghana* 82 C4
Waal →, *Neths.* 17 C5
Waalwijk, *Neths.* 17 C5
Waat, *Sudan* 81 F3
Wabana, *Canada* 103 C9
Wabasca →, *Canada* 104 B5
Wabasca-Desmarais, *Canada* 104 B6
Wabash, *U.S.A.* 108 E3
Wabash →, *U.S.A.* 108 G1
Wabi →, *Ethiopia* 81 F5
Wabigoon L., *Canada* 105 D10
Wabowden, *Canada* 105 C9
Wąbrzeźno, *Poland* 45 E5
Wabu Hu, *China* 59 A11
Wabuk Pt., *Canada* 102 A2
Wabush, *Canada* 103 B6
Wąchock, *Poland* 45 G8
Wächtersbach, *Germany* 25 E5
Waco, *U.S.A.* 113 K6
Waconichi, L., *Canada* 102 B5
Wad Ban Naqa, *Sudan* 81 D3
Wad Banda, *Sudan* 81 E2
Wad el Haddad, *Sudan* 81 E3
Wad en Nau, *Sudan* 81 E3
Wad Hamid, *Sudan* 81 D3

Wad Medanî, Sudan ... 81 E3
Wad Thana, Pakistan ... 68 F2
Wadai, Africa ... 76 E5
Wadayama, Japan ... 55 G7
Waddeneilanden, Neths. ... 17 A5
Waddenzee, Neths. ... 17 A5
Waddington, U.S.A. ... 111 B9
Waddington, Mt., Canada ... 104 C3
Waddy Pt., Australia ... 95 C5
Wadebridge, U.K. ... 13 G3
Wadena, Canada ... 105 C8
Wadena, U.S.A. ... 112 B7
Wädenswil, Switz. ... 25 H4
Wadern, Germany ... 25 F2
Wadeye, Australia ... 92 B4
Wadhams, Canada ... 104 C3
Wādī as Sīr, Jordan ... 75 D4
Wadi Gemāl, Egypt ... 80 C4
Wadi Halfa, Sudan ... 80 C3
Wadian, China ... 59 A9
Wadlew, Poland ... 45 G6
Wadowice, Poland ... 45 J6
Wadsworth, Nev., U.S.A. ... 114 G4
Wadsworth, Ohio, U.S.A. ... 110 E3
Waegwan, S. Korea ... 57 G15
Wafangdian, China ... 57 E11
Wafrah, Si. Arabia ... 70 D5
Wageningen, Neths. ... 17 C5
Wager B., Canada ... 101 B11
Wagga Wagga, Australia ... 95 F4
Waghete, Indonesia ... 63 E9
Wagin, Australia ... 93 F2
Wagner, U.S.A. ... 112 D5
Wagon Mound, U.S.A. ... 113 G2
Wagoner, U.S.A. ... 113 H7
Wagrowiec, Poland ... 45 F4
Wah, Pakistan ... 68 C5
Wahai, Indonesia ... 63 E7
Wahiawa, U.S.A. ... 106 H15
Wāḥid, Egypt ... 75 E1
Wahnai, Afghan. ... 68 C1
Wahni, Ethiopia ... 81 E4
Wahoo, U.S.A. ... 112 E6
Wahpeton, U.S.A. ... 112 B6
Waiau →, N.Z. ... 91 K4
Waibeem, Indonesia ... 63 E8
Waiblingen, Germany ... 25 G5
Waidhofen an der Thaya, Austria ... 26 C8
Waidhofen an der Ybbs, Austria ... 26 D7
Waigeo, Indonesia ... 63 E8
Waihi, N.Z. ... 91 G5
Waihou →, N.Z. ... 91 G5
Waika, Dem. Rep. of the Congo ... 86 C2
Waikabubak, Indonesia ... 63 F5
Waikari, N.Z. ... 91 K4
Waikato →, N.Z. ... 91 G5
Waikerie, Australia ... 95 E3
Waikokopu, N.Z. ... 91 H6
Waikouaiti, N.Z. ... 91 L3
Wailuku, U.S.A. ... 106 H16
Waimakariri →, N.Z. ... 91 K4
Waimate, N.Z. ... 91 L3
Wainganga →, India ... 66 K11
Waingapu, Indonesia ... 63 F6
Waini →, Guyana ... 124 B7
Wainwright, Canada ... 105 C6
Waiouru, N.Z. ... 91 H5
Waipara, N.Z. ... 91 K4
Waipawa, N.Z. ... 91 H6
Waipiro, N.Z. ... 91 H7
Waipu, N.Z. ... 91 F5
Waipukurau, N.Z. ... 91 J6
Wairakei, N.Z. ... 91 H6
Wairarapa, L., N.Z. ... 91 J5
Wairoa, N.Z. ... 91 H6
Waitaki →, N.Z. ... 91 L3
Waitara, N.Z. ... 91 H5
Waitsburg, U.S.A. ... 114 C5
Waiuku, N.Z. ... 91 G5
Wajima, Japan ... 55 F8
Wajir, Kenya ... 86 B5
Waka, Ethiopia ... 81 F4
Wakasa, Japan ... 55 G7
Wakasa-Wan, Japan ... 55 G7
Wakatipu, L., N.Z. ... 91 L2
Wakaw, Canada ... 105 C7
Wakayama, Japan ... 55 G7
Wakayama □, Japan ... 55 H7
Wake Forest, U.S.A. ... 109 H6
Wake I., Pac. Oc. ... 96 F8
WaKeeney, U.S.A. ... 112 F5
Wakefield, N.Z. ... 91 J4
Wakefield, U.K. ... 12 D6
Wakefield, Mass., U.S.A. ... 111 D13
Wakefield, Mich., U.S.A. ... 112 B10
Wakkanai, Japan ... 54 B10
Wakkerstroom, S. Africa ... 89 D5
Wakool, Australia ... 95 F3
Wakool →, Australia ... 95 F3
Wakre, Indonesia ... 63 E8
Wakuach, L., Canada ... 103 A6
Walamba, Zambia ... 87 E2
Wałbrzych, Poland ... 45 H3
Walbury Hill, U.K. ... 13 F6
Walcha, Australia ... 95 E5
Walchen, Neths. ... 17 C3
Walcott, U.S.A. ... 114 F10
Wałcz, Poland ... 45 E3
Waldbröl, Germany ... 24 E3
Waldburg Ra., Australia ... 93 D2
Waldeck, Germany ... 24 D5
Walden, Colo., U.S.A. ... 114 F10
Walden, N.Y., U.S.A. ... 111 E10
Waldkirch, Germany ... 25 G3
Waldkirchen, Germany ... 25 G9
Waldkraiburg, Germany ... 25 G8

Waldport, U.S.A. ... 114 D1
Waldron, U.S.A. ... 113 H7
Waldviertel, Austria ... 26 C8
Walebing, Australia ... 93 F2
Walembele, Ghana ... 82 C4
Walensee, Switz. ... 25 H5
Wales □, U.K. ... 13 E3
Walewale, Ghana ... 83 C4
Walgett, Australia ... 95 E4
Walgreen Coast, Antarctica ... 5 D15
Walker, U.S.A. ... 112 B7
Walker, L., Canada ... 103 B6
Walker L., Canada ... 105 C9
Walker L., U.S.A. ... 114 G4
Walkerston, Australia ... 94 C4
Walkerton, Canada ... 102 D3
Wall, U.S.A. ... 112 D3
Walla Walla, U.S.A. ... 114 C4
Wallace, Idaho, U.S.A. ... 114 C6
Wallace, N.C., U.S.A. ... 109 H7
Wallaceburg, Canada ... 102 D3
Wallachia = Valahia, Romania ... 43 F9
Wallal, Australia ... 95 D4
Wallam Cr. →, Australia ... 95 D4
Wallambin, L., Australia ... 93 F2
Wallangarra, Australia ... 95 D5
Wallaroo, Australia ... 95 E2
Walldürn, Germany ... 25 F5
Wallenhorst, Germany ... 24 C4
Wallenpaupack, L., U.S.A. ... 111 E9
Wallingford, U.S.A. ... 111 E12
Wallis & Futuna, Is., Pac. Oc. ... 96 J10
Wallowa, U.S.A. ... 114 D5
Wallowa Mts., U.S.A. ... 114 D5
Walls, U.K. ... 14 A7
Wallula, U.S.A. ... 114 C4
Wallumbilla, Australia ... 95 D4
Walmsley, L., Canada ... 105 A7
Walney, I. of, U.K. ... 12 C4
Walnut Creek, U.S.A. ... 116 H4
Walnut Ridge, U.S.A. ... 113 G9
Walpole, Australia ... 93 F2
Walpole, U.S.A. ... 111 D13
Wals, Austria ... 26 D5
Walsall, U.K. ... 13 E6
Walsenburg, U.S.A. ... 113 G2
Walsh, U.S.A. ... 113 G3
Walsh →, Australia ... 94 B3
Walsrode, Germany ... 24 C5
Walterboro, U.S.A. ... 109 J5
Walters, U.S.A. ... 113 H5
Waltershausen, Germany ... 24 E6
Waltham, U.S.A. ... 111 D13
Waltman, U.S.A. ... 114 E10
Walton, U.S.A. ... 111 D9
Walton-on-the-Naze, U.K. ... 13 F9
Walvis Bay, Namibia ... 88 C1
Walvisbaai = Walvis Bay, Namibia ... 88 C1
Wamba, Dem. Rep. of the Congo ... 86 B2
Wamba, Kenya ... 86 B4
Wamba, Nigeria ... 83 D6
Wamego, U.S.A. ... 112 F6
Wamena, Indonesia ... 63 E9
Wamsutter, U.S.A. ... 114 F9
Wamulan, Indonesia ... 63 E7
Wan Xian, China ... 56 E8
Wana, Pakistan ... 68 C3
Wanaaring, Australia ... 95 D3
Wanaka, N.Z. ... 91 L2
Wanaka L., N.Z. ... 91 L2
Wan'an, China ... 59 D10
Wanapitei L., Canada ... 102 C3
Wandel Sea = McKinley Sea, Arctic ... 4 A7
Wandérama, Ivory C. ... 82 D4
Wanderer, Zimbabwe ... 87 F3
Wandhari, Pakistan ... 68 F2
Wanding, China ... 58 E2
Wandoan, Australia ... 95 D4
Wanfu, China ... 57 D12
Wang →, Thailand ... 64 D2
Wang Kai, Sudan ... 81 F2
Wang Noi, Thailand ... 64 E3
Wang Saphung, Thailand ... 64 D3
Wang Thong, Thailand ... 64 D3
Wanga, Dem. Rep. of the Congo ... 86 B2
Wangal, Indonesia ... 63 F8
Wanganella, Australia ... 95 F3
Wanganui, N.Z. ... 91 H5
Wangaratta, Australia ... 95 F4
Wangary, Australia ... 95 E2
Wangcang, China ... 58 A6
Wangcheng, China ... 59 C9
Wangdu, China ... 56 E8
Wangen, Germany ... 25 H5
Wangerooge, Germany ... 24 B3
Wangi, Kenya ... 86 C5
Wangiwangi, Indonesia ... 63 F6
Wangjiang, China ... 59 B11
Wangmo, China ... 58 E6
Wangolodougou, Ivory C. ... 82 D3
Wangqing, China ... 57 C15
Wankaner, India ... 68 H4
Wanless, Canada ... 105 C8
Wannian, China ... 59 C11
Wanning, China ... 64 C8
Wanon Niwat, Thailand ... 64 D4
Wanquan, China ... 56 D8
Wanrong, China ... 56 G6
Wanshan, China ... 58 D7
Wanshengchang, China ... 58 C6
Wantage, U.K. ... 13 F6
Wanyuan, China ... 58 A7
Wanzai, China ... 59 C10
Wapakoneta, U.S.A. ... 108 E3
Wapato, U.S.A. ... 114 C3

Wapawekka L., Canada ... 105 C8
Wapikopa L., Canada ... 102 B2
Wapiti →, Canada ... 104 B5
Wappingers Falls, U.S.A. ... 111 E11
Wapsipinicon →, U.S.A. ... 112 E9
Warab □, Sudan ... 81 F2
Warangal, India ... 66 L11
Waraseoni, India ... 69 J9
Waratah, Australia ... 94 G4
Waratah B., Australia ... 95 F4
Warburg, Germany ... 24 D5
Warburton, Vic., Australia ... 95 F4
Warburton, W. Austral., Australia ... 93 E4
Warburton Ra., Australia ... 93 E4
Ward, N.Z. ... 91 J5
Ward →, Australia ... 95 D4
Ward Mt., U.S.A. ... 116 H8
Warden, S. Africa ... 89 D4
Wardha, India ... 66 J11
Wardha →, India ... 66 K11
Ware, Canada ... 104 B3
Ware, U.S.A. ... 111 D12
Waregem, Belgium ... 17 D3
Wareham, U.S.A. ... 111 E14
Waremme, Belgium ... 17 D5
Warialda, Australia ... 95 D5
Wariap, Indonesia ... 63 E8
Warin Chamrap, Thailand ... 64 E5
Warka, Poland ... 45 G8
Warkopi, Indonesia ... 63 E8
Warm Springs, U.S.A. ... 115 G5
Warman, Canada ... 105 C7
Warmbad, Namibia ... 88 D2
Warmbad, S. Africa ... 89 C4
Warmińsko-Mazurskie □, Poland ... 44 D8
Warminster, U.K. ... 13 F5
Warminster, U.S.A. ... 111 F9
Warnemünde, Germany ... 24 A8
Warner Mts., U.S.A. ... 114 F3
Warner Robins, U.S.A. ... 109 J4
Warnow →, Germany ... 24 A8
Waroona, Australia ... 93 F2
Warracknabeal, Australia ... 95 F3
Warragul, Australia ... 95 F4
Warrego →, Australia ... 95 E4
Warrego Ra., Australia ... 94 C4
Warren, Australia ... 95 E4
Warren, Ark., U.S.A. ... 113 J8
Warren, Mich., U.S.A. ... 108 D4
Warren, Minn., U.S.A. ... 112 A6
Warren, Ohio, U.S.A. ... 110 E4
Warren, Pa., U.S.A. ... 110 E5
Warrenpoint, U.K. ... 15 B5
Warrensburg, Mo., U.S.A. ... 112 F8
Warrensburg, N.Y., U.S.A. ... 111 C11
Warrenton, S. Africa ... 88 D3
Warrenton, U.S.A. ... 116 D3
Warri, Nigeria ... 83 D6
Warrina, Australia ... 95 D2
Warrington, U.K. ... 12 D5
Warrington, U.S.A. ... 109 K2
Warrington □, U.K. ... 12 D5
Warrnambool, Australia ... 95 F3
Warroad, U.S.A. ... 112 A7
Warruwi, Australia ... 94 A1
Warsa, Indonesia ... 63 E9
Warsak Dam, Pakistan ... 68 B4
Warsaw = Warszawa, Poland ... 45 F8
Warsaw, Ind., U.S.A. ... 108 E3
Warsaw, N.Y., U.S.A. ... 110 D6
Warsaw, Ohio, U.S.A. ... 110 F3
Warstein, Germany ... 24 D4
Warszawa, Poland ... 45 F8
Warta, Poland ... 45 G5
Warta →, Poland ... 45 F1
Warthe = Warta →, Poland ... 45 F1
Waru, Indonesia ... 63 E8
Warwick, Australia ... 95 D5
Warwick, U.K. ... 13 E6
Warwick, N.Y., U.S.A. ... 111 E10
Warwick, R.I., U.S.A. ... 111 E13
Warwickshire □, U.K. ... 13 E6
Wasaga Beach, Canada ... 110 B4
Wasagaming, Canada ... 105 C9
Wasatch Ra., U.S.A. ... 114 F8
Wasbank, S. Africa ... 89 D5
Wasco, Calif., U.S.A. ... 117 K7
Wasco, Oreg., U.S.A. ... 114 D3
Wase, Nigeria ... 83 D6
Waseca, U.S.A. ... 112 C8
Wasekamio L., Canada ... 105 B7
Wash, The, U.K. ... 12 E8
Washago, Canada ... 110 B5
Washburn, N. Dak., U.S.A. ... 112 B4
Washburn, Wis., U.S.A. ... 112 B9
Washim, India ... 66 J10
Washington, U.K. ... 12 C6
Washington, D.C., U.S.A. ... 108 F7
Washington, Ga., U.S.A. ... 109 J4
Washington, Ind., U.S.A. ... 108 F2
Washington, Iowa, U.S.A. ... 112 E9
Washington, Mo., U.S.A. ... 112 F9
Washington, N.C., U.S.A. ... 109 H7
Washington, N.J., U.S.A. ... 111 F10
Washington, Pa., U.S.A. ... 110 F4
Washington, Utah, U.S.A. ... 115 H7
Washington □, U.S.A. ... 114 C3
Washington, Mt., U.S.A. ... 111 B13
Washington Court House, U.S.A. ... 108 F4
Washington I., U.S.A. ... 108 C2
Washougal, U.S.A. ... 116 E4
Wasian, Indonesia ... 63 E8

Wasilków, Poland ... 45 E10
Wasilla, U.S.A. ... 100 B5
Wasior, Indonesia ... 63 E8
Waskaganish, Canada ... 102 B4
Waskaiowaka, L., Canada ... 105 B9
Waskesiu Lake, Canada ... 105 C7
Wasserburg, Germany ... 25 G8
Wasserkuppe, Germany ... 24 E5
Wassy, France ... 19 D11
Waswanipi, Canada ... 102 C4
Waswanipi, L., Canada ... 102 C4
Watampone, Indonesia ... 63 E6
Water Park Pt., Australia ... 94 C5
Water Valley, U.S.A. ... 113 H10
Waterberge, S. Africa ... 89 C4
Waterbury, Conn., U.S.A. ... 111 E11
Waterbury, Vt., U.S.A. ... 111 B12
Waterbury L., Canada ... 105 B8
Waterdown, Canada ... 110 C5
Waterford, Canada ... 110 D4
Waterford, Ireland ... 15 D4
Waterford, Calif., U.S.A. ... 116 H6
Waterford, Pa., U.S.A. ... 110 E5
Waterford □, Ireland ... 15 D4
Waterford Harbour, Ireland ... 15 D5
Waterhen L., Canada ... 105 C9
Waterloo, Belgium ... 17 D4
Waterloo, Ont., Canada ... 102 D3
Waterloo, Qué., Canada ... 111 A12
Waterloo, S. Leone ... 82 D2
Waterloo, Ill., U.S.A. ... 112 F9
Waterloo, Iowa, U.S.A. ... 112 D8
Waterloo, N.Y., U.S.A. ... 110 D8
Watermeet, U.S.A. ... 112 B10
Waterton Lakes Nat. Park, U.S.A. ... 114 B7
Watertown, Conn., U.S.A. ... 111 E11
Watertown, N.Y., U.S.A. ... 111 C9
Watertown, S. Dak., U.S.A. ... 112 C6
Watertown, Wis., U.S.A. ... 112 D10
Waterval-Boven, S. Africa ... 89 D5
Waterville, Maine, U.S.A. ... 109 C11
Waterville, N.Y., U.S.A. ... 111 D9
Waterville, Pa., U.S.A. ... 110 E7
Waterville, Wash., U.S.A. ... 114 C3
Watervliet, U.S.A. ... 111 D11
Wates, Indonesia ... 63 G14
Watford, Canada ... 110 D3
Watford, U.K. ... 13 F7
Watford City, U.S.A. ... 112 B3
Wathaman →, Canada ... 105 B8
Wathaman L., Canada ... 105 B8
Watheroo, Australia ... 93 F2
Wating, China ... 56 G4
Watkins Glen, U.S.A. ... 110 D8
Watling I. = San Salvador I., Bahamas ... 121 B5
Watonga, U.S.A. ... 113 H5
Watrous, Canada ... 105 C7
Watrous, U.S.A. ... 113 H2
Watsa, Dem. Rep. of the Congo ... 86 B2
Watseka, U.S.A. ... 108 E2
Watson, Australia ... 93 F5
Watson, Canada ... 105 C8
Watson Lake, Canada ... 104 A3
Watsontown, U.S.A. ... 110 E8
Watsonville, U.S.A. ... 116 J5
Wattiwarriganna Cr. →, Australia ... 95 D2
Wattwil, Switz. ... 25 H5
Watuata = Batuata, Indonesia ... 63 F6
Watubela, Kepulauan, Indonesia ... 63 E8
Watubela Is. = Watubela, Kepulauan, Indonesia ... 63 E8
Wau = Wâw, Sudan ... 81 F2
Waubamik, Canada ... 110 A4
Waubay, U.S.A. ... 112 C6
Wauchope, N.S.W., Australia ... 95 E5
Wauchope, N. Terr., Australia ... 94 C1
Wauchula, U.S.A. ... 109 M5
Waukarlycarly, L., Australia ... 92 D3
Waukegan, U.S.A. ... 108 D2
Waukesha, U.S.A. ... 108 D1
Waukon, U.S.A. ... 112 D9
Waupaca, U.S.A. ... 112 C10
Waupun, U.S.A. ... 112 D10
Waurika, U.S.A. ... 113 H6
Wausau, U.S.A. ... 112 C10
Wautoma, U.S.A. ... 112 C10
Wauwatosa, U.S.A. ... 108 D2
Waveney →, U.K. ... 13 E9
Waverley, N.Z. ... 91 H5
Waverly, Iowa, U.S.A. ... 112 D8
Waverly, N.Y., U.S.A. ... 111 E8
Wavre, Belgium ... 17 D4
Wâw, Sudan ... 81 F2
Wawa, Canada ... 102 C3
Wawa, Nigeria ... 83 D5
Wawa, Sudan ... 80 C3
Wawanesa, Canada ... 105 D9
Wawona, U.S.A. ... 116 H7
Waxahachie, U.S.A. ... 113 J6
Way, L., Australia ... 93 E3
Waycross, U.S.A. ... 109 K4
Wayi, Sudan ... 81 F3
Wayland, U.S.A. ... 110 D7
Wayne, Nebr., U.S.A. ... 112 D6
Wayne, W. Va., U.S.A. ... 108 F4
Waynesboro, Ga., U.S.A. ... 109 J4
Waynesboro, Miss., U.S.A. ... 109 K1
Waynesboro, Pa., U.S.A. ... 108 F7
Waynesboro, Va., U.S.A. ... 108 F6
Waynesburg, U.S.A. ... 108 F5
Waynesville, U.S.A. ... 109 H4
Waynoka, U.S.A. ... 113 G5

Wazirabad, Pakistan ... 68 C6
Wda →, Poland ... 44 E5
We, Indonesia ... 62 C1
Weald, The, U.K. ... 13 F8
Wear →, U.K. ... 12 C6
Weatherford, Okla., U.S.A. ... 113 H5
Weatherford, Tex., U.S.A. ... 113 J6
Weaverville, U.S.A. ... 114 F2
Webb City, U.S.A. ... 113 G7
Webequie, Canada ... 102 B2
Webo = Nyaake, Liberia ... 82 E3
Webster, Mass., U.S.A. ... 111 D13
Webster, N.Y., U.S.A. ... 110 C7
Webster, S. Dak., U.S.A. ... 112 C6
Webster City, U.S.A. ... 112 D8
Webster Springs, U.S.A. ... 108 F5
Weda, Indonesia ... 63 D7
Weda, Teluk, Indonesia ... 63 D7
Weddell I., Falk. Is. ... 128 G4
Weddell Sea, Antarctica ... 5 D1
Wedderburn, Australia ... 95 F3
Wedel, Germany ... 24 B5
Wedemark, Germany ... 24 C5
Wedgeport, Canada ... 103 D6
Wedza, Zimbabwe ... 87 F3
Wee Waa, Australia ... 95 E4
Weed, U.S.A. ... 114 F2
Weed Heights, U.S.A. ... 116 G7
Weedsport, U.S.A. ... 111 C8
Weedville, U.S.A. ... 110 E6
Weenen, S. Africa ... 89 D5
Weener, Germany ... 24 B3
Weert, Neths. ... 17 C5
Węgierska-Górka, Poland ... 45 J6
Węgliniec, Poland ... 45 G2
Węgorzewo, Poland ... 44 D8
Węgorzyno, Poland ... 44 E2
Węgrów, Poland ... 45 F9
Wehda □, Sudan ... 81 F3
Wei He →, Hebei, China ... 56 F8
Wei He →, Shaanxi, China ... 56 G6
Weichang, China ... 57 D9
Weichuan, China ... 56 G7
Weida, Germany ... 24 E8
Weiden, Germany ... 25 F8
Weifang, China ... 57 F10
Weihai, China ... 57 F12
Weil, Germany ... 25 H3
Weilburg, Germany ... 24 E4
Weilheim, Germany ... 25 H7
Weimar, Germany ... 24 E7
Weinan, China ... 56 G5
Weingarten, Germany ... 25 H5
Weinheim, Germany ... 25 F4
Weining, China ... 58 D5
Weipa, Australia ... 94 A3
Weir →, Australia ... 95 D4
Weir →, Canada ... 105 B10
Weir River, Canada ... 105 B10
Weirton, U.S.A. ... 110 F4
Weiser, U.S.A. ... 114 D5
Weishan, Shandong, China ... 57 G9
Weishan, Yunnan, China ... 58 E3
Weissenburg, Germany ... 25 F6
Weissenfels, Germany ... 24 D7
Weisswasser, Germany ... 24 D10
Wéitra, Austria ... 26 C7
Weixi, China ... 58 D2
Weixin, China ... 58 D5
Weiyuan, China ... 56 G3
Weiz, Austria ... 26 D8
Weizhou Dao, China ... 58 G7
Wejherowo, Poland ... 44 D5
Wekusko L., Canada ... 105 C9
Welch, U.S.A. ... 108 G5
Weldya, Ethiopia ... 81 E4
Welega □, Ethiopia ... 81 F3
Welkite, Ethiopia ... 81 F4
Welkom, S. Africa ... 88 D4
Welland, Canada ... 102 D4
Welland →, U.K. ... 13 E7
Wellesley Is., Australia ... 94 B2
Wellingborough, U.K. ... 13 E7
Wellington, Australia ... 95 E4
Wellington, Canada ... 110 C7
Wellington, N.Z. ... 91 J5
Wellington, S. Africa ... 88 E2
Wellington, Somst., U.K. ... 13 G4
Wellington, Telford & Wrekin, U.K. ... 13 E5
Wellington, Colo., U.S.A. ... 112 E2
Wellington, Kans., U.S.A. ... 113 G6
Wellington, Nev., U.S.A. ... 116 G7
Wellington, Ohio, U.S.A. ... 110 E2
Wellington, Tex., U.S.A. ... 113 H4
Wellington, I., Chile ... 122 H3
Wellington, L., Australia ... 95 F4
Wells, U.K. ... 13 F5
Wells, Maine, U.S.A. ... 111 C14
Wells, N.Y., U.S.A. ... 111 C10
Wells, Nev., U.S.A. ... 114 F6
Wells, L., Australia ... 93 E3
Wells, Mt., Australia ... 92 C4
Wells Gray Prov. Park, Canada ... 104 C4
Wells-next-the-Sea, U.K. ... 12 E8
Wells River, U.S.A. ... 111 B12
Wellsboro, U.S.A. ... 110 E7
Wellsburg, U.S.A. ... 110 F4
Wellsville, Mo., U.S.A. ... 110 D7
Wellsville, N.Y., U.S.A. ... 110 D7
Wellsville, Ohio, U.S.A. ... 110 F4
Wellsville, Utah, U.S.A. ... 114 F8
Wellton, U.S.A. ... 115 K6
Welmel, Wabi →, Ethiopia ... 81 F5
Welo □, Ethiopia ... 81 E4
Wels, Austria ... 26 C7
Welshpool, U.K. ... 13 E4
Welwyn Garden City, U.K. ... 13 F7

Wem, U.K. ... 12 E5
Wembere →, Tanzania ... 86 C3
Wemindji, Canada ... 102 B4
Wen Xian, China ... 56 G7
Wenatchee, U.S.A. ... 114 C3
Wenchang, China ... 64 C8
Wencheng, China ... 59 D13
Wenchi, Ghana ... 82 D4
Wenchow = Wenzhou, China . 59 D13
Wenchuan, China ... 58 B4
Wenden, China ... 117 M13
Wendeng, China ... 57 F12
Wendesi, Indonesia ... 63 E8
Wendo, Ethiopia ... 81 F4
Wendover, U.S.A. ... 114 F6
Weng'an, China ... 58 D6
Wengcheng, China ... 59 E9
Wengyuan, China ... 59 E10
Wenjiang, China ... 58 B4
Wenling, China ... 59 C13
Wenlock →, Australia ... 94 A3
Wenshan, China ... 58 F5
Wenshang, China ... 56 G9
Wenshui, China ... 56 F7
Wensleydale, U.K. ... 12 C6
Wensu, China ... 60 B3
Wensum →, U.K. ... 12 E8
Wentworth, Australia ... 95 E3
Wentzel L., Canada ... 104 B6
Wenut, Indonesia ... 63 E8
Wenxi, China ... 56 G6
Wenxian, China ... 56 H3
Wenzhou, China ... 59 D13
Weott, U.S.A. ... 114 F2
Wepener, S. Africa ... 88 D4
Werda, Botswana ... 88 D3
Werdau, Germany ... 24 E8
Werder, Germany ... 24 C8
Werdohl, Germany ... 24 D3
Wereilu, Ethiopia ... 81 E4
Weri, Indonesia ... 63 E8
Werneck, Germany ... 25 F6
Wernigerode, Germany ... 24 D6
Werra →, Germany ... 24 D5
Werrimull, Australia ... 95 E3
Werris Creek, Australia ... 95 E5
Wertach →, Germany ... 25 G6
Wertheim, Germany ... 25 F5
Wertingen, Germany ... 25 G6
Wesel, Germany ... 24 D2
Weser →, Germany ... 24 B4
Weser-Ems □, Germany ... 24 C3
Weserbergland, Germany ... 24 C5
Wesiri, Indonesia ... 63 F7
Weslemkoon L., Canada ... 110 A7
Wesleyville, Canada ... 103 C9
Wesleyville, U.S.A. ... 110 D4
Wessel, C., Australia ... 94 A2
Wessel Is., Australia ... 94 A2
Wesselburen, Germany ... 24 A4
Wessington Springs, U.S.A. . 112 C5
West, U.S.A. ... 113 K6
West →, U.S.A. ... 111 D12
West Baines →, Australia ... 92 C4
West Bank □, Asia ... 75 C4
West Bend, U.S.A. ... 108 D1
West Bengal □, India ... 69 H13
West Berkshire □, U.K. ... 13 F6
West Beskids = Západné
  Beskydy, Europe ... 27 B12
West Branch, U.S.A. ... 108 C3
West Branch Susquehanna →,
  U.S.A. ... 111 F8
West Bromwich, U.K. ... 13 E6
West Burra, U.K. ... 14 A7
West Canada Cr. →, U.S.A. . 111 C10
West Cape Howe, Australia . 93 G2
West Chazy, U.S.A. ... 111 B11
West Chester, U.S.A. ... 111 G9
West Columbia, U.S.A. ... 113 L7
West Covina, U.S.A. ... 117 L9
West Des Moines, U.S.A. ... 112 E8
West Dunbartonshire □, U.K. . 14 F4
West End, Bahamas ... 120 A4
West Falkland, Falk. Is. ... 122 J4
West Fargo, U.S.A. ... 112 B6
West Farmington, U.S.A. ... 110 E4
West Fjord = Vestfjorden,
  Norway ... 8 C15
West Fork Trinity →, U.S.A. . 113 J6
West Frankfort, U.S.A. ... 112 G10
West Hartford, U.S.A. ... 111 E12
West Haven, U.S.A. ... 111 E12
West Hazleton, U.S.A. ... 111 F9
West Helena, U.S.A. ... 113 H9
West Hurley, U.S.A. ... 111 E10
West Ice Shelf, Antarctica ... 5 C7
West Indies, Cent. Amer. ... 121 D7
West Jordan, U.S.A. ... 114 F8
West Lorne, Canada ... 110 D3
West Lothian □, U.K. ... 14 F5
West Lunga →, Zambia ... 87 E1
West Memphis, U.S.A. ... 113 H9
West Midlands □, U.K. ... 13 E6
West Milton, U.S.A. ... 110 F5
West Milton, U.S.A. ... 110 E8
West Monroe, U.S.A. ... 113 J8
West Newton, U.S.A. ... 110 F5
West Nicholson, Zimbabwe . 87 G2
West Palm Beach, U.S.A. ... 109 M5
West Plains, U.S.A. ... 113 G9
West Point, N.Y., U.S.A. ... 111 E11
West Point, Nebr., U.S.A. ... 112 E6
West Point, Va., U.S.A. ... 108 G7
West Pt. = Ouest, Pte. de l',
  Canada ... 103 C7
West Pt., Australia ... 95 F2

West Road →, Canada ... 104 C4
West Rutland, U.S.A. ... 111 C11
West Schelde =
  Westerschelde →, Neths. .. 17 C3
West Seneca, U.S.A. ... 110 D6
West Siberian Plain, Russia .. 52 C11
West Sussex □, U.K. ... 13 G7
West-Terschelling, Neths. ... 17 A5
West Valley City, U.S.A. ... 114 F8
West Virginia □, U.S.A. ... 108 F5
West-Vlaanderen □, Belgium . 17 D2
West Walker →, U.S.A. ... 116 G7
West Wyalong, Australia ... 95 E4
West Yellowstone, U.S.A. ... 114 D8
West Yorkshire □, U.K. ... 12 D6
Westall Pt., Australia ... 95 E1
Westbrook, U.S.A. ... 109 D10
Westbury, Australia ... 94 G4
Westby, U.S.A. ... 112 A2
Westend, U.S.A. ... 117 K9
Westerland, Germany ... 9 J13
Westerly, U.S.A. ... 111 E13
Western □, Ghana ... 82 D4
Western □, Kenya ... 86 B3
Western □, S. Leone ... 82 D2
Western □, Zambia ... 87 F1
Western Australia □, Australia 93 E2
Western Cape □, S. Africa ... 88 E3
Western Dvina = Daugava →,
  Latvia ... 9 H21
Western Ghats, India ... 66 N9
Western Isles □, U.K. ... 14 D1
Western Sahara ■, Africa ... 78 D3
Western Samoa = Samoa ■,
  Pac. Oc. ... 91 B13
Westernport, U.S.A. ... 108 F6
Westerschelde →, Neths. ... 17 C3
Westerstede, Germany ... 24 B3
Westerwald, Germany ... 24 E3
Westfield, Mass., U.S.A. ... 111 D12
Westfield, N.Y., U.S.A. ... 110 D5
Westfield, Pa., U.S.A. ... 110 E7
Westhill, U.K. ... 14 D6
Westhope, U.S.A. ... 112 A4
Westland Bight, N.Z. ... 91 K3
Westlock, Canada ... 104 C6
Westmar, Australia ... 95 D4
Westmeath □, Ireland ... 15 C4
Westminster, U.S.A. ... 108 F7
Westmont, U.S.A. ... 110 F6
Westmorland, U.S.A. ... 117 M11
Weston, Oreg., U.S.A. ... 114 D4
Weston, W. Va., U.S.A. ... 108 F5
Weston I., Canada ... 102 B4
Weston-super-Mare, U.K. ... 13 F5
Westover, U.S.A. ... 110 F6
Westport, Canada ... 111 B8
Westport, Ireland ... 15 C2
Westport, N.Z. ... 91 J3
Westport, N.Y., U.S.A. ... 111 B11
Westport, Oreg., U.S.A. ... 116 D3
Westport, Wash., U.S.A. ... 116 D2
Westray, Canada ... 105 C8
Westray, U.K. ... 14 B5
Westree, Canada ... 102 C3
Westville, U.S.A. ... 111 C9
Westwood, U.S.A. ... 114 F3
Wetar, Indonesia ... 63 F7
Wetaskiwin, Canada ... 104 C6
Wete, Tanzania ... 84 F7
Wetherby, U.K. ... 12 D6
Wethersfield, U.S.A. ... 111 E12
Wetteren, Belgium ... 17 D3
Wetzlar, Germany ... 24 E4
Wewoka, U.S.A. ... 113 H6
Wexford, Ireland ... 15 D5
Wexford □, Ireland ... 15 D5
Wexford Harbour, Ireland ... 15 D5
Weyburn, Canada ... 105 D8
Weyer Markt, Austria ... 26 D7
Weyhe, Germany ... 24 C4
Weyib →, Ethiopia ... 81 F5
Weymouth, Canada ... 103 D6
Weymouth, U.K. ... 13 G5
Weymouth, U.S.A. ... 111 D14
Weymouth, C., Australia ... 94 A3
Wha Ti, Canada ... 100 B8
Whakatane, N.Z. ... 91 G6
Whale →, Canada ... 103 A6
Whale Cove, Canada ... 105 A10
Whales, B. of, Antarctica ... 5 D12
Whalsay, U.K. ... 14 A8
Whangamomona, N.Z. ... 91 H5
Whangarei, N.Z. ... 91 F5
Whangarei Harb., N.Z. ... 91 F5
Wharfe →, U.K. ... 12 D6
Wharfedale, U.K. ... 12 C5
Wharton, N.J., U.S.A. ... 111 F10
Wharton, Pa., U.S.A. ... 110 E6
Wharton, Tex., U.S.A. ... 113 L6
Wheatland, Calif., U.S.A. ... 116 F5
Wheatland, Wyo., U.S.A. ... 112 D2
Wheatley, Canada ... 110 D2
Wheaton, Md., U.S.A. ... 108 F7
Wheaton, Minn., U.S.A. ... 112 C6
Wheelbarrow Pk., U.S.A. ... 116 H10
Wheeler, Oreg., U.S.A. ... 114 D2
Wheeler, Tex., U.S.A. ... 113 H4
Wheeler →, Canada ... 103 A6
Wheeler L., U.S.A. ... 109 H2
Wheeler Pk., N. Mex., U.S.A. 115 H11
Wheeler Pk., Nev., U.S.A. ... 115 G6
Wheeler Ridge, U.S.A. ... 117 L8
Wheeling, U.S.A. ... 110 F4
Whernside, U.K. ... 12 C5
Whiskey Jack L., Canada ... 105 B8
Whistleduck Cr. →, Australia 94 C2

Whistler, Canada ... 104 C4
Whitby, Canada ... 110 C6
Whitby, U.K. ... 12 C7
White →, Ark., U.S.A. ... 113 J9
White →, Ind., U.S.A. ... 108 F2
White →, S. Dak., U.S.A. ... 112 D5
White →, Tex., U.S.A. ... 113 J4
White →, Utah, U.S.A. ... 114 F9
White →, Vt., U.S.A. ... 111 C12
White →, Wash., U.S.A. ... 116 C4
White, L., Australia ... 92 D4
White B., Canada ... 103 C8
White Bird, U.S.A. ... 114 D5
White Butte, U.S.A. ... 112 B3
White City, U.S.A. ... 114 E2
White Cliffs, Australia ... 95 E3
White Hall, U.S.A. ... 112 F9
White Haven, U.S.A. ... 111 E9
White Horse, Vale of, U.K. ... 13 F6
White I., N.Z. ... 91 G6
White L., Canada ... 111 A8
White L., U.S.A. ... 113 L8
White Mountain Peak, U.S.A. 115 G4
White Mts., Calif., U.S.A. ... 116 H8
White Mts., N.H., U.S.A. ... 111 B13
White Nile = Nîl el Abyad →,
  Sudan ... 81 D3
White Nile Dam = Khazzân
  Jabal al Awliyâ, Sudan ... 81 D3
White Otter L., Canada ... 102 C1
White Pass, U.S.A. ... 116 D5
White Plains, U.S.A. ... 111 E11
White River, S. Africa ... 89 D5
White River, U.S.A. ... 112 D4
White Rock, Canada ... 116 A4
White Russia = Belarus ■,
  Europe ... 46 F4
White Sea = Beloye More,
  Russia ... 50 C4
White Sulphur Springs, Mont.,
  U.S.A. ... 114 C8
White Sulphur Springs, W. Va.,
  U.S.A. ... 108 G5
White Swan, U.S.A. ... 116 D6
White Volta →, Ghana ... 83 D4
Whitecliffs, N.Z. ... 91 K3
Whitecourt, Canada ... 104 C5
Whiteface Mt., U.S.A. ... 111 B11
Whitefield, U.S.A. ... 111 B13
Whitefish, U.S.A. ... 114 B6
Whitefish L., Canada ... 105 A7
Whitefish Point, U.S.A. ... 108 B3
Whitegull, L., Canada ... 103 A7
Whitehall, Mich., U.S.A. ... 108 D2
Whitehall, Mont., U.S.A. ... 114 D7
Whitehall, N.Y., U.S.A. ... 111 C11
Whitehall, Wis., U.S.A. ... 112 C9
Whitehaven, U.K. ... 12 C4
Whitehorse, Canada ... 104 A1
Whitemark, Australia ... 94 G4
Whiteplains, Liberia ... 82 D2
Whiteriver, U.S.A. ... 115 K9
Whitesand →, Canada ... 104 A5
Whitesands, S. Africa ... 88 E3
Whitesboro, N.Y., U.S.A. ... 111 C9
Whitesboro, Tex., U.S.A. ... 113 J6
Whiteshell Prov. Park, Canada . 105 D9
Whitesville, U.S.A. ... 110 D7
Whiteville, U.S.A. ... 109 H6
Whitewater, U.S.A. ... 108 D1
Whitewater Baldy, U.S.A. ... 115 K9
Whitewater L., Canada ... 102 B2
Whitewood, Australia ... 94 C3
Whitewood, Canada ... 105 C8
Whithorn, U.K. ... 14 G4
Whitianga, N.Z. ... 91 G5
Whitman, U.S.A. ... 111 D14
Whitney, Canada ... 102 C4
Whitney, Mt., U.S.A. ... 115 J8
Whitney Point, U.S.A. ... 111 D9
Whitstable, U.K. ... 13 F9
Whitsunday I., Australia ... 94 C4
Whittier, U.S.A. ... 117 M8
Whittlesea, Australia ... 95 F4
Wholdaia L., Canada ... 105 A8
Whyalla, Australia ... 95 E2
Wiarton, Canada ... 102 D3
Wiawso, Ghana ... 82 D4
Wiay, U.K. ... 14 D1
Wiązów, Poland ... 45 H4
Wibaux, U.S.A. ... 112 B2
Wichian Buri, Thailand ... 64 E3
Wichita, U.S.A. ... 113 G6
Wichita Falls, U.S.A. ... 113 J5
Wick, U.K. ... 14 C5
Wicked Pt., Canada ... 110 C7
Wickenburg, U.S.A. ... 115 K7
Wickepin, Australia ... 93 F2
Wickham, Australia ... 92 D2
Wickham, C., Australia ... 94 F3
Wickliffe, U.S.A. ... 110 E3
Wicklow, Ireland ... 15 D5
Wicklow □, Ireland ... 15 D5
Wicklow Hd., Ireland ... 15 D6
Wicklow Mts., Ireland ... 15 C5
Widawa →, Poland ... 45 G5
Widawka →, Poland ... 45 G6
Widgeegoara Cr. →, Australia . 95 D4
Widgiemooltha, Australia ... 93 F3
Widnes, U.K. ... 12 D5
Więcbork, Poland ... 44 E4
Wiehl, Germany ... 24 E3
Wiek, Germany ... 24 A9
Wielbark, Poland ... 44 E7
Wieleń, Poland ... 45 F3
Wielichowo, Poland ... 45 F3

Wieliczka, Poland ... 45 J7
Wielkopolskie □, Poland ... 45 F4
Wieluń, Poland ... 45 G5
Wien, Austria ... 27 C9
Wiener Neustadt, Austria ... 27 D9
Wieprz →, Poland ... 45 G8
Wieprza →, Poland ... 44 D3
Wieruszów, Poland ... 45 G5
Wiesbaden, Germany ... 25 E4
Wiesental, Germany ... 25 F4
Wiesloch, Germany ... 25 F4
Wieżyca, Poland ... 44 D5
Wigan, U.K. ... 12 D5
Wiggins, Colo., U.S.A. ... 112 E2
Wiggins, Miss., U.S.A. ... 113 K10
Wight, I. of □, U.K. ... 13 G6
Wigry, Jezioro, Poland ... 44 D10
Wigston, U.K. ... 13 E6
Wigton, U.K. ... 12 C4
Wigtown, U.K. ... 14 G4
Wigtown B., U.K. ... 14 G4
Wil, Switz. ... 25 H5
Wilber, U.S.A. ... 112 E6
Wilberforce, Canada ... 110 A6
Wilberforce, C., Australia ... 94 A2
Wilburton, U.S.A. ... 113 H7
Wilcannia, Australia ... 95 E3
Wilcox, U.S.A. ... 110 E6
Wildbad, Germany ... 25 G4
Wildeshausen, Germany ... 24 C4
Wildon, Austria ... 26 E8
Wildrose, U.S.A. ... 117 J9
Wildspitze, Austria ... 26 E3
Wilga →, Poland ... 45 G8
Wilge →, S. Africa ... 89 D4
Wilhelm II Coast, Antarctica . 5 C7
Wilhelmsburg, Austria ... 26 C8
Wilhelmshaven, Germany ... 24 B4
Wilhelmstal, Namibia ... 88 C2
Wilkes-Barre, U.S.A. ... 111 E9
Wilkie, Canada ... 105 C7
Wilkinsburg, U.S.A. ... 110 F5
Wilkinson Lakes, Australia ... 93 E5
Willandra Creek →, Australia . 95 E4
Willapa B., U.S.A. ... 114 C2
Willapa Hills, U.S.A. ... 116 D3
Willard, U.S.A. ... 110 D8
Willard, Ohio, U.S.A. ... 110 E2
Willcox, U.S.A. ... 115 K9
Willemstad, Neth. Ant. ... 121 D6
Willet, U.S.A. ... 111 D9
William →, Canada ... 105 B7
William 'Bill' Dannely Res.,
  U.S.A. ... 109 J2
William Creek, Australia ... 95 D2
Williams, Australia ... 93 F2
Williams, Ariz., U.S.A. ... 115 J7
Williams, Calif., U.S.A. ... 116 F4
Williams Harbour, Canada ... 103 B8
Williams Lake, Canada ... 104 C4
Williamsburg, Ky., U.S.A. ... 109 G3
Williamsburg, Pa., U.S.A. ... 110 F6
Williamsburg, Va., U.S.A. ... 108 G7
Williamson, N.Y., U.S.A. ... 110 C7
Williamson, W. Va., U.S.A. ... 108 G4
Williamsport, U.S.A. ... 110 E7
Williamston, U.S.A. ... 109 H7
Williamstown, Australia ... 95 F3
Williamstown, Ky., U.S.A. ... 108 F3
Williamstown, Mass., U.S.A. . 111 D11
Williamstown, N.Y., U.S.A. ... 111 C9
Willimantic, U.S.A. ... 111 E12
Willingboro, U.S.A. ... 108 E8
Willis Group, Australia ... 94 B5
Williston, S. Africa ... 88 E3
Williston, Fla., U.S.A. ... 109 L4
Williston, N. Dak., U.S.A. ... 112 A3
Williston L., Canada ... 104 B4
Willits, U.S.A. ... 114 G2
Willmar, U.S.A. ... 112 C7
Willoughby, U.S.A. ... 110 E3
Willow Bunch, Canada ... 105 D7
Willow L., Canada ... 104 A5
Willow Wall, The, China ... 57 C12
Willowick, U.S.A. ... 110 E3
Willowlake →, Canada ... 104 A4
Willowmore, S. Africa ... 88 E3
Willows, U.S.A. ... 116 F4
Willowvale = Gatyana, S. Africa 89 E4
Wills, L., Australia ... 92 D4
Wills Cr. →, Australia ... 94 C3
Willsboro, U.S.A. ... 111 B11
Willunga, Australia ... 95 F2
Wilmette, U.S.A. ... 108 D2
Wilmington, Australia ... 95 E2
Wilmington, Del., U.S.A. ... 108 F8
Wilmington, N.C., U.S.A. ... 109 H7
Wilmington, Ohio, U.S.A. ... 108 F4
Wilmington, Vt., U.S.A. ... 111 D12
Wilmslow, U.K. ... 12 D5
Wilpena Cr. →, Australia ... 95 E2
Wilsall, U.S.A. ... 114 D8
Wilson, N.C., U.S.A. ... 109 H7
Wilson, N.Y., U.S.A. ... 110 C6
Wilson, Pa., U.S.A. ... 111 F9
Wilson →, Australia ... 92 C4
Wilson Bluff, Australia ... 93 F4
Wilson Inlet, Australia ... 93 G2
Wilsons Promontory, Australia 95 F4
Wilster, Germany ... 24 B5
Wilton, U.S.A. ... 112 B4
Wilton →, Australia ... 94 A1
Wiltshire □, U.K. ... 13 F6
Wiltz, Lux. ... 17 E5
Wiluna, Australia ... 93 E3

Wimborne Minster, U.K. ... 13 G6
Wimereux, France ... 19 B8
Wimmera →, Australia ... 95 F3
Winam G., Kenya ... 86 C3
Winburg, S. Africa ... 88 D4
Winchendon, U.S.A. ... 111 D12
Winchester, U.K. ... 13 F6
Winchester, Conn., U.S.A. ... 111 E11
Winchester, Idaho, U.S.A. ... 114 C5
Winchester, Ind., U.S.A. ... 108 E3
Winchester, Ky., U.S.A. ... 108 G3
Winchester, N.H., U.S.A. ... 111 D12
Winchester, Nev., U.S.A. ... 117 J11
Winchester, Tenn., U.S.A. ... 109 H2
Winchester, Va., U.S.A. ... 108 F6
Wind →, U.S.A. ... 114 E9
Wind River Range, U.S.A. ... 114 E9
Windau = Ventspils, Latvia . 9 H19
Windber, U.S.A. ... 110 F6
Winder, U.S.A. ... 109 J4
Windermere, U.K. ... 12 C5
Windhoek, Namibia ... 88 C2
Windischgarsten, Austria ... 26 D7
Windom, U.S.A. ... 112 D7
Windorah, Australia ... 94 D3
Window Rock, U.S.A. ... 115 J9
Windrush →, U.K. ... 13 F6
Windsor, Australia ... 95 E5
Windsor, N.S., Canada ... 103 D7
Windsor, Ont., Canada ... 102 D3
Windsor, U.K. ... 13 F7
Windsor, Colo., U.S.A. ... 112 E2
Windsor, Conn., U.S.A. ... 111 E12
Windsor, Mo., U.S.A. ... 112 F8
Windsor, N.Y., U.S.A. ... 111 D9
Windsor, Vt., U.S.A. ... 111 C12
Windsor & Maidenhead □, U.K. 13 F7
Windsorton, S. Africa ... 88 D3
Windward Is., W. Indies ... 121 D7
Windward Passage = Vientos,
  Paso de los, Caribbean ... 121 C5
Winefred L., Canada ... 105 B6
Winejok, Sudan ... 81 F2
Winfield, U.S.A. ... 113 G6
Wingate Mts., U.S.A. ... 92 B5
Wingham, Australia ... 95 E5
Wingham, Canada ... 102 D3
Winisk, Canada ... 102 A2
Winisk →, Canada ... 102 A2
Winisk L., Canada ... 102 B2
Wink, U.S.A. ... 113 K3
Winkler, Canada ... 105 D9
Winklern, Austria ... 26 E5
Winlock, U.S.A. ... 116 D4
Winneba, Ghana ... 83 D4
Winnebago, L., U.S.A. ... 108 D1
Winnecke Cr. →, Australia ... 92 C5
Winnemucca, U.S.A. ... 114 F5
Winnemucca L., U.S.A. ... 114 F4
Winnett, U.S.A. ... 114 C9
Winnfield, U.S.A. ... 113 K8
Winnibigoshish, L., U.S.A. ... 112 B7
Winnipeg, Canada ... 105 D9
Winnipeg →, Canada ... 105 C9
Winnipeg, L., Canada ... 105 C9
Winnipeg Beach, Canada ... 105 C9
Winnipegosis, Canada ... 105 C9
Winnipegosis L., Canada ... 105 C9
Winnipesaukee, L., U.S.A. ... 111 C13
Winnsboro, La., U.S.A. ... 113 J9
Winnsboro, S.C., U.S.A. ... 109 H5
Winnsboro, Tex., U.S.A. ... 113 J7
Winokapau, L., Canada ... 103 B7
Winona, Minn., U.S.A. ... 112 C9
Winona, Miss., U.S.A. ... 113 J10
Winooski, U.S.A. ... 111 B11
Winooski →, U.S.A. ... 111 B11
Winschoten, Neths. ... 17 A7
Winsen, Germany ... 24 B6
Winsford, U.K. ... 12 D5
Winslow, Ariz., U.S.A. ... 115 J8
Winslow, Wash., U.S.A. ... 116 C4
Winsted, U.S.A. ... 111 E11
Winston-Salem, U.S.A. ... 109 G5
Winter Garden, U.S.A. ... 109 L5
Winter Haven, U.S.A. ... 109 M5
Winter Park, U.S.A. ... 109 L5
Winterberg, Germany ... 24 D4
Winterhaven, U.S.A. ... 117 N12
Winters, U.S.A. ... 116 G5
Wintersville, U.S.A. ... 110 F4
Winterswijk, Neths. ... 17 C6
Winterthur, Switz. ... 25 H4
Winthrop, U.S.A. ... 114 B3
Winton, Australia ... 94 C3
Winton, N.Z. ... 91 M2
Wipper →, Germany ... 24 D7
Wirrulla, Australia ... 95 E1
Wisbech, U.K. ... 13 E8
Wisconsin □, U.S.A. ... 112 C10
Wisconsin →, U.S.A. ... 112 D9
Wisconsin Rapids, U.S.A. ... 112 C10
Wisdom, U.S.A. ... 114 D7
Wishaw, U.K. ... 14 F5
Wishek, U.S.A. ... 112 B5
Wisła, Poland ... 45 J5
Wisła →, Poland ... 44 D5
Wisłok →, Poland ... 45 H8
Wisłoka →, Poland ... 45 H8
Wismar, Germany ... 24 B7
Wissant, France ... 19 B8
Wissembourg, France ... 19 C14
Wisznice, Poland ... 45 G10
Witbank, S. Africa ... 89 D4
Witdraai, S. Africa ... 88 D3

Witham, *U.K.* 13 F8
Witham ➤, *U.K.* 12 E7
Withernsea, *U.K.* 12 D8
Witkowo, *Poland* 45 F4
Witney, *U.K.* 13 F6
Witnica, *Poland* 45 F1
Witnossob ➤, *Namibia* 88 D3
Wittdün, *Germany* 24 A4
Witten, *Germany* 24 D3
Wittenberge, *Germany* 24 B7
Wittenburg, *Germany* 24 B7
Wittenheim, *France* 19 E14
Wittenoom, *Australia* 92 D2
Wittingen, *Germany* 24 C6
Wittlich, *Germany* 25 F2
Wittmund, *Germany* 24 B3
Wittow, *Germany* 24 A9
Wittstock, *Germany* 24 B8
Witvlei, *Namibia* 88 C2
Witzenhausen, *Germany* 24 D5
Wkra ➤, *Poland* 45 F7
Władysławowo, *Poland* 44 D5
Wleń, *Poland* 45 G2
Wlingi, *Indonesia* 63 H15
Włocławek, *Poland* 45 F6
Włodawa, *Poland* 45 G10
Włoszczowa, *Poland* 45 H6
Woburn, *U.S.A.* 111 D13
Wodian, *China* 56 H7
Wodonga = Albury-Wodonga,
  Australia 95 F4
Wodzisław Śląski, *Poland* 45 H5
Wœrth, *France* 19 D14
Woinbogoin, *China* 58 A2
Woippy, *France* 19 C13
Wojcieszow, *Poland* 45 H2
Wokam, *Indonesia* 63 F8
Woking, *U.K.* 13 F7
Wokingham □, *U.K.* 13 F7
Wolbrom, *Poland* 45 H6
Wołczyn, *Poland* 45 G5
Woldegk, *Germany* 24 B9
Wolf ➤, *Canada* 104 A2
Wolf Creek, *U.S.A.* 114 C7
Wolf L., *Canada* 104 A2
Wolf Point, *U.S.A.* 112 A2
Wolfe I., *Canada* 102 D4
Wolfeboro, *U.S.A.* 111 C13
Wolfen, *Germany* 24 D8
Wolfenbüttel, *Germany* 24 C6
Wolfratshausen, *Germany* 25 H7
Wolfsberg, *Austria* 26 E7
Wolfsburg, *Germany* 24 C6
Wolgast, *Germany* 24 A9
Wolhusen, *Switz.* 25 H4
Wolin, *Poland* 44 E1
Wollaston, Is., *Chile* 128 H3
Wollaston L., *Canada* 105 B8
Wollaston Lake, *Canada* 105 B8
Wollaston Pen., *Canada* 100 B8
Wollongong, *Australia* 95 E5
Wolmaransstad, *S. Africa* 88 D4
Wołomin, *Poland* 45 F8
Wołów, *Poland* 45 G3
Wolseley, *S. Africa* 88 E2
Wolsey, *U.S.A.* 112 C5
Wolstenholme, C., *Canada* ... 98 C12
Wolsztyn, *Poland* 45 F3
Wolvega, *Neths.* 17 B6
Wolverhampton, *U.K.* 13 E5
Wondai, *Australia* 95 D5
Wongalarroo L., *Australia* 95 E3
Wongan Hills, *Australia* 93 F2
Wŏnju, *S. Korea* 57 F14
Wonosari, *Indonesia* 63 G14
Wonosobo, *Indonesia* 63 G13
Wonowon, *Canada* 104 B4
Wŏnsan, *N. Korea* 57 E14
Wonthaggi, *Australia* 95 F4
Wood Buffalo Nat. Park,
  Canada 104 B6
Wood Is., *Australia* 92 C3
Wood L., *Canada* 105 B8
Woodah I., *Australia* 94 A2
Woodbourne, *U.S.A.* 111 E10
Woodbridge, *Canada* 110 C5
Woodbridge, *U.K.* 13 E9
Woodburn, *U.S.A.* 114 D2
Woodenbong, *Australia* 95 D5
Woodend, *Australia* 95 F3
Woodford, *Australia* 95 D5
Woodfords, *U.S.A.* 116 G7
Woodlake, *U.S.A.* 116 J7
Woodland, *Calif., U.S.A.* 116 G5
Woodland, *Maine, U.S.A.* ... 109 C12
Woodland, *Pa., U.S.A.* 110 F6
Woodland, *Wash., U.S.A.* ... 116 E4
Woodland Caribou Prov. Park,
  Canada 105 C10
Woodridge, *Canada* 105 D9
Woodroffe, Mt., *Australia* 93 E5
Woods, L., *Australia* 94 B1
Woods, L. of the, *Canada* 105 D10
Woodstock, *Australia* 94 B4
Woodstock, *N.B., Canada* 103 C6
Woodstock, *Ont., Canada* ... 102 D3
Woodstock, *U.K.* 13 F6
Woodstock, *Ill., U.S.A.* 112 D10
Woodstock, *Vt., U.S.A.* 111 C12
Woodsville, *U.S.A.* 111 B13
Woodville, *N.Z.* 91 J5
Woodville, *Miss., U.S.A.* 113 K9
Woodville, *Tex., U.S.A.* 113 K7
Woodward, *U.S.A.* 113 G5
Woody, *U.S.A.* 117 K8
Woody ➤, *Canada* 105 C8

Woolamai, C., *Australia* 95 F4
Wooler, *U.K.* 12 B5
Woolgoolga, *Australia* 95 E5
Woomera, *Australia* 95 E2
Woonsocket, *R.I., U.S.A.* 111 E13
Woonsocket, *S. Dak., U.S.A.* . 112 C5
Wooramel ➤, *Australia* 93 E1
Wooramel Roadhouse, *Australia* 93 E1
Wooster, *U.S.A.* 110 F3
Worcester, *S. Africa* 88 E2
Worcester, *U.K.* 13 E5
Worcester, *Mass., U.S.A.* ... 111 D13
Worcester, *N.Y., U.S.A.* 111 D10
Worcestershire □, *U.K.* 13 E5
Wörgl, *Austria* 26 D5
Workington, *U.K.* 12 C4
Worksop, *U.K.* 12 D6
Workum, *Neths.* 17 B5
Worland, *U.S.A.* 114 D10
Wormhout, *France* 19 B9
Worms, *Germany* 25 F4
Worsley, *Canada* 104 B5
Wörth, *Germany* 25 F8
Wortham, *U.S.A.* 113 K6
Wörther See, *Austria* 26 E7
Worthing, *U.K.* 13 G7
Worthington, *Minn., U.S.A.* . 112 D7
Worthington, *Pa., U.S.A.* ... 110 F5
Wosi, *Indonesia* 63 E7
Wou-han = Wuhan, *China* ... 59 B10
Wousi = Wuxi, *China* 59 B13
Wowoni, *Indonesia* 63 E6
Wrangel I. = Vrangelya, Ostrov,
  Russia 51 B19
Wrangell, *U.S.A.* 104 B2
Wrangell Mts., *U.S.A.* 100 B5
Wrath, C., *U.K.* 14 C3
Wray, *U.S.A.* 112 E3
Wrekin, The, *U.K.* 13 E5
Wrens, *U.S.A.* 109 J4
Wrexham, *U.K.* 12 D4
Wrexham □, *U.K.* 12 D4
Wriezen, *Germany* 24 C10
Wright = Paranas, *Phil.* 61 F6
Wright, *U.S.A.* 112 D2
Wright Pt., *Canada* 110 C3
Wrightson Mt., *U.S.A.* 115 L8
Wrightwood, *U.S.A.* 117 L9
Wrigley, *Canada* 100 B7
Wrocław, *Poland* 45 G4
Wronki, *Poland* 45 F3
Września, *Poland* 45 F4
Wschowa, *Poland* 45 G3
Wu Jiang ➤, *China* 58 C6
Wu'an, *China* 56 F8
Wubin, *Australia* 93 F2
Wubu, *China* 56 F6
Wuchang, *China* 57 B14
Wucheng, *China* 56 F9
Wuchuan, *Guangdong, China* . 59 G8
Wuchuan, *Guizhou, China* ... 58 C7
Wuchuan, *Nei Monggol Zizhiqu,*
  China 56 D6
Wudi, *China* 57 F9
Wuding, *China* 58 E4
Wuding He ➤, *China* 56 F6
Wudinna, *Australia* 95 E2
Wudu, *China* 56 H3
Wufeng, *China* 59 B8
Wugang, *China* 59 D8
Wugong Shan, *China* 59 D9
Wuhan, *China* 59 B10
Wuhe, *China* 57 H9
Wuhsi = Wuxi, *China* 59 B13
Wuhu, *China* 59 B12
Wujiang, *China* 59 B13
Wukari, *Nigeria* 83 D6
Wulajie, *China* 57 B14
Wulanbulang, *China* 56 D6
Wular L., *India* 69 B6
Wulehe, *Ghana* 83 D5
Wulian, *China* 57 G10
Wuliang Shan, *China* 58 E3
Wuliaru, *Indonesia* 63 F8
Wuling Shan, *China* 58 C7
Wulong, *China* 58 C6
Wulumuchi = Ürümqi, *China* . 50 B3
Wum, *Cameroon* 83 D7
Wuming, *China* 58 F7
Wun Rog, *Sudan* 81 F2
Wundowie, *Australia* 93 F2
Wuning, *China* 59 C10
Wunnummin L., *Canada* 102 B2
Wunsiedel, *Germany* 25 E8
Wunstorf, *Germany* 24 C5
Wuntho, *Burma* 67 H19
Wuping, *China* 59 E11
Wuppertal, *Germany* 24 D3
Wuppertal, *S. Africa* 88 E2
Wuqing, *China* 57 E9
Wurtsboro, *U.S.A.* 111 E10
Würzburg, *Germany* 25 F5
Wurzen, *Germany* 24 D8
Wushan, *China* 56 G3
Wushishi, *Nigeria* 83 D6
Wusuli Jiang = Ussuri ➤, *Asia* 54 A7
Wutach ➤, *Germany* 25 H4
Wutai, *China* 56 E7
Wuting = Huimin, *China* 57 F9
Wutong, *China* 59 E8
Wutonghaolai, *China* 57 C11
Wutongqiao, *China* 58 C4
Wuwei, *Anhui, China* 59 B11
Wuwei, *Gansu, China* 60 C5
Wuxi, *Jiangsu, China* 59 B13
Wuxi, *Sichuan, China* 58 B7
Wuxiang, *China* 56 F7

Wuxuan, *China* 58 F7
Wuxue, *China* 59 C10
Wuyang, *China* 56 H7
Wuyi, *Hebei, China* 56 F8
Wuyi, *Zhejiang, China* 59 C12
Wuyi Shan, *China* 59 D11
Wuyishan, *China* 59 D12
Wuyo, *Nigeria* 83 C7
Wuyuan, *Jiangxi, China* 59 C11
Wuyuan, *Nei Monggol Zizhiqu,*
  China 56 D5
Wuzhai, *China* 56 E6
Wuzhi Shan, *China* 64 C7
Wuzhong, *China* 56 E4
Wuzhou, *China* 59 F8
Wyaaba Cr. ➤, *Australia* 94 B3
Wyalkatchem, *Australia* 93 F2
Wyalusing, *U.S.A.* 111 E8
Wyandotte, *U.S.A.* 108 D4
Wyandra, *Australia* 95 D4
Wyangala, L., *Australia* 95 E4
Wyara, L., *Australia* 95 D3
Wycheproof, *Australia* 95 F3
Wye ➤, *U.K.* 13 F5
Wyemandoo, *Australia* 93 E2
Wyk, *Germany* 24 A4
Wymondham, *U.K.* 13 E9
Wymore, *U.S.A.* 112 E6
Wyndham, *Australia* 92 C4
Wyndham, *N.Z.* 91 M2
Wynne, *U.S.A.* 113 H9
Wynyard, *Australia* 94 G4
Wynyard, *Canada* 105 C8
Wyola L., *Australia* 93 E5
Wyoming, *Canada* 110 D2
Wyoming □, *U.S.A.* 114 E10
Wyomissing, *U.S.A.* 111 F9
Wyong, *Australia* 95 E5
Wyrzysk, *Poland* 45 E4
Wyśmierzyce, *Poland* 45 G7
Wysoka, *Poland* 45 E4
Wysokie, *Poland* 45 H9
Wysokie Mazowieckie, *Poland* . 45 F9
Wyszków, *Poland* 45 F8
Wyszogród, *Poland* 45 F7
Wytheville, *U.S.A.* 108 G5
Wyżyna Małopolska, *Poland* . 45 H7

X

Xaçmaz, *Azerbaijan* 49 K9
Xai-Xai, *Mozam.* 89 D5
Xainza, *China* 60 C3
Xangongo, *Angola* 88 B2
Xankändi, *Azerbaijan* 70 B5
Xanlar, *Azerbaijan* 49 K8
Xanten, *Germany* 24 D2
Xánthi, *Greece* 41 E8
Xánthi □, *Greece* 41 E8
Xanthos, *Turkey* 39 E11
Xanxerê, *Brazil* 127 B5
Xapuri, *Brazil* 124 F5
Xar Moron He ➤, *China* 57 C11
Xarrë, *Albania* 40 G4
Xau, L., *Botswana* 88 C3
Xátiva, *Spain* 33 G4
Xavantina, *Brazil* 127 A5
Xenia, *U.S.A.* 108 F4
Xeropotamos ➤, *Cyprus* 36 E11
Xertigny, *France* 19 D13
Xhora, *S. Africa* 89 E4
Xhumo, *Botswana* 88 C3
Xi Jiang ➤, *China* 59 F9
Xi Xian, *Henan, China* 59 A10
Xi Xian, *Shanxi, China* 56 F6
Xia Xian, *China* 56 G6
Xiachengzi, *China* 57 B16
Xiachuan Dao, *China* 59 G9
Xiaguan, *China* 60 D5
Xiajiang, *China* 59 D10
Xiajin, *China* 56 F9
Xiamen, *China* 59 E12
Xi'an, *China* 56 G5
Xian Xian, *China* 56 E9
Xianfeng, *China* 58 C7
Xiang Jiang ➤, *China* 59 C9
Xiangcheng, *Henan, China* ... 56 H8
Xiangcheng, *Henan, China* ... 56 H7
Xiangcheng, *Sichuan, China* . 58 C2
Xiangdu, *China* 58 F6
Xiangfan, *China* 59 A9
Xianggang = Hong Kong □,
  China 59 F10
Xianghuang Qi, *China* 56 C7
Xiangning, *China* 56 G6
Xiangquan, *China* 56 F7
Xiangquan He = Sutlej ➤,
  Pakistan 68 E4
Xiangshan, *China* 59 C13
Xiangshui, *China* 57 G10
Xiangtan, *China* 59 D9
Xiangxiang, *China* 59 D9
Xiangyun, *China* 58 E3
Xiangzhou, *China* 58 F7
Xianju, *China* 59 C13
Xianning, *China* 59 C10
Xianshui He ➤, *China* 58 B3
Xiantao, *China* 59 B9
Xianyang, *China* 56 G5
Xianyou, *China* 59 E12

Xiaojin, *China* 58 B4
Xiaolan, *China* 59 F9
Xiaoshan, *China* 59 B13
Xiaoyi, *China* 56 F6
Xiapu, *China* 59 D12
Xiawa, *China* 57 C11
Xiayi, *China* 56 G9
Xichang, *China* 58 D4
Xichong, *China* 58 B5
Xichou, *China* 58 E5
Xichuan, *China* 56 H6
Xide, *China* 58 C4
Xiemahe, *China* 59 B8
Xieng Khouang, *Laos* 64 C4
Xifei He ➤, *China* 56 H9
Xifeng, *Gansu, China* 56 G4
Xifeng, *Guizhou, China* 58 D6
Xifeng, *Liaoning, China* 57 C13
Xifengzhen = Xifeng, *China* .. 56 G4
Xigazê, *China* 60 D3
Xihe, *China* 56 G3
Xihua, *China* 56 H8
Xilaganí, *Greece* 41 F9
Xiliao He ➤, *China* 57 C12
Xilin, *China* 58 E5
Xilókastron, *Greece* 38 C4
Xime, *Guinea-Biss.* 82 C2
Xin Jiang ➤, *China* 59 C11
Xin Xian = Xinzhou, *China* .. 56 E7
Xinavane, *Mozam.* 89 D5
Xinbin, *China* 57 D13
Xincai, *China* 59 A10
Xinchang, *China* 59 C13
Xincheng, *Guangxi Zhuangzu,*
  China 58 E7
Xincheng, *Jiangxi, China* 59 D10
Xindu, *China* 58 B5
Xinfeng, *Guangdong, China* .. 59 E10
Xinfeng, *Jiangxi, China* 59 D11
Xinfeng, *Jiangxi, China* 59 E10
Xinfengjiang Skuiku, *China* .. 59 F10
Xing Xian, *China* 56 E6
Xing'an, *Guangxi Zhuangzu,*
  China 59 E8
Xingan, *Jiangxi, China* 59 D10
Xingcheng, *China* 57 D11
Xingguo, *China* 59 D10
Xinghe, *China* 56 D7
Xinghua, *China* 57 H10
Xinghua Wan, *China* 59 E12
Xinglong, *China* 57 D9
Xingning, *China* 59 E10
Xingping, *China* 56 G5
Xingren, *China* 58 E5
Xingshan, *China* 59 B8
Xingtai, *China* 56 F8
Xingu ➤, *Brazil* 122 D5
Xingwen, *China* 58 C5
Xingyang, *China* 56 G7
Xinhe, *China* 56 F8
Xinhua, *China* 59 D8
Xinhuang, *China* 58 D7
Xinhui, *China* 59 F9
Xining, *China* 60 C5
Xinjian, *China* 59 C10
Xinjiang, *China* 56 G6
Xinjiang Uygur Zizhiqu □,
  China 60 B3
Xinjie, *China* 58 D3
Xinjin = Pulandian, *China* ... 57 E11
Xinjin, *China* 58 B4
Xinkai He ➤, *China* 57 C12
Xinle, *China* 56 E8
Xinlitun, *China* 57 D12
Xinlong, *China* 58 B3
Xinmin, *China* 57 D12
Xinning, *China* 59 D8
Xinping, *China* 58 E3
Xinshao, *China* 59 D8
Xintai, *China* 57 G9
Xintian, *China* 59 E9
Xinxian, *China* 59 B10
Xinxiang, *China* 56 G7
Xinxing, *China* 59 F9
Xinyang, *China* 59 A10
Xinye, *China* 59 A9
Xinyi, *China* 59 F8
Xinyu, *China* 59 D10
Xinzhan, *China* 57 C14
Xinzheng, *China* 56 G7
Xinzhou, *Hubei, China* 59 B10
Xinzhou, *Shanxi, China* 56 E7
Xinzo de Limia, *Spain* 34 C3
Xiongyuecheng, *China* 57 D12
Xiping, *Henan, China* 56 H8
Xiping, *Henan, China* 56 H6
Xiping, *Zhejiang, China* 59 C12
Xique-Xique, *Brazil* 125 F10
Xisha Qundao = Paracel Is.,
  S. China Sea 62 A4
Xishui, *Guizhou, China* 58 C6
Xishui, *Hubei, China* 59 B10
Xitole, *Guinea-Biss.* 82 C2
Xiu Shui ➤, *China* 59 C10
Xiuning, *China* 59 C12
Xiuren, *China* 59 E8
Xiushan, *China* 58 C7
Xiushui, *China* 59 C10
Xiuwen, *China* 58 D6
Xiuyan, *China* 57 D12
Xixabangma Feng, *China* 67 E14
Xixia, *China* 56 H6
Xixiang, *China* 56 H4
Xiyang, *China* 56 F7
Xizang Zizhiqu □, *China* 60 C3
Xlendi, *Malta* 36 C1

Xu Jiang ➤, *China* 59 D11
Xuan Loc, *Vietnam* 65 G6
Xuan'en, *China* 58 C7
Xuanhan, *China* 58 B6
Xuanhua, *China* 56 D8
Xuanwei, *China* 58 C5
Xuanzhou, *China* 59 B12
Xuchang, *China* 56 G7
Xudat, *Azerbaijan* 49 K9
Xuefeng Shan, *China* 59 D8
Xuejiaping, *China* 59 B8
Xun Jiang ➤, *China* 59 F8
Xun Xian, *China* 56 G8
Xundian, *China* 58 E4
Xunwu, *China* 59 E10
Xunyang, *China* 56 H5
Xunyi, *China* 56 G5
Xupu, *China* 59 D8
Xúquer ➤, *Spain* 33 F4
Xushui, *China* 56 E8
Xuwen, *China* 59 G8
Xuyen Moc, *Vietnam* 65 G6
Xuyong, *China* 58 C5
Xuzhou, *China* 57 G9
Xylophagou, *Cyprus* 36 E12

Y

Ya Xian, *China* 64 C7
Yaamba, *Australia* 94 C5
Ya'an, *China* 58 C4
Yaapeet, *Australia* 95 F3
Yabassi, *Cameroon* 83 E6
Yabelo, *Ethiopia* 81 G4
Yablanitsa, *Bulgaria* 41 C8
Yablonovy Ra. = Yablonovyy
  Khrebet, *Russia* 51 D12
Yablonovyy Khrebet, *Russia* .. 51 D12
Yabrai Shan, *China* 56 E2
Yabrūd, *Syria* 75 B5
Yacheng, *China* 64 C7
Yacuiba, *Bolivia* 126 A3
Yacuma ➤, *Bolivia* 124 F5
Yadgir, *India* 66 L10
Yadkin ➤, *U.S.A.* 109 H5
Yadrin, *Russia* 48 C8
Yaeyama-Rettō, *Japan* 55 M1
Yagaba, *Ghana* 83 C4
Yağcılar, *Turkey* 39 B10
Yagodnoye, *Russia* 51 C15
Yahila, *Dem. Rep. of the Congo* 86 B1
Yahk, *Canada* 104 D5
Yahotyn, *Ukraine* 47 G6
Yahuma, *Dem. Rep. of*
  the Congo 84 D4
Yahyalı, *Turkey* 72 C6
Yaita, *Japan* 55 F9
Yaiza, *Canary Is.* 37 F6
Yajiang, *China* 58 B3
Yajua, *Nigeria* 83 C7
Yakima, *U.S.A.* 114 C3
Yakima ➤, *U.S.A.* 114 C3
Yako, *Burkina Faso* 82 C4
Yakobi I., *U.S.A.* 104 B1
Yakoruda, *Bulgaria* 40 D7
Yakovlevka, *Russia* 54 B6
Yaku-Shima, *Japan* 55 J5
Yakumo, *Japan* 54 C10
Yakutat, *U.S.A.* 100 C6
Yakutia = Sakha □, *Russia* .. 51 C13
Yakutsk, *Russia* 51 C13
Yala, *Thailand* 65 J3
Yale, *U.S.A.* 110 C2
Yalgoo, *Australia* 93 E2
Yalinga, *C.A.R.* 84 C4
Yalkubul, Punta, *Mexico* 119 C7
Yalleroi, *Australia* 94 C4
Yalobusha ➤, *U.S.A.* 113 J9
Yalong Jiang ➤, *China* 58 D3
Yalova, *Turkey* 41 F13
Yalta, *Ukraine* 47 K8
Yalu Jiang ➤, *China* 57 E13
Yalvaç, *Turkey* 72 C4
Yam Ha Melah = Dead Sea,
  Asia 75 D4
Yam Kinneret, *Israel* 75 C4
Yamada, *Japan* 55 H5
Yamagata, *Japan* 54 E10
Yamagata □, *Japan* 54 E10
Yamaguchi, *Japan* 55 G5
Yamaguchi □, *Japan* 55 G5
Yamal, Poluostrov, *Russia* ... 50 B8
Yamal Pen. =
  Poluostrov, *Russia* 50 B8
Yamanashi □, *Japan* 55 G9
Yamba, *Australia* 95 D5
Yambarran Ra., *Australia* 92 C5
Yambéring, *Guinea* 82 C2
Yâmbiô, *Sudan* 81 G2
Yambol, *Bulgaria* 41 D10
Yamdena, *Indonesia* 63 F8
Yame, *Japan* 55 H5
Yamethin, *Burma* 67 J20
Yamma-Yamma, L., *Australia* . 95 D3
Yamoussoukro, *Ivory C.* 82 D3
Yampa ➤, *U.S.A.* 114 F9
Yampi Sd., *Australia* 92 C3
Yampil, *Moldova* 47 H5
Yampol = Yampil, *Moldova* .. 47 H5
Yamrukchal = Botev, *Bulgaria* 41 D8
Yamuna ➤, *India* 69 G9
Yamunanagar, *India* 68 D7
Yamzho Yumco, *China* 60 D4
Yan, *Nigeria* 83 C7

Yana →, Russia ... 51 B14
Yanagawa, Japan ... 55 H5
Yanai, Japan ... 55 H6
Yan'an, China ... 56 F5
Yanbian, China ... 58 D3
Yanbu 'al Baḥr, Si. Arabia ... 70 F3
Yanchang, China ... 56 F6
Yancheng, Henan, China ... 56 H8
Yancheng, Jiangsu, China ... 57 H11
Yanchep Beach, Australia ... 93 F2
Yanchi, China ... 56 F4
Yanchuan, China ... 56 F6
Yanco Cr. →, Australia ... 95 F4
Yandoon, Burma ... 67 L19
Yanfeng, China ... 58 E3
Yanfolila, Mali ... 82 C3
Yang Xian, China ... 56 H4
Yang-Yang, Senegal ... 82 B1
Yangambi, Dem. Rep. of the Congo ... 86 B1
Yangbi, China ... 58 E2
Yangcheng, China ... 56 G7
Yangch'ü = Taiyuan, China ... 56 F7
Yangchun, China ... 59 F8
Yanggao, China ... 56 D7
Yanggu, China ... 56 F8
Yangjiang, China ... 59 G8
Yangliuqing, China ... 57 E9
Yangon = Rangoon, Burma ... 67 L20
Yangping, China ... 59 B8
Yangpingguan, China ... 56 H4
Yangquan, China ... 56 F7
Yangshan, China ... 59 E9
Yangshuo, China ... 59 E8
Yangtse = Chang Jiang →, China ... 59 B13
Yangtze Kiang = Chang Jiang →, China ... 59 B13
Yangxin, China ... 59 C10
Yangyang, S. Korea ... 57 E15
Yangyuan, China ... 56 D8
Yangzhong, China ... 59 A12
Yangzhou, China ... 59 A12
Yanhe, China ... 58 C7
Yanji, China ... 57 C15
Yanjin, China ... 58 C5
Yanjing, China ... 58 C2
Yankton, U.S.A. ... 112 D6
Yanonge, Dem. Rep. of the Congo ... 86 B1
Yanqi, China ... 60 B3
Yanqing, China ... 56 D8
Yanshan, Hebei, China ... 57 E9
Yanshan, Jiangxi, China ... 59 C11
Yanshan, Yunnan, China ... 58 F5
Yanshou, China ... 57 B15
Yantabulla, Australia ... 95 D4
Yantai, China ... 57 F11
Yanting, China ... 58 B5
Yanwa, China ... 58 D2
Yanyuan, China ... 58 D3
Yanzhou, China ... 56 G9
Yao Xian, China ... 56 G5
Yao Yai, Ko, Thailand ... 65 J2
Yao'an, China ... 58 E3
Yaodu, China ... 58 A5
Yaoundé, Cameroon ... 83 E7
Yaowan, China ... 57 G10
Yap I., Pac. Oc. ... 96 G5
Yapen, Indonesia ... 63 E9
Yapen, Selat, Indonesia ... 63 E9
Yapero, Indonesia ... 63 E9
Yappar →, Australia ... 94 B3
Yaqui →, Mexico ... 118 B2
Yar-Sale, Russia ... 50 C8
Yaraka, Australia ... 94 C3
Yaransk, Russia ... 48 B8
Yarbasan, Turkey ... 39 C10
Yardımcı Burnu, Turkey ... 39 E12
Yare →, U.K. ... 13 E9
Yaremcha, Ukraine ... 47 H3
Yarensk, Russia ... 50 C5
Yarfa, Si. Arabia ... 80 C4
Yarí →, Colombia ... 124 D4
Yarkand = Shache, China ... 60 C2
Yarker, Canada ... 111 B8
Yarkhun →, Pakistan ... 69 A5
Yarmouth, Canada ... 103 D6
Yarmūk →, Syria ... 75 C4
Yaroslavl, Russia ... 46 D10
Yarqa, W. →, Egypt ... 75 F2
Yarra Yarra Lakes, Australia ... 93 E2
Yarram, Australia ... 95 F4
Yarraman, Australia ... 95 D5
Yarras, Australia ... 95 E5
Yartsevo, Sib., Russia ... 51 C10
Yartsevo, Smolensk, Russia ... 46 E7
Yarumal, Colombia ... 124 B3
Yasawa Group, Fiji ... 91 C7
Yaselda, Belarus ... 47 F4
Yashi, Nigeria ... 83 C6
Yashikera, Nigeria ... 83 D5
Yashkul, Russia ... 49 G7
Yasin, Pakistan ... 69 A5
Yasinski, L., Canada ... 102 B4
Yasinya, Ukraine ... 47 H3
Yasothon, Thailand ... 64 E5
Yass, Australia ... 95 E4
Yāsūj, Iran ... 71 D6
Yatağan, Turkey ... 39 D10
Yatakala, Niger ... 83 C5
Yates Center, U.S.A. ... 113 G7
Yathkyed L., Canada ... 105 A9
Yatsushiro, Japan ... 55 H5
Yatta Plateau, Kenya ... 86 C4

Yavari →, Peru ... 124 D4
Yávaros, Mexico ... 118 B3
Yavatmal, India ... 66 J11
Yavne, Israel ... 75 D3
Yavoriv, Ukraine ... 47 H2
Yavorov = Yavoriv, Ukraine ... 47 H2
Yavuzeli, Turkey ... 72 D7
Yawatahama, Japan ... 55 H6
Yawri B., S. Leone ... 82 D2
Yaxi, China ... 58 D6
Yazd, Iran ... 71 D7
Yazd □, Iran ... 71 D7
Yazd-e Khvāst, Iran ... 71 D7
Yazıköy, Turkey ... 39 E9
Yazman, Pakistan ... 68 E4
Yazoo →, U.S.A. ... 113 J9
Yazoo City, U.S.A. ... 113 J9
Ybbs, Austria ... 26 C8
Yding Skovhøj, Denmark ... 11 J3
Ye Xian = Laizhou, China ... 57 F10
Ye Xian, China ... 56 H7
Yebyu, Burma ... 64 E2
Yechŏn, S. Korea ... 57 F15
Yecla, Spain ... 33 G3
Yécora, Mexico ... 118 B3
Yedintsy = Edineţ, Moldova ... 43 B12
Yedseram →, Nigeria ... 83 C7
Yefremov, Russia ... 46 F10
Yeghegnadzor, Armenia ... 73 C11
Yegorlyk →, Russia ... 49 G5
Yegorlykskaya, Russia ... 49 G5
Yegoryevsk, Russia ... 46 E10
Yegros, Paraguay ... 126 B4
Yehuda, Midbar, Israel ... 75 D4
Yei, Sudan ... 81 G3
Yei, Nahr →, Sudan ... 81 F3
Yejmiadzin, Armenia ... 49 K7
Yekaterinburg, Russia ... 50 D7
Yekaterinodar = Krasnodar, Russia ... 49 H4
Yelabuga, Russia ... 48 C11
Yelan, Russia ... 48 E6
Yelarbon, Australia ... 95 D5
Yelatma, Russia ... 48 C5
Yelets, Russia ... 47 F10
Yélimané, Mali ... 82 B2
Yelizavetgrad = Kirovohrad, Ukraine ... 47 H7
Yell, U.K. ... 14 A7
Yell Sd., U.K. ... 14 A7
Yellow Sea, China ... 57 G12
Yellowhead Pass, Canada ... 104 C5
Yellowknife, Canada ... 104 A6
Yellowknife →, Canada ... 104 A6
Yellowstone →, U.S.A. ... 112 B3
Yellowstone L., U.S.A. ... 114 D8
Yellowstone National Park, U.S.A. ... 114 D9
Yelnya, Russia ... 46 E7
Yelsk, Belarus ... 47 G5
Yelwa, Nigeria ... 83 C5
Yemen ■, Asia ... 74 E3
Yen Bai, Vietnam ... 58 G5
Yenagoa, Nigeria ... 83 E6
Yenakiyeve, Ukraine ... 47 H10
Yenakiyevo = Yenakiyeve, Ukraine ... 47 H10
Yenangyaung, Burma ... 67 J19
Yenbo = Yanbu 'al Baḥr, Si. Arabia ... 70 F3
Yenda, Australia ... 95 E4
Yende Millimou, Guinea ... 82 D2
Yendéré, Burkina Faso ... 82 C4
Yendi, Ghana ... 83 D4
Yéni, Niger ... 83 C5
Yenice, Ankara, Turkey ... 72 C5
Yenice, Aydın, Turkey ... 39 D10
Yenice, Çanakkale, Turkey ... 39 B9
Yenice, Edirne, Turkey ... 41 F10
Yenice →, Turkey ... 72 D6
Yenifoça, Turkey ... 39 C8
Yenihisar, Turkey ... 39 D9
Yeniköy, Bursa, Turkey ... 41 F13
Yeniköy, Çanakkale, Turkey ... 39 B8
Yeniköy, Kütahya, Turkey ... 39 C11
Yenipazar, Turkey ... 39 D10
Yenisaía, Greece ... 41 E8
Yenişehir, Turkey ... 41 F13
Yeniseysk, Russia ... 51 D10
Yenisey →, Russia ... 50 B9
Yeniseyskiy Zaliv, Russia ... 50 B9
Yennádhi, Greece ... 36 C9
Yenne, France ... 21 C9
Yenotayevka, Russia ... 49 G8
Yenyuka, Russia ... 51 D13
Yeo →, U.K. ... 13 G5
Yeo, L., Australia ... 93 E3
Yeo I., Canada ... 110 A3
Yeola, India ... 66 J9
Yeoryioúpolis, Greece ... 36 D6
Yeovil, U.K. ... 13 G5
Yepes, Spain ... 34 F7
Yeppoon, Australia ... 94 C5
Yeráki, Greece ... 38 D4
Yerbent, Turkmenistan ... 50 F6
Yerbogachen, Russia ... 51 C11
Yerevan, Armenia ... 49 K7
Yerington, U.S.A. ... 114 G4
Yerkesik, Turkey ... 39 D10
Yerköy, Turkey ... 72 C6
Yermak, Kazakstan ... 50 D8
Yermo, U.S.A. ... 117 L10
Yerólakkos, Cyprus ... 36 D12
Yeropol, Russia ... 51 C17
Yeropótamos →, Greece ... 36 D6
Yeroskipos, Cyprus ... 36 E11
Yershov, Russia ... 48 E9

Yerushalayim = Jerusalem, Israel ... 75 D4
Yerville, France ... 18 C7
Yes Tor, U.K. ... 13 G4
Yesan, S. Korea ... 57 F14
Yeşilhisar, Turkey ... 72 C6
Yeşilırmak →, Turkey ... 72 B7
Yeşilkent, Turkey ... 72 D7
Yeşilköy, Turkey ... 41 F12
Yeşilova, Turkey ... 39 D11
Yeşilyurt, Manisa, Turkey ... 39 C10
Yeşilyurt, Muğla, Turkey ... 39 D10
Yesnogorsk, Russia ... 46 E9
Yeso, U.S.A. ... 113 H2
Yessentuki, Russia ... 49 H6
Yessey, Russia ... 51 C11
Yeste, Spain ... 33 G2
Yetman, Australia ... 95 D5
Yeu, Î. d', France ... 18 F4
Yevlakh = Yevlax, Azerbaijan ... 49 K8
Yevlax, Azerbaijan ... 49 K8
Yevpatoriya, Ukraine ... 47 K7
Yeya →, Russia ... 47 J10
Yeysk, Russia ... 47 J10
Yezd = Yazd, Iran ... 71 D7
Yezerishche, Belarus ... 46 E5
Yhati, Paraguay ... 126 B4
Yhú, Paraguay ... 127 B4
Yi →, Uruguay ... 126 C4
Yi 'Allaq, G., Egypt ... 75 E2
Yi He →, China ... 57 G10
Yi Xian, Anhui, China ... 59 C11
Yi Xian, Hebei, China ... 56 E8
Yi Xian, Liaoning, China ... 57 D11
Yialí, Greece ... 39 E9
Yialiás →, Cyprus ... 36 D12
Yi'allaq, G., Egypt ... 80 A3
Yialousa, Cyprus ... 36 D13
Yiáltra, Greece ... 38 C4
Yianisádhes, Greece ... 36 D8
Yiannitsa, Greece ... 40 F6
Yibin, China ... 58 C5
Yichang, China ... 59 B8
Yicheng, Henan, China ... 59 B9
Yicheng, Shanxi, China ... 56 G6
Yichuan, China ... 56 F6
Yichun, Heilongjiang, China ... 60 B7
Yichun, Jiangxi, China ... 59 D10
Yidu, China ... 57 F10
Yidun, China ... 58 B2
Yifag, Ethiopia ... 81 E4
Yifeng, China ... 59 C10
Yihuang, China ... 59 D11
Yijun, China ... 56 G5
Yıldız Dağları, Turkey ... 41 E11
Yıldızeli, Turkey ... 72 C7
Yiliang, Yunnan, China ... 58 D5
Yiliang, Yunnan, China ... 58 E4
Yilong, China ... 58 B6
Yimen, China ... 58 E4
Yimianpo, China ... 57 B15
Yinchuan, China ... 56 E4
Yindarlgooda, L., Australia ... 93 F3
Ying He →, China ... 56 H9
Ying Xian, China ... 56 E7
Yingcheng, China ... 59 B9
Yingde, China ... 59 E9
Yingjiang, China ... 58 E1
Yingjing, China ... 58 B2
Yingkou, China ... 57 D12
Yingshan, Henan, China ... 59 B9
Yingshan, Hubei, China ... 59 B10
Yingshan, Sichuan, China ... 58 B6
Yingshang, China ... 59 A11
Yingtan, China ... 59 C11
Yining, China ... 50 E9
Yinjiang, China ... 58 C7
Yinmabin, Burma ... 67 H19
Yiofiros →, Greece ... 36 D7
Yioúra, Nótios Aiyaíon, Greece ... 38 D6
Yioúra, Thessalía, Greece ... 38 B6
Yipinglang, China ... 58 E3
Yirba Muda, Ethiopia ... 81 F4
Yirga Alem, Ethiopia ... 81 F4
Yirol, Sudan ... 81 F3
Yirrkala, Australia ... 94 A2
Yishan, China ... 58 E7
Yishui, China ... 57 G10
Yithion, Greece ... 38 E4
Yitong, China ... 57 C13
Yiwu, China ... 59 C13
Yixing, China ... 59 B12
Yiyang, Henan, China ... 56 G7
Yiyang, Hunan, China ... 59 C9
Yiyang, Jiangxi, China ... 59 C11
Yizhang, China ... 59 E9
Yizheng, China ... 59 A12
Yli-Kitka, Finland ... 8 C23
Ylitornio, Finland ... 8 C20
Ylivieska, Finland ... 8 D21
Yngaren, Sweden ... 11 F10
Yoakum, U.S.A. ... 113 L6
Yobe □, Nigeria ... 83 C7
Yog Pt., Phil. ... 63 B6
Yogan, Togo ... 83 D5
Yoğuntaş, Turkey ... 41 E11
Yogyakarta, Indonesia ... 62 F4
Yoho Nat. Park, Canada ... 104 C5
Yojoa, L. de, Honduras ... 120 D2
Yŏju, S. Korea ... 57 F14
Yokadouma, Cameroon ... 84 D2
Yokkaichi, Japan ... 55 G8
Yoko, Cameroon ... 83 D7
Yokohama, Japan ... 55 G9
Yokosuka, Japan ... 55 G9
Yokote, Japan ... 54 E10
Yola, Nigeria ... 83 D7

Yolaina, Cordillera de, Nic. ... 120 D3
Yoloten, Turkmenistan ... 71 B9
Yom →, Thailand ... 62 A2
Yonago, Japan ... 55 G6
Yonaguni-Jima, Japan ... 55 M1
Yŏnan, N. Korea ... 57 F14
Yonezawa, Japan ... 54 F10
Yong Peng, Malaysia ... 65 L4
Yong Sata, Thailand ... 65 J2
Yongamp'o, N. Korea ... 57 E13
Yong'an, China ... 59 E11
Yongcheng, China ... 56 H9
Yŏngch'ŏn, S. Korea ... 57 G15
Yongchun, China ... 59 E12
Yongde, China ... 58 E2
Yongdeng, China ... 56 F2
Yongding, China ... 59 E11
Yŏngdŏk, S. Korea ... 57 F15
Yŏngdŭngpo, S. Korea ... 57 F14
Yongfeng, China ... 59 D10
Yongfu, China ... 58 E7
Yonghe, China ... 56 F6
Yŏnghŭng, N. Korea ... 57 E14
Yongji, China ... 56 G6
Yongjia, China ... 59 C13
Yŏngju, S. Korea ... 57 F15
Yongkang, Yunnan, China ... 58 E2
Yongkang, Zhejiang, China ... 59 C13
Yongnian, China ... 56 F8
Yongning, Guangxi Zhuangzu, China ... 58 F7
Yongning, Ningxia Huizu, China ... 56 E4
Yongping, China ... 58 E2
Yongqing, China ... 56 E9
Yongren, China ... 58 D3
Yongsheng, China ... 58 D3
Yongshun, China ... 58 C7
Yongtai, China ... 59 E12
Yŏngwŏl, S. Korea ... 57 F15
Yongxin = Jinggangshan, China ... 59 D10
Yongxing, China ... 59 D9
Yongxiu, China ... 59 C10
Yongzhou, China ... 59 D8
Yonibana, S. Leone ... 82 D2
Yonkers, U.S.A. ... 111 F11
Yonne □, France ... 19 E10
Yonne →, France ... 19 D9
York, Australia ... 93 F2
York, U.K. ... 12 D6
York, Ala., U.S.A. ... 113 J10
York, Nebr., U.S.A. ... 112 E6
York, Pa., U.S.A. ... 108 F7
York, C., Australia ... 94 A3
York, City of □, U.K. ... 12 D6
York, Kap, Greenland ... 4 B4
York, Vale of, U.K. ... 12 C6
York Haven, U.S.A. ... 110 F8
York Sd., Australia ... 92 C4
Yorke Pen., Australia ... 95 E2
Yorkshire Wolds, U.K. ... 12 C7
Yorkton, Canada ... 105 C8
Yorkville, U.S.A. ... 116 G3
Yoro, Honduras ... 120 C2
Yoron-Jima, Japan ... 55 L4
Yorosso, Mali ... 82 C4
Yos Sudarso, Pulau = Dolak, Pulau, Indonesia ... 63 F9
Yosemite National Park, U.S.A. ... 116 H7
Yosemite Village, U.S.A. ... 116 H7
Yoshkar Ola, Russia ... 48 B8
Yŏsu, S. Korea ... 57 G14
Yotvata, Israel ... 75 F4
You Jiang →, China ... 58 F6
You Xian, China ... 59 D9
Youbou, Canada ... 116 B2
Youghal, Ireland ... 15 E4
Youghal B., Ireland ... 15 E4
Youkounkoun, Guinea ... 82 C2
Young, Australia ... 95 E4
Young, Canada ... 105 C7
Young, Uruguay ... 126 C4
Younghusband, L., Australia ... 95 E2
Younghusband Pen., Australia ... 95 F2
Youngstown, Canada ... 105 C6
Youngstown, N.Y., U.S.A. ... 110 C5
Youngstown, Ohio, U.S.A. ... 110 E4
Youngsville, U.S.A. ... 110 E5
Youngwood, U.S.A. ... 110 F5
Youxi, China ... 59 D12
Youyang, China ... 58 C7
Youyu, China ... 56 D7
Yozgat, Turkey ... 72 C6
Ypané →, Paraguay ... 126 A4
Yport, France ... 18 C7
Ypres = Ieper, Belgium ... 17 D2
Yreka, U.S.A. ... 114 F2
Yssingeaux, France ... 21 C8
Ystad, Sweden ... 11 J7
Ysyk-Köl, Kyrgyzstan ... 50 E8
Ythan →, U.K. ... 14 D7
Ytterhogdal, Sweden ... 10 B8
Ytyk-Kyuyel, Russia ... 51 C14
Yu Jiang →, China ... 58 F7
Yu Xian = Yuzhou, China ... 56 G7
Yu Xian, Hebei, China ... 56 E8
Yu Xian, Shanxi, China ... 56 E7
Yuan Jiang →, Hunan, China ... 59 C8
Yuan Jiang →, Yunnan, China ... 58 F4
Yuan'an, China ... 59 B8
Yuanjiang, Hunan, China ... 59 C9
Yuanjiang, Yunnan, China ... 58 F4
Yuanli, Taiwan ... 59 E13
Yüanli, Taiwan ... 59 E13
Yüanlin, Taiwan ... 59 F13
Yuanling, China ... 59 C8
Yuanmou, China ... 58 D3

Yuanqu, China ... 56 G6
Yuanyang, Henan, China ... 56 G7
Yuanyang, Yunnan, China ... 58 F4
Yuba →, U.S.A. ... 116 F5
Yuba City, U.S.A. ... 116 F5
Yūbari, Japan ... 54 C10
Yubdo, Ethiopia ... 81 F4
Yūbetsu, Japan ... 54 B11
Yubo, Sudan ... 81 F2
Yucatán □, Mexico ... 119 C7
Yucatán, Canal de, Caribbean ... 120 B2
Yucatán, Península de, Mexico ... 98 H11
Yucatan Basin, Cent. Amer. ... 98 H11
Yucatan Str. = Yucatán, Canal de, Caribbean ... 120 B2
Yucca, U.S.A. ... 117 L12
Yucca Valley, U.S.A. ... 117 L10
Yucheng, China ... 56 F9
Yuci, China ... 56 F7
Yudu, China ... 59 E10
Yuechi, China ... 58 B6
Yuendumu, Australia ... 92 D5
Yueqing, China ... 59 C13
Yueqing Wan, China ... 59 D13
Yuexi, Anhui, China ... 59 B11
Yuexi, Sichuan, China ... 58 C4
Yueyang, China ... 59 C9
Yugan, China ... 59 C11
Yugoslavia ■, Europe ... 40 C4
Yuhuan, China ... 59 C13
Yuhuan Dao, China ... 59 C13
Yujiang, China ... 59 C11
Yukhnov, Russia ... 46 E8
Yukon →, U.S.A. ... 100 B3
Yukon Territory □, Canada ... 100 B6
Yüksekova, Turkey ... 73 D11
Yukta, Russia ... 51 C11
Yukuhashi, Japan ... 55 H5
Yulara, Australia ... 93 E5
Yule →, Australia ... 92 D2
Yuleba, Australia ... 95 D4
Yuli, Nigeria ... 83 D7
Yuli, Taiwan ... 59 F13
Yulin, Guangxi Zhuangzu, China ... 59 F8
Yulin, Hainan, China ... 65 C7
Yulin, Shaanxi, China ... 56 E5
Yuma, Ariz., U.S.A. ... 117 N12
Yuma, Colo., U.S.A. ... 112 E3
Yuma, B. de, Dom. Rep. ... 121 C6
Yumbe, Uganda ... 86 B3
Yumbi, Dem. Rep. of the Congo ... 86 C2
Yumen, China ... 60 C4
Yumurtalık, Turkey ... 72 D6
Yun Gol Gaoyuan, China ... 58 E3
Yun Ho →, China ... 57 E9
Yun Ling, China ... 58 D2
Yun Xian, Hubei, China ... 59 A8
Yun Xian, Yunnan, China ... 58 E3
Yuna, Australia ... 93 E2
Yunak, Turkey ... 72 C4
Yunan, China ... 59 F8
Yuncheng, Henan, China ... 56 G8
Yuncheng, Shanxi, China ... 56 G6
Yunfu, China ... 59 F9
Yungas, Bolivia ... 124 G5
Yungay, Chile ... 126 D1
Yunhe, China ... 59 C12
Yunkai Dashan, China ... 59 F8
Yunlin, Taiwan ... 59 F13
Yunlong, China ... 58 E2
Yunmeng, China ... 59 B9
Yunnan □, China ... 58 E4
Yunquera de Henares, Spain ... 32 E1
Yunt Dağı, Turkey ... 39 C9
Yunta, Australia ... 95 E2
Yunxi, China ... 56 H6
Yunxiao, China ... 59 F11
Yuping, China ... 58 D7
Yupyongdong, N. Korea ... 57 D15
Yuqing, China ... 58 D6
Yurga, Russia ... 50 D9
Yurimaguas, Peru ... 124 E3
Yuryev-Polskiy, Russia ... 46 D10
Yuryevets, Russia ... 48 B6
Yuscarán, Honduras ... 120 D2
Yushan, China ... 59 C12
Yushanzhen, China ... 58 C7
Yushe, China ... 56 F7
Yushu, Jilin, China ... 57 B14
Yushu, Qinghai, China ... 60 C4
Yusufeli, Turkey ... 73 B9
Yutai, China ... 56 G9
Yutian, China ... 57 E9
Yuxarı Qarabağ = Nagorno-Karabakh, Azerbaijan ... 70 B5
Yuxi, China ... 58 E4
Yuyao, China ... 59 B13
Yuzawa, Japan ... 54 E10
Yuzha, Russia ... 48 B6
Yuzhno-Sakhalinsk, Russia ... 51 E15
Yuzhou, China ... 56 G7
Yvelines □, France ... 19 D8
Yverdon-les-Bains, Switz. ... 25 J2
Yvetot, France ... 18 C7
Yzeure, France ... 19 F10

Z

Zaanstad, Neths. ... 17 B4
Zāb al Kabīr →, Iraq ... 70 C4
Zāb aş Şağīr →, Iraq ... 70 C4
Žabalj, Serbia, Yug. ... 42 E5
Zabari, Serbia, Yug. ... 40 B5
Zabarjad, Egypt ... 80 C4

Zabaykalsk, Russia ... 51 E12
Zabki, Poland ... 45 F8
Ząbkowice Śląskie, Poland ... 45 H3
Žabljak, Montenegro, Yug. ... 40 C3
Żabłudów, Poland ... 45 F9
Żabno, Poland ... 45 H7
Zābol, Iran ... 71 D9
Zābol □, Afghan. ... 66 D5
Zābolī, Iran ... 71 E9
Zabré, Burkina Faso ... 83 C4
Zábřeh, Czech Rep. ... 27 B9
Zabrze, Poland ... 45 H5
Zabzuga, Ghana ... 83 D5
Zacapa, Guatemala ... 120 D2
Zacapu, Mexico ... 118 D4
Zacatecas, Mexico ... 118 C4
Zacatecas □, Mexico ... 118 C4
Zacatecoluca, El Salv. ... 120 D2
Zachary, U.S.A. ... 113 K9
Zachodnio-Pomorskie □, Poland ... 44 E2
Zacoalco, Mexico ... 118 C4
Zacualtipán, Mexico ... 119 C5
Zadar, Croatia ... 29 D12
Zadawa, Nigeria ... 83 C7
Zadetkyi Kyun, Burma ... 65 G1
Zadonsk, Russia ... 47 F10
Zafarqand, Iran ... 71 C7
Zafora, Greece ... 39 E8
Zafra, Spain ... 35 G4
Zagań, Poland ... 45 G2
Zagaoua, Chad ... 79 E10
Zagarė, Lithuania ... 44 B10
Zagazig, Egypt ... 80 H7
Zāgheh, Iran ... 71 C6
Zaglivérion, Greece ... 40 F7
Zagnanado, Benin ... 83 D5
Zagorá, Greece ... 38 B5
Zagorje, Slovenia ... 29 B11
Zagórów, Poland ... 45 F4
Zagorsk = Sergiyev Posad, Russia ... 46 D10
Zagórz, Poland ... 45 J9
Zagreb, Croatia ... 29 C12
Zāgros, Kūhhā-ye, Iran ... 71 C6
Zagros Mts. = Zāgros, Kūhhā-ye, Iran ... 71 C6
Žagubica, Serbia, Yug. ... 40 B5
Zaguinaso, Ivory C. ... 82 C3
Zagyva →, Hungary ... 42 C5
Zāhedān, Fārs, Iran ... 71 D7
Zāhedān, Sīstān va Balūchestān, Iran ... 71 D9
Zahlah, Lebanon ... 75 B4
Zahna, Germany ... 24 D8
Záhony, Hungary ... 42 B7
Zainsk, Russia ... 48 C11
Zaïre = Congo →, Africa ... 84 F2
Zaječar, Serbia, Yug. ... 40 C6
Zaka, Zimbabwe ... 89 C5
Zakamensk, Russia ... 51 D11
Zakataly = Zaqatala, Azerbaijan ... 49 K8
Zakháro, Greece ... 38 D3
Zakhodnya Dzvina = Daugava →, Latvia ... 9 H21
Zākhū, Iraq ... 70 B4
Zákinthos, Greece ... 38 D2
Zákinthos □, Greece ... 38 D2
Zakopane, Poland ... 45 J6
Zakroczym, Poland ... 45 F7
Zákros, Greece ... 36 D8
Zala, Ethiopia ... 81 F4
Zala □, Hungary ... 42 D1
Zala →, Hungary ... 42 D2
Zalaegerszeg, Hungary ... 42 D1
Zalakomár, Hungary ... 42 D2
Zalalövő, Hungary ... 42 D1
Zalamea de la Serena, Spain ... 35 G5
Zalamea la Real, Spain ... 35 H4
Zalău, Romania ... 42 C8
Zalec, Slovenia ... 29 B12
Zaleshchiki = Zalishchyky, Ukraine ... 47 H3
Zalew Wiślany, Poland ... 44 D6
Zalewo, Poland ... 44 E6
Zalingei, Sudan ... 79 F10
Zalishchyky, Ukraine ... 47 H3
Zama L., Canada ... 104 B5
Zambeke, Dem. Rep. of the Congo ... 86 B2
Zambeze →, Africa ... 87 F4
Zambezi = Zambeze →, Africa ... 87 F4
Zambezi, Zambia ... 85 G4
Zambezia □, Mozam. ... 87 F4
Zambia ■, Africa ... 87 F2
Zamboanga, Phil. ... 61 H5
Zambrów, Poland ... 45 F9
Zametchino, Russia ... 48 D6
Zamfara □, Nigeria ... 83 C6
Zamfara →, Nigeria ... 83 C5
Zamora, Mexico ... 118 D4
Zamora, Spain ... 34 D5
Zamora □, Spain ... 34 D5
Zamość, Poland ... 45 H10
Zamtang, China ... 58 A3
Zan, Ghana ... 83 D4
Záncara →, Spain ... 33 F1
Zandvoort, Neths. ... 17 B4
Zanesville, U.S.A. ... 110 G2
Zangābād, Iran ... 70 B5
Zangue →, Mozam. ... 87 F4
Zanjān, Iran ... 71 B6
Zanjān □, Iran ... 71 B6
Zanjān →, Iran ... 71 B6
Zannone, Italy ... 30 B6
Zante = Zákinthos, Greece ... 38 D2
Zanthus, Australia ... 93 F3

Zanzibar, Tanzania ... 86 D4
Zaouiet El-Kala = Bordj Omar Driss, Algeria ... 78 C7
Zaouiet Reggâne, Algeria ... 78 C6
Zaoyang, China ... 59 A9
Zaozhuang, China ... 57 G9
Zap Suyu = Zāb al Kabīr →, Iraq ... 70 C4
Zapadna Morava →, Serbia, Yug. ... 40 C5
Zapadnaya Dvina = Daugava →, Latvia ... 9 H21
Zapadnaya Dvina, Russia ... 46 D7
Západné Beskydy, Europe ... 27 B12
Zapadni Rodopi, Bulgaria ... 40 E7
Zapala, Argentina ... 128 D2
Zapaleri, Cerro, Bolivia ... 126 A2
Zapata, U.S.A. ... 113 M5
Zapatón →, Spain ... 35 F4
Zaporizhzhya, Ukraine ... 47 J8
Zaporozhye = Zaporizhzhya, Ukraine ... 47 J8
Zaqatala, Azerbaijan ... 49 K8
Zara, Turkey ... 70 B3
Zaragoza, Coahuila, Mexico ... 118 B4
Zaragoza, Nuevo León, Mexico ... 119 C5
Zaragoza, Spain ... 32 D4
Zaragoza □, Spain ... 32 D4
Zarand, Kermān, Iran ... 71 D8
Zarand, Markazī, Iran ... 71 C6
Zărandului, Munții, Romania ... 42 D7
Zaranj, Afghan. ... 66 D2
Zarasai, Lithuania ... 9 J22
Zarate, Argentina ... 126 C4
Zarautz, Spain ... 32 B2
Zaraysk, Russia ... 46 E10
Zard, Kūh-e, Iran ... 71 C6
Zāreh, Iran ... 71 C6
Zari, Nigeria ... 83 C7
Zaria, Nigeria ... 83 C6
Zarki, Poland ... 45 H6
Žarkon, Greece ... 38 B4
Zarneh, Iran ... 70 C5
Zărneşti, Romania ... 43 E10
Zarós, Greece ... 36 D6
Żarów, Poland ... 45 H3
Zarqā', Nahr az →, Jordan ... 75 C4
Zarrīn, Iran ... 71 C7
Zaruma, Ecuador ... 124 D3
Żary, Poland ... 45 G2
Zarza de Granadilla, Spain ... 34 E4
Zarzis, Tunisia ... 79 B8
Zas, Spain ... 34 B2
Zaskar →, India ... 69 B7
Zaskar Mts., India ... 69 C7
Zastron, S. Africa ... 88 E4
Zatec, Czech Rep. ... 26 A6
Zaterechnyy, Russia ... 49 H7
Zator, Poland ... 45 J6
Zavala, Bos.-H. ... 40 D1
Zavāreh, Iran ... 71 C7
Zave, Zimbabwe ... 89 B5
Zavetnoye, Russia ... 49 G6
Zavidovići, Bos.-H. ... 42 F3
Zavitinsk, Russia ... 51 D13
Zavodovski, I., Antarctica ... 5 B1
Zavolzhsk, Russia ... 48 B6
Zavolzhye, Russia ... 48 B6
Zawadzkie, Poland ... 45 H5
Zawichost, Poland ... 45 H8
Zawidów, Poland ... 45 G2
Zawiercie, Poland ... 45 H6
Zāwiyat al Bayḍā = Al Bayḍā, Libya ... 79 B10
Zāwyet Shammas, Egypt ... 80 A2
Zāwyet Um el Rakham, Egypt ... 80 A2
Zāwyet Ungeîla, Egypt ... 80 A2
Zāyā, Iraq ... 70 C5
Zāyandeh →, Iran ... 71 C7
Zaysan, Kazakstan ... 50 E9
Zaysan, Oz., Kazakstan ... 50 E9
Zayü, China ... 58 C1
Zazafotsy, Madag. ... 89 C8
Zázrivá, Slovak Rep. ... 27 B12
Zbarazh, Ukraine ... 47 H3
Zbąszyń, Poland ... 45 F2
Zbąszynek, Poland ... 45 F2
Zblewo, Poland ... 44 E5
Žďár nad Sázavou, Czech Rep. ... 26 B8
Zdolbuniv, Ukraine ... 47 G4
Ždrelo, Serbia, Yug. ... 40 B5
Zduńska Wola, Poland ... 45 G5
Zduny, Poland ... 45 G4
Zeballos, Canada ... 104 D3
Zebediela, S. Africa ... 89 C4
Zebila, Ghana ... 83 C4
Zeebrugge, Belgium ... 17 C3
Zeehan, Australia ... 94 G4
Zeeland □, Neths. ... 17 C3
Zeerust, S. Africa ... 88 D4
Zefat, Israel ... 75 C4
Zege, Ethiopia ... 81 E4
Zégoua, Mali ... 82 C3
Zehdenick, Germany ... 24 C9
Zeil, Mt., Australia ... 92 D5
Zeila, Somali Rep. ... 74 E3
Zeist, Neths. ... 17 B5
Zeitz, Germany ... 24 D8
Zelechów, Poland ... 45 G8
Zelengora, Bos.-H. ... 40 C2
Zelenodolsk, Russia ... 48 C9
Zelenogorsk, Russia ... 46 B5
Zelenograd, Russia ... 46 D9
Zelenogradsk, Russia ... 9 J19
Zelenokumsk, Russia ... 49 H6
Železná Ruda, Czech Rep. ... 26 B6

Železnik, Serbia, Yug. ... 40 B4
Železovce, Slovak Rep. ... 27 C11
Zelina, Croatia ... 29 C13
Zell, Baden-W., Germany ... 25 H3
Zell, Rhld-Pfz., Germany ... 25 E3
Zell am See, Austria ... 26 D5
Zella-Mehlis, Germany ... 24 E6
Zelów, Poland ... 45 G6
Zeltweg, Austria ... 26 D7
Zémio, C.A.R. ... 86 A2
Zempléni-hegység, Hungary ... 42 B6
Zemplínska širava, Slovak Rep. ... 27 C15
Zemun, Serbia, Yug. ... 40 B4
Zengbé, Cameroon ... 83 D7
Zengcheng, China ... 59 F9
Zenica, Bos.-H. ... 42 F2
Žepče, Bos.-H. ... 42 F3
Zeraf, Bahr ez →, Sudan ... 81 F3
Zerbst, Germany ... 24 D8
Zerków, Poland ... 45 F4
Zermatt, Switz. ... 25 J3
Zernez, Switz. ... 25 J6
Zernograd, Russia ... 49 G5
Zerqan, Albania ... 40 E4
Zestaponi, Georgia ... 49 J6
Zetel, Germany ... 24 B3
Zeulenroda, Germany ... 24 E7
Zeven, Germany ... 24 B5
Zevenaar, Neths. ... 17 C6
Zévio, Italy ... 28 C8
Zeya, Russia ... 51 D13
Zeya →, Russia ... 51 D13
Zeytinbaği, Turkey ... 41 F12
Zeytindağ, Turkey ... 39 C9
Zghartā, Lebanon ... 75 A4
Zgierz, Poland ... 45 G6
Zgorzelec, Poland ... 45 G2
Zguriţa, Moldova ... 43 B13
Zhabinka, Belarus ... 47 F3
Zhailma, Kazakstan ... 50 D7
Zhambyl = Taraz, Kazakstan ... 50 E8
Zhangaqazaly, Kazakstan ... 50 E7
Zhangbei, China ... 56 D8
Zhangguangcai Ling, China ... 57 B15
Zhangjiakou, China ... 56 D8
Zhangping, China ... 59 E11
Zhangpu, China ... 59 E11
Zhangshu, China ... 59 C10
Zhangwu, China ... 57 C12
Zhangye, China ... 56 F2
Zhangzhou, China ... 59 E11
Zhanhua, China ... 57 F10
Zhanjiang, China ... 59 G8
Zhannetty, Ostrov, Russia ... 51 B16
Zhanyi, China ... 58 E4
Zhanyu, China ... 57 B12
Zhao Xian, China ... 56 F8
Zhao'an, China ... 59 F11
Zhaocheng, China ... 56 F6
Zhaojue, China ... 58 C4
Zhaoping, China ... 59 E8
Zhaoqing, China ... 59 F9
Zhaotong, China ... 58 D4
Zhaoyuan, Heilongjiang, China ... 57 B13
Zhaoyuan, Shandong, China ... 57 F11
Zharkovskiy, Russia ... 46 E7
Zhashkiv, Ukraine ... 47 H6
Zhashui, China ... 56 H5
Zhayyq →, Kazakstan ... 50 E6
Zhdanov = Mariupol, Ukraine ... 47 J9
Zhecheng, China ... 56 G8
Zhegao, China ... 59 B11
Zhejiang □, China ... 59 C13
Zheleznogorsk-Ilimskiy, Russia ... 51 D11
Zheltyye Vody = Zhovti Vody, Ukraine ... 47 H7
Zhen'an, China ... 56 H5
Zhenba, China ... 58 A6
Zhenfeng, China ... 58 E5
Zheng'an, China ... 58 C6
Zhengding, China ... 56 E8
Zhengyang, China ... 59 A10
Zhengyangguan, China ... 59 A11
Zhengzhou, China ... 56 G7
Zhenhai, China ... 59 C13
Zhenjiang, China ... 59 A12
Zhenkang, China ... 58 F2
Zhenlai, China ... 57 B12
Zhenning, China ... 58 D5
Zhenping, Henan, China ... 56 H7
Zhenping, Shaanxi, China ... 58 B7
Zhenxiong, China ... 58 D5
Zhenyuan, Gansu, China ... 56 G4
Zhenyuan, Guizhou, China ... 58 D7
Zherdevka, Russia ... 48 E5
Zherong, China ... 59 D12
Zhetiqara, Kazakstan ... 50 D7
Zhezqazghan, Kazakstan ... 50 E7
Zhicheng, China ... 59 B8
Zhidan, China ... 56 F5
Zhigansk, Russia ... 51 C13
Zhigulevsk, Russia ... 48 D9
Zhijiang, Hubei, China ... 59 B8
Zhijiang, Hunan, China ... 58 D7
Zhijin, China ... 58 D5
Zhilinda, Russia ... 51 C12
Zhirnovsk, Russia ... 48 E7
Zhitomir = Zhytomyr, Ukraine ... 47 G5
Zhizdra, Russia ... 46 F8
Zhlobin, Belarus ... 47 F6
Zhmerinka = Zhmerynka, Ukraine ... 47 H5
Zhmerynka, Ukraine ... 47 H5

Zhob, Pakistan ... 68 D3
Zhob →, Pakistan ... 68 C3
Zhodino = Zhodzina, Belarus ... 46 E5
Zhodzina, Belarus ... 46 E5
Zhokhova, Ostrov, Russia ... 51 B16
Zhongdian, China ... 58 D2
Zhongdong, China ... 58 F6
Zhongdu, China ... 58 E7
Zhongning, China ... 56 F3
Zhongshan, Guangdong, China ... 59 F9
Zhongshan, Guangxi Zhuangzu, China ... 59 E8
Zhongtiao Shan, China ... 56 G6
Zhongwei, China ... 56 F3
Zhongxiang, China ... 59 B9
Zhongyang, China ... 56 F6
Zhoucun, China ... 57 F9
Zhouning, China ... 59 D12
Zhoushan, China ... 59 B14
Zhoushan Dao, China ... 59 C14
Zhouzhi, China ... 56 G5
Zhovti Vody, Ukraine ... 47 H7
Zhovtneve, Ukraine ... 47 J7
Zhovtnevoye = Zhovtneve, Ukraine ... 47 J7
Zhu Jiang →, China ... 59 F9
Zhuanghe, China ... 57 E12
Zhucheng, China ... 57 G10
Zhugqu, China ... 56 H3
Zhuhai, China ... 59 F9
Zhuji, China ... 59 C13
Zhukovka, Russia ... 46 F7
Zhumadian, China ... 56 H8
Zhuo Xian = Zhuozhou, China ... 56 E8
Zhuolu, China ... 56 D8
Zhuozhou, China ... 56 E8
Zhuozi, China ... 56 D7
Zhushan, China ... 59 A8
Zhuxi, China ... 58 A7
Zhuzhou, China ... 59 D9
Zhytomyr, Ukraine ... 47 G5
Zi Shui →, China ... 59 C9
Žiar nad Hronom, Slovak Rep. ... 27 C11
Zīārān, Iran ... 71 B6
Ziarat, Pakistan ... 68 D2
Zibo, China ... 57 F10
Zichang, China ... 56 F5
Zidarovo, Bulgaria ... 41 D11
Ziębice, Poland ... 45 H4
Zielona Góra, Poland ... 45 G2
Zierikzee, Neths. ... 17 C3
Ziesar, Germany ... 24 C8
Zifta, Egypt ... 80 H7
Zigey, Chad ... 79 F9
Zigong, China ... 58 C5
Ziguinchor, Senegal ... 82 C1
Zihuatanejo, Mexico ... 118 D4
Zijin, China ... 59 F10
Zile, Turkey ... 72 B6
Zillah, Libya ... 79 C9
Žilina, Slovak Rep. ... 27 B11
Žilinský □, Slovak Rep. ... 27 B12
Zillah, Libya ... 79 C9
Zillertaler Alpen, Austria ... 26 D4
Zima, Russia ... 51 D11
Zimapán, Mexico ... 119 C5
Zimba, Zambia ... 87 F2
Zimbabwe, Zimbabwe ... 87 G3
Zimbabwe ■, Africa ... 87 F3
Zimi, S. Leone ... 82 D2
Zimnicea, Romania ... 43 G10
Zimovniki, Russia ... 49 G6
Zinder, Niger ... 83 C6
Zinga, Tanzania ... 87 D4
Zingst, Germany ... 24 A8
Ziniaré, Burkina Faso ... 83 C4
Zinnowitz, Germany ... 24 A9
Zion National Park, U.S.A. ... 115 H7
Zirbitzkogel, Austria ... 26 D7
Zirc, Hungary ... 42 C2
Žiri, Slovenia ... 29 B11
Žirje, Croatia ... 29 E12
Zirl, Austria ... 26 D4
Zirndorf, Germany ... 25 F6
Ziros, Greece ... 36 D8
Zirreh, Gowd-e, Afghan. ... 66 E3
Zisterdorf, Austria ... 27 C9
Zitácuaro, Mexico ... 118 D4
Žitava →, Slovak Rep. ... 27 C11
Zitište, Serbia, Yug. ... 42 E5
Zitong, China ... 58 B5
Zítsa, Greece ... 38 B2
Zittau, Germany ... 24 E10
Zitundo, Mozam. ... 89 D5
Živinice, Bos.-H. ... 42 F3
Ziwa Magariba □, Tanzania ... 86 C3
Ziway, L., Ethiopia ... 81 F4
Zixi, China ... 59 D11
Zixing, China ... 59 D9
Ziyang, Shaanxi, China ... 56 H5
Ziyang, Sichuan, China ... 58 B5
Ziyuan, China ... 59 D8
Ziyun, China ... 58 E6
Zlarin, Croatia ... 29 E12
Zlatar, Croatia ... 29 B13
Zlatar, Serbia, Yug. ... 40 C3
Zlataritsa, Bulgaria ... 41 C10
Zlatibor, Serbia, Yug. ... 40 C3
Zlatitsa, Bulgaria ... 41 D8
Zlatna, Romania ... 43 D8
Zlatna Panega, Bulgaria ... 41 C12
Zlatni Pyasŭtsi, Bulgaria ... 41 C12
Zlatograd, Bulgaria ... 41 E9
Zlatoust, Russia ... 50 D6
Zletovo, Macedonia ... 40 E6
Zlín, Czech Rep. ... 27 B10

Zlínský □, Czech Rep. ... 27 B10
Złocieniec, Poland ... 44 E3
Złoczew, Poland ... 45 G5
Złot, Serbia, Yug. ... 40 B5
Złotoryja, Poland ... 45 G2
Złotów, Poland ... 44 E4
Zmeinogorsk, Russia ... 50 D9
Żmigród, Poland ... 45 G3
Zmiyev, Ukraine ... 47 H9
Znamenka = Znamyanka, Ukraine ... 47 H7
Znamyanka, Ukraine ... 47 H7
Znin, Poland ... 45 F4
Znojmo, Czech Rep. ... 26 C9
Zobeyrī, Iran ... 70 C5
Zobia, Dem. Rep. of the Congo ... 86 B2
Zoetermeer, Neths. ... 17 B4
Zogang, China ... 58 C1
Zogno, Italy ... 28 C6
Zogqên, China ... 58 A2
Zolochev = Zolochiv, Ukraine ... 47 H3
Zolochiv, Ukraine ... 47 H3
Zolotonosha, Ukraine ... 47 H7
Zomba, Malawi ... 87 F4
Zongo, Dem. Rep. of the Congo ... 84 D3
Zonguldak, Turkey ... 72 B4
Zongyang, China ... 59 B11
Zonqor Pt., Malta ... 36 D2
Zonza, France ... 21 G13
Zorgo, Burkina Faso ... 83 C4
Zorita, Spain ... 35 F5
Zorleni, Romania ... 43 D12
Zornitsa, Bulgaria ... 41 D10
Zorritos, Peru ... 124 D1
Zory, Poland ... 45 H5
Zorzor, Liberia ... 82 D3
Zossen, Germany ... 24 C9
Zou Xiang, China ... 56 G9
Zouar, Chad ... 79 D9
Zouan-Hounien, Ivory C. ... 82 D3
Zouérate = Zouîrât, Mauritania ... 78 D3
Zouîrât, Mauritania ... 78 D3
Zourika, Niger ... 83 B6
Zourma, Burkina Faso ... 83 C4
Zoushan Dao, China ... 59 B14
Zoutkamp, Neths. ... 17 A6
Zrenjanin, Serbia, Yug. ... 42 E5
Zuarungu, Ghana ... 83 C4
Zuba, Nigeria ... 83 D6
Zubayr, Yemen ... 81 D5
Zubtsov, Russia ... 46 D8
Zuénoula, Ivory C. ... 82 D3
Zuera, Spain ... 32 D4
Zufār, Oman ... 74 D5
Zug □, Switz. ... 25 H4
Zugdidi, Georgia ... 49 J5
Zugersee, Switz. ... 25 H4
Zugspitze, Germany ... 25 H6
Zuid-Holland □, Neths. ... 17 C4
Zuidbeveland, Neths. ... 17 C3
Zuidhorn, Neths. ... 17 A6
Zújar, Spain ... 35 H8
Zújar →, Spain ... 35 G5
Zukowo, Poland ... 44 D5
Zula, Eritrea ... 81 D4
Zülpich, Germany ... 24 E2
Zumaia, Spain ... 32 B2
Zumárraga, Spain ... 32 B2
Zumbo, Mozam. ... 87 F3
Zummo, Nigeria ... 83 D7
Zumpango, Mexico ... 119 D5
Zungeru, Nigeria ... 83 D6
Zunhua, China ... 57 D9
Zuni, U.S.A. ... 115 J9
Zunyi, China ... 58 D6
Zuo Jiang →, China ... 58 F6
Zuozhou, China ... 58 F6
Županja, Croatia ... 42 E3
Zur, Kosovo, Yug. ... 40 D4
Zurbātīyah, Iraq ... 70 C5
Zürich, Switz. ... 25 H4
Zürich □, Switz. ... 25 H4
Zürichsee, Switz. ... 25 H4
Zuromin, Poland ... 45 E6
Zut, Croatia ... 29 E12
Zutphen, Neths. ... 17 B6
Zuwārah, Libya ... 79 B8
Zūzan, Iran ... 71 C8
Žužemberk, Slovenia ... 29 C11
Zvenigorodka = Zvenyhorodka, Ukraine ... 47 H6
Zvenyhorodka, Ukraine ... 47 H6
Zverinogolovskoye, Russia ... 50 D7
Zvezdets, Bulgaria ... 41 D11
Zvishavane, Zimbabwe ... 87 G3
Zvolen, Slovak Rep. ... 27 C12
Zvonce, Serbia, Yug. ... 40 D6
Zvornik, Bos.-H. ... 42 F4
Zwedru = Tchien, Liberia ... 82 D3
Zweibrücken, Germany ... 25 F3
Zwenkau, Germany ... 24 D8
Zwettl, Austria ... 26 C8
Zwickau, Germany ... 24 E8
Zwierzyniec, Poland ... 45 H9
Zwiesel, Germany ... 25 F9
Zwoleń, Poland ... 45 G8
Zwolle, Neths. ... 17 B6
Zwolle, U.S.A. ... 113 K8
Zychlin, Poland ... 45 F6
Żyrardów, Poland ... 45 F7
Zyryan, Kazakstan ... 50 E9
Zyryanka, Russia ... 51 C16
Zyryanovsk = Zyryan, Kazakstan ... 50 E9
Żywiec, Poland ... 45 J6
Zyyi, Cyprus ... 36 E12

KEY TO WORLD MAP PAGES

NORTH AMERICA

ARCTIC OCEAN
4

Arctic Circle

NORTH

8

100-101

104-105

14

15

102-103

12-13

108-109

18-19

110-111

34-35

20-21

ATLANTIC

37

116-117

32-33

37

OCEAN

37

114-115

112-113

106

Tropic of Cancer

118-119

120-121

PACIFIC
OCEAN
96-97

78-79

Equator

SOUTH
AMERICA

AFRIC

124-125

Tropic of Capricorn

PACIFIC OCEAN

126-127

128